Criminal Justice in Action

Seventh Edition

LARRY K. GAINES

California State University
San Bernardino

ROGER LEROY MILLER

Institute for University Studies
Arlington, Texas

WADSWORTH
CENGAGE Learning™

Australia • Brazil • Japan • Korea • Mexico • Singapore • Spain • United Kingdom • United States

WADSWORTH
CENGAGE Learning

Criminal Justice in Action, 7th Edition
Larry K. Gaines and **Roger LeRoy Miller**

Editor-in-Chief: Michelle Julet

Senior Publisher: Linda Schreiber Ganster

Senior Acquisitions Editor:
Carolyn Henderson Meier

Senior Developmental Editor: Bob Jucha

Assistant Editor: Rachael McDonald

Editorial Assistant: Virginette Acacio

Senior Marketing Manager:
Michelle Williams

Marketing Assistant: Jack Ward

Marketing Communications Manager:
Heather Baxley

Senior Content Project Manager:
Ann Borman

Photo Researcher: Anne Sheroff

Copyeditor: Pat Lewis

Indexer: Terry Casey

Media Editor: Andy Yap

Manufacturing Coordinator: Judy Inouye

Art Director: Maria Epes

Interior Designer: Riezebos Holzbaur

Cover Designer: Riezebos Holzbaur/
Tim Heraldo

Cover Image: Graeme Outerbridge/
Photolibrary.com

Compositor: Parkwood Composition
Service

Library of Congress Control Number: 2011942457

Student Edition ISBN-13: 978-1-111-83557-6
Student Edition ISBN-10: 1-111-83557-8

Annotated Instructor's Edition: ISBN-13: 978-0-8400-2921-8
Annotated Instructor's Edition: ISBN-10: 0-8400-2921-7

Wadsworth Cengage Learning
20 Davis Drive
Belmont, CA 94002-3098
USA

Cengage Learning products are represented in Canada
by Nelson Education, Ltd.

For your course and learning solutions, visit **academic.cengage.com**
Purchase any of our products at your local college store or at our
preferred online store **www.cengagebrain.com**

Printed in the United States of America
1 2 3 4 5 6 7 14 13 12 11

CONTENTS IN BRIEF

CONTENTS

David McNew/Getty Images

Part Two: The Police and Law Enforcement

CHAPTER 7
POLICE AND THE CONSTITUTION: THE RULES OF LAW ENFORCEMENT 214

Toledo Blade/Dave Zapotosky

Part Three: Criminal Courts

CHAPTER 8
COURTS AND THE QUEST FOR JUSTICE 252

AP Photo/Francisco Kjolseth, Pool

CHAPTER 9
PRETRIAL PROCEDURES: THE ADVERSARY SYSTEM IN ACTION 284

CHAPTER 10
THE CRIMINAL TRIAL 318

CHAPTER 11
PUNISHMENT AND SENTENCING 354

Part Four: Corrections

CHAPTER 12
PROBATION AND COMMUNITY CORRECTIONS 396

CHAPTER 13
PRISONS AND JAILS 426

Part Five: Special Issues

CHAPTER 17
TODAY'S CHALLENGES: IMMIGRATION, CYBER CRIME, AND WHITE-COLLAR CRIME 574

AP Photo/ICE

Features of Special Interest

Badge: Rasmus Rasmusson/iStockphoto; Handcuffs: Photodisc; Gavel: Shutterstock; Scale: James Stadl/iStockphoto

ANTI-TERRORISM IN ACTION

MYTH vs. REALITY

CJ IN ACTION

PREFACE TO THE SEVENTH EDITION

As Americans, we place great demands on our criminal justice system. We expect law enforcement agencies to prevent and deter crime, keeping us safe as we go about our daily lives. We expect the criminal courts to tackle complicated questions of guilt and innocence, punishing the guilty and ensuring that the innocent go free. We expect corrections officials to maintain order over a system that invites disorder, while at the same time rehabilitating those thought by many to be beyond rehabilitation.

The challenge of meeting such demands falls to the men and women who make up the criminal justice workforce. For more than a decade and over the course of six editions, *Criminal Justice in Action* has provided students with an engaging and comprehensive guide to understanding these challenges. In this, our seventh edition, the tradition continues. Combining a solid pedagogical foundation and numerous real-life examples, *Criminal Justice in Action* offers students insight into the world of crime and justice that goes well beyond the clichés of Hollywood or the rhetoric of politicians. With the help and advice of the many criminal justice professors who have adopted this best-selling textbook over the years, we believe we have created an invaluable introduction to the field.

IN THEIR OWN WORDS: CAREER ADVICE FROM CJ PRACTITIONERS

We are well aware that many students using this text are interested in a criminal justice career. Consequently, each chapter of the seventh edition of *Criminal Justice in Action* includes a **page-long Careers in CJ feature.** This feature consists of two parts. First, the criminal justice practitioner presents a personal account of his or her profession, as well as hard-earned career advice. Second, the student is provided with "Fast Facts" about the profession, such as required training and annual salary. Careers covered in this edition include crime scene photographer, probation officer, and border patrol agent.

The enhanced Careers in CJ features are only one aspect of our commitment to helping interested students get their foot in the CJ door. A **dedicated Careers in Criminal Justice Web site** contains self-exploration and profiling activities for students, helping them investigate the numerous career opportunities in law enforcement, the courts, the corrections systems, or any other aspect of American crime and justice. The site also offers students tips on résumé writ-

ing, interviewing techniques, and other practicalities of the job search.

MAJOR CHANGES TO THE SEVENTH EDITION

As with previous editions of *Criminal Justice in Action,* each chapter in the seventh edition begins with a **new "ripped from the headlines" vignette** that introduces the themes to be covered in the pages that follow. Furthermore, the text continues to reflect the ever-changing nature of our topic, with **more than one hundred new real-life crime examples** and **more than seventy new references to recent research involving crime and criminal behavior.** The text also includes hundreds of updated statistical measures of crime, figures, and photographs. The two most extensive changes to the seventh edition, however, are a new feature that puts the student "in the shoes" of criminal justice professionals and a new chapter that expands the students' understanding of crime in the twenty-first century.

- The popular "You Be the Judge" feature has been expanded to include the spectrum of criminal justice employees. So, as part of **this new You Be the _____ feature,** students will assume a number of different professional positions—including a sheriff's deputy, a defense attorney, and a probation officer—and be asked to make a difficult decision based on the law and the facts of the situation in which they find themselves.

- An extensively **revised** Chapter 17 now includes **new sections on the criminalization of immigration law** and **the challenges of white-collar crime,** as well as an **updated section on cyber crime.** The inclusion of these controversial subjects makes the seventh edition of *Criminal Justice in Action* our most comprehensive version to date.

CONCENTRATED CRITICAL THINKING

The new You Be the _____ feature continues our commitment to developing **students' abilities to think critically** about criminal justice. Indeed, each feature and most photograph captions in the textbook end with a question that requires an innovative, inquisitive response. Other critical thinking tools in *Criminal Justice in Action,* Seventh Edition, include:

- **Learning Objectives.** At the beginning of each chapter, students are introduced to up to ten *learning objectives*

(LOs) for that chapter. For example, in Chapter 5, "Law Enforcement Today," Learning Objective 8 (LO8) asks students to "Identify the duties of the FBI." The area of text that furnishes the information required to make this determination is marked with a square LO8 graphic, and, finally, the correct answer is found in the chapter-ending materials. This constant *active learning* will greatly expand students' understanding of dozens of crucial criminal justice topics.

- **Self Assessment Boxes.** Students are not, however, required to wait until they have finished reading a chapter to engage in self-assessment. We have placed a *self assessment* box at the end of each major section of each chapter. Three to five sentences long, these items require students to fill in the blanks, thereby reinforcing the most important points in the section they have just read. (All answers are found at the end of each chapter.)

- **CJ in Action Features.** Each of the *chapter-ending* CJ in Action features introduces students to a controversial topic from the chapter and provides them with "for" and "against" arguments related to that topic. Then, using information and knowledge gained from the chapter, the student is asked to write a short essay giving her or his opinion on the controversy. These features not only help students improve their writing and critical thinking skills, but they also act as a review for the material in the chapter. The seventh edition of *Criminal Justice in Action* includes many new such chapter-ending features, covering topics such as hate crimes and the election of judges.

CHAPTER-BY-CHAPTER ORGANIZATION OF THE TEXT

This edition's seventeen chapters blend the principles of criminal justice with current research and high-interest examples of what is happening in the world of crime and crime prevention right now. What follows is a summary of each chapter, along with a description of some of the revisions to the Seventh Edition.

PART 1: THE CRIMINAL JUSTICE SYSTEM

Chapter 1 provides an *introduction* to the criminal justice system's three major institutions: law enforcement, the courts, and corrections. The chapter also answers conceptual questions such as "what is crime?" and "what are the values of the American criminal justice system?"

- A **new** Comparative Criminal Justice feature ("Unveiling France") highlights the differences in criminal justice systems by examining a new French law that is unlikely to be adopted in the United States.

- The chapter closes with a section entitled **"Criminal Justice Today,"** which has been revised to reflect, on the one hand, growing fears of a recession-driven spike in criminal activity and, on the other hand, statistical evidence that these fears are—for now—unfounded.

Chapter 2 focuses on *criminology*, giving students insight into why crime occurs before shifting their attention toward how society goes about fighting it. The chapter addresses the most widely accepted and influential criminological hypotheses, including choice theories, trait theories, sociological theories, social process theories, and social conflict theories.

- Students will also become acquainted with **emerging and alternative** theories of criminology, including **new** analyses of the **role of the victim** in the criminal equation and the connection between **illegal drugs and crime,** so crucial to a full understanding of criminality in the United States today.

- A **new** Anti-Terrorism in Action feature ("Lessons in Profiling") explores the latest efforts by criminologists to understand the "terrorist mind" and create a useful profile of potential terrorists.

Chapter 3 furnishes students with an understanding of two areas fundamental to criminal justice: (1) the *practical definitions* of crime, such as the difference between felonies and misdemeanors and different degrees of criminal conduct, and (2) the various modes of *measuring* crime, including the FBI's Uniform Crime Reports and the U.S. Department of Justice's National Crime Victimization Survey.

- To give students an idea of how crime statistics shape our perception of crime in the United States, the chapter includes a section entitled **"Crime Trends Today,"** which has been **expanded** to show the historical and contemporary links between violent crime rates and factors such as guns, gangs, illegal drugs, the economy, and the national birth rate.

- The **updated** chapter-ending CJ in Action feature ("Legalizing Marijuana") asks students to determine whether the legalization of marijuana has any benefits to offer American society or would only make an already bad situation worse.

Chapter 4 lays the foundation of *criminal law*. It addresses constitutional law, statutory law, and other sources of

American criminal law before shifting its focus to the legal framework that allows the criminal justice system to determine and punish criminal guilt.

- A **new** chapter-opening vignette ("Deadly Heat") describes the fate of James Arthur Ray, found criminally responsible for the deaths of two participants in a sweat lodge ceremony he led as part of a five-day retreat near Sedona, Arizona.

- A **new** A Question of Ethics feature ("Kidney Compensation") explores the ethical considerations underpinning the U.S. ban on selling kidneys, and asks students to consider whether this criminal law does more harm than good.

PART 2: THE POLICE AND LAW ENFORCEMENT

Chapter 5 acts as an *introduction* to law enforcement in the United States today. This chapter offers a detailed description of the country's numerous local, state, and federal law enforcement agencies and examines the responsibilities and duties that come with a career in law enforcement.

- As part of a **new** discussion on the landscape of **policing today,** students will learn about the strategies that make up **intelligence**-led policing, the challenges of **anti-terrorism,** and "Law Enforcement 2.0," in which law enforcement agents gather information about criminal activity by accessing social networks on the Internet.

- A **new** chapter-ending *CJ in Action* feature asks students to consider the positives and negatives of government efforts to encourage diversity in local police departments.

Chapter 6 puts students on the streets and gives them a gritty look at the many *challenges of being a law enforcement officer.* It starts with a discussion of the importance of discretion in law enforcement and then moves on to policing strategies and issues in modern policing, such as use of force, corruption, and the "thin blue line."

- A **new** You Be the Sheriff's Deputy feature ("Threat Level") addresses the subject of police use of deadly force by placing the student in a dangerous situation where such force may—or may not—be called for.

- A **new** CJ and Technology feature ("Self-Surveillance") describes how some law enforcement agencies are considering a drastic measure to curb employee misconduct: placing small cameras on the heads of police officers to record their every move.

Chapter 7 examines the sometimes uneasy *relationship between law enforcement and the U.S. Constitution* by explaining the rules of being a police officer. Particular emphasis is placed on the Fourth, Fifth, and Sixth Amendments, giving students an understanding of crucial concepts such as probable cause, reasonableness, and custodial interrogation.

- An **updated** section entitled "Video and Digital Surveillance" illuminates the constitutional issues surrounding law enforcement use of closed-circuit television (CCTV) cameras as crime-fighting tools. The discussion includes a **new** CJ and Technology feature ("Backscatter X-Ray Scanners") that introduces students to the surprising ability of new devices to see through walls.

- In the context of racial profiling, a **new** discussion of Arizona's proposed law S.B. 1070, which requires that state and local police officers check the immigration status of any person detained if the officer has a "reasonable suspicion" that the suspect is in the United Sates unlawfully.

PART 3: CRIMINAL COURTS

Chapter 8 takes a big-picture approach in describing the *American court system,* giving students an overview of the basic principles of our judicial system, the state and federal court systems, and the role of judges in the criminal justice system.

- The court system's ability to live up to societal expectations of truth and justice, a running theme of the third part of this textbook, is explored by comparing our system to Italy's. This chapter's **new** opening vignette makes the comparison by examining the fate of Amanda Knox, an American exchange student who successfully fought to clear her name after being convicted of murder in Perugia, Italy.

- A **new** discussion designed to give students an understanding of **how the U.S. Supreme Court "makes" criminal justice policy** through judicial review. The discussion focuses on a recent case in which the Court invalidated a federal law banning the Internet sale of "crush" videos, which show the brutal slaughter of small animals, on First Amendment grounds.

Chapter 9 provides students with a rundown of *pretrial procedures* and highlights the role that these procedures play in America's *adversary system.* Thus, pretrial procedures such as establishing bail and plea bargaining are presented as part of the larger "battle" between the prosecution and the defense.

- A **new** CJ and Technology feature ("Neurological Lie Detection") reports on the progress being made to create a polygraph reliable enough to be used in criminal court.

- The question of how harshly to treat a certain class of female criminals arises in a **new** You Be the Prosecutor feature ("A Battered Woman"). The exercise requires students to decide the charges, if any, that should be brought against a wife who murders her extremely violent and abusive husband while he sleeps.

Chapter 10 puts the student in the courtroom and gives her or him a strong understanding of the steps of the *criminal trial.* The chapter also attempts to answer the fascinating but ultimately frustrating question, "Are criminal trials in this country fair?"

- Three **new** Figures use excerpts from actual court records to give students a first-hand understanding of three crucial aspects of the criminal trial: jury selection, the opening statement, and cross-examination.
- The student's understanding of the special features of American criminal trials is enhanced by an **updated** Anti-Terrorism in Action feature ("Trying Times") that explores the pros and cons of trying suspected terrorists in civilian criminal court.

Chapter 11 links the many different *punishment options* for those who have been convicted of a crime with the theoretical justifications for those punishments. The chapter also examines punishment in the policy context, weighing the public's desire for ever-harsher criminal sanctions against the consequences of such governmental strategies.

- A **new** Comparative Criminal Justice feature ("Blood Money") explains the Pakistani practice of *diyat,* in which a criminal offender provides financial compensation to her or his victim's family in lieu of incarceration or any other form of punishment.
- A **new** You Be the Juror feature ("Life or Death?") asks students to decide whether a man who has been found guilty of a grisly triple murder that involved a mother and two children should be sentenced to death or given a life prison term without parole.

PART 4: CORRECTIONS

Chapter 12 makes an important point, and one that is often overlooked in the larger discussion of the American corrections system: not all of those who are punished need to be placed behind bars. This chapter explores the *community corrections* options, from probation to intermediate sanctions such as intensive supervision and home confinement.

- A **new** discussion of innovative probations strategies focuses on Hawaii's attempt to encourage compliance through "swift and certain" punishment and a California ballot initiative that requires certain low-level drug offenders in that state to receive treatment in the community rather than be incarcerated.
- A **new** CJ in Action feature ("Involuntary Commitment of the Mentally Ill") uses the case of Jared Loughner, who went on a killing spree in Tucson, Arizona, in January 2011, to broach the issue of involuntary confinement. Should mentally ill persons be locked up against their will in the absence of criminal behavior?

Chapter 13 focuses on *prisons and jails.* Record-high rates of incarceration have pushed these institutions to the forefront of the criminal justice system, and this chapter explores the various issues—such as the emergence of private prisons—that have resulted from the prison population boom.

- A **new** section entitled **"Downsizing America's Prisons"** describes efforts by certain states to reduce their prison populations in an effort to lower the unfeasible costs of their corrections systems.
- A **new** Mastering Concepts feature gives students a clear idea of the different roles that prisons and jails play in the American corrections system.

Chapter 14 is another example of our efforts to get students "into the action" of the criminal justice system, this time putting them in the uncomfortable position of being behind bars. It also answers the question, "What happens when the inmate is released back into society?"

- **New** sections on **female correctional guards** and **women's prisons,** providing insight into the challenges faced by women on both sides of prison bars.
- A **new** CJ and Technology feature ("Cell Phones behind Bars") that describes the havoc these electronic devices can wreak on the operational safety of a prison or jail.

PART 5: SPECIAL ISSUES

Chapter 15 examines the *juvenile justice system,* giving students a comprehensive description of the path taken by delinquents from first contact with police to trial and punishment. The chapter contains a strong criminological component as well, scrutinizing the various theories of why certain juveniles turn to delinquency and what steps society can take to stop them from doing so before it is "too late."

- A **new** discussion of the U.S. Supreme Court's 2010 ruling that juveniles who commit crimes that do not involve murder may not be sentenced to life in prison without the possibility of parole.
- A **new** section, **"Bullied to Death,"** that addresses the growing national awareness of the negative con-

sequences of bullying, as well as a critique of the steps taken by government officials and school administrators to prevent this harmful behavior.

Chapter 16 begins with a brief introduction to the historical and social forces behind international terrorism. We then move to an in-depth discussion of the terrorist threat to the United States and the steps that our government is taking to protect its citizens against that threat. The chapter ends with a close look at the question, "How many freedoms are Americans willing to give up to further the fight against terrorism?"

- What effect will Osama bin Laden's death have on homeland security? A **new** section explores the **state of international terrorism** and identifies the dangers posed by this still potent force.

- The **danger posed by homegrown terrorists** in American also continues to grow, and an **updated** section in this chapter explains how law enforcement and homeland security officials in the United States are responding to this latest challenge.

Chapter 17 concludes the text by taking an expanded look at three crucial criminal justice topics: (1) immigration law, (2) cyber crime, and (3) white-collar crime.

- A **new** section on **the criminalization of immigration law** provides students with the basics of immigration law and an understanding of how the actions of federal immigration agents are impacting local law enforcement and crime prevention.

- Another **new** section on **white-collar crime** describes the myriad of wrongdoing covered by this umbrella term and provides an overview of recent law enforcement efforts to combat economic crimes. The section also includes a **new** Myth v. Reality feature ("Soft on White-Collar Crime") that challenges the popular notion that the criminal justice system is "soft" when it comes to punishing white-collar criminals.

SPECIAL FEATURES

Supplementing the main text of *Criminal Justice in Action*, Seventh Edition, are nearly ninety eye-catching, instructive, and penetrating special features. These features, described below with examples, have been designed to enhance the student's understanding of a particular criminal justice issue.

CAREERS IN CJ:
As stated before, many students reading this book are planning a career in criminal justice. We have provided them with an insight into some of these careers by offering first-person accounts of what it is like to work as a criminal justice professional.

- In Chapter 5, William Howe gives career advice to those students interested in following in his footsteps as a detective.

- In Chapter 12, Peggy McCarthy, a probation officer, provides an inside look at the many duties involved with her profession, from assisting in the arrest of hardened criminals to helping defendants make "a positive change in their lives."

ANTI-TERRORISM IN ACTION:
This new feature focuses on various law enforcement strategies to promote homeland security.

- "A Close Call" (Chapter 1) gives an inside look at how local and federal law enforcement agents joined forces to thwart a homeland security threat that, in the words of one expert, "was closer to going operational" than any other terrorist plot on U.S. soil since September 11, 2001.

- "Timed Out" (Chapter 7) raises the question of whether terrorist suspects should be afforded the same *Miranda* rights as other criminal suspects.

MASTERING CONCEPTS:
Some criminal justice topics require additional explanation before they become crystal clear in the minds of students. This feature helps students to master many of the essential concepts in the textbook.

- In Chapter 7, these features help students understand the legal differences between a police stop and a police frisk, and the various exceptions to the requirement that a police officer must have a warrant before making an arrest.

- In Chapter 15, the feature compares and contrasts the juvenile justice system with the criminal justice system.

YOU BE THE _____:
This new feature, as noted earlier in the Preface, puts students into the position of a criminal justice actor in a hypothetical case or situation that is based on a real-life event. The facts of the case or situation are presented with alternative possible outcomes, and the student is asked to "be the _____" and make a decision. Students can then consult Appendix B at the end of the text to learn what actually happened in the offered scenario.

- You Be the Police Officer, "Discretion and Domestic Violence" (Chapter 6) asks students to make a difficult decision involving a domestic violence situation in which the victim does not want to press charges against her abusive husband.

- You Be the Defense Attorney, "A Gang Murder" (Chapter 10), challenges the student to create reasonable doubt in the minds of jurors who will decide the fate of her or his client, who is on trial for murdering a fellow gang member.

CJ AND TECHNOLOGY:
Advances in technology are constantly transforming the face of criminal justice. In these features, which appear in nearly every chapter, students learn of one such emergent technology and are asked to critically evaluate its effects.

- This feature in Chapter 1 explores biometrics, or the science of identifying a person through his or her unique physical characteristics, such as the face, eyes, or vein patterns of the hand.
- This feature in Chapter 16 describes how predator drones are able to "take out" terrorist suspects in hostile, foreign environments and raises the question of whether the use of such devices is sound policy.

COMPARATIVE CRIMINAL JUSTICE:
The world offers a dizzying array of different criminal customs and codes, many of which are in stark contrast to those accepted in the United States. This feature provides dramatic and sometimes perplexing examples of foreign criminal justice practices in order to give students a better understanding of our domestic ways.

- "The World's Oldest Profession" (Chapter 3) presents this startling fact: in Belgium, on any given day, more people are legally paying for sex than are going to the movies. What does this say about the American tradition of criminalizing prostitution?
- "The Great Firewall of China" (Chapter 17) describes China's efforts to limit and control the use of the Internet through criminal laws to an extent that is unimaginable to most Americans.

A QUESTION OF ETHICS:
Ethical dilemmas occur in every profession, but the challenges facing criminal justice professionals often have repercussions beyond their own lives and careers. In this feature, students are asked to place themselves in the shoes of police officers, prosecutors, defense attorneys, and other criminal justice actors facing ethical dilemmas: Will they do the right thing?

- In "The 'Dirty Harry' Problem" (Chapter 6), a police detective is trying to save the life of a young girl who has been buried alive with only enough oxygen to survive for a few hours. Is he justified in torturing the one person—the kidnapper—who knows where the girl is buried?
- In "Keeping a Secret" (Chapter 9), a client confesses to his defense attorney that he committed a crime for which another man has been convicted. The rules of attorney-client privilege hold that defense attorneys may not divulge such confidences. Should those rules always be followed?

LANDMARK CASES:
Rulings by the United States Supreme Court have shaped every area of the criminal justice system. In this feature, students learn about and analyze the most influential of these cases.

- In Chapter 4's *Lawrence v. Texas* (2003), the Supreme Court invalidated state laws that criminalized certain homosexual behavior.
- In Chapter 15's *In re Gault* (1967), the Supreme Court held that juveniles are entitled to many of the same due process rights granted to adult offenders—a decision that caused a seismic shift in America's juvenile justice system.

MYTH VERSUS REALITY:
Nothing endures like a good myth. In this feature, we try to dispel some of the more enduring myths in the criminal justice system while at the same time asking students to think critically about their consequences.

- "Race Stereotyping and Crime" (Chapter 3) challenges the perceived wisdom that members of certain minority groups, particularly African Americans, are prone to violence and therefore more likely to be criminals than other racial or ethnic groups.
- "Are Too Many Criminals Found Not Guilty by Reason of Insanity?" (Chapter 4) dispels the notion that the criminal justice is "soft" because it lets scores of "crazy" defendants go free due to insanity.

EXTENSIVE STUDY AIDS

Criminal Justice in Action, Seventh Edition, includes a number of pedagogical devices designed to complete the student's active learning experience. These devices include:

- Concise **chapter outlines** at the beginning of each chapter. The outlines give students an idea of what to expect in the pages ahead, as well as a quick source of review when needed.
- Dozens of **key terms** and a **running glossary** focus students' attention on major concepts and help them master the vocabulary of criminal justice. The chosen

terms are boldfaced in the text, allowing students to notice their importance without breaking the flow of reading. On the same page that a key term is highlighted, a margin note provides a succinct definition of the term. For further reference, a glossary at the end of the text provides a full list of all the key terms and their definitions. This edition includes over forty new key terms.

- Each chapter has at least six **figures,** which include graphs, charts, and other forms of colorful art that reinforce a point made in the text. This edition includes eleven new figures.

- Hundreds of **photographs** add to the overall readability and design of the text. Each photo has a caption, and **most of these captions include a critical-thinking question** dealing with the topic at hand. This edition includes more than one hundred new photos.

- At the end of each chapter, students will find five **Questions for Critical Analysis.** These questions will help the student assess his or her understanding of the just-completed chapter, as well as develop critical-thinking skills.

- Our teaching/learning package offers numerous opportunities for using online technology in the classroom. In the margins of each chapter, students will find **links to various Web sites** that illuminate a particular subject in the corresponding text.

ANCILLARY MATERIALS

Wadsworth provides a number of supplements to help instructors use *Criminal Justice in Action,* Seventh Edition, in their courses and to aid students in preparing for exams. Supplements are available to qualified adopters. Please consult your local Wadsworth/Cengage sales representative for details.

FOR THE INSTRUCTOR

- **Annotated Instructor's Edition.** This essential resource features teaching tips, discussion tips, and technology tips to help professors engage students with the course material. Prepared by Julia Campbell, University of Nebraska at Kearney.

- **Instructor's Resource Manual with Test Bank.** The manual includes learning objectives, key terms, a detailed chapter outline, a chapter summary, discussion topics, student activities, and a test bank. Each chapter's test bank contains questions in multiple-choice, true/false, fill-in-the-blank, and essay formats, with a full answer key. The test bank is coded to the learning objectives

that appear in the main text, and includes the page numbers in the main text where the answers can be found. Finally, each question in the test bank has been carefully reviewed by experienced criminal justice instructors for quality, accuracy, and content coverage. Our Instructor Approved seal, which appears on the front cover, is our assurance that you are working with an assessment and grading resource of the highest caliber. The manual is available for download on the password-protected website and can also be obtained by e-mailing your local Cengage Learning representative. Prepared by Julia Campbell, University of Nebraska at Kearney.

- **Online Lesson Plans.** The Lesson Plans bring accessible, masterful suggestions to every lesson. This supplement includes a sample syllabus, learning objectives, lecture notes, discussion topics, in-class activities, a detailed lecture outline, assignments, media tools, and "What if . . ." scenarios. Current events and real-life examples in the form of articles, Web sites, and video links are incorporated into the class discussion topics, activities, and assignments. The lecture outlines are correlated with PowerPoint slides for ease of classroom use. Lesson Plans are available on the PowerLecture resource and the instructor Web site. Prepared by Nathan R. Moran, Midwestern State University.

- **Online PowerPoints.** Helping you make your lectures more engaging while effectively reaching your visually oriented students, these handy Microsoft PowerPoint® slides outline the chapters of the main text in a classroom-ready presentation. Available for download on the password-protected instructor book companion website, the presentations and can also be obtained by e-mailing your local Cengage Learning representative. The PowerPoint® slides are updated to reflect the content and organization of the new edition of the text. Prepared by Nathan R. Moran, Midwestern State University.

- **PowerLecture DVD with ExamView.** This one-stop digital library and presentation tool includes preassembled Microsoft® PowerPoint® lecture slides linked to the learning objectives for each chapter. Also included are an electronic copy of the Instructor's Resource Manual with Testbank, the Lesson Plans, ExamView® computerized testing, and more. Based on the learning objectives outlined at the beginning of each chapter, the enhanced PowerLecture lets you bring together text-specific lecture outlines and art from this text, along with new video clips, animations, and learning modules from the web or your own materials—culminating in a powerful, personalized, media-enhanced presentation. PowerLecture also integrates ExamView®—a computerized test bank available for PC and Macintosh computers—software for customizing tests of up to 250 items that can be delivered in print or online. With ExamView you can create, deliver, and customize tests and study guides in minutes. You can easily edit and import your own questions and graphics, change test layouts, and reorganize questions. And, using ExamView's complete word-processing capabilities, you can enter an unlimited number of new questions or edit existing questions.

- **WebTutor™ on Blackboard® and WebCT®.** Jump-start your course with customizable, rich, text-specific content within your Course Management System. Whether you want to web-enable your class or put an entire course online, WebTutor delivers. WebTutor offers a wide array of resources, including media assets, test banks, practice quizzes linked to chapter learning objectives, and additional study aids. Visit www.cengage.com/webtutor to learn more.

- *The Wadsworth Criminal Justice Video Library.* So many exciting new videos—so many great ways to enrich your lectures and spark discussion of the material in this text. Your Cengage Learning representative will be happy to provide details on our video policy by adoption size. The library includes these selections and many others.

- *ABC® Videos.* ABC videos feature short, high-interest clips from current news events as well as historic raw footage going back 40 years. Perfect for discussion starters or to enrich your lectures and spark interest in the material in the text, these brief videos provide students with a new lens through which to view the past and present, one that will greatly enhance their knowledge and understanding of significant events and open up to them new dimensions in learning. Clips are drawn from such programs as *World News Tonight, Good Morning America, This Week, PrimeTime Live, 20/20,* and *Nightline,* as well as numerous ABC News specials and material from the Associated Press Television News and British Movietone News collections.

- *Cengage Learning's "Introduction to Criminal Justice Video Series" features videos supplied by the BBC Motion Gallery.* These short, high-interest clips from CBS and BBC news programs—everything from nightly news broadcasts and specials to *CBS News Special Reports, CBS Sunday Morning, 60 Minutes,* and more—are perfect classroom discussion starters. Designed to enrich your lectures and spark interest in the material in the text, these brief videos provide students with a new lens through which to view the past and present, one that will greatly enhance

their knowledge and understanding of significant events and open up to them new dimensions in learning.

- **Classroom Activities for Criminal Justice.** This valuable booklet contains both tried-and-true favorites and exciting new projects; activities are drawn from across the spectrum of criminal justice subjects and can be customized to fit any course.

- **Internet Activities for Criminal Justice.** This useful booklet helps familiarize students with Internet resources and allows instructors to integrate resources into their course materials.

FOR THE STUDENT

- **CengageNOW.** This unique, interactive online resource has the student take a chapter pretest and then offers him or her a personalized study plan. Once the student has completed the personalized study plan, a posttest evaluates her or his improved comprehension of chapter content.

- *Cengage Learning's Criminal Justice CourseMate* brings course concepts to life with interactive learning, study, and exam preparation tools that support the printed textbook. CourseMate includes an integrated eBook, quizzes mapped to chapter Learning Objectives, flashcards, videos, and more, and EngagementTracker, a first-of-its-kind tool that monitors student engagement in the course. The accompanying instructor website offers access to password-protected resources such as an electronic version of the instructor's manual and PowerPoint® slides. Web Quizzes were prepared by Pamela Donovan, Bloomsburg University.

- **Study Guide.** An extensive student guide has been developed for this edition. Because students learn in different ways, the guide includes a variety of pedagogical aids to help them. Each chapter is outlined and summarized, major terms and figures are defined, and self-tests are provided. Prepared by Janine Kremling, California State University, San Bernardino.

- **Careers in Criminal Justice Web Site: www. cengage. com/criminaljustice/careers.** This unique Web site gives students information on a wide variety of career paths, including requirements, salaries, training, contact information for key agencies, and employment outlooks. Several important tools help students investigate the criminal justice career choices that are right for them.

— *Career Profiles:* Video testimonials from a variety of practicing professionals in the field as well as information on many criminal justice careers, including job descriptions, requirements, training, salary and benefits, and the application process.

— *Interest Assessment:* Self-assessment tool to help students decide which careers suit their personalities and interests.

— *Career Planner:* Résumé-writing tips and worksheets, interviewing techniques, and successful job search strategies.

— *Links for Reference:* Direct links to federal, state, and local agencies where students can get contact information and learn more about current job opportunities.

• ***Handbook of Selected Supreme Court Cases,* Third Edition.** This supplementary handbook covers almost forty landmark cases, with a full case citation, an introduction, a summary from WestLaw, and excerpts and the decision for each case.

• **Current Perspectives: Readings from InfoTrac®.** These readers, designed to give you a deeper taste of special topics in criminal justice, include free access to InfoTrac® College Edition. The timely articles are selected by experts in each topic from within InfoTrac College Edition.

— *Cybercrime*

— *Introduction to Criminal Justice*

— *Forensics and Criminal Investigations*

— *Community Corrections*

— *Policy in Criminal Justice*

— *Technology and Criminal Justice*

— *Law and Courts*

— *Ethics in Criminal Justice*

— *Corrections*

— *Victimology*

— *Policy in Criminal Justice*

— *Terrorism and Homeland Security*

— *New Technologies and Criminal Justice*

— *Racial Profiling*

— *White Collar Crime*

— *Crisis Management and National Emergency Response*

— *Juvenile Justice*

• **CLeBook.** CLeBook allows students to access Cengage Learning textbooks in an easy-to-use online format. Highlight, take notes, bookmark, search your text, and (in some titles) link directly into multimedia: CLeBook combines the best aspects of paper books and ebooks in one package.

• **Course360—Online Learning to the Next Degree. Course360** from Cengage Learning is a complete turn-key solution that teaches course outcomes through student interaction in a highly customizable online learning environment. **Course360** blends relevant content with rich media and builds upon your course design, needs, and objectives. With a wide variety of media elements including audio, video, interactives, simulations, and more, **Course360** is the way today's students learn.

ACKNOWLEDGMENTS

Throughout the creation of the seven editions of this text, we have been aided by hundreds of experts in various criminal justice fields and by professors throughout the country, as well as by numerous students who have used the text. We list below the reviewers for this Seventh Edition, followed by the class-test participants and reviewers for the first six editions. We sincerely thank all who participated on the revision of *Criminal Justice in Action.* We believe that the Seventh Edition is even more responsive to the needs of today's criminal justice instructors and students alike because we have taken into account the constructive comments and criticisms of our reviewers and the helpful suggestions of our survey respondents.

REVIEWERS FOR THE SEVENTH EDITION

We are grateful for the participation of the reviewers who read and reviewed portions of our manuscript throughout its development, and for those who gave us valuable insights through their responses to our survey.

Lorna Alvarez-Rivera
Ohio University

Scott Brantley
Chancellor University

Sheri Chapel
Ridley-Lowell Business and Technical Institute and Keystone College

Gerald Hildebrand
Austin Community College

Jason R. Jolicoeur
Cincinnati State Technical and Community College

Paul Klenowski
Clarion University

Janine Kremling
California State University at San Bernardino

CLASS-TEST PARTICIPANTS

We also want to acknowledge the participation of the professors and their students who agreed to class-test portions of the text. Our thanks go to:

Tom Arnold
College of Lake County

Paula M. Broussard
University of Southwestern Louisiana

Mike Higginson
Suffolk Community College

Andrew Karmen
John Jay College of Criminal Justice

Fred Kramer
John Jay College of Criminal Justice

Anthony P. LaRose
Western Oregon University

Anne Lawrence
Kean University

Jerry E. Loar
Walters State Community College

Phil Reichel
University of Northern Colorado

Albert Sproule
Allentown College

Gregory B. Talley
Broome Community College

Karen Terry
John Jay College of Criminal Justice

Angelo Tritini
Passaic County Community College

Gary Uhrin
Westmoreland County Community College

Robert Vodde
Fairleigh Dickinson University

REVIEWERS OF THE FIRST, SECOND, THIRD, FOURTH, FIFTH AND SIXTH EDITIONS

We appreciate the assistance of the following reviewers whose guidance helped create the foundation for this best seller. We are grateful to all.

Angela Ambers-Henderson
Montgomery County
Community College

Gaylene Armstrong
Southern Illnois University

Judge James Bachman
Bowling Green State University

Tom Barclay
University of South Alabama

Julia Beeman
University of North Carolina
at Charlotte

Lee Roy Black
California University of Pennsylvania

Anita Blowers
University of North Carolina
at Charlotte

Stefan Bosworth
Hostos Community College

Michael E. Boyko
Cuyahoga Community College

John Bower
Bethel College

Steven Brandl
University of Wisconsin–Milwaukee

Charles Brawner III
Heartland Community College

Timothy M. Bray
University of Texas–Dallas

Susan Brinkley
University of Tampa

Paula Broussard
University of Southwestern Louisiana

Michael Brown
Ball State College

Theodore Byrne
California State University,
Dominguez Hills

Patrick Buckley
San Bernardino Valley College

Joseph Bunce
Montgomery College–Rockville

James T. Burnett
SUNY, Rockland Community College

Ronald Burns
Texas Christian University

Paul Campbell
Wayne State College

Dae Chang
Wichita State University

Steven Chermak
Indiana University

Charlie Chukwudolue
Northern Kentucky University

Monte Clampett
Asheville-Buncombe Community
College

John Cochran
University of South Florida

Ellen G. Cohn
Florida International University

Mark Correia
University of Nevada–Reno

Corey Colyer
West Virginia University

Theodore Darden
College of Du Page

John del Nero
Lane Community College

Richard H. De Lung
Wayland Baptist University

John Dempsey
Suffolk County Community College

Tom Dempsey
Christopher Newport University

Joyce Dozier
Wilmington College

Frank J. Drummond
Modesto Junior College

M. G. Eichenberg
Wayne State College

Frank L. Fischer
Kankakee Community College

Linda L. Fleischer
The Community College
of Baltimore County

Aric Steven Frazier
Vincennes University

Frederick Galt
Dutchess Community College

Phyllis Gerstenfeld
California State University Stanislaus

James Gilbert
University of Nebraska–Kearney

Dean Golding
West Chester University
of Pennsylvania

Debbie Goodman
Miami-Dade Community College

Cecil Greek
Florida State University

Donald Grubb
Northern Virginia Community College

Sharon Halford
Community College of Aurora

Michael Hallett
Middle Tennessee State University

Mark Hansel
Moorhead State University

Pati Hendrickson
Tarleton State University

Michelle Heward
Weber State University

Dennis Hoffman
University of Nebraska–Omaha

Richard Holden
Central Missouri State University

Ronald Holmes
University of Louisville

Marilyn Horace-Moore
Eastern Michigan University

Matrice Hurrah
Shelby State Community College

Robert Jerin
Endicott College

Nicholas Irons
County College of Morris

Michael Israel
Kean University

J. D. Jamieson
Southwest Texas State University

James Jengeleski
Shippensburg University

Paul Johnson
Weber State University

Casey Jordan
Western Connecticut State
University

Matthew Kanjirathinkal
Texas A & M University–Commerce

Bill Kelly
University of Texas–Austin

David Kotajarvi
Lakeshore Technical College

John H. Kramer
Pennsylvania State University

Kristen Kuehnle
Salem State University

Karl Kunkel
Southwest Missouri State

James G. Larson
National University

Barry Latzer
John Jay College of Criminal Justice

Deborah Laufersweiler-Dwyer
University of Arkansas at Little Rock

Paul Lawson
Montana State University

Nella Lee
Portland State University

Walter Lewis
St. Louis Community College–
Meramec

Larry Linville
Northern Virginia Community College

Faith Lutze
Washington State University

Richard Martin
Elgin Community College

Richard H. Martin
University of Findlay

William J. Mathias
University of South Carolina

Janet McClellan
Southwestern Oregon
Community College

Pat Murphy
State University of New York–
Geneseo

Rebecca Nathanson
Housatonic Community
Technical College

Ellyn Ness
Mesa Community College

Kenneth O'Keefe
Prairie State College

Michael Palmiotto
Wichita State University

Rebecca D. Petersen
University of Texas, San Antonio

Gary Prawel
Monroe Community College

Mark Robarge
Mansfield University

Matt Robinson
Appalachian State University

Debra Ross
Buffalo State College

William Ruefle
University of South Carolina

Gregory Russell
Washington State University

John Scheb II
University of Tennessee–Knoxville

Melinda Schlager
University of Texas at Arlington

Ed Selby
Southwestern College

Larry Snyder
Herkimer County Community College

Ronald Sopenoff
Brookdale Community College

Domenick Stampone
Raritan Valley Community College

Katherine Steinbeck
Lakeland Community College

Hallie Stephens
Southeastern Oklahoma
State University

Kathleen M. Sweet
St. Cloud State University

Gregory Talley
Broome Community College

Karen Terry
John Jay College of
Criminal Justice

Amy B. Thistlethwaite
Northern Kentucky University

Rebecca Titus
New Mexico Junior College

Lawrence F. Travis III
University of Cincinnati

Kimberly Vogt
University of Wisconsin–La Crosse

Robert Wadman
Weber State University

Ron Walker
Trinity Valley Community College

John Wyant
Illinois Central College

Others were instrumental in bringing this Seventh Edition to fruition. We continue to appreciate the extensive research efforts of Shawn G. Miller and the additional legal assistance of William Eric Hollowell. Robert Jucha, our developmental editor, provided equal parts elbow grease and creative energy; it was a pleasure to work with him. Editor Carolyn Hendersen Meier supplied crucial guidance to the project through her suggestions and recommendations. At the production end, we once again feel fortunate to have enjoyed the services of our tireless production manager, Ann Borman, who oversaw virtually all aspects of this book. How she was able to make all of the schedules on time never ceased to amaze us. Additionally, we wish to thank the designer of this new edition, RHDG of San Francisco, who has created what we believe to be the most dazzling and student-friendly design of any text in the field. Photo researcher Anne Sheroff went to great lengths to satisfy our requests, and we sincerely appreciate her efforts. We are also thankful for the services of all those at Parkwood Composition who worked on the Seventh Edition, particularly Debbie Mealey. The eagle eyes of Pat Lewis, Loretta Palagi, and Kristi Wiswell who shared the duties of proofreading and copy editing, were invaluable.

A special word of thanks must also go to the team responsible for the extensive multimedia package included in this project, including media editor for Criminal Justice, Andy Yap, and writer Robert C. De Lucia of John Jay College of Criminal Justice. In addition, we appreciate the work of Julia Campbell of the University of Nebraska–Kearney, who created annotations for the *Annotated Instructor's Edition*, revised the *Instructor's Resource Manual*, and Nathan Moran of Midwestern State University who created the *Lesson Plans* and *PowerPoints*. We also appreciate the work of Janine Kremling of California State University, San Berndino for revising the Study Guide and Pamela Donovan of Bloomsburg Unviersity for revising the web quizzing. We are also grateful for the aid of assistant editor Rachel McDonald and editorial assistant Virginette Acacio who ensured the timely publication of supplements. A final thanks to all of the great people in marketing and advertising who helped to get the word out about the book, including marketing manager Michelle Williams, who has been tireless in her attention to this project, and marketing communications manager Heather Baxley for keeping everything on track.

Any criminal justice text has to be considered a work in progress. We know that there are improvements that we can make. Therefore, write us with any suggestions that you may have.

L. K. G.
R. L. M.

DEDICATION

This book is dedicated to my good friend and colleague, Lawrence Walsh, of the Lexington, Kentucky Police Department. When I was a rookie, he taught me about policing. When I became a researcher, he taught me about the practical applications of knowledge. He is truly an inspiring professional in our field.

L.K.G.

To Mac,

from whom I learned
so much.

R.L.M.

CHAPTER

1

Criminal Justice Today

AP Photo/*Springfield News-Sun*, Marshall Gorby

LEARNING OBJECTIVES

After reading this chapter, you should be able to . . .

LO 1 Describe the two most common models of how society determines which acts are criminal.

LO 2 Define *crime* and identify the different types of crime.

LO 3 Outline the three levels of law enforcement.

LO 4 List the essential elements of the corrections system.

LO 5 Explain the difference between the formal and informal criminal justice processes.

LO 6 Describe the layers of the "wedding cake" model.

LO 7 Contrast the crime control and due process models.

LO 8 List the major issues in criminal justice today.

The eight learning objectives labeled LO 1 through LO 8 are designed to help improve your understanding of the chapter.

WARNING SIGNS

During his time at Pima Community College in Tucson, Arizona, Jared Loughner was hardly a model student. Over a seven-month stretch in 2010, Loughner had no fewer than seven contacts with campus police. In one classroom incident, which led an officer to suggest that school administrators "keep an eye" on Loughner, he blurted out that dynamite ought to be strapped to baby suicide bombers. In another, Loughner confronted a teacher for giving him a B in her Pilates course. Following a bizarre argument over the meaning of the "number 6," math instructor Ben McGahee began watching Loughner out of the corner of his eye. "I was afraid he was going to pull out a weapon," said McGahee.

College officials finally suspended Loughner in late September after he made a YouTube video describing Pima as "my genocide school" and calling it "one of the biggest scams in America." The suspension did little to curtail Loughner's pattern of disturbing behavior. He had a 9-millimeter bullet tattooed on his right shoulder. He posted incomprehensible tutorials concerning U.S. currency on the Internet. He purchased a Glock 19 semiautomatic pistol and took pictures of himself posing with the gun while wearing only a bright red G-string.

Then, at 5 A.M. on the morning of January 8, 2011, Loughner posted a chilling message on his Myspace page: "Goodbye. Dear friends . . . please don't be mad at me." Several hours later, he opened fire with his Glock 19 into a crowd that had gathered outside a supermarket to "meet-and-greet" Arizona congresswoman Gabrielle Giffords. Before being wrestled to the ground, Loughner killed six of the attendees and wounded thirteen, including Giffords, who was shot in the head. "It wasn't a case of 'Gee, no one saw this coming,'" said Randy Borum, a violent crime expert at the University of South Florida, referring to Loughner's behavior leading up to the tragedy. "People saw it. But the question then was, what do you do about it? Who do you call?"

Jared Loughner has been charged with killing six people and injuring thirteen during an attempt to assassinate Arizona Representative Gabrielle Giffords.

Richard B. Levine/Newscom

By all accounts, Pima Community College officials had taken the threat posed by Jared Loughner seriously. The school's Behavior Assessment Committee had identified him as a "person of concern," which led to his eventual suspension. Just a week before Loughner's shooting rampage, college police commander Manny Amado announced plans to circulate the twenty-two-year-old's photo to staff members as a precautionary measure.[1] The problem, perhaps, was that Pima officials had failed to warn local law enforcement about Loughner's behavior. Even if they had issued such a warning, though, it seems unlikely that it would have been heeded. "Students get kicked out of school for a multitude of reasons," says security expert Dan Borelli. "That doesn't necessarily mean that they're going to go kill somebody."[2]

The Loughner case raises several other interesting issues. First, a number of observers believe that his odd behavior in the months leading up to the massacre can be attributed to a form of delusional thinking known as schizophrenia. In Chapter 2, we will address the question of whether mental illness causes criminal behavior. Second, if Loughner is truly mentally ill, how should he be punished for his actions? In Chapter 4, you will learn about the insanity defense and its place in American criminal courts. Finally, if Loughner is ultimately found guilty on several charges of murder and attempted murder, should he be put to death? As we shall see in Chapter 11, capital punishment is one of the most hotly debated topics in criminal justice.

As you proceed through this textbook, you will see that few aspects of the criminal justice system are ever simple, even though you may have clear opinions about them. In this first chapter, we will introduce you to the criminal justice system by discussing its structure, the values that it is designed to promote, and the most challenging issues it faces today.

WHAT IS CRIME?

Three years before he opened fire on Gabrielle Giffords and his other victims, Jared Loughner was arrested on a minor drug charge related to marijuana use. For all his "creepy," "very hostile," and "suspicious" behavior, this was the only *criminal* wrongdoing in Loughner's past. Throughout this textbook, the word *crime* will be used only to describe a certain category of behavior that goes beyond making inappropriate comments in a classroom or on the Internet. In general, a crime can be defined as a wrong against society proclaimed by law and, if committed under certain circumstances, punishable by society.

One problem with this definition, however, is that it obscures the complex nature of societies. A society is not static—it evolves and changes, and its concept of criminality evolves and changes as well. Different societies can have vastly different ideas of what constitutes a crime. In 2010, for example, Thai police arrested Thanthawut Thaweevarodomkul for operating a Web site that allegedly disparaged King Bhumibol Adulyadej. Thailand's criminal code prohibits anyone from "defaming" or "insulting" a member of the country's royal family. Such legislation protecting public figures from criticism would not be allowed in the United States because of our country's long tradition of free speech. (See the feature *Comparative Criminal Justice—Unveiling France* on the following page to learn about another foreign criminal law that runs counter to America's legal traditions.)

LO 1 To more fully understand the concept of crime, it will help to examine the two most common models of how society "decides" which acts are criminal: the consensus model and the conflict model.

THE CONSENSUS MODEL

The term *consensus* refers to general agreement among the majority of any particular group. Thus, the consensus model rests on the assumption that as people gather together to form a society, its members will naturally come to a basic agreement with regard to shared norms and values. Those individuals whose actions deviate from the established norms and values are considered to pose a threat to the well-being of society as a whole and must be sanctioned (punished). The society passes laws to control and prevent unacceptable behavior, thereby setting the boundaries for acceptable behavior within the group.[3]

The consensus model, to a certain extent, assumes that a diverse group of people can have similar morals. In other words, they share an ideal of what is "right" and "wrong." Consequently, as public attitudes toward morality change, so do laws. In sixteenth-century America, a person found guilty of *adultery* (having sexual relations with someone other than one's spouse) could expect to be publicly whipped, branded, or even executed. Furthermore, a century ago, one could walk into a pharmacy and purchase heroin. Today, social attitudes have shifted to consider adultery a personal issue, beyond the reach of the state, and to consider the sale of heroin a criminal act.

THE CONFLICT MODEL

Some people reject the consensus model on the ground that moral attitudes are not constant or even consistent. In large, democratic societies such as the United States, different groups of citizens have widely varying opinions on controversial issues of morality and criminality such as abortion, the war on drugs, immigration, and assisted suicide.

Crime An act that violates criminal law and is punishable by criminal sanctions.

Consensus Model A criminal justice model in which the majority of citizens in a society share the same values and beliefs. Criminal acts are acts that conflict with these values and beliefs and that are deemed harmful to society.

Morals Principles of right and wrong behavior, as practiced by individuals or by society.

Discussion Tip: Ask students to debate the idea that society's definition of criminality evolves and changes. At what point does deviant behavior cross the line and become criminal? Can students cite examples of these changes from their own lifetimes? Are there any behaviors, presently legal, that students believe may be criminalized at some point in the future?

The **Crime and Courts** page of msnbc.com offers an interesting selection of the day's top criminal justice news stories. Find this Web site by visiting the *Criminal Justice CourseMate* at **cengagebrain.com** and selecting the *Web links* for this chapter.

Critical Thinking Skill Development: Have students respond to "Questions for Critical Analysis" number one on page 29, in which they consider the consensus model. (LO 1)

UNVEILING FRANCE

As of March 2011, a new French law prohibits any person from wearing "a garment aimed at concealing his [or her] face in a public area." Although the wording of the prohibition seems quite broad, in practice it is meant to target a very specific segment of France's population: Muslim women who cover themselves with a *burqa* (head-to-toe robe) or a *niqab* (face veil). The law imposes a fine of $190 for covering one's own face in this manner, while forcing a woman to wear a *burqa* or *niqab* is punishable by a year in prison or a $19,000 fine.

Given that many Muslim women, in France and elsewhere, voluntarily hide their faces, the law has faced harsh criticism for restricting religious and cultural freedom. "It is important for Western countries to avoid impeding Muslim citizens from practicing religion as they see fit—for instance, by dictating what clothes a Muslim woman should wear," said U.S. president Barack Obama. Roughly 80 percent of the French public supports the ban, however. Politicians in that country claim that extreme Muslim fundamentalists force their wives and daughters to wear *burqas* and *niqabs,* and that concealing "one's face under the all-body veil is contrary to public social order."

Opponents of the ban point out that only 2,000 French women—out of a total national population of about 65 million—dress in this manner. The new law, they insist, places suspicion on all of France's 5 million Muslims. "It's upsetting," says Zaima Dendoune, who works as a religion teacher at a Muslim school near Paris. "One thing we are not is terrorists."

FOR CRITICAL ANALYSIS

Because the First Amendment to the U.S. Constitution forbids any law "prohibiting the free exercise of religion," a *burqa/niqab* ban in this country is highly unlikely. Still, American law does criminalize certain religious behavior, such as *polygamy* (having more than one legal spouse) and the use of certain hallucinogenic drugs in Native American ceremonies. Under what circumstances is society justified in restricting religious behavior through criminal law?

Conflict Model A criminal justice model in which the content of criminal law is determined by the groups that hold economic, political, and social power in a community.

Teaching Tip: In a written assignment, ask students which model (consensus or conflict) they subscribe to and why? (LO 1)

These groups and their elected representatives are constantly coming into conflict with one another. According to the conflict model, then, the most politically powerful segments of society—based on class, income, age, and race—have the most influence on criminal laws and are therefore able to impose their values on the rest of the community.

Consequently, what is deemed criminal activity is determined by whichever group happens to be holding power at any given time. Because certain groups do not have access to political power, their interests are not served by the criminal justice system. To give one example, with the exception of Oregon and Washington State, physician-assisted suicide is illegal in the United States. Although opinion polls show that the general public is evenly divided on the issue,[4] several highly motivated interest groups have been able to convince lawmakers that the practice goes against America's shared moral and religious values. This line of thinking is evident in the case of eighty-eight-year-old Roy Charles Laird, who, in 2010, fatally shot his ill, long-suffering wife, Clara, at her nursing home in Seal Beach, California. According to their daughter, Laird performed a "mercy killing" out of love and concern.[5] According to Orange County officials, however, his actions were criminal, and, whatever his motivation, Laird faces a fifty-year prison sentence for murder.

AN INTEGRATED DEFINITION OF CRIME

LO 2 Considering both the consensus and conflict models, we can construct a definition of crime that will be useful throughout this textbook. For our purposes, crime is an action or activity that is:

1. Punishable under criminal law, as determined by the majority or, in some instances, by a powerful minority.

2. Considered an *offense against society as a whole* and prosecuted by public officials, not by victims and their relatives or friends.

3. Punishable by sanctions based on laws that bring about the loss of personal freedom or life.

At this point, it is important to understand the difference between crime and deviance, or behavior that does not conform to the norms of a given community or society. Deviance is a subjective concept. For example, some segments of society may think that smoking marijuana or killing animals for clothing and food is deviant behavior. Deviant acts become crimes only when society as a whole, through its legislatures, determines that those acts should be punished—as is the situation today in the United States with using illegal drugs but not with eating meat. Furthermore, not all crimes are considered particularly deviant—little social disapprobation is attached to those who fail to follow the letter of parking laws. In essence, criminal law reflects those acts that we, as a society, agree are so unacceptable that steps must be taken to prevent them from occurring.

In 2010, the federal government and several state governments banned the sale of Four Loko, here being enjoyed by college students in Fort Collins, Colorado. The drink, known as "blackout in a can," combines the alcohol content of nearly six beers with a strong dose of caffeine. Why might society demand that the sale of this product be made a criminal offense?
Matthew Staver/Landov

TYPES OF CRIME

The manner in which crimes are classified depends on their seriousness. Federal, state, and local legislation has provided for the classification and punishment of hundreds of thousands of different criminal acts, ranging from jaywalking to first degree murder. For general purposes, we can group criminal behavior into six categories: violent crime, property crime, public order crime, white-collar crime, organized crime, and high-tech crime.

VIOLENT CRIME Crimes against persons, or *violent crimes,* have come to dominate our perspectives on crime. There are four major categories of violent crime:

- Murder, or the unlawful killing of a human being.
- Sexual assault, or *rape,* which refers to coerced actions of a sexual nature against an unwilling participant.
- Assault and battery, two separate acts that cover situations in which one person physically attacks another (battery) or, through threats, intentionally leads another to believe that he or she will be physically harmed (assault).
- Robbery, or the taking of funds, personal property, or any other article of value from a person by means of force or fear.

As you will see in Chapter 4, these violent crimes are further classified by *degree,* depending on the circumstances surrounding the criminal act. These circumstances include the intent of the person committing the crime, whether a weapon was used, and (in cases other than murder) the level of pain and suffering experienced by the victim.

PROPERTY CRIME The most common form of criminal activity is *property crime,* or those crimes in which the goal of the offender is some form of economic gain or the damaging of property. Pocket picking, shoplifting, and the stealing of any property that is not accomplished by force are covered by laws against larceny, also known as *theft.*

Deviance Behavior that is considered to go against the norms established by society.

Murder The unlawful killing of one human being by another.

Sexual Assault Forced or coerced sexual intercourse (or other sexual acts).

Assault A threat or an attempt to do violence to another person that causes that person to fear immediate physical harm.

Battery The act of physically contacting another person with the intent to do harm, even if the resulting injury is insubstantial.

Robbery The act of taking property from another person through force, threat of force, or intimidation.

Larceny The act of taking property from another person without the use of force with the intent of keeping that property.

Discussion Tip: Have students debate the concept of victimless crimes. Why are public order crimes referred to as victimless crimes? Ask students if they believe there are any "true" victimless offenses. (LO 2)

Burglary refers to the unlawful entry of a structure with the intention of committing a serious crime such as theft. *Motor vehicle theft* describes the theft or attempted theft of a motor vehicle, including all cases in which automobiles are taken by persons not having lawful access to them. *Arson* is also a property crime. It involves the willful and malicious burning of a home, automobile, commercial building, or any other construction.

PUBLIC ORDER CRIME The concept of public order crimes is linked to the consensus model discussed earlier. Historically, societies have always outlawed activities that are considered contrary to public values and morals. Today, the most common public order crimes include public drunkenness, prostitution, gambling, and illicit drug use. These crimes are sometimes referred to as *victimless crimes* because they often harm only the offender. As you will see throughout this textbook, however, that term is rather misleading. Public order crimes may create an environment that gives rise to property and violent crimes.

WHITE-COLLAR CRIME Business-related crimes are popularly referred to as white-collar crimes. The term *white-collar crime* is broadly used to describe an illegal act or series of acts committed by an individual or business entity using some nonviolent means to obtain a personal or business advantage. As you will see in Chapter 17, when we consider the topic in much greater detail, certain property crimes fall into this category when committed in a business context. Although the extent of this criminal activity is difficult to determine with any certainty, the Association of Certified Fraud Examiners estimates that white-collar crime costs businesses worldwide as much as $2.9 trillion a year.[6]

ORGANIZED CRIME White-collar crime involves the use of legal business facilities and employees to commit illegal acts. For example, a bank teller can't embezzle unless he or she is first hired as a legal employee of the bank. In contrast, organized crime describes illegal acts by illegal organizations, usually geared toward satisfying the public's demand for unlawful goods and services. Organized crime broadly implies a conspiratorial and illegal relationship among any number of persons engaged in unlawful acts. More specifically, groups engaged in organized crime employ criminal tactics such as violence, corruption, and intimidation for economic gain. The hierarchical structure of organized crime operations often mirrors that of legitimate businesses, and, like any corporation, these groups attempt to capture a sufficient percentage of any given market to make a profit. For organized crime, the traditional preferred markets are gambling, prostitution, illegal narcotics, and loan sharking (lending funds at higher-than-legal interest rates), along with more recent ventures into counterfeiting and credit-card scams.

HIGH-TECH CRIME The newest variation on crime is directly related to the increased presence of computers in everyday life. The Internet, with approximately 1.5 billion users worldwide, is the site of numerous *cyber crimes*, such as selling pornographic materials, soliciting minors, and defrauding consumers through bogus financial investments. The dependence of businesses on computer operations has left corporations vulnerable to sabotage, fraud, embezzlement, and theft of proprietary data. Figure 1.1 on the facing page describes several of the most common

Angelo Spata, center, was one of more than 110 suspects arrested by law enforcement agents in January 2011 as part of a massive crackdown on organized crime. According to a government official, most of the arrests were for standard mob activities. What criminal activity would that description cover?
AP Photo/Louis Lanzano

FIGURE 1.1 Types of Cyber Crime

Cyber Crimes against Persons and Property

- *Cyber Fraud:* Any misrepresentation knowingly made over the Internet with the intention of deceiving another person.
- *Identity Theft:* The appropriation of identity information, such as a person's name, driver's license, or Social Security number, to illegally access the victim's financial resources.
- *Cyberstalking:* Use of the Internet, e-mail, or any other form of electronic communication to attempt to contact and/or intimidate another person.

Cyber Crimes in the Business World

- *Hacking/Cracking:* The act of employing one computer to gain illegal access to the information stored on another computer.
- *Malware Production:* The creation of programs harmful to computers, such as worms, Trojan horses, and viruses.
- *Intellectual Property Theft:* The illegal appropriation of property that results from intellectual creative processes, such as films, video games, and software, without compensating its owners.

Cyber Crimes against the Community

- *Online Child Pornography:* The illegal selling, posting, and distributing of material depicting children engaged in sexually explicit conduct.
- *Online Gambling:* The use of the Internet to conduct gambling operations that would be illegal if carried out in the "real" world.

cyber crimes, and we will address this particular criminal activity in much greater detail in Chapter 17.

SELFASSESSMENT

Fill in the blanks and check your answers on page 28.

A criminal act is a wrong against _____ and therefore is "avenged," or prosecuted, by _____ _____, not by the individual victims of a crime. A crime is not the same as an act of _____, the term for behavior that is nonconformist but not necessarily criminal. Murder, assault, and robbery are labeled _____ crimes because they are committed against persons. The category of crime that includes larceny, motor vehicle theft, and arson is called _____ crime. When a criminal acts to gain an illegal business advantage, he or she has committed what is commonly known as a _____-_____ crime.

THE CRIMINAL JUSTICE SYSTEM

Defining which actions are to be labeled "crimes" is only the first step in safeguarding society from criminal behavior. Institutions must be created to apprehend alleged wrongdoers, to determine whether these persons have indeed committed crimes, and to punish those who are found guilty according to society's wishes. These institutions combine to form the **criminal justice system.** As we begin our examination of the American criminal justice system in this introductory chapter, it is important to have an idea of its purpose.

THE PURPOSE OF THE CRIMINAL JUSTICE SYSTEM

In 1967, the President's Commission on Law Enforcement and Administration of Justice stated that the criminal justice system is obliged to enforce accepted standards of conduct so as to "protect individuals and the community."[7] Given this general mandate,

Criminal Justice System The interlocking network of law enforcement agencies, courts, and corrections institutions designed to enforce criminal laws and protect society from criminal behavior.

we can further separate the purpose of the modern criminal justice system into three general goals:

1. To control crime
2. To prevent crime
3. To provide and maintain justice

CONTROLLING AND PREVENTING CRIME Though many observers differ on the precise methods of reaching them, the first two goals are fairly straightforward. By arresting, prosecuting, and punishing wrongdoers, the criminal justice system attempts to *control* crime. In the process, the system also hopes to *prevent* new crimes from taking place. The prevention goal is often used to justify harsh punishments for wrongdoers, which some see as deterring others from committing similar criminal acts.

MAINTAINING JUSTICE The third goal—providing and maintaining justice—is more complicated, largely because *justice* is a difficult concept to define. Broadly stated, justice means that all individuals are equal before the law and that they are free from arbitrary arrest or seizure as defined by the law. In other words, the idea of justice is linked with the idea of fairness. Above all, we want our laws and the means by which they are carried out to be fair.

Justice and fairness are subjective terms, which is to say that people may have different concepts of what is just and fair. If a woman who has been beaten by her husband retaliates by killing him, what is her just punishment? Reasonable persons could disagree, with some thinking that the homicide was justified and that she should be treated leniently. Others might insist that she should not have taken the law into her own hands. Police officers, judges, prosecutors, prison administrators, and other employees of the criminal justice system must decide what is "fair." Sometimes, their course of action is obvious, but often, as we shall see, it is not.

Society places the burden of controlling crime, preventing crime, and determining fairness on those citizens who work in the three main institutions of the criminal justice system: law enforcement, courts, and corrections. In the next section, we take an introductory look at these institutions and their role in the criminal justice system as a whole.

Justice The quality of fairness that must exist in the processes designed to determine whether individuals are guilty of criminal wrongdoing.

Federalism A form of government in which a written constitution provides for a division of powers between a central government and several regional governments. In the United States, the division of powers between the federal government and the fifty states is established by the Constitution.

THE STRUCTURE OF THE CRIMINAL JUSTICE SYSTEM

To understand the structure of the criminal justice system, you must understand the concept of **federalism,** which means that government powers are shared by the national (federal) government and the states. The framers of the U.S. Constitution, fearful of tyranny and a too-powerful central government, chose the system of federalism as a compromise. The appeal of federalism was that it established a strong national government capable of handling large-scale problems while allowing for state powers and local traditions. For example, earlier in the chapter we noted that physician-assisted suicide, though banned in most of the country, is legal in Oregon and Washington State. Several years ago, the federal government challenged the decision made by voters in these two states to allow the practice. The United States Supreme Court sided with the states, ruling that the principle of federalism supported their freedom to differ from the majority viewpoint in this instance.[8]

The Constitution gave the national government certain express powers, such as the power to coin money, raise an army, and regulate interstate commerce. All other powers were left to the states, including police power, which allows the states to enact whatever laws are necessary to protect the health, morals, safety, and welfare of their citizens. As the American criminal justice system has evolved, the ideals of federalism have ebbed somewhat. In particular, the powers of the national government have expanded significantly. (For a better understanding of how federalism works, see the feature *You Be the Senator—Banning Texting While Driving* below.)

LAW ENFORCEMENT The ideals of federalism can be clearly seen in the local, state, and federal levels of law enforcement. Though agencies from the different levels cooperate if the need arises, they have their own organizational structures and tend to operate independently of one another. We briefly introduce each level of law enforcement here and cover them in more detail in Chapters 5, 6, and 7.

Local Law Enforcement On the local level, the duties of law enforcement agencies are

LO 3

split between counties and municipalities. The chief law enforcement officer of most counties is the county sheriff. The sheriff is usually an elected post, with a two- or four-year term. In some areas, where city and county governments have merged, there is a county police force, headed by a chief of police. As Figure 1.2 on the following page shows, the bulk of all police officers in the United States are employed on a local level. The majority of these work in departments that consist of fewer than 10 officers, though a large city such as New York may have a police force of about 38,000.

Local police are responsible for the "nuts and bolts" of law enforcement work. They investigate most crimes and attempt to deter crime through patrol activities. They

Teaching Tip: Invite representatives from municipal and county law enforcement agencies to visit the classroom. Ask them to talk about their respective agencies, jurisdictions, and the challenges they face working together to address crime in your community. (LO 3)

YOU BE THE SENATOR

Banning Texting While Driving

THE SITUATION According to a recent poll, one in five American drivers—and half of those between the ages of sixteen and twenty-four—admits to having texted on a cell phone, BlackBerry, or other electronic device while driving. Texting while behind the wheel makes our roads less safe—one study found that such behavior is twice as risky as driving with a 0.08 blood alcohol level, the general standard for drunk driving. The U.S. Transportation Department estimates that every year nearly 6,000 people are killed and another 530,000 are injured in car crashes connected to "distracted driving," which often involves cell phones or other mobile devices.

THE LAW Thirty states ban texting while driving. Punishments vary: in California, the offense warrants a $20 fine, while in Utah it can result in three months in jail. The effectiveness of these state laws is somewhat questionable, however. In Missouri, state patrol officers, finding it difficult to determine when a person was texting behind the wheel, cited only eight offenders in the first five months after that state's prohibition went into effect. Furthermore, texting bans did nothing to reduce the number of auto accidents in four states surveyed between 2009 and 2010, as most drivers appeared to be ignoring the laws.

YOUR DECISION Suppose that you are a U.S. senator representing your home state, and a colleague introduces a bill that would give the federal government the power to force all states to ban texting while driving. Would you support this bill? Why or why not? What are the benefits and drawbacks of letting each state decide its own response to this problem?

To see how the U.S. Senate has responded to state texting bans, go to Example 1.1 in Appendix B.

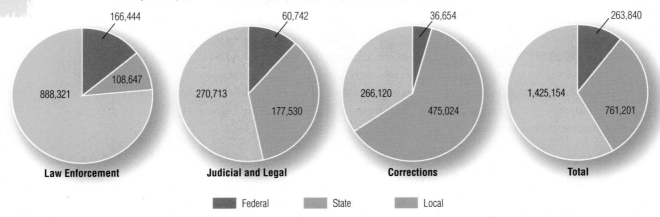

Source: Bureau of Justice Statistics, *Justice Expenditure and Employment in the United States, 2007* (Washington, D.C.: U.S. Department of Justice, September 2010), Table 2.

apprehend criminals and participate in trial proceedings, if necessary. Local police are also charged with "keeping the peace," a broad set of duties that includes crowd and traffic control and the resolution of minor conflicts between citizens. In many areas, local police have the added obligation of providing social services such as dealing with domestic violence and child abuse.

State Law Enforcement Hawaii is the only state that does not have a state law enforcement agency. Generally, there are two types of state law enforcement agencies, those designated simply as "state police" and those designated as "highway patrols." State highway patrols concern themselves mainly with infractions on public highways and freeways. Other state law enforcers include fire marshals, who investigate suspicious fires and educate the public on fire prevention; and fish, game, and watercraft wardens, who police a state's natural resources and often oversee its firearms laws. Some states also have alcoholic beverage control officers, as well as agents who investigate welfare and food stamp fraud.

Federal Law Enforcement The enactment of new national anti-terrorism, gun, drug, and violent crime laws over the past forty years has led to an expansion in the size and scope of the federal government's participation in the criminal justice system. The Department of Homeland Security, which we will examine in detail in Chapters 5 and 16, combines the police powers of twenty-four federal agencies to protect the United States from terrorist attacks. Other federal agencies with police powers include the Federal Bureau of Investigation (FBI), the Drug Enforcement Administration (DEA), the U.S. Secret Service, and the Bureau of Alcohol, Tobacco, Firearms and Explosives (ATF). In fact, almost every federal agency, including the postal and forest services, has some kind of police power.

Unlike their local and state counterparts, federal law enforcement agencies operate throughout the United States. In November 2010, for example, the FBI conducted a nationwide sweep to remove children from the illegal sex trade, rescuing sixty-nine teenage prostitutes and arresting more than 880 suspects in cities from Miami to Detroit to Seattle. Federal agencies are also available to provide support for overworked local police departments, as was necessary several years ago when agents from the ATF joined forces with the Coatesville (Pennsylvania) Police Department to combat a series of arson attacks that had plagued the city for fifteen months.

Technology Tip: Students are often unaware of how many different agencies handle state law enforcement. Have students go online and research the state law enforcement agencies operating in your area. Chart the duties of the various agencies in class. (LO 3)

Group Activities: Have students work in groups to research one of the federal agencies mentioned in the text. If time allows, let each group present its findings to the class. (LO 3)

CAREERS IN CJ

FASTFACTS

CRIME SCENE PHOTOGRAPHER, JOB DESCRIPTION:

- Photograph physical evidence and crime scenes related to criminal investigations.

- Also must be able to compose reports; testify in court; understand basic computer software and terminology; operate film and print processors; recognize, evaluate, and correct problems with Photo Lab systems in order to meet quality control standards; produce color correct images; train other personnel.

WHAT KIND OF TRAINING IS REQUIRED?

- One year in a law enforcement or commercial photography OR a degree or certificate in photography and darkroom techniques OR some combination of the above training or experience totaling one year.

- Must be willing to work irregular hours, second and/or third shifts, weekends, holidays, and evenings.

ANNUAL SALARY RANGE? BENEFITS?

- $45,780–$53,290

For additional information on a career as a crime scene/forensic photographer, visit: **www.crime-scene-investigator.net**

Also see Steven Staggs, *Crime Scene and Evidence Photographer's Guide*, 2nd edition.

DIANA TABOR
CRIME SCENE PHOTOGRAPHER

As a kid, one of my favorite books was *The Hardy Boys Detective Handbook.* Years later, a friend of mine was going to Lake Superior State University to major in criminal justice, and I read the handbook to learn what it was about. When I saw the major in *criminalistics,* I knew that was what I wanted to do.

DIRTY WORK Criminalistics is the application of forensic science, crime scene documentation, and evidence collection at the scene, which then directly includes crime scene photography. A crime scene photographer's job is invaluable to those who are not present at the scene, yet need to be able to observe the scene as accurately as possible. I like the variety of my work. No two scenes are exactly alike, and the conditions pose different challenges. I have photographed scenes in cramped mobile homes, spacious homes, and out in the woods where we had to hike because there were no roads leading directly to the scene. I've been really hot and sweaty, fogging up the viewfinder. Then I have been so cold that I had to go sit in the van to let my hands and the camera warm up because they had stopped working.

I do wonder what the people at the gas stations think when we come in there after we're done to clean up and get something to drink. Fingerprint powder gets everywhere—I have found that nothing less than a shower really gets rid of it completely. It is sometimes difficult to accept that there is nothing to prevent the crime that has already happened, but I take pride in representing the victim when he or she cannot speak.

REAL LIFE I tend to get aggravated at the speed depicted in television shows such as the *CSI* series. From the scene to the lab, criminalistics is time-intensive and often laborious, and cases take weeks to work instead of hours or days, like they show on television. I try to wear clothes I won't be upset ruining, and we tend to wear coveralls at scenes, so there's a big difference between how we look and how the actors look. I don't know that television gives anyone a realistic view of life. If people expect to have the high-tech equipment, amazing wardrobe, and impressive vehicles used in these shows, they will be disappointed. If they expect to work with others who are passionate about their job and display an intense attention to detail, then they are in the right place.

CAREER ADVICE A bachelor's degree is not always required, but it is helpful. There are also good associate's degrees in photography that serve as a foundation for crime scene photography. As important as school and relevant coursework are, an internship is possibly the most useful step in becoming a crime scene photographer. An internship allows you to see if this is what you truly are interested in and gives you good connections and first-hand experiences that cannot be gained in a classroom. It also provides a valuable opportunity to learn if you can handle the graphic nature of the work. A potential employer knows that the applicant with internship experience understands what the job really entails as opposed to what it's like on a television show.

AUTHENTIC DETECTIVE METHODS FOR SOLVING MYSTERIES
THE HARDY BOYS' DETECTIVE HANDBOOK
By FRANKLIN W. DIXON
in consultation with CAPTAIN D. A. SPINA
Cover art by Rudi Nappi

FBI agents confer at the crime scene where Jared Loughner went on a shooting rampage, described in the opening of this chapter. Why were federal law enforcement officers able to investigate a criminal act that took place in Tucson, Arizona?
Gary C. Caskey/UPI/Landov

THE COURTS The United States has a *dual court system,* which means that we have two independent judicial systems, one at the federal level and one at the state level. In practice, this translates into fifty-two different court systems: one federal court system and fifty different state court systems, plus that of the District of Columbia. The federal system consists of district courts, circuit courts of appeals, and the United States Supreme Court. The state systems include trial courts, intermediate courts of appeals, and state supreme courts.

The *criminal court* and its work group—the judge, prosecutors, and defense attorneys—are charged with the weighty responsibility of determining the innocence or guilt of criminal suspects. We will cover these important participants, their roles in the criminal trial, and the court system as a whole in Chapters 8, 9, 10, and 11.

LO 4 **CORRECTIONS** Once the court system convicts and sentences an offender, she or he is delegated to the corrections system. (Those convicted in a state court will be under the control of that state's corrections system, and those convicted of a federal crime will find themselves under the control of the federal corrections system.) Depending on the seriousness of the crime and their individual needs, offenders are placed on probation, incarcerated, or transferred to community-based correctional facilities.

- *Probation,* the most common correctional treatment, allows the offender to return to the community and remain under the supervision of an agent of the court known as a probation officer. While on probation, the offender must follow certain rules of conduct. When probationers fail to follow these rules, they may be incarcerated.
- If the offender's sentence includes a period of incarceration, he or she will be remanded to a correctional facility for a certain amount of time. *Jails* hold those convicted of minor crimes with relatively short sentences, as well as those awaiting trial or involved in certain court proceedings. *Prisons* house those convicted of more serious crimes with longer sentences. Generally speaking, counties and municipalities administer jails, while prisons are the domain of federal and state governments.
- *Community-based corrections* have increased in popularity as jails and prisons have been plagued with problems of funding and overcrowding. Community-based correctional facilities include halfway houses, residential centers, and work-release centers. They operate on the assumption that all convicts do not need, and are not benefited by, incarceration in jail or prison.

The majority of those inmates released from incarceration are not finished with the corrections system. The most frequent type of release from a jail or prison is *parole,* in which an inmate, after serving part of his or her sentence in a correctional facility, is allowed to serve the rest of the term in the community. Like someone on probation, a parolee must conform to certain conditions of freedom, with the same consequences if these conditions are not followed. Issues of probation, incarceration, community-based corrections, and parole will be covered in Chapters 12, 13, and 14.

THE CRIMINAL JUSTICE PROCESS

In its 1967 report, the President's Commission on Law Enforcement and Administration of Justice asserted that the criminal justice system is not a hodgepodge of random actions. It is rather a continuum—an orderly progression of events—some of which, like arrest and trial, are highly visible and some of which, though of great importance, occur out of public view.[9]

The commission's assertion that the criminal justice system is a "continuum" is one that many observers would challenge.[10] Some liken the criminal justice system to a sports team, which is the sum of an indeterminable number of decisions, relationships, conflicts, and adjustments.[11] Such a volatile mix is not what we generally associate with a "system." For most, the word system indicates a certain degree of order and discipline. That we refer to our law enforcement agencies, courts, and correctional facilities as part of a "system" may reflect our hopes rather than reality.

THE ASSEMBLY LINE Just as there is an idealized image of the criminal justice system as a smooth continuum, there also exists an idealized version of the *criminal justice process,* or the procedures through which the criminal justice system meets the expectations of society. Professor Herbert Packer, for example, compared the idealized *criminal justice process* to an assembly line,

> down which moves an endless stream of cases, never stopping, carrying the cases to workers who stand at fixed stations and who perform on each case as it comes by the same small but essential operation that brings it one stop closer to being a finished product, or, to exchange the metaphor for the reality, a closed file.[12]

As Packer himself was wont to point out, the daily operations of criminal justice are not nearly so perfect. In this textbook, the criminal justice process will be examined as the end product of many different decisions made by police officers, courtroom workers, and correctional administrators. It should become clear that, in fact, the criminal justice process functions as a continuous balancing act between its formal and informal nature.

FORMAL VERSUS INFORMAL CRIMINAL JUSTICE In Herbert Packer's

LO 5

image of assembly-line justice, each step of the *formal criminal justice process* involves a series of "routinized operations" with the end goal of getting the criminal defendant from point A (her or his arrest by law enforcement) to point B (the criminal trial) to point C (if guilty, her or his punishment).[13] In reality, however, each of these steps is influenced by a series of decisions that must be made by those who work in the criminal justice system. This discretion—which can be defined as the authority to choose between and among alternative courses of action—leads to the development of the *informal criminal justice process,* discussed below.

Discretionary Basics One New York City defense attorney called his job "a pressure cooker." That description could apply to the entire spectrum of the criminal justice process. Law enforcement agencies do not have the staff or funds to investigate *every* crime, so they must decide where to direct their limited resources. Increasing caseloads and a limited amount of time in which to dispose of them constrict many of our nation's courts. Overcrowding in prisons and jails affects both law enforcement agencies and the courts—there is simply not enough room for all convicts.

The criminal justice system uses discretion to alleviate these pressures. Police decide whether to arrest a suspect; prosecutors decide whether to prosecute; magistrates decide whether there is sufficient probable cause for a case to go to a jury; and judges decide on sentencing, to mention only some of the occasions when discretion is used. (See Figure 1.3 on the following page for a description of some of the most important discretionary decisions.) Collectively, these decisions are said to produce an *informal criminal justice system* because

"It is the spirit and not the form of the law that keeps justice alive."

—Earl Warren,
American jurist
(1891–1974)

System A set of interacting parts that, when functioning properly, achieve a desired result.

Discretion The ability of individuals in the criminal justice system to make operational decisions based on personal judgment instead of formal rules or official information.

FIGURE 1.3 Discretion in the Criminal Justice System

Criminal justice officials must make decisions every day concerning their duties. The officials listed below, whether they operate on a local, state, or federal level, rely heavily on discretion when meeting the following responsibilities.

Police	Judges
• Enforce Laws • Investigate specific crimes • Search people or buildings • Arrest or detain people	• Set conditions for pretrial release • Accept pleas • Dismiss charges • Impose sentences

Prosecutors	Correctional Officials
• File charges against suspects brought to them by the police • Drop cases • Reduce charges	• Assign convicts to prison or jail • Punish prisoners who misbehave • Reward prisoners who behave well

Critical Thinking Skill Development: Ask students to consider Figure 1.3, which lists areas in the criminal justice process where discretion may be used. How much discretion do students feel is needed in the criminal justice system? What are the drawbacks of giving criminal justice professionals too much or too little discretion? (LO 5)

"Wedding Cake" Model A wedding cake–shaped model that explains how different cases receive different treatment in the criminal justice system. The cases at the "top" of the cake receive the most attention, while those cases at the "bottom" are disposed of quickly and largely ignored by the media.

FIGURE 1.4
The Wedding Cake Model

1. The "celebrity" cases

2. Serious or "high-profile" felonies

3. Less serious or "ordinary" felonies

4. Misdemeanors

Steven Miric/iStockphoto

discretion is informally exercised by the individual and is not enclosed within the rigid confines of the law. Even if prosecutors believe that a suspect is guilty, they may decide not to prosecute if the case is weak or if they know that the police erred in the investigative process. In most instances, prosecutors will not squander the scarce resource of court time on a case they might not win. Some argue that the informal process has made our criminal justice system more just. Given the immense pressure of limited resources, the argument goes, only rarely will an innocent person end up before a judge and jury.[14]

Discretionary Values Of course, not all discretionary decisions are dictated by the scarcity of resources. Sometimes, discretion is based on policy considerations. For example, many participants in Hempfest, an annual festival in Seattle, Washington, smoke marijuana in public without fear of arrest because that city's police department de-emphasizes minor drug possession offenses.[15] Furthermore, employees of the criminal justice system may make decisions based on their personal values, which, depending on what those values are, may make the system less just in the eyes of some observers. For that reason, discretion is closely connected to questions of *ethics* in criminal justice and will be discussed in that context throughout this textbook.

The "Wedding Cake" Model of Criminal Justice Some believe that the prevailing informal approach to criminal justice creates a situation in which all cases are not treated equally. As anecdotal evidence, they point to a cultural landmark in the American criminal justice system—the highly publicized O. J. Simpson trial of 1995, during which the wealthy, famous defendant had an experience far different from that of most double-murder suspects. To describe this effect, criminal justice researchers Lawrence M. Friedman and Robert V. Percival came up with a "wedding cake" model of criminal justice.[16] This model posits that discretion comes to bear depending on the relative importance of a particular case to the decision makers. Like any wedding cake, Friedman and Percival's model has the smallest layer at the top and the largest at the bottom (see Figure 1.4 alongside).

LO 6

1. The "top" layer consists of a handful of "celebrity" cases that attract the most attention and publicity. Recent examples of top-level cases include the trials of Brian David Mitchell, convicted of kidnapping fourteen-year-old Elizabeth Smart in Salt Lake City, Utah; Rachel Wade of Pinellas Park, Florida, who was sentenced to twenty-seven years in prison for murdering a romantic rival (see the photo on the facing page); and Casey Anthony, found not guilty by a Clearwater, Florida, jury of killing and burying her two-year-old daughter, Caylee.

2. The second layer consists of "high-profile" felonies. A *felony* is a serious crime such as murder, rape, or burglary. This layer includes crimes committed by persons with criminal records, crimes in which the victim was seriously injured, and crimes in which a weapon was used, as well as crimes in which

the offender and victim were strangers. These types of felonies are considered "high profile" because they usually draw a certain amount of public attention, which puts pressure on the prosecutors to bring such a case to trial instead of accepting a guilty plea for a lesser sentence.

3. The third layer consists of "ordinary" felonies, which include less violent crimes such as burglaries and thefts or even robberies in which no weapon was used. Because of the low profile of the accused—usually a first-time offender who has had a prior relationship with his or her victim—these "ordinary" felonies often do not receive the full formal process of a trial.

4. Finally, the fourth layer consists of *misdemeanors,* or crimes less serious than felonies. Misdemeanors include petty offenses such as shoplifting, disturbing the peace, and violations of local ordinances. More than three-quarters of all arrests made by police are for misdemeanors.

The irony of the wedding cake model is that the cases on the top level come closest to meeting our standards of ideal criminal justice. In these celebrity trials, we get to see committed (and expensive) attorneys argue minute technicalities of the law, sometimes for days on end. The further one moves down the layers of the cake, the more informal the process becomes. Though many of the cases in the second layer are brought to trial, only rarely does this occur for the less serious felonies in the third level of the wedding cake. By the fourth level, almost all cases are dealt with informally, and the end goal appears to be speed rather than what can be called "justice."

Public fascination with celebrity cases obscures a truth of the informal criminal justice process: trial by jury is relatively rare (only about 5 percent of those arrested for felonies go to trial). Most cases are disposed of with an eye more toward convenience than ideals of justice or fairness. Consequently, the summary of the criminal justice system provided by the wedding cake model is much more realistic than the impression many Americans have obtained from the media.

Why do high-profile trials, such as the one involving Rachel Wade, left, give the public an unrealistic view of the average criminal trial?
ZUMA Press/Newscom

SELFASSESSMENT

Fill in the blanks and check your answers on page 28.

To protect against a too-powerful central government, the framers of the U.S. Constitution relied on the principle of _____ to balance power between the national government and the states. Consequently, the United States has a _____ court system—one at the federal level and one at the _____ level. At every level, the criminal justice system relies on the _____ of its employees to keep it from being bogged down by formal rules. Some critics think that this freedom to make decisions leads to the "_____ _____" model of criminal justice, in which only the "top" layer of criminal court cases meets ideal standards.

VALUES OF THE CRIMINAL JUSTICE SYSTEM

If the general conclusion of the wedding cake model—that some defendants are treated differently from others—bothers you, then you probably question the values of the system. Just as individuals have values—a belief structure governing individual conduct—our criminal justice system can be said to have values, too. These values form the foundation for Herbert Packer's two models of the criminal justice system, which we discuss next.

CRIME CONTROL AND DUE PROCESS: TO PUNISH OR PROTECT?

In his landmark book *The Limits of the Criminal Sanction,* Packer introduced two models for the American criminal justice system: the crime control model and the due process model.[17] The underlying value of the crime control model is that the most important function of the criminal justice process is to punish and repress criminal conduct. Though not in direct conflict with crime control, the underlying values of the due process model focus more on protecting the civil rights of the accused through legal restraints on the police, courts, and corrections. Civil rights are those rights guaranteed to all Americans in the U.S. Constitution.

THE CRIME CONTROL MODEL Under the crime control model, law enforcement must be counted on to control criminal activity. "Controlling" criminal activity is at best difficult, and probably impossible. For the crime control model to operate successfully, Packer writes, it

> must produce a high rate of apprehension and conviction, and must do so in a context where the magnitudes being dealt with are very large and the resources for dealing with them are very limited.[18]

LO 7

In other words, the system must be quick and efficient. In the ideal crime control model, any suspect who most likely did not commit a crime is quickly jettisoned from the system, while those who are transferred to the trial process are convicted as quickly as possible. It was in this context that Packer referred to the criminal justice process as an assembly line.

The crime control model also assumes that the police are in a better position than the courts to determine the guilt of arrested suspects. Therefore, not only should judges operate on a "presumption of guilt" (that is, any suspect brought before the court is more likely guilty than not), but as few restrictions as possible should be placed on police investigative and fact-gathering activities. The crime control model relies on the informality in the criminal justice system, as discussed earlier.

THE DUE PROCESS MODEL Packer likened the due process model to an obstacle course instead of an assembly line. Rather than expediting cases through the system, as is preferable in the crime control model, the due process model strives to make it more difficult to prove guilt. It rests on the belief that it is more desirable for society that ninety-nine guilty suspects go free than that a single innocent person be condemned.[19]

The due process model is based on the assumption that the absolute efficiency that is the goal of the crime control model can be realized only if the power of the state is absolute. Because fairness, and not efficiency, is the ultimate goal of the due process model, it rejects the idea of a criminal justice system with unlimited powers. As a practical matter, the model also argues that human error in any process is inevitable. Therefore, the criminal justice system should recognize its own fallibility and take all measures necessary to ensure that this fallibility does not impinge on the rights of citizens.

Finally, whereas the crime control model relies heavily on the police, the due process model relies just as heavily on the courts and their role in upholding the legal procedures of establishing guilt. The due process model is willing to accept that a person who is factually guilty will go free if the criminal justice system does not follow legally prescribed procedures in proving her or his culpability.[20] Therefore, the due process model relies on formality in the criminal justice system. *Mastering Concepts* on the facing page provides a further comparison of the two models.

Civil Rights The personal rights and protections guaranteed by the Constitution, particularly the Bill of Rights.

Crime Control Model A criminal justice model that places primary emphasis on the right of society to be protected from crime and violent criminals.

Due Process Model A criminal justice model that places primacy on the right of the individual to be protected from the power of the government.

Technology Tip: Ask students to go online and research the civil rights guaranteed to all Americans in the United States Constitution. If time allows, quiz students on the Bill of Rights. How many students can identify all ten?

MASTERING CONCEPTS

CRIME CONTROL MODEL VERSUS DUE PROCESS MODEL

Crime Control Model

Due Process Model

Goal	Goal
• Deter crime by arresting and incarcerating criminals as quickly and efficiently as possible.	• Protect the individual charged with a crime against the immense and sometimes possibly unjust power of the state.

Methods	Methods
• Allow the police to "do their jobs" by limiting the amount of judicial oversight of law enforcement tactics.	• Assure the constitutional rights of those accused of crimes, at the hands of both the law enforcement officers who make the arrest and the prosecutors who prosecute the defendant in criminal court.
• Limit the number of rights and protections enjoyed by defendants in court.	• Whenever possible, allow nonviolent convicts to serve their sentences in the community rather than behind bars.
• Incarcerate criminals for lengthy periods of time by imposing harsh sentences, including the death penalty.	• Protect the civil rights of all inmates, and focus on rehabilitation rather than punishment in prisons and jails.

WHICH MODEL PREVAILS TODAY?

Although both the crime control and the due process models have always represented the American criminal justice system to some degree, during certain periods one model takes precedence over the other. In general, when crime rates are high, the public demands that politicians get "tough on crime," and the criminal justice system responds by favoring crime control values. When crime rates are in decline, politicians allow the court system to favor due process values. As the second decade of the twenty-first century begins, however, the crime control/due process balance is in flux. Crime rates continue to drop, rates of imprisonment continue to grow (although more slowly than in the past), and a weak economy clashes with homeland security concerns to create a tumultuous criminal justice landscape.

Critical Thinking Skill Development: In a short writing assignment, ask students to compare and contrast Packer's two models. Which model do students believe dominates the criminal justice system today? Which model do students believe should dominate? (LO 7)

SELF ASSESSMENT

Fill in the blanks and check your answers on page 28.

The _____ _____ model of criminal justice places great importance on high rates of apprehension and conviction of criminal suspects. In contrast, the _____ _____ model emphasizes the rights of the _____ over the powers of the state.

Gun Control Efforts by a government to regulate or control the sale of guns.

CRIMINAL JUSTICE TODAY

Over the course of a few months in the autumn of 2010, residents of Killeen, Texas, twice found themselves dealing with the terrible ordeal of a child abduction. First, on October 18, an eleven-year-old girl disappeared while walking to a bus stop. Then, on December 10, a nine-year-old girl, also on her way to meet a bus, vanished. Both girls were eventually found, but not before they had been sexually assaulted. Extensive local television coverage of the incidents raised stress levels in the area, particularly among parents of young children. "I don't let my kids near the door," said Megan Hall, who lives near one of the abduction sites. "I'm just ready to get out of here. It's just crazy."[21]

Such a reaction is understandable, but it may not be necessary. Only about one hundred children are abducted by strangers each year in this country—a very small num-

LO 8

ber, given the population size of those under the age of eighteen in the United States.[22] Almost every time a young child is kidnapped, however, the story receives maximum coverage on television news and the Internet. As a result, according to one expert, "[There] is a persistent perception that every child is a potential victim to the stranger lurking around the corner."[23]

CRIME: THE BOTTOM LINE

When it comes to crime in the United States, perception is often far from reality. A recent Gallup poll, for example, found that two-thirds of the respondents believed crime is on the rise.[24] In fact, as we will discuss more fully in Chapter 3, most Americans are as safe today as they have been in decades. In 2010, violent crime in the United States dropped for the third straight year, and property crime for the seventh straight year, with both indicators nearing record lows.

Professor Richard Rosenfeld of the University of Missouri–St. Louis points out that the good news regarding crime is a "puzzle," albeit a "welcome" one.[25] As we will also see in Chapter 3, most crime experts assume that poor economic conditions lead to higher crime rates. This assumption has proved wrong over the past few years, as the declining crime rates have occurred simultaneously with an extreme economic downturn. Still, Professor James Alan Fox of Northeastern University believes that the weak economy could "come back to haunt us" by producing an environment ripe for crime, marked by shrinking police department budgets and reduced social services for the young, unemployed, and uneducated.[26]

A potential customer examines tactical rifles for sale at Shot Show in Las Vegas, one of the nation's largest weapon bazaars. Why are some Americans against private ownership of firearms, despite dozens of laws designed to regulate the safe use of guns in this country? Isaac Brekken/*New York Times*/Redux Pictures

GUN SALES AND GUN CONTROL Alfred Blumstein of Carnegie Mellon University in Pittsburgh suggests that the most serious threat to America's positive crime outlook is not the economy but an increase in the number of guns in high-crime neighborhoods.[27] Overall, about 30,000 people are killed by gunfire in the United States each year, and illegally obtained firearms are a constant concern for law enforcement officials. At the same time, legal ownership of guns is widespread, with almost one-third of American households possessing at least one gun.[28] A few years ago, the United States Supreme Court further solidified the legal basis for this practice by ruling that the U.S. Constitution protects an individual's right to "bear arms."[29] The Court's decision has done little to lessen the debate over **gun control**, or the policies that the government implements to keep firearms out of the hands of the wrong people. We will take a closer look at this divisive topic in the *CJ in Action* feature at the end of this chapter.

THE ILLEGAL DRUGS PROBLEM Many observers blamed the explosion of violent crime that shook this country in the late 1980s and early 1990s on the widespread use and sale of crack cocaine at the time.[30] Today, fears of a resurgence of drug-related crime are growing because of the situation in Mexico. As we will see in Chapter 3, that country is experiencing an intense wave of violence as criminal cartels (organizations) battle each other for control of the illegal drug trade. Unfortunately, the repercussions of these "drug wars" are starting to be felt in the United States. Officials in Phoenix, Arizona—located about 180 miles from the border—blame Mexican cartels for their city's escalating kidnapping rate and for violent murders such as that of Martin Alejandro Cota-Monroy, who was found beheaded in his apartment in October 2010.[31] Nationwide, the U.S. government has determined that the Mexican cartels "maintain drug distribution networks or supply drugs to distributors" in more than 230 American cities, including Billings, Montana, and Anchorage, Alaska.[32]

Drugs and Crime Criminologists have long studied the link between crime and drugs. In general, offenders who use greater amounts of alcohol and illegal drugs have significantly higher crime rates than those who are less involved with these substances.[33] Actually, alcohol falls under the broadest possible definition of a drug, which is any substance that modifies biological, psychological, or social behavior. In popular terminology, however, the word *drug* has a more specific connotation. When people speak of the "drug" problem, or the war on "drugs," or "drug" abuse, they are referring specifically to illegal psychoactive drugs, which affect the brain and alter consciousness or perception. Almost all of the drugs that we will be discussing in this textbook, such as marijuana, cocaine, heroin, and amphetamines, are illegal and psychoactive.

Drug Use in the United States The main source of drug use data is the National Survey on Drug Use and Health, conducted annually by the National Institute on Drug Abuse (see Figure 1.5 alongside). According to the survey, only about 9 percent of those questioned had used an illegal drug in the past month. Even so, this means that a significant number of Americans—nearly 22 million—are regularly using illegal drugs, and the figure mushrooms when users of legal substances such as alcohol (131 million users) and tobacco (70 million users) are included.[34] Furthermore, illegal drug use appears to be increasing in this country, particularly among young people. Drug abuse often leads to further criminal behavior in adolescents, as we will see when we look at the juvenile justice system in Chapter 15. In general, the growing market for illegal drugs causes significant damage both in the United States and in countries such as Mexico that supply America with its "fix."

Discussion Tip: Place students in small groups to discuss the issue of guns and illegal drugs. How serious do students perceive these issues to be? What tactics do students think are most effective in addressing these issues? (LO 8)

Drug Any substance that modifies biological, psychological, or social behavior; in particular, an illegal substance with those properties.

Psychoactive Drugs Chemicals that affect the brain, causing changes in emotions, perceptions, and behavior.

FIGURE 1.5 **Drug Use in the United States**
According to the National Survey on Drug Use and Health, nearly 22 million Americans, or about 9 percent of those over twelve years old, can be considered "illicit drug users." As you can see, most of these people used marijuana exclusively. Furthermore, eighteen- to twenty-five-year-olds were more likely to have used illegal drugs than any other segment of the population.

Source: National Survey on Drug Use and Health, 2010.

LAW ENFORCEMENT IN THE UNITED STATES: TRADITIONS AND TECHNOLOGY

The effect of law enforcement on crime rates has always been open to debate. Some observers believe that the police are powerless to counter such forces as a declining economy or the numerous social conditions—discussed in the next chapter—that contribute to criminal behavior.[35] Even with this skepticism in mind, however, it would be difficult to deny the crucial role that law enforcement has played in making America a safer place. The crime wave of the late 1980s and early 1990s forced police departments to become more creative, resulting in a crackdown on "quality of life" crimes, such as public urination and vandalism, and a recommitment to a strategy known as "community policing." In Chapter 6, we will take a closer look at both the successes and the failures of these efforts.

THE SCOURGE OF STREET GANGS For many local law enforcement agencies, particularly those in large metropolitan areas, success is measured by their ability to control street gangs—groups of people who band together to engage in violent, unlawful, or criminal activity. According to the most recent data, there are 27,900 gangs in the United States with approximately 774,000 members.[36] Police departments across the country report high levels of gang involvement in firearm possession and trafficking, vandalism and graffiti, auto theft, and illegal drug sales.[37] According to research conducted by the National Gang Intelligence Center, criminal gangs are responsible for 80 percent of the street crime in this country.[38]

To combat major problems such as gangs, guns, and illegal drugs, law enforcement agents continue to rely on the traditional police powers of search, seizure, arrest, and interrogation, the intricacies of which we will discuss in Chapter 7. Each individual police officer is also constantly learning on the job, a process that allows him or her to develop a "sixth sense" about how to detect, investigate, and deter criminal behavior. In addition, law enforcement agencies are becoming much more efficient at managing and analyzing data. Many local police departments are now able to closely track crimes in their jurisdiction with computerized mapping systems. As we will see in Chapter 6, police administrators can react to this information by deploying police officers to the areas where they are most needed.

DNA PROFILING Police investigators are also enjoying the benefits of perhaps the most effective new crime-fighting tool since fingerprint identification: DNA profiling. This technology allows law enforcement agents to identify a suspect from body fluid evidence, such as blood, saliva, or semen, or biological evidence, such as hair strands or fingernail clippings. For example, DNA evidence identified Raul Aragonez, Jr., as the primary suspect in the kidnapping and sexual assault of the two young girls in Killeen, Texas, mentioned on page 20. As we will see in Chapter 6, by collecting DNA from persons convicted of certain felonies and storing that information in databases, investigators have been able to reach across hundreds of miles and back in time to catch wrongdoers.

For all its benefits as a crime-fighting tool, DNA profiling has also forced the criminal justice system to face some of its shortcomings. As of July 2011, DNA evidence had freed 272 people who had been arrested by law enforcement and convicted by the courts.[39] Incompetent and even dishonest police work has often been a contributing factor in the incarceration of these ultimately innocent suspects. In nearly every chapter of this textbook, you will be exposed to exciting new technologies that have the potential to make the criminal justice system more efficient and just. As you will see in the following discussion of *biometrics,* however, technology can be a double-edged sword, providing challenges to the same society that it may ultimately benefit.

Street Gang A group of people, usually three or more, who share a common identity and engage in illegal activities.

Teaching Tip: Ask students to consider the advantages that DNA profiling has provided the criminal justice system. Are there any disadvantages to the widespread use of this procedure?

The science of biometrics involves identifying a person through her or his unique physical characteristics. In the criminal justice context, the term *biometrics* refers to the various technological devices that read these characteristics and report the identity of the subject to the authorities. Today, there are four leading biometric technologies:

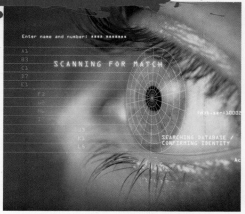

Varie/Alt/Corbis

1. *Fingerprint readers* take photographic images of fingerprints to determine patterns based on the points where the ridges of the fingertips begin, terminate, or split. These patterns are then mathematically encoded and the information stored.

2. *Iris recognition systems* capture about 240 minute details of the eye in a similar manner.

3. *Face recognition systems* use a camera to record from thirty to eighty "markers" on a subject's face, such as cheekbone formations, the width of the nose bridge, and the space between the eyes.

4. *Hand geometry scanners* take and store as many as ninety different measurements, such as vein patterns, distance between knuckles, and the length and width of fingers.

The use of biometrics is becoming more common in law enforcement. More than 2,100 sheriff's departments in twenty-seven states are using iris recognition technology. Many take digital pictures of the eyes of Alzheimer's patients and children to help identify the subjects should they become lost or be abducted. Law enforcement officials in New Mexico scan the irises of convicted sex offenders to keep them from avoiding detection under false names. Experts predict that face recognition systems will eventually allow hidden cameras to check the identities of thousands of people shopping in a mall or taking a stroll in a city park. Furthermore, someday police officers will be able to take a photo of a suspect and instantaneously check the biometric markers against a database of millions for an identifying match.

THINKING ABOUT BIOMETRICS
Do you have any concerns about a technology that would enable the government to identify thousands of people with the sweep of a camera? What would be the benefits and drawbacks of a database that contained biometric information on every person in the United States?

HOMELAND SECURITY AND THE PATRIOT ACT

Without question, the attacks of September 11, 2001—when terrorists hijacked four commercial airlines and used them to kill nearly three thousand people in New York City, northern Virginia, and rural Pennsylvania—were the most significant events of the first decade of the 2000s as far as crime fighting is concerned. As we will see throughout this textbook, the resulting **homeland security** movement has touched nearly every aspect of criminal justice. This movement has the ultimate goal of protecting America from **terrorism**, which can be broadly defined as the random use of staged violence to achieve political goals.

Homeland Security
A concerted national effort to prevent terrorist attacks within the United States and reduce the country's vulnerability to terrorism.

Terrorism The use or threat of violence to achieve political objectives.

The need to respond to the terrorist threat led American politicians and police officials to turn sharply toward crime control principles, as discussed on page 18. In particular, the Patriot Act,[40] passed six weeks after the 9/11 attacks, strengthened the ability of federal law enforcement agents to investigate and incarcerate suspects. The 342-page piece of legislation is difficult to summarize, but some of its key provisions include the following:

Technology Tip: Ask students to go online and explore your local emergency management agency and its partners. How is the threat of terrorism addressed locally? Do students feel that your community is prepared in the event of a terrorist attack?

- An expansion of the definition of what it means to "engage in terrorist activity" to include providing "material support" through such activities as fund-raising or operating Web sites for suspected terrorist organizations.
- Greater leeway for law enforcement agents to track Internet use, access private financial records, and wiretap those suspected of terrorist activity.
- A reduction in the amount of evidence law enforcement agents need to gather before taking a terrorist suspect into custody.

In addition to this kind of legislative action, billions of dollars have been funneled into America's homeland security apparatus, with the majority of the funds going to federal agencies under the control of the Department of Homeland Security. As the feature *Anti-Terrorism in Action—A Close Call* below shows, local police departments are also crucial

ANTI-TERRORISM **IN ACTION**

A CLOSE CALL

Very few people have ever heard of the homegrown American Islamic terrorist group Jam'yyat Al-Islam Al Saheeh (JIS). If not for a dropped cell phone, however, JIS might well be as notorious as al Qaeda. The cell phone in question belonged to Gregory Patterson, who, along with Levar Haney Washington and Hammad Riaz Samana, robbed a string of gas stations in Torrance, California, in 2005. Local police had few clues concerning the robberies until they found the cell phone, which led to the arrest of the men and a search of Washington's apartment. Much to the officers' surprise, this search uncovered a cache of terrorist materials: bulletproof vests, knives, jihadist literature, and the addresses of potential bombing targets such as National Guard facilities, army recruitment centers, and Jewish synagogues in Southern California.

Stuck in Folsom Prison

The Torrance police immediately contacted federal counterterrorism officials stationed in nearby Los Angeles. The ensuing investigation led the FBI to Kevin Lamar James, who was serving a ten-year sentence for armed robbery in Sacramento's Folsom Prison. While at Folsom, James had converted to Islam and formed JIS, a small group that eventually

included fellow inmate Washington. On his release, Washington immediately began recruiting co-conspirators at his mosque in Inglewood. Two signed up—Patterson and Samana. The trio began robbing gas stations to finance their operations.

All four men were charged with conspiracy to levy war against the U.S. government through terrorism. Although Samana was found unfit to stand trial for psychiatric reasons, the other three pleaded guilty. In 2008, Washington and Patterson received sentences of 22 years and 151 months, respectively. A year later, James had sixteen years added to his existing prison term. Law enforcement officials still shudder at what might have happened had a Torrance police officer not found that cell phone. According to Los Angeles Police Department deputy chief Michael Downing, JIS "was closer to going operational at the time than anyone since 9/11."

FOR CRITICAL ANALYSIS Following the JIS arrests, an FBI spokesperson said, "This case serves as an example of how local officers are serving in the front lines in the war against terrorism." How does this case "serve as an example" of the importance of local police officers in anti-terrorism efforts?

Argus/Shutterstock

FIGURE 1.6 Prison and Jail Populations in the United States, 1985–2010

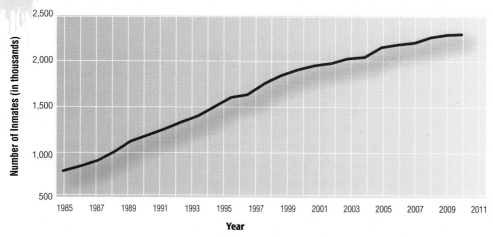

Sources: Bureau of Justice Statistics, *Correctional Populations in the United States, 1995* (Washington, D.C.: U.S. Department of Justice, June 1997), Table 1.1, page 12; and Bureau of Justice Statistics, *Prisoners in 2010* (Washington, D.C.: U.S. Department of Justice, 2011), 2.

participants in this area of law enforcement. The worry, discussed in Chapters 5 and 16, is that the homeland security burden on local police will become too great—especially if criminal activity related to the economic downturn continues to stretch their already limited resources.

CRIME AND PUNISHMENT

In this textbook, you will be exposed to a great deal of statistical data. While each number should help your understanding of the criminal justice system, it is best to keep in mind the warning of the writer William W. Watt, who said, "Do not put your faith in what statistics say until you have carefully considered what they do not say." What, for example, are we to make of the following? From 1991 to 2010, the violent crime rate in the United States fell an impressive 47 percent.[41] During the same time period, however, the number of people in American prisons nearly doubled.[42] If fewer people are committing crimes, why are so many more winding up in prison?

THE GROWING PRISON POPULATION We will take a closer look at this question in Chapter 13. For now, though, it may help to know that the present criminal justice landscape has been greatly influenced by a number of "get tough on crime" laws passed by federal, state, and local politicians in response to the crime wave of the late 1980s and early 1990s. These sentencing laws—discussed in Chapter 11—made it more likely that a person arrested for a crime would wind up behind bars and that, once there, he or she would not be back in the community for a very long while. As a result, the incarcerated population has been growing steadily for more than two decades, reaching yet another new high of nearly 2.4 million in 2010 (see Figure 1.6 above).[43]

Within these general statistics, a bleak picture of minority incarceration emerges. Even though African Americans make up only 13 percent of the general population in the United States, the number of black men in state and federal prisons (563,500) is significantly larger than the number of white men (479,000).[44] In federal prisons, one in every three inmates is Hispanic,[45] a ratio that has increased dramatically over the past decade as law enforcement and homeland security agencies have focused on immigration law violations, a subject we will consider in Chapter 17. The question of whether

Critical Thinking Skill Development: Ask students to consider that while the violent offending rate has fallen, the number of incarcerated offenders has grown. How can this trend be explained?

Inmates walk between buildings at the Washington Corrections Center in Shelton, Washington. What are some of the reasons for the dramatic increase in the American prisoner population since the 1980s?

AP Photo/Elaine Thompson

these figures reflect purposeful bias on the part of certain members of the criminal justice community will be addressed at various points in this textbook.

THE ECONOMICS OF INCARCERATION The last few years have presented criminal justice experts with another statistical anomaly to ponder. Although the overall prison population in the United States continued to rise, 2009 marked the first time in nearly four decades that the number of inmates in state prisons decreased from the previous year. This drop—of nearly four-tenths of a percent—reflected the fact that twenty-seven states managed to reduce their prison rolls over that twelve-month stretch.[46] In addition, in 2009 the number of people locked up in the nation's jails declined for the first time in three decades, by nearly 18,000.[47]

These figures do not necessarily indicate that the due process model, which favors rehabilitation over incarceration, is beginning to dominate the American criminal justice system. Rather, as Ram Cnaan, a professor at the University of Pennsylvania, notes, it reflects a painful truth about prison and jail inmates: "They simply cost too much."[48] For many states and counties, corrections is the most expensive item in their shrinking budgets, outpacing important services such as education and health care. Consequently, state and local officials are looking for ways to bring corrections spending under control. One way of doing this is to grant early release to nonviolent offenders. Another is to divert offenders from correctional facilities through special courts that promote rehabilitation rather than punishment for drug offenses, domestic violence, and other specific crimes. We will examine these policies and their ramifications on the nation's prisons and jails in Chapters 12 and 13.

SELFASSESSMENT

Fill in the blanks and check your answers on page 28.

Despite public perceptions to the contrary, crime rates in the United States have steadily _____ over the past several years. At the same time, prison inmate populations in this country have _____ consistently for several decades, although in 2009 the number of inmates in _____ prisons declined for the first time since the early 1970s. Legislation known as the _____ Act was the initial, and most comprehensive, reaction to the _____ attacks against the United States on September 11, 2001.

CJ IN ACTION

GUN CONTROL VERSUS GUN RIGHTS

"I have a Glock 9 millimeter and I'm a pretty good shot," Arizona congresswoman Gabrielle Giffords told an interviewer in 2010.[49] A year later, as we saw in this chapter's introduction, Jared Loughner used his own Glock handgun to kill six people and wound thirteen others, including Giffords, in front of a Tucson supermarket, a tragic incident that revived the debate over gun control. The vast majority of Americans who own guns are law-abiding citizens who keep their firearms at home for self-protection. This chapter's *CJ in Action* feature deals with the thorny issue of how best to protect the rights of this group while at the same time limiting the harm done by the illegal or improper use of firearms in the United States.

AS AMERICAN AS . . .

The Second Amendment to the U.S. Constitution states, "A well regulated Militia, being necessary to the security of a free State, the right of the people to keep and bear Arms, shall not be infringed." In recent years, the United States Supreme Court has tried to clarify this somewhat unclear language. Over the course of two separate rulings, the Court has stated that the Second Amendment provides individuals with a constitutional right to bear arms, and that this right must be recognized at all levels of government—federal, state, and local.[50]

Although the Supreme Court emphasized in both cases that states could continue to prohibit certain individuals—such as criminals and the mentally ill—from legally purchasing firearms, critics of our nation's relatively lax gun laws were disappointed with the results. Pointing out that Jared Loughner, an obviously disturbed individual, was able to easily (and legally) purchase his weapon at a Sportsman's Warehouse outlet, they continue to argue for greater restrictions on gun ownership. Opponents of stricter gun control laws reject the notion that firearms themselves are to blame for violent crime. Said one gun seller, "That's like pointing a finger at Ford and blaming them for car deaths."[51]

THE CASE FOR MORE RESTRICTIVE GUN LAWS

- Guns kill. Each year, more than 30,000 people in the United States die from gun violence, including about 17,000 suicides and 12,000 murders.[52]
- Guns in a household are more likely to harm the occupants than protect them. A household that

contains guns is three times more likely to be the site of a fatal shooting and five times more likely to experience a suicide than households that have no firearms.[53] Common sense tells us that when a person is in a fit of rage, experiencing depression, or under the influence of drugs or alcohol, easy access to a firearm greatly increases the chances of a gun-related injury or death.

- The importance of guns for self-protection is overstated. Less than 1 percent of all gun deaths involve self-defense, with the rest being accidents, suicides, and homicides.[54]

THE CASE AGAINST MORE RESTRICTIVE GUN LAWS

- Gun control laws do not decrease crime, for the simple reason that someone who is going to commit a crime with a gun is probably going to obtain that firearm illegally. So, for example, fifteen years after a Washington, D.C., ban went into effect in 1977, the city's murder rate had increased 300 percent.[55] As one observer points out, "the D.C. gun control laws irrationally prevent[ed] only law-abiding citizens from owning handguns."[56]
- Handguns offer protection from criminal attacks beyond that provided by public law enforcement.
- About a quarter of a billion handguns are privately and legally owned in this country. Putting restrictions on that ownership would create a huge new criminal class in this country, not to mention the anger toward the government that such measures would provoke.

YOUR OPINION—WRITING ASSIGNMENT

In 2011, Texas' legislature strongly considered passing a law that would allow students and faculty to bring firearms onto college campuses.[57] At the time, such actions were prohibited throughout the nation. Do you believe that people who legally own guns should be able to bring them on college campuses? If Texas does pass this law, should the federal government or the U.S. Supreme Court overturn it? Before responding, you can review our discussions in this chapter concerning:

- Consensus and conflict models of crime (pages 5–6).
- Federalism and the structure of the criminal justice system (pages 10–11).
- Gun sales and gun control (page 20).

Your answer should include at least three full paragraphs.

CHAPTER SUMMARY

LO 1 Describe the two most common models of how society determines which acts are criminal. The consensus model argues that the majority of citizens will agree on which activities should be outlawed and punished as crimes. It rests on the assumption that a diverse group of people can have similar morals. In contrast, the conflict model argues that in a diverse society, the dominant groups exercise power by codifying their value systems into criminal laws.

LO 2 Define *crime* and identify the different types of crime. Crime is any action punishable under criminal statutes and is considered an offense against society. Therefore, alleged criminals are prosecuted by the state rather than by victims. Crimes are punishable by sanctions that bring about a loss of personal freedom or, in some cases, fines. There are six groups of crimes: (a) violent crimes—murder, rape, assault, battery, and robbery; (b) property crimes—pocket picking, shoplifting, larceny/theft, burglary, and arson; (c) public order crimes—public drunkenness, prostitution, gambling, and illicit drug use; (d) white-collar crime—fraud and embezzlement; (e) organized crime—crime undertaken by a number of persons who operate their activities much as legal businesses do; and (f) high-tech crime—sabotage, fraud, embezzlement, and theft of proprietary data from computer systems, as well as cyber crimes, such as selling child pornography over the Internet.

LO 3 Outline the three levels of law enforcement. Because we have a federal system of government, law enforcement occurs at the (a) national, or federal, level and the (b) state level and within the states at (c) local levels. Because crime is mostly a local concern, most employees in the criminal justice system work for local governments. Agencies at the federal level include the FBI, the DEA, and the U.S. Secret Service, among others.

LO 4 List the essential elements of the corrections system. Criminal offenders are placed on probation, incarcerated in a jail or prison, transferred to community-based corrections facilities, or released on parole.

LO 5 Explain the difference between the formal and informal criminal justice processes. The formal criminal justice process involves the somewhat mechanical steps that are designed to guide criminal defendants from arrest to possible punishment. For every step in the formal process, though, someone has discretion, and such discretion leads to an informal process. Even when prosecutors believe that a suspect is guilty, they have the discretion not to prosecute, for example.

LO 6 Describe the layers of the "wedding cake" model. The top layer consists of celebrity cases, which are most highly publicized; the second layer involves high-profile felonies, such as rape and murder; the third layer consists of property crimes, such as larcenies and burglaries; and the fourth layer consists of misdemeanors.

LO 7 Contrast the crime control and due process models. The crime control model assumes that the criminal justice system is designed to protect the public from criminals. Thus, its most important function is to punish and repress criminal conduct. The due process model presumes that the accused are innocent and provides them with the most complete safeguards, usually within the court system.

LO 8 List the major issues in criminal justice today. (a) Fear of crime; (b) understanding why crime rates are falling; (c) the impact of an extended recession on crime rates; (d) gun sales and gun control; (e) use of illegal drugs; (f) street gangs; (g) DNA profiling; (h) homeland security and the Patriot Act; (i) America's massive inmate population; (j) possible bias against minorities in the criminal justice system; and (k) cost-cutting measures in the corrections system.

SELF ASSESSMENT ANSWER KEY

Page 9: i. society; **ii.** public officials/the government; **iii.** deviance; **iv.** violent; **v.** property; **vi.** white-collar

Page 17: i. federalism; **ii.** dual; **iii.** state; **iv.** discretion; **v.** "wedding cake"

Page 19: i. crime control; **ii.** due process; **iii.** individual

Page 26: i. decreased; **ii.** increased; **iii.** state; **iv.** Patriot; **v.** terrorist

KEY TERMS

assault 7

battery 7

burglary 8

civil rights 18

conflict model 6

consensus model 5

crime 5

crime control model 18

criminal justice system 9

deviance 7

discretion 15

drug 21

due process model 18

federalism 10

gun control 20

homeland security 23

justice 10

larceny 7

morals 5

murder 7

organized crime 8

psychoactive drugs 21

public order crime 8

robbery 7

sexual assault 7

street gang 22

system 15

terrorism 23

"wedding cake" model 16

white-collar crime 8

QUESTIONS FOR CRITICAL ANALYSIS

1. How is it possible to have a consensus about what should or should not be illegal in a country with several hundred million adults from all races, religions, and walks of life?

2. What would be some of the drawbacks of having the victims of a crime, rather than the state (through its public officials), prosecute criminals?

3. Do you agree that public order crimes such as prostitution and illegal gambling are "victimless" crimes? Why or why not?

4. In 2010, lawmakers in Arkansas and New York considered passing laws against "distracted walkers," or pedestrians who use cell phones, iPods, and other electronic gadgets while walking on city streets. What would be some of the reasons for instituting these kinds of laws? What is your opinion of any law that prohibits "distracted walking" (or "jogging" or "bicycling")?

5. As noted earlier in the chapter, over the past several years crime rates have decreased even as the American economy has suffered through the "Great Recession." One theory for this development is that as overall economic activity slows, more people who would otherwise be at work are unemployed and thus are spending more time at home. Consequently, their residences are no longer easy targets for burglaries, and because they themselves are at home, they are no longer victimized by street robberies. What is your opinion of this theory? What other explanation could there be for decreasing crime rates during a recession?

CourseMate *For Online Help*

For online help and access to resources that accompany *Criminal Justice Today,* go to www.cengagebrain.com/shop/ISBN/1111835578. Click "Access Now," where you will find flashcards, an online quiz, and other helpful study aids. If you have an access code for CourseMate, log in and go to the chapter of your choice for additional online study aids.

NOTES

1. "College Was on Alert for Giffords' Shooting Suspect," *Associated Press* (February 15, 2011).

2. Quoted in Eileen Sullivan, "Loners Like Tucson Gunman 'Fly below the Radar,'" *Associated Press* (January 17, 2011).

3. Herman Bianchi, *Justice as Sanctuary: Toward a New System of Crime Control* (Bloomington: Indiana University Press, 1994), 72.

4. "Americans Split on Doctor-Assisted Suicide," *Associated Press* (May 29, 2007).

5. Quoted in Tony Barboza and Alan Zarembo, "Is It Mercy or Is It Murder?" *Los Angeles Times* (November 24, 2010), A1.

6. *2010 Report to the Nations: Occupational Fraud and Abuse* (Austin, TX: Association of Certified Fraud Examiners, 2010), 8.

7. President's Commission on Law Enforcement and Administration of Justice, *The Challenge of Crime in a Free Society* (Washington, D.C.: Government Printing Office, 1967), 7.

8. *Gonzales v. Oregon,* 546 U.S. 243 (2006). Many United States Supreme Court cases will be cited in this book, and it is important to understand these citations. *Gonzales v. Oregon* refers to the parties in the case that the Court is reviewing. "U.S." is the abbreviation for *United States Reports,* the official publication of United States Supreme Court decisions. "546" refers to the volume of the *United States Reports* in which the case appears, and "243" is the page number. The citation ends with the year the case was decided in parentheses. Most, though not all, Supreme Court case citations in this book will follow this formula.

9. President's Commission on Law Enforcement and Administration of Justice.

10. John Heinz and Peter Manikas, "Networks among Elites in a Local Criminal Justice System," *Law and Society Review* 26 (1992), 831–861.

11. James Q. Wilson, "What to Do about Crime: Blaming Crime on Root Causes," *Vital Speeches* (April 1, 1995), 373.

12. Herbert Packer, *The Limits of the Criminal Sanction* (Stanford, CA: Stanford University Press, 1968), 154–173.

13. *Ibid.*

14. Daniel Givelber, "Meaningless Acquittals, Meaningful Convictions: Do We Reliably Acquit the Innocent?" *Rutgers Law Review* 49 (Summer 1997), 1317.

15. William Yardley, "In Likely Obama Pick, Some Find Hope for Shift in Drug Policy," *New York Times* (February 16, 2009), A13.

16. Lawrence M. Friedman and Robert V. Percival, *The Roots of Justice* (Chapel Hill, NC: University of North Carolina Press, 1981).

17. Packer, 154–173.

18. *Ibid.*

19. Givelber, 1317.

20. Guy-Uriel E. Charles, "Fourth Amendment Accommodations: (Un)Compelling Public Needs, Balancing Acts, and the Fiction of Consent," *Michigan Journal of Race and Law* (Spring 1997), 461.

21. Quoted in Anthony Scott, "Residents Keep Watch on Area after Abduction," *Killeen (TX) Herald* (December 18, 2010), at **www.kdh-news.com/news/story.aspx?s=47685**.

22. Office of Juvenile Justice and Delinquency Prevention, "National Estimates of Missing Children: An Overview," in *National Incidence Studies of Missing, Abducted, Runaway, and Thrownaway Children* (Washington, D.C.: U.S. Department of Justice, 2002), 7.

23. Steven J. Wernick, "In Accordance with a Public Outcry: Zoning Sex Offenders through Residence Restrictions in Florida," *Florida Law Review* (2006), 1153.

24. Gallup, "Americans Still Perceive Crime as on the Rise" (November 18, 2010), at **www.gallup.com/poll/144827/Americans-Perceive-Crime-Rise.aspx**.

25. Quoted in Pete Yost, "Violent, Other Crimes Drop in U.S.—But Why?" *Associated Press* (September 13, 2010).

26. *Ibid.*

27. Alfred Blumstein, "The Crime Drop in America: An Exploration of Some Recent Crime Trends," *Journal of Scandinavian Studies in Criminology and Crime Prevention* (December 2006), 17–35.

28. James Lindgren, "Fall from Grace: Arming America and the Bellesiles Scandal," *Yale Law Journal* 111 (2002), 2203.

29. *District of Columbia v. Heller,* 554 U.S. 570 (2008).

30. James Alan Fox and Jack Levin, *The Will to Kill: Making Sense of Senseless Murder* (Needham, MA: Allyn & Bacon, 2001), 33–37.

31. Amanda Lee Myers, "Arizona Beheading Raises Fears of Drug Violence," *Associated Press* (October 29, 2010).

32. National Drug Intelligence Center, *National Drug Threat Assessment 2009* (Washington, D.C.: U.S. Department of Justice, December 2008), 45, 58–59.

33. *ADAM II: 2009 Annual Report* (Washington, D.C.: Office of National Drug Control Policy, 2009).

34. Substance Abuse and Mental Health Services Administration, *Results from the 2009 National Survey on Drug Use and Health: Vol. 1: Summary of National Findings* (Washington, D.C.: National Institute on Drug Abuse, 2010), at **www.oas.samhsa.gov/nsduh/2k9ResultsP.pdf**.

35. David H. Bayley, *Police for the Future* (New York: Oxford University Press, 1994), 3–7.

36. Office of Juvenile Justice and Delinquency Prevention, *Highlights of the 2008 National Youth Gang Survey* (Washington, D.C.: U.S. Department of Justice, March 2010), 1.

37. Bureau of Justice Assistance, *2009 National Gang Threat Assessment* (Washington, D.C.: U.S. Department of Justice, 2009), iii.

38. *Ibid.*

39. See **www.innocenceproject.org**.

40. Uniting and Strengthening America by Providing Appropriate Tools Required to Intercept and Obstruct Terrorism (USA PATRIOT) Act of 2001, Pub. L. No. 107-56, 115 Stat. 272 (2001).

41. Federal Bureau of Investigation, *Crime in the United States,* 2010 (Washington, D.C.: U.S. Department of Justice, 2011), at **www.fbi.gov/about-us/cjis/ucr/crime-in-the-u.s/2010/crime-in-the-u.s.-2010/tables10tbl01.xls**.

42. Bureau of Justice Statistics, *Prisoners in 1996,* (Washington, D.C.: U.S. Department of Justice, June 1997), 1; and Bureau of Justice Statistics, *Prisoners in 2010* (Washington, D.C.: U.S. Department of Justice, December 2011), 1.

43. *Prison Inmates at Midyear 2008—Statistical Tables,* Table 1, page 2; and Jail Inmates at Midyear 2008—Statistical Tables, Table 1, page 2.

44. Bureau of Justice Statistics, *Prisoners in 2009* (Washington, D.C.: U.S. Department of Justice, December 2010), Appendix Table 12, page 27.

45. Federal Bureau of Prisons, "Inmate Breakdown," at **www.bop. gov/news/ quick.jsp#2**.

46. *Prison Count 2010: State Population Declines for the First Time in 38 Years* (Washington, D.C.: Pew Center on the States, April 2010), 1.

47. Bureau of Justice Statistics, *Jail Inmates at Midyear 2009—Statistical Tables* (Washington, D.C.: U.S. Department of Justice, June 2010), 1.

48. Quoted in *Associated Press,* "U.S. Prison Population Rises despite a Drop in 20 States" (December 9, 2009).

49. Quoted in Jo Becker and Michael Luo, "In Tucson, Guns Have a Broad Constituency," *New York Times* (January 11, 2011), A1.

50. *District of Columbia v. Heller,* 554 U.S. 570 (2008); and *McDonald v. Chicago,* 561 U.S. _____ (2010).

51. Quoted in Adam Magourney, "In an Ocean of Firearms, Tucson Is Far Away," *New York Times* (January 20, 2011), A15.

52. Michael Grunwald, "The Tucson Tragedy: Fire Away," *Time* (January 24, 2011), 36–37.

53. David Kairys, "The Origin and Development of the Governmental Handgun Cases," *Connecticut Law Review* (2000), 1166.

54. Grunwald, 38.

55. Paul H. Blackman, "Effects of Restrictive Handgun Laws," *New England Journal of Medicine* (1992), 1157.

56. Quoted in David Nakamura and Robert Barnes, "Appeals Court Rules D.C. Handgun Ban Unconstitutional," *Washington Post* (March 10, 2007), A1.

57. Quoted in Jim Vertuno, "Texas Poised to Pass Bill Allowing Guns on Campus," *Associated Press* (February 20, 2011).

CHAPTER ONE APPENDIX

HOW TO READ CASE CITATIONS AND FIND COURT DECISIONS

Many important court cases are discussed throughout this book. Every time a court case is mentioned, you will be able to check its citation using the endnotes on the final pages of the chapter. Court decisions are recorded and published on paper and on the Internet. When a court case is mentioned, the notation that is used to refer to, or to *cite*, the case denotes where the published decision can be found.

Decisions of state courts of appeals are usually published in two places, the state reports of that particular state and the more widely used *National Reporter System* published by West Group. Some states no longer publish their own reports. The *National Reporter System* divides the states into the following geographic areas: Atlantic (A. or A.2d), North Eastern (N.E. or N.E.2d), North Western (N.W. or N.W.2d), Pacific (P., P.2d, or P.3d), Southern (So. or So.2d), and South Western (S.W., S.W.2d, or S.W.3d). The 2d and 3d in these abbreviations refer to the *Second Series* and *Third Series,* respectively.

Federal trial court decisions are published unofficially in West's *Federal Supplement* (F.Supp. or F.Supp.2d), and opinions from the circuit courts of appeals are reported unofficially in West's *Federal Reporter* (F., F.2d, or F.3d). Opinions from the United States Supreme Court are reported in the *United States Reports* (U.S.), the *Lawyers' Edition of the Supreme Court Reports* (L.Ed.), West's *Supreme Court Reporter* (S.Ct.), and other publications. The *United States Reports* is the official publication of United States Supreme Court decisions. It is published by the federal government. Many early decisions are missing from these volumes. The citations of the early volumes of the United States Reports include the names of the actual reporters, such as Dallas, Cranch, or Wheaton. *McCulloch v. Maryland,* for example, is cited as 17 U.S. (4 Wheat.) 316. Only after 1874 did the present citation system, in which cases are cited based solely on their volume and page numbers in the *United States Reports,* come into being. The *Lawyers' Edition of the Supreme Court Reports* is an unofficial and more complete edition of Supreme Court decisions. West's *Supreme Court Reporter* is an unofficial edition of decisions dating from October 1882. These volumes contain headnotes and numerous brief editorial statements of the law involved in the case.

Citations to decisions of state courts of appeals give the name of the case; the volume, name, and page number of the state's official report (if the state publishes its own reports); and the volume, unit, and page number of the *National Reporter.* Federal court citations also give the name of the case and the volume, name, and page number of the reports. In addition to the citation, this textbook lists the year of the decision in parentheses. Consider, for example, the case *Miranda v. Arizona,* 384 U.S. 436 (1966). The Supreme Court's decision in this case may be found in volume 384 of the *United States Reports* on page 436. The case was decided in 1966.

CHAPTER

2

Michael Nagle/Redux

Causes of Crime

CHAPTER OUTLINE

- Theory in Criminology
- Exploring the Causes of Crime
- Further Study: Expanding Criminology
- The Link between Drugs and Crime
- Criminology from Theory to Practice
- CJ in Action—The Link between Violent Video Games and Crime

LEARNING OBJECTIVES

After reading this chapter, you should be able to . . .

LO 1 Discuss the difference between a hypothesis and a theory in the context of criminology.

LO 2 Explain why classical criminology is based on choice theory.

LO 3 Contrast positivism with classical criminology.

LO 4 List and describe the three theories of social structure that help explain crime.

LO 5 List and briefly explain the three branches of social process theory.

LO 6 Describe how life course criminology differs from the other theories addressed in this chapter.

LO 7 Discuss the connection between offenders and victims of crime.

LO 8 Contrast the medical model of addiction with the criminal model of addiction.

LO 9 Explain the theory of the chronic offender and its importance for the criminal justice system.

The nine learning objectives labeled LO 1 through LO 9 are designed to help improve your understanding of the chapter.

MAD or BAD?

Rodnika Hall finally decided she wanted nothing more to do with her boyfriend, Lee Allen. The nineteen-year-old Hall moved from New Orleans, her hometown, to Lafayette, Louisiana, putting 140 miles between herself and eighteen-year-old Allen. The two shared an infant daughter, however, and Hall agreed to let the girl spend a weekend with her father. When Hall went to retrieve the child on September 27, 2010, Allen attacked her with a knife and stabbed her to death.

This was not the first time that Allen had acted violently toward Hall. In November 2009, he had punched Hall in the face and struck her with a stick. Then, in June 2010, Allen again attacked his girlfriend, beating her about the face and body and dragging her by the hair along a sidewalk. In both instances, Allen was arrested, charged with minor crimes, and released. In the paperwork for these arrests, the New Orleans police noted that Allen was suffering from schizophrenia, a chronic and severe brain disorder that can lead to erratic, uncontrollable behavior. According to Allen's sister, Zina, he had been taking several medications to treat his condition, but none had been effective.

Orleans Parish prosecutors eventually charged Allen with second degree murder, which carries a mandatory sentence of life in prison. It was too little, too late for Hall's family and friends, who believed that the criminal justice system should have acted earlier to protect her from a mentally ill and obviously dangerous individual. "[The authorities] knew something was wrong with that boy," said Dianne Hall, Rodnika's aunt. "Rodnika reported him too many times for them not to."

In September 2010, Lee Allen, a New Orleans resident who suffered from various mental illnesses, stabbed his ex-girlfriend Rodnika Hall to death. Orleans Parish Sheriff's Department

Criminology The scientific study of crime and the causes of criminal behavior.

The Greek roots of the word *schizophrenia* indicate a mind that has been "torn apart." Today, this particular form of mental illness retains a stigma of brutality. Certainly, the general public associates schizophrenia with violent behavior such as Lee Allen's murder of Rodnika Hall or, on a much larger scale, Jared Loughner's January 2011 shooting spree in Tucson, Arizona, discussed in the introduction to the previous chapter. (Loughner's bizarre behavior, also detailed in Chapter 1, led many to believe that he had been an undiagnosed schizophrenic before the attack.) In fact, persons suffering from the disease are at an unusually high risk for committing suicide or harming others.[1] Psychiatrist E. Fuller Torrey estimates that schizophrenics commit about 1,000 homicides each year.[2] Further research shows that even moderate use of alcohol or drugs significantly increases the chances that a schizophrenic will behave violently.[3]

The study of crime, or **criminology**, is rich with different theories as to why people commit crimes. In this chapter, we will discuss the most influential of these theories, some of which complement each other and some of which do not. We will also look at the various factors most commonly, if not always correctly, associated with criminal behavior. Finally, this chapter will address the question of relevance: What effect do theories of why wrongdoing occurs have on efforts to control and prevent crime?

THEORY IN CRIMINOLOGY

Criminologists, or researchers who study the causes of crime, warn against using models to predict violent behavior. After all, about 2.4 million Americans—1 percent of the adult population—have been diagnosed with schizophrenia, and the vast majority of them will never commit a violent crime. In the case of Lee Allen, there was certainly a *correlation* between his mental illness and the murder of Rodnika Hall, but it is not correct to say that Allen's schizophrenia alone *caused* the crime to occur. As mentioned earlier, substance abuse has a crucial impact on the criminal activity of schizophrenics, as do other factors such as age, income, and failure to take prescribed medication.[4] **Correlation** between two variables means that they tend to vary together. **Causation,** in contrast, means that one variable is responsible for the change in the other.

Hence, criminologists find themselves in a quandary. They can say that there is a strong correlation between schizophrenia and violent behavior. That is, schizophrenia makes violent behavior more likely. But they cannot say what actually caused Lee Allen and Jared Loughner to commit their crimes without knowing much more about their backgrounds and environments, and possibly not even then. Consequently, the question that is the underpinning of criminology—what causes crime?—has yet to be definitively answered.

THE ROLE OF THEORY

Criminologists have, however, uncovered a wealth of information concerning a different, and more practically applicable, inquiry: Given a certain set of circumstances, why do individuals commit criminal acts? This information has allowed criminologists to develop a number of *theories* concerning the causes of crime. Most of us tend to think of a *theory* as some sort of guess or a **LO 1** statement that is lacking in credibility. In the academic world, and therefore for our purposes, a **theory** is an explanation of a happening or circumstance that is based on observation, experimentation, and reasoning. Scientific and academic researchers observe facts and their consequences to develop *hypotheses* about what will occur when a similar fact pattern is present in the future. A **hypothesis** is a proposition that can be tested by researchers or observers to determine if it is valid. If enough authorities do find the hypothesis valid, it will be accepted as a theory. See Figure 2.1 alongside for an example of this process, known as the *scientific method,* in action.

THE FALLIBILITY OF THEORY

The path to accepted theory in criminology is not an easy one. Several years ago, for example, "maverick" economist Steven D. Levitt and co-author John Donohue proposed a somewhat shocking theory to help explain the dramatic drop in crime rates during the 1990s: legalized abortion.[5]

FIGURE 2.1

The Scientific Method
The scientific method is a process through which researchers test the accuracy of a hypothesis. This simple example should provide an idea of how the scientific method works.

Observation: I left my home at 7:00 this morning, and I was on time for class.

Hypothesis: If I leave home at 7:00 every morning, then I will never be late for class.
(Hypotheses are often presented in this "If . . . , then . . ." format.)

Test: For three straight weeks, I left home at 7:00 every morning. Not one time was I late for class.

Verification: Four of my neighbors have the same morning class. They agree that they are never late if they leave by 7:00 A.M.

Theory: As long as I leave home at 7:00 A.M., I don't have to worry about being late for class.

Prediction: Tomorrow morning I'll leave at 7:00, and I will be on time for my class.

Note that even a sound theory supported by the scientific method such as this one does not *prove* that the prediction will be correct. Other factors not accounted for in the test and verification stages, such as an unexpected traffic accident, may disprove the theory. Predictions based on complex theories such as the criminological ones we will be discussing in this chapter are often challenged in such a manner.

A THEORY PRESENTED Levitt and Donohue based their theory on several assumptions. First, as we shall soon see, young males commit more crimes than any other members of American society. Consequently, laws legalizing abortion that were passed in the early 1970s would lead to fewer boys being born in those years and fewer young males existing two decades later. In addition, the researchers hypothesized, women who were most likely to have abortions were the same type of women—young, minority, poor, and unmarried—most likely to give birth to future criminals. Finally, legalized abortion arguably gave women the ability to choose the timing of motherhood, thus providing their male children with more stable home lives. So, not only did legalized abortion lead to fewer young males in the 1990s, but also those young males who did exist had, on the whole, less exposure to the risk factors that lead to crime.[6]

A THEORY REJECTED As might be expected, both supporters and opponents of legalized abortion found much to dislike about this theory. Among criminologists, however, its shortcomings have more to do with data than politics. According to Franklin E. Zimring of the University of California at Berkeley, there is no evidence that the population at risk for crime decreased in the fifteen years after abortion became legal. In fact, he points out, by the end of the 1970s, the number of births to "at risk" mothers—young, minority, poor, and unmarried—*increased.*[7] By Levitt and Donohue's own reasoning, then, crime rates should have increased from 1991 to 2000. Instead, the rates plummeted during that time period. Zimring also notes that, as late as 1993, a number of respected criminologists, relying on the same reasoning as Levitt and Donohue concerning the connection between youth population and crime, were wrongly predicting that the decade ahead would see an explosion of criminal activity.[8]

SELF ASSESSMENT

Fill in the blanks and check your answers on page 62.
Researchers who study the causes of crime are called _____. These researchers test hypotheses, or educated guesses, using the _____ method. If a hypothesis proves valid, it can be used to support a _____, or explanation based on observation and reasoning, that explains a possible cause of crime.

EXPLORING THE CAUSES OF CRIME

As you read this chapter, keep in mind that theories are not the same as facts, and most, if not all, of the criminological theories described in these pages have their detractors. Over the past century, however, a number of theories of crime have gained wide, if not total, acceptance and are deserving of our attention. These include choice theories, trait theories, sociological theories, social process theories, and social conflict theories.

CRIME AND FREE WILL: CHOICE THEORIES OF CRIME

For the purposes of the American criminal justice system, the answer to why a person commits a crime is rather straightforward: because that person chooses to do so. This application of choice theory to criminal law is not absolute. If a defendant can prove that she or he lacked the ability to make a rational choice, in certain circumstances the defendant will not be punished as harshly for a crime as would normally be the case. But such allowances are relatively recent. From the early days of this country, the general presumption in criminal law has been that behavior is a consequence of free will.

LO 2

Critical Thinking Skill Development: Ask students to respond to "Questions for Critical Analysis" number one on page 62, in which they consider the differences between causes and correlations.

Technology Tip: Ask students to go online and read Levitt and Donohue's paper on the impact of legalized abortion on crime in the *Quarterly Journal of Economics* at **pricetheory.uchicago.edu/ levitt/Papers/DonohueLevitt TheImpactOfLegalized2001.pdf**.

Choice Theory A school of criminology that holds that wrongdoers act as if they weigh the possible benefits of criminal or delinquent activity against the expected costs of being apprehended. When the benefits are greater than the expected costs, the offender will make a rational choice to commit a crime or delinquent act.

THEORIES OF CLASSICAL CRIMINOLOGY An emphasis on free will and human rationality in the realm of criminal behavior has its roots in classical criminology. Classical theorists believed that crime was an expression of a person's rational decision-making process: before committing a crime, a person would weigh the benefits of the crime against the costs of being apprehended. Therefore, if punishments were stringent enough to outweigh the benefits of crime, they would dissuade people from committing the crime in the first place.

The earliest popular expression of classical theory came in 1764 when the Italian Cesare Beccaria (1738–1794) published his *Essays on Crime and Punishments*. Beccaria criticized existing systems of criminal law as irrational and argued that criminal procedures should be more consistent with human behavior. He believed that, to be just, criminal law should reflect three truths:

1. All decisions, including the decision to commit a crime, are the result of rational choice.
2. Fear of punishment can have a deterrent effect on the choice to commit crime.
3. The more swift and certain punishment is, the more effective it will be in controlling crime.[9]

Beccaria believed that any punishment that purported to do anything other than deter crime was cruel and arbitrary. This view was shared by his contemporary, Britain's Jeremy Bentham (1748–1832). In 1789, Bentham pronounced that "nature has placed man under the governance of two sovereign masters, *pain* and *pleasure*." Bentham applied his theory of utilitarianism to the law by contending that punishment should use the threat of pain against criminal individuals to assure the pleasure of society as a whole. As a result, Bentham felt that punishment should have four goals:

1. To prevent all crime.
2. When it cannot prevent crime, to assure that a criminal will commit a lesser crime to avoid a harsher punishment.
3. To give the criminal an incentive not to harm others in the pursuit of crime.
4. To prevent crime at the least possible cost to society.[10]

POSITIVISM AND MODERN RATIONAL THEORY By the end of the nineteenth century, the positivist school of criminologists had superseded classical criminology. According to positivism, criminal behavior is determined by biological, psychological, and social forces and is beyond the control

LO 3 of the individual. The Italian physician Cesare Lombroso (1835–1909), an early adherent of positivism who is known as the "Father of Criminology," believed that criminals were throwbacks to the savagery of early humankind and could therefore be identified by certain physical characteristics such as sharp teeth and large jaws. He also theorized that criminality was similar to mental illness and could be genetically passed down from generation to generation in families that had cases of insanity, syphilis, epilepsy, and even deafness. Such individuals, according to Lombroso and his followers, had no free choice when it came to wrongdoing—their criminality had been predetermined at birth.

Positivist theory lost credibility as crime rates began to climb in the 1970s. If crime was caused by external factors, critics asked, why had the

Classical Criminology A school of criminology based on the belief that individuals have free will to engage in any behavior, including criminal behavior. To deter criminal behavior, society must hold wrongdoers responsible for their actions by punishing them.

Utilitarianism An approach to ethical reasoning in which the "correct" decision is the one that results in the greatest amount of good for the greatest number of people affected by that decision.

Positivism A school of the social sciences that sees criminal and delinquent behavior as the result of biological, psychological, and social forces. Because wrongdoers are driven to deviancy by external factors, they should not be punished but treated to lessen the influence of those factors.

In April 2010, Daniel Baker, left, was arrested for killing Marina Aksman with an aluminum baseball bat. Vernon Hill (Illinois) police believe that Baker was angry with Aksman for her efforts to break up the relationship between Aksman's daughter, Kristina, and him. According to theories of classical criminology, what decision did Baker make before committing his crime?
Bryce Harman/MCT/Landov

proactive social programs of the 1960s not brought about a decrease in criminal activity? An updated version of classical criminology, known as *rational choice theory,* found renewed acceptance. James Q. Wilson, one of the most prominent critics of the positivist school, sums up rational choice theory as follows:

> At any given moment, a person can choose between committing a crime and not committing it. The consequences of committing a crime consist of rewards (what psychologists call "reinforcers") and punishments; the consequences of not committing the crime also entail gains and losses. The larger the ratio of the net rewards of crime to the net rewards of [not committing a crime], the greater the tendency to commit a crime.[11]

According to rational choice theory, we can hypothesize that criminal actions, including acts of violence and even murder, are committed *as if* individuals had this ratio in mind.

THE SEDUCTION OF CRIME   In expanding on rational choice theory, sociologist Jack Katz has stated that the "rewards" of crime may be sensual as well as financial. The inherent danger of criminal activity, according to Katz, increases the "rush" a criminal experiences on successfully committing a crime. Katz labels the rewards of this "rush" the *seduction of crime.*[12] For example, the National Coalition for the Homeless documented nearly 900 unprovoked attacks against the homeless in the decade that ended in 2010, including 244 fatalities.[13] In most of these incidents, the assailants were "thrill offenders" who kicked, punched, or set on fire homeless persons for the sport of it. Katz believes that such seemingly "senseless" crimes can be explained by rational choice theory only if the intrinsic (inner) reward of the crime itself is considered.

CHOICE THEORY AND PUBLIC POLICY   The theory that wrongdoers choose to commit crimes is a cornerstone of the American criminal justice system. Because crime is seen as the end result of a series of rational choices, policymakers have reasoned that severe punishment can deter criminal activity by adding another variable to the decision-making process. Supporters of the death penalty—now used by thirty-four states and the federal government—emphasize its deterrent effects, and legislators have used harsh mandatory sentences to control illegal drug use and trafficking.

"BORN CRIMINAL": BIOLOGICAL AND PSYCHOLOGICAL THEORIES OF CRIME

As we have seen, Cesare Lombroso believed in the "criminal born" man and woman and was confident that he could distinguish criminals by their apelike physical features. Such far-fetched notions have long been relegated to scientific oblivion. Nevertheless, many criminologists do believe that *trait theories* have validity. These theories suggest that certain *biological* or *psychological* traits in individuals could incline them toward criminal behavior given a certain set of circumstances. Biology is a very broad term that refers to the scientific study of living organisms, while psychology pertains more specifically to the study of the mind and its processes. "All behavior is biological," pointed out geneticist David C. Rowe. "All behavior is represented in the brain, in its biochemistry, electrical activity, structure, and growth and decline."[14]

GENETICS AND CRIME   Criminologists who study biological theories of crime often focus on the effect that *genes* have on human behavior. Genes are coded sequences of DNA that control every aspect of our biology, from the color of our eyes and hair to the type of emotions we have. Every person's genetic makeup is determined by genes inherited from his or her parents. Consequently, when scientists study ancestral or evo-

Biology   The science of living organisms, including their structure, function, growth, and origin.

Psychology   The scientific study of mental processes and behavior.

lutionary developments, they are engaging in genetics, a branch of biology that deals with traits that are passed from one generation to another through genes.

Twin Studies Genetics is at the heart of criminology's "nurture versus nature" debate. In other words, are traits such as aggressiveness and antisocial behavior, both of which often lead to criminality, a result of a person's environment (nurture) or her or his genes (nature)? To tip the balance toward "nature," a criminologist must be able to prove that, all other things being equal, the offspring of aggressive or antisocial parents are at risk to exhibit those same traits.

Many criminologists have turned to *twin studies* to determine the relationship between genetics and criminal behavior. If the "nature" argument is correct, then twins should exhibit similar antisocial tendencies. The problem with twin studies is that most twins grow up in the same environment, so it is difficult, if not impossible, to determine whether their behavior is influenced by their genes or by their surroundings. To overcome this difficulty, criminologists compare identical twins, known as MZ twins, and fraternal twins of the same gender, known as DZ twins. Because MZ twins are genetically identical while DZ twins share only half of their genes, the latter should be less likely to have similar behavior patterns than the former.

Adoption Studies The results of such twin studies have been decidedly mixed. Some show that MZ pairs are considerably more likely to exhibit similar criminal behavior than DZ pairs,[15] but others discredit this hypothesis.[16] Because of the inconsistencies of twin studies, some criminologists have turned to *adoption studies,* which eliminate the problem of family members sharing the same environment. A number of well-received adoption studies have shown a correlation between rates of criminality among adopted children and antisocial or criminal behavior by their biological parents.[17]

Furthermore, such studies have shown a genetic basis for such traits as attention deficit hyperactivity disorder (ADHD) and aggressiveness, both of which have been linked to antisocial behavior and crime.[18] Keep in mind, however, that no single gene or trait has been proved to lead to criminality. As a result, the best that genetics can do is raise the possibility for a predisposition toward aggression or violence in an individual based on her or his family background.[19]

HORMONES AND AGGRESSION Chemical messengers known as hormones have also been the subject of much criminological study. Criminal activity in males has been linked to elevated levels of hormones—specifically, testosterone, which controls secondary sex characteristics and has been associated with traits of aggression. Testing of inmate populations shows that those incarcerated for violent crimes exhibit higher testosterone levels than other prisoners.[20] Elevated testosterone levels have also been used to explain the age-crime relationship, as the average testosterone level of men under the age of twenty-eight is double that of men between thirty-one and sixty-six years old.[21]

A very specific form of female violent behavior is believed to stem from hormones. In 2010, defense attorneys for Stephanie Rochester of Superior, Colorado,

Genetics The study of how certain traits or qualities are transmitted from parents to their offspring.

Hormone A chemical substance, produced in tissue and conveyed in the bloodstream, that controls certain cellular and body functions such as growth and reproduction.

Testosterone The hormone primarily responsible for the production of sperm and the development of male secondary sex characteristics such as the growth of facial and pubic hair and the change of voice pitch.

Teaching Tip: To demonstrate the importance of trait theories in criminal justice, ask students to locate an example of a defendant who used a biological or psychological condition as a criminal defense. Have students share their examples with the class.

In 2011, Christopher Gribble, right, was convicted of murdering a Mount Vernon, New Hampshire, woman with a machete. Gribble's attorneys claimed that he was suffering from mental illness at the time of the crime. If true, should this fact have any bearing on Gribble's guilt or innocence?
AP Photo/Don Himsel, Pool

claimed that their client was not responsible for smothering her six-month-old son to death because she was suffering from *postpartum psychosis* at the time of her action. This temporary illness, believed to be caused partly by the hormonal changes that women experience after childbirth, triggers abnormal behavior in a small percentage of new mothers.[22]

THE BRAIN AND CRIME The study of brain activity, or *neurophysiology*, has also found a place in criminology. Cells in the brain known as *neurons* communicate with each other by releasing chemicals called **neurotransmitters.** Criminologists have isolated three neurotransmitters that seem to be particularly related to aggressive behavior:

1. Serotonin, which regulates moods, appetite, and memory.
2. Norepinephrine, which regulates sleep-wake cycles and controls how we respond to anxiety, fear, and stress.
3. Dopamine, which regulates perceptions of pleasure and reward.[23]

Researchers have established that, under certain circumstances, low levels of serotonin and high levels of norepinephrine are correlated with aggressive behavior.[24] Dopamine plays a crucial role in drug addiction, as we shall see later in the chapter.

In addition, research seems to have found a strong connection betwen violent behavior and damage to a part of the brain known as the *frontal lobe*.[25] Located in the part of the brain just behind the forehead, the frontal lobe appears to regulate our ability to behave properly in social situations. Thus, people whose frontal lobes do not function properly—due to birth defect or injury—tend to act more impulsively and violently. Experts testifying in court often use frontal lobe trauma to explain the horrific actions of defendants. In 2010, for example, defense attorneys emphasized damage to Kemar Johnston's frontal lobe—caused by a childhood playground accident—when successfully arguing that their client should not be executed for torturing, mutilating, and murdering two teenagers in Cape Coral, Florida.

Neurotransmitter A chemical that transmits nerve impulses between nerve cells and from nerve cells to the brain.

See **Crime Times** for an online publication dedicated to understanding the role brain dysfunction plays in criminal behavior. Find this Web site by visiting the *Criminal Justice CourseMate* at **cengagebrain. com** and selecting the *Web links* for this chapter.

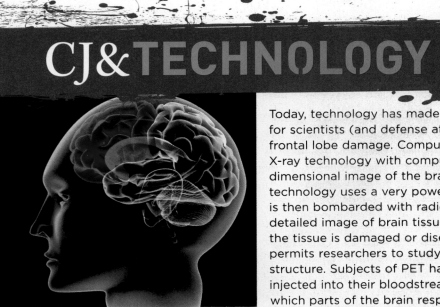

CJ&TECHNOLOGY Mapping the Brain

Today, technology has made it relatively easy (if not always inexpensive) for scientists (and defense attorneys) to show brain irregularities such as frontal lobe damage. Computer axial tomography (CAT) scans combine X-ray technology with computer technology to provide an exact three-dimensional image of the brain. Magnetic resonance imaging (MRI) technology uses a very powerful magnet to create a magnetic field, which is then bombarded with radio waves. These waves can provide a very detailed image of brain tissue, allowing doctors to determine whether the tissue is damaged or diseased. Positron emission tomography (PET) permits researchers to study the function of the brain rather than its structure. Subjects of PET have a small amount of radioactive matter injected into their bloodstream, which is then measured to determine which parts of the brain respond to various activities and functions. Finally, single photon emission computer tomography (SPECT) measures levels of a sugar called glucose in certain areas of the brain. Because

Yakobchuk Vasyl, 2009. Used under license from Shutterstock.com glucose gives the brain the energy to function, tracing which areas of the brain "light up" under SPECT gives scientists clues as to the subject's thoughts and emotions.

THINKING ABOUT BRAIN-SCANNING DEVICES

The techniques discussed above are able to determine chemical and structural problems that indicate a person is suffering from schizophrenia, a brain disease discussed in the opening to this chapter. Given the correlation between schizophrenia and violent behavior, how could brain scanners be used to prevent crime? What would be some of the problems with using these devices to identify potential criminals before they had in fact committed any crimes?

PSYCHOLOGY AND CRIME Like biological theories of crime, psychological theories of crime operate under the assumption that individuals have traits that make them more or less predisposed to criminal activity. To a certain extent, however, psychology rests more heavily on abstract ideas than does biology. Even Sigmund Freud (1856–1939), perhaps the most influential of all psychologists, considered the operations of the mind to be, like an iceberg, mostly hidden.

Freud's Psychoanalytic Theory For all his accomplishments, Freud rarely turned his attention directly toward the causes of crime. His psychoanalytic theory, however, has provided a useful approach for thinking about criminal behavior. According to Freud, most of our thoughts, wishes, and urges originate in the *unconscious* region of the mind, and we have no control—or even awareness of—these processes. Freud believed that, on an unconscious level, all humans have criminal tendencies and that each of us is continually struggling against these tendencies.

To explain this struggle, Freud devised three abstract systems that interact in the brain: the *id,* the *ego,* and the *superego.* The id is driven by a constant desire for pleasure and self-gratification through sexual and aggressive urges. The ego, in contrast, stands for reason and common sense, while the superego "learns" the expectations of family and society and acts as the conscience. When the three systems fall into disorder, the id can take control, causing the individual to act on his or her antisocial urges and, possibly, commit crimes.[26]

Social Psychology and "Evil" Behavior Another crucial branch of psychology—*social psychology*—focuses on human behavior in the context of how human beings relate to and influence one another. Social psychology rests on the assumption that the way we view ourselves is shaped to a large degree by how we think others view us. Generally, we act in the same manner as those we like or admire because we want them to like or admire us. Thus, to a certain extent, social psychology tries to explain the influence of crowds on individual behavior.

About three decades ago, psychologist Philip Zimbardo highlighted the power of group behavior in dramatic fashion. Zimbardo randomly selected some Stanford University undergraduate students to act as "guards" and other students to act as "inmates" in an artificial prison environment. Before long, the students began to act as if these designations were real, with the "guards" physically mistreating the "inmates," who rebelled with equal violence. Within six days, Zimbardo was forced to discontinue

Discussion Tip: Place students into small groups and ask them to respond to "Questions for Critical Analysis" number three on page 62, in which they consider the treatment of the mentally ill.

Psychoanalytic Theory Sigmund Freud's theory that attributes our thoughts and actions to unconscious motives.

Technology Tip: To increase students' understanding of social psychology, ask them to visit **www.zimbardo.com/zimbardo.html** and click on "prison experiment" to learn more about the controversial Stanford experiment exploring group behavior.

Critical Thinking Skill Development: In a written assignment, ask students to consider how trait theories translate into criminal justice policy. Have them contrast these policies to those that have their roots in classical criminology. (LO 3)

> The **American Society of Criminology** will keep you updated on the hot issues in criminology. Find its Web site by visiting the *Criminal Justice CourseMate* at **cengagebrain. com** and selecting the *Web links* for this chapter.

the experiment out of fear for its participants' safety.[27] One of the basic assumptions of social psychology is that people are able to justify improper or even criminal behavior by convincing themselves that it is actually acceptable behavior. This delusion, researchers have found, is much easier to accomplish with the support of others behaving in the same manner.[28] (To learn how social psychology is influencing an important aspect of homeland security, see the feature *Anti-Terrorism in Action—Lessons in Profiling* below.)

TRAIT THEORY AND PUBLIC POLICY Whereas choice theory justifies punishing wrongdoers, biological and psychological views of criminality suggest that antisocial behavior should be identified and treated before it manifests itself in first-time or further criminal activity. Though the focus on treatment diminished somewhat in the 1990s, rehabilitation practices in corrections have made somewhat of a comeback over the past few years. The primary motivation for this new outlook, as we will see in Chapters 11 through 14, is the pressing need to divert nonviolent offenders from the nation's overburdened prison and jail system.

ANTI-TERRORISM IN ACTION

LESSONS IN PROFILING

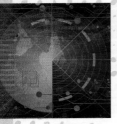

Argus/Shutterstock

The instructor at the front of a lecture hall in Davie, Florida, was addressing about sixty local police officers and law enforcement officials. "When you see a bunch of guys in red, what do you know?" he asked the audience. "They are Bloods," responded many in the audience, who dealt with street gangs regularly. "When you have a Muslim that wears a headband, regardless of color or insignia, basically what that is telling you is 'I am willing to be a martyr,'" the instructor insisted. Similarly, a New York City Police Department handbook identifies "wearing traditional Islamic clothing" and "growing a beard" as signs that an individual is moving toward dangerous radicalization.

Such views support the traditional terrorist profile often relied on by law enforcement agencies, which focuses on young males from Muslim backgrounds. Many terrorism experts, however, feel that this profile is both too broad and too narrow. It is too broad because the vast majority of Muslim Americans who wear headbands and have beards are not potential terrorists. It is too narrow because it does not encompass the realm of potential suspects. In the years since September 2001, well-known Islamic terrorists have included a white American (John Lindh) and a Hispanic American (José Padilla). In 2011, Colleen LaRose, a forty-six-year-old blonde woman from Michigan who went by the Internet moniker "JihadJane," pleaded guilty to several terrorism-related charges.

The Terrorist Mind

Criminologists, using interviews with former extremists and close study of online propaganda, are slowly developing a better understanding of the terrorist mind. Jerrold M. Post, a professor at George Washington University in Washington, D.C., has identified several risk factors for terrorism. These include a strong sense of victimization and alienation, a belief that one's ethnic or religious group is under attack, and the desire to "change things" through violence. Research also shows that the possibility of extremist action is greatly intensified by group support, particularly from the "virtual community of hatred" on the Internet. Potential terrorists caught up in the group dynamic are generally more likely to take risks, because those risks are shared and therefore less frightening. Furthermore, once a person becomes a member of a group, he or she feels pressure to agree with the others in the group, even when the consensus is to take violent action.

FOR CRITICAL ANALYSIS How can the psychological indicators described above be of practical assistance to police officers trying to prevent terrorist activity in their communities? Why might law enforcement agents be more likely to rely on physical markers such as Muslim dress and facial hair than on the terrorist profile provided by criminologists?

SOCIOLOGICAL THEORIES OF CRIME

The problem with trait theory, many criminologists contend, is that it falters when confronted with certain crime patterns. Why is the crime rate in Detroit, Michigan, twenty-five times that of Sioux Falls, South Dakota? Do high levels of air pollution cause an increase in abnormal brain activity or higher levels of testosterone? As no evidence has been found that would suggest that such biological factors can be so easily influenced, several generations of criminologists have instead focused on social and physical environmental factors in their study of criminal behavior.

THE CHICAGO SCHOOL The importance of sociology in the study of criminal behavior was established by a group of scholars who were associated with the Sociology Department at the University of Chicago in the early 1900s. These sociologists, known collectively as the Chicago School, gathered empirical evidence from the slums of the city that showed a correlation between conditions of poverty, such as inadequate housing and poor sanitation, and high rates of crime. Chicago School members Ernest Burgess (1886–1966) and Robert Ezra Park (1864–1944) argued that neighborhood conditions, be they of wealth or poverty, had a much greater determinant effect on criminal behavior than ethnicity, race, or religion.[29] The methods and theories of the Chicago School, which stressed that humans are social creatures whose behavior reflects their environment, have had a profound effect on criminology over the past century.

The study of crime as correlated with social structure revolves around three specific theories: (1) social disorganization theory, (2) strain theory, and (3) cultural deviance theory.

SOCIAL DISORGANIZATION THEORY Park and Burgess introduced an *ecological* analysis of crime to criminology. Just as ecology studies the relationships

LO 4
between animals and their environments, the two Chicago School members studied the relationship between inner-city residents and their environment. In addition, Clifford Shaw and Henry McKay, contemporaries of the Chicago School and researchers in juvenile crime, popularized the idea of ecology in criminology through social disorganization theory. This theory states that crime is largely a product of unfavorable conditions in certain communities.[30]

Disorganized Zones Studying juvenile delinquency in Chicago, Shaw and McKay discovered certain "zones" that exhibited high rates of crime. These zones were characterized by "disorganization," or a breakdown of the traditional institutions of social control such as family, school systems, and local businesses. In contrast, in the city's "organized" communities, residents had developed certain agreements about fundamental values and norms. Shaw and McKay found that residents in high-crime neighborhoods had to a large degree abandoned these fundamental values and norms. Also, a lack of social controls had led to increased levels of antisocial, or criminal, behavior.[31] According to social disorganization theory, ecological factors that lead to crime in these neighborhoods are perpetuated by continued elevated levels of high school dropouts, unemployment, deteriorating infrastructures, and single-parent families. (See Figure 2.2 on the following page to better understand social disorganization theory.)

The Value of Role Models In the late 1990s, sociologist Elijah Anderson of the University of Pennsylvania took Shaw and McKay's theories one step further. According to Anderson, residents in high-crime, African American "disorganized" zones separate themselves into two types of families: "street" and "decent." "Street" families are characterized by a lack

Group Activities: Place students into small groups and ask them to generate a chart comparing and contrasting classical criminology, positivism, and the sociological theories. The chart should include the major tenets of each school, as well as examples of social policy derived from each. (LO2–LO4)

Teaching Tip: Ask students to brainstorm a list of local community programs that fit with the perspective that changing neighborhood conditions can decrease crime. How effective do students feel such programs to be? (LO 4)

Social Disorganization Theory The theory that deviant behavior is more likely in communities where social institutions such as the family, schools, and the criminal justice system fail to exert control over the population.

FIGURE 2.2 The Stages of Social Disorganization Theory

Social disorganization theory holds that crime is related to the environmental pressures that exist in certain communities or neighborhoods. These areas are marked by the desire of many of their inhabitants to "get out" at the first possible opportunity. Consequently, residents tend to ignore the important institutions in the community, such as businesses and education, causing further erosion and an increase in the conditions that lead to crime.

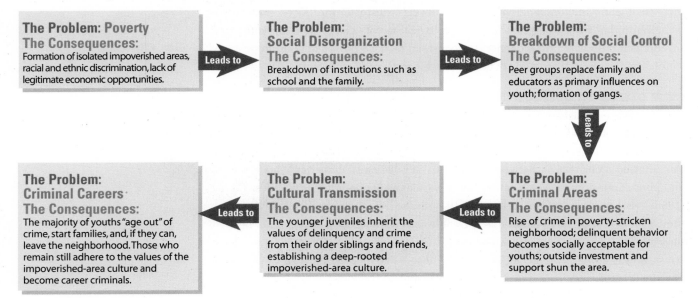

The Problem: Poverty
The Consequences:
Formation of isolated impoverished areas, racial and ethnic discrimination, lack of legitimate economic opportunities.

Leads to

The Problem: Social Disorganization
The Consequences:
Breakdown of institutions such as school and the family.

Leads to

The Problem: Breakdown of Social Control
The Consequences:
Peer groups replace family and educators as primary influences on youth; formation of gangs.

Leads to

The Problem: Criminal Careers
The Consequences:
The majority of youths "age out" of crime, start families, and, if they can, leave the neighborhood. Those who remain still adhere to the values of the impoverished-area culture and become career criminals.

Leads to

The Problem: Cultural Transmission
The Consequences:
The younger juveniles inherit the values of delinquency and crime from their older siblings and friends, establishing a deep-rooted impoverished-area culture.

Leads to

The Problem: Criminal Areas
The Consequences:
Rise of crime in poverty-stricken neighborhood; delinquent behavior becomes socially acceptable for youths; outside investment and support shun the area.

Source: Adapted from Larry J. Siegel, *Criminology*, 10th ed. (Belmont, CA: Thomson/Wadsworth, 2009), 180.

---

of consideration for others and poorly disciplined children. In contrast, "decent" families are community minded, instill values of hard work and education in their children, and generally have "hope for the future."[32]

Spending time in these disadvantaged areas, Anderson discovered that most "decent" families included an older man who held a steady job, performed his duties as husband and father, and was interested in the community's well-being. When external factors such as racial discrimination and lack of employment opportunities reduce the presence of these traditional role models, Anderson theorizes, "street" codes fill the void and youth violence escalates.[33] In a study released in 2010, criminologists Eric A. Stewart and Ronald L. Simons tested Anderson's theories. They studied the behavior of more than seven hundred African American adolescents and found that, indeed, in disorganized neighborhoods where a violent street culture dominates, juveniles are much more likely to commit acts of violent delinquency.[34]

STRAIN THEORY Another self-perpetuating aspect of disorganized neighborhoods is that once residents gain the financial means to leave a high-crime community, they usually do so. This desire to escape the inner city is related to the second branch of social structure theory: **strain theory.** Most Americans have similar life goals, which include gaining a certain measure of wealth and financial freedom. The means of attaining these goals, however, are not universally available. Many citizens do not have access to the education or training necessary for financial success. This often results in frustration and anger, or *strain.*

Strain theory has its roots in the works of French sociologist Emile Durkheim (1858–1917) and his concept of *anomie* (derived from the Greek word for "without norms"). Durkheim believed that *anomie* resulted when social change threw behavioral norms into a flux, leading to a weakening of social controls and an increase in deviant

Strain Theory The assumption that crime is the result of frustration felt by individuals who cannot reach their financial and personal goals through legitimate means.

Anomie A condition in which the individual suffers from the breakdown or absence of social norms. According to this theory, this condition occurs when a person is disconnected from these norms or rejects them as inconsistent with his or her personal goals.

behavior.[35] Another sociologist, American Robert K. Merton, expanded on Durkheim's ideas in his own theory of strain. Merton believed that *anomie* was caused by a social structure in which all citizens have similar goals without equal means to achieve them.[36] One way to alleviate this strain is to gain wealth by the means that are available to the residents of disorganized communities: drug trafficking, burglary, and other criminal activities.

In the 1990s, Robert Agnew of Emory University in Atlanta, Georgia, updated this line of criminology with his *general strain theory,* or GST.[37] Agnew reasoned that of all "strained" individuals, very few actually turn to crime to relieve the strain. GST tries to determine what factors, when combined with strain, actually lead to criminal activity. By the early 2000s, Agnew and other criminologists settled on the factor of negative emotionality, a term used to cover personality traits of those who are easily frustrated, quick to lose their tempers, and disposed to blame others for their own problems.[38] Thus, GST mixes strain theory with aspects of psychological theories of crime.

Discussion Tip: Have students brainstorm examples of crimes that could result from the conditions highlighted by strain theory. Have them discuss the potential shortcomings of this theory as well. (LO 4)

CULTURAL DEVIANCE THEORY Combining elements of social disorganization and strain theories, cultural deviance theory asserts that people adapt to the values of the subculture to which they belong. A subculture (a subdivision that exists within the dominant culture) has its own standards of behavior, or norms. By definition, a disorganized neighborhood is isolated from society at large, and the strain of this isolation encourages the formation of subcultures within the slum. According to cultural deviance theory, members of low-income subcultures are more likely to conform to value systems that celebrate behavior, such as violence, that directly confronts the value system of society at large and therefore draws criminal sanctions.

Cultural Deviance Theory A branch of social structure theory based on the assumption that members of certain subcultures reject the values of the dominant culture through deviant behavior patterns.

Subculture A group exhibiting certain values and behavior patterns that distinguish it from the dominant culture.

Social Process Theories A school of criminology that considers criminal behavior to be the predictable result of a person's interaction with his or her environment. According to these theories, everybody has the potential for wrongdoing. Those who act on this potential are conditioned to do so by family or peer groups, or institutions such as the media.

SOCIAL STRUCTURE THEORY AND PUBLIC POLICY If criminal behavior can be explained by the conditions in which certain groups of people live, then it stands to reason that changing those conditions can prevent crime. Indeed, government programs to decrease unemployment, reduce poverty, and improve educational facilities in low-income neighborhoods have been justified as part of large-scale attempts at crime prevention.

FAMILY, FRIENDS, AND THE MEDIA: SOCIAL PROCESSES OF CRIME

Some criminologists find class theories of crime overly narrow. Surveys that ask people directly about their criminal behavior have shown that the criminal instinct is pervasive in middle- and upper-class communities, even if it is expressed differently. Anybody, these criminologists argue, has the potential to act out criminal behavior, regardless of class, race, or gender.

Philip Zimbardo conducted a well-known, if rather unscientific, experiment to make this point. Zimbardo placed an abandoned automobile with its hood up on the campus of Stanford University. The car remained in place, untouched, for a week. Then, the psychologist smashed the car's window with a sledgehammer. Within minutes, passersby had joined in the destruction of the automobile, eventually stripping its valuable parts.[39] Social process theories function on the same basis as Zimbardo's "interdependence of decisions experiment": the potential for criminal behavior exists in everyone and will be realized depending on an individual's interaction with various institutions and processes of society. Social process theory has three main branches: (1) learning theory, (2) control theory, and (3) labeling theory.

Learning Theory The hypothesis that delinquents and criminals must be taught both the practical and the emotional skills necessary to participate in illegal activity.

Control Theory A series of theories that assume that all individuals have the potential for criminal behavior, but are restrained by the damage that such actions would do to their relationships with family, friends, and members of the community. Criminality occurs when these bonds are broken or nonexistent.

Teaching Tip: In a written assignment, ask students to react to data which suggests a link between television violence and aggression in children. Should violence in television and movies be limited by the federal government? Why or why not?

Discussion Tip: Ask students to discuss Lauritsen's finding that adolescents from single-parent households were victimized at higher rates than their counterparts from two-parent households. How does Lauritsen's study reflect a control theory perspective?

LEARNING THEORY Popularized by Edwin Sutherland in the 1940s, learning

LO 5

theory contends that criminal activity is a learned behavior. In other words, a criminal is taught both the practical methods of crime (such as how to pick a lock) and the psychological aspects of crime (how to deal with the guilt of wrongdoing). Sutherland's *theory of differential association* held that individuals are exposed to the values of family and peers such as school friends or co-workers. If the dominant values one is exposed to favor criminal behavior, then that person is more likely to mimic such behavior.[40] Sutherland concentrated particularly on familial relations, believing that a child was more likely to commit crimes if she or he saw an older sibling or a parent doing so. A good deal of data backs these theories. In a recent survey, a high percentage of boys involved in aggressive delinquent behavior reported having friends who sold drugs or carried a knife or gun.[41] Furthermore, according to the U.S. Department of Justice, nearly 50 percent of inmates in state prisons have relatives who have also been incarcerated.[42]

More recently, learning theory has been expanded to include the growing influence of the media. In the latest in a long series of studies, psychologists at the University of Michigan's Institute for Social Research released data in 2003 showing that exposure to high levels of televised violence erodes a natural aversion to violence and increases aggressive behavior among young children.[43] Such findings have spurred a number of legislative attempts to curb violence on television.[44] (The controversy surrounding the violent attributes of another medium—video games—is the subject of the *CJ in Action* feature at the end of this chapter.)

CONTROL THEORY Criminologist Travis Hirschi focuses on the reasons why individuals do not engage in criminal acts, rather than why they do. According to Hirschi, social bonds promote conformity to social norms. The stronger these social bonds—which include attachment to, commitment to, involvement with, and belief in societal values—the less likely that any individual will commit a crime.[45] Control theory holds that although we all have the potential to commit crimes, most of us are dissuaded from doing so because we care about the opinions of our family and peers. James Q. Wilson and George Kelling describe control theory in terms of the "broken windows" effect. Neighborhoods in poor condition are filled with cues of lack of social control (for example, broken windows) that invite further vandalism and other deviant behavior.[46] If these cues are removed, according to Wilson and Kelling, so is the implied acceptance of crime within a community.

Janet Lauritsen, a criminologist at the University of Missouri–St. Louis, contends that familial control is more important than run-down surroundings in predicting whether crime will occur. Lauritsen found that adolescents residing in two-parent households were victims of crime at similar rates, regardless of the levels of disadvantage in the neighborhoods in which they lived. By contrast, adolescents from single-parent homes who lived in highly disorganized neighborhoods were victimized at much higher rates than their counterparts in more stable locales. In Lauritsen's opinion, the support of a two-parent household offers crucial protection for children, whatever the condition of their neighborhood.[47]

LABELING THEORY James Caston was a big fan of the James Gang, a group of outlaws famous for robbing trains, banks, and stagecoaches in southern and midwestern states near the end of the nineteenth century. Consequently, Caston decided to name his first two sons after gang members "Jesse" and "Frank." Today, both brothers are serving life sentences in a Louisiana state prison for murder. "We never had a chance," said Jesse James Caston when asked about the influence of his name.[48]

CAREERS IN CJ

FAST FACTS

SOCIAL WORKER JOB DESCRIPTION:

- Assist people by helping them cope with issues in their everyday lives, deal with their relationships, and solve personal and family problems.
- Assist families that have serious domestic conflicts, sometimes involving child or spousal abuse.
- Specialize in serving a particular population or working in a specific setting.
- Conduct research, advocate for improved services, engage in systems design, or develop policies.

WHAT KIND OF TRAINING IS REQUIRED?

- While a B.A. in social work is the minimum requirement, a master's degree in social work or a related field has become the standard for many positions.
- Essential qualities: emotionally mature, objective, and sensitive to people and their problems; able to handle responsibility, work independently, and maintain good working relationships with clients and co-workers.

ANNUAL SALARY RANGE? BENEFITS?

- $32,500–$56,500

For additional information on a career as a social worker, visit:
www.socialworkers.org

SUSAN KNOLLS
SOCIAL WORKER

I think if you ask any social worker why they chose this profession, most of them would say they didn't; it chose them. It starts from when you are very young and you want to make sure that everyone is okay, so you stay up in the middle of the night worrying about others and wanting to help in any way you can. That said, I do actually remember the moment when I formally decided to become a social worker. It was after I had taken a year off from college and traveled around the United States and Europe. I remember thinking how incredibly fortunate I was and how I wanted to give back to the world some of what had been given to me.

PROTECTING CHILDREN I work mostly in child protection services, and the children are my favorite part of the job. Granted, some of them have a lot of issues and can be difficult to work with; it's often depressing to watch some of the horrible things going on in their lives. They are a resilient bunch, however, and many of them are smart and funny and can make me laugh even in the direst of circumstances. One of the real tangible rewards of my line of social work is when one of "my" kids gets adopted into a good family situation. I love watching a child who has been through so much finally get the life that, I feel, he or she absolutely deserves.

A HOUSE CALL There is never a dull day in the world of child protection! For instance, when I was still pretty new to the job, our office received an anonymous report that there was a man at the home of a mother I was working with in Boulder County, Colorado. This guy had a history of violence and a restraining order, and he was not supposed to be anywhere near the place. So, my boss and I went to the house to check out the situation. We knocked on the door and a very small, sweet-looking grandmother answered. We asked her if the man was at the home. She told us he wasn't, and we could search the house if we didn't believe her. Even though she hardly seemed like the person to tell a lie, my boss took her up on her offer.

At first, we didn't find anything. Then, my boss noticed a swinging hanger in a closet. He asked me to "check it out." I went to the closet, where I saw nothing but a pile of blankets on the floor. I began peeling them away until, wouldn't you know, I saw the back of a man lying on the floor of the closet! He scared the devil out of me! I looked at him and said, "What are you doing in there? You come out of there right now!" as if I were scolding a child. Luckily, he seemed more embarrassed than angry. Looking back, it was a very dumb—and dangerous—thing for us to do, especially without someone from law enforcement present. It worked out, however, as we reported the guy to his probation officer and he wound up back in jail.

CAREER ADVICE In child protection work, many people hold different degrees, including bachelor's and master's degrees in the fields of social work, psychology, sociology, and counseling. Some of my co-workers are licensed clinical social workers (LCSWs) and certified addiction counselors (CACs). I feel that a bachelor's degree in social work (BSW) is the ideal degree for someone just coming into child protection because it gives you a good, well-rounded foundation in social justice, substance abuse, mental illness, and child development on which to rely during your practice.

The Caston brothers serve as a rather literal example of a third social process theory. **Labeling theory** focuses on perceptions of criminal behavior rather than the behavior itself. Labeling theorists study how being labeled a criminal—a "whore" or a "junkie" or a "thief"—affects that person's future behavior. Sociologist Howard Becker contends that deviance is

> a consequence of the application by others of rules and sanctions to an offender. The deviant is one to whom that label has successfully been applied; deviant behavior is behavior that people so label.[49]

Such labeling, some criminologists believe, becomes a self-fulfilling prophecy. Someone labeled a "junkie" will begin to consider himself or herself a deviant and continue the criminal behavior for which he or she has been labeled. Following this line of reasoning, the criminal justice system is engaged in artificially creating a class of criminals by labeling victimless crimes such as drug use, prostitution, and gambling as "criminal."

SOCIAL PROCESS THEORY AND PUBLIC POLICY Because adult criminals are seen as too "hardened" to unlearn their criminal behavior, crime prevention policies associated with social process theory focus on juvenile offenders. Many youths, for example, are diverted from the formal juvenile justice process to keep them from being labeled "delinquent." Furthermore, many schools have implemented programs that attempt to steer children away from crime by encouraging them to "just say no" to drugs and stay in school. As we shall see in Chapter 6, implementation of Wilson and Kelling's "broken windows" principles has been credited with lowering the violent crime rate in New York and in a number of other major cities.

SOCIAL CONFLICT THEORIES

A more recent movement in criminology focuses not on psychology, biology, or sociology, but on *power*. Those who identify power—seen as the ability of one person or group of persons to control the economic and social positions of other people or groups—as the key component in explaining crime entered the mainstream of American criminology during the 1960s. These theorists saw social ills such as poverty, racism, sexism, and destruction of the environment as the "true crimes," perpetrated by the powerful, or ruling, classes. Burglary, robbery, and even violent crimes were considered justifiable reactions by the powerless against laws that were meant to repress, not protect, them. Supporters of these ideas aligned themselves with Marxist, radical, conflict, and feminist schools of criminology. Collectively, they have constructed the **social conflict theories** of crime causation.

MARXISM VERSUS CAPITALISM The genesis of social conflict theory can be found in the political philosophy of a German named Karl Marx (1818–1883). Marx believed that capitalist economic systems necessarily produce income inequality and lead to the exploitation of the working classes.[50] Consequently, social conflict theory is often associated with a critique of our capitalist economic system.

Capitalism is seen as leading to high levels of violence and crime because of the disparity of income that results. The poor commit property crimes for reasons of need and because, as members of a capitalist society, they desire the same financial rewards as everybody else. They commit violent crimes because of the frustration and rage they feel when these rewards seem unattainable. Laws, instead of reflecting the values of society as a whole, reflect only the values of the segment of society that has achieved power and is willing to use the criminal justice system as a tool to keep that power.[51] Thus, the harsh penalties for "lower-class" crimes such as burglary can be seen as a means of protecting the privileges of the "haves" from the aspirations of the "have-nots."

It is important to note that, according to social conflict theory, power is not synonymous with wealth. Women and members of minority groups can be wealthy and yet still be disassociated from the benefits of power in our society. Richard Quinney, one of the most influential social conflict theorists of the past forty years, encompasses issues of race, gender, power, and crime in a theory known as the social reality of crime.[52] For Quinney, along with many of his peers, criminal law does not reflect a universal moral code, but instead is a set of "rules" through which those who hold power can control and subdue those who do not. Any conflict between the "haves" and the "have-nots," therefore, is bound to be decided in favor of the "haves," who make the law and control the criminal justice system. Following this reasoning, Quinney sees violations of the law not as inherently criminal acts, but rather as political ones—as revolutionary acts against the power of the state.

ISSUES OF RACE AND GENDER Those who perceive the criminal justice system as an instrument of social control point to a number of historical studies and statistics to support their argument. In the nineteenth century, nearly three-quarters of female inmates had been incarcerated for sexual misconduct. They were sent to institutions such as New York's Western House of Refuge at Albion to be taught the virtues of "true" womanhood.[53] Today, about 69 percent of the approximately 48,000 Americans arrested for prostitution each year are women.[54] After the Civil War (1861–1865), many African Americans were driven from the South by "Jim Crow laws" designed to keep them from attaining power in the postwar period. Today, the criminal justice system performs a similar function. One out of every eight black men in their twenties is in prison or jail on any given day,[55] and African American males are incarcerated at about 6.5 times the rate of white males.[56]

Apparent injustices only add to the sense of oppression in minority communities. In November 2010, for example, Bay Area Rapid Transit (BART) police officer Johannes Mehserle was sentenced to twenty-four months in prison for the death of African American Oscar Grant III. Nearly two years earlier, Mehserle had shot a prone and unresisting Grant in the back during an incident at a BART station in Oakland, California. Although Mehserle was able to convince a jury that he had mistakenly pulled his gun, many Oakland residents felt that Grant's race contributed to Mehserle's relatively light punishment (see the photo at right.)

SOCIAL CONFLICT THEORY AND PUBLIC POLICY Given its radical nature, social conflict theory has had a limited impact on public policy. Even in the aftermath of situations in which class conflict has had serious and obvious repercussions, such as the Los Angeles riots of 1991, few observers feel that enough has been accomplished to improve the conditions that led to the violence. Indeed, many believe that the best hope for a shift in the power structure is the employment of more women and minorities in the criminal justice system itself. (See *Mastering Concepts* on the following page for a review of the theories discussed so far in this chapter.)

> **"The common argument that crime is caused by poverty is a kind of slander on the poor."**
>
> **—H. L. Mencken, American journalist (1956)**

Social Reality of Crime The theory that criminal laws are designed by those in power to help them keep power at the expense of those who do not have power.

Riot police subdue a protester following the sentencing of Johannes Mehserle for killing Oscar Grant III. If you were a proponent of social conflict theory, how would you interpret Grant's death and Mehserle's punishment?
AP Photo/Noah Berger

Fill in the blanks and check your answers on page 62.

_____ theory holds that criminals make a deliberate decision to commit a crime after weighing the possible rewards or punishments of the act. _____ theories of crime suggest that the origins of criminal behavior can be found in the body, while _____ theories focus on the disorders of the mind. A criminologist who studies the effect of community or neighborhood conditions on criminal activity is testing _____ theories of crime, while one who concentrates on the influence of friends and family is analyzing _____ _____ theories of criminal behavior.

MASTERINGCONCEPTS

The Causes of Crime

Choice Theories

Key Concept: Crime is the result of rational choices made by those who decide to engage in criminal activity for the rewards—financial and otherwise—that it offers.

Key Question: Do offenders really make rational, considered choices when it comes to crime, or are their decisions irrational and therefore difficult to influence?

Model Legislation: Alaska's new animal cruelty law makes "knowingly inflicting severe and prolonged physical pain or suffering" on an animal a Class C felony, punishable by up to five years in prison. The goal of this legislation is to give potential animal abusers a strong reason to refrain from such behavior.

Biological and Psychological Trait Theories

Key Concept: Criminal behavior is explained by the biological and psychological attributes of an individual.

Key Question: If the secrets of criminal behavior are contained in the body and the mind, will scientists soon be able to predict future crimes by better understanding biological and psychological traits?

Model Legislation: The federal Mentally Ill Offender Treatment and Crime Reduction Act provides $10 million for crisis intervention training programs that help law enforcement officers identify and properly respond to individuals with mental illnesses.

Sociological Theories

Key Concept: Crime is not something one is "born to do." Rather, crime is the result of the social conditions under which a person finds himself or herself.

Key Question: Can the government reduce crime by taking steps to reduce certain aspects of disadvantaged neighborhoods such as poverty, poor schools, unemployment, and racial discrimination?

Model Legislation: In Illinois, the Work Opportunity Tax Credit provides tax savings to employers who hire ex-convicts. This strategy assumes that if someone has a steady job, she or he is less likely to commit crimes.

Social Process Theories

Key Concept: Family, friends, and peers have the greatest impact on an individual's behavior, and it is the interactions with these groups that ultimately determine whether a person will become involved in criminal behavior.

Key Question: Can at-risk youths be discouraged from delinquency and crime by removing negative influences from the environments in which they live?

Model Legislation: In response to findings that the hours from 3 P.M. to 6 P.M. are the peak time for violent behavior by adolescents, California passed the After School Education and Safety Program Act. The legislation aims to keep students off the streets each afternoon by providing them with educational and recreational programs at schools.

Social Conflict Theories

Key Concept: Through criminal laws, the dominant members of society control the minority members, using institutions such as the police, courts, and prisons as tools of oppression.

Key Question: As more members of minority groups and women gain positions of power in the criminal justice system, will the criminal justice system become more "just"?

Model Legislation: More than twenty states have passed laws prohibiting racial profiling, which, as you will learn in Chapter 7, refers to the police tactic of using race to identify a person as a criminal suspect.

FURTHER STUDY: EXPANDING CRIMINOLOGY

The five theories described so far form the bedrock of criminological study. The field is in no way limited to these concepts, however. Each year, criminologists conduct hundreds of studies, some of them expanding on already established theories and others heading in different directions entirely. Over the past few decades, for example, increased arrest and incarceration rates of African Americans have sparked interest in *racial threat theory*. First developed to describe the reaction of many whites to the growing social, economic, and political power of blacks in the 1960s,[57] today the theory focuses on the amount of control the criminal justice system exerts on the African American community. Racial threat theory is based on the hypothesis that as the size of a minority group increases, members of the majority group take steps to repress that group.[58] This hypothesis has found support in a number of studies that link increases in the proportion of black residents to increases in the size and funding of local police departments, as well as higher arrest and incarceration rates for African Americans, in the same area.[59]

> **"It is not racism that makes whites uneasy about blacks moving into their neighborhoods . . . it is fear. Fear of crime, of drugs, of gangs, of violence."**
>
> —James Q. Wilson, criminologist (1992)

Two other emerging strands of criminology that we will examine in this section are life course theories and victimology.

LOOKING BACK TO CHILDHOOD: LIFE COURSE THEORIES OF CRIME

If a child enjoys pulling wings off butterflies or dunking the family cat in the bath, should society take notice? Yes, according to a study released in 2008 that suggests a link between childhood abuse of animals and adult violence.[60] Indeed, perhaps the most **LO 6** influential "new" criminological theory fills what has been a gaping hole in the study of the causes of crime. As Francis T. Cullen and Robert Agnew put it, "throughout much of the history of American criminology, scholars simply ignored the fact that humans have a childhood."[61] Instead, the bulk of research on youthful offending has focused on teenagers. Nevertheless, childhood may hold the key to many questions criminologists have been asking for years.

Many of the other theories we have studied in this chapter tend to attribute criminal behavior to factors—such as unemployment or poor educational performance—that take place long after an individual's personality has been established. Practitioners of life course criminology believe that lying, stealing, bullying, and other conduct problems that occur in childhood are the strongest predictors of future criminal behavior and have been seriously undervalued in the examination of why crime occurs.[62]

SELF-CONTROL THEORY Focusing on childhood behavior raises the question of whether conduct problems established at a young age can be changed over time. Michael Gottfredson and Travis Hirschi, whose 1990 publication *A General Theory of Crime* is one of the foundations of life course criminology, think not.[63] Gottfredson and Hirschi believe that criminal behavior is linked to "low self-control," a personality trait that is formed before a child reaches the age of ten and can usually be attributed to poor parenting.[64]

Someone with low self-control is generally impulsive, thrill seeking, and likely to solve problems with violence rather than his or her intellect. Gottfredson and Hirschi

Teaching Tip: Ask students to reflect on how life course theories of crime differ from classical criminology, positivism, and the sociological theories. Can criminality really be traced to childhood? If one subscribes to life course criminology, how can crime be reduced? (LO 6)

Life Course Criminology The study of crime based on the belief that behavioral patterns developed in childhood can predict delinquent and criminal behavior later in life.

think that once low self-control has been established, it will persist. In other words, childhood behavioral problems are not "solved" by positive developments later in life, such as healthy personal relationships or a good job.[65] Thus, these two criminologists ascribe to what has been called the *continuity theory of crime*, which essentially says that once negative behavior patterns have been established, they cannot be changed.

THE POSSIBILITY OF CHANGE Not all of those who practice life course criminology follow the continuity theory. Terrie Moffitt, for example, notes that youthful offenders can be divided into two groups. The first group are life-course-persistent offenders: they are biting playmates at age five, skipping school at ten, stealing cars at sixteen, committing violent crimes at twenty, and perpetrating fraud and child abuse at thirty.[66] The second group are adolescent-limited offenders: as the name suggests, their "life of crime" is limited to the teenage years.[67] So, according to Moffitt, change is possible, if not for the life-course-persistent offenders (who are saddled with psychological problems that lead to continued social failure and misconduct), then for the adolescent-limited offenders.

Robert Sampson and John Laub take this line of thinking one step further. While acknowledging that "antisocial behavior is relatively stable" from childhood to old age, Sampson and Laub have gathered a great deal of data showing, in their opinion, that offenders may experience "turning points" when they are able to veer off the road from a life of crime.[68] A good deal of research in this area has concentrated on the positive impact of getting married, having children, and finding a job,[69] but other turning points are also being explored.

John F. Frana of Indiana State University and Ryan D. Schroeder of the University of Louisville argue that military service can act as a "rehabilitative agent."[70] Several researchers have studied the role that religion and spirituality can play as "hooks for change."[71] Furthermore, particularly for drug abusers, the death of a loved one or friend from shared criminal behavior can provide a powerful incentive to discontinue that behavior.

VICTIMOLOGY AND VICTIMS OF CRIME

Since its founding days, criminology has focused almost exclusively on one-half of the crime equation: the offender. If you review our discussion of criminology up to this point, you will find little mention of the other half: the victim. Indeed, it was not until after World War II (1939–1945) that the scientific study of crime victims began to appeal to academicians, and only in the last several decades has victimology become an essential component of criminology.[72] The growing emphasis on the victim has had a profound impact on the police, the courts, and corrections administrators in this country. Accordingly, Andrew Karmen, a professor of sociology at the John Jay College of Criminal Justice in New York City, has defined *victimology* as the study of "relationships between victims and offenders [and] the interactions between victims and the criminal justice system."[73]

THE RISKS OF VICTIMIZATION Anybody can be a victim of crime. This does not mean, however, that everybody is at an equal risk of being victimized. For example, because mental illnesses such as schizophrenia (see page 34) interfere with a person's ability to make smart decisions in risky situations, those who suffer from such disabilities are eleven times more likely to be the victims of violent crimes than nonsufferers.[74]

To better explain the circumstances surrounding victimization, in the late 1970s, criminologists Larry Cohen and Marcus Felson devised the *routine activities theory*. According to Cohen and Felson, most criminal acts require the following:

1. A likely offender.
2. A suitable target (a person or an object).
3. The absence of a capable guardian—that is, any person (not necessarily a law enforcement agent) whose presence or proximity prevents a crime from happening.[75]

When these three factors are present, the likelihood of crime rises. Cohen and Felson believe that routine activities often contribute to this "perfect storm" of criminal opportunity. So, when a person leaves for work, her or his home becomes a suitable target for a likely offender because the guardian is absent.

REPEAT VICTIMIZATION Cohen and Felson also hypothesize that offenders attach "values" to suitable targets, and the higher the value, the more likely that target is going to be the subject of a crime.[76] A gold watch, for example, would obviously have a higher value for a thief than a plastic watch and therefore is more likely to be stolen. Similarly, people who are perceived to be weak or unprotected can have high value for criminals. Law enforcement officials in southern Florida, for example, believe that illegal immigrants in the area have high victimization rates because criminals know they are afraid to report crimes to authorities for fear of being removed from the country.

Resources such as the National Crime Victimization Survey, which you will learn more about in the next chapter, provide "victimologists" with an important tool for determining which types of people are most valued as potential victims. The data clearly show that a small percentage of victims are involved in a disproportionate number of crimes. This statistic has led many observers to champion an approach to crime analysis known as **repeat victimization.** This theory is based on the premise that certain people are more likely to be victims of crimes than others and, therefore, past victimization is a strong predictor of future victimization.[77]

THE VICTIM-OFFENDER CONNECTION Early on the morning of August 14, 2010, a lone gunman shot eight people outside a nightclub in Buffalo, New York. Of the eight victims, four of whom died, seven had previously been arrested or convicted of a crime.[78] This incident underscores an important point: criminals and victims are often the same people. Recently gathered data show, for example, that 92 percent of murder suspects and 72 percent of murder victims in Chicago have previously been convicted of a crime.[79] Of Baltimore's 234 murder victims in 2008, 194 had criminal records.[80]

LO 7

"The notion that [violent crimes] are random bolts of lightning, which is the commonly held image, is not the reality at all," says David Kennedy, a professor at New York's John Jay College of Criminal Justice.[81] Kennedy's point is further made by Figure 2.3 on the following page, which shows that the most vulnerable demographic groups—particularly young, low-income African American males—are also those with the highest rates of criminality. Given that victims and offenders appear to be drawn from the same pool of individuals, some criminologists have begun applying the theories we have discussed in this chapter to patterns of victimization.[82] For example, studies have shown that someone with low self-control (see page 51) is at greater risk for victimization as well as for offending.[83]

Mourners carry a photo of Bobby Tillman at his November 2010 funeral in College Park, Georgia. Tillman, 18, was beaten to death after being randomly attacked outside a house party. How does randomness fit, if at all, into the routine activities theory of crime victimization?
AP Photo/*Atlanta Journal & Constitution*, Brant Sanderlin

Repeat Victimization The theory that certain people and places are more likely to be subject to criminal activity and that past victimization is therefore a valuable crime prevention tool because it is a strong indicator of future victimization.

Teaching Tip: Invite a local victim advocate to visit the classroom. Ask him or her to talk about the role of victim advocacy in today's criminal justice process. In your community, what types of victimization are most common? What challenges do advocates face when victims are also offenders? (LO 7)

FIGURE 2.3

Crime Victims in the United States
According to the U.S. Department of Justice, African Americans, households with annual incomes of less than $7,500, and young people between the ages of twelve and fifteen are most likely to be victims of violent crime in this country.

Source: Bureau of Justice Statistics, *Criminal Victimization, 2009* (Washington, D.C.: U.S. Department of Justice, October 2010), 4, 5.

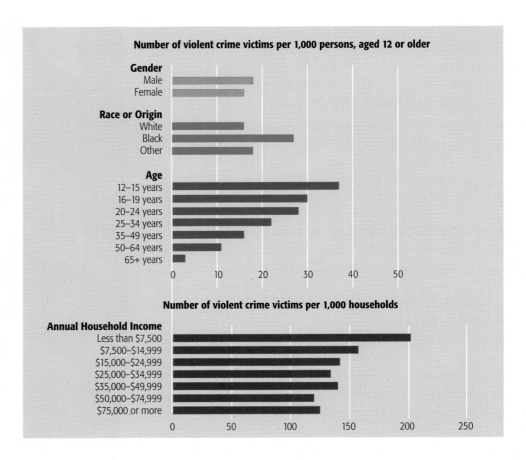

Number of violent crime victims per 1,000 persons, aged 12 or older

Gender
Male
Female

Race or Origin
White
Black
Other

Age
12–15 years
16–19 years
20–24 years
25–34 years
35–49 years
50–64 years
65+ years

0   10   20   30   40   50

Number of violent crime victims per 1,000 households

Annual Household Income
Less than $7,500
$7,500–$14,999
$15,000–$24,999
$25,000–$34,999
$35,000–$49,999
$50,000–$74,999
$75,000 or more

0   50   100   150   200   250

SELFASSESSMENT

Fill in the blanks and check your answers on page 62.
Supporters of _____ course theories of crime believe that stealing, bullying, and other conduct problems that occur during _____ can, in some instances, predict adult offending. These criminologists often find evidence of low self-_____ in future delinquents. _____ is the study of the relationship between victims and offenders in the criminal justice system. The theory of _____ victimization holds that past victimization is a strong predictor of future victimization.

THE LINK BETWEEN DRUGS AND CRIME

Earlier in this chapter, we discussed the difference between correlations and causes. As you may recall, criminologists are generally reluctant to declare that any one factor causes a certain result. Richard B. Felson of Penn State University and Keri B. Burchfield of Northern Illinois University, however, believe that alcohol consumption has a causal effect on victimization under certain circumstances.[84] Felson and Burchfield found that "frequent and heavy" drinkers are at a great risk of assault when they are drinking, but do not show abnormal rates of victimization when sober. They hypothesize that consuming alcohol leads to aggressive and offensive behavior, particularly in men, which in turn triggers violent reactions from others.

In Chapter 1, we learned that nearly 22 million Americans regularly use illegal drugs such as marijuana and cocaine, with another 200 million using legal drugs such as

Teaching Tip: Ask students to react to the first paragraph of the section "The Link Between Drugs and Crime." Do students view illegal drugs and alcohol as being correlated with criminal offending, or as a cause of criminal offending? Why?

alcohol and nicotine. Here, we will discuss two questions concerning these habits. First, why do people use drugs? Second, what are the consequences for the criminal justice system?

THE CRIMINOLOGY OF DRUG USE

At first glance, the reason people use drugs, including legal drugs such as alcohol, is obvious: such drugs give the user pleasure and provide a temporary escape for those who may feel tension or anxiety. Ultimately, though, such explanations are unsatisfactory because they fail to explain why some people use drugs while others do not.

THEORIES OF DRUG USE Several of the theories we discussed earlier in the chapter have been used by experts to explain drug use. *Social disorganization theory* (pages 43–44) holds that rapid social change can cause people to become disaffiliated from mainstream society, causing them to turn to drugs. *Subculture theory* (page 45), particularly as applied to adolescents, sees drug use as the result of peer pressure. *Control theory* (page 46) suggests that a lack of social control, as provided by entities such as the family or school, can lead to antisocial behavior.

Do you feel that the behavior of celebrities such as socialite Paris Hilton, who was arrested for cocaine possession in Las Vegas on August 27, 2010, "teaches" adolescents that such behavior is acceptable or even desirable? Explain your answer. AP Photo/Mark Damon

DRUGS AND THE "LEARNING PROCESS" Focusing on the question of why first-time drug users become habitual users, sociologist Howard Becker sees three factors in the "learning process." He believes first-time users:

1. Learn the techniques of drug use.
2. Learn to perceive the pleasurable effects of drug use.
3. Learn to enjoy the social experience of drug use.[85]

Becker's assumptions are evident in the widespread belief that positive images of drug use in popular culture "teach" adolescents that such behavior is not only acceptable but desirable. The entertainment industry, in particular, has been criticized for glamorizing various forms of drug use.

DRUG ADDICTION AND DEPENDENCY

Another theory rests on the assumption that some people possess overly sensitive drug receptors in their brains and are therefore biologically disposed toward drug use.[86] Though there is little conclusive evidence that biological factors can explain initial drug experimentation, scientific research has provided a great deal of insight into patterns of long-term drug use.

DRUG USE AND DRUG ABUSE In particular, science has aided in understanding the difference between drug *use* and drug *abuse*. **Drug abuse** can be defined as the use of any drug—licit or illicit—that causes either psychological or bodily harm to the abuser or to third parties. Just as most people who drink beer or wine avoid abusing alcohol, most users of illegal substances are not abusers. For most drugs except nicotine, only between 7 and 20 percent of all users suffer from compulsive abuse.[87]

Drug Abuse The use of drugs that results in physical or psychological problems for the user, as well as disruption of personal relationships and employment.

Despite their relatively small numbers, drug abusers have a disparate impact on the drug market. The 20 percent of Americans, for example, who drink the most consume more than 80 percent of all alcoholic beverages sold in the United States. The data are similar for illicit substance abusers, leading to the conclusion that, to a large extent, abusers and addicts sustain the market for illegal drugs.

ADDICTION BASICS The most extreme abusers are addicted to, or physically dependent on a drug. To understand the basics of addiction and physical dependence, you must understand the role of *dopamine* in the brain. Dopamine, mentioned earlier in the chapter on page 40, is the neurotransmitter responsible for delivering pleasure signals to brain nerve endings in response to behavior—such as eating good food or engaging in sex—that makes us feel good. The bloodstream delivers drugs to the area of the brain that produces dopamine, thereby triggering the production of a large amount of the substance in the brain. Over time, the continued use of drugs physically changes the nerve endings, called *receptors.* To continue operating in the presence of large amounts of dopamine, the receptors become less sensitive, meaning that greater amounts of any particular drug are required to create the amount of dopamine needed for the same levels of pleasure. When the supply of the drug is cut off, the brain strongly feels the lack of dopamine stimulation, and the abuser will suffer symptoms of withdrawal until the receptors readjust.[88]

Addiction and physical dependence are interrelated, though not exactly the same. Those who are physically dependent on a drug suffer withdrawal symptoms when they stop using it, but after a certain time period, they are generally able to emerge without further craving. Addicts, in contrast, continue to feel a need for the drug long after withdrawal symptoms have passed. For many years, researchers have been striving to determine if some people are more likely than others to become addicts for biological reasons. In 2008, a group of researchers from Peking University in China made significant headway toward doing so by showing that many addicts share a particular set of *enzymes,* or proteins that trigger chemical reactions in the body.[89]

THE DRUG-CRIME RELATIONSHIP

Of course, because many drugs are illegal, anybody who sells, uses, or in any way promotes the use of these drugs is, under most circumstances, breaking the law. The drug-crime relationship goes beyond the language of criminal drug statutes, however. About 37 percent of state prisoners and 33 percent of jail inmates incarcerated for a violent crime were under the influence of alcohol at the time of their arrest.[90] Similarly, according to one recent study, more than two-thirds of all arrestees in ten major American cities tested positive for illicit drugs when apprehended.[91] As we will see throughout this textbook, the prosecution of illegal drug users and suppliers has been one of the primary factors in the enormous growth of the American correctional industry.

MODELS OF EXPLANATION Epidemiologist Paul Goldstein has devised three models to explain the relationship between drugs and crime:

- The *psychopharmacological model* holds that individuals act violently or criminally as a direct result of the drugs they have ingested.
- The *economically impulsive model* holds that drug abusers commit crimes to get the funds to purchase drugs.
- The *systemic model* suggests that violence is a by-product of the interpersonal relationships within the drug-using community, such as when a dealer is assaulted by a buyer for selling "bad" drugs.[92]

New forms of drug-related crime are appearing, as well. According to federal data, the number of people seeking treatment for abuse of painkillers increased 400 percent from 1998 to 2008.[93] The increased demand for these **prescription drugs** has, in the words of one Maine law enforcement official, led to "home invasions, robberies, assaults, homicides, thefts—all kinds of crime."[94] From 2007 to 2010, more than 1,800 pharmacy robberies occurred in the United States, with the offenders targeting prescription drugs such as the painkillers oxycodone and hydrocodone, and the antianxiety agent Xanax.[95]

Prescription Drugs Medical drugs that require a physician's permission for purchase.

The strength of the drug-crime relationship has provided justification for increased law enforcement efforts to criminalize drug use by harshly punishing offenders of controlled substance laws. (To learn about a country where the violent crime caused by the drug trade has reached catastrophic levels, see the feature *Comparative Criminal Justice—A Real War on Drugs* below.)

COMPARATIVE CRIMINAL JUSTICE

A REAL WAR ON DRUGS

For most of the past decade, Mexico and its citizens have suffered through a bloody and seemingly endless "war on drugs." Each year, illegal drugs worth from $25 to $40 billion are smuggled over the border into the United States, and various cartels are willing to fight—and kill—for their cut. From 2007 to 2011, more than 35,000 Mexicans were murdered in drug-related slayings. "I really characterize this as a civil war," says Howard Campbell of the University of Texas at El Paso. "We're seeing all the casualties of a war, people murdered, people wounded, people fleeing their homes, disintegration and chaos."

MAKING THINGS WORSE?

Mexico's leaders have not stood idly by in the face of this carnage. Mistrustful of corrupt local police, the federal government has sent tens of thousands of federal troops to the areas where the drug trade is most active, primarily along the U.S.–Mexican border. Although numerous drug kingpins have been captured, these efforts have apparently only exacerbated the problem.

The disruption of the cartels has led to more violence as gang members try to fill the power vacuum. In 2010, Ciudad Juárez—across the Rio Grande from El Paso, Texas—experienced more than 3,000 murders, making it one of the most dangerous cities in the world. Included in that tally were a pregnant American consulate worker and her husband, gunned down while driving in their car. One frustrated Juárez resident predicts that the violence "is going to continue until one of the cartels takes control of the country."

FOR CRITICAL ANALYSIS

According to Tony Garza, who spent six years (2002–2008) as the U.S. ambassador to Mexico, the country would not "be experiencing this level of violence were the United States not the largest consumer of illicit drugs and the main supplier of weapons to the cartels." The U.S. government has provided Mexico with $1.4 billion in aid to use in its war on drugs, and numerous American federal, state, and local law enforcement agencies are working with their Mexican counterparts to stem the violence. Is the United States morally obligated to provide this financial and tactical aid? What other steps could our government take to weaken the link between illegal drugs and crime in Mexico?

A soldier stands guard over fifty tons of burning marijuana seized from drug dealers by the Mexican army.
Keith Dannemiller/Corbis

Medical Model of Addiction
An approach to drug addiction that treats drug abuse as a mental illness and focuses on treating and rehabilitating offenders rather than punishing them.

Criminal Model of Addiction
An approach to drug abuse that holds that drug offenders harm society by their actions to the same extent as other criminals and should face the same punitive sanctions.

Chronic Offender A delinquent or criminal who commits multiple offenses and is considered part of a small group of wrongdoers who are responsible for a majority of the antisocial activity in any given community.

Discussion Tip: In small groups, have students debate the two models of addiction: the medical model and the criminal model. Which model do students think represents the most effective approach to combating addiction and offending in today's society? (LO 8)

MODELS OF ADDICTION Is criminal conviction and incarceration the best way for society to deal with addicts? Those who follow the medical model of addiction believe that addicts are not criminals, but mentally or physically ill individuals who are

LO 8 forced into acts of petty crime to "feed their habit." Those who believe in the *enslavement theory of addiction* advocate treating addiction as a disease and hold that society should not punish addicts but rather attempt to rehabilitate them, as would be done for any other unhealthy person.[96] Although a number of organizations, including the American Medical Association, recognize alcoholism and other forms of drug dependence as diseases, the criminal justice system tends to favor the criminal model of addiction over the medical model. The criminal model holds that illegal drug abusers and addicts endanger society with their behavior and should be punished the same as persons who commit non-drug-related crimes.[97]

SELFASSESSMENT

Fill in the blanks and check your answers on page 62.
Drug _____ is defined as the use of any drug that causes harm to the user or a third party. People who are _____, meaning that they desire the drug long after use has stopped, need greater amounts of the drug to stimulate a neurotransmitter in the brain called _____. Those who believe that drug offenders should be rehabilitated support the _____ model of addiction, while those who believe such offenders should be punished just like any other wrongdoers support the _____ model of addiction.

CRIMINOLOGY FROM THEORY TO PRACTICE

You have almost completed the only chapter in this textbook that deals primarily with theory. The chapters that follow will concentrate on the more practical and legal aspects of the criminal justice system: how law enforcement agencies fight crime, how our court systems determine guilt or innocence, and how we punish those who are found guilty. Criminology can, however, play a crucial role in the criminal justice system. "A lot of my colleagues just want to write scholarly articles for scholarly journals," notes Professor James Alan Fox of Northeastern University in Boston. "But I think if you're in a field with specialized knowledge that can be useful to the community, you should engage the public and policymakers."[98]

CRIMINOLOGY AND THE CHRONIC OFFENDER

Perhaps the most useful criminological contribution to crime fighting in the past half century was *Delinquency in a Birth Cohort*, published by the pioneering trio of Marvin Wolfgang, Robert Figlio, and Thorsten Sellin in 1972. This research established the idea of the chronic offender, or career criminal, by showing that a small group of juvenile offenders—6 percent—was responsible for a disproportionate amount of the violent crime attributed to a group of nearly 10,000 young males: 71 percent of the murders, 82 percent of the robberies, 69 percent of the aggravated assaults, and 73 percent of the rapes.[99]

Further research has supported the idea of a "chronic 6 percent,"[100] and law enforce-

LO 9 ment agencies and district attorneys' offices have devised specific strategies to apprehend and prosecute repeat offenders, with dozens of local police agencies forming career criminal units to deal with the problem. Legislators have also reacted to this research: habitual offender laws that provide harsher sentences for repeat offenders have become quite popular. We will discuss these statutes, including the controversial "three-strikes-and-you're-out" laws, in Chapter 11.

CRIMINOLOGY AND THE CRIMINAL JUSTICE SYSTEM

There is a sense, however, that criminology has not done enough to make our country a safer place. Eminent criminologist James Q. Wilson, for one, has criticized his peers for trying to understand crime rather than reduce it.[101] Many criminal justice practitioners also argue that too much of the research done by criminologists is inaccessible to them. As Sarah J. Hart, director of the National Institute of Justice, has noted, an overwhelmed police chief simply does not have the time or patience to wade through the many scientific journals in which crime research appears.[102]

This criticism may be too harsh, however. As we discuss further in Chapter 6, Wilson himself (in collaboration with George Kelling) developed the "broken windows" theory, which reshaped police strategy in the 1990s. Furthermore, as we will also see in Chapter 6, criminological theories about the areas in which crime takes place, also known as *applied geography*, have led dozens of police departments to adopt computer-based crime mapping prevention strategies.[103] The routine activities theory, introduced on page 52, helped convince local authorities across the nation to offer afterschool programs, designed to provide students with a safe environment under protective adult supervision.[104] Following the premises of the medical model of addiction (page 58), state and federal governments spend $15 billion on substance abuse services each year, in part to keep abusers from becoming or staying involved in crime.[105] Indeed, in the opinion of many observers, researchers know more today about "what works" in criminology than at any other time in our nation's history.[106]

Research shows that offenders who commit robberies, residential burglaries, and vehicle thefts are more likely to target the areas where they live or have lived in the past, rather than unfamiliar neighborhoods. How can such information help law enforcement officers such as this Camden (New Jersey) police officer prevent crime?
AP Photo/Mel Evans

Teaching Tip: As students complete the chapter, ask them to write a short essay on the relationship between criminological theory and criminal justice policy. (LO 9)

SELFASSESSMENT

Fill in the blanks and check your answers on page 62.
In 1972, Marvin Wolfgang and his colleagues established the idea of the _____ offender, by showing that a _____ percentage of offenders is often responsible for a disproportionately _____ amount of crime. Research on this subject has led law enforcement agencies to focus resources on _____ offenders.

CJ IN ACTION

THE LINK BETWEEN VIOLENT VIDEO GAMES AND CRIME

There was little mystery as to *who* killed Kimmie Daily. Tyler Savage admitted to law enforcement officers that on August 17, 2010, he convinced the sixteen-year-old girl to follow him to a vacant lot in Puyallup, Washington, where he attacked and murdered her. The mystery was *why* he did it. Eighteen-year-old Savage had a clean record and could provide no motive for investigators. The only clue came from Savage's confession that after killing Daily, he returned home to play the online fantasy video game *Dungeons and Dragons.* "The defendant admitted some kind of connection between the murder and the video game," Pierce County prosecutor Mark Lindquist said. "I'm not clear at this point what exactly that connection is."[107]

Savage is not the only young man to attribute his violent behavior to video games. In recent years, both seventeen-year-old Daniel Petric of Wellington, Ohio, who shot his parents, killing his mother, and twenty-one-year-old Patrick Morris of Klamath Falls, Oregon, who murdered Diego Aguilar with a shotgun, blamed their criminal behavior on violent video games, a topic we now address in this chapter's *CJ in Action* feature.

THE M GENERATION

Video games—representing a $20 billion industry—have saturated American youth culture. A recent study from the Pew Internet and American Life Project found that 97 percent of children ages twelve to seventeen play video games regularly,[108] and further research suggests that half of this group has experience with games rated "M" (mature) for excessive sex and violence, a category supposedly restricted for sale to those over the age of seventeen.[109] Such statistics worry those, including many scientists and criminologists, who believe that exposure to violent video games increases aggressiveness in certain players, leading to antisocial and criminal behavior. This concern is fueled by anecdotal evidence of the link between video games and crime, provided by the actions of offenders such as Tyler Savage, Daniel Petric, and Patrick Morris.

THE CASE FOR A LINK BETWEEN VIOLENT VIDEO GAMES AND CRIME

- Studies using magnetic resonance imaging (MRI; see page 40) show that, immediately after playing a violent video game, teenagers exhibit increased brain activity in the areas of the brain related to aggressive behavior and decreased brain activity in the areas of the brain related to self-control.[110]

- Research has found that violent video games, especially those of the first-person shooter type, not only desensitize players to real violence, but also train them to commit real acts of violence.[111]

- A consortium of health organizations has concluded that "well over 1,000 studies . . . point overwhelmingly to a causal connection between media violence and aggressive behavior in some children."[112]

www.x-box.com

THE CASE AGAINST A LINK BETWEEN VIOLENT VIDEO GAMES AND CRIME

- No legal authority has found that any of the studies cited above prove that violent video games actually cause crime. At best, they show a correlation between the games and aggressiveness, which does not always lead to violence.

- The studies cited cast video games as an easy scapegoat, failing to account for the many other possible factors in criminal behavior, such as parental control, socioeconomic status, and hormonal imbalance, that have been discussed in this chapter.

- Over the past fifteen years, as sales of violent video games have skyrocketed, arrests for juvenile violent crimes have decreased.[113]

YOUR OPINION—WRITING ASSIGNMENT

Do you think that the correlation between video games and violent behavior is strong enough to support laws that restrict a minor's ability to purchase or play them? If so, what issues would you make sure were addressed in the legislation? If not, why do you think such a law is unnecessary? Furthermore, what role should parental responsibility play in this debate? Before responding, you can review our discussion in this chapter concerning:

- The difference between causation and correlation (page 35).

- Social process theories of crime, particularly learning theory and control theory (pages 45 and 46).

- Life course theories of crime (pages 51–52).

Your answer should include at least three full paragraphs.

CHAPTER SUMMARY

LO 1
Discuss the difference between a hypothesis and a theory in the context of criminology. A hypothesis is a proposition, usually presented in an "If . . . , then . . ." format, that can be tested by researchers. If enough different authorities are able to test and verify a hypothesis, it will usually be accepted as a theory. Because theories can offer explanations for behavior, criminologists often rely on them when trying to determine the causes of criminal behavior.

LO 2
Explain why classical criminology is based on choice theory. Choice theory holds that those who commit crimes choose to do so. Classical criminology is based on a model of a person rationally making a choice before committing a crime—weighing the benefits against the costs.

LO 3
Contrast positivism with classical criminology. Whereas classical theorists believe criminals make rational choices, those of the positivist school believe that criminal behavior is determined by psychological, biological, and social forces that the individual cannot control.

LO 4
List and describe the three theories of social structure that help explain crime. Social disorganization theory states that crime is largely a product of unfavorable conditions in certain communities, or zones of disorganization. The strain theory argues that most people seek increased wealth and financial security and that the strain of not being able to achieve these goals through legal means leads to criminal behavior. Finally, cultural deviance theory asserts that people adapt to the values of the subculture—which has its own standards of behavior—to which they belong.

LO 5
List and briefly explain the three branches of social process theory. (a) Learning theory, which contends that people learn to be criminals from their family and peers. (b) Control theory, which holds that most of us are dissuaded from a life of crime because we place importance on the opinions of family and peers. (c) Labeling theory, which holds that a person labeled a "junkie" or a "thief" will respond by becoming or remaining whatever she or he is labeled.

LO 6
Describe how life course criminology differs from the other theories addressed in this chapter. The five other theories addressed in this chapter link criminal behavior to factors—such as unemployment or poor schools—that affect an individual long after his or her personality has been established. Life course theories focus on behavioral patterns of childhood such as bullying, lying, and stealing as predictors of future criminal behavior.

LO 7
Discuss the connection between offenders and victims of crime. To a certain extent, those who are at the greatest risk of becoming criminal offenders are also those at the greatest risk of becoming victims of crimes. For this reason, young, low-income African American males are disproportionately represented in American prisons and jails and in victim statistics. In many major cities, law enforcement agencies have adjusted their strategies to account for the high percentage of violent crime victims who have criminal records themselves.

LO 8
Contrast the medical model of addiction with the criminal model of addiction. Those who support the former believe that addicts are not criminals, but mentally or physically ill individuals who are forced into acts of petty crime to "feed their habit." Those in favor of the criminal model of addiction believe that abusers and addicts endanger society with their behavior and should be treated like any other criminals.

LO 9
Explain the theory of the chronic offender and its importance for the criminal justice system. A chronic offender is a juvenile or adult who commits multiple offenses. According to research conducted by Marvin Wolfgang and others in the 1970s, chronic offenders are responsible for a disproportionately large percentage of all crime. In the decades since, law enforcement agencies and public prosecutors have developed strategies to identify and convict chronic offenders with the goal of lessening overall crime rates. In addition, legislators have passed laws that provide longer sentences for chronic offenders in an attempt to keep them off the streets.

SELF ASSESSMENT ANSWER KEY

KEY TERMS

anomie 44

biology 38

causation 35

choice theory 36

chronic offender 58

classical criminology 37

control theory 46

correlation 35

criminal model of addiction 58

criminologist 35

criminology 34

cultural deviance theory 45

drug abuse 55

genetics 39

hormone 39

hypothesis 35

labeling theory 48

learning theory 46

life course criminology 51

medical model of addiction 58

neurotransmitter 40

positivism 37

prescription drugs 57

psychoanalytic theory 41

psychology 38

repeat victimization 53

social conflict theories 48

social disorganization theory 43

social process theories 45

social reality of crime 49

strain theory 44

subculture 45

testosterone 39

theory 35

utilitarianism 36

victimology 52

QUESTIONS FOR CRITICAL ANALYSIS

1. Research shows that when levels of single-family mortgage foreclosures rise in a neighborhood, so do levels of violent crime. Explain the correlation between these two sets of statistics. Why is it false to say that single-family mortgage foreclosures *cause* violent crimes to occur?

2. Why would someone who subscribes to choice theory (see pages 36–38) believe that increasing the harshness of a penalty for a particular crime would necessarily lead to fewer such crimes being committed?

3. Consider the following statement: "The government should protect the public from mentally ill persons who are potentially dangerous, even if that means hospitalizing those persons against their will." Do you agree or disagree? Why?

4. How does the routine activities theory (see page 52) explain high burglary rates in neighborhoods where a high percentage of residents commute long distances to work?

5. How can law enforcement agencies employ the premise of the repeat victimization theory to devise crime prevention strategies?

NOTES

1. Louise Arsenault *et al.*, "Mental Disorders and Violence in a Total Birth Cohort: Results from the Dunedin Study," *Archives of General Psychology* (2000), 982.

2. E. Fuller Torrey and Mary Zdanowicz, "Why Deinstitutionalization Turned Deadly," *Wall Street Journal* (August 4, 1998), A18.

3. Jeffrey W. Swanson *et al.*, "Alternative Pathways to Violence in Persons with Schizophrenia: The Role of Childhood Antisocial Behavior Problems," *Law and Human Behavior* (June 2008), 228–240.

4. Tony Leys, "Crimes Distort Reality of Schizophrenia," *Des Moines (IA) Register* (March 7, 2010), A1.

5. John J. Donohue and Steven D. Levitt, "The Impact of Legalized Abortion on Crime," *Quarterly Journal of Economics* (2000), 379–420.

6. *Ibid.*, 381.

7. Franklin E. Zimring, *The Great American Crime Decline* (New York: Oxford University Press, 2007), 94–97.

8. *Ibid.*, 165.

9. James Q. Wilson and Richard J. Hernstein, *Crime and Human Nature: The Definitive Study of the Causes of Crime* (New York: Simon & Schuster, 1985), 515.

10. Jeremy Bentham, *An Introduction to the Principles of Morals and Legislation,* ed. W. Harrison (Oxford: Basil Blackwell, 1948).

11. Wilson and Hernstein, 44.

12. Jack Katz, *Seductions of Crime: Moral and Sensual Attractions of Doing Evil* (New York: Basic Books, 1988).

13. National Coalition for the Homeless, "Hate Crimes and Violence against People Experiencing Homelessness," at **www.nationalhomeless.org/factsheets/hate-crimes.html**.

14. David C. Rowe, *Biology and Crime* (Los Angeles: Roxbury, 2002), 2.

15. Sarnoff A. Mednick and Karl O. Christiansen, eds., *Biosocial Bases in Criminal Behavior* (New York: Gardner Press, 1977).

16. David C. Rowe, "Genetic and Environmental Components of Antisocial Behavior: A Study of 265 Twin Pairs," *Criminology* 24 (1986), 513–532.

17. Raymond R. Crowe, "An Adoption Study of Antisocial Personality," *Archives of General Psychiatry* (1974), 785–791; Sarnoff A. Mednick, William F. Gabrielli, and Barry Hutchings, "Genetic Influences on Criminal Convictions: Evidence from an Adoption Cohort," *Science* (1994), 891–894; and Remi J. Cadoret, "Adoption Studies," *Alcohol Health & Research World* (Summer 1995), 195–201.

18. Gail S. Anderson, *Biological Influences on Criminal Behavior* (Boca Raton, FL: CRC Press, 2007), 105–118.

19. *Ibid.*, 118.

20. L. E. Kreuz and R. M. Rose, "Assessment of Aggressive Behavior and Plasma Testosterone in Young Criminal Population," *Psychosomatic Medicine* 34 (1972), 321–332.

21. H. Persky, K. Smith, and G. Basu, "Relation of Psychological Measures of Aggression and Hostility to Testosterone Production in Men," *Psychosomatic Medicine* 33 (1971), 265, 276.

22. Benjamin J. Sadock, Harold I. Kaplan, and Virginia A. Sadock, *Kaplan & Sadock's Synopsis of Psychiatry* (Philadelphia: Lippincott Williams & Wilkins, 2007), 865.

23. Robert J. Meadows and Julie Kuehnel, *Evil Minds: Understanding and Responding to Violent Predators* (Upper Saddle River, NJ: Pearson Prentice Hall, 2005), 156–157.

24. *Ibid.*, 157, 169.

25. Anderson, 210–216.

26. David G. Myers, *Psychology,* 7th ed. (New York: Worth Publishers, 2004), 576–577.

27. Philip Zimbardo, "Pathology of Imprisonment," *Society* (April 1972), 4–8.

28. David Canter and Laurence Alison, "The Social Psychology of Crime: Groups, Teams, and Networks," in *The Social Psychology of Crime: Groups, Teams, and Networks,* ed. David Canter and Laurence Alison (Hanover, NH: Dartmouth, 2000), 3–4.

29. Robert Park, Ernest Burgess, and Roderic McKenzie, *The City* (Chicago: University of Chicago Press, 1929).

30. Clifford R. Shaw, Henry D. McKay, and Leonard S. Cottrell, *Delinquency Areas* (Chicago: University of Chicago Press, 1929).

31. Clifford R. Shaw and Henry D. McKay, *Report on the Causes of Crime*, vol. 2: *Social Factors in Juvenile Delinquency* (Washington, D.C.: National Commission on Law Observance and Enforcement, 1931).

32. Elijah Anderson, *Code of the Street: Decency, Violence and the Moral Life of the Inner City* (New York: W. W. Norton, 2000), 35–65.

33. *Ibid.*, 180.

34. Eric A. Stewart and Ronald L. Simons, "Race, Code of the Street, and Violent Delinquency: A Multilevel Investigation of Neighborhood Street Culture and Individual Norms of Violence," *Criminology* (May 2010), 569–603.

35. Emile Durkheim, *The Rules of Sociological Method,* trans. Sarah A. Solovay and John H. Mueller (New York: Free Press, 1964).

36. Robert K. Merton, *Social Theory and Social Structure* (New York: Free Press, 1957). See the chapter on "Social Structure and Anomie."

37. Robert Agnew, "Foundation for a General Strain Theory of Crime and Delinquency," *Criminology* 30 (1992), 47–87.

38. Robert Agnew, Timothy Brezina, John Paul Wright, and Francis T. Cullen, "Strain, Personality Traits, and Delinquency: Extending General Strain Theory," *Criminology* (February 2002), 43–71.

39. Philip G. Zimbardo, "The Human Choice: Individuation, Reason, and Order versus Deindividuation, Impulse, and Chaos," in *Nebraska Symposium on Motivation,* ed. William J. Arnold and David Levie (Lincoln, NE: University of Nebraska Press, 1969), 287–293.

40. Edwin H. Sutherland, *Criminology,* 4th ed. (Philadelphia: Lippincott, 1947).

41. Marcia Polansky, Augusta M. Villanueva, and Jeffrey Bonfield, "Responses to Violence Related Questionnaires by Delinquent, Truant, and State-Dependent Boys Receiving Treatment in an Extended Day Program," *Journal of Offender Rehabilitation* 47 (2008), 407, 415–416.

42. Prepared for Kevin Johnson, "For Many of USA's Inmates, Crime Runs in the Family," *USA Today* (January 29, 2008), 1A.

43. L. Rowell Huesmann, Jessica Moise-Titus, Cheryl-Lynn Podolski, and Leonard D. Eron, "Longitudinal Relations between Children's Exposure to TV Violence and Their Aggressive and Violent Behavior in Young Adulthood: 1977–1992," *Developmental Psychology* (March 2003), 201.

44. Telecommunications Act of 1996, 47 U.S.C. Section 303 (1999).

45. Travis Hirschi, *Causes of Delinquency* (Berkeley: University of California Press, 1969).

46. James Q. Wilson and George L. Kelling, "Broken Windows," *Atlantic Monthly* (March 1982), 29.

47. Janet L. Lauritsen, *How Families and Communities Influence Youth Victimization* (Washington, D.C.: Office of Juvenile Justice and Delinquency Prevention, 2003).

48. Quoted in Johnson, 1A.

49. Howard S. Becker, *Outsiders: Studies in the Sociology of Deviance* (New York: Free Press, 1963).

50. Lawrence L. Shornack, "Conflict Theory and the Family," *International Social Science Review* 62 (1987), 154–157.

51. Robert Meier, "The New Criminology: Continuity in Criminology Theory," *Journal of Criminal Law and Criminology* 67 (1977), 461–469.

52. Richard Quinney, *The Social Reality of Crime* (Boston: Little, Brown, 1970).

53. Nicole Hahn Rafter, *Partial Justice: Women, Prisons, and Social Control* (New Brunswick, NJ: Transaction Publishers, 1990).

54. Federal Bureau of Investigation, *Crime in the United States,* 2010 (Washington D.C.: U.S. Department of Justice, 2011), at **www.fbi.gov/about-us/cjis/ucr/crime-in-the-u.s/2010/crime-in-the-u.s.-2010/tables/10tbl42.xls**.

55. The Sentencing Project, at **www.sentencingproject.org/IssueAreaHome.aspx?IssueID=3**.

56. Bureau of Justice Statistics, *Bulletin: Prisoners in 2009* (Washington, D.C.: U.S. Department of Justice, December 2010), 9.

57. Hubert M. Blalock, *Toward a Theory of Minority-Group Relations* (New York: Capricorn Books, 1967).

58. *Ibid.*

59. These studies are discussed in Ted Chiricos, Kelly Welch, and Marc Gertz, "Racial Typification of Crime and Support for Punitive Measures," *Criminology* (May 1, 2004), 359–390.

60. Christopher Hensey, "The Effect of Inmates' Self-Reported Childhood and Adolescent Animal Cruelty," *International Journal of Offender Therapy and Comparative Criminology* (April 2008), 175–184.

61. Francis T. Cullen and Robert Agnew, *Criminological Theory, Past to Present: Essential Readings,* 2d ed. (Los Angeles: Roxbury Publishing Co., 2003), 12.

62. *Ibid.,* 443.

63. Michael R. Gottfredson and Travis Hirschi, *A General Theory of Crime* (Stanford, CA: Stanford University Press, 1990).

64. *Ibid.,* 90.

65. *Ibid.*

66. Terrie Moffitt, "Adolescent-Limited and Life-Course-Persistent Antisocial Behavior: A Developmental Taxonomy," *Psychological Review* 100 (1993), 679–680.

67. *Ibid.,* 674.

68. Robert J. Sampson and John H. Laub, *Crime in the Making: Pathways and Turning Points through Life* (Cambridge, MA: Harvard University Press, 1993), 11.

69. *Ibid.;* John H. Laub and Robert J. Sampson, *Shared Beginnings, Divergent Lives: Delinquent Boys to Age 70* (Cambridge, MA: Harvard University Press, 2003); and Derek A. Kreager, Ross L. Matsueda, and Elena A. Erosheva, "Motherhood and Criminal Desistance in Disadvantaged Neighborhoods," *Criminology* (February 2010), 221–257.

70. John F. Frana and Ryan D. Schroeder, "Alternatives to Incarceration," *Justice Policy Journal* (Fall 2008), available at **www.cjcj.org/files/alternatives_to.pdf.**

71. Peggy C. Giordano, Monica A. Longmore, Ryan D. Schroeder, and Patrick M. Seffrin, "A Life-Course Perspective on Spirituality and Desistance from Crime," *Criminology* (February 2008), 99–132.

72. Ezzat A. Fattah, "Victimology: Past, Present, and Future," *Criminologie* (2000), 18.

73. Andrew Karmen, *Crime Victims: An Introduction to Victimology* (Belmont, CA: Wadsworth, 2003).

74. Linda A. Teplin *et al.,* "Crime Victimization in Adults with Severe Mental Illness: Comparison with the National Crime Victimization Survey," *Archives of General Psychiatry* (August 2005), 911–921.

75. Larry Cohen and Marcus Felson, "Social Change and Crime Rate Trends: A Routine Activity Approach," *American Sociological Review* (1979), 588–608.

76. *Ibid.*

77. Ron W. Glensor, Ken J. Peak, and Mark E. Correia, "Focusing on Prey Rather Than Predators," in *Contemporary Policing: Controversies, Challenges, and Solutions,* ed.

Quint C. Thurman and Jihong Zhao (Los Angeles: Roxbury Publishing Co., 2004), 91–92.

78. T. J. Pignataro and Patrick LaKamp, "7 of 8 Shooting Victims Had a Criminal Past," *Buffalo (NY) News* (August 22, 2010), A1.

79. Angela Rozas, "Crime Up for City in 2008," *Chicago Tribune* (January 17, 2009), 12.

80. Peter Hermann, "Statistics Tell a Violent Story That We've Heard Before," *Baltimore Sun* (January 4, 2009), 6A.

81. Quoted in Kevin Johnson, "Criminals Target Each Other, Trend Shows," *USA Today* (August 31, 2007), 1A.

82. Christopher J. Schreck, Eric A. Stewart, and D. Wayne Osgood, "A Reappraisal of the Overlap of Violent Offenders and Victims," *Criminology* (October 2008), 871–906.

83. *Ibid.,* 876–877.

84. Richard B. Felson and Keri B. Burchfield, "Alcohol and the Risk of Physical and Sexual Assault Victimization," *Criminology* (November 1, 2004), 837.

85. Becker.

86. Myers, 75–76.

87. Peter B. Kraska, "The Unmentionable Alternative: The Need for and Argument against the Decriminalization of Drug Laws," in *Drugs, Crime, and the Criminal Justice System,* ed. Ralph Weisheit (Cincinnati, OH: Anderson Publishing, 1990).

88. Anthony A. Grace, "The Tonic/Phasal Model of Dopamine System Regulation," *Drugs and Alcohol* 37 (1995), 111.

89. Li Chuan-Yun, Mao Xizeng, and Wei Liping, "Genes and (Common) Pathways Underlying Drug Addiction," *Public Library of Science,* at **www.ploscompbiol.org/article/info%3Adoi%2F10.1371%2Fjournal.pcbi.0040002.**

90. Bureau of Justice Statistics, "Alcohol and Crime: Data from 2002 to 2008," at **bjs.ojp.usdoj.gov/content/acf/29_prisoners_and_alcoholuse.cfm and bjs.ojp.usdoj.gov/content/acf/30_jails_and_alcoholuse .cfm.**

91. *ADAM II: 2009 Annual Report* (Washington, D.C.: Office of National Drug Policy, June 2010), Figure 3.3, page 23.

92. Paul J. Goldstein, "The Drugs/Violence Nexus: A Tripartite Conceptual Framework," *Journal of Drug Issues* 15 (1985), 493–506.

93. Substance Abuse and Mental Health Services Administration, *The TEDS Report: Substance Abuse Treatment Admissions Involving Abuse of Pain Relievers: 1998 to 2008* (Washington, D.C.: U.S. Department of Health and Human Services, July 15, 2010), 1.

94. Quoted in Abby Goodnough, "A Wave of Addiction and Crime, with the Medicine Cabinet to Blame," *New York Times* (September 24, 2010), A14.

95. Abby Goodnough, "Pharmacies Besieged by Addicted Thieves," *New York Times* (February 7, 2011), A1.

96. James A. Inciardi, *The War on Drugs: Heroin, Cocaine, and Public Policy* (Palo Alto, CA: Mayfield, 1986), 148.

97. *Ibid.,* 106.

98. Quoted in Timothy Egan, "After Seven Deaths, Digging for an Explanation," *New York Times* (June 25, 2006), 12.

99. Marvin Wolfgang, Robert Figlio, and Thorsten Sellin, *Delinquency in a Birth Cohort* (Chicago: University of Chicago Press, 1972).

100. Lawrence W. Sherman, "Attacking Crime: Police and Crime Control," in *Modern Policing,* ed. Michael Tonry and Norval Morris (Chicago: University of Chicago Press, 1992), 159.

101. James Q. Wilson, "What to Do about Crime," *Commentary* (September 1994), 25–34.

102. Sarah J. Hart, "A New Way of Doing Business at the NIJ," *Law Enforcement News* (January 15/31, 2002), 9.

103. Cynthia Lum, "Translating Police Research into Practice," *Ideas in American Policing* (Washington, D.C.: Police Foundation, August 2009), 2.

104. Amanda Brown Cross *et al.,* "The Impact of After-School Programs on the Routine Activities of Middle-School Students: Results from a Randomized, Controlled Trial," *Criminology & Public Policy* (May 2009), 393–397.

105. Benedict Carey, "Drug Rehabilitation or Revolving Door?" *New York Times* (December 23, 2008), D1.

106. Richard Rosenfeld, "Book Review: *The Limits of Crime Control," Journal of Criminal Law and Criminology* (Fall 2002).

107. Quoted in Joel Moreno, "Detective: Murder Motive May Have Been Video Game Fantasy," *Seattle Post-Intelligencer* (August 26, 2010), at **www.seattlepi.com/local/425695_murder25.html.**

108. Amanda Lenhart *et al., Teens, Video Games & Civics* (Washington, D.C.: Pew Internet & American Life Project, 2008), 1.

109. David Walsh *et al.,* "Tenth Annual MediaWise Video Game Report Card" (2005), at **www.mediafamily.org/research/report_vgrc_2005.shtml.**

110. Lee Bowman, "A Way to Lose Self-Control? Violent Games Shown to Have Effects on Brain," *Chicago Sun-Times* (December 4, 2006), 14.

111. David Grossman and Gloria DeGaetano, *Stop Teaching Our Kids to Kill: A Call to Action against TV, Movie and Video Game Violence* (New York: Crown, 1999), 4.

112. Quoted in Kevin Saunders, "A Disconnect between Law and Neuroscience: Modern Brain Science, Media Influences, and Juvenile Justice," *Utah Law Review* (2005), 705.

113. Office of Juvenile Justice and Delinquency Prevention, "Juvenile Arrest Trends," *Statistical Briefing Book,* at **www.ojjdp.gov/ojstatbb/crime/JAR_Display.asp?ID=qa05201.**

David McNew/Getty Images

Defining and Measuring Crime

LEARNING OBJECTIVES

After reading this chapter, you should be able to . . .

LO 1 Discuss the primary goals of civil law and criminal law and explain how these goals are realized.

LO 2 Explain the differences between crimes *mala in se* and *mala prohibita.*

LO 3 Identify the publication in which the FBI reports crime data and list the two main ways in which the data are reported.

LO 4 Distinguish between Part I and Part II offenses as defined in the Uniform Crime Report (UCR).

LO 5 Describe some of the shortcomings of the UCR as a crime-measuring tool.

LO 6 Distinguish between the National Crime Victimization Survey (NCVS) and self-reported surveys.

LO 7 Identify the three factors most often used by criminologists to explain changes in the nation's crime rate.

LO 8 Explain why issues of race and ethnicity tend to be overstated when it comes to crime trends.

LO 9 Discuss the prevailing explanation for the rising number of women incarcerated in the United States.

The nine learning objectives labeled LO 1 through LO 9 are designed to help improve your understanding of the chapter.

CHAPTER OUTLINE

- Classification of Crimes
- The Uniform Crime Report
- Alternative Measuring Methods
- Crime Trends in the United States
- CJ in Action—Legalizing Marijuana

HIGHWAYS to HELL?

Patty Peterson was last seen alive more than five years ago at a truck stop in Tulsa, Oklahoma. Then, in 2009, a hiker stumbled across Peterson's skeleton near a rest stop in Lupton, Arizona, just across the state border from New Mexico. She had been beaten to death, her skull crushed on the right side and her nose broken. When Peterson's remains were finally identified in September 2010, her name was added to a growing—and disturbing—list of crime victims. According to data compiled by the Federal Bureau of Investigation (FBI), over the past four decades at least 459 people have died at the hands of serial killers who operate along the nation's highways.

Many of these victims share a common profile. Like Peterson, they are women involved in high-risk activities such as substance abuse and prostitution who spend time at truck stops or gas stations. They are picked up, and then sexually assaulted, murdered, and discarded along interstates and highways. The prime suspects in these crimes, as identified by the FBI, are long-haul truck drivers, who have the ability to abduct a woman in one state, dispose of her body in another, return to the highway, and disappear. Given the mobile nature of these suspects and the long distances involved, it has proved very difficult for local and state law enforcement agencies to track them down and link them to any criminal activity.

For these reasons, several years ago the FBI started the Highway Serial Killings Initiative. As part of this program, local police departments send information about unsolved murders that fit the "roadside serial killer" profile to the FBI. Analysts at

the agency then process the data and send out e-mail alerts when evidence matches a known suspect with a known victim. "It's a great resource for us," says George Cronin of the Pennsylvania State Police. "For a long time, police departments were operating in a bubble [and did not know] what was going on in neighboring jurisdictions."

For nearly four decades, federal law enforcement agents have been gathering information on murders that occur at truck stops and other locations along the nation's highways.

Thinkstock Images/Comstock Images/Getty Images

Crunching numbers is rarely considered exciting police work. As the Highway Serial Killings Initiative shows, however, it can be a crucial aspect of law enforcement. Using a definition of serial killing that identifies offenders as those who "murder two or more victims . . . in separate events,"[1] FBI analysts have gathered information on two hundred potential serial killers. Using technology such as GPS (global positioning system) devices in trucks and credit-card retrieval records, experts track each suspect and create timelines of his movements. To date, the program has helped solve more than two dozen murders, including that of Monica Massaro, who was killed while sleeping in her bedroom by a trucker named Adam Lane. (Massaro's home was located near a truck stop off Interstate 78 in Hunterdon County, New Jersey.)

As we will see in this chapter, definitions and measurements of crime are tools that both the police and other members of the community can use to help fight crime. We will start our examination of these subjects with an overview of how crimes are classified, move on to the various methods of measuring crime, and end with a discussion of some statistical trends that give us a good idea of the "state of crime" in the United States today.

CLASSIFICATION OF CRIMES

The huge body of the law can be broken down according to various classifications. Three of the most important distinctions are those between (1) civil law and criminal law, (2) felonies and misdemeanors, and (3) crimes *mala in se* and *mala prohibita*.

CIVIL LAW AND CRIMINAL LAW

All law can be divided into two categories: civil law and criminal law. As U.S. criminal law has evolved, it has diverged from U.S. civil law. These two categories of law are distinguished by their primary goals. The criminal justice system is concerned with protecting society from harm by preventing and prosecuting crimes. A crime is an act so reprehensible that it is considered a wrong against society as a whole, as well as against the individual victim. Therefore, the state prosecutes a person who commits a criminal act. If the state is able to prove that a person is guilty of a crime, the government will punish her or him with imprisonment or fines, or both.

Civil law, which includes all types of law other than criminal law, is concerned with disputes between private individuals and between entities. Proceedings in civil lawsuits

LO 1 are normally initiated by an individual or a corporation (in contrast to criminal proceedings, which are initiated by public prosecutors). Such disputes may involve, for example, the terms of a contract, the ownership of property, or an automobile accident. Under civil law, the government provides a forum for the resolution of *torts*—or private wrongs—in which the injured party, called the plaintiff, tries to prove that a wrong has been committed by the accused party, or the defendant. (Note that the accused party in both criminal and civil cases is known as the *defendant*.)

GUILT AND RESPONSIBILITY A criminal court is convened to determine whether the defendant is *guilty*—that is, whether the defendant has, in fact, committed the offense charged. In contrast, civil law is concerned with responsibility, a much more flexible concept. For example, after William Hensley died of an allergic reaction to bee stings, a civil court partially blamed emergency room physician Allen Retirado for his death. When Hensley was brought unconscious to St. Clare's Hospital in Sussex Borough, New Jersey, Retirado had mistakenly attributed his condition to heat stroke. Even though Retirado was never charged with any crime, the civil court decided that he was liable, or legally responsible, for Hensley's death because of his improper diagnosis.

Most civil cases involve a request for monetary damages to compensate for the wrong that has been committed. Thus, in 2010, the civil court ordered Allen Retirado to pay nearly $1 million to William Hensley's family as compensation for the financial and emotional consequences of his death. (See *Mastering Concepts* on the following page for a comparison of civil and criminal law.)

THE BURDEN OF PROOF Although criminal law proceedings are completely separate from civil law proceedings in the modern legal system, the two systems do have some similarities. Both attempt to control behavior by imposing sanctions on those who violate society's definition of acceptable behavior. Furthermore, criminal and civil law often supplement each other. In certain instances, a victim may file a civil suit against an individual who is also the target of a criminal prosecution by the government.

Critical Thinking Skill Development: In a short written assignment, ask students to respond to "Questions for Critical Analysis" number one on page 92, which regards the roles of criminal and civil law in the criminal justice system. (LO 1)

Civil Law The branch of law dealing with the definition and enforcement of all private or public rights, as opposed to criminal matters.

Plaintiff The person or institution that initiates a lawsuit in civil court proceedings by filing a complaint.

Defendant In a civil court, the person or institution against whom an action is brought. In a criminal court, the person or entity who has been formally accused of violating a criminal law.

Liability In a civil court, legal responsibility for one's own or another's actions.

Discussion Tip: Have students discuss the differences between criminal guilt and civil responsibility. Is it easier to establish one's "innocence" in criminal or civil court? Why? (LO 1)

MASTERINGCONCEPTS

Civil Law versus Criminal Law

Issue	Civil Law	Criminal Law
Area of concern	Rights and duties between individuals	Offenses against society as a whole
Wrongful act	Harm to a person or business entity	Violation of a statute that prohibits some type of activity
Party who brings suit	Person who suffered harm (plaintiff)	The state (prosecutor)
Party who responds	Person who supposedly caused harm (defendant)	Person who allegedly committed a crime (defendant)
Standard of proof	Preponderance of the evidence	Beyond a reasonable doubt
Remedy	Damages to compensate for the harm	Punishment (fine or incarceration)

Critical Thinking Skill Development: Have students work together to respond to "Questions for Critical Analysis" number two on page 92, in which they consider the various manslaughter classifications.

Beyond a Reasonable Doubt The degree of proof required to find the defendant in a criminal trial guilty of committing the crime. The defendant's guilt must be the only reasonable explanation for the criminal act before the court.

Preponderance of the Evidence The degree of proof required to decide in favor of one side or the other in a civil case. In general, this requirement is met when a plaintiff proves that a fact more likely than not is true.

Felony A serious crime, usually punishable by death or imprisonment for a year or longer.

Because the burden of proof is much greater in criminal trials than civil ones, it is almost always easier to win monetary damages than a criminal conviction. In 2008, for example, truck driver George Albright was found not guilty of any criminal wrongdoing in connection with a traffic accident near Columbia, Missouri, that left four women dead. In 2010, however, a civil court decided that Albright was responsible for the death of Anita Gibbs, one of the four crash victims, and ordered that $32.25 million in damages be paid to Gibbs's family. In the earlier trial, the criminal court did not find enough evidence to prove beyond a reasonable doubt (the burden of proof in criminal cases) that Albright was guilty of any crime. Nevertheless, the civil trial established by a preponderance of the evidence (the burden of proof in civil cases) that Albright was responsible for Gibbs's death. (In the civil case, the plaintiffs were able to show that Albright falsified his trucking logs to indicate that he had gotten sufficient rest before the accident.)

FELONIES AND MISDEMEANORS

Depending on their degree of seriousness, crimes are classified as *felonies* or *misdemeanors*. Felonies are serious crimes punishable by death or by imprisonment in a federal or state penitentiary for one year or longer (though some states, such as North Carolina, consider felonies to be punishable by at least two years' incarceration). The Model Penal Code, a general guide for criminal law that you will learn more about in the next chapter, provides for four degrees of felony:

1. Capital offenses, for which the maximum penalty is death.
2. First degree felonies, punishable by a maximum penalty of life imprisonment.
3. Second degree felonies, punishable by a maximum of ten years' imprisonment.
4. Third degree felonies, punishable by a maximum of five years' imprisonment.[2]

> ## "Crime, like virtue, has its degrees."
>
> **—Jean Racine, French playwright (1639–1699)**

DEGREES OF CRIME Though specifics vary from state to state, some general rules apply when grading crimes. For example, most jurisdictions punish a burglary that involves a nighttime forced entry into a home more seriously than one that takes place during the day and involves a nonresidential building or structure. Furthermore, the seriousness of any crime is, to a large extent, determined by the mental state of the offender. That is, the law punishes those who plan and intend to do harm more harshly than it does those who act wrongfully because of strong emotions or other extreme circumstances. We will address the importance of mental state in crime more extensively in the next chapter, but here we can see how it affects the degrees of murder.

Murder in the first degree occurs under two circumstances:

1. When the crime is *premeditated,* or considered (contemplated) beforehand by the offender, instead of being a spontaneous act of violence.
2. When the crime is *deliberate,* meaning that it was planned and decided on after a process of decision making. Deliberation does not require a lengthy planning process. A person can be found guilty of first degree murder even if she or he made the decision to murder only seconds before committing the crime.

Second degree murder, generally punishable by fifteen years to life in prison, occurs when no premeditation or deliberation was present, but the offender did have malice aforethought toward the victim. In other words, the offender acted with wanton disregard of the consequences of his or her actions. The difference between first and second degree murder is clearly illustrated in a case involving a California man who beat a neighbor to death with a partially full brandy bottle. The crime took place after Ricky McDonald, the victim, complained to Kazi Cooksey, the offender, about the noise coming from a late-night barbecue Cooksey and his friends were holding. The jury could not find sufficient evidence that Cooksey's actions were premeditated, but he certainly acted with wanton disregard of his victim's safety. Therefore, the jury convicted Cooksey of second degree murder rather than first degree murder.

TYPES OF MANSLAUGHTER A homicide committed without malice toward the victim is known as *manslaughter* and is usually punishable by up to fifteen years in prison. Voluntary manslaughter occurs when the intent to kill may be present, but malice was lacking. Voluntary manslaughter covers crimes of passion, in which the emotion of an argument between two friends may lead to a homicide. Voluntary manslaughter can also occur when the victim provoked the offender to act violently.

Involuntary manslaughter covers incidents in which the offender's acts may have been careless, but she or he had no intent to kill. In 2010, for example, Jeanette Lawrence (see the photo alongside) was convicted of involuntary manslaughter for her role in the death of eighteen-month-old Ava Patrick. A year earlier, Lawrence lost track of Ava at the day-care center she operated in Olathe, Missouri. Unattended, the child suffocated when her neck got caught in the slats of a wooden fence. Although Lawrence certainly did not intend for Ava to die, she was held criminally responsible and sentenced to forty-one months in prison.

DEGREES OF MISDEMEANOR Under federal law and in most states, any crime that is not a felony is considered a misdemeanor. Misdemeanors are crimes punishable by a fine or by confinement for up to a year. If imprisoned, the guilty party goes to a local jail instead of a penitentiary. Disorderly conduct and trespassing are common misdemeanors. Like felonies, misdemeanors are graded by level of seriousness. In Illinois, for example, misdemeanors are either Class A (confinement for up to a year), Class B (not more than six months), or Class C (not more than thirty days).

Most states similarly distinguish between *gross misdemeanors,* which are offenses punishable by thirty days to a year in jail, and *petty misdemeanors,* or offenses punishable by fewer than thirty days in jail. Whether a crime is a felony or a misdemeanor can also determine whether the case is tried in a magistrate's court (for example, by a justice

Malice Aforethought
A depraved state of mind in which the offender's behavior reflected a wanton disregard for the well-being of his or her victim.

Voluntary Manslaughter
A homicide in which the intent to kill was present in the mind of the offender, but malice was lacking. Most commonly used to describe homicides in which the offender was provoked or otherwise acted in the heat of passion.

Involuntary Manslaughter
A negligent homicide, in which the offender had no intent to kill his or her victim.

Misdemeanor A criminal offense that is not a felony; usually punishable by a fine and/or a jail term of less than one year.

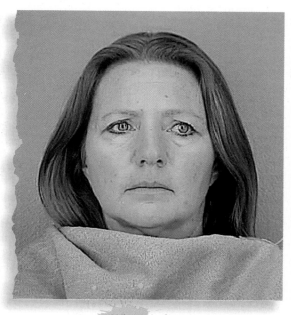

Why was former day-care center operator Jeanette Lawrence, pictured here, convicted of involuntary manslaughter rather than murder or voluntary manslaughter for her role in the death of eighteen-month-old Ava Patrick?
Johnson County Sheriff's Office

Infraction In most jurisdictions, a noncriminal offense for which the penalty is a fine rather than incarceration.

Mala in Se A descriptive term for acts that are inherently wrong, regardless of whether they are prohibited by law.

Mala Prohibita A descriptive term for acts that are made illegal by criminal statute and are not necessarily wrong in and of themselves.

of the peace) or in a general trial court (for example, a superior court). Probation and community service are often imposed on those who commit misdemeanors, especially juveniles.

INFRACTIONS The least serious form of wrongdoing is often called an infraction and is punishable only by a small fine. Even though infractions such as parking tickets or traffic violations technically represent illegal activity, they generally are not considered "crimes." Therefore, infractions rarely lead to jury trials and are deemed to be so minor that they do not appear on the offender's criminal record. In some jurisdictions, the terms *infraction* and *petty offense* are interchangeable. In others, however, they are different. Under federal guidelines, for example, an infraction can be punished by up to five days of prison time, while a petty offender is only liable for a fine.[3] Finally, those who string together a series of infractions (or fail to pay the fines that come with such offenses) are in danger of being criminally charged. In Illinois, having three or more speeding violations in one year is considered criminal behavior.[4]

MALA IN SE AND MALA PROHIBITA

Criminologists often express the social function of criminal law in terms of *mala in se* or *mala prohibita* crimes. A criminal act is referred to as *mala in se* if it would be considered wrong even if there were no law prohibiting it. *Mala in se* crimes are said to go against "natural laws"—that is, against the "natural, moral, and public" principles of a society. Murder, rape, and theft are examples of *mala in se* crimes. These crimes are generally the same from country to country or culture to culture. In contrast, the term *mala prohibita* refers to acts that are considered crimes only because they have been codified as such through statute—"human-made" laws. A *mala prohibita* crime is considered wrong only because it has been prohibited. It is not inherently a wrong, though it may reflect the moral standards of a society at a given time. Thus, the definition of a *mala prohibita* crime can vary from country to country and even from state to state. Bigamy, or the offense of having two legal spouses, could be considered a *mala prohibita* crime.

LO 2

MAKING THE DISTINCTION Some observers question the distinction between *mala in se* and *mala prohibita*. In many instances, it is difficult to define a "pure" *mala in se* crime. That is, it is difficult to separate a crime from the culture that has deemed it a crime.[5] Even murder, under certain cultural circumstances, is not considered a criminal act. In a number of poor, traditional areas of the Middle East and Asia, the law excuses "honor killings" in which men kill female family members suspected of sexual indiscretion. Our own legal system excuses homicide in extreme situations, such as self-defense or when a law enforcement agent kills in the course of upholding the law. Therefore, "natural" laws can be seen as culturally specific. Similar difficulties occur in trying to define a "pure" *mala prohibita* crime. (For an example of how different cultures have different views on crime, see the feature *Comparative Criminal Justice—The World's Oldest Profession* on the facing page.)

THE DRUG DILEMMA In spite of these difficulties, the *mala in se/mala prohibita* split can help explain seeming contradictions in criminal law. Take the law's treatment of *stimulants*, which are drugs that act on the nervous system to produce feelings of well-being and euphoria. *Nicotine*, a naturally occurring substance in the tobacco plant, and *caffeine*, found in coffee, tea, and soft drinks, are both stimulants. So are *cocaine*, an active ingredient in the South American coca plant, and *amphetamine,* developed in the 1920s to treat asthma sufferers. Nicotine and caffeine are considered **licit drugs,** or socially acceptable substances, if used by adults. In contrast, cocaine and many amphetamines are considered **illicit drugs,** or drugs whose sale and use have been made illegal. The most widely used drug in the United States is *alcohol,* consumed, at least occasionally, by approximately two-thirds of adult Americans.[6]

Licit Drugs Legal drugs or substances, such as alcohol, caffeine, and nicotine.

Illicit Drugs Certain drugs or substances whose use or sale has been declared illegal.

COMPARATIVE CRIMINAL JUSTICE

THE WORLD'S OLDEST PROFESSION

The Netherlands has a well-deserved reputation as a place of tolerance, or *gedoogbeleid.* Many activities banned elsewhere, such as same-sex marriage, abortion, euthanasia, and the sale of marijuana, are protected under Dutch law. Another widely proscribed enterprise—prostitution—was made legal in 2000 after decades of *gedoogbeleid* permitted the practice to flourish with a wink and a nod from law enforcement. By legalizing the sex trade, Dutch politicians hoped to offer protection to the women engaged in what is often a dangerous profession. The legislation treats prostitutes like any other workers, allowing the state to collect taxes on their profits in return for health care, unemployment insurance, and pensions.

Common Practice

The situation in the Netherlands is hardly unique. Prostitution is legal (though heavily regulated) in more than 150 countries, including most members of the European Union. In contrast, state laws have made the buying and selling of sex acts illegal in most of the United States—the exception being seven rural counties in Nevada. To a certain extent, these laws are designed to prevent the illegal activities that are said to go along with prostitution, such as organized crime, drug use, trafficking in women from disadvantaged countries, and the spread of sexually transmitted disease. The main driving force behind the state laws, however, is public morality: prostitution is widely believed to go against America's "social fabric."

As it turns out, perhaps morals in the United States and the Netherlands are not so different after all. The Dutch government recently took a number of steps to restrict prostitution. By 2011, officials in the country's capital, Amsterdam, had closed one-third of

the brothels in the city's infamous "red light" district, in some cases renting the vacated buildings to young designers and artists. Besides trying to change the city's image, officials were worried by signs of organized crime and human trafficking: approximately 80 percent of the women working in Dutch brothels are from other, poorer countries.

FOR CRITICAL ANALYSIS

Is prostitution a *mala in se* crime or a *mala prohibita* crime? Explain your answer and discuss whether the practice should be legalized more broadly in the United States. Furthermore, what is your opinion of a Swedish law that makes the selling of sex legal but the buying of sex a crime? What would such legislation accomplish in the United States? What problems would it cause?

Josje has worked for twenty years as a prostitute in the red light district of Amsterdam, capital of the Netherlands.
Anoek de Groot/AFP/Getty Images

Distinguishing between Licit and Illicit Drugs Why has society prohibited the use of certain drugs, while allowing the use of others? The answer cannot be found in the risk of harm caused by the substances. Just as with illicit drugs, many licit drugs, if abused, can have serious consequences for the health of the user or of others. Improper consumption of the nonprescription pain reliever Tylenol (acetaminophen) is a leading cause of liver failure in the United States today,[7] and nearly 34,000 Americans are killed in alcohol-related car crashes each year.[8] Nor is illegality linked to the addictive quality of the drug. According to the American Medical Association, nicotine is the most habit-forming substance, with over two-thirds of people who smoke cigarettes becoming "hooked."[9] The next most addictive drug is heroin, followed by cocaine, alcohol, amphetamines, and marijuana, in that order. The drug most widely associated with violent behavior, especially domestic violence, is alcohol.[10] One professor of preventive medicine has concluded that "there are no scientific . . . or medical bases on which the legal distinctions between various drugs are made."[11]

Discussion Tip: Ask students to consider the way that licit and illicit drugs are defined in our country. What changes do students predict in the way substances like over-the-counter medicines, cigarettes, and alcohol will be categorized in the future?

Society and the Law If drug laws are not based on science or medicine, on what are they based? The answers lies in the concept of *mala prohibita:* certain drugs are characterized as illicit while others are not because of presiding social norms and values. The general attitude of American society toward drugs has changed dramatically over the past century and a half. With the notable exception of alcohol, many drugs were considered useful, medicinal substances in the 1800s. Cocaine was promoted as a remedy for dozens of ailments. Coca-Cola, introduced in 1886, was marketed as providing the benefits of cocaine without the dangers of alcohol.[12]

As these attitudes have changed, the law has changed as well. Today, licit and illicit drugs are regulated under the Controlled Substances Act (CSA), which is part of the Comprehensive Drug Abuse Prevention and Control Act of 1970.[13] The CSA specifies five hierarchical categories for drugs and the penalties for the manufacture, sale, distribution, possession, or consumption of these drugs, based on the substances' medical use, potential for abuse, and addictive qualities (see Figure 3.1 below). The CSA explicitly excludes "distilled spirits, wine, malt beverages, and tobacco" from the legal definition of

FIGURE 3.1 **Schedules of Narcotics as Defined by the Federal Controlled Substances Act**

The Comprehensive Drug Abuse Prevention and Control Act of 1970 continues to be the basis for the regulation of drugs in the United States. Substances named by the act were placed under direct regulation of the Drug Enforcement Administration (DEA). The act "ranks" drugs from I to V, with Schedule I drugs being the most heavily controlled and carrying the most severe penalties for abuse.

	Criteria	Examples
SCHEDULE I	Drugs with high abuse potential that are lacking therapeutic utility or adequate safety for use under medical supervision.	Marijuana, heroin, LSD, peyote, PCP, mescaline
SCHEDULE II	Drugs with high abuse potential that are accepted in current medical practice despite high physical and psychological dependence potential.	Opium, cocaine, morphine, Benzedrine, methadone, methamphetamine
SCHEDULE III	Drugs with moderate abuse potential that are utilized in current medical practice despite dependence potential.	Barbiturates, amphetamine
SCHEDULE IV	Drugs with low abuse potential that are accepted in current medical practice despite limited dependence potential.	Valium, Darvon, phenobarbital
SCHEDULE V	Drugs with minimal abuse potential that are used in current medical practice despite limited dependence potential.	Cough medicine with small amounts of narcotic

Source: The Comprehensive Drug Abuse Prevention and Control Act of 1970.

a "controlled substance."[14] Therefore, alcohol and tobacco are legal not because they have pharmacological effects that are considerably different or safer than those of illicit drugs, but rather because the law, as supported by society, says so.[15]

SELFASSESSMENT

_____ law is concerned with disputes between private individuals and other entities, whereas criminal law involves the _____'s duty to protect society by preventing and prosecuting crimes. A _____ is a serious crime punishable by more than a year in prison or the death penalty, while a person found guilty of a _____ will usually spend less than a year in jail or pay a fine. _____ _____ _____ occurs when a homicide is premeditated and deliberate. If there is no premeditation or malice on the part of the offender toward the victim, the homicide is classified as _____.

THE UNIFORM CRIME REPORT

Suppose that a firefighter dies while fighting a fire at an office building. Later, police discover that the building manager intentionally set the fire. All of the elements of the crime of arson have certainly been met, but can the manager be charged with murder? In some jurisdictions, the act might be considered a form of manslaughter, but according to the U.S. Department of Justice, arson-related deaths and injuries of police officers and firefighters due to the "hazardous natures of their professions" are not murders.[16]

The distinction is important because the Department of Justice provides us with the most far-reaching and oft-cited set of national crime statistics. Each year, the depart-

LO 3
ment releases the Uniform Crime Report (UCR). Since its inception in 1930, the UCR has attempted to measure the overall rate of crime in the United States by organizing "offenses known to the police."[17] To produce the UCR, the FBI relies on the voluntary participation of local law enforcement agencies. These agencies— approximately 17,500 in total, covering 95 percent of the population—base their information on three measurements:

1. The number of persons arrested.
2. The number of crimes reported by victims, witnesses, or the police themselves.
3. The number of law enforcement officers.[18]

Once this information has been sent to the FBI, the agency presents the crime data in two important ways:

1. As a *rate* per 100,000 people. In 2010, for example, the crime rate was 3,346. In other words, for every 100,000 inhabitants of the United States, 3,346 *Part I offenses* (explained on the next page) were reported to the FBI. This statistic is known as the *crime rate* and is often cited by media sources when discussing the level of crime in the United States.

2. As a *percentage* change from the previous year or other time periods. From 2009 to 2010, there was a 6.5 percent decrease in the violent crime rate and a 3.3 percent decrease in the property crime rate.[19]

The Department of Justice publishes these data annually in *Crime in the United States.* Along with the basic statistics, this publication offers an exhaustive array of crime information, including breakdowns of crimes committed by city, county, and other geographic

Uniform Crime Report (UCR) An annual report compiled by the FBI to give an indication of criminal activity in the United States. The FBI collects data from local, state, and federal law enforcement agencies in preparing this report.

Technology Tip: Have students explore the Uniform Crime Report online at **www.fbi.gov/about-us/cjis/ucr/ucr**. Ask them to locate the crime rates for your county. How do those crime rates compare to other locations in your state? To major cities in the United States? (LO 3)

The Federal Bureau of Investigation posts many of its statistical findings, including the Uniform Crime Report. Find its Web site by visiting the *Criminal Justice CourseMate* at **cengagebrain.com** and selecting the *Web links* for this chapter.

designations and by the demographics (gender, race, age) of the individuals who have been arrested for crimes.

PART I OFFENSES

The UCR divides the criminal offenses it measures into two major categories: Part I and Part II offenses. **Part I offenses** are those crimes that, due to their seriousness and frequency, are recorded by the FBI to give a general idea of the "crime picture" in the United States in any given year. For a description of the seven Part I offenses, see Figure 3.2 below.

Part I offenses are those most likely to be covered by the media and, consequently, inspire the most fear of crime in the population. These crimes have come to dominate crime coverage to such an extent that, for most Americans, the first image that comes to mind at the mention of "crime" is one person physically attacking another person or a robbery taking place with the use or threat of force.[20] Furthermore, in the stereotypical crime, the offender and the victim usually do not know each other.

Given the trauma of violent crimes, this perception is understandable, but it is not accurate. According to UCR statistics, a relative or other acquaintance of the victim commits at least 44 percent of the homicides in the United States.[21] Furthermore, as is evident from Figure 3.2, the majority of Part I offenses committed are property crimes. Notice that 60 percent of all reported Part I offenses are larceny/thefts, and another 21 percent are burglaries.[22]

PART II OFFENSES

LO 4 Not only do violent crimes represent the minority of Part I offenses, but Part I offenses are far outweighed by **Part II offenses,** which include all crimes recorded by the FBI that do not fall into the category of Part I offenses. While information gathered on Part I offenses reflects those offenses "known," or reported to the FBI by local agencies, Part II offenses are measured only by arrest data. In 2010, the FBI recorded about

FIGURE 3.2 Part I Offenses

Every month local law enforcement agencies voluntarily provide information on serious offenses in their jurisdiction to the FBI. These serious offenses, known as Part I offenses, are defined here. (Arson is not included in the national crime report data, but it is sometimes considered a Part I offense nonetheless, so its definition is included here.) As the graph shows, most Part I offenses reported by local police departments in any given year are property crimes.

Murder. The willful (nonnegligent) killing of one human being by another.

Forcible rape. The carnal knowledge of a female forcibly and against her will. Included are rapes by force and attempted rapes.

Robbery. The taking or attempting to take anything of value from the care, custody, or control of a person or persons by force or threat of force or violence and/or by putting the victim in fear.

Aggravated assault. An unlawful attack by one person on another for the purpose of inflicting severe or aggravated bodily injury. This type of assault is usually accompanied by the use of a weapon or by means likely to produce death or great bodily harm.

Burglary—breaking or entering. The unlawful entry of a structure to commit a felony or a theft. Attempted forcible entry is included.

Larceny/theft (except motor vehicle theft). The unlawful taking, carrying, leading, or riding away of property from the possession or constructive possession of another.

Motor vehicle theft. The theft or attempted theft of a motor vehicle.

Arson. Any willful or malicious burning or attempt to burn, with or without intent to defraud, a dwelling house, public building, motor vehicle or aircraft, personal property of another, and the like.

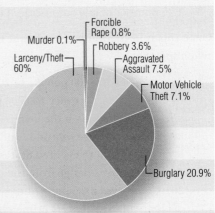

Larceny/Theft 60%
Murder 0.1%
Forcible Rape 0.8%
Robbery 3.6%
Aggravated Assault 7.5%
Motor Vehicle Theft 7.1%
Burglary 20.9%

Sources: Federal Bureau of Investigation, *Crime in the United States, 2010* (Washington, D.C.: U.S. Department of Justice, 2011), at **www.fbi.gov/about-us/cjis/ucr/crime-in-the-u.s/2010/crime-in-the-u.s.-2010/offense-definitions** and **www.fbi.gov/about-us/cjis/ucr/crime-in-the-u.s/2010/crime-in-the-u.s.-2010/tables/10tbl01.xls**.

2.1 million arrests for Part I offenses in the United States. That same year, nearly 11 million arrests for Part II offenses took place.[23] In other words, a Part II offense was over five times more common than a Part I offense (for a description of Part II offenses and their rates, see Figure 3.3 below). Such statistics have prompted Marcus Felson, a professor at Rutgers University School of Criminal Justice, to comment that "most crime is very ordinary."[24]

THE UCR: A FLAWED METHOD?

LO 5
Even though the UCR is the predominant source of crime data in the country, there are numerous questions about the accuracy of its findings. These criticisms focus on the methods that local law enforcement agencies use to collect the UCR statistics and report them to the FBI.

Discussion Tip: Discuss the various flaws in the UCR with your students. Which shortcomings are related to the UCR itself and which flaws are due to human error and dishonesty? (LO 5)

FIGURE 3.3 Part II Offenses

Offense	Estimated Annual Arrests	Offense	Estimated Annual Arrests
Drug abuse violations	1,638,846	Offenses against family and children	111,062
Driving under the influence	1,412,223	Stolen property	94,802
Other assaults	1,292,449	Forgery and counterfeiting	78,101
Disorderly conduct	615,172	Sex offenses (except forcible rape and prostitution)	72,628
Liquor laws	512,790	Prostitution and commercialized vice	62,668
Drunkenness	560,718	Vagrancy	32,033
Fraud	187,887	Embezzlement	16,616
Vandalism	252,753	Gambling	9,941
Weapons	159,020	Suspicion	1,166
Curfew and loitering law violations	94,797	All other offenses	3,720,402

Curfew and loitering law violations (persons under age eighteen)—Offenses relating to violations of local curfew or loitering ordinances.

Disorderly conduct—Breach of the peace.

Driving under the influence—Driving or operating any vehicle or common carrier while drunk or under the influence of liquor or narcotics.

Drug abuse violations—State and/or local offenses relating to the unlawful possession, sale, use, growing, and manufacturing of narcotic drugs. The following drug categories are specified: opium or cocaine and their derivatives (morphine, heroin, codeine); marijuana; synthetic narcotics—manufactured narcotics that can cause true addiction (Demerol, methadone); and dangerous nonnarcotic drugs (barbiturates, Benzedrine).

Drunkenness—Offenses relating to drunkenness or intoxication. Excluded is "driving under the influence."

Embezzlement—Misappropriation or misapplication of funds or property entrusted to one's care, custody, or control.

Forgery and counterfeiting—Making, altering, uttering, or possessing, with intent to defraud, anything false in the semblance of that which is true. Attempts are included.

Fraud—Fraudulent conversion and obtaining funds or property by false pretenses. Included are confidence games and bad checks, except forgeries and counterfeiting.

Gambling—Promoting, permitting, or engaging in illegal gambling.

Liquor laws—State and/or local liquor law violations, except "drunkenness" and "driving under the influence." Federal violations are excluded.

Offenses against family and children—Nonsupport, neglect, desertion, or abuse of family and children.

Other assaults (simple)—Assaults and attempted assaults where no weapon is used and that do not result in serious or aggravated injury to the victim.

Prostitution and commercialized vice—Sex offenses of a commercialized nature, such as prostitution, keeping a bawdy house, or procuring or transporting women for immoral purposes. Attempts are included.

Sex offenses (except forcible rape, prostitution, and commercialized vice)—Statutory rape and offenses against chastity, common decency, morals, and the like. Attempts are included.

Stolen property: buying, receiving, possessing—Buying, receiving, and possessing stolen property, including attempts.

Suspicion—No specific offense; suspect released without formal charges being placed.

Vagrancy—Vagabondage, begging, loitering, and the like.

Vandalism—Willful or malicious destruction, injury, disfigurement, or defacement of any public or private property, real or personal, without consent of the owner or persons having custody or control.

Weapons: carrying, possessing, and the like—All violations of regulations or statutes controlling the carrying, using, possessing, furnishing, and manufacturing of deadly weapons or silencers. Included are attempts.

All other offenses—All violations of state or local laws not specifically identified as Part I or Part II offenses, except traffic violations.

Sources: Federal Bureau of Investigation, *Crime in the United States, 2010* (Washington, D.C.: U.S. Department of Justice, 2011), at **www.fbi.gov/about-us/cjis/ucr/crime-in-the-u.s/2010/crime-in-the-u.s.-2010/tables/10tbl29.xls** and **www.fbi.gov/about-us/cjis/ucr/crime-in-the-u.s/2010/crime-in-the-u.s.-2010/offense-definitions**.

DISCRETIONARY DISTORTIONS For the UCR to be accurate, citizens must report criminal activity to the police, and the police must then pass this information on to the FBI. Criminologists have long been aware that neither citizens nor police can be expected to perform these roles with consistency.[25] Citizens may not report a crime for any number of reasons, including fear of reprisal, embarrassment, or a personal bias in favor of the offender. Many also feel that police cannot do anything to help them in the aftermath of a crime, so they do not see the point of involving law enforcement agents in their lives. Surveys of crime victims reveal that only 49 percent of violent crimes and 39 percent of property crimes are reported to the police.[26] In general, people seem more willing to notify police about robberies and aggravated assaults by strangers than about rapes or violence that occurs within the family context.[27] Studies have also shown that police underreport crimes in certain instances, such as when the offense has occurred within a family or the victim does not want the offender to be charged.

Furthermore, the FBI and local law enforcement agencies do not always interpret Part I offenses in the same manner. FBI guidelines, for example, define forcible rape as the "carnal knowledge" of a woman "forcibly and against her will." Although some local agencies may strictly adhere to this definition, others may define rape more loosely—listing any assault on a woman as a rape. Furthermore, different jurisdictions have different definitions of rape. In Alabama, rape occurs only in cases where the woman offers "earnest resistance" to sexual intercourse,[28] and in a number of other jurisdictions, the courts require proof that the victim physically opposed her attacker's advances. A number of jurisdictions have also expanded their definition of the crime to include the possibility that males can be raped.

CLEARANCE DISTORTIONS The factors just listed influence the arrest decision, as police officers are more likely to make arrests that can be *cleared*. **Clearance of an arrest** occurs when the suspect is charged with a particular crime and turned over to the court for trial. With law enforcement agents in different jurisdictions operating under different definitions of rape, or any other crime, their reports to the FBI for UCR purposes may be misleading. Indeed, when a police department in Alabama and a police department in Oregon both report a rape to the federal agency, they may not be describing the same act. Given that the UCR incorporates reports from 17,000 different local agencies, varying methods of defining offenses could have a significant effect on the overall outcome.

THE NATIONAL INCIDENT-BASED REPORTING SYSTEM

In the 1980s, well aware of the various criticisms of the UCR, the Department of Justice began seeking ways to revise its data-collecting system. The result was the National Incident-Based Reporting System (NIBRS). In the NIBRS, local agencies collect data on each single crime occurrence within twenty-two offense categories made up of forty-six specific crimes called Group A offenses (see Figure 3.4 on the facing page for a list of NIBRS offense categories). These data are recorded on computerized record systems provided—though not completely financed—by the federal government.

The NIBRS became available to local agencies in 1989. Twenty-two years later, 36 states have been NIBRS certified, with about 40 percent of the agencies in those states using the new system.[29] Even in its limited form, however, criminologists have responded enthusiastically to the NIBRS because the system provides information about four "data sets"—offenses, victims, offenders, and arrestees—unavailable through the UCR. The NIBRS also

FIGURE 3.4 NIBRS Offense Categories

The NIBRS collects data on each single incident and arrest within these twenty-two offense categories made up of forty-six specific crimes, called Group A offenses.

1. **Arson**
2. **Assault Offenses**—Aggravated Assault, Simple Assault, Intimidation/Stalking
3. **Bribery**
4. **Burglary/Breaking and Entering**
5. **Counterfeiting/Forgery**
6. **Destruction/Damage/Vandalism of Property**
7. **Drug/Narcotic Offenses**—Drug/Narcotic Violations, Drug Equipment Violations
8. **Embezzlement**
9. **Extortion/Blackmail**
10. **Fraud Offenses**—False Pretenses/Swindle/Confidence Game, Credit Card/ATM Fraud, Impersonation, Welfare Fraud, Wire Fraud
11. **Gambling Offenses**—Betting/Wagering, Operating/Promoting/ Assisting Gambling, Gambling Equipment Violations, Sports Tampering
12. **Homicide Offenses**—Murder and Nonnegligent Manslaughter, Negligent Manslaughter, Justifiable Homicide
13. **Kidnapping/Abduction**
14. **Larceny/Theft Offenses**—Pocket Picking, Purse Snatching, Shoplifting, Theft from Building, Theft from Coin-Operated Machine or Device, Theft from Motor Vehicle, Theft of Motor Vehicle Parts or Accessories, All Other Larceny
15. **Motor Vehicle Theft**
16. **Pornography/Obscene Material**
17. **Prostitution Offenses**—Prostitution, Assisting or Promoting Prostitution
18. **Robbery**
19. **Sex Offenses, Forcible**—Forcible Rape, Forcible Sodomy, Sexual Assault with an Object, Forcible Fondling
20. **Sex Offenses, Nonforcible**—Incest, Statutory Rape
21. **Stolen Property Offenses (Receiving and the Like)**
22. **Weapon Law Violations**

Source: The Federal Bureau of Investigation.

presents a more complete picture of crime by monitoring all criminal "incidents" reported to the police, not just those that lead to an arrest.[30] Furthermore, because jurisdictions involved with the NIBRS must identify bias motivations of offenders, the procedure is very useful in studying hate crimes, a topic we will address in the next chapter.

SELFASSESSMENT

Fill in the blanks and check your answers on page 92.

To produce its annual _____ _____ _____, the FBI relies on the cooperation of law enforcement agencies across the nation. The FBI often presents its findings to the public in terms of a crime _____, or the frequency with which offenses occur for every 100,000 inhabitants of the United States. Although _____ _____ offenses are more likely to be covered by the media, _____ _____ offenses are much more common in the American crime landscape.

ALTERNATIVE MEASURING METHODS

The UCR is generally considered the "official" record of crime in the United States, but it is only one of many sources of crime data in this country. Law enforcement professionals and academics also rely on victim surveys and self-reported surveys to collect such data, and we discuss these two popular crime measurement methods in this section.

VICTIM SURVEYS

One alternative method of data collecting attempts to avoid the distorting influence of the "intermediary," or the local police agencies. In **victim surveys,** criminologists or other researchers ask the victims of crime directly about their experiences, using techniques such as interviews or e-mail and phone surveys. The first large-scale victim survey took place in 1966, when members of 10,000 households answered questionnaires as part of the President's Commission on Law Enforcement and the Administration of Justice. The results indicated a much higher victimization rate than had been previously

Teaching Tip: Ask students to brainstorm the advantages and disadvantages of victim surveys as compared to the UCR. Which data collection tool do students feel yields a more accurate picture of criminal offending? (LO 6)

Victim Surveys A method of gathering crime data that directly surveys participants to determine their experiences as victims of crime.

expected, and researchers felt the process gave them a better understanding of the dark figure of crime, or the actual amount of crime that occurs in the country.

Criminologists were so encouraged by the results of the 1966 experiment that the federal government decided to institute an ongoing victim survey. The result was the National Crime Victimization Survey (NCVS), which started in 1972. Conducted by the U.S. Bureau of the Census in cooperation with the Bureau of Justice Statistics of the Justice Department, the NCVS conducts an annual survey of more than 40,000 households with nearly 75,000 occupants over twelve years of age. Participants are interviewed twice a year concerning their experiences with crimes in the prior six months. As you can see in Figure 3.5 below, the questions cover a wide array of possible victimization.

LO 6

Supporters of the NCVS highlight a number of aspects in which the victim survey is superior to the UCR:

1. It measures both reported and unreported crime.
2. It is unaffected by police bias and distortions in reporting crime to the FBI.
3. It does not rely on victims directly reporting crime to the police.[31]

Most important, some supporters say, is that the NCVS gives victims a voice in the criminal justice process.

SELF-REPORTED SURVEYS

Based on many of the same principles as victim surveys, but focusing instead on offenders, self-reported surveys are a third source of data for criminologists. In this form of data collection, persons are asked directly—through personal interviews or questionnaires, or over the telephone—about specific criminal activity to which they may have been a party. Self-reported surveys are most useful in situations in which the group to be studied is already gathered in an institutional setting, such as a juvenile facility or a

FIGURE 3.5 Sample Questions from the NCVS (National Crime Victimization Survey)

36a. Was something belonging to YOU stolen, such as:
a. Things that you carry, like luggage, a wallet, purse, briefcase, book—
b. Clothing, jewelry, or cell phone—
c. Bicycle or sports equipment—
d. Things in your home—like a TV, stereo, or tools—
e. Things from outside your home, such as a garden hose or lawn furniture—
f. Things belonging to children in the household—
g. Things from a vehicle, such as a package, groceries, camera, or CDs—
h. Did anyone ATTEMPT to steal anything belonging to you?

41a. Has anyone attacked or threatened you in any of these ways:
a. With any weapon, for instance, a gun or knife—
b. With anything like a baseball bat, frying pan, scissors, or stick—
c. By something thrown, such as a rock or bottle—
d. Include any grabbing, punching, or choking,
e. Any rape, attempted rape, or other type of sexual attack—
f. Any face-to-face threats—OR
g. Any attack or threat or use of force by anyone at all? Please mention it even if you are not certain it was a crime.

42a. People often don't think of incidents committed by someone they know. Other than the incidents already mentioned, did you have something stolen from you OR were you attacked or threatened by:
a. Someone at work or school—
b. A neighbor or friend—
c. A relative or family member—
d. Any other person you've met or known?

43a. Incidents involving forced or unwanted sexual acts are often difficult to talk about. Have you been forced or coerced to engage in unwanted sexual activity by—
a. someone you didn't know before—
b. a casual acquaintance—OR
c. someone you know well?

44a. During the last 6 months (other than any incidents already mentioned), did you call the police to report something that happened to YOU which you thought was a crime?

45a. During the last 6 months (other than any incidents already mentioned), did anything which you thought was a crime happen to YOU, but you did NOT report to the police?

Source: U.S. Department of Justice, *National Crime Victimization Survey 2006* (Washington, D.C.: Bureau of Justice Statistics, 2008).

prison. One of the most widespread self-reported surveys in the United States, the Drug Use Forecasting Program, collects information on narcotics use from arrestees who have been brought into booking facilities.

Because there is no penalty for admitting to criminal activity in a self-reported survey, subjects tend to be more forthcoming in discussing their behavior. Researchers interviewing a group of male students at a state university, for example, found that a significant number of them admitted to committing minor crimes for which they had never been arrested.[32] This fact points to the most striking finding of self-reported surveys: the dark figure of crime, referred to earlier as the *actual* amount of crime that takes place, appears to be much larger than the UCR or NCVS would suggest.

Critical Thinking Skill Development: Ask students to respond to "Questions for Critical Analysis" number four on page 92, in which they discuss the best method of uncovering the dark figure of crime.

CJ&TECHNOLOGY Transdermal Alcohol Testing

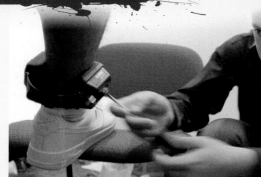

AP Photo/Steve Marcus/*Las Vegas Sun*

Sweat, it seems, is one source of self-reported data that never lies, at least when it comes to alcohol consumption. That's the logic behind the Secure Continuous Remote Alcohol Monitor, otherwise known as the SCRAM bracelet or the "bling with a ping." This eight-ounce bracelet, usually worn around the subject's ankle, relies on a process called *transdermal alcohol testing* to measure the levels of alcohol vapor that show up in perspiration when alcohol has been consumed. The measurements are then transmitted and posted on a Web site via wireless modem, allowing the subject to prove—or disprove—that he or she remains sober. The SCRAM bracelet gained notoriety several years ago when actress and socialite Lindsay Lohan voluntarily donned one to show her commitment to sobriety. Most wearers, however, are not celebrities but rather offenders who are required by a court to undergo the testing after an arrest for drunk driving, domestic violence, or some other alcohol-related wrongdoing.

THINKING ABOUT TRANSDERMAL ALCOHOL TESTING
Coming soon: passive transdermal detectors in steering wheels. These devices will measure the sweat on the driver's hands to determine whether she or he has been ingesting drugs or alcohol. How could this technology be used to keep someone from driving under the influence?

SELFASSESSMENT
Fill in the blanks and check your answers on page 92.
_____ surveys rely on those who have been the subject of criminal activity to discuss the incidents with researchers. _____-_____ surveys ask participants to detail their own criminal behavior. Both methods show that the _____ _____ of crime, or the actual amount of crime that takes place in this country, is much _____ than official crime data would suggest.

CRIME TRENDS IN THE UNITED STATES

The UCR, NCVS, and other statistical measures we have discussed so far in this chapter, though important, represent only the tip of the iceberg of crime data. Thanks to the efforts of government law enforcement agencies, educational institutions, and private individuals, more information on crime is available today than at any time in the nation's history. Pure statistics do not always tell the whole story, however, and crime rates often fail to behave in the ways criminologists predict. In this section, we will look at how crime patterns in the United States have shifted over the past five decades and how trends from the immediate past may or may not help us understand what to expect in the immediate future.

ON THE RISE: CRIME IN THE 1960s AND 1970s

The United States has suffered two episodes of large-scale crime increases since the early 1960s. The first, long term and relatively gradual, lasted through the 1970s. The second, shorter and more dramatic, peaked in 1991. In attempting to explain the first increase, experts relied to a large extent on what Franklin Zimring calls the three "usual suspects" of crime fluctuation:

LO 7

1. *Imprisonment,* based on the principle that (a) an offender in prison or jail is unable to commit a crime on the street, and (b) a potential offender on the street will not commit a crime because he or she does not want to wind up behind bars.
2. *Youth populations,* because offenders commit fewer crimes as they grow older.
3. The *economy,* because when legitimate opportunities to earn income become scarce, some people will turn to illegitimate methods such as crime.[33]

In many ways, evidence from the first episode of increased crime in the 1970s supports the influence of each of these "usual suspects." For example, levels of imprisonment in the United States were relatively low during the 1960s. By the early 1970s, public outcry at violent crime rates that had doubled in the previous decade started a "get tough on crime" political movement that resulted in harsher sentences for a wider range of offenders.[34] In fact, 1972 would mark the last time for thirty years that the number of Americans behind bars dropped, leading many to believe that the massive expansion of the corrections industry has played a crucial role in subsequent reductions in crime.

AGE AND CRIME: THE PEAK YEARS Writing in 1974, criminologist James Q. Wilson pointed out a trend that seemed to have an obvious connection to the crime increases of the era. Between 1960 and 1973, the number of Americans between the ages of eighteen and twenty-four increased by 13 million, bringing the total to more than 40 million.[35] Wilson found these data highly relevant because the strongest statistical determinant of criminal behavior appears to be age. Numerous studies show that criminal behavior peaks in the teenage years. Indeed, juvenile arrest rates did increase in the 1960s and early 1970s before leveling off for the remainder of the decade.[36] As Figure 3.6 on the facing page shows, the eighteen- to twenty-four-year-old group targeted by Wilson remains responsible for a greater percentage of total arrests than any other age group.

Why is the crime rate dramatically higher for young people? There is no single, simple answer. As noted in Chapter 2, biological theories of crime point to high testosterone levels in young males, which increase rates of aggression and violence (see pages

Group Activities: Ask students to work in groups to brainstorm potential explanations for the two large-scale crime increases in the last fifty years. Based on those explanations, ask students if they would predict another increase in the near future. Why or why not? (LO 7)

Critical Thinking Skill Development: In a short written assignment, ask students to evaluate Wilson's statement that the strongest statistical determinant of crime is age. What impact does age have on criminal offending and the crime rate?

39–40). Adolescents are also more susceptible to peer pressure, and studies show that juvenile delinquents tend to socialize with other juvenile delinquents.[37] In Chapter 15, we will take a much closer look at the many *risk factors* that are associated with youthful offending.

CRIME AND THE ECONOMY The 1970s were also a difficult period for the American economy, and criminologists have pointed to high unemployment rates and falling wages as contributing to the crime increases of that decade.[38] While few observers would question the existence of some correlation between crime and the economy, the overall equation is not quite so simple. The 1960s, for example, were a time of concurrent general economic prosperity and increasing crime rates.[39] Indeed, none of the "usual suspects"—imprisonment, demographics, and the economy—has consistently mirrored crime trends. In Chapter 13, we will look at the often contradictory relationship between incarceration and crime. Furthermore, later in this chapter we will see that predictions based on youth populations and the economy have often been wrong—sometimes spectacularly so.

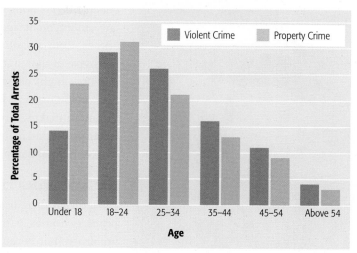

FIGURE 3.6 Percentage of Arrests by Age

As this graph shows, the majority of those persons arrested for property crimes in the United States are under twenty-five years old, and more violent crimes are committed by eighteen- to twenty-four-year-olds than by any other age group.

Source: Federal Bureau of Investigation, *Crime in the United States, 2010* (Washington, D.C.: U.S. Department of Justice, 2011), at **www.fbi.gov/about-us/cjis/ucr/crime-in-the-u.s/2010/crime-in-the-u.s.-2010/tables/10tbl38.xls**.

DRUG WARS: CRIME IN THE 1980s

Another reason often cited for the crime increases of the 1970s was rising heroin use, particularly in America's inner cities. The drug–crime relationship, which we first examined in Chapter 2 (see pages 56–58), also appeared to be a leading factor in the crime spike of the late 1980s and early 1990s. Those years saw the introduction of crack cocaine, which is more powerful than the powdered form of the drug and quickly became a staple of the illegal drug market.

THE IMPACT OF CRACK According to Professor Alfred Blumstein of Pittsburgh's Carnegie Mellon University, the introduction of crack cocaine set off a series of events with disastrous consequences for young, low-income males. First, drug kingpins hired them to sell the drug on the street. Because firearms were necessary to protect a dealer's territory, the crack trade led to a flood of handguns in America's poorer neighborhoods. These handguns then began to spread to the rest of the youth population and were used to commit crimes such as homicide and robbery.[40] Further research by Blumstein showed that the homicide rates by young offenders in large cities began to increase in 1985 and began to fall in 1993, a trend that reflected the ebb and flow of crime rates in general at that time.[41]

THE METHAMPHETAMINE SCOURGE Although nothing as dramatic and far-reaching as the crack cocaine epidemic has occurred in the 2000s, the drug–crime relationship can still be seen in concentrated geographic areas. Many of these crime pockets have formed as a result of the manufacture and sale of methamphetamine (meth), a highly addictive stimulant to the central nervous system. Meth is relatively easy to make in home laboratories using the ingredients of common cold medicines and

Teaching Tip: If possible, invite a narcotics officer to visit the classroom. Ask her or him to describe which illegal drugs are most prevalent in your region, and to discuss how the illegal drug trade has impacted local crime rates.

Methamphetamine (meth) A synthetic stimulant that creates a strong feeling of euphoria in the user and is highly addictive.

Drug Enforcement Administration agents photograph evidence at a meth lab in Liverpool, Ohio. Why have methamphetamine production and use flourished in poor, rural areas?
AP Photo/Wayne Maris/*East Liverpool Review*

⊗ The **Drug Policy Alliance** is critical of the tactics used in this country to combat illegal drug use. To see its Web site, visit the *Criminal Justice CourseMate* at **cengagebrain. com** and select the *Web links* for this chapter.

farm chemicals. Consequently, the drug provides a "cheap high" for the consumer and has become the scourge of many poor rural areas, particularly in the western half of the United States.

Meth can be devastating to a community because of the numerous side effects that go along with the drug's production and use. In Hawaii, for example, law enforcement agencies report that a wide range of violent and property crimes, from assault to robbery to auto theft, can be linked to high levels of meth use in that state.[42] In addition, children who have been taken away from parents caught using or making the substance, known as "meth orphans," are overwhelming local foster homes and social services in affected areas. Finally, the meth-making process results in between five and seven pounds of toxic waste per pound of finished product. When this waste is discarded, the resulting environmental damage can be severe.[43]

AN ALTERNATIVE VIEW Some observers have questioned the conclusion that drug use causes crime. Instead, they believe that the violent and property crimes associated with illicit drugs take place "not because the drugs are drugs [but because] the drugs are illegal."[44] Ninety years ago, when alcohol was illegal in this country, the criminal gangs that controlled the alcohol trade used methods of violence similar to those associated with today's drug gangs. The fact that we

> no longer have drive-by shootings, turf wars and "cement shoes" in the alcohol business [is because] alcohol today is legal—not because alcohol no longer intoxicates people, not because alcohol is no longer addicting, and not because alcohol dealers have suddenly developed a social conscience.[45]

The controversial issue of how the criminal justice system should respond to the use and abuse of the most common illegal drug—marijuana—is the subject of the *CJ in Action* feature at the end of this chapter.

LOOKING GOOD: CRIME IN THE 1990s AND 2000s

In 1995, James Q. Wilson, noting that the number of young males was set to increase dramatically over the next decade, predicted that "30,000 more young muggers, killers, and thieves" would be on the streets by 2000. "Get ready," he warned.[46] Other criminologists offered their own dire projections. John DiIulio foresaw a swarm of "juvenile superpredators" on the streets,[47] and James A. Fox prophesied a "blood bath" by 2005.[48] Given previous data, these experts could be fairly confident in their predictions. Fortunately for the country, they were wrong. As is evident from Figure 3.7 on the facing page, starting in 1994 the United States experienced a steep crime decline that we are still enjoying, though to a somewhat lesser degree, today.

THE GREAT CRIME DECLINE The crime statistics of the 1990s are startling. Even with the upswing at the beginning of the decade, from 1990 to 2000 the homicide rate dropped 39 percent, the robbery rate 44 percent, the burglary rate 41 percent, and the auto theft rate 37 percent. By most measures, this decline was the longest and deepest of the twentieth century.[49] In retrospect, the 1990s seem to have encompassed a "golden era" for the leading indicators of low crime rates. The economy was robust. The incarceration rate was skyrocketing. Plus, despite the misgivings of James Q. Wilson and many of his colleagues, the percentage of the population in the high-risk age bracket in 1995 was actually lower than it had been in 1980.[50]

FIGURE 3.7 Violent Crime in the United States, 1990–2010

According to statistics gathered each year by the FBI, American violent crime rates dropped steadily in the second half of the 1990s, leveled off for several years, and now have begun to decrease anew.

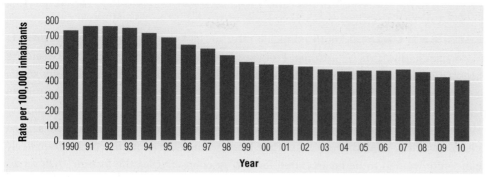

Source: Federal Bureau of Investigation.

Several other factors also seemed to favor lower crime rates. Police tactics, many of which we will discuss in Chapter 6, became more effective—thanks in no small part to "zero-tolerance" policies inspired by Wilson's writings. Furthermore, many of those most heavily involved in the crack cocaine boom of the late 1980s had been killed or imprisoned, or were no longer offending. Without their criminal activity, the United States became a much safer place.[51]

A "WELCOME PUZZLE" In the early years of the 2000s, the nation's crime rate flattened for a time before resuming its downward trend. By 2010, property crime rates had dropped for the seventh straight year, and violent crime rates had shrunk to their lowest levels since the early 1970s. Given that, in recent years, the economy has been mired in a recession, with unemployment running at unusually high levels, the positive crime figures have come as something of a surprise. Richard Rosenfeld, president of the American Society of Criminology, calls the trend "one of those welcome puzzles" and suggests that his colleagues reconsider "under what conditions economic activity influences crime."[52] Again, as in the 1990s, law enforcement is receiving much of the credit for these positive trends, particularly information-based policing techniques that use computer programs to focus crime prevention tactics on "hot spots" of criminal activity.[53]

THE IMMEDIATE FUTURE Not all of the experts are confident that crime rates will continue to decline. Elliott Currie, a criminologist at the University of California at Irvine, believes that if the economy continues to falter, behavior will change and crime rates will inevitably rise. "If you put people in really lousy conditions," he says, "they'll begin to think differently about school, drugs, or gangs."[54] Furthermore, to alleviate financial pressures on strained budgets, local governments are reducing their police forces, and, as we will see in Chapter 13, states are releasing prisoners. Both strategies could have negative consequences for crime in the United States.[55] In general, however, when considering crime rate predictions, it is probably a good idea to heed the warning of Ralph Taylor, a professor of criminal justice at Philadelphia's Temple University. When experts claim confidence in their ability to see into the country's crime future, says Taylor, "they don't know what they're talking about."[56]

Critical Thinking Skill Development: Ask students to consider which factors coincided with the great crime decline of the 1990s. With these factors in mind, would students predict an increase or decrease in crime rates in the near future?

CRIME, RACE, AND POVERTY

One group has noticeably failed to benefit from the positive crime trends of the past fifteen years: young African American males. According to data compiled by criminologists James A. Fox of Northeastern University in Boston and Marc L. Swatt of the University of

Nebraska at Omaha, from 2002 to 2007 the number of murders committed by black males under the age of eighteen rose 43 percent. Over the same time period, the number of young black males who were victims of murder also increased significantly, by 31 percent. In both categories, levels for young white males remained the same or declined.[57]

RACE AND CRIME Youth homicide rates are not the only area in which there is a "worrisome divergence"[58]—to use Professor Fox's term—in crime trends between the races. Official crime data seem to indicate a strong correlation between minority status and crime: African Americans—who make up 13 percent of the population—constitute 38 percent of those arrested for violent crimes and 29 percent of those arrested for property crimes.[59] A black man is almost twelve times more likely than a white man to be sent to prison for a drug-related conviction, while black women are about five times more likely than white women to be incarcerated for a drug offense.[60] (See the feature *Myth versus Reality—Race Stereotyping and Drug Crime* on the facing page.) Furthermore, 1 in every 300 black females living in the United States is incarcerated in prison or jail, compared with about 1 in every 1,100 white women and 1 in every 700 Hispanic females.[61]

Critical Thinking Skill Development: Ask students to respond to "Questions for Critical Analysis" number five on page 92, which concerns the links between race, class, and crime.

The racial differences in the crime rate are one of the most controversial areas of the criminal justice system. At first glance, crime statistics seem to support the idea that

LO 8 the subculture of African Americans in the United States is disposed toward criminal behavior. Not all of the data, however, support that assertion. A recent research project led by sociologist Robert J. Sampson of Harvard University collected extensive data on more than 11,000 residents living in 180 Chicago neighborhoods. Sampson and his colleagues found that 60 percent of the "gap" in levels of violence between whites and African Americans could be attributed to neighborhood and family conditions. In other words, regardless of race, a person would have a much higher risk of violent behavior if he or she lived in a poverty-stricken, disorganized neighborhood or in a household run by a single parent.[62]

CLASS AND CRIME Indeed, a wealth of information suggests that income level is more important than skin color when it comes to crime trends. A 2002 study of nearly 900 African American children (400 boys and 467 girls) from neighborhoods with varying income levels showed that family earning power had the only significant correlation with violent behavior.[63] More recent research conducted by William A. Pridemore of Indiana University found a "positive and significant association" between poverty and homicide.[64] Lack of education, another handicap most often faced by low-income citizens, also seems to correlate with criminal behavior. Forty-one percent of all inmates in state and federal prisons failed to obtain a high school education, compared with 18 percent of the population at large.[65]

It might seem logical that those without the financial means to acquire the consumer goods and services that dominate our society would turn to illegal methods to "steal" purchasing power. But, logic aside, many criminologists are skeptical of such an obvious class-crime relationship. After all, poverty does not *cause* crime. The majority of residents in low-income neighborhoods are law-abiding. Furthermore, self-reported surveys indicate that high-income citizens are involved in all sorts of criminal activities[66] and are far more likely

By some measures, black citizens are twice as likely as whites to live in poverty and hold low-wage jobs. What is your opinion of the theory that economic disadvantage, rather than skin color, accounts for the disproportionate number of African Americans in U.S. prisons, such as these inmates at Florida's Dade County Correctional Facility?
Joe Sohm/Visions of America/Newscom

In response to the crack-related violence that spread like wildfire through the nation's inner cities in the 1980s (see page 83), President Ronald Reagan vowed to escalate the "war on drugs." As a consequence, law enforcement efforts focused on arresting and incarcerating the wrongdoers in those communities, most of whom were African American. Even though this urban violence has largely subsided, the tactics continue: every year between 1980 and 2007, blacks were arrested on drug charges at rates between 2.8 and 5.5 times higher than whites. Today, even though African Americans make up about 13 percent of the U.S. population, they represent more than 50 percent of sentenced drug offenders.

THE MYTH African Americans are sent to prison for drug crimes in greater numbers than whites because more of them buy, sell, and use drugs.

THE REALITY The use of illegal drugs by blacks and whites in the United States is roughly equal. According to data gathered by the federal government, about 9.6 percent of African Americans and about 8.8 percent of whites admit to using drugs within the previous month. Given the relatively smaller population of blacks in this country, this means that African Americans who use drugs are arrested at about three times the rate of whites who use drugs. Furthermore, although blacks account for only 28 percent of all drug arrests, they represent 49 percent of those convicted of drug crimes and 44 percent of all Americans sentenced for drug crimes.

Finally, more than four out of every five drug arrests are for possession of the banned substance, not for its sale or manufacture. Thus, the racial disparity in arrests cannot be due to a large class of African American drug dealers.

Although these statistics leave the criminal justice system open to charges of institutionalized racism, the disparities are more likely the result of practical considerations. "There is as much cocaine in the Stock Exchange as there is in the black community," admits one Chicago police chief. "But those guys are harder to catch. Those deals are done in office buildings [and] in someone's home. But the guy standing on the corner, he's almost got a sign on his back. These guys are just arrestable." In addition, residents of low-income neighborhoods are unlikely to hire expensive legal help to contest police action. Quite simply, the inner city is an easy place for police to rack up impressive arrest numbers with little fear for consequences if mistakes are made.

FOR CRITICAL ANALYSIS Heather Mac Donald, a crime expert at the Manhattan Institute in New York, suggests that the racial disparities in the "war on drugs" make sense because the urban street trade often leads to violence and other crimes that harm inner-city communities. Drug use by whites, in contrast, generally takes place in suburban homes, hidden from view, without the same level of negative side effects. What is your opinion of Mac Donald's theory?

to commit white-collar crimes, which are not included in national crime statistics. These facts tend to support the theory that high crime rates in low-income communities are at least partly the result of a greater willingness of police to arrest poor citizens and of the court system to convict them.

ETHNICITY AND CRIME Another point to remember when reviewing statistical studies of minority offenders and victims is that they tend to focus on race, which distinguishes groups based on physical characteristics such as skin color, rather than *ethnicity*, which denotes national or cultural background. Thus, the bulk of criminological research in this area has focused on the differences between European Americans and African Americans, both because the latter have been the largest minority group in the United States for most of its history and because the racial differences between the two groups are easily identifiable. Americans of Hispanic descent have either been excluded from many crime studies or been linked with whites or blacks based on racial characteristics. Other minority groups, such as Asian Americans, Native Americans, and immigrants from the South Pacific or Eastern Europe, have been similarly underreported in crime studies.

CAREERS IN CJ

Courtesy of F. W. Gill

F. W. GILL
GANG INVESTIGATOR

My full job title is school resource officer and juvenile investigator. Mainly, I work with school administrators and try to help school districts establish safety procedures. I also investigate crimes that occur on or near campus, and if a criminal incident has taken place I have the authority to contact the juvenile offender's parents or, in the worst-case scenario, make an arrest. Of course, in dealing with middle and high school students, I've seen a lot of young people get sucked into the world of gangs. So, in the early 1990s I decided to put my experience with students to work and joined the Alameda County, California, district attorney's gang violence and suppression task force.

LISTEN AND LEARN The problem, for most of these kids, is that nobody cares. Their parents don't, or can't, get involved in their children's lives. (How many times have I heard parents deny that their son or daughter is a gang banger, even though it's obvious?) Teachers are in the business of teaching and don't, or can't, take the time to get to know their most troubled students. So, when I'm dealing with gang members, the first thing I do is listen. I don't lecture them, I don't tell them that they are throwing away their lives. I just listen. You'd be amazed how effective this can be—these kids, who look so tough on the outside, just want an adult to care.

LOST AND FOUND Not that there is any magic formula for convincing a gang member to go straight. It is very difficult to get someone to change his or her lifestyle. If they don't want to change—really want to change—then nothing I can say or do is going to make much of a difference. Unfortunately, there are many lost causes. I've even had a couple of cases in which a juvenile was afraid to leave the gang because his father was a gang member, and he insisted that the boy stay in the gang. I have had some success in convincing gang members to turn their lives around by joining the military. The military provides discipline and a new outlook on life, things that these kids badly need. The way I look at it, in some cases, war is the best shot these kids have at saving their own lives.

A WELCOME CALL One day several years ago I received a call from the producer of *America's Most Wanted*. She told me that I had been recommended for the first responder "All Star" contest by a former student at Castro Valley High School. The former student told the people at the show that I had persuaded him to stay out of a gang and that he would "either be dead or in jail" if not for my influence. Calling *America's Most Wanted* was his way of saying "thank you." Today, that former student is in training and on his way to becoming a law enforcement officer.

CAREER ADVICE First, you have to accept that a career in law enforcement means lots of hard work. Then, you should take advantage of your local police department's ride-along program, if one is offered, to find out if you are intrigued by the world of the police officer. At first, law enforcement can be tough: few days off, constant night shifts, working in bad weather, missing important events like birthdays, holidays, graduations, and family get-togethers with your loved ones. But, if you stick with it, your perseverance will be rewarded. I have not worked a Christmas or New Year's Eve in over two decades. In all, it's been a good career and a good life.

FAST FACTS

YOUTH INTERVENTION SPECIALIST/GANG INVESTIGATOR JOB DESCRIPTION:

- Conducts assessments and refers at-risk youth to appropriate activities, programs, or agencies as an alternative to becoming involved in criminal activity.
- Assists in problem resolution with at-risk youth; counsels youth and parents.
- Serves as a liaison between the police department, schools, other agencies, and the community regarding gang and other youth-related matters.
- Conducts research and analyzes data regarding gang trends.

WHAT KIND OF TRAINING IS REQUIRED?

- At a minimum, a high school diploma and any combination of training, education, and experience equivalent to 3–5 years' social service employment involving youth.
- Also must have valid driver's license, and pass a background check and polygraph test.
- Preferred candidates will have a bachelor's degree in counseling, criminal justice, or other social science-related field. Bilingual(English/Spanish) skills are desired.

ANNUAL SALARY RANGE?

- $40,000–$49,000

For additional information on a career as a gang investigator, visit: **www.nagia.org/Home/tabid/36/Default.aspx.**

This state of affairs will more than likely change in the near future. Latinos are the fastest-growing minority group in the U.S. prison population, and, because of immigration offenses, they now account for 40 percent of those convicted of federal crimes.[67] In fact, criminologists have already begun to focus on issues of Hispanic criminality. For example, Robert Sampson's research project, mentioned earlier on page 86, found lower rates of violence among Mexican Americans than among either whites or blacks living in Chicago. The authors theorize that strong social ties in immigrant populations create an environment that is incompatible with crime.[68]

WOMEN AND CRIME

To put it bluntly, crime is an overwhelmingly male activity. More than 65 percent of all murders involve a male victim and a male perpetrator, and in only 2.4 percent of homicides are both the offender and the victim female.[69] Only 12 percent of the national jail population and 7 percent of the national prison population are female, and in 2010 only 25 percent of all arrests involved women.[70] These statistics, however, fail to convey the startling rate at which the female presence in the criminal justice system has been increasing. In 1970, there were about 6,000 women in federal and state prisons, but today, there are more than 113,000.[71]

There are two possible explanations for these increases. Either (1) the life circumstances and behavior of women have changed dramatically in the past forty years, or (2) the criminal justice system's attitude toward women has changed over that time period.[72] In the 1970s, when female crime rates started surging upward, many observers accepted the former explanation. "You can't get involved in a bar fight if you're not allowed in the bar," said feminist theorist Freda Adler in 1975.[73] It has become clear, however, that a significant percentage of women arrested are involved in a narrow band of wrongdoing, mostly drug- and alcohol-related offenses or property crimes.[74] Research shows that as recently as the 1980s, many of the women now in prison would not have been arrested or would have received lighter sentences for their crimes.[75] Consequently, more scholars are convinced that rising female criminality is the result of a criminal justice system that is "more willing to incarcerate women."[76]

LO 9

A tribal officer takes a suspect into custody on the Oneida Indian Reservation in Hobart, Wisconsin. By some measures, Native Americans are the victims of violent crime at twice the national average. Why, then, do many crime studies fail to provide specific statistics concerning this group, instead focusing only on whites, African Americans, and Hispanics?
AP Photo/Mike Roemer

Group Activities: Have students work in groups to discuss possible explanations for the dramatic increase in female offending. Why do students believe women are more likely to be arrested now than they were in the past? (LO 9)

SELFASSESSMENT

Fill in the blanks and check your answers on page 92.
According to many experts, the three factors that most strongly affect national crime figures are the rate at which offenders are _____, the percentage of the population that is _____ the age of twenty-four, and the economy. In the late 1980s and early 1990s, however, rising crime rates seemed to be fueled by the illegal _____ trade—in particular, the demand for _____ _____. Despite continued declining crime rates in the 2000s, young _____ _____ males continue to experience high levels of offending and victimization.

CJ IN ACTION

LEGALIZING MARIJUANA

As of January 1, 2011, in the words of one observer, "jaywalkers may have more to fear from California cops than potheads do."[77] The statement is a wry comment on a new state law that reduces the penalty for possession of one ounce (28.5 grams) or less of marijuana to the equivalent of a traffic ticket.[78] California is now one of thirteen states that have similarly reduced the penalty for possession of a small amount of marijuana for personal use. Fourteen states, also including California, allow the legal use of marijuana for medical purposes. These trends reflect a growing "get soft" movement regarding the nation's marijuana laws that we now address in this chapter's *CJ in Action* feature.

A STEP TOO FAR?

By making the possession of a small amount of marijuana an infraction (see page 72) rather than a crime, California has *decriminalized* this particular activity. Several months before this new law went into effect, California voters rejected a ballot initiative, known as Proposition 19, that would have gone a step further by legalizing the growing, selling, and use of marijuana for those older than twenty-one.[79] In this instance, the majority of Californians were not ready for *legalization,* which in this context refers to the removal of most criminal sanctions on the sale and production of an illegal drug. The question is, will Americans ever be ready for legalized marijuana?

THE CASE FOR LEGALIZATION

- The "peace dividend" of legalization would be substantial. On the one hand, 850,000 Americans are arrested each year on marijuana-related charges. Removing these offenders from the criminal justice system would save U.S. taxpayers billions of dollars annually.[80] On the other hand, the country would reap a windfall in taxes on the controlled sale of a previously illegal drug. One Harvard University economist has estimated that the net economic gain to the United States for legalizing marijuana would be between $10.1 billion and $13.9 billion a year.[81]

- Legalization would lead to the end of violent crime associated with marijuana dealing, as black market organizations would be put out of business or forced to rely on less profitable criminal activities.

- Legalization would result in a more efficient criminal justice system, as scarce law enforcement resources would be diverted away from marijuana offenses and the pressure on both overloaded courts and overcrowded prisons would be alleviated.[82]

THE CASE AGAINST LEGALIZATION

- Most public health officials are opposed to legalization of marijuana because they believe it will increase the number of people addicted to the drug, contribute to more automobile accidents, and harm the school performance of college students.[83]

- Evidence exists that marijuana acts as a "gateway" drug that leads young people to experiment with more dangerous drugs such as cocaine and heroin.[84]

- Minors can often easily obtain legal but controlled drug products such as cigarettes and alcohol. If marijuana is legalized, we can expect that minors would have greater access to it as well.

YOUR OPINION—WRITING ASSIGNMENT

One commentator has compared the debate over what to do about illegal drugs to the problem that Goldilocks faced on entering the house of the Three Bears.[85] The first bed that Goldilocks tried, Mama Bear's bed, was too soft. The second, Papa Bear's bed, was too hard. Only the third, Baby Bear's bed, was just right. Surely, some suggest, there is a "Baby Bear's bed" way for America to regulate drugs—something between the "too soft" option of legalization and the "too hard" system under which we now function.

What would be your "Baby Bear" solution to the issue of marijuana legalization? Or, do you think that our current strict antidrug laws are adequate and might even benefit from being strengthened? Or, conversely, do you think that legalization would be the proper policy to follow? Before responding, you can review our discussions in this chapter concerning

- *Mala in se* and *mala prohibita* crimes on pages 72–74.

- Self-reported surveys and the dark figure of crime on pages 80–81.

- Illegal drugs and crime on pages 83–84.

Your answer should include at least three full paragraphs.

Getty Images

CHAPTER SUMMARY

LO 1
Discuss the primary goals of civil law and criminal law and explain how these goals are realized. Civil law is designed to resolve disputes between private individuals and other entities such as corporations. In these disputes, one party, called the plaintiff, tries to gain monetary damages by proving that the accused party, or defendant, is to blame for a tort, or wrongful act. In contrast, criminal law exists to protect society from criminal behavior. To that end, the government prosecutes defendants, or persons who have been charged with committing a crime.

LO 2
Explain the differences between crimes *mala in se* and *mala prohibita*. A criminal act is *mala in se* if it is inherently wrong, while a criminal act *mala prohibita* is illegal only because it is prohibited by the laws of a particular society. It is sometimes difficult to distinguish between these two sorts of crimes because it is difficult to define a "pure" *mala in se* crime—that is, it is difficult to separate a crime from the culture that has deemed it a crime.

LO 3
Identify the publication in which the FBI reports crime data and list the two main ways in which the data are reported. Every year the FBI releases the Uniform Crime Report (UCR), in which it presents different crimes as (a) a rate per 100,000 people and (b) a percentage change from the previous year.

LO 4
Distinguish between Part I and Part II offenses as defined in the Uniform Crime Report (UCR). Part I offenses are always felonies and include the most violent crimes. Part II offenses include all other crimes recorded in the UCR. They can be either misdemeanors or felonies and constitute the majority of crimes committed.

LO 5
Describe some of the shortcomings of the UCR as a crime-measuring tool. To collect its data, the Uniform Crime Report (UCR) relies on citizens reporting crimes to the police and the police passing this information on to the FBI. If either fails to do so, the UCR will not accurately reflect criminal activity in the United States. Furthermore, the FBI and local law enforcement agencies do not always define crimes in the same manner, leading to inconsistencies in the data.

LO 6
Distinguish between the National Crime Victimization Survey (NCVS) and self-reported surveys. The NCVS involves an annual survey of more than 40,000 households conducted by the Bureau of the Census along with the Bureau of Justice Statistics. The survey queries citizens on crimes that have been committed against them. As such, the NCVS includes crimes not necessarily reported to police. Self-reported surveys, in contrast, involve asking individuals about criminal activity to which they may have been a party.

LO 7
Identify the three factors most often used by criminologists to explain changes in the nation's crime rate. (a) Levels of incarceration, because an offender behind bars cannot commit any additional crimes and the threat of imprisonment acts as a deterrent to criminal behavior; (b) the size of the youth population, because those under the age of twenty-four commit the majority of crimes in the United States; and (c) the health of the economy, because when income and employment levels fall, those most directly affected may turn to crime for financial gain.

LO 8
Explain why issues of race and ethnicity tend to be overstated when it comes to crime trends. Criminologists have found that the most consistent indicators of criminal behavior are circumstances such as low family earning power and the absence of a parent. In addition, failure to obtain a high school diploma appears to have a positive correlation with criminal activity, regardless of the race or ethnicity of the individual. Finally, some believe that high arrest rates in low-income minority neighborhoods can be attributed to a willingness of police to arrest residents of these communities and of the court system to convict them.

LO 9
Discuss the prevailing explanation for the rising number of women incarcerated in the United States. Experts believe that many women are arrested and given harsh punishment for activity that would not have put them behind bars several decades ago. For the most part, this activity is nonviolent: the majority of female arrestees are involved in drug- and alcohol-related offenses and property crimes.

SELF ASSESSMENT ANSWER KEY

Page 75: **i.** Civil; **ii.** state/government; **iii.** felony; **iv.** misdemeanor; **v.** First degree murder; **vi.** manslaughter

Page 79: **i.** Uniform Crime Report; **ii.** rate; **iii.** Part I; **iv.** Part II

Page 81: **i.** Victim; **ii.** Self-reported; **iii.** dark figure; **iv.** greater/larger

Page 89: **i.** imprisoned/incarcerated; **ii.** under; **iii.** drug; **iv.** crack cocaine; **v.** African American

KEY TERMS

beyond a reasonable doubt   **70**
civil law   **69**
clearance of an arrest   **78**
dark figure of crime   **80**
defendant   **69**
felony   **70**
illicit drugs   **73**
infraction   **72**

involuntary manslaughter   **71**
liability   **69**
licit drugs   **73**
mala in se   **72**
mala prohibita   **72**
malice aforethought   **71**
methamphetamine (meth)   **83**
misdemeanor   **71**

Part I offenses   **76**
Part II offenses   **76**
plaintiff   **69**
preponderance of the evidence   **70**
self-reported survey   **80**
Uniform Crime Report (UCR)   **75**
victim surveys   **79**
voluntary manslaughter   **71**

QUESTIONS FOR CRITICAL ANALYSIS

1. Give an example of how one person could be involved in a civil lawsuit and a criminal lawsuit for the same action.

2. Two fathers, John and Phil, get in a heated argument following a dispute between their sons in a Little League baseball game. They come to blows, and John strikes Phil in the temple, killing him. Will John be charged with voluntary manslaughter or involuntary manslaughter? What other details might you need to be sure of your answer?

3. Why is murder considered a *mala in se* crime? What argument can be made that murder is not a *mala in se* crime?

4. Assume that you are a criminologist who wants to determine the extent to which high school students engage in risky behavior such as abusing alcohol and illegal drugs, carrying weapons, and contemplating suicide. How would you go about gathering these data?

5. What are some of the problems with the assumption that there is a link between race and criminal behavior? What are some of the problems with the assumption that there is a link between poverty and criminal behavior?

CourseMate *For Online Help*

For online help and access to resources that accompany *Criminal Justice Today*, go to www.cengagebrain.com/shop/ISBN/1111835578. Click "Access Now," where you will find flashcards, an online quiz, and other helpful study aids. If you have an access code for CourseMate, log in and go to the chapter of your choice for additional online study aids.

NOTES

1. Federal Bureau of Investigation, "Serial Murder," at **www.fbi.gov/stats-services/publications/serial-murder/serial-murder-1#two.**

2. Model Penal Code Section 1.04 (2).

3. *Federal Criminal Rules Handbook*, Section 2.1 (West 2008).

4. 625 Illinois Compiled Statutes Annotated Section 5/16-104 (West 2002).

5. Johannes Andenaes, "The Moral or Educative Influence of Criminal Law," *Journal of Social Issues* 27 (Spring 1971), 17, 26.

6. National Center for Health Statistics, *Health, United States, 2006* (Washington, D.C.:

Centers for Disease Control and Prevention, 2006), Table 68, page 276.

7. Richard T. Bosshardt, "Not All Types of Hepatitis Infectious," *Orlando Sentinel* (September 19, 2001), J9.

8. National Highway Traffic Safety Administration, *Highlights of 2009 Motor*

Vehicle Crashes (Washington, D.C.: U.S. Department of Transportation, August 2010), Table 3, page 2.

9. John Slade, "Health Consequences of Smoking: Nicotine Addiction," *Hearings before the Subcommittee on Health and the Environment of the House Committee on Energy and Commerce* (Washington, D.C.: U.S. Government Printing Office, 1988), 163–164.

10. Ethan Nadelmann, "Should We Legalize Drugs? History Answers: Yes," *Hofstra Law Review* 18 (1990), 41.

11. Steven Jonas, "Solving the Drug Problem: A Public Health Approach to the Reduction of the Use and Abuse of Both Legal and Recreational Drugs," *Hofstra Law Review* 18 (1990), 753.

12. David F. Musto, *The American Disease: Origins of Narcotic Control* (New York: Oxford University Press, 1987), 1.

13. Codified as amended at 21 U.S.C. Sections 801–966 (1994).

14. Uniform Controlled Substances Act (1994), Section 201(h).

15. Douglas N. Husak, *Drugs and Rights* (New York: Cambridge University Press, 2002), 21.

16. Federal Bureau of Investigation, *Uniform Crime Reporting Handbook* (Washington, D.C.: U.S. Department of Justice, 2004), 74.

17. Federal Bureau of Investigation, *Crime in the United States, 2010* (Washington, D.C.: U.S. Department of Justice, 2011), at **www.fbi.gov/about-us/cjis/ucr/crime-in-the-u.s/2010/crime-in-the-u.s.-2010/index-page**.

18. *Ibid.*

19. *Ibid.,* at **www.fbi.gov/about-us/cjis/ucr/crime-in-the-u.s/2010/crime-in-the-u.s.-2010/tables/10tbl01.xls**.

20. Jeffery Reiman, *The Rich Get Richer and the Poor Get Prison*, 4th ed. (Boston: Allyn & Bacon, 1995), 59–60.

21. *Crime in the United States, 2010,* at **www.fbi.gov/about-us/cjis/ucr/crime-in-the-u.s/2010/crime-in-the-u.s.-2010/tables/10shrtbl10.xls**.

22. *Ibid.,* at **www.fbi.gov/about-us/cjis/ucr/crime-in-the-u.s/2010/crime-in-the-u.s.-2010/tables/10tbl01.xls**.

23. *Ibid.,* at **www.fbi.gov/about-us/cjis/ucr/crime-in-the-u.s/2010/crime-in-the-u.s.-2010/tables/10tbl29.xls**.

24. Marcus Felson, *Crime in Everyday Life* (Thousand Oaks, CA: Pine Forge Press, 1994), 3.

25. Donald J. Black, "Production of Crime Rates," *American Sociological Review* 35 (1970), 733–748.

26. Bureau of Justice Statistics, *Crime Victimization, 2009* (Washington, D.C.: U.S. Department of Justice, October 2010), 2.

27. Eric P. Baumer and Janet L. Lauritsen, "Reporting Crime to the Police, 1973–2005: A Multivariate Analysis of Long-Term Trends in the National Crime Survey (NCS) and National Crime Victimization Survey (NCVS)," *Criminology* (February 2010), 134–141.

28. Alabama Code Sections 13A-6-60(8), 13A-6-61(a)(1) (1994).

29. *Crime in the United States, 2010,* at **www.fbi.gov/about-us/cjis/ucr/crime-in-the-u.s/2010/crime-in-the-u.s.-2010/about-cius**.

30. David Hirschel, "Expanding Police Ability to Report Crime: The National Incident-Based Reporting System," *In Short: Toward Criminal Justice Solutions* (Washington, D.C.: National Institute of Justice, July 2009), 1–2.

31. Victor E. Kappeler, Mark Blumberg, and Gary W. Potter, *The Mythology of Crime and Criminal Justice*, 2d ed. (Prospect Heights, IL: Waveland Press, 1993), 31.

32. Peter B. Wood, Walter R. Grove, James A. Wilson, and John K. Cochran, "Nonsocial Reinforcement and Criminal Conduct: An Extension of Learning Theory," *Criminology* 35 (May 1997), 335–366.

33. Franklin E. Zimring, *The Great American Crime Decline* (New York: Oxford University Press, 2007), 45–72.

34. David Garland, *The Culture of Control: Crime and Social Control in Contemporary Society* (Chicago: University of Chicago Press, 2001), 12–14.

35. James Q. Wilson, *Thinking about Crime* (New York: Basic Books, 1974), 12.

36. Howard N. Snyder and Melissa Sickmund, *Juvenile Offenders and Victims: A National Report* (Washington, D.C.: Office of Juvenile Justice and Delinquency Prevention, August 1995), 104–105.

37. Delbert S. Elliot and Scott Menard, "Delinquent Friends and Delinquent Behavior: Temporal Development Patterns," in Rolf Loeber and David P. Farrington, eds., *Delinquency and Crime: Current Theories* (Thousand Oaks, CA: Sage Publications, 1996), 47–66.

38. Bill McCarthy, "New Economics of Sociological Criminology," *Annual Review of Sociology* 28 (August 2002), 417, 426.

39. Zimring, 63.

40. Alfred Blumstein and Joel Wallman, eds., *The Crime Drop in America* (New York: Cambridge University Press, 2000), 39.

41. *Ibid.*

42. National Drug Intelligence Center, *Hawaii: High Intensity Drug Trafficking Area Market Analysis 2010* (Washington, D.C.: U.S. Department of Justice, May 2010), 6.

43. National Drug Intelligence Center, *National Drug Threat Assessment* (Washington, D.C.: U.S. Department of Justice, February 2010), 7.

44. Daniel K. Benjamin and Roger LeRoy Miller, *Undoing Drugs: Beyond Legalization* (New York: Basic Books, 1991), 110.

45. *Ibid.,* 110–111.

46. James Q. Wilson, "Concluding Essay in Crime," in James Q. Wilson and Joan Petersilia, eds., *Crime* (San Francisco: Institute for Contemporary Studies Press, 1995), 507.

47. John DiIulio, *How to Stop the Coming Crime Wave* (New York: Manhattan Institute, 1996), 4.

48. James Fox, *Trends in Juvenile Violence* (Boston: Northeastern University Press, 1996), 1.

49. Zimring, 6.

50. *Ibid.,* 197–198.

51. *Ibid.,* 82.

52. Quoted in Pete Yost, "Violent Crime Falls for Third Straight Year," *San Jose Mercury News* (September 15, 2010), 2B.

53. Heather Mac Donald, "A Crime Theory Demolished," *Wall Street Journal* (January 4, 2010), at **online.wsj.com/article/SB10001424052748703580900457463802405573590.html**.

54. Quoted in Gregory Rodriguez, "Hard Times and Crime? Just You Wait," *Los Angeles Times* (May 25, 2009), A3.

55. Mac Donald.

56. Quoted in Alfred Lubrano, "Violent Crime in Philadelphia Decreased in 2007," *Philadelphia Inquirer* (September 16, 2008), A6.

57. James Alan Fox and Marc L. Swatt, *The Recent Surge in Homicides Involving Young Black Males and Guns: Time to Reinvest in Prevention and Crime Control* (December 2008), 2, available at **www.jfox.neu.edu/Documents/Fox%20Swatt%20Homicide%20Report%20Dec%2029%202008.pdf**.

58. Quoted in Erik Eckholm, "Murders by Black Teenagers Rise This Decade, Bucking a Trend," *New York Times* (December 29, 2008), A12.

59. *Crime in the United States, 2010,* at **www.fbi.gov/about-us/cjis/ucr/crime-in-the-u.s/2010/crime-in-the-u.s.-2010/tables/table-43**.

60. *Targeting Blacks: Drug Law Enforcement and Race in the United States* (New York: Human Rights Watch, May 2008), 3.

61. Bureau of Justice Statistics, *Prison Inmates at Midyear 2009—Statistical Tables* (Washington, D.C.: U.S. Department of Justice, June 2010), 2.

62. Robert J. Sampson, Jeffrey Morenoff, and Stephen W. Raudenbush, "Social Anatomy of Racial and Ethnic Disparities in Violence," *American Journal of Public Health* 95 (2005), 224–232.

63. Eric A. Stewart, Ronald L. Simons, and Rand D. Donger, "Assessing Neighborhood and Social Psychological Influence on Childhood Violence in an African American Sample," *Criminology* (November 2002), 801–829.

64. William Alex Pridemore, "A Methodological Addition to the Cross-National Empirical Literature on Social Structure and Homicide: A First Test of the Poverty-Homicide Thesis," *Criminology* (February 2008), 133.

65. Caroline Wolf Harlow, *Education and Correctional Populations* (Washington, D.C.: Bureau of Justice Statistics, January 2003), 1.

66. Charles Tittle and Robert Meier, "Specifying the SES/Delinquency Relationship," *Criminology* 28 (1990), 270–301.

67. Mark Hugo Lopez and Michael T. Light, *A Rising Share: Hispanics and Federal Crime*

(Washington, D.C.: Pew Hispanic Center, February 2009), i–iv.

68. Sampson, Morenoff, and Raudenbush. 231.

69. See **www.ojp.usdoj.gov/bjs/homicide/gender.htm**.

70. Bureau of Justice Statistics, *Jail Inmates at Midyear 2009—Statistical Tables* (Washington, D.C.: U.S. Department of Justice, June 2010), Table 6, page 9; Bureau of Justice Statistics, *Prison Inmates at Midyear 2009—Statistical Tables*, Table 1, page 4; and *Crime in the United States, 2010*, at **www.fbi.gov/about-us/cjis/ucr/crime-in-the-u.s/2010/crime-in-the-u.s.-2010/persons-arrested**.

71. Bureau of Justice Statistics, *Prisoners in 2009* (Washington, D.C.: U.S. Department of Justice, December 2010), Table 1, page 2.

72. Jennifer Schwartz and Bryan D. Rookey, "The Narrowing Gender Gap in Arrests: Assessing Competing Explanations Using Self-Report, Traffic Fatality, and Official Data on Drunk Driving, 1980–2004," *Criminology* (August 2008), 637–638.

73. Quoted in Barry Yeoman, "Violent Tendencies: Crime by Women Has Skyrocketed in Recent Years," *Chicago Tribune* (March 15, 2000), 3.

74. *Crime in the United States, 2010*, at **www.fbi.gov/about-us/cjis/ucr/crime-in-the-u.s/2010/crime-in-the-u.s.-2010/tables/10tbl42.xls**.

75. Schwarz and Rookey, 637–671.

76. Meda Chesney-Lind, "Patriarchy, Prisons, and Jails: A Critical Look at Trends in Women's Incarceration," *Prison Journal* (Spring/Summer 1991), 57.

77. Andrew Ferguson, "How Marijuana Got Mainstreamed," *Time* (November 22, 2010), 32.

78. See California Senate Bill 1449, at **www.leginfo.ca.gov/pub/09-10/bill/sen/sb_1401-1450/sb_1449_bill_20100405_amended_sen_v98.html**.

79. "California Pot Initiative Fails," *The Week* (November 12, 2010), 7.

80. Walter Simpson, "A Joint Venture," *Buffalo News* (February 27, 2011), G1.

81. Jeffrey A. Miron, "The Budgetary Implications of Marijuana Prohibition" (June 2005), at **www.prohibitioncosts.org/mironreport.html**.

82. James A. Inciardi and Duane C. McBride, "Debating the Legalization of Drugs," in *Handbook of Drug Control in the United States,* ed. James A. Inciardi (New York: Greenwood Press, 1990), 285–289.

83. Shari Roan, "Health Gets Lost in Pot Debate," *Los Angeles Times* (October 10, 2010), A1.

84. Michael T. Lynskey *et al.,* "Escalation of Drug Use in Early-Onset Cannabis Users vs. Co-twin Controls," *Journal of the American Medical Association* (2003), 427–433.

85. Stephen Mudford, "Drug Legalization and the 'Goldilocks' Problem: Thinking about Costs and Control of Drugs," in *Searching for Alternatives: Drug Control Policy in the United States,* ed. Melvin B. Krauss and Edward P. Lazear (Stanford, CA: Hoover Institution Press, 1991), 31.

CHAPTER

4

Inside Criminal Law

Michael Appleton/New York Times/Redux Pictures

CHAPTER OUTLINE

LEARNING OBJECTIVES

After reading this chapter, you should be able to . . .

LO 1 Explain precedent and the importance of the doctrine of *stare decisis.*

LO 2 List the four written sources of American criminal law.

LO 3 Explain the two basic functions of criminal law.

LO 4 Delineate the elements required to establish *mens rea* (a guilty mental state).

LO 5 Explain how the doctrine of strict liability applies to criminal law.

LO 6 List and briefly define the most important excuse defenses for crimes.

LO 7 Describe the four most important justification criminal defenses.

LO 8 Distinguish between substantive and procedural criminal law.

LO 9 Explain the importance of the due process clause in the criminal justice system.

The nine learning objectives labeled LO 1 through LO 9 are designed to help improve your understanding of the chapter.

DEADLY HEAT

As a nationally known self-help guru, financial wizard, and motivational speaker, James Arthur Ray prides himself on being right. Ray was tragically wrong, however, on an autumn day in 2009 when he told more than fifty participants in a sweat lodge ceremony he was leading, "You are not going to die. You might think you are, but you're not going to die." About halfway through the two-hour ceremony, the final event of Ray's five-day "Spiritual Warrior" retreat near Sedona, Arizona, people began to vomit and pass out in the extreme heat. When it was over, despite Ray's reassuring words, Kirby Brown, James Shore, and Liz Neuman never regained consciousness and died in a local hospital. Twenty other participants required medical treatment, suffering from burns, dehydration, kidney failure, and respiratory arrest.

"I did everything I could to help," Ray told an interviewer following the incident. "I held people's hands, I stroked their hair, I talked to them, I held the IV for paramedics." According to some witnesses, Ray was not quite so helpful during the ceremony. Beverly Bunn, who was inside the sweat lodge, said that people were gasping for air, collapsing, and crying out for water while Ray, positioned near the entrance, "did nothing. He just stood there." Megan Frederickson, an employee at the Angel Valley Retreat (the site of the sweat lodge), admitted that before the ceremony, Ray told her not to worry if participants vomited or fainted, because such responses were to be expected.

After a four-month investigation, law enforcement officials decided that the sweat lodge was, in fact, a crime scene. On February 3, 2010, Yavapai County sheriff's deputies arrested Ray and charged him with three counts of manslaughter for the deaths of Brown, Shore, and Neuman. In June 2011, a Campe Verde jury found Ray guilty of three counts of the lesser crime of negligent homicide. Several months later, judge Warren Darrow sentenced him to two years in prison.

James Arthur Ray—shown here in a Campe Verde, Arizona, courtroom—was convicted of three charges of negligent homicide for his actions during a sweat lodge ceremony over which he presided.

AP Photo/Ross D. Franklin, Pool

Was James Arthur Ray treated fairly? Nobody involved with the situation believes that he wanted any of the Spiritual Warriors to die. The sweat lodge, built in 2008, had been used numerous times previously without incident. "This was a terrible accident," said Luis Ri, Ray's attorney, "but it was an accident, not a criminal act."[1] In this chapter, we will learn that a defendant usually must have a guilty state of mind, or *mens rea*, to have committed a crime. Ray may have acted irresponsibly, but he certainly had no intent to injure or kill.

At the same time, society needs to protect its citizens from harm, even if that harm was not intentionally inflicted. According to the criminal code of Arizona, a person is guilty of negligent homicide if he or she negligently causes the death of another person.[2] Later in the chapter, we define *negligence* as ignoring a foreseeable risk. Given the circumstances of the sweat lodge ceremony, Arizona officials felt that Ray *should have known* that he was placing others in grave danger, and therefore he had committed a criminal act. As this example suggests, criminal law must be flexible enough to encompass behavior that is not marked by criminal intent yet still poses a threat to society and therefore, in the eyes of some, merits punishment. In this chapter, we will examine how these "threats to society" are identified and focus on the guidelines that determine how the criminal justice system resolves and punishes criminal guilt.

THE DEVELOPMENT OF AMERICAN CRIMINAL LAW

⊘ See the **Legal Information Institute** for an overview of criminal law and links to an extensive number of documents relating to criminal justice. Find this Web site by visiting the *Criminal Justice CourseMate* at **cengagebrain. com** and selecting the *Web links* for this chapter.

Given the various functions of *law,* a single definition of this term is difficult to establish. To the Greek philosopher Aristotle (384–322 B.C.E.), law was a "pledge that citizens of a state will do justice to one another." Aristotle's mentor, Plato (427–347 B.C.E.), saw the law as primarily a form of social control. The British jurist Sir William Blackstone (1723–1780) described law as "a rule of civil conduct prescribed by the supreme power in a state, commanding what is right, and prohibiting what is wrong." In the United States, jurist Oliver Wendell Holmes, Jr. (1841–1935), contended that law was a set of rules that allowed one to predict how a court would resolve a particular dispute.

THE CONCEPTION OF LAW

Although these definitions vary in their particulars, they are all based on the following general observation: law consists of enforceable rules governing relationships among individuals and between individuals and their society.[3] Searching back into history, several sources for modern American law can be found in the rules laid out by ancient societies. One of the first known examples of written law was created during the reign of Hammurabi (1792–1750 B.C.E.), the sixth king of the ancient empire of Babylon. The Code of Hammurabi set out crimes and their punishments based on *lex Talionis,* or "an eye for an eye." This concept of retribution is still important and will be discussed in Chapter 11.

Technology Tip: Have students learn more about Hammurabi's Code online from Fordham University's Ancient History Sourcebook at **www.fordham.edu/ halsall/ancient/hamcode.asp**.

Another ancient source of law can be found in the Mosaic Code of the Israelites (1200 B.C.E.). According to tradition, Moses—acting as an intermediary for God—presented the code to the tribes of Israel. The two sides entered into a covenant, or contract, in which the Israelites agreed to follow the code and God agreed to protect them as the chosen people. Besides providing the basis for Judeo-Christian teachings, the Mosaic Code is also reflected in modern American law, as evident in similar prohibitions against murder, theft, adultery, and perjury.

"**Justice?—You get justice in the next world. In this world you have the law.**"

—**William Gaddis, American novelist**

Modern law also owes a debt to the Code of Justinian, promulgated throughout the Roman Empire in the sixth century. This code collected many of the laws that Western society had produced. It was influential in the development of the legal systems of the European continent. To some extent, it also influenced the common law of England.

ENGLISH COMMON LAW

The English system of law as it stands today was solidified during the reign of Henry II (1154–1189). Henry sent judges on a specific route throughout the country, known as a circuit. These circuit judges established a **common law** in England. In other words, they solidified a national law in which legal principles applied to all citizens equally, no matter where they lived or what the local customs had dictated in the past. When confusion about any particular law arose, the circuit judges could draw on English traditions, or they could borrow from legal decisions made in other European countries. Once a circuit judge made a ruling, other circuit judges faced with similar cases generally followed that ruling. Each interpretation became part of the law on the subject and served as a legal **precedent**—a decision that furnished an example or authority for deciding

LO 1 subsequent cases involving similar legal principles or facts. Over time, a body of general rules that prescribed social conduct and that was applied

Common Law The body of law developed from custom or judicial decisions in English and U.S. courts and not attributable to a legislature.

Precedent A court decision that furnishes an example or authority for deciding subsequent cases involving similar facts.

throughout the entire English realm was established, and subsequently it was passed on to British colonies, including those in the New World that would eventually become the thirteen original United States.

What is important about the formation of the common law is that it developed from the customs of the populace rather than simply the will of a ruler. As such, the common law came to reflect the social, religious, economic, and cultural values of the people. All the while, a system of sheriffs, courts, juries, and lawyers accompanied the development of the common law.

STARE DECISIS

The practice of deciding new cases with reference to precedents is the basis for a doctrine called *stare decisis* ("to stand on decided cases"). Under this doctrine, judges are obligated to follow the precedents established within their jurisdictions.[4] For example, any decision of a particular state's highest court will control the outcome of future cases on that issue brought before all of the lower courts within that same state (unless preempted by the federal Constitution). All United States Supreme Court decisions on issues involving the U.S. Constitution are binding on *all* courts because the U.S. Constitution is the supreme law of the land and the Court is its final interpreter.

The doctrine of *stare decisis* helps the court system to be more efficient. It allows judges to refer back to previous cases with similar facts in making a ruling on the case at hand. This does not mean, however, that the system is rigid. The United States Supreme Court, for example, will sometimes rule against precedent set in a previous Court decision. It does so when there have been sufficient changes in society to warrant departing from the doctrine of *stare decisis*. In general, however, the judicial system is slow to change, and courts rarely alter major points of law. The doctrine of *stare decisis* leads to stability in the law, allowing people to predict how the law will be applied in given circumstances.

SELFASSESSMENT

Fill in the blanks and check your answers on page 128.
American law has its roots in English _____ law, which represents a set of legal principles that apply equally to all citizens. Under this legal system, once a judge made a ruling, other judges faced with similar cases followed this _____ . Today, the doctrine of _____ _____ reflects the tradition of relying on decided cases to settle new ones.

WRITTEN SOURCES OF AMERICAN CRIMINAL LAW

Originally, common law was *uncodified*. That is, it relied primarily on judges following precedents, and the body of the law was not written down in any single place. Uncodified

LO 2

law, however, presents a number of drawbacks. For one, if the law is not recorded in a manner or a place in which the citizenry has access to it, then it is difficult, if not impossible, for people to know exactly which acts are legal and which acts are illegal. Furthermore, citizens have no way of determining or understanding the procedures that must be followed to establish innocence or guilt. Consequently, U.S. history has seen the development of several written sources of American criminal law, also known as "substantive" criminal law. These sources include:

Stare Decisis (pronounced *ster*-ay dih-*si-ses*). A common law doctrine under which judges are obligated to follow the precedents established under prior decisions.

Discussion Tip: Ask students to work in small groups to consider the doctrine of *stare decisis*. Why is this doctrine so important to our understanding of criminal law? Does *stare decisis* lead to stability or instability in the law? (LO 1)

Teaching Tip: Bring a copy of your state constitution to class. Also, direct your students' attention to the United States Constitution in Appendix A of this textbook. Allow students to review the documents and discuss their content. (LO 2)

1. The U.S. Constitution and the constitutions of the various states.
2. Statutes, or laws, passed by Congress and by state legislatures, plus local ordinances.
3. Regulations, created by regulatory agencies, such as the federal Food and Drug Administration.
4. Case law (court decisions).

We describe each of these important written sources of law in the following pages.

CONSTITUTIONAL LAW

The federal government and the states have separate written constitutions that set forth the general organization and powers of, and the limits on, their respective governments. **Constitutional law** is the law as expressed in these constitutions.

The U.S. Constitution is the supreme law of the land. As such, it is the basis of all law in the United States. Any law that violates the Constitution, as ultimately determined by the United States Supreme Court, will be declared unconstitutional and will not be enforced. The Tenth Amendment, which defines the powers and limitations of the federal government, reserves to the states all powers not granted to the federal government. Under our system of federalism (see Chapter 1), each state also has its own constitution. Unless they conflict with the U.S. Constitution or a federal law, state constitutions are supreme within their respective borders. (You will learn more about how constitutional law applies to our criminal justice system in later chapters.)

George Washington, standing at right, presided over the constitutional convention of 1787. The convention resulted in the U.S. Constitution, the source of a number of laws that continue to form the basis of our criminal justice system today.
The Granger Collection

STATUTORY LAW

Statutes enacted by legislative bodies at any level of government make up another source of law, which is generally referred to as statutory law. *Federal statutes* are laws that are enacted by the U.S. Congress. *State statutes* are laws enacted by state legislatures, and statutory law also includes the ordinances passed by cities and counties. A federal statute, of course, applies to all states. A state statute, in contrast, applies only within that state's borders. City or county ordinances (statutes) apply only to those jurisdictions where they are enacted. As noted earlier, statutory law found by the Supreme Court to violate the U.S. Constitution will be overturned. In the late 1980s, for example, the Court ruled that any state laws banning the burning of the American flag were unconstitutional because they impinged on the individual's right to freedom of expression.[5] (To learn how one federal statute regulates a particular type of medical crime, see the feature *A Question of Ethics—Kidney Compensation* on the following page.)

Constitutional Law Law based on the U.S. Constitution and the constitutions of the various states.

Statutory Law The body of law enacted by legislative bodies.

THE INFLUENCE OF COMMON LAW Even though the body of statutory law has expanded greatly since the beginning of this nation, thus narrowing the applicability of common law doctrines, there is significant overlap between statutory law and common law. For example, many statutes essentially codify existing common law rules. Therefore, the courts, when interpreting the statutes, often rely on the common law as a guide to what the legislators intended.

In some instances, statutory law has brought common law principles more in line with modern criminal theory. Under common law, for example, the law of rape applied only when the victim was a female. Today, many states recognize that both genders may be the targets of sexual assault. Under common law, burglary was defined as the breaking into and entering of a dwelling during the nighttime. State legislatures, in contrast, generally have defined burglary as occurring at any time. They also have extended it to apply to structures beyond dwellings and even to automobiles.

MODEL PENAL CODE Until the mid-twentieth century, state criminal statutes were disorganized, inconsistent, and generally inadequate for modern society. In 1952, the American Law Institute began to draft a uniform penal code in hopes of solving this problem. The first Model Penal Code was released ten years later and has had a broad effect on state statutes.[6] Though not a law itself, the code defines the general principles of criminal responsibility and codifies specific offenses. It is the source for many of the definitions of crime in this textbook. The majority of the states have adopted parts of the Model Penal Code into their statutes, and some states, such as New York, have adopted a large portion of the Code.[7]

It is important to keep in mind that there are essentially fifty-two different criminal codes in this country—one for each state, the District of Columbia, and the federal government. Even if a state has adopted a large portion of the Model Penal Code, there may be certain discrepancies. Indeed, a state's criminal code often reflects specific values of its citizens, which may not be in keeping with those of the majority of other states. Alaska, Arizona, and Vermont, for example, are the only states that do not require citizens to obtain a permit to carry a concealed firearm. Sometimes, old laws remain on the books even though they are clearly outdated and are rarely, if ever, enforced. In Oklahoma, a person can be sentenced to thirty days in jail for "injuring fruit, melons or flowers in the daytime,"[8] and several counties in North Carolina prohibit swearing.[9]

Model Penal Code A statutory text created by the American Law Institute that sets forth general principles of criminal responsibility and defines specific offenses. States have adopted many aspects of the Model Penal Code, which is not itself a law, into their criminal codes.

Critical Thinking Skill Development: In a short written assignment, ask students to discuss the Model Penal Code. How has the Model Penal Code contributed to criminal law in the United States?

A QUESTION OF ETHICS: *Kidney Compensation*

THE SITUATION Located on each side of the spine, just above the waist, kidneys are small, bean-shaped organs that perform crucial functions such as keeping blood healthy and excreting urine. At any given time, more than 80,000 Americans with faulty kidneys need a new kidney to be transplanted into their bodies. Until this happens, they must rely on an expensive, painful process called dialysis to survive. Each year, about 4,500 people in the United States die while waiting for a healthy kidney.

THE ETHICAL DILEMMA Each person has two kidneys but can manage with just one, meaning that, at least theoretically, there is a huge supply of the organs for transplant. In reality, however, the supply of available healthy kidneys is severely limited. Sometimes, an organ donor who has died can provide the necessary transplant, or a living person may choose to donate a kidney to a person in need. Even so, as the lengthy waiting list suggests, the supply of available kidneys does not come close to meeting demand. There is a way to alleviate this shortage: allow people to sell one of their kidneys for transplantation. However, in the United States, as in most of the world, the exchange of any bodily organ for money or other kinds of payment is a crime. Under the 1984 National Organ Transplant Act, anybody who sells a kidney faces a $50,000 fine and five years in prison. This law is based on the idea that it is immoral to sell one's organs. As George Anas, a professor of health, law, bioethics, and human rights at Boston University, puts it, "We do not want to live in a society in which the rich live off the bodies of the poor."

WHAT IS THE SOLUTION? Iran is the only country in the world that has a government-regulated, open market for kidneys. Donors receive between $2,000 and $4,000 for each organ, and Iran has no waiting list for those needing transplants. Do you think that we should adopt this system in the United States? Why or why not? What ethical concerns do you have about the sale of kidneys? (Keep in mind that Americans are allowed to sell their blood, sperm, and, to infertile women, eggs.)

BALLOT INITIATIVES On a state and local level, voters can write or rewrite criminal statutes through a form of direct democracy known as the ballot initiative. In this process, a group of citizens draft a proposed law and then gather a certain number of signatures to get the proposal on that year's ballot. If a majority of the voters approve the measure, it is enacted into law. Currently, twenty-four states and the District of Columbia accept ballot initiatives, and these special elections have played a crucial role in shaping criminal law in those jurisdictions. In the mid-1990s, for example, California voters approved a "three-strikes" measure (discussed in Chapter 11) that increased penalties for third-time felons, transforming the state's criminal justice system in the process. In 2010, as we saw in the previous chapter, California voters rejected a ballot initiative that would have legalized the production and possession of small amounts of marijuana. That same year, however, Arizona voters used the process to require that their state join fourteen other states and Washington, D.C., in allowing the use of marijuana for medicinal purposes.[10]

ADMINISTRATIVE LAW

A third source of American criminal law consists of administrative law—the rules, orders, and decisions of *regulatory agencies*. A regulatory agency is a federal, state, or local government agency established to perform a specific function. The Occupational Safety and Health Administration (OSHA), for example, oversees the safety and health of American workers. The Environmental Protection Agency (EPA) is concerned with protecting the natural environment, and the Food and Drug Administration (FDA) regulates food and drugs produced in the United States.

Disregarding certain laws created by regulatory agencies can be a criminal violation. Federal statutes, such as the Clean Water Act, authorize a specific regulatory agency, such as the EPA, to enforce regulations to which criminal sanctions are attached.[11] So, after an explosion on the Deepwater Horizon drilling rig on April 20, 2010, allowed 205 million gallons of crude oil to leak into the Gulf of Mexico, the EPA opened an investigation to determine if any criminal activity had contributed to the environmental disaster.

CASE LAW

As is evident from the earlier discussion of the common law tradition, another basic source of American law consists of the rules of law announced in court decisions, or precedents. These rules of law include interpretations of constitutional provisions, of statutes enacted by legislatures, and of regulations created by administrative agencies. Today, this body of law is referred to variously as the common law, judge-made law, or case law.

Case law relies to a certain extent on how courts interpret a particular statute. If you wanted to learn about the coverage and applicability of a particular statute, for example, you would need to locate the statute and study it. You would also need to see how the courts in your jurisdiction have interpreted the statute—in other words, what precedents have been established in regard to that statute. The use of precedent means that judge-made law varies from jurisdiction to jurisdiction. (For a summary of the four different sources of American law, see Figure 4.1 on the next page.)

Ballot Initiative A procedure in which the citizens of a state, by collecting enough signatures, can force a public vote on a proposed change to state law.

Administrative Law The body of law created by administrative agencies (in the form of rules, regulations, orders, and decisions) in order to carry out their duties and responsibilities.

Case Law The rules of law announced in court decisions. Case law includes the aggregate of reported cases that interpret judicial precedents, statutes, regulations, and constitutional provisions.

Group Activities: Take a class trip to your university's library. Have a librarian speak with the students about where legal references can be found in your library. Where should students go to research federal law, state law, and administrative law?

SELFASSESSMENT

Fill in the blanks and check your answers on page 128.

The U.S. _____ is the supreme law of this country. Any law that violates this document will be declared _____ by the United States Supreme Court. Laws enacted by legislative bodies are known as _____, while the body of law created by judicial decisions is known as _____ law.

FIGURE 4.1 Sources of American Law

1 **Constitutional law**   The law as expressed in the U.S. Constitution and the various state constitutions. The U.S. Constitution is the supreme law of the land. State constitutions are supreme within state borders to the extent that they do not violate the U.S. Constitution or a federal law.

2 **Statutory law**   Laws or ordinances created by federal, state, and local legislatures and governing bodies. None of these laws can violate the U.S. Constitution or the relevant state constitution. Uniform laws, when adopted by a state legislature, become statutory law in that state.

3 **Administrative law**   The rules, orders, and decisions of federal or state government administrative agencies. Federal administrative agencies are created by enabling legislation enacted by the U.S. Congress. Agency functions include rulemaking, investigation and enforcement, and adjudication.

4 **Case law and common law doctrines**   Judge-made law, including interpretations of constitutional provisions, of statutes enacted by legislatures, and of regulations created by administrative agencies. The common law—the doctrines and principles embodied in case law—governs all areas not covered by statutory law (or agency regulations issued to implement various statutes).

THE PURPOSES OF CRIMINAL LAW

LO 3 Why do societies need laws? Many criminologists believe that criminal law has two basic functions: one relates to the legal requirements of a society, and the other pertains to the society's need to maintain and promote social values.

PROTECT AND PUNISH:
THE LEGAL FUNCTION OF THE LAW

The primary legal function of the law is to maintain social order by protecting citizens from *criminal harm*. This term refers to a variety of harms that can be generalized to fit into two categories:

1. Harms to individual citizens' physical safety and property, such as the harm caused by murder, theft, or arson.
2. Harms to society's interests collectively, such as the harm caused by unsafe foods or consumer products, a polluted environment, or poorly constructed buildings.[12]

The first category is self-evident, although even murder has different degrees, or grades, of offense to which different punishments are assigned. The second, however, has proved more problematic, for it is difficult to measure society's "collective" interests.

Often, laws passed to reduce such harms seem overly intrusive and marginally necessary. An extreme example would seem to be the Flammable Fabrics Act, which makes it a crime for a retailer to willfully remove a precautionary instruction label from a mattress that is protected with a chemical fire retardant.[13] Yet even in this example, a criminal harm is conceivable. Suppose a retailer removes the tags before selling a large number of mattresses to a hotel chain. Employees of the chain then unknowingly wash the mattresses with an agent that lessens their flame-resistant qualities. After the mattresses have been installed in rooms, a guest falls asleep while smoking a cigarette, starting a fire that burns down the entire hotel and causes several deaths.[14]

MAINTAIN AND TEACH:
THE SOCIAL FUNCTION OF THE LAW

If criminal laws against acts that cause harm or injury to others are almost universally accepted, the same cannot be said for laws that criminalize "morally" wrongful activities

Discussion Tip: Have students debate the two categories of criminal harm. Does all crime fit into at least one of these categories? Why or why not? (LO 3)

that may do no obvious, physical harm outside the families of those involved. Why criminalize gambling or prostitution if the participants are consenting?

EXPRESSING PUBLIC MORALITY

The answer lies in the social function of criminal law. Many observers believe that the main purpose of criminal law is to reflect the values and norms of society, or at least of those segments of society that hold power. Legal scholar Henry Hart has stated that the only justification for criminal law and punishment is "the judgment of community condemnation."[15]

Take, for example, the misdemeanor of bigamy, which occurs when someone knowingly marries a second person without terminating her or his marriage to an original husband or wife. Apart from moral considerations, there would appear to be no victims in a bigamous relationship, and indeed many societies have allowed and continue to allow bigamy to exist. In the American social tradition, however, as John L. Diamond of the University of California's Hastings College of the Law points out:

> Marriage is an institution encouraged and supported by society. The structural importance of the integrity of the family and a monogamous marriage requires unflinching enforcement of the criminal laws against bigamy. The immorality is not in choosing to do wrong, but in transgressing, even innocently, a fundamental social boundary that lies at the core of social order.[16]

When discussing the social function of criminal law, it is important to remember that a society's views of morality change over time. Seventeenth-century Puritan New England society not only had strict laws against adultery, but also considered lying and idleness to be criminal acts.[17] Today, such acts may carry social stigmas, but only in certain extreme circumstances do they elicit legal sanctions. Furthermore, criminal laws aimed at minority groups, which were once widely accepted in the legal community as well as society at large, have increasingly come under question. (See the feature *Landmark Cases—Lawrence v. Texas* on the following page.)

TEACHING SOCIETAL BOUNDARIES Some scholars believe that criminal laws not only express the expectations of society, but "teach" them as well. Professor Lawrence M. Friedman of Stanford University thinks that just as parents teach children behavioral norms through punishment, criminal justice "'teaches a lesson' to the people it punishes, and to society at large." Making burglary a crime, arresting burglars, putting them in jail—each step in the criminal justice process reinforces the idea that burglary is unacceptable and is deserving of punishment.[18]

This teaching function can also be seen in traffic laws. There is nothing "natural" about most traffic laws: Americans drive on the right side of the street, the British on the left side, with no obvious difference in the results. These laws, such as stopping at intersections, using headlights at night, and following speed limits, do lead to a more orderly flow of traffic and fewer accidents—certainly socially desirable goals. The laws can also be updated when needed. Over the past few years, several states have banned the use of handheld cell phones while driving because of the safety hazards associated with that

Several years ago, Louisiana and New Mexico became the last two states to criminalize cockfighting, a form of gambling entertainment in which trained roosters battle, often to the death. How do prohibitions against such practices, which may be favored by a minority, reflect the social function of criminal law?
Al Bello/Getty Images

Group Activities: Ask students to work together to brainstorm a list of statutes that criminalize "morally" wrongful activities. In cases where there is no apparent victim, ask students to discuss why it is important that such behaviors be outlawed. (LO 3)

Critical Thinking Skill Development: Ask students to respond to "Questions for Critical Analysis" number one on page 129, in which they consider the social function of the law. (LO 3)

Discussion Tip: Ask students to work with a partner to brainstorm laws that "teach" individuals the expectations of society (for example, laws that regulate speeding or noise). If time allows, ask students to share their results with the class. (LO 3)

behavior. Various forms of punishment for breaking traffic laws teach drivers the social order of the road.

SELFASSESSMENT

Fill in the blanks and check your answers on page 128.

The _____ function of the law is to protect citizens from _____ harm by assuring their physical safety. The _____ function of the law is to teach citizens proper behavior and express public _____ by codifying the norms and values of the community.

LANDMARK CASES: *Lawrence v. Texas*

Police officers in Houston arrested John Geddes Lawrence and Tyron Garner for violating a Texas law that prohibits individuals of the same sex from engaging in "deviate sexual intercourse." Lawrence and Garner challenged the law as unconstitutional because it banned sexual practices—in this case, sodomy—by homosexual couples that are lawful when performed by a man and a woman. The Texas Supreme Court upheld the statute, relying on the United States Supreme Court's decision in *Bowers v. Hardwick* (1986), which preserved a similar state law (since repealed) in Georgia. Lawrence and Garner appealed to the Supreme Court, in essence telling the highest court in the land that it had been mistaken when it ruled on the *Bowers* case and asking it to reconsider.

> *Lawrence v. Texas*
> **United States Supreme Court**
> **522 U.S. 1064 (2003)**
> www.law.cornell.edu/supct/html/02-102.ZS.html

IN THE WORDS OF THE COURT . . .
JUSTICE KENNEDY, MAJORITY OPINION

* * * *

The laws involved in *Bowers* and here are, to be sure, statutes that purport to do no more than prohibit a particular sexual act. Their penalties and purposes, though, have more far-reaching consequences, touching upon the most private human conduct, sexual behavior, and in the most private of places, the home. The statutes do seek to control a personal relationship that, whether or not entitled to formal recognition in the law, is within the liberty of persons to choose without being punished as criminals.

This, as a general rule, should counsel against attempts by the State, or a court, to define the meaning of the relationship or to set its boundaries absent injury to a person or abuse of an institution

the law protects. It suffices for us to acknowledge that adults may choose to enter upon this relationship in the confines of their homes and their own private lives and still retain their dignity as free persons. * * * The liberty protected by the Constitution allows homosexual persons the right to make this choice.

* * * *

When homosexual conduct is made criminal by the law of the State, that declaration in and of itself is an invitation to subject homosexual persons to discrimination both in the public and in the private spheres. The central holding of *Bowers* has been brought in question by this case, and it should be addressed. Its continuance as precedent demeans the lives of homosexual persons.

* * * *

The petitioners are entitled to respect for their private lives. The State cannot demean their existence or control their destiny by making their private sexual conduct a crime.

DECISION

Overturning its earlier Bowers decision, the Court ruled that the Texas antisodomy law was unconstitutional, at the same time invalidating similar statutes in three other states—Kansas, Missouri, and Oklahoma.

FOR CRITICAL ANALYSIS

Nine states still have laws on the books that make sodomy illegal for both heterosexual and homosexual partners. How do you think one of these laws would fare if brought before the Supreme Court today? Have the morals of American society changed to the extent that any law criminalizing consensual sexual conduct between adults is outdated?

For more information and activities related to this case, visit the *Criminal Justice CourseMate* at <u>cengagebrain.com</u> and select the *Web links* for this chapter.

Douglas Toombs/Shutterstock

THE ELEMENTS OF A CRIME

In fictional accounts of police work, the admission of guilt is often portrayed as the crucial element of a criminal investigation. Although an admission is certainly useful to police and prosecutors, it alone cannot establish the innocence or guilt of a suspect. Criminal law normally requires that the *corpus delicti,* a Latin phrase for "the body of the crime," be proved before a person can be convicted of wrongdoing.[19] *Corpus delicti* can be defined as "proof that a specific crime has actually been committed by someone."[20] It consists of the basic elements of any crime, which include (1) *actus reus,* or a guilty act; (2) *mens rea,* or a guilty intent; (3) concurrence, or the coming together of the criminal act and the guilty mind; (4) a link between the act and the legal definition of the crime; (5) any attendant circumstances; and (6) the harm done, or result of the criminal act. (See *Mastering Concepts* below for an example showing some of the various elements of a crime.)

CRIMINAL ACT: *ACTUS REUS*

Suppose Mr. Smith walks into a police department and announces that he just killed his wife. In and of itself, the confession is insufficient for conviction unless the police find Mrs. Smith's corpse, for example, with a bullet in her brain and establish through evidence that Mr. Smith fired the gun. (This does not mean that an actual dead body has to be found in every homicide case. Rather, it is the fact of the death that must be established in such cases.)

Most crimes require an act of *commission,* meaning that a person must *do* something in order to be accused of a crime. The prohibited act is referred to as the *actus reus,* or guilty act. Furthermore, the act of commission must be voluntary. For example, if Mr. Smith had an epileptic seizure while holding a hunting rifle and accidentally shot his wife, he normally would not be held criminally liable for her death. (To better understand this principle, see the feature *You Be the Judge—A Voluntary Act?* on the following page.)

Corpus Delicti The body of circumstances that must exist for a criminal act to have occurred.

Actus Reus (pronounced *ak*-tus *ray*-uhs). A guilty (prohibited) act. The commission of a prohibited act is one of the two essential elements normally required for criminal liability, the other element being the intent to commit a crime.

Critical Thinking Skill Development: Ask students to reflect on James Arthur Ray's story at the beginning of the chapter. Ask students to discuss whether they believe a *corpus delicti* can be established in that case. Why or why not?

MASTERING CONCEPTS
THE ELEMENTS OF A CRIME

Camilo Torres, 2009. Used under license from Shutterstock.com

Carl Robert Winchell walked into the SunTrust Bank in Volusia County, Florida, and placed a bag containing a box on a counter. Announcing that the box held a bomb, he demanded to be given an unspecified amount of cash. After receiving several thousand dollars in cash, Winchell fled, leaving the box behind. A Volusia County Sheriff's Office bomb squad subsequently determined that the box did not in fact contain any explosive device. Winchell was eventually arrested and charged with robbery.

Winchell's actions were criminal because they satisfy the three elements of a crime:

1. *Actus Reus:* Winchell **physically** committed the crime of bank robbery.
2. *Mens Rea:* Winchell **intended** to commit the crime of bank robbery.
3. *Concurrence:* Winchell's intent to rob the bank and his use of the false bomb threat* **came together** to create a criminal act.

*Note that the fact that there was no bomb in the box has no direct bearing on the three elements of the crime. It could, however, lead to Winchell's receiving a lighter punishment than if he had used a real bomb.

Attempt The act of taking substantial steps toward committing a crime while having the ability and the intent to commit the crime, even if the crime never takes place.

Mens Rea (pronounced *mehns ray*-uh). Mental state, or intent. A wrongful mental state is usually as necessary as a wrongful act to establish criminal liability.

A LEGAL DUTY In some cases, an act of *omission* can be a crime, but only when a person has a legal duty to perform the omitted act. One such legal duty is assumed to exist based on a "special relationship" between two parties, such as a parent and child, adult children and their aged parents, and spouses.[21] Those persons involved in contractual relationships with others, such as physicians and lifeguards, must also perform legal duties to avoid criminal penalty. Hawaii, Minnesota, Rhode Island, Vermont, and Wisconsin have even passed "duty to aid" statutes requiring their citizens to report criminal conduct and help victims of such conduct if possible.[22] Another example of a criminal act of omission is failure to file a federal income tax return when required by law to do so.

A PLAN OR ATTEMPT The guilty act requirement is based on one of the premises of criminal law—that a person is punished for harm done to society. Planning to kill someone or to steal a car may be wrong, but the thoughts do no harm and are therefore not criminal until they are translated into action. Of course, a person can be punished for *attempting* murder or robbery, but normally only if he or she took substantial steps toward the criminal objective and the prosecution can prove that the desire to commit the crime was present. Furthermore, the punishment for an **attempt** normally is less severe than if the act had succeeded.

MENTAL STATE: *MENS REA*

A wrongful mental state—*mens rea*—is usually as necessary as a wrongful act in determining guilt. The mental state, or requisite *intent*, required to establish guilt of a crime is indicated in the applicable statute or law. For theft, the wrongful act is the taking of another person's property, and the required mental state involves both the awareness that the property belongs to another and the desire to deprive the owner of it.

YOU BE THE JUDGE

A Voluntary Act?

THE FACTS On a bright, sunny afternoon, Emil was driving on Delaware Avenue in Buffalo, New York. As he was making a turn, Emil suffered an epileptic seizure and lost control of his automobile. The car careened onto the sidewalk and struck a group of six schoolgirls, killing four of them. Emil knew that he was subject to epileptic attacks that rendered him likely to lose consciousness.

THE LAW An "act" committed while one is unconscious is in reality not an act at all. It is merely a physical event or occurrence over which the defendant has no control—that is, such an act is involuntary. If the defendant voluntarily causes the loss of consciousness by, for example, using drugs or alcohol, however, then he or she will usually be held criminally responsible for any consequences.

YOUR DECISION Emil was charged in the deaths of the four girls. He asked the court to dismiss the charges, as he was unconscious at the time of the accident and therefore had not committed a voluntary act. In your opinion, is there an *actus reus* in this situation, or should the charges against Emil be dismissed?

To see how the appellate court in New York ruled in this case, go to Example 4.1 in Appendix B.

THE CATEGORIES OF MENS REA A guilty mental state includes elements of

LO 4

purpose, knowledge, negligence, and recklessness.[23] A defendant is said to have *purposefully* committed a criminal act when he or she desires to engage in certain criminal conduct or to cause a certain criminal result. For a defendant to have *knowingly* committed an illegal act, he or she must be aware of the illegality, must believe that the illegality exists, or must correctly suspect that the illegality exists but fail to do anything to dispel (or confirm) his or her belief. Criminal negligence involves the mental state in which the defendant grossly deviates from the standard of care that a reasonable person would use under the same circumstances. The defendant is accused of taking an unjustified, substantial, and foreseeable risk that resulted in harm. In Texas, for example, a parent commits a felony if she or he fails to secure a loaded firearm or leaves it in such a manner that it could easily be accessed by a child.[24]

A defendant who commits an act recklessly is more blameworthy than one who is criminally negligent. The Model Penal Code defines criminal recklessness as "consciously disregard[ing] a substantial and unjustifiable risk."[25] Some courts, particularly those adhering to the Model Penal Code, will not find criminal recklessness on the part of a defendant who was subjectively unaware of the risk when she or he acted.

During the trial of James Arthur Ray discussed at the beginning of this chapter, prosecutors presented a witness who testified that Ray did nothing to help those who became ill or lost consciousness in the sweat lodge. This testimony, if true, would help establish that the defendant was aware of the dangers faced by the ceremony participants and that, therefore, his actions were reckless rather than simply negligent. (See Figure 4.2 on the following page for more information on the different categories of *mens rea*.)

Negligence A failure to exercise the standard of care that a reasonable person would exercise in similar circumstances.

Recklessness The state of being aware that a risk does or will exist and nevertheless acting in a way that consciously disregards this risk.

CRIMINAL LIABILITY Intent plays an important part in allowing the law to differentiate among varying degrees of criminal liability for similar, though not identical, guilty acts. The role of intent is clearly seen in the different classifications of homicide, defined generally as the willful killing of one human being by another. It is important to emphasize the word *willful*, as it precludes deaths caused by accident or negligence and those deemed justifiable. A death that results from negligence or accident generally is considered a private wrong and a matter for civil law. Nevertheless, some statutes allow for culpable negligence, which permits certain negligent homicides to be criminalized. As we saw in Chapter 3, when the act of killing is willful, deliberate, and premeditated (planned beforehand), it is considered first degree murder. When premeditation does not exist but intent does, the act is considered second degree murder.

Different degrees of criminal liability for various categories of homicide lead to different penalties. The distinction between murder and manslaughter is evident in the case of three men involved in a brawl outside a Boston nightclub during which José "Danny" Alicea was beaten to death. According to witnesses, the men attacked Alicea after a request for a cigarette turned into a heated argument, beating and kicking him so badly that he lost consciousness and died two days later from massive head trauma. Prosecutors charged Daniel Ek, Johan Garcia, and Anthony Villalobos with second degree murder, but the jury decided that the defendants did not *intend* Alicea's death. That is, they may have wanted to hurt Alicea, but they did not want to kill him. Consequently, in 2011 the jurors found the three men guilty of involuntary manslaughter, and they received sentences ranging from four-and-a-half to six years in prison. In contrast, had Ek, Garcia, and Villalobos been convicted of second degree murder, they would have faced maximum sentences of life in prison.

Critical Thinking Skill Development: Ask students to debate the concept of recklessness. When does merely careless behavior become reckless, and therefore criminal? (LO 4)

FIGURE 4.2 *Mens Rea* and Homicide

The concept of *mens rea* is a tool that the criminal justice system uses to ensure fairness in punishment. In the three examples described here, the defendant's state of mind while committing the crime was a crucial factor in determining a just sentence. The first two cases occurred in California, and the third took place in Washington.

Crime: George Tang arranged to sell two pounds of marijuana to Chad Dias. Tang's girlfriend, Christine Chan, accompanied him to the site of the deal because she feared for his safety. Dias and a friend conspired to rob Tang after the transaction, but ended up seriously wounding him. Because Chan had witnessed the incident, they shot her in the back of the neck, killing her "execution style."

Level of *mens rea:* *Purposefulness.* Even though Dias did not initially intend to kill Chan, or even know that she would be present, he formed this state of mind before committing the crime. Purposefulness (or premeditation) does not require long, drawn-out planning. It can arise in an instant.

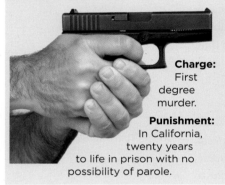

Charge: First degree murder.

Punishment: In California, twenty years to life in prison with no possibility of parole.

Crime: Marjorie Knoller owned two dangerous, aggressive dogs that continuously terrorized her neighbors. Finally, one day the dogs attacked Diane Whipple in the hallway of Knoller's building, killing the young woman.

Level of *mens rea:* Recklessness. Knoller did not intend for Whipple to die. Nevertheless, she was conscious of the substantial risk that her animals posed to others, and she refused to take steps to control them, such as indoor confinement or muzzles.

Charge: Second degree murder.

Punishment: In California, fifteen years to life in prison.

Crime: Albert Rios was sitting beside his backyard fire pit with his seven-month-old son on his lap when he passed out from drinking too much. By the time he woke up, the boy had fallen into the pit and burned to death.

Level of *mens rea:* *Negligence.* In the previous example, Knoller knew and disregarded the risk posed by her dogs. Here, Rios was unconscious and thus unaware of the same sort of risk. Because a reasonable person in his situation would have taken steps to protect his infant son, the law considers him criminally negligent.

Charge: Second degree manslaughter.

Punishment: In Washington, twenty-one to twenty-seven months in prison.

Left, Rob Wilson, Shutterstock.com; top, Mark Strozier/iStockphoto; bottom, Selahattin Bayram/iStockphoto

STRICT LIABILITY For certain crimes, criminal law holds the defendant to be guilty even if intent to commit the offense is lacking. These acts are known as **strict liability crimes** and generally involve endangering the public welfare in some way.[26] Drug-control statutes, health and safety regulations, and traffic laws are all strict liability laws.

Protecting the Public To a certain extent, the concept of strict liability is inconsistent with the traditional principles of criminal law, which hold that *mens rea* is required for an act to be criminal. The goal of strict liability laws is to protect the public by eliminating the possibility that wrongdoers could claim ignorance or mistake to absolve themselves of criminal responsibility.[27] Thus, a person caught dumping waste in a protected pond or driving 70 miles per hour in a 55 miles-per-hour zone cannot plead a lack of intent in his or her defense.

LO 5

The principle is often applied in more serious situations as well. Several years ago twenty-year-old Kieran Hunt of Piscataway, New Jersey, was charged with a first degree felony after he accidentally injected his friend, eighteen-year-old Justin Warfield, with a fatal dose of heroin. Because Hunt had no intention of killing Warfield, in many jurisdictions he would have been charged with involuntary manslaughter. Under New Jersey law, however, strict liability is imposed on anybody who helps another person obtain drugs that lead to a fatal overdose. As a result, Hunt's *mens rea* concerning Warfield's death was irrelevant.[28]

Protecting Minors One of the most controversial strict liability crimes is **statutory rape,** in which an adult engages in a sexual relationship with a minor. In most states, even if the minor consents to the sexual act, the crime still exists because, being underage, he or she is considered incapable of making a rational decision on the matter.[29] Therefore, statutory rape has been committed even if the adult was unaware of the minor's age or was misled to believe that the minor was older.

James Menard's mother, right, reaches to hug him at the end of his 2011 trial in Collier County, Florida, for the murder of Jake Couture. Among other charges, Menard was found guilty of armed trespass before he shot Couture. Why did this make him eligible to be convicted of felony-murder? Lexey Swall/*Naples Daily News*

ACCOMPLICE LIABILITY Under certain circumstances, a person can be charged with and convicted of a crime that he or she did not actually commit. This occurs when the suspect has acted as an *accomplice,* helping another person commit the crime. Generally, to be found guilty as an accomplice, a person must have the "dual intent" (1) to aid the person who committed the crime and (2) that such aid would lead to the commission of the crime.[30] As for the *actus reus,* the accomplice must have helped the primary actor in either a physical sense (for example, by providing the getaway car) or a psychological sense (for example, by encouraging her or him to commit the crime).[31]

In some states, a person can be convicted as an accomplice even without intent if the crime was a "natural and probable consequence" of his or her actions.[32] This principle has led to a proliferation of **felony-murder** legislation. Felony-murder is a form of first degree murder that applies when a person participates in any of a list of serious felonies that results in the unlawful killing of a human being. Under felony-murder law, a person can be convicted as an accomplice to an intentional killing, even when there is no intent. So, for example, if a person intentionally burns down a building, unintentionally killing an inhabitant, he or she will be charged with first degree murder because, in most jurisdictions, arson is a felony.

The felony-murder rule can have odd consequences. Several years ago, for example, Devon Gallagher and his older brother attempted to rob a discount grocery store in Fort Myers, Florida, using a handgun. The shop manager fired at them and killed the older boy. Because Gallagher was involved in a felony (armed robbery) that resulted in a death, he was convicted of first degree murder, even though the victim was his accomplice. These kinds of laws have come under criticism because they punish individuals for acts committed by others. Nevertheless, the criminal codes of more than thirty states include some form of the felony-murder rule.[33]

Statutory Rape A strict liability crime in which an adult engages in a sexual act with a minor. The difference in age between the two participants automatically criminalizes the behavior of the older participant, regardless of whether the younger one consented.

Felony-Murder An unlawful homicide that occurs during the attempted commission of a felony. Regardless of the actor's intent or the circumstances surrounding the death, the homicide is automatically considered first degree murder.

CONCURRENCE

According to criminal law, there must be *concurrence* between the guilty act and the guilty intent. In other words, the guilty act and the guilty intent must occur together.[34] Suppose, for example, that a woman intends to murder her husband with poison in order to collect his life insurance. Every evening, this woman drives her husband home from work. On the night she plans to poison him, however, she swerves to avoid a cat crossing the road and runs into a tree. She survives the accident, but her husband is killed. Even though her intent was realized, the incident would be considered an accidental death because she had not planned to kill him by driving the car into a tree.

Critical Thinking Skill Development: Ask students to respond to "Questions for Critical Analysis" number two on page 129, in which they consider the felony-murder rule.

CAUSATION

Discussion Tip: Ask students to consider the concept of causation. Should a defendant be held liable for murder regardless of how long it takes the victim to die?

Criminal law also requires that the criminal act cause the harm suffered. In 1989, for example, nineteen-year-old Mike Wells shook his two-year-old daughter, Christina, so violently that she suffered brain damage. Soon after the incident, Wells served prison time for aggravated child abuse. Seventeen years later, in 2006, Christina died. When a coroner ruled that the cause of death was the earlier brain injury, Pasco County (Florida) authorities decided that, despite the passage of time, Wells was criminally responsible for his daughter's death. In 2010, Wells pleaded guilty to second degree murder and received a fifteen-year prison sentence.

ATTENDANT CIRCUMSTANCES

Attendant Circumstances
The facts surrounding a criminal event. With some crimes, these facts must be proved to convict the defendant of the underlying crime. With other crimes, proving these facts can increase the penalty associated with the underlying crime.

In certain crimes, attendant circumstances—also known as accompanying circumstances—are relevant to the *corpus delicti*. Most states, for example, differentiate between simple assault and the more serious offense of aggravated assault depending on the attendant circumstance of whether the defendant used a weapon such as a gun or a knife while committing the crime. Criminal law also classifies degrees of property crimes based on the attendant circumstance of the amount stolen. According to federal statutes, the theft of less than $1,000 from a bank is a misdemeanor, while the theft of any amount over $1,000 is a felony.[35] (To get a better understanding of the role of attendant circumstances in criminal statutes, see Figure 4.3 below.)

REQUIREMENTS OF PROOF AND INTENT Attendant circumstances must be proved beyond a reasonable doubt, just like any other element of a crime.[36] Furthermore, the *mens rea* of the defendant regarding each attendant circumstance must be proved as well. Consider, for example, the Portland (Oregon) City Code provision stating that it is "unlawful for any person on a public street or in a public place to carry a firearm upon his [or her] person . . . unless all ammunition has been removed from the chamber."[37] The condition that the firearm be loaded is an attendant circumstance to the crime of carrying the weapon in a public place and must be proved beyond a reasonable doubt. If the gun is not loaded, then there can be no crime. Furthermore, the prosecution must prove that the defendant *knew* that the gun was loaded.[38] If a legislature wants to remove such knowledge from the definition of the crime, it must say so in the statute, thus making the "loadedness" of the gun a *strict liability* (see the previous discussion) attendant circumstance.

Group Activities: Have students work in small groups to generate a list of arguments both for and against the creation of hate crime laws. Why might determining motive be difficult when prosecuting a hate crime?

HATE CRIME LAWS In most cases, a person's motive for committing a crime is irrelevant—a court will not try to read the accused's mind. Over the past few decades, however, nearly every state and the federal government have passed *hate crime laws* that make the suspect's motive an important attendant circumstance to his or her criminal

FIGURE 4.3 Attendant Circumstances in Criminal Law

Most criminal statutes incorporate three of the elements we have discussed in this section: the act (*actus reus*), the intent (*mens rea*), and attendant circumstances. This diagram of Wisconsin's false imprisonment statute should give you an idea of how these elements combine to create the totality of a crime.

| Intent | Act | Attendant Circumstances |

Whoever intentionally confines or restrains another without the person's consent is guilty of false imprisonment.

Source: Wisconsin Statutes Section 940.30 (2001).

act. In general, hate crime laws provide for greater sanctions against those who commit crimes motivated by bias against a person based on race, ethnicity, religion, gender, sexual orientation, disability, or age. The concept of a hate crime as measurable, definable criminal behavior is a relatively new one and, as we will see in the *Criminal Justice in Action* feature at the end of this chapter, has its detractors.

HARM

For most crimes to occur, some harm must have been done to a person or to property. A certain number of crimes are actually categorized depending on the harm done to the victim, regardless of the intent behind the criminal act. Take two offenses, both of which involve one person hitting another in the back of the head with a tire iron. In the first instance, the victim dies, and the offender is charged with murder. In the second, the victim is only knocked unconscious, and the offender is charged with battery. Because the harm in the second instance was less severe, so was the crime with which the offender was charged, even though the act was exactly the same. Furthermore, most states have different degrees of battery depending on the extent of the injuries suffered by the victim.

Many acts are deemed criminal if they could do harm that the laws try to prevent. Such acts are called inchoate offenses. They exist when only an attempt at a criminal act was made. If Jenkins solicits Peterson to murder Jenkins's business partner, this is an inchoate offense on the part of Jenkins, even though Peterson fails to carry out the act. Conspiracies also fall into the category of inchoate offenses. In 2003, the United States Supreme Court ruled that a person could be convicted of criminal conspiracy even though police intervention made the completion of the illegal plan impossible.[39]

SELFASSESSMENT

Fill in the blanks and check your answers on page 128.

Proof that a crime has been committed is established through the elements of the crime, which include the _____, or the physical act of the crime; the _____ _____, or the intent to commit the crime; and the _____ of the guilty act and the guilty intent. With _____ _____ crimes, the law determines that a defendant is guilty even if he or she lacked the _____ to perform a criminal act. _____ circumstances are those circumstances that accompany the main criminal act in a criminal code, and they must be proved _____ _____ _____ _____, just like any other elements of a crime.

DEFENSES UNDER CRIMINAL LAW

When Tammy Gibson of Tacoma, Washington, saw a convicted sex offender named William A. Baldwin talking to her ten-year-old daughter, she leaped into action. Grabbing a baseball bat, she went after Baldwin, striking him repeatedly in the arm. A local judge rejected Gibson's excuse that her victim "got what was coming to him" and sentenced the overly protective mother to three months behind bars for committing assault. A number of other defenses for wrongdoing, however, can be raised in the course of a criminal trial. These defenses generally rely on one of two arguments: (1) the defendant is not responsible for the crime, or (2) the defendant was justified in committing the crime.

CRIMINAL RESPONSIBILITY AND THE LAW

The idea of responsibility plays a significant role in criminal law. In certain circumstances, the law recognizes that even though an act is inherently criminal, society will not punish the actor because he or she does not have the requisite mental condition.

Hate Crime Law A statute that provides for greater sanctions against those who commit crimes motivated by bias against an individual or a group based on race, ethnicity, religion, gender, sexual orientation, disability, or age.

Inchoate Offenses Conduct deemed criminal without actual harm being done, provided that the harm that would have occurred is one the law tries to prevent.

Technology Tip: Have students go online and locate a recent example of an inchoate offense. Examples might include foiled school shootings, murder-for-hire schemes, or terrorism plots. Ask students what they feel the appropriate punishment should be for planning these crimes, even when the acts are not carried out.

In March 2011, a New Jersey judge found Jenny Erazo-Rodriguez not guilty by reason of insanity for fatally strangling her four-year-old daughter and attempting to murder her six-year-old daughter. Erazo-Rodriguez claimed that God had ordered the deaths of her children. Why is someone like Erazo-Rodriguez "not responsible" for behavior that would otherwise be considered criminal?

Robert Sciarrino/*Star-Ledger*

Infancy A condition that, under early American law, excused young wrongdoers of criminal behavior because presumably they could not understand the consequences of their actions.

Insanity A defense for criminal liability that asserts a lack of criminal responsibility. According to the law, a person cannot have the requisite state of mind to commit a crime if she or he did not know at the time of the act that it was wrong, or did not know the nature and quality of the act.

M'Naghten **Rule** A common law test of criminal responsibility, derived from *M'Naghten's* Case in 1843, that relies on the defendant's inability to distinguish right from wrong.

LO 6 In other words, the law "excuses" the person for his or her behavior. Insanity, intoxication, and mistake are the most important excuse defenses today, but we start our discussion of the subject with one of the first such defenses recognized by American law: infancy.

INFANCY Under the earliest state criminal codes of the United States, children younger than seven years of age could never be held legally accountable for crimes. Those between seven and fourteen years old were presumed to lack the capacity for criminal behavior, while anyone over the age of fourteen was tried as an adult. Thus, early American criminal law recognized infancy as a defense in which the accused's wrongdoing is excused because he or she is too young to fully understand the consequences of his or her actions.

With the creation of the juvenile justice system in the early 1900s, the infancy defense became redundant, as youthful delinquents were automatically treated differently from adult offenders. Today, most states either designate an age (eighteen or under) under which wrongdoers are sent to juvenile court or allow prosecutors to decide whether a minor will be charged as an adult on a case-by-case basis. We will explore the concept of infancy as it applies to the modern American juvenile justice system in much greater detail in Chapter 15.

INSANITY After Ashley Von Hadnagy fatally stabbed Riga Quaglino, her eighty-five-year-old grandmother, she told investigators that the voice of Cuban revolutionary leader Fidel Castro had ordered her to kill Quaglino. In 2010, a St. Tammany Parish (Louisiana) judge found that Von Hadnagy's severe mental problems kept her from knowing that her actions were wrong. As a result, Von Hadnagy was sent to a psychiatric hospital rather than prison. Thus, insanity may be a defense to a criminal charge when the defendant's state of mind is such that she or he cannot claim legal responsibility for her or his actions.

Measuring Sanity The general principle of the insanity defense is that a person is excused for his or her criminal wrongdoing if, as a result of a mental disease or defect, he or she

- Does not perceive the physical nature or consequences of his or her conduct;
- Does not know that his or her conduct is wrong or criminal; or
- Is not sufficiently able to control his or her conduct so as to be held accountable for it.[40]

Although criminal law has traditionally accepted the idea that an insane person cannot be held responsible for criminal acts, society has long debated what standards should be used to measure sanity for the purposes of a criminal trial. This lack of consensus is reflected in the diverse tests employed by different American jurisdictions to determine insanity. The tests include the following:

1. *The* M'Naghten *rule.* Derived from an 1843 British murder case, the **M'Naghten rule** states that a person is legally insane and therefore not criminally responsible if, at the time of the offense, he or she was not able to distinguish between right

and wrong.[41] As Figure 4.4 below shows, half of the states still use a version of the *M'Naghten* rule.

2. *The ALI/MPC test.* In the early 1960s, the American Law Institute (ALI) included an insanity standard in its Model Penal Code (MPC), discussed earlier in the chapter. Also known as the substantial-capacity test, the ALI/MPC test requires that the defendant lack "substantial capacity" to either "appreciate the wrongfulness" of his or her conduct or to conform that conduct "to the requirements of the law."[42]

3. *The irresistible-impulse test.* Under the irresistible-impulse test, a person may be found insane even if he or she was aware that a criminal act was "wrong," provided that some "irresistible impulse" resulting from a mental deficiency drove him or her to commit the crime.[43]

The ALI/MPC test is considered the easiest standard of the three for a defendant to meet because the defendant needs only to show a lack of "substantial capacity" to be released from criminal responsibility. Defense attorneys generally consider it more difficult to prove that the defendant could not distinguish "right" from "wrong" or that he or she was driven by an irresistible impulse.

Determining Competency In 1981, John Hinckley was found not guilty of the attempted murder of President Ronald Reagan by reason of insanity. Due to the media attention garnered by this and other high-visibility cases, many Americans see the insanity defense as an easy means for violent criminals to "cheat" the criminal justice system. In fact, this public perception is faulty. The insanity defense is rarely entered and is even less likely to result in an acquittal, as it is difficult to prove.[44] (See the feature *Myth versus Reality—*

Substantial-Capacity Test (ALI/MPC Test) From the Model Penal Code, a test that states that a person is not responsible for criminal behavior if when committing the act "as a result of mental disease or defect he [or she] lacks substantial capacity either to appreciate the wrongfulness of his [or her] conduct or to conform his [or her] conduct to the requirements of the law."

Irresistible-Impulse Test A test for the insanity defense under which a defendant who knew his or her action was wrong may still be found insane if he or she was unable, as a result of a mental deficiency, to control the urge to complete the act.

FIGURE 4.4 Insanity Defenses

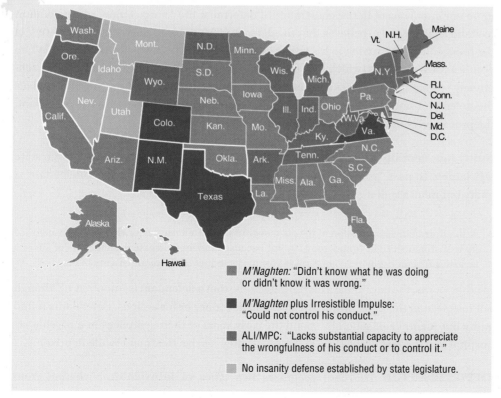

- **M'Naghten:** "Didn't know what he was doing or didn't know it was wrong."
- **M'Naghten plus Irresistible Impulse:** "Could not control his conduct."
- **ALI/MPC:** "Lacks substantial capacity to appreciate the wrongfulness of his conduct or to control it."
- No insanity defense established by state legislature.

Source: Bureau of Justice Statistics, *The Defense of Insanity: Standards and Procedures, State Court Organization, 1998* (Washington, D.C.: U.S. Department of Justice, June 2000), Table 38.

Critical Thinking Skill Development: Ask students to work together to respond to "Questions for Critical Analysis" number three on page 129, in which they consider the insanity defense. (LO 6)

To many Americans, it seems likely that any person who commits a gruesome murder or any other sort of violent crime has psychological problems. The question, then, is, how do we balance the need to punish such a person with the possibility that he or she may be seriously ill?

THE MYTH The American system of criminal justice answers this question by stating that a person may not be tried for an offense if that person cannot be held legally responsible for her or his actions. Because of the publicity surrounding the insanity defense, many people are under the impression that it is a major loophole in our system, allowing criminals to be "let off" no matter how heinous their crimes.

THE REALITY In fact, the insanity defense is raised in only about 1 percent of felony trials, and it is successful only one out of every four times it is raised. The reason: it is extremely difficult to prove insanity under the law. For example, Andre Thomas

cut out the hearts of his wife, their young son, and her thirteen-month-old daughter. Before his murder trial, Thomas pulled his right eye out of its socket. (Several years later, while on death row, he ripped out the other eye and apparently ate it.) Nonetheless, prosecutors were able to convince a Texas jury that Brown understood the difference between right and wrong at the time of the murders, and an appeals court upheld the conviction. Thomas is "clearly 'crazy,'" said one of the appellate judges who heard his case, "but he is also 'sane' under Texas law."

Even if Thomas had succeeded with the insanity defense, he would not have been "let off" in the sense that he would have been set free. Many defendants found not guilty by reason of insanity spend more time in mental hospitals than criminals who are convicted of similar acts spend in prison.

FOR CRITICAL ANALYSIS What do the relatively limited use and success rate of the insanity defense indicate about the impact of public opinion on criminal law?

Are Too Many Criminals Found Not Guilty by Reason of Insanity? above.) Psychiatry is far more commonly used in the courtroom to determine the "competency" of a defendant to stand trial. If a judge believes that the defendant is unable to understand the nature of the proceedings or to assist in his or her own defense, the trial will not take place. When **competency hearings** (which may also take place after the initial arrest and before sentencing) reveal that the defendant is in fact incompetent, the court may decide to place the defendant under treatment. Once competency has been restored to the defendant, the proceedings may recommence.[45]

Guilty But Mentally Ill Public backlash against the insanity defense caused seven state legislatures to pass "guilty but mentally ill" statutes. Under these laws, a defendant is guilty but mentally ill if

> at the time of the commission of the act constituting the offense, he [or she] had the capacity to distinguish right from wrong . . . but because of mental disease or defect he [or she] lacked sufficient capacity to conform his [or her] conduct to the requirements of the law.[46]

In other words, the laws allow a jury to determine that a defendant is "mentally ill," though not insane, and therefore criminally responsible for her or his actions. Defendants found guilty but mentally ill generally spend the early years of their sentences in a psychiatric hospital and the rest of the time in prison, or they receive treatment while in prison.

INTOXICATION The law recognizes two types of intoxication, whether from drugs or from alcohol: *voluntary* and *involuntary.* Involuntary intoxication occurs when a person is physically forced to ingest or is injected with an intoxicating substance, or

Competency Hearing A court proceeding to determine whether the defendant is mentally well enough to understand the charges filed against him or her and cooperate with a lawyer in presenting a defense. If a judge believes the defendant to be incompetent, the trial cannot take place.

Intoxication A defense for criminal liability in which the defendant claims that the taking of intoxicants rendered him or her unable to form the requisite intent to commit a criminal act.

is unaware that a substance contains drugs or alcohol. Involuntary intoxication is a viable defense to a crime if the substance leaves the person unable to form the mental state necessary to understand that the act committed while under the influence was wrong.[47] In Colorado, for example, the murder conviction of a man who shot a neighbor was overturned on the basis that the jury in the initial trial was not informed of the possibility of involuntary intoxication. At the time of the crime, the man had been taking a prescription decongestant that contained phenylpropanolamine, which has been known to cause psychotic episodes.

Voluntary drug or alcohol intoxication is also used to excuse a defendant's actions, though it is not a defense in itself. Rather, it is used when the defense attorney wants to show that the defendant was so intoxicated that *mens rea* was negated. In other words, the defendant could not possibly have had the state of mind that a crime requires. Many courts are reluctant to allow voluntary intoxication arguments to be presented to juries, however. After all, the defendant, by definition, voluntarily chose to enter an intoxicated state.

Teaching Tip: Have students consider the defense of intoxication. What is the difference between voluntary and involuntary intoxication? Which is more likely to be successful before a judge or a jury in a criminal trial? Why? (LO 6)

Twelve states have eliminated voluntary intoxication as a possible defense, a step that has been criticized by many legal scholars but was upheld by the United States Supreme Court in *Montana v. Egelhoff* (1996).[48] The case concerned a double murder committed by James Allen Egelhoff, who was extremely drunk at the time of the crime. Egelhoff was convicted on two counts of deliberate homicide, which is defined by Montana law as "knowingly" or "purposefully" causing the death of another human being.[49] Egelhoff appealed his conviction, arguing that the state statute prohibiting evidence of voluntary intoxication kept his attorneys from showing the jury that he was too inebriated to "knowingly" or "purposefully" commit the murders.[50] The Court allowed Egelhoff's conviction, ruling that states were constitutionally within their rights to abolish the voluntary intoxication defense.

> "You know how it is, Dr. Ellsworth. You go to a party, have a few drinks, somebody gets killed."
>
> **—Letter from a death row inmate to Professor Phoebe Ellsworth, University of Michigan**

MISTAKE Everyone has heard the saying, "Ignorance of the law is no excuse." Ordinarily, ignorance of the law or a *mistaken idea* about what the law requires is not a valid defense.[51] For example, Gilbert A. Robinson appealed a conviction for possession of sexually explicit photographs of teenage boys by claiming that he did not know that such an act had become illegal. Chief Judge Juan R. Torruella del Valle of the Fifth Circuit Court of Appeals upheld Robinson's conviction, stating that child pornography is "inherently deleterious" and that the "probability of regulation is so great that anyone who is aware that he is in possession of [it] . . . must be presumed to be aware of the regulation."[52]

Mistake of Law In some states, however, that rule has been modified to allow for a mistake-of-law defense. People who claim that they honestly did not know that they were breaking a law may have a valid defense if (1) the law was not published or reasonably known to the public or (2) the person relied on an official statement of the law that was erroneous.[53]

Discussion Tip: Have students discuss the mistake defense. When can ignorance be used as a criminal defense? When can it not be used? Can students find an example of a real-life case involving the mistake defense? (LO 6)

Mistake of Fact A *mistake of fact,* as opposed to a *mistake of law,* operates as a defense if it negates the mental state necessary to commit a crime. If, for example, Oliver mistakenly walks off with Julie's briefcase because he thinks it is his, there is no theft. Theft requires knowledge that the property belongs to another. The mistake-of-fact defense has proved very controversial in rape and sexual assault cases, in which the accused claims that the sex was consensual while the alleged victim claims it was coerced.

In some instances, mistake of fact is not an excuse but does allow for a lighter sentence. Several years ago, a Skagit County (Washington) judge sentenced teenage hunter Tyler Kales to thirty days in juvenile detention and 120 hours of community service for shooting and killing a hiker he mistook for a bear. Normally, of course, homicide with a firearm brings a much harsher punishment.

JUSTIFICATION CRIMINAL DEFENSES AND THE LAW

In certain instances, a defendant will accept responsibility for committing an illegal act, but contend that—given the circumstances—the act was justified. In other words, even

LO 7 though the guilty act and the guilty intent are present, the particulars of the case relieve the defendant of criminal liability. In 2010, for example, there were 665 "justified" killings of those who were in the process of committing a felony: 387 were killed by law enforcement officers and 278 by private citizens.[54] Four of the most important justification defenses are duress, self-defense, necessity, and entrapment.

DURESS Duress exists when the *wrongful* threat of one person induces another person to perform an act that she or he would otherwise not perform. In such a situation, duress is said to negate the *mens rea* necessary to commit a crime. For duress to qualify as a defense, the following requirements must be met:

1. The threat must be of serious bodily harm or death.
2. The harm threatened must be greater than the harm caused by the crime.
3. The threat must be immediate and inescapable.
4. The defendant must have become involved in the situation through no fault of his or her own.[55]

When ruling on the duress defense, courts often examine whether the defendant had the opportunity to avoid the threat in question. Two narcotics cases illustrate this point. In the first, the defendant claimed that an associate threatened to kill him and his wife unless he participated in a marijuana deal. Although this contention was proved true during the course of the trial, the court rejected the duress defense because the defendant made no apparent effort to escape, nor did he report his dilemma to the police. In sum, the drug deal was avoidable—the defendant could have made an effort to extricate himself, but he did not, thereby surrendering the protection of the duress defense.[56]

In the second case, a taxi driver in Bogotá, Colombia, was ordered by a passenger to swallow cocaine-filled balloons and take them to the United States. The taxi driver was warned that if he refused, his wife and three-year-old daughter would be killed. After a series of similar threats, the taxi driver agreed to transport the drugs. On arriving at customs at the Los Angeles airport, the defendant consented to have his stomach X-rayed, which led to discovery of the contraband and his arrest. During his trial, the defendant told the court that he was afraid to notify the police in Colombia because he believed them to be corrupt. The court accepted his duress defense, on the grounds that it met the four requirements listed

Duress Unlawful pressure brought to bear on a person, causing the person to perform an act that he or she would not otherwise perform.

Before the bomb attached to his neck detonated and killed him, Brian Douglas Wells claimed that it had been placed there by men who forced him to rob a bank in Summit Township, Pennsylvania. If this were true, and if he had survived, would Wells have been able to claim duress as a defense? Would it make any difference if, unbeknownst to Wells, the bomb around his neck was a fake, incapable of causing him harm?
AP Photo/Janet B. Campbell/ Erie Times-News

on the previous page and the defendant had notified American authorities when given the opportunity to do so.[57]

JUSTIFIABLE USE OF FORCE—SELF-DEFENSE A person who believes he or she is in danger of being harmed by another is justified in defending himself or herself with the use of force, and any criminal act committed in such circumstances can be justified as self-defense. Other situations that also justify the use of force include the defense of one's dwelling, the defense of other property, and the prevention of a crime. In all these situations, it is important to distinguish between deadly and nondeadly force. Deadly force is likely to result in death or serious bodily harm.

The Amount of Force Generally speaking, people can use the amount of nondeadly force that seems necessary to protect themselves, their dwellings, or other property or to prevent the commission of a crime. Deadly force can be used in self-defense if there is a *reasonable belief* that imminent death or bodily harm will otherwise result, if the attacker is using unlawful force (an example of lawful force is that exerted by a police officer), if the defender has not initiated or provoked the attack, and if there is no other possible response or alternative way out of the life-threatening situation.[58] Deadly force normally can be used to defend a dwelling only if the unlawful entry is violent and the person believes deadly force is necessary to prevent imminent death or great bodily harm. In some jurisdictions, it is also a viable defense if the person believes deadly force is necessary to prevent the commission of a felony (such as arson) in the dwelling.

The Duty to Retreat When a person is outside the home or in a public space, the rules for self-defense change somewhat. Until relatively recently, almost all jurisdictions required someone who is attacked under these circumstances to "retreat to the wall" before fighting back. In other words, under this duty to retreat one who is being assaulted may not resort to deadly force if she or he has a reasonable opportunity to "run away" and thus avoid the conflict. Only when this person has run into a "wall," literally or otherwise, may deadly force be used in self-defense.

Recently, however, several states have changed their laws to eliminate this duty to retreat. For example, a Florida law did away with the duty to retreat outside the home, stating that citizens have "the right to stand [their] ground and meet force with force, including deadly force," if they "reasonably" fear for their safety.[59] The Florida law also allows a person to use deadly force against someone who unlawfully intrudes into her or his house (or vehicle), even if that person does not fear for her or his safety.[60] At least sixteen states have adopted "stand your ground" laws similar to Florida's.

NECESSITY In 2009, Jennifer Greenwood of North Pole, Alaska, was charged with felony driving while intoxicated. In her defense, she claimed that, on the night in question, she had no choice but to drive drunk because she needed to warn her boyfriend's parents that he planned to burn down their house. A local judge, noting Greenwood's two earlier DUI convictions, sentenced her to forty-eight months in prison and suspended her driver's license for life. Under different circumstances, however, the necessity defense can be used to justify otherwise illegal behavior.

According to the Model Penal Code, the necessity defense is viable if "the harm or evil sought to be avoided by such conduct is greater than that sought to be prevented by the law defining the offense charged."[61] In another driving case from 2009, for example, Jason Blair of Brooksville, Florida, successfully used the necessity defense to justify leaving the scene of a car accident involving a death. After accidentally hitting a pedestrian

Self-Defense The legally recognized privilege to protect one's self or property from injury by another. The privilege of self-defense covers only acts that are reasonably necessary to protect one's self or property.

Duty to Retreat The requirement that a person claiming self-defense prove that she or he first took reasonable steps to avoid the conflict that resulted in the use of deadly force. Generally, the duty to retreat (1) applies only in public spaces and (2) does not apply when the force used in self-defense was nondeadly.

Necessity A defense against criminal liability in which the defendant asserts that circumstances required her or him to commit an illegal act.

Teaching Tip: Ask students respond to "Questions for Critical Analysis" number four on page 129, in which they consider "stand your ground" laws. (LO 7)

Technology Tip: Have students go online and find cases in which the necessity defense was used. Ask students to share their findings with the class and then debate the success of this particular criminal defense. (LO 7)

who later died from injuries suffered in the collision, Blair claimed that he heard someone yell, "I'm going to kill you." Fearing for his life, Blair fled the scene. A jury agreed that a "greater evil" existed—a threat to his own life—and acquitted Blair of a crime that carries a maximum of thirty years in state prison.[62] The one crime for which the necessity defense is not acceptable under any circumstances is murder.[63]

ENTRAPMENT Entrapment is a justification defense that criminal law allows when a police officer or government agent deceives a defendant into wrongdoing. Although law enforcement agents can legitimately use various forms of subterfuge—such as informants or undercover agents—to gain information or apprehend a suspect in a criminal act, the law places limits on these strategies. Police cannot persuade an innocent person to commit a crime, nor can they coerce a suspect into doing so, even if they are certain she or he is a criminal.

The guidelines for determining entrapment were established in the 1932 case of *Sorrells v. United States.*[64] The case, which took place during Prohibition, when the sale of alcoholic beverages was illegal, involved a federal law enforcement agent who repeatedly urged the defendant to sell him bootleg whiskey. The defendant initially rejected the agent's overtures, stating that he "did not fool with whiskey." Eventually, however, he sold the agent a half-gallon of the substance and was summarily convicted of violating the law. The United States Supreme Court held that the agent had improperly induced the defendant to break the law and reversed his conviction.

This case set the precedent for focusing on the defendant's outlook in entrapment cases. In other words, the Court decided that entrapment occurs if a defendant who is not predisposed to commit the crime is convinced to do so by an agent of the government.[65] (For an overview of justification and excuse defenses, see Figure 4.5 on the facing page.)

SELFASSESSMENT

Fill in the blanks and check your answers on page 128.
Criminal law recognizes that a defendant may not be _____ for a criminal act if her or his mental state was impaired, by either _____—the psychological inability to separate right from wrong—or _____ due to drugs or alcohol. Defendants may also claim that they were _____ in committing an act either because they were under _____ to perform an act that they would not otherwise have performed or because they were acting in _____-_____ to protect themselves from deadly harm. _____ occurs when a government agent deceives a defendant into committing a crime.

PROCEDURAL SAFEGUARDS

To this point, we have focused on substantive criminal law, which defines the acts that the government will punish. We will now turn our attention to procedural criminal law. (The section that follows will provide only a short overview of criminal procedure. In later chapters, many other constitutional issues will be examined in more detail.) Criminal law brings the force of the state, with all its resources, to bear against the individual.

LO 8

Criminal procedures, drawn from the ideals stated in the Bill of Rights, are designed to protect the constitutional rights of individuals and to prevent the arbitrary use of power by the government.

Entrapment A defense in which the defendant claims that he or she was induced by a public official—usually an undercover agent or police officer—to commit a crime that he or she would otherwise not have committed.

Substantive Criminal Law Law that defines the rights and duties of individuals with respect to one another.

Procedural Criminal Law Rules that define the manner in which the rights and duties of individuals may be enforced.

FIGURE 4.5 Justification and Excuse Defenses

Justification Defenses: Based on a defendant admitting that he or she committed the particular criminal act, but asserting that, under the circumstances, the criminal act was justified.

	The defendant must prove that:	Example
DURESS	She or he performed the criminal act under the use or threat of use of unlawful force against her or his person that a reasonable person would have been unable to resist.	A mother assists her boyfriend in committing a burglary after he threatens to kill her children if she refuses to do so.
SELF-DEFENSE	He or she acted in a manner to defend himself or herself, others, or property, or to prevent the commission of a crime.	A husband awakes to find his wife standing over him, pointing a shotgun at his chest. In the ensuing struggle, the firearm goes off, killing the wife.
NECESSITY	The criminal act he or she committed was necessary in order to avoid a harm to himself or herself or another that was greater than the harm caused by the act itself.	Four people physically remove a friend from her residence on the property of a religious cult, arguing that the crime of kidnapping was justified in order to remove the victim from the damaging influence of cult leaders.
ENTRAPMENT	She or he was encouraged by agents of the state to engage in a criminal act she or he would not have engaged in otherwise.	The owner of a boat marina agrees to allow three federal drug enforcement agents, posing as drug dealers, to use his dock to unload shipments of marijuana from Colombia.

Excuse Defenses: Based on a defendant admitting that she or he committed the criminal act, but asserting that she or he cannot be held criminally responsible for the act due to lack of criminal intent.

	The defendant must prove that:	Example
INFANCY	Because he or she was under a statutorily determined age, he or she did not have the maturity to make the decisions necessary to commit a criminal act.	A thirteen-year-old takes a handgun from his backpack at school and begins shooting at fellow students, killing three. (In such cases, the offender is often processed by the juvenile justice system rather than the criminal justice system.)
INSANITY	At the time of the criminal act, he or she did not have the necessary mental capacity to be held responsible for his or her actions.	A man with a history of mental illness pushes a woman in front of an oncoming subway train, which kills her instantly.
INTOXICATION	She or he had diminished control over her or his actions due to the influence of alcohol or drugs.	A woman who had been drinking malt liquor and vodka stabs her boyfriend to death after a domestic argument. She claims to have been so drunk as to not remember the incident.
MISTAKE	He or she did not know that his or her actions violated a law (this defense is very rarely even attempted), or that he or she violated the law believing a relevant fact to be true when, in fact, it was not.	A woman, thinking that her divorce in another state has been finalized when it has not, marries for a second time, thereby committing bigamy.

THE BILL OF RIGHTS

For various reasons, proposals related to the rights of individuals were rejected during the framing of the U.S. Constitution in 1787. In fact, the original constitution contained only three provisions that referred to criminal procedure. Article I, Section 9, Clause 2, states that the "Privilege of the Writ of Habeas Corpus shall not be suspended." As will be discussed in Chapter 10, a writ of *habeas corpus* is an order that requires jailers to bring a person before a court or judge and explain why the person is being held in prison. Article I, Section 9, Clause 3, holds that no "Bill of Attainder or ex post facto Law shall be passed." A bill of attainder is a legislative act that targets a particular person or group for punishment without a trial, while an *ex post facto* law operates retroactively, making an event or action illegal though it took place before the law was passed. Finally, Article III, Section 2, Clause 3, maintains that the "Trial of all Crimes" will be by jury and "such Trial shall be held in the State where the said crimes shall have been committed."

Critical Thinking Skill Development: Have students generate a short written assignment in which they identify the constitutional amendment they feel is most critical in safeguarding individual due process rights. Have students explain the reasons for their selection. (LO 9)

Why do most citizens accept certain steps taken by the federal government that restrict our individual freedoms—such as limiting the amount of liquids and gels passengers can carry on airplanes to prevent such substances from being used in terrorist attacks?
AP Photo/Gene Blyth

AMENDING THE CONSTITUTION The need for a written declaration of rights of individuals eventually caused the first Congress to draft twelve amendments to the Constitution and submit them for approval by the states. Ten of these amendments, commonly known as the **Bill of Rights,** were adopted in 1791. Since then, seventeen more amendments have been added.

The Bill of Rights, as interpreted by the United States Supreme Court, has served as the basis for procedural safeguards of the accused in this country. These safeguards include the following:

1. The Fourth Amendment protection from unreasonable searches and seizures.
2. The Fourth Amendment requirement that no warrants for a search or an arrest can be issued without probable cause.
3. The Fifth Amendment requirement that no one can be deprived of life, liberty, or property without "due process" of law.
4. The Fifth Amendment prohibition against *double jeopardy* (trying someone twice for the same criminal offense).
5. The Fifth Amendment guarantee that no person can be required to be a witness against (incriminate) himself or herself.
6. The Sixth Amendment guarantees of a speedy trial, a trial by jury, a public trial, the right to confront witnesses, and the right to a lawyer at various stages of criminal proceedings.
7. The Eighth Amendment prohibitions against excessive bails and fines and cruel and unusual punishments. (For the full text of the Bill of Rights, see Appendix A.)

EXPANDING THE CONSTITUTION The Bill of Rights initially offered citizens protection only against the federal government. Shortly after the end of the Civil War, in 1868, three-fourths of the states ratified the Fourteenth Amendment to expand the protections of the Bill of Rights. For our purposes, the most important part of the amendment reads:

> No State shall make or enforce any law which shall abridge the privileges or immunities of citizens of the United States, nor shall any State deprive any person of life, liberty, or property, without due process of law; nor deny to any person within its jurisdiction the equal protection of the laws.

The United States Supreme Court did not immediately interpret the Fourteenth Amendment as extending the procedural protections of the Bill of Rights to people who had been charged with breaking state criminal law. Indeed, it would be nearly a hundred years before those accused of crimes on the state level would enjoy all the same protections as those accused of breaking federal laws.[66] As these protections are crucial to criminal justice procedures in the United States, they will be afforded much more attention in Chapter 6, with regard to police action, and in Chapter 10, with regard to the criminal trial.

DUE PROCESS

Both the Fifth and Fourteenth Amendments provide that no person should be deprived of "life, liberty, or property without due process of law." This **due process clause** basically requires that the government not act unfairly or arbitrarily. In other words, the government cannot rely on individual judgment and impulse when making decisions, but must stay within the boundaries of reason and the law. Of course, disagreements as to the meaning of these provisions have plagued courts, politicians, and citizens since this nation was founded, and will undoubtedly continue to do so.

To understand due process, it is important to consider its two types: procedural due process and substantive due process.

LO 9 **PROCEDURAL DUE PROCESS** According to **procedural due process,** the law must be carried out by a *method* that is fair and orderly. It requires that certain procedures be followed in administering and executing a law so that an individual's basic freedoms are never violated.

For example, Hank Skinner, currently residing on Texas's death row for committing a triple murder in 1993, believes new DNA testing of evidence from the crime scene will prove his innocence (see the photo below). Texas officials, however, refused to allow the tests, saying that Skinner's defense attorneys did not file a proper request. Skinner then sued the state, claiming that it is only fair that he be given every chance to prove his innocence. In 2011, the United States Supreme Court gave Skinner a partial victory on procedural due process grounds. The Court ruled that Skinner and other inmates did have the right to bring lawsuits demanding DNA testing of evidence relevant to their cases. At the same time, the justices cautioned that there can be no guarantees that the inmates will win these suits, as the outcome will depend on the circumstances of each case.[67]

SUBSTANTIVE DUE PROCESS Fair procedures would obviously be of little use if they were used to administer unfair laws. For example, suppose a law requires everyone to wear a red shirt on Mondays. You wear a blue shirt on Monday, and you are arrested, convicted, and sentenced to one year in prison. The fact that all proper procedures were followed and your rights were given their proper protections would mean very little because the law that you broke was unfair and arbitrary.

Thus, **substantive due process** requires that the laws themselves be reasonable. The idea is that if a law is unfair or arbitrary, even if properly passed by a legislature, it must be declared unconstitutional. In the 1930s, for example, Oklahoma instituted the Habitual Criminal Sterilization Act. Under this statute, a person who had been convicted of three felonies could be "rendered sexually sterile" by the state (that is, the person would no longer be able to produce children). The United States Supreme Court held that the law was unconstitutional, as there are "limits to the extent which a legislatively represented majority may conduct biological experiments at the expense of the dignity and personality and natural powers of a minority."[68]

Teaching Tip: To reinforce the differences between procedural due process and substantive due process, ask students to complete a written assignment in which they define the two terms. Then, have students identify an issue which serves as an example of each form of due process. (LO 8)

Due Process Clause The provisions of the Fifth and Fourteenth Amendments to the Constitution that guarantee that no person shall be deprived of life, liberty, or property without due process of law. Similar clauses are found in most state constitutions.

Procedural Due Process A provision in the Constitution that states that the law must be carried out in a fair and orderly manner.

Substantive Due Process The constitutional requirement that laws used in accusing and convicting persons of crimes must be fair.

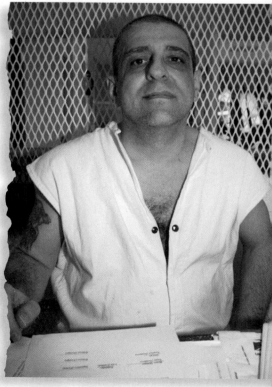

Why did Hank Skinner, shown here in a West Livingston prison, believe that his procedural due process rights were being violated by the state of Texas?

AP Photo/Michael Graczyk

CAREERS IN CJ

ELLEN KALAMA CLARK
SUPERIOR COURT JUDGE

I was an attorney in private practice when I was asked to serve as a Court Commissioner *pro tem.* I did that for a few years, then was appointed as a full-time court commissioner and did that for six years. (Court commissioners in Washington are judicial officers who handle only certain types of cases, such as juvenile and family law.) I thought becoming a trial judge would be an interesting challenge, and I especially wanted to be able to handle trials, jury trials, and criminal matters.

COURTROOM DECORUM One thing about my job, it is never dull. Attorneys come up with some very interesting arguments. As for the cases and the parties, just when you think you've heard it all, something else comes in the door that you never, in a million years, could have made up. It is also great to see the system in action, and to be able to interact with jurors and learn about their perceptions of the criminal justice system. There are light moments, as well. When I took the bench, I was going to be a stickler for proper courtroom decorum, including NO CELL PHONES in the courtroom. On my first day, a cell phone started ringing. I gave a stern lecture about turning off all cell phones, and the ringing stopped, although I had not seen anyone in the courtroom make any suspicious movements. I felt pretty good about being in control, until my judicial assistant slipped me a note indicating that MY cell phone had rung, but not to worry because she had turned it off.

A GREAT SUCCESS STORY My favorite thing about my work is making a difference in people's lives. This is especially true in juvenile court, which is my favorite assignment. For example, early one morning I was walking to the juvenile court building when I saw a group of teenage boys heading toward me. Some of them I recognized from being in court, and they recognized me. A couple avoided eye contact, one looked me straight in the eye rather defiantly, and the last one kind of smirked. As we got closer to each other, the last boy—a tall, stocky kid—stopped, and the group just about blocked the sidewalk. It made me nervous. The boy then leaned forward toward me and said, not in an intimidating manner but certainly meaning to get my attention, "Hey, Judge." I said good morning. He then broke into a big smile and said, "I got my GED [general equivalency diploma]! And I'm staying out of trouble." I didn't remember his name or his offense, but I was absolutely thrilled that he had accomplished those things, that he would want me to know that, and that he was bragging about it in front of his friends. I consider this a great success story.

CAREER ADVICE There is not just one way to become a judge. I started as a *pro tem* commissioner, then a full-time commissioner, then a trial judge. Some other judges have come from lower courts to the superior courts. Some have come from positions as government attorneys (either prosecutor or defense) and others from private practice. No matter what path is taken, judicial officers do a lot of reading, writing, analyzing, and public speaking, so do things that will increase your skills in these areas. You also need to realize that, as a lawyer or judicial officer, you will primarily be dealing with people having some crisis in their lives, such as a facing a criminal charge or being a victim. Dealing with these folks takes patience, as well as the ability to set boundaries.

FAST FACTS

**JUDGE
JOB DESCRIPTION:**

- Preside over trials and hearings in federal, state, and local courts.
- Rule on the admissibility of evidence, monitor the testimony of witnesses, and settle disputes between prosecutors and defense attorneys
- When standard procedures do not already exist, judges establish new rules based on their own knowledge of the law.
- Ensure that all proceedings are fair and protect the legal rights of everyone involved.

WHAT KIND OF TRAINING IS REQUIRED?

- A law degree and several years of legal experience.
- Judges are either appointed or elected.
- Federal administrative law judges must pass examinations administered by the U.S. Office of Personnel Management.

ANNUAL SALARY RANGE?

- $93,000–$162,000

For additional information on a career as a trial judge, visit: **www.abanet.org/jd/ncstj.**

In 1944, during World War II, the U.S. Supreme Court upheld the federal government's ability to forcibly place Japanese Americans in internment camps, as shown here. The Court agreed that such a drastic step was necessary to prevent these citizens from spying on behalf of Japan. Why might the Court be more willing to infringe on due process protections in times of war or international conflict? Library of Congress

THE JUDICIAL SYSTEM'S ROLE IN DUE PROCESS As the last two examples suggest, the United States Supreme Court often plays the important role of ultimately deciding when due process has been violated and when it has not. Throughout this textbook, you will see how the Court has used due process principles numerous times to protect rights such as the right to a jury trial,[69] the right of the accused to confront witnesses at trial,[70] and the right to be free from cruel and unusual punishment,[71] among others.

The due process clause does not, however, automatically doom laws that may infringe on procedural or substantive rights. In certain circumstances, the lawmaking body may be able to prove that its interests are greater than the due process rights of the individual, and in those cases the statute may be upheld. Several years ago, for example, a U.S. appellate court upheld the immediate suspension of a kindergarten student who said "I'm going to shoot you" to classmates during recess. Although a school generally must follow certain steps before suspending a student, the court felt that in this instance the kindergarten's interest in limiting this kind of violent speech was more important than the student's due process rights.[72]

Critical Thinking Skill Development: Ask students to respond to "Questions for Critical Analysis" number five on page 129, in which they consider whether individual due process rights can be violated in a constitutionally acceptable manner under certain circumstances. (LO 9)

DUE PROCESS AND NATIONAL SECURITY The U.S. court system, including the Supreme Court, is often more likely to defer to the government in times of national crisis. The Court was powerless in 1861, when President Abraham Lincoln suspended certain constitutional guarantees against arbitrary arrest.[73] During World War II, in perhaps its most widely criticized decision of the twentieth century, the Court gave its approval to the federal government's rounding up of Japanese American citizens and confining them in "relocation" camps (see the photo above).[74] At the same time, thousands of Italian Americans and German Americans were also interned.

Similarly, the controversies concerning the anti-terrorism strategies that we will discuss in this textbook have their basis in due process concerns. Law enforcement officials at all levels of government have been faced with the difficult task of striking the proper balance between the due process rights of suspected terrorists and the need to protect the public. Some observers feel that the federal government, in particular, has overstepped the bounds of the Constitution by limiting access to counsel, the right to trial, and a number of other due process rights. The feature *Anti-Terrorism in Action—Rights or Wrong?* below provides an introduction to the crucial issue of balancing national security and individual freedoms, which will be discussed throughout the textbook and covered extensively in Chapter 16.

SELFASSESSMENT

Fill in the blanks and check your answers on page 128.

The basis for procedural safeguards for the accused is found in the _____ _____ _____ of the U.S. Constitution. According to these safeguards, no person shall be deprived of life or liberty without _____ _____ (due process) of law. This means that the _____ by which the law is carried out must be fair and orderly and the laws themselves must be _____. The _____ _____ _____ _____ ultimately decides whether these rights have been violated.

ANTI-TERRORISM IN ACTION

RIGHTS OR WRONG?

On March 23, 2003, Abdullah al-Kidd, a U.S. citizen and former college football player, was arrested at Dulles International Airport in Washington, D.C., before he could board a flight to Saudi Arabia. Al-Kidd was strip-searched and shackled, and spent the next two weeks detained in federal prisons in Idaho, Oklahoma, and Virginia. At times, he was left naked and shivering, taunted by corrections officials and fellow inmates alike. Then, as quickly as he had been apprehended, he was released without ever being charged with any criminal wrongdoing.

The Material Witness Law

As you have seen, the due process clause of the U.S. Constitution states that no person may be deprived of "life, liberty, or property" without the government taking certain steps to ensure fairness. Nonetheless, al-Kidd was deprived of his liberty for two weeks even though there was no proof that he had committed a crime. (The trip to Saudi Arabia was for study.) He was not allowed a lawyer, nor was he given any indication as to why he was being detained. How is this possible?

In the aftermath of the September 11, 2001, terrorist attacks, federal law enforcement agents arrested nearly seventy terrorist suspects, almost all of them Muslims such as al-Kidd, under the federal *material witness* law. This law is designed to allow the government to detain individuals who have witnessed, though not necessarily participated in, crimes so that they can testify at trial. In al-Kidd's case, federal agents had connected him to Sami Omar al-Hussayen, whom they were investigating on computer terrorism charges. Al-Kidd was never asked to testify, however, and al-Hussayen was never convicted. It seemed obvious, in retrospect, that al-Kidd was held as a material witness because officials could think of no other way to arrest him, given his lack of criminal wrongdoing.

FOR CRITICAL ANALYSIS Abdullah al-Kidd eventually sued the federal government for violating his rights, and in 2011 his case reached the United States Supreme Court. During oral arguments, a government lawyer admitted that "certain individuals will be harmed" by this use of the material witness law, but contended that such aggressive measures were necessary to ensure homeland security. What is your opinion of this argument? Should certain suspects be afforded fewer—or no—due process rights because of the great danger posed by terrorism?

CJ IN ACTION

HATE CRIME LAWS

During nineteen-year-old Jeffrey Conroy's trial for fatally stabbing Ecuadoran immigrant Marcelo Lucero, New York district attorney Megan O'Donnell spent nearly as much time describing Conroy's racism as she spent on the crime itself. Conroy and his friends did not go to the Long Island village of Patchogue for a "party," she told the jury. Instead, "they were looking for blood—specifically, Mexican blood."[75] O'Donnell also focused on evidence pointing to Conroy's white supremacist beliefs, particularly his Nazi swastika tattoo. As a result, in the spring of 2010, Conroy was convicted of manslaughter *as a hate crime* and given the maximum sentence of twenty-five years in prison. The philosophy behind hate crime legislation, which punishes the defendant not only for acts but also for motives, is the subject of this chapter's *CJ in Action* feature.

PUNISHING BIAS

Nearly every state and the federal government have hate crime laws that, as noted earlier in the text, apply when the underlying crime is committed because of the victim's race, color, religion, ancestry, national origin, political affiliation, gender, sexual orientation, age, or disability. These laws are based on a model created by the Anti-Defamation League (ADL) in 1981. The ADL model was centered on the concept of "penalty enhancement": just as someone who robs a convenience store using a gun will face a greater penalty than if he or she had been unarmed, so will someone who commits a crime because of prejudice against her or his victim or victims.[76]

Critics of hate crime laws feel that such "penalty enhancements" rest on shaky legal grounds. It is one thing to prove that a robber used a gun, but it is another thing to prove what was in a defendant's mind. Furthermore, should evidence as seemingly irrelevant as Jeffrey Conroy's swastika tattoo have any bearing on how many years he spends behind bars? Despite these misgivings, the United States Supreme Court has upheld the constitutionality of hate crime laws as long as the prohibited motive (1) is specifically listed as an attendant circumstance (see page 112) in the legislation and (2) is proved beyond a reasonable doubt during the trial.[77]

THE CASE FOR HATE CRIME LAWS

- Hate crimes target groups, not just an individual—if one Hispanic person on Long Island is attacked, for example, then all Hispanics on Long Island suffer intimidation and fear. Thus, such acts need to be punished more harshly.

- Historically, the groups listed in hate crime legislation have received inadequate protection from the American criminal justice system. Hate crime laws redress these shortcomings.

- Hate crime laws do not punish a defendant's speech or beliefs, which are protected by the U.S. Constitution. Rather, they allow jurors to learn whether the defendant's speech or beliefs were the reason for the choice of victim.

THE CASE AGAINST HATE CRIME LAWS

- Hate crime laws punish political views that, though unpopular and even appalling, are protected by the First Amendment, which states that the government shall make no law "abridging the freedom of speech."

- For the most part, motive is irrelevant in criminal law. Defendants are punished for what they did, not for why they did it.

- Hate crime laws indicate that some victims are worthy of more protection than others. It is unjust that Jeffrey Conroy might have received a lesser sentence if his victim had been white rather than Hispanic.[78]

Michael Lee/iStockphoto

WRITING ASSIGNMENT— YOUR OPINION

Harold, who is white, is at a party, and he is drunk. He sees Mary, his ex-girlfriend, talking with James, who is African American. Harold knows that Mary and James have been dating for several weeks. Harold shouts racial epithets at James and is thrown out of the party. Later that night, Harold stalks James and attacks him with a baseball bat.

Did Harold commit a hate crime deserving of a harsher penalty? How does this case influence your opinion of hate crime laws in general? Before responding, you can review our discussion in this chapter concerning

- The purposes of criminal law (pages 104–106)

- *Mens rea* and criminal acts (pages 108–110)

- Attendant circumstances (pages 112–113)

Your answer should include at least three full paragraphs.

CHAPTER SUMMARY

LO 1
Explain precedent and the importance of the doctrine of *stare decisis*. Precedent is a common law concept in which one decision becomes the example or authority for deciding future cases with similar facts. Under the doctrine of *stare decisis,* judges in a particular jurisdiction are bound to follow precedents of that same jurisdiction. The doctrine of *stare decisis* leads to efficiency in the judicial system.

LO 2
List the four written sources of American criminal law. (a) The U.S. Constitution and state constitutions; (b) statutes passed by Congress and state legislatures (plus local ordinances); (c) administrative agency regulations; and (d) case law.

LO 3
Explain the two basic functions of criminal law. The primary function is to protect citizens from harms to their safety and property and from harms to society's interest collectively. The second function is to maintain and teach social values as well as social boundaries—for example, speed limits and laws against bigamy.

LO 4
Delineate the elements required to establish *mens rea* (a guilty mental state). (a) Purpose, (b) knowledge, (c) negligence, or (d) recklessness.

LO 5
Explain how the doctrine of strict liability applies to criminal law. Strict liability crimes do not allow the alleged wrongdoer to claim ignorance or mistake to avoid criminal responsibility—for example, exceeding the speed limit and statutory rape.

LO 6
List and briefly define the most important excuse defenses for crimes. Insanity—different tests of insanity can be used, including (a) the *M'Naghten* rule (right-wrong test); (b) the ALI/MPC test, also known as the substantial-capacity test; and (c) the irresistible-impulse test. **Intoxication**—voluntary and involuntary, the latter being a possible criminal defense. **Mistake**—sometimes valid if the law was not published or reasonably known or if the alleged offender relied on an official statement of the law that was erroneous. Also, a mistake of fact may negate the mental state necessary to commit a crime.

LO 7
Describe the four most important justification criminal defenses. **Duress**—requires that (a) the threat is of serious bodily harm or death, (b) the harm is greater than that caused by the crime; (c) the threat is immediate and inescapable; and (d) the defendant became involved in the situation through no fault of his or her own. **Justifiable use of force**—the defense of one's person, dwelling, or property, or the prevention of a crime. **Necessity**—justifiable if the harm sought to be avoided is greater than that sought to be prevented by the law defining the offense charged. **Entrapment**—that the criminal action was induced by certain governmental persuasion or trickery.

LO 8
Distinguish between substantive and procedural criminal law. The former concerns questions about what acts are actually criminal. The latter concerns procedures designed to protect the constitutional rights of individuals and to prevent the arbitrary use of power by the government.

LO 9
Explain the importance of the due process clause in the criminal justice system. The due process clause acts to limit the power of government. In the criminal justice system, the due process clause requires that certain procedures be followed to ensure the fairness of criminal proceedings and that all criminal laws be reasonable and in the interest of the public good.

SELF ASSESSMENT ANSWER KEY

Page 100: i. common; **ii.** precedent; **iii.** *stare decisis*

Page 103: i. Constitution; **ii.** unconstitutional; **iii.** statutes; **iv.** case/judge-made/common

Page 106: i. legal; **ii.** criminal; **iii.** social; **iv.** morality

Page 113: i. *actus reus;* **ii.** *mens rea;* **iii.** concurrence; **iv.** strict liability; **v.** intent/*mens rea*/mental state; **vi.** Attendant; **vii.** beyond a reasonable doubt

Page 120: i. responsible; **ii.** insanity; **iii.** intoxication; **iv.** justified; **v.** duress; **vi.** self-defense; **vii.** Entrapment

Page 125: i. Bill of Rights; **ii.** due process; **iii.** procedures; **iv.** reasonable/fair; **v.** United States Supreme Court

KEY TERMS

actus reus   107
administrative law   103
attempt   108
attendant circumstances   112
ballot initiative   103
Bill of Rights   122
case law   103
common law   99
competency hearing   116
constitutional law   101
corpus delicti   107
due process clause   123
duress   118
duty to retreat   119

entrapment   120
felony-murder   111
hate crime law   113
inchoate offenses   113
infancy   114
insanity   114
intoxication   116
irresistible-impulse test   115
mens rea   108
M'Naghten rule   114
Model Penal Code   102
necessity   119
negligence   109
precedent   99

procedural criminal law   120
procedural due process   123
recklessness   109
self-defense   119
stare decisis   100
statutory law   101
statutory rape   111
strict liability crimes   110
substantial-capacity test
    (ALI/MPC test)   115
substantive criminal law   120
substantive due process   123

QUESTIONS FOR CRITICAL ANALYSIS

1. Give an example of a criminal law whose main purpose seems to be teaching societal boundaries rather than protecting citizens from harm. By searching the Internet, can you find examples of other countries where this behavior is *not* considered criminal? How is the behavior perceived in those countries?

2. Keith lends his car to Jermaine, who drives with two other friends to the home of a marijuana dealer. The three men break into the home, intending to steal a safe full of cash. The drug dealer is unexpectedly at home, however, and in a struggle Jermaine winds up murdering him. What rule allows local prosecutors to charge Keith with first degree murder? Why?

3. Sylvia escapes from a mental hospital in Cheyenne, Wyoming, and murders Richard, the first person she sees, with a knife. When she is apprehended by the police, she claims that Richard was a space alien and that it was her duty, as an earthling, to kill him. What defenses are available to Sylvia when she goes to trial? What are the chances that these defenses will succeed?

4. Critics have derogatorily labeled the "stand your ground laws" passed by Florida and many other states (see page 119) "license to kill" laws. Why would they do so? What is your opinion of these laws?

5. Suppose that Louisiana's legislature passes a law allowing law enforcement officers to forcibly remove residents from their homes in the face of an imminent hurricane. Why might a court uphold this law even though, in most circumstances, such forcible removal would violate the residents' due process rights? If you were a judge, would you uphold Louisiana's new law?

CourseMate *For Online Help*

NOTES

1. Quoted in DeeDee Correll, "Sweat Lodge Guru Is Held in Three Deaths," *Los Angeles Times* (February 4, 2010), 1.

2. Arizona Revised Statutes Section 31-1102(A).

3. Roger LeRoy Miller and Gaylord A. Jentz, *Business Law Today, Comprehensive Edition*, 7th ed. (Cincinnati, OH: South-Western, 2007), 2–3.

4. *Neff v. George*, 364 Ill. 306, 4 N.E.2d 388, 390, 391 (1936).

5. *Texas v. Johnson*, 491 U.S. 397 (1989).

6. Joshua Dressler, *Understanding Criminal Law*, 2d ed. (New York: Richard D. Irwin, 1995), 22–23.

7. *Ibid.*, 23.

8. Oklahoma Statutes Section 211771 (2008).

9. Jim Yardley, "Unmarried and Living Together, Till the Sheriff Do Us Part," *New York Times* (March 25, 2000), A7.

10. "Arizona Voters OK Medical-Marijuana Bill," *Boston Globe* (November 15, 2010), 2.

11. Clean Water Act Section 309, 33 U.S.C.A. Section 1319 (1987).

12. Joel Feinberg, *The Moral Limits of the Criminal Law: Harm to Others* (New York: Oxford University Press, 1984), 221–232.

13. Flammable Fabrics Act, 15 U.S.C. Section 1196 (1994).

14. Stuart P. Green, "Why It's a Crime to Tear the Tag Off a Mattress," *Emory Law Journal* 46 (Fall 1997), 1533–1614.

15. Henry M. Hart, Jr., "The Aims of the Criminal Law," *Law & Contemporary Problems* 23 (1958), 405–406.

16. John L. Diamond, "The Myth of Morality and Fault in Criminal Law Doctrine," *American Criminal Law Review* 34 (Fall 1996), 111.

17. Lawrence M. Friedman, *Crime and Punishments in American History* (New York: Basic Books, 1993), 34.

18. *Ibid.*, 10.

19. Thomas A. Mullen, "Rule without Reason: Requiring Independent Proof of the *Corpus Delicti* as a Condition of Admitting Extrajudicial Confession," *University of San Francisco Law Review* 27 (1993), 385.

20. *Hawkins v. State*, 219 Ind. 116, 129, 37 N.E.2d 79 (1941).

21. David C. Biggs, "'The Good Samaritan Is Packing': An Overview of the Broadened Duty to Aid Your Fellowman, with the Modern Desire to Possess Concealed Weapons," *University of Dayton Law Review* 22 (Winter 1997), 225.

22. Terry Halbert and Elaine Ingulli, *Law and Ethics in the Business Environment*, 6th ed. (Mason, OH: South-Western Cengage Learning, 2009), 8.

23. Model Penal Code Section 2.02.

24. Texas Penal Code Section 46.13 (1995).

25. Model Penal Code Section 2.02(c).

26. *Black's Law Dictionary*, 1423.

27. *United States v. Dotterweich*, 320 U.S. 277 (1943).

28. New Jersey Statutes Annotated Section 2C:35-9 (West 2004).

29. *State v. Stiffler*, 763 P.2d 308, 311 (Idaho Ct.App. 1988).

30. *State v. Harrison*, 425 A.2d 111 (1979).

31. Richard G. Singer and John Q. LaFond, *Criminal Law: Examples and Explanations* (New York: Aspen Law & Business, 1997), 322.

32. *State v. Linscott*, 520 A.2d 1067 (1987).

33. Adam Liptak, "Serving Life for Providing Car to Killers," *New York Times* (December 4, 2007), A1.

34. *Morissette v. United States*, 342 U.S. 246, 251–252 (1952).

35. Federal Bank Robbery Act, 18 U.S.C.A. Section 2113.

36. *In re Winship*, 397 U.S. 358, 364, 368–369 (1970).

37. Portland (Oregon) City Code, 14.32.010(C).

38. *Oregon v. Andrews*, 27 P.3d 137 (Or.Ct.App. 2001).

39. *United States v. Jiminez Recio*, 537 U.S. 270 (2003).

40. Paul H. Robinson, *Criminal Law Defenses* (St. Paul, MN: West, 2008), Section 173, Ch. 5Bl.

41. *M'Naghten's* Case, 10 Cl.&F. 200, Eng.Rep. 718 (1843). Note that the name is also spelled M'Naughten and McNaughten.

42. Model Penal Code Section 401 (1952).

43. Joshua Dressler, *Cases and Materials on Criminal Law*, 2d ed. (St. Paul, MN: West Group, 1999), 599.

44. Stephen Lally, "Making Sense of the Insanity Plea," *Washington Post Weekly Edition* (December 1, 1997), 23.

45. Bruce J. Winick, "Presumptions and Burdens of Proof in Determining Competency to Stand Trial: An Analysis of *Medina v. California* and the Supreme Court's New Due Process Methodology in Criminal Cases," *University of Miami Law Review* 47 (1993), 817.

46. South Carolina Code Annotated Section 17-24-20(A) (Law. Co-op. Supp. 1997).

47. Lawrence P. Tiffany and Mary Tiffany, "Nosologic Objections to the Criminal Defense of Pathological Intoxication: What Do the Doubters Doubt?" *International Journal of Law and Psychiatry* 13 (1990), 49.

48. 518 U.S. 37 (1996).

49. Montana Code Annotated Section 45-5-102 (1997).

50. Montana Code Annotated Section 45-2-203 (1997).

51. Kenneth W. Simons, "Mistake and Impossibility, Law and Fact, and Culpability: A Speculative Essay," *Journal of Criminal Law and Criminology* 81 (1990), 447.

52. *United States v. Robinson*, 119 F.3d 1205 (5th Cir. 1997).

53. *Lambert v. California*, 335 U.S. 225 (1957).

54. Federal Bureau of Investigation, *Crime in the United States*, 2010 (Washington, D.C.: U.S. Department of Justice, 2011), at **www.fbi.gov/about-us/cjis/ucr/crime-in-the-u.s/2010/crime-in-the-u.s.-2010/tables/10shrtbl14.xls**, and **www.fbi.gov/about-us/cjis/ucr/crime-in-the-u.s/2010/crime-in-the-u.s.-2010/tables/10shrtbl15.xls**.

55. Craig L. Carr, "Duress and Criminal Responsibility," *Law and Philosophy* 10 (1990), 161.

56. *United States v. May*, 727 F.2d 764 (1984).

57. *United States v. Contento-Pachon*, 723 F.2d 691 (1984).

58. *People v. Murillo*, 587 N.E.2d 1199, 1204 (Ill. App.Ct. 1992).

59. Florida Statutes Section 776.03 (2005).

60. *Ibid.*

61. Model Penal Code Section 3.02.

62. John Frank, "Hit-Run Driver Acquitted," *St. Petersburg (Fla.) Times* (February 4, 2009), 1B.

63. *People v. Petro*, 56 P.2d 984 (Cal.Ct.App. 1936); and *Regina v. Dudley and Stephens*, 14 Q.B.D. 173 (1884).

64. 287 U.S. 435 (1932).

65. Kenneth M. Lord, "Entrapment and Due Process: Moving toward a Dual System of Defenses," *Florida State University Law Review* 25 (Spring 1998), 463.

66. Henry J. Abraham, *Freedom and the Court: Civil Liberties in the United States*, 7th ed. (New York: Oxford University Press, 1998), 38–41.

67. *Skinner v. Switzer*, 131 S.Ct. 1289 (2011).

68. *Skinner v. Oklahoma*, 316 U.S. 535, 546–547 (1942).

69. *Duncan v. Louisiana*, 391 U.S. 145 (1968).

70. *Pointer v. Texas*, 380 U.S. 400 (1965).

71. *Robinson v. California*, 370 U.S. 660 (1962).

72. "*S.G.V. Sayreville Board of Education et al.*, No. 02-2384," *New Jersey Law Journal* (July 14, 2003), 139.

73. Alfred H. Kelley and Winfred A. Harbison, *The American Constitution: Its Origins and Developments*, 7th ed. (New York: Norton, 1991), 441–448.

74. *Korematsu v. United States*, 323 U.S. 214 (1944).

75. Quoted in Manny Fernandez, "Prosecutors Describe 'Hunt' for Hispanic Victim," *New York Times* (March 19, 2010), 18.

76. Steve M. Freeman, "Hate Crime Laws: Punishment Which Fits the Crime," *Annual Survey of American Law* 4 (1992/1993), 581–585.

77. *Wisconsin v. Mitchell*, 508 U.S. 476 (1993); and *Apprendi v. New Jersey*, 530 U.S. 466 (2000).

78. Richard Cohen, "When Thought Becomes a Crime," *Washington Post* (October 19, 2010), at **www.realclearpolitics.com/articles/2010/10/19/punish_crime_not_thought_107629.html**.

CHAPTER

5

Law Enforcement Today

Rod Lamkey Jr./AFP/Getty Images

LEARNING OBJECTIVES

After reading this chapter, you should be able to . . .

LO 1 List the four basic responsibilities of the police.

LO 2 Tell how the patronage system affected policing.

LO 3 Indicate the results of the Wickersham Commission.

LO 4 Explain how intelligence-led policing works and how it benefits modern police departments.

LO5 Identify the differences between the police academy and field training as learning tools for recruits.

LO 6 Describe the challenges facing women who choose law enforcement as a career.

LO 7 Indicate some of the most important law enforcement agencies under the control of the Department of Homeland Security.

LO 8 Identify the duties of the FBI.

LO 9 Analyze the importance of private security today.

The nine learning objectives labeled LO 1 through LO 9 are designed to help improve your understanding of the chapter.

"PRIMED, PREPARED, and PRECISE"

Over the course of twenty years in law enforcement, Feris Jones had not once fired her gun in the line of duty. Then, on the evening of October 23, 2010, Winston Cox burst into Sabine's Hallway Beauty Salon, where the fifty-year-old New York police officer was getting her hair done. Brandishing a .44-caliber revolver, Cox herded the four women present—including Jones—into a back bathroom. "This ain't no joke!" Cox shouted, as he collected the women's valuables in a black bag. "This is a robbery! I will kill you!"

When Cox returned to the main room of the Brooklyn salon, Jones decided to take action. She pulled out her Smith & Wesson five-shot pistol, told the other women to get down, and identified herself as a police officer. Cox responded by opening fire, which Jones returned in kind. At a distance of about twelve feet, all four of Cox's shots missed. Jones, thanks to hundreds of hours of training, had better results. Of her five rounds, two bullets struck Cox—one fracturing his right middle finger and another grazing his left hand—and a third shattered the salon doorknob, blocking a potential avenue of escape. The would-be robber finally did get free by kicking out a window, but police were easily able to track him down, thanks in part to the trail of blood he left behind.

Until the incident at the beauty salon, Jones had spent most of her time at the New York Police Department behind a desk. Following this display of bravery and marksmanship, however, she was promoted to the rank of detective. "Her quick thinking and sharp aim stopped an armed robbery, or worse," said New York mayor Michael Bloomberg at Jones's promotion ceremony. "She was primed, prepared, and precise." Afterward, a reporter asked Jones if she ordinarily took her weapon to a beauty salon. "I'm always armed," the newly minted detective said, with a smile.

New York police officer Feris Jones accepts congratulations for her promotion to the rank of detective. Several weeks earlier, Jones had foiled a robbery attempt at a Brooklyn beauty salon. AP Photo/Frank Franklin II

Teaching Tip: Before beginning the chapter, poll the class to see how many students intend to make policing a career after graduation. What attracts these students to the field of law enforcement?

O fficer Feris Jones certainly did not expect to find herself in a firefight when she went for a routine Saturday night haircut. She probably did not expect to become the focus of so much media attention either. Her promotion ceremony was broadcast live in New York City, and the story of the "Salon Hero's Brave Stand" was an Internet sensation. In many ways, though, the public's response to Detective Jones was not surprising at all. Police officers are the most visible representatives of our criminal justice system. Indeed, they symbolize the system for many Americans who may never see the inside of a courtroom or a prison cell. The police are entrusted with immense power to serve and protect the public good: the power to use weapons and the power to arrest. But that same power alarms many citizens, who fear that it may be turned arbitrarily against them. The role of the police is constantly debated as well. Is their primary mission to fight crime, or should they also be concerned with the social conditions that presumably lead to crime?

This chapter will lay the foundation for our study of law enforcement agents and the work that they do. It includes a short history of policing, followed by a discussion of police recruitment and an examination of the many different agencies that make up the law enforcement system. We will also look at the issues facing members of minority groups and women who choose to follow careers in policing, as well as the subject of private security. We start, however, by answering a basic—though hardly simple—question: What do police do?

THE RESPONSIBILITIES OF THE POLICE

As we begin our examination of police and policing, you should understand that the realities of law enforcement rarely match the depiction of the profession in the popular media. For the most part, the incidents that make up a police officer's daily routine would not make it on to television dramas such as the *CSI* series or *Hawaii Five-O*. Besides catching criminals, police spend a great deal of time on such mundane tasks as responding to noise complaints, confiscating firecrackers, and poring over paperwork. Sociologist Egon Bittner warned against the tendency to see the police primarily as agents of law enforcement and crime control. A more inclusive accounting of "what the police do," Bittner believed, would recognize that they provide "situationally justified force in society."[1] In other words, the function of the police is to solve any problem that may *possibly*, though not *necessarily*, require the use of force.

Within Bittner's rather broad definition of "what the police do," we can pinpoint four basic responsibilities of the police:

LO 1
1. To enforce laws.
2. To provide services.
3. To prevent crime.
4. To preserve the peace.

As will become evident over the next two chapters, there is a great deal of debate among legal and other scholars and law enforcement officers over which responsibilities deserve the most police attention and what methods should be employed by the police in meeting those responsibilities.

Critical Thinking Skill Development: In small groups, have students respond to "Questions for Critical Analysis" number one on page 165, in which they consider the responsibilities of the police. (LO 1)

ENFORCING LAWS

In the public mind, the primary role of the police is to enforce society's laws—hence, the term *law enforcement officer*. In their role as "crime fighters," police officers have a clear mandate to seek out and apprehend those who have violated the law. The crime-fighting responsibility is so dominant that all police activity—from the purchase of new automobiles to a plan to hire more minority officers—must often be justified in terms of its law enforcement value.[2]

Police officers also see themselves primarily as crime fighters, or "crook catchers," a perception that often leads people into what they believe will be an exciting career in law enforcement. Although the job certainly offers challenges unlike any other, police officers normally do not spend the majority of their time in law enforcement duties. After surveying a year's worth of dispatch data from the Wilmington (Delaware) Police Department, researchers Jack Greene and Carl Klockars found that officers spent only about half of their time enforcing the law or dealing with crimes. The rest of their time was spent on order maintenance, service provision, traffic patrol, and medical assistance.[3] Furthermore, information provided by the Uniform Crime Report shows that most arrests are made for "crimes of disorder" or public annoyances rather than violent or property crimes.[4] In 2010, for example, police made nearly 11 million arrests for drunkenness, liquor law violations, disorderly conduct, vagrancy, loitering, and other minor offenses, but only about 550,000 arrests for violent crimes.[5] (In Indonesia, some government officials have taken the concept of "crimes of disorder" to extremes, as described in the feature *Comparative Criminal Justice—Morality Police* below.)

PROVIDING SERVICES

The popular emphasis on crime fighting and law enforcement tends to overshadow the fact that a great deal of a police officer's time is spent providing services for the community. The motto "To Serve and Protect" has been adopted by thousands of local police departments, and the *Law Enforcement Code of Ethics* recognizes the duty "to serve the community" in its first sentence.[6] The services that police provide are numerous—a partial list would include directing traffic, performing emergency medical procedures, counseling those involved in domestic disputes, providing directions to tourists, and finding lost children.

Along with firefighters, police officers are among the first public servants called to conduct search and rescue operations. This particular duty adds considerably to the dangers faced by law enforcement agents. For example, in June 2010 deputy Eddie Wotipka of the Harris County (Texas) Sheriff's Department accidentally drowned after responding to a call to rescue a dog that had fallen into a canal. As we will see in the next section, a majority of police departments have adopted a strategy called *community policing* that requires officers to provide assistance in areas that have not been their domain until recently.[7] Along these lines, police are expected to deal with the problems of the homeless and the mentally ill to a greater extent than in past decades.

PREVENTING CRIME

Perhaps the most controversial responsibility of the police is to *prevent* crime, terrorist related or otherwise. According to Jerome Skolnick, co-director of the Center for Research in Crime and Justice at the New York University School of Law, there are

COMPARATIVE CRIMINAL JUSTICE

MORALITY POLICE

In Chapter 1, we saw that France recently took steps to keep women from wearing head scarves. In some Muslim nations, governments have the opposite concern: how to *force* women to do so. Officials in the small province of Aceh, located on the northern tip of the Indonesian island of Sumatra, have addressed this problem by forming the *Wilayatul Hisbah*. Consisting of 6,300 agents, this special "virtue and vice" squad is responsible for enforcing *sharia,* a code of law based on the religious tenets of Islam. These morality police not only reprimand women who do not properly cover themselves, but also discourage "overly sexual" forms of dress (such as tight jeans) and public displays of affection by unmarried couples.

Nur Aminah, a female officer who organizes patrols to ensure that Aceh men perform their required Friday prayers, feels that she is doing good by helping fellow Muslims follow God's laws. "If you don't follow guidance from the Holy Qur'an [the sacred writings of Islam], it will backfire on you," she says. Not everyone agrees. "It amazes me that in a modern world with sophisticated law and order, we would even consider doing this," says Norma Manalu, the director of Aceh's Human Rights Coalition. "It's barbaric," she adds.

FOR CRITICAL ANALYSIS

Under what circumstances, if any, do American law enforcement officers act as "morality police"? Can you think of any situations in which American law enforcement officers *should* act as morality police, but do not? Explain.

two predictable public responses when crime rates begin to rise in a community. The first is to punish convicted criminals with stricter laws and more severe penalties. The second is to demand that the police "do something" to prevent crimes from occurring in the first place. Is it, in fact, possible for the police to "prevent" crimes? The strongest response that Professor Skolnick is willing to give to this question is "maybe."[8]

On a limited basis, police can certainly prevent some crimes. If a rapist is dissuaded from attacking a solitary woman because a patrol car is cruising the area, then the police officer behind the wheel has prevented a crime. Furthermore, exemplary police work can have a measurable effect. The nation's two largest cities—New York and Los Angeles—have both experienced sharp declines in crime in recent years, a trend many attribute in large part to aggressive and innovative law enforcement.[9] In general, however, the deterrent effects of police presence are unclear. Carl Klockars has written that the "war on crime" is a war that the police cannot win because they cannot control the factors—such as unemployment, poverty, immorality, inequality, political change, and lack of educational opportunities—that contribute to criminal behavior in the first place.[10]

Local and state law enforcement officers consider the best way to get a young bull moose off the grounds of a motel in Fargo, North Dakota. What are the drawbacks and benefits of having police officers provide services to the community that have little to do with fighting crime?
AP Photo/The Forum, Michael Vosburg

PRESERVING THE PEACE

To a certain extent, the fourth responsibility of the police, that of preserving the peace, is related to preventing crime. Police have the legal authority to use the power of arrest, or even force, in situations in which no crime has yet occurred, but might occur in the immediate future.

In the words of James Q. Wilson, the police's peacekeeping role (which Wilson believes is the most important role of law enforcement officers) often takes on a pattern of simply "handling the situation."[11] For example, when police officers arrive on the scene of a loud late-night house party, they may feel the need to disperse the party and even arrest some of the partygoers for disorderly conduct. By their actions, the officers have lessened the chances of serious and violent crimes taking place later in the evening. The same principle is often used when dealing with domestic disputes, which, if escalated, can lead to homicide. Such situations are in need of, to use Wilson's terminology again, "fixing up," and police can use the power of arrest, or threat, or coercion, or sympathy, to do just that.

The basis of Wilson and George Kelling's zero-tolerance theory is similar: street disorder—such as public drunkenness, urination, and loitering—signals to both law-abiding citizens and criminals that the law is not being enforced and therefore leads to more violent crime. Hence, if police preserve the peace and "crack down" on the minor crimes that make up street disorder, they will in fact be preventing serious crimes that would otherwise occur in the future.[12]

"That's the only thing that made me feel safe last night when I came home from work."

—Penny Baily, resident of Indianapolis, commenting on the police car patrolling her neighborhood

Teaching Tip: In a short written assignment, ask students to reflect on the link between preserving the peace and preventing crime. Do students believe that Wilson and Kelling's zero-tolerance theory is an effective crime prevention tactic?

Both the public and law enforcement officers themselves believe that the police's primary job is to _____ laws. A large and crucial part of policing, however, involves providing _____ such as directing traffic. The ability of the police to actually _____ crime is a matter of great debate, and some experts believe that the most important role of a police officer is to _____ the peace.

A SHORT HISTORY OF THE AMERICAN POLICE

> "Every society gets the kind of criminal it deserves. What is equally true is that every community gets the kind of law enforcement it insists on."
>
> —Robert Kennedy, U.S. attorney general (1964)

Although modern society relies on law enforcement officers to control and prevent crime, in the early days of this country police services had little to do with crime control. The policing efforts in the first American cities were directed toward controlling certain groups of people (mostly slaves and Native Americans), delivering goods, regulating activities such as buying and selling in the town market, maintaining health and sanitation, controlling gambling and vice, and managing livestock and other animals.[13] Furthermore, these police services were for the most part performed by volunteers, as a police force was an expensive proposition. Often, the volunteers were organized using the **night watch system,** brought over from England by colonists in the seventeenth century. Under this system, all physically fit males were required to offer their services to protect the community on a rotating nightly basis.[14]

Night Watch System An early form of American law enforcement in which volunteers patrolled their community from dusk to dawn to keep the peace.

THE EVOLUTION OF AMERICAN LAW ENFORCEMENT

The night watch system did not ask much of its volunteers, who were often required to do little more than loudly announce the time and the state of the weather. Furthermore, many citizens avoided their duties by hiring others to "go on watch" in their place, and those who did serve frequently spent their time on watch sleeping and drinking.[15] Eventually, as the populations of American cities grew in the late eighteenth and early nineteenth centuries, so did the need for public order and the willingness to devote public resources to the establishment of formal police forces. The night watch system was insufficient to meet these new demands, and its demise was inevitable.

Technology Tip: Ask students to go online and research the life of Sir Robert Peel and his contributions to American policing. Have them describe some of the ways in which the English roots of policing are still visible today.

EARLY POLICE DEPARTMENTS In 1829, the British home secretary Sir Robert "Bobbie" Peel took a dramatic step to organize law enforcement in London—then as now one of the largest cities in the Western world. He pushed the Metropolitan Police Act through Parliament, forming the London Metropolitan Police. One thousand strong at first, the members of this police force were easily recognizable in their uniforms that featured blue coats and top hats. Under Peel's direction, the "bobbies," as the police were called in honor of their founder, did not carry any firearms and were assigned to specific areas, or "beats," to prevent crime. Peel also believed that the police should be organized along military lines under the control of local, elected officials.[16]

London's police operation was so successful that it was soon imitated in smaller towns throughout England and, eventually, in the United States. In 1833, Philadelphia became the first city to employ both day and night watchmen. Five years later, working from Peel's model, Boston formed the first organized police department, consisting of six full-time officers. In 1844, New York City laid the foundation for the modern police department by combining its day and night watches under the control of a single police chief. By the onset of the Civil War in 1861, a number of American cities, including Baltimore, Boston, Chicago, Cincinnati, New Orleans, and Philadelphia, had similarly consolidated police departments, modeled on the Metropolitan Police of London.[17]

THE POLITICAL ERA Like their modern counterparts, many early police officers were hard working, honest, and devoted to serving and protecting the public. On the whole, however, in the words of historian Samuel Walker, "The quality of American police service in the nineteenth century could hardly have been worse."[18] This poor quality can be attributed to the fact that the recruitment and promotion of police officers were intricately tied to the politics of the day. Police officers received their jobs as a result of political connections, not because of any particular skills or knowledge. Whichever political party was in power in a given city would hire its own cronies to run the police department. Consequently, the police were often more concerned with serving the interests of the political powers than with protecting the citizens.[19]

Corruption was rampant during this *political era* of policing, which lasted roughly from 1840 to 1930. Police salaries were relatively low, and many police officers saw their positions as opportunities to make extra income through any number of illegal activities. Bribery was common, as police would use their close proximity to the people to request

LO 2

"favors," which went into the police officers' own pockets or into the coffers of the local political party as "contributions."[20] This was known as the **patronage system,** or the "spoils system," because to the political victors went the spoils.

The political era also saw police officers take an active role in providing social services for their bosses' constituents. In many instances, this role even took precedence over law enforcement duties. Politicians realized that they could attract more votes by offering social services to citizens than by arresting them, and they required the police departments under their control to act accordingly.

THE REFORM ERA The abuses of the political era of policing did not go unnoticed. Nevertheless, it was not until 1929 that President Herbert Hoover appointed the national Commission on Law Observance and Enforcement to assess the American criminal justice system. The Wickersham Commission, named after its chairman, George Wickersham, focused on two areas of American policing that were in need of reform: (1) police brutality

LO 3

and (2) "the corrupting influence of politics." According to the commission, this reform should come about through higher personnel standards, centralized police administrations, and the increased use of technology.[21] Reformers of the time took the commission's findings as a call for the professionalization of American police and initiated the progressive (or *reform*) era in American policing.

Professionalism and Administrative Reforms Many of the Wickersham Commission's recommendations echoed the opinions of one of its contributors—August Vollmer, the police chief of Berkeley, California, from 1905 to 1932.[22] Along with his protégé O. W. Wilson, Vollmer promoted a style of policing known as the **professional model.** Under the professional model, police chiefs, who had been little more than figureheads during the political era, took more control over their departments. A key to these efforts was the

A horse-drawn police wagon used by the New York City Police Department, circa 1886. Why might this new form of transportation have represented a "revolution" for early American police forces?
Corbis/Bettmann

Patronage System A form of corruption in which the political party in power hires and promotes police officers, receiving job-related "favors" in return.

Professional Model A style of policing advocated by August Vollmer and O. W. Wilson that emphasizes centralized police organizations, increased use of technology, and a limitation of police discretion through regulations and guidelines.

Critical Thinking Skill Development: Have students consider the issues plaguing law enforcement during the political era of policing. What social issues can students identify which may have contributed to the corruption taking place during this era? (LO 2)

reorganization of police departments in many major cities. To improve their control over operations, police chiefs began to add midlevel positions to the force. These new officers, known as majors or assistant chiefs, could develop and implement crime-fighting strategies and more closely supervise individual officers. Police chiefs also tried to consolidate their power by bringing large areas of a city under their control so that no local ward, neighborhood, or politician could easily influence a single police department.

The professionalism trend benefited law enforcement agents in a number of ways. Salaries and working conditions improved, and for the first time, women and members of minority groups were given opportunities—albeit limited—to serve.[23] At the same time, police administrators controlled officers to a much greater extent than in the past, expecting them to meet targets for arrests and other numerical indicators that were seen as barometers of effectiveness. Any contact with citizens that did not explicitly relate to law enforcement was considered "social work" and discouraged.[24] As police expert Chris Braiden puts it, American police officers were expected to "park their brains at the door of the stationhouse" and simply "follow orders like a robot."[25] The isolation of officers from the public was made complete by an overreliance on the patrol car, a relatively new technological innovation at the time. In the political era, officers walked their beats, interacting with citizens. In the reform era, they were expected to stay inside their "rolling fortresses," driving from one call to the next without wasting time or resources on public relations.[26]

CJ&TECHNOLOGY High-Tech Cop Cars

Project 54: DuraTech USA Inc.

When patrol cars came into common use by police departments in the 1930s, they changed the face of American policing. Eight decades later, the technology associated with patrol cars continues to evolve. Project 54, a voice-recognition system developed at the University of New Hampshire, allows police officers to "multitask" without having to divert their attention from the road or take a hand off the wheel. The officer simply presses a button, and all the technological equipment in the car becomes voice activated. Four Andrea digital array microphones positioned in the cab of the automobile cancel all noise except the sound of the officer's voice. So, for example, if the officer witnesses a hit-and-run accident, he or she simply says the word "pursuit" to activate the automobile's siren and flashing lights. Then the officer can call for an ambulance and run a check on the suspect's license plate—all by voice command.

Other recent innovations include Automatic License Plate Recognition, a three-camera computer-operated system that performs a "20-millisecond" background check on every license plate it sees, and the StarChase launcher, a small, laser-guided cannon that shoots a small, sticky radio transmitter at a fleeing vehicle. Once the offending car has been "tagged" with this device, police can track the fugitive at a safe distance without the need for a dangerous, high-speed pursuit.

THINKING ABOUT POLICE AUTOMOBILE TECHNOLOGY

Approximately 75 percent of all patrol cars in the United States are equipped with on-board computers. How might these computers pose a danger to the police officer driving the car and to other drivers or pedestrians? How does the University of New Hampshire's Project 54 help alleviate this danger?

Turmoil in the 1960s and 1970s By the 1950s, America prided itself on having the most modern and professional police force in the world. As efficiency became the goal of the reform-era police chief, however, relations with the community suffered. Instead of being members of the community, police officers were now seen almost as intruders, patrolling the streets in the anonymity of their automobiles. The drawbacks of this perception—and of the professional model in general—became evident in the 1960s, one of the most turbulent decades in American history. The civil rights movement, though not inherently violent, intensified feelings of helplessness and impoverishment in African American communities. These frustrations resulted in civil unrest, and many major American cities experienced race riots in the middle years of the decade. Concurrently, America was experiencing rising crime rates and often violent protests against U.S. involvement in the war in Vietnam (1964-1975).

> **"He may be a very nice man. But I haven't got the time to figure that out. All I know is, he's got a uniform and a gun and I have to relate to him that way."**
>
> **—James Baldwin, American author (1971)**

By the early 1970s, many observers believed that poor policing was contributing to the national turmoil. The National Advisory Commission on Civil Disorders stated bluntly that poor relations between the police and African American communities were partly to blame for the violence that plagued many of those communities.[27] In striving for professionalism, the police appeared to have lost touch with the citizens they were supposed to be serving. To repair their damaged relations with a large segment of the population, police would have to rediscover their community roots.

THE COMMUNITY ERA The beginning of the *community era* may be traced to several government initiatives that took place in 1968. Of primary importance was the Omnibus Crime Control and Safe Streets Act, which was passed that year.[28] Under this act, the federal government provided state and local police departments with funds to create a wide variety of police-community programs. Most large-city police departments established entire units devoted to community relations, implementing programs that ranged from summer recreation activities for inner-city youths to "officer-friendly" referral operations that encouraged citizens to come to the police with their crime concerns.

In the 1970s, as this vital rethinking of the role of the police was taking place, the country was hit by a crime wave. Thus, police administrators were forced to combine efforts to improve community relations with aggressive and innovative crime-fighting strategies. As we will see in Chapter 6 when we discuss these strategies in more depth, the police began to focus on stopping crimes before they occur, rather than concentrating only on solving crimes that have already been committed. A dedication to such proactive strategies led to widespread acceptance of *community policing* in the 1980s and 1990s.

Community policing is based on the notion that meaningful interaction between officers and citizens will lead to a partnership in preventing and fighting crime.[29] Though the idea of involving members of the community in this manner is hardly new—a similar principle was set forth by Sir Robert Peel in the 1820s—community policing has had a major impact on the culture of American law enforcement by asking the average police officer to be a problem solver as well as a crime fighter.[30] (See Figure 5.1 on the following page for an overview of the three eras of policing described in this section.)

POLICING TODAY: INTELLIGENCE, TERRORISM, AND TECHNOLOGY

To effectively prevent crime using the community policing model, police administrators needed to better understand crime patterns. To better understand crime patterns, police

FIGURE 5.1 The Three Eras of American Policing

George L. Kelling and Mark H. Moore have separated the history of policing in the United States from 1840 to 2000 into three distinct periods. Below is a brief summarization of these three eras.

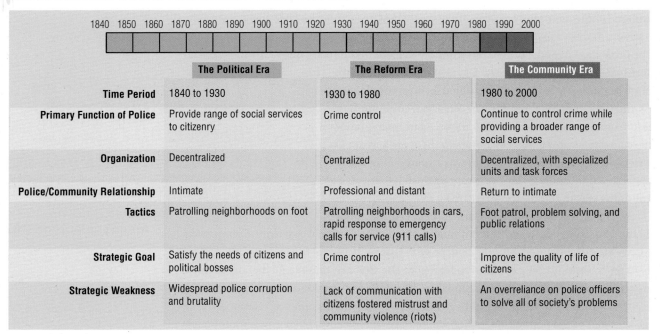

	The Political Era	The Reform Era	The Community Era
Time Period	1840 to 1930	1930 to 1980	1980 to 2000
Primary Function of Police	Provide range of social services to citizenry	Crime control	Continue to control crime while providing a broader range of social services
Organization	Decentralized	Centralized	Decentralized, with specialized units and task forces
Police/Community Relationship	Intimate	Professional and distant	Return to intimate
Tactics	Patrolling neighborhoods on foot	Patrolling neighborhoods in cars, rapid response to emergency calls for service (911 calls)	Foot patrol, problem solving, and public relations
Strategic Goal	Satisfy the needs of citizens and political bosses	Crime control	Improve the quality of life of citizens
Strategic Weakness	Widespread police corruption and brutality	Lack of communication with citizens fostered mistrust and community violence (riots)	An overreliance on police officers to solve all of society's problems

Sources: Adapted from George L. Kelling and Mark H. Moore, "From Political to Reform to Community: The Evolving Strategy of Police," in *Community Policing: Rhetoric or Reality,* ed. Jack R. Greene and Stephen D. Mastrofski (New York: Praeger Publishers, 1991), 14–15, 22–23; plus authors' updates. Reproduced with permission of Greenwood Publishing Group, Inc., Westport, Connecticut.

administrators needed more information about those patterns. As a result, the process of collecting, analyzing, and mapping such crime data has become a hallmark of policing in the twenty-first century.

INTELLIGENCE-LED POLICING "Humans are not nearly as random as we think," says Jeff Brantingham, an anthropologist at the University of California, Los Angeles. "In a sense, crime is just a physical process, and if you can explain how offenders move and how they mix with their victims, you can understand an incredible amount."[31] Brantingham and his colleagues are working on computer programs that will be able to predict when and where crimes are likely to occur. This approach is known as predictive policing, or intelligence-led policing, because it relies on data—or intelligence—concerning past crime patterns to predict future crime patterns.

LO 4

Intelligence-Led Policing
An approach that measures the risk of criminal behavior associated with certain individuals or locations so as to predict when and where such criminal behavior is most likely to occur in the future.

For example, suppose that a city has been plagued by random gunfire each New Year's Eve. In any given year, police administrators could determine where such incidents have occurred in previous years and send more police officers to those areas. In theory, the police would then be better able to deter random gunfire and respond more quickly when shots are fired.[32] This kind of intelligence-led policing should also help police administrators do "more with less," an important consideration as police budgets shrink around the country.[33] Thus, in this example, instead of blanketing the city with officers on New Year's Eve, police administrators would only need to deploy a small force in the areas most likely to experience gunfire.

Teaching Tip: In a short written assignment, ask students to define intelligence-led policing. What advantages does intelligence-led policing provide police agencies? (LO 4)

THE CHALLENGES OF ANTI-TERRORISM If the importance of intelligence-based policing was not evident before September 11, 2001, the tragic events of that day made it clear that the nation's law enforcement agencies could not simply react to the crime of terrorism. With such a high toll in human lives, such attacks needed to be prevented. Within two years of September 11, about 90 percent of the nation's local police departments and sheriff's offices serving large cities (250,000 residents or more) had written plans to deal with terrorist attacks.[34] Today, a similar percentage of these agencies are also gathering intelligence related to terrorism,[35] a task that represents a significant shift for the local law enforcement community. Police officers have traditionally been trained to gather evidence and solve crimes after they have been committed.

Counterterrorism, in contrast, involves a much more proactive approach. The transition has not always been smooth, as many local police administrators resent having to expend scarce resources on anti-terrorism instead of traditional crime fighting. In many ways, even though more than ten years have passed since September 11, 2001, law enforcement is still adjusting to the massive demands and challenges of homeland security. We will discuss these struggles, as well as numerous successes, in the chapter that follows and in Chapter 16. (See the feature *Anti-Terrorism in Action—Foreign Exchange* below to learn how advice from abroad is helping American law enforcement pass the tests of homeland security.)

Critical Thinking Skill Development: Working in small groups, ask students to discuss the ways in which law enforcement agencies have been required to adapt since September 11, 2001. How is terrorism prevention different from traditional policing?

ANTI-TERRORISM IN ACTION

FOREIGN EXCHANGE

Argus/Shutterstock

Like most law enforcement agents in the United States, the men and women of the Washington, D.C., Metropolitan Police Department's Special Operations Division had been trained to "shoot for the chest" when dealing with an armed suspect. The chest, after all, is the broadest part of the body and offers the best chance for single shot success. Now, Commander Cathy Lanier was telling them to aim for the head, because hitting the chest could detonate the explosives strapped to a suicide bomber's torso.

Lanier picked up this piece of hard-earned wisdom when, like thousands of other American law enforcement officials in recent years, she traveled to Israel—the "Harvard of anti-terrorism," in the words of U.S. Capitol police chief Terrance Gainer. Even though the crime rate in Israel is low compared with the United States, acts of terrorism are commonplace, thanks to a long-simmering land dispute with Palestine. Consequently, Israeli law enforcement agents are experts at dealing with suicide bombers and understanding the psychology of Islamic fundamentalism. They are also expert at interrupting the flow of information and explosives between terrorist cells, gathering intelligence, and other anti-terrorism strategies.

In addition to acting as host, Israel has sent many of its law enforcement agents to the United States to run anti-terrorism seminars. Much of what the Americans have learned in these exchanges is, like aiming for the head, counterintuitive to what they have been taught previously. For example, a bomb scene in the United States will be roped off for days to allow for evidence gathering, but in Israel the site is cleared as quickly as possible. "It is very important for [the Israelis to] get back to business as usual," noted Sterling P. Owen IV, chief of police in Knoxville, Tennessee. "They do not want their lives and businesses to be disrupted." "We've paid in blood for our experience," says Mickey Levy of the Jerusalem police, speaking of the damage caused by suicide bombers. "We don't want the American people or the American police to pay as we have."

FOR CRITICAL ANALYSIS Several years ago, officials of the Los Angeles Police Department (LAPD) decided to put some of the lessons learned from their Israeli counterparts to the test at the Emmy Awards ceremony. Using special devices that can detect explosives in clothing, officers checked everyone entering the event. At one point, an officer noticed four cylindrical tubes under the jacket of a man waiting to buy tickets. LAPD officers swooped in, pinned the man to the ground, and swept him away. The tubes turned out to be binoculars. How can this mistake serve as a cautionary tale for transferring Israeli anti-terrorism strategies to the United States?

LAW ENFORCEMENT 2.0 Fortunately, just as more intelligence has become crucial to police work, the means available to gather such intelligence have also increased greatly. As you will see in Chapter 16, nearly every successful anti-terrorism investigation has relied on information gathered from the Internet. More and more often, traditional criminals are also getting caught on the Web. In 2010, for example, Robert Lewis Crose, a fugitive who managed to evade California authorities for more than twelve years, was arrested in northern Montana after complaining about the cold weather there on his Facebook page. Indeed, more than 60 percent of American law enforcement agencies use social networking sites during crime investigations, and 40 percent also employ social media such as Twitter for community outreach and to notify the public of crime problems.[36]

As the leaders of the reform movement envisioned, technology also continues to improve the capabilities of officers in the field. As we saw earlier in this section, the modern police car is quickly evolving into a command center on wheels, and police officers also enjoy the use of mobile fingerprint readers, less lethal weapons such as laser beams (discussed in Chapter 6), and dozens of other technological innovations.

Some law enforcement veterans are concerned that the "art" of policing is being lost in an era of intelligence-led policing and increased reliance on technology. "If it becomes all about the science," says Los Angeles Police Department Deputy Chief Michael Downing, "I worry we'll lose the important nuances."[37] As the remainder of this chapter and the two that follow show, however, the human element continues to dominate all aspects of policing in America.

SELFASSESSMENT

Fill in the blanks and check your answers on page 164.

During the _____ era of American policing, which lasted roughly from 1840 to 1930, police officers used the _____ system to enrich themselves. The _____ era, which followed, saw the modernization of our nation's law enforcement system through innovations like Vollmer and Wilson's _____ model of policing. Following the national turmoil of the 1960s and early 1970s, _____ era strategies encouraged a partnership between citizens and the police. Today, _____-led policing efforts attempt to make law enforcement agencies more efficient and better able to prevent future _____ attacks.

RECRUITMENT AND TRAINING: BECOMING A POLICE OFFICER

In 1961, police expert James H. Chenoweth commented that the methods used to hire police officers had changed little since 1829 when the Metropolitan Police of London was created.[38] The past half-century, however, has seen a number of improvements in the way that police administrators handle the task of **recruitment,** or the development of a pool of qualified applicants from which to select new officers. Efforts have been made to diversify police rolls, and recruits in most police departments undergo a substantial array of tests and screens—discussed below—to determine their aptitude. Furthermore, annual starting salaries that can exceed $70,000, along with the opportunities offered by an interesting profession in the public service field, have attracted a wide variety of applicants to police work. (To learn what a police officer can expect to earn in his or her first year on the job, see Figure 5.2 on the facing page.)

Recruitment The process by which law enforcement agencies develop a pool of qualified applicants from which to select new members.

BASIC REQUIREMENTS

The selection process involves a number of steps, and each police department has a different method of choosing candidates. Most agencies, however, require at a minimum that a police officer:

- Be a U.S. citizen.
- Not have been convicted of a felony.
- Have or be eligible to have a driver's license in the state where the department is located.
- Be at least twenty-one years of age.
- Meet weight and eyesight requirements.

In addition, few departments will accept candidates older than forty-five years of age.

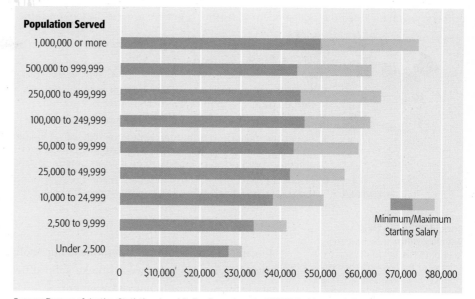

FIGURE 5.2 Average Annual Salary for Entry-Level Officers by Size of Population Served

Source: Bureau of Justice Statistics, *Local Police Departments, 2007* (Washington, D.C.: U.S. Department of Justice, December 2010), Table 7, page 12.

BACKGROUND CHECKS AND TESTS Beyond these minimum requirements, police departments usually engage in extensive background checks, including drug tests; a review of the applicant's educational, military, and driving records; credit checks; interviews with spouses, acquaintances, and previous employers; and a background search to determine whether the applicant has been convicted of any criminal acts.[39] Police agencies generally require certain physical attributes in applicants: normally, they must be able to pass a physical agility or fitness test. (For an example of one such test, see Figure 5.3 on the following page.)

In some departments, the applicant must take a polygraph (lie-detector) exam in conjunction with the background check. The results of the polygraph exam are often compared with the information from the background check to ensure that the applicant has not been deceptive. In addition, according to the International Association of Chiefs of Police, more than one-third of American police agencies now review an applicant's social media activity on sources such as Facebook, MySpace, and Twitter.[40] In one instance, the Middletown (New Jersey) Police Department rejected an applicant because he had posted photos of himself with "scantily clad women" online.

EDUCATIONAL REQUIREMENTS One of the most dramatic differences between today's police recruits and those of several generations ago is their level of education. In the 1920s, when August Vollmer began promoting the need for higher education in police officers, few had attended college. Today, 82 percent of all local police departments require at least a high school diploma, and 9 percent require a degree from a two-year college.[41] Recruits with college or university experience are generally thought to have an advantage in hiring and promotion.

Not all police observers believe that education is a necessity for police officers, however. In the words of one police officer, "effective street cops learn their skills on the

Technology Tip: Have students go online and locate at least one law enforcement agency currently hiring sworn officers. Have them record both the requirements and the starting salary for the position. If time allows, have students share their findings with the class.

The **Oakland Police Academy,** located in Auburn Hills, Michigan, is a full-service police training facility. To access its Web site, visit the *Criminal Justice CourseMate* at **cengagebrain.com** and select the *Web links* for this chapter.

FIGURE 5.3 Physical Agility Exam for the Henrico County (Virginia) Division of Police

Those applying for the position of police officer must finish this physical agility exam within 3 minutes, 30 seconds. During the test, applicants are required to wear the equipment (with a total weight of between 9 and 13 pounds) worn by patrol officers, which includes the police uniform, leather gun belt, firearm, baton, portable radio, and ballistics vest.

1. Applicant begins test seated in a police vehicle, door closed, seat belt fastened.
2. Applicant must exit vehicle and jump or climb a six-foot barrier.
3. Applicant then completes a one-quarter mile run or walk, making various turns along the way, to simulate a pursuit run.
4. Applicant must jump a simulated five-foot culvert/ditch.
5. Applicant must drag a "human simulator" (dummy) weighing 175 pounds a distance of 50 feet (to simulate a situation in which an officer is required to pull or carry an injured person to safety).
6. Applicant must draw his or her weapon and fire five rounds with the strong hand and five rounds with the weak hand.

Critical Thinking Skill Development: Ask students to debate the value of higher education for law enforcement officers. Should police agencies require a college degree? Why or why not?

job, not in a classroom."[42] By emphasizing a college degree, say some, police departments discourage those who would make solid officers but lack the education necessary to apply for positions in law enforcement.

TRAINING

Probationary Period A period of time at the beginning of a police officer's career during which she or he may be fired without cause.

Field Training The segment of a police recruit's training in which he or she is removed from the classroom and placed on the beat, under the supervision of a senior officer.

If an applicant successfully navigates the application process, he or she will be hired on a *probationary* basis. During this **probationary period,** which can last from six to eighteen months depending on the department, the recruit is in jeopardy of being fired without cause if he or she proves inadequate to the challenges of police work. Almost every state requires that police recruits pass through a training period while on probation. During this time, they are taught the basics of police work and are under constant supervision by superiors. The training period usually has two components: the police academy and field training. On average, local police departments serving populations of 250,000 or more require 1,648 hours of training—972 hours in the classroom and 676 hours in the field.[43]

LO 5

ACADEMY TRAINING The *police academy,* run by either the state or a police agency, provides recruits with a controlled, militarized environment in which they receive their introduction to the world of the police officer. They are taught the laws of search, seizure, arrest, and interrogation; how and when to use weapons; the procedures of securing a crime scene and interviewing witnesses; first aid; self-defense; and other essentials of police work. Nine in ten police academies also provide terrorism-related training to teach recruits how to respond to terrorist incidents, including those involving weapons of mass destruction.[44] Academy instructors evaluate the recruits' performance and send intermittent progress reports to police administrators.

A recruit performs pushups under duress at the Cleveland Police Academy. Why are police academies an important part of the learning process for a potential police officer? MARVIN FONG/*Cleveland Plain Dealer*/Landov

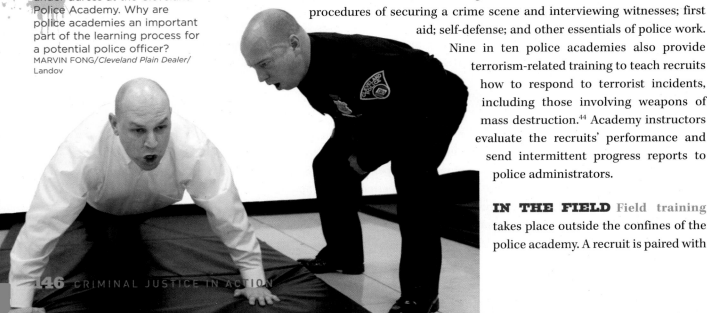

IN THE FIELD Field training takes place outside the confines of the police academy. A recruit is paired with

an experienced police officer known as a field training officer (FTO). The goal of field training is to help rookies apply the concepts they have learned in the academy "to the streets," with the FTO playing a supervisory role to make sure that nothing goes awry. According to many, the academy introduces recruits to the formal rules of police work, but field training gives the rookies their first taste of the informal rules. In fact, the initial advice to recruits from some FTOs is often along the lines of "O.K., kid. Forget everything you learned in the classroom. You're in the real world now." Nonetheless, the academy is a critical component in the learning process, as it provides rookies with a road map to the job.

Group Activities: If possible, take students on a field trip to a nearby police training academy. Tour the facility and learn more about the training requirements in your state. (LO 5)

SELFASSESSMENT

Fill in the blanks and check your answers on page 164.
Most police agencies require that recruits be at least _____-_____ years of age and have no prior _____ convictions. During the _____ period, which can last as long as eighteen months, a recruit will attend a _____ _____ to learn the rules of police work in an institutional setting. Then, she or he will leave the classroom and partner with an experienced officer for _____ _____.

WOMEN AND MINORITIES IN POLICING TODAY

For many years, the typical American police officer was white and male. As recently as 1968, African Americans represented only 5 percent of all sworn officers in the United States, and the percentage of "women in blue" was even lower.[45] Only within the past thirty years has this situation been addressed, and only within the past twenty years have many police departments actively tried to recruit women, African Americans, Hispanics, Asian Americans, and members of other minority groups. The result, as you will see, has been a steady though not spectacular increase in the diversity of the nation's police forces. When it comes to issues of gender, race, and ethnicity, however, mere statistics rarely tell the entire story.

Discussion Tip: Have students debate the concept that diverse police agencies offer improved community relations. Why is diversity a critical component for a successful police department?

ANTIDISCRIMINATION LAW AND AFFIRMATIVE ACTION

To a certain extent, external forces have driven law enforcement agencies to increase the number of female and minority recruits. The 1964 Civil Rights Act and its 1972 amendments guaranteed members of minority groups and women equal access to jobs in law enforcement, partly by establishing the Equal Employment Opportunity Commission (EEOC) to ensure fairness in hiring practices. The United States Supreme Court has also ruled on several occasions that discrimination by law enforcement agencies violates federal law.[46] In legal terms, discrimination occurs when hiring and promotion decisions are based on individual characteristics such as gender or race, and not on job-related factors.

CONSENT DECREES Since the early 1970s, numerous law enforcement agencies have instituted affirmative action programs to increase the diversity of their employees. These programs are designed to give women and members of minority groups certain advantages in hiring and promotion to remedy the effects of past discrimination and prevent future discrimination. Often, affirmative action programs are established voluntarily. Sometimes, however, they are the result of lawsuits brought by employees or

Discrimination The illegal use of characteristics such as gender or race by employers when making hiring or promotion decisions.
Affirmative Action A hiring or promotion policy favoring those groups, such as women, African Americans, or Hispanics, who have suffered from discrimination in the past or continue to suffer from discrimination.

potential employees who believe that the employer has discriminated against them. In such instances, if the court finds that discrimination did occur, it will implement a *consent decree* to remedy the situation. Under a consent decree, the law enforcement agency often agrees to meet certain numerical goals in hiring women and members of minority groups. If it fails to meet these goals, it is punished with a fine or some other sanction.[47]

RECRUITING CHALLENGES Over the past two decades, the EEOC has brought about two dozen discrimination lawsuits against local and state law enforcement agencies on behalf of wronged individuals. In almost every case, the agency agreed to resolve the problem through a consent decree.[48] As the Rochester (New York) Police Department (RPD) has learned, however, simply being willing to increase diversity in recruiting may not be enough. The RPD is operating under a voluntary consent decree that requires at least one in four new hires to come from a minority group. Despite an affirmative action program and a population of potential recruits that is 52 percent nonwhite, from 2005 to 2010 the RPD added only 21 members of minority groups to its force, out of a total of 186 new hires.[49]

In some instances, creative recruiting methods can bolster diversity. For example, Vermont's Step Up to Law Enforcement program provides women interested in law enforcement with a series of courses designed to make the application process less intimidating. The curriculum includes preparation for the physical and written exams, along with lectures on the challenges facing women police officers. In its first four years, twenty of the program's graduates were hired by local police departments or state correctional facilities.[50] Nonetheless, too often the "multiple hurdles" of the police recruiting process discourage or disqualify women and minorities despite efforts to attract them. In the *CJ in Action* feature at the end of this chapter, we will examine the controversial practice of lowering these hurdles to help diversify American police departments.

WORKING WOMEN: GENDER AND LAW ENFORCEMENT

In 1987, about 7.6 percent of all local police officers were women. Twenty years later, that percentage had risen to almost 12 percent.[51] That increase seems less impressive, however, when one considers that women make up more than half of the population of the United States, meaning that they are severely underrepresented in law enforcement.

ADDED SCRUTINY There are several reasons for the low levels of women serving as police officers. First, relatively few women hold leadership positions in American policing. More than half of this country's large police departments have no women in their highest ranks,[52] and fewer than 1 percent of the police chiefs in the United States

LO 6 are women.[53] Consequently, female police officers have few superiors who might be able to mentor them in what can be a hostile work environment. In addition to the dangers and pressures facing all law enforcement agents, which we will discuss in the next chapter, women must deal with an added layer of scrutiny. Many male police officers feel that their female counterparts are mentally soft, physically weak, and generally unsuited for the rigors of the job. At the same time, male officers often try to protect female officers by keeping them out of hazardous situations, thereby denying the women the opportunity to prove themselves.[54]

Women in law enforcement also face the problem of *tokenism,* or the belief that they have been hired or promoted to fulfill diversity requirements and have not earned their positions. Tokenism creates pressure to prove the stereotypes wrong. As one female officer told researcher Teresa Lynn Wertsch:

Technology Tip: Have student visit the Los Angeles Police Department (LAPD) online at **www.joinlapd. com**. What special efforts does the LAPD make to attract minority men and women to the field of policing?

Since the formation of the earliest police departments in the nineteenth century, policing has been seen as "man's work." Only men were considered to have the physical strength necessary to deal with the dangers of the street.

THE MYTH The perception that women are not physically strong enough to be effective law enforcement officers prevails both in the public mind and within police forces themselves. Criminologist Susan Martin has found that policewomen are under "constant pressure to demonstrate their competence and effectiveness vis-à-vis their male counterparts." One female police officer describes her experience:

> I got a call. They send another male officer and then another male officer. The attitude is—get a guy. I'm there with the one male officer and when the other guy shows up, the first male officer says to the second, this is right in front of me—"I'm glad you came."

THE REALITY As we saw at the opening of this chapter, female police officers such as Feris Jones of the New York Police Department are certainly capable of acts of bravery and physical prowess. In fact, a number of studies have shown that policewomen can be as effective as men in most situations, and often more so. Citizens appear to prefer dealing with a female police officer rather than a male during service calls—especially those that involve domestic violence. In general, policewomen are less aggressive and more likely to reduce the potential for a violent situation by relying on verbal skills rather than their authority as law enforcement agents. According to a study conducted by the National Center for Women and Policing, payouts in lawsuits for claims of brutality and misconduct involving male officers exceed those involving females by a ratio of 43 to 1.

FOR CRITICAL ANALYSIS Do you believe that female police officers can be just as effective as men in protecting citizens from criminal behavior? Why or why not?

A female member of the Los Angeles Police Department stands guard outside the county courthouse during a high-profile trial.
Kim Kulish/Corbis

The guys can view you as a sex object instead of a professional. It makes me try harder to put up more fronts and play more of the macho, boy role rather than accept that I am a female. . . . You can't be meek or mild, too quiet. You can't be too loud or boisterous because then you would be a dike, too masculine. I wish it didn't have to be this way, but you're either a bitch, a dike, or a slut.[55]

In fact, most of the negative attitudes toward women police officers are based on prejudice rather than actual experience. A number of studies have shown that there is very little difference between the performances of men and women in uniform.[56] (For more on this topic, see the feature *Myth versus Reality—Women Make Bad Cops* above.)

SEXUAL HARASSMENT The female officer quoted above observed that male officers see her as a "sex object." Anecdotal evidence suggests that this attitude is commonplace in police departments and often leads to **sexual harassment** of female police officers. Sexual harassment refers to a pattern of behavior that is sexual in nature, such as inappropriate touching or lewd jokes, and is unwelcome by its target.[57] Despite having to deal with problems such as sexual harassment, outdated stereotypes, and tokenism,

Discussion Tip: Ask student to work together in groups to discuss the challenges facing women in the field of law enforcement. Why do students feel women continue to be underrepresented as police officers? (LO 6)

Sexual Harassment A repeated pattern of unwelcome sexual advances and/or obscene remarks in the workplace. Under certain circumstances, sexual harassment is illegal and can be the basis for a civil lawsuit.

female police officers have generally shown that they are capable law enforcement officers, willing to take great risks if necessary to do their job. The names of more than 250 women are included on the National Law Enforcement Memorial in Washington, D.C., including 10 killed on duty in 2009 and 2010.[58]

MINORITY REPORT: RACE AND ETHNICITY IN LAW ENFORCEMENT

Critical Thinking Skill Development: Ask students to respond to "Questions for Critical Analysis" number three on page 165, in which they discuss the problem of double marginality.

As Figure 5.4 below shows, like women, members of minority groups have been slowly increasing their presence in local police departments since the late 1980s. Specifically, in 2007, African American officers comprised about 12 percent of the nation's police officers; Hispanic officers, about 10 percent; and other minority groups such as Asians, American Indians, and Pacific Islanders, about 3 percent.[59] By some measures, members of minority groups are better represented than women in policing. Cities such as Detroit and Washington have local police departments that closely match their civilian populations in terms of diversity, and in recent years, a majority of police recruits in New York City have been members of minority groups. In other areas, such as promotion, minorities in law enforcement continue to seek parity.[60]

Double Marginality The double suspicion that minority law enforcement officers face from their white colleagues and from members of the minority community to which they belong.

DOUBLE MARGINALITY According to Peter C. Moskos, a professor at the John Jay College of Criminal Justice in New York, "black and white police officers remain two distinct shades of blue, with distinct attitudes toward each other and the communities they serve."[61] While that may be true, minority officers generally report that they have good relationships with their white fellow officers.[62] Often, though, members of minority groups in law enforcement—particularly African Americans and Hispanics—do face the problem of double marginality. This term refers to a situation in which minority officers are viewed with suspicion by both sides:

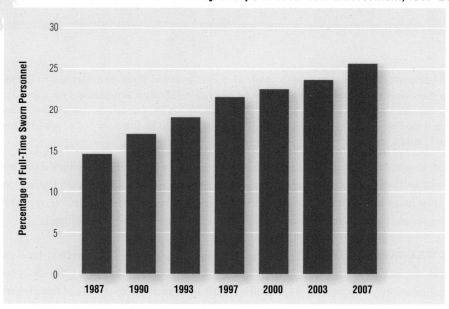

FIGURE 5.4 **Members of Minority Groups in Local Law Enforcement, 1987–2007**

Note: Includes blacks or African Americans, Hispanics or Latinos, Asians, Native Hawaiians or other Pacific Islanders, American Indians, Alaska Natives, and persons identifying two or more races.

Source: Bureau of Justice Statistics, *Local Police Departments, 2007* (Washington, D.C.: U.S. Department of Justice, December 2010), Figure 9, page 14.

1. White police officers believe that minority officers will give members of their own race or ethnicity better treatment on the streets.
2. Those same minority officers face hostility from members of their own community who are under the impression that black and Hispanic officers are traitors to their race or ethnicity.

In response, minority officers may feel the need to act more harshly toward minority offenders to prove that they are not biased in favor of their own racial or ethnic group.[63]

THE BENEFITS OF A DIVERSE POLICE FORCE In 1986, Supreme Court justice John Paul Stevens spoke for many in the criminal justice system when he observed that "an integrated police force could develop a better relationship [with a racially diverse citizenry] and therefore do a more effective job of maintaining law and order than a force composed of white officers."[64] Indeed, despite the effects of double marginality, African American officers may have more credibility in a predominantly black neighborhood than white police officers, leading to better community-police relations and a greater ability to solve and prevent crimes. Certainly, in the Mexican American communities typical of border states such as Arizona, Texas, and California, many Hispanic officers are able to gather information that would be very difficult for non-Spanish-speaking officers to collect. Finally, however, the best argument for a diverse police force is that members of minority groups represent a broad source of talent in this country, and such talent can only enhance the overall effectiveness of American law enforcement.

SELFASSESSMENT

Fill in the blanks and check your answers on page 164.
In the past, women and members of minority groups in law enforcement have suffered from _____, or hiring practices that exclude potential employees based on their gender, race, or ethnicity. To remedy this situation, many law enforcement agencies have instituted _____ _____ programs to diversify their workforces. In some instances, a court will issue a _____ _____, under which an agency agrees to reach certain numerical hiring goals or be penalized.

LAW ENFORCEMENT AGENCIES

On July 30, 2010, John McCluskey, Tracy Province, and Daniel Renwick escaped from a prison facility near Kingman, Arizona. Within a week, Renwick was apprehended after a shootout with a Rifle (Colorado) police officer. On August 9, federal U.S. Marshals and local law enforcement agents arrested Tracy Province outside a church in Meeteetse, Wyoming. Finally, on August 19, a team from the Apache County Sheriff's Office, the Arizona Department for Public Safety, and the U.S. Forest Service captured McCluskey at a campground in northeastern Arizona. Agents from the Federal Bureau of Investigation (FBI) and the U.S. Border Patrol also participated in the three-week manhunt, as did officers from state police agencies in Colorado, Montana, and Wyoming and dozens of local police and sheriff's departments.

As the nationwide search to recapture McCluskey, Province, and Renwick shows, Americans are served by a multitude of police organizations. Overall, there are about 11,400 law enforcement agencies in the United States, employing more than 577,000 people.[65] For the most part, these agencies operate on three different levels: local, state, and federal. Each level has its own set of responsibilities, which we shall discuss starting with local police departments.

Teaching Tip: If possible, invite a panel of law enforcement officers to visit the classroom. Include local, state, and federal officers, and let students compare and contrast their respective roles in fighting crime.

MUNICIPAL LAW ENFORCEMENT AGENCIES

According to the FBI, there are 2.3 state and local police officers for every 1,000 citizens in the United States.[66] This average somewhat masks the discrepancies between the police forces in urban and rural America. The vast majority of all police officers work in small and medium-sized police departments (see Figure 5.5 in the margin below). While the New York City Police Department employs about 38,000 police personnel, 50 percent of all local police departments have ten or fewer law enforcement officers.[67]

Of the three levels of law enforcement, municipal agencies have the broadest authority to apprehend criminal suspects, maintain order, and provide services to the community. Whether the local officer is part of a large force or the only law enforcement officer in the community, he or she is usually responsible for a wide spectrum of duties, from responding to noise complaints to investigating homicides. Much of the criticism of local police departments is based on the belief that local police are too underpaid or poorly trained to handle these various responsibilities. Reformers have suggested that residents of smaller American towns would benefit from greater statewide coordination of local police departments.[68]

SHERIFFS AND COUNTY LAW ENFORCEMENT

The **sheriff** is a very important figure in American law enforcement. Almost every one of the more than three thousand counties in the United States (except those in Alaska) has a sheriff. In every state except Rhode Island and Hawaii, sheriffs are elected by members of the community for two- or four-year terms and are paid a salary set by the state legislature or county board.

As elected officials who do not necessarily need a background in law enforcement, modern sheriffs resemble their counterparts from the political era of policing in many ways. Simply stated, the sheriff is also a politician. When a new sheriff is elected, she or he will sometimes repay political debts by appointing new deputies or promoting those who have given her or him support. This high degree of instability and personnel turnover in many states is seen as one of the weaknesses of county law enforcement.[69]

SIZE AND RESPONSIBILITY OF SHERIFFS' DEPARTMENTS Like municipal police forces, sheriffs' departments vary in size. The largest is the Los Angeles County Sheriff's Department, with more than 8,400 deputies. Of the 3,067 sheriffs' departments in the country, thirteen employ more than 1,000 officers, while nineteen have only one.[70]

The image of the sheriff as a powerful figure patrolling vast expanses is not entirely misleading. Most sheriffs' departments are assigned their duties by state law. About 80 percent of all sheriffs' departments have the primary responsibility for investigating violent crimes in their jurisdictions. Other common responsibilities of a sheriff's department include:

- Investigating drug crimes.
- Maintaining the county jail.
- Carrying out civil and criminal processes within county lines, such as serving eviction notices and court summonses.
- Keeping order in the county courthouse.
- Collecting taxes.
- Enforcing orders of the court, such as overseeing the isolation of a jury during a trial.[71]

Sheriff The primary law enforcement officer in a county, usually elected to the post by a popular vote.

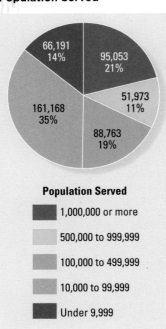

FIGURE 5.5 **Full-Time Police Personnel, by Size of Population Served**

66,191 14%

95,053 21%

51,973 11%

161,168 35%

88,763 19%

Population Served

- 1,000,000 or more
- 500,000 to 999,999
- 100,000 to 499,999
- 10,000 to 99,999
- Under 9,999

Source: Bureau of Justice Statistics, *Local Police Departments, 2007* (Washington, D.C.: U.S. Department of Justice, December 2010), Table 3, page 9.

It is easy to confuse sheriffs' departments and local police departments. Both law enforcement agencies are responsible for many of the same tasks, including crime investigation and routine patrol. There are differences, however. Sheriffs' departments are more likely to be involved in county court and jail operations and to perform certain services such as search and rescue. Local police departments, for their part, are more likely to perform traffic-related functions than are sheriffs' departments.[72]

THE COUNTY CORONER Another elected official on the county level is the coroner, or medical examiner. Duties vary from county to county, but the coroner has a general mandate to investigate "all sudden, unexplained, unnatural, or suspicious deaths" reported to the office. The coroner is ultimately responsible for determining the cause of death in these cases. Coroners also perform autopsies and assist other law enforcement agencies in homicide investigations.[73] For example, after pop star Michael Jackson died under mysterious circumstances in 2009, the Los Angeles County coroner determined that the cause of death was a lethal mixture of propofol administered by Conrad Murray, the singer's personal physician.

A local police officer operates a roadblock as part of the search for Jason Lee Wheeler, who killed one Lake County (Florida) sheriff's deputy and wounded two others. Why would local law enforcement agencies seek the aid of federal law enforcement agencies in a situation such as this one?
AP Photo/Phil Sandlin

STATE POLICE AND HIGHWAY PATROLS

The most visible state law enforcement agency is the state police or highway patrol agency. Historically, state police agencies were created for three reasons:

1. To assist local police agencies, which often did not have adequate resources or training to handle their law enforcement tasks.
2. To investigate criminal activities that crossed jurisdictional boundaries (such as when bank robbers committed a crime in one county and then fled to another part of the state).
3. To provide law enforcement in rural and other areas that did not have local or county police agencies.

Coroner The medical examiner of a county, usually elected by popular vote.

THE DIFFERENCE BETWEEN STATE POLICE AND HIGHWAY PATROLS Today, there are twenty-three state police agencies and twenty-six highway patrols in the United States. State police agencies have statewide jurisdiction and are authorized to perform a wide variety of law enforcement tasks. Thus, they provide the same services as city or county police departments and are restricted only by the boundaries of the state. In contrast, highway patrols have limited authority. Their duties are generally defined either by their jurisdiction or by the specific types of offenses they have the authority to control. As their name suggests, most highway patrols concentrate primarily on regulating traffic. Specifically, they enforce traffic laws and investigate traffic accidents. Furthermore, they usually limit their activity to patrolling state and federal highways.

Teaching Tip: To avoid confusion, ask students to contrast the functions of the state police and the highway patrol. While both have statewide jurisdiction, they are separate agencies with different sets of duties.

A Connecticut State Police officer provides advice for a motorist stuck in a snowstorm on Interstate 84 in East Hartford. In what ways do state law enforcement officers supplement the efforts of local police officers?

AP Photo/Jessica Hill

Trying to determine what state agency has which duties can be confusing. The Washington State Highway Patrol, despite its name, also has state police powers. In addition, thirty-five states have investigative agencies that are independent of the state police or highway patrol. Such agencies are usually found in states with highway patrols, and they have the primary responsibility of investigating criminal activities. For example, in addition to its highway patrol, Oklahoma runs a State Bureau of Investigation and a State Bureau of Narcotics and Dangerous Drugs. Each state has its own methods of determining the jurisdictions of these various organizations.

LIMITED-PURPOSE LAW ENFORCEMENT AGENCIES Even with the agencies just discussed, a number of states have found that certain law enforcement areas need more specific attention. As a result, a wide variety of limited-purpose law enforcement agencies have sprung up in the fifty states. For example, most states have an alcoholic beverage control commission (ABC), or a similarly named organization, which monitors the sale and distribution of alcoholic beverages. The ABC monitors alcohol distributors to ensure that all taxes are paid on the beverages and is responsible for revoking or suspending the liquor licenses of establishments that have broken relevant laws.

Many states have fish and game warden organizations that enforce all laws relating to hunting and fishing. Motor vehicle compliance (MVC) agencies monitor interstate carriers or trucks to make sure that they are in compliance with state and federal laws. MVC officers generally operate the weigh stations that are commonly found on interstate highways. Other limited-purpose law enforcement agencies deal with white-collar and computer crime, regulate nursing homes, and provide training to local police departments.

⊘ Nearly every law enforcement agency hosts a Web site. To find the home pages of the **Pennsylvania State Police** and the **Washington State Patrol,** visit the *Criminal Justice CourseMate* at **cengagebrain. com** and select the *Web links* for this chapter.

Group Activities: Place students in small groups to research the limited-purpose law enforcement agencies operating in your state. If time allows, have them share their findings with the class.

FEDERAL LAW ENFORCEMENT AGENCIES

Statistically, employees of federal agencies do not make up a large part of the nation's law enforcement force. In fact, the New York City Police Department has about one-third as many employees as all of the federal law enforcement agencies combined. Nevertheless, the influence of these federal agencies is substantial. Unlike local police departments, which must deal with all forms of crime, federal agencies have been authorized, usually by Congress, to enforce specific laws or attend to specific situations. The U.S. Coast Guard, for example, patrols the nation's waterways, while U.S. Postal Inspectors investigate and prosecute crimes perpetrated through the use of the U.S. mails.

As mentioned in Chapter 1, the most far-reaching reorganization of the federal government since World War II took place about a decade ago. These changes, particularly the formation of the Department of Homeland Security, have had a significant effect on federal law enforcement. (See Figure 5.6 on the facing page for the current federal law enforcement "lineup.") In Chapter 16, we will take a close look at just how profound this effect has been. Here, you will learn the basic elements of the most important federal law enforcement agencies, which are grouped according to the federal department or bureau to which they report.

FIGURE 5.6 Federal Law Enforcement Agencies

A number of federal agencies employ law enforcement officers who are authorized to carry firearms and make arrests. The most prominent ones are under the control of the U.S. Department of Homeland Security, the U.S. Department of Justice, or the U.S. Department of the Treasury.

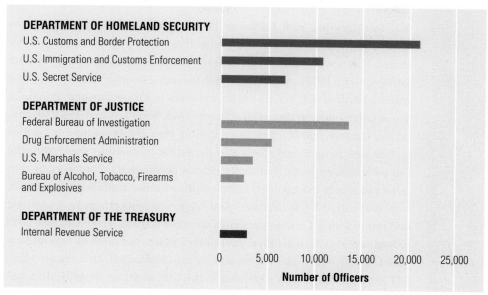

DEPARTMENT OF HOMELAND SECURITY
U.S. Customs and Border Protection
U.S. Immigration and Customs Enforcement
U.S. Secret Service

DEPARTMENT OF JUSTICE
Federal Bureau of Investigation
Drug Enforcement Administration
U.S. Marshals Service
Bureau of Alcohol, Tobacco, Firearms and Explosives

DEPARTMENT OF THE TREASURY
Internal Revenue Service

0   5,000   10,000   15,000   20,000   25,000
Number of Officers

Sources: U.S. Department of Homeland Security, U.S. Department of Justice, and U.S Department of the Treasury.

THE DEPARTMENT OF HOMELAND SECURITY About thirteen months after the September 11, 2001, terrorist attacks, President George W. Bush signed the Homeland Security Act.[74] This legislation created the Department of Homeland Security (DHS), a new cabinet-level department designed to coordinate federal efforts to protect the United States against international and domestic terrorism. The new department has no new agencies. Instead, twenty-two existing agencies were shifted under the control of the secretary of homeland security, a post now held by Janet Napolitano. For example, the Transportation Security Administration, which was formed in 2001 to revive the Federal Air Marshals program placing undercover federal agents on commercial flights, was moved from the Department of Transportation to the DHS. U.S. Customs

LO 7 and Border Protection, U.S. Immigration and Customs Enforcement, and the U.S. Secret Service are the three most visible agencies under the direction of the DHS.

U.S. Customs and Border Protection (CBP) One of the most important effects of the Homeland Security Act was the termination of the Immigration and Naturalization Service (INS), which had monitored and policed the flow of immigrants into the United States since 1933. Many of the INS's duties have been transferred to U.S. Customs and Border Protection (CBP), which polices the flow of goods and people across the United States' international borders. In general terms, this means that the agency has two primary goals: (1) to keep illegal immigrants, drugs, and drug traffickers from crossing our borders, and (2) to facilitate the smooth flow of legal trade and travel. Consequently, CBP officers are stationed at every port of entry and exit to the United States. The officers have widespread authority to investigate and search all international passengers, whether they arrive on airplanes, ships, or other forms of transportation.

The U.S. Border Patrol, a branch of the CBP, has the burden of policing both the Mexican and Canadian borders between official ports of entry. In 2009, Border Patrol

See the **U.S. Department of Homeland Security** for information on how this branch of federal law enforcement is fighting terrorism. Find this Web site by visiting the *Criminal Justice CourseMate* at **cengagebrain.com** and selecting the *Web links* for this chapter.

Discussion Tip: Have students discuss the creation of the Department of Homeland Security. What are the advantages of creating a new federal department in this instance? Are there any disadvantages? (LO 7)

U.S. Customs and Border Protection (CBP) The federal agency responsible for protecting U.S. borders and facilitating legal trade and travel across those borders.

Border Patrol agents make their rounds of the United States' shared boundary with Mexico on all-terrain vehicles (ATVs). What is the difference between U.S. Customs and Border Protection, which oversees the Border Patrol, and U.S. Immigration and Customs Enforcement?

James Tourtellotte/CBP.gov

U.S. Immigration and Customs Enforcement (ICE) The federal agency that enforces the nation's immigration and customs laws.

U.S. Secret Service A federal law enforcement organization with the primary responsibility of protecting the president, the president's family, the vice president, and other important political figures.

Technology Tip: Have students learn more about the Federal Bureau of Investigation online at **www.fbi.gov**. (LO 8)

agents caught nearly 560,000 people entering the country illegally and confiscated 4.75 million pounds of narcotics.[75] Today, more than 21,000 Border Patrol agents guard 19,000 miles of land and sea borders, about double the number of ten years earlier.

U.S. Immigration and Customs Enforcement (ICE) The CBP shares responsibility for locating and apprehending those persons illegally in the United States with special agents from **U.S. Immigration and Customs Enforcement (ICE).** While the CBP focuses almost exclusively on the nation's borders, ICE has a broader mandate to investigate and to enforce our country's immigration and customs laws. Simply stated, the CBP covers the borders, and ICE covers everything else. The latter agency's duties include detaining illegal aliens and deporting (removing) them from the United States, ensuring that those without permission do not work or gain other benefits in this country, and disrupting human trafficking operations.

Recently, ICE has become more aggressive in its efforts to apprehend and remove illegal immigrants with criminal records. From October 2009 to September 2010, ICE officers conducted numerous raids on several New York City hideouts of the violent street gang La Mara Salvatrucha, arresting 285 gang members who were also in the United States illegally. In total, ICE removes about 30,000 illegal immigrants from this country each year.[76] As we shall see in Chapter 16, both the CBP and ICE are crucial elements of the nation's anti-terrorism strategy.

The U.S. Secret Service When it was created in 1865, the **U.S. Secret Service** was primarily responsible for combating currency counterfeiters. In 1901, the agency was given the added responsibility of protecting the president of the United States, the president's family, the vice president, the president-elect, and former presidents. These duties have remained the cornerstone of the agency, with several expansions. After a number of threats against presidential candidates in the 1960s and early 1970s, including the shootings of Robert Kennedy of New York and Governor George Wallace of Alabama, in 1976 Secret Service agents became responsible for protecting those political figures as well.

In addition to its special plainclothes agents, the agency also directs two uniformed groups of law enforcement officers. The Secret Service Uniformed Division protects the grounds of the White House and its inhabitants, and the Treasury Police Force polices the Treasury Building in Washington, D.C. This responsibility includes investigating threats against presidents and those running for presidential office. To aid its battle against counterfeiters and forgers of government bonds, the agency has the use of a laboratory at the Bureau of Engraving and Printing in the nation's capital.

THE DEPARTMENT OF JUSTICE The U.S. Department of Justice, created in 1870, is still the primary federal law enforcement agency in the country. With the responsibility of enforcing criminal law and supervising the federal prisons, the Justice Department plays a leading role in the American criminal justice system. To carry out its responsibilities to prevent and control crime, the department has a number of law enforcement agencies, including the Federal Bureau of Investigation, the federal Drug Enforcement Administration, the Bureau of Alcohol, Tobacco, Firearms and Explosives, and the U.S. Marshals Service.

The Federal Bureau of Investigation (FBI) Initially created in 1908 as the Bureau of Investigation, this agency was renamed the Federal Bureau of Investigation (FBI) in 1935. One of the primary investigative agencies of the federal government, the FBI has

LO 8 jurisdiction over nearly two hundred federal crimes, including white-collar crimes, espionage (spying), kidnapping, extortion, interstate transportation of stolen property, bank robbery, interstate gambling, and civil rights violations. With its network of agents across the country and the globe, the FBI is also uniquely positioned to combat worldwide criminal activity such as terrorism and drug trafficking. The agency also provides valuable support to local and state law enforcement agencies.

The FBI's Identification Division maintains a large database of fingerprint information and offers assistance in finding missing persons and identifying the victims of fires, airplane crashes, and other disfiguring disasters. The services of the FBI Laboratory, the largest crime laboratory in the world, are available at no cost to other agencies. Finally, the FBI's National Crime Information Center (NCIC) provides lists of stolen vehicles and firearms, missing license plates, vehicles used to commit crimes, and other information to local and state law enforcement officers who may access the NCIC database. The FBI employs about 34,000 people and has a budget of approximately $7.9 billion.

The Drug Enforcement Administration (DEA) With a $2.6 billion budget and about 5,200 special agents, the Drug Enforcement Administration (DEA) is one of the most important law enforcement agencies in the country. The mission of the DEA is to enforce domestic drug laws and regulations and to assist other federal and foreign agencies in combating illegal drug manufacture and trade on an international level. The agency also enforces the provisions of the Controlled Substances Act (see pages 74–75), which governs the manufacture, distribution, and dispensing of legal drugs, such as prescription drugs.

DEA agents often work in conjunction with local and state authorities to prevent illicit drugs from reaching communities. The agency also conducts extensive operations with law enforcement entities in other drug-producing countries. Recently, for example, the DEA joined forces with the Mexican military to combat that country's powerful drug cartels. In November 2010, acting on information from DEA agents, Mexican authorities sent 660 marines to Matamoros—just across the U.S. border from Brownsville, Texas—to apprehend drug boss Antonio Ezequiel Cárdenas Guillén, also known as Tony Tormenta, or Tony the Storm.[77] (Guillén was killed in the ensuing firefight.)

Like the FBI, the DEA operates a network of six regional laboratories used to test and categorize seized drugs. Local law enforcement agencies have access to the DEA labs and often use them to ensure that information about particular drugs that will be presented in court is accurate and up to date. In recent years Congress has given the FBI more authority to enforce drug laws, and the two agencies now share a number of administrative controls.

The Bureau of Alcohol, Tobacco, Firearms and Explosives (ATF) As its name suggests, the Bureau of Alcohol, Tobacco, Firearms and Explosives (ATF) is primarily concerned with the illegal sale, possession, and use of firearms and the control of untaxed tobacco and liquor products. The Firearms Division of the agency has

Federal Bureau of Investigation (FBI) The branch of the Department of Justice responsible for investigating violations of federal law. The bureau also collects national crime statistics and provides training and other forms of aid to local law enforcement agencies.

Drug Enforcement Administration (DEA) The federal agency responsible for enforcing the nation's laws and regulations regarding narcotics and other controlled substances.

Technology Tip: Have students learn more about the Drug Enforcement Administration online at **www.dea.gov**.

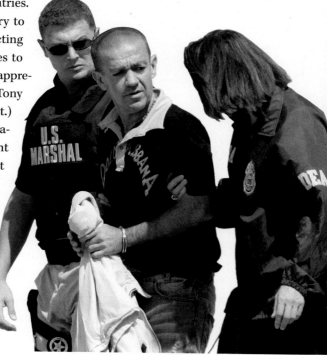

A Colombian fugitive is escorted by a U.S. Marshal and a U.S. DEA agent at his arrival in Florida to face drug trafficking and money laundering charges in federal court. How do the duties of DEA and FBI agents differ? How are they similar?
AP Photo/Alan Diaz

CAREERS IN CJ

FASTFACTS

FBI AGENT JOB DESCRIPTION:

- Primary role is to oversee intelligence and investigate crimes. Agents might track the movement of stolen goods across state lines, examine accounting and business records, listen to legal wiretaps, and conduct undercover investigations.

- Special agent careers are divided into five career paths: intelligence, counterintelligence, counterterrorism, criminal, and cyber.

WHAT KIND OF TRAINING IS REQUIRED?

- Bachelor's and/or master's degree, plus 3 years of work experience. U.S. citizen, 23–36 years old.

- Critical skills required in one or more of the following areas: accounting, finance, computer science/IT, engineering, foreign language(s), law, law enforcement, intelligence, military, and/or physical sciences.

- A written and oral examination, medical and physical examinations, a psychological assessment, and an exhaustive background investigation.

ANNUAL SALARY RANGE?

- $61,100–$69,900

For additional information on a career as an FBI agent, visit **www.fbijobs.gov**.

ARNOLD E. BELL
FEDERAL BUREAU OF INVESTIGATION (FBI) AGENT

As an FBI agent, I work for the largest investigative arm of the U.S. Department of Justice. Since September 11, 2001, our primary focus has shifted from criminal work to counterterrorism. This has been a difficult transformation for many of us "old-timers" because we grew up in the Bureau doing criminal work. We all recognize, however, the importance of this new challenge, and, despite the difficulties, I believe we have been successful in fulfilling both missions.

WORKING THE CYBER BEAT I came to the FBI from the U.S. Army, where I worked as a crewman on a UH-1 helicopter and subsequently as a special agent with the U.S. Army Criminal Investigation Command. My work experience in the U.S. Army and degree from St. Leo College (now University) provided the educational foundation that allowed entry into the FBI. As I have ascended up the ranks, though, I have been able to receive significant management and cyber-related training.

Coming out of the FBI Academy in Quantico, I was assigned to our Los Angeles division, where I spent the next twelve years. It was a particularly interesting time to be working in Los Angeles, which was experiencing a boom in bank robberies. During the most intense stretches, we were averaging between five and seven bank robberies a day! When I wasn't chasing down a bank robber, I had my hands full with hunting down fugitives, working against organized crime, and dealing with public corruption. I am currently assigned to the FBI's cyber division as an assistant section chief. The primary mission of my division is to combat cyber-based terrorism and hostile-intelligence operations conducted via the Internet, and to address general cyber crime.

FROM HERE TO CHINA I have had the good fortune to be involved with many exciting and high-profile assignments over my career. In particular, I remember working on an international kidnapping case involving a teenage boy from San Marino, California, who was abducted a week before Christmas in 1998. The crime immediately took top priority in my squad, and we worked twenty-hour days from the moment the kidnapping was called in until we rescued the boy more than two weeks later. On Christmas Day, I took a couple hours off to be with my kids, and then I was back in the office. It could have been worse: several of my colleagues had their leaves canceled due to the urgency of the case. Nobody complained, however—we knew the stakes.

The case required close coordination with the People's Republic of China, as the ransom calls had been traced to the southeastern coast of that immense country. Ultimately, we coordinated a money drop in the city of Fuzhou, China, and simultaneously raided a home in Temple City, California, where we rescued the young victim. I was the first person into the Temple City home, where we arrested two persons. We also apprehended four suspects in China and recovered all the ransom money. The reunion between the boy and his mother is burned into my memory forever. He talked with little emotion as he was taken to the hospital for examination. Upon the sight of his mother, however, both of them broke down in tears—as did I, my partner, and the San Marino Police detective who had been working with us. The feeling I experienced at that moment validated my decision to become a law enforcement officer.

the responsibility of enforcing the Gun Control Act of 1968, which sets the circumstances under which firearms may be sold and used in this country. The bureau also regulates all gun trade between the United States and foreign nations and collects taxes on all firearm importers, manufacturers, and dealers. In keeping with these duties, the ATF is also responsible for policing the illegal use and possession of explosives. Furthermore, the ATF is charged with enforcing federal gambling laws.

Because it has jurisdiction over such a wide variety of crimes, especially those involving firearms and explosives, the ATF is a constant presence in federal criminal investigations. So, following Jared Loughner's January 2011 shooting rampage in Tucson, Arizona, that left six people dead and Congresswoman Gabrielle Giffords critically injured, the ATF investigated how Loughner obtained the handgun used in the attack. Furthermore, the ATF is engaged in an ongoing and crucial operation to keep American firearms out of the hands of Mexican drug cartels. The ATF has also formed multijurisdictional antigang task forces with other federal and local law enforcement agencies to investigate gang-related crimes involving firearms.

The U.S. Marshals Service The oldest federal law enforcement agency is the U.S. Marshals Service. In 1789, President George Washington assigned thirteen U.S. Marshals to protect his attorney general. That same year, Congress created the office of the U.S. Marshals and Deputy Marshals. Originally, the U.S. Marshals acted as the main law enforcement officers in the western territories. Following the Civil War (1861–1865), when most of these territories had become states, these agents were assigned to work for the U.S. district courts, where federal crimes are tried. The relationship between the U.S. Marshals Service and the federal courts continues today and forms the basis for the officers' main duties, which include:

1. Providing security at federal courts for judges, jurors, and other courtroom participants.
2. Controlling property that has been ordered seized by federal courts.
3. Protecting government witnesses who put themselves in danger by testifying against the targets of federal criminal investigations. This protection is sometimes accomplished by relocating the witnesses and providing them with different identities.
4. Transporting federal prisoners to detention institutions.
5. Investigating violations of federal fugitive laws.[78]

THE DEPARTMENT OF THE TREASURY The Department of the Treasury, formed in 1789, is mainly responsible for all financial matters of the federal government. It pays all the federal government's bills, borrows funds, collects taxes, mints coins, and prints paper currency. The largest bureau of the Treasury Department, the Internal Revenue Service (IRS), is concerned with violations of tax laws and regulations. The bureau has three divisions, only one of which is involved in criminal investigations. The examination branch of the IRS audits the tax returns of corporations and individuals. The collection division attempts to collect taxes from corporations or citizens who have failed to pay the taxes they owe. Finally, the criminal investigation division investigates cases of tax evasion and tax fraud. Criminal investigation agents can make arrests.

The IRS has long played a role in policing criminal activities such as gambling and selling drugs for one simple reason: those who engage in such activities almost never report any illegally gained income on their tax returns. Therefore, the IRS is able to apprehend them for tax evasion. The most famous example took place in the early 1930s, when the IRS finally arrested famed crime boss Al Capone—responsible for numerous violent crimes—for not paying his taxes.

Technology Tip: Have students learn more about the Bureau of Alcohol, Tobacco, Firearms and Explosives online at **www.atf.gov**.

Technology Tip: Have students learn more about the U.S. Marshals Service online at **www.usmarshals.gov**.

Technology Tip: Have students learn more about the various bureaus operating under the Department of the Treasury by evaluating their organizational chart online at **www.treasury.gov/bureaus**.

SELFASSESSMENT

Fill in the blanks and check your answers on page 164.
Municipal police departments and _____ departments are both considered "local" organizations and have many of the same responsibilities. On the state level, the authority of the _____ _____ is usually limited to enforcing traffic laws. Nationally, the _____ has jurisdiction over all federal crimes, while the _____ focuses on federal drug laws and the _____ regulates the illegal sale and possession of guns.

Critical Thinking Skill Development: The text explains that private security officers have "many, if not most" of the same crime prevention powers as sworn law enforcement officers. Ask students to discuss this statement. What role do private security officers play in the justice process? (LO 9)

Private Security The practice of private corporations or individuals offering services traditionally performed by police officers.

PRIVATE SECURITY

LO 9 Even with increasing numbers of local, state, and federal law enforcement officers, the police do not have the ability to prevent every crime. Recognizing this, many businesses and citizens have decided to hire private guards for their properties and homes. In fact, according to the Freedonia Group, an industry-research firm, demand for **private security** generated revenues of $48 billion in 2010.[79] More than 10,000 firms employing around 1.1 million people provide private security services in this country, compared with about 700,000 public law enforcement agents.

PRIVATIZING LAW ENFORCEMENT

In the eyes of the law, a private security guard is the same as any other private person when it comes to police powers such as being able to arrest or interrogate a person suspected of committing a crime. Ideally, a security guard—lacking the training of a law enforcement agent—should only observe and report criminal activity unless use of force is needed to prevent a felony.[80]

A private security guard makes the rounds near the Food Court at Landmark Mall in Alexandria, Virginia. Why is being visible such an important aspect of many private security jobs? Newhouse News Service/Landov

CITIZENS' ARRESTS Any private citizen (including private security guards) may perform a "citizen's arrest" under certain circumstances. The California Penal Code, for example, allows a private person to arrest another:

- For a public offense committed in his or her presence.
- When the person arrested has committed a felony, even if it was not in the arrester's presence, if he or she has reasonable cause to believe that the person committed the felony.[81]

Obviously, these are not very exacting standards, and, in reality, private security guards have many, if not most, of the same powers to prevent crime that a police officer does.

THE DETERRENCE FACTOR As a rule, however, private security is not designed to replace law enforcement. It is intended to deter crime rather than stop it.[82] A uniformed security guard patrolling a shopping mall parking lot or a bank lobby has one primary function—to convince a potential criminal to search out a shopping mall or bank that does not have private security. For the same reason, many citizens hire security personnel to drive marked cars through their neighborhoods, making them a less attractive target for burglaries, robberies, vandalism, and other crimes.

PRIVATE SECURITY TRENDS

Despite the proliferation of private security, many questions remain about this largely unregulated industry. Several years ago, Jessie Walker, a sixty-four-year-old security guard for Markman's Diamonds & Fine Jewelry in West Knoxville, Tennessee, was charged with aggravated assault for shooting Kevin Bowman and Elizabeth Day. Walker had intervened when he heard the couple arguing in the store's parking lot. When the altercation continued, Walker eventually drew his handgun and shot Bowman and Day, neither of whom was armed, sending them to the hospital in critical condition. The only requirement for becoming a weapons-licensed security guard in Tennessee is eight hours of training.[83]

LACK OF STANDARDS As there are no federal regulations regarding private security, each state has its own rules for employment as a security guard. In several states, including California and Florida, prospective guards must have at least forty hours of training. Twenty-nine states, however, have no specific training requirements, and ten states do not regulate the private security industry at all. By comparison, Spain mandates 160 hours of theoretical training, 20 hours of practical training, and 20 hours of annual continuing education for anybody hoping to find employment as a security guard.[84]

The quality of employees is also a problem for the U.S. private security industry. Given the low pay (see Figure 5.7 below) and lack of benefits such as health insurance, paid vacation time, and sick days, the industry does not always attract highly qualified and motivated recruits.[85] "At those wages," notes one industry specialist, "you're competing with McDonald's."[86] To make matters worse, fewer than half of the states require a fingerprint check for applicants, making it relatively easy for a person with a criminal record in one state to obtain a security guard position in another.[87]

The security industry is finding it much easier to uncover past convictions of employees and job applicants thanks to the Private Security Officer Employment Authorization Act of 2004.[88] The legislation, which authorizes the FBI to provide background checks for

Critical Thinking Skill Development: In a written assignment, have students respond to "Questions for Critical Analysis" number five on page 165, in which they consider the steps that could be implemented to increase professionalism in the private security industry.

FIGURE 5.7 Average Salaries in Law Enforcement

In New York City, servers in restaurants, landscapers, hotel desk clerks, and domestic workers all earn more than private security guards. Nationwide, as this figure shows, security guards are the lowest paid of the "protective service occupations."

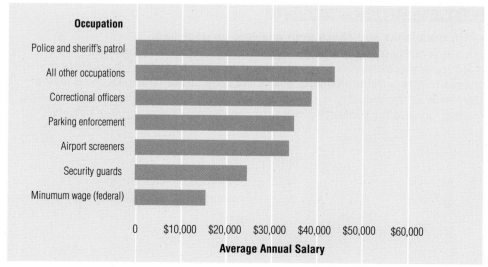

Source: Bureau of Labor Statistics.

security firms, was spurred by congressional concern over possible terrorist attacks on shipping ports, water treatment facilities, telecommunications facilities, power plants, and other strategic targets that are often secured by private guards. In the first year of this program, the FBI found that 990,000 of the estimated 9 million applicants for private security positions (about 11 percent) had criminal records.[89]

CONTINUED GROWTH IN THE INDUSTRY Issues surrounding private security promise to gain even greater prominence in the criminal justice system, as indicators point to higher rates of growth for the industry. The Hallcrest Report II, a far-reaching overview of private security trends funded by the National Institute of Justice, identifies four factors driving this growth:

1. An increase in fear on the part of the public triggered by media coverage of crime.
2. The problem of crime in the workplace. According to the University of Florida's National Retail Security Survey, American retailers lose about $34 billion a year because of shoplifting and employee theft.[90]
3. Budget cuts in states and municipalities that have forced reductions in the number of public police, thereby raising the demand for private ones.
4. A rising awareness of private security products (such as home burglar alarms) and service as cost-effective protective measures.[91]

Another reason for the industry's continued health is terrorism. Private security is responsible for protecting more than three-fourths of the nation's likely terrorist targets such as power plants, financial centers, dams, malls, oil refineries, and transportation hubs. When several dozen private security guards were caught sleeping on the job at the John F. Kennedy International Airport in Queens, New York, in December 2010, the incident was greeted not with chuckles but with alarm. Nine of the employees, who are responsible for guarding the tarmac, inspecting vehicles, and providing other security services at the airport, lost their jobs.

To avoid this kind of negative publicity, private security companies are becoming more professional, with better screened and trained employees. "The importance of [the industry] has resulted in a crackdown on those who think they can sit around and do nothing," says Gregory A. Thomas, an expert in public safety and formerly a senior manager at Columbia University's National Center for Disaster Preparedness.[92]

SELFASSESSMENT

Fill in the blanks and check your answers on page 164.

Private security is designed to _____ crime rather than to prevent it. The majority of states require _____ hours of training and _____ background checks before a person can become a security guard. This perceived lack of standards in the industry is changing, however, as private security companies are responsible for protecting many of the country's likely _____ targets.

Discussion Tip: Ask students to compare and contrast the duties of police with those performed by private security officers. Is there any overlap in the area of preserving the peace (see page 137)? Should some duties be shifted from one group to the other? (LO 9)

Discussion Tip: Ask students to discuss the reasons that experts predict the private security industry will continue to grow. As this aspect of the criminal justice system continues to grow, do students see other trends emerging in this field? (LO 9)

CJ IN ACTION

AFFIRMATIVE ACTION IN LAW ENFORCEMENT

About a quarter of the 38,000 residents of Lima, Ohio, are African American, but only two of the nearly eighty members of the city's police force are black. According to members of Lima's African American community, this disparity has created a poisonous atmosphere in which white police officers routinely harass and physically abuse black citizens. Tensions reached a boiling point a few years ago when white police officers accidentally shot and killed an African American woman named Tarika Wilson during a botched drug raid.[93] Following Wilson's death, Lima officials vowed to increase minority representation in the police department. In this *CJ in Action* feature, we will attempt to answer two questions concerning such affirmative action strategies. First, do they work? Second, and just as important, are they fair?

STRATEGIES FOR DIVERSITY

For potential female police officers, the physical fitness test often poses the greatest barrier to hiring. In California, for example, all applicants must scale a six-foot wall to be considered for a police job. Officials estimate that this requirement eliminates half of the women who apply.[94] Some police departments, however, adjust their physical fitness tests to level the playing field. The Champaign (Illinois) Police Department, for example, requires male applicants to run 1.5 miles in thirteen minutes and female applicants to complete the course in sixteen minutes.[95] Thus, affirmative action programs represent an "active effort" to support the employment of women and members of minority groups in law enforcement.[96]

THE CASE FOR AFFIRMATIVE ACTION IN LAW ENFORCEMENT

- For most of the nation's history, women and minorities suffered from widespread discrimination in policing. Affirmative action remedies these past wrongs.

- The existence of a diverse police force improves community-police relations and makes it easier for all officers to do their jobs because it assures the community that the police will not act in a discriminatory manner.

- Affirmative action works. In Pittsburgh, the percentage of female police officers rose from 1 percent to 27 percent after an affirmative action program went into effect, but it began to decline as soon as the program ended.[97] In Chicago, the African American share of new police hires rose from 10 percent to 40 percent in just two years after the implementation of a consent decree.[98]

THE CASE AGAINST AFFIRMATIVE ACTION IN LAW ENFORCEMENT

- A stigma is attached to persons perceived to have benefited from affirmative action. "I don't want to be in a department where I was hired because of my skin color," said one African American applicant in Dayton. "I want it because I earned it."[99]

- Public safety requires that all police officers be the most competent and skilled, regardless of their gender, race, or ethnicity.

- There are no "special skills" unique to women or minority law enforcement agents. Studies show that, for the most part, "cops act like cops."[100]

AP Photo/Alex Brandon

WRITING ASSIGNMENT—YOUR OPINION

The city of Springfield wants to test seventy-seven of its police officers for possible promotion to lieutenant. The exam—part written multiple choice and part oral—is specifically designed to avoid bias against minority candidates. Of the seventy-seven candidates, forty-three are white, nineteen are black, and fifteen are Hispanic. All of the top ten performers on the exam, immediately eligible for promotion, are white.

A city official argues that these results should be disregarded because black and Hispanic candidates have been unfairly excluded from the opportunity for promotion. What do you think of this argument? Would it be fair to the successful white candidates to invalidate the results? What would be in the best interests of the citizens of Springfield? Before responding, you can review our discussions in this chapter concerning:

- The reform era of policing (pages 139–141).

- Antidiscrimination law and affirmative action (pages 147–148).

- Gender, race, and ethnicity in law enforcement (pages 148–151).

Your answer should include at least three full paragraphs.

CHAPTER SUMMARY

LO 1 List the four basic responsibilities of the police. (a) To enforce laws, (b) to provide services, (c) to prevent crime, and (d) to preserve the peace.

LO 2 Tell how the patronage system affected policing. During the political era of policing (1840–1930), bribes paid by citizens and business owners often went into the coffers of the local political party. This became known as the patronage system.

LO 3 Indicate the results of the Wickersham Commission. The Wickersham Commission of 1929 called for reform to eliminate police brutality and the corrupting influence of politics. The result was the professionalization of American police, sometimes called the progressive era in American policing. Potential police officers began to be trained in institutes of higher learning. Another result was the increased use of technology in police work.

LO 4 Explain how intelligence-led policing works and how it benefits modern police departments. Intelligence-led policing uses past crime patterns to predict when and where crime will occur in the future. In theory, intelligence-led policing allows police administrators to use fewer resources because it removes costly and time-consuming "guesswork" from the law enforcement equation.

LO 5 Identify the differences between the police academy and field training as learning tools for recruits. The police academy is a controlled environment where police recruits learn the basics of policing from instructors in classrooms. In contrast, field training takes place in the "real world": the recruit goes on patrol with an experienced police officer.

LO 6 Describe the challenges facing women who choose law enforcement as a career. Many male officers believe that their female counterparts are not physically or mentally strong enough for police work, which puts pressure on women officers to continually prove themselves. Female officers must also deal with tokenism, or the stigma that they were hired only to fulfill diversity requirements, and sexual harassment in the form of unwanted advances or obscene remarks.

LO 7 Indicate some of the most important law enforcement agencies under the control of the Department of Homeland Security. (a) U.S. Customs and Border Protection, which polices the flow of goods and people across the United States' international borders and oversees the U.S. Border Patrol; (b) U.S. Immigration and Customs Enforcement, which investigates and enforces our nation's immigration and customs laws; and (c) the U.S. Secret Service, which protects high-ranking federal government officials and federal property.

LO 8 Identify the duties of the FBI. The FBI has jurisdiction to investigate hundreds of federal crimes, including white-collar crime, kidnapping, bank robbery, and civil rights violations. The FBI is also heavily involved in combating terrorism and drug-trafficking operations in the United States and around the world. Finally, the agency provides support to state and local law enforcement agencies through its crime laboratories and databases.

LO 9 Analyze the importance of private security today. In the United States, businesses and citizens spend billions of dollars each year on private security. Heightened fear of crime and increased crime in the workplace have fueled the growth in spending on private security.

SELF ASSESSMENT ANSWER KEY

Page 138: i. enforce; **ii.** services; **iii.** prevent; **iv.** preserve

Page 144: i. political; **ii.** patronage; **iii.** reform; **iv.** professional; **v.** community; **vi.** intelligence; **vii.** terrorist

Page 147: i. twenty-one; **ii.** felony; **iii.** probationary; **iv.** police academy; **v.** field training

Page 151: i. discrimination; **ii.** affirmative action; **iii.** consent decree

Page 160: i. sheriffs'; **ii.** highway patrol; **iii.** Federal Bureau of Investigation (FBI); **iv.** Drug Enforcement Administration (DEA); **v.** Bureau of Alcohol, Tobacco, Firearms and Explosives (ATF)

Page 162: i. deter; **ii.** zero; **iii.** no; **iv.** terrorist

KEY TERMS

affirmative action **147**

coroner **153**

discrimination **147**

double marginality **150**

Drug Enforcement Administration (DEA) **157**

Federal Bureau of Investigation (FBI) **157**

field training **146**

intelligence-led policing **142**

night watch system **138**

patronage system **139**

private security **160**

probationary period **146**

professional model **139**

recruitment **144**

sexual harassment **149**

sheriff **152**

U.S. Customs and Border Protection (CBP) **155**

U.S. Immigration and Customs Enforcement (ICE) **156**

U.S. Secret Service **156**

QUESTIONS FOR CRITICAL ANALYSIS

1. Which of the four basic responsibilities of the police do you think is most important? Why?

2. Increased professionalism in police forces has been made possible by two-way radios, telephones, and automobiles. In what way has society not benefited from this increased professionalism? Explain your answer.

3. Review the discussion of double marginality on pages 150–151. Why would members of a minority community think that police officers of the same race or ethnicity were "traitors"? What can police departments do to dispel this misperception?

4. One of the major differences between a local police chief and a sheriff is that the sheriff is elected, while the police chief is appointed. What are some of the possible problems with having a law enforcement official who, like any other politician, is responsible to voters? What are some of the possible benefits of this situation?

5. What strategies could be implemented to improve the quality and performance of the private security industry?

CourseMate *For Online Help*

For online help and access to resources that accompany *Criminal Justice Today*, go to www.cengagebrain.com/shop/ISBN/1111835578. Click "Access Now," where you will find flashcards, an online quiz, and other helpful study aids. If you have an access code for CourseMate, log in and go to the chapter of your choice for additional online study aids.

NOTES

1. Egon Bittner, *The Functions of Police in a Modern Society*, Public Health Service Publication No. 2059 (Chevy Chase, MD: National Institute of Mental Health, 1970), 38–44.

2. Carl Klockars, "The Rhetoric of Community Policing," in *Community Policing: Rhetoric or Reality*, ed. Jack Greene and Stephen Mastrofski (New York: Praeger Publishers, 1991), 244.

3. Jack R. Greene and Carl B. Klockars, "What Do Police Do?" in *Thinking about Police*, 2d ed., ed. Carl B. Klockars and Stephen D. Mastrofski (New York: McGraw-Hill, 1991), 273–284.

4. John S. Dempsey and Linda S. Forst, *An Introduction to Policing*, 6th ed. (Clifton Park, NY: Delmar Cengage Learning, 2012), 380–381.

5. Federal Bureau of Investigation, *Crime in the United States, 2010* (Washington, D.C.: U.S. Department of Justice, 2011), at www.fbi.gov/about-us/cjis/ucr/crime-in-the-u.s/2010/crime-in-the-u.s.-2010/tables/10tbl29.xls.

6. Reprinted in *The Police Chief* (January 1990), 18.

7. Jeffrey M. Wilson, *Community Policing in America* (New York: Routledge, 2006), 7–16.

8. Jerome H. Skolnick, "Police: The New Professionals," *New Society* (September 5, 1986), 9–11.

9. Heather Mac Donald, "A Crime Theory Demolished," *Wall Street Journal* (January 4, 2010), at online.wsj.com/article/SB10001424052748703580904574638024055735590.html.

10. Klockars, 250.

11. James Q. Wilson, *Varieties of Police Behavior: The Management of Law and Order in Eight Communities* (Cambridge, MA: Harvard University Press, 1968).

12. James Q. Wilson and George L. Kelling, "Broken Windows," *Atlantic Monthly* (March 1982), 29.

13. M. K. Nalla and G. R. Newman, "Is White-Collar Crime Policing, Policing?" *Policing and Society* 3 (1994), 304.

14. Mitchell P. Roth, *Crime and Punishment: A History of the Criminal Justice System*, 2d ed. (Belmont, CA: Wadsworth Cengage Learning, 2011), 65.

15. *Ibid.*

16. Peter K. Manning, *Police Work* (Cambridge, MA: MIT Press, 1977), 82.

17. Mark H. Moore and George L. Kelling, "'To Serve and Protect': Learning from Police History," *Public Interest* 70 (1983), 53.

18. Samuel Walker, *The Police in America: An Introduction* (New York: McGraw-Hill, 1983), 7.

19. Moore and Kelling, 54.

20. Mark H. Haller, "Chicago Cops, 1890–1925," in *Thinking about Police,* ed. Carl Klockars and Stephen Mastrofski (New York: McGraw-Hill, 1990), 90.

21. William J. Bopp and Donald O. Shultz, *A Short History of American Law Enforcement* (Springfield, IL: Charles C Thomas, 1977), 109–110.

22. Roger G. Dunham and Geoffrey P. Alpert, *Critical Issues in Policing: Contemporary Issues* (Prospect Heights, IL: Waveland Press, 1989).

23. Ken Peak and Emmanuel P. Barthe, "Community Policing and CompStat: Merged, or Mutually Exclusive?" *The Police Chief* (December 2009), 73.

24. *Ibid.*, 74.

25. Quoted in *ibid.*

26. Peter K. Manning, "The Police: Mandate, Strategies, and Appearances," in *Crime and Justice in American Society*, ed. Jack D. Douglas (Indianapolis, IN: Bobbs-Merrill, 1971), 149–163.

27. National Advisory Commission on Civil Disorder, *Report* (Washington, D.C.: U.S. Government Printing Office, 1968), 157–160.

28. 18 U.S.C.A. Sections 2510–2521.

29. Jayne Seagrave, "Defining Community Policing," *American Journal of Police* 1 (1996), 1–22.

30. Peak and Barthe, 78.

31. Quoted in Joel Rubin, "Stopping Crime before It Starts," *Los Angeles Times* (August 21, 2010), A17.

32. Colleen McCue, Andre Parker, Paul J. McNulty, and David McCoy, "Doing More with Less: Data Mining in Police Deployment Decisions," *Violent Crime Newsletter* (Washington, D.C.: U.S. Department of Justice, Spring 2004), 4–5.

33. Charlie Beck and Colleen McCue, "Predictive Policing: What Can We Learn from Wal-Mart and Amazon about Fighting Crime in a Recession?" *The Police Chief* (November 2009), 19.

34. Bureau of Justice Statistics, *Local Police Departments, 2003* (Washington, D.C.: U.S. Department of Justice, May 2006), i; and Bureau of Justice Statistics, *Sheriffs' Offices, 2003* (Washington, D.C.: U.S. Department of Justice, May 2006), i.

35. Bureau of Justice Statistics, *Local Police Departments, 2007* (Washington, D.C.: U.S. Department of Justice, December 2010), Text table 4, page 32.

36. David J. Robert, "Technology's Impact on Law Enforcement—Community Interaction," *The Police Chief* (February 2011), 78.

37. Quoted in Rubin, A17.

38. James H. Chenoweth, "Situational Tests: A New Attempt at Assessing Police Candidates," *Journal of Criminal Law, Criminology and Police Science* 52 (1961), 232.

39. *Local Police Departments, 2007*, 11.

40. Kevin Johnson, "Cops Get Screened for Digital Dirt," *USA Today* (November 12, 2010), 1A.

41. *Local Police Departments, 2007*, Table 5, page 11.

42. D. P. Hinkle, "College Degree: An Impractical Prerequisite for Police Work," *Law and Order* (July 1991), 105.

43. *Local Police Departments, 2007*, 12.

44. Bureau of Justice Statistics, *State and Local Law Enforcement Training Academies, 2006* (Washington, D.C.: U.S. Department of Justice, February 2009), 7.

45. National Advisory Commission on Civil Disorder, *Report* (Washington, D.C.: U.S. Government Printing Office, 1968), Chapter 11.

46. *Griggs v. Duke Power Co.*, 401 U.S. 424 (1971); and *Abermarle Paper Co. v. Moody*, 422 U.S. 405 (1975).

47. Gene L. Scaramella, Steven M. Cox, and William P. McCamey, *Introduction to Policing* (Thousand Oaks, CA: Sage Publications, 2011), 30–31.

48. Lucas Sullivan, "Black Applicants Protest Lowering Scores," *Dayton (OH) Daily News* (March 6, 2011), A13.

49. Brian Sharp, "Minority Recruiting Poses Test for Police," *Democrat and Chronicle (Rochester, NY)* (March 29, 2010), 1.

50. Lianne M. Tuomey and Rachel Jolly, "Step Up to Law Enforcement: A Successful Strategy for Recruiting Women into the Law Enforcement Profession," *The Police Chief* (June 2009), 70, 73.

51. *Local Police Departments, 2007*, 14.

52. National Center for Women and Policing, *Equality Denied: The Status of Women in Policing: 2001* (Washington, D.C.: U.S. Government Printing Office, 2002), 4.

53. Jacqueline Mroz, "Female Police Chiefs: A Novelty No More," *New York Times* (April 6, 2008), 3.

54. Scaramella, Cox, and McCamey, 318.

55. Quoted in Teresa Lynn Wertsch, "Walking the Thin Blue Line: Policewomen and Tokenism Today," *Women and Criminal Justice* (1998), 35–36.

56. Katherine Stuart van Wormer and Clemens Bartollas, *Women and the Criminal Justice System,* 3d ed. (Upper Saddle River, NJ: Pearson Education, 2011), 318–319.

57. Susan L. Webb, *The Global Impact of Sexual Harassment* (New York: Master Media Limited, 1994), 26.

58. Dempsey and Forst, 204.

59. *Local Police Departments, 2007*, 14.

60. David Alan Sklansky, "Not Your Father's Police Department: Making Sense of the New Demographics of Law Enforcement," *Journal of Criminal Law and Criminology* (Spring 2006), 1209–1243.

61. Peter C. Moskos, "Two Shades of Blue: Black and White in the Blue Brotherhood," *Law Enforcement Executive Forum* (2008), 57.

62. Scaramella, Cox, and McCamey, 324.

63. Dempsey and Forst, 183.

64. *Wygant v. Jackson Board of Education*, 476 U.S. 314 (1986).

65. *Crime in the United States, 2010*, at **www.fbi.gov/about-us/cjis/ucr/crime-in-the-u.s/2010/crime-in-the.u.s.-2010/tables/10tbl70.xls/view**.

66. *Ibid.*, at **www.fbi.gov/about-us/cjis/ucr/crime-in-the-u.s/2010/crime-in-the-u.s.-2010/tables/10tbl71.xls**.

67. *Local Police Departments, 2007*, Table 3, page 9.

68. G. Robert Blakey, "Federal Criminal Law," *Hastings Law Journal* 46 (April 1995), 1175.

69. Vern L. Folley, *American Law Enforcement* (Boston: Allyn & Bacon, 1980), 228.

70. *Sheriffs' Offices, 2003*, 2.

71. *Ibid.*, 15–18.

72. Bureau of Justice Statistics, *Sheriffs' Departments, 1997* (Washington, D.C.: U.S. Department of Justice, February 2000), 14.

73. Bureau of Justice Statistics, *Medical Examiners and Coroners' Offices, 2004* (Washington, D.C.: U.S. Department of Justice, June 2007), 1.

74. Pub. L. No. 107-296, 116 Stat. 2135.

75. "Securing America's Borders: CBP Fiscal Year 2009 in Review Fact Sheet," at **www.cbp.gov/xp/cgov/newsroom/news_releases/archives/2009_news_releases/nov_09/11242009_5.xml**.

76. *U.S. Department of Homeland Security FY 2009 Annual Financial Report* (Washington, D.C.: U.S. Department of Homeland Security, 2010), 12.

77. Nick Miroff and William Booth, "Mexico's Marines Team with U.S. DEA," at **www.washingtonpost.com/wp-dyn/content/article/2010/12/03/AR2010120307106.html**.

78. United States Marshals Service, "Fact Sheet," at **www.justice.gov/marshals/duties/factsheets/general-1209.html**.

79. *Private Security Services* (Cleveland, OH: Freedonia Group, November 2010), 15.

80. John B. Owens, "Westec Story: Gated Communities and the Fourth Amendment," *American Criminal Law Review* (Spring 1997), 1138.

81. California Penal Code Section 837 (West 1995).

82. Bruce L. Benson, "Guns, Crime, and Safety," *Journal of Law and Economics* (October 2001), 725.

83. "Private Protective Services: Armed Security Officer/Guard Requirements," at **state.tn.us/commerce/boards/pps/asgoReqs.shtml**.

84. Jeremy Bagott, "Security Standards Putting Public at Risk," *Chicago Tribune* (February 24, 2003), 15.

85. Mimi Hall, "Private Security Guards: Homeland Defense's Weak Link," *USA Today* (January 23, 2003), A1.

86. Brock N. Meeks, "Are 'Rent-a-Cops' Threatening Security?" *MSNBC Online* (March 9, 2005).

87. "Don Walker, CPP, Former President of ASIS International, Testifies before U.S. House of Representatives' Subcommittee on Crime, Terrorism and Homeland Security," *Business Wire* (March 31, 2004).

88. Pub. L. No. 108-458, Section 6402(d)(2) (2004).

89. David Bates, "New Law Allows Nationwide Checks by Security Firms," *Government Security News*, at **www.gsnmagazine.com/feb_05/security_checks.html**.

90. National Retail Federation, "Retail Fraud, Shoplifting Rates Decrease, According to National Retail Security Survey," at **www.nrf.com/modules.php?name=News&op=viewlive&sp_id=945**.

91. William C. Cunningham, John J. Strauchs, and Clifford W. Van Meter, *The Hallcrest Report II: Private Security Trends, 1970 to 2000* (Boston: Butterworth-Heinemann, 1990), 236.

92. Quoted in Dennis Wagner, "Private Security Guards Play Key Roles Post-9/11," *Arizona Republic* (January 22, 2006), A1.

93. Christopher Maag, "Police Shooting of Mother and Infant Exposes a City's Racial Tension," *New York Times* (January 30, 2008), A11.

94. Liz Tascio, "Women Recruits Meet High Standard," *Contra Coast Times* (March 16, 2003), 4.

95. "DOJ Decides Suit Is a Bad Fit," *Law Enforcement News* (October 31, 2001), 1.

96. Dempsey and Forst, 188.

97. Kim Lonsway *et al.*, "Under Scrutiny: The Effect of Consent Decrees on the Representation of Women in Sworn Law Enforcement," National Center for Women and Policing (2003), at **www.womenandpolicing.org/pdf/Fullconsentdecreestudy.pdf**.

98. Justin McCrary, "The Effect of Court-Ordered Hiring Quotas on the Composition and Quality of Police," National Bureau of Economic Research (2006), at **www.nber.org/papers/w12368**.

99. Quoted in Sullivan.

100. Sklansky, 1224–1228.

CHAPTER

6

Stephen Brashear/Getty Images

Challenges to Effective Policing

LEARNING OBJECTIVES

After reading this chapter, you should be able to . . .

LO 1 Explain why police officers are allowed discretionary powers.

LO 2 List the three primary purposes of police patrol.

LO 3 Indicate some investigation strategies that are considered aggressive.

LO 4 Describe how forensic experts use DNA fingerprinting to solve crimes.

LO 5 Explain why differential response strategies enable police departments to respond more efficiently to 911 calls.

LO 6 Explain community policing and its contribution to the concept of problem-oriented policing.

LO 7 Determine when police officers are justified in using deadly force.

LO 8 Identify the three traditional forms of police corruption.

LO 9 Explain what an ethical dilemma is and name four categories of ethical dilemmas that a police officer typically may face.

The nine learning objectives labeled LO 1 through LO 9 are designed to help improve your understanding of the chapter.

OPEN **WOUNDS**

According to Seattle police officer Ian Birk, while patrolling on the night of August 30, 2010, he "clearly saw" John T. Williams carrying a knife with a three-inch blade "in the open position." In response, Birk got out of his car, drew his handgun, and repeatedly and loudly ordered Williams to put the knife down. When Williams failed to do so, Birk shot at him four times from a distance of about nine feet, killing him. Video recordings from Birk's car measured an interval of approximately four seconds between the first command to drop the knife and the first gunshot. Later, Birk explained that although four seconds may seem like a short time to most people, he had been trained to recognize that it was long enough for Williams to attack him with the knife. "I was not left with any reasonable alternative but to fire at Mr. Williams," Birk said.

As is customary with such shootings, the Seattle Police Department launched an investigation into the incident. Its findings did not support Birk's version of the events. First, witnesses said that Williams, a street alcoholic and woodcarver well known in downtown Seattle, made no threatening movement toward the police officer or anyone else. Second, an autopsy showed that the bullets hit Williams in the side, indicating that he had not been facing Birk when he was shot. Third, and most damning, when police recovered Williams's knife, they found it in a closed position. The department's Firearms Review Board eventually ruled that the shooting was unjustified and relieved Birk of his badge and gun pending further review.

For the local Native American community, this action did not go far enough. They pointed out that Williams, a member of the Canadian Ditidaht tribe, was partially deaf and may not have heard Birk's instructions. Furthermore, if Birk had felt threatened, why didn't he call for backup or use his patrol car as cover? "It's not just about John Williams," said Jack Thompson, chief of the Ditidaht tribe. "It's about the way people are treated on the street. I'm sure this could have been avoided."

Protestors in downtown Seattle show their displeasure with the shooting of John T. Williams by police officer Ian Birk.
AP Photo/Ted S. Warren

Following John T. Williams's death, Seattle police chief John Diaz said of encounters between police and civilians, "We can't get them right 99 percent of the time. We have to get them right 100 percent of the time."[1] For many observers, Diaz's police force had been operating far below this lofty goal. In April 2010, a gang detective was caught on video kicking a Latino man while saying, "I'm going to beat the . . . Mexican piss out of you, Homey."[2] That June, another video showed an officer punching a teenage African American girl in the face following a jaywalking dispute. Finally, Williams was just one of five civilians shot by Seattle police officers in 2010, and one of three who died.

Ideally, police would like to be seen as an integral part of the community, with the same goals of crime prevention and public safety as everybody else. When the relationship between police officers and those they serve is marked by ill will and mistrust, these goals become more difficult to reach. Most Americans cannot imagine the on-the-job situations that the average law enforcement officer faces. As one-time police officer and later professor James Fyfe explained, by telling police officers that we expect them to eradicate crime, we are putting them in a "no win war." Like some soldiers in such combat, Fyfe adds, "they commit atrocities."[3] In this chapter, we will examine some of these "atrocities," such as police brutality and corruption. We will also consider the possible causes of police misconduct and review the steps that are being taken to limit these problems. Our discussion begins with an in-depth look at *discretion,* or the use of one's judgment to make the most appropriate choice in any given situation. As we first noted in Chapter 1, discretion is a crucial aspect of law enforcement work.

THE ROLE OF DISCRETION IN POLICING

One of the ironies of law enforcement is that patrol officers—often the lowest-paid members of an agency with the least amount of authority—have the greatest amount of

LO 1

discretionary power. Part of the explanation for this is practical. Patrol officers spend most of the day on the streets, beyond the control of their supervisors. Usually, only two people are present when a patrol officer must make a decision: the officer and the possible wrongdoer. In most cases, the law enforcement officer has a great deal of freedom to take the action that he or she feels the situation requires.[4]

Discussion Tip: Ask students to debate the role of discretion in policing. What are the advantages and disadvantages of allowing patrol officers wide-ranging discretion on the job? (LO 1)

Sometimes, in hindsight, a police officer's actions may seem indefensible. Certainly, Seattle police officer Ian Birk appears to have made a grave mistake in shooting John T. Williams, as discussed in this chapter's opening. Note, however, that Birk's decision was made in a split second, under stressful circumstances, and without the benefit of the evidence that came to light following the shooting.

JUSTIFICATION FOR POLICE DISCRETION

Despite the possibility of mistakes, courts generally have upheld the patrol officer's freedom to decide "what law to enforce, how much to enforce it, against whom, and on what occasions."[5] This judicial support of police discretion is based on the following factors:

- Police officers are considered trustworthy and are therefore assumed to make honest decisions, regardless of contradictory testimony by a suspect.
- Experience and training give officers the ability to determine whether certain activity poses a threat to society, and to take any reasonable action necessary to investigate or prevent such activity.
- Due to the nature of their jobs, police officers are extremely knowledgeable in human, and by extension criminal, behavior.
- Police officers may find themselves in danger of personal, physical harm and must be allowed to take reasonable and necessary steps to protect themselves.[6]

Dr. Anthony J. Pinizzotto, a psychologist with the Federal Bureau of Investigation (FBI), and Charles E. Miller, an instructor in the bureau's Criminal Justice Information Services Division, take the justification for discretion one step further. These two experts argue that many police officers have a "sixth sense" that helps them handle on-the-job challenges. Pinizzotto and Miller believe that although "intuitive policing" is often difficult to explain to those outside law enforcement, it is a crucial part of policing and should not be discouraged by civilian administrators.[7]

FACTORS OF POLICE DISCRETION

There is no doubt that subjective factors influence police discretion. The officer's beliefs, values, personality, and background all enter into his or her decisions. To a large extent, however, a law enforcement agent's actions are determined by the rules of policing set down in the U.S. Constitution and enforced by the courts. These rules are of paramount importance and will be discussed in great detail in Chapter 7.

Teaching Tip: Present students with a scenario in which a law enforcement officer would be called on to use her or his discretion. Have students write down how they would respond, and then compare responses from the class. What factors influenced the students' responses? (LO 1)

MAKING THE DECISION Assuming that most police officers stay on the right side of the Constitution in most instances, four other factors generally enter the discretion equation in any particular situation. First, and most important, is the nature of the criminal act. The less serious a crime, the more likely a police officer is to ignore it. A person driving 60 miles per hour in a 55-miles-per-hour zone, for example, is much less likely to be ticketed than someone doing 80 miles per hour. A second element often considered is the attitude of the wrongdoer toward the officer. A motorist who is belligerent toward a highway patrol officer is much more likely to be ticketed than one who is contrite and apologetic. Third, the relationship between the victim and the offender can influence the outcome. If the parties are in a familial or other close relationship, police officers may see the incident as a personal matter and be hesitant to make an arrest.

Policy A set of guiding principles designed to influence the behavior and decision making of police officers.

The fourth factor of the discretion equation is departmental policy.[8] A **policy** is a set of guiding principles that law enforcement agents must adhere to in stated situations. If a police administrator decides that all motorists who exceed the speed limit by 10 miles per hour will be ticketed, that policy will certainly influence the patrol officer's decisions. Policies must be flexible enough to allow for officer discretion, but at the same time be specific enough to provide the officer with a clear sense of her or his duties and obligations.

DISCRETION AND HIGH-SPEED PURSUITS On March 24, 2010, Henrico County (Virginia) police ordered Darryl Harris to stop at a traffic checkpoint. Harris refused and led officers on a high-speed chase. Although such drastic action is often necessary, the results can be tragic. This particular chase ended when Harris ran a stop sign and crashed his car into a van driven by Apostle Anthony Taylor, a local pastor. Taylor was killed on impact. In fact, about 35 percent of all police chases end in car crashes, causing 360 fatalities each year. One-third of the victims are third parties—drivers of other cars or pedestrians who were merely innocent bystanders.[9] In response to these deaths, 94 percent of the nation's local police departments have implemented police pursuit policies, with 61 percent restricting the discretion of officers to engage in a high-speed chase.[10] The success of such policies can be seen in the results from Los Angeles, which features more high-speed chases than any other city in the country by a wide margin.

Several years ago, a United States Supreme Court ruling supported a police officer's discretionary use of a ramming technique to end a high-speed chase. Why are courts generally supportive of police discretion as long as it is reasonably applied?

SVLumagraphica/Shutterstock

In 2003, Los Angeles police officers were ordered to conduct dangerous pursuits only if the fleeing driver was suspected of a serious crime. Within a year, the number of high-speed pursuits decreased by 62 percent, and injuries to third parties dropped by 58 percent.[11]

While police departments are trying to limit the use of high-speed chases, the United States Supreme Court has shown that it will support a police officer's discretionary use of the tactic. In 1998, the Court held that an officer can be sued in civil court for damages caused by a high-speed pursuit only if her or his conduct was so outrageous that it "shocks the conscience."[12] Then, in 2007, the Court ruled in favor of a Georgia police officer who intentionally caused a crash involving the plaintiff, a nineteen-year-old who was trying to avoid arrest by driving 90 miles per hour on a two-lane road. Even though the plaintiff was paralyzed in the accident, the Court held that the officer was justified in his drastic effort to protect other drivers.[13]

DISCRETION AND DOMESTIC VIOLENCE

Police have a great deal of discretion in deciding whether to make an arrest. Basically, if a police officer has a good reason (known as *probable cause*) to believe that a person has committed or is about to commit a crime, the officer can arrest that suspect. As noted earlier, police officers have a tendency to avoid making an arrest when the dispute involves a "family matter" such as domestic violence.

A number of explanations have been suggested for this leniency. Many police officers see domestic violence as the responsibility of social-service providers, not law enforcement. Officers may also be uncomfortable with the intensely private nature of domestic disputes, so they leave the resolution to the parties involved.[14] Finally, even when a police officer does arrest the abuser, the victim often refuses to press charges, and prosecutors are also hesitant to follow through on these cases by taking them to court.[15] (See the feature *You Be the Police Officer—Discretion and Domestic Violence* below.)

Technology Tip: Have students go online to learn more about police discretion and high speed pursuits from the National Institute of Justice at **www.ncjrs.gov/pdffiles/164831.pdf**.

Domestic Violence The act of willful neglect or physical violence that occurs within a familial or other intimate relationship.

YOU BE THE POLICE OFFICER
Discretion and Domestic Violence

THE SITUATION You are a police officer responding to a 911 call made by a neighbor of Pam and Bill Adams. According to the neighbor, Pam and Bill are on the street in front of their home, screaming at each other. You know that Pam has reported abuse at the hands of her husband numerous times, but this will be your first visit to the Adams's home. When you arrive at the residence, you find Pam by herself in the living room, crying. She tells you that Bill has left. She also tells you that he punched her in the face, kicked her in the legs, and tried to strangle her. You don't see any marks on Pam's face or neck. There are bruises on her legs, but they appear to be several days old and healing. You ask her if she wants to file a complaint against her husband. "No," Pam says. "That is just going to make the situation worse." Instead, she asks you to "find Bill and tell him to stop hitting me."

THE LAW Even without a warrant (which you will learn about in the next chapter), a police officer can make an arrest for a crime that he or she did not witness. There must be sufficient evidence, however, for the officer to be reasonably sure that the crime did occur and was committed by the suspect in question.

YOUR DECISION Use your discretion to address this situation. Do you believe that Bill has assaulted Pam? What further steps might you need to take before you can make this determination? Depending on the results of your investigation, will you arrest Bill for assaulting his wife? Be aware that you can arrest Bill even if Pam says that she does not want you to and refuses to cooperate in the process.

[To see how a police officer in the village of Cornwall-on-Hudson, New York, reacted in a similar situation, go to Example 6.1 in Appendix B.]

Rasmus Rasmusson/iStockphoto/iStockphoto/Photodisc/Shutterstock/James Stadl/iStockphoto

In light of this apparent reluctance, in the 1970s jurisdictions began passing legislation that severely limits police discretion in domestic violence cases. Today, twenty-three states have **mandatory arrest laws** that require a police officer to arrest a person who has abused someone related by blood or marriage.[16] The theory behind mandatory arrest policies is relatively straightforward: they act as a deterrent to criminal behavior. Costs are imposed on the person who is arrested. He or she must go to court and face the possibility of time in jail. Statistically, these laws appear to have met their goals. Researchers have found significantly higher arrest rates for domestic violence offenders in states with mandatory arrest laws than in states without them.[17]

Even so, mandatory arrest laws do not always trump police discretion. In a 2005 case, the United States Supreme Court refused to allow a civil lawsuit against Castle Rock (Colorado) police officers who failed to enforce a court order mandating that Jessica Gonzales's estranged husband keep at least one hundred yards away from her house at all times. (He eventually kidnapped and killed their three daughters.) In the decision, Justice Antonin Scalia pointed out that there is a "well established tradition of police discretion [that] has long coexisted with apparently mandatory arrest statutes."[18]

SELFASSESSMENT

Fill in the blanks and check your answers on page 208.
In general, a law enforcement officer has a great deal of _____ when it comes to his or her duties. When a police administration wants to curtail this freedom of action, it can institute a departmental _____ to guide the officer's decision making in certain situations, such as high-speed chases. With regard to domestic violence, many states have passed _____ _____ legislation to further restrict police discretion in this area.

POLICE ORGANIZATION AND FIELD OPERATIONS

After the Milwaukee Police Department changed its high-speed pursuit policy to further limit officers' discretion in chase situations, a city detective observed that many members of the force were demoralized. "They feel as though they are minimized as professionals" and not trusted to make good decisions, he said.[19] For American police officers, this situation exemplifies one of their frustrations: although they give orders on the streets, they must take orders at the station house.

The model of the modern police department is bureaucratic. In a **bureaucracy**, formal rules govern an individual's actions and relationships with co-employees. The ultimate goal of any bureaucracy is to reach its maximum efficiency—in the case of a police department, to provide the best service for the community within the confines of its limited resources such as staff and budget. Although some police departments are experimenting with alternative structures based on a partnership between management and the officers in the field,[20] most continue to rely on the hierarchical structure described below.

THE STRUCTURE OF THE POLICE DEPARTMENT

Each police department is organized according to its environment: the size of its jurisdiction, the type of crimes it must deal with, and the demographics of the population it must police. A police department in a racially diverse city often faces different challenges than a department in a homogeneous one. Geographic location also influences police organization. The makeup of the police department in Miami, Florida, for example, is partially determined by the fact that the city is a gateway for illegal drugs smuggled from Central and South America. Consequently, the department directs a high percentage of its resources to special drug-fighting units. It has also formed cooperative partnerships with federal agencies such as the FBI and U.S. Customs and Border Protection in an effort to stop the flow of narcotics and weapons into the South Florida area.

CHAIN OF COMMAND Whatever the size or location of a police department, it needs a clear rank structure and strict accountability to function properly.[21] One of the goals of the police reformers, especially beginning in the 1950s, was to lessen the corrupting influence of politicians. The result was a move toward a militaristic organization of police.[22] As you can see in Figure 6.1 on the following page, a typical police department is based on a chain of command that leads from the police chief down through the various levels of the department. In this formalized structure, all persons are aware of their place in the chain and of their duties and responsibilities within the organization.

Delegation of authority is a critical component of the chain of command, especially in larger departments. The chief of police delegates authority to division chiefs, who delegate authority to commanders, and on down through the organization. This structure creates a situation in which nearly every member of a police department is directly accountable to a superior. As was the original goal of police reformers, these links encourage discipline and control and lessen the possibility that any individual police employee will have the unsupervised freedom to abuse her or his position.[23] In keeping with the need to delegate authority, police departments in large cities divide their jurisdictions into *precincts*. The precinct commander is then held responsible by his or her superiors at police headquarters for the performance of the officers in the precinct.

LAW ENFORCEMENT IN THE FIELD To a large extent, the main goal of any police department is the most efficient organization of its *field services*. Also known as "operations" or "line services," field services include patrol activities, investigations, and special operations. According to Henry M. Wrobleski and Karen M. Hess, most police departments are "generalists." Thus, police officers are assigned to general areas and perform all field service functions within the boundaries of their beats. Larger departments may be more specialized, with personnel assigned to specific types of crime, such as illegal drugs or white-collar crime, rather than geographic locations. Smaller departments, which make up the bulk of local law enforcement agencies, rely almost exclusively on general patrol.[24]

POLICE ON PATROL:
THE BACKBONE OF THE DEPARTMENT

Every police department has a patrol unit, and patrol is usually the largest division in the department. More than two-thirds of the sworn officers, or those officers authorized to make arrests and use force, in local police departments in the United States have patrol duties.[25]

A lieutenant (in the white shirt) gives instructions to two sergeants. On his left, a patrol officer appears to be awaiting instructions. How do the delegation of authority and the chain of command contribute to police efficiency?
Elyse Rieder/Photo Researchers

Delegation of Authority The principles of command on which most police departments are based, in which personnel take orders from and are responsible to those in positions of power directly above them.

Sworn Officer A law enforcement agent who has been authorized to make arrests and use force, including deadly force, against civilians.

▷ **Live Scanner Broadcasts** allows you to listen in on radio reports from police officers in the field over the Internet. To find its Web site, visit the *Criminal Justice CourseMate* at **cengagebrain.com** and select the *Web links* for this chapter.

FIGURE 6.1 The Command Chain of the Lombard (Illinois) Police Department

The Lombard (Illinois) Police Department is made up of more than seventy sworn law enforcement officers and about thirty-five civilians. As you can see, the chain of command runs from the chief of police down to crossing guards and part-time clerks.

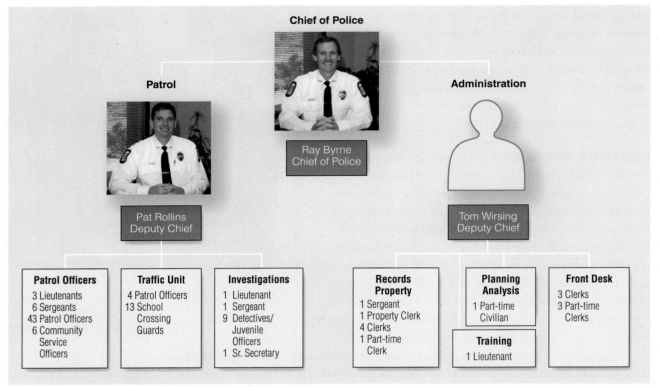

Chief of Police

Ray Byrne
Chief of Police

Patrol

Pat Rollins
Deputy Chief

Administration

Tom Wirsing
Deputy Chief

Patrol Officers	**Traffic Unit**	**Investigations**	**Records Property**	**Planning Analysis**	**Front Desk**
3 Lieutenants	4 Patrol Officers	1 Lieutenant	1 Sergeant	1 Part-time Civilian	3 Clerks
6 Sergeants	13 School Crossing Guards	1 Sergeant	1 Property Clerk		3 Part-time Clerks
43 Patrol Officers		9 Detectives/ Juvenile Officers	4 Clerks	**Training**	
6 Community Service Officers		1 Sr. Secretary	1 Part-time Clerk	1 Lieutenant	

Source: Lombard Police Department.

"Life on the street" is not easy. Patrol officers must be able to handle any number of difficult situations, and experience is often the best and, despite training programs, the only teacher. As one patrol officer commented:

> You never stop learning. You never get your street degree. The person who says . . . they've learned it all is the person that's going to wind up dead or in a very compromising position. They've closed their minds.[26]

It may take a patrol officer years to learn when a gang is "false flagging" (trying to trick rival gang members into the open) or what to look for in a suspect's eyes to sense if he or she is concealing a weapon. This learning process is the backdrop to a number of different general functions that a patrol officer must perform on a daily basis.

THE PURPOSE OF PATROL In general, patrol officers do not spend most of their shifts chasing, catching, and handcuffing suspected criminals. The vast majority of patrol shifts are completed without a single arrest.[27] Officers spend a great deal of time meeting with other officers, completing paperwork, and patrolling with the goal of preventing crime in general rather than focusing on any specific crime or criminal activity.

LO 2 As police accountability expert Samuel Walker has noted, the basic purposes of the police patrol have changed very little since 1829, when Sir Robert Peel founded the modern police department. These purposes include:

1. The deterrence of crime by maintaining a visible police presence.
2. The maintenance of public order and a sense of security in the community.
3. The twenty-four-hour provision of services that are not crime related.[28]

The first two goals—deterring crime and keeping order—are generally accepted as legitimate police functions. The third, however, has been more controversial.

COMMUNITY CONCERNS As noted in Chapter 5, the community era saw a resurgence of the patrol officer as a provider of community services, many of which have little to do with crime. The extent to which noncrime incidents dominate patrol officers' time is evident in the Police Services Study, a survey of 26,000 calls to police in sixty different neighborhoods. The study found that only one out of every five calls involved the report of criminal activity.[29] (See Figure 6.2 on the next page for the results of another survey of crime calls.)

There is some debate over whether community services should be allowed to dominate patrol officers' duties. The question, however, remains: If the police do not handle these problems, who will? Few cities have the financial resources to hire public servants to deal specifically with, for example, finding shelter for homeless persons. Furthermore, the police are the only public servants on call twenty-four hours a day, seven days a week, making them uniquely accessible to citizen needs.

Given that most patrol shifts end without an officer making a single arrest, what activities take up most of a patrol officer's time?
David Turnley/Corbis

PATROL ACTIVITIES To recap, the purposes of police patrols are to prevent and deter crime and also to provide social services. How can the police best accomplish these goals? Of course, each department has its own methods and strategies, but William Gay, Theodore Schell, and Stephen Schack are able to divide routine patrol activity into four general categories:

1. *Preventive patrol.* By maintaining a presence in a community, either in a car or on foot, patrol officers attempt to prevent crime from occurring. This strategy, which O. W. Wilson called "omnipresence," was a cornerstone of early policing philosophy and still takes up roughly 40 percent of patrol time.
2. *Calls for service.* Patrol officers spend nearly a quarter of their time responding to 911 calls for emergency service or other citizen problems and complaints.
3. *Administrative duties.* Paperwork takes up nearly 20 percent of patrol time.
4. *Officer-initiated activities.* Incidents in which the patrol officer initiates contact with citizens, such as stopping motorists and pedestrians and questioning them, account for 15 percent of patrol time.[30]

The category estimates made by Gay, Schell, and Schack are not universally accepted. Professor of law enforcement Gary W. Cordner argues that administrative duties account for the largest percentage of patrol officers' time. According to Cordner, when officers are not consumed with paperwork and meetings, they are either answering calls for service (which takes up 67 percent of the officers' time on the street) or initiating activities themselves (the remaining 33 percent).[31]

"NOISE, BOOZE, AND VIOLENCE" Indeed, there are dozens of academic studies that purport to answer the question of how patrol officers spend their days and nights. Perhaps it is only fair, then, to give a police officer the chance to describe the duties patrol officers perform. In the words of Anthony Bouza, a former police chief:

Group Activities: Invite a local police officer to the classroom. Ask students to interview the officer about his or her patrol activities. What activities comprise most of his or her shift? Are there activities that he or she must complete that seem inappropriate for law enforcement? (LO 2)

FIGURE 6.2 Calls for Service

Over a period of two years, the Project on Policing Neighborhoods gathered information on calls for service in Indianapolis, Indiana, and St. Petersburg, Florida. As you can see, the largest portion of these calls involved disputes where no violence or threat of violence existed. Be aware also that nearly two-thirds of the nonviolent dispute calls and nearly half of the assault calls answered by police dealt with domestic confrontations.

Description of Violation	Percentage of Total Calls
NONSERIOUS CRIME CALLS	
Nonviolent disputes	42
Public disorder (examples: drunk, disorderly, begging, prostitution)	22
Assistance (examples: missing persons, traffic accident, damaged property)	10
Minor violations (examples: shoplifting, trespassing, traffic/parking offense, refusal to pay)	4
SERIOUS CRIME CALLS	
Assaults (examples: using violence against a person, kidnapping, child abuse)	26
Serious theft (examples: motor vehicle theft, burglary, purse snatching)	5
General disorder (examples: illicit drugs, fleeing police, leaving the scene of an accident)	2

Source adapted from: Stephen D. Mastrofski, Jeffrey B. Snipes, Roger B. Parks, and Christopher D. Maxwell, "The Helping Hand of the Law: Police Control of Citizens on Request," *Criminology* 38 (May 2000), Table 5, page 328.

Getty Images

> **"One night ... it was so slow that three patrol cars showed up for a dispute between two crackheads over a shopping cart."**
>
> —**Marcus Laffey,**
> New York police officer

[Patrol officers] hurry from call to call, bound to their crackling radios, which offer no relief—especially on summer weekend nights. . . . The cops jump from crisis to crisis, rarely having time to do more than tamp one down sufficiently and leave for the next. Gaps of boredom and inactivity fill the interims, although there aren't many of these in the hot months. Periods of boredom get increasingly longer as the nights wear on and the weather gets colder.[32]

Bouza paints a picture of a routine beat as filled with "noise, booze, violence, drugs, illness, blaring TVs, and human misery." This may describe the situation in high-crime neighborhoods, but it certainly does not represent the reality for the majority of patrol officers in the United States. Duties that all patrol officers have in common, whether they work in Bouza's rather nightmarish city streets or in the quieter environment of rural America, include controlling traffic, conducting preliminary investigations, making arrests, and patrolling public events.

POLICE INVESTIGATIONS

Investigation is the second main function of police, along with patrol. Whereas patrol is primarily preventive, investigation is reactive. After a crime has been committed and the patrol officer has gathered the preliminary information from the crime scene, the responsibility of finding "who dunnit" is delegated to the investigator, generally known as the **detective.** The most common way for someone to become a detective is to be promoted from patrol officer. Detectives have not been the focus of nearly as much reform attention as their patrol counterparts, mainly because the scope of the detective's job is limited to law enforcement, with less emphasis given to social services or order maintenance.

DETECTIVES IN ACTION The detective's job is not quite as glamorous as it is sometimes portrayed by the media. Detectives spend much of their time investigating common crimes such as burglaries and are more likely to be tracking down stolen property than a murderer. They must also prepare cases for trial, which involves a great deal of time-consuming

Teaching Tip: Invite a local detective to visit your classroom. Ask her or him to discuss the the educational and professional requirements for becoming a detective. Then, ask her or him to describe a typical day on the job.

Detective The primary police investigator of crimes.

CAREERS IN CJ

MARTHA BLAKE
FORENSIC SCIENTIST

In high school, I was interested in science, but didn't want to end up being a technician doing the same thing every day. I was looking in college catalogues and came across criminalistics at U.C. Berkeley. The coursework included such courses as microscopy, instrumental analysis, trace evidence, criminal law, and statistics, and it sounded fascinating. I decided in my senior year of high school to become a forensic scientist.

TAKING NOTES Working in a crime lab, I enjoy the variety and the challenge of the types of physical evidence that are examined and evaluated. I am most happy, though, examining "questioned documents," which are written communications whose authenticity or origin is in question. A bank robbery note could be a questioned document, for example, as could writing on a wall, a stolen check, a threat/extortion letter, or medical records. When I was hired as a forensic document examiner in 1990, there were numerous bank robberies in San Francisco with demand notes, usually hand-printed with text like "This is a robbery, give me all the $100s, $50s, and $20s in your drawer or I will shoot you." The notes interested me, so I started "collecting" them by copying the writing down on note cards.

I have about one hundred bank robbery notes in my collection. My favorite is fictional, from the Woody Allen movie *Take the Money and Run*. In the process of trying to rob a bank, the hapless Allen character hands the teller a note that says, "I have a gub," causing mass confusion. I've also seen a note that said, "You have 5½ seconds to do what I say." How do you count to 5½? My collection is not just for laughs, however. Once I was able to match a note from my collection to a new one that had just come in from a fresh bank robbery. Thanks to my "hobby," the police were able to arrest the suspect.

COURT WORK As quality assurance manager at the San Francisco Police Department's crime lab, I am often called to criminal court to testify about evidence that has passed through our lab. I am always nervous when I testify, and I think it is healthy to be a little nervous. As an expert witness, the most challenging part of my testimony is describing my findings to a jury of primarily nonscientists in a way that will make my testimony understandable and credible. I've found that juries tend to understand evidence that is part of their lives. Everyone can identify the writing of a family member or spouse, so describing how handwriting is identified is not too hard. Explaining how DNA analysis works is more difficult.

CAREER ADVICE Be sure you are interested in forensic science for the right reasons, and not because it looks cool or glamorous on TV. Successful forensic careers are shaped by hard work—attending seminars, presenting research, and striving for certification in a specialty such as forensic biology, questioned documents, and firearms identification. A good foundation in chemistry is essential; other useful degrees include biology, biochemistry, and physics.

FASTFACTS

FORENSIC SCIENTIST, JOB DESCRIPTION:

- Examine, test, and analyze tissue samples, chemical substances, physical materials, and ballistics evidence collected at crime scene.

- Reconstruct crime scene to determine relationships among pieces of evidence.

- Prepare reports or presentations of findings, investigative methods, or laboratory techniques.

- Testify as an expert witness on evidence or laboratory techniques in trials or hearings.

WHAT KIND OF TRAINING IS REQUIRED?

- Bachelor's degree in science, particularly chemistry, biology, biochemistry, or physics.

- Certification programs (usually 2 years additional study) can help prospective applicants specialize as forensic consultants, fingerprint technicians, forensic investigators, laboratory technicians, and fingerprint examiners.

ANNUAL SALARY RANGE? BENEFITS?

- $25,100–$65,000

For additional information on a career as a forensic scientist, visit: **www.aafs.org**.

paperwork. Furthermore, a landmark Rand Corporation study estimated that more than 97 percent of cases that are "solved" can be attributed to a patrol officer making an arrest at the scene, witnesses or victims identifying the perpetrator, or detectives undertaking routine investigative procedures that could easily be performed by clerical personnel.[33] For example, it was not detective work but an informant's tip that led to the arrest several years ago of two men responsible for twenty-four random attacks—seven of which resulted in death—over a period of nearly fifteen months in the Phoenix, Arizona, area. "There is no Sherlock Holmes," said one investigator. "The good detective on the street is the one who knows all the weasels and one of the weasels will tell him who did it."[34]

THE DETECTION FUNCTION A detective division in the larger police departments usually has a number of sections. These sections often include crimes against persons, such as homicide or sexual assault, and crimes against property, such as burglary and robbery. Many departments have separate detective divisions that deal exclusively with *vice,* a broad term that covers a number of public order crimes such as prostitution, gambling, and pornography. In the past, vice officers have also been primarily responsible for narcotics violations, but many departments now devote entire units to that particular social and legal problem.

The ideal case for any detective, of course, is one in which the criminal stays on the scene of the crime, has the weapon in her or his hands when apprehended, and, driven by an overriding sense of guilt, confesses immediately. Such cases are, needless to say, rare. University of Cincinnati criminal justice professor John E. Eck, in attempting to improve the understanding of the investigative process, concluded that investigators face three categories of cases:

- *Unsolvable cases,* or weak cases that cannot be solved regardless of investigative effort.
- *Solvable cases,* or cases with moderate evidence that can be solved with considerable investigative effort.
- *Already solved cases,* or cases with strong evidence that can be solved with minimum investigative effort.[35]

Eck found that the "unsolvable cases," once identified as such, should not be investigated because the effort would be wasted, and that the "already solved cases" require little additional effort or time on the part of detectives. Therefore, Eck concluded, the investigation resources of a law enforcement agency should primarily be aimed at "solvable cases." Further research by Steven G. Brandl and James Frank found that detectives had relatively high success rates in investigating burglary and robbery cases for which a moderate level of evidence was available.[36] Thus, the Rand study cited above may be somewhat misleading, in that investigators can routinely produce positive results as long as they concentrate on those cases that potentially can be solved. (To learn the factors that help law enforcement agents solve cases, see Figure 6.3 on the facing page.)

AGGRESSIVE INVESTIGATION STRATEGIES

LO 3 Detective bureaus also have the option of implementing more aggressive strategies. For example, if detectives suspect that a person was involved in the robbery of a Mercedes-Benz parts warehouse, one of them might pose as a "fence"—or purchaser of stolen goods. In what is known as a "sting" operation, the suspect is deceived into thinking that the detective (fence) wants to buy stolen car parts. After the transaction takes place, the suspect can be arrested.

Technology Tip: Have students visit the Bureau of Labor Statistics online to learn more about a career as a detective at **www.bls.gov/oco/ocos160.htm**.

FIGURE 6.3 Solvability Factors

During their investigations of crimes, officers with the Rochester (New York) Police Department pay close attention to the solvability factors listed here. Without the answers to at least some of these questions, the chances of determining who committed the crime are minimal.

1. Are there any eyewitnesses to the crime?
2. Has the suspect been identified by name or otherwise?
3. Where did the crime occur?
4. Is a description of the suspect available?
5. If the crime is a property crime, does the stolen property have any recognizable marks, numbers, or other identifiable characteristics?
6. Do the particulars of the crime match any other crimes committed recently?
7. Is there significant physical evidence (bodily fluids, hair, fingerprints) at the crime scene?
8. Has a vehicle involved with the crime been identified?
9. Will additional investigative work or media assistance increase the probabiliy of solving the crime?
10. Is it possible that someone other than the suspect is responsible for the crime?

Source: Adapted from Ronald F. Becker, *Criminal Investigation*, 2d ed. (Sudbury, MA: Jones and Bartlett Publishers, 2005), 145.

UNDERCOVER OPERATIONS Perhaps the most dangerous and controversial operation a law enforcement agent can undertake is to go *undercover*, or to assume a false identity in order to obtain information concerning illegal activities. Though each department has its own guidelines on when undercover operations are necessary, all that is generally required is the suspicion that illegal activity is taking place. (As you may recall from the discussion of entrapment in Chapter 4, police officers are limited in what they can do to convince the target of an undercover operation to participate in the illegal activity.) Today, undercover officers are most commonly used to infiltrate large-scale narcotics operations or those run by organized crime. Undercover operations, though extremely dangerous, can yield impressive results. In April 2010, evidence gathered by an FBI agent who infiltrated the Michigan-based militia organization Hutaree led to the arrest of seven of the group's members for plotting to kill law enforcement officers.

CONFIDENTIAL INFORMANTS In some situations, a detective bureau may not want to take the risk of exposing an officer to undercover work or may believe that an outsider cannot infiltrate an organized crime network. When the police need access and information, they have the option of turning to a **confidential informant (CI)**. A CI is a person who is involved in criminal activity and gives information about that activity and those who engage in it to the police. The United States Supreme Court, in *Rovario v. United States* (1957),[37] held that the state has a confidential informant privilege, which means that it is not required to disclose the identity of an informant unless a court finds that such information is needed to determine the guilt or innocence of a suspect.

CLEARANCE RATES AND COLD CASES

The ultimate goal of all law enforcement activity is to *clear* a crime, or secure the arrest and prosecution of the offender. Even a cursory glance at **clearance rates,** which show the percentage of reported crimes that have been cleared, reveals that investigations succeed only part of the time. In 2010, just 65 percent of homicides and 47 percent of

Critical Thinking Skill Development: Have students work in small groups to discuss the advantages and disadvantages of the aggressive patrol strategies discussed in this section of the text. When are tactics such as these necessary? (LO 3)

Confidential Informant (CI) A human source for police who provides information concerning illegal activity in which he or she is involved.

Clearance Rate A comparison of the number of crimes cleared by arrest and prosecution with the number of crimes reported during any given time period.

By posing as a "Muggable Mary," this undercover New York detective is offering herself as bait to lure would-be muggers. What might be some of the deterrent effects on potential muggers of this sort of police strategy?
Corbis/Bettmann

Cold Case A criminal investigation that has not been solved after a certain amount of time.

Forensics The application of science to establish facts and evidence during the investigation of crimes.

total violent crimes were solved, while police cleared only 18 percent of property crimes.[38] To a large extent, the different clearance rates for different crimes reflect the resources that a law enforcement agency expends on each type of crime. The police generally investigate a murder or a rape more vigorously than the theft of an automobile or a computer.

DECLINING CLEARANCE RATES Despite the best efforts of detectives and other police officers, the clearance rate for violent crimes has been dropping for decades. In the early 1960s, the clearance rate for homicides was as high as 91 percent.[39] According to law enforcement officials, the main reason for this decline is a change in the demographics of murder. Fifty years ago, the majority of killers and victims knew each other, and investigations focused on finding clues to this relationship. Today, police are dealing with a large number of impersonal and anonymous drug- and gang-related slayings, and the clues no longer exist. "With the gangs and the drugs," said one expert, "we don't have that ability to establish motive, opportunity, and means."[40]

UNSOLVED CASES As a result of low clearance rates, police departments are saddled with an increasing number of cold cases, or criminal investigations that are not cleared after a certain amount of time. (The length of time before a case becomes "cold" varies from department to department. In general, a cold case must be "somewhat old" but not "so old that there can be no hope of ever solving it".[41]) More than 80 percent of large-city police departments have cold case squads dedicated to unsolved crimes.[42]

Without these squads, cold cases can have a domino effect within a police department. Detectives will continue to work on the older case even as newer cases present themselves, making it even less likely that the newer cases will be solved (and more likely that the offender will remain free to commit more crimes).[43] Thus, cold case squads are essential for the smooth functioning of law enforcement.

FORENSIC INVESTIGATIONS AND DNA

Although the crime scene typically offers a wealth of evidence, some of it is incomprehensible to a patrol officer or detective without assistance. For that aid, law enforcement officers rely on experts in forensics, or the practice of using science and technology to investigate crimes. Forensic experts apply their knowledge to items found at the crime scene to determine crucial facts such as:

- The cause of death or injury.
- The time of death or injury.
- The type of weapon or weapons used.
- The identity of the crime victim, if that information is unavailable.
- The identity of the offender (in the best-case scenario).[44]

To assist forensic experts, many police departments operate or are affiliated with crime laboratories. As we noted in the previous chapter, the FBI also offers the services of its crime lab, the largest in the world, to agencies with limited resources.

CRIME SCENE FORENSICS The first law enforcement agent to reach a crime scene has the important task of protecting any trace evidence from contamination. Trace evidence is generally very small—often invisible to the naked human eye—and often requires technological aid for detection. Hairs, fibers, blood, fingerprints, broken glass, and footprints are all examples of trace evidence. A study released by the National Institute of Justice in 2010 confirmed that when police are able to link such evidence to a suspect, the likelihood of a conviction rises dramatically.[45] Police will also search a crime scene for bullets and spent cartridge casings. These items can provide clues as to how far the shooter was from the target. They can also be compared with information stored in national firearms databases to determine, under some circumstances, the gun used and its most recent owner. The study of firearms and its application to solving crimes goes under the general term ballistics.

The Human Fingerprint For more than a century, the most important piece of trace evidence has been the human fingerprint. Because no two fingerprints are alike, they are considered reliable sources of identification. Forensic scientists compare a fingerprint lifted from a crime scene with that of a suspect and declare a match if there are between eight and sixteen "points of similarity." This method of identification is not infallible, however. It is often difficult to lift a suitable print from a crime scene, and researchers have uncovered numerous cases in which innocent persons were convicted based on evidence obtained through faulty fingerprinting procedures.[46]

Bloodstain Pattern Analysis Many of those working in the field will tell you that forensics is as much art as science. Some of the most creative "artists" in forensics are those who engage in *bloodstain pattern analysis.* Specialists can learn a great deal about a violent crime by examining where blood landed at the scene, the size and consistency of the drops, and the pattern of the blood spatter.

A skilled bloodstain pattern analyst can, in some instances, even re-create the crime, determining the type of weapon, the movements of the victim and the assailant, the timing of the action, and other relevant details.[47] Several years ago, for example, Paul Foglia was convicted of murder in large part because of a bloodstain on his shoe. An expert from the New Jersey State Police determined not only that the blood belonged to victim Elizabeth Lott, but also that the "impact stain" was caused by "medium-velocity force blunt trauma" such as a swung baseball bat or club.[48]

THE DNA REVOLUTION The technique of DNA fingerprinting, or using a suspect's DNA to match the suspect to a crime, emerged in the mid-1990s and has now all but replaced fingerprint evidence in many types of criminal investigations. The shift has been a boon to crime fighters: one law enforcement agent likened DNA fingerprinting to "the finger of God pointing down" at a guilty suspect.[49]

DNA, which is the same in each cell of a person's body, provides a "genetic blueprint" or "code" for every living organism. DNA fingerprinting is useful in criminal investigations because no two people, save for identical twins, have the same genetic code. Therefore, lab technicians, using the process described in Figure 6.4 on the next page, can compare the DNA sample of a suspect to the evidence found at the crime scene. If the match is negative, it is certain that the two samples did not come from the same source. If the match is positive, the lab will determine the odds that the DNA sample could have come from someone other than the suspect. Those odds are so high—sometimes reaching 30 billion to one—that a match is practically conclusive.[50]

LO 4

Trace Evidence Evidence such as a fingerprint, blood, or hair found in small amounts at a crime scene.
Ballistics The study of firearms, including the firing of the weapon and the flight of the bullet.
DNA Fingerprinting The identification of a person based on a sample of her or his DNA, the genetic material found in the cells of all living things.

Technology Tip: Have students learn more about careers in forensics online at the American Academy of Forensic Sciences at **www.aafs.org/choosing-career**.

FIGURE 6.4 Unlocking Evidence in DNA

Deoxyribonucleic acid, or DNA, is the genetic material that carries the code for all living cells. Through DNA profiling, a process explained here, forensic scientists test DNA samples to see if they match the DNA profile of a known criminal or other test subject.

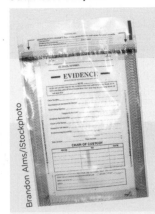

1. DNA samples can be taken from a number of sources, including saliva, blood, hair, or skin. These samples are labeled and shipped to a forensic lab.

2. The DNA is extracted from the cells of the sample using complex proteins known as enzymes. An electrical charge is then sent through the resulting DNA fragments to separate them according to size.

3. Another set of enzymes is added to the now separate DNA fragments. These enzymes attach themselves to different categories of genetic material within the DNA fragments and become distinct when exposed to photographic film. The "photograph" of this visible pattern is the DNA fingerprint.

4. Crime lab technicians will look for thirteen points on the DNA fingerprint called "markers." These thirteen markers are then compared with a suspect's DNA or with DNA found at a crime scene. If a match is found for each of the thirteen markers, there is almost no chance that the two DNA samples came from different persons.

The initial use of DNA to establish criminal guilt took place in Britain in 1986. The FBI used it for the first time in the United States two years later. The process begins when forensic technicians gather blood, semen, skin, saliva, or hair from the scene of a crime. Blood cells and sperm are rich in DNA, making them particularly useful in murder and rape cases, but DNA has also been extracted from sweat on dirty laundry, skin cells on eyeglasses, and saliva on used envelope seals. Once a suspect is identified, her or his DNA can be used to determine whether she or he can be placed at the crime scene. In 2011, for example, investigators connected Aaron Thomas, the "East Coast Rapist," to a series of sexual assaults that took place from Rhode Island to Virginia by obtaining Thomas's DNA sample from a discarded cigarette.

DNA IN ACTION The ability to "dust" for genetic information on such a wide variety of evidence, as well as that evidence's longevity and accuracy, greatly increases the chances that a crime will be solved (review the solvability factors in Figure 6.3 on page 181). Indeed, police no longer need a witness or even a suspect in custody to solve crimes. What they do need is a piece of evidence and a database.

In 2010, for example, Samuel Roshard Cole was convicted of abducting and raping a woman in Petersburg, Virginia, eight years earlier. During most of that time, law enforcement had been unable to identify a suspect in the case. When Cole was arrested for an unrelated charge in 2008, however, he was required to provide authorities with a sample of his DNA. Technicians entered the sample into the state's database, where it matched DNA evidence taken from the earlier rape victim's T-shirt.

Databases and Cold Hits The identification of Samuel Roshard Cole is an example of what police call a **cold hit,** which occurs when law enforcement finds a suspect "out of nowhere" by comparing DNA evidence from a crime scene against the contents of a database. The largest and most important database is the National Combined DNA Index System (CODIS). Operated by the FBI since 1998, CODIS gives local and state law enforcement agencies access to the DNA profiles of those who have been convicted of various crimes. CODIS contains DNA records of nearly 10 million people, and as of July 2011, the database had produced 149,200 cold hits nationwide.[51]

Cold Hit The establishment of a connection between a suspect and a crime, often through the use of DNA evidence, in the absence of an ongoing criminal investigation.

New Developments The investigative uses of DNA fingerprinting are expanding rapidly. Taking advantage of a new technique known as "touch DNA," investigators can collect evidence from surfaces that are not marked by obvious clues such as bloodstains or well-preserved fingerprints. With this technique, forensic scientists can gather enough microscopic cells to test for the presence of DNA by scraping a piece of food or an article of clothing. In addition, although CODIS was designed to help police solve murders and rapes, it is becoming increasingly useful in identifying suspects in burglaries and other property crimes. A recent study funded by the National Institute of Justice found that twice as many suspects were arrested when DNA fingerprinting was added to property crime investigations.[52]

How did "familial DNA" lead investigators to Lonnie Franklin, Jr., left, shown here in a Los Angeles courtroom? Why might privacy advocates criticize this method of using DNA to identify criminal suspects? AP Photo/Irfan Khan, Pool

Because relatives have similar DNA, law enforcement agents are now conducting "familial searches" of parents, siblings, and other relatives to gain more information about suspects. One such search led to the 2010 arrest of Los Angeles's "Grim Sleeper"— so called because there was a fourteen-year gap between the murders he committed in the 1980s and those in the 2000s. Investigators were able to narrow their focus to Lonnie Franklin, Jr., after DNA evidence from various Grim Sleeper crime scenes exhibited similarities to the DNA of Lonnie's son Christopher, who had recently been convicted on a weapon's charge (see the photo above). Forensic experts are also raising the possibility that DNA will be able to act as a "genetic witness." That is, a DNA sample taken from a crime scene soon may be able to provide law enforcement with a physical description of a suspect, including her or his eye, skin, and hair color and age.[53]

An Imperfect Science Even though DNA fingerprinting has proved to be the most reliable form of forensic science, the process is not infallible. Human error, as always, can distort results. A crime lab in Houston, Texas, was shut down twice in the first decade of the 2000s because of contaminated DNA and other problems that resulted in the release of six wrongly convicted men from prison.[54] Furthermore, the rush to collect and analyze DNA has overwhelmed crime lab technicians, causing evidence to sit untested for long periods of time due to lack of resources. The Houston crime lab, for example, has four thousand rape kits containing DNA samples waiting to be tested—some date back to the 1980s. Finally, privacy and civil rights advocates protest that DNA collection has gone too far. Authorities now collect samples from those who have been convicted of nonviolent crimes and, in some instances, from those who have merely been arrested for a crime but not convicted. (We will examine the controversy surrounding that practice in the *CJ in Action* feature at the end of the chapter.)

Technology Tip: Have students learn more about false convictions and the science of DNA online at the Innocence Project's Web site: **www.innocenceproject.org**. (LO 4)

SELFASSESSMENT

Fill in the blanks and check your answers on page 208.
_____ officers make up the backbone of a police department. One of their primary functions is to _____ crime by maintaining a visible _____ in the community. _____, in contrast, investigate crimes that have already occurred. In the past two decades, _____, or the science of crime investigation, has been revolutionized by the technique of _____ _____, in which crime labs use samples of a person's genetic material to match suspects to crimes.

POLICE STRATEGIES: WHAT WORKS

No matter how "miraculous" DNA fingerprinting may appear, the technology does have its limitations. Forensic evidence, including DNA fingerprinting, is the primary factor in only about 30 percent of solved cold cases.[55] Furthermore, any evidence, forensic or otherwise, can only help police solve a crime that has already taken place. It does little to prevent crime that has yet to occur. Finally, law enforcement's ability to take advantage of DNA fingerprinting is being hampered by extensive budget cuts. The state crime lab in Kansas, for example, is facing a backlog of nearly one thousand cases, while the state has reduced the number of technicians who work there by one-fifth.[56]

Police departments are facing the same financial pressures. Across the nation, many are being forced to reduce staff to levels not seen since the 1980s. The results can be disheartening: two months after Camden, New Jersey, laid off more than 160 officers in January 2011, violent crime in the city rose 19 percent, and aggravated assaults with firearms increased by 259 percent.[57] Some departments have taken drastic steps in the face of budget cuts. After losing 300 officers, the Fresno (California) Police Department began utilizing volunteers to perform duties such as collecting evidence and interviewing witnesses.[58] For the most part, however, police administrators are refocusing on two bulwarks of police crime prevention—responding to calls for service and providing effective patrols.

RESPONSE TIME TO 911 CALLS

Even though law enforcement officers do not like to think of themselves as being at the "beck and call" of citizens, that is the operational basis of much police work. All police departments practice **incident-driven policing,** in which calls for service are the primary instigators of action. Between 40 and 60 percent of police activity is the result of 911 calls or other citizen requests, which means that police officers in the field initiate only about half of such activity.[59]

RESPONSE TIME AND EFFICIENCY The speed with which the police respond to calls for service has traditionally been seen as a crucial aspect of crime fighting and crime prevention. In incident-driven policing, the ideal scenario is as follows: a citizen sees a person committing a crime and calls 911, and the police arrive quickly and catch the perpetrator in the act. Alternatively, a citizen who is the victim of a crime, such as a mugging, calls 911 as soon as possible, and the police arrive to catch the mugger before she or he can flee the immediate area of the crime. Although such scenarios are quite rare in real life, **response time,** or the time elapsed between the instant a call for service is received and the instant the police arrive on the scene, has become a benchmark for police efficiency.

IMPROVING RESPONSE TIME EFFICIENCY Many police departments have come to realize that overall response time is not as critical as response time for the most important calls. For this reason, since the mid-1990s, a number of metropolitan areas have introduced 311 nonemergency call systems to reduce the strain on 911 operations.[60] Another popular method of improving performance in this area is a **differential response** strategy, in which the police distinguish among different calls for service so that they can respond more quickly to the most serious incidents. Suppose, for example, that a police department receives two calls for service at the same time. The first caller reports that a burglar is in her house, and the second says that he has returned home from work to find his automobile missing. If the depart-

LO 5

Incident-Driven Policing A reactive approach to policing that emphasizes a speedy response to calls for service.

Response Time The rapidity with which calls for service are answered.

Differential Response A strategy for answering calls for service in which response time is adapted to the seriousness of the call.

Discussion Tip: Have students work in small groups to discuss the advantages of differential response. Then have them consider the possible problems that could arise as a result of this practice. (LO 5)

ment employs differential response, the burglary in progress—a "hot" crime—will receive immediate attention. The missing automobile—a "cold" crime that could have been committed several hours earlier—will receive attention "as time permits," and the caller may even be asked to make an appointment to come to the police station to formally report the theft. (See Figure 6.5 below for possible responses to calls to a 911 operator.)

There is some evidence that response time is linked to departmental resources. After an 11 percent reduction in the number of sworn officers in January 2010, the Tulsa (Oklahoma) Police Department's average response time for top-priority calls was 18 percent slower than in the previous year.[61] Also in 2010, after the Los Angeles Sheriff's Department budget was cut by $128 million, 911 emergency response times dropped by a full minute.[62] Another worry is that the 911 system has become outdated because it cannot locate mobile phones or VOIP (voice-over-Internet protocol) services. The technology can only provide dispatchers with the address at which phone service is registered. If, as often occurs, the call is not coming from a landline and the caller cannot provide the location, the dispatcher will be unable to send law enforcement to the scene of the emergency.

An operator takes a 911 call at the Sumter City–County Law Enforcement Center in Sumter, South Carolina. What does the importance of 911 systems tell us about the way that much police activity is initiated?
AP Photo/*The Item*, Keith Gedamke

PATROL STRATEGIES

Earlier in this chapter, we noted that the majority of police officers are assigned to patrol duties. Most of these officers work **general patrol,** making the rounds of a specific area with the purpose of carrying out the various patrol functions. Every police department in the United States patrols its jurisdiction using automobiles. In addition, 53 percent

General Patrol A patrol strategy that relies on police officers monitoring a certain area with the goal of detecting crimes in progress or preventing crime due to their presence. Also known as *random* or *preventive patrol.*

FIGURE 6.5 Putting the Theory of Differential Response into Action

Differential response strategies are based on a simple concept: treat emergencies like emergencies and nonemergencies like nonemergencies. As you see, calls for service that involve "hot crimes" will be dealt with immediately, while those that report "cold crimes" will be dealt with at some point in the future.

"HOT" CALLS FOR SERVICE—IMMEDIATE RESPONSE	
Complaint to 911 Officer	**Rationale**
"I just got home from work and I can see someone in my bedroom through the window."	Possibility that the intruder is committing a crime.
"My husband has a baseball bat, and he says he's going to kill me."	Crime in progress
"A woman in a green jacket just grabbed my purse and ran away."	Chances of catching the suspect are increased with immediate action.

"COLD" CALLS FOR SERVICE—ALTERNATIVE RESPONSE	
"I got to my office about two hours ago, but I just noticed that the fax machine was stolen during the night."	The crime occurred at least two hours earlier.
"The guy in the apartment above me has been selling pot for years, and I'm sick and tired of it."	Not an emergency situation.
"My husband came home late two nights ago with a black eye, and I finally got him to admit that he didn't run into a doorknob. Larry Smith smacked him."	Past crime with a known suspect who is unlikely to flee.

Source: Adapted from John S. Dempsey and Linda S. Forst, *An Introduction to Policing,* 6th ed. (Clifton Park, NY: Delmar Cengage Learning, 2011), 260–261.

utilize foot patrols, 32 percent bicycle patrols, 16 percent motorcycle patrols, 4 percent boat patrols, and 1 percent horse patrols.[63]

General patrols are *random* because the officers spend a substantial amount of their shifts hoping to notice any crimes that may be occurring. In contrast, **directed patrols** are specifically designed to deal with crimes that commonly occur in certain locations and under circumstances that provide police with opportunity for preparation. The Pittsburgh (Pennsylvania) Police Department's recent decision to set up weekend traffic checkpoints and send undercover detectives into "nuisance" bars in some of the city's high-violence neighborhoods is a good example of a directed patrol.

Directed Patrol A patrol strategy that is designed to focus on a specific type of criminal activity at a specific time.

Teaching Tip: In a short writing assignment, ask students to explain the value of directed patrols. Which do students feel is more effective in fighting crime—general patrols or directed patrols?

TESTING GENERAL PATROL THEORIES IN KANSAS CITY Some observers have compared a patrol officer to a scarecrow because of the hope that the officer's presence alone will deter any would-be criminals from attempting a crime.[64] This theory was tested in the Kansas City Preventive Patrol Experiment of 1972 and 1973. With the cooperation of the local police department, a team of researchers chose three areas, each comprising five beats with similar crime statistics. (A *beat*, in this instance, is the area that a police officer or group of police officers regularly patrol.) Over the course of twelve months, the police applied different patrol strategies to each designated area:

- On the *control* beats, normal preventive measures were taken, meaning that a single automobile drove the streets when not answering a call for service.
- On the *proactive* beats, the level of preventive measures was increased, with automobile patrols being doubled or tripled.
- On the *reactive* beats, preventive patrol was eliminated entirely, and patrol cars only answered calls for service.

Before, during, and after the experiments, the researchers also interviewed residents of the three designated areas to determine their opinion of police service and fear of crime.

The results of the Kansas City experiment were somewhat shocking. Researchers found that increasing or decreasing preventive patrol had little or no impact on crimes, public opinion, the effectiveness of the police, police response time, traffic accidents, or reports of crime to police.[65]

Critical Thinking Skill Development: Ask students to write a short paper on the Kansas City Experiment. What was learned in Kansas City, and how does it impact our perceptions of preventive police patrol?

INTERPRETING THE KANSAS CITY EXPERIMENT Criminologists were, and continue to be, somewhat divided on how to interpret these results. For some, the Kansas City experiment and other similar data prove that patrol officers, after a certain threshold, are not effective in preventing crime and that scarce law enforcement resources should therefore be diverted to other areas. "It makes about as much sense to have police patrol routinely in cars to fight crime as it does to have firemen patrol routinely in fire trucks to fight fire," said University of Delaware professor Carl Klockars.[66]

Others saw the experiment as proving only one conclusion in a very specific set of circumstances and were unwilling to accept the results as universal. Professor James Q. Wilson, for example, argues that the study showed only that random patrols in marked police cars were of questionable value and that it proved nothing about other types of police presence such as foot patrols or patrols in unmarked vehicles.[67]

PREDICTIVE POLICING AND CRIME MAPPING

In the previous chapter, we discussed how predictive, or intelligence-led, policing strategies help law enforcement agencies anticipate patterns of criminal activity, allowing them to respond to, or even prevent, crime more effectively. Predictive policing is also increasingly attractive to police administrators because, at least in theory, it requires fewer resources than traditional policing. "With predictive policing, we have the tools to put the cops at the right place at the right time," said George Gascon, formerly the chief of police for the San Francisco Police Department, "and we can do so with less."[68]

> ## "Why aren't we thinking more about 'wheredunit' rather than 'whodunit'?"
>
> **—Lawrence Sherman,**
> American criminologist

FINDING "HOT SPOTS" Predictive policing strategies are strongly linked with directed patrols, which seek to improve on general patrols by targeting specific high-crime areas already known to law enforcement.[69] The target areas for directed patrols are often called **hot spots** because they contain greater numbers of criminals and have higher-than-average levels of victimization. Data gathered in Seattle over a fourteen-year period, for example, showed that 5 percent of the city's blocks accounted for 50 percent of its reported crime.[70] Similarly, a Minneapolis study found that 3 percent of the addresses in the city accounted for half of all calls for service.[71]

Needless to say, police administrators are no longer sticking pins in maps to determine where hot spots exist. Rather, police departments are using **crime mapping** technology to locate and identify hot spots and "cool" them down. Crime mapping uses geographic information systems (GIS) to track criminal acts as they occur in time and space. Once sufficient information has been gathered, it is analyzed to predict future crime patterns.

THE RISE OF COMPSTAT Computerized crime mapping was popularized when the New York Police Department launched CompStat in the mid-1990s. Still in use, CompStat starts with police officers reporting the exact location of crime and other crime-related information to department officials. These reports are then fed into a computer, which prepares grids of a particular city or neighborhood and highlights areas with a high incidence of serious offenses. (See Figure 6.6 on the next page for an example of a GIS crime map.) In New York and many other cities, the police department holds "Crime Control Strategy Meetings" during which precinct commanders are held accountable for CompStat's data-based reports in their districts. In theory, this system provides the police with accurate information about patterns of crime and gives them the ability to "flood" hot spots with officers at short notice. About two-thirds of large departments now employ some form of computerized crime mapping,[72] and Wesley Skogan, a criminologist at Northwestern University, believes that CompStat and similar technologies are the most likely cause of recent declines in big-city crime.[73]

ARREST STRATEGIES

Like patrol strategies, arrest strategies can be broken into two categories that reflect the intent of police administrators. **Reactive arrests** are those arrests made by police officers, usually on general patrol, who observe a criminal act or respond to a call for service. **Proactive arrests** occur when the police take the initiative to target a particular type of criminal or behavior. Proactive arrests are often associated with directed patrols of hot spots, and thus are believed by many experts to have a greater influence on an area's crime rates.[74]

THE BROKEN WINDOWS EFFECT To a certain extent, the popularity of proactive theories was solidified by a magazine article that James Q. Wilson and George L. Kelling wrote in 1982.[75] In their piece, entitled "Broken Windows," Wilson and Kelling argued

Hot Spots Concentrated areas of high criminal activity that draw a directed police response.

Crime Mapping Technology that allows crime analysts to identify trends and patterns of criminal behavior within a given area.

Reactive Arrests Arrests that come about as part of the ordinary routine of police patrol and responses to calls for service.

Proactive Arrests Arrests that occur because of concerted efforts by law enforcement agencies to respond to a particular type of criminal or criminal behavior.

Discussion Tip: Ask students to compare reactive and proactive arrests as crime prevention strategies. Do students believe one is more effective in preventing crime than the other?

FIGURE 6.6 A GIS Crime Map for a Neighborhood in New Orleans

This crime map shows the incidence of various crimes during a two-week period in a neighborhood near downtown New Orleans.

that reform-era policing strategies focused on violent crime to the detriment of the vital police role of promoting the quality of life in neighborhoods. As a result, many communities, particularly in large cities, had fallen into a state of disorder and disrepute, with two very important consequences. First, these neighborhoods—with their broken windows, dilapidated buildings, and lawless behavior by residents—send out "signals" that criminal activity is tolerated. Second, this disorder spreads fear among law-abiding citizens, dissuading them from leaving their homes or attempting to improve their surroundings.

Thus, the **broken windows theory** is based on "order maintenance" of neighborhoods by cracking down on "quality-of-life" crimes such as panhandling, public drinking and urinating, loitering, and graffiti painting. Only by encouraging directed arrest strategies with regard to these quality-of-life crimes, the two professors argued, could American cities be rescued from rising crime rates.

SUPPORTERS AND CRITICS Like CompStat, the implementation of Wilson and Kelling's theory as a police strategy has been given a great deal of credit for crime decreases in American cities (particularly New York) over the past three decades.[76] It has remained in favor among police administrators, despite debate in the academic community over whether the tactics have any measurable impact on violent crime in blighted neighborhoods.[77] Critics insist that instituting "zero-tolerance" arrest policies for lesser crimes in low-income neighborhoods not only discriminates against the poor and minority groups but also fosters a strong mistrust of police.[78]

COMMUNITY POLICING AND PROBLEM SOLVING

In "Broken Windows," Wilson and Kelling insisted that, to reduce fear and crime in high-risk neighborhoods, police had to rely on the cooperation of citizens. For all its drawbacks, the political era of policing (see Chapter 5) did have characteristics that observers such

Broken Windows Theory Wilson and Kelling's theory that a neighborhood in disrepair signals that criminal activity is tolerated in the area. Thus, by cracking down on quality-of-life crimes, police can reclaim the neighborhood and encourage law-abiding citizens to live and work there.

Teaching Tip: In a short paper, have students explain why cracking down on "quality of life" crimes might lead to a reduction in the number of serious felonies.

as Wilson and Kelling have come to see as advantageous. During the nineteenth century, the police were much more involved in the community than they were after the reforms. Officers performed many duties that today are associated with social services, such as operating soup kitchens and providing lodging for homeless people. They also played a more direct role in keeping public order by "running in" drunks and intervening in minor disturbances.[79] To a certain extent, community policing advocates a return to this understanding of the police mission.

RETURN TO THE COMMUNITY

Community policing can be defined as an approach that promotes community-police partnerships, proactive problem solving, and community engagement to address issues such as fear of crime and the causes of such fear in a particular area.[80] During the reform era, police were more detached from the community. They did their jobs to the best of their ability but were more concerned with making arrests or speedily answering calls for service than learn-

LO 6 ing about the problems or concerns of the citizenry. In their efforts to eliminate police corruption, administrators put more emphasis on segregating the police from the public than on cooperatively working with citizens to resolve community problems. Under community policing, patrol officers have much more freedom to improvise. They are expected to develop personal relationships with residents and to encourage those residents to become involved in making the community a safer place.

The strategy of increasing police presence in the community has been part of, in the words of George Kelling, a "quiet revolution" in American law enforcement.[81] Today, nearly two-thirds of police departments mention community policing in their mission statements, and a majority of the departments in large cities offer community police training for employees.[82] Nevertheless, despite, or maybe because of, its "feel good" associations, community policing has been the target of several criticisms. First, more than half of the police chiefs and sheriffs in a survey conducted by the National Institute of Justice were unclear about the actual meaning of "community policing,"[83] leading one observer to joke that Professor Kelling's revolution is even quieter than expected.[84] Second, since its inception, community policing has been criticized—not the least by police officials—as having more to do with public relations than with actual crime fighting.[85]

PROBLEM-ORIENTED POLICING

A drawback inherent in most police strategies can be summed up with the truism, "Catch a thief, there will always be another one to take his [or her] place." In other words, common street criminals such as burglars, auto thieves, and shoplifters are so numerous that arresting one seems to have little or no impact.[86] By itself, community policing may not offer much hope for solving this dilemma. But having law enforcement establish a cooperative presence in the community is a crucial part of a strategy that focuses on long-term crime prevention. Introduced by Herman Goldstein of the Police Executive Research Forum in the 1970s, problem-oriented policing is based on the premise that police departments devote too many of their resources to reacting to calls for service and too few to "acting on their own initiative to prevent or reduce community problems."[87] To rectify this situation, problem-oriented policing moves

A Drug Enforcement Administration special agent adjusts a fifth-grader's helmet at an elementary school in Tucson, Arizona, as part of the school's Red Ribbon Week, a series of events dedicated to drug prevention and education. How can establishing friendly relations with citizens help law enforcement agencies reduce crime?

James Wood/*Arizona Daily Star*

Discussion Tip: Ask students to discuss why community policing might be seen as a "public relations" gambit rather than a serious anti-crime strategy. (LO 6)

Community Policing
A policing philosophy that emphasizes community support for and cooperation with the police in preventing crime. Community policing stresses a police role that is less centralized and more proactive than reform-era policing strategies.

Problem-Oriented Policing
A policing philosophy that requires police to identify potential criminal activity and develop strategies to prevent or respond to that activity.

> ### "We have a hard enough time dealing with real crime, let alone somebody's fantasy of it."
>
> —Los Angeles patrol officer, complaining about the difficulty in implementing community policing programs

beyond simply responding to incidents and attempts instead to control or even solve the root causes of criminal behavior.

Goldstein's theory encourages police officers to stop looking at their work as a day-to-day proposition. Rather, they should try to shift the patterns of criminal behavior in a positive direction. For example, instead of responding to a 911 call concerning illegal drug use by simply arresting the offender—a short-term response—the patrol officers should also look at the long-term implications of the situation. They should analyze the pattern of similar arrests in the area and interview the arrestee to determine the reasons, if any, that the site was selected for drug activity.[88] Then additional police action should be taken to prevent further drug sales at the identified location. (For an example of problem-oriented policing in action, see Figure 6.7 below.)

LOCAL POLICE AND ANTI-TERRORISM

The policing strategies we have just covered are designed to meet the traditional challenges of law enforcement—street crime, property crime, and violent crime. Over the past decade, however, local police departments have had to confront what, for them, is a

FIGURE 6.7 Problem-Oriented Policing in Action

Proponents of problem-oriented policing often use the acronym SARA (scanning, analysis, response, assessment) to describe how the strategy works. Here is an example of how SARA can be applied to a particular situation.

S (Scanning): The (fictional) city of Nash Bay has a burglary problem. In *scanning* the problem, the Nash Bay Police Department discovers something interesting about its burglary patterns. The burglaries that occurred in Nash Bay's inner city took place during the day, from the front of the dwelling, and usually involved easy-to-carry items such as cash and jewelry. In Nash Bay's wealthier suburbs, however, the burglaries occurred at night, involved rear entries, and targeted electronic devices, such as laptops and flatscreen TVs.

A (Analysis): By *analyzing* this information, the police concluded that the inner-city burglaries were probably committed mostly by juveniles and young adults who (1) would not invite suspicion if seen on the streets and (2) knew who was away at work during the day. Furthermore, these criminals operated on foot. In contrast, the suburban burglaries involved outsiders who needed automobiles to reach their targets and to carry away their loot. These criminals were most likely targeting homes with no lights, suggesting that the owners were absent.

R (Response): Nash Bay's police administrators *responded* by increasing levels of foot patrols in the inner city during daylight hours and ordered the officers to keep an eye out for suspicious groups of loitering young people. The suburbs received increased numbers of police cruisers, with the officers on the lookout for slow-moving automobiles. In both areas, police officers went door to door to educate residents on the burglary threats and suggest the purchase of burglar alarms.

A (Assessment): Three months after these steps, an *assessment* showed that burglary rates had dropped significantly in both sections of Nash Bay, an unlikely result if the police had responded similarly to what turned out to be two different problems.

Source: Adapted from Ronald V. Clarke, "Defining Police Strategies," in Quint C. Thurman and Jihong Zhao, eds., *Contemporary Policing: Controversies, Challenges, and Solutions* (Los Angeles: Roxbury Publishing Co., 2004), 18–24.

new challenge—terrorism. Many experts believe that local police officers are well suited for counterterrorism duties because of their sheer numbers—more than 730,000 in the United States—and their unmatched knowledge of local communities.[89]

To this end, each year the Department of Homeland Security provides local police departments with billions of dollars in anti-terrorism funding. For the most part, these funds must be used for equipment directly related to combating terrorism. For the Providence (Rhode Island) Police Department, located at the head of Narragansett Bay, this meant the purchase of a 27-foot patrol boat, an automated underwater inspection system, and a portable small-craft intrusion barrier. Over the past few years, Providence officials have also obtained a fleet of SUVs for emergency response, two bomb containment vehicles (one of which is specifically for canine units), scuba gear, protective suits for all officers, and a great deal more. Furthermore, the department spent millions of dollars to secure its headquarters with a video surveillance system, 159 concrete posts, and 220 feet of guardrails.[90] Providence police officers have attended classes in terrorism prevention and suicide bombings. They have traveled to New Mexico to attend terrorist bombing school and have studied unconventional weapons along with the intricacies of hidden explosive laboratories.[91]

Even some of the maxims of community policing have made their way into anti-terrorism strategies. Following a national trend, Providence police administrators have worked to improve relations with local Muslim leaders. The goal in these efforts is to protect Arab American communities from hate crimes and other racially tinged incidents and to share information about possible terrorist sympathizers.[92] Another important aspect of counterterrorism efforts—cooperation between local and federal law enforcement agencies—will be covered in detail in Chapter 16.

SELFASSESSMENT

Fill in the blanks and check your answers on page 208.

Without exception, modern police departments practice _____-driven policing, in which officers respond to calls for _____ such as 911 phone calls after a crime has occurred. Along the same lines, most patrol officers work _____ patrols, in which they cover designated areas and react to the incidents they encounter. _____ patrols, which often focus on "hot spots" of crime, and _____ arrest policies, which target a particular type of criminal behavior, have both been shown to be very effective. _____ policing, a popular strategy in which officers are encouraged to develop partnerships with citizens, is only one of the tactics used to combat _____, the latest challenge facing local police departments.

"US VERSUS THEM": ISSUES IN MODERN POLICING

Each year, the Guardian Civil League, a group of experienced Philadelphia police officers, presents a program called "Steer Straight" to Philadelphia Police Academy cadets. The purpose of the course is to warn the cadets about the various self-imposed hazards of policing, including domestic violence, improper use of force, alcohol abuse, corruption, and racial insensitivity—in other words, all the things that could get them fired. "It takes one slip to lose everything you've worked so hard for," cautions Inspector Cynthia Dorsey, a veteran officer with the department's internal affairs division.[93] The Steer Straight program covers many of the on-the-job issues that make law enforcement such a challenging and often difficult career. When faced with these issues, sometimes police officers

Discussion Tip: Ask students to discuss the role of local police departments in national anti-terrorism efforts. Even though terrorism is seen as a mostly federal effort, what important role do local police officers play preventing future terrorist attacks?

Critical Thinking Skill Development: Ask students to respond to "Questions for Critical Analysis" number two on page 209, in which they consider local counterterrorism efforts.

make the right decisions, and sometimes they make the wrong ones. Indeed, it may often be difficult to tell the two apart.

POLICE SUBCULTURE

During a recent Steer Straight presentation, Philadelphia cadets were shown a video, taken by a local news station, showing about a dozen of the city's police officers kicking and punching three suspects at a traffic stop. Eventually, four of the officers were fired and several others demoted. "Don't even think about privacy," a Philadelphia official warned the cadets. "You are going to have to remember that everybody is watching you."[94] Mistrust of the media and of civilians is one of the hallmarks of police subculture, a broad term used to describe the basic assumptions and values that permeate law enforcement agencies and are taught to new members of a law enforcement agency as the proper way to think, perceive, and act. Every organization has a subculture, with values shaped by the particular aspects and pressures of that organization. In the police subculture, those values are formed in an environment characterized by danger, stress, boredom, and violence.

> "The police subculture permits and sometimes demands deception of courts, prosecutors, defense attorneys, and defendants."
>
> —**Jerome Skolnick,**
> criminologist

Police Subculture The values and perceptions that are shared by members of a police department and, to a certain extent, by all law enforcement agents.

Socialization The process through which a police officer is taught the values and expected behavior of the police subculture.

Blue Curtain A metaphorical term used to refer to the value placed on secrecy and the general mistrust of the outside world shared by many police officers.

Police Cynicism The suspicion that citizens are weak, corrupt, and dangerous. This outlook is the result of a police officer being constantly exposed to civilians at their worst and can negatively affect the officer's performance.

THE CORE VALUES OF POLICE SUBCULTURE From the first day on the job, rookies begin the process of socialization, in which they are taught the values and rules of police work. This process is aided by a number of rituals that are common to the law enforcement experience. Police theorist Harry J. Mullins believes that the following rituals are critical to the police officer's acceptance, and even embrace, of police subculture:

- Attending a police academy.
- Working with a senior officer, who passes on the "lessons" of police work and life to the younger officer.
- Making the initial felony arrest.
- Using force to make an arrest for the first time.
- Using or witnessing deadly force for the first time.
- Witnessing major traumatic incidents for the first time.[95]

Each of these rituals makes it clear to the police officer that this is not a "normal" job. The only other people who can understand the stresses of police work are fellow officers, and consequently law enforcement officers tend to insulate themselves from civilians. Eventually, the insulation breeds mistrust, and the police officer develops an "us versus them" outlook toward those outside the force. In turn, this outlook creates what sociologist William Westly called the blue curtain, also known as the "blue wall of silence" or simply "the code."[96] This curtain separates the police from the civilians they are meant to protect.

POLICE CYNICISM A cynic is someone who universally distrusts human motives and expects nothing but the worst from human behavior. Police cynicism is characterized by a rejection of the ideals of truth and justice—the very values that an officer is sworn to uphold.[97] As cynical police officers lose respect for the law, they replace legal rules with those learned in the police subculture, which are believed to be more reflective of "reality." The implications for society can be an increase in police misconduct, corruption, and brutality.[98]

Police cynicism is exacerbated by a feeling of helplessness—to report another officer's wrongdoing is a severe breach of the blue wall of silence. As one officer said:

> If you were to challenge somebody for something that was going on, they would say: "Listen, if the supervisor isn't saying anything, what the hell are you interjecting for? What are you, a rat?" You've gotta work with a lot of these guys. You go on a gun job, the next thing you know, you got nobody following you up the stairs.[99]

The officer's statement highlights one of the reasons why the police subculture resonates beyond department walls—he has basically admitted that he will not report wrongdoing by his peers. In this manner, the police subculture influences the actions of police officers, sometimes to the detriment of society. In the next two sections, we will examine two areas of the law enforcement work environment that help create the police subculture and must be fully understood if the cynical nature of the police subculture is ever to be changed: (1) the dangers of police work and (2) the need for police officers to establish and maintain authority.

THE PHYSICAL DANGERS OF POLICE WORK

Near 11 P.M. on the night of January 29, 2010, Gilbert (Arizona) police lieutenant Eric Shuhandler pulled over a pickup truck for a traffic violation. A passenger, perhaps aware that a warrant was out for his arrest, fatally shot Shuhandler in the face. One of the strongest tenets of the police code is justice for fallen comrades, and both suspects were apprehended after a dramatic midnight chase in which more than fifty law enforcement officers pursued the truck through the Phoenix suburbs and into the nearby mountains. As this incident shows, there is no such thing as a "routine" traffic stop. For that matter, police officers learn early in their careers that nothing about their job is "routine"—they face the threat of physical harm every day.

OFFICERS KILLED AND ASSAULTED According to the Officer Down Memorial Page, Eric Shuhandler was one of 160 law enforcement agents who died in the line of duty in 2010, and one of fifty-nine who were killed by hostile gunfire.[100] In addition, about 53,000 assaults were committed against police officers that year, with 26 percent of these assaults resulting in an injury.[101] These numbers are hardly surprising. As police experts John S. Dempsey and Linda S. Forst point out, police "deal constantly with what may be the most dangerous species on this planet—the human being."[102]

At the same time, Dempsey and Forst note that according to data compiled by the federal government, citizens and the police come into contact about 43.5 million times a year.[103] Given this figure, the police have relatively low death and injury rates. Dempsey and Forst attribute the statistical safety of police work to two factors. First, as the offender who shot Eric Shuhandler learned, most criminals are aware that relentless efforts will be made to catch and prosecute anyone who harms a police officer. Second, police officers take extraordinary precautions to protect their physical safety, including wearing protective **body armor** underneath their clothing.[104] The body armor most widely used by American police officers is made of Kevlar, a high-strength fiber discovered in 1964 by a chemist named Stephanie Kwolek. Low-level Kevlar can stop .357 and .9mm shots, while high-level "tactical armor" can deflect rifle and machine gun bullets. Seventy-five percent of all police departments require their officers to wear body armor,[105] which has saved at least 3,100 law enforcement lives since 1987.[106]

AUTOMOBILE CRASHES In 2010, seventy-two police officers were killed in traffic-related incidents—more than were killed by firearms. This marked the thirteenth consecutive

Critical Thinking Skill Development: Ask students to reflect on the experiences that rookie police officers encounter on the job. Is it possible for young officers to avoid becoming cynical about their work? How can officers be trained to operate without becoming part of the blue wall of silence?

Technology Tip: Students can learn more about fallen officers online at the National Law Enforcement Officers Memorial Fund Web site: **www.nleomf.com**.

Body Armor Protective covering that is worn under a police officer's clothing and designed to minimize injury from being hit by a fired bullet.

A fellow officer pays his respects during the 2010 funeral of Chattachoochee Hills, Georgia, police officer Mike Vogt, who was shot and killed while on patrol. Besides physical violence, what are some of the other occupational threats that police officers face on a daily basis?

AP Photo/Brant Sanderlin

year that traffic incidents were the leading cause of line-of-duty deaths.[107] One reason for the fatalities is that a number of law enforcement officers do not take simple precautions when behind the wheel. A recent study conducted by the National Highway Traffic Safety Administration found that 42 percent of police officers killed in vehicle crashes were not wearing seat belts.[108]

Also, as Craig Floyd of the National Law Enforcement Officers Memorial Fund points out, nearly every police officer will be involved in a high-speed automobile response or chase during her or his career, but only 10 percent will be involved in a gunfight. Yet firearms training is common, while driver training is not. Furthermore, although great strides have been made in protective body armor for police officers, the same cannot be said for safety measures in patrol cars.[109]

STRESS AND THE MENTAL DANGERS OF POLICE WORK

In addition to physical dangers, police work entails considerable mental pressure and stress. Professor John Violanti and his colleagues at the University of Buffalo have determined that police officers experience unusually high levels of *cortisol*, otherwise known as the "stress hormone," which is associated with serious health problems such as diabetes and heart disease.[110] "Intervention is necessary to help officers deal with this difficult and stressful occupation," says Violanti. "[Police officers] need to learn how to relax, how to think differently about things they experience as a cop."[111]

Stressors The aspects of police work and life that lead to feelings of stress.

POLICE STRESSORS The conditions that cause stress—such as worries over finances or relationships—are known as **stressors.** Each profession has its own set of stressors, but police are particularly vulnerable to occupational pressures and stress factors such as the following:

- The constant fear of being a victim of violent crime.
- Exposure to violent crime and its victims.
- The need to comply with the law in nearly every job action.
- Lack of community support.
- Negative media coverage.

Critical Thinking Skill Development: Discuss with your class the various physical and mental dangers of police work. What strategies can officers employ to deal with the dangers of the job? What types of programs should agencies employ to keep officers physically and mentally healthy?

Police face a number of internal pressures as well, including limited opportunities for career advancement, excessive paperwork, and low wages and benefits.[112] The unconventional hours of shift work can also interfere with an officer's private life and contribute to lack of sleep. Each of these is a primary stressor associated with police work.[113]

THE CONSEQUENCES OF POLICE STRESS Police stress can manifest itself in different ways. The University of Buffalo study cited above found that the stresses of law enforcement often lead to high blood pressure and heart problems.[114] Other research shows that police officers are three times more likely to suffer from alcoholism than the average American.[115] If stress becomes overwhelming, an officer may suffer from **burnout,** becoming listless and ineffective as a result of mental and physical exhaustion. Another problem related to stress is *post-traumatic stress disorder (PTSD)*. Often recognized in war veterans and rape victims, PTSD is a reaction to a stressor that evokes significant stress. For police officers, such stressors might include the death of a fellow agent or the shooting of a civilian. An officer suffering from PTSD will:

1. Re-experience the traumatic event through nightmare and flashbacks.
2. Become less and less involved in the outside world by withdrawing from others and refusing to participate in normal social interactions.
3. Experience "survival guilt," which may lead to loss of sleep and memory impairment.[116]

The effects of stress can be seen most tragically in the high rate of suicide among law enforcement officers—three times higher than in the general population.[117]

Burnout A mental state that occurs when a person suffers from exhaustion and has difficulty functioning normally as a result of overwork and stress.

AUTHORITY AND THE USE OF FORCE

If the police subculture is shaped by the dangers of the job, it often finds expression through authority. The various symbols of authority that decorate a police officer—including the uniform, badge, nightstick, and firearm—establish the power she or he holds over civilians. For better or for worse, both police officers and civilians tend to equate terms such as *authority* and *respect* with the ability to use force.

Near the beginning of the twentieth century, a police officer stated that his job was to "protect the good people and treat the crooks rough."[118] Implicit in the officer's statement is the idea that to do the protecting, he had to do some roughing up as well. This attitude toward the use of force is still with us today. Indeed, it is generally accepted that not only is police use of force inevitable, but that police officers who are unwilling to use force in certain circumstances cannot do their jobs effectively.

Discussion Tip: Ask students to reflect on the statistics presented in the text regarding use of force by police officers. Are students surprised by the data? Does it support the perceptions they may have formed through popular media?

THE "MISUSE" OF FORCE In general, the use of physical force by law enforcement personnel is very rare, occurring in only about 1.6 percent of the 43.5 million annual police-public encounters mentioned earlier. Still, the Department of Justice estimates that law enforcement officers threaten to use force or use force in encounters with 700,000 Americans a year, and 14.8 percent of those incidents result in an injury.[119] Federal authorities also report that about 650 deaths occur in the process of an arrest on an annual basis.[120] Of course, police officers are often justified in using force to protect themselves and other citizens. As we noted earlier, they are the targets of tens of thousands of assaults each year.

"No one takes into consideration the human being behind the cop."

—Colleague of New York police officer Michael W. Pigott, who committed suicide in 2008 after having ordered the fatal Tasering of an emotionally disturbed suspect

At the same time, few observers would be naïve enough to believe that the police are *always* justified in the use of force. A 2009 survey of emergency room physicians found that 98 percent believed that they had treated patients who were victims of excessive police force.[121] How, then, is "misuse" of force to be defined? One attempt to define excessive force that has been lauded by legal scholars, if not necessarily by police officers, was offered by the Christopher Commission. Established in Los Angeles in 1991 after the beating of African American motorist Rodney King, the commission advised that "an officer may resort to force only where he or she faces a credible threat, and then may only use the minimum amount necessary to control the subject."[122]

To provide guidance for officers in this tricky area, nearly every law enforcement agency designs a *use of force matrix*. As the example in Figure 6.8 on the next page shows, such a matrix presents officers with the proper force options for different levels of contact with a civilian.

TYPES OF FORCE To comply with the various, and not always consistent, laws concerning the use of force, a police officer must understand that there are two kinds of force: *nondeadly force* and *deadly force*. Most force used by law enforcement is nondeadly force. In most states, the use of nondeadly force is regulated by the concept of reasonable force, which allows the use of nondeadly force when a reasonable person would assume that such force was necessary. In contrast, deadly force is force that an objective police officer realizes will place the subject in direct threat of serious injury or death.

THE UNITED STATES SUPREME COURT AND USE OF FORCE The United States Supreme Court set the limits for the use of deadly force by law enforcement officers in *Tennessee v. Garner* (1985).[123] The case involved an incident in which Memphis police officer Elton Hymon shot and killed a suspect who was trying to climb over a fence after stealing ten dollars from a residence. Hymon testified that he had been trained to shoot to keep a suspect from escaping, and indeed Tennessee law at the time allowed police officers to apprehend fleeing suspects in this manner.

In reviewing the case, the Court focused not on Hymon's action but on the Tennessee statute itself, ultimately finding it unconstitutional:

> When the suspect poses no immediate threat to the officer and no threat to others, the use of deadly force is unjustified. . . . It is not better that all felony suspects die than that they escape.[124]

Reasonable Force The degree of force that is appropriate to protect the police officer or other citizens and is not excessive.

Deadly Force Force applied by a police officer that is likely or intended to cause death.

Teaching Tip: Ask students to consider an officer's need to use force on the job. How can one determine if an unacceptable level of force has been used? (LO 7)

FIGURE 6.8 **The San Diego Police Department's Use of Force Matrix**
The San Diego Police Department has a mission to "train its officers in the use of the safest, most humane restraint procedures and force options currently known." As part of this mission, the department provides its officers with this use of force matrix, which details the appropriate response to various forms of suspect behavior.

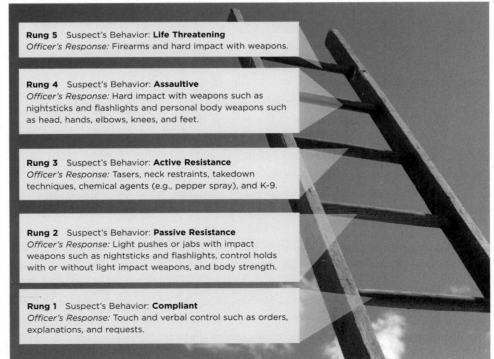

Rung 5 Suspect's Behavior: **Life Threatening**
Officer's Response: Firearms and hard impact with weapons.

Rung 4 Suspect's Behavior: **Assaultive**
Officer's Response: Hard impact with weapons such as nightsticks and flashlights and personal body weapons such as head, hands, elbows, knees, and feet.

Rung 3 Suspect's Behavior: **Active Resistance**
Officer's Response: Tasers, neck restraints, takedown techniques, chemical agents (e.g., pepper spray), and K-9.

Rung 2 Suspect's Behavior: **Passive Resistance**
Officer's Response: Light pushes or jabs with impact weapons such as nightsticks and flashlights, control holds with or without light impact weapons, and body strength.

Rung 1 Suspect's Behavior: **Compliant**
Officer's Response: Touch and verbal control such as orders, explanations, and requests.

S.P. Rayner/iStockphoto

Source: San Diego Police Department.

The Court's decision forced twenty-three states to change their fleeing felon rules, but it did not completely eliminate police discretion in such situations. Police officers still may

LO 7 use deadly force if they have probable cause to believe that the fleeing suspect poses a threat of serious injury or death to the officers or others. (We will discuss the concept of probable cause in the next chapter.) In essence, the Court recognized that police officers must be able to make split-second decisions without worrying about the legal ramifications. Four years after the *Garner* case, the Court tried to clarify this concept in *Graham v. Connor* (1989), stating that the use of any force should be judged by the "reasonableness of the moment."[125] In 2004, the Court modified this rule by suggesting that an officer's use of force could be "reasonable" even if, by objective measures, the force was not needed to protect the officer or others in the area.[126] (See the feature *You Be the Sheriff's Deputy—Threat Level* below.)

Teaching Tip: In a short written assignment, ask students to describe the circumstances under which the use of deadly force is acceptable. (LO 7)

LESS LETHAL WEAPONS Regardless of any legal restrictions, violent confrontations between officers and suspects are inevitable. To decrease the likelihood that such confrontations will result in death or serious injury, many police departments use *less lethal weapons,* which are designed to subdue but not seriously harm suspects. The most common less lethal weapon is Oleoresin Capsicum, or OC pepper spray, which is used by 97 percent of all local police departments.[127] An organic substance that combines ingredients such as resin and cayenne pepper, OC causes a sensation similar to having sand or

YOU BE THE SHERIFF'S DEPUTY

Threat Level

THE SITUATION You receive a call from dispatch telling you that Lee Dylan, a mentally unstable man, has just escaped from a local jail where he was being held on suspicion of committing a nonviolent felony. Driving toward the jail, you see a man matching Dylan's description running down a back alley. Jumping out of your car, you and your partner follow on foot. Eventually, you and your partner corner the man, who is indeed Dylan, in a construction site. Dylan, who is of average height and build, grabs a loose brick and makes threatening motions with it. You pull your gun and, along with your partner, move toward Dylan. You yell, "Drop the brick!" He screams, "You're going to have to kill me!" and rushes at you.

THE LAW The use of force by a law enforcement agent—even deadly force—is based on the concept of reasonableness. In other words, would a reasonable police officer in this officer's shoes have been justified in using force?

YOUR DECISION Does Dylan pose a threat of serious bodily harm to you or your partner? How you answer this question will determine the type of force you use against him. Keep in mind that almost all police officers experience an adrenaline rush in stressful situations, and this may influence your reaction.

[To see how a law enforcement officer in Cincinnati reacted in similar circumstances, go to Example 6.2 in Appendix B.]

Rasmus Rasmusson/iStockphoto/iStockphoto/Photodisc/Shutterstock/James Stadl/iStockphoto

needles in the eyes when sprayed into a suspect's face. Other common less lethal weapons include tear gas, water cannons, and **conducted energy devices (CEDs)**, which rely on an electrical shock to incapacitate uncooperative suspects.

The best-known, and most controversial, CED is the Taser—a handheld electrical stun gun that fires blunt darts up to 21 feet at speeds of 200 to 220 feet per second. The darts deliver 50,000 volts into the target for a span of about five seconds. Nationally, about 16,000 police departments deploy Tasers, and a 2009 study by the National Institute of Justice showed that, when used properly, the devices increase the safety of both officers and suspects.[128]

Nevertheless, according to the human rights organization Amnesty International, as of 2011 more than 400 people have died in the United States after being Tasered. Often, these deaths occurred because the target had a weakened heart or was in ill health because of drug use.[129] To reduce the use of Tasers, several police departments have instituted use of force matrixes like the one in Figure 6.8 on page 198.[130] In addition, some law enforcement agencies are considering the use of *active denial systems,* or laser beams that, when directed at a target's eyes, tend to stop all violent or undesired activity.[131]

SELFASSESSMENT

Fill in the blanks and check your answers on page 208.
Like any organization, a police department has a _____ that determines the values of its employees. In law enforcement, these values are shaped by the _____ dangers, such as assault, and mental dangers, such as high levels of _____, that officers face every day. Laws regulating police use of force rely on two concepts: _____ force, which is the amount of force that a rational person would consider necessary in a given situation, and _____ force, which is a level of force that will place the subject in grave bodily danger.

POLICE MISCONDUCT AND ETHICS

If police culture is, as we noted earlier, marked by a certain mistrust of the public, it is only fair to note that the reverse is often true as well. Community anger recently surfaced in Houston where, on May 11, 2010, police sergeant Jeffrey Cotton was acquitted in the shooting of an unarmed man, Robert Tolan. Cotton had fired his weapon after another officer mistook Tolan for a car thief. During the incident, the police also forced Tolan's mother against a garage door. "They are police officers and all they have to say is 'I fear for my life' and that gives them a free pass," said Tolan's father on the day of Cotton's acquittal.[132]

Police are held to a high standard of behavior that can be summarized by the umbrella term **professionalism.** A professional law enforcement agent is expected to be honest, committed to ideals of justice, respectful of the law, and intolerant of misconduct by his or her fellow officers. When police act unprofessionally, or are perceived to have done so, then their relationship with the community will inevitably suffer.

RACIAL AND ETHNIC BIASES IN POLICING

Anger in Houston following Jeffrey Cotton's acquittal was particularly strong among the city's African American citizens. Robert Tolan is black, and two weeks earlier the family of another young African American, Chad Holley, had come forward with a videotape showing Holley being beaten by eight police officers. "That's just the way Houston's always been policed," said one black citizen,[133] reflecting the belief of many members of minority groups that the United States has a "just us" system, not a justice system.

PERCEIVED BIAS In the next chapter's discussion of racial profiling, we will see that many African Americans believe that they are often targeted for a particular "offense"—DWB, or "driving while black." To a certain extent, statistics bear out these suspicions. A recent Justice Department study reports that although police pull over black, white, and Hispanic drivers at similar rates, blacks and Hispanics are almost three times more likely to be searched following the stop.[134]

The same study found that police officers are more than three times more likely to use force when coming into contact with African Americans than with whites and more than twice as likely with Hispanics as with whites.[135] Furthermore, self-reported surveys consistently show that members of minority groups are more likely to feel that the police discriminate against them, particularly when contacts with law enforcement occur in predominantly white neighborhoods.[136] (See Figure 6.9 below.) These data reinforce the notion that police bias is responsible for the disproportionate numbers of minorities in American prisons and jails discussed throughout this textbook.

Teaching Tip: Ask students to respond to "Questions for Critical Analysis" number four on page 209, in which they consider the impact of cultural differences on police use of force.

POLICE ATTITUDES AND DISCRETION Although everyone would agree that some individual officers may be influenced by prejudice, the greater police presence and arrest rates in minority neighborhoods should not be accepted as automatic evidence of law enforcement discrimination. As we learned earlier in the chapter, the primary operational tactic of all metropolitan police forces is responding to calls for service. According to research by law enforcement expert Richard J. Ludman, the greater police presence in these communities is mainly the result of calls for service from residents, which, in turn, are caused by higher local crime rates. Indeed, Randall Kennedy believes that such "selective law enforcement" should be, and for the most part is, welcomed by those who live in high-crime areas and appreciate the added protection.[137]

FIGURE 6.9 Perceptions of Police Bias

Several years ago, a *New York Times*/CBS News poll asked nearly two thousand Americans, "Have you ever felt you were stopped by the police just because of your race or ethnic background?" As the results show, members of minority groups are much more likely than whites to respond positively to this question.

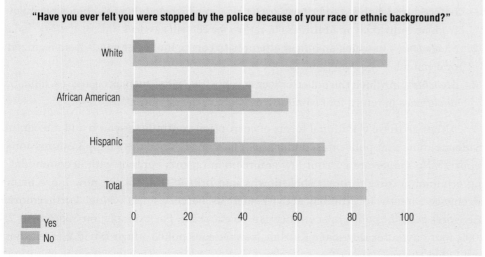

"Have you ever felt you were stopped by the police because of your race or ethnic background?"

Yes
No

Source adapted from: *New York Times*/CBS News Poll, July 7–14, 2008, at **graphics8.nytimes.com/packages/pdf/politics/20080716_POLL.pdf**.

Furthermore, as several experts point out, cultural differences often exist between police officers and the residents of the neighborhoods they patrol. One survey found that police working in minority areas perceived higher levels of abuse and less respect from those citizens than from those in nonminority areas.[138] In looking at police abuse in Inglewood, California, the *Los Angeles Times* found that most of the victims claimed they were assaulted after "contempt of cop" incidents, such as not immediately following orders or verbally challenging the officer.[139] Judging someone's demeanor is often a subjective task and can be influenced by a lack of communication between two people of different backgrounds—another reason why it is so important for police departments to attract members of minority groups, as noted in our discussion of recruiting strategies in the previous chapter.

POLICE CORRUPTION

Police *corruption* has been a concern since the first organized American police departments. As you recall from Chapter 5, a desire to eradicate, or at least limit, corruption was one of the motivating factors behind the reform movement of policing. For general purposes, **police corruption** can be defined as the misuse of authority by a law enforcement officer "in a manner designed to produce personal gain."

In the 1970s, a police officer named Frank Serpico went public about corruption in the New York Police Department. City authorities responded by establishing the Knapp Commission to investigate Serpico's claims. The inquiry uncovered widespread institutionalized corruption in the department. In general, the Knapp Commission report divided corrupt police officers into two categories: "grass eaters" and "meat eaters." "Grass eaters" are involved in passive corruption—they simply accept the payoffs and opportunities that police work can provide. As the name implies, "meat eaters" are more aggressive in their quest for personal gain, initiating and going to great lengths to carry out corrupt schemes.[140]

TYPES OF CORRUPTION Specifically, the Knapp Commission's investigation identified three basic, traditional types of police corruption:

1. *Bribery,* in which the police officer accepts money or other forms of payment **LO 8** in exchange for "favors," which may include allowing a certain criminal activity to continue or misplacing a key piece of evidence before a trial. Related to bribery are *payoffs,* in which an officer demands payment from an individual or a business in return for certain services.
2. *Shakedowns,* in which an officer attempts to coerce money or goods from a citizen or criminal.
3. *Mooching,* in which the police officer accepts free "gifts" such as cigarettes, liquor, or services in return for favorable treatment of the gift giver.[141]

Although these traditional forms of corruption continue, research and anecdotal evidence show that police misconduct has "hardened" since the Knapp Commission's report.[142] No longer are corrupt law enforcement agents content with accommodating criminal activity through shakedowns and bribes. Officers are now more likely to engage directly in criminal activity such as narcotics trafficking. Furthermore, the worst cases of police misconduct can be shocking. For example, on September 2, 2005, four days after Hurricane Katrina, New Orleans police officer David Warren shot and killed Henry Glover, after mistaking him for a looter. To cover up this shooting, another officer burned Glover's body in a car, and a third wrote a false arrest report

Discussion Tip: Ask students about the prevalence of police corruption. Do they think such behavior is widespread? Why or why not? What type of corruption do they feel is most common? (LO 8)

on the incident. In 2010, all three were found guilty of various crimes, and Warren was sentenced to at least twenty-five years in prison for manslaughter (see the photo alongside).

CORRUPTION IN POLICE SUBCULTURE

There is no single reason why police misconduct occurs. Certain types of officers do, however, seem more likely to engage in corruption—the young, the relatively uneducated (lacking a college degree), those with records of prior criminality and citizens' complaints, and those unlikely to be promoted.[143] Lawrence Sherman has identified several stages in the moral decline of these "bad cops."[144]

In the first stage, the officers accept minor gratuities, such as the occasional free meal from a restaurant on their beats. These gratuities gradually evolve into outright bribes, in which the officers receive the gratuity for overlooking some violation. For example, a law officer may accept pay from a bar owner to ensure that the establishment is not investigated for serving alcohol to minors. In the final stage, officers no longer passively accept bribes but actively seek them out. The officers may even force the other party to pay for unwanted police services. This stage often involves large amounts of money and may entail protection of or involvement in drug, gambling, or prostitution organizations.

Relatives and friends of Henry Glover react with relief after a New Orleans jury found police officer David Warren guilty of manslaughter. How does the kind of misconduct that Warren and two of his fellow officers engaged in undermine public confidence in the police?
AP Photo/Gerald Herbert

POLICE ACCOUNTABILITY

Even in a police department with excellent recruiting methods, state-of-the-art ethics and discretionary training programs, and a culturally diverse workforce that nearly matches the makeup of the community, the problems discussed earlier in this chapter are bound to occur. The question then becomes—given the inevitability of excessive force, corruption, and other misconduct—*who shall police the police?*

INTERNAL INVESTIGATIONS "The minute the public feels that the police department is not investigating its own alleged wrongdoing well, the police department will not be able to function credibly in even the most routine of matters," says Sheldon Greenberg, a professor of police management at Johns Hopkins University.[145] The mechanism for these investigations within a police department is the internal affairs unit (IAU). In many smaller police departments, the police chief conducts internal affairs investigations, while midsized and large departments have a team of internal affairs officers. The New York Police Department's IAU has an annual budget of nearly $62 million and consists of 650 officers.

As much as police officers may resent internal affairs units, most realize that it is preferable to settle disciplinary matters in house. The alternatives may be worse. Police officers are criminally liable for any crimes they might commit, and city and state governments can be held civilly liable for wrongdoing by their police officers. The taxpayers of Pennsylvania, for example, have paid nearly $13 million to settle several civil claims against a single officer, state trooper Samuel J. Nassan III. In 2011, Nassan was a defendant in two more lawsuits, stemming from incidents in which he allegedly beat one civilian following a traffic stop and fatally shot another during a car chase.[146]

Technology Tip: Have students experience a civilian review board in action by visiting the New York City Civilian Complaint Review Board online at **www.nyc.gov/html/ccrb**. When and how should a complaint be filed? How are complaints against the police processed in New York City?

Internal Affairs Unit (IAU)
A division within a police department that receives and investigates complaints of wrongdoing by police officers.

"**History tells us there will always be bad cops.**"

—**Christopher Dunn,**
New York Civil Liberties Union (2010)

> **Citizens Alert** is a Chicago-based organization that advocates for victims of police brutality and harassment in that city. To find its Web site, visit the *Criminal Justice CourseMate* at **cengagebrain. com** and select the *Web links* for this chapter.

Citizen Oversight The process by which citizens review complaints brought against individual police officers or police departments.

Ethics The rules or standards of behavior governing a profession; aimed at ensuring the fairness and rightness of actions.

CITIZEN OVERSIGHT Despite the large sums involved, such civil suits are unlikely to deter police corruption for two reasons. First, the misbehaving officers do not pay the damages out of their own pockets. Second, in the vast majority of cases, the offending officers do not face disciplinary measures within the department.[147] Mounting frustration over this lack of accountability has led many communities to turn to an external procedure for handling citizens' complaints known as **citizen oversight.**

In this process, citizens—people who are not sworn officers and, by inference, not biased in favor of law enforcement officers—review allegations of police misconduct or brutality. According to data gathered by police accountability expert Samuel Walker, nearly one hundred cities now operate some kind of review procedure by an independent body.[148] For the most part, citizen review boards can only recommend action to the police chief or other executive. They do not have the power to discipline officers directly. Police officers generally resent this intrusion by civilians, and most studies have shown that civilian review boards are not widely successful in their efforts to convince police chiefs to take action against their subordinate officers.[149]

CJ&TECHNOLOGY Self-Surveillance

Korhan Hasim Isik/iStockphoto

One form of citizen oversight that has been highly successful in curbing police misconduct is cheap video. Every week, it seems, video taken by citizens using a handheld camera, cell phone, or some other device goes "viral" online, flooding the Internet with examples of police brutality or some other form of misbehavior. "All of our people should be conducting themselves like they are being recorded all the time," says Robin Larson of the Broward County (Florida) Sheriff's Department.

Indeed, law enforcement agents may soon be under constant surveillance—by their own superiors. Police departments in Aberdeen (South Dakota), Cincinnati, Fort Smith (Arkansas), and San Jose are conducting an experiment in which officers wear tiny cameras near their ears. The device sees everything the officer sees, and records it. Police administrators hope that this system will help protect officers against unfounded charges of misconduct. "There is no doubt in my mind that this is the wave of the future in policing," says Cincinnati police chief Tom Streicher.

THINKING ABOUT SELF-SURVEILLANCE

Dennis Kenney, a professor at New York's John Jay College of Criminal Justice, warns that this technology "raises tremendous privacy concerns." What are some of those concerns?

ETHICS IN LAW ENFORCEMENT

Police corruption is intricately connected with the ethics of law enforcement officers. **Ethics** has to do with fundamental questions of the fairness, justice, rightness, or wrongness of any action. Given the significant power that police officers hold, society expects very high standards of ethical behavior from them. These expectations are summed up in the *Police Code of Conduct*, which was developed by the International Association of Chiefs of Police in 1989.

To some extent, the *Police Code of Conduct* is self-evident: "A police officer will not engage in acts of corruption or bribery." In other aspects, it is idealistic, perhaps unreasonably so: "Officers will never allow personal feelings, animosities, or friendships to influence official conduct." The police working environment—rife with lying, cheating, lawbreaking, and violence—often does not allow for such ethical absolutes.

ETHICAL DILEMMAS Some police actions are obviously unethical, such as the behavior of a Pennsylvania officer who paid a woman he was dating $500 to pretend to be an eyewitness in a murder trial. The majority of ethical dilemmas that a police officer will face are not so clear cut. Criminologists Joycelyn M. Pollock and Ronald F. Becker define an ethical dilemma as a situation in which law enforcement officers:

LO 9

- Do not know the right course of action;
- Have difficulty doing what they consider to be right; and/or
- Find the wrong choice very tempting.[150]

Because of the many rules that govern policing—the subject of the next chapter—police officers often find themselves tempted by a phenomenon called **noble cause corruption**. This type of corruption occurs when, in the words of John P. Crank and Michael A. Caldero, "officers do bad things because they believe the outcomes will be good."[151] Examples include planting evidence or lying in court to help convict someone the officer knows to be guilty and the situation discussed in the feature *A Question of Ethics—The "Dirty Harry" Problem* below.

ELEMENTS OF ETHICS Pollock and Becker, both of whom have extensive experience as ethics instructors for police departments, further identify four categories of ethical dilemmas, involving discretion, duty, honesty, and loyalty.[152]

Critical Thinking Skill Development: Have students work in groups to discuss ethics in policing. How can officers be taught to practice good ethics? Can ethics be learned, or is ethical behavior an inherent quality? (LO 9)

Noble Cause Corruption Knowing misconduct by a police officer with the goal of attaining what the officer believes is a "just" result.

A QUESTION OF ETHICS: *The "Dirty Harry" Problem*

THE SITUATION A young girl has been kidnapped by a psychotic killer named Scorpio. Demanding a $200,000 ransom, Scorpio has buried the girl alive, leaving her with just enough oxygen to survive for a few hours. Detective Harry Callahan manages to find Scorpio, but the kidnapper stubbornly refuses to reveal the location of the girl. Callahan comes to the conclusion that the only way he can get this information from Scorpio in time is to beat it out of him.

THE ETHICAL DILEMMA The U.S. Constitution, as interpreted by the United States Supreme Court, forbids the torture of criminal suspects. Following proper procedure, Callahan should arrest Scorpio and advise him of his constitutional rights. If Scorpio requests an attorney, Callahan must comply. If the attorney then advises Scorpio to remain silent, there is nothing Callahan can do. Of course, after all this time, the girl will certainly be dead.*

WHAT IS THE SOLUTION? What should Detective Callahan do? According to the late Carl B. Klockars of the University of Delaware, "Each time a police officer considers deceiving a suspect into confessing by telling him that his [or her] fingerprints were found at the scene or that a conspirator has already confessed, each time a police officer considers adding some untrue details to his [or her] account of a probable cause to legitimate a crucial stop or search [that police officer] faces" the same problem as Detective Callahan. Are police ever justified in using unlawful methods, no matter what good may ultimately be achieved?

* This scenario is taken from *Dirty Harry* (1971), one of the most popular police dramas of all time. In the film, Detective Callahan, played by Clint Eastwood, shoots Scorpio and then tortures him. Although Callahan eventually gets the information he needs, it is too late to save the girl.

Larry A. Godwin, director of the Memphis (Tennessee) Police Department, cooperated with federal law enforcement agents in a probe of his own department. The effort—named Tarnished Blue—led to the arrests of nearly twenty Memphis police officers for robbing drug dealers and conspiring to sell drugs. Why is strong leadership important in ensuring the ethical integrity of a police department?

AP Photo/Mark Humphrey

Duty The moral sense of a police officer that she or he should behave in a certain manner.

- *Discretion.* The law provides rigid guidelines for how police officers must act and how they cannot act, but it does not offer guidelines for how officers *should act* in many circumstances. As mentioned at the beginning of this chapter, police officers often use discretion to determine how they should act, and ethics plays an important role in guiding discretionary actions.
- *Duty.* The concept of discretion is linked with **duty,** or the obligation to act in a certain manner. Society, by passing laws, can make a police officer's duty clearer and, in the process, help eliminate discretion from the decision-making process. But an officer's duty will not always be obvious, and ethical considerations can often supplement "the rules" of being a law enforcement agent.
- *Honesty.* Of course, honesty is a critical attribute for an ethical police officer. A law enforcement agent must make hundreds of decisions in a day, and most of them require him or her to be honest in order to properly do the job.
- *Loyalty.* What should a police officer do if he or she witnesses a partner using excessive force on a suspect? The choice often sets loyalty against ethics, especially if the officer does not condone the violence.

Although an individual's ethical makeup is determined by a multitude of personal factors, police departments can create an atmosphere that is conducive to professionalism. Brandon V. Zuidema and H. Wayne Duff, both captains with the Lynchburg (Virginia) Police Department, believe that law enforcement administrators can encourage ethical policing by:

1. Incorporating ethics into the department's mission statement.
2. Conducting internal training sessions in ethics.
3. Accepting "honest mistakes" and helping the officer learn from those mistakes.
4. Adopting a zero-tolerance policy toward unethical decisions when the mistakes are not so honest.[153]

SELFASSESSMENT

Fill in the blanks and check your answers on page 208.

Police officers are held to high standards of _____, meaning that they are expected to be honest and respectful of the law. Misconduct such as accepting bribes or shaking down citizens is known as _____, and such behavior is investigated by _____ _____ units within police departments. In matters of ethics, a police officer is often guided by his or her sense of _____, or the obligation to act in a certain manner, and feeling of _____ toward fellow officers.

CJ IN ACTION

THE DNA JUGGERNAUT

In August 2003, Katie Sepich, a graduate student at the University of New Mexico, was raped and strangled to death. Using a tiny amount of skin tissue from under Sepich's fingernails, the police were able to recover the DNA of her attacker. Authorities did not find a match until four years later, when Gabriel Avila was found guilty of burglary and was forced to provide a DNA sample. As it turned out, Avila had been arrested for other crimes just weeks after killing Sepich, and if his DNA had been taken at that point, he would quickly have been identified as her murderer. Collecting DNA from a person who has been arrested but not convicted of a crime is controversial, however, as we discuss in this chapter's *CJ in Action*.

EXPANDING DNA SAMPLING

Today, forty-six states collect DNA from all persons convicted of a felony. In addition, sixteen states gather DNA from those found guilty of a misdemeanor, and thirty-five do the same for juvenile felony offenders.[154] Eighteen states—including New Mexico, in the wake of the Katie Sepich situation—and the federal government are taking the process one step further. They have passed legislation that allows for DNA fingerprinting of those who have not been convicted of a felony but have merely been arrested.[155] Supporters of this strategy see it as similar, if not identical, to the common practice of recording the actual fingerprints of all arrestees.

THE CASE FOR COLLECTING DNA FROM ARRESTEES

- The more comprehensive our DNA data banks, the higher the number of cold hits and other matches by law enforcement agencies. As a Virginia prosecutor puts it, "enhanced databases increase the chances of solving crimes."[156]

- Such measures are preventive, as they increase the odds that individuals who have committed violent crimes and are subsequently arrested on separate, less serious charges will wind up behind bars. One study conducted in Chicago identified fifty-three murders and rapes that could have been prevented by DNA fingerprinting of arrestees.[157]

- The public interest in law enforcement is more important than the privacy interests of individuals who have been arrested for criminal behavior.

THE CASE AGAINST COLLECTING DNA FROM ARRESTEES

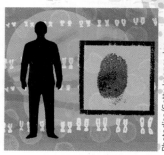

Photodisc/Getty Images, Inc.

- Our criminal justice system is based on the premise that someone is innocent until proven guilty. An arrest does not equal guilt, and a person should not suffer the consequences of guilt until it has been proved in court. In California alone, each year approximately 50,000 people are arrested for felonies and never charged with a crime, and thousands more are tried and not convicted.[158]

- Crime labs are already overwhelmed by growing DNA databases. Under these new laws, such databases will be deluged with millions of samples, costing taxpayers billions of dollars and causing unacceptable delays in getting lab results to police.

- Forty percent of DNA profiles in the federal database belong to African Americans, and, given a greater law enforcement emphasis on immigration offenses, Hispanics could dominate such databases in the future.[159] Consequently, the system will exacerbate the perception by many that our criminal justice system is inherently biased.

YOUR OPINION—WRITING ASSIGNMENT

Although most states would limit DNA fingerprinting to those arrested for felonies and serious misdemeanors, South Carolina has considered applying the procedure to people arrested for any crime, including lesser misdemeanors such as shoplifting, vandalism, and jaywalking.[160] What is your opinion of collecting DNA from arrestees, in general? What do you think of South Carolina's proposed law? From what you have learned about police strategies and the police subculture, what impact do you think the spread of these laws would have on criminal investigations in this country? Before responding, you can review our discussions in this chapter concerning:

- Police strategies, particularly problem-oriented policing (pages 191–192).

- Detective investigations and DNA (pages 182–185).

- Police ethics (pages 204–206).

Your answer should include at least three full paragraphs.

CHAPTER SUMMARY

LO 1 **Explain why police officers are allowed discretionary powers.** Police officers are considered trustworthy and able to make honest decisions. They have experience and training. They are knowledgeable in criminal behavior. Finally, they must have the discretion to take reasonable steps to protect themselves.

LO 2 **List the three primary purposes of police patrol.** (a) The deterrence of crime, (b) the maintenance of public order, and (c) the provision of services that are not related to crime.

LO 3 **Indicate some investigation strategies that are considered aggressive.** Using undercover officers is considered an aggressive (and often dangerous) investigative technique. The use of informants is also aggressive, but involves danger for those who inform.

LO 4 **Describe how forensic experts use DNA fingerprinting to solve crimes.** Law enforcement agents gather trace evidence such as blood, semen, skin, or hair from the crime scene. Because these items are rich in DNA, which provides a unique genetic blueprint for every living organism, crime labs can create a DNA profile of the suspect and test it against other such profiles of known criminals stored in databases. If the profiles match, then law enforcement agents have found a strong suspect for the crime.

LO 5 **Explain why differential response strategies enable police departments to respond more efficiently to 911 calls.** A differential response strategy allows a police department to distinguish among calls for service so that officers may respond to important calls more quickly. Therefore, a "hot" crime, such as a burglary in progress, will receive more immediate attention than a "cold" crime, such as a missing automobile that disappeared several days earlier.

LO 6 **Explain community policing and its contribution to the concept of problem-oriented policing.** Community policing involves proactive problem solving and a community-police partnership in which the community engages itself along with the police to address crime and the fear of crime in a particular geographic area. By establishing a cooperative presence in a community, police officers are better able to recognize the root causes of criminal behavior there and apply problem-oriented policing methods when necessary.

LO 7 **Determine when police officers are justified in using deadly force.** Police officers must make a reasonable judgment in determining when to use force that will place the suspect in threat of injury or death. That is, given the circumstances, the officer must reasonably assume that the use of such force is necessary to avoid serious injury or death to the officer or someone else.

LO 8 **Identify the three traditional forms of police corruption.** The three traditional forms are bribery, shakedowns, and mooching.

LO 9 **Explain what an ethical dilemma is and name four categories of ethical dilemmas that a police officer typically may face.** An ethical dilemma is a situation in which police officers (a) do not know the right course of action, (b) have difficulty doing what they consider to be right, and/or (c) find the wrong choice very tempting. The four types of ethical dilemmas involve (a) discretion, (b) duty, (c) honesty, and (d) loyalty.

SELF ASSESSMENT ANSWER KEY

Page 174: i. discretion; **ii.** policy; **iii.** mandatory arrest

Page 185: i. Patrol; **ii.** deter; **iii.** presence; **iv.** Detectives; **v.** forensics; **vi.** DNA fingerprinting

Page 193: i. incident; **ii.** service; **iii.** general; **iv.** Directed; **v.** proactive; **vi.** Community; **vii.** terrorism

Page 200: i. subculture; **ii.** physical; **iii.** stress; **iv.** reasonable; **v.** deadly

Page 206: i. professionalism; **ii.** corruption; **iii.** internal affairs; **iv.** duty; **v.** loyalty

KEY TERMS

QUESTIONS FOR CRITICAL ANALYSIS

1. Mandatory arrest laws regarding domestic violence have had two unintended consequences. First, more women are being arrested for assault. Second, more dual arrests are occurring, in which police officers arrest both parties in a domestic violence incident. Why are these trends a natural consequence of limiting police discretion in this area?

2. As noted on page 193, the federal government dispenses billions of dollars to local police departments each year to aid in fighting terrorism. In many instances, this is a "use it or lose it" proposition—if an agency declines the funds because it has no practical anti-terrorism needs, then the funds are diverted elsewhere. How might this practice lead to inefficiency in counterterrorism spending by local police departments?

3. Relate the concept of "broken windows" to high-crime neighborhoods and potential ways to combat crime in such neighborhoods.

4. How might cultural differences between police officers and residents of the neighborhoods they patrol contribute to increased use of officer force in those neighborhoods?

5. How does the police subculture contribute to police corruption?

CourseMate *For Online Help*

For online help and access to resources that accompany *Criminal Justice Today*, go to www.cengagebrain.com/shop/ISBN/1111835578. Click "Access Now," where you will find flashcards, an online quiz, and other helpful study aids. If you have an access code for CourseMate, log in and go to the chapter of your choice for additional online study aids.

NOTES

1. Quoted in Kim Murphy, "Shooting by Police Stirs Anger in Seattle," *Los Angeles Times* (September 17, 2010), A10.

2. *Ibid.*

3. Quoted in Gordon Witkin, "When the Bad Guys Are Cops," *U.S. News and World Report* (September 11, 1995), 22.

4. A. J. Reiss, Jr., "Police Organization in the Twentieth Century," in *Modern Policing*, ed. Michael Tonry and Norval Morris (Chicago: University of Chicago Press, 1992), 51–98.

5. Kenneth Culp David, *Police Discretion* (St. Paul, MN: West Publishing Co., 1975).

6. C. E. Pratt, "Police Discretion," *Law and Order* (March 1992), 99–100.

7. "More than a Hunch," *Law Enforcement News* (September 2004), 1.

8. Herbert Jacob, *Urban Justice* (Boston: Little, Brown, 1973), 27.

9. Larry Copeland, "Chases by Police Yield High Fatalities," *USA Today* (April 23, 2010), 3A.

10. Bureau of Justice Statistics, *Local Police Departments, 2003* (Washington, D.C.: U.S. Department of Justice, May 2006), 24.

11. Jack Richter, "Number of Police Pursuits Drop Dramatically in Los Angeles," *Los Angeles Police Department Press Release* (August 20, 2003).

12. *County of Sacramento v. Lewis,* 523 U.S. 833 (1998).

13. *Scott v. Harris,* 550 U.S. 372 (2007).

14. L. Craig Parker, Robert D. Meier, and Lynn Hunt Monahan, *Interpersonal Psychology for Criminal Justice* (St. Paul, MN: West Publishing Co., 1989), 113.

15. Paul C. Friday, Vivian B. Lord, M. Lyn Exum, and Jennifer L. Hartman, *Evaluating the Impact of a Specialized Domestic Violence Police Unit* (Charlotte, NC: University of North Carolina, 2006), 6.

16. National Institute of Justice, Table 1: States with Mandatory Arrest, "Domestic Violence Cases: What Research Shows about Arrest and Dual Arrest Rates," at **www.nij.gov/ publications/dv-dual-arrest-222679/ exhibits/table1.htm.**

17. David Hirschel, Eve Buzawa, April Pattavina, and Don Faggiani, "Domestic Violence and Mandatory Arrest Laws: To What Extent Do They Influence Police Arrest Decisions?" *Journal of Criminal Law and Criminology* (Fall 2007), 255–298.

18. *Town of Castle Rock v. Gonzales,* 545 U.S. 748, 760 (2005).

19. Quoted in Copeland.

20. H. Nees, "Policing 2001," *Law and Order* (January 1990), 257–264.

21. Peter K. Manning, *Police Work: The Social Organization of Policing,* 2d ed. (Prospect Heights, IL: Waveland Press, 1997), 96.

22. Samuel Walker, *The Police in America: An Introduction,* 2d ed. (New York: McGraw-Hill, 1992), 16.

23. George L. Kelling and Mark H. Moore, "From Political to Reform to Community: The Evolving Strategy of Police," in *Community Policing: Rhetoric or Reality,* ed. Jack Greene and Stephen Mastrofski (New York: Praeger Publishers, 1988), 13.

24. Henry M. Wrobleski and Karen M. Hess, *Introduction to Law Enforcement and Criminal Justice,* 7th ed. (Belmont, CA: Wadsworth/Thomson Learning, 2003), 119.

25. Bureau of Justice Statistics, *Local Police Departments, 2007* (Washington, D.C.: U.S. Department of Justice, December 2010), 6.

26. Connie Fletcher, "What Cops Know," *On Patrol* (Summer 1996), 44–45.

27. David H. Bayley, *Police for the Future* (New York: Oxford University Press, 1994), 20.

28. Walker, 103.

29. Eric J. Scott, *Calls for Service: Citizens Demand an Initial Police Response* (Washington, D.C.: National Institute of Justice, 1981), 28–30.

30. William G. Gay, Theodore H. Schell, and Stephen Schack, *Routine Patrol: Improving Patrol Productivity,* vol. 1 (Washington, D.C.: National Institute of Justice, 1977), 3–6.

31. Gary W. Cordner, "The Police on Patrol," in *Police and Policing: Contemporary Issues,* ed. Dennis Jay Kenney (New York: Praeger Publishers, 1989), 60–71.

32. Anthony V. Bouza, *The Police Mystique: An Insider's Look at Cops, Crime, and the Criminal Justice System* (New York: Plenum Press, 1990), 27.

33. Peter W. Greenwood and Joan Petersilia, *The Criminal Investigation Process: Summary and Policy Implications* (Santa Monica, CA: Rand Corporation, 1975).

34. Fletcher, 46.

35. John E. Eck, *Solving Crimes: The Investigation of Burglary and Robbery* (Washington, D.C.: Police Executive Research Forum, 1983).

36. Steven G. Brandl and James Frank, "The Relationship between Evidence, Detective Effort, and the Disposition of Burglary and Robbery Investigations," *American Journal of Police* 1 (1994), 149–168.

37. 353 U.S. 53 (1957).

38. Federal Bureau of Investigation, *Crime in the United States, 2010* (Washington, D.C.: U.S. Department of Justice, 2011), at **www.fbi.gov/about-us/cjis/ucr/crime -in-the-u.s/2010/crime-in-the-u.s.-2010 /tables/10tbl25.xls.**

39. Karen Hawkins, "More Are Getting Away with Murder," *Associated Press* (December 8, 2008).

40. Quoted in *ibid.*

41. James M. Cronin, Gerard R. Murphy, Lisa L. Spahr, Jessica I. Toliver, and Richard E. Weger, *Promoting Effective Homicide Investigations* (Washington, D.C.: Police Executive Research Forum, August 2007), 102–103.

42. Timothy G. Keel, "Homicide Investigations: Identifying Best Practices," *FBI Law Enforcement Bulletin* (February 2008), 5.

43. Hawkins.

44. Ronald F. Becker, *Criminal Investigations,* 2d ed. (Sudbury, MA: Jones & Bartlett, 2004), 7.

45. Joseph Peterson, Ira Sommers, Deborah Baskin, and Donald Johnson, *The Role and Impact of Forensic Evidence in the Criminal Justice Process* (Washington, D.C.: National Institute of Justice, September 2010), 8–9.

46. Simon A. Cole, "More Than Zero: Accounting for Error in Latent Fingerprinting Identification," *Journal of Criminal Law and Criminology* (Spring 2005), 985–1078.

47. Stuart H. James, Paul E. Kish, and T. Paulette Sutton, *Principles of Bloodstain Pattern Analysis: Theory and Practice* (Boca Raton, FL: Taylor & Francis Group, 2005), 1–3.

48. Jim Lockwood, "Scientist: Blood on the Shoe Was from Victim," *Star-Ledger (Newark, NJ)* (February 15, 2008), 21.

49. Quoted in "New DNA Database Helps Crack 1979 N.Y. Murder Case," *Miami Herald* (March 14, 2000), 18A.

50. Judith E. Lewter, "The Use of Forensic DNA in Criminal Cases in Kentucky as Compared with Other Selected States," *Kentucky Law Journal* (1997–1998), 223.

51. "CODIS—NDIS Statistics," at **www.fbi. gov/about-us/lab/codis/ndis-statistics.**

52. Nancy Ritter, "DNA Solves Property Crimes (But Are We Ready for That?)," *NIJ Journal* (October 2008), 2–12.

53. Evan Pellegrino, "UA Team Adds Precision to DNA Forensics," *Arizona Daily Star* (March 3, 2009), A1; and Gautam Naik, "To Sketch a Thief: Genes Draw Likeness of Suspects," *Wall Street Journal* (March 29, 2009), A9.

54. Alex Johnson, "Already under Fire, Crime Labs Cut to the Bone" (February 23, 2010), at **www.msnbc.msn.com/id/35319938/ ns/us_news-crime_and_courts.**

55. Hawkins.

56. Johnson.

57. Barbara Boyer and Darran Simon, "Statistics Say Crime Is Up in Camden since Police Layoffs," *Philadelphia Inquirer* (March 3, 2011), B1.

58. Jesse McKinley, "Police Departments Turn to Volunteers," *New York Times* (March 2, 2011), A13.

59. Wrobleski and Hess, 173.

60. National Institute of Justice, *Managing Calls to the Police with 911/311 Systems* (Washington, D.C.: U.S. Department of Justice, February 5, 2005).

61. Stephanie Simon, "In Lean Times, Police Cuts Spark Debate over Safety," *Wall Street Journal* (April 26, 2010), at **online.wsj. com/article/SB1000142405274870450890457519235109010 7196.html.**

62. Robert Faturechi, "Deputies' 911 Response Times Grow," *Los Angeles Times* (September 6, 2010), AA1.

63. *Local Police Departments, 2007,* Table 12, page 15.

64. Dale O. Cloninger, "Enforcement Risks and Deterrence: A Reexamination," *Journal of Socio-Economics* 23 (1994), 273.

65. George L. Kelling, Tony Pate, Duane Dieckman, and Charles Brown, *The Kansas City Preventive Patrol Experiment: A Summary Report* (Washington, D.C.: The Police Foundation, 1974), 3–4.

66. Carl B. Klockars and Stephen D. Mastrofski, "The Police and Serious Crime," in *Thinking about Police,* ed. Carl B. Klockars and Stephen Mastrofski (New York: McGraw-Hill, 1990), 130.

67. James Q. Wilson, *Thinking about Crime* (New York: Basic Books, 1983), 65–66.

68. Quoted in Beth Pearsall, "Predictive Policing: The Future of Law Enforcement," *NIJ Journal* (June 2010), at **www.nij.gov/ journals/266/predictive.htm.**

69. Lawrence W. Sherman, "Policing for Crime Prevention," in *Contemporary Policing: Controversies, Challenges, and Solutions*, ed. Quint C. Thurman and Jihong Zhao (Los Angeles: Roxbury Publishing Co., 2004), 62.

70. Jerry Ratcliffe, *Intelligence-Led Policing* (Portland, OR: Willan, 2008), 50.

71. *Ibid.*

72. David Weisburd and Cynthia Lum, "The Diffusion of Computerized Crime Mapping in Policing: Linking Research and Practice," *Police Practice and Research* 6 (2005), 419–434.

73. Quoted in "New Model Police," *Economist* (June 9, 2007), 29.

74. Sherman, 63–66.

75. *Ibid.*, 65.

76. William Sousa and George L. Kelling, "Of 'Broken Windows,' Criminology, and Criminal Justice," in *Police Innovation: Contrasting Perspectives*, ed. David L. Weisburd and Anthony A. Braga (New York: Cambridge University Press, 2006), 77–97.

77. Anthony A. Braga and Brenda J. Bond, "Policing Crime and Disorder Hot Spots: A Randomized Controlled Trial," *Criminology* (August 2008), 579.

78. Ralph B. Taylor, "Incivilities Reduction Policing, Zero Tolerance, and the Retreat from Coproduction: Weak Foundations and Strong Pressures," in *Police Innovation: Contrasting Perspectives*, ed. David L. Weisburd and Anthony A. Braga (New York: Cambridge University Press, 2006), 133–153.

79. Mark H. Moore and George L. Kelling, "'To Serve and Protect': Learning from Police History," *Public Interest* (Winter 1983), 54–57.

80. A. Steven Deitz, "Evaluating Community Policing: Quality Police Service and Fear of Crime," *Policing: An International Journal of Police Strategies and Management* 20 (1997), 83–100.

81. George Kelling, "Police and Community: The Quiet Revolution," in *Perspectives in Policing* (Washington, D.C.: National Institute of Justice, 1988).

82. *Local Police Departments, 2003*, 19.

83. National Institute of Justice Preview, *Community Policing Strategies* (Washington, D.C.: Office of Justice Programs, November 1995), 1.

84. Jihong Zhao and Quint C. Thurman, "Community Policing: Where Are We Now?" *Crime and Delinquency* (July 1997), 345–357.

85. Robert C. Trojanowicz and David Carter, "The Philosophy and Role of Community Policing," at **www.cj.msu.edu/~people/cp/cpphil.html**.

86. Tom Casady, "Beyond Arrest: Using Crime Analysis to Prevent Crime," *The Police Chief* (September 2008), 24.

87. Herman Goldstein, "Improving Policing: A Problem-Oriented Approach," *Crime and Delinquency* 25 (1979), 236–258.

88. Bureau of Justice Assistance, *Problem-Oriented Drug Enforcement: A Community-Based Approach for Effective Policing* (Washington, D.C.: Office of Justice Programs, 1993), 5.

89. Matthew C. Waxman, *Police and National Security: American Local Law Enforcement and Counter-Terrorism after 9/11* (New York: Columbia Law School Public Law & Legal Theory Working Paper Group, 2008), 7 (available at **ssrn.com/abstract=1305268**).

90. David Johnston, "With Crime Up, a City's Police Force Questions the Focus on Terror," *New York Times* (July 24, 2008), A14, A19.

91. *Ibid.*, A19.

92. National Institute of Justice, Nicole J. Henderson, Christopher W. Ortiz, Naomi F. Sugie, and Joel Miller, *Policing in Arab-American Communities after 9/11* (Washington, D.C.: U.S. Department of Justice, July 8, 2008), 1–10.

93. Quoted in "Philadelphia Cadets Get Straight Talk about Job," *Associated Press* (June 29, 2009).

94. *Ibid.*

95. Harry J. Mullins, "Myth, Tradition, and Ritual," *Law and Order* (September 1995), 197.

96. William Westly, *Violence and the Police: A Sociological Study of Law, Custom, and Morality* (Cambridge, MA: MIT Press, 1970).

97. Wallace Graves, "Police Cynicism: Causes and Cures," *FBI Law Enforcement Bulletin* (June 1996), 16–21.

98. Robert Regoli, *Police in America* (Washington, D.C.: R. F. Publishing, 1977).

99. Bob Herbert, "A Cop's View," *New York Times* (March 15, 1998), 17.

100. The Officer Down Memorial Page, "Honoring Officers Killed in the Year 2010," at **www.odmp.org/year.php?year=2010**.

101. Federal Bureau of Investigation, *Law Enforcement Officers Killed and Assaulted* (Washington, D.C.: U.S. Department of Justice, 2011), at **www.fbi.gov/about-us/cjis/ucr/leoka/leoka-2010/officers-assaulted/officers-assaulted**.

102. John S. Dempsey and Linda S. Forst, *An Introduction to Policing*, 6th ed. (Clifton Park, NY: Delmar Cengage Learning, 2011), 170.

103. Bureau of Justice Statistics, *Contacts between Police and the Public, 2005* (Washington, D.C.: U.S. Department of Justice, April 2007), 1.

104. Dempsey and Forst, 170.

105. *Local Police Departments, 2007*, Table 16, page 19.

106. Rebecca Kanable, "No Excuses: Break Mental and Physical Barriers to Body Armor Wear Compliance," *Law Enforcement Technology* (October 2010), 42–43.

107. The Officer Down Memorial Page; and Craig W. Floyd and Kevin P. Morrison, "Officer Safety on Our Roadways: What the Numbers Say about Saving Lives," *The Police Chief* (July 2010), 28.

108. National Highway Traffic Safety Administration, *Characteristics of Law Enforcement Officers' Fatalities in Motor Vehicle Crashes* (Washington, D.C.: U.S. Department of Transportation, January 2011), Figure 15, page 25.

109. Rebecca Kanable, "Going Home at Night," *Law Enforcement Technology* (January 2009), 23–24.

110. University of Buffalo, "Impact of Stress on Police Officers' Physical and Mental Health," *Science Daily* (September 29, 2008), at **www.sciencedaily.com/releases/2008/09/080926105029.htm**.

111. Quoted in *ibid.*

112. Gail A. Goolsakian, *et al.*, *Coping with Police Stress* (Washington, D.C.: National Institute of Justice, 1985).

113. J. L. O'Neil and M. A. Cushing, *The Impact of Shift Work on Police Officers* (Washington, D.C.: Police Executive Research Forum, 1991), 1.

114. "Impact of Stress on Police Officers' Physical and Mental Health."

115. James Hibberd, "Police Psychology," *On Patrol* (Fall 1996), 26.

116. M. J. Horowitz, N. Wilner, N. B. Kaltreider, and W. Alvarez, "Signs and Symptoms of Post Traumatic Stress Disorder," *Archives of General Psychiatry* 37 (1980), 85–92.

117. Laurence Miller, "Practical Strategies for Preventing Officer Suicide," *Law and Order* 3 (2006), 90–92.

118. Lawrence M. Friedman, *Crime and Punishment in American History* (New York: Basic Books, 1993), 362.

119. *Contacts between Police and the Public, 2005*, 1.

120. Bureau of Justice Statistics, *Arrest-Related Deaths in the United States, 2003–2005* (Washington, D.C.: U.S. Department of Justice, October 2007), 1.

121. H. Range Hutson, Deirdre Anglin, Phillip Rice, Demetrious N. Kyriacou, Michael Guirguis, and Jared Strote, "Excessive Use of Force by Police: A Survey of Academic Emergency Physicians," *Emergency Medicine Journal* (January 2009), 20–22.

122. Independent Commission on the Los Angeles Police Department, *Report of the Independent Commission on the Los Angeles Police Department* (1991), ix.

123. 471 U.S. 1 (1985).

124. 471 U.S. 1, 11 (1985).

125. 490 U.S. 386 (1989).

126. *Brosseau v. Haugen*, 543 U.S. 194 (2004).

127. *Local Police Departments, 2007*, Table 14, page 17.

128. Bruce Taylor *et al.*, *Comparing Safety Outcomes in Police Use-of-Force Cases for Law Enforcement Agencies That Have Deployed Conducted Energy Devices and a Matched Comparison Group That Have*

Not: A Quasi-Experimental Evaluation (Washington, D.C.: National Institute of Justice, September 2009).

129. "Taser Training Called Dangerous," *The (Jackson, MS) Clarion-Ledger* (February 12, 2011), A1.

130. Michael E. Miller, "Taser Use and the Use-of-Force Continuum: Examining the Effect of Policy Change," *The Police Chief* (September 2010), 72–75.

131. Jonathan Kozlowski, "Beaming Pain Confusion," *Law Enforcement Technology* (August 2009), 58–61.

132. Quoted in James C. McKinley, Jr., "In Houston, Tough Questions on Race," *New York Times* (May 15, 2010), A9.

133. Quoted in *ibid.*

134. *Contacts between Police and the Public, 2005,* 1.

135. *Ibid.,* Table 9, page 8.

136. Eric A. Stewart, Eric P. Baumer, Rod K. Brunson, and Ronald L. Simons, "Neighborhood Racial Context and Perceptions of Police-Based Racial Discrimination among Black Youth," *Criminology* (August 2009), 847–886.

137. Randall L. Kennedy, "*McClesky v. Kemp,* Race, Capital Punishment, and the Supreme Court," *Harvard Law Review* 101 (1988), 1436–1438.

138. Douglas A. Smith, "Minorities and the Police: Attitudinal and Behavioral Questions," in *Race and Criminal Justice,* ed. Michael J. Lynch and E. Britt Patterson (New York: Harrow & Heston, 1991), 28–30.

139. Matt Lait and Scott Glover, "Inglewood Police Accused of Abuse in Other Cases," *Los Angeles Times* (July 15, 2002), A1.

140. Bouza, 72.

141. Knapp Commission, *Report on Police Corruption* (New York: Brazilier, 1973).

142. *Commission to Investigate Allegations of Police Corruption and the Anti-Corruption Procedures of the Police Department* (New York: The Commission, 1994), 36.

143. Robert J. Kane and Michael D. White, "Bad Cops: A Study of Career-Ending Misconduct among New York City Police Officers," *Criminology & Public Policy* (November 2009), 764.

144. Lawrence W. Sherman, "Becoming Bent: Moral Careers of Corrupt Policemen," in *Police Corruption: A Sociological Perspective,* ed. Lawrence W. Sherman (Garden City, NY: Doubleday, 1974), 191–208.

145. Quoted in Jennifer Dukes and Loren Keller, "Can Police Be Police to Selves?" *Omaha World-Herald* (February 22, 1998), 1A.

146. Rich Lord, "State Trooper Faces Another Civil Lawsuit," *Pittsburgh Post-Gazette* (February 21, 2011), B1.

147. National Research Council of the National Academies, *Fairness and Effectiveness in Policing: The Evidence* (Washington, D.C.: National Academies Press, 2004), 279, 289.

148. "Roster of Civilian Oversight Agencies in the U.S.," National Association for Civilian Oversight of Law Enforcement, at **www. nacole.org**.

149. Hazel Glenn Beh, "Municipal Liability for Failure to Investigate Citizen Complaints against Police," *Fordham Urban Law Journal* 23 (Winter 1998), 209.

150. Jocelyn M. Pollock and Ronald F. Becker, "Ethics Training Using Officers' Dilemmas," *FBI Law Enforcement Bulletin* (November 1996), 20–28.

151. Quoted in Thomas J. Martinelli, "Dodging the Pitfalls of Noble Cause Corruption and the Intelligence Unit," *The Police Chief* (October 2009), 124.

152. Pollock and Becker.

153. Brandon V. Zuidema and H. Wayne Duff, "Organizational Ethics through Effective Leadership," *Law Enforcement Bulletin* (March 2009), 8–9.

154. Solomon Moore, "FBI and States Vastly Expanding Databases of DNA," *New York Times* (April 19, 2009), 1.

155. National Conference of State Legislatures, "State Laws on DNA Banks," at **www.ncsl. org/programs/cj/dnadatabanks.htm**.

156. Quoted in Ellen Sorokin, "Attorney General Hopefuls Favor More DNA Collection," *Washington Times* (August 7, 2001), C1.

157. Referenced in Eileen Sullivan, "Feds to Collect DNA from Every Person They Arrest," *Associated Press* (April 16, 2008).

158. Tania Simoncelli and Barry Steinhardt, "California's Proposition 69: A Dangerous Precedent for Criminal DNA," *Journal of Law, Medicine, and Ethics* (Summer 2006), 208.

159. Moore, 19.

160. Yvonne M. Wenger, "Proposal Expands DNA Use by Police," *Post and Courier (Charleston, SC)* (January 3, 2007), 1.

CHAPTER

7

Police and the Constitution

The Rules of Law Enforcement

Toledo Blade/Dave Zapotosky

LEARNING OBJECTIVES

After reading this chapter, you should be able to . . .

LO 1 Outline the four major sources that may provide probable cause.

LO 2 Explain the exclusionary rule and the exceptions to it.

LO 3 Distinguish between a stop and a frisk, and indicate the importance of the case *Terry v. Ohio*.

LO 4 List the four elements that must be present for an arrest to take place.

LO 5 List the four categories of items that can be seized by use of a search warrant.

LO 6 Explain when searches can be made without a warrant.

LO 7 Describe the plain view doctrine and indicate one of its limitations.

LO 8 Recite the *Miranda* warning.

LO 9 Indicate situations in which a *Miranda* warning is unnecessary.

LO 10 List the three basic types of police identification.

The ten learning objectives labeled LO 1 through LO 10 are designed to help improve your understanding of the chapter.

HOUSE CALL

Jeremy Fisher obviously did not want the police, or anybody else, to bother him. Not only had he locked the back door to his home in Brownstown, Michigan, but he had also shoved a couch against the front door to block access. Still, Officer Christopher Goolsby and his partner felt that they needed to look inside. They had just received a call that someone was "going crazy" at Fisher's residence, and when they arrived at the home, they found "considerable chaos": a smashed pickup truck in the driveway, a damaged fence post on the side lawn, three broken windows in the house, and blood on the hood of the truck and on one of the doors of the house.

The officers knocked on the front door, but Fisher did not answer. They could hear him screaming, however, and they caught sight of him bleeding from a cut on his hand. Goolsby yelled to Fisher, asking if he needed medical attention, but Fisher responded with a profanity. The officer then pushed the front door partway open and entered the home. The first thing he saw was Fisher pointing a rifle at him. Goolsby quickly retreated and called for backup. Fisher was eventually arrested and charged under Michigan law with assault with a dangerous weapon and possession of a firearm during the commission of a felony.

During his trial, Fisher argued that Goolsby did not have a right to enter his house and, therefore, any evidence gathered during this entry could not be used against him. Several years ago, the case reached the United States Supreme Court, which rejected Fisher's claims and sided with the police. According to the Court, requiring police officers to "walk away" from situations such as the one they encountered at Fisher's house would not "meet the needs of law enforcement or the demands of public safety."

Through its decisions, the United States Supreme Court determines the guidelines that law enforcement agents must follow when entering a home and searching and detaining its inhabitants.
Photo by Justin Sullivan/Getty Images

Jeremy Fisher's argument that the police officers overstepped the boundaries of their authority was not a fanciful one. The "right of a man to retreat to his own home" is one of the cornerstones of the U.S. Constitution.[1] Generally, law enforcement agents cannot enter any sort of dwelling without written permission from a judge called a *warrant,* which you will learn about later in the chapter. This warrant requirement has several exceptions, however, including "the need to assist persons who are seriously injured or threatened with such injury."[2] Given the circumstances in *Michigan v. Fisher,* the Supreme Court found that the police officers were reasonable in believing that Fisher could have posed a threat to himself or someone else in the house.[3]

In the last chapter, we discussed the importance of discretion in the criminal justice system. Certainly, as in this case, police officers have a great deal of discretion to make the decisions they feel are necessary to protect themselves and the public. This discretion is not absolute, however. For the most part, a law enforcement agent's actions are determined by the rules for policing set down in the U.S. Constitution and enforced by the courts. In this chapter, we will examine the extent to which police behavior is controlled by the law, starting with a discussion of the constitutional principles on which such control is grounded.

THE FOURTH AMENDMENT

In *Michigan v. Fisher,* the Supreme Court did not address whether Jeremy Fisher was guilty or innocent of the charges against him. That was for the trial court to decide. Rather, the Court ruled that Officer Christopher Goolsby had not overstepped the boundaries of his authority in entering and "searching" Fisher's house. To understand these boundaries, law enforcement officers must understand the Fourth Amendment, which reads as follows:

> The right of the people to be secure in their persons, houses, papers, and effects, against unreasonable searches and seizures, shall not be violated, and no Warrants shall issue, but upon probable cause, supported by Oath or affirmation, and particularly describing the place to be searched, and the persons or things to be seized.

This amendment contains two critical legal concepts: a prohibition against *unreasonable searches and seizures* and the requirement of *probable cause* to issue a warrant (see Figure 7.1 below).

REASONABLENESS

Law enforcement personnel use searches and seizures to look for and collect the evidence they need to convict individuals suspected of crimes. As you have just read, when police are conducting a search or seizure, they must be *reasonable.* Though courts have spent innumerable hours scrutinizing the word, no specific meaning for *reasonable* exists. A thesaurus can provide useful synonyms—logical, practical, sensible, intelligent, plausible—but because each case is different, those terms are relative.

In the *Fisher* case, the Supreme Court rejected the argument that the search had been so unreasonable as to violate the Fourth Amendment's prohibition against unreasonable searches and seizures. That does not mean that the police officers' actions would have been reasonable under any circumstances. What if there had been no evidence of carnage at Jeremy Fisher's home and he had been quietly watching television when the police officers arrived? In this situation, Officer Goolsby's conduct would almost certainly have been considered unreasonable, as American courts go to great lengths to protect against overzealous searches of homes. The Supreme Court has even ruled that homicide detectives cannot enter a house containing a dead body without a judge's permission, unless an emergency requires them to enter immediately.[4]

Searches and Seizures The legal term, as found in the Fourth Amendment to the U.S. Constitution, that generally refers to the searching for and the confiscating of evidence by law enforcement agents.

Probable Cause Reasonable grounds to believe the existence of facts warranting certain actions, such as the search or arrest of a person.

Teaching Tip: In a short written assignment, have students answer "Questions for Critical Analysis" number one on page 248, in which they discuss the two most important legal concepts contained in the Fourth Amendment.

FIGURE 7.1 The Meaning of Unreasonable Searches and Seizures and Probable Cause

AP Photo/Denis Poroy

UNREASONABLE SEARCHES AND SEIZURES The Fourth Amendment provides that individuals have the right to be "secure in their persons" against "unreasonable searches and seizures" conducted by government agents. In practice, this means that law enforcement officers are generally required to obtain a search warrant prior to any search and seizure. Basically, the search warrant is the acknowledgment by a judge that probable cause exists for law enforcement officers to search for or take a person or property. In other words, the search and seizure must be "reasonable."

PROBABLE CAUSE Before a search can take place or an individual can be arrested, the requirement of probable cause must be met. Probable cause exists if there is a substantial likelihood that (1) a crime was committed and (2) the individual committed the crime. Note that probable cause involves a likelihood—not just a possibility—that the suspect committed the crime. Probable cause must exist before police can get an arrest warrant or a search warrant from a judge.

PROBABLE CAUSE

The concept of reasonableness is linked to probable cause. The Supreme Court has ruled, for example, that any arrest or seizure is unreasonable unless it is supported by probable cause.[5] The burden of probable cause requires more than mere suspicion on a police officer's part. The officer must know of facts and circumstances that would reasonably lead to "the belief that an offense has been or is being committed."[6]

SOURCES OF PROBABLE CAUSE If no probable cause existed when a police officer took a certain action, it cannot be retroactively applied. If, for example, a police officer stops a person for jaywalking and then (without the help of a drug-sniffing dog) finds several ounces of marijuana in that person's pocket, the arrest for marijuana possession would probably be disallowed. Remember, suspicion does not equal probable cause. If, however, an informant had tipped the officer off that the person was a drug dealer, probable cause might exist and the arrest could be valid. Informants are one of several sources that may provide probable cause. Others include:

Teaching Tip: Invite a campus or local police officer to class. Ask the officer to discuss the process of establishing probable cause. How does the officer determine when he or she has grounds to make an arrest? What information is the officer required to present in court to establish that probable cause existed? (LO 1)

1. *Personal observation.* Police officers may use their personal training, experience, and expertise to infer probable cause from situations that may not be obviously criminal. If, for example, a police officer observes several people in a car slowly circling a certain building in a high-crime area, that officer may infer that the people are "casing" the building in preparation for a burglary. Probable cause could be established for detaining the suspects.

   LO 1

2. *Information.* Law enforcement officers receive information from victims, eyewitnesses, informants, and official sources such as police bulletins or broadcasts. Such information, as long as it is believed to be reliable, is a basis for probable cause.

3. *Evidence.* In certain circumstances, which will be examined later in this chapter, police have probable cause for a search or seizure based on evidence—such as a shotgun—in plain view.

4. *Association.* In some circumstances, if the police see a person with a known criminal background in a place where criminal activity is openly taking place, they have probable cause to stop that person. Generally, however, association is not adequate to establish probable cause.[7]

In March 2010, Monroe Township police officer Thomas Lucasiewicz used his nose—literally—to establish probable cause for one of the biggest pot busts in New Jersey history. While on patrol in Middlesex County, Lucasiewicz noticed the strong scent of burning marijuana. Following the smell, he found his way to a house that had dark smoke billowing from the chimney. Inside, where a gardener had been foolishly burning excess product, investigators eventually found more than a thousand marijuana plants and fifty pounds of packaged pot (see the photo on the facing page).

Findlaw has a handy summary of the many laws regarding police procedure that can be traced to the Fourth Amendment. Find its Web site by visiting the *Criminal Justice CourseMate* at **cengagebrain. com** and selecting the *Web links* for this chapter.

THE PROBABLE CAUSE FRAMEWORK In a sense, the concept of probable cause allows police officers to do their job effectively. Most arrests are made without a warrant because most arrests are the result of quick police reaction to the commission of a crime. Indeed, it would not be practical to expect a police officer to obtain a warrant before making an arrest on the street. Thus, probable cause provides a framework that limits the situations in which police officers can make arrests, but also gives officers the freedom to act within that framework. In 2003, the Supreme Court reaffirmed this freedom by ruling that Baltimore (Maryland) police officers acted properly when they arrested all three passengers of a car in which cocaine had been hidden in the back seat. "A reasonable officer," wrote Chief Justice William H. Rehnquist, "could conclude that there was probable cause to believe" that the defendant, who had been sitting in the front seat, was in "possession" of the illicit drug despite his protestations to the contrary.[8]

Once an arrest is made, the arresting officer must prove to a judge that probable cause existed. In *County of Riverside v. McLaughlin* (1991),[9] the Supreme Court ruled that this judicial determination of probable cause must be made within forty-eight hours after the arrest, even if this two-day period includes a weekend or holiday.

THE EXCLUSIONARY RULE

Historically, the courts have looked to the Fourth Amendment for guidance in regulating the activity of law enforcement officers, as the language of the Constitution does not expressly do so. The courts' most potent legal tool in this endeavor is the **exclusionary rule,** which prohibits the use of illegally seized evidence. According to this rule, any evidence obtained by an

LO 2

unreasonable search or seizure is inadmissible (may not be used) against a defendant in a criminal trial.[10] Even highly incriminating evidence, such as a knife stained with the victim's blood, usually cannot be introduced at a trial if illegally obtained. Furthermore, any physical or verbal evidence police are able to acquire by using illegally obtained evidence is known as the **fruit of the poisoned tree** and is also inadmissible. For example, if the police use the existence of the bloodstained knife to get a confession out of a suspect, that confession will be excluded as well.

The Supreme Court began applying the exclusionary rule to evidence in federal courts nearly a century ago, in 1914.[11] About fifty years later, the Court decided to apply the rule to state court evidence as well,[12] meaning that these Fourth Amendment requirements extend to all of the nation's law enforcement officers. One of the implications of the exclusionary rule is that it forces police to gather evidence properly. If they follow appropriate procedures, they are more likely to be rewarded with a conviction. If they are careless or abuse the rights of the suspect, they are unlikely to get a conviction. A strict application of the exclusionary rule, therefore, will permit guilty people to go free because of police carelessness or innocent errors.

THE "INEVITABLE DISCOVERY" EXCEPTION Critics of the exclusionary rule have long maintained that the costs to society of losing critical evidence are higher than the benefits of deterring police misconduct. Several Supreme Court decisions have mirrored this view and provided exceptions to the exclusionary rule. The **"inevitable discovery" exception** was established in the wake of the disappearance of ten-year-old Pamela Powers of Des Moines, Iowa, on Christmas Eve, 1968. The primary suspect in the case, a religious fanatic named Robert Williams, was tricked by a detective into leading police to the site where he had buried Powers. The detective convinced Williams that if he did not lead police to the body, he would soon forget where it was buried. This would deny his victim a "Christian burial." Initially, in *Brewer v. Williams* (1977),[13] the Court ruled that the evidence (Powers's body) had been obtained illegally because Williams's attorney had not been present during the interrogation that led to his admission. Several years later, in *Nix v. Williams* (1984),[14] the Court reversed itself, ruling that the evidence was admissible because the body would have eventually ("inevitably") been found by lawful means.

What were the circumstances that provided Monroe Township (New Jersey) police officer Thomas Lucasiewicz, right, with probable cause to initiate one of the largest marijuana busts in state history?
AP Photo/Mel Evans

Exclusionary Rule A rule under which any evidence that is obtained in violation of the accused's rights under the Fourth, Fifth, and Sixth Amendments, as well as any evidence derived from illegally obtained evidence, will not be admissible in criminal court.

Fruit of the Poisoned Tree Evidence that is acquired through the use of illegally obtained evidence and is therefore inadmissible in court.

"Inevitable Discovery" Exception The legal principle that illegally obtained evidence can be admissible in court if police using lawful means would have "inevitably" discovered it.

Why do critics of Arizona's S.B. 1070, such as this protester, believe that the law will lead to racial profiling of Hispanics in that state? Do you agree with these criticisms? Why or why not?
AP Photo/Ross D. Franklin

THE "GOOD FAITH" EXCEPTION The scope of the exclusionary rule has been further diminished by two cases involving faulty warrants. In the first, *United States v. Leon* (1984),[15] the police seized evidence on authority of a search warrant that had been improperly issued by a judge. In the second, *Herring v. United States* (2009),[16] due to a computer error, police officers detained a man on the mistaken belief that he was subject to an arrest warrant. As a result, they found that the suspect was carrying illegal drugs and an unregistered firearm.

In both cases, the Court allowed the evidence to stand under a "good faith" exception to the exclusionary rule. Under this exception, evidence acquired by a police officer using a technically invalid warrant is admissible if the officer was unaware of the error. In these two cases, the Court said that the officers acted in "good faith." By the same token, if police officers use a search warrant that they know to be technically incorrect, the good faith exception does not apply, and the evidence can be suppressed.

SELF ASSESSMENT

Fill in the blanks and check your answers on page 248.
The Fourth Amendment contains two critically important restrictions on police authority: a prohibition against _____ searches and seizures and a requirement of _____ _____ that a crime has been committed before a warrant for a search or seizure can be issued. Judges rely on the _____ rule to keep _____ that has been improperly obtained by the police out of criminal courts.

STOPS AND FRISKS

On April 23, 2010, Arizona governor Jan Brewer signed one of the toughest state immigration laws in the nation. Known as S.B. 1070, the new law requires a state law enforcement officer to check the immigration status of any person detained if the officer has "reasonable suspicion" to believe that person is in the country illegally.[17] The law aroused considerable controversy because of concern about what factors might trigger a police officer's reasonable suspicion of a person's illegal immigration status (see the photo alongside).

Latino groups and lawmakers, in particular, worry that police will target Arizona residents who look Hispanic or have Hispanic surnames. This tactic is called **racial profiling** because the police action is based on the race, nationality, or national origin of the suspect rather than on evidence or information that the suspect has broken the law.

Supporters of S.B. 1070 point out that the statute specifically forbids racial profiling and applies only after police have legally stopped a suspect for a different reason, such as a traffic stop. Regardless, Georgetown University law professor David Cole believes that such profiling is "inevitable" under the new Arizona law. "People don't wear signs saying that they are illegal immigrants," Cole points out. "So police officers will not stop white people, and will stop Latinos, especially poor Latinos."[18] Already, seven lawsuits have been filed to keep S.B. 1070 from being implemented, and the law's fate may ultimately rest on the courts' view of its reasonable suspicion provision. When such reasonable suspicion does exist, police officers are well within their rights to *stop and frisk* a suspect. In a stop and frisk, law enforcement officers (1) briefly detain a person they reasonably believe to be suspicious, and (2) if they believe the person to be armed, proceed to pat down, or "frisk," that person's outer clothing.[19]

THE ELUSIVE DEFINITION OF REASONABLE SUSPICION

Like so many elements of police work, the decision of whether to stop a suspect is based on the balancing of conflicting priorities. On the one hand, a police officer feels a sense of urgency to act when he or she believes that criminal activity is occurring or is about to occur. On the other hand, law enforcement agents do not want to harass innocent individuals, especially if doing so runs afoul of the U.S. Constitution. In stop-and-frisk law, this balancing act rests on the fulcrum of reasonable suspicion.

Discussion Tip: Ask students to react to the discussion of S.B. 1070 in the text. In their opinion, does S.B. 1070 represent a form of racial profiling? Why or why not?

TERRY V. OHIO The precedent for the ever-elusive definition of a "reasonable" suspicion in stop-and-frisk situations was established in *Terry v. Ohio* (1968).[20] In that case, a detective named McFadden observed two men (one of whom was Terry) acting strangely

LO 3

in downtown Cleveland. The men would walk past a certain store, peer into the window, and then stop at a street corner and confer. While they were talking, another man joined the conversation and then left quickly. Several minutes later the three men met again at another corner a few blocks away. Detective McFadden believed the trio was planning to break into the store. He approached them, told them who he was, and asked for identification. After receiving a mumbled response, the detective frisked the three men and found handguns on two of them, who were tried and convicted of carrying concealed weapons.

Critical Thinking Skill Development: Ask students to explain the difference between reasonable suspicion and probable cause. Why do stops require reasonable suspicion rather than probable cause? (LO 3)

The Supreme Court upheld the conviction, ruling that Detective McFadden had reasonable cause to believe that the men were armed and dangerous and that swift action was necessary to protect himself and other citizens in the area.[21] The Court accepted McFadden's interpretation of the unfolding scene as based on objective facts and practical conclusions. It therefore concluded that his suspicion was reasonable. In contrast, critics of Arizona's S.B. 1070, described above, believe that the law will result in state police officers stopping citizens for reasons—their skin color or general appearance—that are not reasonable. We will take a closer look at the issue of racial profiling by law enforcement agents in the *CJ in Action* feature at the end of the chapter.

THE "TOTALITY OF THE CIRCUMSTANCES" TEST For the most part, the judicial system has refrained from placing restrictions on police officers' ability to make stops. In the *Terry* case, the Supreme Court did say that an officer must have "specific and articulable facts" to support the decision to make a stop, but added that the facts may be "taken together with rational inferences."[22] The Court has consistently ruled that because of their practical experience, law enforcement agents are in a unique position to make such inferences and should be given a good deal of freedom in doing so.

Teaching Tip: Ask students to generate a brief written assignment in which they discuss when a stop can be made. Have them list the circumstances that would justify a stop and then list the circumstances that would not. (LO 3)

In the years since the *Terry* case was decided, the Court has settled on a "totality of the circumstances" test to determine whether a stop is based on reasonable suspicion.[23] In 2002, for example, the Court ruled that a U.S. Border Patrol agent's stop of a minivan in Arizona was reasonable.[24] On being approached by the Border Patrol car, the driver had stiffened, slowed down his van, and avoided making eye contact with the agent. Furthermore, the children in the van waved at the officer in a mechanical manner, as if ordered to do so. The agent pulled over the van and found 128 pounds of marijuana. In his opinion, Chief Justice

William Rehnquist pointed out that such conduct might have been unremarkable on a busy city highway, but on an unpaved road thirty miles from the Mexican border it was enough to reasonably arouse the agent's suspicion.[25] The justices also made clear that the need to prevent terrorist attacks is part of the "totality of the circumstances" and, therefore, law enforcement agents will have more leeway to make stops near U.S. borders.

INFORMANTS AND REASONABLE SUSPICION A "bare-bones" anonymous tip is at the opposite end of the reasonable suspicion spectrum from a situation that meets the "totality of the circumstances" test. In 2000, the Supreme Court overturned a conviction based on such a "bare-bones" tip. An anonymous caller had told the Miami–Dade County (Florida) police that a young African American male standing at a bus stop was illegally carrying a handgun. Even though the information was correct, the police officer who made the stop and subsequent arrest had no reason other than the anonymous tip to suspect criminal activity.[26]

This restriction does not prevent tips from informants from being valuable resources for police officers. The Court has held that a tip from a *known* informant who had provided reliable information in the past is sufficient to justify a *Terry* stop, even if there is no other supporting evidence to make the stop.[27] Furthermore, an anonymous tip can pass the "totality of the circumstances" test if it is specific enough and the police verify it with their own observations.[28]

A STOP

The terms *stop* and *frisk* are often used in concert, but they describe two separate acts. A **stop** takes place when a law enforcement officer has reasonable suspicion that a criminal activity is about to take place. Because an investigatory stop is not an arrest, there are limits to the extent police can detain someone who has been stopped. For example, in one situation an airline traveler and his luggage were detained for ninety minutes while the police waited for a drug-sniffing dog to arrive. The Supreme Court ruled that the initial stop of the passenger was constitutional, but that the ninety-minute wait was excessive.[29]

In 2004, the Court held that police officers could require suspects to identify themselves during a stop that is otherwise valid under the *Terry* ruling.[30] The case involved a Nevada rancher who was fined $250 for refusing to give his name to a police officer investigating a possible assault. The defendant argued that such requests force citizens to incriminate themselves against their will, which is prohibited, as we shall see later in the chapter, by the Fifth Amendment. Justice Anthony Kennedy wrote, however, that "asking questions is an essential part of police investigations" that would be made much more difficult if officers could not determine the identity of a suspect.[31] The ruling validated "stop-and-identify" laws in twenty states and numerous cities and towns.

A FRISK

The Supreme Court has stated that a **frisk** should be a protective measure. Police officers cannot conduct a frisk as a "fishing expedition" simply to try to find items besides weapons, such as illegal narcotics, on a suspect.[32] A frisk does not necessarily follow a stop and in fact may occur only when the officer is justified in thinking that the safety of police officers or other citizens may be endangered.

Stop A brief detention of a person by law enforcement agents for questioning. The agents must have a reasonable suspicion of the person before making a stop.

Frisk A pat-down or minimal search by police to discover weapons. It is conducted for the express purpose of protecting the officer or other citizens, rather than finding evidence of illegal substances for use in a trial.

A police officer frisks a suspect in Lockhart, Texas. What is the main purpose behind a frisk? When are police justified in frisking someone who has been detained?
John Boykin/PhotoEdit

Again, the question of reasonable suspicion is at the heart of determining the legality of frisks. In the *Terry* case, the Court accepted that Detective McFadden reasonably believed that the three suspects posed a threat. The suspects' refusal to answer McFadden's questions, though within their rights because they had not been arrested, provided him with sufficient motive for the frisk. In 2009, the Court extended the "stop and frisk" authority by ruling that a police officer could order a passenger in a car that had been pulled over for a traffic violation to submit to a pat-down.[33] To do so, the officer must have a reasonable suspicion that the suspect may be armed and dangerous.

Teaching Tip: Ask students to respond to "Questions for Critical Analysis" number three on page 248, in which they apply what they have learned about stop and frisks to a hypothetical case.

SELFASSESSMENT

Fill in the blanks and check your answers on page 248.
A police officer can make a _____ , which is not the same as an arrest, if she or he has a _____ suspicion that a criminal act is taking place or is about to take place. Then, the officer has the ability to _____ the suspect for weapons as a protective measure.

ARRESTS

As in the *Terry* case, a stop and frisk may lead to an **arrest.** An arrest is the taking into custody of a citizen for the purpose of detaining him or her on a criminal charge. It is important to understand the difference between a stop and an arrest. In the eyes of the law, a stop is a relatively brief intrusion on a citizen's rights, whereas an arrest—which involves a deprivation of liberty—is deserving of a full range of constitutional protections, which we shall discuss throughout the chapter (see *Mastering Concepts—The Difference between a Stop and an Arrest* below). Consequently, while a stop can be made based on reasonable suspicion, a law enforcement officer needs probable cause, as defined earlier, to make an arrest.[34]

Arrest To take into custody a person suspected of criminal activity.

MASTERINGCONCEPTS

THE DIFFERENCE BETWEEN A STOP AND AN ARREST

Both stops and arrests are considered seizures because both police actions involve the restriction of an individual's freedom to "walk away." Both must be justified by a showing of reasonableness as well. You should be aware, however, of the differences between a stop and an arrest. **During a stop,** police can interrogate the person and make a limited search of his or her outer clothing. If anything occurs during the stop, such as the discovery of an illegal weapon, then officers may arrest the person. **If an arrest is made,** the suspect is now in police custody and is protected by the U.S. Constitution in a number of ways that will be discussed later in the chapter.

PhotoDisc

	STOP	ARREST
Justification	Reasonable suspicion only	Probable cause
Warrant	None	Required in some, but not all, situations
Intent of Officer	To investigate suspicious activity	To make a formal charge against the suspect
Search	May frisk, or "pat down," for weapons	May conduct a full search for weapons or evidence
Scope of Search	Outer clothing only	Area within the suspect's immediate control or "reach"

ELEMENTS OF AN ARREST

When is somebody under arrest? The easy—and incorrect—answer would be whenever the police officer says so. In fact, the state of being under arrest is dependent not only on the actions of the law enforcement officers but also on the perception of the suspect. Suppose Mr. Jones is stopped by plainclothes detectives, driven to the police station, and detained for three hours for questioning. During this time, the police never tell Mr. Jones he is under arrest, and in fact, he is free to leave at any time. But if Mr. Jones or any other reasonable person *believes* he is not free to leave, then, according to the Supreme Court, that person is in fact under arrest and should receive the necessary constitutional protections.[35]

Criminal justice professor Rolando V. del Carmen of Sam Houston State University has identified four elements that must be present for an arrest to take place:

Discussion Tip: Ask students to consider the elements of an arrest. Is it possible for someone to be legally under arrest without the officer indicating that he or she is under arrest? What role does the suspect's perception play during the proceedings? (LO 4)

1. The *intent* to arrest. In a stop, though it may entail slight inconvenience and a short detention period, there is no intent on the part of the law enforcement officer to take the person into custody. Therefore, there is no arrest. As intent is a subjective term, it is sometimes difficult to determine whether the police officer intended to arrest. In situations when the intent is unclear, courts often rely—as in our hypothetical case of Mr. Jones—on the perception of the arrestee.[36]

   LO 4

2. The *authority* to arrest. State laws give police officers the authority to place citizens under custodial arrest, or take them into custody. Like other state laws, the authorization to arrest varies among the fifty states. Some states, for example, allow off-duty police officers to make arrests, while others do not.

3. *Seizure or detention.* A necessary part of an arrest is the detention of the subject. Detention is considered to have occurred as soon as the arrested individual submits to the control of the officer, whether peacefully or under the threat or use of force.

4. The *understanding* of the person that she or he has been arrested. Through either words—such as "you are now under arrest"—or actions, the person taken into custody must understand that an arrest has taken place. When a suspect has been forcibly subdued by the police, handcuffed, and placed in a patrol car, he or she is believed to understand that an arrest has been made. This understanding may be lacking if the person is intoxicated, insane, or unconscious.[37]

ARRESTS WITH A WARRANT

When law enforcement officers have established probable cause to arrest an individual who is not in police custody, they obtain an **arrest warrant** for that person. An arrest warrant contains information such as the name of the person suspected and the crime he or she is suspected of having committed. (See Figure 7.2 on the facing page for an example of an arrest warrant.) Judges or magistrates issue arrest warrants after first determining that the law enforcement officers have indeed established probable cause.

Arrest Warrant A written order, based on probable cause and issued by a judge or magistrate, commanding that the person named on the warrant be arrested by the police.

Exigent Circumstances Situations that require extralegal or exceptional actions by the police. In these circumstances, police officers are justified in not following procedural rules, such as those pertaining to search and arrest warrants.

ENTERING A DWELLING There is a perception that an arrest warrant gives law enforcement officers the authority to enter a dwelling without first announcing themselves. This is not accurate. In *Wilson v. Arkansas* (1995),[38] the Supreme Court reiterated the common law requirement that police officers must knock and announce their identity and purpose before entering a dwelling. Under certain conditions, known as **exigent circumstances,** law enforcement officers need not announce themselves. These circumstances include situations in which the officers have a reasonable belief of any of the following:

- The suspect is armed and poses a strong threat of violence to the officers or others inside the dwelling.
- Persons inside the dwelling are in the process of destroying evidence or escaping because of the presence of the police.
- A felony is being committed at the time the officers enter.[39]

According to Peter Kraska, a professor at Eastern Kentucky University, the number of no-knock police raids based on exigent circumstances has increased from 2,000 to 3,000 per year in the mid-1980s to 70,000 to 80,000 per year today.[40] Critics worry that with these tactics police are increasingly endangering citizens, some of whom may be innocent.[41] Infamously, in 2006 Atlanta undercover police officers fatally shot a ninety-two-year-old woman during a botched no-knock drug raid.

THE WAITING PERIOD The Supreme Court severely weakened the practical impact of the "knock and announce" rule with its decision in *Hudson v. Michigan* (2006).[42] In that case, Detroit police did not knock before entering the defendant's home with a warrant. Instead, they announced themselves and then waited only three to five seconds before making their entrance, not the fifteen to twenty seconds suggested by a prior Court ruling.[43] Hudson argued that the drugs found during the subsequent search were inadmissible because the law enforcement agents did not follow proper procedure. By a 5–4 margin, the Court disagreed. In his majority opinion, Justice Antonin Scalia stated that an improper "knock and announce" is not unreasonable enough to provide defendants with a "get-out-of-jail-free card" by disqualifying evidence uncovered on the basis of a valid search warrant.[44] Thus, the exclusionary rule, discussed earlier in this chapter, would no longer apply under such circumstances. Legal experts still advise, however, that police observe a reasonable waiting period after knocking and announcing to be certain that any evidence found during the subsequent search will stand up in court.[45]

ARRESTS WITHOUT A WARRANT

Arrest warrants are not always required, and in fact, most arrests are made on the scene without a warrant.[46] A law enforcement officer may make a **warrantless arrest** if:

1. The offense is committed in the presence of the officer; or
2. The officer has knowledge that a crime has been committed and probable cause to believe the crime was committed by a particular suspect.[47]

The type of crime also comes to bear in questions of arrests without a warrant. As a general rule, officers can make a warrantless arrest for a crime they did not see if they have probable cause to believe that a felony has been committed. For misdemeanors, the crime must have been committed in the presence of the officer for a warrantless arrest to be valid. According to a 2001 Supreme Court ruling, even an arrest for a misdemeanor

FIGURE 7.2 Example of an Arrest Warrant

United States District Court

DISTRICT OF_____

UNITED STATES OF AMERICA
V.

WARRANT FOR ARREST

CASE NUMBER:

To: The United States Marshal
and any Authorized United States Officer

YOU ARE HEREBY COMMANDED to arrest_____
name

and bring him or her forthwith to the nearest magistrate to answer a(n)

☐ Indictment ☐ Information ☐ Complaint ☐ Order of Court ☐ Violation Notice ☐ Probation Violation Petition

charging him or her with (brief description of offense)

in violation of Title_____ United States Code, Section(s)_____

Name of Issuing Officer   Title of Issuing Officer

Signature of Issuing Officer   Date and Location

Bail fixed at $ by_____
Name of Judicial Officer

RETURN

This warrant was received and executed with the arrest of the above-named defendant at_____

DATE RECEIVED   NAME AND TITLE OF ARRESTING OFFICER   SIGNATURE OF ARRESTING OFFICER

DATE OF ARREST

Technology Tip: Have students read the Supreme Court's decision in *Hudson v. Michigan* online at **www.supremecourtus.gov/opinions/05pdf/04-1360.pdf**. Then, have them discuss whether the exclusionary rule should apply when an improper "knock and announce" has taken place. Why or why not?

Warrantless Arrest An arrest made without first seeking a warrant for the action. Such arrests are permitted under certain circumstances, such as when the arresting officer has witnessed the crime or has probable cause that the suspect has committed a felony.

that involves "gratuitous humiliations" imposed by a police officer "exercising extremely poor judgment" is valid as long as the officer can satisfy probable cause requirements.[48] That case involved a Texas mother who was handcuffed, taken away from her two young children, and placed in jail for failing to wear her seat bet.

In certain situations, warrantless arrests are unlawful even though a police officer can establish probable cause. In *Payton v. New York* (1980),[49] for example, the Supreme Court held that when exigent circumstances do not exist and the suspect does not give consent to enter a dwelling, law enforcement officers cannot force themselves in for the purpose of making a warrantless arrest. In contrast, in the situation discussed at the opening of this chapter, exigent circumstances (such as the smashed truck in the driveway and blood on a house door and the suspect's person) provided the police officers with compelling reasons to enter Jeremy Fisher's house and arrest him without a warrant.

The *Payton* ruling was expanded to cover the homes of third parties when, in *Steagald v. United States* (1981),[50] the Court ruled that if the police wish to arrest a criminal suspect in another person's home, they cannot enter that home to arrest the suspect without first obtaining a search warrant, a process we will discuss in the following section.

SELFASSESSMENT

Fill in the blanks and check your answers on page 248.
An arrest occurs when a law enforcement agent takes a suspect into _____ on a criminal charge. If the officer has prior knowledge of the suspect's criminal activity, she or he must obtain a _____ from a judge or magistrate before making the arrest. Officers can, however, make _____ arrests if an offense is committed in their presence or they have _____ _____ to believe that a crime was committed by the particular subject.

LAWFUL SEARCHES AND SEIZURES

How far can law enforcement agents go in searching and seizing private property? Consider the steps taken by Jenny Stracner, an investigator with the Laguna Beach (California) Police Department. After receiving information that a suspect, Greenwood, was engaged in drug trafficking, Stracner enlisted the aid of the local trash collector in procuring evidence. Instead of taking Greenwood's trash bags to be incinerated, the collector agreed to give them to Stracner. The officer found enough drug paraphernalia in the garbage to obtain a warrant to search the suspect's home. Subsequently, Greenwood was arrested and convicted on narcotics charges.[51]

Remember, the Fourth Amendment is quite specific in forbidding unreasonable searches and seizures. Were Stracner's search of Greenwood's garbage and her seizure of its contents "reasonable"? The Supreme Court thought so, holding that Greenwood's garbage was not protected by the Fourth Amendment.[52]

THE ROLE OF PRIVACY IN SEARCHES

A crucial concept in understanding search and seizure law is *privacy.* By definition, a **search** is a governmental intrusion on a citizen's reasonable expectation of privacy. The recognized standard for a "reasonable expectation of privacy" was established in *Katz v. United States* (1967).[53] The case dealt with the question of whether the defendant was justified in his expectation of privacy in the calls he made from a public phone booth. The Supreme Court held that "the Fourth Amendment protects people, not places," and Katz prevailed.

Search The process by which police examine a person or property to find evidence that will be used to prove guilt in a criminal trial.

In his concurring opinion, Justice John Harlan, Jr., set a two-pronged test for a person's expectation of privacy:

1. The individual must prove that she or he expected privacy, and
2. Society must recognize that expectation as reasonable.[54]

Accordingly, the Court agreed with Katz's claim that he had a reasonable right to privacy in a public phone booth. (Remember, however, that the *Terry* case allows for conditions under which a person's privacy rights are overcome by a reasonable suspicion on the part of a law enforcement officer that a threat to public safety exists.)

A LEGITIMATE PRIVACY INTEREST In contrast, in *California v. Greenwood* (1988),[55] described above, the Court did not believe that the suspect had a reasonable expectation of privacy when it came to his garbage bags. The Court noted that when we place our trash on a curb, we expose it to any number of intrusions by "animals, children, scavengers, snoops, and other members of the public."[56] In other words, if Greenwood had truly intended for the contents of his garbage bags to remain private, he would not have left them on the side of the road. To give another example, the Court also upheld the search in a case in which a drug-sniffing dog was used to detect marijuana in the trunk of a car after the driver was stopped for speeding. The Court ruled that no one has a legitimate privacy interest in possessing illegal drugs or other contraband such as explosives in the trunk of his or her car.[57]

GENETIC PRIVACY Does a person have a legitimate privacy interest in spit left on a sidewalk? Or the saliva on a discarded cigarette butt or a half-eaten cinnamon roll? DNA fingerprinting technology, discussed in the previous chapter, has made the question relevant. The items just listed, along with hundreds of other examples of "abandoned DNA," have been used by law enforcement to link suspects to violent crimes.

The case of Rolando Gallego offers a good example of how "abandoned DNA" works. Sheriff's deputies in Sacramento, California, were convinced that Gallego was responsible for the murder of his aunt fifteen years earlier, but they did not have enough evidence to compel him to give them a DNA sample. Instead, two deputies followed Gallego and collected a cigarette butt he had dropped on the pavement. DNA from saliva on this sample matched that from blood on a towel found at the crime scene, and a judge eventually sentenced Gallego to sixteen years to life in prison for the murder.

Critics of these tactics claim that the use of "abandoned DNA" is an unforeseen loophole in the probable cause requirement that essentially allows police officers to search anyone at any time without the suspect's knowledge. Most courts, however, have followed the *Greenwood* decision mentioned above in accepting the procedure. Upholding the conviction of a rapist who had been identified by spit on the street, the Massachusetts Court of Appeals concluded that the "expectorating defendant had no reasonable expectation of privacy in his spittle."[58] Although some legal experts see a difference between garbage, which can be "destroyed before it is released into the world," and DNA evidence, which often cannot, the practice of "surreptitious sampling" will continue to be fruitful for law enforcement unless the Supreme Court eventually rules otherwise.[59]

SEARCH AND SEIZURE WARRANTS

To protect against charges that they have unreasonably infringed on privacy rights during a search, law enforcement officers can obtain a **search warrant**. (See Figure 7.3 on the next page for an example of a search warrant.) Similar to an arrest warrant, a search

Group Activities: Have students brainstorm locations on campus where they would have a high expectation of privacy, as well as places where they would have a low expectation of privacy. Ask them to share their lists with the class. Do all students agree on how much privacy should be afforded in specific locations?

Critical Thinking Skill Development: Ask students to consider the claim that there is no expectation of privacy regarding "abandoned DNA." Do students agree with this view? Why or why not?

Search Warrant A written order, based on probable cause and issued by a judge or magistrate, commanding that police officers or criminal investigators search a specific person, place, or property to obtain evidence.

FIGURE 7.3 Example of a Search Warrant

United States District Court

DISTRICT OF_____

In the Matter of the Search of
(Name, address or brief description of person or property to be searched)

SEARCH WARRANT

CASE NUMBER:

TO:_____ and any Authorized Officer of the United States

Affidavit(s) having been made before me by_____ who has reason to
                                              Affiant
believe that ☐ on the person of or ☐ on the premises known as (name, description and/or location)

in the_____District of_____there is now
concealed a certain person or property, namely (describe the person or property)

I am satisfied that the affidavit(s) and any recorded testimony establish probable cause to believe that the person or property so described is now concealed on the person or premises above-described and establish grounds for the issuance of this warrant.

YOU ARE HEREBY COMMANDED to search on or before_____
                                                                        Date
(not to exceed 10 days) the person or place named above for the person or property specified, serving this warrant and making the search (in the daytime — 6:00 A.M. to 10:00 P.M.) (at any time in the day or night as I find reasonable cause has been established) and if the person or property be found there to seize same, leaving a copy of this warrant and receipt for the person or property taken, and prepare a written inventory of the person or property seized and promptly return this warrant to_____
as required by law.   U.S. Judge or Magistrate

_____ at _____
Date and Time Issued   City and State

_____   _____
Name and Title of Judicial Officer   Signature of Judicial Officer

warrant is a court order that authorizes police to search a certain area. Before a judge or magistrate will issue a search warrant, law enforcement officers must provide:

- Information showing probable cause that a crime has been or will be committed.
- Specific information on the premises to be searched, the suspects to be found and the illegal activities taking place at those premises, and the items to be seized.

The purpose of a search warrant is to establish, before the search takes place, that a *probable cause to search* justifies infringing on the suspect's reasonable expectation of privacy.

PARTICULARITY OF SEARCH WARRANTS The members of the First Congress specifically did not want law enforcement officers to have the freedom to make "general, exploratory" searches through a person's belongings.[60] Consequently, the Fourth Amendment requires that a warrant describe with "particularity" the place to be searched and the things—either people or objects—to be seized.

This "particularity" requirement places a heavy burden on law enforcement officers. Before going to a judge to ask for a search warrant, they must prepare an affidavit in which they provide specific, written information on the property that they wish to search and seize. They must know the specific address of any place they wish to search. General addresses of apartment buildings or office complexes are not sufficient. Furthermore, courts generally frown on vague descriptions of goods to be seized. "Stolen goods" would most likely be considered unacceptably imprecise, while "1 MacBook Pro laptop computer" would be preferred.

A seizure is the act of taking possession of a person or property by the government because of a (suspected) violation of the law. In general, four categories of items can be seized by use of a search warrant:

LO 5

1. Items resulting from the crime, such as stolen goods.
2. Items that are inherently illegal for anybody to possess (with certain exceptions), such as narcotics and counterfeit currency.
3. Items that can be called "evidence" of the crime, such as a bloodstained sneaker or a ski mask.
4. Items used in committing the crime, such as an ice pick or a printing press used to make counterfeit bills.[61]

(For more on the role probable cause plays in the search warrant process, see the feature *You Be the Judge—A Valid Search?* on the facing page.)

REASONABLENESS DURING A SEARCH AND SEIZURE No matter how "particular" a warrant is, it cannot provide for all the conditions that are bound to come up during its service. Consequently, the law gives law enforcement officers the ability to act "reasonably" during a search and seizure in the event of unforeseeable circumstances. For example, if a police officer is searching an apartment for a stolen MacBook Pro laptop computer and notices a vial of crack cocaine sitting on the suspect's bed, that contraband is considered to be in "plain view" and can be seized.

Affidavit A written statement of facts, confirmed by the oath or affirmation of the party making it and made before a person having the authority to administer the oath or affirmation.

Seizure The forcible taking of a person or property in response to a violation of the law.

Teaching Tip: If time allows, invite a campus police officer to visit the classroom. Ask him or her to discuss campus policies for searches of dormitories and student property on campus. Allow time for students to ask questions.

Note that if law enforcement officers have a search warrant that authorizes them to search for a stolen laptop computer, they would not be justified in opening small drawers. Because a computer could not fit in a small drawer, an officer would not have a basis for reasonably searching one. Hence, officers are restricted in terms of where they can look by the items they are searching for.

SEARCHES AND SEIZURES WITHOUT A WARRANT

Although the Supreme Court has established the principle that searches conducted without warrants are *per se* (by definition) unreasonable, it has set "specifically established" exceptions to the rule.[62] In fact, most searches, like most arrests, take place in the absence of a judicial order. Warrantless searches and seizures can be lawful when police are in "hot pursuit" of a subject or when they search bags of trash left at the curb for regular collection. Because of the magnitude of smuggling activities in "border areas" such as airports, seaports, and international boundaries, a warrant normally is not needed to search property in those places. Furthermore, in 2006 the Court held unanimously that police officers do not need a warrant to enter a private home in an emergency, such as

LO 6 when they reasonably fear for the safety of the inhabitants.[63] The two most important circumstances in which a warrant is not needed, though, are (1) searches incidental to an arrest and (2) consent searches.

SEARCHES INCIDENTAL TO AN ARREST The most frequent exception to the warrant requirement involves searches incidental to arrests, so called because nearly every time police officers make an arrest, they also search the suspect. As long as the original arrest was based on probable cause, these searches are valid for two reasons, established by the Supreme Court in *United States v. Robinson* (1973):

Searches Incidental to Arrests Searches for weapons and evidence that are conducted on persons who have just been arrested. The fruit of such searches is admissible if any items found are within the immediate vicinity or control of the suspect.

YOU BE THE JUDGE
A Valid Search?

THE SITUATION Detective Jones receives an anonymous tip that there is a high volume of foot traffic in and out of a house at 312 Elm Street between 4 P.M. and 12 A.M. every night. Because each visitor stays for only a short time, the tipster believes that someone is selling drugs from the residence. Jones drives by the house at 2 A.M. and picks up a garbage bag from the front driveway. In it, he finds a small amount of marijuana. The next morning, Jones appears before you at the courthouse and asks for a search warrant to get inside the house at 312 Elm Street.

THE LAW A search warrant shall be issued if there is probable cause to believe that criminal activity is taking place within the area to be searched.

YOUR DECISION In this case, Detective Jones does not want to arrest the resident of 312 Elm Street for drug possession. Rather, he believes that someone is dealing drugs out of the house. Do you believe that, based on the evidence of drug dealing Jones has provided, there is probable cause to justify issuing the search warrant? Why or why not?

[To see what a judge in St. Lucie County, Florida, did in a similar situation, go to Example 7.1 in Appendix B.]

Rasmus Rasmusson/iStockphoto/Photodisc/Shutterstock/James Stadl/iStockphoto

1. The need for a police officer to find and confiscate any weapons a suspect may be carrying.
2. The need to protect any evidence on the suspect's person from being destroyed.[64]

Law enforcement officers are, however, limited in the searches they may make during an arrest. These limits were established by the Supreme Court in *Chimel v. California* (1969).[65] In that case, police arrived at Chimel's home with an arrest warrant but not a search warrant. Even though Chimel refused their request to "look around," the officers searched the entire three-bedroom house for nearly an hour, finding stolen coins in the process. Chimel was convicted of burglary and appealed, arguing that the evidence of the coins should have been suppressed.

The Supreme Court held that the search was unreasonable. In doing so, the Court established guidelines as to the acceptable extent of searches incidental to an arrest. Primarily, the Court ruled that police may search any area within the suspect's "immediate control" to confiscate any weapons or evidence that the suspect could destroy. The Court found, however, that there was no justification

> for routinely searching rooms other than that in which the arrest occurs—or, for that matter, for searching through all desk drawers or other closed or concealed areas in that room itself. Such searches, in the absence of well-recognized exceptions, may be made only under the authority of a search warrant.[66]

The exact interpretation of the "area within immediate control" has been left to individual courts, but in general it has been taken to mean the area within the reach of the arrested person. Thus, the Court is said to have established the "arm's reach doctrine" in its *Chimel* decision.

SEARCHES WITH CONSENT Consent searches, the second most common type of warrantless searches, take place when individuals voluntarily give law enforcement officers permission to search their persons, homes, or belongings. The most relevant factors in determining whether consent is voluntary are

1. The age, intelligence, and physical condition of the consenting suspect;
2. Any coercive behavior by the police, such as the language used to request consent; and
3. The length of the questioning and its location.[67]

If a court finds that a person has been physically threatened or otherwise coerced into giving consent, the search is invalid.[68] Furthermore, the search consented to must be reasonable. Several years ago, the North Carolina Supreme Court invalidated a consent search that turned up a packet of cocaine. As part of this search, the police had pulled down the suspect's underwear and shone a flashlight on his groin. The court ruled that a reasonable person in the defendant's position would not consent to such an intrusive examination.[69]

The Citizen's Decision The standard for consent searches was set in *Schneckcloth v. Bustamonte* (1973),[70] in which, after being asked, the defendant told police officers to "go ahead" and search his car. A packet of stolen checks found in the trunk was ruled valid evidence because the driver consented to the search. Numerous court decisions have also supported the "knock and talk" strategy, in which the law enforcement agent simply walks up to the door of a residence, knocks, and asks to come in and talk to the resident.[71] The officer does not need reasonable suspicion or probable cause that a crime has taken place in this situation because the decision to cooperate rests with the civilian.

The Intimidation Factor Critics of consent searches hold that such searches are rarely voluntary because most people are intimidated by police and will react to a request for permission to make a search as if it were an order.[72] Furthermore, most people are unaware that they have the option *not* to comply with a request for a search. Thus, if a police officer asks to search an individual's car after issuing a speeding ticket, the individual is well within her or his rights to refuse. According to the United States Supreme Court in *Florida v. Bostick* (1991),[73] so long as police officers do not improperly coerce a suspect to cooperate, they are not *required* to inform the person that he or she has a choice in the matter.

Consequently, in *Ohio v. Robinette* (1996),[74] the Court held that police officers do *not* need to notify people that they are "free to go" after an initial stop when no arrest is involved. Similarly, in 2002, the Court ruled that the inside of a bus is not an inherently coercive environment and thus officers do not need to advise passengers that they can refuse to be searched.[75] The significance of this line of cases is underscored by data presented in connection with the *Robinette* ruling: in the two years leading up to that case, four hundred Ohio drivers were convicted of narcotics offenses that resulted directly from search requests that could have been denied but were not.[76] (For an overview of the circumstances under which warrantless searches are allowed, see Figure 7.4 below.)

SEARCHES OF AUTOMOBILES

In *Carroll v. United States* (1925),[77] the Supreme Court ruled that the law would distinguish among automobiles, homes, and persons in questions involving police searches. In the years since its *Carroll* decision, the Court has established that the Fourth Amendment

Critical Thinking Skill Development: Ask students to discuss the concept of searches by consent. Is a request by an officer to search inherently intimidating and therefore always coercive? Should officers be required to tell citizens that they have the right to refuse a search? (LO 6)

FIGURE 7.4 Exceptions to the Requirement That Officers Have a Search Warrant

In many instances, it would be impractical for police officers to leave a crime scene, go to a judge, and obtain a search warrant before conducting a search. Therefore, under the following circumstances, a search warrant is not required.

INCIDENT TO LAWFUL ARREST
Police officers may search the area within immediate control of a person after they have arrested him or her.

CONSENT
Police officers may search a person without a warrant if that person voluntarily agrees to be searched and has the legal authority to authorize the search.

STOP AND FRISK
Police officers may frisk, or "pat down," a person if they suspect that the person may be involved in criminal activity or pose a danger to those in the immediate area.

HOT PURSUIT
If police officers are in "hot pursuit" or chasing a person they have probable cause to believe committed a crime, and that person enters a building, the officers may search the building without a warrant.

AUTOMOBILE EXCEPTION
If police officers have probable cause to believe that an automobile contains evidence of a crime, they may, in most instances, search the vehicle without a warrant.

PLAIN VIEW
If police officers are legally engaged in police work and happen to see evidence of a crime in "plain view," they may seize it without a warrant.

ABANDONED PROPERTY
Any property, such as a hotel room that has been vacated or contraband that has been discarded, may be searched and seized by police officers without a warrant.

BORDER SEARCHES
Law enforcement officers on border patrol do not need a warrant to search vehicles crossing the border.

does not require police to obtain a warrant to search automobiles or other movable vehicles when they have probable cause to believe that a vehicle contains contraband or evidence of criminal activity.[78] The reasoning behind such leniency is straightforward: requiring a warrant to search an automobile places too heavy a burden on police officers. By the time the officers could communicate with a judge and obtain the warrant, the suspects could have driven away and destroyed any evidence. Consequently, the Court has consistently held that someone in a vehicle does not have the same reasonable expectation of privacy as someone at home or even in a phone booth.

WARRANTLESS SEARCHES OF AUTOMOBILES For nearly three decades, police officers believed that if they lawfully arrested the driver of a car, they could legally make a warrantless search of the car's entire front and back compartments. This understanding was based on the Supreme Court's ruling in *New York v. Benton* (1981),[79] which seemed to allow this expansive interpretation of the "area within immediate control" with regard to automobiles. In *Arizona v. Gant* (2009), however, the Court announced that its *Benton* decision had been misinterpreted. Such warrantless searches are allowed only if (1) the person being arrested is close enough to the car to grab or destroy evidence or a weapon inside the car or (2) the arresting officer reasonably believes that the car contains evidence pertinent to the same crime for which the arrest took place.[80]

So, for example, police will no longer be able to search an automobile for contraband if the driver has been arrested for failing to pay previous speeding tickets—unless the officer reasonably believes the suspect has the ability to reach and destroy any such contraband. As you can imagine, the law enforcement community has reacted negatively to this new, more demanding set of rules.[81] Police officers, however, still can conduct a warrantless search of an automobile based on circumstances other than the incidental-to-an-arrest doctrine. These circumstances include probable cause of criminal activity, consent of the driver, and "protective searches" to search for weapons if police officers have a reasonable suspicion that such weapons exist.[82]

PRETEXTUAL STOPS Despite the Supreme Court's ruling in the *Gant* case, police officers still have a great deal of leeway during automobile stops. In *Whren v. United States* (1996),[83] the Supreme Court ruled that the "true" motivation of police officers in making traffic stops was irrelevant as long as they had probable cause to believe that a traffic law had been broken. In that case, police stopped a car they believed was transporting drugs in order to issue a speeding citation. The Court said that the fact that the officers were using the speeding ticket as a pretext to stop the car (and would not have stopped the driver otherwise) did not matter because the driver actually was speeding.

One year later, in *Maryland v. Wilson* (1997),[84] the Court further expanded police power by ruling that an officer may order passengers as well as the driver out of a car during a traffic stop. The Court reasoned that the danger to an officer is increased when there is a passenger in the automobile.

Teaching Tip: If possible, invite a highway patrol officer to visit your class. Ask the officer to discuss the "movable vehicle" exception to search warrants. What reason must an officer have to stop a vehicle? Once stopped, what level of privacy does the driver have? What level of privacy does a passenger have? (LO 6)

Early on the morning of September 21, 2010, New York police officers pulled over professional football player Braylon Edwards for having excessive tinting on his car windows. The officers then arrested him for driving while intoxicated. Why might this be considered a "pretextual stop"? What is your opinion of such tactics by police?
AP Photo/Louis Lanzano

CAREERS IN CJ

Photo Courtesy of William Howe

FAST FACTS

POLICE DETECTIVE JOB DESCRIPTION

- Collect evidence and obtain facts pertaining to criminal cases.
- Conduct interviews, observe suspects, examine records, and help with raids and busts. Some detectives are assigned to multi-agency task forces that deal with specific types of crime, like drug trafficking or gang activity.

WHAT KIND OF TRAINING IS REQUIRED?

- 2–5 years' experience as a police patrol officer is required before testing to become a detective.
- Larger departments require 60 units of college credit or an associate's degree.

ANNUAL SALARY RANGE AND BENEFITS

- $43,920–$76,350
- Paid vacation, sick leave, medical and life insurance, pension plans, plus special allowances for uniforms.

For additional information on a career as a police detective, visit:

www.bls.gov/oco/ocos160.htm.

WILLIAM HOWE
POLICE DETECTIVE

When I left the Army in 1973, the only teaching job I could find at that time was as a substitute teacher in the Detroit area. In my one year of sub teaching, I was assaulted five times, my car was vandalized four times, and I was set afire by a student throwing a paper airplane doused in lighter fluid at me during a lecture. I quickly saw that I needed to find a safer job—that of a police officer seemed to fit the bill.

RIDING SHOTGUN My first day as an officer with the Battle Creek (Michigan) Police Department, I found myself riding with a real "cowboy." Our first call just after dark was a silent alarm at a McDonald's near the highway. This was my first code run with potentially serious consequences. My knees were shaking so badly I sensed the whole car shook. On arrival I could hardly exit the car to talk to the manager about the false alarm. But I have had this feeling before . . . like every single time I walked into a junior high school classroom as a substitute teacher. I would get over the fear of the priority call, yet I knew I would never get over the terror of the junior high classroom. I had made the right career decision.

DETECTIVE WORK Each crime scene, each major accident, each time you are called to investigate you are presented with a puzzle with various pieces missing. When you discover and interpret the interlocking missing pieces together in a successful prosecution, there is no better feeling. The payoff is when you get the opportunity to show off your completed "puzzle" to the jury and they agree that the pieces fit. When I once thrilled at the chase of the bad guy through the alleys and neighborhoods, I now enjoy even more pursuing them with the mental skills I have developed—accident reconstruction, fingerprint identification, and the interpretation of crime scenes. This can be every bit as rewarding as the foot pursuit, not to mention ever so much easier on the body.

Having been in police work for thirty-five years, I have been assaulted only four times on the job (two of which were at gunpoint). This confirmed for me, once and for all, the importance of being able to use your mind rather than your size to, first, talk your way out of trouble, and, second, talk the bad guys into going along with your plans for them. It also confirmed for me that I had chosen a safer career field.

CAREER ADVICE Today's police officer must have exemplary skills in reading and writing. I recommend creative writing classes, and speech classes are a high priority, in particular. How can you be an effective police officer if you cannot write an articulate police report or address a jury without getting butterflies in your stomach? Furthermore, I strongly suggest that any student interested in becoming a detective take courses in chemistry, physical sciences, botany, anatomy and physiology, communication, administration, and the behavioral sciences. These classes increase your chances of job promotion and lateral movement. Finally, I firmly believe that the patrol position is the backbone of any police agency and that the best place for a career in law enforcement to start is on the street.

CONTAINERS WITHIN A VEHICLE In keeping with the principles of the "movable vehicle" exception, the Supreme Court has also provided law enforcement agents with a great deal of leeway for warrantless searches of containers within a vehicle. In one case, Washington, D.C., detectives received a reliable tip that a man known as the "Bandit" was selling drugs from his car. Without first getting a warrant, the detectives searched the Bandit's trunk and found heroin in a closed paper bag. The Court refused to suppress the evidence, ruling that in such situations police officers can search every part of the vehicle that might contain the items they are seeking, as long as they have probable cause to believe that the items are somewhere in the car.[85]

Nevertheless, there are limits to what can be searched. As Justice John Paul Stevens stated in his opinion, "probable cause to believe that undocumented aliens are being transported in a van will not justify a warrantless search of a suitcase" in that van.[86] By the same token, if the tipster had told the police specifically that "Bandit has a bag of heroin in his trunk," they would not have been justified in searching the front area of the car without a warrant or probable cause.[87]

THE PLAIN VIEW DOCTRINE

The Constitution, as interpreted by our courts, provides very little protection to contraband *in plain view*. For example, suppose a traffic officer pulls over a person for speeding, looks in the driver's side window, and clearly sees what appears to be a bag of heroin resting on the passenger seat. In this instance, under the plain view doctrine, the officer would be justified in seizing the drugs without a warrant.

The plain view doctrine was first enunciated by the Supreme Court in *Coolidge v. New Hampshire* (1971).[88] The Court ruled that law enforcement officers may make a warrantless seizure of an item if four criteria are met:

LO 7

1. The item is positioned so as to be detected easily by an officer's sight or some other sense.
2. The officer is legally in a position to notice the item in question.
3. The discovery of the item is inadvertent. That is, the officer had not intended to find the item.
4. The officer immediately recognizes the illegal nature of the item. No interrogation or further investigation is allowed under the plain view doctrine.

Advances in technology that allow law enforcement agents to "see" beyond normal human capabilities have raised new issues in regard to plain view principles. *Thermal imagers,* for example, measure otherwise invisible levels of infrared radiation. These devices are particularly effective in detecting marijuana plants grown indoors because of the heat thrown off by the "grow lights" that the plants need to survive. The question for the courts has been whether a warrantless search of a dwelling through its walls by means of a thermal imager violates Fourth Amendment protections of privacy. According to the Supreme Court, an item is not in plain view if law enforcement agents need the aid of technology to "see" it.[89] Thus, information from a thermal imager is not by itself justification for a warrantless search.

ELECTRONIC SURVEILLANCE

During the course of a criminal investigation, law enforcement officers may decide to use electronic surveillance, or electronic devices such as wiretaps or hidden microphones ("bugs"), to monitor and record conversations, observe movements, and trace or record telephone calls.

Plain View Doctrine The legal principle that objects in plain view of a law enforcement agent who has the right to be in a position to have that view may be seized without a warrant and introduced as evidence.

Electronic Surveillance The use of electronic equipment by law enforcement agents to record private conversations or observe conduct that is meant to be private.

Technology Tip: Have students visit *ABC News* online to learn more about the Supreme Court's ruling in *Kyllo v. United States* at **abcnews.go.com/US/ story?id=93127&page=1**. What was the Court's rationale regarding the use of thermal imaging technology without a search warrant? (LO 7)

BASIC RULES: CONSENT AND PROBABLE CAUSE Given the invasiveness of electronic surveillance, the Supreme Court has generally held that the practice is prohibited by the Fourth Amendment. In *Burger v. New York* (1967),[90] however, the Court ruled that it was permissible under certain circumstances. That same year, *Katz v. United States* (discussed on pages 226–227) established that recorded conversations are inadmissible as evidence unless certain procedures are followed.

In general, law enforcement officers can use electronic surveillance only if:

1. Consent is given by one of the parties to be monitored; or
2. There is a warrant authorizing the use of the devices.[91]

Teaching Tip: Take a few moments to discuss the statutes in your state that govern electronic surveillance. Is your campus in a state which allows one-party consent, or are officers required to secure a search warrant before monitoring conversations between private parties?

Note that the consent of only one of the parties being monitored is needed to waive the reasonable expectation of privacy. The Court has ruled that people whose conversations have been recorded by supposed friends who turn out to be police informers have not been subjected to an unreasonable search.[92] Therefore, at least theoretically, a person always assumes the risk that whatever he or she says to someone else may be monitored by the police. A number of states, however, have statutes that forbid private citizens from tape-recording another person's conversation without her or his knowledge. In Maryland, for example, such an act is a felony.

If consent exists, then law enforcement officers are not required to obtain a warrant before engaging in electronic surveillance. In most other instances, however, a warrant is required. For the warrant to be valid, it must:

1. Detail with "particularity" the conversations that are to be overheard.
2. Name the suspects and the places that will be under surveillance.
3. Show probable cause to believe that a specific crime has been or will be committed.[93]

Once the specific information has been gathered, the law enforcement officers must end the electronic surveillance immediately.[94] In any case, the surveillance cannot last more than thirty days without a judicial extension. In Chapter 16, we will look at the thorny issues of electronic surveillance in the age of homeland security.

VIDEO AND DIGITAL SURVEILLANCE When Marat Mikhaylich stole a livery taxicab to flee the scene of a bank robbery he had just committed in Edison, New Jersey, he probably thought that he had successfully evaded the police. The next morning, however, on March 29, 2011, he was arrested in Queens, New York, after a police department security camera detected the stolen car's license plates. In fact, the New York Police Department has 238 cameras—130 mounted on police cars—equipped with Automatic License Plate Recognition (ALPR) technology.[95] These computerized cameras first convert photo images of license plates into text. Then, the numbers are checked against databases that contain records of the license plates of stolen cars and automobiles driven by known drug dealers, wanted felons, and sex offenders. In heavy-traffic areas, ALPR units can check tens of thousands of license plates each hour.[96]

FORCE MULTIPLYING Many Americans, and not just wanted bank robbers, would be surprised to learn how often their movements are under the watchful eyes of law enforcement. Along with ALPR, many cities are blanketed with closed circuit television (CCTV) cameras that record and transmit all activity in a targeted area. The images are monitored in real time so that law enforcement personnel can investigate any suspicious or criminal activity captured by the cameras. Law enforcement can also now follow a suspect by placing a global positioning system (GPS) device on the suspect's car. The device transmits a signal to a satellite that tells police the current location and velocity of the targeted vehicle. Furthermore, police departments in Houston and Miami are testing unmanned aerial vehicles (UAVs), or surveillance drones, that can record video images and listen in on cell phone conversations from high above city streets.

Local police departments welcome these surveillance systems because they act as "force multipliers." In other words, by using surveillance technology, a police department can expand its capabilities without a significant increase in personnel. Speaking of CCTV, Brian Harvey, a deputy chief with the Dallas Police Department, says, "One camera operator can cover a lot more area than field officers can."[97]

Critical Thinking Skill Development: Ask students to respond to "Questions for Critical Analysis" number five on page 248, in which they ponder the constitutionality of ALPR and CCTV.

Privacy Concerns Critics of the rapid spread of CCTV cameras and other forms of high-tech surveillance contend that they infringe on individual privacy, allowing law enforcement to create "digital dossiers" on people without probable cause.[98] Traditionally, however, courts have ruled that the mere tracking of a person or a vehicle on public streets does not constitute a search, as people have no expectation of privacy in such situations.[99] While upholding the police's ability to electronically follow automobiles using GPS devices, federal judge Richard Posner stated that the Fourth Amendment "cannot sensibly be read to mean that police shall be no more efficient in the 21st century than they were in the 18th." Posner added, "There is a tradeoff between security and privacy, and it often favors security."[100]

CJ&TECHNOLOGY Backscatter X-Ray Scanners

American Science and Engineering, Inc.

With the proliferation of a piece of machinery known as the "Z Backscatter," law enforcement agencies have yet another piece of surveillance technology at their disposal. The Z Backscatter is a scanning device that sends a narrow stream of X-rays at and through objects and then "reads" the X-rays as they bounce back. Dense material such as steel absorbs the rays and therefore does not show up on the scan. Less dense materials, such as human bodies, drugs, or explosives, scatter the rays and allow an image to be recorded. The result resembles a black-and-white photograph that gives a strong indication of what is inside an automobile or cargo container. Law enforcement agencies recently began purchasing Z Backscatters and mounting them on the back of nondescript vans, allowing for drive-by X-ray vision. The Border Patrol has used this technology to discover 1,500 pounds of marijuana and five illegal immigrants hidden in a large truck, while other agencies have discovered amphetamines in a car bumper and barrels packed with sticks of dynamite.

THINKING ABOUT BACKSCATTER X-RAY SCANNERS

In the words of one observer, "From a privacy perspective [the Z Backscatter is] one of the most intrusive technologies conceivable." Do you agree? Why or why not? In what ways, if at all, do you think that the courts should limit the use of this technology?

A search is a governmental intrusion on the _____ of an individual. To protect these rights, law enforcement agents must procure a _____ _____ before examining a suspect's home or personal possessions. During a properly executed search, officers may _____ any items that may be used as evidence or that are inherently illegal to possess. Law enforcement agents do not need a judge's prior approval to conduct a search incidental to an _____ or when the subject of the search gives his or her _____.

THE INTERROGATION PROCESS AND *MIRANDA*

Teaching Tip: Ask students to close their textbooks and recite (or write down) the *Miranda* warning. How many know the warning by memory? (LO 8)

After the Pledge of Allegiance, there is perhaps no recitation that comes more readily to the American mind than the *Miranda* warning:

LO 8 You have the right to remain silent. If you give up that right, anything you say can and will be used against you in a court of law. You have the right to speak with an attorney and to have the attorney present during questioning. If you so desire and cannot afford one, an attorney will be appointed for you without charge before questioning.

The *Miranda* warning is not a mere prop. It strongly affects one of the most important aspects of any criminal investigation—the **interrogation,** or questioning of a suspect from whom the police want to get information concerning a crime and perhaps a confession.

Interrogation The direct questioning of a suspect to gather evidence of criminal activity and to try to gain a confession.

THE LEGAL BASIS FOR *MIRANDA*

The Fifth Amendment guarantees protection against self-incrimination. In other words, as we shall see again in Chapter 10, a defendant cannot be required to provide information about his or her own criminal activity. A defendant's choice *not* to incriminate himself or herself cannot be interpreted as a sign of guilt by a jury in a criminal trial. A confession, or admission of guilt, is by definition a statement of self-incrimination. How, then, to reconcile the Fifth Amendment with the critical need of law enforcement officers to gain confessions? The answer lies in the concept of **coercion,** or the use of physical or psychological duress to obtain a confession.

Coercion The use of physical force or mental intimidation to compel a person to do something—such as confess to committing a crime—against her or his will.

SETTING THE STAGE FOR *MIRANDA* The Supreme Court first recognized that a confession could not be physically coerced in a 1936 case concerning a defendant who was beaten and whipped until he confessed to a murder.[101] It was not until 1964, however, that the Court specifically recognized that the accused's due process rights should be protected during interrogation. That year, the Court heard the case of *Escobedo v. Illinois,*[102] which involved a convicted murderer who had incriminated himself during a four-hour questioning session at a police station. Police officers ignored the defendant's requests to speak with his lawyer, who was actually present at the station while his client was being interrogated. The Court overturned the conviction, setting forth a five-pronged test in the process. This test established that if police are interrogating a suspect in custody, they cannot deny the suspect's request to speak with an attorney and must warn the suspect of his or her constitutional right to remain silent under the Fifth Amendment. If any one of the five prongs was not satisfied, the suspect had effectively been denied his or her right to counsel under the Sixth Amendment.[103]

Teaching Tip: In a short writing assignment, have students explain why the *Miranda* warnings are necessary to protect against improper coercion of criminal suspects.

THE *MIRANDA* CASE The limitations of the *Escobedo* decision quickly became apparent. All five of the prongs had to be satisfied for the defendant to enjoy the

A Los Angeles police officer reads a handcuffed "suspect" his *Miranda* rights during a training exercise. Does a police officer need to take this action every time he or she arrests a suspect? If not, under what circumstances must an officer administer the *Miranda* warning?

Kim Kulish/Corbis

Miranda Rights The constitutional rights of accused persons taken into custody by law enforcement officials, such as the right to remain silent and the right to counsel.

Custody The forceful detention of a person, or the perception that a person is not free to leave the immediate vicinity.

Custodial Interrogation The questioning of a suspect after that person has been taken into custody. In this situation, the suspect must be read his or her *Miranda* rights before interrogation can begin.

Sixth Amendment protections it offered. In fact, the accused rarely requested counsel, rendering the *Escobedo* test irrelevant no matter what questionable interrogation methods the police used to elicit confessions. Consequently, two years later, the Supreme Court handed down its *Miranda* decision,[104] establishing the *Miranda* **rights** and introducing the concept of what University of Columbia law professor H. Richard Uviller called *inherent coercion*. This terms refers to the assumption that even if a police officer does not lay a hand on a suspect, the general atmosphere of an interrogation is in and of itself coercive.[105]

Though the *Miranda* case is best remembered for the procedural requirement it spurred, at the time the Supreme Court was more concerned about the treatment of suspects during interrogation. (See the feature *Landmark Cases*—Miranda v. Arizona on the facing page.) The Court found that routine police interrogation strategies, such as leaving suspects alone in a room for several hours before questioning them, were inherently coercive. Therefore, the Court reasoned, every suspect needed protection from coercion, not just those who had been physically abused. The *Miranda* warning is a result of this need. In theory, if the warning is not given to a suspect before an interrogation, the fruits of that interrogation, including a confession, are invalid.

WHEN A *MIRANDA* WARNING IS REQUIRED

As we shall see, a *Miranda* warning is not necessary under several conditions, such as when no questions are asked of the suspect. Generally, *Miranda* requirements apply only when a suspect is in **custody.** In a series of rulings since *Miranda,* the Supreme Court has defined custody as an arrest or a situation in which a reasonable person would not feel free to leave.[106] Consequently, a **custodial interrogation** occurs when a suspect is under arrest or is deprived of her or his freedom in a significant manner. Remember, a *Miranda* warning is only required before a custodial interrogation takes place. For example, if four police officers enter a suspect's bedroom at 4:00 A.M., wake him, and form a circle around him, then they must give him a *Miranda* warning before questioning. Even though the suspect has not been arrested, he will "not feel free to go where he please[s]."[107]

WHEN A *MIRANDA* WARNING IS NOT REQUIRED

A *Miranda* warning is not necessary in a number of situations:

1. When the police do not ask the suspect any questions that are *testimonial* in nature. Such questions are designed to elicit information that may be used against the suspect in court. Note that "routine booking questions," such as the suspect's name, address, height, and eye color, do not require a *Miranda* warning. Even though answering these questions may provide incriminating evidence (especially if the person answering is a prime suspect), the Supreme Court has held that they are absolutely necessary if the police are to do their jobs.[108] (Imagine the officer not being able to ask a suspect her or his name.)

2. When the police have not focused on a suspect and are questioning witnesses at the scene of a crime.

LO 9

LANDMARK CASES: *Miranda v. Arizona*

AP/Wide World

Ernesto Miranda

Ernesto Miranda, a produce worker, was arrested in Phoenix, Arizona, in 1963 and charged with kidnapping and rape. After being identified by the victim in a lineup, Miranda was taken into an interrogation room and questioned for two hours by detectives. At no time was Miranda informed that he had a right to have an attorney present. When the police emerged from the session, they had a signed statement by Miranda confessing to the crimes. He was subsequently convicted and sentenced to twenty to thirty years in prison. After the conviction was confirmed by the Arizona Supreme Court, Miranda appealed to the United States Supreme Court, claiming that he had not been warned that any statement he made could be used against him, and that he had a right to counsel during the interrogation. The *Miranda* case was one of four examined by the Court that dealt with the question of coercive questioning.

Miranda v. Arizona
United States Supreme Court
384 U.S. 436 (1966)
laws.findlaw.com/US/384/436.html

IN THE WORDS OF THE COURT . . .
CHIEF JUSTICE WARREN, MAJORITY OPINION
* * * *

The cases before us raise questions which go to the roots of our concepts of American criminal jurisprudence: the restraints society must observe consistent with the Federal Constitution in prosecuting individuals for crime. More specifically, we deal with the admissibility of statements obtained from an individual who is subjected to custodial police interrogation and the necessity for procedures which assure that the individual is accorded his privilege under the Fifth Amendment to the Constitution not to be compelled to incriminate himself.
* * * *

As for the procedural safeguards to be employed, unless other fully effective means are devised to inform accused persons of their right of silence and to assure a continuous opportunity to exercise it,

the following measures are required. Prior to any questioning, the person must be warned that he has a right to remain silent, that any statement he does make may be used as evidence against him, and that he has a right to the presence of an attorney, either retained or appointed. The defendant may waive effectuation of these rights, provided the waiver is made voluntarily, knowingly and intelligently. * * * The mere fact that he may have answered some questions or volunteered some statements on his own does not deprive him of the right to refrain from answering any further inquiries until he has consulted with an attorney and thereafter consents to be questioned.
* * * *

It is obvious that such an interrogation environment is created for no purpose other than to subjugate the individual to the will of his examiner. This atmosphere carries its own badge of intimidation. To be sure, this is not physical intimidation, but it is equally destructive of human dignity. The current practice of incommunicado interrogation is at odds with one of our Nation's most cherished principles—that the individual may not be compelled to incriminate himself. Unless adequate protective devices are employed to dispel the compulsion inherent in custodial surroundings, no statement obtained from the defendant can truly be the product of his free choice.

DECISION
The Court overturned Miranda's conviction, stating that police interrogations are, by their very nature, coercive and therefore deny suspects their constitutional right against self-incrimination by "forcing" them to confess. Consequently, any person who has been arrested and placed in custody must be informed of his or her right to be free from self-incrimination and to be represented by counsel during any interrogation. In other words, suspects must be told that they *do not have to* answer police questions. To accomplish this, the Court established the *Miranda* warning, which must be read prior to questioning a suspect in custody.

FOR CRITICAL ANALYSIS
What is meant by the phrase "coercion can be mental as well as physical"? What role does the concept of "mental coercion" play in Chief Justice Warren's opinion?

For more information and activities related to this case, visit the *Criminal Justice CourseMate* at <u>cengagebrain.com</u> and select the *Web links* for this chapter.

3. When a person volunteers information before the police have asked a question.
4. When the suspect has given a private statement to a friend or some other acquaintance. *Miranda* does not apply to these statements so long as the government did not orchestrate the situation.
5. During a stop and frisk, when no arrest has been made.
6. During a traffic stop.[109]

WAIVING MIRANDA Suspects can *waive* their Fifth Amendment rights and speak to a police officer, but only if the waiver is made voluntarily. Silence on the part of a suspect does not mean that his or her *Miranda* protections have been relinquished. To waive their rights, suspects must state—either in writing or orally—that they understand those rights and that they will voluntarily answer questions without the presence of counsel.

To ensure that the suspect's rights are upheld, prosecutors are required to prove by a preponderance of the evidence that the suspect "knowing and intelligently" waived his or her *Miranda* rights.[110] To make the waiver perfectly clear, police will ask suspects two questions in addition to giving the *Miranda* warning:

1. Do you understand your rights as I have read them to you?
2. Knowing your rights, are you willing to talk to another law enforcement officer or me?

If the suspect indicates that she or he does not want to speak to the officer, thereby invoking her or his right to silence, the officer must *immediately* stop any questioning.[111] Similarly, if the suspect requests a lawyer, the police can ask no further questions until an attorney is present.[112]

CLEAR INTENT The suspect must be absolutely clear about her or his intention to stop the questioning or have a lawyer present. In *Davis v. United States* (1994),[113] the Supreme Court upheld the interrogation of a suspect after he said, "Maybe I should talk to a lawyer." The Court found that this statement was too ambiguous, saying that it did not want to force police officers to "read the minds" of suspects who make vague declarations. Along these same lines, in *Berghuis v. Thompkins* (2010),[114] the Court upheld the conviction of a suspect who implicated himself in a murder after remaining mostly silent during nearly three hours of police questioning. The defendant claimed that he had invoked his *Miranda* rights by being uncommunicative with the interrogating officers. The Court disagreed, saying that silence is not enough—a suspect must actually state that he or she wishes to cut off questioning for the *Miranda* protections to apply.

THE LAW ENFORCEMENT RESPONSE TO *MIRANDA*

When the *Miranda* decision was first handed down, many people, particularly police officials, complained that it distorted the Constitution by placing the rights of criminal suspects above the rights of society as a whole.[115] In the four and a half decades since the ruling, however, law enforcement agents

What aspects of the situation shown in this photo indicate that the Aspen (Colorado) police officer is required to "Mirandize" the suspect before asking him any questions, even if he never formally places the suspect under arrest?
Photo by Chris Hondros/Getty Images

have adapted to the *Miranda* restrictions, and strategies to work within their boundaries have become a standard part of police training.

POLICING AROUND MIRANDA After an extensive on-site study of police interrogation tactics, Richard A. Leo, a criminologist at the University of San Francisco law school, noted a pattern of maneuvers that officers use to convince suspects to voluntarily waive their *Miranda* rights. Leo identifies three such strategies:

- The *conditioning* strategy is geared toward creating an environment in which the suspect is encouraged to think positively of the interrogator and thus is conditioned to cooperate. The interrogator will offer the suspect coffee or a cigarette and make pleasant small talk. These steps are intended to lower the suspect's anxiety level and generate a sense of trust that is conducive to a *Miranda* waiver and confession.
- The *de-emphasizing strategy* tries to downplay the importance of *Miranda* protections, giving the impression that the rights are unimportant and can be easily waived. For example, one officer told a suspect, "I need to advise you of your rights. It's a formality. I'm sure you've watched television with the cop shows and you hear them say their rights so you can probably recite this better than I can, but it's something I need to do and we can get this out of the way before we talk about what happened."
- When using the *persuasion* strategy, an officer will explicitly try to convince the suspect to waive her or his rights. Commonly, the detective will tell suspects that waiving the rights is the only way they will be able to get their side of the story out. Otherwise, the detective continues, only the victim's side of the story will be considered during the trial.[116]

Sometimes, officers go too far with their interrogation strategies and infringe on a suspect's rights. About twenty years ago, for example, police officers questioned seventeen-year-old Jonathan Doody overnight for more than twelve straight hours concerning the killing of nine people outside a Buddhist temple in Phoenix, Arizona. Although the officers told Doody at the outset that he had the right to remain silent, they reacted to his silence aggressively. At one point, when Doody refused to answer the same questions for the fourteenth time, a frustrated detective responded:

> Say something. Say something, Jonathan. Come on, man, this is ridiculous. Say something. What's your name? What's your name, Jonathan? Jonathan, what's your name? What's your last name?[117]

Finally, at 4 A.M., Doody confessed to his involvement in the killings and was eventually convicted on nine counts of murder. In 2010, however, a federal appeals court overturned the conviction, holding that the officers had effectively "de-Mirandized" Doody during the long and stressful interrogation session and therefore his confession was inadmissible in court.[118] (To learn why some observers would like to "de-Mirandize" an entire class of suspects, see the feature *Anti-Terrorism in Action—Timed Out* on the following page.)

THE FUTURE OF *MIRANDA*

In 2000, the Supreme Court made a strong ruling in favor of the continued importance of *Miranda*. In *Dickerson v. United States*,[119] the Court rejected the application of a little-known law passed by Congress in 1968 that allowed police in federal cases to use

Technology Tip: After students read about Jonathan Doody in the text, have them go online and learn more about false confessions from the Innocence Project: www. innocenceproject.org/understand/ False-Confessions.php.

See **Officer.com** for a wealth of information on the interrogation process and other law enforcement issues. Find this Web site by visiting the *Criminal Justice CourseMate* at **cengagebrain.com** and selecting the *Web links* for this chapter.

incriminatory statements even if the suspect had not been read the warning. "*Miranda* has become embedded in routine police practice to the point where the warnings have become part of our national culture," wrote then Chief Justice William Rehnquist in his opinion. The chief justice added that *Miranda* was a "constitutional rule" that Congress could not overturn by passing a law.[120]

Critical Thinking Skill Development: It has been speculated that the *Miranda* warning has become such a part of the American culture that most citizens can recite it from memory. With this in mind, ask students whether they believe the *Miranda* warning is still necessary. Given the level of knowledge regarding the *Miranda* warning, should the exclusionary rule still apply to situations in which it was omitted or improperly cited?

THE EROSION OF MIRANDA Despite these strong words, many legal scholars believe that a series of Supreme Court rulings have eroded *Miranda's* protections. "It's death by a thousand cuts," says Jeffrey L. Fisher of the National Association of Criminal Defense Lawyers, who believes the Court is "doing everything it can to ease the admissibility of confessions that police wriggle out of suspects."[121] In this chapter, we have seen how, in recent years, the Court has expanded the "good faith" exception to the exclusionary rule (page 220) and required suspects to be more explicit in waiving their *Miranda* rights (page 238). Figure 7.5 on the facing page provides a rundown of other Court rulings that have weakened *Miranda* over the past several decades.

One such decision, issued in 2004, is crucial to understanding the Supreme Court's present position on this subject. The case involved a Colorado defendant who voluntarily told the police the location of his gun (which, being an ex-felon, he was not allowed to possess) without being read his rights.[122] The Court upheld the conviction, finding that the *Miranda* warning is merely *prophylactic*. In other words, it is only intended to prevent violations of the Fifth Amendment. Because only the gun, and not the defendant's testimony, was presented at trial, the police had not violated the

ANTI-TERRORISM IN ACTION

TIMED OUT

After the federal government took Faisal Shahzad into custody, FBI agents interrogated him for three hours before delivering a *Miranda* warning. Shahzad was suspected of parking a sport-utility vehicle loaded with explosives in New York City's Times Square on May 1, 2010, a crime to which he later confessed. Four months earlier, federal officers had conducted about fifty minutes of questioning before "Mirandizing" Umar Farouk Abdulmutallab, who had attempted to set off a bomb on an international flight headed for Detroit. In these two instances, federal law enforcement agents relied on the rarely used public-safety exception to the *Miranda* requirements. As you can see in Figure 7.5 on the facing page, this exception, established by the United States Supreme Court in 1984, allows officers to dispense with *Miranda* warnings if they feel there is an imminent threat of danger to the public.

According to officials, the strategy worked. Both Shahzad and Abdulmutallab provided valuable information and were read their *Miranda* rights only after the possibility of further immediate terrorist attacks had been ruled out. Still, the federal government was widely denounced for its handling of the two cases. Critics believe that suspects such as Shahzad and Abdulmutallab should be considered military prisoners, thereby denying them constitutional protections and allowing for interrogation unimpeded by *Miranda* limitations. "Treating terrorists like civilians damages our ability to gather crucial intelligence," said Jeff Sessions, a Republican senator from Alabama.

FOR CRITICAL ANALYSIS About a week after Faisal Shahzad's capture, President Barack Obama asked Congress to pass a law that would allow investigators to question terrorism suspects indefinitely without informing them of their *Miranda* rights. What is your opinion of having a "terrorism exception" to the *Miranda* warning? What might be some of the unintended consequences of such an exception?

Argus/Shutterstock

FIGURE 7.5 Supreme Court Decisions Eroding *Miranda* Rights

New York v. Quarles (467 U.S. 649 [1984]). **This case established the "public-safety" exception to the *Miranda* rule.** It concerned a police officer who, after feeling an empty shoulder holster on a man he had just arrested, asked the suspect the location of the gun without informing him of his *Miranda* rights. The Court ruled that the gun was admissible as evidence and that the need for police officers to protect the public is more important than a suspect's *Miranda* rights.

Moran v. Burbine (475 U.S. 412 [1986]). **This case established that police officers are not required to tell suspects undergoing custodial interrogation that their attorney is trying to reach them.** The Court ruled that events that the suspect could have no way of knowing about have no bearing on his ability to waive his *Miranda* rights.

Arizona v. Fulminante (499 U.S. 279 [1991]). **In this very important ruling, the Court held that a conviction is not automatically overturned if the suspect was coerced into making a confession.** If the other evidence introduced at the trial is strong enough to justify a conviction without the confession, then the fact that the confession was illegally gained can be, for all intents and purposes, ignored.

Texas v. Cobb (532 U.S. 162 [2001]). When a suspect refuses to waive his or her *Miranda* rights, a police officer cannot lawfully continue the interrogation until the suspect's attorney arrives on the scene. In this case, however, **the Court held that a suspect may be questioned without having a lawyer present if the interrogation does not focus on the crime for which he or she was arrested,** even though it does touch on another, closely related, offense.

Florida v. Powell (559 U.S. ___ [2010]). Florida's version of the *Miranda* warning informs suspects that they have a right "to talk with an attorney," but does not clearly inform them of the right to a lawyer during any police interrogation. The Court upheld Florida's warning, **ruling that different jurisdictions may use whatever version of the *Miranda* warning they please, as long as it reasonably conveys the essential information about a suspect's rights.**

defendant's constitutional rights. In essence, the Court was ruling that the "fruit of the poisoned tree" doctrine, discussed earlier in this chapter, does not bar the admission of physical evidence that is discovered based on voluntary statements by a suspect who has not been "Mirandized."[123]

RECORDING CONFESSIONS *Miranda* may eventually find itself obsolete regardless of any decisions made in the courts. A relatively new trend in law enforcement has been for agencies to record interrogations and confessions digitally. Fourteen states and thousands of local police departments now require that all interrogations of those who are suspected of committing serious felonies be recorded. In many instances, these policies were established as a result of faulty interrogations. The Detroit Police Department, for example, implemented its videotaping policy after a mentally ill man spent seventeen years in prison after having confessed to a rape that he did not commit. Some scholars have suggested that recording all custodial interrogations would satisfy the Fifth Amendment's prohibition against coercion and thus render the *Miranda* warning unnecessary.

Discussion Tip: Some states require that all police interrogations be recorded either digitally or on videotape. What are the advantages of recording confessions? Are there disadvantages to this practice?

SELFASSESSMENT

Fill in the blanks and check your answers on page 248.

Miranda requirements apply only when law enforcement agents have the suspect in _____. The *Miranda* warning is only required _____ a custodial interrogation takes place. A suspect can _____ his or her *Miranda* rights, but this must be done "knowingly and intentionally." If the suspect indicates that he or she does not wish to speak, the police officer must _____ stop any questioning. The suspect can also end questioning any time by requesting the presence of an _____.

THE IDENTIFICATION PROCESS

A confession is a form of self-identification; the suspect has identified herself or himself as the guilty party. If police officers are unable to gain a confession, they must use other methods to link the suspect with the crime. In fact, to protect against false admissions, police must use these other methods even if the suspect confesses.

ESSENTIAL PROCEDURES

LO 10 Unless police officers witness the commission of the crime themselves, they must establish the identity of the suspect using three basic types of identification procedures:

1. *Showups,* which occur when a suspect who matches the description given by witnesses is apprehended near the scene of the crime within a reasonable amount of time after the crime has been committed. The suspect is usually returned to the crime scene for possible identification by witnesses.
2. *Photo arrays,* which occur when no suspect is in custody but the police have a general description of the person. Witnesses and victims are shown "mug shots" of people with police records that match the description. Police will also present witnesses and victims with pictures of people they believe might have committed the crime.
3. *Lineups,* which entail lining up several physically similar people, one of whom is the suspect, in front of a witness or victim. The police may have each member of the lineup wear clothing similar to that worn by the criminal and say a phrase that was used during the crime. These visual and oral cues are designed to help the witness identify the suspect.

As with the other procedures discussed in this chapter, constitutional law governs the identification process, though some aspects are more tightly restricted than others. The Sixth Amendment right to counsel, for example, does not apply during showups or photo arrays. In showups, the police often need to establish a suspect quickly, and it would be unreasonable to expect them to wait for an attorney to arrive. According to the Supreme Court in *United States v. Ash* (1973),[124] however, the police must be able to prove this need for immediate identification, perhaps by showing that it was necessary to keep the suspect from fleeing the state.

As for photo arrays, courts have found that any procedure that does not require the suspect's presence does not require the presence of his or her attorney.[125] The lack of an attorney does not mean that police can "steer" a witness toward a positive identification with statements such as "Are you sure this isn't the person you saw robbing the grocery store?" Such actions would violate the suspect's due process rights.

NONTESTIMONIAL EVIDENCE

Some observers feel that the standard booking procedure—the process of recording information about the suspect immediately after arrest—infringes on a suspect's Fifth Amendment rights.

Booking The process of entering a suspect's name, offense, and arrival time into the police log following her or his arrest.

Billy Wayne Miller, shown here, spent twenty-two years in a Texas prison after being falsely identified at 3 A.M., standing on his front porch in his underwear, by a woman who had just been raped and was sitting in a police car. There were no fingerprints or biological evidence linking Miller to the crime. Why do you think many police departments discourage the use of showups— also known as "drive-bys"—to identify criminal suspects?
Nathan Hunsinger/DMN Photo Staff

During booking, the suspect is photographed and fingerprinted, and blood samples may be taken. If these samples lead to the suspect's eventual identification, according to some, they amount to self-incrimination. In *Schmerber v. California* (1966),[126] however, the Supreme Court held that such tests are not the equivalent of *testimonial* self-incrimination (where the suspect testifies verbally against himself or herself) and therefore do not violate the Fifth Amendment.

What are some of the possible drawbacks of using traditional lineups to help victims or witnesses identify suspects?
© Rich Legg/iStockphoto

Using similar legal reasoning, the Court has also determined that voice and handwriting samples gathered by police may be used to identify a suspect.[127] Because alcohol dissipates quickly in the bloodstream, courts consistently allow the police to draw blood from suspected drunk drivers without consent or a search warrant.[128]

SELFASSESSMENT

Fill in the blanks and check your answers on page 248.
Police employ several methods to _____ a suspect, or link that suspect to the crime. They will show witnesses a _____ _____ of suspect "mug shots" or present a number of physically similar persons, one of whom is the suspect, in a _____. The United States Supreme Court has determined that standard _____ procedures, during which police record information on the suspect, do not violate the Fifth Amendment.

Discussion Tip: Place students in small groups to discuss the idea that nontestimonial evidence, which can lead to a suspect's identification, is a form of self-incrimination. Do students believe that booking procedures jeopardize a suspect's Fifth Amendment rights? (LO 10)

CJ IN ACTION

RACIAL PROFILING AND THE CONSTITUTION

The Los Angeles police officer, confronted with complaints that he engaged in racial profiling, spoke with candor that he would soon regret. Unaware that the conversation was being recorded, the officer responded that he "couldn't do [his] job without racially profiling."[129] Particularly in the age of terrorism, when community suspicion rests heavily on Arab and Muslim Americans, the practice of racial profiling remains a controversial subject. In this *CJ in Action* feature, we will explore the difficult question of whether this police tactic can be justified.

THE *WHREN* EFFECT

As noted earlier in the chapter, the Fourth Amendment protects persons against "unreasonable searches and seizures." Intuitively, it would seem that when the police search or detain a person because of his or her race, an unreasonable search or seizure has taken place. The United States Supreme Court, however, made it practically impossible to prove "racist intent" on the part of law enforcement agents with its decision in *Whren v. United States* (1996),[130] discussed on page 232.

In that case, the Court ruled that the subjective intentions of the police, including any motives based on racial stereotyping or bias, are irrelevant as far as the Fourth Amendment is concerned.[131] As long as police have objective probable cause to believe a traffic violation or other wrongdoing has occurred, any other reasons for the stop should be ignored. Thus, if a suspect was driving over the speed limit or was not wearing a seat belt, then a police officer's decision to stop that driver is constitutional, even if the "real" reason for the stop was the driver's race.

THE CASE FOR RACIAL PROFILING

- Crime rates are racially disproportionate. Young African American males are often more likely than other age and racial groups to commit drug-related crimes. Hispanics are more likely than other ethnic groups to have violated immigration laws. To ignore such evidence in the name of cultural sensitivity does a disservice to law-abiding citizens of all races.[132]

- Racial profiling sometimes can seem to work. In the late 1990s, New York's Street Crime Unit was disbanded after racking up 45,000 stops and frisks, only 22 percent of which led to arrests and 90 percent of which involved members of a minority group.[133] The unit's actions did, however, result in the seizure of 2,500 illegal guns, leading some to argue that the "hassle factor" was offset by "great gains."[134]

- Racial profiling is necessary to protect against terrorist acts, which, at present, have mostly been committed by men of Middle Eastern background. "We're at war with a terrorist network," says one commentator. "Are we really supposed to ignore the one identifiable fact that we know about them?"[135]

THE CASE AGAINST RACIAL PROFILING

- Racial profiling is indistinguishable from racism and humiliates thousands of innocent people.

- If members of minority groups are more likely to be carrying illegal drugs than are whites, then police should find drugs more often on them than on whites after a stop and search. In fact, such "hit rates" are remarkably similar among the races.[136]

- If terrorist groups know in advance that law enforcement agencies are focusing on certain races or ethnic groups, they will simply select individuals of different races or ethnic groups for future attacks.

YOUR OPINION—WRITING ASSIGNMENT

Several years ago, the FBI released photos of two dark-skinned men who had "exhibited unusual behavior" on a Washington State ferryboat. The men had been taking pictures of the boat and asking questions about its structural details. The FBI was heavily criticized for profiling MEWCs—Middle Easterners with cameras. Do you think that there are any circumstances, such as those that existed in Washington, under which a suspect's race or ethnicity can be used to establish reasonable suspicion or probable cause? Or, do you think that law enforcement should always be "color blind"? Before responding, you can review our discussions in this chapter concerning:

- Probable cause (pages 218–219).

- The definition of reasonable suspicion (pages 221–222).

- Arrests (pages 223–226).

Your answer should include at least three full paragraphs.

CHAPTER SUMMARY

LO 1 **Outline the four major sources that may provide probable cause.** (a) Personal observation, usually due to an officer's personal training, experience, and expertise; (b) information, gathered from informants, eyewitnesses, victims, police bulletins, and other sources; (c) evidence, which often has to be in plain view; and (d) association, which generally must involve a person with a known criminal background who is seen in a place where criminal activity is openly taking place.

LO 2 **Explain the exclusionary rule and the exceptions to it.** This rule prohibits illegally seized evidence, or evidence obtained by an unreasonable search and seizure in an inadmissible way, from being used against the accused in criminal court. Exceptions to the exclusionary rule are the "inevitable discovery" exception established in *Nix v. Williams* and the "good faith" exception established in *United States v. Leon* and *Herring v. United States*.

LO 3 **Distinguish between a stop and a frisk, and indicate the importance of the case** *Terry v. Ohio.* Though the terms *stop* and *frisk* are often used in concert, a stop is the separate act of detaining a suspect when an officer reasonably believes that a criminal activity is about to take place. A frisk is the physical "pat-down" of a suspect. In *Terry v. Ohio,* the Supreme Court ruled that an officer must have "specific and articulable facts" before making a stop, but those facts may be "taken together with rational inferences."

LO 4 **List the four elements that must be present for an arrest to take place.** (a) Intent, (b) authority, (c) seizure or detention, and (d) the understanding of the person that he or she has been arrested.

LO 5 **List the four categories of items that can be seized by use of a search warrant.** (a) Items resulting from a crime, such as stolen goods; (b) inherently illegal items; (c) evidence of the crime; and (d) items used in committing the crime.

LO 6 **Explain when searches can be made without a warrant.** Searches and seizures can be made without a warrant if they are incidental to an arrest (but they must be reasonable); when they are made with voluntary consent; when they involve the "movable vehicle" exception; when property has been abandoned; and when items are in plain view, under certain restricted circumstances (see *Coolidge v. New Hampshire*).

LO 7 **Describe the plain view doctrine and indicate one of its limitations.** Under the plain view doctrine, police officers are justified in seizing an item if (a) the item is easily seen by an officer who is legally in a position to notice it; (b) the discovery of the item is unintended; and (c) the officer, without further investigation, immediately recognizes the illegal nature of the item. An item is not in plain view if the law enforcement agent needs to use technology such as a thermal imager to "see" it.

LO 8 **Recite the *Miranda* warning.** You have the right to remain silent. If you give up that right, anything you say can and will be used against you in a court of law. You have the right to speak with an attorney and to have the attorney present during questioning. If you so desire and cannot afford one, an attorney will be appointed for you without charge before questioning.

LO 9 **Indicate situations in which a *Miranda* warning is unnecessary.** (a) When no questions that are testimonial in nature are asked of the suspect; (b) when there is no suspect and witnesses in general are being questioned at the scene of a crime; (c) when a person volunteers information before the police ask anything; (d) when a suspect has given a private statement to a friend without the government orchestrating it; (e) during a stop and frisk when no arrests have been made; and (f) during a traffic stop.

LO 10 **List the three basic types of police identification.** (a) Showups, (b) photo arrays, and (c) lineups.

SELF ASSESSMENT

ANSWER KEY

KEY TERMS

affidavit **228**

arrest **223**

arrest warrant **224**

booking **244**

coercion **237**

consent searches **230**

custodial interrogation **238**

custody **238**

electronic surveillance **234**

exclusionary rule **219**

exigent circumstances **224**

frisk **222**

fruit of the poisoned tree **219**

"good faith" exception **220**

"inevitable discovery" exception **219**

interrogation **237**

Miranda rights **238**

plain view doctrine **234**

probable cause **217**

racial profiling **220**

search **226**

search warrant **227**

searches and seizures **217**

searches incidental to arrests **229**

seizure **228**

stop **222**

warrantless arrest **225**

QUESTIONS FOR CRITICAL ANALYSIS

1. What are the two most significant legal concepts contained in the Fourth Amendment, and why are they important?

2. How might an unscrupulous police officer take advantage of the good faith exception to the exclusionary rule?

3. Suppose that a police officer stops a person who "looks funny." The person acts strangely, so the police officer decides to frisk him. The officer feels a bulge in the suspect's coat pocket, which turns out to be a bag of cocaine. Would the arrest for cocaine possession hold up in court? Why or why not?

4. In Chapter 4, you learned that force—even deadly force—can be used to protect against attack in one's home. In this chapter, you learned that the police can, at times, enter a home without knocking or announcing themselves. Under what circumstances could the combination of these two legal concepts prove extremely dangerous for a law enforcement agent?

5. Using ALPR (see page 235), a CCTV camera reads the license plate of a stolen car parked in the garage beneath a football stadium. In court, the defendant—charged with auto theft—claims that the search methods are unconstitutional. What will the judge rule?

CourseMate *For Online Help*

NOTES

1. *Illinois v. Rodriguez*, 497 U.S. 177 (1990).

2. *Brigham City v. Stuart*, 547 U.S. 398, 403 (2006).

3. *Michigan v. Fisher*, 130 S.Ct. 546 (2009).

4. *Thompson v. Louisiana*, 469 U.S. 17 (1984).

5. *Michigan v. Summers*, 452 U.S. 692 (1981).

6. *Brinegar v. United States*, 338 U.S. 160 (1949).

7. Rolando V. del Carmen, *Criminal Procedure for Law Enforcement Personnel* (Monterey, CA: Brooks/Cole Publishing Co., 1987), 63–64.

8. *Maryland v. Pringle*, 540 U.S. 366 (2003).

9. 500 U.S. 44 (1991).

10. *United States v. Leon*, 468 U.S. 897 (1984).

11. *Weeks v. United States*, 232 U.S. 383 (1914).

12. *Mapp v. Ohio*, 367 U.S. 643 (1961).

13. 430 U.S. 387 (1977).

14. 467 U.S. 431 (1984).

15. 468 U.S. 897 (1984).

16. 555 U.S. 135 (2009).

17. Arizona Revised Statutes Sections 11-1051(B), 13-1509, 13-2929(C).

18. Quoted in Arian Campo-Flores, "Will Arizona's New Immigration Law Lead to Racial Profiling?" *Newsweek* (April 27, 2010), at **www.newsweek.com/2010/04/26/will-arizona-s-new-immigration-law-lead-to-racial-profiling.html**.

19. Karen M. Hess and Henry M. Wrobleski, *Police Operation: Theory and Practice* (St. Paul, MN: West Publishing Co., 1997), 122.

20. 392 U.S. 1 (1968).

21. *Ibid.*, 20.

22. *Ibid.*, 21.

23. See *United States v. Cortez*, 449 U.S. 411 (1981); and *United States v. Sokolow*, 490 U.S. 1 (1989).

24. *United States v. Arvizu*, 534 U.S. 266 (2002).

25. *Ibid.*, 270.

26. *Florida v. J.L.*, 529 U.S. 266, 274 (2000).

27. *Adams v. Williams*, 407 U.S. 143 (1972).

28. *Alabama v. White*, 496 U.S. 325 (1990).

29. *United States v. Place*, 462 U.S. 696 (1983).

30. *Hibel v. Sixth Judicial District Court*, 542 U.S. 177 (2004).

31. *Ibid.*, 182.

32. *Minnesota v. Dickerson*, 508 U.S. 366 (1993).

33. *Arizona v. Johnson*, 555 U.S. ___ (2009).

34. Rolando V. del Carmen and Jeffrey T. Walker, *Briefs of Leading Cases in Law Enforcement*, 2d ed. (Cincinnati, OH: Anderson, 1995), 38–40.

35. *Florida v. Royer*, 460 U.S. 491 (1983).

36. See also *United States v. Mendenhall*, 446 U.S. 544 (1980).

37. del Carmen, 97–98.

38. 514 U.S. 927 (1995).

39. Linda J. Collier and Deborah D. Rosenbloom, *American Jurisprudence*, 2d ed. (Rochester, NY: Lawyers Cooperative Publishing, 1995), 122.

40. Quoted in Ron Barnett and Paul Alongi, "Critics Knock No-Knock Police Raids," *USA Today* (February 14, 2011), 3A.

41. Radley Balko, *Overkill: The Rise of Paramilitary Police Raids in America* (Washington, D.C.: Cato Institute, 2006), 2–15.

42. 547 U.S. 586 (2006).

43. *United States v. Banks*, 540 U.S. 31, 41 (2003).

44. *Hudson v. Michigan*, 547 U.S. 586, 593 (2006).

45. Tom Van Dorn, "Violation of Knock-and-Announce Rule Does Not Require Suppression of All Evidence Found in Search," *The Police Chief* (October 2006), 10.

46. Wayne R. LeFave and Jerold H. Israel, *Criminal Procedure* (St. Paul, MN: West Publishing Co., 1985), 141–144.

47. David Orlin, Jacob Thiessen, Kelli C. McTaggart, Lisa Toporek, and James Pearl, "Warrantless Searches and Seizures," in "Twenty-sixth Annual Review of Criminal Procedure," *Georgetown Law Journal* 85 (April 1997), 847.

48. *Atwater v. City of Lago Vista*, 532 U.S. 318, 346–347 (2001).

49. 445 U.S. 573 (1980).

50. 451 U.S. 204 (1981).

51. *California v. Greenwood*, 486 U.S. 35 (1988).

52. *Ibid.*

53. 389 U.S. 347 (1967).

54. *Ibid.*, 361.

55. 486 U.S. 35 (1988).

56. *Ibid.*

57. *Illinois v. Caballes*, 543 U.S. 405 (2005).

58. *Commonwealth v. Cabral*, 69 Mass.App.Ct. 68, 866 N.E.2d 429 (2008).

59. Amy Harmon, "Lawyers Fight Gene Material Gained on the Sly," *New York Times* (April 3, 2008), A1..

60. *Coolidge v. New Hampshire*, 403 U.S. 443, 467 (1971).

61. del Carmen, 158.

62. *Katz v. United States*, 389 U.S. 347, 357 (1967).

63. *Brigham City v. Stuart*, 547 U.S. 398 (2006).

64. 414 U.S. 234–235 (1973).

65. 395 U.S. 752 (1969).

66. *Ibid.*, 763.

67. Carl A. Benoit, "Questioning 'Authority': Fourth Amendment Consent Searches," *FBI Law Enforcement Bulletin* (July 2008), 24.

68. *Bumper v. North Carolina*, 391 U.S. 543 (1968).

69. *State v. Stone*, 362 N.C. 50, 653 S.E.2d 414 (2007).

70. 412 U.S. 218 (1973).

71. Jayme W. Holcomb, "Knock and Talks," *FBI Law Enforcement Bulletin* (August 2006), 22–32.

72. Ian D. Midgley, "Just One Question before We Get to *Ohio v. Robinette*: 'Are You Carrying Any Contraband . . . Weapons, Drugs, Constitutional Protections . . . Anything Like That?'" *Case Western Reserve Law Review* 48 (Fall 1997), 173.

73. 501 U.S. 429 (1991).

74. 519 U.S. 33 (1996).

75. *United States v. Drayton*, 536 U.S. 194 (2002).

76. Linda Greenhouse, "Supreme Court Upholds Police Methods in Vehicle Drug Searches," *New York Times* (November 19, 1996), A23.

77. 267 U.S. 132 (1925).

78. *United States v. Ross*, 456 U.S. 798, 804–809 (1982); and *Chambers v. Maroney*, 399 U.S. 42, 44, 52 (1970).

79. 453 U.S. 454 (1981).

80. *Arizona v. Gant*, 556 U.S. ___ (2009).

81. Adam Liptak, "Justices Significantly Cut Back Officers' Searches of Cars of People They Arrest," *New York Times* (April 22, 2009), A12.

82. Dale Anderson and Dave Cole, "Search and Seizure after *Arizona v. Gant*," *Arizona Attorney* (October 2009), 15.

83. 517 U.S. 806 (1996).

84. 519 U.S. 408 (1997).

85. *United States v. Ross*, 456 U.S. 798 (1982).

86. *Ibid.*, 824.

87. *California v. Acevedo*, 500 U.S. 565 (1991).

88. 403 U.S. 443 (1971).

89. *Kyollo v. United States*, 533 U.S. 27 (2001).

90. 388 U.S. 42 (1967).

91. 18 U.S.C. Sections 2510(7), 2518(1)(a), 2516 (1994).

92. *Lee v. United States*, 343 U.S. 747 (1952).

93. Christopher K. Murphy, "Electronic Surveillance," in "Twenty-Sixth Annual Review of Criminal Procedure," *Georgetown Law Journal* (April 1997), 920.

94. *United States v. Nguyen*, 46 F.3d 781, 783 (8th Cir. 1995).

95. Al Baker, "Camera Scans of Car Plates Are Reshaping Police Inquiries," *New York Times* (April 12, 2011), A17.

96. Tyson E. Hubbard, "Automatic License Plate Recognition: An Exciting New Enforcement Tool with Potentially Scary Consequences," *Syracuse Science & Technology Law Reporter* (Spring 2008), 3–5.

97. Quoted in Rebecca Kanable, "Dallas' First Year with CCTV," *Law Enforcement Technology* (February 2008), 35.

98. Sharon B. Franklin, "Watching the Watchers: Establishing Limits on Public Video Surveillance," *Champion* (April 2008), 40.

99. *United States v. Knotts,* 460 U.S. 276 (1983).

100. *United States v. Garcia,* 474 F.3d 994, 998 (2007).

101. *Brown v. Mississippi,* 297 U.S. 278 (1936).

102. 378 U.S. 478 (1964).

103. *Ibid.,* 490–491.

104. *Miranda v. Arizona,* 384 U.S. 436 (1966).

105. H. Richard Uviller, *Tempered Zeal* (Chicago: Contemporary Books, 1988), 188–198.

106. *Orozco v. Texas,* 394 U.S. 324 (1969); *Oregon v. Mathiason,* 429 U.S. 492 (1977); and *California v. Beheler,* 463 U.S. 1121 (1983).

107. *Orozco,* 325.

108. *Pennsylvania v. Muniz,* 496 U.S. 582 (1990).

109. del Carmen, 267–268.

110. *Moran v. Burbine,* 475 U.S. 412 (1986).

111. *Michigan v. Mosley,* 423 U.S. 96 (1975).

112. *Fare v. Michael C.,* 442 U.S. 707, 723–724 (1979).

113. 512 U.S. 452 (1994).

114. 560 U.S. ___ (2010).

115. Patrick Malone, "You Have the Right to Remain Silent: *Miranda* after Twenty Years," *American Scholar* 55 (1986), 367.

116. Richard A. Leo, "The Impact of *Miranda* Revisited," *Journal of Criminal Law and Criminology* 86 (Spring 1996), 621–692.

117. *Doody v. Schriro,* 596 F.3d 620, 624 (9th Cir. 2010).

118. *Ibid.,* 620.

119. 530 U.S. 428 (2000).

120. *Ibid.,* 443.

121. Quoted in Jesse J. Holland, "High Court Trims *Miranda* Warning Rights Bit by Bit," *Associated Press* (August 2, 2010).

122. *United States v. Patane,* 542 U.S. 630 (2004).

123. *Ibid.,* 640.

124. 413 U.S. 300 (1973).

125. *United States v. Barker,* 988 F.2d 77, 78 (9th Cir. 1993).

126. 384 U.S. 757 (1966).

127. *United States v. Dionisio,* 410 U.S. 1 (1973); and *United States v. Mara,* 410 U.S. 19 (1973).

128. *State v. Johnson,* 774 N.W.2d 340 (Iowa 2008).

129. Quoted in Joel Rubin, "Get Tougher on Profiling, LAPD Told," *Los Angeles Times* (November 14, 2010), A1.

130. 517 U.S. 806 (1996).

131. *Ibid.,* 813.

132. Dinesh D'Souza, *The End of Racism: Principles for a Multicultural Society* (New York: Free Press, 1995), 260–261.

133. Melanie Lefkowitz, "Policy Set on the Street," *Newsday* (March 14, 2002), A3.

134. James Q. Wilson and Heather Mac Donald, "Profiles in Courage," *Wall Street Journal* (January 10, 2002), A12.

135. Michael Kinsley, "When Is Racial Profiling Okay?" *Washington Post* (September 30, 2001), A1.

136. Bureau of Justice Statistics, *Contacts between Police and the Public,* 2005 (Washington, D.C.: U.S. Department of Justice, April 2007).

CHAPTER

8

AP Photo/Carlos Osorio

Courts and the Quest for Justice

LEARNING OBJECTIVES

After reading this chapter, you should be able to . . .

LO 1 Define and contrast the four functions of the courts.

LO 2 Define *jurisdiction* and contrast geographic and subject-matter jurisdiction.

LO 3 Explain the difference between trial and appellate courts.

LO 4 Outline the several levels of a typical state court system.

LO 5 Outline the federal court system.

LO 6 Explain briefly how a case is brought to the Supreme Court.

LO 7 List the actions that a judge might take prior to an actual trial.

LO 8 Explain the difference between the selection of judges at the state level and at the federal level.

LO 9 List and describe the members of the courtroom work group.

The nine learning objectives labeled LO 1 through LO 9 are designed to help improve your understanding of the chapter.

INNOCENT **ABROAD?**

Shortly after police discovered the bloody, lifeless body of twenty-one-year-old British student Meredith Kercher in her apartment in Perugia, Italy, local prosecutors focused on Amanda Knox, Kercher's twenty-year-old American roommate, as the primary suspect. They believed that Knox, Knox's Italian boyfriend Raffaele Sollecito, and an African immigrant named Rudy Guede had engaged in a "drug-fueled" orgy in the apartment. After the trio forced Kercher to have sex with them, Sollecito and Guede held her down "while the American slit her throat."

Knox, then a junior at the University of Washington, maintained that she had spent the night in question at Sollecito's apartment, where the two had smoked hashish and watched a movie. Initially, this report meshed with Guede's admission that he and Kercher had been alone that evening. Guede claimed that while he was using the bathroom, a stranger had sneaked into the apartment and killed the British woman. Then, after unsuccessfully trying to avoid arrest by fleeing to Germany, Guede changed his story to implicate Knox and Sollecito. The main piece of concrete evidence against Knox was a knife found in Sollecito's kitchen. Authorities claimed that this murder weapon had traces of DNA belonging to both Knox—not surprisingly, given how much time she spent with her boyfriend—and, more damningly, the murder victim.

During Knox's trial, her attorneys argued that the trace amounts of "mystery" DNA on the knife were so small that it was impossible to determine their origin. Furthermore, the lawyers pointed out, the shape of the blade did not match a knife-shaped bloodstain on Kercher's bed. Nonetheless, on December 4, 2009, more than two years after Kercher's death, an Italian jury found Knox guilty of murder and sentenced her to twenty-six years in prison. The verdict caused an outcry among Knox's supporters, including many in the American media. One CBS News commentator called the trial "the railroad job from hell."

American student Amanda Knox, convicted of murdering her British roommate, is led through an Italian court before her appeal hearing in December 2010.
Giuseppe Bellini/Getty Images

Critics of Amanda Knox's guilty verdict were not shy about condemning Italy's criminal justice system. First, they pointed out, Italian police questioned Knox for more than fifty-three hours without providing her access to an attorney—a situation that, as we learned in Chapter 7, would not be allowed in the United States. Then, Knox was held in an Italian jail for more than a year before being charged with a crime. The jury in her trial deliberated for only two days a week, which, in addition to a long summer break, added to the overall length of the proceedings. More important, the jury was not *sequestered,* or shielded from the influence of a local media that reveled in lurid and possibly untrue tales of Knox's unseemly behavior as a foreign student caught in a whirlpool of drugs, booze, and sex.

"I am innocent. Raffaele [Sollecito] is innocent," Knox told an Italian judge on December 11, 2010, during an appeal. "It doesn't do justice to Meredith [Kercher] and her loved ones to take our lives from us."[1] In October 2011, the Italian appeals court agreed, throwing out the convictions of Knox and Sollecito. Echoing the thoughts of many, one commentator concluded that Knox, who spent more than four years in jail, "now has her justice."[2]

Would the American courts have treated Knox more fairly? Famed jurist Roscoe Pound characterized "justice" as society's demand "that serious offenders be convicted and punished," while at the same time "the innocent and unfortunate are not oppressed."[3] We can expand on this noble, if idealistic, definition. Citizens expect their

Discussion Tip: Before beginning this chapter, ask students to describe what they believe is the purpose of the court system. If the students indicate that the court has multiple objectives, ask them which they think is the most important. (LO 1)

courts to discipline the guilty, provide deterrents for illegal activities, protect civil liberties, and rehabilitate criminals—all simultaneously. Over the course of the next four chapters, we shall examine these lofty goals and the extent to which they can be reached. We start with a discussion of how courts in the United States work.

FUNCTIONS OF THE COURTS

Simply stated, a court is a place where arguments are settled. The argument may be between the federal government and a corporation accused of violating environmental regulations, between business partners, between a criminal and the state, or between any number of other parties. The court provides an environment in which the basis of the argument can be decided through the application of the law.

Courts have extensive powers in our criminal justice system: they can bring the authority of the state to seize property and to restrict individual liberty. Given that the rights to own property and to enjoy personal freedom are enshrined in the U.S. Constitution, a court's *legitimacy* in taking such measures must be unquestioned by society. This legitimacy is based on two factors: impartiality and independence.[4] In theory, each party involved in a courtroom dispute must have an equal chance to present its case and must be secure in the belief that no outside factors are going to influence the decision rendered by the court. In reality, as we shall see over the next four chapters, it does not always work that way.

DUE PROCESS AND CRIME CONTROL IN THE COURTS

As mentioned in Chapter 1, the criminal justice system has two sets of underlying values: due process and crime control. Due process values focus on protecting the rights of the individual, whereas crime control values stress the punishment and repression of criminal conduct.[5] The competing nature of these two value systems is often evident in the nation's courts.

THE DUE PROCESS FUNCTION The primary concern of early American courts was to protect the rights of the individual against the power of the state. Memories of injustices suffered at the hands of the British monarchy were still strong, and most of the procedural rules that we have discussed in this textbook were created with the express purpose of giving the individual a "fair chance" against the government in any courtroom proceedings. Therefore, the due process function of the courts is to protect individuals from the unfair advantages that the government—with its immense resources—automatically enjoys in legal battles.

Seen in this light, constitutional guarantees such as the right to counsel, the

LO 1

Why is it important that American criminal courtrooms, such as this one in Cape May, New Jersey, are places of impartiality and independence? AP Photo/*The Press of Atlantic City,* Dale Gerhard

right to a jury trial, and protection from self-incrimination are equalizers in the "contest" between the state and the individual. The idea that the two sides in a courtroom dispute are adversaries is, as we shall discuss in the next chapter, fundamental in American courts.

THE CRIME CONTROL FUNCTION Advocates of crime control distinguish between the court's obligation to be fair to the accused and its obligation to be fair to society.[6] The crime control function of the courts emphasizes punishment and retribution—criminals must suffer for the harm done to society, and it is the courts' responsibility to see that they do so. Given this responsibility to protect the public, deter criminal behavior, and "get criminals off the streets," the courts should not be concerned solely with giving the accused a fair chance. Rather than using due process rules as "equalizers," the courts should use them as protection against blatantly unconstitutional acts. For example, a detective who beats a suspect with a tire iron to get a confession has obviously infringed on the suspect's constitutional rights. If, however, the detective uses trickery to gain a confession, the court should allow the confession to stand because it is not in society's interest that law enforcement agents be deterred from outwitting criminals.

THE REHABILITATION FUNCTION

A third view of the court's responsibility is based on the "medical model" of the criminal justice system. In this model, criminals are analogous to patients, and the courts perform the role of physicians who dispense "treatment."[7] The criminal is seen as sick, not evil, and therefore treatment is morally justified. Of course, treatment varies from case to case, and some criminals require harsh penalties such as incarceration. In other cases, however, it may not be in society's best interest for the criminal to be punished according to the formal rules of the justice system. Perhaps the criminal can be rehabilitated to become a productive member of society and thus save taxpayers the costs of incarceration or other punishment.

THE BUREAUCRATIC FUNCTION

To a certain extent, the crime control, due process, and rehabilitation functions of a court are secondary to its bureaucratic function. In general, a court may have the goal of protecting society or protecting the rights of the individual, but on a day-to-day basis that court has the more pressing task of dealing with the cases brought before it. Like any bureaucracy, a court is concerned with speed and efficiency, and loftier concepts such as justice can be secondary to a judge's need to wrap up a particular case before six o'clock so that administrative deadlines can be met. Indeed, many observers feel that the primary adversarial relationship in the courts is not between the two parties involved but between the ideal of justice and the reality of bureaucratic limitations.[8]

SELFASSESSMENT

Fill in the blanks and check your answers on page 280.
The _____ _____ function of American courts is to protect _____ from the unfair advantages that the government enjoys during legal proceedings. In contrast, the _____ _____ function of the courts emphasizes punishment—criminals must suffer for the harm they do to _____. A third view of the court system focuses on the need to _____ a criminal, in much the same way as a doctor would treat a patient.

THE BASIC PRINCIPLES OF THE AMERICAN JUDICIAL SYSTEM

One of the most often cited limitations of the American judicial system is its complex nature. In truth, the United States does not have a single judicial system, but fifty-two different systems—one for each state, the District of Columbia, and the federal government. As each state has its own unique judiciary with its own set of rules, some of which may be in conflict with the federal judiciary, it is helpful at this point to discuss some basics—jurisdiction, trial and appellate courts, and the dual court system.

JURISDICTION

In Latin, *juris* means "law," and *diction* means "to speak." Thus, jurisdiction literally refers to the power "to speak the law." Before any court can hear a case, it must have jurisdiction over the persons involved in the case or its subject matter. The jurisdiction of every court, even the United States Supreme Court, is limited in some way.

GEOGRAPHIC JURISDICTION One limitation is geographic. Generally, a court can exercise its authority over residents of a certain area. A state trial court, for example, normally has jurisdictional authority over crimes committed in a particular area of the state,

LO 2 such as a county or a district. A state's highest court (often called the state supreme court) has jurisdictional authority over the entire state, and the United States Supreme Court has jurisdiction over the entire country. (As the feature *Myth versus Reality—Reservation Rules* on the next page shows, a jurisdictional "void" on tribal land in the United States has had dire consequences for the Native American population.)

For the most part, criminal jurisdiction is determined by legislation. The U.S. Congress or a state legislature can determine what acts are illegal within the geographic boundaries it controls, thus giving federal or state courts jurisdiction over those crimes. What happens, however, when more than one court system has jurisdiction over the same criminal act?

Federal versus State Jurisdiction Most criminal laws are state laws, so the majority of all criminal trials are heard in state courts. Many acts that are illegal under state law, however, are also illegal under federal law. As a general rule, when Congress "criminalizes" behavior that is already prohibited under a state criminal code, the federal and state courts both have jurisdiction over that crime unless Congress states otherwise in the initial legislation. Thus, concurrent jurisdiction, which occurs when two different court systems have simultaneous jurisdiction over the same case, is quite common.

Less common is the situation in which federal law and state law contradict each other. As we saw in Chapter 3, fifteen states allow the use of marijuana for medicinal purposes (see the photo alongside), even though federal law considers the possession, sale, or distribution of marijuana a crime. This contradiction can place citizens of those states in a perilous position.

In 2005, the United State Supreme Court ruled that federal authorities can prosecute users of medical marijuana in

Jurisdiction The authority of a court to hear and decide cases within an area of the law or a geographic territory.

Concurrent Jurisdiction The situation that occurs when two or more courts have the authority to preside over the same criminal case.

At the Dr. Reefer dispensary in Boulder, Colorado, a saleswoman bags some medical marijuana for a customer. How does medical marijuana represent a situation in which federal and state law is contradictory?

Chris Hondros/Getty Images

Thanks to freedom from state antigambling laws and "sin" taxes on alcohol and cigarettes, Native American reservations are often considered somewhat outside the law. Indeed, Vernon Roanhorse, a Navajo tribal official, calls his reservation a "lawless land." The problems, however, go much deeper than casinos and cheap cigarettes.

THE MYTH In its earliest days, the U.S. government treated the various Native American tribes as individual sovereign nations. Ever since, the American government has allowed American Indians a considerable amount of self-rule. Consequently, many non-Native Americans believe that tribal leaders enjoy complete jurisdiction over all events that occur on tribal lands, including crimes.

THE REALITY There is no single justice system for the 464 tribes that operate in the United States. Some have their own police departments, while others rely on federal or state law enforcement agents. Tribes do run their own court systems, but federal law denies tribal courts criminal jurisdiction over defendants who are not American Indians or who are from a different tribe. Furthermore, serious felonies including violent crimes such as rape and murder are automatically under federal jurisdiction. For these crimes, tribal authorities must rely on federal agents to investigate and U.S. attorneys to prosecute.

The federal government's record in this area has been dismal. A congressional report issued in December 2010 stated that, for the previous five years, federal prosecutors declined to take action on about 50 percent of all cases referred to them by the tribes. Without a strong threat of arrest and punishment, crime has flourished in Native American jurisdictions. Violent crime rates on reservations are twice the national average, and one in three American Indian women will be a victim of sexual assault during her lifetime. More than 80 percent of Native American rape victims identify their assailant as non-Native American, placing these suspects out of the reach of tribal jurisdiction and into the hands of the often unresponsive federal criminal justice system.

FOR CRITICAL ANALYSIS In July 2010, President Barack Obama signed the Tribal Law and Order Act. Among other provisions, the new law increases the maximum prison sentence that tribal courts can impose from one to three years. The legislation also provides for the appointment of additional U.S. assistant attorneys to prosecute reservation crime in federal courts. How might these two steps reduce the amount of violent crime in the Native American community?

states that permit it.[9] Although President Barack Obama has indicated that his administration will not prosecute medical marijuana users in states where the practice is legal, there is no guarantee that future presidents will continue this policy.

Discussion Tip: Asks students to debate the concept of concurrent jurisdiction. Consider a scenario that involves a single offender who has committed offenses in multiple states. Which court should prosecute first, and why? (LO 2)

State versus State Jurisdiction Multiple states can also claim jurisdiction over the same defendant or criminal act, depending on state legislation and the circumstances of the crime. For example, if Billy is standing in State A and shoots Frances, who is standing in State B, the two states could have concurrent jurisdiction to try Billy for murder. Similarly, if a property theft takes places in State A but police recover the stolen goods in State B, concurrent jurisdiction could exist. Some states have also passed laws stating that they have jurisdiction over their own citizens who commit crimes in other states, even if there is no other connection between the home state and the criminal act.[10]

Consequently, rules of jurisdiction can give a state court power over an individual who has had only minor contact with that state. Consider the case of Phillip R. Greaves II, of Pueblo, Colorado. In 2010, Greaves touched off national outrage by publishing a book about pedophilia (sexual desire felt by adults for children). Although his territory was far from Colorado, a law enforcement agent in Polk County, Florida, ordered a copy of *The Pedophile's Guide to Love and Pleasure: A Child-Lover's Code of Conduct* using the Internet. As soon as the book arrived, Polk County officials claimed jurisdiction over Greaves and issued a warrant for his arrest on charges of distributing obscene material in Florida. Cooperating with the Florida officials, Colorado law enforcement agents *extradited* Greaves to Florida. Extradition is the formal process by which one legal authority, such as a state or a nation, transfers a fugitive or a suspect to another legal authority that has a valid claim on that person. Greaves was consequently found guilty and sentenced to two years' probation.

Multiple Trials When different courts share jurisdiction over the same defendant, multiple trials can result. In late 2007, for example, professional football player Michael Vick was convicted in federal court for operating a dogfighting ring and was sentenced to twenty-three months in federal prison. Nearly a year into his sentence, Vick traveled to Surry County, Virginia—where his crimes had taken place—and pleaded guilty to similar state charges, receiving as punishment a suspended sentence (discussed in Chapter 12). Similarly, from 2007 to 2010, religious sect leader Warren Jeffs appeared in the courts of three different states—Arizona, Texas, and Utah—to face charges related to sex with underage girls. Because officials in each state had probable cause that he had committed crimes within state limits, each state had jurisdiction over him and the right to conduct a criminal trial.

Although some believe that such multiple trials are a waste of taxpayer money, state and county prosecutors often argue that local victims of crimes deserve the "sense of closure" that comes with criminal proceedings.[11] In addition, as we will see in Chapter 10, guilty verdicts can be appealed and reversed, and extra convictions serve as "insurance" against that possibility. In most situations, however, convictions in one jurisdiction end the prosecution of the same case in another jurisdiction.

INTERNATIONAL JURISDICTION Under international law, each country has the right to create and enact criminal law for its territory. Therefore, the notion that a nation has jurisdiction over any crimes committed within its borders is well established. The situation becomes more delicate when one nation feels the need to go outside its own territory to enforce its criminal law. International precedent does, however, provide several bases for expanding jurisdiction across international borders. For example, anti-terrorism efforts have been aided by the principle that the United States has jurisdiction over persons who commit crimes against Americans even when the former are citizens of foreign countries and live outside the United States. Some behavior, such as piracy and genocide, is considered a crime against all nations collectively and, according to the principles of *universal jurisdiction,* can be prosecuted by any nation with custody of the wrongdoer (see the photo alongside).

Furthermore, a nation can arrest one of its citizens for breaking its criminal laws when the act takes place on foreign soil.[12] Thus, the PROTECT (Prosecuting Remedies and Tools Against the Exploitation of Children Today) Act of 2003 makes it a crime for any U.S. citizen to travel abroad and have sex with a minor.[13] The legislation explicitly allows American courts to exercise jurisdiction when the prohibited behavior— the sex act itself—occurs in a foreign country.[14]

Extradition The process by which one jurisdiction surrenders a person accused or convicted of violating another jurisdiction's criminal law to the second jurisdiction.

Teaching Tip: Ask students to respond to "Questions for Critical Analysis" number two on page 281, in which they consider geographic jurisdiction. (LO 2)

In February 2011, Somali pirates killed Scott and Jean Adam, the American couple shown here, off the coast of Oman in the Arabian Sea. Why do American law enforcement authorities have the power to arrest the pirates, even though they are foreign citizens and the alleged crime took place far from the United States?
Splash News/SvQuest/Newscom

To facilitate the process of international jurisdiction, the United States has entered into extradition treaties with a number of countries. In these treaties, the nations agree to extradite fugitives to each other following a formal request. For example, operating under an extradition treaty, in 2009 the Mexican government sent 107 criminal suspects—mostly alleged murderers and drug traffickers—to the United States.[15]

Teaching Tip: Does your area have a drug court, domestic violence court, teen court, or other subject-matter specific court? If so, take some time in your lecture to discuss this local resource and how it supplements your local justice system. (LO 2)

SUBJECT-MATTER JURISDICTION Jurisdiction over subject matter also acts as a limitation on the types of cases a court can hear. State court systems include courts of *general* (unlimited) *jurisdiction* and courts of *limited jurisdiction.* Courts of general jurisdiction have no restrictions on the subject matter they may address, and therefore deal with the most serious felonies and civil cases. Courts of limited jurisdiction, also known as lower courts, handle misdemeanors and civil matters under a certain amount, usually $1,000. To alleviate caseload pressures in lower courts, many states have created special subject-matter courts that only dispose of cases involving a specific crime. For example, a number of jurisdictions have established drug courts to handle an overload of illicit narcotics arrests, and in 2008 California created the first court specifically designed for crimes involving U.S. military veterans.

TRIAL AND APPELLATE COURTS

Trial Courts Courts in which most cases usually begin and in which questions of fact are examined.

Appellate Courts Courts that review decisions made by lower courts, such as trial courts; also known as *courts of appeals.*

Opinions Written statements by the judges expressing the reasons for the court's decision in a case.

Dual Court System The separate but interrelated court system of the United States, made up of the courts on the national level and the courts on the state level.

Another distinction is between courts of original jurisdiction and courts of appellate, or review, jurisdiction. Courts having *original jurisdiction* are courts of the first instance, or trial courts. Almost every case begins in a trial court. It is in this court that a trial (or a guilty plea) takes place, and the judge imposes a sentence if the defendant is found guilty. Trial courts are primarily concerned with *questions of fact.* They are designed to determine exactly what events occurred that are relevant to questions of the defendant's guilt or innocence.

LO 3

Courts having *appellate jurisdiction* act as reviewing courts, or appellate courts. In general, cases can be brought before appellate courts only on appeal by one of the parties in the trial court. (Note that because of constitutional protections against being tried twice for the same crime, prosecutors who lose in criminal trial court *cannot* appeal the verdict.) An appellate court does not use juries or witnesses to reach its decision. Instead, its judges make a decision on whether the case should be *reversed* and *remanded,* or sent back to the court of original jurisdiction for a new trial. Appellate judges present written explanations for their decisions, and these opinions of the court are the basis for a great deal of the precedent in the criminal justice system.

It is important to understand that appellate courts do not determine the defendant's guilt or innocence—they only make judgments on questions of procedure. In other words, they are concerned with *questions of law* and normally accept the facts as established by the trial court. Only rarely will an appeals court question a jury's decision. Instead, the appellate judges will review the manner in which the facts and evidence were provided to the jury and rule on whether errors were made in the process.

Teaching Tip: Ask students to create a chart that illustrates the differences between trial and appellate courts. Who has the right to appeal the trial court's decision and at what point can this appeal be made? (LO 3)

THE DUAL COURT SYSTEM

As we saw in Chapter 1, America's system of federalism allows the federal government and the governments of the fifty states to hold authority in many areas. As a result, the federal government and each of the fifty states, as well as the District of Columbia, have their own separate court systems. Because of the split between the federal courts and the state courts, this is known as the dual court system. (See Figure 8.1 on the facing page to get a better idea of how federal and state courts operate as distinct yet parallel entities.)

FIGURE 8.1 The Dual Court System

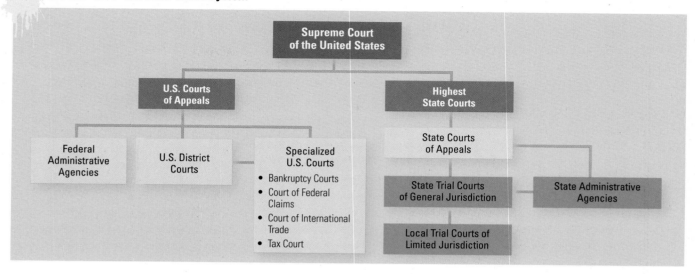

Federal and state courts both have limited jurisdiction. Generally, federal courts preside over cases involving violations of federal law, and state courts preside over cases involving violations of state law. The distinction is not always clear, however. Federal courts have jurisdiction over more than four thousand crimes, many of which also exist in state criminal codes. Furthermore, the federal government and each of the fifty states have their own specific court procedures, complicating situations of concurrent jurisdiction. For example, Jared Loughner, charged under both federal and Arizona law for his shooting spree in Tucson on January 8, 2011, is expected to mount an insanity defense (discussed in Chapter 4). Unlike federal courts, however, Arizona courts do not allow a finding of not guilty by reason of insanity. In that state, a defendant is either guilty, not guilty, or *guilty but insane*. Consequently, Loughner could receive very different penalties depending on the venue of his criminal trial.

Discussion Tip: Ask students to work together in small groups to discuss the dual court system. What are the advantages to a court system that is constructed in this way? Are there any disadvantages?

SELFASSESSMENT

Fill in the blanks and check your answers on page 280.

Before any court can hear a case, it must have _____ over the persons involved or the _____ _____ of the dispute. Almost every case begins in a _____ court, which is primarily concerned with determining the facts of the dispute. After this first trial, the participants can, under some circumstances, ask an _____ court to review the proceedings for errors in applying the law. The American court system is called a _____ court system because _____ courts address violations of federal law and _____ courts address violations of state law.

STATE COURT SYSTEMS

Typically, a state court system includes several levels, or tiers, of courts. State courts may include (1) lower courts, or courts of limited jurisdiction; (2) trial courts of general jurisdiction; (3) appellate courts; and (4) the state's highest court. As previously mentioned,

LO 4 each state has a different judicial structure, in which different courts have different jurisdictions, but there are enough similarities to allow for a general discussion. Figure 8.2 on the following page shows a typical state court system.

FIGURE 8.2 A Typical State Court System

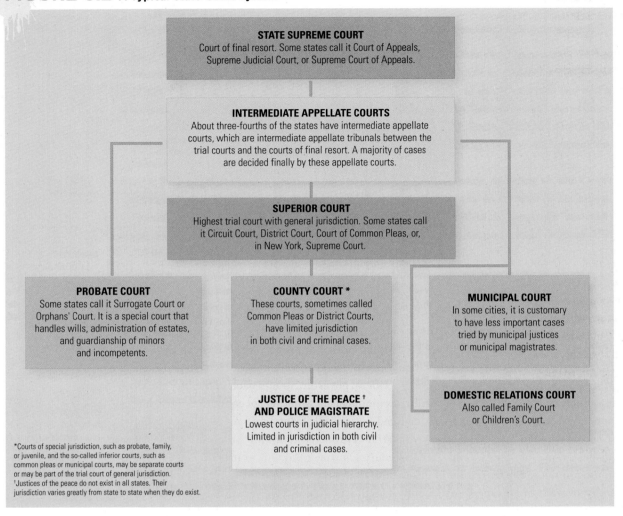

STATE SUPREME COURT
Court of final resort. Some states call it Court of Appeals, Supreme Judicial Court, or Supreme Court of Appeals.

INTERMEDIATE APPELLATE COURTS
About three-fourths of the states have intermediate appellate courts, which are intermediate appellate tribunals between the trial courts and the courts of final resort. A majority of cases are decided finally by these appellate courts.

SUPERIOR COURT
Highest trial court with general jurisdiction. Some states call it Circuit Court, District Court, Court of Common Pleas, or, in New York, Supreme Court.

PROBATE COURT
Some states call it Surrogate Court or Orphans' Court. It is a special court that handles wills, administration of estates, and guardianship of minors and incompetents.

COUNTY COURT *
These courts, sometimes called Common Pleas or District Courts, have limited jurisdiction in both civil and criminal cases.

MUNICIPAL COURT
In some cities, it is customary to have less important cases tried by municipal justices or municipal magistrates.

**JUSTICE OF THE PEACE †
AND POLICE MAGISTRATE**
Lowest courts in judicial hierarchy. Limited in jurisdiction in both civil and criminal cases.

DOMESTIC RELATIONS COURT
Also called Family Court or Children's Court.

*Courts of special jurisdiction, such as probate, family, or juvenile, and the so-called inferior courts, such as common pleas or municipal courts, may be separate courts or may be part of the trial court of general jurisdiction.
†Justices of the peace do not exist in all states. Their jurisdiction varies greatly from state to state when they do exist.

COURTS OF LIMITED JURISDICTION

Group Activities: Ask students to work together in small groups to create a chart that illustrates how the state court system functions in your state. (LO 4)

Most states have local trial courts that are limited to trying cases involving minor criminal matters, such as traffic violations, prostitution, and drunk and disorderly conduct. Although these minor courts usually keep no written record of the trial proceedings and cases are decided by a judge rather than a jury, defendants have the same rights as those in other trial courts. The majority of all minor criminal cases are decided in these lower courts. Courts of limited jurisdiction can also be responsible for the preliminary stages of felony cases. Arraignments, bail hearings, and preliminary hearings often take place in these lower courts.

MAGISTRATE COURTS One of the earliest courts of limited jurisdiction was the justice court, presided over by a *justice of the peace,* or JP. In the early days of this nation, JPs were found everywhere in the country. One of the most famous JPs was Judge Roy Bean, the "hanging judge" of Langtry, Texas, who presided over his court at the turn of the twentieth century. Today, more than half the states have abolished justice courts, though JPs still serve a useful function in some cities and rural areas, notably in Texas. The jurisdiction of justice courts is limited to minor disputes between private individuals and to crimes punishable by small fines or short jail terms. The equivalent of a county JP in a city is known as a **magistrate** or, in some states, a municipal court judge. Magistrate

Magistrate A public civil officer or official with limited judicial authority within a particular geographic area, such as the authority to issue an arrest warrant.

courts have the same limited jurisdiction as do justice courts in rural settings. In most jurisdictions, magistrates are responsible for providing law enforcement agents with search and seizure warrants, discussed in Chapter 7.

SPECIALTY COURTS As mentioned earlier, many states have created specialty courts that have jurisdiction over very narrowly defined areas of criminal justice. Not only do these courts remove many cases from the existing court systems, but they also allow court personnel to become experts in a particular subject. Specialty courts include:

1. Drug courts, which deal only with illegal substance crimes.
2. Gun courts, which have jurisdiction over crimes that involve the illegal use of firearms.
3. Juvenile courts, which specialize in crimes committed by minors. (We will discuss juvenile courts in more detail in Chapter 15.)
4. Domestic courts, which deal with crimes of domestic violence, such as child and spousal abuse.
5. Mental health courts, which focus primarily on the treatment and rehabilitation of offenders with mental health problems.

As we will see in Chapter 12, many state and local governments are searching for cheaper alternatives to locking up nonviolent offenders in prison or jail. Because specialty courts offer a range of treatment options for wrongdoers, these courts are becoming increasingly popular in today's more budget-conscious criminal justice system. For example, about two thousand drug courts are now operating in the United States, a number that is expected to increase as the financial benefits of diverting drug law violators from correctional facilities become more attractive to politicians.

An offender collects trash as part of his participation in the Albany County (Wyoming) Drug Court. What are the benefits of drug courts and other specialty courts? AP Photo/*Laramie Boomerang*, Aaron Ontiveroz

Specialty Courts Lower courts that have jurisdiction over one specific area of criminal activity, such as illegal drugs or domestic violence.

TRIAL COURTS OF GENERAL JURISDICTION

State trial courts that have general jurisdiction may be called county courts, district courts, superior courts, or circuit courts. In Ohio, the name is the court of common pleas and in Massachusetts, the trial court. (The name sometimes does not correspond with the court's functions. For example, in New York the trial court is called the supreme court, whereas in most states the supreme court is the state's highest court.) Courts of general jurisdiction have the authority to hear and decide cases involving many types of subject matter, and they are the setting for criminal trials (discussed in Chapter 10).

Teaching Tip: If time allows, take students on a field trip to your local courthouse. Let students meet members of the courtroom work group and spend some time observing the workings of the criminal court.

STATE COURTS OF APPEALS

Every state has at least one court of appeals (known as an appellate, or reviewing, court), which may be an intermediate appellate court or the state's highest court. About three-fourths have intermediate appellate courts. The highest appellate court in a state is usually called the supreme court, but in both New York and Maryland, the highest state court is called the court of appeals. The decisions of each state's highest court on all questions of state law are final. Only when issues of federal law or constitutional procedure are involved can the United States Supreme Court overrule a decision made by a state's highest court.

THE FEDERAL COURT SYSTEM

LO 5 The federal court system is basically a three-tiered model consisting of (1) U.S. district courts (trial courts of general jurisdiction) and various courts of limited jurisdiction, (2) U.S. courts of appeals (intermediate courts of appeals), and (3) the United States Supreme Court.

Unlike state court judges, who are usually elected, federal court judges—including the justices of the Supreme Court—are appointed by the president of the United States, subject to the approval of the Senate. All federal judges receive lifetime appointments (because under Article III of the Constitution they "hold their offices during Good Behavior").

U.S. DISTRICT COURTS

On the lowest tier of the federal court system are the U.S. district courts, or federal trial courts. These are the courts in which cases involving federal laws begin, and a judge or jury decides the case (if it is a jury trial). Every state has at least one federal district court, and there is one in the District of Columbia. The number of judicial districts varies over time, primarily owing to population changes and corresponding caseloads. At the present time, there are ninety-four judicial districts. The federal system also includes other trial courts of limited jurisdiction, such as the Tax Court and the Court of International Trade.

U.S. COURTS OF APPEALS

In the federal court system, there are thirteen U.S. courts of appeals—also referred to as U.S. circuit courts of appeals. The federal courts of appeals for twelve of the circuits hear appeals from the district courts located within their respective judicial circuits (see Figure 8.3 on the facing page). The Court of Appeals for the Thirteenth Circuit, called the Federal Circuit, has national appellate jurisdiction over certain types of cases, such as cases in which the U.S. government is a defendant. The decisions of the circuit courts of appeals are final unless a further appeal is pursued and granted. In that case, the matter is brought before the Supreme Court.

THE UNITED STATES SUPREME COURT

Alexander Hamilton, writing in *Federalist Paper* No. 78 (1788), predicted that the United States Supreme Court would be the "least dangerous branch" of the federal government because it had neither the power of the purse nor the power of the sword (that is, it could not raise any revenue, and it lacked an enforcement agency).[16] Unless the other two branches of the government—the president and Congress—would accept its decisions, the Court would be superfluous.

In the Supreme Court's earliest years, it appeared that Hamilton's prediction would come true. The first chief justice of the Supreme Court, John Jay, resigned to become

Teaching Tip: Have students identify the U.S. District Court closest to your campus. If time allows, tour the facility with your class. (LO 5)

⊗ The **Supreme Court of the United States** provides an up-to-date record of its decisions and the most important issues that it considers. Visit the Court's Web site by accessing the *Criminal Justice CourseMate* at **cengagebrain.com** and selecting the *Web links* for this chapter.

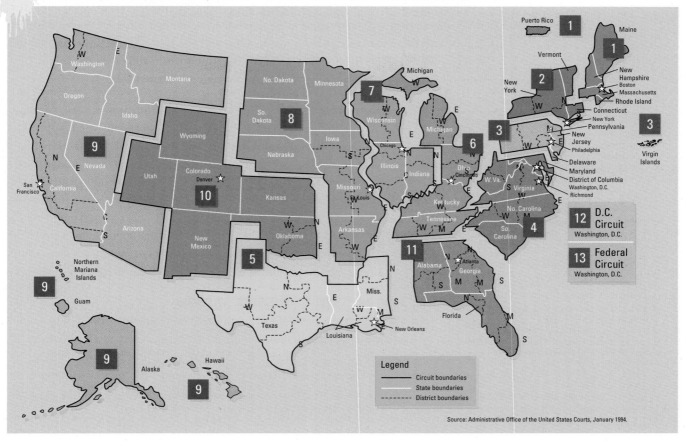

Source: Administrative Office of the United States Courts, January 1994.

governor of New York because he thought the Court would never play an important role in American society. The next chief justice, Oliver Ellsworth, quit to become an envoy to France. In 1801, when the federal capital was moved to Washington, D.C., no one remembered to include the Supreme Court in the plans. It did not have its own meeting space until 1835.[17]

INTERPRETING AND APPLYING THE LAW Despite these early bouts of inconsequence, the Supreme Court has come to dominate the country's legal culture. Although the Court reviews a minuscule percentage of the cases decided in the United States each year, its decisions profoundly affect our lives. The impact of Court decisions on the criminal justice system is equally far reaching: *Gideon v. Wainwright* (1963)[18] established every American's right to be represented by counsel in a criminal trial; *Miranda v. Arizona* (1966)[19] transformed pretrial interrogations; *Furman v. Georgia* (1972)[20] ruled that the death penalty was unconstitutional; and *Gregg v. Georgia* (1976)[21] spelled out the conditions under which it could be allowed. As you have no doubt noticed from references in this textbook, the Court has addressed nearly every important facet of criminal law.

Judicial Review The Supreme Court "makes" criminal justice policy in two important ways: through *judicial review* and through its authority to interpret the law. Judicial review refers to the power of the Court to determine whether a law or action by the other branches of the government is constitutional. For example, in the late 1990s Congress passed a law restricting Internet sales of "crush" videos, which showed women crushing small animals

Judicial Review The power of a court—particularly the United States Supreme Court—to review the actions of the executive and legislative branches and, if necessary, declare those actions unconstitutional.

to death with their bare feet or high heels.[22] The wording of the statute prohibited the sale of videos showing any form of graphic violence against animals. Several years after the law's passage, Robert Stevens of Pittsville, Virginia, was sentenced to three years in prison for distributing videos that featured pit bull fights. In 2010, the Supreme Court overturned Stevens's conviction and invalidated the federal law as unconstitutional on the ground that it violated the First Amendment's protections of freedom of expression.[23]

Statutory Interpretation As the final interpreter of the Constitution, the Supreme Court must also determine the meaning of certain statutory provisions when applied to specific situations. In the previous chapter, you learned that a law enforcement officer must immediately stop questioning a suspect who invokes her or his *Miranda* rights (see page 237). In *Maryland v. Shatzer* (2010),[24] the Court considered a situation in which a sexual abuse suspect invoked his *Miranda* rights, spent more than two years in prison (for an unrelated crime), and then waived his *Miranda* rights. The Court rejected the suspect's claim that due to his much earlier action, the later waiver, although made willingly, "did not count." Instead, the Court decided on a new rule: a *Miranda* invocation is good for only fourteen days. After that, a suspect must clearly reestablish her or his right to silence.

JURISDICTION OF THE SUPREME COURT The United States Supreme Court consists of nine justices—a chief justice and eight associate justices. The Supreme Court has original, or trial, jurisdiction only in rare instances (set forth in Article III, Section 2, of the Constitution). In other words, only rarely does a case originate at the Supreme Court level. Most of the Court's work is as an appellate court. It has appellate authority over cases decided by the U.S. courts of appeals, as well as over some cases decided in the state courts when federal questions are at issue.

WHICH CASES REACH THE SUPREME COURT? There is no absolute right to appeal to the United States Supreme Court. Although thousands of cases are filed with the Supreme Court each year, in 2010–2011 the Court heard only eighty-five. With a **writ of certiorari** (pronounced sur-shee-uh-*rah*-ree), the Supreme Court orders a lower court to send it the record of a case for review. A party can petition the Supreme Court to issue a writ of *certiorari*, but whether the Court will do so is entirely within its discretion. More than 90 percent of the petitions for writs of *certiorari* (or "certs," as they are popularly called) are denied. A denial is not a decision on the merits of a case, nor does it indicate agreement with the lower court's opinion. Therefore, the denial of the writ has no value as a precedent.

The Court will not issue a writ unless at least four justices approve of it. This is called the **rule of four.** Although the justices are not required to give their reasons for refusing to hear a case, most often the discretionary decision is based on whether the legal issue involves a "substantial federal question." Often, such questions arise when lower courts split on a particular issue. For example, in recent years different federal and state courts have produced varying opinions on the question of whether police officers can search the contents of cell phones incident to an arrest.[25] To

Writ of *Certiorari* A request from a higher court asking a lower court for the record of a case. In essence, the request signals the higher court's willingness to review the case.

Rule of Four A rule of the United States Supreme Court that the Court will not issue a writ of *certiorari* unless at least four justices approve of the decision to hear the case.

John G. Roberts, Jr., pictured here, is the seventeenth chief justice of the United States Supreme Court. What does it mean to say that Roberts and the eight associate members of the Court "make criminal justice policy"?
AP Photo/Lawrence Jackson, File

LO 6

clear up confusion on this increasingly important matter, the Court will likely hear a case involving cell phone searches in the near future. Practical considerations aside, if the justices feel that a case does not address an important federal law or constitutional issue, they will vote to deny the writ of *certiorari*.

SUPREME COURT DECISIONS Like all appellate courts, the Supreme Court normally does not hear any evidence. The Court's decision in a particular case is based on the written record of the case and the written arguments (briefs) that the attorneys submit. The attorneys also present oral arguments—arguments presented in person rather than on paper—to the Court, after which the justices discuss the case in *conference*. The conference is strictly private—only the justices are allowed in the room.

When the Court has reached a decision, the chief justice, if in the majority, assigns the task of writing the Court's opinion to one of the justices. When the chief justice is not in the majority, the most senior justice voting with the majority assigns the writing of the Court's opinion. The opinion outlines the reasons for the Court's decision, the rules of law that apply, and the decision.

Often, one or more justices who agree with the Court's decision may do so for different reasons than those outlined in the majority opinion. These justices may write concurring opinions setting forth their own legal reasoning on the issue. Frequently, one or more justices disagree with the Court's conclusion. These justices may write dissenting opinions outlining the reasons why they feel the majority erred. Although a dissenting opinion does not affect the outcome of the case before the Court, it may be important later. In a subsequent case concerning the same issue, a justice or attorney may use the legal reasoning in the dissenting opinion as the basis for an argument to reverse the previous decision and establish a new precedent.

SELFASSESSMENT

Fill in the blanks and check your answers on page 280.
The lowest tier of the federal court system contains U.S. _____ courts, also known as federal trial courts. Appeals from this lower tier are heard in the thirteen U.S. _____ courts of appeals. A decision handed down by a court in this second tier is final unless the United States _____ Court issues a writ of _____, indicating that it has agreed to review the case.

JUDGES IN THE COURT SYSTEM

Supreme Court justices are the most visible and best-known American jurists, but in many ways they are unrepresentative of the profession as a whole. Few judges enjoy three-room office suites fitted with a fireplace and a private bath, as do the Supreme Court justices. Few judges have four clerks to assist them. Few judges get a yearly vacation that stretches from July through September. Most judges, in fact, work at the lowest level of the system, in criminal trial courts, where they are burdened with overflowing caseloads and must deal daily with the pettiest of criminals.

One attribute a Supreme Court justice and a criminal trial judge in any small American city do have in common is the expectation that they will be just. Of all the participants in the criminal justice system, no single person is held to the same high standards as the judge. From her or his lofty perch in the courtroom, the judge is counted on to be "above the fray" of the bickering defense attorneys and prosecutors. When the other courtroom contestants rise at the entrance of the judge, they are placing the burden of justice squarely on the judge's shoulders.

Teaching Tip: In a written assignment, ask students to respond to "Questions for Critical Analysis" number three on page 281, in which they consider the process by which cases go before the United States Supreme Court. (LO 6)

Oral Arguments The verbal arguments presented in person by attorneys to an appellate court. Each attorney presents reasons why the court should rule in his or her client's favor.

Concurring Opinions Separate opinions prepared by judges who support the decision of the majority of the court but who want to make or clarify a particular point or to voice disapproval of the grounds on which the decision was made.

Dissenting Opinions Separate opinions in which judges disagree with the conclusion reached by the majority of the court and expand on their own views about the case.

Teaching Tip: Take a few moments to find out if students are familiar with our sitting United States Supreme Court justices. Can students name all nine? What about State Supreme Court justices in your area?

THE ROLES AND RESPONSIBILITIES OF TRIAL JUDGES

One of the reasons that judicial integrity is considered so important is the amount of discretionary power a judge has over the court proceedings. As you can see in Figure 8.4 below, nearly every stage of the trial process includes a decision or action to be taken by the presiding judge.

Critical Thinking Skill Development: Ask students to debate the concept that a judge may be conflicted between administering justice and ensuring that proper legal procedures have been followed. Which ideal do students feel is most important, and why?

BEFORE THE TRIAL A great deal of the work done by a judge takes place before

LO 7

the trial even starts, free from public scrutiny. These duties, some of which you have seen from a different point of view in the section on law enforcement agents, include determining the following:

1. Whether there is sufficient probable cause to issue a search or arrest warrant.
2. Whether there is sufficient probable cause to authorize electronic surveillance of a suspect.
3. Whether enough evidence exists to justify the temporary incarceration of a suspect.
4. Whether a defendant should be released on bail, and if so, the amount of the bail.
5. Whether to accept pretrial motions by prosecutors and defense attorneys.
6. Whether to accept a plea bargain.

During these pretrial activities, the judge takes on the role of the *negotiator*.[26] As most cases are decided through plea bargains rather than through trial proceedings, the judge often offers his or her services as a negotiator to help the prosecution and the defense "make a deal." The amount at which bail is set is often negotiated as well. Throughout the trial process, the judge usually spends a great deal of time in his or her *chambers*, or office, negotiating with the prosecutors and defense attorneys.

FIGURE 8.4 The Role of the Judge in the Criminal Trial Process

In the various stages of a felony case, judges must undertake the actions described here.

David Young-Wolff/Stone/Getty Images

1. Pre-Arrest
- Decide whether law enforcement officers have provided sufficient probable cause to justify a search or arrest warrant.

2. Initial Appearance
- Inform the suspect of the charges against him or her and of his or her rights.
- Review the charges to see if probable cause exists that the suspect committed the crime; if not, the judge will dismiss the case.
- Set the amount of bail (or deny bail) and determine any other conditions of pretrial release.

3. Preliminary Hearing
- Based on evidence provided by the prosecution and defense, decide whether there is probable cause that the suspect committed the crime.
- Continue to make sure that the defendant's constitutional rights are not being violated.

4. Arraignment
- Ensure that the defendant has been informed of the charges against him or her.
- Ensure that the defendant understands the plea choices before him or her (to plead guilty, not guilty, or *nolo contendere*).

5. Plea Bargain
- Assist with the plea bargaining process, if both sides are willing to "make a deal."
- If the defendant decides to plead guilty in return for charges being lessened, ensure that the defendant understands the nature of the plea bargain and has not been pressured into pleading guilty by his or her attorney.

6. Pretrial Motions
- Rule on pretrial motions presented by the defense.
- Decide whether to grant continuances (the postponement of the trial to allow more time for gathering evidence).

7. Trial
- Ensure that proper procedure is followed in jury selection.
- "Officiate" at the trial, making sure that both the prosecutor and the defense follow procedural rules in presenting evidence and questioning witnesses.
- Explain points of law that affect the case to the jury.
- Provide jury instructions, or instruction to jurors on the meaning of the laws applicable to the case.
- Receive the jury's final verdict of guilty or not guilty.

8. Sentencing
- If the verdict is "guilty," impose the sentence on the convict.

DURING THE TRIAL When the trial starts, the judge takes on the role of *referee*. In this role, she or he is responsible for seeing that the trial unfolds according to the dictates of the law and that the participants in the trial do not overstep any legal or ethical bounds. In this role, the judge is expected to be neutral, determining the admissibility of testimony and evidence on a completely objective basis. The judge also acts as a *teacher* during the trial, explaining points of law to the jury. If the trial is not a jury trial, then the judge must also make decisions concerning the guilt or innocence of the defendant. If the defendant is found guilty, the judge must decide on the length of the sentence and the type of sentence. (Different types of sentences, such as incarceration, probation, and other forms of community-based corrections, will be discussed in Chapters 11 and 12.)

Teaching Tip: If possible, invite a local judge to visit the classroom. Ask the judge to describe the most rewarding and challenging aspects of her or his work.

THE ADMINISTRATIVE ROLE Judges are also *administrators* and are responsible for the day-to-day functioning of their courts. A primary administrative task of a judge is scheduling. Each courtroom has a **docket,** or calendar of cases, and it is the judge's responsibility to keep the docket current. This entails not only scheduling the trial, but also setting pretrial motion dates and deciding whether to grant attorneys' requests for *continuances,* or additional time to prepare for the trial. Judges must also keep track of the immense paperwork generated by each case and manage the various employees of the court. In some instances, judges are even responsible for the budgets of their courtrooms.[27] In 1939, Congress, recognizing the burden of such tasks, created the Administrative Office of the United States Courts to provide administrative assistance for federal court judges.[28] Most state court judges, however, do not have the luxury of similar aid, though they are supported by a court staff.

Docket The list of cases entered on a court's calendar and thus scheduled to be heard by the court.

CJ&TECHNOLOGY "Tweeting" on Trial

For the most part, nothing happens in a courtroom without the judge's approval. As you will see in the next chapter, the judge keeps a particularly close eye on the members of the jury, who are supposed to reach their decision based solely on the evidence presented at trial. In recent years, however, the judge's control is being challenged by technology. Jurors can, and do, use small (and easily hidden) wireless devices to text, tweet, blog, take photos, and conduct Internet research on the case before them. "Dozens of people a day are sending tweets or Facebook updates from courthouses all over America," says one social networking expert. This technology also poses a problem for witnesses, who are supposed to testify in court without knowing anything about what has occurred during the trial. For this reason, many judges have banned journalists from blogging live during a trial. The judges fear that witnesses waiting to testify might follow the proceedings on their cell phones from the courthouse lobby.

Stockbyte/Getty Images, Keith Binns, iStockphoto

THINKING ABOUT WIRELESS DEVICES IN THE COURTROOM

Recently, during a criminal trial in California, a juror complained on his blog that the defense attorney was "whacked out" and "acting stupid" and posted a photo of the alleged murder weapon—a fifteen-inch saw-toothed knife—taken with his cell phone camera. How might this behavior threaten the integrity of the courtroom?

SELECTION OF JUDGES

In the federal court system, all judges are appointed by the president and confirmed by

LO 8

the Senate. It is difficult to make a general statement about how judges are selected in state court systems, however, because the procedure varies widely from state to state. In some states, such as New Jersey, all judges are appointed by the governor and confirmed by the upper chamber of the state legislature. In other states, such as Alabama, **partisan elections** are used to choose judges. In these elections, a judicial candidate declares allegiance to a political party, usually the Democrats or the Republicans, before the election. States such as Kentucky that conduct **nonpartisan elections** do not require a candidate to affiliate herself or himself with a political party in this manner. Finally, some states, such as Missouri, select judges based on a subjective definition of merit.

The two key concepts in discussing methods of selecting judges are *independence* and *accountability.*[29] Those who feel that judicial fairness is dependent on the judges' belief that they will not be removed from office as the result of an unpopular ruling support methods of selection that include appointment.[30] In contrast, some observers feel that judges are "politicians in robes" who make policy decisions every time they step to the bench. Following this line of thought, judges should be held accountable to those who are affected by their decisions and therefore should be chosen through elections, as legislators are.[31] The most independent, and therefore least accountable, judges are those who hold lifetime appointments. They are influenced neither by the temptation to make popular decisions to impress voters nor by the need to follow the ideological or party line of the politicians who provided them with their posts.

APPOINTMENT OF JUDGES Article II, Section 2, of the Constitution authorizes the president to appoint the justices of the Supreme Court with the advice and consent of the Senate. Subsequent laws enacted by Congress provide that the same procedure is used for appointing judges to the lower federal courts as well.

On paper, the appointment process is relatively simple. After selecting a nominee, the president submits the name to the Senate for approval. The Senate Judiciary Committee then holds hearings and makes its recommendation to the Senate, where a majority vote is needed to confirm the nomination. In practice, the process does not always proceed smoothly. Given the importance of the Supreme Court in shaping the nation's laws and values, the appointment process for its justices is highly politicized. Presidents choose candidates who reflect the political beliefs of their party, and members of the opposing party in the Senate do their best to discredit these individuals. In recent years, heated debate over controversial issues such as abortion and gay rights has characterized the proceedings to the point that one commentator likens them to elections rather than the appointments envisioned by the nation's founders.[32]

Five states, as well as Puerto Rico, employ similar selection methods, with the governor offering nominees for the approval of the state legislature. Judges in these states, as would be expected, serve longer terms than their counterparts in nonappointment judicial systems.[33] They are also regarded as products of *patronage,* as are judges appointed to federal positions by the president. In other words, appointed judges often obtain their positions because they belong to the same political party as the president (or governor, at the state level) and also have been active in supporting the candidates and ideology of the party in power. One of the most prevalent criticisms of appointing judges is that the system is based on "having friends in high places" rather than on merit.[34]

Partisan Elections Elections in which candidates are affiliated with and receive support from political parties. The candidates are listed in conjunction with their party on the ballot.

Nonpartisan Elections Elections in which candidates are presented on the ballot without any party affiliation.

Group Activities: Ask students to work together to research how judges are chosen in your area. What qualities do students feel a candidate for the bench should possess? What level of experience or expertise do they feel is necessary? What factors should exclude someone from consideration? (LO 8)

ELECTION OF JUDGES Most states moved from an appointive to an elective system for judges in the mid-nineteenth century. The reasoning behind the move was to make judges more representative of the communities in which they served. Today, all but eleven states choose at least some of their judges through elections.[35] Nearly 90 percent of all state judges face elections at some point in their judicial careers.[36] Even though the practice is widespread, as we will see in the *CJ in Action* feature at the end of the chapter, many observers feel that judicial elections raise unavoidable questions about the impartiality that lies at the heart of the profession.

MERIT SELECTION In 1940, Missouri became the first state to combine appointment and election in a single merit selection. When all jurisdiction levels are counted, nineteen states and the District of Columbia now utilize the **Missouri Plan**, as merit selection has been labeled. The Missouri Plan consists of three basic steps:

- When a vacancy on the bench arises, candidates are nominated by a nonpartisan committee of citizens.
- The names of the three most qualified candidates are sent to the governor or executive of the state judicial system, and that person chooses who will be the judge.
- A year after the new judge has been installed, a "retention election" is held so that voters can decide whether the judge deserves to keep the post.[37]

The goal of the Missouri Plan is to eliminate partisan politics from the selection procedure, while at the same time giving the citizens a voice in the process. (For a review of the selection processes, see *Mastering Concepts—The Selection of State and Federal Judges* below.)

> **Justice at Stake** is an organization dedicated to fair and impartial courts in the United States. Find its Web site by visiting the *Criminal Justice CourseMate* at **cengagebrain.com** and selecting the *Web links* for this chapter.

Missouri Plan A method of selecting judges that combines appointment and election. Under the plan, the state governor or another government official selects judges from a group of nominees chosen by a nonpartisan committee. After a year on the bench, the judges face a popular election to determine whether the public wishes to keep them in office.

MASTERING CONCEPTS

THE SELECTION OF STATE AND FEDERAL JUDGES

FEDERAL JUDGES	STATE JUDGES	
1. The president nominates a candidate to the U.S. Senate. 2. The Senate Judiciary Committee holds hearings concerning the qualifications of the candidate and makes its recommendation to the full Senate. 3. The full Senate votes to confirm or reject the president's nominee.	**Partisan Elections** • Judicial candidates, supported by and affiliated with political parties, place their names before the voters for consideration for a particular judicial seat. • The electorate votes to decide who will retain or gain the seat. **Executive Apointment** • The governor nominates a candidate to the state legislature. • The legislature votes to confirm or reject the governor's nominee.	**Nonpartisan Elections** • Judicial candidates, not supported by or affiliated with political parties, place their names before the voters for consideration for a particular judicial seat. • The electorate votes to decide who will retain or gain the seat. **Missouri Plan** • A nominating commission provides a list of worthy candidates. • An elected official (usually the governor) chooses from the list submitted by the commission. • A year later, a "retention election" is held to allow voters to decide whether the judge will stay on the bench.

THE REMOVAL OF JUDGES Besides losing an election, sitting judges can be removed from office for judicial misconduct, or behavior that diminishes public confidence in the judiciary. Nearly every state has a *judicial conduct commission,* which consists of lawyers, judges, and other prominent citizens and is often a branch of the state's highest court. This commission investigates charges of judicial misconduct and may recommend removal if warranted. The final decision to discipline a judge generally is made by the state supreme court.[38] Several state judges are removed from office each year. Recent examples include Nevada District Judge Elizabeth Halverson, who lost her seat for a wide range of misconduct that included sleeping on the job, cursing at her staff, and ordering an assistant to give her foot and back massages.

Such transgressions, however deplorable, would be unlikely to result in a similar outcome if committed by a federal judge. Appointed under Article II of the U.S. Constitution, federal judges can be removed from office only if found guilty of "Treason, Bribery, or other high Crimes and Misdemeanors." Before a federal judge can be impeached, the U.S. House of Representatives must be presented with specific charges of misconduct and vote on whether these charges merit further action. If the House votes to impeach by a simple majority (more than 50 percent), the U.S. Senate—presided over by the chief justice of the United States Supreme Court—holds a trial on the judge's conduct. At the conclusion of this trial, a two-thirds majority vote is required in the Senate to remove the judge. This disciplinary action is extremely rare: only eight federal judges have been impeached and convicted in the nation's history. Most recently, in 2010 U.S. District Court Judge G. Thomas Porteous was removed from office for accepting tens of thousands of dollars in cash from lawyers to pay gambling debts and then lying about his misbehavior to federal investigators. (See the feature *Comparative Criminal Justice—Back to School* below to learn about France's preferred method for producing ethical judges.)

COMPARATIVE CRIMINAL JUSTICE

BACK TO SCHOOL

Elections for judges are extremely rare outside the United States. Indeed, only two nations—Japan and Switzerland—engage in the practice, and then only in very limited situations. To the rest of the world, according to one expert, "American adherence to judicial elections is as incomprehensible as our rejection of the metric system." Much more common, for example, is the French system, crafted to provide extensive training for potential judges.

French judicial candidates must pass two exams. The first, open to law school graduates only, combines oral and written sections and lasts at least four days. In some years, only 5 percent of the applicants overcome this hurdle. Not surprisingly, the pressure is intense. "It gives you nightmares for years afterwards," says Jean-Marc Baissus, a judge in Toulouse. "You come out of [the exam] completely shattered." Those who do survive the first test enter a two-year program at the École Nationale de la Magistrature, a judicial training academy. This school is similar to a police training academy in the United States, in that candidates spend half of their time in the classroom and the other half in the courtroom.

At the end of this program, judicial candidates are subject to a second examination. Only those who pass the exam may become judges. The result, in the words of Mitchell Lasser, a law professor at Cornell University, is that French judges "actually know what the hell they are doing. They've spent years in school taking practical and theoretical courses on how to be a judge." The French also pride themselves on creating judges who are free from the kind of political pressures faced by American judges who must go before the voters.

FOR CRITICAL ANALYSIS

Do you think that the French system of training judges is superior to the American system of electing them? Before explaining your answer, consider that French judges lack the practical courtroom experience of American judges, many of whom served as lawyers earlier in their careers.

DIVERSITY ON THE BENCH

One criticism of merit selection is that the members of the selection committee, who are mostly white, upper-class attorneys, nominate mostly white, upper-class attorneys.[39] In South Carolina, which uses this method to select most members of the judiciary, only 16 of the state's 186 judges are African American, and only 5 of its 46 circuit court judges are women. "There's a perception that [the selection process] is tied to the good-old-boys network rather than picking the best person for the seat," says one observer.[40] The lack of diversity is particularly striking given that almost 30 percent of South Carolina's population is black, a pattern that is repeated in other states. Arizona's population, for example, is 40 percent nonwhite, but the state has no minority supreme court justices and minorities hold less than 20 percent of other state judgeships.[41]

The federal judiciary shows a similar pattern. Of the nearly 1,300 federal judges in this country, 8 percent are African American, 5 percent are Hispanic, and less than 1 percent are Asian American. Furthermore, only 15 percent are women.[42] Of the 111 justices who have served on the United States Supreme Court, two have been African American: Thurgood Marshall (1970–1991) and Clarence Thomas (1991–present). In 2009, Sonia Sotomayor became the first Hispanic appointed to the Court and the third woman, following Sandra Day O'Connor (1981 to 2006) and Ruth Bader Ginsburg (1993–present). A year later, Elena Kagan became the fourth woman appointed to the Court.

THE IMPACT OF PAST DISCRIMINATION

Edward Chen, a federal judge for the Northern District of California, identifies a number of reasons for the low minority representation on the bench. Past discrimination in law schools has limited the pool of experienced minority attorneys who have the political ties, access to "old boy" networks, and career opportunities that lead to judgeships.[43] Only recently, as increased numbers of minorities have graduated from law schools, have rates of minority judges begun to creep slowly upward. Traditionally, efforts to diversify American judges by race, ethnicity, and gender have been met with resistance from those who argue that because judges must be impartial, it makes no difference whether a judge is black, Asian, Hispanic, or white.[44]

Sherrilyn A. Ifill of the University of Maryland School of Law rejects this argument. She believes that "diversity on the bench" can only enrich our judiciary by introducing a variety of voices and perspectives into what are perhaps the most powerful positions in the criminal justice system. By the same token, Ifill credits the lack of diversity in many trial and appeals courts with a number of harmful consequences, such as more severe sentences for minority youths than for white youths who have committed similar crimes, disproportionate denial of bail to minority defendants, and the disproportionate imposition of the death penalty on minority defendants accused of killing white victims.[45]

Federal judge Audrey B. Collins's grandmother was a slave, and she experienced racism firsthand when, in the 1950s, hers was the first African American family to move into an all-white neighborhood in Chester, Pennsylvania. What are some of the benefits of having judges with a wide range of experiences on the bench?
Lawrence K. Ho/MCT/Newscom

SELFASSESSMENT

Fill in the blanks and check your answers on page 281.

In the federal court system, judges are appointed by the _____ and confirmed by the _____. In state court systems, however, the selection process varies. Some states mirror the federal system, with the _____ making judicial appointments with the approval of the legislature. Others conduct either _____ elections, in which political parties openly support judicial candidates, or _____ elections, in which the candidate is not affiliated with any political group. Finally, a number of states rely on _____ selection, which combines appointment and election. Federal judges can be removed only through the process of _____, while state judges face removal if they engage in serious _____.

Teaching Tip: While much attention is paid to judges and attorneys, the courtroom work group is comprised of many individuals. If time allows, invite your local court clerk, court reporter, or bailiff to visit the classroom. Let students interview these individuals about their roles in the justice process. (LO 9)

Courtroom Work Group The social organization consisting of the judge, prosecutor, defense attorney, and other court workers. The relationships among these persons have a far-reaching impact on the day-to-day operations of any court.

A stenotype machine, such as the one shown in use here, allows court reporters to press more than one key at a time to keep up with the often fast-paced action of the courtroom. Why do you think it is necessary for court reporters to produce written records of criminal trials?
Michael Newman/PhotoEdit

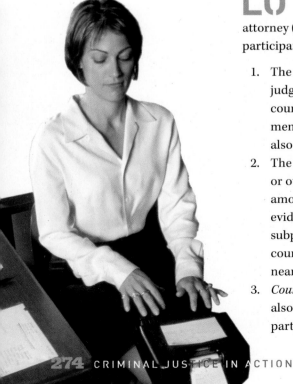

THE COURTROOM WORK GROUP

Television dramas often depict the courtroom as a battlefield, with prosecutors and defense attorneys spitting fire at each other over the loud and insistent protestations of a frustrated judge. Consequently, many people are somewhat disappointed when they witness a real courtroom at work. Rarely does anyone raise his or her voice, and the courtroom professionals appear—to a great extent—to be cooperating with each other. In Chapter 6, we discussed the existence of a police subculture, based on the shared values of law enforcement agents. A courtroom subculture exists as well, centered on the courtroom work group.

The most important feature of any work group is that it is a *cooperative* unit, whose members establish shared values and methods that help the group efficiently reach its goals. Though cooperation is not a concept usually associated with criminal courts, it is in fact crucial to the adjudication process.

MEMBERS OF THE COURTROOM WORK GROUP

LO 9 The courtroom work group is made up of those individuals who are involved with the defendant from the time she or he is arrested until sentencing. The most prominent members are the judge, the prosecutor, and the defense attorney (the latter two will be discussed in detail in the next chapter). Three other court participants complete the work group:

1. The *bailiff of the court* is responsible for maintaining security and order in the judge's chambers and the courtroom. Bailiffs lead the defendant in and out of the courtroom and attend to the needs of the jurors during the trial. A bailiff, often a member of the local sheriff's department but sometimes an employee of the court, also delivers summonses in some jurisdictions.

2. The *clerk of the court* has an exhausting list of responsibilities. Any plea, motion, or other matter to be acted on by the judge must go through the clerk. The large amount of paperwork generated during a trial, including transcripts, photographs, evidence, and any other records, is maintained by the clerk. The clerk also issues subpoenas for jury duty and coordinates the jury selection process. In the federal court system, judges select clerks, while state clerks are either appointed or, in nearly a third of the states, elected.

3. *Court reporters* record every word that is said during the course of the trial. They also record any *depositions,* or pretrial question-and-answer sessions in which a party or a witness answers an attorney's questions under oath.

FORMATION OF THE COURTROOM WORK GROUP

The premise of the work group is based on constant interaction that fosters relationships among the members. As legal scholar David W. Neubauer describes:

> Every day, the same group of courthouse regulars assembles in the same courtroom, sits or stands in the same places, and performs the same tasks as the day before. The types of defendants and the nature of the crimes they are accused of committing also remain constant. Only the names of the victim, witnesses, and defendants are different.[46]

After a period of time, the members of a courtroom work group learn how the others operate. The work group establishes patterns of behavior and norms, and cooperation allows the adjudication process to function informally and smoothly.[47] In some cases, the members of the work group may even form personal relationships, which only strengthen the courtroom culture.

One way in which the courtroom work group differs from a traditional work group at a company such as Facebook, Inc., is that each member answers to a different sponsoring organization. Although the judge has ultimate authority over a courtroom, he or she is not the "boss" of the attorneys. The prosecutor is hired by the district attorney's office, the defense attorney by a private individual or the public defender's office, and the judge by the court system itself. (See Figure 8.5 on the following page for an overview of the relationships among the main participants in the courtroom work group.)

Three trial lawyers confer as the judge waits at the Sedgwick County Courthouse in Wichita, Kansas. How is working in a courtroom similar to working in a corporate office? How is it different?
Jaime Oppenheimer/MCT/Landov

Discussion Tip: Have students work in small groups to discuss how the personality and work ethic of a judge can impact the workings of the court.

THE JUDGE IN THE COURTROOM WORK GROUP

The judge is the dominant figure in the courtroom and therefore exerts the most influence over the values and norms of the work group. A judge who runs a "tight ship" follows procedure and restricts the freedom of attorneys to deviate from regulations, while a *"laissez-faire"* judge allows more leeway to members of the work group. A judge's personal philosophy also affects the court proceedings. If a judge has a reputation for being "tough on crime," both prosecutors and defense attorneys will alter their strategies accordingly. In fact, a lawyer may be able to manipulate the system to "shop" for a judge whose philosophy best fits the attorney's goals in a particular case.[48] If a lawyer is caught trying to influence the assignment of judges, however, she or he is said to be "corrupting judicial independence" and may face legal proceedings.

Although preeminent in the work group, a judge must still rely on other members of the group. To a certain extent, the judge is the least informed member of the trio. Like a juror, the judge learns the facts of the case as they are presented by the attorneys. If the attorneys do not properly present the facts, then the judge is hampered in making rulings. Furthermore, if a judge deviates from the norms of the work group—by, for example, refusing to grant continuances—the other members of the work group can "discipline" the judge. Defense attorneys and prosecutors can request further continuances, fail to produce

> **"A judge is not supposed to know anything about the facts . . . until they have been presented in evidence and explained to him at least three times."**
>
> **—Lord Chief Justice Parker,** British judge (1961)

FIGURE 8.5 The Courtroom Work Group and Incentives to Cooperate

The major figures of the courtoom work group—judges, prosecutors, and defense attorneys—benefit from a certain degree of cooperation. As you can see, one of the primary considerations of each of the three principals is to dispose of cases as quickly as possible.

Defense Attorney's obligations to the Judge
- Be prepared
- Negotiate pleas when justified
- Refrain from engaging in time-consuming arguments with prosecutor
- Refrain from filing time-consuming motions

Judge's obligation to the Defense Attorney
- Grant continuances when extra time is needed to prepare case or to get client to pay fees

Judge's obligation to the Prosecutor
- Grant continuances when extra time is needed to prepare case

Prosecutor's obligations to the Judge
- Be prepared
- Negotiate pleas when justified
- Refrain from engaging in time-consuming arguments with defense attorney

All images ©Royalty-Free/Corbis

JUDGE

Official Responsibility: To make sure that proper legal procedure is followed before, during, and after a trial

Job Pressures: Large caseloads, little time; the administrative burden of managing case dockets

DEFENSE ATTORNEY

Official Responsibility: To advocate for the client's innocence

Job Pressures: Earning a living by having a large number of clients; get best outcome for client with limited resources

Defense Attorney's obligations to the Prosecutor
- Persuade clients to accept "reasonable" plea bargains
- Negotiate a sentence that is favorable to client

PROSECUTOR

Official Responsibility: To convict those guilty of crimes against society

Job Pressures: More cases than time to dispose of all of them; satisfy public expectations that criminals will be punished

Prosecutor's obligations to the Defense Attorney
- Provide access to witnesses, police reports, and other information that is unavailable due to limited resources
- Be accommodating when extra time is needed to prepare case

witnesses in a timely manner, and slow down the proceeding through a general lack of preparedness. The delays caused by such acts can ruin a judge's calendar—especially in large courts—and bring pressure from the judge's superiors.

ASSEMBLY-LINE JUSTICE

In discussing the goals of the courtroom work group, several general concepts figure prominently—efficiency, cooperation, rapidity, and socialization. One aim of the work group, however, is glaring in its absence: justice. One of the main criticisms of the American court system is that it has sacrificed the goal of justice for efficiency. Some observers claim that only the wealthiest can afford to receive justice as promised by the Constitution, while the rest of society is left with a watered-down version of *assembly-line justice.*

THE IMPACT OF EXCESSIVE CASELOADS Given the caseloads that most courts face, some degree of assembly-line justice seems inevitable. A quick survey of

CAREERS IN CJ

Photo Courtesy of Shawn Davis

FAST FACTS

**BAILIFF
JOB DESCRIPTION:**

- Maintain order and provide security in the courtroom during trials.
- Open and close court, call cases, call witnesses, and the like.
- Serve eviction orders, civil lawsuits, garnishments, or asset seizures.
- Escort and guard juries, prevent juries from having contact with the public.

WHAT KIND OF TRAINING IS REQUIRED?

- At a minimum, a high school diploma or GED.
- Supplemental training, either at a 2- or 4-year college, vocational school, or police academy, with an emphasis in criminal justice.

ANNUAL SALARY RANGE?

- $30,000–$38,000

For additional information on a career as a bailiff, visit:
www.criminaljusticeusa.com/ bailiff.html

Photo Disc/Getty Images

SHAWN DAVIS
BAILIFF

I moved to the Scioto County (Ohio) Common Pleas Court as a bailiff after spending eight years with the local sheriff's office, working mostly as a deputy. At first, I was in awe of the courtroom and court procedures, which seem very confusing if you do not know exactly what is going on. A welcome aspect of the new job was the respect I got from inmates. When I was working the jail as a deputy, the inmates would regularly curse at me and fail to follow orders. Just a few weeks before I moved over to the courtroom as a bailiff, I had a very unpleasant incident with an inmate who refused to leave his cell. My colleagues and I had no choice but to use force on him, which made him furious. He even threatened to "get" me and members of my family after he was released. Then, coincidentally, this same inmate had to appear in the courtroom where I had just been assigned as bailiff. He was very respectful and apologetic. Many of the inmates are under the mistaken impression that if they behave and are polite to the court employees, they will get a better deal from the judge.

DOUBLE DUTY Basically, there are two kinds of bailiffs: administrative bailiffs and criminal bailiffs. An administrative bailiff will handle paperwork, set up court dates, and answer questions about filings that the attorneys may have. A criminal bailiff is responsible for bringing the court to session, directing jurors, and overseeing court security, which involves keeping everybody—judges, attorneys, jurors, spectators, witnesses, and defendants—safe. In my case, I do double duty as an administrative and criminal bailiff. Because I enjoy an excellent working relationship with "my" judge, Howard H. Harcha III, I also sometimes take care of pretrial concerns for him when he is out of the office. Indeed, the level of trust that I have developed with Judge Harcha is the aspect of my job that I take the most pride in.

Violence in the courtroom is rare. As I said before, most inmates are on their best behavior in front of the judge. It can flare up in an instant, however, and you have to be constantly on guard. One time, an inmate under my control made a run for it as we were transporting him back to the jail from his court appearance. His leg shackles broke, giving him a short-lived sense of freedom. We were able to tackle him in front of the courthouse just before he could jump into a waiting convertible. We later learned that the accomplice—the inmate's brother—was supposed to bring a handgun and shoot us as part of the escape plan. Another time, a defendant started taking off his shirt and tried to attack the victim, who had just given testimony. He was quickly tackled, cuffed, and carted off to jail.

CAREER ADVICE Education is key. I did not have my college degree when I started working as a bailiff. I have since earned a bachelor's degree in administration of criminal justice. An education makes it much easier to deal with the public and attorneys on a daily basis. Training in areas such as security procedures, self-defense, and personal safety is also very important if you want to make it home to see your family at the end of the day. You can get this type of training through a state's bailiff associations and state supreme courts. Also, the U.S. Marshals and other law enforcement agencies provide training courses—for example, I attended a training session at the U.S. Marshals Service Basic Training Academy in Glynco, Georgia.

Discussion Tip: Ask students to discuss the concept of assembly-line justice. When is it most likely to occur? Which cases are most likely to be affected?

the nation's court system provides clear examples of the extent of the problem and its consequences. Many, if not most, state courts are consistently behind on their dockets.[49] After watching a judge in Lynwood (Washington) Municipal Court handle more than one hundred misdemeanor cases in four hours, a researcher noted that each defendant got less time before the judge "than it takes to get a hamburger from a McDonald's drive-through."[50]

Though the situation is less extreme in the federal court system, those courts are also burdened by heavy caseloads. From 2001 to 2010, the number of criminal cases filed in federal court increased by nearly 22 percent, driven mostly by drug, immigration, and sex offender prosecutions.[51] Because of dramatic increases in immigration cases in recent years, federal courts along the U.S.-Mexico border have become so overwhelmed that officials' ability to deal with other crimes is limited. For a time in 2010, federal prosecutors in Arizona even stopped bringing charges against smugglers caught with less than 500 pounds of marijuana.[52] The lack of resources to deal with excessive caseloads is generally recognized as one of the most critical issues facing both federal and state law enforcement agencies and courtrooms.[53]

THE COURTROOM WORK GROUP AND OVERLOADED COURTS A judge's worth is increasingly measured by her or his ability to keep the "assembly line" of cases moving, rather than by the quality of her or his judicial work. Consequently, the judicial process is accused of being "careless and haphazard" and of routinely supporting decisions made on the basis of incomplete information. Though definitive statistics on the subject have never been adequately gathered, many observers feel that assembly-line justice affects the actions of others in the criminal justice system as well:

- Beyond filling out a crime report, police officers often do not investigate misdemeanors and less serious felonies unless the offender was caught in the act.
- Police officers often are encouraged to obtain confessions—using whatever means necessary—from defendants, rather than find incriminating evidence, because a confession is more likely to lead to conviction.
- Prosecutors often press charges for misdemeanors and nonviolent felonies only when the case is a "slam dunk"—that is, when conviction is certain.
- To wrap up cases quickly, prosecutors generally bargain reduced sentences for guilty verdicts. As a result, criminals spend less time in prison than is in society's best interests.[54]

If the public is under the impression that police, judges, and lawyers are more interested in speed than in justice, the pressure of caseloads may also lead to loss of respect for the criminal justice system as a whole.

SELFASSESSMENT

Fill in the blanks and check your answers on page 281.
The three most prominent members of the courtroom work group are the _____, the _____, and the _____ _____. As a rule, these professionals must _____ with each other to ensure the smooth functioning of the court system. A condition known as _____ exists when courtroom work groups sacrifice justice for the sake of efficiency.

CJ IN ACTION

ELECTING JUDGES

The three actors, dressed as inmates in orange jumpsuits with their faces obscured, speak one at a time. "I was convicted of stabbing my victims with a kitchen knife," says the first. "Of shooting my ex-girlfriend and murdering her sister in front of our child," says the second. "Of sexual assault on a mom and her ten-year-old daughter," says the third, before adding with a laugh, "And I slashed their throats." The actors go on to state that Justice Thomas Kilbride "sided with us over law enforcement or victims on appeal."[55] When this television advertisement aired in the fall of 2010, during Kilbride's reelection campaign for his seat on the Illinois Supreme Court, watchdog groups criticized it as misleading.[56] The ad also contributed to the continuing controversy over judicial elections, the subject of this chapter's *CJ in Action* feature.

POPULARITY AND ACCOUNTABILITY

Judge Thomas Kilbride had angered special interest groups in Illinois with a vote on medical malpractice suits. Yet the attack ads against him focused on crime—a subject more likely to anger voters and, at least theoretically, get them to the polls. Proponents of judicial elections insist that unless judges are regularly forced to submit themselves to the will of the electorate, there is no way to hold them accountable for their actions. Critics, such as Hans A. Linde, a retired justice of the Oregon Supreme Court, counter that, "'Judicial accountability' has a virtuous ring to it until one asks, accountability for what?"[57] The answer to Linde's rhetorical question, at least in his mind, is that the public will hold a judge accountable for making unpopular rulings, but not necessarily for making "incorrect" ones. If Linde's assertion is true, the negative impact will fall most heavily on defendants in criminal trials, who are among the most unpopular participants in the judicial process.

THE CASE FOR JUDICIAL ELECTIONS

- In a democracy, voters have the right to select government officials such as judges who make important policy decisions.

- Elections ensure that the people have a measure of control over the judiciary. If a judge repeatedly makes unpopular decisions involving the punishment of criminals or other important issues, he or she deserves to be voted out of office.

- Campaigning requires judges to interact with the community, thereby broadening their perspective. One judicial candidate noted that he was forced to "leave his comfort zone of similarly minded lawyers" and talk to "nurses in Pearland [Texas], stay-at-home moms in Galveston, shrimpers in Chambers County, doctors in Houston's vast medical center, [and] farmers in Sealy."[58]

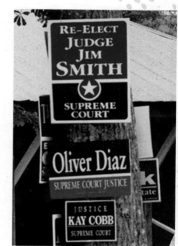

AP Photo/Rogelio Solis

THE CASE AGAINST JUDICIAL ELECTIONS

- Judges are not like politicians. They must be neutral in applying the law to the facts, regardless of any political consequences. In other words, "courts are supposed to do what is right, not what is popular."[59]

- The need to raise funds for judges' election campaigns raises concerns of undue influence by major contributors such as lawyers and other special interests. In one poll, more than a quarter of 2,428 state judges felt that campaign contributions had some influence on judges' decisions.[60] In another, nearly 80 percent of citizens agreed with the statement: "Elected judges are influenced by having to raise campaign funds."[61]

- Voters not only lack knowledge of the issues of a judicial election, but do not even know who the candidates are. A poll in Michigan found that nine out of ten voters could not identify a single sitting supreme court justice.[62]

YOUR OPINION— WRITING ASSIGNMENT

Under what circumstances, if any, should a judge be required to remove himself or herself from a trial because of statements made or contributions accepted during a campaign? Note that, according to the Model Code of Judicial Conduct, "A judge shall disqualify himself or herself in a proceeding in which the judge's impartiality might reasonably be questioned."[63] Before completing this assignment, you can review our discussions in this chapter concerning:

- The legitimacy of courts (page 255).

- The roles and responsibilities of trial judges (pages 268–269).

- Selection of judges (pages 270–272).

Your answer should be at least three full paragraphs.

CHAPTER SUMMARY

LO 1 **Define and contrast the four functions of the courts.** The four functions are (a) due process, (b) crime control, (c) rehabilitation, and (d) bureaucratic. The most obvious contrast is between the due process and crime control functions. The former is mainly concerned with the procedural rules that allow each accused individual to have a "fair chance" against the government in a criminal proceeding. For crime control, the courts are supposed to impose enough "pain" on convicted criminals to deter criminal behavior. For the rehabilitation function, the courts serve as "doctors" who dispense "treatment." In their bureaucratic function, courts are more concerned with speed and efficiency.

LO 2 **Define *jurisdiction* and contrast geographic and subject-matter jurisdiction.** Jurisdiction relates to the power of a court to hear a particular case. Courts are typically limited in geographic jurisdiction—for example, to a particular state. Some courts are restricted in subject matter, such as a small claims court, which can hear only cases involving civil matters under a certain monetary limit.

LO 3 **Explain the difference between trial and appellate courts.** Trial courts are courts of the first instance, where a case is first heard. Appellate courts review the proceedings of a lower court. Appellate courts do not have juries.

LO 4 **Outline the several levels of a typical state court system.** (a) At the lowest level are courts of limited jurisdiction, (b) next are trial courts of general jurisdiction, (c) then appellate courts, and (d) finally, the state's highest court.

LO 5 **Outline the federal court system.** (a) At the lowest level are the U.S. district courts in which trials are held, as well as various minor federal courts of limited jurisdiction; (b) next are the U.S. courts of appeals, otherwise known as circuit courts of appeals; and (c) finally, the United States Supreme Court.

LO 6 **Explain briefly how a case is brought to the Supreme Court.** Cases decided in U.S. courts of appeals, as well as cases decided in the highest state courts (when federal questions arise), can be appealed to the Supreme Court. If at least four justices approve of a case filed with the Supreme Court, the Court will issue a writ of *certiorari*, ordering the lower court to send the Supreme Court the record of the case for review.

LO 7 **List the actions that a judge might take prior to an actual trial.** Trial judges may do the following before an actual trial: (a) issue search or arrest warrants, (b) authorize electronic surveillance of a suspect, (c) order the temporary incarceration of a suspect, (d) decide whether a suspect should be released on bail and the amount of that bail, (e) accept or reject pretrial motions by prosecutors and defense attorneys, and (f) accept or reject a plea bargain.

LO 8 **Explain the difference between the selection of judges at the state level and at the federal level.** The president nominates all judges at the federal level, and the Senate must approve the nominations. A similar procedure is used in some states. In other states, all judges are elected on a partisan ballot or on a nonpartisan ballot. Some states use merit selection, or the Missouri Plan, in which a citizen committee nominates judicial candidates, the governor or executive of the state judicial system chooses among the top three nominees, and a year later a "retention election" is held.

LO 9 **List and describe the members of the courtroom work group.** (a) The judge; (b) the prosecutor, who brings charges in the name of the people (the state) against the accused; (c) the defense attorney; (d) the bailiff, who is responsible for maintaining security and order in the judge's chambers and the courtroom; (e) the clerk, who accepts all pleas, motions, and other matters to be acted on by the judge; and (f) court reporters, who record what is said during a trial as well as at depositions.

SELF ASSESSMENT ANSWER KEY

Page 256: **i.** due process; **ii.** individuals; **iii.** crime control; **iv.** society; **v.** rehabilitate

Page 261: **i.** jurisdiction; **ii.** subject matter; **iii.** trial; **iv.** appellate; **v.** dual; **vi.** federal; **vii.** state

Page 264: **i.** limited; **ii.** general; **iii.** appeals

Page 267: **i.** district; **ii.** circuit; **iii.** Supreme; **iv.** *certiorari*

KEY TERMS

appellate courts **260**

concurrent jurisdiction **257**

concurring opinions **267**

courtroom work group **274**

dissenting opinions **267**

docket **269**

dual court system **260**

extradition **259**

impeachment **272**

judicial misconduct **272**

judicial review **265**

jurisdiction **257**

magistrate **262**

Missouri Plan **271**

nonpartisan elections **270**

opinions **260**

oral arguments **267**

partisan elections **270**

rule of four **266**

specialty courts **263**

trial courts **260**

writ of *certiorari* **266**

QUESTIONS FOR CRITICAL ANALYSIS

1. "The primary adversarial relationship in the courts is not between the plaintiff (prosecutor, or state) and defendant, but rather between the ideal of justice and the reality of bureaucratic limitations." Explain why you agree or disagree with this statement.

2. In 2010, authorities in Thailand extradited Russian citizen and alleged international arms dealer Viktor Bout to the United States. The evidence against Bout included an audio recording of a conversation he had with American agents posing as Colombian rebels. During this conversation, Bout agreed to furnish the "revolutionaries" with weapons for the purpose of killing American pilots. How does this evidence give the United States jurisdiction over Bout?

3. In late 2009, the United States Supreme Court "denied cert" in the case of Yasin Muhammed Basardh, a Yemeni citizen still in the custody of the U.S. military even though he had been ruled innocent of terrorism charges by a U.S. court. What does it mean for the Court to "deny cert"? In this instance, what might be some of the reasons for the Court's refusal to consider Basardh's case?

4. Why do federal judges have more job security than state judges? How does this give them more freedom to make unpopular decisions?

5. Why is cooperation so important in the courtroom work group?

CourseMate *For Online Help*

For online help and access to resources that accompany *Criminal Justice Today,* go to www.cengagebrain.com/shop/ISBN/1111835578. Click "Access Now," where you will find flashcards, an online quiz, and other helpful study aids. If you have an access code for CourseMate, log in and go to the chapter of your choice for additional online study aids.

NOTES

1. Quoted in Alessandro Rizzo, "Amanda Knox Makes Emotional Address in Appeal," *Seattle Times* (December 12, 2010), B10.

2. Timothy Egan, "Lessons from the Amanda Knox Case," *New York Times* (October 3, 2011), at **opinionator.blogs.nytimes.com/2011/10/03/justice-in-perugia**.

3. Roscoe Pound, "The Administration of Justice in American Cities," *Harvard Law Review* 12 (1912).

4. Russell Wheeler and Howard Whitcomb, *Judicial Administration: Text and Readings* (Englewood Cliffs, NJ: Prentice Hall, 1977), 3.

5. Herbert Packer, *The Limits of the Criminal Sanction* (Stanford, CA: Stanford University Press, 1968), 154–173.

6. Herbert Packer, "The Courts, the Police and the Rest of Us," *Criminal Law, Criminology & Political Science* 57 (1966), 238–239.

7. Larry J. Siegel, Criminology: *Instructor's Manual,* 6th ed. (Belmont, CA: West/Wadsworth Publishing Co., 1998), 440.

8. Gerald F. Velman, "Federal Sentencing Guidelines: A Cure Worse Than the Disease," *American Criminal Law Review* 29 (Spring 1992), 904.

9. *Gonzales v. Raich,* 545 U.S. 1 (2005).

10. Wayne R. LaFave, "Section 4.6. Multiple Jurisdiction and Multiple Prosecution," *Substantive Criminal Law,* 2d ed. (C.J.S. Criminal Section 254), 2007.

11. William Wan, "Snipers to Be Tried in Maryland," *Baltimore Sun* (May 11, 2005), 1A.

12. *Jones v. United States,* 137 U.S. 202 (1890).

13. Pub. L. No. 108-21, 117 Stat. 650 (2003).

14. 18 U.S.C. Section 2423(c) (2005).

15. William Finnegan, "Silver or Lead," *The New Yorker* (May 31, 2010), 46.

16. Alexander Hamilton, *Federalist Paper* No. 78, in *The Federalist Papers,* ed. Clinton Rossiter (New York: New American Library, 1961), 467–470.

17. G. Edward White, *History of the Supreme Court,* vols. 3–4: *The Marshall Court and Cultural Change* (New York: Oxford University Press, 1988), 157–200.

18. 372 U.S. 335 (1963).

19. 384 U.S. 436 (1966).

20. 408 U.S. 238 (1972).

21. 428 U.S. 153 (1976).

22. 18 U.S.C. Section 48 (1999).

23. *United States v. Stevens,* 559 U.S. _____ (2010).

24. 559 U.S. _____ (2010).

25. Carl Milazzo, "Searching Cell Phones Incident to Arrest: 2009," *The Police Chief* (May 2009), 12.

26. Barry R. Schaller, *A Vision of American Law: Judging Law, Literature, and the Stories We Tell* (Westport, CT: Praeger, 1997).

27. Harlington Wood, Jr., "Judiciary Reform: Recent Improvements in Federal Judicial Administration," *American University Law Review* 44 (June 1995), 1557.

28. Pub. L. No. 76-299, 53 Stat. 1223, codified as amended at 28 U.S.C. Sections 601–610 (1988 & Supp. V 1993).

29. Patrick Emery Longan, "Judicial Professionalism in a New Era of Judicial Selection," *Mercer Law Review* (Spring 2005), 913.

30. Andrew F. Hanssen, "Learning about Judicial Independence: Institutional Change in the State Courts," *Journal of Legal Studies* (2004), 431–474.

31. Brian P. Anderson, "Judicial Elections in West Virginia," *West Virginia Law Review* (Fall 2004), 243.

32. Richard Davis, *Electing Justice: Fixing the Supreme Court Nomination Process* (New York: Oxford University Press, 2005), 6–9.

33. Daniel R. Deja, "How Judges Are Selected: A Survey of the Judicial Selection Process in the United States," *Michigan Bar Journal* 75 (September 1996), 904.

34. Edmund V. Ludwig, "Another Case against the Election of Trial Judges," *Pennsylvania Lawyer* 19 (May/June 1997), 33.

35. "Fair and Independent Courts: A Conference on the State of the Judiciary," *Georgetown Law Journal* (April 2007), 1104.

36. David K. Scott, "Zero-Sum Judicial Elections: Balancing Free Speech and Impartiality through Recusal Reform," *Brigham Young University Law Review* (2009), 481, 485.

37. James E. Lozier, "The Missouri Plan a.k.a. Merit Selection Is the Best Solution for Selecting Michigan's Judges," *Michigan Bar Journal* 75 (September 1996), 918.

38. John Gardiner, "Preventing Judicial Misconduct: Defining the Role of Conduct Organizations," *Judicature* 70 (1986), 113–121.

39. Richard A. Watson and Rondal G. Downing, *The Politics of the Bench and Bar: Judicial Selection under the Missouri Nonpartisan Court Plan* (New York: John Wiley & Sons, 1969).

40. Quoted in Robert Hehre, "League Looks to Diversify Courts," *The Post and Courier (Charleston, SC)* (October 4, 2010), at **www.postandcourier.com/news/2010/oct/04/league-looks-to-diversify-courts**.

41. Ciara Torres-Spelliscy, Monique Chase, and Emma Greenman, *Improving Judicial Diversity,* 2d ed. (New York: Brennan Center for Justice, 2010), 1.

42. Russell Wheeler, *The Changing Face of the Federal Judiciary* (Washington, D.C.: The Brookings Institution, August 2009), Appendix table 1, page 11.

43. Edward M. Chen, "The Judiciary, Diversity, and Justice for All," *California Law Review* (July 2003), 1109.

44. Theresa B. Beiner, "The Elusive (but Worthwhile) Quest for a Diverse Bench in the New Millennium," *University of California at Davis Law Review* (February 2003), 599.

45. Sherrilyn A. Ifill, "Racial Diversity on the Bench: Beyond Role Models and Public Confidence," *Washington and Lee Law Review* (Spring 2000), 405.

46. David W. Neubauer, *America's Courts and the Criminal Justice System,* 5th ed. (Belmont, CA: Wadsworth Publishing Co., 1996), 41.

47. Alissa P. Worden, "The Judge's Role in Plea Bargaining: An Analysis of Judges' Agreement with Prosecutors' Sentencing Recommendations," *Justice Quarterly* 10 (1995), 257–278.

48. Kimberly Jade Norwood, "Shopping for Venue: The Need for More Limits," *University of Miami Law Review* 50 (1996), 295–298.

49. State Court Statistics Project, *State Court Caseload Statistics: An Analysis of 2008 State Court Caseloads* (National Center for State Courts, 2010), Table 1, pages 44-45.

50. Robert C. Boruchowitz, Malia N. Brink, and Maureen Dimino, *Minor Crimes, Massive Waste* (Washington, D.C.: National Association of Criminal Defense Lawyers, April 2009), 32.

51. United States Courts, "Judicial Caseload Indicators," at **www.uscourts.gov/Viewer.aspx?doc=/uscourts/Statistics/FederalJudicialCaseloadStatistics/2010/front/IndicatorsMar10.pdf**.

52. Amanda Lee Myers, "Courts Need $40 Million for Obama's Border Plan," *Houston Chronicle* (June 30, 2010), A6.

53. *2004 Annual Report to the Director* (Washington, D.C.: The Administrative Office of the U.S. Courts, 2005), 3.

54. Malcom Feeley, *Felony Arrests: Their Prosecutions and Disposition in New York Courts* (New York: Vera Institute, 1981), xii.

55. FactCheck.org, "Court Watch: Mudfest 2010 (October 29, 2010), at **www.factcheck.org/2010/10/court-watch-mudfest-2010**.

56. *Ibid.*

57. Quoted in Daniel Burke, "Code of Judicial Conduct Canon 7B(1)(c): Toward the Proper Regulation of Speech in Judicial Campaigns," *Georgetown Journal of Legal Ethics* 81 (Summer 1993), 181.

58. Martin J. Siegel, "In Defense of Judicial Election (Sort Of)," *Litigation* (Summer 2010), 24–25.

59. Owen Fiss, "The Right Degree of Independence," in *The Law As It Could Be* (New York: New York University Press, 2003), 61.

60. Justice at Stake Campaign, "Justice at Stake—State Judges Frequency Questionnaire" (2002), at **www.justiceatstake.org/media/cms/JASJudgesSurveyResults_EA8838C0504A5.pdf**.

61. Referenced in Thomas J. Moyer, "Commission on the 21st Century Judiciary," *Akron Law Review* (2005), 556.

62. William Ballenger, "In Judicial Wilderness, Even Brickley's Not Safe," *Michigan Politics* 28 (1996), 1–3.

63. *Model Code of Judicial Conduct,* Canon 3(E)(1) (2007).

CHAPTER

9

Pretrial Procedures

The Adversary System in Action

AP Photo/Francisco Kjolseth, Pool

LEARNING OBJECTIVES

After reading this chapter, you should be able to ...

LO 1 List the different names given to public prosecutors and indicate the general powers that they have.

LO 2 Contrast the prosecutor's roles as an elected official and as a crime fighter.

LO 3 Delineate the responsibilities of defense attorneys.

LO 4 Indicate the three types of defense allocation programs.

LO 5 List the three basic features of an adversary system of justice.

LO 6 Identify the steps involved in the pretrial criminal process.

LO 7 Indicate the three influences on a judge's decision to set bail.

LO 8 Explain how a prosecutor screens potential cases.

LO 9 Indicate the ways that both defense attorneys and prosecutors can induce plea bargaining.

The nine learning objectives labeled LO 1 through LO 9 are designed to help improve your understanding of the chapter.

TO SLEEP NO MORE

Michael Jackson, like many who suffer from insomnia, would ask for some milk when he had trouble sleeping. But, the famous pop singer was not referring to the nutritious liquid that comes from cows. Rather, he wanted a dose of a white solution called *propofol,* a powerful anesthetic used to render patients unconscious during surgery. For six weeks in the spring and summer of 2009, Dr. Conrad Murray, Jackson's personal physician, administered propofol to the singer daily, despite growing concerns that his patient was addicted to the drug. On the morning of June 25, Murray tried to help Jackson sleep using milder sedatives. When that did not work, Jackson again demanded his "milk," and Murray again provided it. Within twelve minutes, the fifty-year-old singer was dead.

Murray initially informed paramedics that he had given Jackson only one sedative—the antianxiety drug lorazepam—and failed to mention anything about propofol. "That [was] a telling omission," said Dr. Bryan A. Liang, a physician and professor at San Diego's California Western School of Law. "He knows he is not supposed to be fooling around with propofol." Because the drug is so powerful, it is generally used only in a hospital setting, where heart monitors and breathing machines can deal with any unexpected side effects. Furthermore, noted another expert, "The concept of using propofol for insomnia is completely crazy. It's like trying to swat a fly with a bomb."

On February 9, 2010, about five months after the Los Angeles County coroner ruled that Jackson died of "acute propofol intoxication," Murray was arrested and charged with involuntary manslaughter. The exact language of the criminal complaint contended that the physician "did unlawfully, and without malice, kill Michael Joseph Jackson" by acting "without due caution." After watching Murray plead not guilty to the manslaughter charge, Joe Jackson, the singer's father, gave his own verdict on what had happened: "My son was murdered."

In 2010, Dr. Conrad Murray, left, was arrested and charged with involuntary manslaughter for providing Michael Jackson with the drugs that led to the pop singer's death.
Irfan Khan/
Reuters/Landov

The police had done their job. They had investigated the circumstances surrounding Michael Jackson's death, interviewed those involved, and recorded the results. Now, the case was in the hands of the lawyers, who got their first chance to square off at a *preliminary hearing* before Judge Michael Pastor in the Los Angeles County Superior Court in early January 2011. As you will learn later in this chapter, the preliminary hearing is designed so that a judge can decide whether enough evidence exists for a case to go to trial. In general, a preliminary hearing is short. It features few, if any, witnesses and has almost a routine feel.

There was nothing routine about this particular pretrial hearing, though. Over the course of six days, Deputy District Attorney David Walgren summoned twenty-two witnesses to show that "[b]ecause of Dr. Murray's actions, Michael's children are left without a father."[1] Joseph Low IV, Murray's defense attorney, dismissed the parade of accusers, hinting that Jackson self-medicated himself to the point of overdose.[2] Eventually, Low asked Pastor to dismiss the charges, arguing that the prosecution had failed to conclusively link Jackson's death to his client's actions. The judge refused, ruling that there was sufficient evidence to try Murray for involuntary manslaughter, the crime for which, in November 2011, he was convicted and sentenced to four years in prison.

"Dueling lawyers" such as Walgren and Low are the main combatants of the American adversary system. Contrary to public perception, however, these struggles start well before the beginning of the criminal trial. Indeed, cases rarely make it as far as trial. Instead, the issue of guilt and innocence is usually settled beforehand through the efforts of the legal representatives of the state and the defendant. Thus, we will start this chapter—which focuses on "negotiated justice"—with a discussion of these key players: the prosecutor and the defense attorney.

THE PROSECUTION

Criminal cases are tried by **public prosecutors,** who are employed by the government. The public prosecutor in federal criminal cases is called a U.S. attorney. In cases tried in state or local courts, the public prosecutor may be referred to as a *prosecuting attorney, state prosecutor, district attorney, county attorney,* or *city attorney.* Given their great auton-

LO 1 omy, prosecutors are generally considered the most dominant figures in the American criminal justice system. In some jurisdictions, the district attorney is the chief law enforcement officer, with broad powers over police operations. Prosecutors have the power to bring the resources of the state against the individual and hold the legal keys to meting out or withholding punishment.[3] Ideally, this power is balanced by a duty of fairness and a recognition that the prosecutor's ultimate goal is not to win cases, but to see that justice is done. In *Berger v. United States* (1935), Justice George Sutherland called the prosecutor

> in a peculiar and very definite sense the servant of the law, the twofold aim of which is that guilt shall not escape or innocence suffer. He may prosecute with earnestness and vigor— indeed, he should do so. But, while he may strike hard blows, he is not at liberty to strike foul ones. It is as much his duty to refrain from improper methods calculated to produce a wrongful conviction as it is to use every legitimate means to bring about a just one.[4]

THE OFFICE OF THE PROSECUTOR

When he or she is acting as an *officer of the law* during a criminal trial, there are limits on the prosecutor's conduct, as we shall see in the next chapter. During the pretrial process, however, prosecutors hold a great deal of discretion in deciding the following:

1. Whether an individual who has been arrested by the police will be charged with a crime.
2. The level of the charges to be brought against the suspect.
3. If and when to stop the prosecution.[5]

There are more than eight thousand prosecutor's offices around the country, serving state, county, and municipal jurisdictions. Even though the **attorney general** is the chief law enforcement officer in any state, she or he has limited (and in some states, no) control over prosecutors within the state's boundaries.

Each jurisdiction has a chief prosecutor, who is sometimes appointed but more often elected. As an elected official, he or she typically serves a four-year term, though in some states, such as Alabama, the term is six years. In smaller jurisdictions, the chief prosecutor has several assistants, and they work closely together. In larger ones, the chief prosecutor may have numerous *assistant prosecutors,* many of whom he or she rarely meets. Assistant prosecutors—for the most part, young attorneys recently graduated from law school—may be assigned to particular sections of the organization, such as criminal prosecutions in general or areas of *special prosecution,* such as narcotics or gang crimes. (See Figure 9.1 on the next page for the structure of a typical prosecutor's office.)

Public Prosecutors Individuals, acting as trial lawyers, who initiate and conduct cases in the government's name and on behalf of the people.

Attorney General The chief law officer of a state; also, the chief law officer of the nation.

Teaching Tip: If possible, invite a local prosecutor to visit your classroom. Ask him or her to describe a typical work day. What does he or she find most rewarding about a career as a prosecutor?

Discussion Tip: Have students debate the advantages and disadvantages of prosecutorial discretion. Should the ability to decide which cases to bring to trial be limited more stringently than is presently the case? What checks and balances are in place to ensure that prosecutors do not abuse their discretion?

FIGURE 9.1 **The Baltimore City State's Attorney's Office**

*F.I.V.E. is an acronym for "Firearms Investigation Violence Enforcement."
Source: Baltimore City State's Attorney's Office.

THE PROSECUTOR AS ELECTED OFFICIAL

The chief prosecutor's autonomy is not absolute. As an elected official, she or he must answer to the voters. (There are exceptions: U.S. attorneys are nominated by the president and approved by the Senate, and chief prosecutors in Alaska, Connecticut, New Jersey, Rhode Island, and the District of Columbia are either appointed or hired as members of the attorney general's office.) The prosecutor may be part of the political machine. In many jurisdictions, the prosecutor must declare a party affiliation and is expected to reward fellow party members with positions in the district attorney's office if elected.

The post is often seen as a "stepping-stone" to higher political office, and many prosecutors have gone on to serve in legislatures or as judges. Sonia Sotomayor (see the photo on the facing page), the first Hispanic member of the United States Supreme Court, started her legal career in 1979 as an assistant district attorney in New York City. While at that job, she first came to public attention by helping to prosecute the "Tarzan Murderer," an athletic criminal responsible for at least twenty burglaries and four killings.

Discussion Tip: Have students debate the pros and cons of electing, rather than appointing, chief prosecutors. (LO 2)

LO 2
Just as judicial elections can raise concerns that judges' decisions may be influenced by politics, as we discussed in the previous chapter, the specter of an upcoming election can cast doubt on the impartiality of a prosecutor's decisions. For example, Spokane County (Washington) prosecutor Steve Tucker found himself in a difficult situation just months before facing the voters in November 2010. That August, sheriff's deputy Brian Hirzel had fatally shot an elderly pastor, Wayne Scott Creach, on Creach's property. If Tucker charged Hirzel in Creach's death, he would lose the support of Spokane's law enforcement community in the upcoming election.

If Tucker did not charge Hirzel, he would be criticized for failing to hold the police accountable for their actions. Despite mounting pressure from the community, Tucker did not announce his decision until after he was reelected by a narrow margin. Then, in January 2011, Tucker declined to prosecute Hirzel, citing a lack of evidence that the deputy acted with an evil intent.[6]

THE PROSECUTOR AS CRIME FIGHTER

Critical Thinking Skill Development: In a written assignment, ask student to respond to "Questions for Critical Analysis" number one on page 315, in which they consider the consequences for prosecutorial misconduct.

One of the reasons the prosecutor's post is a useful first step in a political career is that it is linked to crime fighting. Thanks to savvy public relations efforts and television police dramas such as *Law & Order*—with its opening line, "In the criminal justice system, the people are represented by two separate yet equally important groups: the police who investigate crime and the district attorneys who prosecute the offenders"—prosecutors are generally seen as law enforcement agents. Indeed, the prosecutors and the police do have a symbiotic relationship. Prosecutors rely on police to arrest suspects and gather sufficient evidence, and police rely on prosecutors to convict those who have been apprehended.

POLICE-PROSECUTOR CONFLICT Despite, or perhaps because of, this mutual dependency, the relationship between the two branches of law enforcement is often strained. Part of this can be attributed to different backgrounds. Most prosecutors come from middle- or upper-class families, while police are often recruited from the working class. Furthermore, prosecutors are required to have a level of education that is not attained by most police officers.

More important, however, is a basic divergence in the concept of guilt. For a police officer, a suspect is guilty if he or she has in fact committed a crime. For a prosecutor, a suspect is guilty if enough evidence can be legally gathered to prove such guilt in a court of law. In other words, police officers often focus on *factual guilt*, whereas prosecutors are ultimately concerned with *legal guilt*.[7] Thus, police officers will feel a great deal of frustration when a suspect they "know" to be guilty is set free. Similarly, a prosecutor may become annoyed when police officers do not follow the letter of the law in gathering evidence, thereby greatly reducing the chances of conviction.

ATTEMPTS AT COOPERATION Tension arising from these grievances can hamper crime control efforts. As a result, a number of jurisdictions are trying to achieve better police-prosecutor relations. A key step in the process seems to be improving communications between the two groups. In San Diego, for example, the district attorney has a permanent office in the police department for the express purpose of counseling officers on legal questions. From the office, a deputy district attorney (DDA) acts as a human legal reference book, advising police officers on how to write a search warrant, what steps they can take to help solidify a prosecutor's case, and other issues. The DDA will even sit in on morning briefings, giving updates on how changes in the law may affect police work.

Give several reasons why experience as a prosecutor would make someone such as United States Supreme Court justice Sonia Sotomayor a more effective judge.
AP Photo/Pablo Martinez Monsivais

SELFASSESSMENT

Fill in the blanks and check your answers on page 315.
Public prosecutors initiate and conduct cases on behalf of the _____ against the defendant. During the pretrial process, prosecutors must decide whether to _____ an individual with a particular crime. Ideally, a prosecutor's ultimate goal is not to _____ cases, but rather to see _____ done.

THE DEFENSE ATTORNEY

The media provide most people's perception of defense counsel: the idealistic public defender who nobly serves the poor, the "ambulance chaser," or the celebrity attorney in the $3,000 suit. These stereotypes, though not entirely fictional, tend to obscure the crucial role that the **defense attorney** plays in the criminal justice system. Most persons charged with crimes have little or no knowledge of criminal procedure. Without assistance, they would be helpless in court. By acting as a staunch advocate for her or his client, the defense attorney (ideally) ensures that the government proves every point against that client beyond a reasonable doubt, even for cases that do not go to trial. In sum, the defense attorney provides a counterweight against the state in our adversary system. (See the feature *Myth versus Reality—Are Fingerprint Matches Foolproof?* on the next page to learn more about how defense attorneys fight for their clients.)

Defense Attorney The lawyer representing the defendant.

MYTH vs. REALITY   Are Fingerprint Matches Foolproof?

For nearly a century, police and prosecutors have relied on fingerprint evidence as a powerful tool to link suspects to crimes. Today, however, defense attorneys are challenging this traditional weapon of forensic science, saying that it is not really "science" at all.

THE MYTH No two fingerprints are alike. Therefore, when law enforcement agents match a print taken from a crime scene to a print from a suspect, the suspect must have been at the crime scene.

THE REALITY When forensic scientists compare a fingerprint lifted from a crime scene with one taken from a suspect, they are looking for points of similarity. These experts will usually declare a match if the two samples show between eight and sixteen points of similarity. Many defense attorneys claim that this method is flawed, however.

First, prints found at crime scenes tend to be incomplete, which means that examiners generally compare fragments of fingerprints rather than whole fingerprints. Two fingerprints that clearly are not alike when viewed in their entirety may appear to be identical when only fragments are compared. Second, fingerprint evidence found at crime scenes requires ultraviolet light to make it clear enough to process. Is it scientifically acceptable to compare this "altered" print with a "clean" one obtained from a suspect in controlled circumstances?

An internal audit by the Federal Bureau of Investigation (FBI) found a 0.8 percent error rate for fingerprint matches—a seemingly small number, until one realizes that crime labs handle about 250,000 latent print analyses each year. Thus, there could be as many as 2,000 false matches annually.

Consequently, the FBI decided to review the cases of all state and federal prisoners scheduled for execution whose convictions were based on testimony by its fingerprint examiners. The procedure's credibility was further damaged in 2009, when the National Academy of Sciences released a report that found little established evidence for claims that fingerprint matching is infallible.

Citing this report, in 2010 federal judge Nancy Gertner suggested that all lawyers who appear before her should "vigorously" challenge fingerprint evidence. As might be expected, defense attorneys applauded Gertner's stance. Said one, "The stakes are too high in our society to be using junk science and putting it before juries which think that it's gold."

FOR CRITICAL ANALYSIS Given the strength of the perception that "no two fingerprints are alike," how might a defense attorney raise doubt in a judge's or juror's mind about testimony that a fingerprint lifted from a crime scene matches that of the defendant?

AP Photo/Toby Talbot

THE RESPONSIBILITIES OF THE DEFENSE ATTORNEY

The Sixth Amendment right to counsel is not limited to the actual criminal trial. In a number of instances, the United States Supreme Court has held that defendants are entitled to representation as soon as their rights may be denied, which, as we have seen, includes the custodial interrogation and lineup identification procedures.[8] Therefore, an important responsibility of the defense attorney is to represent the defendant at the various stages of the custodial process, such as arrest, interrogation, lineup, and arraignment. Other responsibilities include:

LO 3

- Investigating the incident for which the defendant has been charged.
- Communicating with the prosecutor, which includes negotiating plea bargains.

- Preparing the case for trial.
- Submitting defense motions, including motions to suppress evidence.
- Representing the defendant at trial.
- Negotiating a sentence, if the client has been convicted.
- Determining whether to appeal a guilty verdict.[9]

DEFENDING THE GUILTY

At one time or another in their careers, all defense attorneys will face a difficult question: Must I defend a client whom I know to be guilty? According to the American Bar Association's code of legal ethics, the answer is almost always, "yes."[10] The most important responsibility of the criminal defense attorney is to be an advocate for her or his client. As such, the attorney is obligated to use all ethical and legal means to achieve the client's desired goal, which is usually to avoid or lessen punishment for the charged crime.

As Supreme Court justice Byron White once noted, defense counsel has no "obligation to ascertain or present the truth." Rather, our adversarial system insists that the defense attorney "defend the client whether he is innocent or guilty."[11] Indeed, if defense attorneys refused to represent clients whom they believed to be guilty, the Sixth Amendment guarantee of a criminal trial for all accused persons would be rendered meaningless.

> **"Look at the stakes. In civil law, if you screw up, it's just money. Here, it's the client—his life, his time in jail—and you never know how much time people have in their life."**
>
> **—Stacey Richman**
> Criminal defense attorney

THE PUBLIC DEFENDER

Generally speaking, there are two different types of defense attorneys: (1) private attorneys, who are hired by individuals, and (2) **public defenders,** who work for the government. The distinction is not absolute, as many private attorneys accept employment as public defenders, too. The modern role of the public defender was established by the Supreme Court's interpretation of the Sixth Amendment in *Gideon v. Wainwright* (1963).[12]

In that case, the Court ruled that no defendant can be "assured a fair trial unless counsel is provided for him," and therefore the state must provide a public defender to those who cannot afford to hire one for themselves. Subsequently, the Court extended this protection to juveniles in *In re Gault* (1967)[13] and those faced with imprisonment for committing misdemeanors in *Argersinger v. Hamlin* (1972).[14] The impact of these decisions has been substantial: about 90 percent of all criminal defendants in the United States are represented by public defenders or other appointed counsel.[15]

ELIGIBILITY ISSUES Although the Supreme Court's *Gideon* decision obligated the government to provide attorneys for poor defendants, it offered no guidance on just how poor the defendant needs to be to qualify for a public defender. In theory, counsel should be provided for those who are unable to hire an attorney themselves without "substantial hardship."[16] In reality, each jurisdiction has its own guidelines, and a defendant refused counsel in one area might be entitled to it in another. A judge in Kittitas County, Washington, to give an extreme example, frequently denies public counsel for college student defendants. This judge believes that any person who chooses to go to school rather than work automatically falls outside the *Gideon* case's definition of indigence.[17]

DEFENSE COUNSEL PROGRAMS In most areas, the county government is responsible for providing indigent defendants with attorneys. Three basic types of programs are used to allocate defense counsel:

Public Defenders Court-appointed attorneys who are paid by the state to represent defendants who are unable to hire private counsel.

Critical Thinking Skill Development: Ask students if they believe that defendants with public defenders are at a disadvantage during the criminal justice process. Is it possible for defendants to "buy" their freedom by hiring private defense counsel?

Teaching Tip: In a written assignment, ask students to respond to "Questions for Critical Analysis" number two on page 315, in which they consider the *Gideon* decision.

CAREERS IN CJ

ANNIKA CARLSTEN
PUBLIC DEFENDER

For me, things started during law school with an internship at Amnesty International, profiling juvenile death penalty cases. This led to work on adult death penalty cases. The vast majority of people sentenced to death in America are represented by public defenders, and I developed a great deal of respect for the nature and importance of the work. So when I finished law school, public defense was the natural choice.

EMOTIONAL INVESTMENTS My very first day on the job, I watched another attorney conduct *voir dire* (see page 327) on a domestic violence assault. I wondered if I would ever be that comfortable and confident in court. Many years later, the cases have started to blur in my memory. That said, I will always remember my very first "not guilty" verdict. I was utterly convinced of my client's innocence, and very emotionally invested in winning the case for him. At the other end of the spectrum, I will never forget having to explain court proceedings to a man only hours after he accidentally shot and killed his child. Nothing in law school prepares you for that conversation. Nothing in life prepares you for that conversation.

JUSTICE FOR ALL The modern court system is heavily geared toward plea bargaining and negotiations, and I love the challenge of being creative within an otherwise rigid system. I love coming up with an alternative resolution that addresses the legal concerns without dehumanizing my client. Some days that can be as small as helping with a letter of apology, or making sure the court takes the time to really hear my client's side of the story. Other days it may mean negotiating a plea deal that is the difference between my client being allowed to stay in this country and being deported.

Most of all, I believe passionately in the idea of what I do, in the principle of equal justice for everyone, regardless of money or circumstance. On a good day, I see that ideal fulfilled. On a great day, I feel like I personally have done something to make it so.

CAREER ADVICE First of all, study everything you can about all sides of the criminal justice story. Thinking like a prosecutor or a police officer helps me see the weaknesses in my case, and in theirs. Read the stories of great defense heroes—listen to their words, and draw inspiration from their passion. Study theater, music, and dance; do whatever it takes to become comfortable in front of a crowd. Don't expect to learn everything in law school. Real life experience is crucial—spend time working within the population you want to represent. You can't effectively represent someone who doesn't trust you, and you can't build a rapport with clients if you don't appreciate the day-to-day realities of their life.

Most importantly, don't be discouraged by people who ask, "How can you defend those people?" Never lose sight of the fact that you are part of a much bigger picture. We are privileged to live in a society of laws, and everyone—everyone, no matter what—is entitled to the presumption of innocence. That presumption is meaningless without public defenders to hold the government accountable.

FASTFACTS

PUBLIC DEFENDER JOB DESCRIPTION:

- Interview low-income applicants for legal services; advise and counsel individuals and groups regarding their legal rights; handle a reasonable caseload; and, where necessary, engage in the negotiation, trial, and/or appeal of legal issues that have a substantial impact on the rights of eligible clients.

- Exercise initiative, sound judgment, and creativity in attempting to solve the legal problems of the poor.

- Engage in outreach and education in the community.

WHAT KIND OF TRAINING IS REQUIRED?

- A law degree and membership in the relevant state bar association.

- Commitment and dedication to the needs of low-income and elderly clients.

ANNUAL SALARY RANGE?

- $44,000–$92,000

For additional information on a career as a public defender, visit: **www.nlada.org/Jobs**.

1. *Assigned counsel programs,* in which local private attorneys are assigned clients on a case-by-case basis by the county.

LO 4

2. *Contracting attorney programs,* in which a particular law firm or group of attorneys is hired to regularly assume the representative and administrative tasks of indigent defense.

3. *Public defender programs,* in which the county assembles a salaried staff of full-time or part-time attorneys and creates a public (taxpayer-funded) agency to provide services.[18]

Much to the surprise of many indigent defendants, these programs are not entirely without cost. Government agencies can charge fees for "free" legal counsel when the fees will not impose a "significant legal financial hardship" on the defendant. Today, more than 80 percent of all local public defender offices charge some form of so-called cost recoupment.[19] Florida, North Carolina, and Virginia have mandatory public defender fees, meaning that judges cannot waive such costs under any circumstances. In Virginia, indigent defendants may be charged up to $1,235 per count for certain felonies.[20]

EFFECTIVENESS OF PUBLIC DEFENDERS Under the U.S. Constitution, a defendant who is paying for her or his defense attorney has a right to choose that attorney without interference from the court.[21] This right of choice does not extend to indigent defendants. According to the United States Supreme Court, "a defendant may not insist on an attorney he cannot afford."[22] In other words, an indigent defendant must accept the public defender provided by the court system. (Note that, unless the presiding judge rules otherwise, a person can waive her or his Sixth Amendment rights and act as her or his own defense attorney.) This lack of control contributes to the widespread belief that public defenders do not provide an acceptable level of defense to indigents.

Statistics show, however, that conviction rates of defendants with private counsel and those represented by publicly funded attorneys are generally the same. The difference comes during sentencing, when a higher percentage of defendants with public defenders are sent to prison.[23]

Unreasonable Caseloads For a month in the summer of 2010, the public defender's office in Springfield, Missouri, closed its doors to new clients. Local judges, who assign indigent defendants to the office, reacted with harsh criticism. "It flies in the face of our Constitution," said one.[24] The public defenders countered that their high caseloads and low staff levels were making it impossible for them to provide constitutionally acceptable levels of service to their clients. According to a report commissioned by the state bar, "Missouri's public defender system has reached a point where what it provides is often nothing more than the illusion of a lawyer."[25]

The American Bar Association recommends that a public defender handle no more than 150 felony cases and 400 misdemeanor cases each year. Nationwide, about three-quarters of all county-based public defender programs exceed these limits.[26] In Minnesota, for example, each public defender averages about 300 felony cases and 760 misdemeanor cases annually.[27] Public defenders in Arizona, Florida, Kentucky, Maryland, Minnesota, and Tennessee have also reacted to high caseloads by limiting new clients. Several years ago, New York City lawmakers passed a law that caps the number of criminal cases for court-appointed

Group Activities: Place students in groups and ask them to research indigent defense counsel programs in your area. What type of programs are used to allocate defense counsel locally? (LO 4)

The **National Association of Criminal Defense Lawyers** represents more than ten thousand lawyers and advocates on a number of issues relating to the criminal justice system. To find its Web site, visit the *Criminal Justice CourseMate* at **cengagebrain.com** and select the *Web links* for this chapter.

"If you are the average poor person, you are going to be herded through the criminal justice system about like an animal is herded through the stockyards."

—Stephen Bright, director of the Southern Center for Human Rights

lawyers.[28] Supporters expressed hope that the legislation would serve as a model to alleviate oppressive client caseloads plaguing public defenders throughout the country.

The Strickland Standard In one Louisiana murder trial, not only did the court-appointed defense attorney spend only eleven minutes preparing for trial on a charge that carries a mandatory life sentence, but she also represented the victim's father and had been representing the victim at the time of his death. Not surprisingly, her defendant was found guilty.[29] Such behavior raises a critical question: When a lawyer does such a poor job, has the client essentially been denied his or her Sixth Amendment right to assistance of counsel? In *Strickland v. Washington* (1984),[30] the Supreme Court set up a two-pronged test to determine whether constitutional requirements have been met. To prove that prior counsel was not sufficient, a defendant must show (1) that the attorney's performance was deficient *and* (2) that this deficiency *more likely than not* caused the defendant to lose the case.

In practice, it has been very difficult to prove the second prong of this test. A prosecutor can always argue that the defendant would have lost the case even if his or her lawyer had not been inept. Several years ago, for example, the U.S. Court of Appeals for the Sixth Circuit declined to overturn the death sentence of Jeffrey Leonard even though his public defender's investigation of the case was so superficial that it did not even uncover Leonard's real name (see the photo alongside). Despite the court's finding that the public defender's performance was so lax as to violate the Constitution, it held that the evidence against Leonard was strong enough that he would have suffered the same fate even if he had enjoyed the services of a relatively competent defense attorney.[31]

THE ATTORNEY-CLIENT RELATIONSHIP

The implied trust between an attorney and her or his client usually is not in question when the attorney has been hired directly by the defendant—as an "employee," the attorney well understands her or his duties. Relationships between public defenders and their clients, however, are often marred by suspicion on both sides. As Northwestern University professor Jonathan D. Casper discovered while interviewing indigent defendants, many of them feel a certain amount of respect for the prosecutor. Like police officers, prosecutors are just "doing their job" by trying to convict the defendant. In contrast, the defendants' view of their own attorneys can be summed up in the following exchange between Casper and a defendant:

> Did you have a lawyer when you went to court the next morning?
> No, I had a public defender.[32]

This attitude is somewhat understandable. Given the caseloads that most public defenders carry, they may have as little as five or ten minutes to spend with a client before appearing in front of a judge. How much, realistically, can a public defender learn about the defendant in that time? Furthermore, the defendant is well aware that the public defender is being paid by the same source as the prosecutor and the judge. "Because you're part of the system, your indigent client doesn't trust you," admitted one court-appointed attorney.[33]

The situation handcuffs the public defenders as well. With so little time to spend on each case, they cannot validate the information provided by their clients. If the defendant says he or she has no prior offenses, the public defender often has no choice but to believe the client. Consequently, many public defenders later find that their clients have

Why did a court of appeals uphold the death sentence of Jeffrey Leonard, shown here, even though his public defender was so incompetent as to be unaware of Leonard's true name?
AP Photo/Kentucky State Dept. of Corrections

deceived them. Along with the high pressures of the job, a client's lack of cooperation and disrespect can limit whatever satisfaction a public defender may find in the profession.

ATTORNEY-CLIENT PRIVILEGE

To defend a client effectively, a defense attorney must have access to all the facts concerning the case, even those that may be harmful to the defendant. To promote the unrestrained flow of information between the two parties, legislatures and lawyers themselves have constructed rules of **attorney-client privilege.** These rules require that communications between a client and his or her attorney be kept confidential, unless the client consents to the disclosure.

THE PRIVILEGE AND CONFESSIONS Attorney-client privilege does not stop short of confessions.[34] Indeed, if, on hearing any statement that points toward guilt, the defense attorney could alert the prosecution or try to resign from the case, attorney-client privilege would be rendered meaningless. Even if the client says, "I have just killed seventeen women. I selected only pregnant women so I could torture them and kill two people at once. I did it. I liked it. I enjoyed it," the defense attorney must continue to do his or her utmost to serve that client.[35]

Without attorney-client privilege, observes legal expert John Kaplan, lawyers would be forced to give their clients the equivalent of the *Miranda* warning before representing them.[36] In other words, lawyers would have to make clear what clients could or could not say in the course of preparing for trial, because any incriminating statement might be used against the client in court. Such a development would have serious ramifications for the criminal justice system.

THE EXCEPTION TO THE PRIVILEGE The scope of attorney-client privilege is not all encompassing. In *United States v. Zolin* (1989),[37] the Supreme Court ruled that lawyers may disclose the contents of a conversation with a client if the client has provided information concerning a crime that has yet to be committed. This exception applies only to communications involving a crime that is ongoing or will occur in the future. If the client reveals a past crime, the privilege is still in effect, and the attorney may not reveal any details of that particular criminal act. (To learn more about the difficult situations that result from attorney-client privilege, see the feature *A Question of Ethics—Keeping a Secret* on the following page.)

SELF ASSESSMENT

Fill in the blanks and check your answers on page 315.
The _____ Amendment states that every person accused of a crime has a right to counsel. There are two types of defense attorneys: (1) _____ attorneys hired by individuals and (2) _____ defenders, provided to _____ defendants by the government. Because of attorney-client _____, any admissions of guilt for past crimes that a client makes to her or his defense attorney are _____, unless the client _____ to their disclosure.

Defense attorney John Amabile makes a point on behalf of his client in a Woburn, Massachusetts, courtroom. Why are the rules of attorney-client privilege necessary for a defense attorney to properly do his or her job?
ZUMA Press/Newscom

Attorney-Client Privilege A rule of evidence requiring that communications between a client and his or her attorney be kept confidential, unless the client consents to disclosure.

Discussion Tip: Have students debate the value of attorney-client privilege. When does this privilege apply? When does it not apply? Are there additional circumstances under which students think the attorney-client privilege should be void?

TRUTH, VICTORY, AND THE ADVERSARY SYSTEM

Adversary System A legal system in which the prosecution and defense are opponents, or adversaries, and present their cases in the light most favorable to themselves. The court arrives at a just solution based on the evidence presented by the contestants and determines who wins and who loses.

In strictly legal terms, three basic features characterize the adversary system:

LO 5

1. A neutral and passive decision maker, either the judge or the jury.
2. The presentation of evidence from both parties.
3. A highly structured set of procedures (in the form of constitutional safeguards) that must be followed in the presentation of that evidence.[38]

Some critics of the American court system believe that it has been tainted by overzealous prosecutors and defense attorneys. Gordon Van Kessel, a professor at Hastings College of Law in California, complains that American lawyers see themselves as "prize fighters, gladiators, or, more accurately, semantic warriors in a verbal battle," and bemoans the atmosphere of "ritualized aggression" that exists in the courts.[39]

Our discussion of the courtroom work group in the last chapter, however, seems to contradict this image of "ritualized aggression." As political scientists Herbert Jacob and James Eisenstein have written, "pervasive conflict is not only unpleasant; it also makes work more difficult."[40] The image of the courtroom work group as "negotiators" rather than "prize fighters" seems to be supported by the fact that more than nine out of every ten cases conclude with negotiated "deals" rather than trials. Jerome Skolnick of the University of California at Berkeley found that work group members grade each other according to "reasonableness"[41]—a concept criminal justice scholar Abraham S. Blumberg embellished by labeling the defense attorney a "double agent." Blumberg believed that a defense attorney is likely to cooperate with the prosecutor in convincing a client to accept a negotiated plea of guilty because the defense attorney's main object is to finish the case quickly so as to collect the fee and move on.[42]

Perhaps, then, the most useful definition of the adversary process tempers Professor Van Kessel's criticism with the realities of the courtroom work group. University of California at Berkeley law professor Malcolm Feeley observes:

A QUESTION OF ETHICS: *Keeping a Secret*

THE SITUATION Factory manager Leo Frank is arrested for raping and killing a young woman named Mary Phagan with whom he worked. Frank is convicted of murder and sentenced to life behind bars. After Frank is imprisoned, a client of attorney Arthur Powell admits to Powell that he, and not Frank, killed Phagan.

THE ETHICAL DILEMMA According to the rules of attorney-client privilege, a defense attorney has an ethical duty *not* to reveal past crimes committed by a client if the client confesses to those crimes in confidence. Note, however, that in most instances an attorney does not face criminal penalties for breaking these rules. At most, an attorney who betrays the confidence of a client needs to worry about a civil lawsuit brought by the client and a reprimand from his or her state bar association (which could include the loss of the attorney's license to practice law in that state).

WHAT IS THE SOLUTION? Should Arthur Powell disclose his client's confession and possibly allow Leo Frank to go free? What are the arguments for and against taking this action? In the actual case, which occurred early in the twentieth century, Powell did not disclose his client's confession, and Frank was subsequently lynched by other inmates in prison. Afterward, an anguished Powell said, "I could not have revealed the information the client had given me in the confidential relationship without violating my oath as an attorney. Such is the law; I did not make the law, but it is my duty and the court's duty to obey the law, so long as it stands."

In the adversary system the goal of the advocate is not to determine truth but to win, to maximize the interests of his or her side within the confines of the norms governing the proceedings. This is not to imply that the theory of the adversary process has no concern for the truth. Rather, the underlying assumption of the adversary process is that truth is most likely to emerge as a by-product of vigorous conflict between intensely partisan advocates, each of whose goal is to win.[43]

Blumberg took a more cynical view when he called the court process a "confidence game" in which "victory" is achieved when a defense attorney—with the implicit aid of the prosecutor and judge—is able to persuade the defendant to plead guilty.[44] As you read the rest of the chapter, which deals with pretrial procedures, keep in mind Feeley's and Blumberg's contentions concerning "truth" and "victory" in the American courts.

Critical Thinking Skill Development: In a written assignment, have students respond to Feeley's assertion that in the adversary system the goal is "not to determine truth but to win." Do students agree with Feeley's assessment? Why or why not? (LO 5)

CJ&TECHNOLOGY Neurological Lie Detection

AP Photo/Cecil Whig, Matthew Given

Almost a hundred years ago, the *New York Times* predicted an end to the American adversary system. "There will be no jury, no horde of detectives and witnesses, no charges and countercharges, and no attorney for the defense," the newspaper stated. This prediction was a reaction to the invention of the polygraph, a lie detector that purports to read a subject's stress levels during questioning to ascertain if the answers are truthful. Today, though widely used in criminal investigations, polygraph results are inadmissible in criminal court and therefore have had minimal impact on the criminal justice system. Nevertheless, scientists have not given up the search for a reliable lie detector. The latest research has focused on neurotechnological lie detection (NTLD), particularly functional magnetic resonance imaging (fMRI) and functional near-infrared neuroimaging (fNIR). Both devices measure blood flow in the brain, on the assumption that we access certain parts of our brains when we lie. Although this theory has yet to be proved, many experts believe that NTLD has the potential to transform the American courtroom—eventually.

THINKING ABOUT NEUROTECHNOLOGICAL LIE DETECTION

In theory, lie detectors would be used primarily on defendants to determine whether they are telling the truth about alleged wrongdoing. But would NTLD, if proved effective, be limited to criminal suspects? How might the pressures of the adversary system tempt prosecutors and defense attorneys to distort the facts of a case?

PRETRIAL DETENTION

LO 6 After an arrest has been made, the first step toward determining the suspect's guilt or innocence is the initial appearance (for an overview of the entire process, see Figure 9.2 on the next page). During this brief proceeding, a magistrate (see Chapter 8) informs the defendant of the charges that have been brought against him or her and explains his or her constitutional rights—particularly, the right to remain silent (under the Fifth Amendment) and the right to be represented by counsel (under the Sixth Amendment). At this point, if the defendant cannot afford to hire a private attorney, a public

Initial Appearance An accused's first appearance before a judge or magistrate following arrest. During the appearance, the defendant is informed of the charges, advised of the right to counsel, told the amount of bail, and given a date for the preliminary hearing.

FIGURE 9.2 **The Steps Leading to a Trial**

Booking After arrest, at the police station, the suspect is searched, photographed, finger-printed, and allowed at least one telephone call. After the booking, charges are reviewed, and if they are not dropped, a complaint is filed and a judge or magistrate examines the case for probable cause.

Initial Appearance The suspect appears before the judge, who informs the suspect of the charges and of his or her rights. If the suspect requests a lawyer, one is appointed. The judge sets bail (conditions under which a suspect can obtain release pending disposition of the case).

Grand Jury A grand jury determines if there is probable cause to believe that the defendant committed the crime. The federal government and about one-third of the states require grand jury indictments for at least some felonies.

Preliminary Hearing A preliminary hearing is a court proceeding in which the prosecutor presents evidence and the judge determines whether there is probable cause to hold the defendant over for trial.

Indictment An indictment is the charging instrument issued by the grand jury.

Information An information is the charging instrument issued by the prosecutor.

Arraignment The suspect is brought before the trial court, informed of the charges, and asked to enter a plea.

Plea Bargain A plea bargain is a prosecutor's promise of concessions (or promise to seek concessions) in return for the defendant's guilty plea. Concessions include a reduced charge and/or a lesser sentence.

Guilty Plea In most jurisdictions, the majority of cases that reach the arraignment stage do not go to trial but are resolved by a guilty plea, often as the result of a plea bargain. The judge sets the case for sentencing.

Trial If the defendant refuses to plead guilty, he or she proceeds to either a jury trial (in most instances) or a bench trial.

Teaching Tip: Assign students to take a trip to the local courthouse and observe some portion of criminal pretrial proceedings. Ask each student to reflect on his or her visit in a reaction paper. Which part of the process (the initial appearance, the arraignment, and so on) did the student observe? How long did the hearing take and what was accomplished? (LO 6)

Discussion Tip: Ask students to debate the value of pretrial detention. Should the public's safety outweigh the personal liberty of individual defendants? Do defendants who find themselves detained prior to trial suffer any disadvantages when the trial begins?

defender may be appointed, or private counsel may be hired by the state to represent the defendant. As the U.S. Constitution does not specify how soon a defendant must be brought before a magistrate after arrest, it has been left to the judicial branch to determine the timing of the initial appearance. The Supreme Court has held that the initial appearance must occur "promptly," which in most cases means within forty-eight hours of booking.[45]

In misdemeanor cases, a defendant may decide to plead guilty and be sentenced during the initial appearance. Otherwise, the magistrate will usually release those charged with misdemeanors on their promise to return at a later date for further proceedings. For felony cases, however, the defendant is not permitted to make a plea at the initial appearance because a magistrate's court does not have jurisdiction to decide felonies. Furthermore, in most cases the defendant will be released only if she or he posts **bail**—an amount paid by the defendant to the court and retained by the court until the defendant returns for further proceedings.

Defendants who cannot afford bail are generally kept in a local jail or lockup until the date of their trial, though many jurisdictions are searching for alternatives to this practice because of overcrowded incarceration facilities. Government statisticians estimate that 62 percent of felony defendants are released before their trials.[46]

Bail The dollar amount or conditions set by the court to ensure that an individual accused of a crime will appear for further criminal proceedings.

THE PURPOSE OF BAIL

Bail is provided for under the Eighth Amendment. The amendment does not, however, guarantee the right to bail. Instead, it states that "excessive bail shall not be required." This has come to mean that in all cases except those involving a capital crime (where bail is prohibited), the amount of bail required must be reasonable compared with the seriousness of the wrongdoing. It does *not* mean that the amount of bail must be within the defendant's ability to pay.

The vagueness of the Eighth Amendment has encouraged a second purpose of bail: to protect the community by preventing the defendant from committing another crime before trial. To achieve this purpose, a judge can set bail at a level the suspect cannot possibly afford. As we shall see, several states and the federal government have passed laws that allow judges to detain suspects deemed a threat to the community without going through the motions of setting relatively high bail.

Discussion Tip: Place students in small groups to discuss the issue of bail. When is bail prohibited? Is this a violation of the Eighth Amendment? Why or why not?

SETTING BAIL

There is no uniform system for pretrial detention. Each jurisdiction has its own *bail tariffs,* or general guidelines concerning the proper amount of bail. For misdemeanors, the police usually follow a preapproved bail schedule created by local judicial authorities. In felony cases, the primary responsibility to set bail lies with the judge. Figure 9.3 alongside shows typical bail amounts for violent offenses.

Bail guidelines can be quite extensive. In Illinois, for example, a judge is required to take thirty-eight different factors into account when setting bail: fourteen involve the crime itself, two refer to the evidence gathered, four to the defendant's record, nine to the defendant's flight risk and immigration status, and nine to the defendant's general character.[47] For the most part, however, judges are free to use such tariffs as loose guidelines, and they have a great deal of discretion in setting bail according to the circumstances in each case.

Extralegal factors may also play a part in bail setting. University of New Orleans political scientist David W. Neubauer has identified three contexts that may influence a judge's decision-making process:[48]

1. *Uncertainty.* To a certain extent, predetermined bail tariffs are unrealistic, given that judges are required to set bail within forty-eight hours of arrest. It is often difficult to get information on the defendant in that period of time, and even if a judge can obtain a "rap sheet," or list of prior arrests ("priors"), she or he will probably not have an opportunity

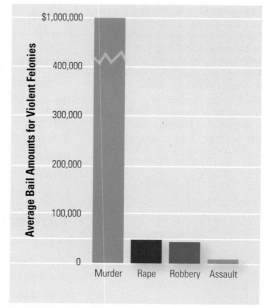

FIGURE 9.3 **Average Bail Amounts for Violent Felonies**
These figures represent the mean bail figures for the seventy-five largest counties in the nation.

Source: Adapted from Bureau of Justice Statistics, *Felony Defendants in Large Urban Counties, 2007* (Washington, D.C.: U.S. Department of Justice, May 2010), Table 7, page 7.

to verify its accuracy. Due to this uncertainty, most judges have no choice but to focus primarily on the seriousness of the crime in setting bail.

2. *Risk.* There is no way of knowing for certain whether a defendant released on bail will return for his or her court date, or whether he or she will commit a crime while free. Judges are aware of the criticism they will come under from police groups, prosecutors, the press, and the public if a crime is committed during that time. Consequently, especially if she or he is up for reelection, a judge may prefer to "play it safe" and set a high bail to detain a suspect or refuse outright to offer bail when legally able to do so. In general, risk aversion also dictates why those who are charged with a violent crime such as murder are usually less likely to be released prior to trial than those who are charged with property crimes such as larceny or motor vehicle theft.

LO 7

3. *Overcrowded jails.* As we will discuss in detail in Chapter 13, many of the nation's jails are overcrowded. This may force a judge to make a difficult distinction between those suspects she or he believes must be detained and those who might need to be detained. To save jail space, a judge might be more lenient in setting bail for members of the latter group.[49]

In the case featured at the beginning of this chapter, Judge Michael Pastor set bail for Dr. Conrad Murray at $75,000, which is three times the standard for involuntary manslaughter in Los Angeles County.[50] Most likely, the publicity surrounding this high-profile case had an impact on the judge's decision.

GAINING PRETRIAL RELEASE

Earlier, we mentioned that many jurisdictions are looking for alternatives to the bail system. One of the most popular options is **release on recognizance (ROR).** This is used when the judge, based on the advice of trained personnel, decides that the defendant is not at risk to "jump" bail and does not pose a threat to the community. The defendant is then released at no cost with the understanding that he or she will return at the time of the trial. The Vera Institute, a nonprofit organization in New York City, introduced the concept of ROR as part of the Manhattan Bail Project in the 1960s, and such programs are now found in nearly every jurisdiction. When properly administered, ROR programs seem to be successful, with less than 5 percent of the participants failing to show for trial.[51]

POSTING BAIL Those suspected of committing a felony, however, are rarely released on recognizance. These defendants may post, or pay, the full amount of the bail in cash to the court. The money will be returned when the suspect appears for trial. Given the large amount of funds required, and the relative lack of wealth of many criminal defendants, a defendant can rarely post bail in cash. Another option is to use personal property as collateral. These **property bonds** are also rare because most courts require property valued at double the bail amount. Thus, if bail is set at $5,000, the defendant (or the defendant's family and friends) will have to produce property valued at $10,000.

BAIL BOND AGENTS If unable to post bail with cash or property, a defendant may arrange for a **bail bond agent** to post a bail bond on the defendant's behalf. The bond agent, in effect, promises the court that he or she will turn over to the court the full amount of bail if the defendant fails to return for further proceedings. The defendant usually must give the bond agent a certain percentage of the bail (frequently 10 percent) in cash. This amount, which is often not returned to the defendant later, is considered payment for the bond agent's assistance and assumption of risk.

Release on Recognizance (ROR) A judge's order that releases an accused from jail with the understanding that he or she will return for further proceedings of his or her own will; used instead of setting a monetary bond.

Property Bond An alternative to posting bail in cash, in which the defendant gains pretrial release by providing the court with property valued at the bail amount as assurance that he or she will return for trial.

Bail Bond Agent A businessperson who agrees, for a fee, to pay the bail amount if the accused fails to appear in court as ordered.

Depending on the amount of the bail bond, the defendant may also be required to sign over to the bond agent rights to certain property (such as a car, a valuable watch, or other asset) as security for the bond.

Although bail bond agents obviously provide a service for which there is demand, the process is widely viewed with distaste. Indeed, the Philippines is the only other nation where bail bonding is an accepted part of the pretrial release process. Four states—Illinois, Kentucky, Oregon, and Wisconsin—have abolished bail bonding for profit. The rationale for such reform focuses on three perceived problems with the practice:

1. Bail bond agents provide opportunities for corruption, as they may improperly influence officials who are involved in setting bail to inflate the bail.
2. Because they can refuse to post a bail bond, bail bond agents are, in essence, making a business decision concerning a suspect's pretrial release. This is considered the responsibility of a judge, not a private individual with a profit motive.[52]
3. About 40 percent of defendants released on bail are eventually found not guilty of any crime. These people, although innocent, have had to pay what amounts to a bribe if they wanted to stay out of jail before their trial.[53]

The states that have banned bail bond agents have established an alternative known as **ten percent cash bail.** This process, pioneered in Chicago in the early 1960s, requires the court, in effect, to take the place of the bond agent. An officer of the court will accept a deposit of 10 percent of the bail amount, refundable when the defendant appears at the assigned time.[54] A number of jurisdictions allow for both bail bond agents and ten percent cash bail, with the judge deciding whether a defendant is eligible for the latter.

PREVENTIVE DETENTION

Judges who believe that suspects pose a danger to the community or are high flight risks have always had the power to detain them by setting bail at a prohibitively high level. This strategy does involve some risk, however. In 2009, a Washington State judge set bail for Maurice Clemons, arrested on charges of assaulting a police officer and raping a child, at $190,000. To the surprise of Pierce County law enforcement and court personnel, Clemons's family was able to raise the bail amount, and Clemons was set free. Six months later, he killed four police officers in a coffee shop near Seattle.

In an attempt to prevent such scenarios, more than thirty states and the federal government have directly authorized judges to act "in the best interests of the community" by passing **preventive detention** legislation. These laws allow judges to deny bail to arrestees with prior records of violence, thus keeping them in custody prior to trial. The federal Bail Reform Act of 1984 similarly states that federal offenders can be held without bail to ensure "the safety of any other person and the community."[55]

Critics of the 1984 act believe that it violates the U.S. Constitution by allowing the freedom of a citizen to be restricted before he or she has been proved guilty in a court of

What is your opinion of legislation that abolishes bail bonding for profit? What other ethical issues are raised by the bail system?
Christine Osborne/Corbis

Ten Percent Cash Bail An alternative to traditional bail in which defendants may gain pretrial release by posting 10 percent of their bond amount to the court instead of seeking a bail bond agent.

Preventive Detention The retention of an accused person in custody due to fears that she or he will commit a crime if released before trial.

See the **Professional Bail Agents of the United States** for a wealth of information about how bail bond agents operate. Find its Web site by visiting the *Criminal Justice CourseMate* at **cengagebrain.com** and selecting the *Web links* for this chapter.

Bounty hunters such as the ones shown here are often paid substantial sums by bail bond agents to capture bond-jumping clients. What services does a bond agent offer a person facing trial?

Hemis/Alamy

law. For many, the act also brings up the troubling issue of *false positives*—erroneous predictions that defendants, if given pretrial release, would commit a crime, when in fact they would not. In *United States v. Salerno* (1987),[56] however, the Supreme Court upheld the act's premise. Then Chief Justice William Rehnquist wrote that preventive detention was not a "punishment for dangerous individuals" but a "potential solution to a pressing social problem." Therefore, "there is no doubt that preventing danger to the community is a legitimate . . . goal." In fact, about 21 percent of released defendants are rearrested before their trials begin, 13 percent for violent felonies.[57]

SELFASSESSMENT

Fill in the blanks and check your answers on page 315.

During the _____ _____, a magistrate informs the defendant of the charges brought against her or him and explains her or his _____ rights. Following this proceeding, the defendant will be detained until trial unless he or she can post _____, the amount of which is determined by the _____. Even if the defendant can afford to pay this amount, he or she may be kept in jail until trial under a _____ detention statute if the court decides that he or she poses a risk to the community.

Group Activities: Asks students to work in groups to debate "Questions for Critical Analysis" number four on page 315, in which they consider the factors that impact the bail decision. (LO 7)

ESTABLISHING PROBABLE CAUSE

Once the initial appearance has been completed and bail has been set, the prosecutor must establish *probable cause.* In other words, the prosecutor must show that a crime was committed and link the defendant to that crime. There are two formal procedures for establishing probable cause at this stage of the pretrial process: preliminary hearings and grand juries.

THE PRELIMINARY HEARING

Preliminary Hearing An initial hearing in which a magistrate decides if there is probable cause to believe that the defendant committed the crime with which he or she is charged.

Discovery Formal investigation by each side prior to trial.

During the **preliminary hearing**, the defendant appears before a judge or magistrate who decides whether the evidence presented is sufficient for the case to proceed to trial. Normally, every person arrested has a right to this hearing within a reasonable amount of time after his or her initial arrest[58]—usually, no later than ten days if the defendant is in custody or within thirty days if he or she has gained pretrial release.

THE PRELIMINARY HEARING PROCESS The preliminary hearing is conducted in the manner of a mini-trial. Typically, a police report of the arrest is presented by a law enforcement officer, supplemented with evidence provided by the prosecutor. Because the burden of proving probable cause is relatively light (compared with proving guilt beyond a reasonable doubt), prosecutors rarely call witnesses during the preliminary hearing, saving them for the trial. During this hearing, the defendant has a right to be represented by counsel, who may cross-examine witnesses and challenge any evidence offered by the prosecutor. In most states, defense attorneys can take advantage of the preliminary hearing to begin the process of **discovery,** in which they are entitled to have access to any evidence in the possession of the prosecution relating to the case.

Discovery is considered a keystone in the adversary process, as it allows the defense to see the evidence against the defendant prior to making a plea.

WAIVING THE HEARING The preliminary hearing often seems rather perfunctory, although in some jurisdictions it replaces grand jury proceedings. It usually lasts no longer than five minutes, and the judge or magistrate rarely finds that probable cause does not exist. For this reason, defense attorneys commonly advise their clients to waive their right to a preliminary hearing. Once a judge has ruled affirmatively, in many jurisdictions the defendant is bound over to the grand jury, a group of citizens called to decide whether probable cause exists. In other jurisdictions, the prosecutor issues an information, which replaces the police complaint as the formal charge against the defendant for the purposes of a trial.

THE GRAND JURY

The federal government and about one-third of the states require a grand jury to make the decision as to whether a case should go to trial. Grand juries are *impaneled*, or created, for a period of time usually not exceeding three months. During that time, the grand jury sits in closed (secret) session and hears only evidence presented by the prosecutor—the defendant cannot present evidence at this hearing. The prosecutor presents to the grand jury whatever evidence the state has against the defendant, including photographs, documents, tangible objects, the testimony of witnesses, and other items. If the grand jury finds that probable cause exists, it issues an indictment (pronounced in-*dyte*-ment) against the defendant.

Like an information in a preliminary hearing, the indictment becomes the formal charge against the defendant. As Figure 9.4 below shows, some states require a grand jury to indict for certain crimes, while in other states a grand jury indictment is optional.

Grand Jury The group of citizens called to decide whether probable cause exists to believe that a suspect committed the crime with which she or he has been charged.

Information The formal charge against the accused issued by the prosecutor after a preliminary hearing has found probable cause.

Indictment A charge or written accusation, issued by a grand jury, that probable cause exists to believe that a named person has committed a crime.

FIGURE 9.4 State Grand Jury Requirements

As you can see, in some states a grand jury indictment is required to charge an individual with a crime, while in others it is either optional or prohibited. When a grand jury is not used, the discretion of whether to charge is left to the prosecutor, who must then present his or her argument at the preliminary hearing (discussed earlier in the chapter).

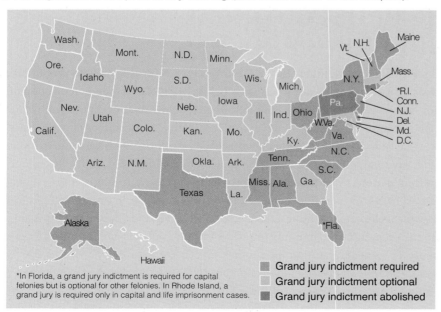

*In Florida, a grand jury indictment is required for capital felonies but is optional for other felonies. In Rhode Island, a grand jury is required only in capital and life imprisonment cases.

- ■ Grand jury indictment required
- □ Grand jury indictment optional
- ■ Grand jury indictment abolished

Source: Bureau of Justice Statistics, *State Court Organization, 2004* (Washington, D.C.: U.S. Department of Justice, August 2006), 215–217.

THE "SHIELD" AND THE "SWORD" The grand jury has a long history in the United States, having been brought over from England by the colonists and codified in the Fifth Amendment to the U.S. Constitution. Historically, it has acted as both a "shield" and a "sword" in the criminal justice process. By giving citizens the chance to review government charges of wrongdoing, it "shields" the individual from the power of the state. At the same time, the grand jury offers the government a "sword"—the opportunity to provide evidence against the accused—in its efforts to fight crime and protect society.[59]

A "RUBBER STAMP" Today, the protective function of the grand jury is in doubt—critics say that the "sword" aspect works too well and the "shield" aspect not at all. Statistically, the grand jury is even more prosecutor friendly than the preliminary hearing. Defendants are indicted at a rate of more than 99 percent,[60] leading to the common characterization of the grand jury as little more than a "rubber stamp" for the prosecution.

Certainly, the procedural rules of the grand jury favor prosecutors. The exclusionary rule (see Chapter 7) does not apply in grand jury investigations, so prosecutors can present evidence that would be disallowed at any subsequent trial. Furthermore, because the grand jury is given only one version of the facts—the prosecution's—it is likely to find probable cause. In the words of one observer, a grand jury would indict a "ham sandwich" if the government asked it to do so.[61] As a result of these concerns, a number of jurisdictions have abolished grand juries.

SELFASSESSMENT

Fill in the blanks and check your answers on page 315.
If a case is to proceed to trial, the prosecutor must establish _____ _____ that the defendant committed the crime in question. One way of doing this involves a _____ hearing, in which a judge or magistrate rules whether the prosecutor has met this burden. In the other method, the decision rests with a group of citizens called a _____ _____ who will hand down an _____ if they believe the evidence is sufficient to support the charges.

THE PROSECUTORIAL SCREENING PROCESS

Some see the high government success rates in pretrial proceedings as proof that prosecutors successfully screen out weak cases before they get to a grand jury or preliminary hearing. If, however, grand juries have indeed abandoned their traditional duties in favor of "rubber stamping" most cases set in front of them, and preliminary hearings are little better, what is to keep prosecutors from using their charging powers indiscriminately? Nothing, say many observers. Once the police have initially charged a defendant with committing a crime, the prosecutor can prosecute the case as it stands, reduce or increase the initial charge, file additional charges, or dismiss the case. In a system of government and law that relies on checks and balances, asked legal expert Kenneth Culp Davis, why should the prosecutor be "immune to review by other officials and immune to review by the courts?"[62] (For information on another prosecutor-friendly system, see the feature *Comparative Criminal Justice—Japan's All-Powerful Prosecutors* on the facing page.)

Though American prosecutors have far-ranging discretionary charging powers, it is not entirely correct to say that they are unrestricted. Controls are indirect and informal, but they do exist.

Critical Thinking Skill Development: In a written assignment, ask students to debate the use of grand juries. What do students think of this process? Do students view grand juries as "shields" or as "rubber stamps"? Are grand juries used in your state? Should they be?

Teaching Tip: Ask students to consider case attrition. What is case attrition, and why does it occur? Can students find an example of case attrition in the local media? (LO 8)

COMPARATIVE CRIMINAL JUSTICE

JAPAN'S ALL-POWERFUL PROSECUTORS

Prosecutors in the United States are generally believed to have a great deal of charging discretion. The discretionary power of American prosecutors, however, does not equal that of their Japanese counterparts. With the ability to "cherry pick" their cases, prosecutors in Japan routinely have annual conviction rates of over 99.9 percent.

The "Confession Mill"

One observer described the Japanese courts as a "confession mill." Unlike the American system, Japan has no arraignment procedure during which the accused can plead guilty or innocent. Instead, the focus of the Japanese criminal justice system is on extracting confessions of guilt: police can hold and question suspects for up to twenty-three days without pressing charges. Furthermore, the suspect has no absolute right to counsel during the interrogation, and police are often able to get confessions that make for open-and-shut convictions. The prosecutor also has the "benevolent" discretion to drop the case altogether if the suspect expresses remorse.

In addition, the extraordinarily high conviction rate is a product of Japanese culture. To fail in an attempt to convict results in a loss of face, not only for the individual prosecutor but also for the court system as a whole. The Japanese Justice Ministry estimates that, to avoid the risk of losing, prosecutors decline to press charges against 35 percent of indictable suspects each year. Japanese judges—there are almost no juries—contribute to the high conviction rate by rarely questioning the manner in which prosecutors obtain confessions.

No Plea Bargaining

Interestingly, given the amount of prosecutorial discretion, the Japanese criminal justice system does not allow for plea bargaining. The Japanese see the practice of "trading" a guilty plea for a lesser sentence as counterproductive, as a defendant may be tempted to confess to crimes she or he did not commit if the prosecution has a strong case. For the Japanese, a confession extracted after, say, twenty-three days of interrogation may be "voluntary," but a confession gained through a promise of leniency is "forced" and therefore in conflict with the system's goals of truth seeking and accuracy.

FOR CRITICAL ANALYSIS

Explain the fundamental differences between the American and Japanese criminal justice systems. Do you think the lack of a comparable adversarial system weakens or strengthens the Japanese system in comparison with the American one?

CASE ATTRITION

Prosecutorial discretion includes the power *not* to prosecute cases. For example, federal prosecutors decline to bring charges in nearly three out of every four computer fraud cases referred to them by investigators.[63] Figure 9.5 on the following page depicts the average outcomes of one hundred felony arrests in the United States. As you can see, of the sixty-five adult arrestees brought before the district attorney, only thirty-five are prosecuted, and only eighteen of these prosecutions lead to incarceration. Consequently, fewer than one in three adults arrested for a felony sees the inside of a prison or jail cell. This phenomenon is known as case attrition, and it is explained in part by prosecutorial discretion.

Case Attrition The process through which prosecutors, by deciding whether to prosecute each person arrested, effect an overall reduction in the number of persons prosecuted.

SCARCE RESOURCES About half of those adult felony cases brought to prosecutors by police are dismissed through a *nolle prosequi* (Latin for "unwilling to pursue"). Why are these cases "nolled," or not prosecuted by the district attorney? In the section on law enforcement, you learned that the police do not have the resources to arrest every lawbreaker in the nation. Similarly, district attorneys do not have the resources to prosecute every arrest. They must choose how to distribute their scarce resources. Several years ago, for example, Contra Costa County (California) district attorney Robert Kochly

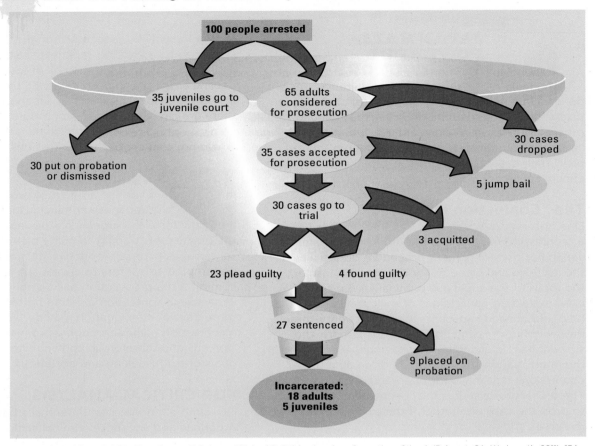

Source: Adapted from Todd R. Clear, George F. Cole, and Michael D. Reisig, *American Corrections,* 9th ed. (Belmont, CA: Wadsworth, 2011), 134.

announced that, due to budget shortfalls, his office would no longer prosecute anyone caught with less than a gram of methamphetamine or cocaine, less than half a gram of heroin, and fewer than five pills of Ecstasy.[64]

In some cases, the decision is made for prosecutors, such as when police break procedural law and negate important evidence. This happens rarely—less than 1 percent of felony arrests are dropped because of the exclusionary rule, and almost all of these are the result of illegal drug searches.[65]

SCREENING FACTORS Most prosecutors have a *screening* process for deciding when to prosecute and when to "noll." This process varies a bit from jurisdiction to jurisdiction, but most prosecutors consider several factors in making the decision:

- The most important factor in deciding whether to prosecute is not the prosecutor's belief in the guilt of the suspect, but whether there is *sufficient evidence for conviction.*[66] If prosecutors have strong physical evidence and a **LO 8** number of reliable and believable witnesses, they are quite likely to prosecute.

- Prosecutors also tend to establish *case priorities.* In other words, everything else being equal, a district attorney will prosecute a rapist instead of a jaywalker because the former presents a greater threat to society than does the latter. A prosecutor will also be more likely to prosecute someone with an extensive record of wrongdoing than a first-time offender. Often, in coordination with the police, a district attorney's office will target a single area of crime, such as illegal drug use or drunk driving.

- Sometimes a case is dropped even when it involves a serious crime and a wealth of evidence exists against the suspect. These situations usually involve *uncooperative victims.* Domestic violence cases are particularly difficult to prosecute because the victims may want to keep the matter private, fear reprisals, or have a strong desire to protect their abuser.[67] In some jurisdictions, as many as 80 percent of domestic violence victims refuse to cooperate with the prosecution.[68]
- *Unreliability of victims* can also affect a charging decision. If the victim in a rape case is a crack addict and a prostitute, while the defendant is the chief executive officer of a large corporation, prosecutors may be hesitant to have a jury decide which one is more trustworthy.
- A prosecutor may be willing to drop a case or reduce the charges against *a defendant who is willing to testify against other offenders.* Federal law encourages this kind of behavior by offering sentencing reductions to defendants who provide "substantial assistance in the investigation or prosecution of another person who has committed an offense."[69]

A prosecutor also has great discretion to interpret the criminal codes under which he or she operates. Michigan, for example, like many other states, has a law that prohibits anyone from gaining unlawful access to a computer system. The legislation is intended to protect against credit-card theft and other forms of computer crime, but Oakland County prosecutor Jessica Cooper recently used it to charge Leon Walker with reading his wife's e-mails without her permission. Despite widespread criticism that she was wasting resources on a private, family matter, Cooper insisted that her decision "ha[d] nothing to do with a husband trying to prove his wife had an affair. It ha[d] to do with hacking."[70] (To get a better idea of the difficulty of some charging decisions, see the feature *You Be the Prosecutor—A Battered Woman* on the following page.)

Technology Tip: Have students go online (**www.ice.gov/doclib/ secure-communities/pdf/ prosecutorial-discretion-memo. pdf**) and review a recent memo issued by John Morton, director of U.S. Immigration and Customs Enforcement (ICE). The memo serves to guide ICE personnel in their use of prosecutorial discretion. According to the memo, when and why should ICE officers use discretion? What factors should they consider? (LO 8)

PROSECUTORIAL CHARGING AND THE DEFENSE ATTORNEY

For the most part, there is little the defense attorney can do when the prosecutor decides to charge a client. If a defense attorney feels strongly that the charge has been made in violation of the defendant's rights, he or she can, however, submit *pretrial motions* to the court requesting that a particular action be taken to protect his or her client. Pretrial motions include the following:

1. Motions to suppress evidence obtained illegally.
2. Motions for a change of venue because the defendant cannot receive a fair trial in the original jurisdiction.
3. Motions to invalidate a search warrant.
4. Motions to dismiss the case because of a delay in bringing it to trial.
5. Motions to obtain evidence that the prosecution may be withholding.

As we shall soon see, defense attorneys sometimes use these pretrial motions to pressure the prosecution into offering a favorable deal for their client.

Discussion Tip: Have students discuss the concept of *nolo contendere*. What are the advantages of entering this plea? What are the disadvantages?

SELFASSESSMENT

Fill in the blanks and check your answers on page 315.

On average, of sixty-five adult arrestees, a district attorney will prosecute only thirty-five. This process, which is known as case _____, requires that the prosecutor _____ all potential cases and dismiss the ones where the likelihood of _____ is weakest. The most important factor in this decision is whether there is sufficient _____ to find the defendant guilty.

PLEADING GUILTY

Arraignment A court proceeding in which the suspect is formally charged with the criminal offense stated in the indictment. The suspect enters a plea (guilty, not guilty, *nolo contendere*) in response.

Nolo Contendere Latin for "I will not contest it." A criminal defendant's plea, in which he or she chooses not to challenge, or contest, the charges brought by the government. Although the defendant may still be sentenced or fined, the plea neither admits nor denies guilt.

Based on the information (delivered during the preliminary hearing) or indictment (handed down by the grand jury), the prosecutor submits a motion to the court to order the defendant to appear before the trial court for an **arraignment**. Due process of law, as guaranteed by the Fifth Amendment, requires that a criminal defendant be informed of the charges brought against her or him and be offered an opportunity to respond to those charges. The arraignment is one of the ways in which due process requirements are satisfied by criminal procedure law.

At the arraignment, the defendant is informed of the charges and must respond by pleading not guilty or guilty. In some but not all states, the defendant may also enter a plea of *nolo contendere,* which is Latin for "I will not contest it." The plea of *nolo contendere* is neither an admission nor a denial of guilt. (The consequences for someone who pleads guilty and for someone who pleads *nolo contendere* are the same in a criminal

YOU BE THE PROSECUTOR

A Battered Woman

THE SITUATION For more than twenty years, John regularly beat his wife, Judy. He even put out cigarettes on her skin and slashed her face with glass. John was often unemployed and forced Judy into prostitution to earn a living. He regularly denied her food and threatened to maim or kill her. Judy left home several times, but John always managed to find her, bring her home, and punish her. Finally, Judy took steps to get John put in a psychiatric hospital. He told her that if anybody came for him, he would "see them coming" and cut her throat before they arrived. That night, Judy shot John three times in the back of the head while he was asleep, killing him. You are the prosecutor with authority over Judy.

THE LAW In your jurisdiction, a person can use deadly force in self-defense if it is necessary to kill an unlawful aggressor to save himself or herself from imminent death. (See page 119 for a review of self-defense.) Voluntary manslaughter is the intentional killing of another human being without malice. It covers crimes of passion. First degree murder is premeditated killing, with malice. (See pages 70–71 for a review of the different degrees of murder.)

YOUR DECISION Will you charge Judy with voluntary manslaughter or first degree murder? Alternatively, do you believe she was acting in self-defense, in which case you will not charge her with any crime? Explain your choice.

[To see how a Rutherford County, North Carolina, prosecutor decided a case with similar facts, go to Example 9.1 in Appendix B.]

trial, but the latter plea cannot be used in a subsequent civil trial as an admission of guilt.) Most frequently, the defendant pleads guilty to the initial charge or to a lesser charge that has been agreed on through *plea bargaining* between the prosecutor and the defendant. If the defendant pleads guilty, no trial is necessary, and the defendant is sentenced based on the crime he or she has admitted committing.

PLEA BARGAINING IN THE CRIMINAL JUSTICE SYSTEM

Plea bargaining most often takes place after the arraignment and before the beginning of the trial. In its simplest terms, it is a process by which the accused, represented by the defense counsel, and the prosecutor work out a mutually satisfactory disposition of the case, subject to court approval. Usually, plea bargaining involves the defendant's pleading guilty to the charges against her or him in return for a lighter sentence, but other variations are possible as well. The defendant can agree to plead guilty in exchange for having the charge against her or him reduced from, say, felony burglary to the lesser offense of breaking and entering. Or a person charged with multiple counts may agree to plead guilty if the prosecutor agrees to drop one or more of the counts. Whatever the particulars, the results of a plea bargain are generally the same: the prosecutor gets a conviction, and the defendant a lesser punishment.

In *Santobello v. New York* (1971),[71] the Supreme Court held that plea bargaining "is not only an essential part of the process but a highly desirable part for many reasons." Some observers would agree, but with ambivalence. They understand that plea bargaining offers the practical benefit of saving court resources, but question whether it is the best way to achieve justice.[72] We will address the question of whether plea bargaining is an acceptable means of determining the defendant's fate in the *CJ in Action* feature at the end of the chapter.

Plea Bargaining The process by which the accused and the prosecutor work out a mutually satisfactory conclusion to the case, subject to court approval.

> "I ain't shot no man, but I take the fault for the other man. . . . I just pleaded guilty because they said if I didn't they would gas me for it, and that is all."
>
> —**Henry Alford,** who claimed that he pleaded guilty to a murder charge only because he faced the threat of the death penalty if the case went to trial

MOTIVATIONS FOR PLEA BARGAINING

Given the high rate of plea bargaining—accounting for 95 percent of criminal convictions in state courts[73]—it follows that the prosecutor, defense attorney, and defendant each have strong reasons to engage in the practice.

PROSECUTORS AND PLEA BARGAINING In most cases, a prosecutor has a single goal after charging a defendant with a crime: conviction. If a case goes to trial, no matter how certain a prosecutor may be that the defendant is guilty, there is always a chance that a jury or judge will disagree. Plea bargaining removes this risk. Furthermore, the prosecutorial screening process described earlier in the chapter is not infallible. Sometimes, a prosecutor will find that the evidence against the accused is weaker than first thought or will uncover new information that changes the complexion of the case. In these situations, the prosecutor may decide to drop the charges or, if he or she still feels that the defendant is guilty, turn to plea bargaining to "save" a questionable case.

The prosecutor's role as an administrator also comes into play. She or he may be interested in the quickest, most efficient manner to dispose of caseloads, and plea bargains reduce the time and money spent on each case. Personal philosophy can affect the proceedings as well. A prosecutor who feels that a mandatory minimum sentence for a particular crime, such as marijuana possession, is too strict may plea bargain in order to lessen the penalty. Similarly, some prosecutors will consider plea bargaining only in certain instances—for burglary and theft, for example, but not for more serious felonies such as rape and murder.[74]

Critical Thinking Skill Development: Ask students to generate a written assignment in which they consider plea bargaining. What are the advantages and disadvantages of plea bargaining? Does the practice represent a "necessary evil"?

DEFENSE ATTORNEYS AND PLEA BARGAINING Political scientist Milton Heumann has said that the most important lesson that a defense attorney learns is that "most of his [or her] clients are guilty."[75] Given this stark reality, favorable plea bargains are often the best a defense attorney can do for clients, aside from helping them to gain acquittals. Some have suggested that defense attorneys have other, less savory motives for convincing a client to plead guilty, such as a desire to increase profit margins by quickly disposing of cases[76] or a wish to ingratiate themselves with the other members of the courtroom work group by showing their "reasonableness."[77]

Why did John Albert Gardner agree to plead guilty to murdering two teenagers? What incentives might the San Diego prosecutors have had for accepting Gardner's guilty plea and declining to seek his execution?
AP Photo/*San Diego Union-Tribune*, Nelvin C. Cepeda, Pool

DEFENDANTS AND PLEA BARGAINING The plea bargain allows the defendant a measure of control over his or her fate. In 2010, for example, John Albert Gardner was convicted of killing fourteen-year-old Amber Dubois and seventeen-year old Chelsea King (see the photo alongside). Despite the violent nature of the crimes, San Diego County prosecutors agreed not to seek the death penalty if Gardner pleaded guilty to both murders. He did so, and a judge sentenced him to life in prison without parole. As Figure 9.6 on the facing page shows, defendants who plea bargain receive significantly lighter sentences on average than those who are found guilty at trial.

VICTIMS AND PLEA BARGAINING One of the major goals of the victims' rights movement has been to increase the role of victims in the plea bargaining process. In recent years, the movement has had some success in this area. About half of the states now allow for victim participation in plea bargaining. Many have laws similar to North Carolina's statute that requires the district attorney's office to offer victims "the opportunity to consult with the prosecuting attorney" and give their views on "plea possibilities."[78] On the federal level, the Crime Victims' Rights Act grants victims the right to be "reasonably heard" during the process.[79]

If they choose, prosecutors can provide victims with more of a voice. After Alfonso Rodriguez, Jr., was arrested for kidnapping Dru Sjodin, a twenty-two-year-old University of North Dakota student, in 2003, federal prosecutors consulted closely with the young woman's family. In early 2004, Sjodin's parents agreed to a deal that prosecutors presented to the suspect: if Rodriguez would plead guilty to kidnapping and murder and tell law enforcement agents the location of Sjodin's body, the government would not seek his execution. Rodriguez spurned the proposition. Eventually, volunteers found Sjodin's remains in a ravine near Crookston, Minnesota. Two years into the federal trial, Rodriguez changed his mind and offered to plead guilty in return for a life sentence. Sjodin's family, speaking through the prosecutors, said, in effect, "too late."[80] On February 8, 2007, Rodriguez received the death penalty for his crimes.

PLEA BARGAINING AND THE ADVERSARY SYSTEM

One criticism of plea bargaining is that it subverts the adversary system, the goal of which is to determine innocence or guilt. Although plea bargaining does value negotiation over conflict, it is important to remember that it does so in a context in which legal guilt has already been established. Even within this context, plea bargaining is not completely divorced from the adversary process.

FIGURE 9.6 Sentencing Outcomes for Guilty Pleas

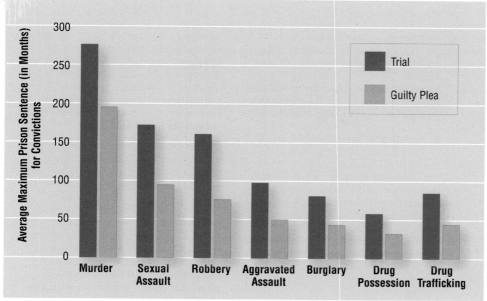

Source: Bureau of Justice Statistics, *Felony Sentences in State Courts, 2006—Statistical Tables* (Washington, D.C.: U.S. Department of Justice, December 2009), Table 4.3.

LO 9 STRATEGIES TO INDUCE A PLEA BARGAIN

Earlier, we pointed out that the most likely reason why a prosecutor does not bring charges is the lack of a strong case. This is also the most common reason why a prosecutor agrees to a plea bargain once charges have been brought. Defense attorneys are well aware of this fact and often file numerous pretrial motions in an effort to weaken the state's case. Even if the judge does not accept the motions, the defense may hope that the time required to process them will wear on the prosecutor's patience. As one district attorney has said, "the usual defense strategy today is to bring in a stack of motions as thick as a Sunday newspaper; defense attorneys hope that we won't have the patience to ride them out."[81]

Prosecutors have their own methods of inducing a plea bargain. The most common is the ethically questionable practice of *overcharging*—that is, charging the defendant with more counts than may be appropriate. There are two types of overcharging:

1. In *horizontal overcharging*, the prosecutor brings a number of different counts for a single criminal incident.
2. In *vertical overcharging*, the prosecutor raises the level of a charge above its proper place. For example, the facts of the case warrant a charge of battery, but the prosecutor charges the defendant with attempted murder.

After overcharging, prosecutors allow themselves to be "bargained down" to the correct charge, giving the defense attorney and the defendant the impression that they have achieved some sort of victory.

PROTECTING THE DEFENDANT

Watching the defense attorney and the prosecutor maneuver in this manner, the defendant often comes to the conclusion that the plea bargaining process is a sort of game with sometimes incomprehensible rules.[82] The Supreme Court is also aware of the potential for taking advantage of the defendant in plea bargaining and has taken steps to protect the accused. (For a summary of notable Supreme Court cases involving plea bargaining procedures, see Figure 9.7 on the following page.) Until *Boykin v.*

Group Activities: Ask students to search online for examples of regional cases where plea bargaining has been used. In each case, have students determine whether the prosecutor employed horizontal or vertical overcharging to encourage the defendant to accept the proposed plea bargain. (LO 9)

FIGURE 9.7 Notable United States Supreme Court Decisions on Plea Bargaining

The constitutional justification of the plea bargain as an accepted part of the criminal justice process has been fortified by these Supreme Court rulings.

Brady v. United States (397 U.S. 742 [1970]). In this case the defendant entered a guilty plea in order to avoid the death penalty. In allowing this action, the Court ruled that **plea bargains are a legitimate part of the adjudication process as long as they are entered into voluntarily and the defendant has full knowledge of the consequences of pleading guilty.**

North Carolina v. Alford (400 U.S. 25 [1970]). Although maintaining he was innocent of the first degree murder with which he was charged, Alford pleaded guilty to second degree murder in order to avoid the possibility of the death penalty that came with the original charges. After being sentenced to thirty years in prison, Alford argued that he was forced to plea bargain because of the threat of the death penalty. The Court refused to invalidate Alford's guilty plea, stating that **plea bargains are valid even if the defendant claims innocence, as long as the plea was entered into voluntarily.**

Santobello v. New York (404 U.S. 257 [1971]). This case focused on the prosecutor's role in the plea bargain process. The Court ruled that **if a prosecutor promises a more lenient sentence in return for the defendant's guilty plea, the promise must be kept.**

Bordenkircher v. Hayes (434 U.S. 357 [1978]). A Kentucky prosecutor told Hayes that if he entered a guilty plea, the prosecutor would recommend a light sentence. If not, he would indict Hayes under the state's habitual offender act, which carried the possibility of life imprisonment. The Court ruled that **prosecutors are within their rights to threaten defendants with harsher sentences in order to induce a guilty plea.**

Ricketts v. Adamson (483 U.S. 1 [1987]). In return for a reduction of charges, Ricketts agreed to plead guilty and to testify against a co-defendant in a murder case. When the co-defendant's conviction was reversed on appeal, Ricketts refused to testify a second time. Therefore, the prosecutor rescinded the offer of leniency. The Court ruled that the prosecutor's action was justified, and that **defendants must uphold their side of the plea bargain in order to receive its benefits.**

United States v. Mezzanatto (513 U.S. 196 [1995]). The Court ruled that a prosecutor can refuse to plea bargain with a defendant unless the defendant agrees that any statements made by him or her during the bargaining process can be used against him or her in a possible trial. In other words, **if the defendant admits to committing the crime during plea bargain negotiations, and then decides to plead not guilty, the prosecution can use the admission as evidence during the trial.**

Alabama (1969),[83] judges would often accept the defense counsel's word that the defendant wanted to plead guilty. In that case, the Court held that the defendant must make a clear statement that he or she accepts the plea bargain. As a result, many jurisdictions now ask the accused to sign a *Boykin* form waiving his or her right to a trial. A statement in which the defendant admits exactly what crime he or she committed must accompany this guilty plea.

Boykin Form A form that must be completed by a defendant who pleads guilty. The defendant states that she or he has done so voluntarily and with full comprehension of the consequences.

GOING TO TRIAL

The pretrial process does not inexorably lead to a guilty plea. Just as prosecutors, defense attorneys, and defendants have reasons to negotiate, they may also be motivated to take a case to trial. If either side is confident in the strength of its arguments and evidence, it will obviously be less likely to accept a plea bargain. Both prosecutors and defense attorneys may favor a trial to gain publicity, and sometimes public pressure after an extremely violent or high-profile crime will force a chief prosecutor (who is, remember, normally an elected official) to take a weak case to trial. Also, some defendants may insist on their right to a trial, regardless of their attorneys' advice. In the next chapter, we will examine what happens to the roughly 5 percent of indictments that do lead to the courtroom.

SELFASSESSMENT

Fill in the blanks and check your answers on page 315.

A _____ _____ occurs when the prosecution and the defense work out an agreement that resolves the case. Generally, a defendant will plead guilty in exchange for a reduction of the _____ against him or her or a lighter _____, or both. To ensure that the defendant understands the terms of the plea, he or she must sign a _____ form waiving his or her right to a _____.

CJ IN ACTION

THE PLEA BARGAIN PUZZLE

In November 2010, when a Colorado Springs judge sentenced Clifford Huery to twelve years behind bars for fatally stabbing Nicholas Murphy, few were happy with the sentence. Because of the lack of evidence against him, Huery was able to bargain his charge down from first degree murder to reckless manslaughter. Murphy's mother called the sentence "not only a slap on the hand for Clifford Huery but a slap in the face to myself and my family."[84] Prosecutor Amy Fitch admitted that the resolution of the case was "sad and frustrating" but claimed it was the best she could obtain under the circumstances.[85] In this *CJ in Action* feature, we will examine the process of plea bargaining, a source of constant frustration for defendants, attorneys, and victims that the American court system apparently cannot live without.

ADVERSARIAL AND INEVITABLE

Those who support plea bargaining often do so because they cannot imagine life without it. In 1970, Supreme Court chief justice Warren Burger warned that "a reduction from 90 percent to 80 percent in guilty pleas requires the assignment of twice the judicial manpower and facilities—judges, court reporters, bailiffs, clerks, jurors, and courtrooms." Burger added, "A reduction to 70 percent trebles this demand."[86] This practicality bothers some observers. "Because of plea bargaining, I guess we can say, 'Gee, the trains run on time,'" notes criminologist Franklin Zimring. "But do we like where they're going?"[87]

THE CASE FOR PLEA BARGAINING

- Plea bargaining provides prosecutors and defense attorneys with the flexibility to quickly dispose of some cases while allocating scarce resources to the cases that require them.

- Because of mandatory minimum sentencing, which you will study in Chapter 11, criminal defendants who go to trial risk very harsh punishment if they lose. Plea bargaining allows them to mitigate that risk and accept a lesser sentence.

- The practice spares victims from reliving the horrors of their victimization as courtroom witnesses.

THE CASE AGAINST PLEA BARGAINING

- Plea bargaining gives innocent people an incentive to plead guilty if they feel that there is even a slight chance that a jury or judge might decide against them.

- Plea bargaining gives prosecutors too much power to coerce defendants, either by overcharging (see page 311) or by bluffing by claiming to have evidence that the prosecutor knows would actually be inadmissible at trial, such as contraband gained by an illegal search.

- The practice allows dangerous criminals to "beat the system" by negotiating for lighter sentences than they deserve. Consequently, it undermines the deterrent effects of punishment and the public's confidence in the criminal justice system.

Photodisc/Getty Images

YOUR OPINION— WRITING ASSIGNMENT

When Kathleen Rice took office as district attorney for Nassau County, New York, she was dismayed to see that one-third of the people arrested for drunken driving in the county had previous convictions for the same offense. "The message was that you can do this as many times as you want and you're always going to be given the option to plead out to the equivalent of a traffic infraction," said Rice.[88] As a result, she instituted a "no deals" policy for drinking-and-driving charges. Not surprisingly, Nassau County's defense attorneys did not react positively to Rice's plan. "People need some degree of hope, and under [her] policies, they're not getting it," complained one.[89]

What is your opinion of "no deals" policies for specific crimes? What impact do such policies have on prosecutors, defense attorneys, and defendants? If you agree with this strategy, to which crimes would you apply it and why? Before responding, you can review our discussions in this chapter concerning:

- Defense attorneys (pages 289–295).

- Case attrition (pages 305–307).

- Plea bargaining (pages 309–312).

Your answer should include at least three full paragraphs.

CHAPTER SUMMARY

LO 1 **List the different names given to public prosecutors and indicate the general powers that they have.** At the federal level, the prosecutor is called the U.S. attorney. In state and local courts, the prosecutor may be referred to as the prosecuting attorney, state prosecutor, district attorney, county attorney, or city attorney. Prosecutors in general have the power to decide when and how the state will pursue an individual suspected of criminal wrongdoing. In some jurisdictions, the district attorney is also the chief law enforcement officer, holding broad powers over police operations.

LO 2 **Contrast the prosecutor's roles as an elected official and as a crime fighter.** In most instances, the prosecutor is elected and therefore may feel obliged to reward members of her or his party with jobs. To win reelection or higher political office, the prosecutor may feel a need to bow to community pressures. As a crime fighter, the prosecutor is dependent on the police, and indeed prosecutors are generally seen as law enforcement agents. Prosecutors, however, generally pursue cases only when they believe there is sufficient legal guilt to obtain a conviction.

LO 3 **Delineate the responsibilities of defense attorneys.** (a) Representation of the defendant during the custodial process; (b) investigation of the supposed criminal incident; (c) communication with the prosecutor (including plea bargaining); (d) preparation of the case for trial; (e) submission of defense motions; (f) representation of the defendant at trial; (g) negotiation of a sentence after conviction; and (h) appeal of a guilty verdict.

LO 4 **Indicate the three types of defense allocation programs.** (a) Assigned counsel programs, which use local private attorneys; (b) contracting attorney programs; and (c) public defender programs.

LO 5 **List the three basic features of an adversary system of justice.** (a) A neutral decision maker (judge or jury); (b) presentation of evidence from both parties; and (c) a highly structured set of procedures that must be used when evidence is presented.

LO 6 **Identify the steps involved in the pretrial criminal process.** (a) Suspect taken into custody or arrested; (b) initial appearance before a magistrate, at which time the defendant is informed of his or her constitutional rights and a public defender may be appointed or private counsel may be hired by the state to represent the defendant; (c) the posting of bail or release on recognizance; (d) preventive detention, if deemed necessary to ensure the safety of other persons or the community, or regular detention, if the defendant is unable to post bail; (e) preliminary hearing (mini-trial), at which the judge rules on whether there is probable cause and the prosecutor issues an information; or in the alternative (f) grand jury hearings, after which an indictment is issued against the defendant if the grand jury finds probable cause; (g) arraignment, in which the defendant is informed of the charges and must respond by pleading not guilty or guilty (or in some cases *nolo contendere*); and (h) plea bargaining.

LO 7 **Indicate the three influences on a judge's decision to set bail.** (a) Uncertainty about the character and past criminal history of the defendant; (b) the risk that the defendant will commit another crime if out on bail; and (c) overcrowded jails, which may influence a judge to release a defendant on bail.

LO 8 **Explain how a prosecutor screens potential cases.** (a) Is there sufficient evidence for conviction? (b) What is the priority of the case? The more serious the alleged crime, the higher the priority. The more extensive the defendant's criminal record, the higher the priority. (c) Are the victims cooperative? Violence against family members often yields uncooperative victims, so these cases are rarely prosecuted. (d) Are the victims reliable? (e) Might the defendant be willing to testify against other offenders?

LO 9 **Indicate the ways that both defense attorneys and prosecutors can induce plea bargaining.** Defense attorneys can file numerous pretrial motions in an effort to weaken the state's case. Prosecutors can engage in horizontal or vertical overcharging so that they can be "bargained down" in the process of plea bargaining.

SELF ASSESSMENT ANSWER KEY

Page 289: i. government/state; **ii.** charge; **iii.** win; **iv.** justice

Page 295: i. Sixth; **ii.** private; **iii.** public; **iv.** poor/indigent; **v.** privilege; **vi.** confidential; **vii.** consents

Page 302: i. initial appearance; **ii.** constitutional; **iii.** bail; **iv.** judge; **v.** preventive

Page 304: i. probable cause; **ii.** preliminary; **iii.** grand jury; **iv.** indictment

Page 308: i. attrition; **ii.** screen; **iii.** conviction; **iv.** evidence

Page 312: i. plea bargain; **ii.** charges; **iii.** sentence; **iv.** *Boykin*; **v.** trial

KEY TERMS

adversary system **296**
arraignment **308**
attorney general **287**
attorney-client privilege **295**
bail **299**
bail bond agent **300**
Boykin form **312**
case attrition **305**

defense attorney **289**
discovery **302**
grand jury **303**
indictment **303**
information **303**
initial appearance **297**
nolo contendere **308**
plea bargaining **309**

preliminary hearing **302**
preventive detention **301**
property bond **300**
public defenders **291**
public prosecutors **287**
release on recognizance (ROR) **300**
ten percent cash bail **301**

QUESTIONS FOR CRITICAL ANALYSIS

1. According to the United States Supreme Court, prosecutors cannot face civil lawsuits for misconduct, even if they have deliberately sent an innocent person to prison. In practical terms, why do you think prosecutors are protected in this manner? Do you think the Supreme Court should lift this immunity for prosecutors? Why or why not?

2. Critics argue that charging low-income defendants fees for the services of public defenders is unconstitutional. Why might this practice go against the Supreme Court's ruling in *Gideon v. Wainwright* (see page 291)?

3. Preventive detention laws (see pages 301–302) raise the troubling issue of *false positives*, or erroneous predictions that defendants, if released before trial, would commit a crime when in fact they would not. Why do you think that legislators, judges, and citizens are willing to accept the possibility of false positives when denying pretrial release to certain defendants?

4. Suppose that a billionaire investment adviser is arrested for defrauding her clients out of millions of dollars. Should she be released on recognizance, released on bail, or denied bail before her trial? Why? How do bail issues for white-collar criminals differ from those for violent criminals?

5. Do you think that a prosecutor should offer a favorable plea bargain to a defendant who provides helpful information concerning a different defendant? What are the pros and cons of this practice?

CourseMate *For Online Help*

For online help and access to resources that accompany *Criminal Justice Today*, go to www.cengagebrain.com/shop/ISBN/1111835578. Click "Access Now," where you will find flashcards, an online quiz, and other helpful study aids. If you have an access code for CourseMate, log in and go to the chapter of your choice for additional online study aids.

NOTES

1. Quoted in Linda Deutsch, "Michael Jackson Doctor to Stand Trial for Involuntary Manslaughter," *Pittsburgh Post-Gazette* (January 12, 2011), C4.

2. Daniel B. Wood, "Michael Jackson Trial: Did Conrad Murray Act as a Doctor or an Enabler?" *Christian Science Monitor* (January 12, 2011), at **www.csmonitor. com/USA/Justice/2011/0112/Michael-Jackson-trial-Did-Conrad-Murray-act-as-a-doctor-or-an-enabler**.

3. Bennett L. Gershman, "Abuse of Power in the Prosecutor's Office," in *Criminal Justice 92/93*, ed. John J. Sullivan and Joseph L. Victor (Guilford, CT: The Dushkin Publishing Group, 1991), 117–123.

4. 295 U.S. 78 (1935).

5. Celesta Albonetti, "Prosecutorial Discretion: The Effects of Uncertainty," *Law and Society Review* 21 (1987), 291–313.

6. Thomas Clouse, "Deputy Won't Face Charges in Shooting," *The (Spokane, WA) Spokesman-Review* (January 22, 2011), 1A.

7. Herbert Packer, *Limits of the Criminal Sanction* (Stanford, CA: Stanford University Press, 1968), 166–167.

8. *Gideon v. Wainwright*, 372 U.S. 335 (1963); *Massiah v. United States*, 377 U.S. 201 (1964); *United States v. Wade*, 388 U.S. 218 (1967); *Argersinger v. Hamlin*, 407 U.S. 25 (1972); and *Brewer v. Williams*, 430 U.S. 387 (1977).

9. Larry Siegel, *Criminology*, 6th ed. (Belmont, CA: West/Wadsworth Publishing Co., 1998), 487–488.

10. Center for Professional Responsibility, *Model Rules of Professional Conduct* (Washington, D.C.: American Bar Association, 2003), Rules 1.6 and 3.1.

11. *United States v. Wade*, 388 U.S. 218, 256–258 (1967).

12. 372 U.S. 335 (1963).

13. 387 U.S. 1 (1967).

14. 407 U.S. 25 (1972).

15. Peter A. Joy and Kevin C. McMunigal, "Client Autonomy and Choice of Counsel," *Criminal Justice* (Fall 2006), 57.

16. American Bar Association, "Providing Defense Services," Standard 5-7.1, at **www. abanet.org/crimjust/standards/defs-vcs_blk.html#7.1**.

17. Robert C. Boruchowitz, "The Right to Counsel: Every Accused Person's Right," *Washington State Bar Association Bar News* (January 2004), at **www.wsba.org/media/publications/barnews/2004/jan-04-boruchowitz.htm**.

18. Bureau of Justice Statistics, *County-Based and Local Public Defender Offices, 2007* (Washington, D.C.: U.S. Department of Justice, September 2010), 3.

19. *Ibid.*, 6.

20. Alicia Bannon, Mitali Nagrecha, and Rebekah Diller, *Criminal Justice Debt: A Barrier to Reentry* (New York: Brennan Center for Justice, October 2010), 12.

21. *United States v. Gonzalez-Lopez*, 548 U.S. 140 (2006).

22. *Wheat v. United States*, 486 U.S. 153, 159 (1988).

23. Bureau of Justice Statistics, *Defense Counsel in Criminal Cases* (Washington, D.C.: U.S. Department of Justice, 2000), 3.

24. Quoted in Monica Davey, "Budget Woes Hit Defense Lawyers for the Indigent," *New York Times* (September 10, 2010), A13.

25. Quoted in *ibid.*

26. *County-Based and Local Public Defender Offices*, 2007, 1.

27. John Brewer, "More Fines and Fewer Trials?" *St. Paul (MN) Pioneer Press* (September 16, 2010), A1.

28. John Eligon, "New Law to Limit Public Defenders' Caseloads in New York City," *New York Times* (April 6, 2009), A19.

29. Catherine Bean, "Indigent Defense: Separate and Unequal," *Champion* (May 2004), 54.

30. 466 U.S. 668 (1984).

31. Adam Liptak, "Despite Flawed Defense, a Death Sentence Stands," *New York Times* (November 2, 2006), A17.

32. Jonathan D. Casper, *American Criminal Justice: The Defendant's Perspective* (Englewood Cliffs, NJ: Prentice Hall, 1972), 101.

33. Quoted in Mark Pogrebin, *Qualitative Approaches to Criminal Justice* (Thousand Oaks, CA: Sage Publications, 2002), 173.

34. *Model Rules of Professional Conduct*, Rule 1.2(c)–(d).

35. Randolph Braccialarghe, "Why Were Perry Mason's Clients Always Innocent?" *Valparaiso University Law Review* (Fall 2004), 65.

36. John Kaplan, "Defending Guilty People," *University of Bridgeport Law Review* (1986), 223.

37. 491 U.S. 554 (1989).

38. Johannes F. Nijboer, "The American Adversary System in Criminal Cases: Between Ideology and Reality," *Cardozo Journal of International and Comparative Law* 5 (Spring 1997), 79.

39. Gordon Van Kessel, "Adversary Excesses in the American Criminal Trial," *Notre Dame Law Review* 67 (1992), 403.

40. James Eisenstein and Herbert Jacob, *Felony Justice* (Boston: Little, Brown, 1977), 24.

41. Jerome Skolnick, "Social Control in the Adversary System," *Journal of Conflict Resolution* 11 (1967), 52–70.

42. Abraham S. Blumberg, "The Practice of Law as Confidence Game: Organizational Cooption of a Profession," *Law and Society Review* 4 (June 1967), 115–139.

43. Malcolm Feeley, "The Adversary System," in *Encyclopedia of the American Judicial System*, ed. Robert J. Janosik (New York: Scribners, 1987), 753.

44. Blumberg, 115.

45. *Riverside County, California v. McLaughlin*, 500 U.S. 44 (1991).

46. Bureau of Justice Statistics, *Pretrial Release of Felony Defendants in State Courts* (Washington, D.C.: U.S. Department of Justice, November 2007), 2.

47. Illinois Annotated Statutes Chapter 725, Paragraph 5/110-5.

48. David W. Neubauer, *America's Courts and the Criminal Justice System*, 5th ed. (Belmont, CA: Wadsworth Publishing Co., 1996), 179–181.

49. Roy Flemming, C. Kohfeld, and Thomas Uhlman, "The Limits of Bail Reform: A Quasi Experimental Analysis," *Law and Society Review* 14 (1980), 947–976.

50. Los Angeles County Superior Court, *Felony Bail Schedule 2011*, at **www.lasuperior-court.org/bail/pdf/felony.pdf**.

51. Wayne H. Thomas, Jr., *Bail Reform in America* (Berkeley, CA: University of California Press, 1976), 4.

52. John S. Goldkamp and Michael R. Gottfredson, *Policy Guidelines for Bail: An Experiment in Court Reform* (Philadelphia: Temple University Press, 1985), 18.

53. Adam Liptak, "Illegal Globally, Bail Profit Remains Pillar of U.S. Justice," *New York Times* (January 28, 2008), A1.

54. Thomas, 7.

55. 18 U.S.C. Sections 3141–3150 (Supp. III 1985).

56. 481 U.S. 739 (1987).

57. Bureau of Justice Statistics, *Felony Defendants in Large Urban Counties, 2004* (Washington, D.C.: U.S. Department of Justice, April 2008), Appendix table F.

58. *Gerstein v. Pugh*, 420 U.S. 103 (1975).

59. Andrew D. Leipold, "Why Grand Juries Do Not (and Cannot) Protect the Accused," *Cornell Law Review* 80 (January 1995), 260.

60. Sam Skolnick, "Grand Juries: Power Shift?" *The Legal Times* (April 12, 1999), 1.

61. New York Court of Appeals Judge Sol Wachtler, quoted in David Margolik, "Law Professor to Administer Courts in State," *New York Times* (February 1, 1985), B2.

62. Kenneth C. Davis, *Discretionary Justice: A Preliminary Inquiry* (Baton Rouge, LA: Louisiana State University Press, 1969), 189.

63. Ryan Blitstein, "Online Crooks Often Escape Prosecution," *San Jose Mercury News* (November 18, 2007), 1A.

64. Henry K. Lee, "D.A. Cuts Efforts on Lesser Crimes," *San Francisco Chronicle* (April 22, 2009), B1.

65. Milton Hirsh and David Oscar Markus, "Fourth Amendment Forum," *Champion* (December 2002), 42.

66. Barbara Boland, Paul Mahanna, and Ronald Scones, *The Prosecution of Felony Arrests, 1988* (Washington, D.C.: Bureau of Justice Statistics, 1992).

67. Richard Felson and Paul-Philippe Pare, *The Reporting of Domestic Violence and Sexual Assault by Nonstrangers to the Police* (Washington, D.C.: U.S. Department of Justice, March 2005), 6.

68. Tom Lininger, "Evidentiary Issues in Federal Prosecutions of Violence against Women," *Indiana Law Review* 36 (2003), 709.

69. 18 U.S.C. Section 3553(e) (2006).

70. Quoted in Jonathan Oosting, "Oakland County Prosecutor: Leon Walker Charged for Hacking, Not Snooping on Cheating Spouse," *Mlive.com* (January 4, 2011), at **www.mlive.com/news/detroit/index. ssf/2011/01/oakland_county_prosecutor_leon.html**.

71. 404 U.S. 257 (1971).

72. Fred C. Zacharias, "Justice in Plea Bargaining," *William and Mary Law Review* 39 (March 1998), 1121.

73. Bureau of Justice Statistics, *State Court Sentencing of Convicted Felons, 2004* (Washington, D.C.: U.S. Department of Justice, July 2004), Table 4.1.

74. Albert W. Alschuler, "The Prosecutor's Role in Plea Bargaining," *University of Chicago Law Review* 36 (1968), 52.

75. Milton Heumann, *Plea Bargaining: The Experiences of Prosecutors, Judges, and Defense Attorneys* (Chicago: University of Chicago Press, 1978), 58.

76. Albert W. Alschuler, "The Defense Attorney's Role in Plea Bargaining," *Yale Law Journal* 84 (1975), 1200.

77. Stephen J. Schulhofer, "Plea Bargaining as Disaster," *Yale Law Journal* 101 (1992), 1987.

78. North Carolina General Statutes Section 15A-832(f) (2003).

79. 18 U.S.C. Section 3771 (2004).

80. Chuck Haga, "Killer Rejected Life-Sentence Plea Bargain," *(Minneapolis, MN) Star Tribune* (February 18, 2007), 1B.

81. Alschuler, "The Prosecutor's Role in Plea Bargaining," 53.

82. Casper, 77–81.

83. 395 U.S. 238 (1969).

84. Quoted in John C. Ensslin, "Springs Man Gets Twelve Years in Prison for Fatal Stabbing," *The (Colorado Springs, CO) Gazette* (November 12, 2010), A1.

85. *Ibid.*

86. Warren Burger, "Address to the American Bar Association Annual Convention," *New York Times* (August 11, 1970), 24.

87. Quoted in "Is Plea Bargaining a Cop-Out?" *Time* (August 28, 1978), at **www. time.com/time/magazine/article/0,9171,916340-3,00.html**.

88. Quoted in Frank Eltman, "D.A. Gets Tough on DWIs," *Grand Rapids (Mich.) Press* (October 1, 2006), A10.

89. *Ibid.*

CHAPTER

10

Press-Register/Bill Starling/Landov

The Criminal Trial

LEARNING OBJECTIVES

After reading this chapter, you should be able to . . .

LO 1 Identify the basic protections enjoyed by criminal defendants in the United States.

LO 2 Explain what "taking the Fifth" really means.

LO 3 List the requirements normally imposed on potential jurors.

LO 4 Contrast challenges for cause and peremptory challenges during *voir dire*.

LO 5 List the standard steps in a criminal jury trial.

LO 6 Explain the difference between testimony and real evidence, between lay witnesses and expert witnesses, and between direct and circumstantial evidence.

LO 7 List possible affirmative defenses.

LO 8 Delineate circumstances in which a criminal defendant may be tried a second time for the same act.

LO 9 List the five basic steps of an appeal.

The nine learning objectives labeled LO 1 through LO 9 are designed to help improve your understanding of the chapter.

STAR WITNESS

The jury had been sitting in a District of Columbia court for nearly two weeks, watching the trial of Ingmar Guandique for the first degree murder of Chandra Levy. In that time, the prosecution had presented thirty-seven witnesses, most of whom were forensic experts who offered detailed testimony about highly technical subjects such as DNA testing and body decomposition. To put it bluntly, the jurors looked bored. One of them even appeared to be nodding off.

Then, witness number thirty-eight took the stand, and the tone of the trial changed. Handcuffed and wearing an orange jail jumpsuit, Armando Morales testified about a conversation he had had with Guandique four years earlier, when the two shared a prison cell in Kentucky. Guandique had been incarcerated for attacking two female joggers in Rock Creek Park in Washington, D.C., during the spring of 2001—about the same time that Levy, a twenty-four-year-old government intern, had disappeared. Morales recalled Guandique's words about Levy, whose body was found in Rock Creek Park a year after she vanished: "I killed that bitch, but I didn't rape her."

"Mr. Morales is a pretty smart guy," Santha Sonenberg, Guandique's public defender, told the jurors. Sonenberg was trying to convince them that Morales, serving a ten-year prison term for gang-related drug and weapons crimes, had made up his testimony to "get in good" with government corrections officials. This strategy didn't work. On November 22, 2010, the jury found Guandique guilty of killing Levy during an attempted robbery and kidnapping, and he was sentenced to sixty years in prison. After the verdict, Susan Levy, Chandra's mother, hugged lead prosecutor Amanda Haines. "Thank you," Levy said "That was a miracle."

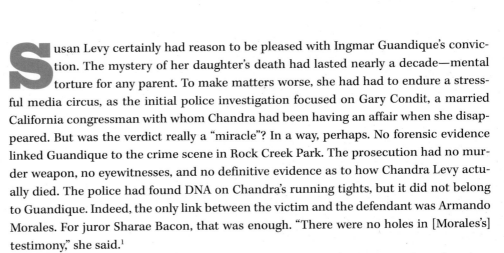

In November 2010, a Washington, D.C., jury found Ingmar Guandique guilty of murdering Chandra Levy ten years earlier.
AP Photo/Jacquelyn Martin, File

Susan Levy certainly had reason to be pleased with Ingmar Guandique's conviction. The mystery of her daughter's death had lasted nearly a decade—mental torture for any parent. To make matters worse, she had had to endure a stressful media circus, as the initial police investigation focused on Gary Condit, a married California congressman with whom Chandra had been having an affair when she disappeared. But was the verdict really a "miracle"? In a way, perhaps. No forensic evidence linked Guandique to the crime scene in Rock Creek Park. The prosecution had no murder weapon, no eyewitnesses, and no definitive evidence as to how Chandra Levy actually died. The police had found DNA on Chandra's running tights, but it did not belong to Guandique. Indeed, the only link between the victim and the defendant was Armando Morales. For juror Sharae Bacon, that was enough. "There were no holes in [Morales's] testimony," she said.[1]

Throughout the proceedings, Guandique's lawyers complained that their client was being made a scapegoat for the prosecution's earlier failures, particularly the embarrassing investigation of Condit.[2] Whenever a defendant, even one with a criminal past, is convicted without direct evidence, the fairness of a criminal trial's result inevitably comes into question. Fairness is, of course, a crucial component of the criminal trial. Protection against the arbitrary abuse of power is at the heart of the U.S. Constitution, and the right to a criminal trial before a jury is one means of ensuring this protection. In this chapter, we will examine the fairness of the criminal trial in the context of the current legal environment. Because "fairness" can only be defined subjectively, we will also make an effort to look into the effect human nature has on the adversary process. Trials may be based on fact finding, but as Judge Jerome Frank once sardonically asserted, when it comes to a jury, "facts are guesses."[3]

SPECIAL FEATURES OF CRIMINAL TRIALS

Civil trials (see Chapter 4) and criminal trials have many similar features. In both types of trials, attorneys from each side select a jury, make their opening statements to the court, examine and cross-examine witnesses, and summarize their positions in closing arguments. The jury is charged (instructed), and if it reaches a verdict, the trial comes to an end.

The principal difference is that in civil trials, the adversaries are persons (including corporations, which are legal persons, and businesses), one of whom often is seeking a remedy in the form of damages from the other. In a criminal trial, it is the state, not the victim **LO 1** of the crime, that brings the action against an alleged wrongdoer. Criminal trial procedures reflect the need to protect criminal defendants against the power of the state by providing them with a number of rights. Many of the significant rights of the accused are spelled out in the Sixth Amendment, which reads, in part, as follows:

> In all criminal prosecutions, the accused shall enjoy the right to a speedy and public trial, by an impartial jury of the State and the district wherein the crime shall have been committed, . . . and to be informed of the nature and cause of the accusation; to be confronted with the witnesses against him; to have compulsory process for obtaining witnesses in his favor; and to have the Assistance of Counsel for his defense.

In the last chapter, we discussed the Sixth Amendment's guarantee of the right to counsel. In this section, we will examine the other important aspects of the criminal trial, beginning with two protections explicitly stated in the Sixth Amendment: the right to a speedy trial by an impartial jury.

A "SPEEDY" TRIAL

As you have just read, the Sixth Amendment requires a speedy trial for those accused of a criminal act. The reason for this requirement is obvious: depending on various factors, the defendant may lose his or her right to move freely and may be incarcerated prior to trial. Also, the accusation that a person has committed a crime jeopardizes that person's reputation in the community. If the defendant is innocent, the sooner the trial is held, the sooner his or her innocence can be established in the eyes of the court and the public.

REASONS FOR DELAY As the preceding chapter made clear, there are numerous reasons for delay in bringing a defendant to trial. In defending the rights of the accused, a defense attorney may use a number of legal tactics, including pretrial motions and plea negotiations. Court congestion also contributes to the problem. Many jurisdictions do not have enough judges and courtroom space to meet the needs of the system. This situation has been aggravated by the increase in drug-related arrests, which threatens to create judicial "gridlock" in certain metropolitan courthouses.[4]

THE DEFINITION OF A SPEEDY TRIAL The Sixth Amendment does not specify what is meant by the term *speedy*. The United States Supreme Court has refused

Critical Thinking Skill Development: Have students discuss the concept of a "speedy trial." How long do students feel is "too long" between the commission of a crime and the start of a criminal trial? Under what circumstances could the start of a criminal trial be delayed with justification? (LO 1)

to quantify "speedy" as well, ruling instead in *Barker v. Wingo* (1972)[5] that only in situations in which the delay is unwarranted and proved to be prejudicial can the accused claim a violation of Sixth Amendment rights.

SPEEDY-TRIAL LAWS To meet constitutional requiements, all fifty states have their own speedy-trial statutes. For example, the Illinois Speedy Trial Act holds that a defendant must be tried within 120 days of arrest unless both the prosecution and the defense agree otherwise.[6] Keep in mind, however, that a defendant does not automatically go free if her or his trial is not "speedy" enough. There must be judicial action, which is rare but does occur in certain extreme circumstances. In 2004, for example, a Philadelphia judge ordered the release of seven men, some of whom had been charged with murder and kidnapping, because they had spent six or more years in jail awaiting trial. According to Pennsylvania law, trials must start within one year of arrest.[7] Nearly half of all criminal trials in state courts are settled within three months of the defendant's arrest. About 12 percent take more than a year to adjudicate.[8]

At the national level, the Speedy Trial Act of 1974[9] (amended in 1979) specifies the following time limits for those in the federal court system:

1. No more than thirty days between arrest and indictment.
2. No more than ten days between indictment and arraignment.
3. No more than sixty days between arraignment and trial.

Federal law allows extra time for hearings on pretrial motions, mental competency examinations, and other procedural actions.

Statutes of Limitations Note that the Sixth Amendment's guarantee of a speedy trial does not apply until a person has been accused of a crime. Citizens are protected against unreasonable delays before accusation by statutes of limitations, which are legislative time limits that require prosecutors to charge a defendant with a crime within a certain amount of time after the illegal act took place. If the statute of limitations on a particular crime is ten years, and the police do not identify a suspect until ten years and one day after the criminal act occurred, then that suspect cannot be charged with that particular offense.

In general, prosecutions for murder and other offenses that carry the death penalty do not have a statute of limitations. This exception provides police with the ability to conduct cold case investigations (see page 182) that last for decades. In 2011, for example, federal law enforcement agents were still interviewing suspects in the arson-related 1964 murder of Frank Morris. Morris died when his Ferriday, Louisiana, shoe shop was set on fire by members of the local Ku Klux Klan. The problem with prosecuting such cases, of course, is that so much time has passed since the criminal act that witnesses may be missing or dead, memories may be unreliable, and other evidence may have been lost.

THE ROLE OF THE JURY

The Sixth Amendment also states that anyone accused of a crime shall be judged by "an impartial jury." In *Duncan v. Louisiana* (1968),[10]

Teaching Tip: Have students consider the idea of statutes of limitations. What is the purpose behind such legislative time limits? Should crimes "expire"? (LO 1)

Statute of Limitations A law limiting the amount of time prosecutors have to bring criminal charges against a suspect after the crime has occurred.

In 2010, because of new evidence, Norfolk County (Massachusetts) prosecutors charged Amy Bishop, center, with murdering her brother Seth in 1986. At the time of the incident, authorities believed Amy's claim that she accidentally killed Seth while unloading a shotgun. Do you agree that statutes of limitations should not apply to murder? Why or why not?
Robin Conn/*The Huntsville Times*/Landov

the Supreme Court solidified this right by ruling that in all felony cases, the defendant is entitled to a jury trial. The Court has, however, left it to the individual states to decide whether juries are required for misdemeanor cases.[11] If the defendant waives her or his right to trial by jury, a bench trial takes place in which a judge decides questions of legality and fact, and no jury is involved.

JURY SIZE The predominant American twelve-person jury is not the result of any one law—the Constitution does not require that the jury be a particular size. Historically, the number was inherited from the size of English juries, which was fixed at twelve during the fourteenth century.

In 1970, responding to a case that challenged Florida's practice of using a six-person jury in all but capital cases, the Supreme Court ruled that the accused did not have the right to be tried by a twelve-person jury. Indeed, the Court labeled the number twelve "a historical accident, wholly without significance except to mystics."[12] In *Ballew v. Georgia* (1978),[13] however, the Court did strike down attempts to use juries with fewer than six members, stating that a jury's effectiveness was severely hampered below that limit. About half the states allow fewer than twelve persons on criminal juries, though only for misdemeanor cases. Only three states—Arizona, Florida, and Utah—use juries with fewer than twelve members for serious felony cases. In federal courts, defendants are entitled to have the case heard by a twelve-member jury unless both parties agree in writing to a smaller jury.

UNANIMITY In most jurisdictions, jury verdicts in criminal cases must be *unanimous* for acquittal or conviction. As will be explained in more detail later, if the jury cannot reach unanimous agreement on whether to acquit or convict the defendant, the result is a *hung jury*, and the judge may order a new trial.

The Supreme Court has held that unanimity is not a rigid requirement. It declared that jury verdicts must be unanimous in federal criminal trials, but has given states leeway to set their own rules.[14] As a result, Louisiana and Oregon continue to require only ten votes for conviction in criminal cases.

THE PRIVILEGE AGAINST SELF-INCRIMINATION

In addition to the Sixth Amendment, which specifies the protections we have just discussed, the Fifth Amendment to the Constitution also provides important safeguards for the defendant. The Fifth Amendment states that no person "shall be compelled in any criminal case to be a witness against himself." Therefore, a defendant has the right not to testify at a trial if to do so would implicate him or her in the crime. Witnesses may also refuse to testify on this ground. For example, if a witness, while testifying, is asked a question and the answer would reveal her or his own criminal wrongdoing, the witness may "take the Fifth." In other words, she or he can refuse to testify on the ground that such testimony may be self-incriminating. Such a refusal rarely occurs, however, as

LO 2 witnesses are often granted *immunity* before testifying, meaning that no information they disclose can be used to bring criminal charges against them. Witnesses who have been granted immunity cannot refuse to answer questions on the basis of self-incrimination.

It is important to note that not only does the defendant have the right to "take the Fifth," but also that the decision to do so should not prejudice the jury in the prosecution's favor. The Supreme Court came to this controversial decision while reviewing *Adamson v. California* (1947),[15] a case involving the convictions of two defendants who had declined to testify in their own defense against charges of robbery, kidnapping, and

Jury Trial A trial before a judge and a jury.

Bench Trial A trial conducted without a jury, in which a judge makes the determination of the defendant's guilt or innocence.

Acquittal A declaration following a trial that the individual accused of the crime is innocent in the eyes of the law and thus is absolved from the charges.

Discussion Tip: Have students work in small groups to discuss bench trials. In what circumstances would a defendant be better served by requesting a bench trial instead of a jury trial? (LO 1)

Teaching Tip: Have students respond to "Questions for Critical Analysis" number one on page 351, in which they consider the privilege against self-incrimination. (LO 2)

murder. The prosecutor in the *Adamson* proceedings frequently and insistently brought this silence to the notice of the jury in his closing argument, insinuating that if the pair had been innocent, they would not have been afraid to testify. The Court ruled that such tactics effectively invalidated the Fifth Amendment by using the defendants' refusal to testify against them. Now judges are required to inform the jury that an accused's decision to remain silent cannot be held against him or her.

Why did the presiding judge choose to import an impartial jury in the high-profile trial of Casey Anthony? What is your opinion of the judge's decision to do so?

AP Photo/Red Huber, Pool

THE PRESUMPTION OF A DEFENDANT'S INNOCENCE

The presumption in criminal law is that a defendant is innocent until proved guilty. The burden of proving guilt falls on the state (the public prosecutor). Even if a defendant did in fact commit the crime, she or he will be "innocent" in the eyes of the law unless the prosecutor can substantiate the charge with sufficient evidence to convince a jury (or judge in a bench trial) of the defendant's guilt.[16] Sometimes, especially when a case involves a high-profile violent crime, pretrial publicity may have convinced many members of the community—including potential jurors—that a defendant is guilty. In these instances, a judge has the authority to change the venue of the trial to ensure an unbiased jury. The judge can also import an impartial jury, as was the case for the high-profile trial of Casey Anthony, charged with killing her two-year-old daughter, Caylee. Although the trial took place in Orlando, Florida, the presiding judge, Belvin Perry, Jr., decided to bring in a jury from Clearwater—about 100 miles away. Perry was worried that Orlando residents would have found it difficult, if not impossible, to act impartially toward Anthony (see the photo alongside). In 2011, the Clearwater jury found Anthony not guilty of first degree murder.

A STRICT STANDARD OF PROOF

In a criminal trial, the defendant is not required to prove his or her innocence. As mentioned earlier, the burden of proving the defendant's guilt lies entirely with the state. Furthermore, the state must prove the defendant's guilt *beyond a reasonable doubt.* In other words, the prosecution must show that, based on all the evidence, the defendant's guilt is clear and unquestionable. In *In re Winship* (1970),[17] a case involving the due process rights of juveniles, the Supreme Court ruled that the Constitution requires the reasonable doubt standard because it reduces the risk of convicting innocent people and therefore reassures Americans of the law's moral force and legitimacy.

This high standard of proof in criminal cases reflects a fundamental social value—the belief that it is worse to convict an innocent individual than to let a guilty one go free. The consequences to the life, liberty, and reputation of an accused person from an erroneous conviction for a crime are substantial, and this has been factored into the process. Placing a high standard of proof on the prosecutor reduces the margin of error in criminal cases (at least in one direction). This strict standard of proof is one of the few protections enjoyed by defendants in military tribunals. The *Anti-Terrorism in Action—Trying Times* feature on the facing page addresses these tribunals, the once and future venue for judging terrorist suspects, most of whom were captured during military operations in Iraq and Afghanistan.

Fill in the blanks and check your answers on page 351.

The defendant in any felony case is entitled to a trial by _____. If the defendant waives this right, a _____ trial takes place, in which the _____ decides questions of law and fact. Another benefit for the defendant is the privilege against _____-_____, which gives her or him the right to "take the Fifth." Perhaps the most important protection for the defendant, however, is the presumption in criminal law that she or he is _____ until proved _____. Thus, the burden is on the _____ to prove the defendant's culpability beyond a _____ _____.

ANTI-TERRORISM IN ACTION

TRYING TIMES

The trial of Ahmed Khalfan Ghailani in a federal court in New York City was a contentious, messy affair. Federal prosecutors charged that Ghailani was an integral member of the 1998 al Qaeda conspiracy that led to the bombing of two American embassies in East Africa. Specifically, prosecutors said that Ghailani helped buy the truck and the explosives used in one of the attacks, which killed 224 people. Ghailani's defense attorneys countered that their client was a "dupe" who had no knowledge of the bombing plot.

Throughout the trial, the prosecution and the defense argued about which witnesses and which evidence should be admitted. Judge Lewis A. Kaplan finally ruled that Hussein Abebe, who may have sold Ghailani some TNT, could not testify because the government learned about him through a coerced interrogation. Kaplan also disallowed Ghailani's statement that he knew about the plot a week beforehand because it was made to military and not civilian investigators. Then, the jury argued about the verdict—one juror even complained to the judge that the others were verbally attacking her. Finally, Ghailani was convicted on one count of conspiracy to destroy government buildings and property and acquitted of more than 280 other counts of conspiracy and murder. On January 24, 2011, Kaplan sentenced Ghailani to life in prison for his crime.

Policy Change

To a certain degree, the Ghailani trial was a test of President Barack Obama's strategy of trying terrorism suspects in civilian criminal courts.

Given the suppression of important evidence and Ghailani's acquittal on almost all the charges, many observers felt it was a test that failed. According to Republican senator Mitch McConnell of Kentucky, the Ghailani verdict was "all the proof we need that the administration's approach to prosecuting terrorists has been deeply misguided and indeed potentially harmful as a matter of national security."

The Obama administration seems to have taken this criticism to heart. In April 2011, federal officials announced that Khalid Shaikh Mohammed and four other defendants accused of plotting the September 11, 2001, terrorist attacks would be tried by military tribunals, rather than by civilian courts as originally intended. In these tribunals, the accused does not have the right to a trial by jury, as guaranteed by the Sixth Amendment. Instead, a panel of at least five military commissioners acts in place of the judge and jury and decides questions of both "fact and law."

Only two-thirds of the panel members need to agree for a conviction, in contrast to the unanimous jury required in criminal trials. Furthermore, evidence that would be inadmissible in criminal court is allowed before these tribunals. In response to complaints that Obama had "flip-flopped" on military tribunals, a White House spokesperson replied, "First and foremost, the president does what is in the best security interests of the United States."

FOR CRITICAL ANALYSIS Do you think that foreigners suspected of terrorist acts should be given the same protections as defendants in U.S. criminal courts? Why or why not?

Argus/Shutterstock

JURY SELECTION

The initial step in a criminal trial involves choosing the jury. The framers of the Constitution ensured that the importance of the jury would not be easily overlooked. The right to a trial by jury is explicitly mentioned no fewer than three times in the Constitution: in Article III, Section 2, in the Sixth Amendment, and again in the Seventh Amendment. The use of a peer jury not only provided safeguards against the abuses of state power that the framers feared, but also gave Americans a chance—and a duty—to participate in the criminal justice system.

In the early years of the country, a jury "of one's peers" meant a jury limited to white, landowning males. Now, as the process has become fully democratized, there are still questions about what "a jury of one's peers" actually means and how effective the system has been in providing the necessary diversity in juries.

Teaching Tip: If possible, invite someone who has served as a juror to visit your classroom. Ask her or him to discuss the experience with your students.

INITIAL STEPS: THE MASTER JURY LIST AND *VENIRE*

The main goal of jury selection is to produce a cross section of the population in the jurisdiction where the crime was committed. As we saw earlier, sometimes a defense attorney may argue that his or her client's trial should be moved to another community to protect against undue prejudice. In practice, judges, mindful of the intent of the Constitution, are hesitant to grant such pretrial motions.

> **"A jury consists of twelve persons chosen to decide who has the better lawyer."**
>
> —**Robert Frost,**
> American poet
> (1874–1963)

A JURY OF PEERS This belief that trials should take place in the community where the crime was committed is central to the purpose of selecting a jury of the defendant's "peers." The United States is a large, diverse nation, and the outlook of its citizens varies accordingly. Two very different cases, one tried in rural Maine and the other in San Francisco, illustrate this point.[18] In Maine, the defendant had accidentally shot and killed a woman standing in her backyard because he had mistaken her white mittens for a deer's tail. His attorney argued that it was the responsibility of the victim to wear bright-colored clothing in the vicinity of hunters during hunting season. The jury agreed, and the defendant was acquitted of manslaughter. In the San Francisco case, two people were charged with distributing sterile needles to intravenous drug users. Rather than denying that the defendants had distributed the needles, the defense admitted the act but insisted that it was necessary to stem the transmission of AIDS and, thus, to save lives. The jury voted 11–1 to acquit, causing a mistrial.

These two outcomes may surprise or even anger people in other parts of the country, but they reflect the values of the regions where the alleged crimes were committed. Thus, a primary goal of the jury selection process is to ensure that the defendant is judged by members of her or his community—peers in the true sense of the word.

Teaching Tip: Have students interview your local county clerk to learn more about the jury selection process. How is the master jury list determined in your area? What limitations, if any, are placed on those who may serve as jurors? (LO 3)

THE MASTER JURY LIST Besides having to live in the jurisdiction where the case is being tried, there are very few restrictions on eligibility to serve on a jury. State legislatures generally set the requirements, and they are similar in most states. For the most part, jurors must be

1. Citizens of the United States.
2. Over eighteen years of age.

LO 3

3. Free of felony convictions.
4. Healthy enough to function in a jury setting.
5. Sufficiently intelligent to understand the issues of a trial.
6. Able to read, write, and comprehend the English language (with one exception—New Mexico does not allow non-English-speaking citizens to be eliminated from jury lists simply because of their lack of English-language skills).

The **master jury list,** sometimes called the *jury pool,* is made up of all the eligible jurors in a community. This list is usually drawn from voter-registration lists or driver's license rolls, which have the benefit of being easily available and timely.

VENIRE The next step in gathering a jury is to draw together the *venire* (Latin for "to come"). The *venire* is composed of all those people who are notified by the clerk of the court that they have been selected for jury duty. Those selected to be part of the *venire* are ordered to report to the courthouse on the date specified by the notice.

Some people are excused from answering this summons. Persons who do not meet the qualifications listed above either need not appear in court or, in some states, must appear only in order to be officially dismissed by court officials. Also, people in some professions, including teachers, physicians, and judges, can receive exemptions due to the nature of their work. Each court sets its own guidelines for the circumstances under which it will excuse jurors from service, and these guidelines can be as strict or as lenient as the court desires.

VOIR DIRE

At the courthouse, prospective jurors are gathered, and the process of selecting those who will actually hear the case begins. This selection process is not haphazard. The court ultimately seeks jurors who are free of any biases that may affect their willingness to listen to the facts of the case impartially. To this end, both the prosecutor and the defense attorney have some input into the ultimate makeup of the jury. Each attorney questions prospective jurors in a proceeding known as *voir dire* (French for "to speak the truth"). During *voir dire,* jurors are required to provide the court with a significant amount of personal information, including home address, marital status, employment status, arrest record, and life experiences.

The *voir dire* process involves both written and oral questioning of potential jurors. Attorneys fashion their inquiries in such a manner as to uncover any biases on the parts of prospective jurors and to find persons who might identify with the plights of their

Group Activities: Ask students to brainstorm a list of characteristics they think a good juror should possess. Ask them to come up with a second list of characteristics they would avoid in selecting jurors.

Master Jury List The list of citizens in a court's district from which a jury can be selected; compiled from voter-registration lists, driver's license lists, and other sources.

Venire The group of citizens from which the jury is selected.

Voir Dire The preliminary questions that the trial attorneys ask prospective jurors to determine whether they are biased or have any connection with the defendant or a witness.

CAREERS IN CJ

Photo Courtesy Collins E. Ijoma

COLLINS E. IJOMA
TRIAL COURT ADMINISTRATOR

My first job in the court system was by accident rather than design. After completing a graduate internship with the Essex County government, I had the opportunity to seek permanent employment with the county-funded judiciary. I was first employed in the Trial Court Administrator's Office in Newark, New Jersey, as the court finance officer in 1983. Much of my education in court administration was gained through the Institute for Court Management of the National Center for State Courts. I pursued this program of professional development from 1984 through 1991 when I graduated as a fellow of ICM.

OPPORTUNITY KNOCKS My initial position offered many opportunities to learn about court management and the workings of a large urban court system. My primary concentration was in human resources, budget, and finance. As a state court, funded by the county, we had to continually justify and fight for positions, space, and equipment. Our court was growing rapidly, and we needed additional resources to allow for an effective and efficient operation. In 1985, I was promoted to director of personnel. I had direct responsibility for all personnel programs, policies, and practices. The knowledge gained combined with experience helped me to successfully seek the position of assistant trial court administrator and my present position as trial court administrator.

As the trial court administrator, I serve principally as the chief administrative officer for the largest trial and municipal court system in New Jersey. We provide technical and managerial support to the court (more than sixty superior court judges and thirty-six municipal court judges) on such matters as personnel, program development, case flow, resources, and facilities management. This description may sound "highfalutin" considering that most people can only describe a court in terms of a judge, one or two courtroom staff, and a few other employees associated with the visible activities in the courthouse. Obviously, there is a lot more going on behind the scenes of which the average citizen is not aware. For example, besides directing case flow for the four major divisions (criminal, civil, family, and probation), the work involved in managing personnel programs for more than 1,200 employees, information systems and technology infrastructure, records of proceedings, coordination of transcription, grand and petit jury operations, and court interpreting, to mention but a few examples, is enormous. The modern court needs dedicated professionals in each of these areas.

ENTHUSIASM AND HOPE One thing that keeps me going and enthused about this profession is the resolve and dedication of our judges and staff. The family division embraces a host of issues, and in some cases those who seek help are hurting and desperate. The court may be their only hope. We are also actively engaged in pursuing new ways to offer and manage dispute resolution. Some of these include drug courts to give nonviolent drug offenders a chance at rehabilitation rather than going to jail, complimentary dispute resolution to reach more satisfactory conclusions in less time and at a lower cost to litigants, and creative uses of volunteers to assist in the work of the court and create a positive connection to the community.

FAST FACTS

TRIAL COURT ADMINISTRATOR JOB DESCRIPTION:

- Oversees court operations, budget and accounting, technology, emergency management, and human resources.
- Oversees court programs and services, ensuring compliance with applicable procedures, policy, regulations, and statutes.
- Establishes and maintains working relationships with judges, state attorneys, public defenders, sheriffs' offices, and the public.

WHAT KIND OF TRAINING IS REQUIRED?

- A B.A. in court administration, management, or a related area, and five years of professional experience in court administration or government administration, plus five years in a supervisory capacity.
- A law degree, master's degree, or certification by the Institute for Court Management may substitute for one year of the nonsupervisory experience.

ANNUAL SALARY RANGE?

- $66,000–$116,000

For additional information on a career as a trial court administrator, visit: **www.ncsconline.org/D_Icm/icmindex.html**

respective sides. As one attorney noted, though a lawyer will have many chances to talk to a jury as a whole, *voir dire* is his or her only chance to talk with the individual jurors. (To better understand the specific kinds of questions asked during this process, see Figure 10.1 below.) Increasingly, attorneys are also conducting virtual *voir dires* on the Internet, using social networking sites such as Myspace and Facebook to learn valuable information about potential jurors.

CHALLENGING POTENTIAL JURORS During *voir dire*, the attorney for each side may exercise a certain number of challenges to prevent particular persons from serving on the jury. Both sides can exercise two types of challenges: challenges "for cause" and peremptory challenges.

Challenges for Cause If a defense attorney or prosecutor concludes that a prospective juror is unfit to serve, the attorney may exercise a challenge for cause and request that that person not be included on the jury. Attorneys must provide the court with a sound,

Discussion Tip: Have students discuss the practice of using a jury consultant to ensure the selection of sympathetic jurors. Taking into consideration the *voir dire* process, are juries still representative of society at large, or are they tailored to produce an outcome favorable to the parties involved in the case?

Challenge for Cause A *voir dire* challenge for which an attorney states the reason why a prospective juror should not be included on the jury.

FIGURE 10.1 Sample Juror Questionnaire

In 2010, Brian David Mitchell went on trial in Salt Lake City, Utah, for kidnapping fourteen-year-old Elizabeth Smart and keeping her in captivity for "nine months of hell." Mitchell held a number of extreme religious views, including the belief that he was a godlike figure who would play a prominent role in the coming "end of the world." As Mitchell's religion would play a significant part in the criminal proceedings, both the prosecution and the defense were interested in the religious beliefs of potential jurors, as this excerpt from the juror questionnaire shows.

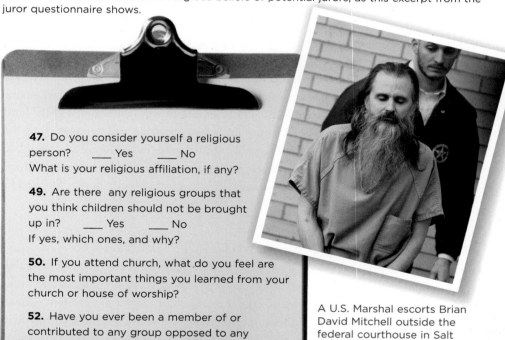

47. Do you consider yourself a religious person? ___ Yes ___ No
What is your religious affiliation, if any?

49. Are there any religious groups that you think children should not be brought up in? ___ Yes ___ No
If yes, which ones, and why?

50. If you attend church, what do you feel are the most important things you learned from your church or house of worship?

52. Have you ever been a member of or contributed to any group opposed to any religious group or sect? ___ Yes ___ No
If yes, what groups and how long have you participated?

A U.S. Marshal escorts Brian David Mitchell outside the federal courthouse in Salt Lake City, Utah.
AP Photo/Colin E. Braley

Paul-Andre Belle-Isle/Shutterstock

legally justifiable reason for why potential jurors are "unfit" to serve. For example, jurors can be challenged for cause if they are mentally incompetent, do not understand English, or are proved to have a prior link—be it personal or financial—with the defendant or victim.

Jurors can also be challenged if they are outwardly biased in some way that would prejudice them for or against the defendant. During jury selection for the 2011 trial of former professional baseball player Barry Bonds, charged with perjury for lying to a federal grand jury about his alleged steroid use, one potential juror was dismissed because he was a fan of the San Francisco Giants, Bonds's team. Another was kept off the jury because she was still "getting over" the rowdy behavior of baseball players she served as an attendant on charter flights.[19] The Supreme Court has ruled that individuals may also be legally excluded from a jury in a capital case if they would under no circumstances vote for a guilty verdict if it carried the death penalty.[20]

At the same time, potential jurors cannot be challenged for cause if they have "general objections" or have "expressed conscientious or religious scruples" against capital punishment.[21] The final responsibility for deciding whether a potential juror should be excluded rests with the judge, who may choose not to act on an attorney's request.

Peremptory Challenges *Voir dire* challenges to exclude potential jurors from serving on the jury without any supporting reason or cause.

Critical Thinking Skill Development: Ask students to respond to "Questions for Critical Analysis" number two on page 351, in which they consider the use of social networking sites in the jury selection process.

Peremptory Challenges Each attorney may also exercise a limited number of **peremptory challenges.** These challenges are based solely on an attorney's subjective reasoning, and the attorney usually is not required to give any legally justifiable reason for wanting to exclude a particular person from the jury. Because of the rather random nature of peremptory challenges, each state limits the number that an attorney may utilize: between five and ten for felony trials (depending on the state) and between ten and twenty for trials that could possibly result in the death penalty (also depending on the state). Once an attorney's peremptory challenges are used up, he or she must accept forthcoming jurors, unless a challenge for cause can be used.

LO 4

An attorney's decision to exclude a juror may sometimes seem whimsical. One state prosecutor who litigated drug cases was known to use a peremptory challenge whenever he saw a potential juror with a coffee mug or backpack bearing the insignia of the local public broadcasting station. The attorney presumed that this was evidence that the potential juror had donated funds to the public station, and that anybody who would do so would be too "liberal" to give the government's case against a drug offender a favorable hearing.[22] Lawyers have been known to similarly reject potential jurors for reasons of demeanor, dress, and posture.

RACE AND GENDER ISSUES IN JURY SELECTION

Teaching Tip: In a written assignment, ask students to consider race and gender in jury selection. How has the Supreme Court ruled on this issue? What are the benefits of having a diverse jury?

For many years, prosecutors used their peremptory challenges as an instrument of segregation in jury selection. Prosecutors were able to keep African Americans off juries in cases in which an African American was the defendant. The argument that African Americans—or members of any other minority group—would be partial toward one of their own was tacitly supported by the Supreme Court. Despite its own assertion, made in *Swain v. Alabama* (1965),[23] that blacks have the same right to appear on a jury as whites, the Court mirrored the apparent racism of society as a whole by protecting the questionable actions of many prosecutors.

THE BATSON REVERSAL The Supreme Court reversed this policy in 1986 with *Batson v. Kentucky*.[24] In that case, the Court declared that the Constitution prohibits prosecutors from using peremptory challenges to strike possible jurors on the basis of race. Under the *Batson* ruling, the defendant must prove that the prosecution's use of a peremptory challenge was racially motivated. Doing so requires a number of legal steps:[25]

1. First, the defendant must make a *prima facie* case that there has been discrimination during *venire*. (*Prima facie* is Latin for "at first sight." Legally, it refers to a fact that is presumed to be true unless contradicted by evidence.)
2. To do so, the defendant must show that he or she is a member of a recognizable racial group and that the prosecutor has used peremptory challenges to remove members of this group from the jury pool.
3. Then, the defendant must show that these facts and other relevant circumstances raise the possibility that the prosecutor removed the prospective jurors solely because of their race.
4. If the court accepts the defendant's charges, the burden shifts to the prosecution to prove that its peremptory challenges were race neutral. If the court finds against the prosecution, it rules that a *Batson* violation has occurred.

The Court has revisited the issue of race a number of times in the years since its *Batson* decision. In *Powers v. Ohio* (1991),[26] it ruled that a defendant may contest race-based peremptory challenges even if the defendant is not of the same race as the excluded jurors. In *Georgia v. McCollum* (1992),[27] the Court placed defense attorneys under the same restrictions as prosecutors when making race-based peremptory challenges. Finally, in 2008, the Court, reaffirming its *Batson* decision of twenty-two years earlier, overturned the conviction of an African American death row inmate because a Louisiana prosecutor improperly picked an all-white jury for his murder trial.[28]

These rulings do not mean that a black defendant can never be judged by a jury made up entirely of whites. Rather, they indicate that attorneys cannot use peremptory challenges to reject a prospective juror because of her or his race. Indeed, there is evidence that African Americans are still being kept off juries, particularly in parts of the South. According to the Louisiana Capital Assistance Center, in that state's Louisiana Parish, blacks are struck from juries at three times the rate of whites.[29] In Houston County, Alabama, from 2005 to 2009, prosecutors removed 80 percent of eligible African Americans from death penalty cases.[30] "Anyone with any sense at all can think up a race-neutral reason [to exclude a potential minority juror] and get away with it," says Atlanta defense attorney Stephen B. Bright.[31]

WOMEN ON THE JURY In *J.E.B. v. Alabama ex rel. T.B.* (1994),[32] the Supreme Court extended the principles of the *Batson* ruling to cover gender bias in jury selection. The case was a civil suit for paternity and child support brought by the state of Alabama. Prosecutors used nine of their ten challenges to remove men from the jury, while the defense made similar efforts to remove women. When challenged, the state defended its actions by referring to what it called the rational belief that men and women might have different views on the issues of paternity and child support. The Court disagreed and held this approach to be unconstitutional.

ALTERNATE JURORS

Because unforeseeable circumstances or illness may necessitate that one or more of the sitting jurors be dismissed, the court may also seat several *alternate jurors* who will hear the entire trial. Depending on the rules of the particular jurisdiction, two or three alternate jurors may be present throughout the trial. If a juror has to be excused in the middle of the trial, an alternate may take his or her place without disrupting the proceedings.

Teaching Tip: In a written assignment, have students explain the *Batson* decision and discuss its impact on jury selection. Then have students explain how *Batson* has evolved since 1986 through subsequent Supreme Court rulings.

The **Constitutional Rights Foundation of Chicago** has created a Web site dedicated to the American jury and its role in our criminal justice system. Find a link to this site by visiting the *Criminal Justice CourseMate* at **cengagebrain. com** and selecting the *Web links* for this chapter.

The _____ is composed of all those people who have been identified as potential jurors for a particular trial. These people are then gathered for the process of _____ _____, in which the prosecution and defense choose the actual members of the jury. Both sides can remove jurors in two ways: (1) through unlimited challenges for _____, which require the attorney to give a reason for the removal, and (2) through a limited number of _____ challenges, for which no reason is necessary. According to the United States Supreme Court, potential jurors cannot be removed for reasons of _____ or _____.

THE TRIAL

Once the jury members have been selected, the judge swears them in and the trial itself can begin. A rather pessimistic truism among attorneys is that every case "has been won or lost when the jury is sworn." This reflects the belief that a juror's values are the major, if not dominant, factor in the decision of guilt or innocence.[33]

LO 5 In actuality, it is difficult to predict how a jury will go about reaching a decision. Despite a number of studies on the question, researchers have not been able to identify any definitive consistent patterns of jury behavior. Sometimes, jurors in a criminal trial will follow instructions to find a defendant guilty unless there is a reasonable doubt, and sometimes they seem to follow instinct or prejudice and apply the law any way they choose.[34]

OPENING STATEMENTS

Attorneys may choose to open the trial with a statement to the jury, though they are not required to do so. In these opening statements, the attorneys give a brief version of the facts and the supporting evidence that they will present during the trial. Because some trials can drag on for weeks or even months, it is extremely helpful for jurors to hear a summary of what will unfold. In short, the opening statement is a kind of "road map" that describes the destination that each attorney hopes to reach and outlines how she or he plans to reach it. The danger for attorneys is that they will offer evidence during the trial that might contradict an assertion made during the opening statement. This may cause jurors to disregard the evidence or shift their own thinking further away from the narrative being offered by the attorney.[35] (For an example of an opening statement, see Figure 10.2 on the facing page.)

THE ROLE OF EVIDENCE

Once the opening statements have been made, the prosecutor begins the trial proceedings by presenting the state's evidence against the defendant. Courts have complex rules about what types of evidence may be presented and how the evidence may be brought out during the trial. Evidence is anything that is used to prove the existence or nonexistence of a fact. For the most part, evidence can be broken down into two categories: testimony and real evidence. Testimony consists of statements by competent witnesses. Real evidence, presented to the court in the form of exhibits, includes any physical items—such as the murder weapon or a bloodstained piece of clothing—that affect the case.

Rules of evidence are designed to ensure that testimony and exhibits presented to the jury are relevant, reliable, and not unfairly prejudicial against the defendant. One of the tasks of the defense attorney is to challenge evidence presented by the prosecution by

---

Group Activities: If possible, take a field trip to a local courthouse and allow students to sit in on a portion of a criminal trial. When you get back to class, have each student reflect on the experience in a short written assignment. (LO 5)

Opening Statements The attorneys' statements to the jury at the beginning of the trial. Each side briefly outlines the evidence that will be offered during the trial and the legal theory that will be pursued.

Evidence Anything that is used to prove the existence or nonexistence of a fact.

Testimony Verbal evidence given by witnesses under oath.

Real Evidence Evidence that is brought into court and seen by the jury, as opposed to evidence that is described for a jury.

FIGURE 10.2 The Opening Statement

Mazoltuv Borukhova was charged with hiring her cousin, Mikhail Mallayev, to kill her husband. In his opening statement, New York prosecutor Brad Leventhal asked the jury why Mallayev would commit such a murder, given that he did not know the victim. He proceeded to answer his own question:

"Because he was hired to do it. He was paid to do it. He's an assassin. A paid assassin. An executioner. A hit man. For who? Who would hire this man, this defendant, to murder in cold blood an innocent victim in the presence of his own daughter? Who could have such strong feelings toward Daniel Malekov that they would hire an assassin to end his life. Who?"

Leventhal then pointed his finger at Borukhova and said,

"Her."

Mazoltuv Borukhova was sentenced to life in prison after being found guilty of hiring a hit man to murder her husband.

Photo Courtesy the Queens District Attorney's office

Source: Janet Malcolm, "Iphigenia in Forest Hills," *The New Yorker* (May 3, 2010), 36.

establishing that the evidence is not reliable. Of course, the prosecutor also tries to demonstrate the irrelevance or unreliability of evidence presented by the defense. The final decision on whether evidence is allowed before the jury rests with the judge, in keeping with his or her role as the "referee" of the adversary system.

LO 6

TESTIMONIAL EVIDENCE A person who is called to testify on factual matters that would be understood by the average citizen is referred to as a **lay witness.** If asked about the condition of a victim of an assault, for example, a lay witness could relate certain facts, such as "she was bleeding from her forehead" or "she was unconscious on the ground for several minutes." A lay witness could not, however, give information about the medical extent of the victim's injuries, such as whether she suffered from a fractured skull or internal bleeding. Coming from a lay witness, such testimony would be inadmissible. When the matter in question requires scientific, medical, or technical skill beyond the scope of the average person, prosecutors and defense attorneys may call an **expert witness** to the stand. The expert witness is an individual who has professional training, advanced knowledge, or substantial experience in a specialized area, such as medicine, computer technology, or ballistics. The rules of evidence state that expert witnesses may base their opinions on three types of information:

1. Facts or data of which they have personal knowledge.
2. Material presented at trial.
3. Secondhand information given to the expert outside the courtroom.[36]

Expert witnesses are considered somewhat problematic for two reasons. First, they may be chosen for their "court presence"—whether they speak well or will appear sympathetic to the jury—rather than their expertise. Second, attorneys pay expert witnesses for their services. Given human nature, the attorneys expect a certain measure of cooperation from an expert they have hired, and an expert witness has an interest in satisfying the attorneys so that he or she will be hired again.[37]

Lay Witness A witness who can truthfully and accurately testify on a fact in question without having specialized training or knowledge.

Expert Witness A witness with professional training or substantial experience qualifying her or him to testify on a certain subject.

Discussion Tip: Ask students to discuss the various forms of evidence that are presented in a criminal trial. Which form of evidence do students find most useful and why?

Direct Evidence Evidence that establishes the existence of a fact that is in question without relying on inference.

Circumstantial Evidence Indirect evidence that is offered to establish, by inference, the likelihood of a fact that is in question.

Under these circumstances, some have questioned whether the courts can rely on the professional nonpartisanship of expert witnesses.[38] Take a recent case in which a Denver court was trying to determine whether a defendant named Timothy Wilkins was competent to stand trial on drug charges. One expert, hired by the defense, said that Wilkins had a verbal IQ of 58 and therefore could not understand the court proceedings. Another expert, hired by the prosecution, said that Wilkins's verbal IQ was 88, well above the cutoff line for competence. The judge rejected both conclusions, writing, "The two sides have canceled each other out."[39]

DIRECT VERSUS CIRCUMSTANTIAL EVIDENCE Two types of testimonial evidence may be brought into court: direct evidence and circumstantial evidence. **Direct evidence** is evidence that has been witnessed by the person giving testimony. "I saw Bill shoot Chris" is an example of direct evidence. **Circumstantial evidence** is indirect evidence that, even if believed, does not establish the fact in question but only the degree of likelihood of the fact. In other words, circumstantial evidence can create an inference that a fact exists.

Suppose, for example, that the defendant owns a gun that shoots bullets of the type found in the victim's body. This circumstantial evidence, by itself, does not establish that the defendant committed the crime. Combined with other circumstantial evidence, however, it may do just that. For instance, if other circumstantial evidence indicates that the defendant had a motive for harming the victim and was at the scene of the crime when the shooting occurred, the jury might conclude that the defendant committed the crime. The prosecutor's successful case against Ingmar Guandique for the murder of Chandra Levy, described in the opening of this chapter, was based entirely on circumstantial evidence.

CJ&TECHNOLOGY The CSI Effect

Cliff Lipson/CBS via Getty Images

Letalvis Cobbins and Lemaricus Davidson, half brothers, were prime suspects in the brutal kidnapping, torture, rape, and murder of a University of Tennessee student named Channon Christian. As part of its case during Cobbins's trial, the prosecution planned to present a key piece of evidence: a strand of hair found on Christian's body. There was only one problem. Because of the family relationship between Cobbins and Davidson, a DNA fingerprinting expert could not say which brother was the source of the hair. The judge in the case was leaning toward keeping the hair from the jury, so as not to confuse the jurors. Prosecutor Leland Price did not like this idea. "If they hear the victim was in that house for twelve hours and we didn't find a fiber, hair, or something, that's going to weigh against us," he said.

Price was worried about the "CSI effect," a phenomenon that takes its name from the popular television series *CSI: Crime Scene Investigation* and its two spin-offs, *CSI: Miami* and *CSI: NY.* According to many prosecutors, the shows have fostered unrealistic notions among jurors as to what forensic science can accomplish as part of a criminal investigation. In reality, the kind of physical evidence used to solve crimes on *CSI* is often not available to the prosecution, which must rely instead on witnesses and circumstantial evidence. Prosecutors such as Price fear that jurors, expecting the high-tech physical clues they have become accustomed to on television, will wrongfully acquit guilty defendants when this expectation is not met. Indeed, one recent study of jurors in Washtenaw County, Michigan, found that nearly half "expected the prosecutor to present scientific evidence in every criminal case."

THINKING ABOUT THE CSI EFFECT

In general, why are prosecutors taking a risk when they present *only* circumstantial evidence to a jury? How might the CSI effect have a positive impact on criminal trials, from the standpoint of both prosecutor preparation and juror interest?

RELEVANCE Evidence will not be admitted in court unless it is relevant to the case being considered. **Relevant evidence** is evidence that tends to prove or disprove a fact in question. Forensic proof that the bullets found in a victim's body were fired from a gun discovered in the suspect's pocket at the time of arrest, for example, is certainly relevant. The suspect's prior record, showing a conviction for armed robbery ten years earlier, is, as we shall soon see, irrelevant to the case at hand and in most instances will be ruled inadmissible by the judge.

Relevant Evidence Evidence tending to make a fact in question more or less probable than it would be without the evidence. Only relevant evidence is admissible in court.

PREJUDICIAL EVIDENCE Evidence may be excluded if it would tend to distract the jury from the main issues of the case, mislead the jury, or cause jurors to decide the issue on an emotional basis.

Real Evidence In most cases involving a violent crime, prosecutors try to offer as much physical evidence of the crime as possible, showing the jury touching photographs of the victim before the crime and graphic photos of the victim after the crime, bloody pieces of clothing, and other evocative items. Defense attorneys usually try to exclude these items on the ground that they unfairly prejudice the jury against the defendant.

Judges generally will permit such evidence so long as it is not blatantly prejudicial. In 2010, for example, Edward B. Fleury faced manslaughter charges after an eight-year-old boy named Christopher Bizilj accidentally shot and killed himself at a gun show sponsored by Fleury. During the trial, Judge Peter A. Velis of Hampden Superior Court in Springfield, Massachusetts, allowed jurors to see a video of the incident, in which a bullet from a 9mm Micro UZI pierces Bizilj's head. Velis, however, turned off the audio track so that jurors would not hear the boy's screams. "The greatest risk in this case is invoking any sympathy" for young Christopher, the judge explained.[40] (See the photo alongside.)

Evil Character Defense attorneys are likely to have some success precluding prosecutors from using prior purported criminal activities or actual convictions to show that the defendant has criminal propensities or an "evil character."[41] This concept is codified in the Federal Rules of Evidence, which state that evidence of "other crimes, wrongs, or acts is not admissible to

During the manslaughter trial of Edward Fleury, prosecutor William Bennet shows the jury a photo of Colin Bizilj, brother of victim Christopher, firing an Uzi machine gun. Why would this photo be considered relevant evidence in Fleury's trial?

AP Photo/*Springfield Republican*, Michael S. Gordon

prove the character of a person in order to show action in conformity therewith." Such evidence is allowed only when it does not apply to character construction and focuses instead on "motive, opportunity, intent, preparation, plan, knowledge, identity, or absence of mistake or accident."[42]

Though this legal concept has come under a great deal of criticism, it is consistent with the presumption-of-innocence standards discussed earlier. Presumably, if a prosecutor is allowed to establish that the defendant has shown antisocial or even violent character traits, this will prejudice the jury against the defendant. While discussing a 1930 murder case, New York Court of Appeals chief judge Benjamin Cardozo addressed the issue thusly:

> With only the rough and ready tests supplied by their experience of life, the jurors were to look into the workings of another's mind, and discover its capacities and disabilities, its urges and inhibitions, in moments of intense excitement. Delicate enough and subtle is the inquiry, even in the most favorable conditions, with every warping influence excluded. There must be no blurring of the issues by evidence illegally admitted and carrying with it in its admission an appeal to prejudice and passion.[43]

THE PROSECUTION'S CASE

Because the burden of proof is on the state, the prosecution is generally considered to have a more difficult task than the defense. The prosecutor attempts to establish guilt beyond a reasonable doubt by presenting the *corpus delicti* ("body of the offense" in Latin) of the crime to the jury. The *corpus delicti* is simply a legal term that refers to the substantial facts that show a crime has been committed. By establishing such facts through the presentation of relevant and nonprejudicial evidence, the prosecutor hopes to convince the jury of the defendant's guilt.[44]

DIRECT EXAMINATION OF WITNESSES Witnesses are crucial to establishing the prosecutor's case against the defendant. The prosecutor will call witnesses to the stand and ask them questions pertaining to the sequence of events that the trial is addressing. This form of questioning is known as **direct examination**. During direct examination, the prosecutor will usually not be allowed to ask *leading questions*—questions that might suggest to the witness a particular desired response.

A leading question might be something like "So, Mrs. Williams, you noticed the defendant threatening the victim with a broken beer bottle?" If Mrs. Williams answers "yes" to this question, she has, in effect, been "led" to the conclusion that the defendant was, in fact, threatening with a broken beer bottle. The fundamental purpose behind testimony is to establish what actually happened, not what the trial attorneys would like the jury to believe happened. (A properly worded query would be, "Mrs. Williams, please describe the defendant's manner toward the victim during the incident.")

HEARSAY When interviewing a witness, both the prosecutor and the defense attorney will make sure that the witness's statements are based on the witness's own knowledge and not hearsay. **Hearsay** can be defined as any testimony given in court about a statement made by someone else. Literally, it is what someone heard someone else say. For the most part, hearsay is not admissible as evidence. It is excluded because the listener may have misunderstood what the other person said, and without the opportunity of cross-examining the originator of the statement, the misconception cannot be challenged.

There are a number of exceptions to the hearsay rule, and as a result, a good deal of hearsay evidence is allowed before the jury. For example, a hearsay statement is usually admissible if there seems to be little risk of a lie. Therefore, a statement made

Direct Examination The examination of a witness by the attorney who calls the witness to the stand to testify.

Hearsay An oral or written statement made by an out-of-court speaker that is later offered in court by a witness (not the speaker) concerning a matter before the court. Hearsay usually is not admissible as evidence.

Group Activities: Present students with a mock-crime scenario. Ask them to imagine that they will be performing the direct examination of a key witness. Have them work in groups to develop questions they will ask the witness. They must avoid asking leading questions.

by someone who believes that his or her death is imminent—a "dying declaration"—is allowed in court even though it is hearsay.[45] The rules of most courts also allow hearsay when the person who made the statement is unavailable to be questioned in court or when the statement is particularly important to the argument being made by one side. Consequently, an admission of guilt by the defendant is often permitted even when it falls under the strict definition of hearsay.[46]

COMPETENCE AND RELIABILITY OF WITNESSES The rules of evidence include certain restrictions and qualifications pertaining to witnesses. Witnesses must have sufficient mental competence to understand the significance of testifying under oath. They must also be reliable in the sense that they are able to give a clear and reliable description of the events in question. If not, the prosecutor or defense attorney will make sure that the jury is aware of these shortcomings.

In a 2011 trial, for example, Devaughndre Broussard was the prosecution's star witness in the trial of Yusuf Bey. Broussard testified that Bey had ordered him to kill journalist Chauncey Bailey, who was investigating Bey's finances. Trying to undermine Broussard's credibility, Bey's defense counsel told the jury that Broussard had already lied numerous times about his involvement in Bailey's murder, was receiving a lesser sentence in exchange for his testimony, and had threatened to "get [Bey's] ass."[47]

CROSS-EXAMINATION

After the prosecutor has directly examined her or his witnesses, the defense attorney is given the chance to question the same witnesses. The Sixth Amendment states, "In all criminal prosecutions, the accused shall enjoy the right . . . to be confronted with witnesses against him." This **confrontation clause** gives the accused, through his or her attorneys, the right to cross-examine witnesses. **Cross-examination** refers to the questioning of an opposing witness during trial, and both sides of a case are allowed to do so (see Figure 10.3 on the next page).

Cross-examination allows the attorneys to test the truthfulness of opposing witnesses and usually entails efforts to create doubt in the jurors' minds that the witness is reliable. Cross-examination is also linked to the problems presented by hearsay evidence. When a witness offers hearsay, the person making the original remarks is not in the court and therefore cannot be cross-examined. If such testimony were allowed, the defendant's Sixth Amendment right to confront witnesses against him or her would be violated.

After the defense has cross-examined a prosecution witness, the prosecutor may want to reestablish any reliability that might have been lost. The prosecutor can do so by again questioning the witness, a process known as *redirect examination*. Following the redirect examination, the defense attorney will be given the opportunity to ask further questions of prosecution witnesses, or recross-examination. Thus, each side has two opportunities to question a witness. The attorneys need not do so, but only after each side has been offered the opportunity will the trial move on to the next witness or the next stage.

MOTION FOR A DIRECTED VERDICT

After the prosecutor has finished presenting evidence against the defendant, the government will inform the court that it has rested the people's case. At this point, the defense may make a **motion for a directed verdict** (now also known as a *motion for judgment as a matter of law* in federal courts). Through this motion, the defense is basically saying that the prosecution has not offered enough evidence to prove that the accused is guilty

truTV is a cable television channel that offers continuous coverage of the most important criminal trials of the day. Find its Web site, which offers news on current and classic trials, by visiting the *Criminal Justice CourseMate* at **cengagebrain.com** and selecting the *Web links* for this chapter.

Critical Thinking Skill Development: Ask students to consider why both the defense and the prosecution have two or more opportunities to question each witness. How is this related to the Sixth Amendment?

Confrontation Clause The part of the Sixth Amendment that guarantees all defendants the right to confront witnesses testifying against them during the criminal trial.

Cross-Examination The questioning of an opposing witness during trial.

Motion for a Directed Verdict A motion requesting that the court grant judgment in favor of the defense on the ground that the prosecution has not produced sufficient evidence to support the state's claim.

FIGURE 10.3 The Cross-Examination

The following is a transcript of a cross-examination of a government witness during a drug trial. Note that the defense attorney is not trying to establish any facts concerning the alleged crime. Instead, she is trying to create a negative picture of the witness in the minds of the jurors.

Defense: "You have thirteen children?"

Witness: "Unh huh" (affirmative)

Defense: "Made by thirteen different women?"

Witness: "Unh huh"

Defense: "Now and you are twenty-four years old?"

Witness: "Yes, m'am."

Defense: "So, out of the twenty-four years that you have been living, twenty years has been on the street, and almost four have been in prison?"

Witness: "Yes, you can say so."

Defense: "And out of the last two years that you have been on the street you had thirteen children?"

Witness: "Yes."

Rich Legg/iStockphoto

Source: www.thesmokinggun.com/archive/years/2009/0813091alfamega1.html.
Text Source: The United States District Court for the Northern District of Georgia Atlanta Division, Transcript of Proceedings Before the Honorable Clarence Cooper, United States District Judge and a Jury, October 8, 1996. Docket Number: 1:95-CR-373-CC

beyond a reasonable doubt. If the judge grants this motion, which rarely occurs, then a judgment will be entered in favor of the defendant, and the trial is over.

THE DEFENDANT'S CASE

Assuming that the motion for a directed verdict is denied, the defense attorney may offer the defendant's case. Because the burden is on the state to prove the accused's guilt, the defense is not required to offer any case at all. It can simply "rest" without calling any witnesses or producing any real evidence and ask the jury to decide the merits of the case on what it has seen and heard from the prosecution.

Discussion Tip: Ask the class to discuss the reasons why a defense attorney would keep her or his client from testifying during a criminal trial. How do students feel this impacts the perceived guilt or innocence of the defendant?

PLACING THE DEFENDANT ON THE STAND If the defense does present a case, its first—and often most important—decision is whether the defendant will take the stand in her or his own defense. Because of the Fifth Amendment protection against self-incrimination, the defendant is not required to testify. Therefore, the defense attorney must make a judgment call. He or she may want to put the defendant on the stand if the defendant is likely to appear sympathetic to the jury or is well spoken and able to aid the defense's case. With a less sympathetic or less effective defendant, the defense attorney may decide that exposing the defendant before the jury presents too large a risk. Also, if the defendant testifies, she or he is open to cross-examination under oath from the prosecutor. In any case, remember that the prosecution cannot comment on a defendant's refusal to testify.[48]

CREATING A REASONABLE DOUBT Defense lawyers most commonly defend their clients by attempting to expose weaknesses in the prosecutor's case. Remember that if the defense attorney can create reasonable doubt concerning the client's guilt in the mind of just a single juror, the defendant has a good chance of gaining an acquittal or at least a *hung jury*, a circumstance explained later in the chapter.

Even if the prosecution can present seemingly strong evidence, a defense attorney may succeed by creating reasonable doubt. In an illustrative case, Jason Korey bragged to his friends that he had shot and killed Joseph Brucker in Pittsburgh, Pennsylvania, and a great deal of circumstantial evidence linked Korey to the killing. The police, however, could find no direct evidence: they could not link Korey to the murder weapon, nor could they match his footprints to those found at the crime scene. Michael Foglia, Korey's defense attorney, explained his client's bragging as an attempt to gain attention, not a true statement. Though this explanation may strike some as unlikely, in the absence of physical evidence it did create doubt in the jurors' minds, and Korey was acquitted. (For a better idea of how this strategy works in court, see the feature *You Be the Defense Attorney—A Gang Murder* below.)

REASONABLE DOUBT AND SEXUAL ASSAULT Creating reasonable doubt is also very effective in cases that essentially rely on the word of the defendant against the word of the victim. In sexual-assault cases, for example, if the defense attorneys can create doubt about the victim's credibility—in other words, raise the possibility that he or she is lying—then they may prevail at trial. According to the Alcohol and Rape Study, carried out by researchers at Rutgers University and the University of New Hampshire, juries acquit about 90 percent of the time when the defendant says the sex was consensual

YOU BE THE DEFENSE ATTORNEY

A Gang Murder

THE SITUATION Your client is Daniel, a twenty-three-year-old member of a violent Los Angeles street gang. Daniel is charged with the first degree murder of Christopher, his best friend and fellow gang member. Christopher was killed because other gang members believed he had "snitched" about their criminal activity. According to prosecutors, Daniel lured Christopher to a garage, where other gang members hit him in the head with a shotgun and then stabbed him more than sixty times. During the trial, José, the prosecution's main witness, who admitted taking part in the stabbing while high on methamphetamine, testified that Daniel kicked Christopher's dead body. In her opening argument, the prosecutor told the jury that even though your client did not stab Christopher, he was just as guilty of murder as those who did.

THE LAW To find a defendant guilty (in this jurisdiction), a jury must find *beyond a reasonable doubt* that he or she committed the crime. For Daniel to be guilty of first degree murder, the prosecution must prove that he acted with "malice aforethought" in luring Christopher to his death in the garage.

YOUR DECISION As a defense attorney, your job is to create reasonable doubt in the jurors' minds about Daniel's intent to lure Christopher to his death. Besides the facts presented above, other important details about this case include the following: (1) José, the prosecution's main witness, was allowed to plead guilty to a lesser charge of voluntary manslaughter in return for his testimony, and (2) José was dating Christopher's sister at the time of the murder. What argument will you make before the jury to create reasonable doubt?

[To see how a Los Angeles defense attorney argued in a case with similar facts, go to Example 10.1 in Appendix B.]

and there is evidence that the alleged victim was drinking alcohol before the incident in question.[49] (The *CJ in Action* feature at the end of this chapter explores issues concerning evidence in sexual-assault cases in more detail.)

OTHER DEFENSE STRATEGIES The defense can choose among a number of strategies to generate reasonable doubt in the jurors' minds. It can present an *alibi defense,* by submitting evidence that the accused was not at or near the scene of the crime at the time the crime was committed. Another option is to attempt an *affirmative defense,* by presenting additional facts to the ones offered by the prosecution. Possible affirmative defenses, which we discussed in detail in Chapter 4, include the following:

LO 7

1. Self-defense   2. Insanity   3. Duress   4. Entrapment

With an affirmative defense strategy, the defense attempts to prove that the defendant should be found not guilty because of certain circumstances surrounding the crime. An affirmative strategy can be difficult to carry out because it forces the defense to prove the reliability of its own evidence, not simply disprove the evidence offered by the prosecution.

The defense is often willing to admit that a certain criminal act took place, especially if the defendant has already confessed. In this case, the primary question of the trial becomes not whether the defendant is guilty, but what the defendant is guilty of. In these situations, the defense strategy focuses on obtaining the lightest possible penalty for the defendant. As we saw in the last chapter, this strategy is responsible for the high percentage of proceedings that end in plea bargains.

REBUTTAL AND SURREBUTTAL

After the defense closes its case, the prosecution is permitted to bring new evidence forward that was not used during its initial presentation to the jury. This is called the **rebuttal** stage of the trial. When the rebuttal stage is finished, the defense is given the opportunity to cross-examine the prosecution's new witnesses and introduce new witnesses of its own. This final act is part of the *surrebuttal*. After these stages have been completed, the defense may offer another motion for a directed verdict, asking the judge to find in the defendant's favor. If this motion is rejected, and it almost always is, the case is closed, and the opposing sides offer their closing arguments.

CLOSING ARGUMENTS

In their **closing arguments,** the attorneys summarize their presentations and argue one final time for their respective cases. In most states, the defense attorney goes first, and then the prosecutor. (In Colorado, Kentucky, and Missouri, the order is reversed.) An effective closing argument includes all of the major points that support the government's or the defense's case. It also emphasizes the shortcomings of the opposing party's case. Jurors will view a closing argument with some skepticism if it merely recites the central points of a party's claim or defense without also responding to the unfavorable facts or issues raised by the other side. Of course, neither attorney wants to focus too much on the other side's position, but the elements of the opposing position do need to be acknowledged and their flaws highlighted. (For an example of opposing closing arguments, see Figure 10.4 on the facing page.)

One danger in the closing arguments is that an attorney will become too emotional and make remarks that are later deemed by appellate courts to be prejudicial. Once both

Teaching Tip: Ask students to search media outlets and locate examples of criminal trials in which the defendant utilized an affirmative defense. Let students share their cases with the class, as well as the outcomes. (LO 7)

Rebuttal Evidence given to counteract or disprove evidence presented by the opposing party.

Closing Arguments Arguments made by each side's attorney after the cases for the plaintiff and defendant have been presented.

Teaching Tip: If possible, take the class to the local courthouse to hear closing arguments in a criminal trial. Ask students to imagine themselves as members of the jury. Would they vote for a conviction? Why or why not?

FIGURE 10.4 Closing Arguments

During the murder trial of Justin Barber for murdering his wife, April, on a Florida beach, the defense claimed that someone else had attacked the couple, killing April and wounding Justin. As proof, Barber's lawyers presented evidence that bullet holes in the defendant's shirt did not align with wounds on his body, thus proving his claim that he had struggled with the assailant. In his closing argument, assistant state's attorney Matthew Foxman contested this evidence:

"[B]ased on what was observed yesterday in the courtroom, and you can see from the image of that, that shirt was big on the defendant. He was practically swimming in it. And bear in mind, he had just drowned his wife, and dragged her 100 yards up the beach. Might that explain a little displacement in the shirt? Then also, I'm not sure the evidence tells you how the defendant might have shot himself, or pulled this shirt when he did it. Not sure how that would happen. But to say that's indicative of a struggle is quite a leap."

Nikolay Mamluke/iStockphoto

The jury found Barber guilty of first degree murder, and a Florida judge sentenced him to life in prison without parole.

Source: For a complete transcript of Foxman's closing argument, go to **www.msnbc.msn.com/id/14740478/ns/ dateline_nbc-crime_reports**.

attorneys have completed their remarks, the case is submitted to the jury, and the attorneys' role in the trial is, for the moment, complete.

SELFASSESSMENT

Fill in the blanks and check your answers on page 351.

Evidence is any object or spoken _____ that can be used in a criminal trial to prove or disprove a _____ related to the crime. Evidence will not be admitted into the trial unless it is _____ and does not unfairly _____ the jury against the defendant by appealing to emotion rather than fact. The prosecution will usually try to build its case through _____ examination of its witnesses, which the defense will counter with a _____ -examination of its own. The defense's main goal is to create _____ _____ concerning the defendant's guilt in the minds of as many jurors as possible.

THE FINAL STEPS OF THE TRIAL AND POSTCONVICTION PROCEDURES

After closing arguments, the outcome of the trial is in the hands of the jury. In this section, we examine the efforts to give jurors the means necessary to make informed decisions about the guilt or innocence of the accused. We also look at the posttrial motions that can occur when the defense feels that the jurors, prosecution, or trial judge made errors that necessitate remedial legal action.

JURY INSTRUCTIONS

Charge The judge's instructions to the jury following the attorneys' closing arguments. The charge sets forth the rules of law that the jury must apply in reaching its decision, or verdict.

Before the jurors begin their deliberations, the judge gives the jury a **charge,** summing up the case and instructing the jurors on the rules of law that apply to the issues in the case. These charges, also called jury instructions, are usually prepared during a special *charging conference* involving the judge and the trial attorneys. In this conference, the attorneys suggest the instructions they would like to see be sent to the jurors, but the judge makes the final decision as to the charges submitted. If the defense attorney disagrees with the charges sent to the jury, he or she can enter an objection, thereby setting the stage for a possible appeal.

Teaching Tip: In a written assignment, ask students to explain the purpose of a charging conference. Who may contribute to the construction of the charge, and how might the wording of the charge impact the outcome of the trial?

THE JUDGE'S ROLE The judge usually begins by explaining basic legal principles, such as the need to find the defendant guilty beyond a reasonable doubt. Then the jury instructions narrow to the specifics of the case at hand, and the judge explains to the jurors what facts the prosecution must have proved to obtain a conviction. If the defense strategy centers on an affirmative defense such as insanity or entrapment, the judge will discuss the relevant legal principles that the defense must have proved to obtain an acquittal. The final segment of the charges discusses possible verdicts. These always include "guilty" and "not guilty," but some cases also allow for the jury to find "guilt by reason of insanity" or "guilty but mentally ill." Juries are often charged with determining the seriousness of the crime as well, such as deciding whether a homicide is murder in the first degree, murder in the second degree, or manslaughter.

"Nothing can ever prepare you for this kind of thing."

—Juror Elizabeth Burbank, following a 2010 trial involving the triple murder of a mother and her two young daughters

UNDERSTANDING THE INSTRUCTIONS A serious problem with jury instructions is that jurors often do not seem to understand them.[50] This situation is hardly surprising, as most average Americans do not have the education or legal background to disentangle the somewhat unfathomable jargon of the law. One study came to the unfortunate conclusion that juries that received no instructions whatsoever were basically as well equipped—or poorly equipped, as the case may be—as juries that did receive instructions.[51]

One solution is to simplify the language of the jury instructions. Several years ago, California became the first state to move in this direction when state officials approved 2,048 pages of new "plain language" criminal jury instructions. So, for example, a juror in California will no longer read, "The law does not undertake to measure in units of time the length of the period during which the thought must be pondered before it can ripen into an intent to kill which is truly deliberate and premeditated." Instead, he or she will read, "The length of time the person spends considering whether to kill does not alone determine whether the killing is deliberate and premeditated."[52]

JURY DELIBERATION

Discussion Tip: Ask students to discuss the issues related to jury instructions. What are the problems associated with this stage of the trial process?

After receiving the charge, the jury begins its deliberations. Jury deliberation is a somewhat mysterious process, as it takes place in complete seclusion. Most of what is known about how a jury deliberates comes from mock trials or interviews with jurors after the verdict has been reached. A general picture of the deliberation process constructed from this research shows that the romantic notion of jurors with high-minded ideals of justice making eloquent speeches is, for the most part, not the reality. In approximately three out of every ten cases, the initial vote by the jury led to a unanimous decision. In 90 percent of the remaining cases, the majority eventually dictated the decision.[53]

RESTRICTING THE JURY One of the most important instructions that a judge normally gives the jurors is that they should seek no outside information during deliberation. The idea is that jurors should base their verdict *only* on the evidence that the judge has deemed admissible. As we saw in Chapter 8, in recent years, technology has made this restriction difficult to enforce. As cell phones have been transformed into small computers, many jurors now have the ability to conduct Internet searches on lawyers or defendants, read news articles on the case, or search for evidence that has been excluded by the judge. This form of electronic juror misconduct can force the judge to declare a *mistrial,* requiring that the proceedings start over again with a different jury.

SEQUESTRATION In extreme cases, the judge will order that the jury be *sequestered,* or isolated from the public, during the trial and deliberation stages of the proceedings. Sequestration is used when deliberations are expected to be lengthy, or the trial is attracting a high amount of interest and the judge wants to keep the jury from being unduly influenced. Juries are usually sequestered in hotels and kept under the watch and guard of officers of the court. The importance of *total* sequestration is reflected in a recent Colorado Supreme Court decision to overturn the death penalty of a man who was sentenced after the jurors consulted a Bible during deliberations. The court held that a Bible constituted an improper outside influence and a reliance on a "higher authority."[54]

Teaching Tip: In a brief written assignment, ask students to discuss the circumstances that could lead a judge to sequester a jury. Can students find a recent example of sequestration to reference in the assignment?

THE VERDICT

Once it has reached a decision, the jury issues a **verdict.** The most common verdicts are guilty and not guilty, though, as we have seen, juries may signify different degrees of guilt if instructed to do so. Following the announcement of a guilty or not guilty verdict, the jurors are discharged, and the jury trial proceedings are finished. (See Figure 10.5 below for a review of the steps of a jury trial.)

Verdict A formal decision made by the jury.

Hung Jury A jury whose members are so irreconcilably divided in their opinions that they cannot reach a verdict.

THE HUNG JURY When a jury in a criminal trial is unable to agree on a unanimous verdict—or a majority in certain states—it returns with no decision. This is known as a **hung jury.** Following a hung jury, the judge will declare a mistrial, and the case will be tried again in front of a different jury if the prosecution decides to pursue the matter a second time. A judge can do little to reverse a hung jury, considering that "no decision" is just as legitimate a verdict as guilty or not guilty. In some states, if there are only a

FIGURE 10.5 The Steps of a Jury Trial

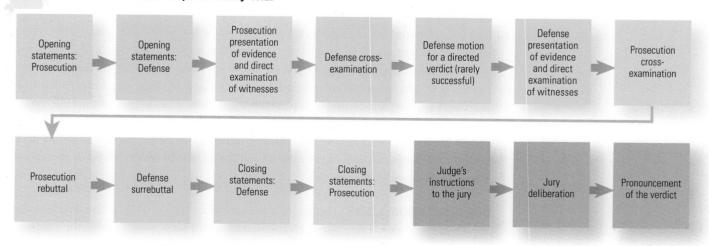

Opening statements: Prosecution → Opening statements: Defense → Prosecution presentation of evidence and direct examination of witnesses → Defense cross-examination → Defense motion for a directed verdict (rarely successful) → Defense presentation of evidence and direct examination of witnesses → Prosecution cross-examination →

Prosecution rebuttal → Defense surrebuttal → Closing statements: Defense → Closing statements: Prosecution → Judge's instructions to the jury → Jury deliberation → Pronouncement of the verdict

Allen Charge An instruction
by a judge to a deadlocked jury
with only a few dissenters that
asks the jurors in the minority
to reconsider the majority
opinion.

Jury Nullification An
acquittal of a defendant by a
jury even though the evidence
presented and the judge's
instructions indicate that the
defendant is guilty.

Appeal The process of seeking
a higher court's review of
a lower court's decision for
the purpose of correcting or
changing this decision.

Critical Thinking Skill
Development: Ask students to
consider the *Allen* Charge. Should
hung juries be sent back into the
jury room by the judge, or is this in
fact a subtle form of coercion?

Discussion Tip: Have the class
debate jury nullification. Should
jurors have the right to question the
laws they are asked to enforce?

few dissenters to the majority view, a judge can send the jury back to the jury room under a set of rules set forth more than a century ago by the Supreme Court in *Allen v. United States* (1896).[55] The *Allen* Charge, as this instruction is called, asks the jurors in the minority to reconsider the majority opinion. Many jurisdictions do not allow *Allen* Charges on the ground that they improperly coerce jurors with the minority opinion to change their minds.[56]

For all of the attention they receive, hung juries are relatively rare. Juries are unable to come to a decision in only about 6 percent of all cases.[57] Furthermore, juries may be more lenient (or easy to "trick") than is generally perceived. One study found that juries were six times more likely than judges (in bench trials) to acquit a person who turns out to be guilty.[58]

JURY NULLIFICATION The last statistic points to a growing concern of a number of criminal justice observers, who question whether jury verdicts are always based on the proper legal principles. Their concern relates to the controversial subject of jury nullification, which occurs when jurors "nullify" the law by acquitting a defendant who may be guilty according to the instruction given to them by the court. In other words, the jury acquits *in spite of* the evidence, rather than *because of* the evidence.[59]

The specter of jury nullification is most often raised in cases that involve issues on which jurors may have strong ideological opinions, such as race, the death penalty, assisted suicide, or drug offenses. Jury nullification is often used to explain anomalies in trial results. For example, juries in the suburbs of Baltimore are about thirty times more likely to convict defendants of felonies than are their counterparts within city limits. The assumption is that the largely African American population of Baltimore is less inclined to trust police officer testimony than are the nearby white suburbanites.[60]

Many observers believe jury nullification is counter to the principles of American law because it allows a jury to "play by its own rules." Others, however, feel that jurors are within their rights when they question not only the facts in the case before them, but also the merits of the laws that the court is asking them to enforce. This argument has been made since the earliest days of the American legal system, when John Adams (1735–1826) said that a juror has not only a right, but a duty, "to find the verdict according to his own best understanding, judgment, and conscience, though in direct opposition to the direction of the court."[61] By this reasoning, jurors who feel that a particular law is unjust, or that the penalty for a law is too severe, are justified in nullifying a guilty verdict.

APPEALS

Even if a defendant is found guilty, the trial process is not necessarily over. In our criminal justice system, a person convicted of a crime has a right to appeal. An appeal is the process of seeking a higher court's review of a lower court's decision for the purpose of correcting or changing the lower court's judgment. A defendant who loses a case in a trial court cannot automatically appeal the conviction. The defendant normally must first be able to show that the trial court acted improperly on a question of law. Common reasons for appeals include the introduction of tainted evidence by the prosecution or faulty jury instructions delivered by the trial judge. In federal courts, about 17 percent of criminal convictions are appealed.[62]

DOUBLE JEOPARDY The appeals process is available only to the defense. If a jury finds the accused not guilty, the prosecution cannot appeal to have the decision reversed. To do so would infringe on the defendant's Fifth Amendment rights against multiple trials for the same offense. This guarantee against being tried a second time for the same crime is known as protection from double jeopardy.

The Limits of Double Jeopardy The prohibition against double jeopardy means that once a criminal defendant is found not guilty of a particular crime, the government may not reindict the person and retry him or her for the same crime. The basic idea behind the double jeopardy clause, in the words of Supreme Court Justice Hugo Black, is that the state should not be allowed to

> make repeated attempts to convict an individual for an alleged offense, thereby subjecting him to embarrassment, expense, and ordeal and compelling him to live in a continuing state of anxiety and insecurity, as well as enhancing the possibility that though innocent he may be found guilty.[63]

The bar against double jeopardy does not preclude a victim from bringing a civil suit against the same person to recover damages. For example, in 2010, Charles Buck was acquitted of killing his wife, Leslie, who eight years earlier had been found dead at the bottom of the stairs of their home in Mystic, Connecticut, with unexplained head injuries. Although prosecutors could not prove Buck's guilt, a wrongful death lawsuit against him filed by Leslie's brother proceeded, unaffected. This was not considered double jeopardy because the wrongful death suit involved a civil claim, not a criminal one. Therefore, Buck was not being tried for the same *crime* more than once.

The Possibility and Risk of Retrial Additionally, a state's prosecution of a crime will not prevent a separate federal prosecution of the same crime, and vice versa. In other words, a defendant found not guilty of violating a state law can be tried in federal court for the same act, if the act is also defined as a crime under federal law. Furthermore, as we saw in Chapter 8 with the example of sex offender Warren Jeffs, double jeopardy does not preclude different states from prosecuting the same person for multiple crimes that take place in different jurisdictions.

LO 8

Note that a hung jury is *not* an acquittal for purposes of double jeopardy. So, if a jury is deadlocked, the government is free to seek a new trial. In another spousal murder case, in June 2010, a jury deliberated for thirty hours but could not decide whether Ryan Widmer of Hamilton Township, Ohio, had drowned his wife, Sarah, in their bathtub (see the photo alongside). Six months later, relying on a new "mystery witness" who heard Widmer admit to killing Sarah, prosecutors opted to try the defendant again for the same crime. At the conclusion of this trial, in February 2011, a jury found Widmer guilty, and he was sentenced to fifteen years to life in prison.

THE APPEAL PROCESS There are two basic reasons for the appeal process. The first is to correct an error made during the initial trial. The second is to review policy. Because of this second function, the appellate courts are an important part of the flexible nature of the criminal justice system. When existing law has ceased to be effective or no longer reflects the values of society, an appellate court can effectively change the law through its decisions and the precedents that it sets.[64] A classic example was the *Miranda v. Arizona* decision (see page 239), which, although it failed to change

Double Jeopardy To twice place at risk (jeopardize) a person's life or liberty. The Fifth Amendment to the U.S. Constitution prohibits a second prosecution in the same court for the same criminal offense.

Do you think that the government should be able to seek a new trial if a jury deadlocks in the previous one, as happened with Ryan Widmer, shown here, who was convicted of murder in his second trial for the same crime? Why or why not?
AP Photo/*The Cincinnati Enquirer*, Cara Owsley

Group Activities: Ask students to create a chart explaining when double jeopardy applies and when it does not. Be sure they include circumstances such as civil claims and hung juries in their charts. (LO 8)

the fate of the defendant (he was found guilty on retrial), had a far-reaching impact on custodial interrogation of suspects.

It is also important to understand that once the appeal process begins, the defendant is no longer presumed innocent. The burden of proof has shifted, and the defendant is obligated to prove that her or his conviction should be overturned. The method of filing an appeal differs slightly among the fifty states and the federal government, but the five basic steps are similar enough for summarization in Figure 10.6 below. For the most part, defendants are not required to exercise their right to appeal. The one exception involves the death sentence. Given the seriousness of capital punishment, the defendant is required to appeal the case, regardless of his or her wishes.

LO 9

Finality The end of a criminal case, meaning that the outcome of the case is no longer susceptible to challenge by prosecutors or the defendant.

> ## "I fell out of my chair and burst into tears because I knew the evidence meant freedom."
>
> **—Dwayne Deal,** describing his reaction after being told that items related to his case would be subjected to DNA analysis. Three weeks later, Deal, who spent nineteen years in prison for rape of a minor, was released.

FINALITY AND WRONGFUL CONVICTIONS

Mandatory death sentence appeals lead to long stints on death row. According to the U.S. Department of Justice, prisoners sentenced to death spend, on average, just over fourteen years awaiting their execution.[65] Such a lengthy appeals process seems contrary to the concept of finality, which exists when the outcome of a criminal case can no longer be challenged by anyone. The benefits of finality are evident—once a case is over, all of the participants can redirect their energy to other activities. Furthermore, cases that drag on for years or even decades can weaken the public's confidence in the criminal justice system. Several aspects of the criminal justice system discussed in this chapter directly promote finality. Statutes of limitations ensure that, after a reasonable amount of time, the government cannot prosecute most crimes. The protection against double jeopardy also protects suspects from the "fear and anxiety" of a second trial.

FIGURE 10.6 The Steps of an Appeal

1. The defendant, or *appellant*, files a **notice of appeal**—a short written statement outlining the basis of the appeal.

2. The appellant transfers the trial court record to the appellate court. This record contains items such as evidence and a transcript of the testimony.

3. Both parties file **briefs.** A brief is a written document that presents the party's legal arguments.

4. Attorneys from both sides present **oral arguments** before the appellate court.

5. Having heard from both sides, the judges of the appellate court retire to deliberate the case and make their decision. As described in Chapter 8, this decision is issued as a **written opinion.** Appellate courts generally do one of the following:

   - **Uphold** the decision of the lower court.
   - **Modify** the lower court's decision by changing only a part of it.
   - **Reverse** the decision of the lower court.
   - **Reverse and remand** the case, meaning that the matter is sent back to the lower court for further proceedings.

At the same time, however, finality also means that there is a point at which a convicted defendant will no longer be able to challenge the verdict, even though he or she may be innocent. For most of American history, finality had the upper hand over innocence as far as postconviction procedures were concerned. Only during the past fifty years have appeals processes provided significant relief for those who wish to revisit aspects of the criminal trial after a final verdict has been delivered. The most serious threat to the primacy of finality, however, is the same DNA fingerprinting that has been a boon to law enforcement, as we saw in Chapter 6. As these techniques have become more effective, they have brought the problem of **wrongful convictions,** which occur when an innocent person is found guilty, into the national spotlight.

DNA EXONERATION DNA exonerates potential wrongdoers the same way it identifies them: by matching genetic material found at a crime scene to that of a suspect. (Or, conversely, by showing that the genetic material does not match the suspect's.) For example, in 1980 Phillip Bivens was convicted of raping and killing a woman in Forrest County, Mississippi. He had admitted to the crimes before recanting, saying that his confession was coerced by police officers. Bivens subsequently spent three decades in prison until a DNA test of the initial rape kit proved his innocence, and in 2010, he was set free. (See the photo below.)

According to the Innocence Project, a New York–based legal group, as of May 2011, 268 convicts have been exonerated by DNA evidence in the United States.[66] Given that state courts convict about 1.1 million adults each year,[67] this number may not seem very significant. People convicted of crimes do not have an automatic right to DNA checks of the evidence in their cases, however. In most instances, the trial judge must approve the request, and if it is rejected, the convict must bring a lawsuit to force the issue.[68] Consequently, the DNA exonerations that have already taken place may represent a "random audit of convictions," meaning that the incidence of wrongful convictions may be a larger problem than the statistics indicate.[69] (Figure 10.7 on the following page shows the most common causes of wrongful convictions.)

HABEAS CORPUS Even after the appeals process is exhausted, a convict many have access to one final procedure, known as *habeas corpus* (Latin for "you have the body"). *Habeas corpus* is a judicial order that commands a corrections official to bring a prisoner before a federal court so that the court can hear the convict's claim that he or she is being held illegally. A writ of *habeas corpus* differs from an appeal in that it can be filed only by someone who is imprisoned. In recent years, defense attorneys have successfully used the *habeas corpus* procedure for a number of their death row clients who have new DNA evidence proving their innocence.[70]

Wrongful Conviction The conviction, either by verdict or by guilty plea, of a person who is factually innocent of the charges.

Habeas Corpus An order that requires corrections officials to bring an inmate before a court or a judge and explain why he or she is being held in prison.

Phillip Bivens, left, is congratulated by his attorney after being exonerated of a thirty-year-old murder conviction. What role did DNA fingerprinting play in his eventual release? Meggan Haller/*New York Times*/Redux Pictures

FIGURE 10.7 Wrongful Convictions and Unreliable Evidence

Phillip Bivens, mentioned on the previous page, not only falsely confessed to the crime that put him behind bars for thirty years, but he also falsely implicated another man, Larry Ruffin, in the crime. False confessions and false informant testimony are two of the four most common reasons found for wrongful convictions later overturned by DNA evidence.

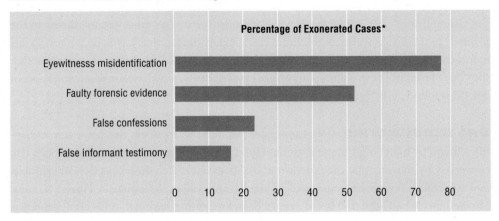

Percentage of Exonerated Cases*

* The total exceeds 100 percent because wrongful convictions can have more than one cause.

Sources: The Innocence Project; and Peter Modaferri, Patricia Robinson, and Phyllis McDonald, "When the Guilty Walk Free: The Role of Police in Preventing Wrongful Convictions," *The Police Chief* (October 2010), Figure 1, page 36.

Teaching Tip: Ask students to generate a short written assignment explaining the *habeas corpus* petition. Under what circumstances can a defendant ask for a *habeas corpus* review of his or her case?

Habeas corpus rules also provide federal judges with an opportunity to review state law. In 2011, for example, U.S. District Judge Mary S. Scriven granted the *habeas corpus* petition of Mackle Shelton, who had been convicted of drug trafficking in Florida. In his petition, Shelton claimed that Florida's drug trafficking law was unfair because it had no *mens rea* requirement. That is, a person could be found guilty of transporting drugs even if he or she was not aware of doing so. Judge Scriven agreed with Shelton and ruled that Florida law, lacking an intent requirement, was unconstitutional.[71] (See pages 108–109 in Chapter 4 for a description of *mens rea* basics.)

SELFASSESSMENT

Fill in the blanks and check your answers on page 351.

Once both the prosecution and the defense have completed their closing arguments, the judge will give the jury a _____ summing up the case and providing instructions on how to proceed. After the jury has _____ and reached a decision, it will announce a _____ of guilty or not guilty. If the jury cannot do so, a _____ jury occurs, and the judge will call a mistrial. If a defendant is convicted, he or she has the option of _____ this outcome based on a showing that the trial court acted improperly on a question of _____, not fact, during the proceedings.

CJ IN ACTION

RAPE SHIELD LAWS

Historically, the courtroom has been a hostile environment for victims of sexual assault. Because of a pervasive attitude labeled the "chastity requirement" by Professor Michelle Anderson of the City University of New York School of Law, rape victims who were perceived to be sexually virtuous were much more likely to be believed by jurors than those who had been sexually active.[72] If a woman had consented to sex before, so the line of thought went, she was more likely to do so again. Consequently, defense attorneys invariably and successfully focused on the accuser's sexual past, convincing juries that consent had been given in the present instance by establishing a pattern of consent in past ones. As we close this chapter, we will examine much-debated legislative efforts to make the courtroom "safe" for rape victims.

"UNCHASTITY" EVIDENCE

Rape shield laws keep specific evidence, including evidence about the victim's reputation and previous sexual conduct, out of the courtroom, except under certain circumstances.[73] Today, every state except Arizona has a rape shield law. (In Arizona, well-established case law, rather than a statute, declares evidence of the accuser's "unchastity" inadmissible.)[74] In 1978, Congress also imposed a rape shield law in federal courts.[75]

Rape shield laws do contain certain exceptions that allow the defense to use evidence of the accuser's prior sexual conduct to undermine the credibility of his or her testimony. For example, Federal Rule 412 states that evidence of "other sexual behavior" or the "sexual disposition" of a rape complainant is inadmissible *unless* it is offered *either* (1) to prove that a person other than the accused was the source of semen, injury, or other physical evidence; *or* (2) to prove consent *and* involves previous sexual behavior by the alleged victim with the defendant. In addition, the defense must show that the exclusion of the evidence would violate the constitutional rights of the defendant.[76]

THE CASE FOR RAPE SHIELD LAWS

- Without these laws, defense attorneys may subject victims of sexual assault to embarrassing and degrading cross-examination concerning their personal lives.

- These laws ensure that defendants are convicted or acquitted based on the relevant evidence, not the prejudices of jurors more focused on the sexual history of the accuser than on the facts of the case.

- These laws encourage victims to report incidents of sexual assault by protecting their privacy.

THE CASE AGAINST RAPE SHIELD LAWS

- The confrontation clause of the Sixth Amendment gives all defendants the right to question their accusers. By limiting this right, rape shield laws leave defendants in sexual-assault cases at the mercy of juries that do not know all the facts.

Photodisc/Getty Images

- In many instances, the victim's prior sexual history is relevant to the issue of whether she or he consented to the incident in question. These facts should not be hidden from the jury simply because they may cause an emotional reaction or deal with sexual issues.

- The many exceptions to rape shield laws, mentioned earlier, have effectively rendered them meaningless. According to the federal government, only 38 percent of those who have been sexually assaulted report the crime to the police.[77]

YOUR OPINION—WRITING ASSIGNMENT

A woman accuses two men of raping her in the back seat of a car. Both defendants claim that the sexual activity was consensual. At their trial, they want to present the following evidence from that night: (1) a fourth person had witnessed the accuser flirting aggressively with numerous men at a local bar; (2) the accuser had openly tried to seduce the older brother of one of the defendants; and (3) another witness had seen the accuser sitting on a soda crate in front of the defendants, one of whom was zipping up his pants.

Given the goals of rape shield laws and their exceptions discussed in this feature, which evidence, if any, concerning the above incident should be admitted before the jury? In cases such as this one, do you feel that rape shield laws properly balance the rights of the accuser and the rights of the accused? Before responding, you can review our discussions in this chapter concerning:

- Relevant and prejudicial evidence (pages 335–336).

- The prosecutor's case (pages 336–337).

- The defendant's case (pages 338–340).

Your answer should include at least three full paragraphs.

CHAPTER SUMMARY

LO 1 **Identify the basic protections enjoyed by criminal defendants in the United States.** According to the Sixth Amendment, a criminal defendant has the right to a speedy and public trial by an impartial jury in the physical location where the crime was committed. Additionally, a person accused of a crime must be informed of the nature of the crime and be confronted with the witnesses against him or her. Further, the accused must be able to summon witnesses in her or his favor and have the assistance of counsel.

LO 2 **Explain what "taking the Fifth" really means.** The Fifth Amendment states that no person "shall be compelled in any criminal case to be a witness against himself." Thus, defendants do not have to testify if their testimony would implicate them in the crime. Witnesses may refuse to testify on this same ground. (Witnesses, though, are often granted immunity and thereafter can no longer take the Fifth.) In the United States, silence on the part of a defendant cannot be used by the jury in forming its opinion about guilt or innocence.

LO 3 **List the requirements normally imposed on potential jurors.** They must be (a) citizens of the United States; (b) over eighteen years of age; (c) free of felony convictions; (d) healthy enough to function on a jury; (e) sufficiently intelligent to understand the issues at trial; and (f) able to read, write, and comprehend the English language.

LO 4 **Contrast challenges for cause and peremptory challenges during *voir dire*.** A challenge for cause occurs when an attorney provides the court with a legally justifiable reason why a potential juror should be excluded—for example, the juror does not understand English. In contrast, peremptory challenges do not require any justification by the attorney and are usually limited to a small number. They cannot, however, be based, even implicitly, on race or gender.

LO 5 **List the standard steps in a criminal jury trial.** (a) Opening statements by the prosecutor and the defense attorney; (b) presentation of evidence, usually in the form of questioning by the prosecutor, known as direct examination; (c) cross-examination by the defense attorney of the same witnesses; (d) at the end of the prosecutor's presentation of evidence, motion for a directed verdict by the defense (also called a motion for judgment as a matter of law in the federal courts), which is normally denied by the judge; (e) presentation of the defendant's case, which may include putting the defendant on the stand and direct examination of the defense's witnesses; (f) cross-examination by the prosecutor; (g) after the defense closes its case, rebuttal by the prosecution, which may involve new evidence that was not used initially by the prosecution; (h) cross-examination of the prosecution's new witnesses by the defense and introduction of new witnesses of its own, called the surrebuttal; (i) closing arguments by both the defense and the prosecution; (j) the charging of the jury by the judge, during which the judge sums up the case and instructs the jurors on the rules of law that apply; (k) jury deliberations; and (l) presentation of the verdict.

LO 6 **Explain the difference between testimony and real evidence, between lay witnesses and expert witnesses, and between direct and circumstantial evidence.** Testimony consists of statements by competent witnesses, whereas real evidence includes physical items that affect the case. A lay witness is an "average person," whereas an expert witness speaks with the authority of one who has professional training, advanced knowledge, or substantial experience in a specialized area. Direct evidence is evidence presented by witnesses as opposed to circumstantial evidence, which can create an inference that a fact exists, but does not directly establish the fact.

LO 7 **List possible affirmative defenses.** (a) Self-defense, (b) insanity, (c) duress, and (d) entrapment.

LO 8 **Delineate circumstances in which a criminal defendant may be tried a second time for the same act.** A defendant who is acquitted in a criminal trial may be sued in a civil case for essentially the same act. When an act is a crime under both state and federal law, a defendant who is acquitted in state court may be tried in federal court for the same act, and vice versa.

LO 9 **List the five basic steps of an appeal.** (a) The filing of a notice of appeal; (b) the transfer of the trial court record to the appellate court; (c) the filing of briefs; (d) the presentation of oral arguments; and (e) the issuance of a written opinion by the appellate judges, upholding the decision of the lower court, modifying part of the decision, reversing the decision, or reversing and remanding the case to the trial court.

SELF ASSESSMENT ANSWER KEY

Page 325: **i.** jury; **ii.** bench; **iii.** judge; **iv.** self-incrimination; **v.** innocent; **vi.** guilty; **vii.** state/prosecutor; **viii.** reasonable doubt

Page 332: **i.** *venire*; **ii.** *voir dire*; **iii.** cause; **iv.** peremptory; **v.** race; **vi.** gender

Page 341: **i.** testimony; **ii.** fact; **iii.** relevant; **iv.** prejudice; **v.** direct; **vi.** cross; **vii.** reasonable doubt

Page 348: **i.** charge; **ii.** deliberated; **iii.** verdict; **iv.** hung; **v.** appealing; **vi.** law

KEY TERMS

acquittal **323**
Allen Charge **344**
appeal **344**
bench trial **323**
challenge for cause **329**
charge **342**
circumstantial evidence **334**
closing arguments **340**
confrontation clause **337**
cross-examination **337**
direct evidence **334**
direct examination **336**

double jeopardy **345**
evidence **332**
expert witness **333**
finality **346**
habeas corpus **347**
hearsay **336**
hung jury **343**
jury nullification **344**
jury trial **323**
lay witness **333**
master jury list **327**
motion for a directed verdict **337**

opening statements **332**
peremptory challenges **330**
real evidence **332**
rebuttal **340**
relevant evidence **335**
statute of limitations **322**
testimony **332**
venire **327**
verdict **343**
voir dire **327**
wrongful conviction **347**

QUESTIONS FOR CRITICAL ANALYSIS

1. Why is it important for the judge to tell jurors that a defendant's decision to remain silent during the trial cannot be taken as a sign of guilt?

2. To supplement the information gained in *voir dire*, many lawyers are going on the Internet to gather information about prospective jurors. Social networking sites such as Facebook can provide lawyers with a great deal of insight. Why do you think some observers believe this practice to be unethical?

3. What does it mean to say that certain evidence is "irrelevant"? Why is it inappropriate for irrelevant evidence to be heard by jurors?

4. Texas has a law called the Timothy Cole Compensation Act, under which people who are wrongfully convicted of crimes may collect $80,000 from the state for each year of unwarranted imprisonment. Do you think this is fair? Why or why not? What are the goals of this kind of legislation?

5. Why is the appeals process so important to the American criminal justice system? What would be some of the consequences if criminal defendants did not have the ability to appeal questionable convictions?

CourseMate *For Online Help*

For online help and access to resources that accompany *Criminal Justice Today*, go to www.cengagebrain.com/shop/ISBN/1111835578. Click "Access Now," where you will find flashcards, an online quiz, and other helpful study aids. If you have an access code for CourseMate, log in and go to the chapter of your choice for additional online study aids.

NOTES

1. Quoted in Keith L. Alexander and Henri E. Cauvin, "Ingmar Guandique Convicted of First-Degree Murder of Former Intern Chandra Levy," *Washington Post* (November 23, 2010), at **www.washingtonpost.com/wp-dyn/content/article/2010/11/22/AR2010112203633.html**.

2. Ben Conery, "Prosecution, Defense Agree: Levy's Murder Probe Botched," *Washington Times* (October 26, 2010), A1.

3. Jerome Frank, *Courts on Trial: Myth and Reality in American Justice* (New York: Atheneum, 1969), 14–33.

4. David L. Cook, Steven R. Schlesinger, Thomas J. Bak, and William T. Rule II, "Criminal Caseload in U.S. District Courts: More Than Meets the Eye," *American University Law Review* 44 (June 1995), 44.

5. 407 U.S. 514 (1972).

6. 725 Illinois Compiled Statutes Section 5/103-5 (1992).

7. L. Stuart Ditzen, "Suspects' Release Stuns City Lawyers: Seven Murder Defendants Were Set Free on a Speedy-Trial Violation," *Philadelphia Inquirer* (August 6, 2004), B1.

8. Bureau of Justice Statistics, *Felony Defendants in Large Urban Counties, 2006* (Washington, D.C.: U.S. Department of Justice, May 2010), Table 10, page 10.

9. 18 U.S.C. Section 3161.

10. 391 U.S. 145 (1968).

11. *Blanton v. Las Vegas*, 489 U.S. 538 (1989).

12. *Williams v. Florida*, 399 U.S. 102 (1970).

13. 435 U.S. 223 (1978).

14. *Apodaca v. Oregon*, 406 U.S. 404 (1972); and *Lee v. Louisiana*, No. 07-1523 (2008).

15. 332 U.S. 46 (1947).

16. Barton L. Ingraham, "The Right of Silence, the Presumption of Innocence, the Burden of Proof, and a Modest Proposal," *Journal of Criminal Law and Criminology* 85 (1994), 559–595.

17. 397 U.S. 358 (1970).

18. James P. Levine, "The Impact of Local Political Cultures on Jury Verdicts," *Criminal Justice Journal* 14 (1992), 163–164.

19. Juliet Macur, "After Day of Questions, Bonds Trial Has a Jury," *New York Times* (March 22, 2011), 10.

20. *Lockhart v. McCree*, 476 U.S. 162 (1986).

21. *Witherspoon v. Illinois*, 391 U.S. 510 (1968).

22. John Kaplan and Jon R. Waltz, *The Trial of Jack Ruby* (New York: Macmillan, 1965), 91–94.

23. 380 U.S. 224 (1965).

24. 476 U.S. 79 (1986).

25. Eric L. Muller, "Solving the *Batson* Paradox: Harmless Error, Jury Representation, and the Sixth Amendment," *Yale Law Journal* 106 (October 1996), 93.

26. 499 U.S. 400 (1991).

27. 502 U.S. 1056 (1992).

28. *Snyder v. Louisiana*, 552 U.S. 472 (2008).

29. Louisiana Capital Assistance Project, "LCAC Projects—Blackstrikes," at **www.thejusticecenter.org/lcac/lcac_projects.html**.

30. *Illegal Racial Discrimination in Jury Selection: A Continuing Legacy* (Montgomery, AL: Equal Justice Initiative, August 2010), 14.

31. Quoted in Shaila Dewan, "Study Finds Blacks Blocked from Southern Juries," *New York Times* (June 2, 2010), 14.

32. 511 U.S. 127 (1994).

33. Harry Kalven and Hans Zeisel, *The American Jury* (Boston: Little, Brown, 1966), 163–167.

34. Douglas D. Koski, "Testing the Story Model of Juror Decision Making," *Sex Offender Law* (June/July 2003), 53–58.

35. Nancy Pennington and Reid Hastie, "The Story Model for Juror Decision Making," in *Inside the Juror: The Psychology of Juror Decision Making* (Cambridge, MA: Harvard University Press, 1983), 192, 194–195.

36. Federal Rule of Evidence 703.

37. Richard A. Epstein, "Judicial Control over Expert Testimony: Of Deference and Education," *Northwestern University Law Review* 87 (1993), 1156.

38. L. Timothy Perrin, "Expert Witnesses under Rules 703 and 803(4) of the Federal Rules of Evidence: Separating the Wheat from the Chaff," *Indiana Law Journal* 72 (Fall 1997), 939.

39. Adam Liptak, "Experts Hired to Shed Light Can Leave U.S. Courts in the Dark," *New York Times* (August 12, 2008), A1.

40. Quoted in Katie Zezima, "Judge Will Allow Jurors to See Video of 8-Year-Old Being Killed by Uzi at Gun Show," *New York Times* (December 8, 2010), A15.

41. Thomas J. Reed, "Trial by Propensity: Admission of Other Criminal Acts Evidenced in Federal Criminal Trials," *University of Cincinnati Law Review* 50 (1981), 713.

42. *Ibid.*

43. *People v. Zackowitz*, 254 N.Y. 192 (1930).

44. Charles McCormick, *Handbook on Evidence* (St. Paul, MN: West Publishing Co., 1987), Chapter 1.

45. Federal Rules of Procedure, Rule 804(b)(2).

46. Arthur Best, *Evidence: Examples and Explanations*, 4th ed. (New York: Aspen Law & Business, 2001), 89–90.

47. Henry K. Lee, "Bey's Defense Tries to Show Killer Acted on His Own," *San Francisco Chronicle* (April 6, 2011), C3.

48. *Griffin v. California*, 380 U.S. 609 (1965).

49. Douglas D. Koski, "Alcohol and Rape Study," *Criminal Law Bulletin* 38 (2002), 21–159.

50. Firoz Dattu, "Illustrated Jury Instructions," *Judicature* 82 (September/October 1998), 79.

51. Walter J. Steele, Jr., and Elizabeth Thornburg, "Jury Instructions: A Persistent Failure to Communicate," *Judicature* 74 (1991), 249–254.

52. Judicial Council of California, *Criminal Jury Instructions* (Eagan, MN: Thomson/West, 2005), no. 521.

53. David W. Broeder, "The University of Chicago Jury Project," *Nebraska Law Review* 38 (1959), 744–760.

54. *People v. Haran*, 109 P.3d 616 (Colo. 2005).

55. 164 U.S. 492 (1896).

56. *United States v. Fioravanti*, 412 F.2d 407 (3d Cir. 1969).

57. William S. Neilson and Harold Winter, "The Elimination of Hung Juries: Retrials and Nonunanimous Verdicts," *International Review of Law and Economics* (March 2005), 2.

58. Joseph L. Gastwirth and Michael D. Sinclair, "Diagnostic Test Methodology in the Design and Analysis of Judge-Jury Agreement Studies," *Jurimetrics Journal* 39 (Fall 1998), 59.

59. Peter Western, "The Three Faces of Double Jeopardy: Reflections on Government Appeals of Criminal Sentences," *Michigan Law Review* 78 (1980), 1001–1002.

60. "Jury Report Needs a Fair Trial," *Baltimore Sun* (August 19, 2008), 1B.

61. Quoted in Jeffrey Abramson, *We, the Jury: The Jury System and the Ideal of Democracy* (New York: Basic Books, 1994), 250.

62. Bureau of Justice Statistics, *Federal Justice Statistics, 2008—Statistical Tables* (Washington, D.C.: U.S. Department of Justice, November 2010), Table 5.2 and Table 6.1.

63. *Green v. United States*, 355 U.S. 184 (1957).

64. David W. Neubauer, *America's Courts and the Criminal Justice System*, 5th ed. (Belmont, CA: Wadsworth Publishing Co. 1996), 254.

65. Bureau of Justice Statistics, *Capital Punishment, 2009* (Washington, D.C.: U.S. Department of Justice, December 2010), 1.

66. The Innocence Project, "Innocence Project Case Files," at **www.innocenceproject.org/know**.

67. Bureau of Justice Statistics, *Felony Sentences in State Courts, 2006—Statistical Tables* (Washington, D.C.: U.S. Department of Justice, December 2009), 1.

68. *Skinner v. Switzer*, 131 S.Ct. 1289 (2011).

69. Richard A. Rosen, "Innocence and Death," *North Carolina Law Review* (December 2003), 69–70.

70. William J. Morgan, Jr., "Justice in Foresight: Past Problems with Eyewitness Identification and Exoneration by DNA Technology," *Southern Regional Black Law Students Association Law Journal* (Spring 2009), 87.

71. National Association of Criminal Defense Lawyers, "Federal Judge Rules Florida's Drug Laws Unconstitutional" (July 27, 2011), at **www.nacdl.org/public.nsf/NewsReleases /2011mn28?OpenDocument**.

72. Michelle J. Anderson, "From Chastity Requirement to Sexuality License: Sexual Consent and a New Rape Shield Law," *George Washington Law Review* (February 2002), 51.

73. Michigan Compiled Laws Annotated Section 750.520j (West 1991).

74. *State ex rel. Pope v. Superior Court*, 545 P.2d 946, 953 (Ariz. 1996).

75. Federal Rule of Evidence 412(a)(1)–(2).

76. Federal Rule of Evidence 412(b)(1)(A)–(C).

77. Bureau of Justice Statistics, *Criminal Victimization, 2005* (Washington, D.C.: U.S. Department of Justice, September 2006), 10.

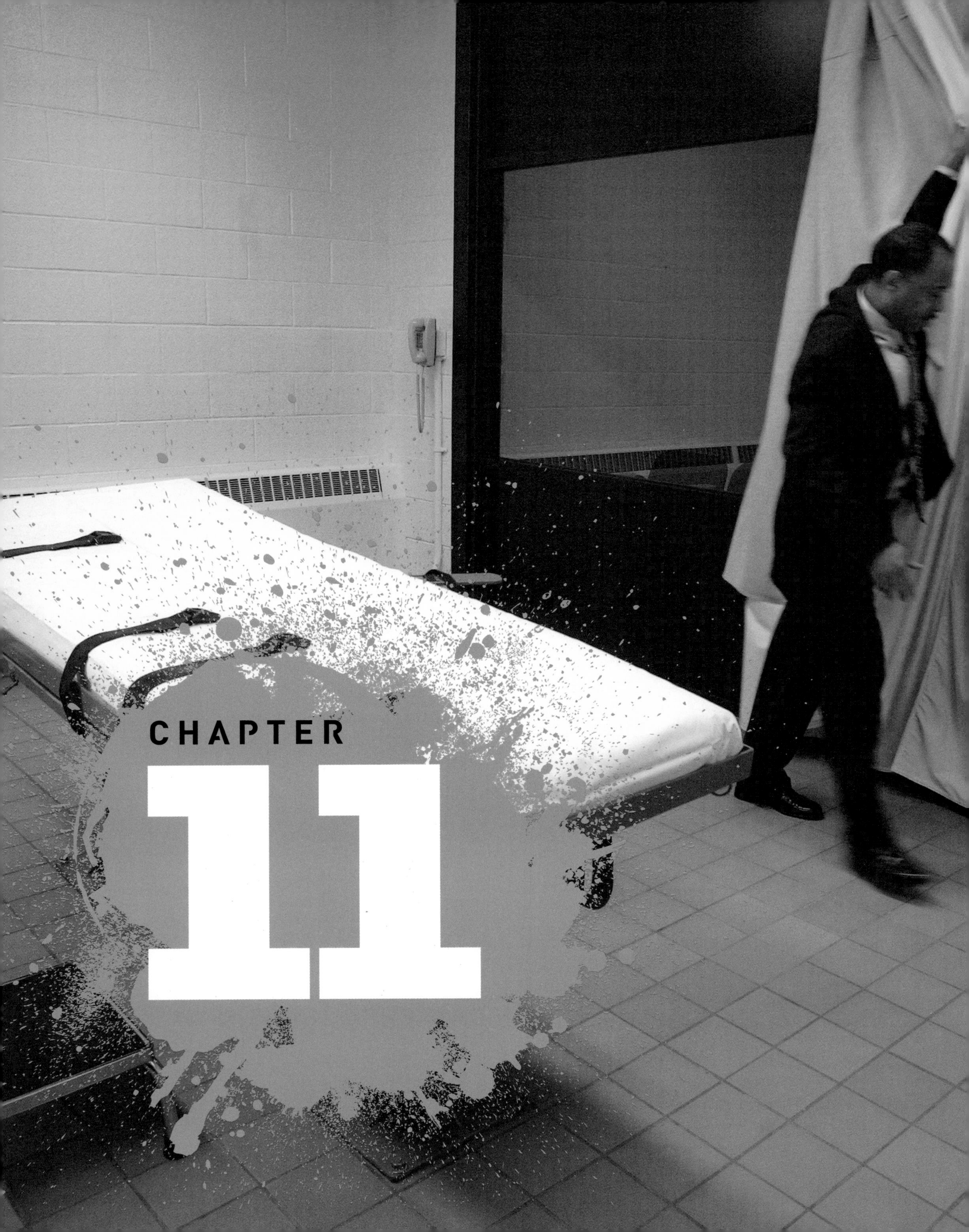

CHAPTER 11

Punishment and Sentencing

AP Photo/Kiichiro Sato, File

LEARNING OBJECTIVES

After reading this chapter, you should be able to . . .

LO 1 List and contrast the four basic philosophical reasons for sentencing criminals.

LO 2 Contrast indeterminate with determinate sentencing.

LO 3 Explain why there is a difference between the sentence imposed by a judge and the actual sentence served by the prisoner.

LO 4 List the six forms of punishment.

LO 5 State who has input into the sentencing decision and list the factors that determine a sentence.

LO 6 Explain some of the reasons why sentencing reform has occurred.

LO 7 Identify the arguments for and against the use of victim impact statements during sentencing hearings.

LO 8 Identify the two stages that make up the bifurcated process of death penalty sentencing.

LO 9 Describe the main issues of the death penalty debate.

The nine learning objectives labeled LO 1 through LO 9 are designed to help improve your understanding of the chapter.

BAD HABITS

The cases of John Patterson and Michael Albanesi were strikingly similar. In late 2008, the Pennsylvania Internet Crimes against Children Task Force raided Patterson's home in West Pittston, and the officers discovered nearly three hundred images of child pornography stored on various hard drives. A year later, the same task force raided Albanesi's home in Wyoming, Pennsylvania, located about three miles from Patterson's residence, and discovered computer hardware with about five hundred images of child pornography. Neither man had a criminal record. Both admitted to having a long history of downloading and trading sexually explicit images of children on the Internet.

When it came to sentencing, however, Patterson's and Albanesi's fates differed greatly. In November 2009, Patterson pleaded guilty to one count of receiving child pornography and was sentenced to eleven years in prison. In April 2010, Albanesi pleaded guilty to 507 counts of possession of child pornography, eleven counts of dissemination, and one count of utilizing a computer to commit his crimes. He was sentenced to twenty-three months behind bars.

Within the criminal justice system, opinions about the proper punishment for child pornography–related crimes vary just as widely as Patterson's and Albanesi's sentences do. A recent poll of federal judges found that 70 percent believe the sentencing requirements for child pornography defendants are too harsh. Ingrid Cronin, a federal public defender, points out that these defendants often receive longer prison terms than those who are caught "actually having sex with a child." Luzerne County (Pennsylvania) detective Chaz Balogh counters that real children are harmed in the production of these images and rejects the argument that merely "curious" users of child porn should be treated with leniency. "Maybe they wouldn't be so curious if they knew they were going to do ten years [in prison]," Balogh insists.

U.S. Representative Debbie Wasserman of Florida, shown here, recently sponsored a bill that provides state and local law enforcement agencies $1 billion to help fight child pornography.
Win McNamee/Getty Images

Why did John Patterson receive a dramatically stiffer punishment than Michael Albanesi for committing essentially the same crime? The main reason is that Patterson was prosecuted in federal court, while Albanesi was tried in a Pennsylvania state court. Federal sentencing guidelines, which you will learn about later in the chapter, tend to be harsher than state requirements. In 2009, the average sentence in federal court for possessing or disseminating child pornography was seven years in prison. That same year, 47 percent of convicted child pornographers in Pennsylvania state court served *no* time behind bars. Instead, they were sentenced to probation or house arrest.[1]

Is the federal approach to child pornography better than Pennsylvania's? A recent study, conducted at a North Carolina prison, found that 85 percent of those convicted of possessing child pornography had also engaged in at least one "hands-on" sexual offense against a minor.[2] This finding would suggest that the harsher federal approach is justified to deter potential abusers. The authors of that study, however, cautioned against a one-size-fits-all approach, pointing out that "we know less about online child pornographers than many other types of offenders."[3] As you can see, punishment and sentencing present some of the most complex issues of the criminal justice system. One scholar has even asserted:

There is no such thing as "accurate" sentencing; there are only sentences that are more or less just, more or less effective. Nothing in the recent or distant history of sentencing reform suggests that anything approaching perfection is attainable.[4]

In this chapter, we will discuss the various attempts to "perfect" the practice of sentencing over the past century. We will also explore the ramifications of these efforts for the American criminal justice system. Whereas previous chapters have concentrated on the prosecutor and defense attorney, this one spotlights the judge and his or her role in making the sentencing decision. We will particularly focus on recent national and state efforts to limit judicial discretion in this area, a trend that has had the overall effect of producing harsher sentences for many offenders. Finally, we will examine the issues surrounding the death penalty, a controversial subject that forces us to confront the basic truth of sentencing: the way we punish criminals says a great deal about the kind of people we are.

THE PURPOSE OF SENTENCING

Professor Herbert Packer has said that punishing criminals serves two ultimate purposes: the "deserved infliction of suffering on evil doers" and "the prevention of crime."[5] Even this straightforward assessment raises several questions. How does one determine the sort of punishment that is "deserved"? How can we be sure that certain penalties "prevent" crime? Should criminals be punished solely for the good of society, or should their well-being also be taken into consideration? Sentencing laws indicate how any given group of people has answered these questions, but do not tell us why they were answered in that manner. To understand why, we must first consider the four basic philosophical reasons for sentencing—retribution, deterrence, incapacitation, and rehabilitation. (For an introduction to these concepts, see Figure 11.1 below.)

Critical Thinking Skill Development: Retribution is the oldest justification for punishment, but many feel it has no place in today's sentencing process. Ask students to consider retribution as an element of sentencing. What is the difference between retribution and revenge? (LO 1)

RETRIBUTION

LO 1
The oldest and most common justification for punishing someone is that he or she "deserved it"—as the Old Testament states, "an eye for an eye and a tooth for a tooth." Under a system of justice that favors **retribution,** a wrongdoer

Retribution The philosophy that those who commit criminal acts should be punished based on the severity of the crime and that no other factors need be considered.

FIGURE 11.1 Sentencing Philosophies

In April 2011, a judge sentenced Eric Stefanski to a five-year prison term for shoplifting $622 worth of clothing from a Macy's department store in Kahului, Hawaii. Although the sentence may seem harsh, Stefanski was a repeat offender participating in a drug court program at the time of his arrest. Thus, his punishment was in keeping with the four main philosophies of sentencing.

Retribution	Punishment is society's means of expressing condemnation of illegal acts such as shoplifting. Repeat offenders should be punished more harshly because of their continuing criminal behavior.
Deterrence	Harsh sentences for shoplifting may convince others not to engage in that behavior. Also, when Stefanski has completed his sentence, he will avoid repeating his crimes because he will want to avoid returning to prison.
Incapacitation	While he is in prison, Stefanski will be unable to commit more crimes.
Rehabilitation	Stefanski's shoplifting may be connected to his substance abuse. While in prison, he can participate in drug treatment programs to address this problem.

who has freely chosen to violate society's rules must be punished for the infraction. Retribution relies on the principle of just deserts, which holds that the severity of the punishment must be in proportion to the severity of the crime. Retributive justice is not the same as *revenge*. Whereas revenge implies that the wrongdoer is punished only with the aim of satisfying a victim or victims, retribution is more concerned with the needs of society as a whole.

The *principle of willful wrongdoing* is central to the idea of retribution. According to this principle, society is morally justified in punishing someone only if that person was aware that he or she committed a crime. Therefore, animals, children, and the mentally incapacitated are not responsible for their criminal actions, even though they may be a threat to the community.[6] Furthermore, the principles of retribution reject any wide-reaching social benefit as a goal of punishment. The philosopher Immanuel Kant (1724–1804), an early proponent of retribution in criminal justice, believed that punishment by a court

> can never be inflicted merely as a means to promote some other good for the criminal himself or for civil society. It must always be inflicted upon him only because he has committed a crime. For a man can never be treated merely as a means to the purposes of another.[7]

In other words, punishment is an end in itself and cannot be justified by any future good that may result from a criminal's suffering.

One problem with retributive ideas of justice lies in proportionality. Whether or not one agrees with the death penalty, the principle behind it is easy to fathom: the punishment (death) often fits the crime (murder). But what about the theft of an automobile? How does one fairly determine the amount of time the thief must spend in prison for that crime? Should the type of car or the wealth of the car owner matter? Theories of retribution often have a difficult time providing answers to such questions.[8]

DETERRENCE

The concept of deterrence (as well as incapacitation and rehabilitation) takes a different approach than does retribution. That is, rather than seeking only to punish the wrongdoer, the goal of sentencing should be to prevent future crimes. By "setting an example," society is sending a message to potential criminals that certain actions will not be tolerated. Jeremy Bentham, a nineteenth-century British reformer who first articulated the principles of deterrence, felt that retribution was counterproductive because it does not serve the community. (See Chapter 2 to review Bentham's utilitarian theories.) He believed that a person should be punished only when doing so is in society's best interests and that the severity of the punishment should be based on its deterrent value, not on the severity of the crime.[9]

GENERAL AND SPECIFIC DETERRENCE Deterrence can take two forms: general and specific. The basic idea of *general deterrence* is that by punishing one person, others will be discouraged from committing a similar crime. *Specific deterrence* assumes that an individual, after being punished once for a certain act, will be less likely to repeat that act because she or he does not want to be punished again.[10]

Both forms of deterrence have proved problematic in practice. General deterrence assumes that a person commits a crime only after a rational decision-making process, in which he or she implicitly weighs the benefits of the crime against the possible costs of the punishment. This is not necessarily the case, especially for young offenders who tend to value the immediate rewards of crime over the possible future consequences. The argument for specific deterrence is somewhat weakened by the fact that a relatively small number of habitual offenders are responsible for the majority of certain criminal acts.

LOW PROBABILITY OF PUNISHMENT Another criticism of deterrence is that for most crimes, wrongdoers are unlikely to be caught, sentenced, and imprisoned. According to the National Crime Victimization Survey, only 49 percent of all violent crimes and 40 percent of all property crimes are even reported to the police.[11] Of those reported, only 45 percent of violent crimes and 18 percent of property crimes result in an arrest.[12] Then, as we saw in Chapter 9, case attrition further whittles down the number of arrestees who face trial and the possibility of imprisonment.

Thus, in general, potential criminals have less to fear from the criminal justice system than one might expect. Professors Paul H. Robinson of the University of Pennsylvania Law School and John M. Darley of Princeton University note that this low probability of punishment could be offset by making the punishment so severe that even the slightest chance of apprehension could act as a deterrent—for example, an eighty-five-year prison term for shoplifting or the loss of a hand for burglary.[13] Our society is, however, unwilling to allow for this possibility.

> "Men are not hanged for stealing horses, but that horses may not be stolen."
>
> —**Marquis de Halifax,**
> *Political Thoughts and Reflections* (1750)

INCAPACITATION

"Wicked people exist," said James Q. Wilson. "Nothing avails except to set them apart from innocent people."[14] Wilson's blunt statement summarizes the justification for *incapacitation* as a form of punishment. As a purely practical matter, incarcerating criminals guarantees that they will not be a danger to society, at least for the length of their prison terms. At some level, the death penalty can also be justified in terms of incapacitation, as it prevents the offender from committing any future crimes.

Incapacitation A strategy for preventing crime by detaining wrongdoers in prison, thereby separating them from the community and reducing criminal opportunities.

THE IMPACT OF INCAPACITATION Several studies do support incapacitation's efficacy as a crime-fighting tool. Criminologist Isaac Ehrlich of the University of Buffalo–SUNY estimated that a 1 percent increase in sentence length will produce a 1 percent decrease in the crime rate.[15] University of Chicago professor Steven Levitt has noticed a trend that further supports incapacitation. He found that violent crime rates rise in communities where inmate litigation over prison overcrowding has forced the early release of some inmates and a subsequent drop in the prison population.[16] More recently, Avinash Singh Bhati of the Urban Institute in Washington, D.C., found that higher levels of incarceration lead to fewer violent crimes but have little impact on property crime rates.[17]

Incapacitation as a theory of punishment does suffer from several weaknesses. Unlike retribution, it offers no proportionality with regard to a particular crime. Giving a burglar a life sentence would certainly ensure that she or he would not commit another burglary. Does that justify such a severe penalty? Furthermore, incarceration protects society only until the criminal is freed. Many studies have shown that, on release, offenders may actually be more likely to commit crimes than before they were imprisoned.[18] In that case, incapacitation may increase likelihood of crime, rather than diminish it.

Group Activities: One of the most common crime fighting strategies of the past few decades in the United States has been increased lengths of incarceration for criminal offenses. Ask students to work in groups to brainstorm the consequences, both intended and unintended, of this policy.

SELECTIVE AND COLLECTIVE INCAPACITATION Some observers believe that strategies of *selective incapacitation* should be favored over strategies of *collective incapacitation* for the best results. With collective incapacitation, all offenders who have committed a similar crime are imprisoned for the same time period, whereas selective incapacitation provides longer sentences for individuals, such as career criminals, who are judged more likely to commit further crimes if and when they are released. The problem with selective incapacitation, however, lies in the difficulty of predicting just who is at the

In a Santa Ana, California, courtroom, Andrew Gallo reacts to his sentence of fifty-one years in prison for killing three people in a drunk driving automobile accident. How do theories of deterrence and incapacitation justify Gallo's punishment?

AP Photo/Mark Rightmire, Pool

greatest risk to commit future crimes. Studies have shown that even the most effective methods of trying to predict future criminality are correct less than half of the time.[19]

REHABILITATION

For most of the past century, **rehabilitation** has been seen as the most "humane" goal of punishment. This line of thinking reflects the view that crime is a "social phenomenon" caused not by the inherent criminality of a person, but by factors in that person's surroundings. By removing wrongdoers from their environment and intervening to change their values and personalities, the rehabilitative model suggests, criminals can be "treated" and possibly even "cured" of their proclivities toward crime. Although studies of the effectiveness of rehabilitation are too varied to be easily summarized, it does appear that, in most instances, criminals who receive treatment are less likely to reoffend than those who do not.[20]

For the better part of the past three decades, the American criminal justice system has been characterized by a notable rejection of many of the precepts of rehabilitation in favor of retributive, deterrent, and incapacitating sentencing strategies that "get tough on crime." Recently, however, more jurisdictions are turning to rehabilitation as a cost-effective (and, possibly, crime-reducing) alternative to punishment, a topic that we will explore more fully in the next chapter. Furthermore, the American public may be more accepting of rehabilitative principles than many elected officials think. A survey by Zogby International, sponsored by the National Council on Crime and Delinquency, found that 87 percent of respondents favored rehabilitative services for nonviolent offenders, both before and after they leave prison.[21]

RESTORATIVE JUSTICE

It would be a mistake to view the four philosophies we have just discussed as being mutually exclusive. For the most part, a society's overall sentencing direction is influenced by all four theories, with political and social factors determining which one is predominant at any one time. Political and social factors can also support new approaches to punishment. The influence of victims, for example, has contributed to the small but growing *restorative justice* movement in this country.

LISTENING TO THE VICTIM Despite the emergence of victim impact statements, which we will discuss later in the chapter, victims have historically been restricted from participating in the punishment process. Such restrictions are supported by the general assumption that victims are focused on vengeance rather than justice. According to criminologists Heather Strang of Australia's Center for Restorative Justice and Lawrence W. Sherman of the University of Pennsylvania, however, this is not always the case. After the initial shock of the crime has worn off, Strang and Sherman have found, victims are

Rehabilitation The philosophy that society is best served when wrongdoers are provided the resources needed to eliminate criminality from their behavioral pattern.

Critical Thinking Skill Development: In a written assignment, ask students to consider rehabilitation as a philosophical foundation of punishment. Why might some view this motivation for punishment as more "humane" than other forms of punishment? Do students believe it is possible to rehabilitate criminal offenders? (LO 1)

more interested in three things that have little to do with revenge: (1) an opportunity to participate in the process, (2) financial reparations, and (3) an apology.[22]

Restorative justice strategies focus on these concerns by attempting to repair the damage that a crime does to the victim, the victim's family, and society as a whole. This outlook relies on the efforts of the offender to "undo" the harm caused by the criminal act through an apology and **restitution,** or monetary compensation for losses suffered by the victim(s). Theoretically, the community also participates in the process by providing treatment programs and financial support that allow both offender and victim to reestablish themselves as productive members of society.[23]

LIMITED IMPACT A study of efforts to improve communications between victims and offenders in Indiana found high levels of satisfaction among both parties. Victims appreciated statements of contrition made by the offender, and offenders appreciated the opportunity to express remorse and "make things right."[24] Despite such results, many criminal justice professionals in this country regard restorative justice as too vague and "touchy-feely" to be useful.[25] Furthermore, its practical impact is limited because federal and state sentencing laws do not include it as an option. Therefore, supporters have to rely on sympathetic judges, prosecutors, and defense attorneys to implement restorative justice theories in court. Finally, many courts are unable or unwilling to enforce restitution orders. Several years ago, Pennsylvania estimated that the amount of unpaid fees, fines, and restitution owed by its citizens exceeded $1.5 billion.[26] (See the feature *Comparative Criminal Justice—Blood Money* below to learn about the significant role that a controversial form of restorative justice plays in Pakistan's criminal justice system.)

Restorative Justice An approach to punishment designed to repair the harm done to the victim and the community by the offender's criminal act.

Restitution Monetary compensation for damages done to the victim by the offender's criminal act.

Discussion Tip: Ask students to reflect on the four philosophical goals of punishment. Which goal do students believe best reflects society's expectations for justice today? Which goal, if any, do they believe should dominate current sentencing practices? (LO 1)

COMPARATIVE CRIMINAL JUSTICE

BLOOD MONEY

After American citizen Raymond Davis shot and killed two men in Lahore, Pakistan, he claimed that he was acting in self-defense during a robbery. Pakistani law enforcement agents disagreed, noting that several of the bullet wounds were in the men's backs. Further adding to the intrigue was the fact that Davis was an employee of the U.S. Central Intelligence Agency. As American officials negotiated for Davis's release, they found themselves considering a form of restitution called *diyat,* which plays a crucial role in Pakistani notions of justice.

In Pakistan, violent crimes such as murder and attempted murder are considered private wrongs rather than wrongs against society. Thus, in most cases, it is the victim or the victim's family that decides the punishment, not the state. Options include (1) forgiveness, (2) retribution equal to the crime, or (3) *diyat,* in which the offender pays financial compensation to the victim or the victim's family. By

some estimates, *diyat* is applied to three in five of the country's homicide cases. Although many criticize the practice for allowing wealthy criminals to escape punishment, the poverty-stricken citizens of Pakistan generally accept *diyat.*

"We are not bitter at all," said Mohammed Nasir after his brother's murderer was set free in exchange for $9,400. "This money will take care of [the victim's] wife and children." Apparently, relatives of the men killed by Raymond Davis felt the same way. On March 16, 2011, Davis was on an airplane back to the United States, having remitted *diyat* for his wrongdoing. One Pakistani official said that the families received $1.1 million each, a figure disputed by the U.S. government.

FOR CRITICAL ANALYSIS

In Chapter 4, you learned that victims of violent crimes or the families of these victims can sue offenders in civil court for monetary awards. How is this different from the Pakistani system of *diyat*? Do you feel that one approach is superior to the other? Why?

SELFASSESSMENT

Fill in the blanks and check your answers on page 392.

The saying "an eye for an eye and a tooth for a tooth" reflects the concept of _____ as a justification for punishment. The goal of _____ is to prevent future crimes by "setting an example," while _____ purports to prevent crime by keeping offenders behind bars. Models of _____ suggest that criminals can be "treated" and possibly even "cured."

THE STRUCTURE OF SENTENCING

Philosophy not only is integral to explaining *why* we punish criminals, but also influences *how* we do so. The history of criminal sentencing in the United States has been characterized by shifts in institutional power among the three branches of the government. When public opinion moves toward more severe strategies of retribution, deterrence, and incapacitation, *legislatures* have responded by asserting their power over determining sentencing guidelines. In contrast, periods of rehabilitative justice are marked by a transfer of this power to the *judicial* and *administrative* branches.

LEGISLATIVE SENTENCING AUTHORITY

Because legislatures are responsible for making laws, these bodies are also initially responsible for passing the criminal codes that determine the length of sentences.

INDETERMINATE SENTENCING For a good part of the past century, goals of rehabilitation dominated the criminal justice system, and legislatures were more likely to enact indeterminate sentencing policies. Penal codes with indeterminate sentences set a minimum and maximum amount of time that a person must spend in prison. For example, the indeterminate sentence for aggravated assault could be three to nine years, or six to twelve years, or twenty years to life. Within these parameters, a judge can prescribe a particular term, after which an administrative body known as the *parole board* decides at what point the offender is to be released. A prisoner is aware that he or she is

LO 2 eligible for *parole* as soon as the minimum time has been served and that good behavior can further shorten the sentence.

DETERMINATE SENTENCING Disillusionment with the ideals of rehabilitation has led to determinate sentencing, or fixed sentencing. As the name implies, in determinate sentencing an offender serves exactly the amount of time to which she or he is sentenced (minus "good time," described below). For example, if the legislature deems that the punishment for a first-time armed robber is ten years, then the judge has no choice but to impose a sentence of ten years, and the criminal will serve ten years minus good time before being freed.

"GOOD TIME" AND TRUTH IN SENTENCING Often, the amount of time prescribed by a judge bears little relation to the amount of time the offender actually spends behind bars. In states with indeterminate sentencing, parole boards have broad

LO 3 powers to release prisoners once they have served the minimum portion of their sentence. Furthermore, all but four states offer prisoners the opportunity to reduce their sentences by doing "good time"—or behaving well—as determined by prison administrators. (See Figure 11.2 on the facing page for an idea of the effects of good-time regulations and other early-release programs on state prison sentences.)

Group Activities: Ask students to form teams and debate the value of indeterminate sentencing versus determinate sentencing. Which do students feel is the more appropriate approach for today's criminal offenders? (LO 2)

Indeterminate Sentencing An indeterminate term of incarceration in which a judge determines the minimum and maximum terms of imprisonment. When the minimum term is reached, the prisoner becomes eligible to be paroled.

Determinate Sentencing A period of incarceration that is fixed by a sentencing authority and cannot be reduced by judges or other corrections officials.

"Good Time" A reduction in time served by prisoners based on good behavior, conformity to rules, and other positive behavior.

FIGURE 11.2 Average Sentence Length and Estimated Time to Be Served in State Prison

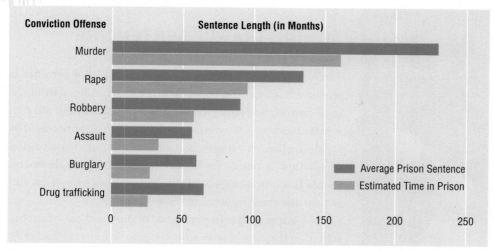

Source: Bureau of Justice Statistics, *National Corrections Reporting Program: Sentence Length of State Prisoners, by Offense, Admission Type, Sex, and Race* (January 20, 2011), "Table 9: First Releases from State Prison, 2008," at **bjs.ojp. usdoj.gov/index.cfm?ty=pbdetail&iid=2056**.

Sentence-reduction programs promote discipline within a correctional institution and reduce overcrowding, so many prison officials welcome them. The public, however, may react negatively to news that a violent criminal has served a shorter term than ordered by a judge and pressure elected officials to "do something." In Illinois, for example, some inmates were serving less than half their sentences by receiving a one-day reduction in their term for each day of "good time." Under pressure from victims' groups, the state legislature passed a **truth-in-sentencing law** that requires murderers and others convicted of serious crimes to complete at least 85 percent of their sentences with no time off for good behavior.[27] As their name suggests, the primary goal of these laws is to provide the public with more accurate information about the actual amount of time an offender will spend behind bars. They have also found support with those who believe that keeping offenders incapacitated for longer periods of time will reduce crime.[28] Today, forty states have instituted some form of truth-in-sentencing laws, though the future of such statutes is in doubt due to the pressure of overflowing prisons.

Truth-in-Sentencing Laws Legislative attempts to ensure that convicts will serve approximately the terms to which they were initially sentenced.

JUDICIAL SENTENCING AUTHORITY

Determinate sentencing is a direct encroachment on the long-recognized power of judges to make the final decision on sentencing. Historically, the judge bore most of the responsibility for choosing the proper sentence within the guidelines set by the legislature. In the twentieth century, this power was reinforced by the rehabilitative ethic. Each offender, it was believed, has a different set of problems and should therefore receive a sentence tailored to her or his particular circumstances. Legislators have generally accepted a judge as the most qualified person to choose the proper punishment.

Between 1880 and 1899, seven states passed indeterminate sentencing laws, and in the next dozen years, another twenty-one followed suit. By the 1960s, every state in the nation allowed its judges the freedom of operating under an indeterminate sentencing system.[29] In the 1970s, however, criticism of indeterminate sentencing began to grow. Marvin E. Frankel, a former federal district judge in New York, gained a great deal of attention when he described sentencing authority as "unchecked" and "terrifying and intolerable for a society that professes devotion to a rule of law."[30] As we shall see, the

Teaching Tip: Ask students to respond to "Questions for Critical Analysis" number two on page 392, in which they consider the impact of truth-in-sentencing laws.

1980s and 1990s saw numerous attempts on both the state and federal levels to limit this judicial discretion.

ADMINISTRATIVE SENTENCING AUTHORITY

Parole is a condition of early release in which a prisoner is released from a correctional facility but is not freed from the legal custody and supervision of the state. Generally, after an inmate has been released on parole, he or she is supervised by a parole officer for a specified amount of time. The decision of whether to parole an inmate lies with the parole board. Parole is a crucial aspect of the criminal justice system and will be discussed in detail in Chapter 14.

For now, it is important to understand the role rehabilitation theories play in *administrative sentencing authority.* The formation in 1910 of the U.S. Parole Commission and similar commissions in the fifty states implied that the judge, though a legal expert, was not trained to determine when an inmate had been rehabilitated. Therefore, the sentencing power should be given to experts in human behavior, who were qualified to determine whether a convict was fit to return to society.[31] The recent repudiation of rehabilitation principles has not spared these administrative bodies. Since 1976, fourteen states and the federal government have abolished traditional parole for their prisoners.[32]

Judge Dee Anna Farnell of the Pinellas County (Florida) Drug Court tells a drug offender that, if she keeps shooting heroin, she's "going to die." What are some of the arguments for giving judges the discretion to make sentencing decisions? ZUMA Press/Newscom

SELFASSESSMENT

Fill in the blanks and check your answers on page 392.

_____ sentences set a minimum and maximum amount of time a convict must spend in prison or jail, whereas _____ sentences reflect the exact length of incapacitation, minus reductions for _____ _____, or behaving well. Historically, the _____ has had most of the responsibility for making sentencing decisions.

INDIVIDUALIZED JUSTICE AND THE JUDGE

During the pretrial procedures and the trial itself, the judge's role is somewhat passive and reactive. She or he is primarily a "procedural watchdog," ensuring that the rights of the defendant are not infringed while the prosecutor and defense attorney dictate the course of action. At a traditional sentencing hearing, however, the judge is no longer an arbiter between the parties. She or he is now called on to exercise the ultimate authority of the state in determining the defendant's fate.

From the 1930s to the 1970s, when theories of rehabilitation held sway over the criminal justice system, indeterminate sentencing practices were guided by the theory of "individualized justice." Just as a physician gives specific treatment to individual patients depending on their particular health needs, the hypothesis goes, a judge needs to consider the specific circumstances of each individual offender in choosing the best form of punishment. Taking the analogy one step further, just as the diagnosis of a qualified physician should not be questioned, a qualified judge should have absolute discretion in making the sentencing decision. *Judicial discretion* rests on the assumption that a judge should be given ample leeway in determining punishments that fit both the crime and the criminal.[33] As we shall see later in the chapter, the growth of determinate sentencing has severely restricted judicial discretion in many jurisdictions.

FORMS OF PUNISHMENT

LO 4 Within whatever legislative restrictions apply, the sentencing judge has a number of options when it comes to choosing the proper form of punishment. These sentences, or *dispositions,* include:

1. *Capital punishment.* Reserved normally for those who commit first degree murder under aggravated circumstances, capital punishment, or the death penalty, is a sentencing option in thirty-four states and in federal courts.

2. *Imprisonment.* Whether for the purpose of retribution, deterrence, incapacitation, or rehabilitation, a common form of punishment in American history has been imprisonment. In fact, it is used so commonly today that judges—and legislators—are having to take factors such as prison overcrowding into consideration when making sentencing decisions. The issues surrounding imprisonment will be discussed in Chapters 13 and 14.

3. *Probation.* One of the effects of prison overcrowding has been a sharp rise in the use of probation, in which an offender is permitted to live in the community under supervision and is not incarcerated. (Probation is covered in Chapter 12.) *Alternative sanctions* (also discussed in Chapter 12) combine probation with other dispositions such as electronic monitoring, house arrest, boot camps, and shock incarceration.

Teaching Tip: Give students a pop quiz in class to be sure that they understand the terms used in this section. Specifically, be sure they can list a few of the alternative sanctions mentioned in the text. (LO 4)

> "I am painfully aware that I have deeply hurt many, many people. . . . I cannot adequately express how sorry I am for what I have done."
>
> **—Bernard Madoff,** after pleading guilty to defrauding investors out of an estimated $65 billion (2009)

4. *Fines.* Fines can be levied by judges in addition to incarceration and probation or independently of other forms of punishment. When a fine is the only punishment, it usually reflects the judge's belief that the offender is not a threat to the community and does not need to be imprisoned or supervised. In some instances, mostly involving drug offenders, a judge can order the seizure of an offender's property, such as his or her home.

5. *Restitution and community service.* Whereas fines are payable to the government, restitution and community service are seen as reparations to the injured party or to the community. Restitution (see page 361) is a direct payment to the victim or victims of a crime. Community service consists of "good works"—such as cleaning up highway litter or tutoring disadvantaged youths—that benefit the entire community.

6. *Apologies.* As we saw earlier in this chapter, when the offender has committed a less serious crime, many judges are turning to restorative justice to provide a remedy. At the heart of restorative justice is the apology. So, for example, a judge in Texas required a teenager who had vandalized thirteen schools to go to each school and apologize to the students and faculty.

In some jurisdictions, judges have a great deal of discretionary power and can impose sentences that do not fall into any of these categories. This "creative sentencing," as it is sometimes called, has produced some interesting results. Teenagers who violate noise ordinances in Fort Lupton, Colorado, are required to spend Friday nights in a courtroom listening to Barry Manilow, opera, and the "Barney" theme song. A judge in Painesville, Ohio, ordered a man who had stolen from a Salvation Army kettle to pass

Discussion Tip: Have students debate the concept of "creative sentencing." Should judges be able to step outside the traditional forms of punishment when determining the appropriate sanction for a criminal offender? Why or why not?

After Jason Householder, left, and John Stockum were convicted of criminal damaging for throwing beer bottles at a car, municipal court judge David Hostetler of Coshocton, Ohio, gave them a choice: jail time or a walk down Main Street in women's clothing. As you can see, they chose the dresses. What reasons might a judge have for handing down this sort of "creative" sentence?

AP Photo/Dante Smith/*Coshocton Tribune*

twenty-four hours as a homeless person. In Harris County, Texas, a man who slapped his wife was sentenced to attend yoga classes. Though these types of punishments are often ridiculed, many judges see them as a viable alternative to incarceration for less dangerous offenders.

THE SENTENCING PROCESS

The decision of how to punish a wrongdoer is the end result of what Yale Law School professor Kate Stith and federal appeals court judge José A. Cabranes call the "sentencing ritual."[34] The two main participants in this ritual are the judge and the defendant, but prosecutors, defense attorneys, and probation officers also play a role in the proceedings. Individualized justice requires that the judge consider all the relevant circumstances in making sentencing decisions. Therefore, judicial discretion is often tantamount to *informed* discretion—without the aid of the other members of the courtroom work group, the judge would not have sufficient information to make the proper sentencing choice.

LO 5

THE PRESENTENCE INVESTIGATIVE REPORT For judges operating under various states' indeterminate sentencing guidelines, information in the **presentence investigative report** is a valuable component of the sentencing ritual. Compiled by a probation officer, the report describes the crime in question, notes the suffering of any victims, and lists the defendant's prior offenses (as well as any alleged but uncharged criminal activity). The report also contains a range of personal data such as family background, work history, education, and community activities—information that is not admissible as evidence during trial. In putting together the presentence investigative report, the probation officer is supposed to gain a "feel" for the defendant and communicate these impressions of the offender to the judge.

The report also includes a sentencing recommendation. In the past, this aspect has been criticized as giving probation officers too much power in the sentencing process, because less diligent judges would simply rely on the recommendation in determining punishment.[35] Consequently, as we shall see, many jurisdictions have moved to limit the influence of the presentence investigative report.

Presentence Investigative Report An investigative report on an offender's background that assists a judge in determining the proper sentence.

THE PROSECUTOR AND DEFENSE ATTORNEY To a certain extent, the adversary process does not end when the guilt of the defendant has been established. Both the prosecutor and the defense attorney are interviewed in the process of preparing the presentence investigative report, and both will try to present a version of the facts consistent with their own sentencing goals. The defense attorney in particular has a duty to make sure that the information contained in the report is accurate and not prejudicial toward his or her client. Depending on the norms of any particular courtroom work group, prosecutors and defense attorneys may petition the judge directly for certain sentences.

Note that this process is not always adversarial. As we saw in Chapter 9, in some instances the prosecutor will advocate leniency and may join the defense attorney in requesting a short term of imprisonment, probation, or some form of intermediate sanction.[36]

SENTENCING AND THE JURY Juries also play an important role in the sentencing process. As we will see later in the chapter, it is the jury, and not the judge, who

Teaching Tip: Invite a probation officer to visit the classroom. Ask him or her to discuss the process of generating a presentence investigative report. What kind of information is commonly included in the report? How is the information gathered? How long does the process generally take? (LO 5)

generally decides whether a convict eligible for the death penalty will in fact be executed. Additionally, six states—Arkansas, Kentucky, Missouri, Oklahoma, Texas, and Virginia—allow juries, rather than judges, to make the sentencing decision even when the death penalty is not an option. In these states, the judge gives the jury instructions on the range of penalties available, and then the jury makes the final decision.[37]

Juries have traditionally been assigned a relatively small role in felony sentencing, largely out of concern that jurors' lack of experience and legal expertise leaves them unprepared for the task. When sentencing by juries is allowed, the practice is popular with prosecutors because jurors are more likely than judges to give harsh sentences, particularly for drug crimes, sexual assault, and theft.[38]

FACTORS OF SENTENCING

The sentencing ritual strongly lends itself to the concept of individualized justice. With inputs—sometimes conflicting—from the prosecutor, attorney, and probation officer, the judge can be reasonably sure of getting the "full picture" of the crime and the criminal. In making the final decision, however, most judges consider two factors above all others: the seriousness of the crime and any mitigating or aggravating circumstances.

THE SERIOUSNESS OF THE CRIME As would be expected, the seriousness of the crime is the primary factor in a judge's sentencing decision. The more serious the crime, the harsher the punishment, for society demands no less. Each judge has his or her own methods of determining the seriousness of the offense. Many judges simply consider the "conviction offense," basing their sentence on the crime for which the defendant was convicted.

Other judges—some mandated by statute—focus instead on the "real offense" in determining the punishment. The "real offense" is based on the actual behavior of the defendant, regardless of the official conviction. For example, through a plea bargain, a defendant may plead guilty to simple assault when in fact he hit his victim in the face with a baseball bat. A judge, after reading the presentence investigative report, could decide to sentence the defendant as if he had committed aggravated assault, which is the "real" offense. Though many prosecutors and defense attorneys are opposed to "real offense" procedures, which can render a plea bargain meaningless, there is a growing belief in criminal justice circles that they bring a measure of fairness to the sentencing decision.[39]

MITIGATING AND AGGRAVATING CIRCUMSTANCES When deciding the severity of punishment, judges and juries are often required to evaluate the *mitigating* and *aggravating circumstances* surrounding the case. **Mitigating circumstances** are those circumstances, such as the fact that the defendant was coerced into committing the crime, that allow a lighter sentence to be handed down. In contrast, **aggravating circumstances,** such as a prior record, blatant disregard for the safety of others, or the use of a weapon, can lead a judge or jury to inflict a harsher penalty than might otherwise be warranted (see Figure 11.3 on the next page).

In 2005, for example, Zacarias Moussaoui pleaded guilty to taking part in the al Qaeda plot that led to the terrorist attacks of September 11, 2001. The defense asked the jury to consider twenty-four mitigating circumstances when deciding whether Moussaoui deserved the death penalty or life in prison. These included Moussaoui's hostile mother and physically abusive father, the racism that he had to face as an

Discussion Tip: In most cases, the jury, not the judge, decides whether a convict will be sentenced to death. Ask students why they think sentencing in capital cases is handled this way.

"Real Offense" The actual offense committed, as opposed to the charge levied by a prosecutor as the result of a plea bargain.

Mitigating Circumstances Any circumstances accompanying the commission of a crime that may justify a lighter sentence.

Aggravating Circumstances Any circumstances accompanying the commission of a crime that may justify a harsher sentence.

Critical Thinking Skill Development: Ask students to work in small groups to debate the idea that "real offenses" rather than "conviction offenses" may be considered in the sentencing process. Do students feel this is a fair practice? Why or why not? (LO 5)

FIGURE 11.3 Aggravating and Mitigating Circumstances

Aggravating Circumstances	Mitigating Circumstances
• An offense involved multiple participants, and the offender was the leader of the group.	• An offender acted under strong provocation, or other circumstances in the relationship between the offender and the victim make the offender's behavior less serious and therefore less deserving of punishment.
• A victim was particularly vulnerable.	• An offender played a minor or passive role in the offense or participated under circumstances of coercion or duress.
• A victim was treated with particular cruelty for which an offender should be held responsible.	• An offender, because of youth or physical impairment, lacked substantial capacity for judgment when the offense was committed.
• The offense involved injury or threatened violence to others and was committed to gratify an offender's desire for pleasure or excitement.	
• The degree of bodily harm caused, attempted, threatened, or foreseen by an offender was substantially greater than average for the given offense.	
• The degree of economic harm caused, attempted, threatened, or foreseen by an offender was substantially greater than average for the given offense.	
• The amount of contraband materials possessed by the offender or under the offender's control was substantially greater than average for the given offense.	

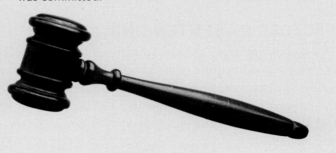

Source: American Bar Association.

African in French society, and his limited knowledge of the September 11 attack plans. For their part, the prosecutors offered seven aggravating circumstances, including the great death and destruction caused by the terrorist attacks, Moussaoui's desire to harm Americans, and his lack of remorse for the victims. In choosing life imprisonment over the death penalty, the jury decided that the mitigating circumstances surrounding the defendant's crimes outweighed the aggravating circumstances.

JUDICIAL PHILOSOPHY Most states spell out mitigating and aggravating circumstances in statutes, but there is room for judicial discretion in applying the law to particular cases. Judges are not uniform, or even consistent, in their opinions of which circumstances are mitigating or aggravating. One judge may believe that a fourteen-year-old is not fully responsible for his or her actions, while another may believe that teenagers should be treated as adults by criminal courts. Those judges who support rehabilitative theories of criminal justice have been found to give more lenient sentences than those who subscribe to theories of deterrence and incapacitation.[40] Furthermore, judges can have different philosophies with regard to different crimes, handing down, for example, harsh penalties for domestic abusers while showing leniency toward drug offenders.

SELFASSESSMENT

Fill in the blanks and check your answers on page 392.
Judges often rely on information contained in the _____ _____ report when making sentencing decisions. The primary factor in the sentencing process is the _____ of the crime for which the defendant was convicted. _____ circumstances allow a lighter sentence to be handed down, while _____ circumstances can lead to the imposition of a harsher penalty.

INCONSISTENCIES IN SENTENCING

For some, the natural differences in judicial philosophies, when combined with a lack of institutional control, raise important questions. Why should a bank robber in South Carolina and a bank robber in Michigan receive different sentences? Even federal indeterminate sentencing guidelines seem overly vague: a bank robber can receive a prison term from one day to twenty years, depending almost entirely on the judge.[41] Furthermore, if judges have freedom to use their discretion, do they not also have the freedom to misuse it?

LO 6 Purported improper judicial discretion is often the first reason given for two phenomena that plague the criminal justice system: *sentencing disparity* and *sentencing discrimination*. Though the two terms are often used interchangeably, they describe different statistical occurrences—the causes of which are open to debate.

Teaching Tip: Take a few extra moments in your lecture to make sure that students understand the difference between sentencing discrimination and sentencing disparity. If possible, use criminal cases from local and national media to support your explanation. (LO 6)

SENTENCING DISPARITY

Justice would seem to demand that those who commit similar crimes should receive similar punishments. **Sentencing disparity** occurs when this expectation is not met in one of three ways:

1. Criminals receive similar sentences for different crimes of unequal seriousness.
2. Criminals receive different sentences for similar crimes.
3. Mitigating or aggravating circumstances have a disproportionate effect on sentences. Prosecutors, for example, reward drug dealers who inform on their associates with lesser sentences. As a result, low-level drug sellers, who have no information to trade for reduced sentences, often spend more time in prison than their better-informed bosses.[42]

Sentencing Disparity A situation in which those convicted of similar crimes do not receive similar sentences.

Most of the blame for sentencing disparities is placed at the feet of the judicial profession. Even with the restrictive presence of the sentencing reforms we will discuss shortly, judges have a great deal of influence over the sentencing decision, whether they are making that decision themselves or instructing the jury on how to do so. Like other members of the criminal justice system, judges are individuals, and their discretionary sentencing decisions reflect that individuality. Besides judicial discretion, several other causes have been offered as explanations for sentencing disparity, including differences between geographic jurisdictions and between federal and state courts.

Critical Thinking Skill Development: Ask students to consider the issue of sentencing disparity. In a written assignment, ask them to identify what they believe causes sentencing disparity. (LO 6)

GEOGRAPHIC DISPARITIES For wrongdoers, the amount of time spent in prison often depends as much on where the crime was committed as on the crime itself. A comparison of the sentences for drug trafficking reveals that someone convicted of the crime in the Northern District of California faces an average of 79 months in prison, whereas a similar offender in northern Iowa can expect an average of 148 months.[43] The average sentences imposed in the Fourth Circuit, which includes North Carolina, South Carolina, Virginia, and West Virginia, are consistently harsher than those in the Ninth Circuit, comprising most of the western states: 57 months longer for firearms violations and 28 months longer for all offenses.[44] Such disparities can be attributed to a number of different factors, including local attitudes toward crime and available financial resources to cover the expenses of incarceration.

FEDERAL VERSUS STATE COURT DISPARITIES Because of different sentencing guidelines, as we saw at the opening of this chapter, the punishment for the same crime in federal and state courts can also be dramatically different. In North Carolina, for example, a defendant charged with trafficking 50 grams of methamphetamine would face a minimum sentence of 90 months and a maximum sentence of 117 months.[45] A person charged with exactly the same crime in a federal court would face a minimum of 120 months and a maximum of life in prison.[46] Figure 11.4 below shows the sentencing disparities for certain crimes in the two systems.

SENTENCING DISCRIMINATION

Sentencing discrimination occurs when disparities can be attributed to extralegal variables such as the defendant's gender, race, or economic standing.

RACE AND SENTENCING At first glance, racial discrimination would seem to be rampant in sentencing practices. Research by Cassia Spohn of Arizona State University and David Holleran of the College of New Jersey suggests that minorities pay a "punishment penalty" when it comes to sentencing.[47] In Chicago, Spohn and Holleran found that convicted African Americans were 12.1 percent and convicted Hispanics were 15.3 percent more likely to go to prison than convicted whites. In Miami, Hispanics were 10.3 percent more likely to be imprisoned than either blacks or whites.[48] Nationwide, about 43 percent of all inmates in state and federal prisons are African American,[49] even though members of that minority group make up only about 13 percent of the country's population and represent less than 30 percent of those arrested.[50]

Interestingly, Spohn and Holleran found that the rate of imprisonment rose significantly for minorities who were young and unemployed. This led them to conclude that the disparities between races were not the result of "conscious" discrimination on the part of the sentencing judges. Rather, faced with limited time to make decisions and limited information about the offenders, the judges would resort to stereotypes, considering

Sentencing Discrimination A situation in which the length of a sentence appears to be influenced by a defendant's race, gender, economic status, or other factor not directly related to the crime he or she committed.

Discussion Tip: Ask students to debate the "punishment penalty" for minorities in sentencing. What role, if any, do students feel race and ethnicity play in the sentencing process?

FIGURE 11.4 Average Maximum Sentences for Selected Crimes in State and Federal Courts

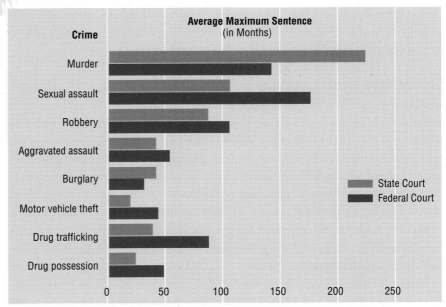

Source: Bureau of Justice Statistics, *Felony Sentences in State Courts, 2006—Statistical Tables* (Washington, D.C.: U.S. Department of Justice, December 2009), Table 1.6, page 9.

not just race, but age and unemployment as well.[51] Another study, published in 2006, found that older judges and judges who were members of minority groups in Pennsylvania were less likely to send offenders to prison, regardless of their race.[52] Such research findings support the argument in favor of diversity among judges, discussed in Chapter 8.

Comparing Sentences In addition, Spohn and Holleran found that none of the offender characteristics (race, age, employment) had an effect on the *length* of the prison sentence.[53] Not all the data support this premise, however. Several years ago, researchers from the University of Nevada at Reno found that African Americans received "significantly higher" minimum and maximum sentences than white defendants for felony convictions and drunk driving in that state.[54] National statistics on the matter are somewhat conflicting. According to the Bureau of Justice Statistics, African Americans' sentences are thirteen months longer, on average, for all violent crimes. Yet, for individual crimes such as sexual assault and drug trafficking, whites, on average, receive longer sentences.[55]

Crack Cocaine Sentencing Few sentencing policies have aroused as many charges of discrimination as those involving crack cocaine. Powder cocaine and crack, a crystallized form of the drug that is smoked rather than inhaled, are chemically identical. Under federal legislation passed in 1986, however, sentences for crimes involving crack are, in some instances, one hundred times more severe than for crimes involving powder cocaine.[56] The law was designed to combat the violence associated with the crack trade in American cities. Instead, say critics, it wound up harming those very areas, particularly African American communities. About 80 percent of federal crack defendants are African American.[57]

In November 2007, the U.S. Sentencing Commission voted to lessen the disparity between crack and powder cocaine sentences. The commission also decided that the changes would be retroactive, meaning that about 25,000 federal inmates were eligible for sentence reductions.[58] As of November 2010, federal judges had reduced the sentences of more than 16,000 of these inmates.[59] Also in 2010, President Barack Obama signed the Fair Sentencing Act, which reduces the legal disparity between the two forms of cocaine to eighteen to one for federal sentencing purposes.[60]

WOMEN AND SENTENCING Few would argue that race or ethnicity should be a factor in sentencing decisions—the system should be "color-blind." Does the same principle apply to women? In other words, should the system be "gender-blind" as well—at least on a policy level? Congress answered that question in the Sentencing Reform Act of 1984, which emphasized the ideal of gender-neutral sentencing.[61] In practice, however, this has not occurred. Women who are convicted of crimes are less likely to go to prison than men, and those who are incarcerated tend to serve shorter sentences. According to government data, on average, a woman receives a sentence that is twenty-nine months shorter than that of a man for a violent crime and nine months shorter for a property crime.[62] One study attributes these differences to the elements of female criminality: in property crimes, women are usually accessories, and in violent crimes, women are usually reacting to physical abuse. In both situations, the mitigating circumstances lead to lesser punishment.[63]

James V. Taylor was sentenced to fifteen years in a Missouri prison for possessing so little crack cocaine that the amount was unweighable. Do you think that individual states should follow the federal government's lead in addressing unequal punishments for crack- and powder-cocaine-related crimes? Why or why not?
AP Photo/Jeff Roberson

Group Activities: Ask students to work in groups to discuss the role that gender plays in sentencing. Should factors such as a history of domestic abuse or the presence of children in the home impact the assigned criminal sentence for a female defendant?

Other evidence also suggests that a *chivalry effect,* or the idea that women should be treated more leniently than men, plays a large role in sentencing decisions. Several self-reported studies have shown that judges may treat female defendants more "gently" than males and that judges are influenced by mitigating factors such as marital status and family background with women that they would ignore with men.[64] In certain situations, however, a woman's gender can work against her. In 2010, Florida prosecutors asked that Emose Oceant receive eighteen years in prison after she was convicted of child abuse. Instead, circuit judge Margaret Steinbeck sentenced Oceant, who had whipped her seven children with boards, belts, and wire hangers, to thirty years behind bars. According to Keith Crew, a professor of sociology and criminology at the University of Northern Iowa, defendants who are seen as bad mothers often "get the hammer" from judges and juries.[65]

SELFASSESSMENT

Fill in the blanks and check your answers on page 392.
Sentencing _____ occurs when similar crimes are punished with dissimilar sentences, while sentencing _____ is the result of judicial consideration of extralegal variables such as the defendant's race or gender.

SENTENCING REFORM

Critical Thinking Skill Development: In a written assignment, ask students to discuss what steps should be taken to eliminate the sentencing inconsistencies discussed in the text. Would more judicial discretion in this area help solve the problem? Would less?

Judicial discretion, then, appears to be a double-edged sword. Although it allows judges to impose a wide variety of sentences to fit specific criminal situations, it appears to fail to rein in a judge's subjective biases, which can lead to disparity and perhaps discrimination. Critics of judicial discretion believe that its costs (the lack of equality) outweigh its benefits (providing individualized justice). As Columbia law professor John C. Coffee noted:

> If we wish the sentencing judge to treat "like cases alike," a more inappropriate technique for the presentation could hardly be found than one that stresses a novelistic portrayal of each offender and thereby overloads the decisionmaker in a welter of detail.[66]

In other words, Professor Coffee feels that judges are given too much information in the sentencing process, making it impossible for them to be consistent in their decisions. It follows that limiting judicial discretion would not only simplify the process but lessen the opportunity for disparity or discrimination. Since the 1970s, this attitude has spread through state and federal legislatures, causing more extensive changes in sentencing procedures than in almost any other area of the American criminal justice system over that time period.

SENTENCING GUIDELINES

Sentencing Guidelines
Legislatively determined guidelines that judges are required to follow when sentencing those convicted of specific crimes. These guidelines limit judicial discretion.

In an effort to eliminate the inequities of disparity by removing judicial bias from the sentencing process, many states and the federal government have turned to sentencing guidelines, which require judges to dispense legislatively determined sentences based on factors such as the seriousness of the crime and the offender's prior record.

STATE SENTENCING GUIDELINES In 1978, Minnesota became the first state to create a Sentencing Guidelines Commission with a mandate to construct and monitor the use of a determinate sentencing structure. The Minnesota Commission left no doubt as to the philosophical justification for the new sentencing statutes, stating unconditionally that retribution was its primary goal.[67] Today, about twenty states employ some form of sentencing guidelines with similar goals.

In general, these guidelines remove discretionary power from state judges by turning sentencing into a mathematical exercise. Members of the courtroom work group are guided by a *grid,* which helps them determine the proper sentence. Figure 11.5 on the following page shows the grid established by the Massachusetts sentencing commission. As in the grids used by most states, one axis ranks the type of crime, while the other refers to the offender's criminal history. In the grid for Massachusetts, the red boxes indicate the "incarceration zone." A prison sentence is required for crimes in this zone. The yellow boxes delineate a "discretionary zone," in which the judge can decide between incarceration or intermediate sanctions, which you will learn about in the next chapter. The green boxes indicate the "intermediate sanction zone," in which only intermediate sanctions are to be levied.

Certain crimes are "staircased" in the Massachusetts grid, meaning that the same crime can result in different punishments based on other factors.[68] For example, assault and battery with a dangerous weapon (A&B DW) resulting in no injury or a minor injury is at offense seriousness level 3. When the crime results in a moderate but not life-threatening injury, it is at offense seriousness level 4. But when the injury is life threatening, the crime is at offense seriousness level 6—squarely in the "incarceration zone" regardless of the defendant's criminal history.

FEDERAL SENTENCING GUIDELINES In 1984, Congress passed the Sentencing Reform Act (SRA),[69] paving the way for federal sentencing guidelines that went into effect three years later. Similar in many respects to the state guidelines, the SRA also eliminated parole for federal prisoners and severely limited early release from prison due to good behavior.[70] The impact of the SRA and the state guidelines has been dramatic. Sentences have become harsher—by the mid-2000s, the average federal prison sentence was fifty months, more than twice as long as in 1984.[71] Furthermore, much of the discretion in sentencing has shifted from the judge to the prosecutor. Because the prosecutor chooses the criminal charge, she or he can, in effect, present the judge with the range of sentences. Defendants and their defense attorneys realize this and are more likely to agree to a plea bargain, which is, after all, a "deal" with the prosecutor.[72]

JUDICIAL DEPARTURES Even in their haste to limit a judge's power, legislators realized that sentencing guidelines could not be expected to cover every possible criminal situation. Therefore, both state and federal sentencing guidelines allow an "escape hatch" of limited judicial discretion known as a departure. Judges in Massachusetts can "depart" from the grid on the next page if a case involves mitigating or aggravating circumstances,[73] and the United States Supreme Court has upheld federal judges' freedom to similarly deviate from the federal guidelines.[74] So, for example, federal judge Jack Weinstein acted properly when, in 2010, he overturned a twenty-year sentence for child pornography, ruling that "unless applied with care," the federal requirements "can lead to unreasonable sentences."[75] As we noted in the opening to this chapter, federal judges often react this way to child pornography punishments. Indeed, they depart downward about 40 percent of the time in child pornography cases—more often than in cases involving any other offense.[76]

MANDATORY SENTENCING GUIDELINES

In an attempt to close even the limited loophole of judicial discretion offered by departures, politicians (often urged on by their constituents) have passed sentencing laws even more contrary to the idea of individualized justice. These mandatory (minimum) sentencing guidelines further limit a judge's power to deviate from determinate sentencing laws by setting firm standards for certain crimes. Forty-six states have mandatory sentencing laws

Teaching Tip: Invite a local judge to visit the classroom and speak about the process of determining the appropriate sanction for a criminal offender. Have the judge discuss what role her or his discretion plays in determining any given sentence and what factors are included in the decision-making process.

The **United States Sentencing Commission** is an independent agency in the judicial branch that establishes sentencing policies for federal courts. To visit its Web site, click on the *Criminal Justice CourseMate* at **cengagebrain.com** and select the *Web links* for this chapter.

Departure A stipulation in many federal and state sentencing guidelines that allows a judge to adjust his or her sentencing decision based on the special circumstances of a particular case.

Mandatory Sentencing Guidelines Statutorily determined punishments that must be applied to those who are convicted of specific crimes.

FIGURE 11.5 Massachusetts's Sentencing Guidelines

Sentencing Guidelines Grid

Level	Illustrative Offenses	Sentence Range				
9	Murder	Life	Life	Life	Life	Life
8	Manslaughter (Voluntary) Rape of a Child with Force Aggravated Rape Armed Burglary	96–144 Months	108–162 Months	120–180 Months	144–216 Months	204–306 Months
7	Armed Robbery Rape Mayhem	60–90 Months	68–102 Months	84–126 Months	108–162 Months	160–240 Months
6	Manslaughter (Involuntary) Armed Robbery (No Gun) A&B DW* (Significant Injury)	40–60 Months	45–67 Months	50–75 Months	60–90 Months	80–120 Months
5	Unarmed Robbery Unarmed Burglary Stalking in Violation of Order Larceny ($50,000 and over)	12–36 Months IS-IV IS-III IS-II	24–36 Months IS-IV IS-III IS-II	36–54 Months	48–72 Months	60–90 Months
4	Larceny (from a Person) A&B DW (Moderate Injury)* B&E** (Dwelling) Larceny ($10,000 to $50,000)	0–24 Months IS-IV IS-III IS-II	3–30 Months IS-IV IS-III IS-II	6–30 Months IS-IV IS-III IS-II	20–30 Months	24–36 Months
3	A&B DW (Minor or No Injury) B&E (Not Dwelling) Larceny ($250 to $10,000)	0–12 Months IS-IV IS-III IS-II IS-I	0–15 Months IS-IV IS-III IS-II IS-I	0–18 Months IS-IV IS-III IS-II IS-I	0–24 Months IS-IV IS-III IS-II	6–24 Months IS-IV IS-III IS-II
2	Assault Larceny (under $250)	IS-III IS-II IS-I	0–6 Months IS-III IS-II IS-I	0–6 Months IS-III IS-II IS-I	0–9 Months IS-IV IS-III IS-II IS-I	0–12 Months IS-IV IS-III IS-II IS-I
1	Driving after Suspended License Disorderly Conduct Vandalism	IS-II IS-I	IS-III IS-II IS-I	IS-III IS-II IS-I	0–3 Months IS-IV IS-III IS-II IS-I	0–6 Months IS-IV IS-III IS-II IS-I
	Criminal History Scale	**A** No/Minor Record	**B** Moderate Record	**C** Serious Record	**D** Violent/Repetitive	**E** Serious Violent

*A&B DW = Assault and Battery, Dangerous Weapon
**B&E = Breaking and Entering

The numbers in each cell represent the range from which the judge selects the maximum sentence (Not More Than).
The minimum sentence (Not Less Than) is two-thirds of the maximum sentence and constitutes the initial parole eligibility date.

www.mass.gov/courts/formsandguidelines/sentencing/grid.html

Sentencing Zones

- Incarceration Zone
- Discretionary Zone (incarceration/intermediate sanction)
- Intermediate Sanction Zone

Intermediate Sanction Levels

IS-IV	24-Hour Restriction
IS-III	Daily Accountability
IS-II	Standard Supervision
IS-I	Financial Accountability

Teaching Tip: Ask students to respond to "Questions for Critical Analysis" number three on page 392, in which they employ this sentencing grid to determine the appropriate sentence for a hypothetical offender.

for crimes such as selling illegal drugs, driving under the influence of alcohol, and committing any crime with a dangerous weapon. In Alabama, for example, any person caught selling illegal drugs must spend at least two years in prison, with five years added to the sentence if the sale takes place within three miles of a school or housing project.[77] Similarly, Congress has set mandatory minimum sentences for more than one hundred crimes, mostly drug offenses.

Habitual offender laws are a form of mandatory sentencing that has become increasingly popular over the past decade. Also known as "three-strikes-and-you're-out" laws, these statutes require that any person convicted of a third felony must serve a lengthy prison sentence. The crime does not have to be of a violent or dangerous nature. Under Washington's habitual offender law, for example, a "persistent offender" is automatically sentenced to life even if the third felony offense happens to be "vehicular assault" (an automobile accident that causes injury), unarmed robbery, or attempted arson, among other lesser felonies.[78] Today, twenty-six states and the federal government employ "three-strikes" statutes, with varying degrees of severity.

Habitual Offender Laws
Statutes that require lengthy prison sentences for those who are convicted of multiple felonies.

"THREE STRIKES" IN COURT The United States Supreme Court paved the way for these three-strikes laws when it ruled in *Rummel v. Estelle* (1980)[79] that Texas's habitual offender statute did not constitute "cruel and unusual punishment" under the Eighth Amendment. Basically, the Court gave each state the freedom to legislate such laws in the manner that it deems proper. Twenty-three years later, in *Lockyer v. Andrade* (2003),[80] the Court upheld California's "three-strikes" law. The California statute allows prosecutors to seek penalties up to life imprisonment without parole on conviction of *any* third felony, including for nonviolent crimes. Leandro Andrade received fifty years in prison for stealing $153 worth of videotapes, his fourth felony conviction. A federal appeals court overturned the sentence, agreeing with Andrade's attorneys that it met the definition of cruel and unusual punishment.[81]

In a bitterly divided 5–4 decision, the Supreme Court reversed. Justice Sandra Day O'Connor, writing for the majority, stated that the sentence was not so "objectively" unreasonable that it violated the Constitution.[82] In his dissent, Justice David H. Souter countered that "[i]f Andrade's sentence is not grossly disproportionate, the principle has no meaning."[83] Basically, the justices who upheld the law said that if the California legislature—and by extension the California voters—felt that the law was reasonable, then the judicial branch was in no position to disagree.

RETHINKING "THREE-STRIKES" LAWS For all the publicity they receive, three-strikes laws are underused in most jurisdictions. Indeed, the majority of all three-strike sentences are handed down in California, which has 8,400 inmates behind bars serving twenty-five years to life as "three-strikers."[84] According to one estimate, the state pays $500 million per year to incarcerate third-strike offenders.[85] This high price tag has caused many California officials to rethink their commitment to the law, particularly when it comes to nonviolent offenders.

For example, the Los Angeles district attorney's office no longer seeks life sentences under the law unless the third-strike crime is violent or serious.[86] At the same time, the California Supreme Court has given trial judges the freedom to depart from these harsh sentences when a defendant's "background, character, and prospects" warrant leniency.[87]

Other states are also reconsidering the wisdom of snaring nonviolent criminals in the net of their three-strikes laws. About a decade ago, Washington judges began departing in three-strikes cases, with dramatic results. From 1994 to 1999, about a hundred defendants

Technology Tip: Have students learn more about the potential consequences of mandatory minimum sentencing practices online at Families against Mandatory Minimums at **www.famm.org/UnderstandSentencing.aspx**. Also, have them brainstorm counterarguments to the opinions expressed on the Web page.

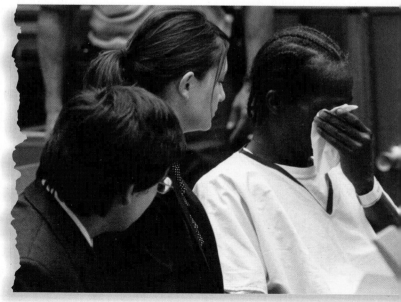

On August 16, 2010, Gregory Taylor, right, wipes away tears following a judge's decision that he be set free after spending thirteen years in prison. Taylor was serving a potential life sentence for stealing food from a Los Angeles church—his "third strike" under California law. Why might prosecutors seek such a harsh sentence for a seemingly minor crime?
AP Photo/Anne Cusack, Pool

Discussion Tip: Ask students to debate habitual offender laws. Are these laws appropriate, and if so, for which offenders?

who had never committed an offense involving serious violence were sentenced to life without parole. Between 2000 and 2007, that number decreased to thirty-nine.[88] Furthermore, Washington governor Chris Gregoire recently pardoned Steven Dozier, who, although he had never caused serious injury or used a weapon, was serving a life sentence for four purse snatching convictions. Dozier was the first "three-striker" to be freed early from prison thanks to an executive pardon, a process we will describe in Chapter 14.

VICTIM IMPACT EVIDENCE

The final piece of the sentencing puzzle involves victims and victims' families. As was mentioned in the previous chapter, crime victims traditionally were banished to the peripheries of the criminal justice system. This situation has changed dramatically with the emergence of the victims' rights movement over the past few decades. Victims are now given the opportunity to testify—in person or through written testimony—during sentencing hearings about the suffering they experienced as the result of the crime. These victim impact statements (VISs) have proved extremely controversial, however, and even the Supreme Court has had a difficult time determining whether they cause more harm than good.

Victim Impact Statement (VIS) A statement to the sentencing body (judge, jury, or parole board) in which the victim is given the opportunity to describe how the crime has affected her or him.

BALANCING THE PROCESS Every state and federal government has some form of victim impact legislation. In general, these laws allow a victim (or victims) to tell his or her "side of the story" to the sentencing body, be it a judge, jury, or parole officer. In nonmurder cases, the victim can personally describe the physical, financial, and emotional impact of the crime. When the charge is murder or manslaughter, relatives or friends can give personal details about the victim and describe the effects of her or his death. In the sentencing phase of the Zacarias Moussaoui trial, discussed earlier in this chapter, the prosecution called thirty-five witnesses to tell the jury how losing loved ones in the September 11 attacks had affected their lives. (As could have been expected, much of this testimony was heartbreaking, such as that of the Indian-born dentist whose sister hanged herself after her husband perished in one of the hijacked planes.) In almost all instances, the goal of the VIS is to increase the harshness of the sentence.

LO 7

Critical Thinking Skill Development: Ask students to consider the role the victim should play in the sentencing process. What are the pros and cons of allowing victims to present victim impact statements prior to sentencing? (LO 7)

Most of the debate surrounding VISs centers on their use in the sentencing phases of death penalty cases. Supporters point out that the defendant has always been allowed to present character evidence in the hopes of dissuading a judge or jury from capital punishment. According to some, a VIS balances the equation by giving survivors a voice in the process. Presenting a VIS is also said to have psychological benefits for victims, who are no longer forced to sit in silence as decisions that affect their lives are made by others.[89] Finally, on a purely practical level, a VIS may help judges and juries make informed sentencing decisions by providing them with an understanding of all of the consequences of the crime. (For an example of a victim impact statement from a recent death penalty case, see Figure 11.6 on the facing page.)

THE RISKS OF VICTIM EVIDENCE Opponents of the use of VISs claim that they interject dangerously prejudicial evidence into the sentencing process, which should be governed by reason, not emotion. The inflammatory nature of VISs, they say, may distract judges and juries from the facts of the case, which should be the only basis for a sentence.[90] Furthermore, critics contend that a VIS introduces the idea of "social value" into the courtroom. In other words, judges and juries may feel compelled

FIGURE 11.6 Victim Impact Statement (VIS)

In 2010, a Connecticut jury convicted Steven Hayes on sixteen counts of kidnapping, rape, and murder resulting from the deaths of Jennifer Hawke-Petit and her two daughters, seventeen-year-old Hayley and eleven-year-old Michaela. During the sentencing phase of the trial, Cynthia Hawke-Renn, Jennifer's sister, gave a VIS via videotape. A portion of the transcript is reprinted here. The jury eventually decided that Hayes deserved the death penalty for his crimes.

> My sister gave me my middle name of Joy. I have always been a joyful person with a bubbly, happy-go-lucky attitude and you have taken that from me. I used to have trust and faith in humanity and you have taken that as well. I used to feel safe in my bed at night as did my children and you have destroyed that also. The very saddest thing in the world to me is that if you had just asked any of them for what you wanted you would have gotten all of it and more. . . . You did not have to murder or rape any of them. . . . We are to resist evil and I have to say I see you only as pure evil.

Along with her two daughters, Jennifer Hawke-Petit was tortured and murdered by Steven Hayes and an accomplice.
ZUMA Press/Newscom

Source: "Cynthia Hawke-Renn Delivers Statement at Hayes Sentencing," *Eyewitness News 3* (December 2, 2010), at **www.wfsb.com/news/25995640/detail.html**.

to base the punishment on the "social value" of the victim (his or her standing in the community, role as a family member, and the like) rather than the circumstances of the crime.

In 1991, the United States Supreme Court gave its approval to the use of VISs, allowing judges to decide whether the statements are admissible on a case-by-case basis just as they do with any other type of evidence.[91] Several years after this decision, Bryan Myers of the University of North Carolina at Wilmington and Jack Arbuthnot of Ohio University decided to test the prejudicial impact of the testimony in question. They ran simulated court proceedings with two groups of mock jurors: one group heard a "family member" give a VIS, while the other group did not. Of those mock jurors who ultimately voted for the death penalty, 67 percent had heard the VIS. In contrast, only 30 percent of those who did not hear it voted to execute the defendant.[92]

Technology Tip: Have students go online to learn more about victim impact statements from the National Center for Victims Rights at **www.ncvc.org/ncvc/main. aspx?dbName=DocumentViewer &DocumentID=32515**.

SELFASSESSMENT

Fill in the blanks and check your answers on page 392.

With the aim of limiting judicial discretion, many states and the federal government have enacted sentencing _____. These laws have greatly _____ the length of prison sentences in the United States. The trend toward longer prison terms has also been influenced by _____ - _____ laws, a form of mandatory sentencing that requires increased punishment for a person convicted of multiple felonies. According to the United States Supreme Court, _____ _____ statements may be presented at sentencing hearings so long as they are not overly prejudicial.

CAREERS IN CJ

Courtesy Anne Seymour

FASTFACTS

VICTIM ADVOCATE JOB DESCRIPTION:

- Provide direct support, advocacy, and short-term crisis counseling to crime victims.

- Coordinate with multiple agencies investigating the crime and providing benefits for victims.

- Act as liaison between victims or witnesses and deputy district attorneys or law enforcement, and provide court support.

WHAT KIND OF TRAINING IS REQUIRED?

- Bachelor's degree in criminal justice, social work/psychology, or related field.

- A minimum of two years' experience in the criminal justice system, one year of which must have involved direct services with victims.

- Ability to recognize and maintain confidentiality in all aspects of position. Skill in multicultural outreach. Multilingual proficiency preferred.

ANNUAL SALARY RANGE?

- $29,000–$44,000

For additional information on a career as victim advocate, visit: **www.ncvc.org/ncvc/Main.aspx.**

ANNE SEYMOUR
NATIONAL VICTIM ADVOCATE

I was involved in politics and working in the California legislature in the early 1980s—right out of graduate school. To be frank, I burned out on running campaigns and applied to a blind ad in the *San Francisco Chronicle*, which brought me to the Mothers Against Drunk Driving (MADD) National Office near Dallas, Texas. Although I was a "creature of fate," I ended up absolutely loving the field of crime victim services. In 1986, I began what is today the National Center for Victims of Crime in Washington, D.C. I decided to continue pursuing this career to ensure that crime victims and survivors have voices, choices, and a true role in justice processes.

REGAINING CONTROL The aspect of my job that I enjoy the most is my direct work with crime victims and survivors. These are people who have been severely traumatized by pain and suffering and

loss, and I consider it a true honor to be able to assist them. I'll never forget the day I met a young survivor who had been abducted, beaten within an inch of her life, raped, and then left to die in the forest. This young woman became one of my closest friends, and I helped her to speak out in her state and at the national level. Every time she does so, she has a powerful impact on our society. So my help in turning a victim/survivor into a stellar victim advocate/activist began on the day I met her, and it continues.

CAREER ADVICE Today, students can actually complete a major or minor in victimology or victim services at several major universities. Many students from social work and criminal justice programs, however, also end up as victim advocates. There are many "ideal" entry-level positions, in both community-based programs (child protective services, children advocacy centers, domestic violence shelters, rape crisis centers, MADD chapters, and the like) and system-based programs (victim assistance in law enforcement, courts, probation, parole, and corrections). I've also noticed that many people get into the victim assistance field because they, themselves, have been hurt by a crime. Along those lines, we have many professional training opportunities to help survivors become great victim advocates, both through the U.S. Department of Justice Office for Victims of Crime (www.ovc.gov) and through community-based training programs offered by domestic violence and rape crisis programs, among others.

Victim advocacy is one of the most exciting and rewarding careers you could ever embark on, though it is not one that you should get into because of the money. (Few victim advocates become rich doing this work!) Every day is unique and different, reflecting the people I assist and the colleagues with whom I interact. I am never, ever bored and never will be. AND I go to bed every single day knowing that I have done at least one thing—and often many more than one!—to promote social justice and to help someone who is hurting. It's an amazing feeling!

CAPITAL PUNISHMENT— THE ULTIMATE SENTENCE

"You do not know how hard it is to let a human being die," Abraham Lincoln (1809–1865) once said, "when you feel that a stroke of your pen will save him." Despite these misgivings, during his four years in office Lincoln approved the execution of 267 soldiers, including those who had slept at their posts.[93] Our sixteenth president's ambivalence toward **capital punishment** is reflected in America's continuing struggle to reconcile the penalty of death with the morals and values of society. Capital punishment has played a role in sentencing since the earliest days of the Republic and—having survived a brief period of abolition between 1972 and 1976—continues to enjoy public support.

Still, few topics in the criminal justice system inspire such heated debate. Death penalty opponents such as legal expert Stephen Bright wonder whether "there comes a time when a society gets beyond some of the more primitive forms of punishment."[94] They point out that two dozen countries have abolished the death penalty since 1985 and that the United States is the only Western democracy that continues the practice. Critics also claim that a process whose subjects are chosen by "luck and money and race" cannot serve the interests of justice.[95] Proponents believe that the death penalty serves as the ultimate deterrent for violent criminal behavior and that the criminals who are put to death are the "worst of the worst" and deserve their fate.

Today, about 3,250 convicts are living on "death row" in American prisons, meaning they have been sentenced to death and are awaiting execution. In the 1940s, as many as two hundred people were put to death in the United States in one year. As Figure 11.7 below shows, the most recent high-water mark was ninety-eight in 1999. Despite declines since then, states and the federal government are still executing convicts at a rate not seen in six decades. Consequently, the questions that surround the death penalty—Is it fair? Is it humane? Does it deter crime?—will continue to mobilize both its supporters and its detractors.

METHODS OF EXECUTION

In its early years, when the United States adopted the practice of capital punishment from England, it also adopted English methods, which included drawing and quartering and boiling the convict alive. By the nineteenth century, these techniques had been

Capital Punishment The use of the death penalty to punish wrongdoers for certain crimes.

Group Activities: Ask students to make a list of all the arguments for and against the death penalty. Consider this a brainstorming activity, rather than a debate. (LO 9)

Technology Tip: Have students research the history of the death penalty in the United States online at the Death Penalty Information Center at **www.deathpenaltyinfo. org/article.php?did=199**.

FIGURE 11.7 Executions in the United States, 1976 to 2010

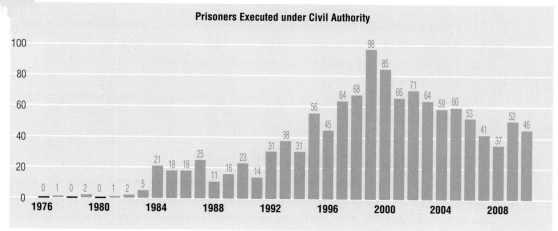

Source: Death Penalty Information Center.

The Virginia Department of Corrections' electric chair is used only at the request of the inmate facing the death sentence. Why has lethal injection replaced the use of the "chair" in most American executions?

AP Photo/Virginia Department of Corrections

See the Web sites of the **Death Penalty Information Center** and **Pro-Death Penalty. com** for opposing views on capital punishment. Find these Web sites by visiting the *Criminal Justice CourseMate* at **cengagebrain.com** and selecting the *Web links* for this chapter.

Teaching Tip: In a writing assignment, have students reflect on *Weems v. United States*. How does the precedent set in this case impact the way the Supreme Court views capital punishment today?

deemed "barbaric" and were replaced by hanging. Indeed, the history of capital punishment in America is marked by attempts to make the act more humane. The 1890s saw the introduction of electrocution as a less painful method of execution than hanging, and in 1890 in Auburn Prison, New York, William Kemmler became the first American to die in an electric chair.

The "chair" remained the primary form of execution until 1977, when Oklahoma became the first state to adopt lethal injection. Today, this method dominates executions in all thirty-four states that employ the death penalty. In the lethal injection process, the condemned convict is given a sedative, followed by a combination of deadly drugs administered intravenously. Sixteen states authorize at least two different methods of execution, meaning that electrocution (eight states), lethal gas (four states), hanging (three states), and the firing squad (three states) are still used on rare occasions.[96]

THE DEATH PENALTY AND THE SUPREME COURT

In 1890, William Kemmler challenged his sentence to die in New York's new electric chair (for murdering his mistress) on the grounds that electrocution infringed on his Eighth Amendment rights against cruel and unusual punishment.[97] Kemmler's challenge is historically significant in that it did not implicate the death penalty itself as being cruel and unusual, but only the method by which it was carried out. Many constitutional scholars believe that the framers never questioned the necessity of capital punishment, as long as due process is followed in determining the guilt of the suspect.[98] Accordingly, the Supreme Court rejected Kemmler's challenge, stating:

> Punishments are cruel when they involve torture or a lingering death; but the punishment of death is not cruel, within the meaning of that word as used in the Constitution. It implies there something inhuman and barbarous, something more than the mere extinguishment of life.[99]

Thus, the Court set a standard that it has followed to this day. No *method* of execution has ever been found to be unconstitutional by the Supreme Court.

For nearly eight decades following its decision in the *Kemmler* case, the Supreme Court was silent on the question of whether capital punishment was constitutional. In *Weems v. United States* (1910),[100] however, the Court made a ruling that would significantly affect the debate on the death penalty. In this case, the defendant had been sentenced to fifteen years of hard labor, a heavy fine, and a number of other penalties for the relatively minor crime of falsifying official records. The Court overturned the sentence, ruling that the penalty was too harsh considering the nature of the offense. Ultimately, in the *Weems* decision, the Court set three important precedents concerning sentencing:

1. Cruel and unusual punishment is defined by the changing norms and standards of society and therefore is not based on historical interpretations.
2. Courts may decide whether a punishment is unnecessarily cruel with regard to physical pain.
3. Courts may decide whether a punishment is unnecessarily cruel with regard to psychological pain.[101]

REFORMING THE DEATH PENALTY

LO 8 In the 1960s, the Supreme Court became increasingly concerned about what it saw as serious flaws in the way the states administered capital punishment. Finally, in 1967, the Court put a moratorium on executions until it could "clean up" the process. The chance to do so came with the *Furman v. Georgia* case, decided in 1972.[102]

THE BIFURCATED PROCESS In its *Furman* decision, by a 5–4 margin, the Supreme Court essentially held that the death penalty, as administered by the states, violated the Eighth Amendment. Justice Potter Stewart was particularly eloquent in his concurring opinion, stating that the sentence of death was so arbitrary as to be comparable to "being struck by lightning."[103] Although the *Furman* ruling invalidated the death penalty for more than six hundred offenders on death row at the time, it also provided the states with a window to make the process less arbitrary, therefore bringing their death penalty statutes up to constitutional standards.

The result was a two-stage, or *bifurcated,* procedure for capital cases. In the first stage, a jury determines the guilt or innocence of the defendant for a crime that has, by state statute, been determined to be punishable by death. If the defendant is found guilty, the jury reconvenes in the second stage and considers all aggravating and mitigating factors to decide whether the death sentence is in fact warranted. (See *Mastering Concepts—The Bifurcated Death Penalty Process* alongside.) Therefore, even if a jury finds the defendant guilty of a crime, such as first degree murder, that *may be* punishable by death, in the second stage it can decide that the circumstances surrounding the crime justify only a punishment of life in prison.

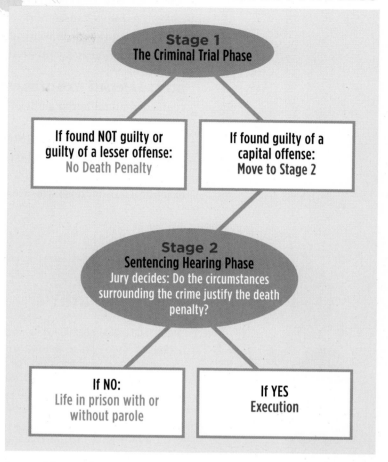

MASTERINGCONCEPTS
THE BIFURCATED DEATH PENALTY PROCESS

Stage 1
The Criminal Trial Phase

If found **NOT guilty** or guilty of a lesser offense:
No Death Penalty

If found **guilty** of a capital offense:
Move to Stage 2

Stage 2
Sentencing Hearing Phase
Jury decides: Do the circumstances surrounding the crime justify the death penalty?

If NO:
Life in prison with or without parole

If YES
Execution

COURT APPROVAL The Supreme Court ruled in favor of Georgia's new bifurcated process in 1976, stating that the process removed the ability of a court to "wantonly and freakishly impose the death penalty."[104] The Court upheld similar procedures in Texas and Florida, establishing a model for all states to follow that would assure them protection from lawsuits based on Eighth Amendment grounds. On January 17, 1977, Gary Gilmore became the first American executed (by Utah) under the new laws, and today thirty-four states and the federal government have capital punishment laws based on the bifurcated process. (Note that state governments are responsible for almost all executions in this country. The federal government has carried out only three death sentences since 1963.)

THE JURY'S ROLE The Supreme Court reaffirmed the important role of the jury in death penalties in *Ring v. Arizona* (2002).[105] The case involved Arizona's bifurcated process: after the jury determined a defendant's guilt or innocence, it would be dismissed, and the judge alone would decide whether execution was warranted. The Court found that this procedure violated the defendant's Sixth Amendment right to a jury trial, ruling that juries must be involved in *both* stages of the bifurcated process. The decision invalidated death penalty laws in Arizona, Colorado, Idaho, Montana, and Nebraska, forcing legislatures in those states to hastily revamp their procedures. (To learn how a jury makes this difficult decision, see the feature *You Be the Juror—Life or Death?* on the following page.)

Some states still allow for a measure of judicial discretion in capital punishment decisions. In Alabama, Delaware, and Florida, the jury only recommends a sentence of

Critical Thinking Skill Development: Ask students to respond to "Questions for Critical Analysis" number four on page 392, regarding the Supreme Court's ruling in *Ring v. Arizona.* (LO 8)

death or life in prison. If the judge feels that the sentence is unreasonable, he or she can override the jury. In 2011, for example, an Alabama jury voted unanimously that Iraq War veteran Courtney Lockhart should spend his life in prison for kidnapping and murdering college freshman Lauren Burk. Nonetheless, Lee County circuit judge Jacob Walker, noting that the jury was unaware of the defendant's extensive criminal history, overrode its recommendation and sentenced Lockhart to death.

MITIGATING CIRCUMSTANCES Several mitigating circumstances will prevent a defendant found guilty of first degree murder from receiving the death penalty.

Insanity In 1986, the United States Supreme Court held that the Constitution prohibits the execution of a person who is insane. The Court failed to provide a test for insanity other than Justice Lewis F. Powell's statement that the Eighth Amendment "forbids the execution only of those who are unaware of the punishment they are about to suffer and

YOU BE THE JUROR

Life or Death?

THE SITUATION Kitty and her two children—six-year-old Rachel and four-year-old Kyle—were asleep in Kitty's bed when her nephew Mills entered the bedroom. He was looking for his aunt's ATM card, which he planned to use to get funds to buy drugs. Someone woke up, and Mills attacked, fatally stabbing Kitty forty-five times and the children six times each. He then stole Kitty's car and bought large amounts of crack cocaine. When apprehended by police, Mills admitted the killings, saying, "I go crazy when I do pills and coke. It brings out the devil in me." You are a member of the jury that found Mills guilty of triple murder and now must decide his punishment. According to state law, Mills is eligible for the death penalty.

THE LAW The jury must weigh the aggravating circumstances against the mitigating circumstances of the crime. If the aggravating factors are greater, the jury will impose the death penalty on Mills. If the mitigating factors are greater, the jury will choose life in prison. (To review aggravating and mitigating circumstances, see page 367.)

YOUR DECISION During the sentencing phase of the trial, the prosecutor provides you with details of Mills's criminal history, which includes twenty-three convictions for various crimes. He also focuses on the extreme physical and psychological pain that Mills inflicted needlessly on his victims. "Imagine [Kitty's] mental anguish as she tried to protect her children from the blade of the knife," the prosecutor says. The defense attorney counters that his client was so high on drugs that he didn't know what he was doing at the time of the murders. The defense attorney also tells you about Mills's difficult childhood, marked by physical abuse from his alcoholic father, and points out that Mills has apologized, taking full responsibility for his actions. "Years from now, when your thought comes back to this trial, you will be comforted knowing that you chose . . . mercy over revenge," he says. After hearing these arguments, do you think the aggravating or mitigating circumstances carry more weight? What will you decide, and why?

[To see whether a Connecticut jury chose the death sentence in similar circumstances, go to Example 11.1 in Appendix B.]

why they are to suffer it."[106] Consequently, each state must come up with its own definition of "insanity" for death penalty purposes. A state may also force convicts on death row to take medication that will make them sane enough to be aware of the punishment they are about to suffer and why they are about to suffer it.[107]

Mentally Handicapped The Supreme Court's change of mind on the question of whether a mentally handicapped convict may be put to death underscores the continuing importance of the *Weems* test (see page 380). In 1989, the Court rejected the argument that execution of a mentally handicapped person was "cruel and unusual" under the Eighth Amendment.[108] At the time, only two states barred execution of the mentally handicapped. Thirteen years later, eighteen states had such laws, and the Court decided that this increased number reflected "changing norms and standards of society." In *Atkins v. Virginia* (2002),[109] the Court used the *Weems* test as the main rationale for barring the execution of the mentally handicapped.

The *Atkins* ruling did not end controversy in this area, however, as it allowed state courts to make their own determinations concerning which inmates qualified as "mentally impaired" for death penalty purposes. Several years ago, for example, Texas executed Bobby Wayne Woods even though some tests showed that his IQ was below 70, a level accepted by many experts as the cutoff point for mental retardation (see the photo alongside). Although Woods's lawyers spent years challenging their client's fate, numerous appellate courts, including the Supreme Court, upheld the right of Texas to execute in this instance.[110]

How does the case of Bobby Wayne Woods, executed by the state of Texas several years ago, show that capital punishment of the mentally handicapped will continue to be a controversial subject?
AP Photo/Texas Department of Criminal Justice

Age Following the *Atkins* case, many observers, including four Supreme Court justices, hoped that the same reasoning would be applied to the question of whether convicts who committed the relevant crime when they were juveniles may be executed. These hopes were realized in 2005 when the Court issued its *Roper v. Simmons* decision, which effectively ended the execution of those who committed crimes as juveniles.[111] As in the *Atkins* case, the Court relied on the "evolving standards of decency" test, noting that a majority of the states, as well as every other civilized nation, prohibited the execution of offenders who committed their crimes before the age of eighteen. The *Roper* ruling required that seventy-two convicted murderers in twelve states be resentenced and took the death penalty "off the table" for dozens of pending cases in which prosecutors were seeking capital punishment for juvenile criminal acts.

STILL CRUEL AND UNUSUAL?

As noted earlier, lethal injection is the dominant form of execution in this country. Most states employ the same three-drug process. First, the sedative sodium thiopental is administered to deaden pain. Then pancuronium bromide, a paralytic, immobilizes the prisoner. Finally, a dose of potassium chloride stops the heart. Members of the law enforcement and medical communities have long claimed that, if performed correctly, this procedure kills the individual quickly and painlessly. Many others, however, contend that the second drug—the paralytic—masks any outward signs of distress and thus keeps observers from knowing whether the inmate suffers extreme pain before death.[112]

Discussion Tip: Ask your students to summarize the ways in which the Supreme Court has limited eligibility for the death penalty since 1986. Do the students feel that capital punishment is now more "just" because of these decisions? Why or why not?

Critical Thinking Skill Development: Ask students to generate an essay in which they discuss the philosophy behind the death penalty. Which of the four basic philosophical justifications for sentencing does the death sentence satisfy?

In 2007, two convicted murderers in Kentucky asked the United States Supreme Court to invalidate the state's lethal injection procedure because of the possibility that it inflicted undetectable suffering. Nearly all of the scheduled executions in the United States were placed on hold while the Court deliberated this issue. In 2008, the Court ruled in *Baze v. Rees* that the mere possibility of pain "does not establish the sort of 'objectively intolerable risk of harm' that qualifies as cruel and unusual" punishment.[113] (See the feature *Landmark Cases*—Baze v. Rees on the facing page.) Though executions resumed shortly after the *Baze* decision, the states that employ the death penalty faced another challenge when the only American producer of sodium thiopental—the first drug used in the cocktail—stopped its production.

By 2011, ten of these states had replaced sodium thiopental in their three-step processes with a similar sedative called pentobarbital, commonly used in this country to euthanize animals. In addition, Ohio now uses a single, very strong dose of pentobarbital to carry out the death penalty.

DEBATING THE SENTENCE OF DEATH

Of the topics covered in this textbook, few inspire such passionate argument as the death penalty. Many advocates believe that execution is "just deserts" for those who commit heinous crimes. In the words of Ernest van den Haag, death is the "only fitting retribution for murder that I can think of."[114] Opponents worry that retribution is simply another word for vengeance and that "the use of the death penalty by the state will increase the acceptance of revenge in our society and will give official sanction to a climate of violence."[115] As the debate over capital punishment continues, it tends to focus on several key issues: deterrence, incapacitation, fallibility, arbitrariness, and discrimination.

LO 9

DETERRENCE Those advocates of the death penalty who wish to show that the practice benefits society often turn to the idea of deterrence. In other words, they believe that by executing convicted criminals, the criminal justice system discourages potential criminals from committing similar violent acts. (When people speak of "deterrence" with regard to the death penalty, they are usually referring to general deterrence rather than specific deterrence.) Deterrence was the primary justification for the frequent public executions carried out in this country before the 1830s and for the brutality of those events.

For Deterrence In 1975, Isaac Ehrlich, an economist then at the University of Chicago, estimated that if all those eligible for the death penalty had been executed, each additional execution that would have taken place between 1933 and 1967 could have saved the lives of as many as eight murder victims.[116] Ehrlich's data were subjected to heavy criticism, but researchers, relying on statistical comparisons of death sentences, executions, and homicide rates in particular geographic areas, continue to find statistical proof of the deterrent effect of capital punishment. Several reports released in the 2000s claim that each convict executed deters between three and eighteen future homicides.[117] "I oppose the death penalty," says Naci Mocan, an economics professor at Louisiana State University. "But my results show that the death penalty [has a deterrent effect]—what am I going to do, hide them?"[118]

Against Deterrence The main problem with studies that support the death penalty, say its critics, is that there are too few executions carried out in the United States each year to adequately determine their impact.[119] Furthermore, each study that "proves" the deterrent effect of the death penalty seems be matched by one that "disproves" the same premise.[120] In 2004, for example, criminal justice professors Lisa Stolzenberg and Stewart J. D'Alessio of Florida International University found no evidence that the number of executions had

LANDMARK CASES: *Baze v. Rees*

Ralph Baze shot and killed two Powell County sheriff's deputies. Ralph Bowling murdered Tina and Eddie Earley in Lexington. For their crimes, the state of Kentucky decided that the two men would be put to death. Baze's and Bowling's lawyers, however, challenged their clients' executions on the ground that Kentucky's method of lethal injection—the three-drug "cocktail" described on page 383—was unreliable and inflicted "unnecessary pain." After the Kentucky Supreme Court rejected this argument, the United States Supreme Court agreed to hear the inmates' appeal. The Court's decision was eagerly awaited, as state governments and courts had placed more than forty executions by lethal injection on hold pending the ruling.

Baze v. Rees
United States Supreme Court
553 U.S. 35 (2008)
www.scotusblog.com/case-files/cases/baze-v-rees

IN THE WORDS OF THE COURT . . .
CHIEF JUSTICE ROBERTS, MAJORITY OPINION
* * * *

We begin with the principle, settled by *Gregg,* that capital punishment is constitutional. It necessarily follows that there must be a means of carrying it out. Some risk of pain is inherent in any method of execution—no matter how humane—if only from the prospect of error in following the required procedure. It is clear, then, that the Constitution does not demand the avoidance of all risk of pain in carrying out executions.
* * * *

Our cases recognize that subjecting individuals to a risk of future harm—not simply actually inflicting pain—can qualify as cruel and unusual punishment. To establish that such exposure violates the Eighth Amendment, however, the conditions presenting the risk must be "sure or very likely to cause serious illness and needless suffering," and give rise to "sufficiently imminent dangers."
* * * *

In applying these standards to the facts of this case, we note at the outset that it is difficult to regard a practice as "objectively intolerable" when it is in fact widely tolerated. Thirty-six States that sanction capital punishment have adopted lethal injection as the preferred method of execution. * * * This broad consensus goes not just to the method of execution, but also to the specific three-drug combination used by Kentucky. Thirty States, as well as the Federal Government, use a series of sodium thiopental, pancuronium bromide, and potassium chloride, in varying amounts.
* * * *

Throughout our history, whenever a method of execution has been challenged in this Court as cruel and unusual, the Court has rejected the challenge. Our society has nonetheless steadily moved to more humane methods of carrying out capital punishment. The firing squad, hanging, the electric chair, and the gas chamber have each in turn given way to more humane methods, culminating in today's consensus on lethal injection.

DECISION
The Court found that the pain caused by any mode of execution, be it accidental or "an inescapable cause of death," does not trigger Eighth Amendment protections against "cruel and unusual punishment." In essence, the Court said that this form of lethal injection, though perhaps not perfect, was acceptable. It therefore upheld the decision of the Kentucky Supreme Court.

FOR CRITICAL ANALYSIS
Do you agree that it would be unreasonable to expect corrections officials to provide death row inmates with a completely painless mode of execution? If a less painful alternative to the three-drug "cocktail" becomes readily available, should the Court require states to use it? Explain your answers.

For more information and activities related to this case, visit the *Criminal Justice CourseMate* at cengagebrain. com and select the *Web links* for this chapter.

Group Activities: Have students go online to research the death penalty in your state. Is capital punishment permitted? What is the method of execution? How many convicted offenders are currently on death row? What were there offenses and how long have they been there?

any effect on the incidence of murder in the Houston, Texas, area over a five-year period.[121] In the end, the deterrence debate follows a familiar pattern. Opponents of the death penalty claim that murderers rarely consider the consequences of their act, and therefore it makes no difference whether capital punishment exists or not. Proponents counter that this proves the death penalty's deterrent value, because if the murderers *had* considered the possibility of execution, they would not have committed their crimes. (For a discussion of the moral component to this argument, see the feature *CJ in Action* at the end of the chapter.)

INCAPACITATION In one sense, capital punishment acts as the ultimate deterrent by rendering those executed incapable of committing further crimes. A study done by Paul Cassell and Stephen Markman analyzed the records of 52,000 state inmates doing time for murder and found that 810 of them had been previously convicted for the same crime. These 810 recidivists had killed 821 people after being released from prison the first time.[122] If, hypothetically, the death penalty was mandatory for those convicted of murder, then 821 innocent lives would have been saved in Cassell and Markman's example, and thousands of others among the general population. Such projections seem to show that by incapacitating dangerous criminals, capital punishment could provide society with measurable benefits.

Of course, the benefits of incapacitation are also available for those offenders sentenced to life without parole as an alternative to execution. Recent studies have found that the repeat murder rate of death-eligible convicts who live the remainder of their lives behind bars is about .002 percent. In the rare instance when one of these offenders is involved in a homicide, the victim is almost always another inmate.[123]

FALLIBILITY According to critics, the incapacitation justification for capital punishment rests on two questionable assumptions: (1) every convicted murderer is likely to recidivate, and (2) the criminal justice system is *infallible*. In other words, the system never convicts someone who is actually not guilty. As of yet, conclusive evidence that an innocent person has been executed in the United States has not been presented to the public. According to the Death Penalty Information Center, however, between 1973, when the Supreme Court had temporarily suspended capital punishment, and April 2011, 138 American men and women who had been convicted of capital crimes and sentenced to death—though not executed—were later found to be innocent. Over that same time period, 1,246 executions took place, meaning that for every nine convicts put to death during that period, about one death row inmate has been found innocent.[124]

The single factor that contributes the most to the criminal justice system's fallibility in this area is widely believed to be unsatisfactory legal representation. Many states and counties cannot or will not allocate adequate funds for death penalty cases, meaning that indigent capital defendants are often provided with a less-than-vigorous defense. The case of convicted murderer Ronald Rompilla highlights the consequences of poor counsel in a capital case. During the sentencing phase of his trial, Rompilla's lawyers made two serious errors. First, they failed to challenge the prosecution's characterization of Rompilla's previous conviction for rape and assault. In fact, they never even looked at the file of that case. Second, they failed to provide the Pennsylvania jury with mitigating factors that would argue against a death sentence, such as their client's troubled childhood, severe alcoholism, and other mental illnesses. Not surprisingly, the jury ordered Rompilla's execution, a sentence that was eventually overturned by the United States Supreme Court due to ineffective counsel.[125]

ARBITRARINESS As noted earlier, one of the reasons it is so difficult to determine the deterrent effect of the death penalty is that it is rarely meted out. Despite the bifurcated process required by the Supreme Court's *Furman* ruling (see pages 380–381), a significant amount of arbitrariness appears to remain in the system. Only 2 percent of all defendants convicted of murder are sentenced to death, and, as we have seen, relatively few of those on death row are ever executed.[126]

The chances of a defendant in a capital trial being sentenced to death seem to depend heavily on, as we have just seen, the quality of the defense counsel and the jurisdiction where the crime was committed. As Figure 11.8 below shows, a convict's likelihood of being executed is strongly influenced by geography. Six states (Alabama, Florida, Missouri, Oklahoma, Texas, and Virginia) account for more than two-thirds of all executions, while sixteen states and the District of Columbia do not provide for capital punishment within their borders. Thus, a person on trial for first degree murder in Idaho has a much better chance of avoiding execution than someone who has committed the same crime in Texas. Dramatic differences can exist even within the same state. Those convicted of death-eligible crimes in Baltimore County, Maryland, are twenty-three times more likely to be sentenced to death than are defendants in similar situations in neighboring Baltimore City.[127]

DISCRIMINATORY EFFECT AND THE DEATH PENALTY

Whether or not capital punishment is imposed arbitrarily, some observers claim that it is not done without bias. A disproportionate number of those executed since 1976—just over one-third—have been African American, and today 42 percent of all inmates on death row are black.[128] Another set of statistics also continues to be problematic: in 250 cases involving interracial murders in which the defendant was executed between 1976 and May 2011, the defendant was African American and the victim was white. Over that same time period, only 15 cases involved a white defendant and a black victim.[129] In fact, although slightly less than half of murder victims are white, three out of every four executions involve white victims (see Figure 11.9 on the next page).

In *McCleskey v. Kemp* (1987),[130] the defense attorney for an African American sentenced to death for killing a white police officer used similar statistics to challenge

Technology Tip: Students can learn more about the relationship between race and capital punishment online at the Death Penalty Information Center at **www.deathpenaltyinfo.org/ documents/FactSheet.pdf**.

FIGURE 11.8 **Executions by State, 1976–2010**

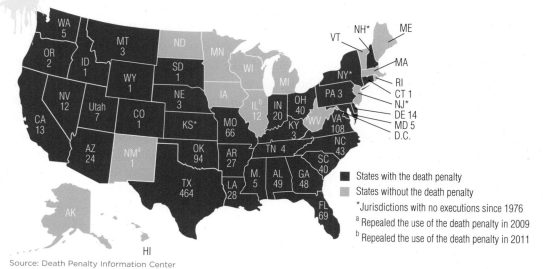

Source: Death Penalty Information Center

FIGURE 11.9 Race and the Death Penalty

As these two graphs show, a disproportionate percentage of executed murderers had white victims.

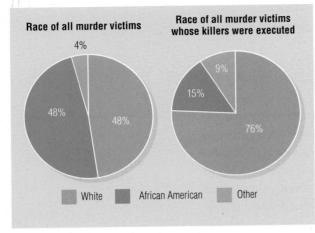

Race of all murder victims

4%
48%
48%

Race of all murder victims whose killers were executed

9%
15%
76%

White   African American   Other

Source: U.S. Bureau of Justice Statistics.

In March 2011, Marvin Mercado, center, was sentenced to eight consecutive life prison terms without the possibility of parole for his role in eight Los Angeles–area murders. Why do you think judges and juries often favor life-without-parole over the death penalty when given the choice?

AP Photo/Nick Ut

Georgia's death penalty law. A study of two thousand Georgia murder cases showed that although African Americans were the victims of six out of every ten murders in the state, more than 80 percent of the cases in which death was imposed involved murders of whites.[131] In a 5–4 decision, the United States Supreme Court rejected the defense's claims, ruling that statistical evidence did not prove discriminatory intent on the part of Georgia's lawmakers.

One of the reasons the study was unpersuasive in the *McClesky* case is that statistics, as we noted in Chapter 3, are often imperfect tools to measure trends. Even though the studies mentioned above show that race has an effect on the probability of receiving the death penalty, to prove discrimination from a legal standpoint, race must be the *only* determinant. Thus, a study must show that race, and not other factors such as the severity of the crime, the criminal history of the defendant, and the quality of the defense attorney, was the determining factor.[132] Research by William M. Holmes of the Criminal Justice Center at the University of Massachusetts in Boston, for example, found that race did not account for wrongful convictions in capital cases. A much more important factor, according to Holmes, was education level, which correlates strongly with income.[133]

THE IMMEDIATE FUTURE OF THE DEATH PENALTY

As Figure 11.7 on page 379 made clear, the number of executions carried out each year in the United States has decreased dramatically since 1999. Other statistics also indicate a decline in death penalty activity. In 2010, only 114 people were sentenced to death, compared with 277 in 1999.[134]

REASONS FOR THE DECLINE IN EXECUTIONS We have already addressed many of the reasons for the diminishing presence of executions in the criminal justice system. The unofficial moratorium on capital punishment that went into effect after the United States Supreme Court agreed to hear the *Baze* case challenging the constitutionality of lethal injections certainly contributed to the low number of executions in 2007 and 2008.

With its earlier decisions in the *Atkins* (2002) and *Roper* (2005) cases, the Court removed the possibility that hundreds of mentally handicapped and juvenile offenders could be sentenced to death. Furthermore, nearly all of the states that allow for the death penalty now permit juries to impose a sentence of life in prison without parole as an alternative to death. In Texas, the number of death sentences imposed each year dropped by about 50 percent after jurors were given the life-without-parole option in 2005, a trend that has been mirrored throughout the United States.[135]

Financial considerations are also starting to color the capital punishment picture. Because of the costs of intensive investigations, extensive *voir dire* (see pages 327–330), and lengthy appellate reviews, pursuing the death penalty can be very expensive. A recent study by the Urban Institute found that the average death penalty trial costs a state $2 million more than a murder trial in which capital punishment is not sought.[136] Taking all of the system's costs into account, Florida spends $24 million per execution, and California spends an extraordinary $250 million per execution.[137] As state budgets come under increased pressure from declining revenues, officials are looking at capital punishment as an area of potential savings.

CONTINUED SUPPORT FOR THE DEATH PENALTY In March 2011, Illinois governor Pat Quinn signed legislation banning the death penalty in his state, saying that it was not possible to fix a system that had put twenty men on death row who were later found innocent.[138] Quinn's decision commuted the death sentences of thirteen Illinois convicts to life in prison without parole. Citing concerns over both innocence and rising costs, Illinois is the third state since 2007 to end capital punishment, following New Jersey and New Mexico. Does this mean society's "standards of decency" are changing to the point that the death sentence is in danger of being completely abolished in the United States? Probably not. Despite its decisions in the 2000s, the Supreme Court has shown no interest in holding that the death penalty itself is unconstitutional. In addition to its *Baze* decision (see page 385), in 2007 the Court made it easier for prosecutors to seek the death penalty by allowing them to remove potential jurors who express reservations about the practice.[139]

Although public support for the death penalty has been steadily dropping since the mid-1990s, one poll taken in 2010 showed that 64 percent of Americans still favor the practice. (That percentage does, however, drop to about 50 percent when the choice is between execution and a sentence of life in prison without parole.)[140] Another poll found that 58 percent of the respondents favored an official moratorium on executions nationwide to consider the problem of wrongful death sentences.[141] In the 2000s, then, Americans seem more interested in making the sentence of death fairer than in doing away with it altogether.

Critical Thinking Skill Development: In a brief written assignment, ask students if they think that the death penalty will be abolished in the United States in the near future. Why or why not? (LO 9)

SELF ASSESSMENT

Fill in the blanks and check your answers on page 392.

By a large margin, _____ _____ is the most widespread method of execution in the United States today. According to the United States Supreme Court's *Weems* decision, "cruel and unusual punishment" under the Eighth Amendment is determined by the changing _____ _____ _____ of society. Following these guidelines, in 2002 the Court barred the execution of the _____ _____, and in 2005 it prohibited the execution of persons who were _____ at the time of their crime.

CJ IN ACTION

THE MORALITY OF THE DEATH PENALTY

Not everyone in Illinois was pleased when, in 2011, Governor Pat Quinn abolished the death penalty. Fifteen years earlier, death row inmate Daniel Ramsey had shot Rachel Williams in the head, killed her twelve-year-old sister, and raped and killed her best friend. "Nobody knows what it's like to hear your sister say, 'Don't shoot me,'" Williams said after the governor's decision, which spared Ramsey's life. "Why should he be able to sit there in prison until he turns over and dies? It's not fair."[142] Like many Americans, Williams does not see the death penalty in terms of the Eighth Amendment, "changing norms and standards," or the bifurcated sentencing process. Rather, she sees it as a matter of right and wrong, a viewpoint we will examine in this *CJ in Action* feature.

THE "LIFE-LIFE TRADE-OFF"

In academic circles, discussion about the morality of the death penalty has generally focused on two concepts. Those who take a *utilitarian* approach believe that the "cost" of each execution is acceptable because of the "benefit" to society, usually expressed in terms of deterrence of future crimes. Those who favor the *deontological* approach reject this cost-benefit analysis on the grounds that an individual's right to life should never be sacrificed, not even for the greater good.

Robert Blecker, a professor at New York Law School, sees such arguments as too esoteric to explain our country's somewhat unique relationship with the death penalty. Blecker believes that, for many Americans, capital punishment is an expression of hatred toward the offender and the "wrongness" of his or her crime.[143] Viewed in this light, the death penalty, still popular in the United States, can be seen as an expression of society's collective moral judgment on those who commit murder.

THE CASE FOR EXECUTION AS A MORAL ACT

- If the death penalty can prevent even a single future murder, then it is morally justifiable and perhaps even required by the government.

- Some crimes are so horrible that executing the person responsible is the only fitting response.

- The victim's family members often say that a murderer's execution brings them a sense of "closure" by allowing them to come to terms with their grief.

THE CASE AGAINST EXECUTION AS A MORAL ACT

- The death penalty is an inherently cruel and barbaric act, and it is improper for the government of a civilized nation to kill its own citizens.

- Just as we would not permit a physician to remove the organs of a living person to save the lives of others who need organ transplants, we should not execute a criminal based on the principle that the act would save the lives of others.[144]

- Problems of arbitrariness, discrimination, and wrongful convictions rob the death penalty of any moral justification, leaving it nothing more than the pointless infliction of violence by the state.

WRITING ASSIGNMENT—YOUR OPINION

Patrick O. Kennedy spent five years on Louisiana's death row for raping his eight-year-old stepdaughter so violently that she required emergency surgery. Louisiana was one of six states that allowed the death penalty for certain sex crimes, mostly involving minors. In 2008, the United States Supreme Court found these laws to be unconstitutional, labeling as "cruel and unusual" any punishment that is not proportionate to the crime.[145] Kennedy's sentence was reduced to life in prison without parole.

Mike Kemp, Getty

How do the arguments concerning the morality of the death penalty apply when the punishment extends to other crimes besides murder? In general, do you think an argument can be made that people who rape children should be executed? Before responding, you can review our discussions in this chapter concerning:

- The purposes of sentencing, particularly retribution, deterrence, and incapacitation (pages 357–360).

- The debate over the death penalty, particularly the discussions of fallibility and arbitrariness (pages 386–387).

- Possible discrimination and the death penalty (pages 387–388).

Your answer should include at least three full paragraphs.

CHAPTER SUMMARY

LO 1 **List and contrast the four basic philosophical reasons for sentencing criminals.** (a) Retribution, (b) deterrence, (c) incapacitation, and (d) rehabilitation. Under the principle of retributive justice, the severity of the punishment is in proportion to the severity of the crime. Punishment is an end in itself. In contrast, the deterrence approach seeks to prevent future crimes by setting an example. Such punishment is based on its deterrent value and not necessarily on the severity of the crime. The incapacitation theory of punishment simply argues that a criminal in prison cannot inflict further harm on society. In contrast, the rehabilitation theory believes that criminals can be rehabilitated in the appropriate prison environment.

LO 2 **Contrast indeterminate with determinate sentencing.** Indeterminate sentencing follows from legislative penal codes that set minimum and maximum amounts of incarceration time. Determinate sentencing carries a fixed amount of time, although this may be reduced for "good time."

LO 3 **Explain why there is a difference between the sentence imposed by a judge and the actual sentence served by the prisoner.** Although judges may decide on indeterminate sentencing, thereafter it is parole boards that decide when prisoners will be released after the minimum sentence is served.

LO 4 **List the six forms of punishment.** (a) Capital (death sentence), (b) imprisonment, (c) probation, (d) fines, (e) restitution and community service, and (f) restorative justice (apologies).

LO 5 **State who has input into the sentencing decision and list the factors that determine a sentence.** The prosecutor, defense attorney, probation officer, and judge provide inputs. The factors considered in sentencing are (a) the seriousness of the crime, (b) mitigating circumstances, (c) aggravating circumstances, and (d) judicial philosophy.

LO 6 **Explain some of the reasons why sentencing reform has occurred.** One reason is sentencing disparity, which is indicative of a situation in which those convicted of similar crimes receive dissimilar sentences (often due to a particular judge's sentencing philosophy). Sentencing discrimination has also occurred on the basis of defendants' gender, race, or economic standing. An additional reason for sentencing reform has been a general desire to "get tough on crime."

LO 7 **Identify the arguments for and against the use of victim impact statements during sentencing hearings.** Proponents of victim impact statements believe that they allow victims to provide character evidence in the same manner as defendants have always been allowed to do and that they give victims a therapeutic "voice" in the sentencing process. Opponents argue that the statements bring unacceptable levels of emotion into the courtroom and encourage judges and juries to make sentencing decisions based on the "social value" of the victim rather than the facts of the case.

LO 8 **Identify the two stages that make up the bifurcated process of death penalty sentencing.** The first stage of the bifurcated process requires a jury to find the defendant guilty or not guilty of a crime that is punishable by execution. If the defendant is found guilty, then, in the second stage, the jury reconvenes to decide whether the death sentence is warranted.

LO 9 **Describe the main issues of the death penalty debate.** Many of those who favor capital punishment believe that it is "just deserts" for the most violent of criminals. Those who oppose it see the act as little more than revenge. There is also disagreement over whether the death penalty acts as a deterrent. The relatively high number of death row inmates who have been found innocent has raised questions about the fallibility of the process, while certain statistics seem to show that execution is rather arbitrary. Finally, many observers contend that capital punishment is administered unfairly with regard to members of minority groups.

SELF ASSESSMENT ANSWER KEY

Page 362: **i.** retribution; **ii.** deterrence; **iii.** incapacitation; **iv.** rehabilitation

Page 364: **i.** Indeterminate; **ii.** determinate; **iii.** good time; **iv.** judge

Page 368: **i.** presentence investigative; **ii.** seriousness; **iii.** Mitigating; **iv.** aggravating

Page 372: **i.** disparity; **ii.** discrimination

Page 377: **i.** guidelines; **ii.** increased; **iii.** three-strikes/habitual offender; **iv.** victim impact

Page 389: **i.** lethal injection; **ii.** norms and standards; **iii.** mentally handicapped; **iv.** juveniles/minors

KEY TERMS

QUESTIONS FOR CRITICAL ANALYSIS

1. Suppose that the U.S. Congress passed a new law that punished shoplifting with a mandatory eighty-five-year prison term. What would be the impact of the new law on shoplifting nationwide? Would such a harsh law be justified by its deterrent effect? What about imposing a similarly extreme punishment on a more serious crime—a mandatory sentence of life in prison for, say, drunk driving? Would such a law be in society's best interest? Why or why not?

2. Why are truth-in-sentencing laws generally popular among victims' rights advocates? Why might these laws not be so popular with prison administrators or government officials charged with balancing a state budget?

3. Harold is convicted of unarmed burglary after a trial in Boston, Massachusetts. He has no prior convictions. According to the grid on page 374, what punishment do the state guidelines require? What would his punishment be if he had a previous conviction for armed robbery, which means that he has a "serious" criminal record?

4. In Alabama, Delaware, and Florida, judges can override sentencing decisions made by juries. What are the arguments for and against giving judges this power? How might these three states be in conflict with the United States Supreme Court's *Ring* decision, described on page 381?

5. Some observers believe that, by abolishing the death penalty, state officials in New Mexico and Illinois have taken away an important bargaining chip for prosecutors to use during plea bargaining. Why might this be the case?

CourseMate *For Online Help*

For online help and access to resources that accompany *Criminal Justice Today*, go to www.cengagebrain.com/shop/ISBN/1111835578. Click "Access Now," where you will find flashcards, an online quiz, and other helpful study aids. If you have an access code for CourseMate, log in and go to the chapter of your choice for additional online study aids.

NOTES

1. Terrie Morgan-Besecker, "Feds, Pa. Differ on Kid Porn," *Times-Leader (Wilkes-Barre, PA)* (January 16, 2011), at **www.times-leader.com/news/Feds_Pa_differ_on_kid_porn_01-16-2011.html**.

2. Michael L. Bourke and Andres E. Hernandez, "The 'Butner Study' Redux: A Report on the Incidence of Hands-On Child Victimization by Child Pornography Offenders," *Journal of Family Violence* (2009), 183–191.

3. *Ibid.*, 188.

4. David Yellen, "Just Deserts and Lenient Prosecutors: The Flawed Case for Real Offense Sentencing," *Northwestern University Law Review* 91 (Summer 1997), 1434.

5. Herbert L. Packer, "Justification for Criminal Punishment," in *The Limits of Criminal Sanction* (Palo Alto, CA: Stanford University Press, 1968), 36–37.

6. Jami L. Anderson, "Reciprocity as a Justification for Retributivism," *Criminal Justice Ethics* (Winter/Spring 1997), 13–14.

7. Immanuel Kant, *Metaphysical First Principles of the Doctrine of Right,* trans. Mary Gregor (Cambridge, UK: Cambridge University Press, 1991), 331.

8. Harold Pepinsky and Paul Jesilow, *Myths That Cause Crime* (Cabin John, MD: Seven Locks Press, 1984).

9. Jeremy Bentham, *An Introduction to the Principles of Morals and Legislation 1789* (New York: Hafner Publishing Corp., 1961).

10. Brian Forst, "Prosecution and Sentencing," in *Crime,* ed. James Q. Wilson and Joan Petersilia (San Francisco: ICS Press, 1995), 376.

11. Bureau of Justice Statistics, *Criminal Victimization, 2009* (Washington, D.C.: U.S. Department of Justice, October 2010), 1.

12. Federal Bureau of Investigation, *Crime in the United States, 2010* (Washington, D.C.: U.S. Department of Justice, 2011), at **www.fbi.gov/about-us/cjis/ucr/crime-in-the-u.s/2010/crime-in-the-u.s.-2010/tables/10tbl25.xls**.

13. Paul H. Robinson and John M. Darley, "The Utility of Desert," *Northwestern University Law Review* 91 (Winter 1997), 453.

14. James Q. Wilson, *Thinking about Crime* (New York: Basic Books, 1975), 235.

15. Isaac Ehrlich, "Participation in Illegitimate Activities: A Theoretical and Empirical Investigation," *Journal of Political Economy* 81 (May/June 1973), 521–564.

16. Steven Levitt, "The Effect of Prison Population Size on Crime Rates," *Quarterly Journal of Economics* 111 (May 1996), 319.

17. Avinash Singh Bhati, *An Information Theoretic Method for Estimating the Number of Crimes Averted by Incapacitation* (Washington, D.C.: Urban Institute, July 2007), 18–33.

18. Todd Clear, *Harm in Punishment* (Boston: Northeastern University Press, 1980).

19. Jan Chaiken, Marcia Chaiken, and William Rhodes, "Predicting Violent Behavior and Classifying Violent Offenders," in *Understanding and Preventing Violence,* ed. Albert J. Reiss, Jr., and Jeffrey A. Roth (Washington, D.C.: National Academy Press, 1994).

20. Robert J. Meadows and Julie Kuehnel, *Evil Minds: Understanding and Responding to Violent Predators* (Upper Saddle River, NJ: Pearson Prentice Hall, 2005), 256–258.

21. Barry Krisberg and Susan Marchionna, *Attitudes of U.S. Voters toward Prisoner Rehabilitation and Reentry Policies* (Oakland, CA: National Council on Crime and Delinquency, April 2006), 1.

22. Heather Strang and Lawrence W. Sherman, "Repairing the Harm: Victims and Restorative Justice," *Utah Law Review* (2003), 15, 18, 20–25.

23. Todd R. Clear, George F. Cole, and Michael D. Reisig, *American Corrections,* 7th ed. (Belmont, CA: Thomson Wadsworth, 2006), 68–69.

24. Mark S. Umbreit, *Victim Meets Offender: The Impact of Restorative Justice and Mediation* (New York: Criminal Justice Press, 1994), 17–19.

25. Leena Kurki, "Restorative and Community Justice in the United States," in *Crime and Justice: A Review of Research,* vol. 27, ed. Michael Tonry (Chicago: University of Chicago Press, 2000), 253–303.

26. Mark Scolforo, "Unpaid Restitution, Fees Exceed $1.55 Billion across Pennsylvania," *Associated Press* (December 24, 2007).

27. Gregory W. O'Reilly, "Truth-in-Sentencing: Illinois Adds Yet Another Layer of 'Reform' to Its Complicated Code of Corrections," *Loyola University of Chicago Law Journal* (Summer 1996), 986, 999–1000.

28. Marc Mauer, "The Truth about Truth-in-Sentencing," *Corrections Today* (February 1, 1996), 1–8.

29. Marvin Zalman, "The Rise and Fall of the Indeterminate Sentence," *Wayne Law Review* 24 (1977), 45, 52.

30. Marvin E. Frankel, *Criminal Sentences: Law without Order* (New York: Hill & Wang, 1972), 5.

31. Jessica Mitford, *Kind and Usual Punishment* (New York: Alfred A. Knopf, 1973), 80–83.

32. Bureau of Justice Statistics, *Truth in Sentencing in State Prisons* (Washington, D.C.: U.S. Department of Justice, 1999).

33. Paul W. Keve, *Crime Control and Justice in America: Searching for Facts and Answers* (Chicago: American Library Association, 1995), 77.

34. Kate Stith and José A. Cabranes, "Judging under the Federal Sentencing Guidelines," *Northwestern University Law Review* 91 (Summer 1997), 1247.

35. Mark M. Lanier and Claud H. Miller III, "Attitudes and Practices of Federal Probation Officers towards Pre-Plea/Trial Investigative Report Policy," *Crime & Delinquency* 41 (July 1995), 365–366.

36. Stith and Cabranes, 1247.

37. Nancy J. King and Rosevelt L. Noble, "Felony Jury Sentencing in Practice: A Three-State Study," *Vanderbilt Law Review* (2004), 1986.

38. Jena Iontcheva, "Jury Sentencing as Democratic Practice," *Virginia Law Review* (April 2003), 325.

39. Julie R. O'Sullivan, "In Defense of the U.S. Sentencing Guidelines Modified Real-Offense System," *Northwestern University Law Review* 91 (1997), 1342.

40. Brian Forst and Charles Wellford, "Punishment and Sentencing: Developing Sentencing Guidelines Empirically from Principles of Punishment," *Rutgers Law Review* 33 (1981).

41. 18 U.S.C. Section 2113(a) (1994).

42. Bob Barr and Eric Sterling, "The War on Drugs: Fighting Crime or Wasting Time?" *American Criminal Law Review* (Fall 2001), 1545.

43. United States Sentencing Commission, "Statistical Information Packet, Fiscal Year 2009, Northern District of California," Table 7, at **www.ussc.gov/Data_and_Statistics/Federal_Sentencing_Statistics/State_District_Circuit/JP2009.htm**; and "Statistical Information Packet, Fiscal Year 2009, Northern District of Iowa," Table 7, at **www.ussc.gov/Data_and_Statistics/Federal_Sentencing_Statistics/State_District_Circuit/2009/ian09.pdf**.

44. United States Sentencing Commission, "Statistical Information Packet, Fiscal Year 2009, Fourth Circuit," Table 7, at **www.ussc.gov/Data_and_Statistics/Federal_Sentencing_Statistics/State_District_Circuit/2009/4c09.pdf**; and "Statistical Information Packet, Fiscal Year 2009, Ninth Circuit," Table 7, at **www.ussc.gov/Data_and_Statistics/Federal_Sentencing_Statistics/State_District_Circuit/2009/9c09.pdf**.

45. Wake Forest University, "North Carolina Penalties for the Illegal Possession and Trafficking of Controlled Substances," at **www.wfu.edu/hr/drug/nc-penalties.html**.

46. Ronald F. Wright, "Federal or State? Sorting as a Sentencing Choice," *Criminal Justice* (Summer 2006), 17.

47. Cassia Spohn and David Holleran, "The Imprisonment Penalty Paid by Young, Unemployed Black and Hispanic Male Offenders," *Criminology* 35 (2000), 281.

48. *Ibid.*, 297.

49. Bureau of Justice Statistics, *Prison Inmates at Midyear 2009—Statistical Tables* (Washington, D.C.: U.S. Department of Justice, June 2010), Table 16, page 19.

50. *Crime in the United States, 2010*, at **www.fbi.gov/about-us/cjis/ucr/crime-in-the-u.s/2010/crime-in-the-u.s.-2010/tables/table-43.**

51. Spohn and Holleran, 301.

52. Brian Johnson, "The Multilevel Context of Criminal Sentencing: Integrating Judge- and County-Level Influences," *Criminology* (May 2006), 259–298.

53. Spohn and Holleran, 291.

54. Jeff German and Cy Ran, "Sentencing Study Finds Disparities You'd Expect," *Las Vegas Sun* (August 13, 2008), 1.

55. Bureau of Justice Statistics, *State Court Sentencing of Convicted Felons, 2004—Statistical Tables* (Washington, D.C.: U.S. Department of Justice, July 2007), Table 2.7.

56. Anti-Drug Abuse Act of 1986, Pub. L. No. 99-570, 100 Stat. 3207 (1986).

57. Solomon Moore, "Justice Department Seeks Equity in Sentences for Cocaine," *New York Times* (April 30, 2009), A17.

58. David Stout, "Retroactively, Panel Reduces Drug Sentences," *New York Times* (December 12, 2007), A1.

59. *U.S. Sentencing Commission Preliminary Crack Cocaine Retroactivity Data Report* (Washington, D.C.: U.S. Sentencing Commission, November 2010), Table 1.

60. Pub. L. No. 111-220, Section 2, 124 Statute 2372.

61. 28 U.S.C. Section 991 (1994).

62. Bureau of Justice Statistics, *Felony Sentences in State Courts, 2006—Statistical Tables* (Washington, D.C.: U.S. Department of Justice, December 2009), Table 3.5, page 20.

63. Clarice Feinman, *Women in the Criminal Justice System*, 3d ed. (Westport, CT: Praeger, 1994), 35.

64. Darrell Steffensmeier, John Kramer, and Cathy Streifel, "Gender and Imprisonment Decisions," *Criminology* 31 (1993), 411.

65. Quoted in Kareem Fahim and Karen Zraick, "Seeing Failure of Mother as Factor in Sentencing," *New York Times* (November 17, 2008), A24.

66. John C. Coffee, "Repressed Issues of Sentencing," *Georgetown Law Journal* 66 (1978), 987.

67. J. S. Bainbridge, Jr., "The Return of Retribution," *ABA Journal* (May 1985), 63.

68. The Massachusetts Court System, "Introduction: Sentencing Guidelines," at **www.mass.gov/courts/formsandguidelines/sentencing/step1.html#step1.**

69. Pub. L. No. 98-473, 98 Stat. 1987, codified as amended at 18 U.S.C. Sections 3551–3742 and 28 U.S.C. Sections 991–998 (1988).

70. Julia L. Black, "The Constitutionality of Federal Sentences Imposed under the Sentencing Reform Act of 1984 after *Mistretta v. United States*," *Iowa Law Review* 75 (March 1990), 767.

71. *Fifteen Years of Guidelines Sentencing: An Assessment of How Well the Federal Criminal Justice System Is Achieving the Goals of Sentencing Reform* (Washington, D.C.: U.S. Sentencing Commission, November 2004), 46.

72. Clear, Cole, and Reisig, 86.

73. Neal B. Kauder and Brian J. Ostrom, *State Sentencing Guidelines: Profiles and Continuum* (Williamsburg, VA: National Center for State Courts, 2008), 15.

74. *United States v. Booker,* 543 U.S. 220 (2005); *Gall v. United States,* 552 U.S. 38 (2007); and *Kimbrough v. United States,* 552 U.S. 85 (2007).

75. Quoted in A. G. Sulzberger, "Defiant Judge Takes on Child Pornography Laws," *New York Times* (May 22, 2010), A1.

76. Tim McGlone, "Leniency Often Granted in Child Porn Cases," *Virginian-Pilot (Norfolk, VA)* (January 16, 2011), at **hamptonroads.com/2011/01/leniency-often-granted-porn-cases.**

77. Alabama Code 1975 Section 20–2–79.

78. Washington Revised Code Annotated Section 9.94A.030.

79. 445 U.S. 263 (1980).

80. 538 U.S. 63 (2003).

81. *Lockyer v. Andrade,* 270 F.3d 743 (9th Cir. 2001).

82. *Lockyer v. Andrade,* 538 U.S. 63, 76 (2003).

83. *Ibid.,* 83.

84. Kim Murphy, "Washington State Revisits Three-Strikes Law," *Los Angeles Times* (August 11, 2009), at **articles.latimes.com/2009/aug/11/nation/na-three-strikes11.**

85. Radha Iyengar, "I'd Rather Be Hanged for a Sheep Than a Lamb: The Unintended Consequences of Three-Strikes' Laws," Working Paper No. 13784 (National Bureau of Economic Research, 2008), 2, at **www.nber.org/papers/w13784.pdf.**

86. Emily Bazelon, "Arguing Three Strikes," *New York Times Magazine* (May 23, 2010), 43.

87. *People v. Williams,* 17 Cal.4th 148, 161 (1998).

88. Murphy.

89. Edna Erez, "Victim Voice, Impact Statements, and Sentencing: Integrating Restorative Justice and Therapeutic Jurisprudence Principles in Adversarial Proceedings," *Criminal Law Bulletin* (September/October 2004), 495.

90. Bryan Myers and Edith Greene, "Prejudicial Nature of Impact Statements," *Psychology, Public Policy, and Law* (December 2004), 493.

91. *Payne v. Tennessee,* 501 U.S. 808 (1991).

92. Bryan Myers and Jack Arbuthnot, "The Effects of Victim Impact Evidence on the Verdicts and Sentencing Judgments of Mock Jurors," *Journal of Offender Rehabilitation* (1999), 95–112.

93. Walter Berns, "Abraham Lincoln (Book Review)," *Commentary* (January 1, 1996), 70.

94. Comments made at the Georgetown Law Center, "The Modern View of Capital Punishment," *American Criminal Law Review* 34 (Summer 1997), 1353.

95. David Bruck, quoted in Bill Rankin, "Fairness of the Death Penalty Is Still on Trial," *Atlanta Constitution-Journal* (July 29, 1997), A13.

96. Bureau of Justice Statistics, *Capital Punishment, 2009* (Washington, D.C.: U.S. Department of Justice, December 2010), Table 2, page 6.

97. Larry C. Berkson, *The Concept of Cruel and Unusual Punishment* (Lexington, MA: Lexington Books, 1975), 43.

98. John P. Cunningham, "Death in the Federal Courts: Expectations and Realities of the Federal Death Penalty Act of 1994," *University of Richmond Law Review* 32 (May 1998), 939.

99. *In re Kemmler,* 136 U.S. 447 (1890).

100. 217 U.S. 349 (1910).

101. Pamela S. Nagy, "Hang by the Neck until Dead: The Resurgence of Cruel and Unusual Punishment in the 1990s," *Pacific Law Journal* 26 (October 1994), 85.

102. 408 U.S. 238 (1972).

103. 408 U.S. 309 (1972) (Stewart, concurring).

104. *Gregg v. Georgia,* 428 U.S. 153 (1976).

105. 536 U.S. 584 (2002).

106. *Ford v. Wainwright,* 477 U.S. 399, 422 (1986).

107. Vidisha Barua, "'Synthetic Sanity': A Way Around the Eighth Amendment?" *Criminal Law Bulletin* (July/August 2008), 561–572.

108. *Penry v. Lynaugh,* 492 U.S. 302 (1989).

109. 536 U.S. 304 (2002).

110. James C. McKinley, "Killer with Low I.Q. Is Executed in Texas," *New York Times* (December 4, 2009), A19.

111. 543 U.S. 551 (2005).

112. *Baze v. Rees,* 217 S.W.3d 207 (Ky. 2006).

113. 553 U.S. 35 (2008).

114. Ernest van den Haag, "The Ultimate Punishment: A Defense," *Harvard Law Review* 99 (1986), 1669.

115. *The Death Penalty: The Religious Community Calls for Abolition* (pamphlet published by the National Coalition to Abolish the Death Penalty and the National Interreligious Task Force on Criminal Justice, 1988), 48.

116. Isaac Ehrlich, "The Deterrent Effect of Capital Punishment: A Question of Life and Death," *American Economic Review* 65 (June 1975), 397–417.

117. Hashem Dezhbakhsh, Paul H. Rubin, and Joanna M. Shepherd, "Does Capital Punishment Have a Deterrent Effect? New Evidence from Postmoratorium Panel

Data," *American Law and Economics Review* 5 (2003), 344–376; H. Naci Mocan and R. Kaj Gittings, "Getting Off Death Row: Commuted Sentences and the Deterrent Effect of Capital Punishment," *Journal of Law and Economics* 46 (2003), 453–478; Joanna M. Shepherd, "Deterrence versus Brutalization: Capital Punishment's Differing Impact among States," *Michigan Law Review* 104 (2005), 203–255; and Paul R. Zimmerman, "State Executions, Deterrence, and the Incidence of Murder," *Journal of Applied Economics* 7 (2005), 163–193.

118. Quoted in Robert Tanner, "Studies Say Death Penalty Deters Crime," *Associated Press* (June 10, 2007).

119. Richard Berk, "Can't Tell: Comments on 'Does the Death Penalty Save Lives?'" *Criminology and Public Policy* (November 2009), 845–851.

120. John J. Donohue and Justin Wolfers, "Uses and Abuses of Empirical Evidence in the Death Penalty Debate," *Stanford Law Review* 58 (2005), 791–845.

121. Lisa Stolzenberg and Stewart J. D'Alessio, "Capital Punishment, Execution Publicity, and Murder in Houston, Texas," *Journal of Criminal Law and Criminology* (Winter 2004), 351–379.

122. Stephen Markman and Paul Cassell, "Protecting the Innocent: A Response to the Bedau-Radelet Study," *Stanford Law Review* 41 (1988), 153.

123. Jonathan R. Sorensen and Rocky L. Pilgrim, "An Actuarial Risk Assessment of Violence Posed by Capital Murder Defendants," *Journal of Criminal Law and Criminology* (Summer 2000), 1251, 1256.

124. Death Penalty Information Center, "Innocence and the Death Penalty," at **www.deathpenaltyinfo.org/innocence-and-death-penalty**.

125. *Rompilla v. Beard*, 545 U.S. 375 (2005).

126. Adam Liptak, "Geography and the Machinery of Death," *New York Times* (February 5, 2007), A10.

127. Raymond Paternoster, Robert Brame, Sarah Bacon, and Andrew Ditchfield, "Justice by Geography and Race: The Administration of the Death Penalty in Maryland 1978–1999," *Maryland's Law Journal on Race, Religion, Gender and Class* (2004), Table 65, page 72.

128. Bureau of Justice Statistics, *Capital Punishment, 2009—Statistical Tables* (Washington, D.C.: U.S. Department of Justice, December 2010), Table 4, page 8, and Table 13, page 15.

129. Death Penalty Information Center, "National Statistics on the Death Penalty and Race," at **www.deathpenaltyinfo.org/race-death-row-inmates-executed-1976#defend**.

130. 481 U.S. 279 (1987).

131. David C. Baldus, George Woodworth, and Charles A. Pulaski, *Equal Justice and the Death Penalty: A Legal and Empirical Analysis* (Boston: Northeastern University Press, 1990), 140–197, 306.

132. Laura Argys and Naci Mocan, *Who Shall Live and Who Shall Die? An Analysis of Prisoners on Death Row in the United States* (Cambridge, MA: National Bureau of Economic Research, February 2003), 22.

133. William M. Holmes, "Who Are the Wrongly Convicted on Death Row?" in *Wrongly Convicted: When Justice Fails*, ed. Saundra Westervelt and John Humphrey (Piscataway, NJ: Rutgers University Press, 2001).

134. Death Penalty Information Center, "The Death Penalty in 2010: Year End Report," at **www.deathpenaltyinfo.org/documents/2010YearEnd-Final.pdf**.

135. David McCord, "What's Messing with Texas Death Sentences?" *Texas Tech Law Review* (Winter 2011), 601–608.

136. Cited in "Saving Lives and Money," *The Economist* (March 14, 2009), 32.

137. Mary Kate Cary, "The Case against the Death Penalty," *U.S. News Weekly* (March 25, 2011), 13.

138. Barbara Goldberg, "State's Budget Woes Aid Death Penalty Opponents," *Chicago Tribune* (March 20, 2011), 22.

139. *Uttecht v. Brown*, 551 U.S. 1 (2007).

140. Gallup, "In U.S. 64% Support Death Penalty in Cases of Murder" (November 8, 2010), at **www.gallup.com/poll/144284/support-death-penalty-cases-murder.aspx**.

141. Richard C. Dieter, *A Crisis of Confidence: Americans' Doubts about the Death Penalty* (Washington, D.C.: Death Penalty Information Center, June 2007), 5, 9.

142. Quoted in Tom Nicario, Stacy St. Clair, and Dahleen Glanton, "Quinn Angers Some Families," *Chicago Tribune* (March 10, 2011), 7.

143. Quoted in Andrea Weigl, "Father Wants Killer to Die," *Raleigh (NC) News & Observer* (April 23, 2007), A1.

144. Claire Finkelstein, "A Contractarian Argument against the Death Penalty," *New York University Law Review* (October 2006), 1283.

145. *Kennedy v. Louisiana*, 554 U.S. 407 (2008).

CHAPTER

12

Brandon Todd/Splash News/Newscom

Probation and Community Corrections

LEARNING OBJECTIVES

After reading this chapter, you should be able to . . .

LO 1 Explain the justifications for community-based corrections programs.

LO 2 Explain several alternative sentencing arrangements that combine probation with incarceration.

LO 3 Specify the conditions under which an offender is most likely to be denied probation.

LO 4 Describe the three general categories of conditions placed on a probationer.

LO 5 Explain why probation officers' work has become more dangerous.

LO 6 Explain the three stages of probation revocation.

LO 7 List the five sentencing options for a judge besides imprisonment and probation.

LO 8 Contrast day reporting centers with intensive supervision probation.

LO 9 List the three levels of home monitoring.

The nine learning objectives labeled LO 1 through LO 9 are designed to help improve your understanding of the chapter.

LIGHT RAP FOR LIL WAYNE?

Usually, judges prefer that a defendant be in attendance for sentencing, but Lil Wayne had a good excuse for his absence from the Yuma County (Arizona) Superior Court. The hip-hop artist, born Dwayne Carter, Jr., was incarcerated 2,600 miles to the east, serving a yearlong sentence at the Rikers Island Prison Complex in New York City on a weapons violation. So, Lil Wayne was forced to watch via video monitor on June 30, 2010, as Judge Mark W. Reeves decided his fate.

Lil Wayne's "appearance" in the Arizona court stemmed from an incident at a U.S. Border Patrol checkpoint near Mexico two and a half years earlier. Led onto the rapper's tour bus by drug-sniffing dogs, law enforcement agents found an ounce of cocaine, nearly four ounces of marijuana, forty-one grams of Ecstasy, and a .40-caliber handgun. Yuma County prosecutors charged Lil Wayne with felony possession of a narcotic drug for sale, possession of dangerous drugs, misconduct involving weapons, and possession of drug paraphernalia. If found guilty on all charges, Lil Wayne faced more than three years in a state prison.

Not wanting to risk a further stay behind bars, Lil Wayne negotiated a deal with Arizona authorities.

He pleaded guilty to one count of possession of a dangerous drug in exchange for the dismissal of the other charges. As part of the plea bargain, Reeves sentenced Lil Wayne to three years' probation only, with the further conditions that he not consume any alcohol, take any illegal drugs, or consort with any individual involved in criminal activity during that time. Lil Wayne's probationary period started the instant he left Rikers Island on November 4, 2010, which didn't stop him from joining fellow rapper Drake onstage in Las Vegas two days later. "I'm fresh from vacation," he told the adoring crowd. "I swear to God ain't nothing, nothing, nothing like home."

The rapper Lil Wayne, shown here in a red baseball cap with his attorneys, was sentenced to probation in Arizona after being found guilty on a drug charge.
AP Photo/*Yuma Sun*, Jared Dort)

Lil Wayne's Arizona sentence sparked skepticism, particularly in light of his previous conviction in New York. Many felt he had been let off easy because of his fame and a high-priced defense attorney. In fact, Judge Reeves was hardly breaking new ground. Defendants found guilty of crimes far more serious than drug possession are routinely given *probation* in this country. A system that initially provided judges with the discretion to show leniency to first-time, minor offenders increasingly allows those who have committed serious crimes to serve their time in the community rather than prison or jail. Just two months after Lil Wayne's release from Rikers Island, Illinois circuit court judge Daniel J. Rozak sentenced a sixty-nine-year-old man who had been found guilty of second degree murder to four years of probation. (The judge based the sentence on the defendant's advanced age, his lack of a criminal record, and the fact that he had been provoked by the victim.) Fifty-one percent of probationers in this country have been convicted of a felony, and about 800,000 have been found guilty of a violent crime such as assault or rape.[1]

Today, about 4.2 million adults are under the supervision of state and federal probation organizations—a figure that has grown by approximately 600,000 over the past decade.[2] In this chapter, we will discuss the strengths and weaknesses of probation and other community or intermediate sanctions such as intensive probation, fines, boot camps, electronic monitoring, and home confinement. Given the scarcity of prison resources, decisions made today concerning these alternative punishments will affect the criminal justice system for decades to come.

THE JUSTIFICATION FOR COMMUNITY CORRECTIONS

LO 1 In the court of popular opinion, retribution and crime control take precedence over community-based correctional programs. America, says University of Minnesota law professor Michael Tonry, is preoccupied with the "absolute severity of punishment" and the "widespread view that only imprisonment counts."[3] Mandatory sentencing guidelines and "three-strikes" laws are theoretically the opposite of community-based corrections.[4] To a certain degree, correctional programs that are administered in the community are considered a less severe, and therefore a less worthy, alternative to imprisonment.

Critical Thinking Skill Development: Ask students to consider the concept of reintegration. How important is the task of building ties between the offender and the community? How much attention should be paid to reintegration in the corrections system? (LO 1)

REINTEGRATION

Supporters of probation and intermediate sanctions reject such views as not only shortsighted, but also contradictory to the aims of the corrections system. A very small percentage of all convicted offenders have committed crimes that warrant life imprisonment or capital punishment. Most, at some point, will return to the community. Consequently, according to one group of experts, the task of the corrections system

> includes building or rebuilding solid ties between the offender and the community, integrating or reintegrating the offender into community life—restoring family ties, obtaining employment and an education, securing in the larger sense a place for the offender in the routine functioning of society.[5]

The **Sentencing Project** is a nonprofit organization that promotes reduced reliance on incarceration and alternative forms of sentencing. To visit its Web site, click on the *Criminal Justice CourseMate* at **cengagebrain.com** and select the *Web links* for this chapter.

Considering that some studies have shown higher recidivism rates for offenders who are subjected to prison culture, a frequent justification of community-based corrections is that they help to reintegrate the offender into society.

Reintegration has a strong theoretical basis in rehabilitative theories of punishment. An offender is generally considered to be "rehabilitated" when he or she no longer represents a threat to other members of the community and therefore is believed to be fit to live in that community. In the context of this chapter and the two that follow, it will also be helpful to see reintegration as a process through which corrections officials such as probation and parole officers provide the offender with incentives to follow the rules of society. These incentives can be positive, such as enrolling the offender in a drug treatment program. They can also be negative—in particular, the threat of return to prison or jail for failure to comply. In all instances, corrections system professionals must carefully balance the needs of the individual offender against the rights of law-abiding members of the community.

Reintegration A goal of corrections that focuses on preparing the offender for a return to the community unmarred by further criminal behavior.

Diversion In the context of corrections, a strategy to divert those offenders who qualify away from prison and jail and toward community-based and intermediate sanctions.

DIVERSION

Another justification for community-based corrections, based on practical considerations, is **diversion.** As you are already aware, many criminal offenses fall into the category of "petty," and it is well-nigh impossible, as well as unnecessary, to imprison every offender for every offense. Community-based corrections are an important means of diverting criminals to alternative modes of punishment so that scarce incarceration

In Dallas, street prostitutes such as the two shown here are often treated as crime victims and offered access to treatment and rehabilitation programs. How might society benefit if such offenders are kept out of jail or prison through these kinds of diversion programs?
AP Photo/LM Otero, File

resources are consumed by only the most dangerous criminals. In his "strainer" analogy, corrections expert Paul H. Hahn likens this process to the workings of a kitchen strainer. With each "shake" of the corrections "strainer," the less serious offenders are diverted from incarceration. At the end, only the most serious convicts remain to be sent to prison.[6] (The concept of diversion is closely linked to that of selective incapacitation, mentioned in Chapter 11.)

The diversionary role of community-based punishments has become more pronounced as prisons and jails have filled up over the past three decades. In fact, probationers now account for about 60 percent of all adults in the American corrections systems. (To learn about another form of diversion, which focuses on the mental health system rather than the criminal justice system, see the *CJ in Action* feature at the end of this chapter.)

THE "LOW-COST ALTERNATIVE"

Not all of the recent expansion of community corrections can be attributed to acceptance of its theoretical underpinnings. Many politicians and criminal justice officials who do not look favorably on ideas such as reintegration and diversion have embraced programs to keep nonviolent offenders out of prison. The reason is simple: economics. The cost of constructing and maintaining prisons and jails, as well as housing and caring for inmates, has placed a great deal of pressure on corrections budgets across the country. Indeed, to cut incarceration costs, states are taking such steps as installing windmills and solar panels to save energy and using medical schools to provide less costly health care.[7]

Community corrections offer an enticing financial alternative to imprisonment. In the federal corrections system, for example, the annual cost of incarcerating an inmate is just over $25,800, compared with about $3,740 for a year of probation.[8] For states, the annual cost is $29,000 for a prison inmate versus $1,250 for a probationer.[9] Not surprisingly, many jurisdictions are adopting policies that favor moving offenders from their cells into the community. In Texas, for example, corrections officials estimate that programs designed to increase the use of probation and intermediate sanctions have saved the state nearly $450 million in prison costs.[10] Officials can also require community-based criminals to pay the bill for their own supervision. In Loudoun County, Virginia, the $12 daily cost of wearing a transdermal alcohol ankle bracelet (see page 81) is covered by the offender.[11]

SELF ASSESSMENT

Fill in the blanks and check your answers on page 423.
The three basic justifications for community corrections are (1) _____, which focuses on building or rebuilding the offender's ties with the community; (2) _____, a strategy that attempts to allocate scarce jail and prison space to only the most dangerous criminals; and (3) _____ considerations, as community corrections are generally _____ expensive than incarceration.

Discussion Tip: Ask students to debate the roll that economics should play in the sentencing of criminal offenders. Why might economics be responsible for the growing number of offenders who are sentenced to community-based corrections rather than prison or jail? (LO1)

PROBATION: DOING TIME IN THE COMMUNITY

As Figure 12.1 alongside shows, probation is the most common form of punishment in the United States. Although it is administered differently in various jurisdictions, probation can be generally defined as

> the legal status of an offender who, after being convicted of a crime, has been directed by the sentencing court to remain in the community under the supervision of a probation service for a designated period of time and subject to certain conditions imposed by the court or by law.[12]

(As you read this chapter, keep in mind the distinction between *probation* and *parole*. Although they sound similar and both involve community supervision of offenders, there are differences. Probation is a sentence handed down by a judge following conviction and usually does not include incarceration. Parole, explained in detail in Chapter 14, is a form of conditional release from prison.)

The theory behind probation is that certain offenders, having been found guilty of a crime, can be treated more economically and humanely by putting them under controls while still allowing them to live in the community. One of the advantages of probation has been that it provides for the rehabilitation of the offender while saving society the costs of incarceration. Despite probation's widespread use, certain participants in the criminal justice system question its ability to reach its rehabilitative goals. Critics point to the immense number of probationers and the fact that many of them are violent felons as evidence that the system is "out of control." Supporters contend that nothing is wrong with probation in principle, but admit that its execution must be adjusted to meet the goals of modern corrections.[13]

THE ROOTS OF PROBATION

In its earliest forms, probation was based on a desire to inject leniency into an often harsh criminal justice system. Nineteenth-century English judges had the power to issue judicial reprieves, or to suspend sentences for a certain amount of time, on the condition of continued good behavior by the defendant. This practice was adopted in the United States, albeit in a different form. American judges used their reprieve power to suspend the imposition of a penalty indefinitely, so long as the offender did not commit a second crime. If another crime was committed, the offender could be punished for both crimes.

In *Ex parte United States* (1916),[14] the United States Supreme Court ruled that such indefinite reprieves were unconstitutional because they limited the ability of the legislative and administrative branches to make and enforce sentencing laws. With this diversion option removed, judges increasingly turned to the model of probation first established in Massachusetts eighty years earlier.

JOHN AUGUSTUS AND THE ORIGINS OF PROBATION The roots of probation can be directly traced to a Boston shoemaker named John Augustus. In 1841, Augustus, who was deeply religious and had considerable wealth, offered to post bail for a man charged with drunkenness. Augustus persuaded the judge to defer sentencing for three weeks, during which time the offender would be in his custody. At the end of this probationary period, the offender was able to convince the judge that he had been reformed and received a fine instead of incarceration.

FIGURE 12.1 Probation in American Corrections
As you can see, the majority of convicts under the control of the American corrections system are on probation.

Prison 21%

Jail 10%

Parole 11%

Probation 58%

Source: Bureau of Justice Statistics, *Correctional Populations in the United States, 2009* (Washington, D.C.: U.S. Department of Justice, December 2010), Table 1, page 2.

Probation A criminal sanction in which a convict is allowed to remain in the community rather than be imprisoned, as long as she or he follows certain conditions set by the court.

Judicial Reprieve Temporary relief or the postponement of a sentence on the authority of a judge.

Teaching Tip: At this point, help students understand the basic differences between probation and parole, as noted in the text. Ask students to make sure that they mean "probation" when they refer to "probation" and "parole" when they refer to "parole."

During the next eighteen years until his death, Augustus bailed out and supervised nearly 1,800 persons in lieu of confinement in the Boston House of Corrections. He carefully screened potential probationers, researching their personal backgrounds before deciding whether to include them in his caseload. Generally, Augustus accepted only first offenders of otherwise good character. During the probationary period, he helped his charges find employment and lodging and aided them in obtaining an education.[15] Augustus can be credited with nearly every aspect of modern probation, from the name itself (from the Latin term *probatio,* or a "period of governing or trial") to presentence investigations, supervision, and revocation.

Augustus's work was continued by a group of volunteer "probation officers" who strived to rescue youths from the dangers of imprisonment. In 1869, the state of Massachusetts passed a law that allowed for probation of juveniles and, nine years later, provided for paid probation officers to be hired by Boston's criminal courts. The law limited probation to "such persons as may reasonably be expected to be reformed without punishment." By 1891, Massachusetts had established the first statewide probation program.[16]

THE EVOLUTION OF PROBATION Even as probation systems have been adopted in each of the fifty states and by the federal government, the basic conflict between "help" and "punishment" has dominated the context of probation. When both criminal justice practitioners and the public hold the rehabilitative model in favor, as was the case for most of the first half of the twentieth century, probation is generally considered a valuable aspect of treatment. When retributive goals come to the fore, however, probation is seen as being in need of reform, as has been the case in the United States since the mid-1970s. (It should be noted, though, that the number of Americans on probation has continued to grow even as its theoretical underpinnings are being challenged.)

SENTENCING CHOICES AND PROBATION

Probation is basically an arrangement between sentencing authorities and the offender. In traditional probation, the offender agrees to comply with certain terms for a specified amount of time in return for serving the sentence in the community. One of the primary benefits for the offender, besides not getting sent to a correctional facility, is that the length of the probationary period is usually considerably shorter than the length of a prison term (see Figure 12.2 on the facing page).

The traditional form of probation is not the only arrangement that can be made. A judge can hand down a **suspended sentence,** under which a defendant who has been

LO 2 convicted and sentenced to be incarcerated is not required to serve the sentence. Instead, the judge puts the offender on notice, keeping open the option of reinstating the original sentence and sending the offender to prison or jail if he or she reoffends. In practice, suspended sentences are quite similar to probation.

ALTERNATIVE SENTENCING ARRANGEMENTS Judges can also combine probation with incarceration. Such sentencing arrangements include:

- *Split sentences.* In **split sentence probation,** also known as *shock probation,* the offender is sentenced to a specific amount of time in prison or jail, to be followed by a period of probation.
- *Shock incarceration.* In this arrangement, an offender is sentenced to prison or jail with the understanding that after a period of time, she or he may petition the

Teaching Tip: Spend a few minutes talking with students about the differences between probation and a suspended sentence. While these two practices appear to be similar, they are not. (LO 2)

Suspended Sentence A judicially imposed condition in which an offender is sentenced after being convicted of a crime, but is not required to begin serving the sentence immediately. The judge may revoke the suspended sentence and remit the offender to prison or jail if he or she reoffends.

Split Sentence Probation A sentence that consists of incarceration in a prison or jail, followed by a probationary period in the community.

FIGURE 12.2 Average Length of Sentence: Prison versus Probation

As you can see, the average probation sentence is much shorter than the average prison sentence for most crimes.

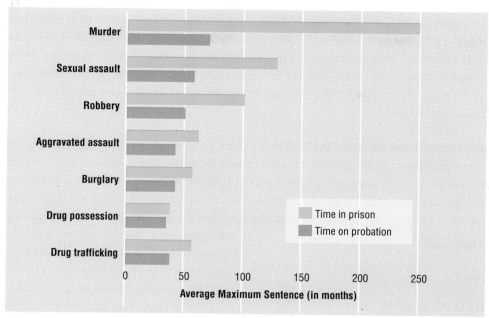

Source: Bureau of Justice Statistics, *Felony Sentences in State Courts, 2006—Statistical Tables* (Washington, D.C.: U.S. Department of Justice, December 2009), Table 1.3.

court to be released on probation. Shock incarceration is discussed more fully later in the chapter.

- *Intermittent incarceration.* With intermittent incarceration, the offender spends a certain amount of time each week, usually during the weekend, in a jail, workhouse, or other government institution.

Split sentences are popular with judges, as they combine the "treatment" aspects of probation with the "punishment" aspects of incarceration. According to the U.S. Department of Justice, about a fifth of all probationers are also sentenced to some form of incarceration.[17]

ELIGIBILITY FOR PROBATION Not every offender is eligible for probation. In Bell County, Texas, for example, juries can recommend probation only for assessed prison sentences of ten years or less. Generally, research has shown that offenders are most likely to be denied probation if they:

LO 3

- Are convicted on multiple charges.
- Were on probation or parole at the time of the arrest.
- Have two or more prior convictions.
- Are addicted to narcotics.
- Seriously injured the victim of the crime.
- Used a weapon during the commission of the crime.[18]

About half of all probationers have been found guilty of a misdemeanor, and about half have been found guilty of a felony.[19] As might be expected, the chances of a felon being sentenced to probation are highly dependent on the seriousness of the crime he or she has committed. Only one in five felons on probation has been convicted of a violent crime.[20]

Discussion Tip: Place students into groups and have them consider the potential advantages and disadvantages of combining probation with incarceration. Which goals of corrections are satisfied by these programs? (LO 2)

Teaching Tip: Interview a local probation officer and share your findings with the class. How many probationers are being served in your area? What are the demographics of this population? For what offenses are offenders typically sentenced to probation? (LO 3)

CONDITIONS OF PROBATION

Teaching Tip: If possible, invite a local judge to visit the classroom. Have him or her detail the most commonly assigned conditions of probation in your area. What are the goals of those conditions? Are they primarily punitive or designed with an eye toward treatment? (LO 4)

A judge may decide to impose certain conditions as part of a probation sentence. These conditions represent a "contract" between the judge and the offender, in which the latter agrees that if she or he does not follow certain rules, probation may be revoked (see Figure 12.3 below). The probation officer usually recommends the conditions of probation, but judges also have the power to set any terms they believe to be necessary. As we saw at the beginning of this chapter, Judge Mark W. Reeves imposed several conditions on Lil Wayne, prohibiting the performer from consuming alcohol and associating with known criminals.

PRINCIPLES OF PROBATION A judge's personal philosophy is often reflected in the probation conditions that she or he creates for probationers. In *In re Quirk* (1997),[21] for example, the Louisiana Supreme Court upheld the ability of a trial judge to impose church attendance as a condition of probation. Though judges have a great deal of discretion in setting the conditions of probation, they do operate under several guiding principles. First, the conditions must be related to the dual purposes of probation, which most federal and state courts define as (1) the rehabilitation of the probationer and (2) the protection of the community. Second, the conditions must not violate the U.S. Constitution, as probationers are generally entitled to the same constitutional rights as other prisoners.[22]

Of course, probationers do give up certain constitutional rights when they consent to the terms of probation. Most probationers, for example, agree to spot checks of their homes for contraband such as drugs or weapons, and they therefore have a diminished expectation of privacy.

In *United States v. Knights* (2001),[23] the United States Supreme Court upheld the actions of deputy sheriffs in Napa County, California, who searched a probationer's home without a warrant or probable cause. The unanimous decision was based on the premise that because those on probation are more likely to commit crimes, law enforcement agents "may therefore justifiably focus on probationers in a way that [they do] not on the ordinary citizen."[24]

TYPES OF CONDITIONS Obviously, probationers who break the law are very likely to have their probation revoked. Other, less serious infractions may also result in revocation. The conditions placed on a probationer fall into three general categories:

FIGURE 12.3 Conditions of Probation

UNITED STATES DISTRICT COURT
FOR THE
DISTRICT OF COLUMBIA

To: _____ No. 84-417

Address: 1440 N St., N.W., #10, Wash., D.C.

In accordance with authority conferred by the United States Probation Law, you have been placed on probation this date, January 25, 2012 for a period of one year by the Hon. Thomas F. Hogan United States District Judge, sitting in and for this District Court at Washington, D.C.

CONDITIONS OF PROBATION

It is the order of the Court that you shall comply with the following conditions of probation:

(1)-You shall refrain from violation of any law (federal, state, and local). You shall get in touch immediately with your probation officer if arrested or questioned by a law enforcement officer.

(2)-You shall associate only with law-abiding persons and maintain reasonable hours.

(3)-You shall work regularly at a lawful occupation and support your legal dependents, if any, to the best of your ability. When out of work you shall notify your probation officer at once. You shall consult him prior to job changes.

(4)-You shall not leave the judicial district without permission of the probation officer.

(5)-You shall notify your probation officer immediately of any change in your place of residence.

(6)-You shall follow the probation officer's instructions.

(7)-You shall report to the probation officer as directed.

(8)-You shall not possess a firearm (handgun or rifle) for any reason.

The special conditions ordered by the Court are as follows:

  Imposition of sentence suspended, one year probation, Fine of $75 on each count.

I understand that the Court may change the conditions of probation, reduce or extend the period of probation, and at any time during the probation period or within the maximum probation period of 5 years permitted by law, may issue a warrant and revoke probation for a violation occurring during the probation period.

I have read or had read to me the above conditions of probation. I fully understand them and I will abide by them.

_____ Date _____
Probationer

You will report as follows: _____ as directed by your Probation Officer

_____ Date _____
U.S. Probation Officer

- *Standard conditions,* which are imposed on all probationers. These include reporting regularly to the probation officer, notifying the agency of any change of address, not leaving the jurisdiction without permission, and remaining employed.
- *Punitive conditions,* which usually reflect the seriousness of the offense and are

LO 4

intended to increase the punishment of the offender. Such conditions include fines, community service, restitution, drug testing, and home confinement (discussed later).
- *Treatment conditions,* which are imposed to reverse patterns of self-destructive behavior. Data show that more than 40 percent of probationers were required to undergo drug or alcohol treatment as part of their sentences, and an additional 18 percent were ordered to seek other kinds of treatment such as anger-control therapy.[25]

See the **Corrections Connection** for information on the corrections industry, including community corrections. Find its Web site by visiting the *Criminal Justice CourseMate* at **cengagebrain.com** and selecting the *Web links* for this chapter.

Some observers feel that judges have too much discretion in imposing overly restrictive conditions that no person, much less one who has exhibited antisocial tendencies, could meet. Citing prohibitions on drinking liquor, gambling, and associating with "undesirables," as well as requirements such as meeting early curfews, the late University of Delaware professor Carl B. Klockars claimed that if probation rules were taken seriously, "very few probationers would complete their terms without violation."[26]

As more than six out of ten federal probationers do complete their terms successfully, Klockars's statement suggests that either probation officers are unable to determine that violations are taking place, or many of them are exercising a great deal of discretion in reporting minor probation violations. Perhaps the officers realize that violating probationers for every single "slip-up" is unrealistic and would add to the already significant problem of jail and prison overcrowding.

> **"For you not to be in prison means you are making a deal with me to follow the rules. If you don't want to follow the rules, tell me now, and I will send you to prison."**
>
> —**Judge Steven Alm,** speaking to a group of probationers in Hawaii

THE SUPERVISORY ROLE OF THE PROBATION OFFICER

The probation officer has two basic roles. The first is investigative and consists of conducting the presentence investigation (PSI), which was discussed in Chapter 11. The second is supervisory and begins as soon as the offender has been sentenced to probation. In smaller probation agencies, individual officers perform both tasks. In larger jurisdictions, the trend has been toward separating the responsibilities, with *investigating officers* handling the PSI and *line officers* concentrating on supervision.

Supervisory policies vary and are often a reflection of whether the authority to administer probation services is *decentralized* (under local, judicial control) or *centralized* (under state, administrative control). In any circumstance, however, certain basic principles of supervision apply. Starting with a preliminary interview, the probation officer establishes a relationship with the offender. This relationship is based on the mutual goal of both parties: the successful completion of the probationary period. Just because the line officer and the offender have the same goal, however, does not necessarily mean that cooperation will be a feature of probation.

Critical Thinking Skill Development: Ask students to discuss the often conflicting goals of probation. Is the primary goal of the probation officer to assist the probationer's rehabilitation, or to protect society from the probationer by controlling his or her movement and behavior?

THE USE OF AUTHORITY The ideal probation officer–offender relationship is based on trust. In reality, this trust often does not exist. Any incentive an offender might have to be completely truthful with a line officer is marred by one simple fact: self-reported

A Washington, D.C., probation officer makes phone curfew checks while her partner watches. Why is trust so often difficult to achieve between probation officers and offenders?

Mark Gail/*The Washington Post*/Getty Images

Authority The power designated to an agent of the law over a person who has broken the law.

Technology Tip: Ask students to go online and learn more about a career as a U.S. Probation Officer at www. uscourts.gov/FederalCourts/ProbationPretrialServices/Officers.aspx.

wrongdoing can be used to revoke probation. Even probation officers whose primary mission is to rehabilitate are under institutional pressure to punish their clients for violating conditions of probation. One officer deals with this situation by telling his clients

> that I'm here to help them, to get them a job, and whatever else I can do. But I tell them too that I have a family to support and that if they get too far off track, I can't afford to put my job on the line for them. I'm going to have to violate them.[27]

In the absence of trust, most probation officers rely on their authority to guide an offender successfully through the sentence. An officer's authority, or ability to influence a person's actions without resorting to force, is based partially on her or his power to revoke probation. It also reflects her or his ability to impose a number of lesser sanctions. For example, if a probationer fails to attend a required alcohol treatment program, the officer can send him or her to a "lockup," or detention center, overnight. To be successful, a probation officer must establish this authority early in the relationship because it is the primary tool for persuading the probationer to behave in a manner acceptable to the community.[28]

THE OFFENDER'S PERSPECTIVE The public perception of probationers is that they are lucky not to be in prison or jail and should be grateful for receiving a "second chance." Although they may not describe their situation in that way, many probationers are willing to comply with the terms of their sentences, if for no other reason than to avoid any further punishments. Such offenders can make a line officer's supervision duties relatively simple.

By the same token, as we discussed in Chapter 2, criminal behavior is often predicated on a lack of respect for authority. This attitude can be incompatible with the supervisory aspects of probation. The average probationer will have eighteen face-to-face meetings with her or his probation officer each year. Those under more restrictive probation conditions may see their supervising officers as many as eighty times a year.[29] Furthermore, to follow the conditions of probation, convicts may have to discontinue activities that they find enjoyable, such as going to a bar for a drink on Saturday night. Consequently, some probationers consider supervision as akin to "baby-sitting" and resist the strict controls imposed on them by the government.

THE CHANGING ENVIRONMENT OF THE PROBATION OFFICER To some extent, today's probation officers function similarly to John Augustus's volunteers (see page 401). They spend a great deal of time in the community, working with businesses, churches, schools, and neighborhood groups on behalf of their clients.

Nevertheless, the profession has seen considerable changes over the past three decades. As noted earlier, probation is being offered to more offenders with violent criminal histories than in the past. Inevitably, this has changed the job description of the probation officer, who must increasingly act as a law enforcement agent rather than

LO 5 concentrating on the rehabilitation of clients. Probation officers now conduct surveillance and search and seizure operations, administer drug tests, and accompany police officers on high-risk law enforcement assignments. Consequently, the work has become more dangerous. According to the National Institute of Corrections, more than half of the probation officers who directly supervise wrongdoers have been victims of a "hazardous incident" that endangered their safety.[30]

As a result, many probation officers are seeking permission to carry guns on the job. Several years ago, for example, the Arizona Probation Officer Association convinced state authorities that probation officers should be able to wield firearms if they so desire. Making a similar argument, Los Angeles probation officer Janis Jones said, "We're not in the '70s anymore. We're not dealing with little dope dealers on the corner selling nickel bags of marijuana." Jones, whose unit collects about a dozen guns a week, added, "These guys are into hard-core, heavy firepower to protect their interests. You feel totally vulnerable [without a gun]."[31] In the federal probation system, eighty-five of the ninety-four federal judicial districts permit their probation officers to carry firearms after receiving proper training, as do thirty-five states.[32]

Discussion Tip: Ask students if they believe probation officers should carry firearms. Why or why not? (LO 5)

REVOCATION OF PROBATION

The probation period can end in one of two ways. Either the probationer successfully fulfills the conditions of the sentence, or the probationer misbehaves and probation is revoked, resulting in a prison or jail term. The decision of whether to revoke after a technical violation—such as failing to report a change of address or testing positive for drug use—is often a judgment call by the probation officer and therefore the focus of controversy.

Technical Violation An action taken by a probationer that, although not criminal, breaks the terms of probation as designated by the court.

REVOCATION TRENDS In the past, a technical violation almost always led to revocation. Today, many probation officers will take that step only if they believe the technical violation in question represents a danger to the community. At the same time, the public's more punitive attitude, along with improved drug-testing methods, has increased the number of conditions imposed on probationers and, consequently, the odds that they will violate one of those conditions.

In the 1980s and 1990s, to some extent, these two trends negated each other: between 1987 and 1996, there was almost no change in the percentage (between 75 and 80 percent) of offenders who successfully completed their probation terms.[33] Today, 65 percent of probationers complete their terms without revocation, a number that has been rising steadily for the past decade.[34] There are indications that this increase may be related to state budget problems and the need to reduce the cost of corrections, as noted earlier in the chapter. To achieve fewer revocations, probation officers must often "look the other way" when confronted with probationer wrongdoing unless a violent crime has occurred. (See the feature *You Be the Probation Officer—A Judgment Call* on the following page to learn more about the issues surrounding revocation.)

THE REVOCATION PROCESS As we have seen, probationers do not always enjoy the same protections under the U.S. Constitution as other members of society. The United States Supreme Court has not stripped these offenders of all rights, however. In *Mempa v. Rhay* (1967),[35] the Court ruled that probationers were entitled to an attorney during the revocation process. Then, in *Morrissey v. Brewer* (1972) and *Gagnon v. Scarpelli* (1973),[36] the Court established a three-stage procedure by which the "limited" due process rights of probationers must be protected in potential revocation situations:

LO 6

Group Activities: Ask students to work together to construct a chart demonstrating the various conditions under which probation can be revoked.

Critical Thinking Skill
Development: Ask students to
consider the probation revocation
process. Which basic due process
rights apply and which do not?
(LO 6)

- *Preliminary hearing.* In this appearance before a "disinterested person" (often a judge), the facts of the violation or arrest are presented, and it is determined whether probable cause for revoking probation exists. This hearing can be waived by the probationer.

- *Revocation hearing.* During this hearing, the probation agency presents evidence to support its claim of violation, and the probationer can attempt to refute this evidence. The probationer has the right to know the charges being brought against him or her. Furthermore, probationers can testify on their own behalf and present witnesses in their favor, as well as confront and cross-examine adverse witnesses. A "neutral and detached" body must hear the evidence and rule on the validity of the proposed revocation.

- *Revocation sentencing.* If the presiding body rules against the probationer, then the judge must decide whether to impose incarceration and for what length of time. In a revocation hearing dealing with technical violations, the judge will often reimpose probation with stricter terms or intermediate sanctions.

In effect, this is a "bare-bones" approach to due process. Most of the rules of evidence that govern regular trials do not apply to revocation hearings. Probation officers are

YOU BE THE
PROBATION OFFICER
A Judgment Call

THE FACTS Your client, Alain, was convicted of selling drugs and given a split sentence—three years in prison and three years on probation. You meet Alain for the first time two days after his release, and you are immediately concerned about his mental health. His mother confirms your worries, telling you that Alain needs help. You refer him to a psychiatric hospital, but the officials there determine that he "does not require mental health treatment at this time." Several weeks later, Alain's mother tells you that he is staying out late at night and "hanging out with the wrong crowd," both violations of his probation agreement. After he tests positive for marijuana, you warn Alain that, after one more violation, you will revoke his probation and send him back to prison. He tells you that he is "feeling agitated" and "having intermittent rage." You refer him to a substance abuse and mental health treatment facility, where he tests positive for marijuana once again.

THE LAW For any number of reasons, but particularly for the failed drug tests, you can start revocation proceedings against Alain. These proceedings will almost certainly conclude with his return to prison.

YOUR DECISION On the one hand, Alain has violated the terms of his probation agreement numerous times. On the other hand, he has been convicted of only one crime—a drug violation—and you have no evidence that he is behaving violently or poses a danger to himself or others. Furthermore, Alain has strong family support and is willing to enter treatment for his substance abuse problems. Do Alain's technical violations cause you to begin the revocation process? Why or why not?

[To see how a Fairfield County, Connecticut, probation officer dealt with a similar situation, go to Example 12.1 in Appendix B.]

Rasmus Rasmusson/iStockphoto/Photodisc/Shutterstock/James Stadl/iStockphoto

not, for example, required to read offenders their *Miranda* rights before questioning them about crimes they may have committed during probation. In *Minnesota v. Murphy* (1984),[37] the Supreme Court ruled that a meeting between probation officer and client does not equal custody and, therefore, the Fifth Amendment protection against self-incrimination does not apply, either.

DOES PROBATION WORK?

On June 2, 2010, apparently as part of a dispute over the sale of a used car, Frederick Hedgepeth fatally shot an elderly couple in Salisbury, North Carolina (see the photo below). At the time of the murders, Hedgepeth was serving his second stint on probation for felony fraud. Indeed, probationers are responsible for a significant amount of crime. Each year, about 375,000 probationers return to prison or jail, many because of criminal behavior.[38] Such statistics raise a critical question—is probation worthwhile?

To measure the effectiveness of probation, one must first establish its purpose. Generally, the goal of probation is to protect public safety. Specifically, it is to prevent *recidivism*—the eventual rearrest of the probationer.[39] Given that most probationers are first-time, nonviolent offenders, the system is not designed to prevent relatively rare outbursts of violence, such as the murders committed by Frederick Hedgepeth.

THE HYBRID APPROACH A good deal of evidence suggests that probation is more effective than incarceration at preventing recidivism. A recent study of drug offenders in Kansas City, Missouri, for example, found that those who went to prison were 2.3 times more likely to be charged with a new offense than those on probation and 2.2 times more likely than the probationers to be sent back to a correctional facility.[40] Such findings are hardly surprising, though, because, by definition, the criminal justice system considers probationers to be lower-risk offenders than prison inmates in the first place.

Perhaps the better question is, Do certain types of probation work better than others? As far as preventing recidivism is concerned, the most effective probation strategy appears to be a mix of supervision (behavior monitoring) and treatment (behavior change). Researchers have labeled this a "hybrid" approach to probation, and numerous studies attest to the benefits of mixing "tough love" and treatment such as drug counseling and continuing education instead of focusing on one or the other.[41] Some experts even claim that supervision, by itself, has no effect on recidivism—a sobering conclusion, considering the resources dedicated to supervised probation.[42]

THE CASELOAD DILEMMA Even the most balanced, "firm but fair" approach to probation can be defeated by the problem of excessive *caseloads*. A *caseload* is the number of clients a probation officer is responsible for at any one time. Heavy probation caseloads seem inevitable: unlike a prison cell, a probation officer can always take "just one more" client. Furthermore, the ideal caseload size is very difficult to determine because different offenders require different levels of supervision.[43]

The consequences of disproportionate probation officer–probationer ratios are self-evident,

"I try to get in the field two to three nights a week to see my offenders. It's really the only way to stop trouble before it happens. Otherwise, it's a free-for-all."

—Kevin Dudley,
Salt Lake City probation officer

Critical Thinking Skill Development: In a written assignment, ask students to answer the authors' question, "Is probation worthwhile?"

Caseload The number of individual probationers or parolees under the supervision of a probation or parole officer.

Do the benefits of our probation system outweigh the risks that probationers such as Frederick Hedgepeth, left, will commit violent crimes? Explain your answer.
Wayne Hinshaw

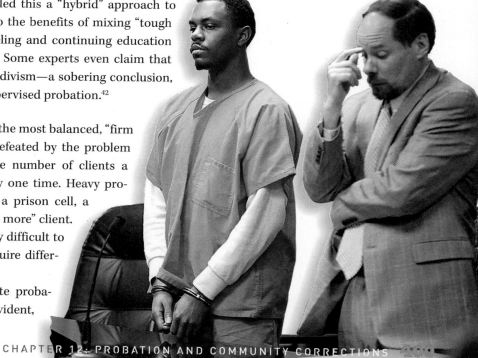

CAREERS IN CJ

Courtesy Peggy McCarthy

PEGGY McCARTHY
LEAD PROBATION OFFICER

I originally thought that I wanted to be a police officer. While I was completing my associate's degree, however, I did an internship with a juvenile probation department. Once I was exposed to probation work, I knew that corrections was the right track for me.

NEVER A DULL MOMENT The best thing about my job is that every day is different. I may be in court first thing in the morning, and then in my office meeting with defendants or developing case plans. In the afternoon, I may be at the jail taking statements for court reports or out in the field seeing my defendants. If I work a late shift, I may be visiting counseling agencies or talking to collateral sources or doing surveillance. I may be organizing a search on a defendant's home or making an arrest. I may be working with the police to solve crimes or locate absconders. Or I may simply be completing administrative duties like filing or returning phone calls to defendants and/or their family members. Anything can happen at any time, and I have to be ready to respond. If a probation officer gets bored, something is wrong.

I take a great deal of pride in assisting defendants with the difficult task of making positive change in their lives. The rewards may be few and far between, but when a defendant with a history of substance abuse stays clean and sober for a year, when a gang-affiliated defendant secures a job and no longer associates with negative peers, or when a defendant who admittedly never liked school obtains a GED or diploma, that is when I realize that what I'm doing day in and day out is 100 percent worthwhile.

FINDING SOMETHING BIG The most memorable day of my career was when my partner and I conducted a home visit on a defendant in Ajo, Arizona. As it happened, though he tried to cover it up, he was obviously in the middle of packaging large amounts of illegal drugs. His actions gave us what we needed to perform a search. My partner started speaking to me in a scrambled code language that I was able to decipher to mean we are about to find something big. And we did—large amounts of cocaine and heroin all neatly packaged and ready to hit the streets. A more thorough search ensued, and, in addition to the drugs, we uncovered a large sum of cash and a lot of drug paraphernalia. As a result of that "routine" daytime home visit, the defendant was sentenced to twenty-eight years in prison.

CAREER ADVICE Any student interested in becoming a probation officer should get as much experience as possible interacting with the criminal population. You can do this by volunteering at a community corrections facility or a juvenile or adult probation department. Or you can work at a correctional facility such as a county jail or a state or federal prison. As for educational requirements, you will need at least a bachelor's degree, preferably in criminal justice, sociology, psychology, or a related social science field. Finally, I would recommend learning how to conduct a good interview—a probation officer spends a lot of his or her time trying to get information out of someone who doesn't want to give it to you.

FAST FACTS

PROBATION OFFICER JOB DESCRIPTION:

- Work with offenders or clients who have been sentenced to probation and will not go to prison or jail for their offense.

- Extensive travel and fieldwork may be required to meet with offenders. May be required to carry a firearm or other weapon for protection.

- Work with the courts. Investigate backgrounds, write presentence reports, and recommend sentences.

- Testify in court as to findings and recommendations. Attend hearings to update the court on offenders' efforts at rehabilitation and compliance with the terms of their sentences.

WHAT KIND OF TRAINING IS REQUIRED?

- Bachelor's degree in criminal justice, social work/psychology, or related field.

- Must be at least 21 years of age, have no felony convictions, and have strong writing and interview skills. Experience in multicultural outreach a plus.

ANNUAL SALARY RANGE?

- $31,500–$51,500

For additional information on a career as a probation officer, visit: **www.careeroverview.com/ probation-officer-careers.html**.

however. When burdened with large caseloads, probation officers find it practically impossible to rigorously enforce the conditions imposed on their clients. Lack of surveillance leads to lack of control, which can undermine the very basis of a probationary system. In Guilford County, North Carolina, where probation officers have caseloads of more than 100 clients each, nearly a fifth of probationers may be unaccounted for at any time.[44] Chicago sex offender Acurie Collier violated the terms of his probation at least forty times before sexually assaulting a thirteen-year-old girl in 2010. Chicago's probation department's sex offender unit has four probation officers overseeing 130 cases—considered a low workload by city standards.[45]

NEW MODELS OF PROBATION

In their efforts to cut the costs and caseloads associated with corrections, a number of jurisdictions are experimenting with new models of probation. Since 2004, for example, Hawaii's Office of the Attorney General has operated Hawaii's Opportunity Probation with Enforcement (HOPE) program under the "swift and certain" principle. The rules of HOPE are simple. Each substance abuse probationer must call the courthouse every day to learn if she or he is required to come in for urine tests for drugs, or *urinalysis*. If drugs are found in the probationer's system during one of these frequent tests, a short jail term—one to two weeks—is automatically served.[46] HOPE has resulted in large reductions in positive drugs tests by probationers, and its 1,500 participants are significantly less likely to be rearrested than those not in the program.[47]

In 2000, with the approval of a ballot initiative, California embarked on an even more ambitious undertaking. The Substance Abuse and Crime Prevention Act changed the state penal code to mandate probation for any first- or second-time drug offender arrested for a crime involving personal use.[48] As a condition of probation, the offender must complete a yearlong drug treatment program followed by six months of aftercare. A study by researchers at the University of California at Los Angeles found that, in the five years following the law's passage, the number of drug possession–related prison admissions in California decreased by 30 percent. During that same period, the state saved nearly $3,000 for each probationer in treatment rather than behind bars.[49]

Teaching Tip: Ask students to respond to "Questions for Critical Analysis" number two on page 423, regarding the HOPE program.

Discussion Tip: Ask students to discuss "Questions for Critical Analysis" number three on page 423, concerning California's Substance Abuse and Crime Prevention Act.

SELFASSESSMENT

Fill in the blanks and check your answers on page 423.
Offenders sentenced to probation serve their sentence in the _____ under the supervision of a _____ _____. If a probationer commits a _____ _____ by failing to follow the _____ of his or her probation, it may be revoked. If revocation occurs, the offender will be sent to _____. To a large extent, the effectiveness of probation programs is measured by _____, or the rate at which offenders are rearrested. In many instances, this effectiveness is compromised by the heavy _____ carried by probation officers.

INTERMEDIATE SANCTIONS

Many observers feel that the most widely used sentencing options—imprisonment and probation—fail to reflect the immense diversity of crimes and criminals. **Intermediate sanctions** provide a number of additional sentencing options for those wrongdoers who require stricter supervision than that supplied by probation, but for whom imprisonment would be unduly harsh and counterproductive.[50] The intermediate sanctions discussed in

Intermediate Sanctions Sanctions that are more restrictive than probation and less restrictive than imprisonment.

this section are designed to match the specific punishment and treatment of an individual offender with a corrections program that reflects that offender's situation.

Dozens of different variations of intermediate sanctions are handed down each year. To cover the spectrum succinctly, two general categories of such sanctions will be discussed in this section: those administered primarily by the courts and those administered primarily by corrections departments, including day reporting centers, intensive supervision probation, shock incarceration, and home confinement. Remember that none of these sanctions are exclusive. They are often combined with imprisonment and probation, and with each other.

JUDICIALLY ADMINISTERED SANCTIONS

The lack of sentencing options is most frustrating for the person who, in the majority of cases, does the sentencing—the judge. Consequently, when judges are given the discretion to "color"

LO 7 a punishment with intermediate sanctions, they will often do so. In addition to imprisonment and probation, a judge has five sentencing options:

1. Fines.
2. Community service.
3. Restitution.
4. Pretrial diversion programs.
5. Forfeiture.

Fines, community service, and restitution were discussed in Chapter 11. In the context of intermediate sanctions, it is important to remember that these punishments are generally combined with incarceration or probation. For that reason, some critics feel the retributive or deterrent impact of such punishments is severely limited. Many European countries, in contrast, rely heavily on fines as the sole sanctions for a variety of crimes. (See the feature *Comparative Criminal Justice—Swedish Day-Fines* on the facing page.)

PRETRIAL DIVERSION PROGRAMS Not every criminal violation requires the courtroom process. Consequently, some judges have the discretion to order an offender into a pretrial diversion program during the preliminary hearing. (Prosecutors can also offer an offender the opportunity to join such a program in return for reducing or dropping the initial charges.) These programs represent an "interruption" of the criminal proceedings and are generally reserved for young or first-time offenders who have been arrested on charges of illegal drug use, child or spousal abuse, or sexual misconduct. Pretrial diversion programs usually include extensive counseling, often in a treatment center. If the offender successfully follows the conditions of the program, the criminal charges are dropped.

DRUG COURTS With more than two thousand in operation, *drug courts* have become the fastest-growing form of pretrial diversion in the country. Though the specific procedures of drug courts vary widely from jurisdiction to jurisdiction, most follow a general pattern. Either after arrest or on conviction, the offender is given the option of entering a drug court program or continuing through the standard courtroom process. Those who choose the former come under the supervision of a judge who will oversee a mixture of treatment and sanctions designed to cure their addiction. When offenders successfully complete the program, the drug court rewards them by dropping all charges against them.

Drug courts operate on the assumption that when a criminal addict's drug use is reduced, his or her drug-fueled criminal activity will also decline. To test this

COMPARATIVE CRIMINAL JUSTICE

SWEDISH DAY-FINES

Few ideals are cherished as highly in our criminal justice system as equality. Most Americans take it for granted that individuals guilty of identical crimes should face identical punishments. From an economic perspective, however, this emphasis on equality renders our system decidedly unequal. Take two citizens, one a millionaire investment banker and the other a checkout clerk earning the minimum wage. Driving home from work one afternoon, each is caught by a traffic officer doing 80 miles per hour in a 55-mile-per-hour zone. The fine for this offense is $150. This amount, though equal for both, has different consequences: it represents mere pocket change for the investment banker, but a significant chunk out of the checkout clerk's weekly paycheck.

Restricted by a "tariff system" that sets specific amounts for specific crimes, regardless of the financial situation of the convict, American judges often refrain from using fines as a primary sanction. They either assume that poor offenders cannot pay the fine or worry that a fine will allow wealthier offenders to "buy" their way out of a punishment.

Paying for Crime

In searching for a way to make fines more effective sanctions, many reformers have seized on the concept of the "day-fine," as practiced in Sweden and several other European countries. In this system, which was established in the 1920s and 1930s, the fine amount is linked to the monetary value of the offender's daily income. Depending on the seriousness of the crime, a Swedish offender will be sentenced to 1 to 120 day-fines or, as combined punishment for multiple crimes, up to 200 day-fines.

For each day-fine unit assessed, the offender is required to pay one-thousandth of her or his annual gross income (minus a deduction for basic living expenses, as determined by the Prosecutor General's Office) to the court. Consequently, the day-fine system not only reflects the degree of the crime, but ensures that the economic burden will be equal for those with different incomes.

Swedish police and prosecutors can levy day-fines without court involvement. As a result, plea bargaining is nonexistent, and more than 80 percent of all offenders are sentenced to intermediate sanctions without a trial. The remaining cases receive full trials, with an acquittal rate of only 6 percent, compared with roughly 30 percent in the United States.

FOR CRITICAL ANALYSIS

Do you think a "day-fine" system would be feasible in the United States? Why might it be difficult to implement in this country?

---

assumption, researchers in Georgia compared reoffending by drug court participants with reoffending by probationers and inmates convicted of drug-related crimes. The study found that graduates of the state's drug court programs had a recidivism rate of 7 percent, compared with 15 percent for the probationers and 29 percent for the inmates.[51] A larger study conducted by the National Institute of Justice produced similar results.[52]

FORFEITURE In 1970, Congress passed the Racketeer Influenced and Corrupt Organizations Act (RICO) in an attempt to prevent the use of legitimate business enterprises as shields for organized crime.[53] As amended, RICO and other statutes give judges the ability to implement forfeiture proceedings in certain criminal cases. **Forfeiture** is a process by which the government seizes property gained from or used in criminal activity. For example, if a person is convicted for smuggling cocaine into the United States from South America, a judge can order the seizure of not only the narcotics, but also the speedboat the offender used to deliver the drugs to a pickup point off the coast of South Florida. In *Bennis v. Michigan* (1996),[54] the Supreme Court ruled that a person's home or car could be forfeited even though the owner was unaware that the property was connected to illegal activity.

Forfeiture The process by which the government seizes private property attached to criminal activity.

Teaching Tip: Ask students to research what happens to property that is forfeited. What are the advantages of forfeiture for law enforcement agencies? For the general public?

Once property is forfeited, the government has several options. It can sell the property, with the proceeds going to the state and/or federal law enforcement agencies involved in the seizure. Alternatively, the government agency can use the property directly in further crime-fighting efforts or award it to a third party, such as an informant. Note that there are two types of forfeiture. The first, criminal forfeiture, involves confiscating property from convicted criminals and is not particularly controversial. The second, civil forfeiture, often targets people who have not even been criminally charged. For that reason, as the feature *A Question of Ethics—False Profit?* below shows, it has received a great deal of criticism.

DAY REPORTING CENTERS

Day Reporting Center (DRC)
A community-based corrections center to which offenders report on a daily basis for treatment, education, and rehabilitation.

First used in Great Britain, **day reporting centers (DRCs)** are mainly tools to reduce jail and prison overcrowding. Although the offenders are allowed to live in the community rather than jail or prison, they must spend all or part of each day at a reporting center. In general, being sentenced to a DRC is an extreme form of supervision. With offenders under a single roof, they are much more easily monitored and controlled.

DRCs are instruments of rehabilitation as well. They often feature treatment programs for drug and alcohol abusers and provide counseling for a number of psychological problems, such as depression and anger management. Many of those found guilty in

A QUESTION OF ETHICS: *False Profit?*

THE SITUATION Michael Coleman and Jacquard Merrit walked into the Montgomery (Alabama) Regional Airport with more than $120,000 in cash stashed in their carry-on bags and pockets. Before they could board their flight to San Antonio, federal law enforcement agents stopped the two men, confiscating their cash and sending them home.

Coleman and Merrit were never charged with any crime. Nonetheless, under its civil asset forfeiture law, the federal government was able to keep the funds. In many jurisdictions, similar laws allow the police to seize property that they suspect has been used to commit a crime, regardless of whether any criminal activity is proved. Here, as one federal agent put it, "No legitimate businessman travels with $120,000 in cash through the airport." Coleman and Merrit's attorney had a different interpretation of the situation: "If you can't prove it's not dope money, you lose it."

THE ETHICAL DILEMMA Civil forfeiture has been very profitable for American law enforcement agencies. The U.S. Justice Department's Assets Forfeiture Fund contains approximately $1.3 billion, and 40 percent of local police executives called funds gained from civil asset forfeiture "necessary as a budget supplement." In 2010, for example, the Greenville (South Carolina) Sheriff's Office spent more than $100,000 in forfeited drug money to buy two helicopters and a Cessna airplane and to upgrade its K-9 unit. The problem, critics say, is that these laws provide law enforcement agencies with a financial incentive to seize property rather than fight crime. Furthermore, the laws punish people who are technically innocent—indeed, 80 percent of those who lose property through civil asset forfeiture are never even charged with wrongdoing. Ethically, this is problematic: If these people have not committed any crime, why are they being punished?

WHAT IS THE SOLUTION? One commentator has described the present system as "nakedly unjust." Do you agree? Why or why not? Proposals to "fix" civil asset forfeiture generally focus on the burden of proof. In Chapter 3, you learned that the government must prove criminal behavior "beyond a reasonable doubt" to secure a conviction in criminal court. Most states and the federal government, however, allow property to be seized if law enforcement shows by a "preponderance of the evidence" or by "clear and convincing evidence" that the property was used in the commission of a crime. As the Coleman and Merrit example shows, these are fairly easy standards to meet. What would be the result if police were required to use the "beyond a reasonable doubt" standard in civil asset forfeiture cases?

the Roanoke (Virginia) Drug Court, for example, are ordered to participate in a yearlong day reporting program. At the center, offenders meet with probation officers, submit to urine tests, and attend counseling and education programs, such as parenting and life-skills classes. After the year has passed, if the offender has completed the program to the satisfaction of the judge and has found employment, the charges will be dropped.[55]

Given that each DRC is unique, evaluating the overall success of this particular intermediate sanction can be difficult. Still, there is evidence of success. A recent study found that participants in the Franklin County, Pennsylvania, DRC reoffend at a rate of 18.2 percent, compared with 47.8 percent for standard probationers.[56] In general, how-ever, the centers appear to have a limited impact on recidivism rates unless they include strong therapeutic programs.[57] The economic benefits of these facilities are more obvi-ous. Officials in Franklin County estimate that by diverting nonviolent offenders from jail to treatment, the DRC program saves the county about $2 million a year.[58]

Group Activities: If possible, take students to visit a nearby day reporting center. What is the purpose of this facility? (LO 8)

INTENSIVE SUPERVISION PROBATION

Over the past several decades, a number of jurisdictions have turned to intensive supervision probation (ISP) to solve the problems associated with burdensome caseloads we discussed earlier in the chapter. ISP offers a more restrictive alternative to regular probation, with higher levels of face-to-face contact between offenders and officers and frequent modes of control such as urine tests for drugs. In New Jersey, for example, ISP officers have caseloads of only 20 offenders (compared with 115 for other probation officers in the state) and are provided with additional resources to help them keep tabs on their charges.[59] Different jurisdictions have different methods of determin-ing who is eligible for ISP, but a majority of states limit ISP to offenders who do not have prior probation violations.

The main goal of ISP is to provide prisonlike control of offenders while keeping them out of prison. With this in mind, one researcher claims that ISP has had "uni-

LO 8 formly dismal" results.[60] In an experiment that compared ISP-eligible probationers in traditional and ISP programs, Joan Petersilia and Susan Turner found that those in ISP programs were more likely to have a technical violation, equally likely to be rearrested and convicted, and more likely to return to prison or jail.[61] One theory is that ISP "causes" these high failure rates—more supervision increases the chances that an offender will be caught breaking conditions of probation. In those ISP programs that have produced low rates of recidivism, a mixture of manageable caseloads and offender access to treatment seems to make the difference.[62]

Intensive Supervision Probation (ISP) A punishment-oriented form of probation in which the offender is placed under stricter and more frequent surveillance and control than in conventional probation by probation officers with limited caseloads.

Shock Incarceration A short period of incarceration that is designed to deter further criminal activity by "shocking" the offender with the hardships of imprisonment.

Critical Thinking Skill Development: Ask students to analyze the theory that ISP "causes" high failure rates. What evidence supports this theory? What evidence seems to contradict it? (LO 8)

SHOCK INCARCERATION

As the name suggests, shock incarceration is designed to "shock" criminals into com-pliance with the law. Following conviction, the offender is first sentenced to a prison or jail term. Then, usually within ninety days, he or she is released and resentenced to pro-bation. The theory behind shock incarceration is that by getting a taste of the brutalities of the daily prison grind, the offender will be shocked into a crime-free existence.

THE VALUE OF SHOCK In the past, shock incarceration was targeted primarily toward youthful, first-time offenders, who were thought to be more likely to be "scared straight" by a short stint behind bars. Recent data show, however, that 20 percent of all adults sentenced to probation spend some time in jail or prison before being released into the community.[63] Critics of shock incarceration are dismayed by this trend. They

Inmates engage in morning calisthenics at the Impact Incarceration Program in Illinois. In theory, why would boot camps like this one benefit first-time nonviolent offenders more than a jail or prison sentence? *Journal Courier*/The Image Works Image

Home Confinement A community-based sanction in which offenders serve their terms of incarceration in their homes.

Electronic Monitoring A technique of probation supervision in which the offender's whereabouts are kept under surveillance by an electronic device.

argue that the practice needlessly disrupts the lives of low-level offenders who would not otherwise be eligible for incarceration and exposes them to the mental and physical hardships of prison life (which we will discuss in Chapter 14).[64] Furthermore, there is little evidence that shock probationers fare any better than regular probationers when it comes to recidivism rates.[65]

BOOT CAMPS The *boot camp* is a variation on traditional shock incarceration. Instead of spending the "shock" period of incarceration in prison or jail, offenders are sent to a boot camp. Modeled on military basic training, these camps are generally located within prisons and jails, though some can be found in the community. The programs emphasize strict discipline, manual labor, and physical training. They are designed to instill self-responsibility and self-respect in participants, thereby lessening the chances that they will return to a life of crime. More recently, boot camps have also emphasized rehabilitation, incorporating such components as drug and alcohol treatment programs, anger-management courses, and vocational training.[66]

The first boot camp opened in Georgia in 1983. At the peak of their popularity in the mid-1990s, about 120 local, state, and federal boot camps housed more than seven thousand inmates. Around that time, however, studies began to show that the camps were not meeting their goals of improving rearrest rates while reducing prison populations and corrections budgets.[67] By 2000, nearly one-third of the boot camps had closed, and in 2005 the Federal Bureau of Prisons announced plans to discontinue its boot camp program. Because of their rehabilitative and disciplinarian features, boot camps remain popular in the juvenile corrections system, and there is some evidence that the programs can have a positive effect when measured by a standard other than recidivism rates. As part of a study released in 2010, researchers Derrick Franke, David Bierie, and Doris L. MacKenzie found that offenders had a relatively positive experience at boot camp. At least, those who served short sentences there left with a higher opinion of the American criminal justice system than did those who spent the same amount of time in prison.[68]

HOME CONFINEMENT AND ELECTRONIC MONITORING

Various forms of home confinement—in which offenders serve their sentences not in a government institution but at home—have existed for centuries. It has often served, and continues to do so, as a method of political control, used by totalitarian regimes to isolate and silence dissidents. For purposes of general law enforcement, home confinement was impractical until relatively recently. After all, one could not expect offenders to keep their promises to stay at home, and the personnel costs of guarding them were prohibitive. In the 1980s, however, with the advent of electronic monitoring, or using technology to guard the prisoner, home confinement became more viable. Today, all fifty states and the federal government have home monitoring programs with about 130,000 offenders participating at any one time.[69]

THE LEVELS OF HOME MONITORING Home monitoring has three general levels of restriction:

1. *Curfew,* which requires offenders to be in their homes at specific hours each day, usually at night.

LO 9

2. *Home detention,* which requires that offenders remain home at all times, with exceptions being made for education, employment, counseling, or other specified activities such as the purchase of food or, in some instances, attendance at religious ceremonies.

3. *Home incarceration,* which requires the offender to remain home at all times, save for medical emergencies.

Under ideal circumstances, home confinement serves many of the goals of intermediate sanctions. It protects the community. It saves public funds and space in correctional facilities by keeping convicts out of institutional incarceration. It meets public expectations of punishment for criminals. Uniquely, home confinement also recognizes that convicts, despite their crimes, play important roles in the community, and allows them to continue in those roles. An offender, for example, may be given permission to leave confinement to care for elderly parents.

Home confinement is also lauded for giving sentencing officials the freedom to match the punishment with the needs of the offender. In Missouri, for instance, the conditions of detention for a musician required him to remain at home during the day, but allowed him to continue his career at night. In addition, he was obliged to make antidrug statements before each performance, to be verified by the manager at the club where he appeared.

TYPES OF ELECTRONIC MONITORING According to some reports, the inspiration for electronic monitoring was a *Spider-Man* comic book in which the hero was trailed by the use of an electronic device on his arm. In 1979, a New Mexico judge named Jack Love, having read the comic, convinced an executive at Honeywell, Inc., to begin developing similar technology to supervise convicts.[70]

Two major types of electronic monitoring have grown out of Love's initial concept. The first is a "programmed contact" program, in which the offender is contacted periodically by telephone or beeper to verify his or her whereabouts. Verification is obtained via a computer that uses voice or visual identification techniques or by requiring the offender to enter a code in an electronic box when called. The second is a "continuously signaling" device, worn around the convict's wrist, ankle, or neck. A transmitter in the device sends out a continuous signal to a "receiver-dialer" device located in the offender's dwelling. If the receiver device does not detect a signal from the transmitter, it informs a central computer, and the police are notified.[71]

TECHNOLOGICAL ADVANCES IN ELECTRONIC MONITORING As electronic monitoring technology has evolved, the ability of community corrections officials to target specific forms of risky behavior has greatly increased. A Michigan court, for example, has begun placing black boxes in the automobiles of repeat traffic law

Offenders who are confined to their homes are often monitored by electronic devices like this one, which fits around the ankle. What are some of the benefits of electronic monitoring as an intermediate sanction?
AP Photo/CP, Tom Hanson

violators. Not only do these boxes record information about the offenders' driving habits for review by probation officers, but they also emit a loud beep when the car goes too fast or stops too quickly. As we saw in Chapter 3, another device—an ankle bracelet—is able to test a person's sweat for alcohol levels and transmit the results over the Internet.

CJ&TECHNOLOGY Global Positioning System (GPS)

AP Photo/Jeff T. Green

San Bernardino County (California) probation officer Nathan Scarano had two reasons to believe that Christopher Henry was involved in a street gang fight earlier that night. First, Henry's face was bloodied. Second, the global positioning system (GPS) device strapped to Henry's ankle placed him at the scene. GPS technology is a form of tracking technology that relies on twenty-four military satellites orbiting thousands of miles above the earth. The satellites transmit signals to each other and to a receiver on the ground, allowing a monitoring station to determine the location of a receiving device to within a few feet. GPS provides a much more precise level of supervision than regular electronic monitoring. A probationer like Henry wears a transmitter, similar to a traditional electronic monitor, around his or her ankle or wrist. This transmitter communicates with a portable tracking device (PTD), a small box that uses the military satellites to determine the probationer's movements.

GPS technology can be used either "actively" to constantly monitor the subject's whereabouts, or "passively" to ensure that the offender remains within the confines of a limited area determined by a judge or probation officer. Inclusion and exclusion zones are also important to GPS supervision. Inclusion zones are areas such as a home or workplace where the offender is expected to be at certain times. Exclusion zones are areas such as parks, playgrounds, and schools where the offender is not permitted to go. GPS-linked computers can alert officials immediately when an exclusion zone has been breached and create a computerized record of the probationer's movements for review at a later time. Despite the benefits of this technology, it is rarely implemented. According to the Bureau of Justice Statistics, in 2009 only about eight thousand probationers were being tracked by GPS.

THINKING ABOUT GPS

How could GPS technology be used to ensure that a convicted sex offender complies with a judge's order to stay away from areas where large numbers of children are present?

Teaching Tip: Ask students to respond to "Questions for Critical Analysis" number four on page 423, in which they consider the impact of GPS technology on community-based corrections.

EFFECTIVENESS OF HOME CONFINEMENT As might be expected, technical problems can limit the effectiveness of an electronic monitoring device. So can tampering by the offender. In one incident, for example, a fourteen-year-old girl in Princeton, West Virginia, who was under house arrest on charges of murdering her father, managed to escape after cutting the electronic monitoring device off her ankle and gluing it on a cat. The possibility of such problems will decrease as tamper-resistant monitoring devices are perfected. One such device contracts if the offender applies heat, which normally loosens some transmitters. If enough heat is applied, the offender's circulation will be cut off.[72]

Because most participants in home confinement programs are low-risk offenders, their recidivism rates are quite low. Indeed, these programs appear to be no more or less effective than those that rely on human supervision, with most of their upside coming from the benefits mentioned earlier, such as cost savings and offender freedom.[73] One concern about home confinement is that offenders are often required to defray program costs, which can be as high as $100 per week. Consequently, those who cannot afford to pay for electronic monitoring may not be eligible. Furthermore, families of offenders confined to the home can experience high levels of stress and a loss of privacy.[74] In general, however, those who successfully complete a home confinement term seem to benefit in areas such as obtaining and holding employment.[75]

WIDENING THE NET

As mentioned above, most of the convicts chosen for intermediate sanctions are low-risk offenders. From the point of view of the corrections official doing the choosing, this makes sense. Such offenders are less likely to commit crimes and attract negative publicity. This selection strategy, however, appears to invalidate one of the primary reasons intermediate sanctions exist: to reduce prison and jail populations. If most of the offenders in intermediate sanctions programs would otherwise have received probation, then the effect on these populations is nullified. Indeed, studies have shown this to be the case.[76]

At the same time, intermediate sanctions broaden the reach of the corrections system. In other words, they increase rather than decrease the amount of control the state exerts over the individual. Suppose a person is arrested for a misdemeanor such as shoplifting and, under normal circumstances, would receive probation. With access to intermediate sanctions, the judge may add a period of home confinement to the sentence. Critics contend that such practices **widen the net** of the corrections system by augmenting the number of citizens who are under the control and surveillance of the state and also *strengthen the net* by increasing the government's power to intervene in the lives of its citizens.[77] Technological advances—such as the black boxes in automobiles, sweat-testing ankle bracelets, and GPS devices mentioned in this chapter—will only accelerate the trend.

French politician Dominique Strauss-Kahn, center, spent four months under house arrest before prosecutors decided not to charge him with sexually assaulting a New York hotel maid in 2011. What are the benefits of home confinement rather than jail for those awaiting a possible criminal trial?
AP Photo/David Karp

Critical Thinking Skill Development: Ask students to respond to "Questions for Critical Analysis" number five on page 423, in which they consider the issue of net widening.

Widen the Net The criticism that intermediate sanctions designed to divert offenders from prison actually increase the number of citizens who are under the control and surveillance of the American corrections system.

SELFASSESSMENT

Fill in the blanks and check your answers on page 423.
Judicially administered sanctions include fines, restitution, and _____, a process in which the government seizes property connected to illegal activity. Offenders may also be sentenced to spend part of their time at _____ _____ _____, where they receive treatment and are more easily _____ by corrections officials. _____ _____, or militaristic programs designed to instill self-responsibility, are a form of _____ incarceration. Home confinement, another intermediate sanction, has become more effective in recent years thanks to technology known as _____ _____.

THE PARADOX OF COMMUNITY CORRECTIONS

Despite their many benefits, including cost savings, treatment options, and the ability to divert hundreds of thousands of nonviolent wrongdoers from prisons and jails, community-based corrections programs suffer from a basic paradox: the more effectively offenders are controlled, the more likely they are to be caught violating the terms of their conditional release. As you may have noticed, the community supervision programs discussed in this chapter are evaluated according to rates of recidivism and revocation, with low levels of each reflecting a successful program. Increased control and surveillance, however, will necessarily raise the level of violations, thus increasing the probability that any single violation will be discovered. Therefore, as factors such as the number of conditions placed on probationers and the technological proficiency of electronic monitoring devices increase, so, too, will the number of offenders who fail to meet the conditions of their community-based punishment.

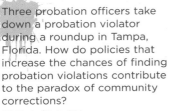

Three probation officers take down a probation violator during a roundup in Tampa, Florida. How do policies that increase the chances of finding probation violations contribute to the paradox of community corrections?
AP Photo/Chris O'Meara

One observer calls this the "quicksand" effect of increased surveillance. Instead of helping offenders leave the corrections system, increased surveillance pulls them more deeply into it.[78] The quicksand effect can be quite strong, according to researchers Barbara Sims of Penn State University–Harrisburg and Mark Jones of East Carolina University. In a study of North Carolina corrections data, Sims and Jones found that 26 percent of the probationers whose probation terms were revoked had been guilty of violations such as failing a single drug test. The researchers believe this strategy is overly punitive—anybody who has tried to quit smoking is aware of the difficulties of breaking an addiction.[79]

CJ IN ACTION

INVOLUNTARY COMMITMENT OF THE MENTALLY ILL

Most people who suffer from mental illness are not criminals, and most criminals are not mentally ill. As we saw in Chapter 2, however, there appears to be a correlation between mental illness and violent behavior. So, under certain circumstances that we will explore in this *CJ in Action* feature, mental health professionals have the same powers as criminal justice professionals—they can restrict the freedom of potentially dangerous individuals for the good of society. As in the criminal justice system, however, this power is fraught with controversy and fears of making the wrong decision.

THE NEED FOR TREATMENT

Jared Loughner's murderous rampage in Tucson, Arizona, on January 8, 2011, did not come as a surprise to everyone. "We have a mentally unstable person in the class that scares the living crap out of me," said one of his classmates at Pima Community College in an e-mail sent to friends.[80] Indeed, details of Loughner's bizarre behavior—described in Chapter 1 (see pages 4–5)—had many wondering why he wasn't being treated for his seemingly obvious mental illness. Although he did not seek help, government officials could have forced him to get it. Arizona, like every other state, has an *involuntary civil commitment* law, under which mentally ill individuals can be held in custody and committed to a psychiatric hospital against their wishes.

Involuntary commitment, like imprisonment for criminals, raises due process concerns because it involves a significant deprivation of liberty.[81] Therefore, states must devise procedures that protect the rights of mentally ill individuals during this process. Ironically, Arizona has a fairly flexible involuntary commitment law. Anyone with knowledge of a person's unstable behavior—such as a parent, teacher, or friend—can petition for a court-ordered mental health evaluation. Then, if the court finds a "need for treatment," the person can be involuntarily committed.[82] When issues of mental health and crime take the national spotlight, one question is inevitably raised: Should we make it easier to involuntarily commit mentally ill individuals, for their safety and our own?

THE CASE FOR LENIENT INVOLUNTARY COMMITMENT STANDARDS

- More lenient standards would allow for the care and rehabilitation of individuals who need treatment and are not receiving it.

- Such standards would protect society from the dangers posed by the untreated mentally ill.

- Treatment before arrest would also prevent many criminal acts from taking place and spare society the costs of incarceration.[83]

THE CASE AGAINST LENIENT INVOLUNTARY COMMITMENT STANDARDS

- Such standards infringe on the rights of the mentally ill. As the United States Supreme Court has stated, "the mere presence of mental illness does not disqualify a person from preferring his home to the comforts of an institution."[84]

- Only a small percentage of people with mental illnesses behave violently, and it is very difficult to predict whether a person will present a future danger. More lenient commitment standards would strip many harmless people of their freedoms unnecessarily.[85]

- States do not have the funds or the capacity to treat a large influx of new psychiatric patients.

YOUR DECISION— WRITING ASSIGNMENT

As you have seen throughout this textbook, substance abuse has a strong connection to criminality. For that reason, the American corrections system routinely mandates substance abuse treatment for those under community supervision or behind bars. But what if alcohol or drug problems could be addressed before the first arrest? Research shows that early treatment improves an addict's ability to stay off drugs and alcohol, and therefore lessens the chances of future wrongdoing.[86]

Would you support a law, similar to Arizona's involuntary commitment law, that would allow concerned parties—family members, co-workers, or friends—to petition a court for involuntary substance abuse treatment? In other words, the law would permit one adult to force another adult, with judicial approval, to get treatment for drug or alcohol abuse. How could such a law be written to balance individual rights and society's need for protection? Would it successfully divert potential offenders from the criminal justice system? Before responding, you can review our discussions in this chapter concerning:

- Diversion (pages 399–400)
- Drug courts (pages 412–413)
- Widening the net (page 419)

Your answer should include at least three full paragraphs.

CHAPTER SUMMARY

LO 1 **Explain the justifications for community-based corrections programs.** One justification involves reintegration of the offender into society. Reintegration restores family ties, encourages employment and education, and secures a place for the offender in the routine functioning of society. Other justifications involve diversion and cost savings. By diverting criminals to alternative modes of punishment, further overcrowding of jail and prison facilities can be avoided, as can the costs of incarcerating the offenders.

LO 2 **Explain several alternative sentencing arrangements that combine probation with incarceration.** With a suspended sentence, a convicted offender is not required to serve the sentence, but the judge has the option of reinstating the sentence if the person reoffends. In addition, there are three other general types of sentencing arrangements: (a) split sentence probation, in which the judge specifies a certain time in jail or prison followed by a certain time on probation; (b) shock incarceration, in which a judge sentences an offender to be incarcerated, but allows that person to petition the court to be released on probation; and (c) intermittent incarceration, in which an offender spends a certain amount of time each week in jail or in a halfway house or another government institution.

LO 3 **Specify the conditions under which an offender is most likely to be denied probation.** The offender (a) has been convicted of multiple charges, (b) was on probation or parole when arrested, (c) has two or more prior convictions, (d) is addicted to narcotics, (e) seriously injured the victim of the crime, or (f) used a weapon while committing the crime.

LO 4 **Describe the three general categories of conditions placed on a probationer.** (a) Standard conditions, such as requiring that the probationer notify the agency of a change of address, not leave the jurisdiction without permission, and remain employed; (b) punitive conditions, such as restitution, community service, and home confinement; and (c) treatment conditions, such as required drug or alcohol treatment.

LO 5 **Explain why probation officers' work has become more dangerous.** One reason is that probation is increasingly offered to felons, even those who have committed violent crimes. Additionally, because there are more guns on the streets, a probationer is more likely to be armed.

LO 6 **Explain the three stages of probation revocation.** (a) The preliminary hearing, usually before a judge, during which the facts of the probation violation are presented; (b) the revocation hearing, during which the probation agency presents its claims of violation and the probationer has an opportunity to refute them; and (c) revocation sentencing, during which a judge decides what to do with the probationer convicted of violating the terms of probation.

LO 7 **List the five sentencing options for a judge besides imprisonment and probation.** (a) Fines, (b) community service, (c) restitution, (d) pretrial diversion programs, and (e) forfeiture.

LO 8 **Contrast day reporting centers with intensive supervision probation.** In a day reporting center, the offender is allowed to remain in the community, but must spend all or part of each day at the reporting center. While at the center, offenders meet with probation officers, submit to drug tests, and attend counseling and education programs. With intensive supervision probation (ISP), more restrictions are imposed, and there is more face-to-face contact between offenders and probation officers. ISP may also include electronic surveillance.

LO 9 **List the three levels of home monitoring.** (a) Curfew, which requires that the offender be at home during specified hours; (b) home detention, which requires that the offender be at home except for education, employment, and counseling; and (c) home incarceration, which requires that the offender be at home at all times except for medical emergencies.

SELF ASSESSMENT ANSWER KEY

KEY TERMS

authority **406**

caseload **409**

day reporting center (DRC) **414**

diversion **399**

electronic monitoring **416**

forfeiture **413**

home confinement **416**

intensive supervision probation (ISP) **415**

intermediate sanctions **411**

judicial reprieve **401**

pretrial diversion program **412**

probation **401**

reintegration **399**

shock incarceration **415**

split sentence probation **402**

suspended sentence **402**

technical violation **407**

widen the net **419**

QUESTIONS FOR CRITICAL ANALYSIS

1. What are the dual purposes of probation (see page 404)? Which is more important? Why?

2. Review our discussion of Hawaii's Opportunity Probation with Enforcement (HOPE) program on page 411. What might explain why second violations of the urine tests are rare?

3. Review our discussion of California's Substance Abuse and Crime Prevention Act on page 411. The program has had one unintended consequence: in its first four years, drug arrests in California increased significantly. Before 2000, these rates had been falling. How might the new law have contributed to this increase in drug crime?

4. How might technology such as GPS-enhanced electronic monitoring ease the caseload burden of probation officers?

5. In your own words, explain what the phrase "widening the net" means. What might be some of the unintended consequences of increasing the number of offenders who are supervised by corrections officers in the community?

CourseMate *For Online Help*

For online help and access to resources that accompany *Criminal Justice Today*, go to www.cengagebrain.com/shop/ISBN/1111835578. Click "Access Now," where you will find flashcards, an online quiz, and other helpful study aids. If you have an access code for CourseMate, log in and go to the chapter of your choice for additional online study aids.

NOTES

1. Bureau of Justice Statistics, *Probation and Parole in the United States, 2009* (Washington, D.C.: U.S. Department of Justice, December 2010), 4.

2. *Ibid.,* Table 2, page 2.

3. Michael Tonry, *Sentencing Matters* (New York: Oxford Press, 1996), 28.

4. Todd Clear and Anthony Braga, "Community Corrections," in *Crime*, ed. James Q. Wilson and Joan Petersilia (San Francisco: ICS Press, 1995), 444.

5. Corrections Task Force of the President's Commission on Law Enforcement and Administration of Justice (1967).

6. Paul H. Hahn, *Emerging Criminal Justice: Three Pillars for a Proactive Justice System* (Thousand Oaks, CA: Sage Publications, 1998), 106–108.

7. "Cutting Costs: How States Are Addressing Corrections Budget Shortfalls," *Corrections Directions* (December 2008), 6.

8. U.S. Courts, "Costs of Imprisonment Far Exceed Supervision Costs," at **www. uscourts.gov/newsroom/2009/costs0-fImprisonment.cfm.**

9. *One in 31: The Long Reach of American Corrections* (Washington, D.C.: The Pew Center on the States, March 2009), 12.

10. Lisa Falkenberg, "Austin Deserves Credit Here," *Houston Chronicle* (April 14, 2011), B1.

11. Frederick Kunkle and Derek Kravitz, "Sweat Becomes Offenders' New Snitch," *Washington Post* (September 25, 2009), A1.

12. Paul W. Keve, *Crime Control and Justice in America* (Chicago: American Library Association, 1995), 183.

13. Andrew R. Klein, *Alternative Sentencing, Intermediate Sanctions and Probation,* 2d ed. (Cincinnati: Anderson Publishing Co., 1997), 72.

14. 242 U.S. 27 (1916).

15. Joan Petersilia, "Probation in the United States," *Perspectives* (Spring 1998), 32–33.

16. Barry A. Krisberg and James F. Austin, "The Unmet Promise of Alternatives to Incarceration," in *Criminal Justice,* ed. John Kaplan, Jerome H. Skolnick, and Malcolm M. Feeley, 5th ed. (Westbury, NY: The Foundation Press, 1991), 537.

17. *Probation and Parole in the United States, 2009,* Appendix table 3, page 24.

18. Joan Petersilia and Susan Turner, *Prison versus Probation in California: Implications for Crime and Offender Recidivism* (Santa Monica, CA: RAND Corporation, 1986).

19. *Probation and Parole in the United States, 2009,* Appendix table 5, page 26.

20. *Ibid.*

21. 705 So.2d 172 (La. 1997).

22. Neil P. Cohen and James J. Gobert, *The Law of Probation and Parole* (Colorado Springs, CO: Shepard's/McGraw-Hill, 1983), Section 5.01, 183–184; Section 5.03, 191–192.

23. 534 U.S. 112 (2001).

24. *Ibid.,* 113.

25. Bureau of Justice Statistics, *Substance Abuse and Treatment for Adults on Probation, 1995* (Washington, D.C.: U.S. Department of Justice, March 1998), 11.

26. Carl B. Klockars, Jr., "A Theory of Probation Supervision," *Journal of Criminal Law, Criminology, and Police Science* 63 (1972), 550–557.

27. *Ibid.,* 551.

28. Hahn, 116–118.

29. Camille Graham Camp and George M. Camp, *The Corrections Yearbook: 1999* (Middletown, CT: Criminal Justice Institute, 1999).

30. National Institute of Corrections, *New Approaches to Staff Safety* (Washington, D.C.: U.S. Department of Justice, March 2003), 16.

31. Nicholas Riccardi, "Probation Dept. Divided over Rule Prohibiting Guns," *Los Angeles Times* (January 2, 1999), B1.

32. Leanne Fiftal Alarid, Paul F. Cromwell, and Rolando V. del Carmen, *Community-Based Corrections,* 7th ed. (Belmont, CA: Thomson Higher Education, 2008), 101; and *Adult and Juvenile Probation and Parole National Firearm Survey,* 2d ed. (Lexington, KY: American Probation and Parole Association, October 2006).

33. Bureau of Justice Statistics, *Special Report, Federal Offenders under Community Supervisions, 1987–1996* (Washington, D.C.: U.S. Department of Justice, August 1998), Table 6, page 5.

34. *Probation and Parole in the United States, 2009,* Table 2, page 3.

35. 389 U.S. 128 (1967).

36. *Morrissey v. Brewer,* 408 U.S. 471 (1972); and *Gagnon v. Scarpelli,* 411 U.S. 778 (1973).

37. 465 U.S. 420 (1984).

38. *Probation and Parole in the United States, 2009,* Tables 2 and 3, page 3.

39. Jennifer L. Skeem and Sarah Manchak, "Back to the Future: From Klockars' Model of Effective Supervision to Evidence-Based Practice in Probation," *Journal of Offender Rehabilitation* 47 (2008), 231.

40. Cassia Spohn and David Holleran, "The Effect of Imprisonment on Recidivism Rates of Felony Offenders: A Focus on Drug Offenders," *Criminology* (May 1, 2002), 329–357.

41. Skeem and Manchak, 226–229.

42. James Bonta, Tanya Rugge, Terri-Lynne Scott, Guy Bourgon, and Annie K. Yessine, "Exploring the Black Box of Community Supervision," *Journal of Offender Rehabilitation* 47 (2008), 248–270.

43. Matthew T. DeMichele, *Probation and Parole's Growing Caseloads and Workload Allocation: Strategies for Managerial Decision Making* (Lexington, KY: American Probation and Parole Association, May 2007).

44. "Probation Gaps Persist," *Greensboro (NC) News and Record* (February 6, 2010), A11.

45. Jason Meisner, "Probation Officer Sued in Rape Case," *Chicago Tribune* (January 27, 2011), 7.

46. Graeme Wood, "Prison without Walls," *The Atlantic* (September 2010), 92–93.

47. Angela Hawkins and Mark Kleiman, *Managing Drug Involved Probationers and Swift and Certain Sanctions: Evaluating Hawaii's HOPE* (Washington, D.C.: U.S. Department of Justice, December 2009), 4.

48. California Penal Code Sections 1210, 1210.1 (West Supp. 2004); and California Health and Safety Code Sections 11999.4–11999.13 (West Supp. 2004).

49. Douglas Longshore, Angela Hawken, Darren Urada, and M. Douglas Anglin, *Evaluation of the Substance Abuse and Crime Prevention Act: SACPA Cost-Analysis Report (First and Second Years)* (Los Angeles: UCLA Integrated Substance Abuse Programs, 2006), 5.

50. Norval Morris and Michael Tonry, *Between Prison and Probation: Intermediate Punishments in a Rational Sentencing System* (Oxford: Oxford University Press, 1990).

51. Cited in "Stay Out of Jail Clean," *The Economist* (February 26, 2011), 38.

52. John Roman, Wendy Townsend, and Avinash Singh Bhati, *Recidivism Rates for Drug Court Graduates: Nationally Based Estimates, Final Report* (Washington, D.C.: Urban Institute and Caliber Associates, July 2003), 27–42.

53. 18 U.S.C. Sections 1961–1968.

54. 516 U.S. 442 (1996).

55. Model State Drug Court Legislation Committee, *Model State Drug Court Legislation: Model Drug Offender Accountability and Treatment Act* (Alexandria, VA: National Drug Court Institute, May 2004), 42.

56. "Franklin County Announcements: New Study Reveals Franklin County Day Reporting Center Reaps Rewards for County" (January 6, 2011), at **www. co.franklin.pa.us/Lists/Franklin%20 County%20Announcements/DispForm. aspx?ID=92.**

57. Adele Harrell, Ojmarrh Mitchell, Alex Hirst, Douglas Marlowe, and Jeffrey Merrill, "Breaking the Cycle of Drugs and Crime: Findings from the Birmingham BTC Demonstration," *Criminology and Public Policy* (March 2002), 189–216.

58. "Fairfield County Studies Day Reporting Center for Jail," *Lancaster (OH) Eagle-Gazette* (October 13, 2010), A1.

59. Kate Coscarelli, "A Model Program for Model Prisoners," *(Newark) Star Ledger* (February 24, 2004), 25.

60. William Burrell, "Caseload Standards for Probation and Parole" (Lexington, KY: American Probation and Parole Association, September 2006), 4, at **www. appa-net.org/ccheadlines/docs/ Caseload_Standards_PP_0906.pdf.**

61. Joan Petersilia and Susan Turner, "Intensive Probation and Parole," *Crime and Justice* 17 (1993), 281–335.

62. Skeem and Manchak, 235–236.

63. *Probation and Parole in the United States, 2009,* Appendix table 3, page 24.

64. Todd R. Clear, George F. Cole, and Michael D. Reisig, *American Corrections,* 7th ed. (Belmont, CA: Thomson Wadsworth, 2006).

65. Ted Palmer, "Programmatic and Nonprogrammatic Aspects of Successful Intervention: New Directions for Research," *Crime and Delinquency* (1995), 100–131.

66. Dale Parent, *Correctional Boot Camps: Lessons from a Decade of Research* (Washington, D.C.: U.S. Department of Justice, June 2003), 6.

67. *Ibid.,* 8, 11–12.

68. Derrick Franke, David Bierie, and Doris L. MacKenzie, "Legitimacy in Corrections:

A Randomized Experiment Comparing a Boot Camp to Prison," *Criminology and Public Policy* (February 2010), 89–114.

69. Robert S. Gable, "Left to Their Own Devices: Should Manufacturers of Offender Monitoring Equipment Be Liable for Design Defect?" *University of Illinois Journal of Law, Technology, and Policy* (Fall 2009), 334.

70. Josh Kurtz, "New Growth in a Captive Market," *New York Times* (December 31, 1989), 12.

71. Edna Erez, Peter R. Ibarra, and Norman A. Lurie, "Electronic Monitoring of Domestic Violence Cases—A Study of Two Bilateral Programs," *Federal Probation* (June 2004), 15–20.

72. Russell Carlisle, "Electronic Monitoring as an Alternative Sentencing Tool," *Georgia State Bar Journal* 24 (1988), 132.

73. Office of Justice Programs, *Home Confinement/Electronic Monitoring Literature Review* (Washington, D.C.: U.S. Department of Justice, 2009).

74. Joseph B. Vaughn, "Planning for Change: The Use of Electronic Monitoring as a Correctional Alternative," in *Intermediate Punishments: Intensive Supervision, Home Confinement, and Electronic Surveillance,* ed. Belinda R. McCarthy (Monsey, NY: Criminal Justice Press, 1987), 158.

75. Terry Baumer and Robert Mendelsohn, *The Electronic Monitoring of Nonviolent Convicted Felons* (Washington, D.C.: National Institute of Justice, 1992).

76. Michael Tonry and Mary Lynch, "Intermediate Sanctions," in *Crime and Justice,* vol. 20, ed. Michael Tonry (Chicago: University of Chicago Press, 1996), 99.

77. Dennis Palumbo, Mary Clifford, and Zoann K. Snyder-Joy, "From Net Widening to Intermediate Sanctions: The Transformation of Alternatives to Incarceration from Benevolence to Malevolence," in *Smart Sentencing: The Emergence of Intermediate Sanctions,* ed. James M. Byrne, Arthur Lurigio, and Joan Petersilia (Newbury Park, CA: Sage, 1992), 231.

78. Keve, 207.

79. Barbara Sims and Mark Jones, "Predicting Success or Failure on Probation: Factors Associated with Felony Probation Outcomes," *Crime and Delinquency* (July 1997), 314–327.

80. Quoted in Carolyn Jones and Casey Newton, "Suspect Seen As Compelled by Delusions, Not Politics," *San Francisco Chronicle* (January 10, 2011), A1.

81. *Addington v. Texas,* 441 U.S. 418, 425 (1979).

82. Arizona Revised Statute Section 36-3701 (Supp. 2000).

83. Andrew P. Wilper *et al.,* "The Health and Health Care of U.S. Prisoners: Results of a National Survey," *American Journal of Public Health* (April 2009), 673–679.

84. *O'Connor v. Donaldson,* 422 U.S. 563, 575 (1975).

85. Jacob Sullum, "The Slippery Slope of Locking Up Loons," *Chicago Sun-Times* (January 19, 2011), 27.

86. David Farabee *et al.,* "The Effectiveness of Coerced Treatment for Drug-Abusing Offenders," *Federal Probation* 2 (1998), 3–7.

CHAPTER

13

Prisons and Jails

Spencer Lowell/Commune Images

LEARNING OBJECTIVES

After reading this chapter, you should be able to . . .

LO 1 Contrast the Pennsylvania and the New York penitentiary theories of the 1800s.

LO 2 List the factors that have caused the prison population to grow dramatically in the last several decades.

LO 3 Explain the three general models of prisons.

LO 4 List and briefly explain the four types of prisons.

LO 5 Describe the formal prison management system, and indicate the three most important aspects of prison governance.

LO 6 List the reasons why private prisons can often be run more cheaply than public ones.

LO 7 Summarize the distinction between jails and prisons, and indicate the importance of jails in the American corrections system.

LO 8 Explain how jails are administered.

LO 9 Indicate some of the consequences of our high rates of incarceration.

The nine learning objectives labeled LO 1 through LO 9 are designed to help improve your understanding of the chapter.

INCARCERATION NATION

How much does it cost to send someone to prison? As a rule, judges ignore costs when they make the sentencing decision. Missouri lawmakers, however, have decided that this question needs to be considered. In August 2010, state corrections officials began providing judges with very specific information about the economics of sentencing. Missouri judges now know, for example, that a three-year prison sentence for someone convicted of endangering the welfare of a child will cost more than $37,000, whereas the price tag for placing that same person on probation would be only $6,770. Similarly, the going rate for a five-year term in state prison for second degree robbery is $50,000, compared with $9,000 for intensive probation over that same time period.

The intent is clear: saddled with an ever-growing corrections budget, Missouri officials would rather that judges keep certain offenders out of expensive prison cells. Other states are also taking steps to reduce their prison populations. California has recently extended the use of good behavior credits to reduce the length of prison terms. Rhode Island has increased its commitment to rehabilitating offenders rather than incarcerating them. Michigan is closing five prisons. The consequences of these new policies, in the words of one corrections expert,

"took us a little bit by surprise." In 2009, the number of inmates in state prisons nationwide declined for the first time since 1972.

To be sure, this decline was very small—less than 1 percent—and does little to threaten America's title as "the globe's leading incarcerator." About 2.3 million Americans are in prison or jail. The United States locks up six times as many of its citizens as Canada does, and seven times as many as most European democracies. Still, the fact that so many state politicians are willing to seek bargains when it comes to corrections represents a sea change in policy thinking. As one Missouri judge puts it, "We live in a what's-it-going-to-cost society now."

About 2.3 million inmates, including these four at the Western Missouri Correctional Center in Cameron, Missouri, are incarcerated in the United States.
Mike Ransdell/MCT/Landov

Cost-cutting tactics aside, the American corrections system is a massive institution and will remain so for the foreseeable future.[1] Indeed, despite the decline in state prison populations noted above, the overall U.S. prison population continues to grow, thanks to more significant annual increases in the number of inmates in federal corrections facilities.[2] Both state and federal prisons exist because America has a dual prison system that parallels its court system. Those offenders sentenced in federal courts for breaking federal law serve their time in federal prisons, and state offenders serve their time in state prisons. The Federal Bureau of Prisons operates more than 100 prisons, and state governments control just over 1,700 prisons.

Throughout this textbook, we have discussed many of the social and political factors that help explain the prison population "boom" of the past forty years. In this chapter and the next, we turn our attention to the incarceration system itself. This chapter focuses on the history and organizational structures of prisons (which generally hold those who have committed serious felonies for long periods of time) and jails (which generally hold those who have committed less serious felonies and misdemeanors, and those awaiting trial, for short periods of time). Though the two terms are often used interchangeably, they refer to two very different institutions, each with its own place in the criminal justice system and its own set of challenging problems.

A SHORT HISTORY OF AMERICAN PRISONS

Today, we view prisons as instruments of punishment. The loss of freedom imposed on inmates is society's retribution for the crimes they have committed. This has not always been the function of incarceration. The prisons of eighteenth-century England, known as "bridewells" after London's Bridewell Palace, actually had little to do with punishment. These facilities were mainly used to hold debtors or those awaiting trial, execution, or banishment from the community. (In many ways, as will be made clear, these facilities resembled the modern jail.) English courts generally imposed one of two sanctions on convicted felons: they turned them loose, or they executed them.[3] To be sure, most felons were released, pardoned either by the court or the clergy after receiving a whipping or a branding.

The correctional system in the American colonies differed very little from that of their motherland. If anything, colonial administrators were more likely to use corporal punishment than their English counterparts, and the death penalty was not uncommon in early America. The one dissenter was William Penn, who adopted the "Great Law" in Pennsylvania in 1682. Based on Quaker ideals of humanity and rehabilitation, this criminal code forbade the use of torture and mutilation as forms of punishment. Instead, felons were ordered to pay restitution of property or goods to their victims. If the offenders did not have sufficient property to make restitution, they were placed in a prison, which was primarily a "workhouse."[4] The death penalty was still allowed under the "Great Law," but only in cases of premeditated murder. Penn proved to be an exception, however, and the path to reform was much slower in the colonies than in England.

Technology Tip: Have students learn more about William Penn's "Great Law" online at the Pennsylvania Historical and Museum Commission's Web site: **www.portal.state.pa.us/portal/server.pt?open=514&o.bjID=998171&mode=2**.

WALNUT STREET PRISON: THE FIRST PENITENTIARY

On William Penn's death in 1718, the "Great Law" was rescinded in favor of a harsher criminal code, similar to those of the other colonies. At the time of the American Revolution, however, the Quakers were instrumental in the first broad swing of the incarceration pendulum from punishment to rehabilitation. In 1776, Pennsylvania passed legislation ordering that offenders be reformed through treatment and discipline rather than simply beaten or executed.[5] Several states, including Massachusetts and New York, quickly followed Pennsylvania's example.

Pennsylvania continued its reformist ways by opening the country's first **penitentiary** in a wing of Philadelphia's Walnut Street Jail in 1790. The penitentiary operated on the assumption that silence and labor provided the best hope of rehabilitating the criminal spirit. Remaining silent would force the prisoners to think about their crimes, and eventually the weight of conscience would lead to repentance. At the same time, enforced labor would attack the problem of idleness—regarded as the main cause of crime by penologists of the time.[6] Consequently, inmates at Walnut Street were isolated from one another in solitary rooms and kept busy with constant menial chores.

Penitentiary An early form of correctional facility that emphasized separating inmates from society and from each other.

Eventually, the penitentiary at Walnut Street succumbed to the same problems that continue to plague institutions of confinement: overcrowding and excessive costs. As an influx of inmates forced more than one person to be housed in a room, maintaining silence became nearly impossible. By the early 1800s, officials could not find work for all of the convicts, so many were left idle.

Discussion Tip: Place students in groups of three or four to discuss the correctional philosophy behind Philadelphia's Walnut Street Jail and other early penitentiaries. Would such tactics work with today's inmate population? (LO 1)

THE GREAT PENITENTIARY RIVALRY: PENNSYLVANIA VERSUS NEW YORK

LO 1 The apparent lack of success at Walnut Street did little to dampen enthusiasm for the penitentiary concept. Throughout the first half of the nineteenth century, a number of states reacted to prison overcrowding by constructing new penitentiaries. Each state tended to have its own peculiar twist on the roles of silence and labor, and two such systems—those of Pennsylvania and New York—emerged to shape the debate over the most effective way to run a prison.

Separate Confinement A nineteenth-century penitentiary system developed in Pennsylvania in which inmates were kept separate from each other at all times, with daily activities taking place in individual cells.

THE PENNSYLVANIA SYSTEM After the failure of Walnut Street, Pennsylvania constructed two new prisons: the Western Penitentiary near Pittsburgh (opened in 1826) and the Eastern Penitentiary in Cherry Hill, near Philadelphia (1829). The Pennsylvania system took the concept of silence as a virtue to new extremes. Based on the idea of **separate confinement,** these penitentiaries were constructed with back-to-back cells facing outward from the center. (See Figure 13.1 below for the layout of the original Eastern Penitentiary.) To protect each inmate from the corrupting influence of the others, prisoners worked, slept, and ate alone in their cells. Their only contact with other human beings came in the form of religious instruction from a visiting clergyman or prison official.[7]

Congregate System A nineteenth-century penitentiary system developed in New York in which inmates were kept in separate cells during the night but worked together in the daytime under a code of enforced silence.

THE NEW YORK SYSTEM If Pennsylvania's prisons were designed to transform wrongdoers into honest citizens, those in New York focused on obedience. When New York's Newgate Prison (built in 1791) became overcrowded, the state authorized the construction of Auburn Prison, which opened in 1816. Auburn initially operated under many of the same assumptions that guided the penitentiary at Walnut Street. Solitary confinement, however, seemed to lead to an inordinate amount of sickness, insanity, and even suicide among inmates, and it was abandoned in 1822. Nine years later, Elam Lynds became warden at Auburn and instilled the **congregate system,** also known as the Auburn system. Like Pennsylvania's separate confinement system, the congregate system was based on silence and labor. At Auburn, however, inmates worked and ate together, with silence enforced by prison guards.[8]

If either state can be said to have "won" the debate, it was New York. The Auburn system proved more popular, and a majority of the new prisons built during the first half of the nineteenth century followed New York's lead, though mainly for economic reasons rather than philosophical ones. New York's penitentiaries were cheaper to build because they did not require so much space. Furthermore, inmates in New York were employed in workshops, whereas those in Pennsylvania toiled alone in their cells. Consequently, the Auburn system was better positioned to exploit prison labor in the early years of widespread factory production.

FIGURE 13.1 The Eastern Penitentiary

As you can see, the Eastern Penitentiary was designed in the form of a "wagon wheel," known today as the radial style. The back-to-back cells in each "spoke" of the wheel faced outward from the center to limit contact between inmates. What was the primary goal of this design?

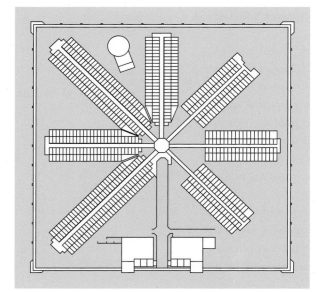

THE REFORMERS AND THE PROGRESSIVES

The Auburn system did not go unchallenged. In the 1870s, a group of reformers argued that fixed sentences, imposed silence, and isolation did nothing to improve prisoners. These critics proposed that penal institutions should offer the promise of early release as a prime tool for rehabilitation. Echoing the views of the Quakers a century earlier, the reformers presented an ideology that would heavily influence American corrections for the next century.

This "new penology" was put into practice at New York's Elmira Reformatory in 1876 (see the photo alongside). At Elmira, good behavior was rewarded by early release, and misbehavior was punished with extended time under a three-grade system of classification. On entering the institution, the offender was assigned a grade of 2. If the inmate followed the rules and completed work and school assignments, after six months he was moved up to grade 1, the necessary grade for release. If, however, the inmate broke institutional rules, he was lowered to grade 3. A grade 3 inmate needed to behave properly for three months before he could return to grade 2 and begin to work back toward grade 1 and eventual release.[9]

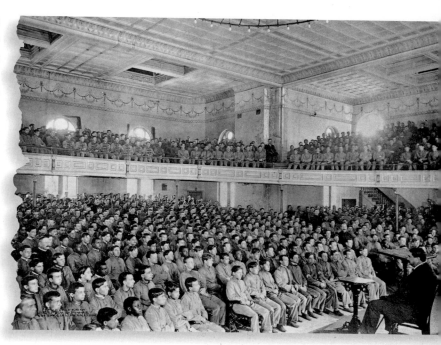

Inmates of the Elmira Reformatory in New York attend a presentation at the prison auditorium. To what extent do you believe that treatment should be a part of the incarceration of criminals? Corbis

Although other penal institutions did not adopt the Elmira model, its theories came into prominence in the first two decades of the twentieth century thanks to the Progressive movement in criminal justice. The Progressives—linked to the positivist school of criminology discussed in Chapter 2—believed that criminal behavior was caused by social, economic, and biological factors and, therefore, a corrections system should have a goal of treatment, not punishment. Consequently, they trumpeted a **medical model** for prisons, which held that institutions should offer a variety of programs and therapies to cure inmates of their "ills," whatever the root causes. The Progressives were largely responsible for the spread of indeterminate sentences (Chapter 11), probation (Chapter 12), community sanctions (Chapter 12), and parole (Chapter 14) in the first half of the twentieth century.

Medical Model A model of corrections in which the psychological and biological roots of an inmate's criminal behavior are identified and treated.

THE REASSERTION OF PUNISHMENT

Even though the Progressives had a great influence on the corrections system as a whole, their theories had little impact on the prisons themselves. Many of these facilities had been constructed in the nineteenth century and were impervious to change. More important, prison administrators usually did not agree with the Progressives and their followers, so the day-to-day lives of most inmates varied little from the congregate system of Auburn Prison.

Academic attitudes began to shift toward the prison administrators in the mid-1960s. Then, in 1974, the publication of Robert Martinson's famous "What Works?" essay provided opponents of the medical model with statistical evidence that rehabilitation efforts did nothing to lower recidivism rates.[10] This is not to say that Martinson's findings went unchallenged. A number of critics argued that rehabilitative programs could be successful.[11] In fact, Martinson himself retracted most of his claims in a little-noticed article published five years after his initial report.[12] Attempts by Martinson and others to "set the record straight" went largely unnoticed, however, as crime rose sharply in the early 1970s. This trend led many criminologists and politicians to champion "get tough" measures to deal with criminals they now considered "incurable." By the end of the 1980s, the legislative, judicial, and administrative strategies that we have discussed throughout this text had positioned the United States for an explosion in inmate populations and prison construction unparalleled in the nation's history.

Discussion Tip: Ask students to debate Martinson's claim (later mostly retracted) that rehabilitation efforts do not significantly affect recidivism. How difficult is it to successfully rehabilitate prisoners? Is rehabilitation a worthwhile objective for the correctional system?

SELFASSESSMENT

Fill in the blanks and check your answers on page 456.

In the early 1800s, Pennsylvania's _____ confinement strategy and New York's _____ system were the two dominant methods of managing prisons in the United States. Both were based on _____ and labor, but New York's system proved more popular because its institutions were _____ to construct and exploited the demand for prison _____. In the second half of the century, the Progressive movement rejected both systems and introduced the _____ model for prisons, which focused on rehabilitation rather than punishment.

THE PRISON POPULATION BOMB

The number of Americans in prison or jail has more than tripled since 1985 (see Figure 13.2 below). These numbers are not only dramatic, but also, say some observers, inexplicable, given the overall crime picture in the United States. According to one theory, incarceration rates and crime rates should move up and down together. Yet violent and property crime rates have been *declining* since the 1990s, even as incarceration rates have been *rising*. "That's the puzzling piece" of the recent drop in state prison populations, says Marc Mauer of the Sentencing Project, a research group based in Washington, D.C. "Why did this [decline] take so long?"[13] (See the feature *Myth versus Reality: Does Putting Criminals in Prison Reduce Crime?* on the facing page.)

FACTORS IN PRISON POPULATION GROWTH

To a large degree, the dramatic growth of inmate populations is a consequence of the *penal harm movement*.[14] Characterized by "get tough" ideologies in sentencing and punishment, this movement has been particularly influential when it comes to the "war"

FIGURE 13.2 The Inmate Population of the United States

The total number of inmates in the United States has risen from 744,208 in 1985 to about 2.3 million in 2010.

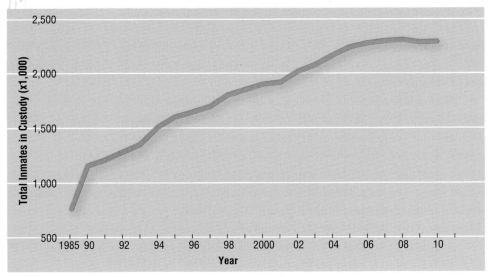

Source: U.S. Department of Justice.

MYTH vs. REALITY   Does Putting Criminals in Prison Reduce Crime?

Since the early 1990s, violent crime rates in the United States have been stable or declining. Yet, during the same period, as Figure 13.2 on the previous page shows, the rate at which Americans are imprisoned has climbed precipitously. The correlation between these two trends is the subject of much discussion among crime experts.

THE MYTH A popular view of incarceration is that "a thug in jail can't shoot your sister." Obviously, a prison inmate is incapable of doing any further harm to the community. By extension, then, as the number of criminals behind bars increases, the crime rate should drop accordingly.

THE REALITY Numerous studies have shown that this is not always the case. Of particular interest to criminologists are data from the 1990s, when, as we saw in Chapter 3, the United States enjoyed one of the most dramatic declines in crime rates in its history. In New York City, for example, between 1993 and 2001 the violent crime rate decreased by 52 percent. During that same time period, the number of felons sentenced to prison from the city declined almost as much—by 42 percent. Nationwide, from 1992 to 2002, the number of state prison inmates increased by 59 percent, and the violent crime rate dropped by 26 percent. As Figure 13.3 at the right shows, however, none of the ten states with the highest percentage increases in prisoners during that decade reaped the benefits of "getting tough." Not one of them had a decrease in crime greater than the national average. In fact, five of the ten saw their violent crime rates *increase.* Canada, for its part, experienced a decline in crime rates similar to the United States in the 1990s without *any* national increase in incarceration levels.

One possible explanation for this phenomenon, offered by criminologist Franklin Zimring, focuses on the types of criminals imprisoned. When prison populations were small, as they were until the 1980s, additional inmates tended to be mostly violent and property crime offenders. The data, as well as common sense, tell us that removing these sorts of criminals from the community has a direct impact on violent and property crime rates. When prison populations expanded in the 1990s, most of the new admissions were drug law offenders and probation violators. These types of criminals have a smaller effect on violent and property crime rates. In fact, their absence from their homes may even contribute to criminal activity. As we discussed in Chapter 2, many criminologists believe that widespread family disruption greatly increases the incidence of crime in a community.

FOR CRITICAL ANALYSIS Many criminologists think that prison has a *criminogenic* effect on inmates. That is, they believe that inmates are more likely to commit crimes after their release from prison than they would have been if they had never been incarcerated in the first place. If this is true, what impact would you expect the criminogenic effect to have on the relationship between crime rates and incarceration rates?

FIGURE 13.3 **States with the Ten Largest Increases in Prison Population, 1992–2002**

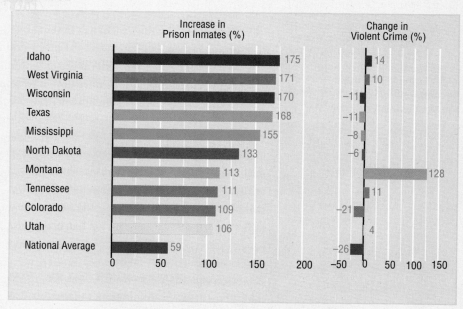

Source: Adapted from Michael Jacobson, *Downsizing Prisons* (New York: NYU Press, 2005), Figure 4.6, page 128.

on drugs. Indeed, much of the growth in the number of Americans behind bars can be attributed to the enhancement and stricter enforcement of the nation's drug laws. There are more people in prison and jail for drug offenses today than there were for *all* offenses in the early 1970s.[15] In 1980, about 19,000 drug offenders were incarcerated in state prisons and 4,800 drug offenders were in federal prisons. Twenty-nine years later,

LO 2 state prisons held about 264,000 inmates who had been arrested for drug offenses, and the number of drug offenders in federal prisons had risen to more than 95,200 (representing about half of all inmates in federal facilities).[16]

Other reasons for the growth in incarcerated populations include:

- *Increased probability of incarceration.* Simply stated, the chance of someone who is arrested going to prison today is much greater than it was thirty years ago. Most of this growth took place in the 1980s, when the likelihood of incarceration in a state prison after arrest increased fivefold for drug offenses, threefold for weapons offenses, and twofold for crimes such as sexual assault, burglary, auto theft, and larceny.[17] For federal crimes, the proportion of convicted defendants being sent to prison rose from 54 percent in 1988 to 86 percent in 2009.[18]

- *Inmates serving more time for each crime.* After the Sentencing Reform Act of 1984, the length of time served by federal convicts for their crimes rose significantly. As noted in Chapter 11, in the fifteen years after the law went into effect, the average time served by inmates in federal prisons rose to fifty months—an increase of more than 50 percent.[19] For drug offenders, the average amount of time served in federal prison escalated from 39.3 months to 62.4 months, while the average prison term for weapons offenses grew from 32.4 months to 64.5 months.[20] State sentencing reform statutes and "truth-in-sentencing" laws have had similar consequences. In the thirty-two states that require their inmates to serve at least 85 percent of their sentences, for example, violent offenders are expected to spend an average of fifteen months more in prison than violent offenders in states without such laws.[21]

- *Federal prison growth.* Thanks in part to federal sentencing policy, the federal prison system is now the largest in the country, with more than 180,000 inmates. In fact, since 1995 the federal prison population has more than doubled, whereas state prison populations have grown by "only" 37 percent.[22] Besides the increase in federal drug offenders already mentioned, this growth can be attributed to efforts by Presidents Bill Clinton and George W. Bush to federalize gun possession crimes. From 1995 to 2003, the number of inmates sent to federal prisons for weapons violations jumped by 120 percent.[23] Furthermore, between 1995 and 2009 immigration law offenders behind bars increased by nearly 600 percent (3,612 to 21,395).[24] As a result of this trend, a third of all federal inmates are now Hispanic.[25]

- *Rising incarceration rates of women.* In 1981, 14,000 women were prisoners in federal and state institutions. By 2009, the number had grown to about 113,500. Women still account for only 7 percent of all prisoners nationwide, but their rates of imprisonment are growing nearly twice as rapidly as those of men.[26]

The **Federal Bureau of Prisons** is the largest incarceration system in the United States. Find its Web site by visiting the *Criminal Justice CourseMate* at **cengagebrain.com** and selecting the *Web links* for this chapter.

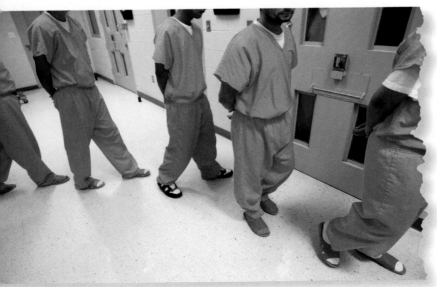

Several Hispanic inmates await health screening at the Val Verde Correctional Facility in Del Rio, Texas. What factor is most responsible for the surge in the number of Hispanics incarcerated by the federal government?
Tom Pennington/MCT/Newscom

DOWNSIZING AMERICA'S PRISONS

The escalation in the U.S. prison population has been accompanied by increased costs. Today, the states together spend more than $50 billion a year to operate their corrections systems—up from $12 billion in 1987.[27] Thirteen states allocate in excess of $1 billion a year for corrections-related services, often spending more on prisons than on education or health care. Nearly 90 percent of this spending goes to operating prisons, as opposed to probation, parole, or other community-based programs.[28] With the severe economic downturn of the past several years, the burden of expensive corrections systems has become too much for many state budgets to bear. Consequently, as we saw in the opening of this chapter, states are increasingly trying to reduce prison costs by revising mandatory-sentencing laws (see pages 373–376), recalculating credits for "good time" (see page 362), and, in extreme situations, closing facilities down.

Nearly thirty states are in the process of changing their laws to cut prison costs.[29] New York, for example, plans to save $250 million a year by repealing a series of harsh drug laws under which anyone convicted of selling two ounces or possessing four ounces of narcotics receives a prison term of fifteen years to life.[30] South Carolina similarly envisions saving $50 million a year by diverting nonviolent drug offenders to community supervision rather than prison and forcing them to pay a fine that would, in part, pay for their own treatment.[31] States are also expanding prison work programs, reducing the costs of incarceration by having inmates perform tasks previously done by private contractors. Florida, for example, has prisoners grow their own food, reducing its corrections budget by $2 million annually.[32]

SELFASSESSMENT

Fill in the blanks and check your answers on page 456.

Of all the factors in the growth of the prison population in the last several decades, stricter enforcement of the nation's _____ laws has had the greatest impact. Other factors contributing to this growth include (1) increased probability of _____, (2) increased _____ of time served in prison, (3) the growth of the _____ prison system, and (4) rising incarceration rates of _____.

▶ As the name implies, **PrisonSucks.com** is highly critical of what it calls the "crime control industry." Find this Web site by clicking on *Criminal Justice CourseMate* at **cengagebrain.com** and selecting the *Web links* for this chapter.

Teaching Tip: Invite a correctional administrator to visit the class and discuss the condition of incarceration in your state. What is the inmate population forecast in your area? How can rising, or falling, incarceration rates be best explained? Has your state taken steps to address prison overcrowding? (LO 2)

THE ROLE OF PRISONS IN SOCIETY

The increase in prison populations also reflects the varied demands placed on penal institutions. As University of Connecticut sociologist Charles Logan once noted, Americans expect prisons to "correct the incorrigible, rehabilitate the wretched . . . restrain the dangerous, and punish the wicked."[33] Basically, prisons exist to make society a safer place. Whether this is to be achieved through retribution, deterrence, incapacitation, or rehabilitation—the four justifications of corrections introduced in Chapter 11—depends on the operating philosophy of the individual penal institution.

Three general models of prisons have emerged to describe the different schools of thought behind prison organization:

- The *custodial model* is based on the assumption that prisoners are incarcerated **LO 3** for reasons of incapacitation, deterrence, and retribution. All decisions within the prison—such as what form of recreation to provide the inmates—are made with an eye toward security and discipline, and the daily routine of the inmates is highly controlled. The custodial model has dominated the most restrictive prisons in the United States since the 1930s.

Critical Thinking Skill Development: Ask students to react to the three models of prisons and the different schools of thought behind prison organization. What do students view as being the proper primary objective of prisons: custody, rehabilitation, or reintegration? (LO 3)

- The *rehabilitation model* stresses the ideals of individualized treatment that we discussed in Chapter 11. Security concerns are often secondary to the well-being of the individual inmate, and a number of treatment programs are offered to aid prisoners in changing their criminal and antisocial behavior. The rehabilitation model came into prominence during the 1950s and enjoyed widespread popularity until it began to lose general acceptance in the 1970s and 1980s.

- In the *reintegration model,* the correctional institution serves as a training ground for the inmate to prepare for existence in the community. Prisons that have adopted this model give the prisoners more responsibility during incarceration and offer halfway houses and work programs (both discussed in Chapter 14) to help them reintegrate into society. This model is becoming more influential, as corrections officials react to problems such as prison overcrowding.[34]

Competing views of the prison's role in society are at odds with these three "ideal" perspectives. Professor Alfred Blumstein argues that prisons create new criminals, especially with regard to nonviolent drug offenders. Not only do these nonviolent felons become socialized to the criminal lifestyle while in prison, but the stigma of incarceration makes it more difficult for them to obtain employment on release. Their only means of sustenance "on the outside" is to apply the criminal methods they learned in prison.[35] A study by criminal justice professors Cassia Spohn of Arizona State University and David Holleran of the College of New Jersey found that convicted drug offenders who were sentenced to prison were 2.2 times more likely to be incarcerated for a new offense than those sentenced to probation.[36]

TYPES OF PRISONS

Prison administrators have long been aware of the need to separate different kinds of offenders. In federal prisons, this led to a system with six levels based on the security needs of the inmates, from level 1 facilities with the lowest amount of security to level 6 with the harshest security measures. (Many states also use the six-level system, an example of which can be seen in Figure 13.4 on the facing page.) To simplify matters, most observers refer to correctional facilities as being one of three levels—minimum, medium, or

Group Activities: Have students research prisons in their home states. Ask them to create a map indicating the location and classification of each facility. How many inmates are housed in the various facilities? If possible, have students identify the design of each institution. (LO 4)

LO 4 maximum. A fourth level—the supermaximum-security prison, known as the "supermax"—is relatively rare and extremely controversial due to its hyperharsh methods of punishing and controlling the most dangerous prisoners.

MAXIMUM-SECURITY PRISONS

In a certain sense, the classification of prisoners today owes a debt to the three-grade system developed at the Elmira Reformatory, discussed earlier in the chapter. Once wrongdoers enter a corrections facility, they are constantly graded on behavior. Those who serve "good time," as we have seen, are often rewarded with early release. Those who compile extensive misconduct records are usually housed, along with violent and repeat offenders, in **maximum-security prisons.** The names of these institutions—Folsom, San Quentin, Sing Sing, Attica—conjure up foreboding images of concrete and steel jungles, with good reason.

Maximum-security prisons are designed with full attention to security and surveillance. In these institutions, inmates' lives are programmed in a militaristic fashion to keep them from escaping or from harming themselves or the prison staff. About a quarter of the prisons in the United States are classified as maximum security, and these institutions house about a third of the country's prisoners.

Maximum-Security Prison A correctional institution designed and organized to control and discipline dangerous felons, as well as prevent escape; characterized by intense supervision, concrete walls, and electrically charged, barbed wire fences.

FIGURE 13.4 Security Levels of Correctional Facilities in Virginia

The security levels of correctional facilities in Virginia are graded from level 1 to level 6. As you can see, level 1 facilities are for those inmates who pose the least amount of risk to fellow inmates, staff members, and themselves. Level 6 facilities are for those who are considered the most dangerous by the Virginia Department of Corrections.

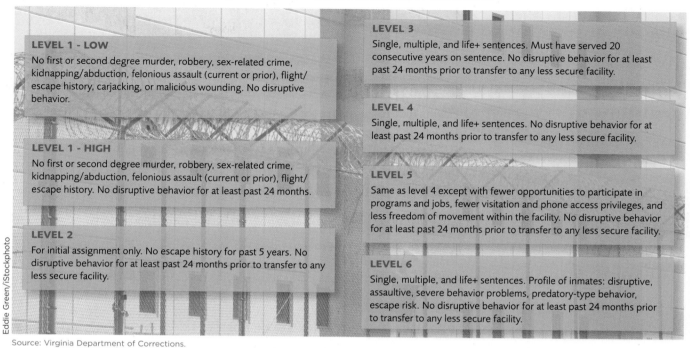

LEVEL 1 - LOW

No first or second degree murder, robbery, sex-related crime, kidnapping/abduction, felonious assault (current or prior), flight/escape history, carjacking, or malicious wounding. No disruptive behavior.

LEVEL 1 - HIGH

No first or second degree murder, robbery, sex-related crime, kidnapping/abduction, felonious assault (current or prior), flight/escape history. No disruptive behavior for at least past 24 months.

LEVEL 2

For initial assignment only. No escape history for past 5 years. No disruptive behavior for at least past 24 months prior to transfer to any less secure facility.

LEVEL 3

Single, multiple, and life+ sentences. Must have served 20 consecutive years on sentence. No disruptive behavior for at least past 24 months prior to transfer to any less secure facility.

LEVEL 4

Single, multiple, and life+ sentences. No disruptive behavior for at least past 24 months prior to transfer to any less secure facility.

LEVEL 5

Same as level 4 except with fewer opportunities to participate in programs and jobs, fewer visitation and phone access privileges, and less freedom of movement within the facility. No disruptive behavior for at least past 24 months prior to transfer to any less secure facility.

LEVEL 6

Single, multiple, and life+ sentences. Profile of inmates: disruptive, assaultive, severe behavior problems, predatory-type behavior, escape risk. No disruptive behavior for at least past 24 months prior to transfer to any less secure facility.

Eddie Green/iStockphoto

Source: Virginia Department of Corrections.

THE DESIGN Maximum-security prisons tend to be large—holding more than a thousand inmates—and they have similar features. The entire operation is usually surrounded by concrete walls that stand twenty to thirty feet high and have also been sunk deep into the ground to deter tunnel escapes. Fences reinforced with razor-ribbon barbed wire that can be electrically charged may supplement these barriers. The prison walls are studded with watchtowers, from which guards armed with shotguns and rifles survey the movement of prisoners below. The designs of these facilities, though similar, are not uniform. Though correctional facilities built using the radial design pioneered by the Eastern Penitentiary still exist, several other designs have become prominent in more recently constructed institutions. For an overview of these designs, including the radial design, see Figure 13.5 on page 439.

Inmates live in cells, most of them with similar dimensions to those found in the I-Max maximum-security prison for women in Topeka, Kansas: eight feet by fourteen feet with cinder block walls.[37] The space contains bunks, a toilet, a sink, and possibly a cabinet or closet. Cells are located in rows of *cell blocks,* each of which forms its own security unit, set off by a series of gates and bars. A maximum-security institution is essentially a collection of numerous cell blocks, each constituting its own prison within a prison.

Inmates' lives are dominated by security measures. Whenever they move from one area of the prison to another, they do so in groups and under the watchful eye of armed correctional officers. Television surveillance cameras may be used to monitor their every move, even when sleeping, showering, or using the toilet. They are subject to frequent pat-downs or strip searches at the guards' discretion. Constant "head counts" ensure that every inmate is where he or she should be. Tower guards—many of whom have orders to shoot to kill in the case of a disturbance or escape attempt—constantly look down on the inmates as they move around outdoor areas of the facility.

Technology Tip: As you begin your discussion on maximum-security prisons, take some time to show students a video clip featuring life inside these facilities. The Cengage video library has a variety of short clips to choose from.

Black Creek/TSI PRISM

Technology has added significantly to the overall safety of maximum-security prisons. Walk-through metal detectors and X-ray body scanners, for example, can detect weapons or other contraband hidden on the body of an inmate. The most promising new technology in this field, however, relies on radio frequency identification (RFID). About the size of two grains of rice, an RFID tag consists of a glass capsule that contains a computer chip, a tiny copper antenna, and an electrical device known as a "capacitor" that transmits the data in the chip to an outside scanner. In the prison context, RFID works as a high-tech head count: inmates wear bracelets tagged with the microchips while correctional officers wear small RFID devices resembling pagers.

Guided by a series of radio transmitters and receivers, the system is able to pinpoint the location of inmates and guards within twenty feet. Every two seconds, radio signals "search out" the location of each inmate and guard, and relay this information to a central computer. On a grid of the prison, an inmate shows up as a yellow dot and a correctional officer as a blue dot. Many RFID systems also store all movements in a database for future reference. "[RFID] completely revolutionizes a prison because you know where everyone is—not approximately but exactly where they are," remarked an official at the National Institute of Justice.

THINKING ABOUT RFID TRACKING

Review the discussion of crime mapping and "hot spots" on pages 189–190 in Chapter 6. Drawing on your knowledge of crime-mapping technology, discuss how RFID technology can reduce violence and other misconduct such as drug sales in prisons.

Supermax Prison A correctional facility reserved for those inmates who have extensive records of misconduct in maximum-security prisons; characterized by extremely strict control and supervision over the inmates, including extensive use of solitary confinement.

Group Activities: Have students work together in small groups to research supermax prisons. What are the advantages of these facilities for corrections administrators? What concerns do critics have regarding supermax prisons?

SUPERMAX PRISONS About thirty states and the Federal Bureau of Prisons (BOP) operate supermax (short for supermaximum security) prisons, which are supposedly reserved for the "worst of the worst" of America's corrections population. Most of the inmates in these facilities are deemed high risks to commit murder behind bars—about a quarter of the occupants of the BOP's U.S. Penitentiary Administrative Maximum (ADX) in Florence, Colorado, have killed other prisoners or assaulted correctional officers elsewhere. In addition, a growing number are either high-profile individuals who would be at constant risk of attack in a general prison population or convicted terrorists such as Zacarias Moussaoui (see page 367), Ted "the Unabomber" Kaczynski, and Terry Nichols, who was involved in the bombing of a federal office building in Oklahoma City in 1995.

A Controlled Environment The main purpose of a supermax prison is to strictly control the inmates' movement, thereby limiting (or eliminating) situations that could lead to breakdowns in discipline. The conditions at California's Security Housing Unit (SHU) at Pelican Bay State Prison are representative of most supermax institutions. Prisoners are confined to their one-person cells for twenty-two and a half hours each day under video camera surveillance. They receive meals through a slot in the door. The cells measure eight by ten feet in size and are windowless. No decorations of any kind are permitted on the walls.[38]

FIGURE 13.5 Prison Designs

Photos Courtesy of Leavenworth Area Development

The Radial Design

The wagon wheel form of the radial design was created with the dual goals of separation and control. Inmates are separated from one another in their cells on the "spokes" of the wheel, and prison officials can control the activities of the inmates from the control center in the "hub" of the wheel.

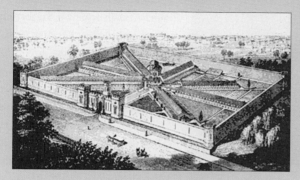

The Telephone-Pole Design

The main feature of this design is a long central corridor that serves as a means for transporting inmates from one part of the facility to another. Branching off from this main corridor are the functional areas of the facility: housing, food services, workshops, a treatment programs room, and other services.

Source: Text adapted from Todd R. Clear, George F. Cole, and Michael D. Reisig, *American Corrections*, 9th ed. (Belmont, CA: Wadsworth Publishing Company, 2010), 267–268.

The Courtyard Style

In the courtyard-style prison, a courtyard replaces the transportation function of the "pole" in the telephone-pole prison. The prison buildings form a square around the courtyard, and to get from one part of the facility to another, the inmates go across the courtyard.

The Campus Style

Some of the newer minimum-security prisons have adopted the campus style, which had previously been used in correctional facilities for women and juveniles. As on a college campus, housing units are scattered among functional units such as the dining room, recreation area, and treatment centers.

For the most part, supermax prisons operate in a state of perpetual lockdown, in which all inmates are confined to their cells and social activities such as meals, recreational sports, and treatment programs are nonexistent. For the ninety minutes of each day that SHU inmates are allowed out of their cells (compared with twelve to sixteen hours in regular maximum-security prisons), they may either shower or exercise in an enclosed, concrete "yard" covered by plastic mesh. Prisoners are strip-searched before and after leaving their cells, and are placed in waist restraints and handcuffs on their way to and from the "yard" and showers.[39]

Supermax Syndrome Many prison officials support the proliferation of supermax prisons because they provide increased security for the most dangerous inmates. These proponents believe that the harsh reputation of the facilities will deter convicts from misbehaving for fear of transfer to a supermax. Nevertheless, the supermax

Lockdown A disciplinary action taken by prison officials in which all inmates are ordered to their quarters and nonessential prison activities are suspended.

Technology Tip: Have students learn more about conditions inside supermax prisons at *ABC News* online: **abcnews.go.com/TheLaw/story?id=3435989&page=1**.

has aroused a number of criticisms. Amnesty International and other human rights groups assert that the facilities violate standards for proper treatment of prisoners. At Wisconsin's Supermax Correctional Facility, for example, the cells are illuminated twenty-four hours a day. Because they have no air-conditioning or windows, average temperatures during the summer top 100 degrees.[40]

Furthermore, while studying prisoners at California's Pelican Bay facility, a Harvard University psychiatrist found that 80 percent suffered from what he called "SHU [security housing unit] syndrome," a condition brought on by long periods of isolation.[41] Further research on SHU syndrome shows that supermax inmates manifest a number of psychological problems, including massive anxiety, hallucinations, and acute confusion.[42] We will take a closer look at the merits and drawbacks of solitary confinement, a method of inmate punishment that extends well beyond supermax prisons, in the *CJ in Action* feature that ends this chapter.

Inside the Northern Correctional Institution, the supermax facility in Somers, Connecticut, a correctional officer escorts a prisoner out of a shower, top left. In what ways does the supermax prison represent the ultimate controlled environment for its inmates?
AP Photo, Steve Miller

MEDIUM- AND MINIMUM-SECURITY PRISONS

Medium-security prisons hold about 40 percent of the prison population and minimum-security prisons 20 percent. Inmates at medium-security prisons have for the most part committed less serious crimes than those housed in maximum-security prisons and are not considered high risks for escaping or causing harm. Consequently, medium-security institutions are not designed for control to the same extent as maximum-security prisons and have a more relaxed atmosphere. These facilities also offer more educational and treatment programs and allow for more contact between inmates. Medium-security prisons are rarely walled, relying instead on high fences. Prisoners have more freedom of movement within the structures, and the levels of surveillance are much lower. Living quarters are less restrictive as well—many of the newer medium-security prisons provide dormitory housing.

A minimum-security prison seems at first glance to be more like a college campus than an incarceration facility. Most of the inmates at these institutions are first-time offenders who are nonviolent and well behaved. A high percentage are white-collar criminals. Indeed, inmates are often transferred to minimum-security prisons as a reward for good behavior in other facilities. Therefore, security measures are lax compared with even medium-security prisons. Unlike medium-security institutions, minimum-security prisons do not have armed guards. Prisoners are provided with amenities such as television sets and computers in their rooms. They also enjoy freedom of movement, and are allowed off prison grounds for educational or employment purposes to

Medium-Security Prison A correctional institution that houses less dangerous inmates and therefore uses less restrictive measures to prevent violence and escapes.

Minimum-Security Prison A correctional institution designed to allow inmates, most of whom pose low security risks, a great deal of freedom of movement and contact with the outside world.

a much greater extent than those held in more restrictive facilities. Some critics have likened minimum-security prisons to "country clubs," but in the corrections system, everything is relative. A minimum-security prison may seem like a vacation spot when compared with the horrors of Sing Sing, but it still represents a restriction of personal freedom and separates the inmate from the outside world. (The feature *Comparative Criminal Justice—Salutary Confinement* below provides a look inside Norway's newest prison, which is based on a theory of punishment that will seem foreign in more ways than one.)

Technology Tip: Have students go online to learn more about the way the Federal Bureau of Prisons classifies its institutions at **www. bop.gov/locations/institutions/ index.jsp**.

SELFASSESSMENT

Fill in the blanks and check your answers on page 456.
Those offenders who have been convicted of violent crimes and repeat offenders are most likely to be sent to _____-security prisons. If a prisoner assaults another inmate or a correctional officer, prison officials may decide to transfer him or her to a _____ prison. Inmates at _____-security prisons have committed less serious felonies and are not considered to pose a serious risk to other prisoners, while _____-security prisons, which resemble college campuses, house mostly first-time, nonviolent offenders.

COMPARATIVE CRIMINAL JUSTICE

SALUTARY CONFINEMENT

In the United States, life behind bars has long been predicated on the *principle of least eligibility,* which holds that the least advantaged members of outside society should lead a better existence than any person living in prison or jail. Although some minimum-security prisons might seem to violate this principle—the federal women's prison in Danbury, Connecticut, for example, has a law library, a jogging track, and a gymnasium that is used for Dancersize, Pilates, and yoga classes—it applies to most U.S. prisons.

By contrast, in Norway incarceration is based on the premise that every correctional facility should, in the words of one official, look "as much like the outside world as possible." The country's new Halden Fengsel prison, for example, is made of bricks and galvanized steel, not concrete. Its cells resemble college dorm rooms and feature flat-screen televisions and minifridges. Inmates share living rooms with wraparound sofas, coffee tables, and stainless-steel countertops. They eat meals and play sports with prison staff, the better to "create a sense of family" on prison grounds.

Halden Fengsel houses some of Norway's most violent criminals, including murderers and rapists. Still, the facility provides prisoners with amenities such as a recording studio, a "kitchen laboratory" for cooking classes, and a two-bedroom house where inmates can host their families for overnight visits. On release, prisoners are given questionnaires asking how their experience at Halden Fengsel could have been improved. "In the Norwegian prison system, there's a focus on human rights and respect," explains Are Høidal, the facility's governor. "We don't see any of this as unusual."

FOR CRITICAL ANALYSIS
What is your opinion of the theory, dominant in Norwegian corrections, that loss of liberty is punishment enough for offenders and that their prison experience should therefore be as pleasant as possible?

PRISON ADMINISTRATION

The security level of a prison generally determines the specific methods used to manage it. There are, however, some general goals of prison administration, summarized by Charles Logan as follows:

> The mission of a prison is to keep prisoners—to keep them in, keep them safe, keep them in line, keep them healthy, and keep them busy—and to do it with fairness, without undue suffering and as efficiently as possible.[43]

Considering the environment of a prison—an enclosed world inhabited by people who are generally violent and angry and would rather be anywhere else—Logan's mission statement is somewhat unrealistic. A prison staff must supervise the daily routines of hundreds or thousands of inmates, a duty that includes providing them with meals, education, vocational programs, and different forms of leisure. The smooth operation of this supervision is made more difficult—if not, at times, impossible—by budgetary restrictions, overcrowding, and continual inmate turnover.

FORMAL PRISON MANAGEMENT

Critical Thinking Skill Development: In a brief written assignment, ask students to compare the management structure of a prison to that of a police department. How are these two systems similar? How are they different? (Police organization was discussed on pages 174–175) (LO 5)

In some respects, the management structure of a prison is similar to that of a police department, as discussed in Chapter 5. Both systems rely on a hierarchical (top-down) **LO 5** *chain of command* to increase personal responsibility. Both assign different employees to specific tasks, though prison managers have much more direct control over their subordinates than do police managers. The main difference is that police departments have a *continuity of purpose* that is sometimes lacking in prison organizations. All members of a police force are, at least theoretically, working to reduce crime and apprehend criminals. In a prison, this continuity is less evident. An employee in the prison laundry service and one who works in the visiting center have little in common. In some instances, employees may even have cross-purposes: a prison guard may want to punish an inmate, while a counselor in the treatment center may want to rehabilitate her or him.

Warden The prison official who is ultimately responsible for the organization and performance of a correctional facility.

Consequently, a strong hierarchy is crucial for any prison management team that hopes to meet Charles Logan's expectations. As Figure 13.6 below shows, the warden (also known as a superintendent) is ultimately responsible for the operation of a prison.

FIGURE 13.6 Organizational Chart for a Typical Correctional Facility

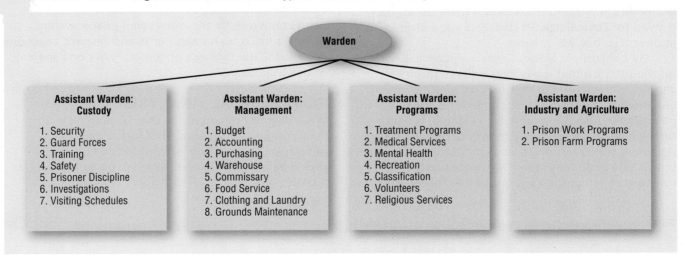

Warden

Assistant Warden: Custody
1. Security
2. Guard Forces
3. Training
4. Safety
5. Prisoner Discipline
6. Investigations
7. Visiting Schedules

Assistant Warden: Management
1. Budget
2. Accounting
3. Purchasing
4. Warehouse
5. Commissary
6. Food Service
7. Clothing and Laundry
8. Grounds Maintenance

Assistant Warden: Programs
1. Treatment Programs
2. Medical Services
3. Mental Health
4. Recreation
5. Classification
6. Volunteers
7. Religious Services

Assistant Warden: Industry and Agriculture
1. Prison Work Programs
2. Prison Farm Programs

He or she oversees deputy wardens, who in turn manage the various organizational lines of the institution. The custodial employees, who deal directly with the inmates and make up more than half of a prison's staff, operate under a militaristic hierarchy, with a line of command passing from the deputy warden to the captain to the correctional officer.

GOVERNING PRISONS

The implications of prison mismanagement can be severe. While studying a series of prison riots, sociologists Bert Useem and Peter Kimball found that breakdown in managerial control commonly preceded such acts of mass violence.[44] During the 1970s, for example, conditions at the State Penitentiary in New Mexico deteriorated significantly. Inmates were increasingly the targets of random and harsh treatment at the hands of the prison staff, while at the same time a reduction in structured activities left prison life "painfully boring."[45] The result, in 1980, was one of the most violent prison riots in the nation's history.

What sort of prison management is most suited to avoid such situations? Although there is no single "best" form of prison management, political scientist John DiIulio believes that, in general, the sound governance of correctional facilities is a matter of order, amenities, and services:

- *Order* can be defined as the absence of misconduct such as murder, assault, and rape. Many observers, including DiIulio, believe that, having incarcerated a person, the state has a responsibility to protect that person from disorder in the correctional institution.
- *Amenities* are those comforts that make life "livable," such as clean living conditions, acceptable food, and entertainment. One theory of incarceration holds that inmates should not enjoy a quality of life comparable to life outside prison. Without the basic amenities, however, prison life becomes unbearable, and inmates are more likely to lapse into disorder.
- *Services* include programs designed to improve an inmate's prospects on release, such as vocational training, remedial education, and drug treatment. Again, many feel that a person convicted of a crime does not deserve to participate in these kinds of programs, but they have two clear benefits. First, they keep the inmate occupied and focused during her or his sentence. Second, they reduce the chances that the inmate will go back to a life of crime after she or he returns to the community.[46]

Teaching Tip: Have students take a field trip to a nearby prison. While touring the facility, have staff talk to students about the challenges of running a safe and orderly prison. (LO 5)

According to DiIulio, in the absence of order, amenities, and services, inmates will come to see their imprisonment as not only unpleasant but unfair, and they will become much more difficult to control.[47] Furthermore, weak governance encourages inmates to come up with their own methods of regulating their lives. As we shall see in the next chapter, the result is usually high levels of violence and the expansion of prison gangs and other unsanctioned forms of authority.

SELFASSESSMENT

Fill in the blanks and check your answers on page 456.

The management of a prison is hierarchical, with the _____ (also known as a superintendent) at the top of the power structure. Unlike other hierarchical systems such as police departments, correctional facilities often lack continuity of _____, meaning that not all employees have the same organizational goals. In general, however, effective governance of a prison requires prison staff to protect prisoners from _____ and provide them with _____ and services.

CAREERS IN CJ

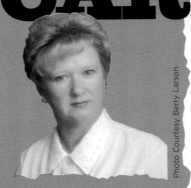

Photo Courtesy Berry Larson.

FAST FACTS

PRISON WARDEN JOB DESCRIPTION:

- A prison warden is the chief managing officer of an adult correctional institution.

- Responsible for custody, feeding, clothing, housing, care, treatment, discipline, training, employment, rehabilitation, and the well-being of offenders.

- Provides institutional staff with effective communications, training, and leadership.

- Addresses citizen groups, legislative committees, the media, and others regarding program and policy issues.

WHAT KIND OF TRAINING IS REQUIRED?

- Bachelor's degree in criminal justice, corrections, law enforcement, or a related field.

- One or more years of work experience in the management of a major division of a correctional institution.

- A background check, drug screening, and/or a polygraph examination may be required.

ANNUAL SALARY RANGE?

- $42,000–$95,000 (depending on size of institution and geographic region)

For additional information on a career as a prison warden, visit: **www.legal-criminal-justice-schools.com/Criminal-Justice-Careers/prison-warden.html.**

BERRY LARSON
WARDEN

I needed a career that met my altruistic needs, a career with a purpose that would have an impact on the lives of others. I had a sister who was involved in drugs and taking the wrong path in life. I couldn't help her, but I wanted to be able to help others make a change in their own lives.

CRISIS SITUATION Before I began my career as a correctional officer for the Arizona Department of Corrections, I had several people question my desire to work inside a prison. Why would I want to stick myself somewhere so unpleasant and stressful? While at the training academy, however, we were taught that "approach determines response." I found that to be very true during my time as a correctional officer. It is all about the way you carry yourself and the way you relate to the inmates. An inmate can tell if you are trying to be someone you are not. They can also tell if you are afraid. I never had to use physical force once in all the time I was a correctional officer—officer presence and nonverbal/verbal communication is usually sufficient to handle any situation, as long as you keep control of your emotions.

For example, the biggest crisis I ever faced as a deputy warden took place one evening when, just after dinner, the inmates separated themselves along racial lines in the yard. The Caucasians stood in one group, the African Americans in another, and the Mexican Americans and Mexican nationals in a third. These factions formed kind of a circle around a smaller group of Native Americans. All of a sudden, the Mexican inmates attacked one of the Native Americans, sparking a short brawl. The correctional staff quickly broke up the fight and sent the inmates back to their dorms. Over the course of the next two days, with the prison population in lockdown, my staff and I conducted countless interviews to figure out what was going on. As it turned out, the inmate who had been attacked was a suspected gang member who wanted to impose segregation in the prison's recreation program. The rest of the inmates opposed this idea and were unified in "taking care" of the troublemaker.

DUTIES AND CHALLENGES As warden of the Arizona State Prison Complex—Lewis, my duties include touring the units; attending special events such as inmate graduations for GED and vocational programs; managing emergency situations such as power outages, fights and assaults, and staff injuries; and eradicating all criminal activity from the facility. Many, if not most, of our inmates came to us in pretty bad shape—little or no education, a substance abuse history, or mental health or behavioral issues. These young men have spent their lives watching television and playing video games and simply do not have the skills to be successful in life. We try to remedy the situation by providing them with educational and vocational programs and "life-skills" classes that promote civil and productive behavior.

CAREER ADVICE If you want to be a warden—the top of the corrections "ladder"—you need to start at the bottom. Experience and education are the keys to corrections success. Begin with a bachelor's degree and then find employment as a correctional officer. Give yourself a well-rounded background by working with male, female, and juvenile offenders at all the different custody levels. You never know what type of correctional facility you may end up administering.

THE EMERGENCE OF PRIVATE PRISONS

In addition to all the other pressures placed on wardens and other prison administrators, they must operate within a budget assigned to them by an overseeing governmental agency. Today, the great majority of all prisons are under the control of federal and state governments, but government-run prisons have not always been the rule. In the nineteenth century, some correctional facilities were not under the control of the state. In fact, the entire Texas prison system was privately operated from 1872 to the late 1880s. For most of the twentieth century, however, private prisons, or prisons run by private business firms to make a profit, could not be found in the United States.

That is certainly not the case today. With corrections exhibiting all appearances of, in the words of one observer, "a recession-proof industry," the American business community has eagerly entered the market. Fourteen private corrections firms operate more than two hundred facilities across the United States. The two largest corrections companies, Corrections Corporation of America (CCA) and the GEO Group, Inc., have contracted to supervise more than 100,000 inmates. More than a decade ago, the Federal Bureau of Prisons (BOP) awarded the first contract paying a private company to operate one of its prisons—the GEO Group received $88 million to run the Taft Correctional Institution in Taft, California. Today, the GEO Group operates nineteen federal corrections facilities. By 2010, private penal institutions housed nearly 130,000 inmates, representing 8 percent of all prisoners in the state and federal corrections systems.[48]

Private Prisons Correctional facilities operated by private corporations instead of the government and, therefore, reliant on profits for survival.

Technology Tip: Have students visit Corrections Corporation of America (CCA) online at **www.correctionscorp.com**. CCA is one of the largest private corrections companies in the United States.

WHY PRIVATIZE?

It would be a mistake to automatically assume that private prisons are less expensive to run than public ones. Nevertheless, the incentive to privatize is primarily financial.

COST EFFICIENCY In the 1980s and 1990s, a number of states and cities reduced operating costs by transferring government-run services such as garbage collection and road maintenance to the private sector. Similarly, private prisons can often be run more cheaply and efficiently than public ones for the following reasons:

LO 6

- *Labor costs.* The wages of public employees account for nearly two-thirds of a prison's operating expenses. Although private corrections firms pay base salaries comparable to those enjoyed by public prison employees, their nonunionized staffs receive lower levels of overtime pay, workers' compensation claims, sick leave, and health-care insurance.
- *Competitive bidding.* Because of the profit motive, private corrections firms have an incentive to buy goods and services at the lowest possible price.
- *Less red tape.* Private corrections firms are not part of the government bureaucracy and therefore do not have to contend with the massive amount of paperwork that can clog government organizations.[49]

In 2005, the National Institute of Justice released the results of a five-year study comparing low-security public and private prisons in California. The government agency found that private facilities cost taxpayers between 6 and 10 percent less than public ones.[50] More recent research conducted at Vanderbilt University found that states saved about $15 million annually when they supplemented their corrections systems with privately managed institutions.[51]

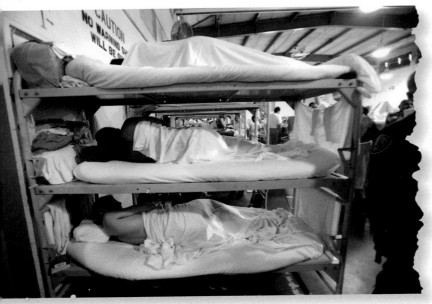

Because of overcrowding, inmates are forced to sleep in bunk beds in a gymnasium at the California Institution for Men in Chino. Why would private prisons be attractive options in this situation? Can you think of any drawbacks to housing prisoners out of state, whether they are kept in private facilities or public ones?
Monica Almeida/*New York Times*/Redux

Group Activities: Ask students to work in small groups to debate the advantages and disadvantages of private prisons. (LO 6)

OVERCROWDING AND OUTSOURCING

Private prisons are becoming increasingly attractive to state governments faced with the competing pressures of tight budgets and overcrowded corrections facilities. Lacking the funds to alleviate overcrowding by building more prisons, state officials are turning to the private institutions for help. Often, the private prison is out of state, which leads to the "outsourcing" of inmates. Hawaii, for example, sends about one-third of its 6,000 inmates to private prisons in Arizona.[52] California, dealing with severe overcrowding and an annual corrections health-care budget of $1.5 billion, has increased the number of its inmates housed out of state to more than 15,000, sending them to private institutions in Arizona, Colorado, Michigan, Minnesota, Missouri, Montana, and Oklahoma.[53]

THE ARGUMENT AGAINST PRIVATE PRISONS

The assertion that private prisons offer economic benefits is not universally accepted. A number of studies have found that private prisons are no more cost-effective than public ones.[54] Furthermore, opponents of private prisons worry that, despite the assurances of corporate executives, private corrections companies will "cut corners" to save costs, denying inmates important security guarantees in the process.

SAFETY CONCERNS Criticism of private prisons is somewhat justified by the anecdotal evidence. Certainly, these institutions have been the setting for a number of unacceptable incidents over the past several years. In August 2009, Hawaii prison officials announced that all of the state's 168 female inmates were being removed from a Kentucky facility operated by CCA. The decision was made in response to allegations of sexual abuse of inmates by CCA correctional officers, at least five of whom had been charged with having sex with inmates in previous years.[55] That same year, the GEO Group was ordered to pay $42.5 million in punitive damages for the death of Gregorio De La Rosa, Jr. According to trial documents, correctional officers watched while two other inmates at the Willacy County State Jail in Raymondville, Texas, beat De La Rosa to death using socks stuffed with padlocks.[56]

Apart from anecdotal evidence, various studies have also uncovered disturbing patterns of misbehavior at private prisons. For example, officials from the BOP discovered higher levels of serious inmate violence and drug abuse at California's Taft Correctional Institute, operated by the GEO Group, than at three similar government-run prisons.[57] In addition, research conducted by Curtis R. Blakely of the University of South Alabama and Vic W. Bumphus of the University of Tennessee at Chattanooga found that a prisoner in a private correctional facility was twice as likely to be assaulted by a fellow inmate as a prisoner in a public one.[58]

FINANCIAL CONCERNS Furthermore, some observers note, if a private corrections firm receives a fee from the state for each inmate housed in its facility, does that not give management an incentive to increase the amount of time each prisoner serves? Though government parole boards make the final decision on an inmate's release from private prisons, the company could manipulate misconduct and good behavior reports to maximize time served and, by extension, higher profits.[59]

PHILOSOPHICAL CONCERNS Other critics see private prisons as inherently unjust, even if they do save tax dollars or provide enhanced services. These observers believe that corrections is not simply another industry, like garbage collection or road maintenance, and that only the government has the authority to punish wrongdoers. In the words of John DiIulio:

> It is precisely because corrections involves the deprivation of liberty, precisely because it involves the legally sanctioned exercise of coercion by some citizens over others, that it must remain wholly within public hands.[60]

Critics of private correctional facilities also believe that private prisons are constitutionally problematic, offering Article I of the U.S. Constitution as support. That passage states that "legislative powers herein granted shall be vested in a Congress of the United States." These powers include the authority to define penal codes and to determine the punishments that will be handed out for breaking federal law. Therefore, a strict interpretation of the Constitution appears to prohibit the passing of this authority from the federal government to a private company.[61]

Critical Thinking Skill Development: Ask students to respond to "Questions for Critical Analysis" number four on page 456, in which they consider whether private prisons are inherently unjust.

THE FUTURE OF PRIVATIZATION IN THE CORRECTIONS INDUSTRY

The continued financial health of the "recession-proof" private prison industry seems assured by two factors. First, as we have noted, shrinking budgets have forced states to look for less costly alternatives to housing inmates in public prisons. Second, as the number of federal prisoners increases, the BOP has turned to private prisons to expand its capacity. Between 2000 and 2010, the number of federal inmates in private prisons more than doubled, from about 15,500 to about 34,000.[62] The current emphasis on imprisoning violators of immigration law seems likely to ensure that this trend will continue.

Teaching Tip: Ask students to consider the assertion that private prisons are "recession proof." Why might this be the case?

SELFASSESSMENT

Fill in the blanks and check your answers on page 456.

The incentive for using private prisons is primarily _____. Prison officials also feel pressure to send inmates to private prisons to alleviate _____ of public correctional facilities. Critics of private prisons claim that as a result of their cost-cutting measures, inmates are denied important _____ guarantees and thus may be put in physical danger. The industry's future seems assured, however, because of increased demand for prison beds for immigration law violators on the part of the _____ government.

JAILS

Although prisons and prison issues dominate the public discourse on corrections, there is an argument to be made that jails are the dominant penal institutions in the United States. In general, a prison is a facility designed to house people convicted of felonies for lengthy periods of time, while a jail is authorized to hold pretrial detainees and offenders who

LO 7

have committed misdemeanors. On any given day, about 765,000 inmates are in jail in this country, and approximately 7 million Americans spend at least a day in jail each year. Furthermore, the jail population increased by 38 percent

Jail A facility, usually operated by the county government, used to hold persons awaiting trial or those who have been found guilty of misdemeanors.

between 1995 and 2010.[63] Nevertheless, jail funding is often the lowest priority for the tight budgets of local governments, leading to severe overcrowding and other dismal conditions.

Many observers see this negligence as having far-reaching consequences for criminal justice. Jail is often the first contact that citizens have with the corrections system. It is at this point that treatment and counseling have the best chance to deter future criminal behavior.[64] By failing to take advantage of this opportunity, says Professor Franklin Zimring of the University of California at Berkeley School of Law, corrections officials have created a situation in which "today's jail folk are tomorrow's prisoners."[65] (To better understand the role that these two correctional institutions play in the criminal justice system, see *Mastering Concepts—The Main Differences between Prisons and Jails* below.)

THE FUNCTION OF JAILS

Critical Thinking Skill Development: More offenders pass through America's jails each year than through its prisons. Have students discuss why jails are such an important part of the criminal justice system. Why don't jails receive the media attention given to prisons? (LO 7)

Until the eighteenth century, all penal institutions existed primarily to hold those charged with a crime until their trial. Although jails still serve this purpose, they have evolved to play a number of different roles in the corrections system, including the following:

- Holding those convicted of misdemeanors.
- Receiving individuals pending arraignment and holding them while awaiting trial (if they cannot post bail), conviction, or sentencing.
- Temporarily detaining juveniles pending transfer to juvenile authorities.
- Holding the mentally ill pending transfer to health facilities.
- Detaining those who have violated conditions of probation or parole and those who have "jumped" bail.
- Housing inmates awaiting transfer to federal or state prisons.
- Operating community-based corrections programs such as home confinement and electronic monitoring.

Increasingly, jails are also called on to handle the overflow from saturated state and federal prisons. In Washington State, for example, corrections officials are forced to rent eight hundred jail cells a day to house convicts who have been sent back to prison for violating the terms of their parole.

MASTERING CONCEPTS

THE MAIN DIFFERENCES BETWEEN PRISONS AND JAILS

	Prisons	Jails
1.	. . . are operated by the federal and state governments.	. . . are operated by county and city governments.
2.	. . . hold inmates who may have lived quite far away before being arrested.	. . . hold mostly inmates from the local community.
3.	. . . house only those who have been convicted of a crime.	. . . house those who are awaiting trial or have recently been arrested, in addition to convicts.
4.	. . . generally hold inmates who have been found guilty of serious crimes and received sentences of longer than one year.	. . . generally hold inmates who have been found guilty of minor crimes and are serving sentences of less than a year.
5.	. . . often offer a wide variety of rehabilitation and educational programs for long-term prisoners.	. . . due to smaller budgets, tend to focus only on the necessities of safety, food, and clothing.

According to sociologist John Irwin, the unofficial purpose of the jail is to manage society's "rabble," so called because

> [they] are not well integrated into conventional society, they are not members of conventional social organizations, they have few ties to conventional social networks, and they are carriers of unconventional values and beliefs.[66]

In Irwin's opinion, "rabble" who act violently are arrested and sent to prison. The jail is reserved for merely offensive rabble, whose primary threat to society lies in their failure to conform to its behavioral norms. Nearly seven out of ten jail inmates, for example, are dependent on or abuse alcohol or drugs.[67] This concept of "rabble" has been used by some critics of American corrections to explain the disproportionate number of poor and minority groups who may be found in the nation's jails at any time.

Teaching Tip: Have students take a field trip to a local jail and write a brief reaction paper after their visit. What is life like inside the jail?

THE JAIL POPULATION

About 88 percent of jail inmates in the United States are male. As in other areas of corrections, however, women are becoming more numerous. Between 2000 and 2010, the adult female jail population increased by 30 percent, compared with a 19 percent increase for males.[68] Jails also follow the general corrections pattern in that, as mentioned, a disproportionate number of their inmates are members of minority groups. (For an overview of the characteristics of the jail population, see Figure 13.7 below.)

PRETRIAL DETAINEES A significant number of those detained in jails technically are not prisoners. They are **pretrial detainees** who have been arrested by the police and, for a variety of reasons that we discussed in Chapter 9, are unable to post bail. Pretrial detainees are, in many ways, walking legal contradictions. According to the U.S. Constitution, they are innocent until proved guilty. At the same time, by being incarcerated while awaiting trial, they are denied a number of personal freedoms and are subjected to the poor conditions of many jails. In *Bell v. Wolfish* (1979), the Supreme Court rejected the notion that this situation

Pretrial Detainees Individuals who cannot post bail after arrest or are not released on their own recognizance and are therefore forced to spend the time prior to their trial incarcerated in jail.

FIGURE 13.7 The Characteristics of America's Jail Population

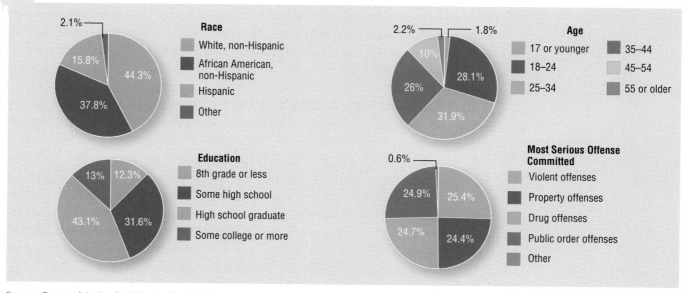

Sources: Bureau of Justice Statistics, *Profile of Jail Inmates, 2002* (Washington, D.C.: U.S. Department of Justice, July 2004), 1–4; and Bureau of Justice Statistics, *Jail Inmates at Midyear 2010—Statistical Tables* (Washington, D.C.: U.S. Department of Justice, April 2011), Table 6, page 7.

is inherently unfair by refusing to give pretrial detainees greater legal protections than sentenced jail inmates have.[69] In essence, the Court recognized that treating pretrial detainees differently from convicted jail inmates would place too much of a burden on corrections officials and was therefore impractical.[70]

SENTENCED JAIL INMATES According to the U.S. Department of Justice, about 40 percent of those in jail have been convicted of their current charges.[71] In other words, they have been found guilty of a crime, usually a misdemeanor, and sentenced to time in jail. The typical jail term lasts between thirty and ninety days, and rarely does a prisoner spend more than one year in jail for any single crime. Often, a judge will credit the length of time the convict has spent in detention waiting for trial—known as **time served**—toward his or her sentence. This practice acknowledges two realities of jails:

1. Terms are generally too short to allow the prisoner to gain any benefit (that is, rehabilitation) from the jail's often limited or nonexistent treatment facilities. Therefore, the jail term can serve no purpose except to punish the wrongdoer. (Judges who believe jail time can serve purposes of deterrence and incapacitation may not agree with this line of reasoning.)
2. Jails are chronically overcrowded, and judges need to clear space for new offenders.

OTHER JAIL INMATES Pretrial detainees and those convicted of misdemeanors make up the majority of the jail population. As mentioned earlier, jail inmates also include felons either waiting for transfer or assigned to jails because of prison overcrowding, probation and parole violators, the mentally ill, and juveniles. In addition, jails can hold those who require incarceration but do not "fit" anywhere else. A material witness or an attorney in a trial who refuses to follow the judge's instructions may, for example, be held in contempt of court and sent to jail.

JAIL ADMINISTRATION

LO 8 Of the nearly 3,370 jails in the United States, more than 2,700 are operated on a county level by an elected sheriff. Most of the remainder are under the control of municipalities, although six state governments (Alaska, Connecticut, Delaware, Hawaii, Rhode Island, and Vermont) manage jails. The capacity of jails varies widely. The Los Angeles County Men's Central Jail holds nearly 7,000 people, but jails that large are the exception rather than the rule. Almost two-thirds of all jails in this country house fewer than 50 inmates.[72]

THE "BURDEN" OF JAIL ADMINISTRATION Given that the public's opinion of jails ranges from negative to indifferent, some sheriffs neglect their jail management duties. Instead, they focus on high-visibility issues such as putting more law enforcement officers on the streets and improving security in schools. In fact, a jail usually receives publicity only after an escape or an incident in which inmates are abused by jailers. Nonetheless, with their more complex and diverse populations, jails are often more difficult to manage than prisons. Jails hold people who have never been incarcerated before, people under the influence of drugs or alcohol at the time of their arrival, the mentally ill, and people who exhibit a range of violent behavior—from nonexistent to extreme—that only adds to the unpredictable atmosphere.[73]

Despite some sheriffs' general apathy toward jails, few would be willing to give up their management duties. As troublesome as they may be, jails can be useful in other

Time Served The period of time a person denied bail (or unable to pay it) has spent in jail prior to his or her trial. If the suspect is found guilty and sentenced to a jail or prison term, the judge will often shorten the duration of the sentence based on the amount of time served as a pretrial detainee.

Critical Thinking Skill Development: Have students discuss the variety of individuals that may be housed in jails at any one time. What risks are involved when housing pretrial detainees, convicts, and the mentally ill in the same facility? What conflicts inevitably emerge when a jail tries to serve so many different functions?

ways. The sheriff appoints a jail administrator, or deputy sheriff, to oversee the day-to-day operations of the facility. The sheriff also has the power to hire other staff members, such as deputy jailers. The sheriff may award these jobs to people who helped her or him get elected, and, in return, jail staffers can prove helpful to the sheriff in future elections. Furthermore, jails pay. In Kentucky, for example, jails receive $30.94 a day for every inmate transferred from the state's consistently overcrowded prison system.[74]

THE CHALLENGES OF OVERCROWDING In many ways, the sheriff is placed in an untenable position when it comes to jail overcrowding. He or she has little control over the number of people who are sent to jail—that power resides with prosecutors and judges. Nevertheless, the jail is expected to find space to hold all comers, regardless of its capacity. A sheriff from Kane County, Utah, describes the situation:

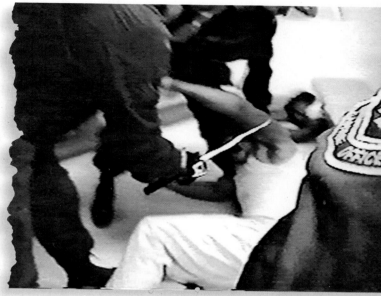

Local sheriff's deputies strike an inmate of the Brazoria County Detention Center in Clute, Texas, with a baton. Guard-on-inmate violence is only one of the problems plaguing the nation's jails, others being inmate-on-inmate violence, poor living conditions, and inadequate health-care facilities. Yet jail problems receive considerably less attention than prison issues. Why might this be the case? AP Photo/*The Brazosport Facts*

> We have people who should get sixty or ninety days, and they just do a weekend and we kick them out. Unless we get a real habitual abuser, we have no choice but to set them free. Most of the time we're pretty sure they will be back in a couple of days with a new offense.[75]

Living Conditions Chronic overcrowding makes the jail experience a miserable one for most inmates. Cells intended to hold one or two people are packed with up to six. Often, inmates are forced to sleep in hallways. In such stressful situations, tempers flare, leading to violent, aggressive behavior. The close proximity and unsanitary living conditions also lead to numerous health problems. In the words of one observer, jail inmates

> share tight space day and night, struggle with human density never before experienced (unless earlier in jail), and search hopelessly for even a moment of solitude. . . . [The congested conditions offer] inmates next to nothing except a stifling idleness that is almost sure to make them worse for the experience. If hard time in prison or jail is time without meaning, there might be no equal to long periods of time in the seriously overcrowded living areas of jails; for above all else (and clearly in comparison to time in prison), jail time is dead time.[76]

Such conditions also raise basic questions of justice: as we noted earlier, many of the inmates in jail have not yet been tried and must be presumed innocent.

A New Trend? Fortunately, at least for some jail managers, the situation seems to be improving. Between June 30, 2008, and June 30, 2009, the nation's jail inmate population dropped for the first time since the early 1980s, a trend that continued in 2010.[77] To a large extent, this decrease was caused by reductions in jail populations in larger counties: two-thirds of jail jurisdictions with a thousand or more inmates reported a decline. Spurred by the same factors that have led to a reduction in state prison inmates, discussed earlier in this chapter, in 2010 U.S. jails averaged only 86 percent capacity, the lowest rate in a decade.[78] Also, jails have continued to add new beds—nearly 17,000 in 2009–2010—which has helped relieve overcrowding, if not pressures on local and state budgets.[79]

Technology Tip: Sheriff Joe Arpaio of Maricopa County in Arizona has gained a national reputation for his jail management style. Visit the Maricopa County Jail online at **www.mcso.org** to learn more about the unique jail programs Arpaio has enacted.

NEW-GENERATION JAILS

For most of the nation's history, the architecture of a jail was secondary to its purpose of keeping inmates safely locked away. Consequently, most jails in the United States continue to resemble those from the days of the Walnut Street Jail in Philadelphia. In

The linear design is similar to that of a hospital in which long rows of rooms are placed along a corridor. What sorts of risks are inherent in this type of jail design?

Courtesy National Corrections Corporation

this *traditional*, or *linear design*, jail cells are located along a corridor (see the photo alongside). To supervise the inmates while they are in their cells, custodial officers must walk up and down the corridor, so the number of prisoners they can see at any one time is severely limited. With this limited supervision, inmates can more easily break institutional rules.

PODULAR DESIGN In the 1970s, planners at the Bureau of Federal Prisons decided to upgrade the traditional jail design with the goal of improving conditions for both the staff and the inmates. The result was the new-generation jail, which differs significantly from its predecessors.[80] The layout of the new facilities makes it easier for the staff to monitor cell-confined inmates. The basic structure of the new-generation jail is based on a podular design. Each "pod" contains "living units" for individual prisoners. These units, instead of lining up along a straight corridor, are often situated in a triangle so that a staff member in the center of the triangle has visual access to nearly all the cells.

Daily activities such as eating and showering take place in the pod, which also has an outdoor exercise area. Treatment facilities are also located in the pod, allowing greater access for the inmates. During the day, inmates stay out in the open and are allowed back in their cells only when given permission. The officer locks the door to the cells from his or her control terminal.

DIRECT SUPERVISION APPROACH The podular design also enables a new-generation jail to be managed using a direct supervision approach.[81] One or more jail officers are stationed in the living area of the pod and are therefore in constant interaction with all prisoners in that particular pod. Some new-generation jails even provide a desk in the center of the living area, which sends a very different message to the prisoners than the traditional control booth. Theoretically, jail officials who have constant contact with inmates will be able to stem misconduct quickly and efficiently and will also be able to recognize "danger signs" from individual inmates and stop outbursts before they occur.

At first, the new-generation jails provoked a great deal of skepticism, as they were seen as inherently "soft" for criminals. A number of empirical results, however, seem to speak to the success of podular design and direct supervision. One study measured inmate behavior in an adult detention facility before and after it was converted to a direct supervision jail. The researchers found a "dramatic reduction" in the number of assaults, batteries, attempted suicides, sex offenses, possession of weapons, and escapees.[82] Today, nearly three hundred new-generation jails are in operation or under construction.

New-Generation Jail A type of jail that is distinguished architecturally from its predecessors by a design that encourages interaction between inmates and jailers and that offers greater opportunities for treatment.

Podular Design The architectural style of the new-generation jail. Each "pod" consists of between twelve and twenty-four one-person cells and a communal dayroom to allow for social interaction.

Direct Supervision Approach A process of prison and jail administration in which correctional officers are in continuous physical contact with inmates during the day.

Group Activities: Have students break into teams to debate the hypothetical construction of a new jail. Have one side attempt to convince "the city council" that a new-generation jail is the most appropriate option, while the other side advocates for the traditional jail design.

SELF ASSESSMENT

Fill in the blanks and check your answers on page 456.

A significant number of the people in jail are not prisoners, but rather _____ _____ who are unable to post bail and await trial. About 40 percent have been _____ of their current charges, meaning that the jail sentence is punishment for a crime—usually a _____ and not a felony. Most jails are operated on a local level by the county _____.

THE CONSEQUENCES OF OUR HIGH RATES OF INCARCERATION

LO 9 For many observers, especially those who support the crime control theory of criminal justice, America's high rate of incarceration has contributed significantly to the drop in the country's crime rates.[83] At the heart of this belief is the fact, which we discussed in Chapter 2, that most crimes are committed by a relatively small group of repeat offenders. Several studies have tried to corroborate this viewpoint, with varying results—estimates of the number of crimes committed each year by habitual offenders range from 3 to 187.[84] If one accepts the higher estimate, each year a repeat offender spends in prison prevents a significant number of criminal acts.

Criminologists, however, note the negative consequences of America's immense prison and jail population. For one, incarceration can have severe social consequences for communities and the families that make up those communities. About 1.7 million minor children—one in 43—have a parent in prison, putting them at greater risk of suffering financial hardship and reduced supervision and discipline.[85] As a result of the deterioration of the family structure, children of inmates are at a higher risk than their peers for antisocial behavior and mental health problems.[86] Our high rates of incarceration also deny one of the basic rights of American democracy—the right to vote—to about 5.3 million Americans with criminal records.[87] A number of states and the federal government *disenfranchise*, or take away the ability to vote, from those convicted of felonies. This has a disproportionate impact on minority groups, weakening their voice in the democratic debate. Today, African American males are incarcerated at a rate more than six times that of white males and almost three times that of Hispanic males.[88] With more black men behind bars than enrolled in the nation's colleges and universities, Marc Mauer of the Sentencing Project believes that the "ripple effect on their communities and on the next generation of kids, growing up with their fathers in prison, will certainly be with us for at least a generation."[89]

Whether our incarceration situation is "good" or "bad" depends to a large extent on one's personal philosophy. In the end, it is difficult to do a definitive cost-benefit analysis for each person incarcerated, weighing the benefits of preventing crimes that might (or might not) have been committed by an inmate against the costs to the convict's family and society. One thing that can be stated with some certainty is that, even with the growing interest in diversion and rehabilitation described in the previous chapter, the American prison system will remain one of the largest in the world for the foreseeable future.

A mother and child wait outside the Donald W. W. Wyatt Detention Facility in Central Falls, Rhode Island. What are the possible consequences of having a parent behind bars for the affected children and for American society as a whole?
Suzanne DeChillo/*New York Times*/Redux

Teaching Tip: Asks students to brainstorm a list of the consequences associated with high rates of incarceration. Then, have them brainstorm ways federal, state, and local officials might address those issues. (LO 9)

CJ IN ACTION

SOLITARY CONFINEMENT: SENSELESS SUFFERING?

"This is going to be a piece of cake," thought Bobby Dellelo after being locked, alone, in a thirteen-by-eight-foot cell at the Massachusetts Correctional Institute as punishment because of a recent prison escape. After all, he had a radio and a television set, and there were no other inmates around to bother him. Within a few months, however, Dellelo began having screaming panic attacks and hallucinating that the white walls of his cell were changing colors. Within a year, the television set began talking directly to him, forcing him to hide it under the bed. Dellelo worried that he was losing his mind.[90] In this *CJ in Action* feature, we will examine the widespread practice of solitary confinement, condemned by critics as inhumane but heralded by supporters as an invaluable tool of prison management.

ENFORCED ISOLATION

Although conditions of solitary confinement vary, in general the term refers to the confinement of an inmate alone in a small cell for most or all of the day with minimal environmental stimulation and social interaction.[91] Most solitary confinement cells measure approximately ten feet by six feet. Furnished with only a sink, toilet, and concrete bed, they have no windows or barred doors that would let in natural light.

As a rule, inmates are not sentenced to solitary confinement by a judge, and the assignment has no connection to the severity of the original offense. Rather, these isolation cells are reserved for prisoners who commit disciplinary violations once in prison or are deemed a security risk to themselves or others. According to estimates, approximately 60,000 inmates—about 4.5 percent of the American prison population—are in solitary confinement at any given time.[92]

THE CASE FOR SOLITARY CONFINEMENT

- Prison officials see the threat of solitary confinement as a vital tool in maintaining order and discipline. Because human contact is one of the few privileges that inmates enjoy, they have a strong incentive to conform to the rules of the institution rather than risk losing that privilege.

- Solitary confinement protects prison staff and inmates alike by removing violent convicts from the general inmate population.

- Solitary confinement can be a form of rehabilitation, as it separates the inmate from negative influences.

THE CASE AGAINST SOLITARY CONFINEMENT

- Solitary confinement causes severe damage to the mental health of prisoners. Researchers have identified a number of resulting symptoms, including intense anxiety, hallucinations, violent fantasies, and reduced impulse control.[93]

- The majority of inmates who suffer the psychological harm of solitary confinement will eventually be returned to society, which will have to bear the burden of their mental illness.

- Because prison officials have unfettered discretion in deciding who gets sent to solitary confinement and for how long, the practice is rife with abuse.

YOUR OPINION—WRITING ASSIGNMENT

To many observers, the drawbacks of solitary confinement lie in its practice, not its principles. Although it may be useful in controlling inmate populations, solitary confinement procedures suffer from failure to properly monitor the medical and psychological state of those in "the Hole," confinement for trivial offenses like "talking back" to corrections officials, and unacceptably long periods of isolation. The courts have shown no inclination to rein in these abuses, as judges tend to be extremely deferential to the decisions and policies of prison officials.

Today, no federal laws control the use of solitary confinement. Only one state, Washington, places a limit—twenty days—on the length of time an inmate may be kept in isolation.[94] If you were to draft a law regulating the use of solitary confinement, what elements would your law contain? Would you, like the courts, give prison officials a "free hand," or would you restrict their discretion? Would you allow prisoners to challenge their solitary confinement in court? Before responding, you can review our discussions in this chapter concerning:

- The three general models of prison organization (pages 435–436).

- Maximum-security and supermax prisons (pages 436–440).

- Prison administration (pages 442–443).

Your answer should include at least three full paragraphs.

CHAPTER SUMMARY

LO 1 Contrast the Pennsylvania and the New York penitentiary theories of the 1800s. Basically, the Pennsylvania system imposed total silence on its prisoners. Based on the concept of separate confinement, penitentiaries were constructed with back-to-back cells facing both outward and inward. Prisoners worked, slept, and ate alone in their cells. In contrast, New York used the congregate system: silence was imposed, but inmates worked and ate together.

LO 2 List the factors that have caused the prison population to grow dramatically in the last several decades. (a) The enhancement and stricter enforcement of the nation's drug laws; (b) increased probability of incarceration; (c) inmates serving more time for each crime; (d) federal prison growth; and (e) rising incarceration rates for women.

LO 3 Explain the three general models of prisons. (a) The custodial model assumes the prisoner is incarcerated for reasons of incapacitation, deterrence, and retribution. (b) The rehabilitation model puts security concerns second and the well-being of the individual inmate first. As a consequence, treatment programs are offered to prisoners. (c) The reintegration model sees the correctional institution as a training ground for preparing convicts to reenter society.

LO 4 List and briefly explain the four types of prisons. (a) Maximum-security prisons, which are designed mainly with security and surveillance in mind. Such prisons are usually large and consist of cell blocks, each of which is set off by a series of gates and bars. (b) Medium-security prisons, which offer considerably more educational and treatment programs and allow more contact between inmates. Such prisons are usually surrounded by high fences rather than by walls. (c) Minimum-security prisons, which permit prisoners to have television sets and computers and often allow them to leave the grounds for educational and employment purposes. (d) Supermaximum-security (supermax) prisons, in which prisoners are confined to one-person cells for up to twenty-two and a half hours per day under constant video camera surveillance.

LO 5 Describe the formal prison management system, and indicate the three most important aspects of prison governance. A formal system is militaristic with a hierarchical (top-down) chain of command; the warden (or superintendent) is on top, then deputy wardens, and last, custodial employees. Sound governance of a correctional facility requires officials to provide inmates with a sense of order, amenities such as clean living conditions and acceptable food, and services such as vocational training and remedial education programs.

LO 6 List the reasons why private prisons can often be run more cheaply than public ones. (a) Labor costs are lower because private prison employees are nonunionized and receive lower levels of overtime pay, sick leave, and health care. (b) Competitive bidding requires the operators of private prisons to buy goods and services at the lowest possible prices. (c) There is less red tape in a private prison facility.

LO 7 Summarize the distinction between jails and prisons, and indicate the importance of jails in the American corrections system. Generally, a prison is for those convicted of felonies who will serve lengthy periods of incarceration, whereas a jail is for those who have been convicted of misdemeanors and will serve less than a year of incarceration. A jail also (a) receives individuals pending arraignment and holds them while awaiting trial, conviction, or sentencing; (b) temporarily holds juveniles pending transfer to juvenile authorities; (c) holds the mentally ill pending transfer to health facilities; (d) detains those who have violated probation or parole and those who have "jumped" bail; and (e) houses those awaiting transfer to federal or state prisons. Approximately 7 million Americans spend time in jail each year.

LO 8 Explain how jails are administered. Most jails are operated at the county level by an elected sheriff, although about 20 percent are under the control of municipalities and six states manage jails themselves. Sheriffs appoint jail administrators (deputy sheriffs) as well as deputy jailers.

LO 9 Indicate some of the consequences of our high rates of incarceration. Some people believe that the reduction in the country's crime rate is a direct result of increased incarceration rates. Others believe that high incarceration rates are having increasingly negative social consequences, such as financial hardships, reduced supervision and discipline of children, and a general deterioration of the family structure when one parent is in prison.

SELF ASSESSMENT ANSWER KEY

Page 432: **i.** separate; **ii.** congregate; **iii.** silence; **iv.** cheaper; **v.** labor; **vi.** medical

Page 435: **i.** drug; **ii.** incarceration/imprisonment; **iii.** length; **iv.** federal; **v.** women

Page 441: **i.** maximum; **ii.** supermax; **iii.** medium; **iv.** minimum

Page 443: **i.** warden; **ii.** purpose; **iii.** disorder; **iv.** amenities

Page 447: **i.** financial; **ii.** overcrowding; **iii.** security/safety; **iv.** federal

Page 452: **i.** pretrial detainees; **ii.** convicted; **iii.** misdemeanor; **iv.** sheriff

KEY TERMS

congregate system **430**

direct supervision approach **452**

jail **447**

lockdown **439**

maximum-security prison **436**

medical model **431**

medium-security prison **440**

minimum-security prison **440**

new-generation jails **452**

penitentiary **429**

podular design **452**

pretrial detainees **449**

private prisons **445**

separate confinement **430**

supermax prison **438**

time served **450**

warden **442**

QUESTIONS FOR CRITICAL ANALYSIS

1. Zebulon Brockway, the superintendent at the Elmira Reformatory in New York (see page 431), believed that criminals were an "inferior class" of human being and should be treated as society's defectives. How were Brockway's theories adopted by the Progressives in the early twentieth century? Why hasn't the Progressives' medical model for prisons been more influential in modern prison management?

2. Some experts predict that America's prison population will soon see significant decreases for the first time in nearly four decades. Would such a decline likely reflect a change in sentencing philosophy in our criminal justice system? If not, what would be the probable reason behind a smaller U.S. prison population?

3. Supermax prisons operate in a state of perpetual lockdown (see page 439). Why might a warden institute a lockdown in a maximum-security prison?

4. Do you agree with the argument that private prisons are inherently injust, no matter what costs they may save taxpayers? Why or why not?

5. Why have pretrial detainees been called "walking legal contradictions" (see page 449)? What are the practical reasons why pretrial detainees will continue to be housed in jails prior to trial, regardless of whether their incarceration presents any constitutional irregularities?

◢ CourseMate *For Online Help*

For online help and access to resources that accompany *Criminal Justice Today*, go to www.cengagebrain.com/shop/ISBN/1111835578. Click "Access Now," where you will find flashcards, an online quiz, and other helpful study aids. If you have an access code for CourseMate, log in and go to the chapter of your choice for additional online study aids.

NOTES

1. Bureau of Justice Statistics, *Prisoners in 2009* (Washington, D.C.: U.S. Department of Justice, December 2010), 1.

2. Bureau of Justice Statistics, *Correctional Populations in the United States, 2009* (Washington, D.C.: U.S. Department of Justice, December 2010), Table 1, page 2.

3. James M. Beattie, *Crime and the Courts in England, 1660–1800* (Princeton, NJ: Princeton University Press, 1986), 506–507.

4. Samuel Walker, *Popular Justice* (New York: Oxford University Press, 1980), 11.

5. Michael Meranze, *Laboratories of Virtue: Punishment, Revolution, and Authority in Philadelphia, 1760–1835* (Chapel Hill, NC: University of North Carolina Press, 1996), 55.

6. Negley K. Teeters, *The Cradle of the Penitentiary: The Walnut Street Jail at Philadelphia, 1773–1835* (Philadelphia: Pennsylvania Prison Society, 1955), 30.

7. Negley K. Teeters and John D. Shearer, *The Prison at Philadelphia's Cherry Hill* (New York: Columbia University Press, 1957), 142–143.

8. Henry Calvin Mohler, "Convict Labor Policies," *Journal of the American Institute of Criminal Law and Criminology* 15 (1925), 556–557.

9. Zebulon Brockway, *Fifty Years of Prison Service* (Montclair, NJ: Patterson Smith, 1969), 400–401.

10. Robert Martinson, "What Works? Questions and Answers about Prison Reform," *Public Interest* 35 (Spring 1974), 22.

11. See Ted Palmer, "Martinson Revisited," *Journal of Research on Crime and Delinquency* (1975), 133; and Paul Gendreau and Bob Ross, "Effective Correctional Treatment: Bibliotherapy for Cynics," *Crime & Delinquency* 25 (1979), 499.

12. Robert Martinson, "New Findings, New Views: A Note of Caution Regarding Sentencing Reform," *Hofstra Law Review* 7 (1979), 243.

13. Quoted in John Schwarz, "Report Finds States Holding Fewer Prisoners," *New York Times* (March 17, 2010), A15.

14. Cheryl L. Jonson, Francis T. Cullen, and Edward J. Latessa, "Cracks in the Penal Harm Movement: Evidence from the Field," *Criminology & Public Policy* (August 2008), 423.

15. Steven D. Levitt, "Understanding Why Crime Fell in the 1990s: Four Factors That Explain the Decline and Six That Do Not," *Journal of Economic Perspectives* (Winter 2004), 177.

16. *Prisoners in 2009*, Appendix table 16a, page 29; and Appendix table 18, page 33.

17. Allen J. Beck, "Growth, Change, and Stability in the U.S. Prison Population, 1980–1995," *Corrections Management Quarterly* (Spring 1997), 9–10.

18. Bureau of Justice Statistics, "Criminal Defendants Sentenced in U.S. District Courts," *Sourcebook of Criminal Justice Statistics Online,* Table 5.25, at **www.albany.edu/sourcebook/pdf/t5252009.pdf**.

19. *Fifteen Years of Guidelines Sentencing: An Assessment of How Well the Federal Criminal Justice System Is Achieving the Goals of Sentencing Reform* (Washington, D.C.: U.S. Sentencing Commission, November 2004), 46.

20. Bureau of Justice Statistics, *Federal Criminal Case Processing, 2002* (Washington, D.C.: U.S. Department of Justice, January 2005), 1.

21. Bureau of Justice Statistics, *Truth in Sentencing in State Prisons* (Washington, D.C.: U.S. Department of Justice, 1999), 7.

22. Bureau of Justice Statistics, *Prison and Jail Inmates, 1995* (Washington, D.C.: U.S. Department of Justice, August 1996), 1; and Bureau of Justice Statistics, *Prisoners in 2009*, Table 1, page 2.

23. Bureau of Justice Statistics, *Prisoners in 2005* (Washington, D.C.: U.S. Department of Justice, November 2006), Table 14, page 10.

24. *Prisoners in 2009*, Appendix table 18, page 33.

25. Federal Bureau of Prisons, "Quick Facts about the Bureau of Prisons" (March 26, 2011), at **www.bop.gov/news/quick.jsp**.

26. *Prisoners in 2009*, Appendix table 5, page 20; and Appendix table 7, page 22.

27. Pew Center on the States, *One in 31: The Long Reach of American Corrections* (Washington, D.C.: The Pew Charitable Trusts, March 2009), 1.

28. Pew Center on the States, *One in 100: Behind Bars in America 2008* (Washington, D.C.: The Pew Charitable Trusts, February 2008), 11.

29. Hal Weitzman, "U.S. States Free Prisoners to Cut Budget Deficits," *Financial Times* (November 14–15, 2009), 5.

30. Deborah Hastings, "States Pull Back after Decades of Get-Tough Laws," *Associated Press* (April 4, 2009).

31. "Prisons Full, Coffers Empty," *The Economist* (July 24, 2010), 28.

32. Robbie Brown and Kim Severson, "Enlisting Prison Labor to Close Budget Gaps," *New York Times* (February 25, 2011), A14.

33. Charles H. Logan, *Criminal Justice Performance Measures in Prisons* (Washington, D.C.: U.S. Department of Justice, 1993), 5.

34. Todd R. Clear and George F. Cole, *American Corrections*, 4th ed. (Belmont, CA: Wadsworth Publishing Co., 1997), 245–246.

35. Alfred Blumstein, "Prisons," in *Crime*, ed. James Q. Wilson and Joan Petersilia (San Francisco: ICS Press, 1995), 392.

36. Cassia Spohn and David Holleran, "The Effect of Imprisonment on Recidivism Rates of Felony Offenders: A Focus on Drug Offenders," *Criminology* (May 1, 2002), 329–357.

37. Tony Izzo, "I-Max Awaits Green," *Kansas City Star* (May 26, 1996), A1.

38. Charles A. Pettigrew, "Technology and the Eighth Amendment: The Problem of Supermax Prisons," *North Carolina Journal of Law and Technology* (Fall 2002), 195.

39. "Facts about Pelican Bay's SHU," *California Prisoner* (December 1991).

40. *Jones-El et al. v. Berge and Lichter*, 164 F.Supp.2d 1096 (2001).

41. Robert Perkinson, "Shackled Justice: Florence Federal Penitentiary and the New Politics of Punishment," *Social Justice* (Fall 1994), 117–123.

42. Terry Kuppers, *Prison Madness: The Mental Health Crisis behind Bars and What We Must Do about It* (San Francisco: Jossey-Bass, 1999), 56–64.

43. Charles H. Logan, "Well Kept: Comparing Quality of Confinement in a Public and Private Prison," *Journal of Criminal Law and Criminology* 83 (1992), 580.

44. Bert Useem and Peter Kimball, *Stages of Siege: U.S. Prison Riots, 1971–1986* (New York: Oxford University Press, 1989).

45. Bert Useem, "Disorganization and the New Mexico Prison Riot of 1980," *American Sociology Review* 50 (1985), 685.

46. John J. DiIulio, *Governing Prisons* (New York: Free Press, 1987), 12.

47. *Ibid.*

48. *Prisoners in 2009*, 9.

49. "A Tale of Two Systems: Cost, Quality, and Accountability in Private Prisons," *Harvard Law Review* (May 2002), 1872.

50. Douglas C. McDonald and Kenneth Carlson, *Contracting for Imprisonment in the Federal Prison System: Cost and Performance of the Privately Operated Taft Correctional Institution* (Cambridge, MA: Abt Associates, Inc., October 2005), vii.

51. Vanderbilt University Law School, "New Study Shows Benefits of Having Privately and Publicly Managed Prisons in the Same State" (November 25, 2008), at **law.vanderbilt.edu/article-search/article-detail/index.aspx?nid=213**.

52. Nelson Daranciang, "Isle Inmates Brought Home," *Honolulu Star-Advertiser* (January 28, 2011), A3.

53. John Tunison, "Baldwin Prisoners Will Be Classified Medium Security," *Grand Rapids (MI) Press* (December 11, 2010), A4.

54. "Behind the Bars: Experts Question Benefits of Private Prisons," *Kentucky Courier Journal* (July 5, 2010), at **www.courier-journal.com/article/20100705/NEWS01/7050312/Behind-Bars-Experts-question-benefits-private-prisons**.

55. Ian Urbina, "Hawaii to Remove Inmates over Sex Abuse Charges," *New York Times* (August 26, 2009), A12.

56. John MacCormack, "Court Upholds Much of Jury Award," *San Antonio Express-News* (April 8, 2009), 5B.

57. Harley G. Lappin *et al., Evaluation of the Taft Demonstration Project: Performance of a Private-Sector Prison and the BOP* (Washington, D.C.: Federal Bureau of Prisons, 2005), 57–59.

58. Curtis R. Blakely and Vic W. Bumphus, "Private and Public Sector Prisons," *Federal Probation* (June 2004), 27.

59. Richard L. Lippke, "Thinking about Private Prisons," *Criminal Justice Ethics* (Winter/Spring 1997), 32.

60. John Dilulio, "Prisons, Profits, and the Public Good: The Privatization of Corrections," in *Criminal Justice Center Bulletin* (Huntsville, TX: Sam Houston State University, 1986).

61. Ira P. Robbins, "Privatization of Prisons, Privatization of Corrections: Defining the Issues," *Vanderbilt Law Review* 40 (1987), 823.

62. *Prisoners in 2009,* Appendix table 19, page 33.

63. Bureau of Justice Statistics, *Prison and Jail Inmates, 1995* (Washington, D.C.: U.S. Department of Justice, August 1996), 1; and Bureau of Justice Statistics, *Jail Inmates at Midyear 2010—Statistical Tables* (Washington, D.C.: U.S. Department of Justice, April 2011), 1.

64. Arthur Wallenstein, "Jail Crowding: Bringing the Issue to the Corrections Center Stage," *Corrections Today* (December 1996), 76–81.

65. Quoted in Fox Butterfield, "'Defying Gravity,' Inmate Population Climbs," *New York Times* (January 19, 1998), A10.

66. John Irwin, *The Jail: Managing the Underclass in American Society* (Berkeley, CA: University of California Press, 1985), 2.

67. Bureau of Justice Statistics, *Substance Dependence, Abuse, and Treatment of Jail Inmates, 2002* (Washington, D.C.: U.S. Department of Justice, July 2005), 1.

68. *Jail Inmates at Midyear 2010—Statistical Tables,* Table 6, page 7.

69. 441 U.S. 520 (1979).

70. *Ibid.,* at 546.

71. *Jail Inmates at Midyear 2010—Statistical Tables,* 1.

72. Bureau of Justice Statistics, *Bulletin* (Washington, D.C.: U.S. Department of Justice, May 2004), 10.

73. Philip L. Reichel, *Corrections: Philosophies, Practices, and Procedures,* 2d ed. (Boston: Allyn & Bacon, 2001), 283.

74. John Cheves, "Cramming in the Inmates," *Lexington (KY) Herald-Leader* (January 13, 2008), A1.

75. Quoted in Greg Burton, "Jail Builders Race to Keep Up with Demand," *Salt Lake City Tribune* (May 8, 1998), N31.

76. Robert G. Lawson, "Turning Jails into Prisons—Collateral Damage from Kentucky's 'War on Crime,'" *Kentucky Law Journal* (2006–2007), 1.

77. *Jail Inmates at Midyear 2010—Statistical Tables,* 2.

78. *Ibid.*

79. *Ibid.*

80. R. L. Miller, "New Generation Justice Facilities: The Case for Direct Supervision," *Architectural Technology* 12 (1985), 6–7.

81. David Bogard, Virginia A. Hutchinson, and Vicci Persons, *Direct Supervision Jails: The Role of the Administrator* (Washington, D.C.: National Institute of Corrections, February 2010), 1–2.

82. Gerald J. Bayens, Jimmy J. Williams, and John Ortiz Smykla, "Jail Type and Inmate

Behavior: A Longitudinal Analysis," *Federal Probation* (September 1997), 54.

83. Dan Seligman, "Lock 'Em Up," *Forbes* (May 23, 2005), 216–217.

84. Franklin E. Zimring and Gordon Hawkins, *Incapacitation: Penal Confinement and the Restraint of Crime* (New York: Oxford University Press, 1995), 38, 40, 145.

85. Sarah Schirmer, Ashley Nellis, and Marc Mauer, *Incarcerated Parents and Their Children* (The Sentencing Project, February 2009), 2.

86. Joseph Murrey *et al., Effects of Parental Imprisonment on Antisocial Behavior and Mental Health: A Systematic Review* (Oslo, Norway: Campbell Systematic Reviews, September 2009), 56–59.

87. The Sentencing Project, "Felony Disenfranchisement," at **www.sentencingproject.org/IssueAreaHome.aspx?IssueID=4.**

88. *Prisoners in 2009,* 9.

89. Quoted in Fox Butterfield, "Study Finds 2.6% Increase in U.S. Prison Population," *New York Times* (July 28, 2003), A8.

90. Atul Gawande, "Hellhole," *The New Yorker* (March 30, 2009), 40.

91. Stuart Grassian, "Psychiatric Effects of Solitary Confinement," *Washington University Journal of Law and Policy* (2006), 327.

92. *The Corrections Yearbook, 2000,* ed. Camille Graham Camp and George M. Camp (New York: Criminal Justice Yearbook, 2000), 26.

93. Bruce Arrigo and Jennifer Leslie Bullock, "The Psychological Effects of Solitary Confinement on Prisoners in Supermax Units," *International Journal of Offender Therapy and Comparative Criminology* (December 2008), 622–640.

94. Washington Revised Code Section 10.64.060 (2005).

CHAPTER

14

William F. Campbell/Time Life Pictures/Getty Images

Behind Bars:

The Life of an Inmate

LEARNING OBJECTIVES

After reading this chapter, you should be able to . . .

LO 1   Explain the concept of prison as a total institution.

LO 2   Describe the possible patterns of inmate behavior, which are driven by the inmate's personality and values.

LO 3   Indicate some of the reasons for violent behavior in prisons.

LO 4   List and briefly explain the six general job categories among correctional officers.

LO 5   Describe the hands-off doctrine of prisoner law and indicate two standards used to determine if prisoners' rights have been violated.

LO 6   Contrast probation, parole, expiration release, pardon, and furlough.

LO 7   Describe typical conditions of parole.

LO 8   Explain the goal of prisoner reentry programs.

LO 9   Indicate typical conditions for release for a paroled child molester.

The nine learning objectives labeled LO 1 through LO 9 are designed to help improve your understanding of the chapter.

THREE**PEAT**

On August 27, 2010, a riot involving about two hundred inmates broke out in the main exercise yard at California's Folsom State Prison. After gas grenades and rubber bullets failed to stop the brawl, correctional officers fired actual bullets into the mass of convicts, sending five of them to the hospital. This tumult should not have surprised anyone, as such outbreaks have become an annual occurrence at the Folsom Prison. Less than a year earlier, in October 2009, eight inmates were injured when a riot broke out in the facility's dining hall. A year before that, in September 2008, five inmates were treated for injuries sustained in yet another disturbance in the exercise yard.

A list of similar episodes could be compiled for many of today's penal institutions, which are often characterized by "grindingly dull routine interrupted by occasional flashes of violence and brutality." The situation is even worse in facilities such as Folsom that are plagued by overcrowding. The prison, built in 1880, houses more than 4,000 inmates even though it was designed to hold only 2,065. According to one Folsom inmate, the daily frustrations born of such congestion are the main reason for the eruptions of violence. "Imagine you have to wait in line to relieve yourself or take a shower," he says. "Then watching someone crowd his way in." Adding to the discomfort is a "no frills" movement in public policy and prison management that has succeeded in removing all amenities from inmates' lives. Many state prisons ban weight lifting, televisions, radios, adult magazines, and conjugal visits. All states and the federal government have limited smoking in their correctional facilities and some institutions spend less than $2 a day per inmate on meals.

California's Folsom State Prison, shown here on a peaceful day, has been the site of several eruptions of violence and brutality in recent years. ZUMA Press/ Newscom

In "Folsom Prison Blues," country singer Johnny Cash told the story of a murderer who laments, "I know I can't be free," as he hears the whistle of a train passing outside his cell window.[1] Most inmates, however, will at some point "be free," following their release from incarceration. The Delancey Street Foundation, a self-supporting rehabilitation program headquartered about two hours south of Folsom State Prison in San Francisco, helps released prisoners adjust to their newfound freedom by offering them a place to live, job training, and employment at one of the businesses owned by the group. Roderick Davis, who has worked at the Delancey Street Restaurant for ten years since his release from prison, credits the foundation for accepting him despite "all the horrible and terrible things I've done in my life." He adds, "Nobody judged me because I did those things."[2]

In this chapter, we will look at the life of the imprisoned convict, starting with the realities of an existence behind bars and finishing with the challenges of returning to free society. Along the way, we will discuss violence in prison, correctional officers, women's prisons, the mechanics of release, and several other issues that are at the forefront of the American corrections system today. To start, we must understand the forces that shape prison culture and how those forces affect the overall operation of the correctional facility.

PRISON CULTURE

Any institution, whether a school, a bank, or a police department, has an organizational culture—a set of values that help the people in the organization understand what actions are acceptable and what actions are unacceptable. According **LO 1** to a theory put forth by the influential sociologist Erving Goffman, prison cultures are unique because prisons are total institutions that encompass every aspect of an inmate's life. Unlike a student or a bank teller, a prisoner cannot leave the institution or have any meaningful interaction with outside communities. Others arrange every aspect of daily life, and all prisoners are required to follow this schedule in the same manner.[3]

Inmates develop their own argot, or language (see Figure 14.1 below). They create their own economy, which, in the absence of currency, is based on the barter of valued items such as food, contraband, and sexual favors. They establish methods of determining power, many of which, as we shall see, involve violence. Isolated and heavily regulated, prisoners create a social existence that is, out of both necessity and design, separate from the outside world.

ADAPTING TO PRISON SOCIETY

On arriving at prison, each convict attends an orientation session and receives a "Resident's Handbook." The handbook provides information such as meal and official count times, disciplinary regulations, and visitation guidelines. The norms and values of the prison society, however, cannot be communicated by the staff or learned from a handbook. As first described by Donald Clemmer in his classic 1940 work, *The Prison Community,* the process of prisonization—or adaptation to the prison culture—advances as the inmate gradually understands what constitutes acceptable behavior in the institution, as defined not by the prison officials but by other inmates.[4]

In studying prisonization, criminologists have focused on two areas: how prisoners **LO 2** change their behavior to adapt to life behind bars, and how life behind bars has changed because of inmate behavior. Sociologist John Irwin has identified several patterns of inmate behavior, each one driven by the inmate's personality and values:

1. Professional criminals adapt to prison by "doing time." In other words, they follow the rules and generally do whatever is necessary to speed up their release and return to freedom.

> ## "One of the most amazing things about prisons is that they 'work' at all."
>
> **—Donald Ray Cressey,** American prison expert (1919–1987)

Total Institution An institution, such as a prison, that provides all of the necessities for existence to those who live within its boundaries.

Prisonization The socialization process through which a new inmate learns the accepted norms and values of the prison culture.

FIGURE 14.1 Prison Slang

Ace Another word for "dollar."

Bang A fight to the death, or shoot to kill.

Base head A cocaine addict.

B.G. "Baby gangster," or someone who has never shot another person.

Booty bandit An incarcerated sexual predator who preys on weaker inmates, called "punks."

Bug A correctional staff member, such as a psychiatrist, who is deemed untrustworthy or unreliable.

Bumpin' titties Fighting.

Catch cold To get killed.

Chiva Heroin.

Dancing on the blacktop Getting stabbed.

Diddler Child molester or pedophile.

Green light Prison gang term for a contract killing.

Hacks Correctional officers.

Jug-up Mealtime.

Lugger An inmate who smuggles in and possesses illegal substances.

Punk An inmate subject to rape, usually more submissive than most inmates.

Ride with To perform favors, including sexual favors, for a convict in return for protection or prison-store goods.

Shank Knife.

Tits-up An inmate who has died.

Topped Committed suicide.

Source: **www.insideprison.com/glossary.asp**.

2. Some convicts, mostly state-raised youths or those frequently incarcerated in juvenile detention centers, are more comfortable inside prison than outside. These inmates serve time by "jailing," or establishing themselves in the power structure of prison culture.

3. Other inmates take advantage of prison resources such as libraries or drug treatment programs by "gleaning," or working to improve themselves to prepare for a return to society.

4. Finally, "disorganized" criminals exist on the fringes of prison society. These inmates may have mental impairments or low levels of intelligence and find it impossible to adapt to prison culture on any level.[5]

The process of categorizing prisoners has a theoretical basis, but it serves a practical purpose as well, allowing administrators to reasonably predict how different inmates will act in certain situations. An inmate who is "doing time" generally does not present the same security risk as one who is "jailing."

WHO IS IN PRISON?

The culture of any prison is heavily influenced by its inmates. Their values, beliefs, and experiences will be reflected in the social order that exists behind bars. As we noted in the last chapter, the past three decades have seen incarceration rates of women and minority groups rise sharply. Furthermore, the arrest patterns of inmates have changed over that time period. A prisoner today is much more likely to have been incarcerated on a drug charge or immigration violation than was the case in the 1980s. Today's inmate is also more likely to behave violently behind bars—a situation that will be addressed shortly.

AN AGING INMATE POPULATION In recent years, the most significant demographic change in the prison population involves age. Though the majority of inmates are still under thirty-four years old, as you can see in Figure 14.2 on the left, the number of state and federal prisoners over the age of forty has increased dramatically since the mid-1990s. Several factors have contributed to this upsurge, including "get tough on crime" measures that impose mandatory sentences (discussed in Chapter 11), high rates of recidivism, higher levels of murder and sex crimes committed by older offenders, and the aging of the U.S. population as a whole.[6]

AN AILING INMATE POPULATION Given that older inmates will experience more health-related problems, prisons and jails are now housing more people with medical issues than in the past. The death rate for state prisoners dying because of poor health increased by 82 percent between 1991 and 2004.[7] About 40 percent of state and federal prisoners suffer from at least one form of illness other than a cold, the most common ailments being arthritis, hypertension, tuberculosis, and asthma.[8] Some states report rates of hepatitis C—an infectious, chronic disease of the liver—as high as 40 percent.[9]

Not surprisingly, corrections budgets are straining under the financial pressures caused by the

FIGURE 14.2 The Aging Prison Population

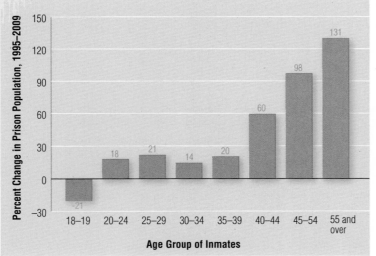

Sources: Bureau of Justice Statistics, *Prisoners in 2003* (Washington, D.C.: U.S. Department of Justice, November 2004), Table 10, page 8; Bureau of Justice Statistics, *Prisoners in 2009* (Washington, D.C.: U.S. Department of Justice, December 2010), Appendix table 13, page 27.

health-care needs of aging inmates. According to the American Civil Liberties Union, it costs three times as much to house an elderly inmate as that of a younger one.[10] In Oklahoma, where the number of prisoners aged fifty and older has increased from 85 to 3,952 over the past two decades, the state's correctional health-care budget nearly doubled between 2000 and 2010.[11] Though forced to cut back on education and social programs for the population at large, California allocates nearly $2 billion a year for sick inmates. These inmates include more than 1,300 prisoners who cost the state in excess of $100,000 per year for medical care each.[12] (The feature *A Question of Ethics—The Million-Dollar Man* below addresses the issue of whether the government is obliged to provide criminals with expensive medical care at taxpayers' expense.)

MENTAL ILLNESS BEHIND BARS Another factor in rising correctional health-care costs is the high incidence of mental illness in American prisons and jails. During the 1950s and 1960s, nearly 600,000 mental patients lived in public hospitals, often against their will. A series of scandals spotlighting the poor medical services and horrendous living conditions in these institutions led to their closure and the elimination of much of the nation's state-run mental health infrastructure.[13] Many mentally ill people now receive no supervision whatsoever, and some inevitably commit deviant or criminal acts.

As a result, in the words of criminal justice experts Katherine Stuart van Wormer and Clemens Bartollas, jails and prison have become "the dumping grounds for people whose bizarre behavior lands them behind bars."[14] Nationwide, 60 percent of jail inmates and 56 percent of state prisoners suffer from some form of mental illness.[15] For reasons that should become clear over the course of this chapter, correctional facilities are not designed to foster mental well-being, and indeed inmates with mental illnesses often find that their problems are exacerbated by the prison environment.[16]

Teaching Tip: Invite a local mental health professional to visit the classroom. Ask her or him to talk about the need for treatment after a diagnosis of mental illness. What does treatment involve? Do students feel that such treatment can be successfully administered in a correctional setting?

A QUESTION OF ETHICS: *The Million-Dollar Man*

Prisoner X is serving fourteen years in a California prison for robbery. He has fallen ill, and only a heart transplant will save his life. Although many Americans who need organ transplants cannot afford such an expensive procedure, the California Department of Corrections is considering whether to spend more than $1 million for Prisoner X's operation and recovery.

THE ETHICAL DILEMMA At the time Prisoner X fell ill, more than 4,100 names were on the national waiting list for a new heart. Many California taxpayers—who would ultimately pay for Prisoner X's operation—were outraged that a convicted criminal could receive a new heart before other, law-abiding patients. In 1976, however, the United States Supreme Court ruled that prisoners have a right to "adequate" medical care, which has been interpreted to mean the same level of care they would receive if they were not behind bars. According to Michael A. Grodin, director of medical ethics at the Boston University School of

Medicine and Public Health, "[B]ecause someone is incarcerated, we have a higher obligation to provide them with health care because we have deprived them of their liberty." As the wife of a patient who was below Prisoner X on the heart transplant waiting list put it, "Since when is it unethical to save someone's life?"

WHAT IS THE SOLUTION? A number of states do not provide their prisoners with organ transplants or will do so only if the prisoner can pay for the operation. What should California do with Prisoner X?* What options do state prison officials have if they decide not to cover the costs of the transplant? Would it be ethical to release Prisoner X or any other inmate simply to avoid the burden of his or her medical bills?

*In the actual case, California did provide Prisoner X with a new heart, but his body rejected the transplanted organ and he died within a year.

REHABILITATION AND PRISON PROGRAMS

In Chapter 11, we saw that rehabilitation is one of the basic theoretical justifications for punishment. **Prison programs,** which include any organized activities designed to foster rehabilitation, benefit inmates in several ways. On a basic level, these programs get prisoners out of their cells and alleviate the boredom that marks prison and jail life. The programs also help inmates improve their health and skills, giving them a better chance of reintegration into society after release. Consequently, nearly every federal and state prison in the United States offers some form of rehabilitation.[17]

Prison programs are limited, however. Many inmates suffering from mental illness would benefit from medication and twenty-four-hour psychiatric care. Yet these services are quite rare behind bars, mostly due to their high costs.[18] In addition, as many state prison systems face budget restraints, rehabilitation programs are increasingly subject to a *cost-benefit* analysis. In other words, for each dollar spent on a program, how many dollars are saved? These savings can be difficult to calculate, but researchers have become skilled at measuring reductions in future criminal behavior—and the costs such behavior would have imposed on society—to determine the usefulness of prison programs.

SUBSTANCE ABUSE TREATMENT As we have seen throughout this textbook, there is a strong link between crime and abuse of drugs and alcohol. According to the National Center on Addiction and Substance Abuse (CASA) at New York's Columbia University, 1.5 million prison and jail inmates in the United States meet the medical criteria for substance abuse or addiction. Also according to CASA, only 11 percent of these inmates have received any type of professional treatment behind bars.[19] The most effective substance abuse programs for prisoners require trained staff, lengthy periods of therapy, expensive medication, and community aftercare, but such programs carry a price tag of nearly $10,000 per inmate. If every eligible prisoner in the United States received such treatment, the cost would be $12.6 billion. Researchers at CASA contend, however, that "the nation would break even in a year" if just one in ten of these inmates remained substance and crime free and employed for one year after release from prison.[20]

VOCATIONAL AND EDUCATIONAL PROGRAMS Even if an ex-convict does stay substance free, he or she will have a difficult time finding a steady paycheck. Employers are only about half as likely to hire job applicants with criminal records as they are those with "clean sheets."[21] To overcome this handicap, more than half of all American prisons offer *vocational* training, or prison programs that provide inmates with skills necessary to find a job. The California Institute for Men at Chino, for example, gives certain convicts the chance to complete a program in commercial diving. Nine out of ten prisons also attempt to educate their inmates, offering literacy training, GED (general equivalency degree) programs, and other types of instruction.[22]

Some evidence suggests that such efforts can have a positive effect on rates of reoffending. The Arkansas Department of Corrections figures that GED programs in its jails have cut the state's recidivism rate by 8 percent.[23] Only about 6 percent of the commercial divers from Chino return to prison within three years, compared with California's 70 percent overall recidivism rate.[24] Proponents of such efforts also point to their potential financial benefits. Researchers at the Washington State Institute for Public Policy estimate that every $1,182 spent for inmate vocational training saves $6,806 in future criminal justice costs and that every $962 spent on inmate education saves $5,306 in future criminal justice costs.[25]

Prison culture is different from the cultures of schools or workplaces because prison is a _____ _____ that dominates every aspect of the inmate's life. Inmates create their own _____, or language, and develop their own _____ based on bartering food, contraband, and sexual favors. In recent decades, the prison culture has been affected by the increased average _____ of inmates, which has led to skyrocketing _____-_____ costs for federal and state corrections systems. Prison programs such as substance abuse treatment and _____ training, which helps improve inmates' job skills, are often justified by _____-benefit analyses.

PRISON VIOLENCE

Prisons and jails are dangerous places to live. Prison culture is predicated on violence—one observer calls the modern institution an "unstable and violent jungle."[26] Prison guards use the threat of violence (and, at times, its reality) to control the inmate population. Sometimes, the inmates strike back. Each year, federal correctional officers are subjected to about eighty assaults and 1,500 less serious attacks such as shoving and pushing.[27] Among the prisoners, violence is used to establish power and dominance. On occasion, this violence leads to death. About fifty-five inmates in state prisons and twenty-five inmates in local jails are murdered by fellow inmates each year.[28] (Note, though, that this homicide rate is lower than the national average.) With nothing but time on their hands, prisoners have been known to fashion deadly weapons out of everyday items such as toothbrushes and mop handles.

VIOLENCE IN PRISON CULTURE

LO 3 Until the 1970s, prison culture emphasized "noninterference" and did not support inmate-on-inmate violence. Prison "elders" would themselves punish any of their peers who showed a proclivity toward assaulting fellow inmates. Today, in contrast, violence is used to establish the prisoner hierarchy by separating the powerful from the weak. Humboldt State University's Lee H. Bowker has identified several other reasons for violent behavior:

- It provides a deterrent against being victimized, as a reputation for violence may eliminate an inmate as a target of assault.
- It enhances self-image in an environment that does not respect other attributes, such as intelligence.
- In the case of rape, it gives sexual relief.
- It serves as a means of acquiring material goods through extortion or outright robbery.[29]

The **deprivation model** can be used to explain the high level of prison violence. According to this model, the stressful and oppressive conditions of prison life lead to aggressive behavior on the part of inmates. Prison researcher Stephen C. Light found that when conditions such as overcrowding worsen, inmate misconduct often increases.[30] In these circumstances, the violent behavior may not have any express purpose—it may just be a means of relieving tension.

RIOTS

The deprivation model is helpful, though less convincing, in searching for the roots of collective violence. As far back as the 1930s, sociologist Frank Tannenbaum noted that harsh prison conditions can cause tension to build among inmates until it eventually

Critical Thinking Skill Development: Ask students to work together to discuss violence in prison. Why is violence so prevalent within correctional facilities? With those causes in mind, how can violence in prison be limited, if not prevented? (LO 3)

Deprivation Model A theory that inmate aggression is the result of the frustration inmates feel at being deprived of freedom, consumer goods, sex, and other staples of life outside the institution.

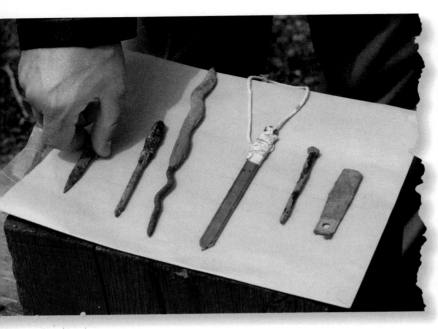

A correctional official displays a set of homemade knives, also known as *shivs,* made by inmates at Attica Correctional Facility in Attica, New York. What are some of the reasons that violence flourishes behind bars?
AP Photo/David Duprey

Relative Deprivation The theory that inmate aggression is caused when freedoms and services that the inmate has come to accept as normal are decreased or eliminated.

"I've seen seven stabbings, about six bashings, and three self-mutilations. Two hangings, one attempted hanging, any number of overdoses. And that's only me, in just seventy days."

—Anonymous jail inmate

explodes in the form of mass violence.[31] Living conditions among prisons are fairly constant, however, so how can the seemingly spontaneous outbreak of prison riots be explained?

LOSS OF INSTITUTIONAL CONTROL

Researchers have addressed the seeming randomness of prison violence by turning to the concept of relative deprivation. These theories focus on the gap between what is expected in a certain situation and what is achieved. Criminologist Peter C. Kratcoski has argued that because prisoners enjoy such meager privileges to begin with, any further deprivation can spark disorder.[32] A number of prison experts have noted that collective violence occurs in response to heightened measures of security at corrections facilities.[33] Thus, the violence occurs in response to an additional reduction in freedom for inmates, who enjoy very little freedom to begin with.

Riots, which have been defined as situations in which a number of prisoners are beyond institutional control for a significant amount of time, are relatively rare. Because of their explosive nature and potential for high casualties, however, riots have a unique ability to focus public attention on prison conditions. The collective violence that took place in 1971 at the Attica Correctional Facility in upstate New York has been described as a turning point in the history of American corrections. A media event, it alerted citizens to the situation in correctional facilities and spurred the prisoners' rights movement.[34]

THE SPECTRUM OF VIOLENCE The Attica prison riot lasted five days in September 1971. Nearly half of the institution's 2,500 inmates seized control of most of the prison, holding thirty-eight correctional officers as hostages. In large measure, the riot was a reaction to the punitive atmosphere in Attica. During negotiations to end the standoff, one inmate complained, "We are men, we are not beasts and we will not be beaten or driven as such."[35] The talks ended abruptly when New York state troopers raided the prison grounds, killing thirty-nine inmates and wounding eighty-eight others. In the wake of the riot, however, New York governor Nelson Rockefeller called for "radical reforms" in the state's corrections system, and twenty-four of the prisoners' original demands for such improvements as better food, more programs, and due process for disciplinary action were met.

The Attica riot has, however, proved to be the exception to the rule. Most riots are disorganized, and the participants have no political agenda. The incidents are marked by extreme levels of inmate-on-inmate violence and can often be attributed, at least in part, to poor living conditions and inadequate prison administration. The worst disturbance in the past forty years, for example, took place at the Penitentiary of New Mexico in Santa Fe in 1980. Prisoners killed thirty-three of their fellow inmates, and nearly two hundred others were tortured, beaten, and raped. The levels of violence—including the use of blowtorches on genitals—

shocked the public. Two weeks *before* the riot, an outside consultant had warned that New Mexico prison officials were playing "Russian roulette with the lives of inmates" by failing to properly staff and train the personnel at the state's penal institutions.[36]

ISSUES OF RACE AND ETHNICITY

The night before the Attica riot erupted, inmates yelled, "[G]et a good night's sleep, whitey. Sleep tight, because tomorrow's the day." Officers in the prison were known to refer to their batons as "nigger sticks."[37] Race plays a major role in prison life, and prison violence is often an outlet for racial tension. As prison populations have changed over the past three decades, with African Americans and Hispanics becoming the majority in many penal institutions, issues of race and ethnicity have become increasingly important to prison administrators and researchers.

SEPARATE WORLDS As early as the 1950s, researchers were noticing different group structures in inmate life. At that time, for example, prisoners at California's Soledad Prison informally segregated themselves according to geography as well as race: Tejanos (Mexicans raised in Texas), Chicanos, blacks from California, blacks from the South and Southwest, and the majority whites all formed separate social worlds.[38]

Leo Carroll, professor of sociology at the University of Rhode Island, has written extensively about how today's prisoners are divided into hostile groups, with race determining nearly every aspect of an inmate's life, including friends, job assignments, and cell location.[39] Carroll's research has also shown how minority groups in prison have seized on race to help form their prison identities.[40]

PRISON SEGREGATION More than four decades ago, the United States Supreme Court put an end to the widespread practice of **prison segregation,** under which correctional officials would place inmates in cells or blocks with those of a similar race or ethnicity.[41] According to the Supreme Court, prison segregation was unconstitutional because government officials were discriminating against individuals based on their skin color. Years after this ruling, however, the California Department of Corrections began implementing an unwritten policy of putting all new and transferred male inmates in cells with inmates of the same race or ethnicity for the first sixty days of incarceration. The goal of this policy was to determine if an inmate was a member of a race-based gang before allowing him to live in integrated quarters.

In 2005, the Supreme Court struck down California's version of prison segregation.[42] The Court did, however, leave prison officials with an "out." They can still segregate prisoners in an "emergency situation."[43] Thus, a year after the decision, when more than two thousand African American and Hispanic inmates at the Pitchless Detention Center in Castaic, California, battled each other for several hours, temporary segregation of the two groups was deemed justified under the circumstances. Even so, segregation proved to be only a short-term remedy. A week later Hispanic inmates threw bunk beds and other items at their African American counterparts in a dayroom in the nearby Los Angeles Men's Central Jail, sparking a disturbance that resulted in the death of a black inmate. As one observer pointed out, racial segregation "will never solve the underlying problems in L.A. County's jails."[44]

PRISON GANGS AND SECURITY THREAT GROUPS (STGS)

In many instances, racial and ethnic identification is the primary focus of the **prison gang**—a clique of inmates who join together in an organizational structure. Gang affiliation is often the cause of inmate-on-inmate violence. Folsom State Prison, discussed

Technology Tip: Have students learn more about what went wrong prior to the Penitentiary of New Mexico prison riot in 1980 online at **www.newmexicohistory.org/filedetails.php?fileID=451**.

Prison Segregation The practice of separating inmates based on a certain characteristic, such as age, gender, type of crime committed, or race.
Prison Gang A group of inmates who band together within the corrections system to engage in social and criminal activities.

Critical Thinking Skill Analysis: Ask students to discuss the role that race plays in prison culture. What effect does race have on inmate behavior? What impact does it have on the management of corrections facilities?

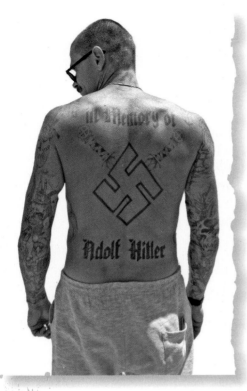

A member of the Aryan Brotherhood in California's Calipatria State Prison. This particular prison gang espouses white supremacy, but for the most part its leadership focuses on illegal activities such as extortion and drug trafficking. Why might an inmate join a prison gang?
Mark Allen Johnson/ZUMA

Security Threat Group (STG) A group of three or more inmates who engage in activity that poses a threat to the safety of other inmates or the prison staff.

Group Activities: Divide the class into groups and have each group prepare an intelligence report on one of the gangs listed in Figure 14.3 on the next page. If time allows, have each group present its report to the class.

in the opening of this chapter, is plagued by various gangs such as the Mexican Mafia, composed of U.S.-born inmates of Mexican descent, and their enemies, a spin-off organization called La Nuestra Familia.

In part, the prison gang is a natural result of life in the modern prison. As one expert says of these gangs:

> Their members have done in prison what many people do elsewhere when they feel personally powerless, threatened, and vulnerable. They align themselves with others, organize to fight back, and enhance their own status and control through their connection to a more powerful group.[45]

In addition to their important role in the social structure of correctional facilities, prison gangs participate in a wide range of illegal economic activities within these institutions, including prostitution, drug selling, gambling, and loan sharking. A study released in 2011 by Alan J. Drury and Matt DeLisi of Iowa State University found that gang members were more likely to be involved in prison misconduct than those offenders who had been convicted of murder.[46]

THE PREVALENCE OF PRISON GANGS Recent research places the rate of gang membership at 11.7 percent in federal prisons, 13.4 percent in state prisons, and 15.6 percent in jails.[47] When the National Gang Crime Research Center surveyed prison administrators, however, almost 95 percent said that gang recruitment took place at their institutions, so the overall prevalence of gangs is probably much higher.[48] Los Angeles correctional officials believe that eight out of every ten inmates in their city jails are gang affiliated.

In many instances, prison gangs are extensions of street gangs. Indeed, investigators believe leaders of the Mexican Mafia put out a contract for (green lighted) the violence in the Los Angeles jails discussed earlier in retaliation for an attack that took place on the city streets. Though the stereotypical gang is composed of African Americans or Hispanics, the majority of large prisons also have white, or "Aryan," gangs. One of the largest federal capital prosecutions in U.S. history, involving thirty-two counts of murder, focused on a major prison gang known as the Aryan Brotherhood. (See Figure 14.3 on the facing page.)

COMBATING PRISON GANGS In their efforts to combat the influence of prison gangs, over the past decade correctional officials have increasingly turned to the security threat group (STG) model. Generally speaking, an STG is an identifiable group of three or more individuals who pose a threat to the safety of other inmates or members of the corrections community.[49] About two-thirds of all prisons have a correctional officer who acts as an STG coordinator.[50] This official is responsible for determining groups of individuals (not necessarily members of a prison gang) that qualify as STGs and taking appropriate measures. In many instances, these measures are punitive. Prison officials, for example, have reduced overall levels of violence significantly by putting gang members in solitary confinement, away from the general prison population. Treatment philosophies also have a place in these strategies. New York prison administrators have increased group therapy and anger-management classes for STGs, a decision they credit for low murder rates in their state prisons.[51]

PRISON RAPE

In contrast to riots, the problem of sexual assault in prisons receives very little attention from media sources. This can be partly attributed to the ambiguity of the subject. The occurrence of rape in prisons and jails is undisputed, but determining exactly how

FIGURE 14.3 **The Top Prison Gangs in the United States**

Certain prison gangs, such as the Crips and the Bloods, are offshoots of street gangs and gained influence behind bars because so many of their members have been incarcerated. Others, such as the Aryan Brotherhood and the Mexican Mafia, formed in prison and expanded to the streets. Listed here are seven of the most dangerous gangs operating in the American prison system today.

Aryan Brotherhood

White

Origins: Prison gang, formed in San Quentin State Prison in 1967, as white protection against blacks.

Allies: Mexican Mafia

Rivals: Black Guerrilla Family

Signs/Symbols: Swastika, SS Lightning bolts, numbers "666" (Satan, evil) and "88" (to signify the eighth letter of the alphabet, or HH), HH for "Heil Hitler," letters "AB," shamrock (a symbol of their original Irish membership), Nordic dagger on shield with lightning bolts.

Black Guerrilla Family

African American

Origins: Prison gang, founded by incarcerated Black Panthers in San Quentin State Prison in the mid-1960s.

Allies: La Nuestra Familia

Rivals: Aryan Brotherhood

Signs/Symbols: Crossed sabers, machetes, rifles, shotguns with the letters "B G F." A black dragon squeezing the life out of a prison guard by a prison tower.

Bloods

African American

Origins: Street gang, formed in Los Angeles in the 1960s, as a defense against the Crips.

Allies: People Nation (Chicago gang), La Nuestra Familia

Rivals: Crips, Aryan Brotherhood

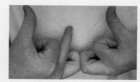

Signs/Symbols: The color red, red bandannas or rags, the word "Piru" (the original Blood gang), crossed-out "c" in words as disrespect for Crips, other anti-Crip graffiti, hand signal spells "blood."

Crips

African American

Origins: Street gang, formed in the Central Avenue area of Los Angeles in the late 1960s.

Allies: Black Guerrilla Family, La Nuestra Familia

Rivals: Bloods, Aryan Brotherhood, Vice Lords

Signs/Symbols: The color blue, blue bandannas and rags, use the letter "c" in place of "b" in writing as disrespect for Bloods, calling each other "Cuzz," calling themselves "Blood Killas" (BK), wearing British Knight (BK) tennis shoes.

Mexican Mafia (EMC)

Mexican American/Hispanic

Origins: Prison gang, formed in Los Angeles in the Deuel Vocational Institution in the late 1950s. Foot soldiers and related Southern California street gangs are called Sureños.

Allies: Aryan Brotherhood

Rivals: Black Guerrilla Family, La Nuestra Familia

Signs/Symbols: The national symbol of Mexico, an eagle and a snake, on a flaming circle, lying on crossed knives. The color blue, the number 13.

Mara Salvatrucha 13 (MS-13)

Hispanic

Origins: Largest street gang in North America, originated in El Salvador and formed in Los Angeles in the 1980s.

Allies: Mexican Mafia

Rivals: MS-18 (LA gang)

Yuri Cortez/AFP/Getty Images

Signs/Symbols: Most Mara Salvatrucha members are covered in tattoos, even on their faces. Common markings include "MS," "13," "Salvadorian Pride," "Devil Horns."

La Nuestra Familia

Mexican American/ Hispanic

Origins: Prison gang, formed in Soledad Prison in the late 1960s, as a reaction to the Mexican Mafia. Based in Northern California, foot soldiers outside of prison are called Norteños.

Allies: Black Guerrilla Family, Bloods, Crips

Rivals: Mexican Mafia, Mara Salvatrucha

Signs/Symbols: Large tattoos, often on the entire back. The initials NF, LNF, ENE, and F. The number 14 for "N," the fourteenth letter in the alphabet, stands for Norte or Norteño. The color red, Nebraska cornhuskers' caps with the letter N. A sombrero with a dagger is a common NF symbol.

Sources: "Gangs or Us," at **www.gangsorus.com/index.html**; and "Prison Gang Profiles," at **www.insideprison.com/prison_gang_profiles.asp**.

widespread the problem is has proved difficult. Prison officials, aware that any sexual contact is prohibited in most penal institutions, are often unwilling to provide realistic figures for fear of negative publicity. Even when they are willing, they may be unable to do so. Most inmates are ashamed of being rape victims and refuse to report sexual assaults.

Consequently, it has been difficult to come up with consistent statistics for sexual assault in prison. Three surveys conducted by federal researchers, for example, provided widely disparate estimates for the number of prison and jail inmates sexually abused in 2008. The first counted 7,444; the second, 90,000; and the third, 216,600.[52]

Whatever the figures, prison rape, like all rape, is considered primarily an act of violence rather than sex. Inmates subject to rape ("punks") are near the bottom of the prison power structure and, in some instances, may accept rape by one particularly powerful inmate in return for protection from others.[53] Abused inmates often suffer from rape trauma syndrome and a host of other psychological ailments, including suicidal tendencies. Many prisons do not offer sufficient medical treatment for rape victims, nor does the prison staff take the necessary measures to protect obvious targets of rape—young, slightly built, nonviolent offenders. Furthermore, correctional officials are rarely held responsible for inmate-on-inmate violence.

SELFASSESSMENT

Fill in the blanks and check your answers on page 497.

Some researchers rely on the _____ model, which focuses on the stressful and oppressive conditions of incarceration, to explain general prison violence. The concept of _____ _____, based on the gap between an inmate's expectations and reality, is used to explain the conditions that lead to prison riots. The strategy of prison _____, in which officials assign inmates of different races to separate living areas, has been used at times to control violence started by prison _____, or criminal organizations that operate behind bars.

CORRECTIONAL OFFICERS AND DISCIPLINE

Ideally, the presence of correctional officers—the standard term used to describe prison guards—has the effect of lessening violence in American correctional institutions. Practically speaking, this is indeed the case. Without correctional officers, the prison would be a place of anarchy. But in the highly regulated, oppressive environment of the prison, correctional officers must use the threat of violence, if not actual violence, to instill discipline and keep order. Thus, the relationship between prison staff and inmates is marked by mutual distrust. Consider the two following statements, the first made by a correctional officer and the second by a prisoner:

> [My job is to] protect, feed, and try to educate scum who raped and brutalized women and children . . . who, if I turn my back, will go into their cell, wrap a blanket around their cellmate's legs, and threaten to beat or rape him if he doesn't give sex, carry contraband, or fork over radios, money, or other goods willingly. And they'll stick a shank in me tomorrow if they think they can get away with it.[54]

> The pigs in the state and federal prisons . . . treat me so violently, I cannot possibly imagine a time I could ever have anything but the deepest, aching, searing hatred for them. I can't begin to tell you what they do to me. If I were weaker by a hair, they would destroy me.[55]

It may be difficult for an outsider to understand the emotions that fuel such sentiments. French philosopher Michel Foucault points out that discipline, both in prison and in the general community, is a means of social organization as well as punishment.[56] Discipline is imposed when a person behaves in a manner that is contrary to the values of the

Teaching Tip: If possible, invite a correctional officer to visit the classroom. Ask her or him to describe a typical day on the job. How does the officer deal with the constant threat of violence from the prison population?

dominant social group. Correctional officers and inmates have different concepts of the ideal structure of prison society, and, as the two quotations just cited demonstrate, this conflict generates intense feelings of fear and hatred, which often lead to violence.

RANK AND DUTIES OF CORRECTIONAL OFFICERS

After local officials shut down the Montague County (Texas) Jail several years ago because it had become something of an "Animal House" behind bars, much of the blame fell on the custodial staff. Security at the facility had become lax, to put it mildly. With little interference, inmates were allowed to have sex with their girlfriends, bring in comfortable furniture from home, take drugs, and chat on cell phones.

To avoid such problems, correctional facilities generally provide their employees with clearly delineated ranks and duties. The custodial staff at most prisons, for example, is organized according to four general ranks—captain, lieutenant, sergeant, and officer. In keeping with the militaristic model, captains are primarily administrators who deal directly with the warden on custodial issues. Lieutenants are the disciplinarians of the prison, responsible for policing and transporting the inmates. Sergeants oversee platoons of officers in specific parts of the prison, such as various cell blocks or work spaces.

Lucien X. Lombardo, professor of sociology and criminal justice at Old Dominion University, has identified six general job categories among correctional officers:[57]

1. *Block officers.* These employees supervise cell blocks containing as many as four hundred inmates, as well as the correctional officers on block guard duty. In general, the block officer is responsible for the well-being of the inmates. He or she makes sure the inmates do not harm themselves or other prisoners and also acts as something of a camp counselor, dispensing advice and seeing that inmates understand and follow the rules of the facility.

LO 4

2. *Work detail supervisors.* In many penal institutions, the inmates work in the cafeteria, the prison store, the laundry, and other areas. Work detail supervisors oversee small groups of inmates as they perform their tasks.

3. *Industrial shop and school officers.* These officers perform maintenance and security functions in workshop and educational programs. Their primary responsibility is to make sure that inmates are on time for these programs and do not cause any disturbances during the sessions.

4. *Yard officers.* Officers who work the prison yard usually have the least seniority, befitting the assignment's reputation as dangerous and stressful. These officers must be constantly on alert for breaches in prison discipline or regulations in the relatively unstructured environment of the prison yard.

5. *Tower guards.* These officers spend their entire shifts, which usually last eight hours, in isolated, silent posts high above the grounds of the facility. Although

In high-security prisons, correctional officers such as these two at the supermax prison in Tamms, Illinois, monitor even the most mundane of inmate activities, including working, exercising, eating, and showering. How might this constant surveillance contribute to tension between correctional officers and prisoners?
John Smierciak/MCT/Landov

Technology Tip: Ask students to go online to locate job postings for prison or jail personnel. Students are encouraged to locate as many different positions in as many different kinds of corrections facilities as possible. Have them compile their lists for a greater understanding of the scope of employment opportunities in the field of corrections. (LO 4)

The **U.S. Department of Labor** offers information about a career as a correctional officer. Find its Web site by visiting the *Criminal Justice CourseMate* at **cengagebrain. com** and selecting the *Web links* for this chapter.

their only means of communication are walkie-talkies or cellular devices, the safety benefits of the position can outweigh the loneliness that comes with the job.

6. *Administrative building assignments.* Officers who hold these positions provide security at prison gates, oversee visitation procedures, act as liaisons for civilians, and handle administrative tasks such as processing the paperwork when an inmate is transferred from another institution.

CJ&TECHNOLOGY — Cell Phones behind Bars

AP Photo/Mel Evans, File

Just because Justin Walker was incarcerated, he wasn't about to go offline. Walker, serving a thirty-year sentence at the Oklahoma State Penitentiary in Granite for killing a sheriff, took several photos of himself with a cell phone. One showed him licking a shank. Another featured him smoking a joint while holding a bag of marijuana and a bottle of liquor. Although controversy erupted in December 2010 after Walker managed to post these photos on Facebook, his technological misconduct was relatively benign. Other inmates have planned escapes, coordinated drug deals, organized prison riots, and even ordered murders, all via cell phone.

Of course, prison and jail inmates are not allowed to have cell phones. Still, California correctional officers confiscated nearly nine thousand cell phones from prisoners in 2010, and nearly every correctional facility in the country struggles to keep them out of the hands of inmates. Attempts to combat the problem with cell phone–sniffing dogs and "managed access," which limits the transmission of calls from prison grounds, have been only marginally successful in solving the problem. "[Cell phones] are everywhere," complains Maryland prison administrator Carl Harmon.

THINKING ABOUT CELL PHONES BEHIND BARS
In recent years, more and more inmates are smuggling smartphones into prisons and jails, thereby gaining access to the Internet. Why would one security expert say, "The smartphone is the most lethal weapon you can get inside a prison"?

DISCIPLINE

As Erving Goffman noted in his essay on the "total institution," in the general society adults are rarely placed in a position where they are "punished" as a child would be.[58] Therefore, the strict disciplinary measures imposed on prisoners come as something of a shock and can provoke strong defensive reactions. Correctional officers who must deal with these responses often find that disciplining inmates is the most difficult and stressful aspect of their job.

Critical Thinking Skill Development: Ask students to respond to "Questions for Critical Analysis" number two on page 497, in which they debate the appropriateness of various disciplinary techniques in prisons.

SANCTIONING PRISONERS As mentioned earlier, one of the first things that an inmate receives on entering a correctional facility is a manual that details the rules of the prison or jail, along with the punishment that will result from rule violations. These handbooks can be quite lengthy—running one hundred pages in some instances—and specific. Not only will a prison manual prohibit obvious misconduct such as violent or sexual activity, gambling, and possession of drugs or currency, but it also addresses matters of daily life such as personal hygiene, dress codes, and conduct during meals.

Correctional officers enforce the prison rules in much the same way that a highway patrol officer enforces traffic regulations. For a minor violation, the inmate may be "let off easy" with a verbal warning. More serious infractions will result in a "ticket," or a report forwarded to the institution's disciplinary committee.[59] The disciplinary committee generally includes several correctional officers and, in some instances, outside citizens or even inmates. Although, as we shall see, the United States Supreme Court has ruled that an inmate must be given a "fair hearing" before being disciplined,[60] in reality he or she has very little ability to challenge the committee's decision. Depending on the seriousness of the violation, sanctions can range from a loss of privileges such as visits from family members to the unpleasantness of solitary confinement, discussed in the previous chapter.

USE OF FORCE Most correctional officers prefer to rely on the "you scratch my back and I'll scratch yours" model for controlling inmates. In other words, as long as the prisoner makes a reasonable effort to conform to institutional rules, the correctional officer will refrain from taking disciplinary steps. Of course, the staff-inmate relationship is not always marked by cooperation, and correctional officers often find themselves in situations where they must use force.

Legitimate Security Interests Generally, courts have been unwilling to put too many restrictions on the use of force by correctional officers. As we saw with police officers in Chapter 6, correctional officers are given great leeway to use their experience to determine when force is warranted. In *Whitley v. Albers* (1986),[61] the Supreme Court held that the use of force by prison officials violates an inmate's Eighth Amendment protections only if the force amounts to "the unnecessary and wanton infliction of pain." Excessive force can be considered "necessary" if the legitimate security interests of the penal institution are at stake. Consequently, an appeals court ruled that when officers at a Maryland prison formed an "extraction team" to remove the leader of a riot from his cell, beating him in the process, the use of force was justified given the situation.[62]

In general, courts have found that the "legitimate security interests" of a prison or jail justify the use of force when the correctional officer is[63]

1. Acting in self-defense.
2. Acting to defend the safety of a third person, such as a member of the prison staff or another inmate.
3. Upholding the rules of the institution.
4. Preventing a crime such as assault, destruction of property, or theft.
5. Preventing an escape effort.

In addition, most prisons and jails have written policies that spell out the situations in which their employees may use force against inmates.

The "Malicious and Sadistic" Standard The judicial system has not, however, given correctional officers total freedom of discretion to apply force. In *Hudson v. McMillan* (1992),[64] the Supreme Court ruled that minor injuries suffered by a convict at the hands of a correctional officer following an argument did violate the inmate's rights, because there was no security concern at the time of the incident. In other words, the issue is

Discussion Tip: Ask students to reflect on the use of force in prisons. According to the Supreme Court, when does the use of force by correctional officers become excessive?

About a quarter of the security staff at Sing Sing Correctional Facility in Ossining, New York—shown here—are women. What are some of the challenges that face female correctional officers who work in a men's maximum security prison?. Susan Farley/*New York Times*/Redux Pictures

Critical Thinking Skill Development: Ask students to debate the placement of female correctional officers in men's prisons. What are the advantages and potential disadvantages of these placements?

"Hands-Off" Doctrine The unwritten judicial policy that favors noninterference by the courts in the administration of prisons and jails.

not *how much* force was used, but whether the officer used the force as part of a good faith effort to restore discipline or acted "maliciously and sadistically" to cause harm. This "malicious and sadistic" standard has been difficult for aggrieved prisoners to meet: in the ten years following the *Hudson* decision, only about 20 percent of excessive force lawsuits against correctional officials were successful.[65]

FEMALE CORRECTIONAL OFFICERS

Security concerns were the main reason that, for many years, prison administrators refused to hire women as correctional officers in men's prisons. The consensus was that women were not physically strong enough to subdue violent male inmates and that their mere presence in the predominantly masculine prison world would cause disciplinary break-downs.[66] As a result, in the 1970s a number of women brought lawsuits against state corrections systems, claiming that they were being discriminated against on the basis of their gender. For the most part, these legal actions were successful in opening the doors to men's prisons for female correctional officers (and vice versa).[67] Today, more than 150,000 women work in correctional facilities, many of them in constant close contact with male inmates.[68]

As it turns out, female correctional officers have proved just as effective as their male counterparts in maintaining discipline in men's prisons.[69] Furthermore, evidence shows that women prison staff can have a calming influence on male inmates, thus lowering levels of prison violence.[70] The primary problem caused by women working in male prisons, it seems, involves sexual misconduct. According to the federal government, nearly 60 percent of prison staff members who engage in sexual misconduct are female, suggesting a disturbing amount of consensual sex with inmates.[71] As we will see in the next section, similar issues exist between male correctional officers and female inmates, though in those cases the sexual contact is much more likely to be coerced.

PROTECTING PRISONERS' RIGHTS

The general attitude of the law toward inmates is summed up by the Thirteenth Amendment to the U.S. Constitution:

> Neither slavery nor involuntary servitude, except as a punishment for crime whereof the party shall have been duly convicted, shall exist within the United States.

In other words, inmates do not have the same guaranteed rights as other Americans. For most of the nation's history, courts have followed the spirit of this amendment by applying the **"hands-off" doctrine** of prisoner law. This (unwritten) doctrine assumes that the care of inmates should be left to prison officials and that it is not the place of judges to intervene in penal administrative matters.

LO 5

At the same time, the United States Supreme Court has stated that "[t]here is no iron curtain between the Constitution and the prisons of this country."[72] Consequently, like so many other areas of the criminal justice system, the treatment of prisoners is based on a balancing act—here, between the rights of prisoners and the security needs the correctional institutions. Of course, as just noted, inmates do not have the same civil rights as do other members of society. In 1984, for example, the Supreme Court ruled that arbitrary searches of prison cells are allowed under the Fourth Amendment because inmates have no reasonable expectation of privacy[73] (see pages 226–227 for a review of this expectation).

THE "DELIBERATE INDIFFERENCE" STANDARD As for those constitutional rights that inmates do retain, in 1976 the Supreme Court established the "deliberate indifference" standard. In the case in question, *Estelle v. Gamble*,[74] an inmate had claimed to be the victim of medical malpractice. In his majority opinion, Justice Thurgood Marshall wrote that prison officials violated a convict's Eighth Amendment rights if they "deliberately" failed to provide him or her with necessary medical care. At the time, the decision was hailed as a victory for prisoners' rights, and it continues to ensure that a certain level of health care is provided. Defining "deliberate" has proved difficult, however. Does it mean that prison officials "should have known" that an inmate was placed in harm's way, or does it mean that officials purposefully placed the inmate in that position?

The Supreme Court seems to have taken the latter position. In *Wilson v. Seiter* (1991),[75] for example, inmate Pearly L. Wilson filed a lawsuit alleging that certain conditions of his confinement—including overcrowding; excessive noise; inadequate heating, cooling, and ventilation; and unsanitary bathroom and dining facilities—were cruel and unusual. The Court ruled against Wilson, stating that he had failed to prove that these conditions, even if they existed, were the result of "deliberate indifference" on the part of prison officials.

"IDENTIFIABLE HUMAN NEEDS" In its *Wilson* decision, the Supreme Court created the "identifiable human needs" standard for determining Eighth Amendment violations. The Court asserted that a prisoner must show that the institution has denied her or him a basic need such as food, warmth, or exercise.[76] The Court mentioned only these three needs, however, forcing the lower courts to determine for themselves what other needs, if any, fall into this category. In 2011, the Court finally revisited the question of cruel and unusual prison conditions with its *Brown v. Plata* decision.[77] In that ruling, the Court asserted that the overcrowding of California's state prisons was so severe that it denied inmates satisfactory levels of mental and physical health care. As a result, California will have to transfer or release 33,000 inmates by mid-2013.

THE FIRST AMENDMENT IN PRISON The First Amendment reads, in part, that the federal government "shall make no law respecting an establishment of religion, or prohibiting the free exercise thereof; or abridging the freedom of speech." In the 1970s, the prisoners' rights movement forced open the "iron curtain" to allow the First Amendment behind bars. In 1974, for example, the Supreme Court held that prison officials can censor inmate mail only if doing so is necessary to maintain prison security.[78] The decade also saw court decisions protecting inmates' access to group worship, instruction by clergy, special dietary requirements, religious publications, and other aspects of both mainstream and nonmainstream religions.[79]

Judges will limit some of these protections when an obvious security interest is at stake. In 2010, for example, a Pennsylvania prison was allowed to continue banning religious headscarves because of legitimate concerns that the scarves could be used to conceal drugs or strangle someone.[80] In general, however, the judicial system's commitment to

Many prisons punish misbehaving inmates by feeding them *nutraloaf*, an unpleasant concoction made of ingredients such as nondairy cheese, powdered milk, seedless raisins, tomato paste, and dehydrated potato flakes. Do you have any concerns about this form of punishment? Explain your answer.
AP Photo/Andy Duback

"Deliberate Indifference" A standard that must be met by inmates trying to prove that their Eighth Amendment rights were violated by a correctional facility. It occurs when prison officials are aware of harmful conditions of confinement but fail to take steps to remedy those conditions.

"Identifiable Human Needs" The basic human necessities that correctional facilities are required by the Constitution to provide to inmates.

freedom of speech and religion behind bars remains strong. (This commitment may have a particularly dangerous side effect, as you can see in the feature *Anti-Terrorism in Action—Prislam* below.)

SELF ASSESSMENT

Fill in the blanks and check your answers on page 497.

Correctional officers known as _____ _____ are responsible for the daily well-being of the inmates in their cells. Perhaps the most stressful and important aspect of a correctional officer's job is enforcing _____ among the inmates. To do so, the officers may use force when a _____ security interest is being served. Courts will not, however, accept any force that is "_____ and sadistic." To prove that prison officials violated the _____ Amendment's prohibitions against cruel and unusual punishment, the inmate must first show that the officials acted with "_____ indifference" in taking or not taking an action.

ANTI-TERRORISM IN ACTION

PRISLAM

Argus/Shutterstock

Islam is the fastest-growing religion in the American prison system. According to one U.S. Justice Department study, about 30,000 to 40,000 federal prisoners convert to Islam each year. For the vast majority of inmates who choose "Prislam," as correctional officials have come to call the practice, the conversion is not political. Rather, the religion acts as a stabilizing force in their lives, helping them break the destructive patterns that caused them to be incarcerated in the first place.

From time to time, however, Prislam finds itself tainted by the specter of radical Islamic terrorism. In May 2009, for example, four Muslim men were accused of planning to bomb synagogues and shoot down military aircraft with Stinger missiles in the New York City area. Two of the plotters—Laguerre Payen and Onta Williams—are believed to have converted while in prison. As we learned in Chapter 1 (see page 24), about a decade ago the Islamic terrorist group Jam'yyat Al-Islam Al Saheeh (JIS), which was formed in Sacramento's Folsom Prison, launched a conspiracy to "kill infidels" in Southern California. Both Richard Reid, the "shoe bomber" who attempted to blow up an international flight in 2001, and José Padilla, convicted in 2007 of aiding terrorists, were prison converts to Islam.

"PEOPLE SHOULD BE WORRIED" Many American Muslims discount the connection between Islamic

inmates and terrorist activity. If a radical prisoner with terrorist tendencies is "an unreformed sociopath who happens to be a Muslim, [then] Islam is not to be blamed for his condition," says Iman Talib Abdur-Rashid, a chaplain in the New York City prison system.

Still, the Federal Bureau of Prisons is taking steps to prevent the radicalization of federal inmates, including monitoring religious meetings and screening written religion materials. The worry is that the degradations and frustrations of prison life will drive unstable prisoners toward terrorism. "People should be worried about us. People in prison feel there is no way out," says Jehmahl, a murderer who converted to Islam while behind bars and subsequently joined JIS. "This is not so much about Islam. I'm radical. Radical means that you're holding no foundation. That's what the suicide bombers do. There's nothing but God left so let's go find a bomb."

FOR CRITICAL ANALYSIS The United States Supreme Court has held that prisoners retain a constitutional right to religious freedom. At the same time, prison administrators may regulate religious activities for security reasons. What steps do you think correctional officials should take to limit the spread of Islamic extremism in the nation's prisons? How could they make use of solitary confinement (see page 454) to deal with this problem?

INSIDE A WOMEN'S PRISON

When the first women's prison in the United States opened in 1839 on the grounds of New York's Sing Sing institution, the focus was on rehabilitation. Prisoners were prepared for a return to society with classes on reading, knitting, and sewing. Early women's reformatories had few locks or bars, and several included nurseries for the inmates' young children. Today, the situation is dramatically different. "Women's institutions are literally men's institutions, only we pull out the urinals," remarks Meda Chesney-Lind, a criminologist at the University of Hawaii.[81] Given the different circumstances surrounding male and female incarceration, this uniformity can have serious consequences for the women imprisoned in this country.

CHARACTERISTICS OF FEMALE INMATES

Male inmates outnumber female inmates by approximately nine to one, and there are only about a hundred women's correctional facilities in the United States. Consequently, most research concerning the American corrections system focuses on male inmates and men's prisons. Enough data exist, however, to provide a useful portrait of women behind bars. Female inmates are typically low income and undereducated, and have a history of unemployment. Like male inmates, female prisoners are disproportionately African American, although the percentage of white female inmates has increased over the past two decades. Female offenders are much less likely than male offenders to have committed a violent offense. Most are incarcerated for a nonviolent drug or property crime (see Figure 14.4 below).

A HISTORY OF ABUSE The single factor that most distinguishes female prisoners from their male counterparts is a history of physical or sexual abuse. A self-reported study conducted by the federal government indicates that 55 percent of female jail inmates have been abused at some point in their lives, compared with only 13 percent of male jail inmates.[82] Fifty-seven percent of women in state prisons and 40 percent of women in federal prisons report some form of past abuse—both figures are significantly higher than those for male prisoners.[83] Health experts believe that these levels of abuse are related to the significant amount of drug and/or alcohol addiction that plagues the

> **Critical Thinking Skill Development:** Ask students to brainstorm the services they feel are needed in women's correctional facilities. Do these services differ from those necessary in men's facilities?

FIGURE 14.4 Offenses of Women in Jail and Prison

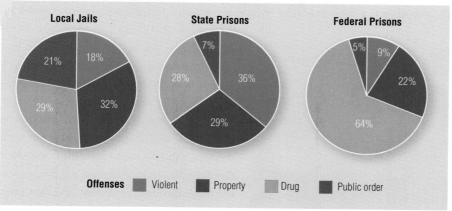

Sources: Bureau of Justice Statistics, *Sourcebook of Criminal Justice*, 3d ed. (Washington, D.C.: U.S. Department of Justice, 2003), Table 6.56, page 519; Bureau of Justice Statistics, *Profile of Jail Inmates, 2002* (Washington, D.C.: Department of Justice, July 2004), Table 4, page 4; and Bureau of Justice Statistics, *Prisoners in 2009* (Washington, D.C.: U.S. Department of Justice, December 2010), Appendix table 17c, page 32.

female prison population, as well as to the mental illness problems that such addictions can cause or exacerbate.[84]

OTHER HEALTH PROBLEMS In fact, about 25 percent of women in state prisons have been diagnosed with mental disorders such as post–traumatic stress disorder (PTSD), depression, and substance abuse. PTSD, in particular, is found in women who have experienced sexual or physical abuse.[85] Furthermore, more women than men enter prisons and jails with health problems due to higher instances of poverty, inadequate health care, and substance abuse.[86] Not only do women prisoners have high rates of breast and cervical cancer, but they are also 50 percent more likely than men to be HIV positive and are at significantly greater risk for lung cancer.[87] The health risks and medical needs are even higher for the 5 percent of the female prison population who enter the correctional facility while pregnant. One study estimates that 20 to 35 percent of women inmates visit the infirmary each day, compared with 7 to 10 percent of male inmates.[88]

THE MOTHERHOOD PROBLEM

Discussion Tip: Ask students to describe the impact that incarceration has on mothers and their children. How can this impact be lessened?

Drug and alcohol use within a women's prison can be a function of the anger and depression many inmates experience due to being separated from their children. An estimated seven out of every ten female prisoners have at least one minor child. About 1.7 million American children have a mother who is under correctional supervision.[89] Given the scarcity of women's correctional facilities, inmates are often housed at great distances from their children. One study found that almost two-thirds of women in federal prison are more than five hundred miles from their homes.[90]

Further research indicates that an inmate who serves her sentence more than fifty miles from her residence is much less likely to receive phone calls or personal visits from family members. For most inmates and their families, the costs of "staying in touch" are too high.[91] This kind of separation can have serious consequences for the children of inmates. When a father goes to prison, his children are likely to live with their mother. When a mother is incarcerated, however, her children are likely to live with other relatives or, in about 11 percent of the cases, be sent to foster care.[92] Only six states—California, Indiana, Nebraska, New York, Ohio, and Washington—provide facilities where inmates and their infant children can live together, and even in these facilities nursery privileges generally end once the child is eighteen months old.

THE CULTURE OF WOMEN'S PRISONS

After spending five years visiting female inmates in the Massachusetts Correctional Institution (MCI) at Framingham, journalist Cristina Rathbone observed that the medium-security facility seemed "more like a high school than a prison."[93] The prisoners were older and tougher than high school girls, but they still divided into cliques, with the "lifers" at the top of the hierarchy and "untouchables" such as child abusers at the bottom. Unlike in men's prisons, where the underground economy revolves around drugs and weapons, at MCI-Framingham the most treasured contraband items are clothing, food, and makeup.[94]

Female inmates at the Women's Eastern Reception, Diagnostic and Correctional Center in Vandalia, Missouri, visit with their daughters and granddaughters. Why is it difficult for many mothers behind bars to see their children?
AP Photo/Whitney Curtis

THE PSEUDO-FAMILY Although both men's and women's prisons are organized with the same goals of control and discipline, the cultures within the two institutions are generally very different. As we have seen, male prison society operates primarily on the basis of power. Deprived of the benefits of freedom, male prisoners tend to create a violent environment that bears little relation to life on the outside.[95] In contrast, researchers have found that women prisoners prefer to re-create their outside identities by forming social networks that resemble high school cliques or, more commonly, the traditional family structure.[96] In these pseudo-families, inmates often play specific roles, with the more experienced convicts acting as "mothers" to younger, inexperienced "daughters." As one observer noted, the younger women rely on their "moms" for emotional support, companionship, loans, and even discipline.[97]

Such a family unit may have a "married" couple at its head, sometimes with a lesbian assuming the role of the father figure. Indeed, homosexuality in women's prisons often manifests itself through the formation of another traditional family model: the monogamous couple.[98] For the most part, sex between inmates plays a different role in women's prisons than in men's prisons. In the latter, rape is an act of aggression and power rather than sex, and "true" homosexuals are relegated to the lowest rungs of the social hierarchy. By contrast, women inmates who engage in sexual activity are not automatically labeled homosexual, and lesbians are not hampered in their social-climbing efforts.[99]

SEXUAL VIOLENCE AND PRISON STAFF Compared with men's prisons, women's prisons have extremely low levels of race-based, gang-related physical aggression.[100] Furthermore, though rates of sexual victimization can be high, most such episodes involve abusive sexual contacts such as unwanted touching rather than sexual assault or rape.[101] One form of serious prison violence that does plague women prisoners, however, is sexual misconduct by prison staff. Although no large-scale study on sexual abuse of female inmates by male correctional officers exists, a number of state-level studies suggest that it is widespread.[102] Given that, in many corrections systems, more than half of all staff members in women's prisons are men, such problems seem inevitable.[103] To start with, security procedures such as the pat down and, in more extreme cases, the strip search become problematic when a female inmate and a male correctional officer are involved. The conditions in most prisons—including lack of privacy, inadequate grievance procedures, and harsh treatment of whistle-blowers—only add to the potential for abuse of power in this area. Dr. Kerry Kupers, who has studied the effects of prison sexual assault, believes that it contributes to the PTSD, depression, anxiety, and other mental illnesses suffered by so many women prisoners.[104]

Critical Thinking Skill Development: In a short essay, have students contrast the disciplinary issues in male and female correctional facilities. Why is there such a disparity in levels of violence in men's and women's corrections facilities?

Teaching Tip: Ask students to respond to "Questions for Critical Analysis" number three on page 497, which concerns the role of male correctional officers in women's prisons.

"He likes for you to bend down [to show your breasts], and then he rubs his hands on his pants and says, 'Look! Look!' to show you that you are turning him on."

—A female inmate describing the behavior of a male correctional officer (2008)

SELF ASSESSMENT

Fill in the blanks and check your answers on page 497.

The majority of female inmates are members of _____ groups who have been arrested for nonviolent _____ or property crimes. On admission to a correctional facility, women report much higher levels of physical and sexual _____ than their male counterparts, and female inmates often suffer from depression because they are separated from their _____. While levels of physical violence are relatively low in women's prisons, female inmates do face a greater threat of sexual assault from _____ _____ than male inmates do.

PAROLE AND RELEASE FROM PRISON

LO 6 At any given time, more than 800,000 Americans are living in the community on **parole,** or the *conditional* release of a prisoner after a portion of his or her sentence has been served. Parole allows the corrections system to continue to supervise an offender who is no longer incarcerated. As long as parolees follow the conditions of their parole, they are allowed to finish their terms outside the prison. If parolees break the terms of their early release, however, they face the risk of being returned to a penal institution.

Parole is based on three concepts:[105]

1. *Grace.* The prisoner has no right to be given an early release, but the government has granted her or him that privilege.
2. *Contract of consent.* The government and the parolee enter into an arrangement whereby the latter agrees to abide by certain conditions in return for continued freedom.
3. *Custody.* Technically, though no longer incarcerated, the parolee is still the responsibility of the state. Parole is an extension of corrections. (The phonetic and administrative similarities between probation and parole can be confusing. See *Mastering Concepts—Probation versus Parole* on the facing page for clarification.)

Because of good-time credits and parole, most prisoners do not serve their entire sentence in prison. In fact, the average felon serves only about half of the term handed down by the court.

OTHER TYPES OF PRISON RELEASE

The vast majority of all inmates leaving prison—about 80 percent—do so through one of the parole mechanisms discussed in the chapter. Of the remaining 20 percent, most are given an **expiration release.**[106] Also known as "maxing out," expiration release occurs when an inmate has served the maximum amount of time on the initial sentence, minus reductions for good-time credits, and is not subjected to community supervision. Another, quite rare unconditional release is a **pardon,** a form of executive clemency. The president (on the federal level) and the governor (on the state level) can grant a pardon, or forgive a convict's criminal punishment. Most states have a board of pardons—affiliated with the parole board—that makes recommendations to the governor in cases in which it believes a pardon is warranted. Most pardons involve obvious miscarriages of justice, though sometimes a governor will pardon an individual to remove the stain of conviction from his or her criminal record.

Certain *temporary releases* also exist. Some inmates, who qualify by exhibiting good behavior and generally proving that they do not represent a risk to society, are allowed to leave the prison on **furlough** for a certain amount of time, usually between a day and a week. At times, a furlough is granted because of a family emergency, such as a funeral. Furloughs can be particularly helpful for an inmate who is nearing release and can use them to ease the readjustment period.

DISCRETIONARY RELEASE

As you may recall from Chapter 11, corrections systems are classified by sentencing procedure—indeterminate or determinate. Indeterminate sentencing occurs when the legislature sets a range of punishments for particular crimes, and the judge and the parole board

Parole The conditional release of an inmate before his or her sentence has expired.

Expiration Release The release of an inmate from prison at the end of his or her sentence without any further correctional supervision.

Pardon An act of executive clemency that overturns a conviction and erases mention of the crime from the person's criminal record.

Furlough Temporary release from a prison for purposes of vocational or educational training, to ease the shock of release, or for personal reasons.

Teaching Tip: Have students consider the various means by which an inmate can be released from prison before his or her expiration date. Ask students to come up with a scenario to serve as an example of each form of release. Ask them to share their examples with the class. (LO 6)

Discussion Tip: Ask students to debate the appropriateness of furloughs. Should inmates be temporarily released in case of a family emergency? (LO 6)

MASTERING CONCEPTS

PROBATION VERSUS PAROLE

Probation and parole have many aspects in common. In fact, probation and parole are so similar that many jurisdictions combine them into a single agency. There are, however, some important distinctions between the two systems, as noted below.

	PROBATION	PAROLE
Basic Definition	An alternative to imprisonment in which a person who has been convicted of a crime is allowed to serve his or her sentence in the community subject to certain conditions and supervision by a probation officer.	An early release from a correctional facility as determined by an administrative body (the parole board), in which the convicted offender is given the chance to spend the remainder of his or her sentence under supervision in the community.
Timing	The offender is sentenced to a probationary term in place of a prison or jail term. If the offender breaks the conditions of probation, he or she is sent to prison or jail. Therefore, probation generally occurs before imprisonment.	Parole is a form of early release. Therefore, parole occurs *after* an offender has spent time behind bars.
Authority	Probation is under the domain of the judiciary. A judge decides whether to sentence a convict to probation, and a judge determines whether a probation violation warrants revocation and incarceration.	Parole falls under the domain of the parole board. This administrative body determines whether the prisoner qualifies for early release and the conditions under which the parole must be served. If a parolee violates these conditions, the parole board decides whether to send her or him back to prison.
Characteristics of Offenders	As a number of studies have shown, probationers are normally less involved in the criminal lifestyle. Most of them are first-time offenders who have committed nonviolent crimes.	Many parolees have spent months or even years in prison and, besides abiding by conditions of parole, must make the difficult transition to "life on the outside."

exercise discretion in determining the actual length of the prison term. For that reason, states with indeterminate sentencing are said to have systems of discretionary release. Until the mid-1970s, all states and the federal government operated in this manner.

ELIGIBILITY FOR PAROLE Under indeterminate sentencing, parole is not a right but a privilege. This is a crucial point, as it establishes the terms of the relationship between the inmate and the corrections authorities during the parole process. In *Greenholtz v. Inmates of the Nebraska Penal and Correctional Complex* (1979),[107] the Supreme Court ruled that inmates do not have a constitutionally protected right to expect parole, thereby giving states the freedom to set their own standards for determining parole eligibility. In most states that have retained indeterminate sentencing, a prisoner is eligible to be considered for parole release after serving a legislatively determined percentage of the minimum sentence—usually one-half or two-thirds—less any good time or other credits.

Not all convicts are eligible for parole. As we saw in Chapter 11, offenders who have committed the most serious crimes often receive life sentences without the possibility of early release. In general, life without parole is reserved for those who have committed first degree murder or are defined by statute as habitual offenders. Today, about 30 percent of convicts serving life sentences have no possibility of parole.[108] Also, officials can

Discretionary Release The release of an inmate into a community supervision program at the discretion of the parole board within limits set by state or federal law.

Critical Thinking Skill Development: Ask students to debate the controversial sentence of life without parole. What do students think about the claim that this form of punishment may be crueler than the death penalty?

Part of the reason Mississippi Governor Haley Barbour agreed to the unusual conditional release of Jamie, left, and Gladys Scott was to save the state from paying Jamie's annual $200,000 medical bill. What is your opinion of Barbour's decision?
AP Photo/Rogelio V. Solis, File

set conditions for parole eligibility. In 2011, for example, Mississippi governor Haley Barbour agreed to the conditional release of sisters Jamie and Gladys Scott, who were both serving life sentences for armed robbery, if Gladys would donate a kidney to Jamie (see the photo alongside).

THE PAROLE BOARD A convict does not apply for parole. Rather, an inmate's case automatically comes up for review a certain number of days—often ninety—before he or she is eligible for parole. The date of eligibility depends on statutory requirements, the terms of the sentence, and the behavior of the inmate in prison. The responsibility of making the parole decision often falls to the **parole board,** whose members are generally appointed by the state governor.

According to the American Correctional Association, the parole board has four basic roles:

1. To decide which offenders should be placed on parole.
2. To determine the conditions of parole and aid in the continuing supervision of the parolee.
3. To discharge the offender when the conditions of parole have been met.
4. If a violation occurs, to determine whether parole privileges should be revoked.[109]

Most parole boards are small, made up of five to seven members. In many jurisdictions, board members' terms are limited to between four and six years. The requirements for board members vary. Nearly half the states have no prerequisites, while others require a bachelor's degree or some expertise in the field of criminal justice.

Parole Board A body of appointed civilians that decides whether a convict should be granted conditional release before the end of his or her sentence.

Parole Grant Hearing A hearing in which the entire parole board or a subcommittee reviews information, meets the offender, and hears testimony from relevant witnesses to determine whether to grant parole.

Critical Thinking Skill Development: Place students into small groups to discuss discretionary parole. What factors should be taken into consideration during this process? Should offenders be released on the basis of "good behavior?"

THE PAROLE HEARING In a system that uses discretionary parole, the actual release decision is made at a **parole grant hearing.** During this hearing, the entire board or a subcommittee reviews relevant information on the convict. Sometimes, but not always, the offender is interviewed. Because the board members have only limited knowledge of each offender, key players in the case are often notified in advance of the parole hearing and asked to provide comments and recommendations. These participants include the sentencing judge, the attorneys at the trial, the victims, and any law enforcement officers who may be involved. After these preparations, the typical parole hearing itself is very short—usually lasting just a few minutes.

If parole is denied, the entire process is replayed at the next "action date," which depends on the nature of the offender's crimes and all relevant laws. In 2010, for example, Mark David Chapman was denied parole for the sixth time. Three decades earlier, Chapman had been convicted of murder for fatally shooting musician John Lennon in New York City and sentenced to twenty years to life in prison. Although Chapman had not had an infraction behind bars since 1994, the three parole board members told him that they still had concerns "about the disregard you displayed for the norms of our society and the sanctity of human life."[110] Chapman's chances for release are also hurt by the continuing wishes of Yoko Ono, Lennon's widow, that parole be denied. (See the feature *You Be the Parole Board Member—Cause for Compassion?* on the facing page to learn more about the process of discretionary release.)

THE EMERGENCE OF MANDATORY RELEASE

The legitimacy of discretionary release relies to a certain extent on the perception of parole decisions by offenders, victims, and the general public. Like judicial discretion (as we discussed in Chapter 11), parole board discretion is criticized when the decisions are seen as arbitrary and unfair and lead to rampant disparity in the release dates of similar offenders. Proponents of discretionary release argue that parole boards must tailor their decisions to the individual case, but such protestations seem to be undermined by the raw data: research done by the Bureau of Justice Statistics has found that most offenders were serving less than a third of their sentences in the early 1990s.[111]

As Michael Tonry noted, such statistics gave the impression that parole board members "tossed darts at a dartboard" to determine who should be released, and when.[112] As a result of this criticism, a majority of states have now implemented determinate sentencing systems, which set minimum mandatory terms without possibility of parole. These systems provide for **mandatory release,** in which offenders leave prison only when their sentences have expired, minus adjustments for good time. No parole board is involved in this type of release, which is designed to eliminate discretion from the process. (Unlike those given an expiration release [discussed on page 482], inmates released under determinate sentencing can still be subject to community supervision, as described under "Parole Supervision" on the next page.)

Discussion Tip: Ask students to debate the advantages and disadvantages of mandatory release, in which offenders leave prison only when their sentences have expired.

Mandatory Release Release from prison that occurs when an offender has served the full length of his or her sentence, minus any adjustments for good time.

YOU BE THE PAROLE BOARD MEMBER

Cause for Compassion?

THE SITUATION Thirty-seven years ago, Susan was convicted of first degree murder and sentenced to life in prison for taking part in a grisly killing spree in Los Angeles. Over the course of two days, Susan and her accomplices killed seven people. Susan stabbed one of the victims—a pregnant woman—sixteen times and wrote the word "PIG" on a door using another woman's blood. During her trial, Susan testified that "I was stoned, man, stoned on acid," at the time of her crimes. Now sixty-one years old, Susan is before your parole board, requesting release from prison. For most of her time behind bars, she has been a model prisoner, and she has apologized numerous times for her wrongdoing. Furthermore, her left leg has been amputated, the left side of her body is paralyzed, and she has been diagnosed with terminal brain cancer.

THE LAW You have a great deal of discretion in determining whether a prisoner should be paroled. Some of the factors you should consider are the threat the prisoner would pose to the community if released, the nature of the offense, and the level of remorse. In addition, California allows for "compassionate release" when an inmate is "terminally ill."

YOUR DECISION Susan obviously poses no threat to the community and is a viable candidate for compassionate release. Should she be set free on parole? Or are some crimes so horrific that the convict should never be given parole, no matter what the circumstances? Explain your vote.

[To see how a California parole board voted in a similar situation, go to Example 14.1 in Appendix B.]

Rasmus Rasmusson/iStockphoto/iStockphoto/Photodisc/Shutterstock/James Stadl/iStockphoto

Parole Guidelines Standards that are used in the parole process to measure the risk that a potential parolee will recidivate.

Parole Contract An agreement between the state and the offender that establishes the conditions under which the latter will be allowed to serve the remainder of her or his prison term in the community.

TRUTH IN SENTENCING The move toward mandatory release is reflected in the popularity of truth-in-sentencing laws, which have been passed by the legislatures of more than forty states. As we noted in Chapter 11 (see page 363), these laws require certain statutorily determined offenders to serve at least 85 percent of their terms. As the name implies, such laws are designed to restore "truth" to the sentencing process by eliminating situations in which offenders are released by a parole board after serving less than the minimum term to which they were sentenced.[113] One method of ensuring truth in sentencing is the use of parole guidelines. Similar to sentencing guidelines (see Chapter 11), parole guidelines attempt to measure a potential parolee's risk of recidivism by considering factors such as the original offense, criminal history, behavior in prison, past employment, substance abuse, and performance under any previous periods of parole or probation. Inmates who score positively in these areas are considered less likely to pose a danger to society and have a better chance of obtaining an early release date.

"ABOLISHING" PAROLE Note that a number of states and the federal government have officially "abolished" parole through legislation. For the most part, however, these laws simply emphasize prison terms that are "truthful," not necessarily "longer." Mechanisms for parole, by whatever name, are crucial to the criminal justice system for several reasons. First, they provide inmates with an incentive to behave properly in the hope of an early release. Second, they reduce the costs related to incarceration by keeping down the inmate population, a critical concern for prison administrators.[114]

PAROLE SUPERVISION

The term *parole* has two meanings. The first, as we have seen, refers to the establishment of a release date. The second relates to the continuing supervision of convicted felons after they have been released from prison.

"Johnny plus alcohol plus women equals trouble."

—Excerpt from parole report on Johnny Robert Eggers, who was released on parole five different times before stabbing a female teenager to death in 1994

LO 7 **CONDITIONS OF PAROLE** Many of the procedures and issues of parole supervision are similar to those of probation supervision. Like probationers, when parolees are granted parole, they are placed under the supervision of parole officers and required to follow certain conditions. Some of these conditions are fairly uniform. All parolees, for example, must comply with the law, and they are generally responsible for reporting to their parole officer at certain intervals. The frequency of these visits, along with the other terms of parole, is spelled out in the parole contract, which sets out the agreement between the state and the paroled offender. Under the terms of the contract, the state agrees to release the inmate under certain conditions, and the future parolee agrees to follow these conditions.

Each jurisdiction has its own standard parole contract, although the parole board can add specific provisions if it sees the need (see Figure 14.5 on the facing page). Besides common restrictions, such as no illegal drug use, no association with known felons, and no change of address without notifying authorities, parolees have on occasion been ordered to lose weight and even to undergo chemical castration. Professional football player Michael Vick, who recently spent eighteen months in federal prison for running a pit bull–fighting operation in Virginia, was prohibited from owning a dog as a condition of his early release.

FIGURE 14.5 Standard Conditions of Parole

1. Upon my release I will report to my parole officer as directed and follow the parole officer's instructions.
2. I will report to my parole officer in person and in writing whenever and wherever the parole officer directs.
3. I agree that the parole officer has the right to visit my residence or place of employment at any reasonable time.
4. I will seek, obtain, and maintain employment throughout my parole term, or perform community service as directed by my parole officer.
5. I will notify my parole officer prior to any changes in my place of residence, in my place of employment, or of any change in my marital status.
6. I will notify my parole officer within 48 hours if at any time I am arrested for any offense.
7. I will not at any time have firearms, ammunition, or any other weapon in my possession or under my control.
8. I will obey all laws, and to the best of my ability, fulfill all my legal obligations, including payment of all applicable child support and alimony orders.
9. I will not leave the state of _____ without prior permission of my parole officer.
10. I will not at any time use, or have in my possession or control, any illegal drug or narcotic.
11. I will not at any time have contact or affiliation with any street gangs or with any members thereof.
12. I understand that my release on parole is based upon the conclusion of the parole panel that there is a reasonable probability that I will live and remain at liberty without violating the law and that my release is not incompatible with the welfare of society. In the event that I engage in conduct in the future which renders this conclusion no longer valid, then my parole will be revoked or modified accordingly.

Source: Connecticut Board of Parole.

PAROLE REVOCATION If convicts follow the conditions of their parole until the *maximum expiration date,* or the date on which their sentence ends, then they are discharged from supervision. A large number—about one-third—return to incarceration before their maximum expiration date, most because they were convicted of a new offense or had their parole revoked (see Figure 14.6 below). Parole revocation is similar in many aspects to probation revocation. If the parolee commits a new crime, then a return to prison is very likely. If, however, the individual breaks a condition of parole, known as a *technical violation,* the parole authorities have discretion as to whether revocation proceedings should be initiated. An example of a technical violation would be failure to report a change in address to parole authorities. As with probation revocation, many observers believe that those who commit technical violations should not be imprisoned, as they have not committed a crime.

Parole Revocation When a parolee breaks the conditions of parole, the process of withdrawing parole and returning the person to prison.

PAROLE AND DUE PROCESS Until 1972, parole officers had the power to arbitrarily revoke parole status for technical violations. A parolee who was returned to prison had little or no recourse. In *Morrissey v. Brewer* (1972),[115] the Supreme Court changed this by holding that a parolee has a "liberty interest" in remaining on parole. In other words, before parolees can be deprived of their liberty, they must be afforded a measure of due process at a parole revocation hearing.

Although this hearing does not provide the same due process protections as a criminal trial, the parolee does have the right to be notified of the charges, to present witnesses, to speak in his or her defense, and to question any hostile witnesses (so long as such questioning would not place them in danger). In the first stage of the hearing, the parole board determines whether there

FIGURE 14.6 Terminating Parole

As you can see, just over half of all parolees successfully complete their terms of parole. The rest are either returned to incarceration or have their supervision terminated administratively for a variety of reasons, including transfer to another jurisdiction, disappearance, or death.

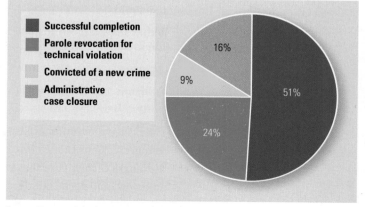

- Successful completion — 51%
- Parole revocation for technical violation — 24%
- Convicted of a new crime — 9%
- Administrative case closure — 16%

Source: Bureau of Justice Statistics, *Probation and Parole in the United States, 2009* (Washington, D.C.: U.S. Department of Justice, December 2010), Table 6, page 6.

is probable cause that a violation occurred. Then, the board decides whether to return the parolee to prison.

SELFASSESSMENT

Fill in the blanks and check your answers on page 497.

Parole refers to the _____ release of an inmate from prison before the end of his or her _____. In jurisdictions that have systems of discretionary release, a _____ makes the parole decision. In contrast, with a _____ release under determinate sentencing, the inmate will not leave prison until her or his sentence has expired, minus good-time credits. Once an inmate has been released from prison, the terms of his or her release are spelled out in a parole _____, and a _____ violation of these terms or the commission of a new crime will almost certainly result in a return to prison.

REENTRY INTO SOCIETY

LO 8

Even though Dominic Cinelli had a lengthy criminal history and was serving three consecutive life sentences for a series of armed robberies, the Massachusetts Parole Board decided that he deserved to be granted parole. Unfortunately, on December 26, 2010, just a year after his release, Cinelli fatally shot Woburn police officer John Maguire during a failed attempt to rob a jewelry store. Ex-inmates such as Cinelli (who also died in the shootout) and the troubles they bring with them present a crucial challenge for the criminal justice system.

Each year, more than 650,000 persons leave prison and return to the community. What steps can be taken to lessen the possibility that these ex-convicts will continue to harm society following their release? Efforts to answer that question have focused on programs that help inmates make the transition from prison to the outside. In past years, these programs would have come under the general heading of "rehabilitation," but today corrections officials and criminologists refer to them as part of the strategy of **prisoner reentry**. The concept of reentry has come to mean many things to many people. For our purposes, keep in mind the words of Joan Petersilia of the University of California at Irvine, who defines *reentry* as encompassing "all activities and programming conducted to prepare ex-convicts to return safely to the community and to live as law abiding citizens."[116] In other words, whereas rehab is focused on the individual offender, *reentry* encompasses the released convict's relationship with society.

BARRIERS TO REENTRY

Perhaps the largest obstacle to successful prisoner reentry is the simple truth that life behind bars is very different from life on the outside. As one inmate explains, the "rules" of prison survival are hardly compatible with good citizenship:

> An unexpected smile could mean trouble. A man in uniform was not a friend. Being kind was a weakness. Viciousness and recklessness were to be respected and admired.[117]

The prison environment also insulates inmates. They are not required to make the day-to-day decisions that characterize a normal existence beyond prison bars. Depending on the length of incarceration, a released inmate must adjust to an array of economic, technological, and social changes that took place while she or he was behind bars. Common acts such as using an ATM or pumping gas may be completely alien to someone who has just completed a long prison term.

Teaching Tip: In a written assignment, ask students to reflect on the challenges parolees face as they attempt to reintegrate into society. What services can be provided to assist offenders with this transition? (LO 8)

Prisoner Reentry A corrections strategy designed to prepare inmates for a successful return to the community and to reduce their criminal activity after release.

CHALLENGES OF RELEASE Other obstacles hamper reentry efforts. Housing can be difficult to secure, as many private property owners refuse to rent to someone with a criminal record, and federal and state laws restrict public housing options for ex-convicts. A criminal past also limits the ability to find employment, as does the lack of job skills of someone who has spent a significant portion of his or her life in prison. Felix Mata, who works with ex-convicts in Baltimore, Maryland, estimates that the average male prisoner returning to that city has only $50 in his pocket and owes $8,000 in child support. Furthermore, these men generally have no means of transportation, no place to live, and no ability to gain employment. At best, most ex-prisoners can expect to earn no more than $10,000 annually the first few years after being released.[118]

These economic barriers can be complicated by the physical and mental condition of the freed convict. We have already discussed the high incidence of substance abuse among prisoners and the health-care needs of aging inmates earlier in this chapter. In addition, one study concluded that as many as one in five Americans leaving jail or prison is seriously mentally ill.[119] (See Figure 14.7 below for a list of the hardships commonly faced by former inmates in their first year out of prison.)

THE THREAT OF RELAPSE All of these problems conspire to make successful reentry difficult to achieve. Perhaps it is not surprising that research conducted by the Pew Center on the States found that 43 percent of ex-prisoners are back in prison or jail within three years of their release dates.[120] These figures highlight the problem of recidivism among those released from incarceration.

Even given the barriers to reentry we have discussed, these rates of recidivism seem improbably high. Regardless of their ability to find a job or housing, many ex-convicts are fated to run afoul of the criminal justice system. Psychologists Edward Zamble and Vernon Quinsey explain the phenomenon as a *relapse process*.[121] Take the hypothetical

Discussion Tip: Have students discuss the relapse process. How can correctional services help ex-convicts avoid this pitfall?

FIGURE 14.7 Prisoner Reentry Issues

Researchers from the Urban Institute in Washington, D.C., asked nearly three hundred former prisoners (all male) in the Cleveland, Ohio, area about the most pressing issues they faced in their first year after release. The answers provide a useful snapshot of the many challenges of reentry.

1. *Housing.* Nearly two-thirds of the men were living with family members, and about half considered their housing situation "temporary." Many were concerned about their living environment: half said that drug dealing was a major problem in their neighborhoods, and almost 25 percent were living with drug and alcohol abusers.

2. *Employment.* After one year, only about one-third of the former inmates had a full-time job, and another 11 percent were working part-time.

3. *Family and friends.* One in four of the men identified family support as the most important thing keeping them from returning to criminality. Another 16 percent said that avoiding certain people and situations was the most crucial factor in their continued good behavior.

4. *Programs and services.* About two-thirds of the former inmates had taken part in programs and services such as drug treatment and continuing education.

5. *Health.* More than half of the men reported suffering from a chronic health condition, and 29 percent showed symptoms of depression.

6. *Substance use.* About half of the men admitted to weekly drug use or alcohol intoxication. Men who had strong family ties and those who were required to maintain telephone contact with their parole officer were less likely to engage in frequent substance use.

7. *Parole violation and recidivism.* More than half of the former inmates reported that they had violated the conditions of their parole, usually by drug use or having contact with other parolees. Fifteen percent of the men returned to prison in the year after release. Four out of five of the returns were the result of a new crime.

Source: Christy A. Visher and Shannon M. E. Courtney, *One Year Out: Experience of Prisoners Returning to Cleveland* (Washington, D.C.: Urban Institute, April 2007), 2.

> **"I don't see prison as prison. I see prison as a cage. A dog cage, or monkey cage. It's an animal cage, period. I refuse. I will not live my life like that anymore."**
>
> —**Alissa,** ex-inmate (2009)

Desistance The process through which criminal activity decreases and reintegration into society increases over a period of time.

Work Release Program Temporary release of convicts from prison for purposes of employment. The offenders may spend their days on the job, but must return to the correctional facility at night and during the weekend.

Halfway House A community-based form of early release that places inmates in residential centers and allows them to reintegrate with society.

Why is it beneficial for prisoners such as these two Colorado state inmates, seen working on mannequin heads during a cosmetology class, to receive job training while still incarcerated?
AP Photo/*The Daily Record,* Jeff Shane

example of an ex-convict who gets in a minor automobile accident while driving from his home to his job one morning. The person in the other car gets out and starts yelling at the ex-convict, who "relapses" and reacts just as he would have in prison—by punching the other person in the face. The ex-convict is then convicted of assault and battery and given a harsh prison sentence because of his criminal record.

PROMOTING DESISTANCE

One ex-inmate compared the experience of being released to entering a "dark room, knowing that there are steps in front of you and waiting to fall."[122] The goal of reentry is to act as a flashlight for convicts by promoting **desistance,** a general term used to describe the continued abstinence from offending and the reintroduction of offenders into society. Certainly, the most important factor in the process is the individual convict. She or he has to *want* to desist and take steps to do so. In most cases, however, ex-inmates are going to need help—help getting an education, help finding and keeping a job, and help freeing themselves from harmful addictions to drugs and alcohol. Corrections officials are in a good position to offer this assistance, and their efforts in doing so form the backbone of the reentry movement.

Preparation for reentry starts behind bars. In addition to the rehabilitation-oriented prison programs discussed earlier in the chapter, most correctional facilities offer "life skills" classes to inmates. This counseling covers topics such as finding and keeping a job, locating a residence, understanding family responsibilities, and budgeting. After release, however, former inmates often find it difficult to continue with educational programs and counseling as they struggle to readjust to life outside prison. Consequently, parole supervising agencies operate a number of programs to facilitate offenders' desistance efforts while, at the same time, protecting the community to the greatest extent possible.

WORK RELEASE AND HALFWAY HOUSES As is made clear in Figure 14.7 on the previous page, work and lodging are crucial components of desistance. Corrections officials have several options in helping certain parolees—usually low-risk offenders—find employment and a place to live during the supervision period. Nearly a third of correctional facilities offer **work release programs,** in which prisoners nearing the end of their sentences are given permission to work at paid employment in the community.[123]

Inmates on work release must either return to the correctional facility in the evening or live in community residential facilities known as **halfway houses.** These facilities, also available to other parolees and those who have finished their sentences, are often remodeled hotels or private homes. They provide a less institutionalized living environment than a prison or jail for a small number of offenders (usually between ten and twenty-five). Halfway houses can be tailored to the needs of the former inmate. Many communities, for example, offer substance-free transitional housing for those whose past criminal behavior was linked to drug or alcohol abuse.

WHAT WORKS IN REENTRY Substance abuse treatment can have a significant impact on desistance. One study in Delaware found that prisoners who received such treatment in the community as a follow-up to prison programs

CAREERS IN CJ

FASTFACTS

HALFWAY HOUSE PROGRAM MANAGER JOB DESCRIPTION:

- Coordinate recreational, educational, and vocational counseling, and other programs for residents.

- Maintain the security of the house and residents.

- Serve as a mediator between the residents and the community and serve as an advocate for the halfway house before community groups.

- Supervise and train staff and communicate with parole officers.

- Prepare budgets, keep records, and maintain and repair the house and equipment.

WHAT KIND OF TRAINING IS REQUIRED?

- A bachelor's degree or master's degree in social work, career counseling, criminal justice, or psychology.

- Also helpful are internships, volunteer work with a halfway house, and community service work with an agency.

ANNUAL SALARY RANGE?

- $29,390–$45,552

For additional information on a career as a halfway house program manager, visit:

www.michigan.gov/careers/
0,1607,7-170-46398-64300--,00
.html

JULIE HOWE
HALFWAY HOUSE PROGRAM MANAGER

My involvement in the criminal justice field started my freshman year of college. I took a criminal justice class, liked it, and just stuck with it. I know my career choice surprised my parents, but I wanted to have an impact on others.

GETTING STARTED My career in the criminal justice field began in 1987 as an employee of Oriana House, a nonprofit, nationally renowned chemical dependency treatment and community corrections agency in Akron, Ohio, that offers a variety of residential and nonresidential programming to offenders within the community. In 1989, on completion of my bachelor of arts degree in sociology/corrections and associate degree in criminal justice, I left Oriana House and became a probation officer. As a probation officer, I was able to examine my career path and expand my knowledge as well as my interest within the criminal justice field. When, in 1992, I returned to Oriana House, I was determined to grow with the agency because I agreed with and trusted its philosophy and mission. Today, I manage the admissions department and our minimum-security jail.

EARNING TRUST Early on in my career, I felt a bit intimidated by the clients simply because of my discomfort, not by their behavior. I started out very stern and learned later that it was better to start strong and to lighten up later rather than the reverse. The clients respect you more and know to take you seriously. My first client as a case manager was a real eye-opener. He was in his fifties and I was in my early twenties. Earning his trust was quite a challenge. In the end he learned to respect me, and I learned different techniques when working with offenders.

CHANGING LIVES My favorite part of my job is that I know that I have an impact on people's lives. If I can assist someone to become sober, responsible, employed, and self-sufficient, I am also having an impact on the community and those whom my clients' lives touch. I never get tired of hearing clients say thanks and knowing their lives are forever changed when they realize their potential and value. I also love that I have the opportunity to influence the behavior of others and shape their future. What an awesome responsibility!

CAREER ADVICE Having a degree in this field is essential, and working hard to get to the next level is rewarding. You have to keep focused; have a goal, and you will achieve success through commitment to the field and your beliefs, honesty to yourself and others, and compassion for what you do. Do this and you will become a leader in your desired field. Work hard, stay true to your beliefs and values, and get involved. Be authentic. I would also advise people to work one day at a time and forget about the stresses or failures of yesterday. Those things you learned yesterday can be used to make today better.

were five times more likely to be drug free after sixty months of freedom than those who did not.[124] Employment aid is also essential. Several years ago, the mayor of Newark, New Jersey, created an Office of Reentry to help ex-inmates find jobs. Of those who are successful, only 10 percent are likely to reoffend.[125] The incentive to reduce recidivism—thereby holding down inmate populations—has spurred a number of states to implement far-reaching desistance programs. The Michigan Prison Reentry Initiative, for example, establishes an individualized "transition plan" for all released inmates. This plan, which includes not only substance abuse treatment and employment aid but transportation, housing, and life skills counseling, is credited with reducing Michigan's recidivism rate among parolees by 33 percent.[126]

"I don't care if we stomp on his civil liberties. Truly, I don't."

—New Jersey politician **Mike Howell,** referring to a law limiting where sex offenders are allowed to live (2008)

Sex Offender Notification Law Legislation that requires law enforcement authorities to notify people when convicted sex offenders are released into their neighborhood or community.

THE SPECIAL CASE OF SEX OFFENDERS

Despite the beneficial impact of reentry efforts, one group of wrongdoers has consistently been denied access to such programs: those convicted of sex crimes. The eventual return of these offenders to society causes such high levels of community anxiety that the criminal justice system has not yet figured out what to do with them. (A Gallup poll found that 66 percent of the respondents were "very concerned" about child molesters, compared with 52 percent who expressed such concern about violent crime and 36 percent about terrorism.[127])

Part of the problem is that efforts to reform sex offenders have produced inconsistent results. In one of the few long-term studies of the issue, researchers found that sex offenders who took part in therapy programs in California were actually more likely to reoffend than those who received no treatment whatsoever.[128] Thus, corrections officials are caught between public demands for protection from "these monsters" and the insistence of medical professionals that sex offenders represent a public health problem, albeit one without any ready solution. Not surprisingly, strategies to control sex offenders on their release from prison have frustrated both the public and medical professionals.

SEX OFFENDER NOTIFICATION LAWS In the summer of 1994, seven-year-old Megan Kanka of Hamilton Township, New Jersey, was raped and murdered by a twice-convicted pedophile (an adult sexually attracted to children) who had moved into her neighborhood after being released from prison on parole. The next year, in response to public outrage, the state passed a series of laws known collectively as the New Jersey Sexual Offender Registration Act, or "Megan's Law."[129] Today, all fifty states and the federal government have their own version of Megan's Law, or a **sex offender notification law,** which requires local law authorities to alert the public when a sex offender has been released into the community.

ACTIVE AND PASSIVE NOTIFICATION No two sex offender notification laws have exactly the same provisions, but all are designed with the goal of allowing the public to learn the identities of convicted sex offenders living in their midst. In general, the laws demand that a paroled sex offender notify local law enforcement authorities on taking up residence in a state. In Georgia, for example, paroled sex offenders are required to present themselves to both the local sheriff and the superintendent of the public school district where they plan to live.[130] This registration process must be renewed every time the parolee changes address.

The authorities, in turn, notify the community of the sex offender's presence through the use of one of two models. Under the "active" model, the authorities directly notify the community or community representatives. Traditionally, this notification has taken the form of bulletins or posters, distributed and posted within a certain distance from the offender's home. Recently, however, a number of states have started using e-mail alerts to fulfill notification obligations. In the "passive" model, information on sex offenders is made open and available for public scrutiny. All fifty states operate Web sites that provide citizens with data on registered sex offenders in their jurisdiction.

CONDITIONS OF RELEASE Generally, sex offenders are supervised by parole officers and are subject to the same threat

LO 9

of revocation as other parolees. Paroled child molesters usually have the following conditions of release:

- Must have no contact with children under the age of sixteen.
- Must continue psychiatric treatment.
- Must receive permission from the parole officers to change residence.
- Must stay a certain distance from schools or parks where children are present.
- Cannot own toys that may be used to lure children.
- Cannot have a job or participate in any activity that involves children.

In addition, of course, they are required to register through the proper authorities. Today, more than 715,000 registered sex offenders live throughout the United States. (Many face further restrictions because of state and local residency laws, a controversial strategy addressed in the *CJ in Action* feature at the end of this chapter.)

CIVIL CONFINEMENT To many, any type of freedom, even if encumbered by notification requirements, is too much freedom for a sex offender. "The issue is, what can you do short of putting them all in prison for the rest of their lives?" complained one policymaker.[131] In fact, many jurisdictions have devised a method to keep sex offenders off the streets for, if not their entire lives, then close to it.

A number of states have passed civil confinement laws that allow corrections officials to keep sex offenders locked up in noncorrectional facilities such as psychiatric hospitals after the conclusion of their prison terms. Under these laws, which we first encountered in Chapter 12 in connection with the mentally ill, corrections officials can keep sexual criminals confined indefinitely, as long as they are deemed a danger to society. Given the recidivism rates of sex offenders, civil confinement laws essentially give the state the power to detain this class of criminal indefinitely—a power upheld by the United States Supreme Court in 2010.[132] (To learn more about this subject, see the feature *Myth versus Reality—Recidivism Rates of Sex Offenders* on the next page.)

Protests by relatives and friends of Donna Jou forced California state officials to delay the scheduled April 2011 release of John Steven Burgess, a convicted sex offender who drugged and accidentally killed Jou four years earlier. Why might notification laws sometimes fail to protect the community from sex offenders such as Burgess? ZUMA Press/Newscom

Teaching Tip: Have students research sex offender notification procedures in your state. How is the public informed of sex offenders living within your community? Are the procedures active or passive?

Civil Confinement The practice of confining individuals against their will if they present a danger to the community.

MYTH vs. REALITY Recidivism Rates of Sex Offenders

In paving the way for extended confinement of sex offenders beyond the terms of their sentences, the United States Supreme Court focused on the high recidivism rates associated with this class of criminal. According to the Supreme Court, "when convicted sex offenders reenter society they are much more likely than any other type of offender to be arrested for a new rape or sexual assault." The unusually high recidivism rates of sex offenders have been used as justification for a wide range of measures designed to control their movements after release from prison. All of this begs the question: Is the justification supported by the facts?

THE MYTH Sex offenders, more than other criminals, are bound to repeat their crimes.

THE REALITY To a certain extent, the myth is correct, in that the medical health profession has had little success in treating the "urges" that lead to sexually deviant behavior. This has not, however, translated into rampant recidivism among sex offenders when compared with other types of offenders. According to a report published by the U.S. Department of Justice in 2002, the released prisoners with the highest rearrest rates were those who committed property crimes such as possession and sale of stolen goods (77.4 percent), larceny (74.6 percent), and burglary (74 percent). The rearrest rates of rapists (46 percent) and those convicted of other forms of sexual assault (41.4 percent) were among the lowest for all crimes. Furthermore, only 2.5 percent of convicted rapists were arrested for another rape within three years of their release.

More recently, Canadian researchers R. Karl Hanson and Kelly Morton-Bourgon analyzed eighty-two recidivism studies on sex offenders and found that 13.7 percent were apprehended for another sex crime after release. On average, the sex offenders were significantly more likely to be rearrested for nonsexual criminal activity, if they were rearrested at all.

FOR CRITICAL ANALYSIS How do these figures affect your opinion of Megan's Laws and other legal steps taken to monitor and control released sex offenders? Do you think the horrible nature of sex crimes, particularly against children, justifies any measures taken to protect the community against these offenders, regardless of the statistics?

SELFASSESSMENT

Fill in the blanks and check your answers on page 497.

Ex-convicts often struggle to succeed after being released from prison because their limited skills make it difficult to find _____. The resulting financial troubles hamper the offender's ability to secure _____, which makes it more likely that he or she will recidivate. One way in which the corrections system tries to reverse this process is by offering _____ programs that include job training and work release opportunities. Corrections officials also promote _____, or the process by which a former inmate stops committing crimes, by allowing certain low-risk offenders to live in _____ houses, where they can receive specialized treatment. Sex offender _____ laws, also known as Megan's laws, mandate that law enforcement officials must alert the public when a sex offender has moved into the community.

CJ IN ACTION

A SECOND LOOK AT RESIDENCY LAWS

In early 2010, more than one hundred convicted sex offenders were living under the Julia Tuttle Causeway, a bridge that connects Miami, Florida, with Miami Beach. Soon thereafter, Dade County officials closed the impromptu camp, which had become an embarrassment. Efforts to relocate the ex-convicts created clusters of sex offenders in two other unhappy neighborhoods, however, and many of the former bridge dwellers remained homeless. "We're damned," said Patrick Weise, a forty-nine-year-old former Julia Tuttle resident who was living in a field.[133] Weise and the other sex offenders were having difficulty finding housing as a result of the county's residency law, an increasingly common and popular method for protecting children that, as we will discuss in this *CJ in Action* feature, may have unexpected consequences.

ZONING RESTRICTIONS FOR SEX OFFENDERS

More than half of the states and hundreds of municipalities have passed residency restrictions for convicted sex offenders. These laws ban sex offenders from living within a certain distance from places where children naturally congregate. In New Jersey, for example, "high-risk" offenders cannot take up residence within 3,000 feet of any school, park or campground, church, theater, bowling alley, library, or convenience store.[134] (For medium- and low-risk offenders, the distances are 2,500 feet and 1,000 feet, respectively.) The overlapping "off-limits zones" created by residency requirements can dramatically limit where a sex offender can find affordable housing, as was the case with Patrick Weise and the other sex offenders living under the bridge in Miami.

THE CASE FOR SEX OFFENDER RESIDENCY RESTRICTIONS

- Forbidding sex offenders from residing near schools and other areas that attract large groups of children decreases their access to these children, thus reducing the risk that they will reoffend. Research conducted by Jeffrey Walker of the University of Arkansas found that child molesters are nearly twice as likely to live near schools as offenders convicted of sexually assaulting adults.[135]

- The residency requirements are reassuring to parents and are generally very popular with the public.

- The right of convicted sex offenders to choose where they live is less important than the protection of law-abiding citizens.

THE CASE AGAINST SEX OFFENDER RESIDENCY RESTRICTIONS

- The laws push sex offenders into less populated areas or homelessness, which makes it much more difficult for law enforcement and corrections agents to keep tabs on them. "Probation and parole supervisors cannot effectively monitor offenders who are living under bridges, in parking lots, in tents at parks or interstate truck stops," says Elizabeth Barnhill of the Iowa Coalition against Sexual Assault.[136]

AP Photo/J. Pat Carter

- The laws are inadequate. Studies have shown that strangers commit only about 10 percent of all sexual offenses against children. The perpetrators of such crimes are much more likely to be family members, friends, or other acquaintances.[137]

- The laws create a false sense of security. If a sex offender wants to get to a child, a residency requirement cannot stop him or her from simply getting in a car or walking to find a victim.

WRITING ASSIGNMENT— YOUR OPINION

The town of Dyersville, Iowa, has one of the strictest residency requirements in the country: no sex offenders can live anywhere within its limits. What is your opinion of this strategy? How do you feel about residency laws in general? Do these regulations constitute extra punishment for convicts who have already, at least in theory, paid their debt for their crimes? As an alternative, should certain sex offenders be sentenced to life in prison without parole, sparing the criminal justice system the need to create awkward laws like residency requirements and civil confinement? Before responding, you can review our discussions in this chapter concerning:

- Parole, particularly the discussion of the reasons for parole (page 482).

- Barriers to reentry (pages 488–490).

- Civil confinement (page 493).

Your answer should include at least three full paragraphs.

CHAPTER SUMMARY

LO 1 **Explain the concept of prison as a total institution.** Though many people spend time in partial institutions—schools, companies where they work, and religious organizations—only in prison is every aspect of an inmate's life controlled, and that is why prisons are called total institutions. Every detail for every prisoner is fully prescribed and managed.

LO 2 **Describe the possible patterns of inmate behavior, which are driven by the inmate's personality and values.** (a) Professional criminals adapt to prison by "doing time" and follow the rules in order to get out quickly. (b) Those who are "jailing" establish themselves within the power structure of prison culture. These are often veterans of juvenile detention centers and other prisons. (c) Those who are "gleaning" are working to improve themselves for return to society. (d) "Disorganized" criminals have mental impairments or low IQs and therefore are unable to adapt to prison culture.

LO 3 **Indicate some of the reasons for violent behavior in prisons.** (a) To separate the powerful from the weak and establish a prisoner hierarchy; (b) to minimize one's own probability of being a target of assault; (c) to enhance one's self-image; (d) to obtain sexual relief; and (e) to obtain material goods through extortion or robbery.

LO 4 **List and briefly explain the six general job categories among correctional officers.** (a) Block officers, who supervise cell blocks or are on block guard duty; (b) work detail supervisors, who oversee the cafeteria, prison store, and laundry, for example; (c) industrial shop and school officers, who generally oversee workshop and educational programs; (d) yard officers, who patrol the prison yard when prisoners are allowed there; (e) tower guards, who work in isolation; and (f) those who hold administrative building assignments, such as prison gate guards and overseers of visitation procedures.

LO 5 **Describe the hands-off doctrine of prisoner law and indicate two standards used to determine if prisoners' rights have been violated.** The hands-off doctrine assumes that the care of prisoners should be left to prison officials and that it is not the place of judges to intervene. Nonetheless, the Supreme Court has created two standards to be used by the courts in determining whether a prisoner's Eighth Amendment protections against cruel and unusual punishment have been violated. Under the "deliberate indifference" standard, prisoners must show that prison officials were aware of harmful conditions at the facility but failed to remedy them. Under the "identifiable human needs" standard, prisoners must show that they were denied a basic need such as food, warmth, or exercise.

LO 6 **Contrast probation, parole, expiration release, pardon, and furlough.** Probation is an alternative to incarceration. Parole is an early release program for those incarcerated. Expiration release occurs when the inmate has served the maximum time for her or his initial sentence minus good-time credits. A pardon can be given only by the president or one of the fifty governors. Furlough is a temporary release while in jail or prison.

LO 7 **Describe typical conditions of parole.** Parolees must not use drugs, not associate with known felons, not change their addresses without notifying authorities, and report to their parole officer at specified intervals. (These terms are usually set out in the parole contract.)

LO 8 **Explain the goal of prisoner reentry programs.** Based on the ideals of rehabilitation, these programs have two main objectives: (a) to prepare a prisoner for a successful return to the community, and (b) to protect the community by reducing the chances that the ex-convict will continue her or his criminal activity after release from prison.

LO 9 **Indicate typical conditions for release for a paroled child molester.** (a) Have no contact with children under the age of sixteen; (b) continue psychiatric treatment; (c) obtain permission from a parole officer to change residence; (d) keep away from schools or parks where children are present; (e) cannot own toys that may be used to lure children; and (f) cannot have a job or participate in any activity that involves children.

SELF ASSESSMENT ANSWER KEY

Page 467: **i.** total institution; **ii.** argot; **iii.** economies; **iv.** age; **v.** health-care; **vi.** vocational; **vii.** cost

Page 472: **i.** deprivation; **ii.** relative deprivation; **iii.** segregation; **iv.** gangs

Page 478: **i.** block officers; **ii.** discipline; **iii.** legitimate; **iv.** malicious; **v.** Eighth; **vi.** deliberate

Page 481: **i.** minority; **ii.** drug; **iii.** abuse; **iv.** children; **v.** correctional officers

Page 488: **i.** conditional; **ii.** sentence; **iii.** parole board; **iv.** mandatory; **v.** contract; **vi.** technical

Page 494: **i.** employment; **ii.** housing; **iii.** reentry; **iv.** desistance; **v.** halfway; **vi.** notification

KEY TERMS

civil confinement **493**
"deliberate indifference" **477**
deprivation model **467**
desistance **490**
discretionary release **483**
expiration release **482**
furlough **482**
halfway house **490**
"hands-off" doctrine **476**
"identifiable human needs" **477**

mandatory release **485**
pardon **482**
parole **482**
parole board **484**
parole contract **486**
parole grant hearing **484**
parole guidelines **486**
parole revocation **487**
prison gang **469**
prison programs **466**

prison segregation **469**
prisoner reentry **488**
prisonization **463**
relative deprivation **468**
security threat group (STG) **470**
sex offender notification law **492**
total institution **463**
work release program **490**

QUESTIONS FOR CRITICAL ANALYSIS

1. How does the process of prisonization differ between male and female inmates?

2. Several years ago, sheriff's deputies ordered one hundred inmates at a Los Angeles County jail to strip naked, removed the mattresses from their cells, and left them with nothing to cover themselves but blankets for twenty-four hours. Are these steps—taken to quell racially motivated violence—morally acceptable? Are they legal?

3. Do you agree with prison policies that prohibit male correctional officers from patting down and strip searching female inmates? Why or why not? Under what circumstances might such policies be unrealistic?

4. In the last chapter, you learned about the principle of least eligibility, which holds that inmates should not receive any benefits that are unavailable to the least advantaged members of outside society. Do you agree with the principle of least eligibility? If so, do you believe that the prison programs such as substance abuse treatment and vocational training should be discontinued? Why or why not? If you disagree with the principle, how can you justify such programs beyond their benefits for individual inmates? Explain your answers.

5. In many jurisdictions, parolees can be stopped and searched by parole or police officers at any time, even if there is no probable cause that the parolee has committed a crime. What is the justification for such a policy?

CourseMate *For Online Help*

For online help and access to resources that accompany *Criminal Justice Today*, go to www.cengagebrain.com/shop/ISBN/1111835578. Click "Access Now," where you will find flashcards, an online quiz, and other helpful study aids. If you have an access code for CourseMate, log in and go to the chapter of your choice for additional online study aids.

NOTES

1. Johnny Cash, "Folsom Prison Blues" (Sun Records, 1955).

2. Roderick Davis, "The Road from Prison to Rehabilitation," *New York Times* (January 21, 2011), at **www.nytimes.com/interactive/2011/01/22/opinion/20110122_Fixes_Delancey.html?emc=eta1**.

3. Erving Goffman, "On the Characteristics of Total Institutions," in *Asylums: Essays on the Social Situation of Mental Patients and Other Inmates* (New York: Doubleday, 1961), 6.

4. Donald Clemmer, *The Prison Community* (Boston: Christopher, 1940).

5. John Irwin, *Prisons in Turmoil* (Boston: Little, Brown, 1980), 67.

6. Robert Aday, *Aging Prisoners: Crisis in American Corrections* (Westport, CT: Praeger, 2003), 1–5.

7. Bureau of Justice Statistics, *Medical Causes of Death in State Prisons* (Washington, D.C.: U.S. Department of Justice, January 2007), 3.

8. Bureau of Justice Statistics, "Medical Problems of Prisoners," April 2008, "Highlights" and Table 2, at **www.ojp.usdoj.gov/bjs/pub/pdf/mpp.pdf**.

9. Rena Fox et al., "Hepatitis C Virus Infection among Prisoners in the California State Correctional System," *Clinical Infectious Diseases* (June 2005), 177–186.

10. Nicholas K. Geranios, "Aging Inmates Straining State Prison System," *Associated Press* (November 10, 2010).

11. Barbara Hoberock, "Golden Years of Prison," *Tulsa World* (January 7, 2011), A1.

12. Marisa Lagos, "Inmates' Medical Parole Proposed," *San Francisco Chronicle* (March 18, 2010), C1.

13. Michael Vitiello, "Addressing the Special Problems of Mentally Ill Prisoners: A Small Piece of the Solution to Our Nation's Prison Crisis," *Denver University Law Review* (Fall 2010), 57–62.

14. Katherine Stuart van Wormer and Clemens Bartollas, *Women and the Criminal Justice System*, 3d ed. (Upper Saddle River, NJ: Pearson Education, 2011), 143.

15. Bureau of Justice Statistics, *Mental Health Problems of Prison and Jail Inmates* (Washington, D.C.: U.S. Department of Justice, September 2006), 1.

16. William Kanapaux, "Guilty of Mental Illness," *Psychiatric Times* (January 1, 2004), at **www.psychiatrictimes.com/forensic-psych/content/article/10168/47631**.

17. Bureau of Justice Statistics, *Census of State and Federal Correctional Facilities, 2005* (Washington, D.C.: U.S. Department of Justice, October 2008), 6.

18. Todd R. Clear, George F. Cole, and Michael D. Reisig, *American Corrections*, 9th ed (Belmont, CA: Wadsworth Cengage Learning, 2011), 381.

19. *Behind Bars II: Substance Abuse and America's Prison Population* (New York: The National Center on Addiction and Substance Abuse at Columbia University, February 2010), 4.

20. *Ibid.,* 83–84.

21. Devah Pager and Bruce Western, *Investigating Prisoner Reentry: The Impact of Conviction Status on the Employment Prospects of Young Men* (Washington, D.C.: National Institute of Justice, October 2009), 6.

22. *Census of State and Federal Correctional Facilities, 2005,* 6.

23. Ron Barnett, "Incarcerated Getting Educated," *USA Today* (September 26, 2008), 2A.

24. Kevin Johnson, "Prison Diving Program Anchors Former Inmates," *USA Today* (July 14, 2008), 4A.

25. Steve Aos, Marna Miller, and Elizabeth Drake, *Evidence-Based Public Policy Options to Reduce Future Prison Construction, Criminal Justice Costs, and Crime Rates* (Olympia, WA: Washington State Institute for Public Policy, 2006), Exhibit 4, page 9.

26. Robert Johnson, *Hard Time: Understanding and Reforming the Prison*, 2d ed. (Belmont, CA: Wadsworth, 1996), 133.

27. Federal Bureau of Prisons report, cited in Kevin Johnson, "Report Points to Prison Security Failures," *USA Today* (June 8, 2009), 3A.

28. "Table 1. Number of State Prisoner Deaths, by Cause of Death, 2001–2007," at **bjs.ojp.usdoj.gov/content/dcrp/tables/dcst07spt1.pdf**; and Bureau of Justice Statistics, *Mortality in Local Jails, 2001–2007* (Washington, D.C.: U.S. Department of Justice, July 2010), Appendix Table 2, page 16.

29. Lee H. Bowker, *Prison Victimization* (New York: Elsevier, 1981), 31–33.

30. Stephen C. Light, "The Severity of Assaults on Prison Officers: A Contextual Analysis," *Social Science Quarterly* 71 (1990), 267–284.

31. Frank Tannenbaum, *Crime and Community* (Boston: Ginn & Co., 1938).

32. Randy Martin and Sherwood Zimmerman, "A Typology of the Causes of Prison Riots and an Analytical Extension to the 1986 Virginia Riot," *Justice Quarterly* 7 (1990), 711–737.

33. Bert Useem, "Disorganization and the New Mexico Prison Riot of 1980," *American Sociological Review* 50 (1985), 677–688.

34. Stuart B. Klein, "Prisoners' Rights to Physical and Mental Health Care: A Modern Expansion of the Eighth Amendment's Cruel and Unusual Punishment Clause," *Fordham University Law Journal* 7 (1978), 1.

35. Herman Badillo and Milton Haynes, *A Bill of No Rights: Attica and the American Prison System* (New York: Outerbridge & Lazard, 1972), 42.

36. Michael S. Serrill and Peter Katel, "New Mexico: The Anatomy of a Riot," *Corrections Magazine* (April 1980), 6–7.

37. Badillo and Haynes, 26.

38. Irwin, 47.

39. Leo Carroll, "Race, Ethnicity, and the Social Order of the Prison," in *The Pains of Imprisonment*, ed. R. Johnson and H. Toch (Beverly Hills, CA: Sage, 1982).

40. Leo Carroll, *Hacks, Blacks, and Cons: Race Relations in a Maximum-Security Prison* (Lexington, MA: Lexington Books, 1988), 78.

41. *Lee v. Washington*, 390 U.S. 333 (1968).

42. *Johnson v. California*, 543 U.S. 499 (2005).

43. *Ibid.,* at 508.

44. Jody Kent, "Race Walls Won't End Jail Riots," *Los Angeles Times* (February 12, 2006), M3.

45. Craig Haney, "Psychology and the Limits of Prison Pain," *Psychology, Public Policy, and Law* (December 1977), 499.

46. Alan J. Drury and Matt DeLisi, "Gangkill: An Exploratory Empirical Assessment of Gang Membership, Homicide Offending, and Prison Misconduct," *Crime & Delinquency* (January 2011), 130–146.

47. *A Study of Gangs and Security Threat Groups in America's Adult Prisons and Jails* (Indianapolis: National Major Gang Task Force, 2002).

48. George W. Knox, *The Problem of Gangs and Security Threat Groups (STGs) in American Prisons Today: Recent Research Findings from the 2004 Prison Gang Survey*, available at **www.ngcrc.com/corr2006.html**.

49. David M. Allender and Frank Marcell. "Career Criminals, Security Threat Groups, and Prison Gangs: An Interrelated Threat," *FBI Law Enforcement Bulletin* (June 2003), 8.

50. Knox.

51. Alan Gomez, "States Make Prisons Far Less Deadly," *USA Today* (August 22, 2008), 3A.

52. David Kaiser and Lovisa Stannow, "Prison Rape and the Government," *The New York Review of Books* (March 24, 2011), at **www.nybooks.com/articles/archives/2011/mar/24/prison-rape-and-government**.

53. James E. Robertson, "The Prison Rape Elimination Act of 2003: A Primer," *Criminal Law Bulletin* (May/June 2004), 270–273.

54. Quoted in John J. DiIulio, Jr., *No Escape: The Future of American Corrections* (New York: Basic Books, 1991), 268.

55. Jack Henry Abbott, *In the Belly of the Beast* (New York: Vintage Books, 1991), 54.

56. Michel Foucault, *Discipline and Punish: The Birth of the Prison* (New York: Pantheon Books, 1977), 128.

57. Lucien X. Lombardo, *Guards Imprisoned: Correctional Officers at Work* (Cincinnati, OH: Anderson Publishing Co., 1989), 51–71.

58. Goffman, 7.

59. Clear, Cole, and Reisig, 333.

60. *Wolff v. McDonnell*, 418 U.S. 539 (1974).

61. 475 U.S. 312 (1986).

62. *Stanley v. Hejirika*, 134 F.3d 629 (4th Cir. 1998).

63. Christopher R. Smith, *Law and Contemporary Corrections* (Belmont, CA: Wadsworth, 1999), Chapter 6.

64. 503 U.S. 1 (1992).

65. Darrell L. Ross, "Assessing *Hudson v. McMillan* Ten Years Later," *Criminal Law Bulletin* (September/October 2004), 508.

66. Van Wormer and Bartollas, 387.

67. Cristina Rathbone, *A World Apart: Women, Prison, and a Life behind Bars* (New York: Random House, 2006), 46.

68. Carl Nink *et al., Women Professionals in Corrections: A Growing Asset* (Centerville, UT: MTC Institute, August 2008), 1.

69. Denise L. Jenne and Robert C. Kersting, "Aggression and Women Correctional Officers in Male Prisons," *Prison Journal* (1996), 442–460.

70. Nink *et al.,* 8–9.

71. Matt Gouras, "Female Prison Guards Often Behind Sex Misconduct," *Associated Press* (March 14, 2010).

72. *Wolff v. McDonnell,* 539.

73. *Hudson v. Palmer,* 468 U.S. 517 (1984).

74. 429 U.S. 97 (1976).

75. 501 U.S. 294 (1991).

76. *Wilson v. Seiter,* 501 U.S. 294, 304 (1991).

77. 563 U.S. ___ (2011).

78. *Procunier v. Martinez,* 416 U.S. 396 (1974).

79. *Cruz v. Beto,* 405 U.S. 319 (1972); *Gittlemacker v. Prasse,* 428 F.2d 1 (3d Cir. 1970); and *Kahane v. Carlson,* 527 F.2d 492 (2d Cir. 1975).

80. Maryclaire Dale, "Court Says Pa. Prison Can Ban Muslim Scarf," *Associated Press* (August 2, 2010).

81. Quoted in Alexandra Marks, "Martha Checks in Today," *Seattle Times* (October 8, 2004), A8.

82. Bureau of Justice Statistics, *Profile of Jail Inmates, 2002* (Washington, D.C.: U.S. Department of Justice, July 2004), 10.

83. Bureau of Justice Statistics, *Prior Abuse Reported by Inmates and Probationers* (Washington, D.C.: U.S. Department of Justice, April 1999), 2.

84. *Caught in the Net: The Impact of Drug Policies on Women and Families* (Washington, D.C.: American Civil Liberties Union, 2004), 18–19.

85. Allen J. Beck and Laura M. Maruschak, *Mental Health Treatment in State Prisons, 2000* (Washington, D.C.: U.S. Department of Justice, July 2001), 1.

86. Barbara Bloom, Barbara Owen, and Stephanie Covington, *Gender Responsive Strategies: Research, Practice, and Guiding Principles for Women Offenders* (Washington, D.C.: National Institute of Corrections, 2003), 6.

87. *Ibid.,* 7.

88. *Ibid.,* 6.

89. Sarah Schirmer, Ashley Nellis, and Marc Mauer, *Incarcerated Parents and Their Children: Trends 1991–2007* (Washington, D.C.: The Sentencing Project, February 2009), 2.

90. Kelly Bedard and Eric Helland, "Location of Women's Prisons and the Deterrent Effect of 'Harder' Time," *International Review of Law and Economics* (June 2004), 152.

91. *Ibid.*

92. Schirmer, Nellis, and Mauer, 5.

93. Rathbone, 4.

94. *Ibid.,* 158.

95. Van Wormer and Bartollas, 137–138.

96. Barbara Bloom and Meda Chesney-Lind, "Women in Prison," in Roslyn Muraskin, ed., *It's a Crime: Women and Justice,* 4th ed. (Upper Saddle River, NJ: Prentice Hall, 2007), 542–563.

97. Piper Kerman, *Orange Is the New Black: My Year in a Women's Prison* (New York: Spiegal and Grau, 2011), 131.

98. Esther Heffernan, *Making It in Prison: The Square, the Cool, and the Life* (New York: Wiley, 1972), 91.

99. Leanne F. Alarid, "Female Inmate Subcultures," in *Corrections Contexts: Contemporary and Classical Readings,* ed. James W. Marquart and Jonathan R. Sorenson (Los Angeles: Roxbury Publishing Co., 1997), 136–137.

100. Barbara Owen *et al., Gendered Violence and Safety: A Contextual Approach to Improving Security in Women's Facilities,* December 2008, 12–14, at **www.ncjrs.gov/pdffiles1/ nij/grants/225340.pdf.**

101. Nancy Wolff, Cynthia Blitz, Jing Shi, Jane Siegel, and Ronet Bachman, "Physical Violence inside Prisons: Rates of Victimization," *Criminal Justice and Behavior* 34 (2007), 588–604.

102. Van Wormer and Bartollas, 146–148.

103. Jocelyn M. Pollock, *Women, Prison and Crime* (Belmont, CA: Wadsworth, 2002), 52.

104. Cited in Bloom, Owen, and Covington, 26.

105. Clear, Cole, and Reisig, 408.

106. Bureau of Justice Statistics, "Reentry Trends in the U.S.," at **bjs.ojp.usdoj.gov/ content/reentry/releases.cfm.**

107. 442 U.S. 1 (1979).

108. Ashley Nellis and Ryan S. King, *No Exit: The Expanding Use of Life Sentences in America* (Washington, D.C.: The Sentencing Project, July 2009), 3.

109. William Parker, *Parole: Origins, Development, Current Practices, and Statutes* (College Park, MD: American Correctional Association, 1972), 26.

110. Quoted in "Chapman Strikes Out Again in Parole Bid," *Chicago Tribune* (September 8, 2010), 15.

111. Bureau of Justice Statistics, *Bulletin* (Washington, D.C.: U.S. Department of Justice, January 1995), 2.

112. Michael Tonry, "Twenty Years of Sentencing Reform: Steps Forward, Steps Backward," *Judicature* 78 (January/February 1995), 169.

113. Marc Mauer, "The Truth about Truth in Sentencing," *Corrections Today* (February 1, 1996), S1.

114. Mark P. Rankin, Mark H. Allenbaugh, and Carlton Fields, "Parole's Essential Role in Bailing Out Our Nation's Criminal Justice Systems," *Champion* (January 2009), 47–48.

115. 408 U.S. 471 (1972).

116. Joan Petersilia, *When Prisoners Come Home: Parole and Prisoner Reentry* (New York: Oxford University Press, 2003), 39.

117. Victor Hassine, *Life without Parole: Living in Prison Today,* ed. Thomas J. Bernard and Richard McCleary (Los Angeles: Roxbury Publishing Co., 1996), 12.

118. John H. Tyler and Jeffrey R. King, "Prison-Based Education and Reentry into the Mainstream Labor Market," in *Barriers to Reentry? The Labor Market for Released Prisoners in Post-Industrial America,* ed. Shawn D. Bushway, Michael A. Stoll, and David F. Weiman (New York: Russell Sage Foundation, 2007), 237.

119. *Ill Equipped: U.S. Prisons and Offenders with Mental Illness* (New York: Human Rights Watch, 2003).

120. Pew Center on the States, *State of Recidivism: The Revolving Door of America's Prisons* (Washington, D.C.: The Pew Charitable Trusts, April 2011), 2.

121. Edward Zamble and Vernon Quinsey, *The Criminal Recidivism Process* (Cambridge, England: Cambridge University Press, 1997).

122. Quoted in Kevin Johnson, "After Years of Solitary, Freedom Is Hard to Grasp," *USA Today* (June 9, 2005), 2A.

123. *Census of State and Federal Correctional Facilities,* 2005, Table 6, page 5.

124. *Behind Bars II: Substance Abuse and America's Prison Population,* 68–69.

125. "They All Come Home," *The Economist* (April 23, 2011), 34.

126. Pew Center on the States, 21.

127. "The Greatest Fear," *The Economist* (August 26, 2006), 25.

128. Janice Marques, Mark Wiederanders, David Day, Craig Nelson, and Alice Ommeren, "Effects of a Relapse Prevention Program on Sexual Recidivism: Final Results from California's Sex Offender Treatment and Evaluation Project (SOTEP)," *Sexual Abuse: A Journal of Research and Treatment* (January 2005), 79–107.

129. New Jersey Revised Statute Section 2C:7-8(c) (1995).

130. Georgia Code Annotated Section 42-9-44.1(b)(1).

131. Abby Goodnough, "After Two Cases in Florida, Crackdown on Molesters," *Law Enforcement News* (May 2004), 12.

132. *United States v. Comstock,* 560 U.S. ___ (2010).

133. Quoted in Robert Samuels, "Julia Tuttle Encampment: For Miami-Dade Sex Offenders, Wandering Awaits," *Miami Herald* (July 27, 2010), A1.

134. New Jersey Statutes Annotated Section 2C: 7-3.

135. Wendy Kock, "Sex-Offender Residency Laws Get a Second Look," *USA Today* (February 26, 2007), 1A.

136. Quoted in Jenifer Warren, "Sex Crime Residency Laws Exile Offenders," *Los Angeles Times* (October 30, 2006), 1.

137. Bureau of Justice Statistics, *Recidivism of Sex Offenders Released from Prison in 1994* (Washington, D.C.: U.S. Department of Justice, November 2003), 36; and Luis Rosell, "Sex Offenders: Pariahs of the 21st Century?" *William Mitchell Law Review* (2005), 419.

CHAPTER

15

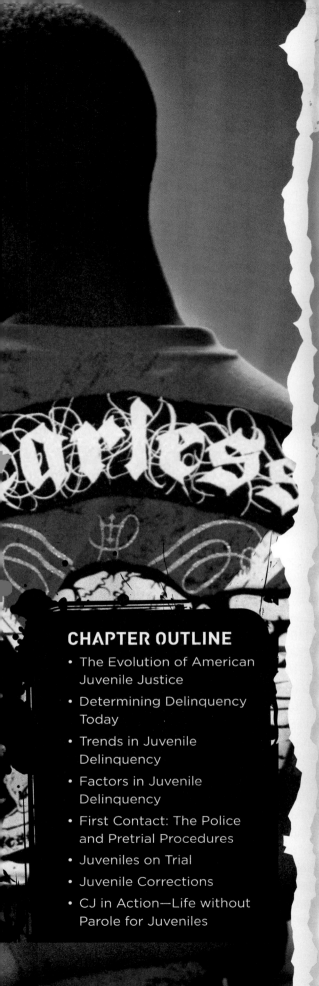

ZUMA Press/Newscom

The Juvenile Justice System

LEARNING OBJECTIVES

After reading this chapter, you should be able to . . .

LO 1 Describe the child-saving movement and its relationship to the doctrine of *parens patriae.*

LO 2 List the four major differences between juvenile courts and adult courts.

LO 3 Identify and briefly describe the single most important Supreme Court case with respect to juvenile justice.

LO 4 Describe the one variable that always correlates highly with juvenile crime rates.

LO 5 Indicate some of the reasons why youths join gangs.

LO 6 List the factors that normally determine what police do with juvenile offenders.

LO 7 Describe the four primary stages of pretrial juvenile justice procedure.

LO 8 Explain the distinction between an adjudicatory hearing and a disposition hearing.

LO 9 List the four categories of residential treatment programs.

The nine learning objectives labeled LO 1 through LO 9 are designed to help improve your understanding of the chapter.

CHAPTER OUTLINE

- The Evolution of American Juvenile Justice
- Determining Delinquency Today
- Trends in Juvenile Delinquency
- Factors in Juvenile Delinquency
- First Contact: The Police and Pretrial Procedures
- Juveniles on Trial
- Juvenile Corrections
- CJ in Action—Life without Parole for Juveniles

FULL OF SOUND AND FURY

Wayne Treacy was in a rage. The fifteen-year-old barely knew Josie Lou Ratley, yet he told his friend Kayla Manson on March 17, 2010, that he was going to "snap [Ratley's] neck." Two hours earlier, in a heated text message exchange, Ratley, also fifteen, had chided Treacy for his interest in the thirteen-year-old Manson, calling him a rapist. When Treacy reacted with threats and profanity, Ratley told him to "go visit ur dead brother." This taunt, referring to the suicide of Treacy's older brother six months earlier, elicited a ferocious response. "UR F——CKING DEAD!" Treacy wrote. "I SWEAR TO GOD I'M GONNA KILL YOU. I'LL F——CKING FIND YOU! YOUR ASS IS COLD DEAD MEAT!"

Treacy then put on a pair of steel-toed boots and biked to the Deerfield Middle School campus in Deerfield, Florida. With Manson's help, he found Ratley waiting at a bus stop. Treacy immediately attacked, grabbing the unsuspecting girl by the neck and pushing her to the sidewalk. Before a teacher stopped him, he slammed Ratley's head on the concrete and kicked her in the head several times. Ratley suffered irreversible brain damage, and, a year later, she was still relearning basic skills such as how to read, write, and dress herself.

While being interrogated by law enforcement agents after the incident, Treacy muttered to himself, "You were supposed to yell at her, you stupid idiot." Later, he told his stepfather, "Whenever I think about what I did, I feel so freaking horrible. Like, you know that guilty . . . my chest gets tight and I get that . . . knotted up feeling in my stomach. It just sucks." Prosecutors eventually charged Treacy as an adult with first degree attempted murder. If convicted, he could spend the next fifty years in prison.

Fifteen-year-old Wayne Treacy, center, appears in the Broward County (Florida) Juvenile Court after critically injuring Josie Lou Ratley.
Michael Francis McElroy/MCT/Landov

Sitting alone in the interrogation room at the Broward County Sheriff's Office following his attack on Josie Lou Ratley, unaware that he was being recorded, Wayne Treacy said, "I'm a monster."[1] After several months at the Broward Main Jail awaiting trial, however, his self-diagnosis had softened. "I don't need prison," he told his parents. "I need counseling. And a lot of it."[2] A difficult question—asked every time a young offender such as Treacy commits a horrific act of violence—lies at the heart of the juvenile justice debate: Should criminal acts by youths be given the same weight as those committed by adults, or should they be seen as "mistakes" that can be "corrected" by care and counseling?

The American juvenile justice system generally operates as an uneasy compromise between "rehabilitation and punishment, treatment and custody."[3] In this chapter, we will discuss the successes and failures of this compromise and examine the aspects of the juvenile justice system that differentiate it from the criminal justice system. As you will see, observers on both sides of the "rehabilitation versus punishment" debate find many flaws with the present system. Some have even begun to call for its dismantling. Others blame social problems such as racism, poverty, and a culture dominated by images of violence for creating a situation that no government agency or policy can effectively control.[4]

Critical Thinking Skill Development: Before beginning the chapter, ask students to share their views on the juvenile justice system. Should violent juveniles be tried as adults? Should we even maintain a separate juvenile justice system?

THE EVOLUTION OF AMERICAN JUVENILE JUSTICE

In a 2003 poll, almost 60 percent of Americans indicated that they favored trying violent youths in adult criminal court instead of juvenile courts, which were perceived as too lenient.[5] To a certain degree, such opinions reflect the view that the American juvenile justice system should return to its early emphasis on punishment and incapacitation. At the beginning of the nineteenth century, juvenile offenders were treated the same as adult offenders—they were judged by the same courts and sentenced to the same severe penalties. This situation began to change soon after, as urbanization and industrialization created an immigrant underclass that was, at least in the eyes of many reformers, predisposed to deviant activity. Certain members of the Progressive movement, known as the child savers, began to take steps to "save" children from these circumstances, introducing the idea of rehabilitating delinquents in the process.

> "When our children make mistakes, are we going to lock them up and throw away the key?"
>
> **—Brian Gowdy,**
> defense attorney (2009)

THE CHILD-SAVING MOVEMENT

LO 1 In general, the child savers favored the doctrine of *parens patriae,* which holds that the state has not only a right but also a duty to care for children who are neglected, delinquent, or in some other way disadvantaged. Juvenile offenders, the child savers believed, required treatment, not punishment, and they were horrified at the thought of placing children in prisons with hardened adult criminals. In 1967, then Supreme Court justice Abe Fortas said of the child savers:

> They believed that society's role was not to ascertain whether the child was "guilty" or "innocent," but "What is he, how has he become what he is, and what had best be done in his interest and in the interest of the state to save him from a downward career." The child—essentially good, as they saw it—was made "to feel that he is the object of [the government's] care and solicitude," not that he was under arrest or on trial.[6]

Child-saving organizations convinced local legislatures to pass laws that allowed them to take control of children who exhibited criminal tendencies or had been neglected by their parents. To separate these children from the environment in which they were raised, the organizations created a number of institutions, the best known of which was New York's House of Refuge. Opening in 1825, the House of Refuge implemented many of the same reformist measures popular in the penitentiaries of the time, meaning that its charges were subjected to the healthful influences of hard study and labor. Although the House of Refuge was criticized for its harsh discipline (which caused many boys to run away), similar institutions sprang up throughout the Northeast during the middle of the 1800s.

Parens Patriae A doctrine that holds that the state has a responsibility to look after the well-being of children and to assume the role of parent if necessary.

Teaching Tip: In a short writing assignment, ask students to reflect on the concept of *parens patriae*. What do they think of the idea that juveniles are not fully responsible for their wrongdoing? Can juvenile offenders be rehabilitated? Is rehabilitation still an appropriate goal for the juvenile justice system? (LO 1)

THE ILLINOIS JUVENILE COURT

The efforts of the child savers culminated with the passage of the Illinois Juvenile Court Act in 1899. The Illinois legislature created the first court specifically for juveniles, guided by the principles of *parens patriae* and based on the belief that children are not fully responsible for criminal conduct and are capable of being rehabilitated.[7]

The Illinois Juvenile Court and those in other states that followed in its path were (and, in many cases, remain) drastically different from adult courts:

- *No juries.* The matter was decided by judges who wore regular clothes instead of

LO 2 black robes and sat at a table with the other participants rather than behind a bench. Because the primary focus of the court was on the child and not the crime, the judge had wide discretion in disposing of each case.
- *Different terminology.* To reduce the stigma of criminal proceedings, "petitions" were issued instead of "warrants." The children were not "defendants," but "respondents," and they were not "found guilty" but "adjudicated delinquent."
- *No adversarial relationship.* Instead of trying to determine guilt or innocence, the parties involved in the juvenile court worked together in the best interests of the child, with the emphasis on rehabilitation rather than punishment.
- *Confidentiality.* To avoid "saddling" the child with a criminal past, juvenile court hearings and records were kept sealed, and the proceedings were closed to the public.

By 1945, every state had a juvenile court system modeled after the first Illinois court. For the most part, these courts were able to operate without interference until the 1960s and the onset of the juvenile rights movement.

JUVENILE DELINQUENCY

After the first juvenile court was established in Illinois, the Chicago Bar Association described its purpose as, in part, to "exercise the same tender solicitude and care over its neglected wards that a wise and loving parent would exercise with reference to his [or her] own children under similar circumstances."[8] In other words, the state was given the responsibility of caring for those minors whose behavior seemed to show that they could not be controlled by their parents. As a result, many **status offenders** found themselves in the early houses of refuge and continue to be placed in state-run facilities today. A status offense is an act that, if committed by a juvenile, is considered illegal and grounds for possible state custody. The same act, if committed by an adult, does not warrant law enforcement action. (See Figure 15.1 below for a list of the most common status offenses.)

In contrast, **juvenile delinquency** refers to conduct that would also be criminal if committed by an adult. According to federal law and the laws of most states, a juvenile delinquent is someone who has not yet reached his or her eighteenth birthday—the age of adult criminal responsibility—at the time of the offense in question. In two states (New York and North Carolina), persons aged sixteen are considered adults, and eleven other states confer adulthood on seventeen-year-olds for purposes of criminal law. Under certain circumstances, discussed later in this chapter, children under these ages can be tried in adult courts and incarcerated in adult prisons and jails. Remember that Wayne Treacy was fifteen years old when he was charged as an adult for the attempted murder of Josie Lou Ratley, described on page 502.

Status Offender A juvenile who has engaged in behavior deemed unacceptable for those under a certain statutorily determined age.

Juvenile Delinquency Behavior that is illegal under federal or state law that has been committed by a person who is under an age limit specified by statute.

Critical Thinking Skill Development: Ask students to respond to "Questions for Critical Analysis" number one on page 533, in which they consider the differences between status offenses and crimes.

FIGURE 15.1 Status Offenses.

1. Smoking cigarettes	**5.** Running away from home
2. Drinking alcohol	**6.** Violating curfew
3. Being truant (skipping school)	**7.** Participating in sexual activity
4. Disobeying teachers	**8.** Using profane language

CONSTITUTIONAL PROTECTIONS AND THE JUVENILE COURT

Though the ideal of the juvenile court seemed to offer the "best of both worlds" for juvenile offenders, in reality the lack of procedural protections led to many children being arbitrarily punished not only for crimes, but for status offenses as well. Juvenile judges were treating all violators similarly, which led to many status offenders being incarcerated in the same institutions as violent delinquents. In response to a wave of lawsuits demanding due process rights for juveniles, the United States Supreme Court issued several rulings in the 1960s and 1970s that significantly changed the juvenile justice system.

KENT v. UNITED STATES The first decision to extend due process rights to children in juvenile courts was *Kent v. United States* (1966).[9] The case concerned sixteen-year-old Morris Kent, who had been arrested for breaking into a woman's house, stealing her purse, and raping her. Because Kent was on juvenile probation, the state sought to transfer his trial for the crime to an adult court (a process to be discussed later in the chapter).

Without giving any reasons for his decision, the juvenile judge consented to this judicial waiver, and Kent was sentenced in the adult court to a thirty- to ninety-year prison term. The Supreme Court overturned the sentence, ruling that juveniles have a right to counsel and a hearing in any instance in which the juvenile judge is considering sending the case to an adult court. The Court stated that, in jurisdiction waiver cases, a child receives "the worst of both worlds," getting neither the "protections accorded to adults" nor the "solicitous care and regenerative treatment" offered in the juvenile system.[10]

IN RE GAULT The *Kent* decision provided the groundwork for *In re Gault* one year later. Considered by many the single most important case concerning juvenile justice, *In re Gault* involved a fifteen-year-old boy who was arrested for allegedly making a lewd phone call while on probation.[11] (See the feature *Landmark Cases: In re Gault* on the following page.) In its decision, the Supreme Court held that juveniles are entitled to many of the same due process rights granted to adult offenders, including notice of charges, the right to counsel, the privilege against self-incrimination, and the right to confront and cross-examine witnesses.

LO 3

OTHER IMPORTANT COURT DECISIONS Over the next ten years, the Supreme Court handed down three more important rulings on juvenile court procedure. The ruling in *In re Winship* (1970)[12] required the government to prove "beyond a reasonable doubt" that a juvenile had committed an act of delinquency, raising the burden of proof from a "preponderance of the evidence." In *Breed v. Jones* (1975),[13] the Court held that the Fifth Amendment's double jeopardy clause prevented a juvenile from being tried in an adult court for a crime that had already been adjudicated in juvenile court. In contrast, the decision in *McKeiver v. Pennsylvania* (1971)[14] represented an instance in which the Court did not move the juvenile court further toward the adult model. In that case, the Court ruled that the Constitution did not give juveniles the right to a jury trial.

A Port Authority (New York) police officer speaks to a girl who has run away from her home. Why is leaving home considered a status offense and not a crime?

James Estrin/*New York Times*/Redux

Group Activities: Have students work together to create a chart illustrating each of the critical juvenile court cases mentioned in the text and its significance. (LO 3)

Discussion Tip: Ask students to discuss the due process rights afforded to juveniles. Which due process rights are not granted to juveniles? (LO 3)

LANDMARK CASES: *In Re Gault*

In 1964, fifteen-year-old Gerald Gault and a friend were arrested for making lewd telephone calls to a neighbor in Gila County, Arizona. Gault, who was on probation, was placed under custody with no notice given to his parents. The juvenile court in his district held a series of informal hearings to determine Gault's punishment. During these hearings, no records were kept, Gault was not afforded the right to counsel, and the complaining witness was never made available for questioning. At the close of the hearing, the judge sentenced Gault to remain in Arizona's State Industrial School until the age of twenty-one. The defendant filed a writ of *habeas corpus,* claiming that he had been denied due process rights at his hearing. Arizona's Supreme Court affirmed the dismissal of this writ, ruling that the proceedings did not infringe on Gault's due process rights, a matter eventually taken up by the United States Supreme Court.

> ### *In re Gault*
> **United States Supreme Court**
> **387 U.S. 1 (1967)**
> **supreme.justia.com/us/387/1/case.html**

IN THE WORDS OF THE COURT . . .
JUSTICE FORTAS, MAJORITY OPINION

* * * *

From the inception of the juvenile court system, wide differences have been tolerated—indeed insisted upon—between the procedural rights accorded to adults and those of juveniles. In practically all jurisdictions, there are rights granted to adults which are withheld from juveniles.

* * * *

Accordingly, the highest motives and most enlightened impulses led to a peculiar system for juveniles, unknown to our law in any comparable context. The constitutional and theoretical basis for this peculiar system is—to say the least—debatable. And in practice, as we remarked in the *Kent* case, the results have not been entirely satisfactory. * * * The absence of substantive standards has not necessarily meant that children receive careful, compassionate, individualized treatment. The absence of procedural rules based upon constitutional principle has not always produced fair, efficient, and effective procedures. Departures from established principles of due process have frequently resulted not in enlightened procedure, but in arbitrariness.

* * * *

Ultimately, however, we confront the reality of that portion of the Juvenile Court process with which we deal in this case. A boy is charged with misconduct. The boy is committed to an institution where he may be restrained of liberty for years. It is of no constitutional consequence—and of limited practical meaning—that the institution to which he is committed is called an Industrial School. The fact of the matter is that, however euphemistic the title, a "receiving home" or an "industrial school" for juveniles is an institution of confinement in which the child is incarcerated for a greater or lesser time. His world becomes "a building with whitewashed walls, regimented routine and institutional hours . . . ." Instead of mother and father and sisters and brothers and friends and classmates, his world is peopled by guards, custodians, state employees, and "delinquents" confined with him for anything from waywardness to rape and homicide. In view of this, it would be extraordinary if our Constitution did not require the procedural regularity and the exercise of care implied in the phrase "due process." Under our Constitution, the condition of being a boy does not justify a kangaroo court.

* * * *

DECISION

The Court held that juveniles were entitled to the basic procedural safeguards afforded by the Fourteenth Amendment, including the right to advance notice of charges, the right to counsel, the right to confront and cross-examine witnesses, and the privilege against self-incrimination. The decision marked a turning point in juvenile justice in this country: no longer would informality and paternalism be the guiding principles of juvenile courts. Instead, due process would dictate the adjudication process, much as in an adult court.

FOR CRITICAL ANALYSIS

What might be some of the negative consequences of the *In re Gault* decision for juveniles charged with committing delinquent acts?

For more information and activities related to this case, visit the *Criminal Justice CourseMate* at <u>cengagebrain. com</u> and select the *Web links* for this chapter.

DETERMINING DELINQUENCY TODAY

In the eyes of many observers, the net effect of the Supreme Court decisions during the 1966–1975 period was to move juvenile justice away from the ideals of the child savers. As a result of these decisions, many young offenders would find themselves in a formalized system that is often indistinguishable from its adult counterpart. But, though the Court has recognized that minors charged with crimes possess certain constitutional rights, it has failed to dictate at what age these rights should be granted. Consequently, the legal status of children in the United States varies depending on where they live, with each state making its own policy decisions on the crucial questions of age and competency.

THE AGE QUESTION

Several years ago, eleven-year-old Jordan Brown of New Galilee, Pennsylvania, apparently shot his father's fiancée, Kenzie Houk, in the head with a shotgun while she slept, killing both Houk and her unborn child. Prosecutors believe that Brown was upset about the impending birth of his half-brother, particularly because he had been asked to vacate his room for the infant. "He looked like a baby in an orange jumpsuit," the fifth-grader's father, Chris, said after the boy's first court appearance.[15]

In Chapter 4 (page 114), we saw that early American criminal law recognized infancy as a defense against criminal charges. At that time, on attaining fourteen years of age, a youth was considered an adult and treated accordingly by the criminal justice system. Today, as Figure 15.2 alongside shows, twenty-two states, including Pennsylvania, and the District of Columbia, do not have age restrictions on prosecuting juveniles as adults. Thus, Pennsylvania officials had the option of prosecuting Brown for murder as an adult, despite his tender years. On March 29, 2010, Judge Dominick Motto decided that, indeed, the boy could be tried for first

Discussion Tip: Ask students to discuss the role that age plays in the decision to prosecute a minor for a criminal offense. What are the age limits for the juvenile courts in your state? Do students feel these age limits are appropriate? Why or why not?

FIGURE 15.2 **The Minimum Age at Which a Juvenile Can Be Tried as an Adult**

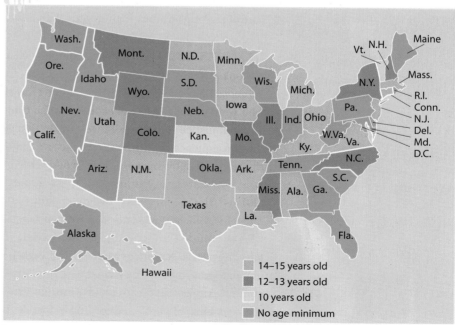

- 14–15 years old
- 12–13 years old
- 10 years old
- No age minimum

Source: National Center for Juvenile Justice.

degree murder in adult court, where he would face the possibility of a life sentence (with the possibility of parole) in adult prison. The judge based his decision on the defendant's lack of remorse and the "execution style" of the killing.[16]

Brown's attorneys had argued that their client would be better served by facing the charges in juvenile court, where he would receive treatment designed for younger offenders. For the most part, when juveniles who remain in juvenile court are found guilty, they receive "limited" sentences. Under these circumstances, they cannot remain incarcerated in juvenile detention centers past their eighteenth or twenty-first birthday. As the Jordan Brown case shows, when the underlying crime is a serious one such as rape or murder, judges and prosecutors are less likely to accept the juvenile justice option.

THE CULPABILITY QUESTION

Critical Thinking Skill Development: In a short writing assignment, have students debate the Supreme Court's statement that juveniles have "diminished culpability." What does this mean? Do students agree with this point of view?

Many researchers believe that by the age of fourteen, an adolescent has the same ability as an adult to make a competent decision.[17] Nevertheless, according to some observers, a juvenile's ability to theoretically understand the difference between "right" and "wrong" does not mean that she or he should be held to the same standards of competency as an adult.

JUVENILE BEHAVIOR A study released in 2003 by the Research Network on Adolescent Development and Juvenile Justice found that 33 percent of juvenile defendants in criminal courts had the same low level of understanding of legal matters as mentally ill adults who had been found incompetent to stand trial.[18]

Legal psychologist Richard E. Redding believes that

adolescents' lack of life experience may limit their real-world decision-making ability. Whether we call it wisdom, judgment, or common sense, adolescents may not have nearly enough.[19]

Juveniles are generally more impulsive, more likely to engage in risky behavior, and less likely to calculate the long-term consequences of any particular action. Furthermore, adolescents are far more likely to respond to peer pressure than are adults. The desire for acceptance and approval may drive them to commit crimes: juveniles are arrested as part of a group at much higher rates than adults.[20]

DIMINISHED GUILT The "diminished culpability" of juveniles was one of the reasons given by the United States Supreme Court in its landmark decision in *Roper v. Simmons* (2005).[21] As we saw in Chapter 11, that case forbade the execution of offenders who were under the age of eighteen when they committed their crimes. In his majority opinion, Justice Anthony Kennedy wrote that because minors cannot fully comprehend the consequences of their actions, the two main justifications for the death penalty—retribution and deterrence—do not "work" with juvenile wrongdoers.[22]

Five years later, the Supreme Court applied the same reasoning in *Graham v. Florida* (2010).[23] The case involved two defendants who had committed violent crimes as juveniles: Joe Sullivan, who raped a woman when he was thirteen, and Terrance Graham, who committed armed burglary at sixteen. Both defendants claimed that their life-without-parole sentences violated the Eighth Amendment's prohibition of "cruel and unusual punishment." By a close 5–4 vote, the Court agreed, holding that juveniles who commit crimes that do not involve murder may not be sentenced to life in prison without the possibility of parole. According to Justice Anthony Kennedy, who wrote the majority opinion, state officials must give these inmates "some meaningful opportunity to obtain release based on demonstrated maturity and rehabilitation."[24] (We will examine this issue more closely in the *CJ in Action* feature at the end of the chapter.)

SELFASSESSMENT

Fill in the blanks and check your answers on page 532.

The age at which a child can be held criminally responsible for his or her actions differs from _____ to _____. Many experts believe that minors should not be held to the same level of competency as adults, partially because they are more _____ and more likely to respond to _____ pressure. This "diminished culpability" was one of the reasons the United States Supreme Court gave for prohibiting the _____ _____ for offenders who were under the age of eighteen when they committed their crimes.

In 2009, sixteen-year-old Morgan Leppert was sentenced to life in prison without parole for killing an elderly disabled man in Palatka, Florida, so that she and her boyfriend could take the victim's money and truck. Does the Supreme Court's ruling in *Graham v. Florida* apply to Leppert's sentence? Why or why not? AP Photo/Patrick C. Leonard, Pool

Critical Thinking Skill Development: Ask students to assess the UCR as a tool to determine juvenile offending rates. What are the advantages and disadvantages of relying solely on official data for a complete understanding of juvenile crime?

TRENDS IN JUVENILE DELINQUENCY

When asked, juveniles will admit to a wide range of illegal or dangerous behavior, including carrying weapons, getting involved in physical fights, driving after drinking alcohol, and stealing or deliberately damaging school property.[25] Has the juvenile justice system been effective in controlling and preventing this kind of misbehavior, as well as more serious acts?

To answer this question, many observers turn to the Federal Bureau of Investigation's Uniform Crime Report (UCR), initially covered in Chapter 3. Because the UCR breaks down arrest statistics by age of the arrestee, it has been considered the primary source of information on the presence of juveniles in America's justice system. This does not mean, however, that the UCR is completely reliable when it comes to measuring juvenile delinquency. The process measures only those juveniles who were caught and therefore does not accurately reflect all delinquent acts in any given year. Furthermore, it measures the number of arrests but not the number of arrestees, meaning that—due to repeat offenders—the number of juveniles actually in the system could be below the number of juvenile arrests.

DELINQUENCY BY THE NUMBERS

With these cautions in mind, UCR findings are quite clear as to the extent of juvenile delinquency in the United States today. In 2010, juveniles accounted for 13.7 percent of violent crime arrests and 12.6 percent of criminal activity arrests in general.[26] According to the 2010 UCR, juveniles were responsible for

- 9 percent of all murder arrests.
- 11 percent of all aggravated assault arrests.
- 14 percent of all forcible rapes.
- 20 percent of all weapons arrests.
- 24 percent of all robbery arrests.
- 23 percent of all Part I property crimes.
- 10 percent of all drug offenses.

THE RISE AND FALL OF JUVENILE CRIME

As Figure 15.3 below shows, juvenile arrest rates for violent crimes have fluctuated dramatically over the past three decades, with highs in the mid-1990s and lows in the early years of this century. Today, the juvenile crime rate has leveled off, although in 2007 the juvenile property crime rate rose for the first time in thirteen years, only to resume its downward trend a year later. In addition, juvenile arrest rates for some crimes—such as fraud and driving under the influence—are still relatively high. The overall situation, however, is not nearly as bleak as it was fifteen years ago.[27]

Although the theory is not universally accepted, many observers see the rise and decline of juvenile arrests as mirroring the rise and decline of crack cocaine.[28] When inner-city youths took advantage of the economic opportunities offered by the crack trade in the 1980s, they found they needed to protect themselves against rival dealers. This led to the proliferation of firearms among juveniles, as well as the formation of violent youth gangs. As the crack "epidemic" has slowed, so have arrest and violent crime rates for juveniles.

Other theories have been put forth as well. Some observers point to the increase in police action against "quality-of-life" crimes such as loitering, which they believe stops juveniles before they have a chance to commit more serious crimes. Similarly, about 80 percent of American municipalities enforce juvenile curfews, which restrict the movement of minors during certain hours, usually after dark.[29] In 2010, law enforcement made nearly 74,000 arrests for curfew and loitering law violations.[30] Furthermore, hundreds of local programs designed to educate children about the dangers of drugs and crime operate across the country. Though the results of such community-based efforts are difficult, if not impossible, to measure—it cannot be assumed that children would have become

FIGURE 15.3 Arrest Rates of Juveniles, 1980 to 2008

After rising dramatically from 1985 to 1994, arrest rates for juveniles fell for nearly a decade before leveling off in recent years.

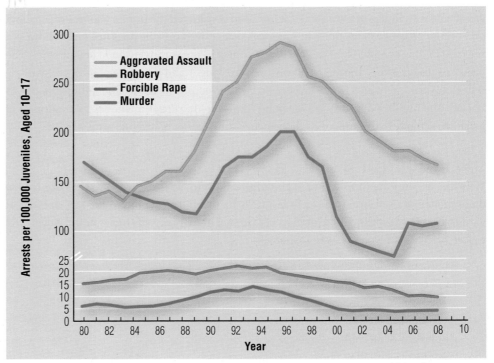

Source: Office of Juvenile Justice and Delinquency Prevention, *Statistical Briefing Book*, at **www.ojjdp.ncjrs.org** /ojstatbb/crime/JAR.asp.

delinquent if they had not participated—these programs are generally considered a crucial element of keeping youth crime under control.[31]

GIRLS IN THE JUVENILE JUSTICE SYSTEM

Though overall rates of juvenile offending have been dropping, one particular group of juveniles has become more involved in the juvenile justice system than ever before. Just as we saw earlier in this textbook that women are the fasting-growing segment of the adult prison population, girls are becoming more and more visible in the institutions that punish juvenile delinquency and crime.

A social worker speaks with two incarcerated teenage girls at the Cobb County Jail in Marietta, Georgia. What are some of the reasons that the arrest rate for female juveniles has increased over the past few decades?
Robin Nelson/PhotoEdit

A GROWING PRESENCE Although girls have for the most part been treated more harshly than boys for status offenses,[32] a "chivalry effect" (see page 372) has traditionally existed in other areas of the juvenile justice system. In the past, police were likely to arrest offending boys while allowing girls to go home to the care of their families for similar behavior. This is no longer the case. According to the Office of Juvenile Justice and Delinquency Prevention, juvenile courts handled twice as many cases involving girls in 2005 as they did in 1985.[33] A particular problem area for girls appears to be the crime of assault. In 2010, females accounted for 24 percent of all juvenile arrests for aggravated assault and 35 percent of those arrests for simple assault, higher percentages than for other violent crimes.[34]

FAMILY-BASED DELINQUENCY Criminologists disagree on whether rising arrest rates for female juveniles reflect a change in behavior or a change in law enforcement practices. A significant amount of data supports the latter proposal, especially research showing that police are much more likely to make arrests in situations involving domestic violence than they were even a decade ago. Experts have found that girls are four times more apt to fight with parents or siblings than are boys, who usually engage in violent encounters with strangers. Consequently, a large percentage of female juvenile arrests for assault arise out of family disputes—arrests that until relatively recently would not have been made.[35]

Evidence also shows that law enforcement agents continue to treat girls more harshly for status offenses. More girls than boys are arrested for the status offense of running away from home, for example, even though studies show that male and female juveniles run away from home with equal frequency.[36] Criminologists who focus on issues of gender hypothesize that such behavior is considered normal for boys, but is seen as deviant for girls and therefore more deserving of punishment.[37]

Teaching Tip: Have students consider the differences in male and female juvenile offending. In a written assignment, ask students to discuss the issues faced by adolescent female offenders.

SCHOOL VIOLENCE AND BULLYING

One Wednesday afternoon in January 2011, seventeen-year-old Robert Butler, Jr., walked into an administrative office at Millard South High School in Omaha, Nebraska, and fatally shot assistant principal Vicki Kaspar. Butler, who had been suspended for misconduct earlier that day, also wounded principal Curtis Case before taking his own life. The incident was every teacher's (and student's and parent's) worst nightmare. Like other episodes of school violence, it received heavy media coverage, fanning fears that our schools are unsafe.

Technology Tip: Ask students to go online and learn more about bullying and its consequences at **www.stopbullying.gov**.

Bullying Overt acts taken by students with the goal of intimidating, harassing, or humiliating other students.

"It wud be easier if he or any1 of them handed me a [expletive] noose."

—Text message from fifteen-year-old **Phoebe Prince,** two hours before she committed suicide in response to bullying (2010)

SAFE SCHOOLS In fact, school-age youths are more than fifty times more likely to be murdered away from school than on a campus.[38] Furthermore, between 1995 and 2009, victimization rates of students for nonfatal crimes at school declined significantly, meaning that, in general, schools are safer today than they were in the recent past.[39] For the most part, these statistics mirror the downward trend of all criminal activity in the United States since the mid-1990s. In addition, since the fatal shootings of fourteen students and a teacher at Columbine High School near Littleton, Colorado, in 1999, many schools have improved security measures. From 1999 to 2007, the percentage of American schools using security cameras to monitor their campuses increased from 19 to 50 percent. Today, 90 percent of public schools control access to school buildings by locking or monitoring their doors.[40]

"BULLIED TO DEATH" Broadly defined as repeated, aggressive behavior with physical (hitting, punching, and spitting) and verbal (teasing, name calling, and spreading false rumors) components, **bullying** has traditionally been seen more as an inevitable rite of passage than as deviant behavior. In recent years, however, society has become more aware of the negative consequences of bullying, underscored by a number of high-profile "bullycides." In January 2010, for example, fifteen-year-old high school sophomore Phoebe Prince hanged herself after months of torment inflicted by a group of fellow students at South Hadley High School in Massachusetts. That September, four teenage boys in different parts of the country committed suicide after being bullied about their sexuality.

According to data gathered by the federal government, 32 percent of students aged twelve to eighteen have been victims of bullying.[41] In particular, gay students are targeted—nine out of ten report being bullied each year.[42] As a response to this problem, forty-five states have passed anti-bullying legislation. These laws focus mostly on "soft" measures, such as training school personnel how to recognize and respond to bullying.[43] As yet, state legislatures have been reluctant to take "harder" measures such as specifically defining bullying as a crime. The six students deemed responsible for Phoebe Prince's death, for example, pleaded guilty to various misdemeanors ranging from criminal harassment to violating Prince's civil rights. According to Brenda High of Pasco, Washington, whose son committed suicide after being bullied, if anti-bullying laws are to have any significant impact, bullying must carry "the same consequences as assault."[44]

CJ&TECHNOLOGY Cyberbullying

Cheryl E. Davis/Shutterstock

Although it is not clear whether bullying in general is more prevalent now than in the past, one form of bullying is definitely on the rise. As the Internet, texting, and social networking sites such as Facebook have become integral parts of youth culture, so, it seems, has cyberbullying. Studies have shown that between one-fifth and one-third of American teenagers are targets of cyberbullying, which occurs when a person uses computers, smartphones, or other electronic devices to inflict willful and repeated emotional harm. Cyberbullying attracted national attention as a result of eighteen-year-old Tyler Clementi's suicide in the fall of 2010. Clementi, a freshman at New Jersey's Rutgers University, jumped off the George Washington Bridge after his roommate secretly recorded a video of Clementi "making out with a dude" and posted it on YouTube.

To many, cyberbullying can be even more devastating than "old school" bullying. Not only does the anonymity of cyberspace seem to embolden perpetrators, causing them to be more vicious than they might be in person, but, as one expert points out, when bullying occurs online, "you can't get away from it."

THINKING ABOUT CYBERBULLYING

How should the criminal justice system respond to cyberbullying, if at all?

SELFASSESSMENT

Fill in the blanks and check your answers on page 532.

The crime rate for juveniles has generally been _____ for more than a decade. Despite this trend, more _____ are getting involved with the juvenile justice system today than at any time in recent history. _____ violence is another area in which crime rates have dropped since the 1990s, thanks, in part, to greater security measures such as surveillance cameras and locked building doors. _____, in both its traditional and electronic forms, remains a problem, however, and is increasingly being addressed by school administrators and state legislators.

FACTORS IN JUVENILE DELINQUENCY

As we discussed in Chapter 2, an influential study conducted by Professor Marvin Wolfgang and several colleagues in the early 1970s introduced the "chronic 6 percent" to criminology. The researchers found that out of one hundred boys, six will become chronic offenders, meaning that they are arrested five or more times before their eighteenth birthdays. Furthermore, Wolfgang and his colleagues determined that these chronic offenders are responsible for half of all crimes and two-thirds of all violent crimes within any given cohort (a group of persons who have similar characteristics).[45] Does this "6 percent rule" mean that no matter what steps society takes, six out of every hundred juveniles are "bad seeds" and will act delinquently? Or does it point to a situation in which a small percentage of children may be more likely to commit crimes under certain circumstances?

Most criminologists favor the second interpretation. In this section, we will examine the four factors that have traditionally been used to explain juvenile criminal behavior and violent crime rates: age, substance abuse, family problems, and gangs. Keep in mind, however, that the factors influencing delinquency are not limited to these topics (see Figure 15.4 on the following page). Researchers are constantly interpreting and reinterpreting statistical evidence to provide fresh perspectives on this very important issue. For example, criminologists continue to debate the consequences of dropping out of high school. Although adolescents who do so are statistically at a

Group Activities: Before beginning this portion of the lecture, ask students to break into groups and brainstorm the factors that they believe lead to juvenile offending. If time allows, revisit the lists once the lectures concerning this material have concluded. (LO 4)

FIGURE 15.4 Risk Factors for Juvenile Delinquency

The characteristics listed here are generally accepted as "risk factors" for juvenile delinquency. In other words if one or more of these factors are present in a juvenile's life, he or she has a greater chance of exhibiting delinquent behavior—though such behavior is by no means a certainty.

Family	• Single parent/lack of parental role model • Parental or sibling drug/alcohol abuse • Extreme economic deprivation • Family members in a gang
School	• Academic frustration/failure • Learning disability • Negative labeling by teachers • Disciplinary problems
Community	• Social disorganization (refer to Chapter 2) • Presence of gangs and obvious drug use in the community • Availability of firearms • High crime/constant feeling of danger • Lack of social and economic opportunities
Peers	• Delinquent friends • Friends who use drugs or who are members of gangs • Lack of "positive" peer pressure
Individual	• Tendency toward aggressive behavior • Inability to concentrate or focus/easily bored/hyperactive • Alcohol or drug use • Fatalistic/pessimistic viewpoint

Aging Out A term used to explain the fact that criminal activity declines with age.

Age of Onset The age at which a juvenile first exhibits delinquent behavior.

Technology Tip: Ask students to learn more about adolescents and substance abuse online at **www.drugwarfacts.org/adolesce.htm**.

higher risk for coming into contact with the juvenile justice system, does leaving school *cause* delinquency and criminal behavior? Or do adolescents drop out of high school for the same reasons that they become involved in crime, such as low self-control and substance abuse?[46]

THE AGE-CRIME RELATIONSHIP

LO 4 Crime statistics are fairly conclusive on one point: the older a person is, the less likely he or she will exhibit criminal behavior. Self-reported studies confirm that most people are involved in some form of criminal behavior—however "harmless"—during their early years. In fact, Terrie Moffitt of Duke University has said that "it is statistically aberrant to refrain from crime during adolescence."[47] So, why do the vast majority of us not become chronic offenders? According to many criminologists, particularly Travis Hirschi and Michael Gottfredson, any group of at-risk persons—regardless of gender, race, intelligence, or class—will commit fewer crimes as they grow older.[48]

This process is known as **aging out** (or, sometimes, *desistance,* a term we first encountered in the previous chapter). Professor Robert J. Sampson and his colleague John H. Laub believe that this phenomenon is explained by certain events, such as marriage, employment, and military service, which force delinquents to "grow up" and forgo criminal acts.[49]

Another view sees the **age of onset,** or the age at which the youth begins delinquent behavior, as a consistent predictor of future criminal behavior. One study compared recidivism rates between juveniles first judged to be delinquent before the age of fifteen and those first adjudicated delinquent after the age of fifteen. Of the seventy-one subjects who made up the first group, 32 percent became chronic offenders. Of the sixty-five who made up the second group, none became chronic offenders.[50] Furthermore, according to the Office of Juvenile Justice and Delinquency Prevention, the earlier a youth enters the juvenile justice system, the more likely he or she will become a violent offender.[51] This research suggests that juvenile justice resources should be concentrated on the youngest offenders, with the goal of preventing crime and reducing the long-term risks for society.

SUBSTANCE ABUSE

As we have seen throughout this textbook, substance abuse plays a strong role in criminal behavior for adults. The same can certainly be said for juveniles. According to the National Survey on Drug Use and Health, more than 11 million Americans between the ages of twelve and twenty consume alcohol on a regular basis, increasing the probability that they will become involved in violent behavior, delinquency, academic problems, and risky sexual behavior.[52] The health consequences of this level of underage drinking are staggering: alcohol is a factor in between 50 and 65 percent of all teenage suicides, and nearly 2,500 youths are killed each year in alcohol-related automobile crashes. At the same time, 10 percent of those between the ages of twelve and seventeen admit using illegal drugs on a regular basis, a number that, as Figure 15.5 alongside shows, rose in 2009 for the first time in several years.

As with adults, substance abuse among juveniles seems to play a major role in offending. About 10 percent of all juvenile arrests involve a drug abuse violation. Nearly all young offenders (94 percent) entering juvenile detention self-report drug use at some point in their lives, and 85 percent have used drugs in the previous six months.[53] According to the Arrestee Drug Abuse Monitoring Program, nearly 60 percent of male juvenile detainees and 46 percent of female juvenile detainees test positive for drug use at the time of their offense.[54] Drug use is a particularly strong risk factor for girls: 75 percent of young women incarcerated in juvenile facilities report regular drug and alcohol use—starting at the age of fourteen—and one study found that 87 percent of female teenage offenders need substance abuse treatment.[55]

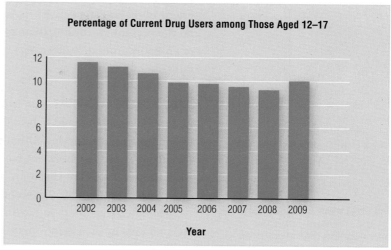

FIGURE 15.5 **Drug Use among Juveniles**
Among Americans aged twelve to seventeen, the percentage who admit to using illegal drugs in the past month dropped each year from 2002 to 2008 before rising in 2009.

Percentage of Current Drug Users among Those Aged 12–17

Source: National Survey on Drug Use and Health, 2003–2010.

CHILD ABUSE AND NEGLECT

Abuse by parents also plays a substantial role in juvenile delinquency. **Child abuse** can be broadly defined as the infliction of physical or emotional damage on a child. Similar though not the same, **child neglect** refers to deprivations—of love, shelter, food, and proper care—children undergo by their parents. According to the National Survey of Children's Exposure to Violence, one in ten children in the United States suffers from mistreatment at the hands of a close family member.[56]

Children in homes characterized by violence or neglect suffer from a variety of physical, emotional, and mental health problems at a much greater rate than their peers.[57] This, in turn, increases their chances of engaging in delinquent behavior. One survey of violent juveniles showed that 75 percent had suffered severe abuse by a family member and 80 percent had witnessed violence in their homes.[58] Cathy Spatz Widom, currently a professor of psychology at John Jay College of Criminal Justice, compared the arrest records of two groups of subjects—one made up of 908 cases of substantiated parental abuse and neglect and the other made up of 667 children who had not been abused or neglected. Widom found that those who had been abused or neglected were 53 percent more likely to be arrested as juveniles than those who had not.[59]

Simply put, according to researchers Janet Currie of Columbia University and Erdal Tekin of Georgia State University, "child maltreatment roughly doubles the probability that an individual engages in many types of crime."[60]

GANGS

When youths cannot find the stability and support they require in the family structure, they will often turn to their peers. This is just one explanation for why juveniles join **youth gangs.** Although jurisdictions may have varying definitions, for general purposes

Child Abuse Mistreatment of children by causing physical, emotional, or sexual damage without any plausible explanation, such as an accident.

Child Neglect A form of child abuse in which the child is denied certain necessities such as shelter, food, care, and love.

Youth Gang A self-formed group of youths with several identifiable characteristics, including a gang name and other recognizable symbols, a geographic territory, and participation in illegal activities.

Teaching Tip: In a short writing assignment, ask students to describe the relationship between child abuse and juvenile delinquency. Why are victims of such abuse at a greater risk for offending?

a youth gang is viewed as a group of three or more persons who (1) self-identify themselves as an entity separate from the community by special clothing, vocabulary, hand signals, and names and (2) engage in criminal activity. Although the first gangs may have appeared in the 1780s, around the time of the American Revolution, there have been four periods of major gang activity in American history: the late 1800s, the 1920s, the 1960s, and the present. According to an exhaustive survey of law enforcement agencies, there are probably around 20,000 gangs with approximately 1 million members in the United States.[61]

WHO JOINS GANGS? The average gang member is seventeen to eighteen years old, though members tend to be older in cities with long traditions of gang activity such as Chicago and Los Angeles. Although it is difficult to determine with any certainty the makeup of gangs as a whole, one recent survey found that 49 percent of all gang members in the United States are Hispanic, 35 percent are African American, and 9 percent are white, with the remaining 7 percent belonging to other racial or ethnic backgrounds.[62]

Though gangs tend to have racial or ethnic characteristics—that is, one group predominates in each gang—many researchers do not believe that race or ethnicity is the dominant factor in gang membership. Instead, gang members seem to come from lower-class or working-class communities, mostly in urban areas but with an increasing number from the suburbs and rural counties. In addition, researchers are finding that adolescents who will eventually join a gang display significantly higher levels of delinquent behavior than those who will never become involved in gang activity.[63]

A very small percentage of youth gang members are female. In many instances, girls associate themselves with gangs, even though they are not considered members. Generally, girls assume subordinate gender roles in youth gangs, providing emotional, physical, and sexual services for the dominant males.[64] Still, almost half of all youth gangs report having female members, and, as in other areas of juvenile crime and delinquency, involvement of girls in gangs is increasing.[65]

WHY DO YOUTHS JOIN GANGS? Gang membership often appears to be linked with status in the community. This tends to be true of both males and females. Many teenagers, feeling alienated from their families and communities, join gangs for the social relationships and the sense of identity a gang can provide.[66]

LO 5

A number of youths, especially those who live in high-crime neighborhoods, see gang membership as a necessity—joining a gang is a form of protection against violence from other gangs. For example, Mara Salvatrucha (MS-13) was formed by the children of immigrants who fled the civil war of El Salvador for Los Angeles in the 1980s. Finding themselves easy prey for the established local gangs, these young Salvadorans started MS-13 as a protective measure. (To see how El Salvador is reacting to high levels of gang violence, see the feature *Comparative Criminal Justice—Extending a Firm Hand* on the facing page.)

Excitement is another attraction of the gang life, as is the economic incentive of enjoying the profits from illegal gang activities such as dealing drugs or robbery. Finally, some teenagers are forced to join gangs by the threat of violence from gang members.

Teaching Tip: Invite a local police officer to visit the classroom. Ask him or her to talk about youth gangs in your community. Which gangs are active in your area, and how does their presence impact local offending rates?

The **National Gang Center** is a government-sponsored organization that researches the problems caused by gangs and proposes methods of solving them. Find its Web site by visiting the *Criminal Justice CourseMate* at **cengagebrain. com** and selecting the *Web links* for this chapter.

Here, a "gangbanger" in South Central Los Angeles identifies himself as a Crip by his hand gestures. What role does identity play in a juvenile's decision to join a gang?
Ted Soqui/Corbis

COMPARATIVE CRIMINAL JUSTICE

EXTENDING A FIRM HAND

Mara Salvatrucha (MS-13) is one of the most powerful and fastest-growing street gangs in the world. In the United States, where MS-13 has about 10,000 members and a presence in forty-two states, the Federal Bureau of Investigation (FBI) has set up a task force to deal exclusively with the gang, and immigration officials routinely deport members back to their home countries in Central America. One of these countries, El Salvador, has responded to the resulting influx of violent gang members with strict antigang legislation.

Over the past decade, Salvadoran politicians passed a series of *mano dura,* or "firm hand," laws designed to crack down on criminal gang activity. These laws made it easier for police to detain suspects who exhibited certain characteristics such as having gang tattoos or loitering in known gang areas. Still, in June 2010, MS-13 members fired on two crowded buses in San Salvador, the country's capital, killing seventeen people and intensifying public outrage over gang violence. In response, three months later Salvadoran president Muaricio Funes signed the country's harshest antigang legislation to date. Under the new law, merely belonging to a gang is punishable by four to six years in prison, even if no other criminal activity is proved.

FOR CRITICAL ANALYSIS

What are the pros and cons of making gang membership illegal? Why does the probable cause requirement of the Fourth Amendment make it unlikely that such a law ever could exist in this country? (See pages 218–219 to review this requirement.)

Gang tattoos cover the body of an MS-13 gang member incarcerated in El Salvador's Ciudad Barrios penitentiary.
Eros Hoagland/Redux

GANGS AND CRIME To a certain extent, the violent and criminal behavior of youths in gangs has been exaggerated by information sources such as the media. In proportion to all gang activities, violence is a rare event. Youth gang members spend most of their time "hanging out" and taking part in other normal adolescent behavior.[67] That having been said, gang members are responsible for a disproportionate amount of violent and nonviolent criminal acts by juveniles. Traditional gang activities such as using and trafficking in drugs, protecting their territory in "turf battles," and graffiti/vandalism all contribute to high crime rates among members.

Nationwide, larger cities report the highest number of gang-related homicides.[68] Consistently, more than half of the murders in Chicago and Los Angeles are attributed to gang violence. Statistics also show high levels of gang involvement in weapons trafficking, burglary, assault, and motor vehicle theft, while more than 50 percent of all youth gangs are believed to be involved in drug sales.[69] Furthermore, a study of criminal behavior among juveniles in Seattle found that gang members were considerably more likely to commit crimes than at-risk youths who shared many characteristics with gang members but were not affiliated with any gang (see Figure 15.6 on the next page).[70] The gang members in Seattle were also much more likely to own firearms or to have friends who owned firearms.

Technology Tip: Have students visit the Federal Bureau of Investigation online and learn more about gang-related crime at **www.fbi.gov/about-us/investigate/vc_majorthefts/gangs**.

FIGURE 15.6 Comparison of Gang and Nongang Delinquent Behavior

Taking self-reported surveys of subjects aged thirteen to eighteen in the Seattle area, researchers for the Office of Juvenile Justice and Delinquency Prevention found that gang members were much more likely to exhibit delinquent behavior.

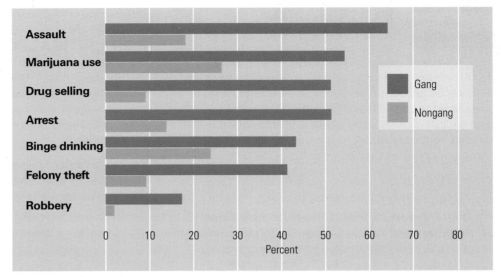

Source: Karl G. Hill, Christina Lui, and J. David Hawkins, *Early Precursors of Gang Membership: A Study of Seattle Youth* (Washington, D.C.: Office of Juvenile Justice and Delinquency Prevention, December 2001), Figure 1, page 2.

GUNS

It is hardly surprising that the gang members in Seattle were much more likely to own firearms or to have friends who did. Studies have shown that youths who are members of gangs are three times as likely to own a handgun as those who are not.[71] Gang members are also much more likely to believe that they need a gun for protection and to be involved in gun-related crimes.[72]

The harmful link between juveniles and guns is hardly limited to gang members, however. Indeed, one explanation for the increase in youth violence in the late 1980s and early 1990s points to the unprecedented access minors had to illegal weapons during that time. According to Carnegie Mellon University's Alfred Blumstein:

> [Y]outh have always fought with each other. But when it's a battle with fists, the dynamics run much more slowly. With a gun, it evolves very rapidly, too fast for a third party to intervene. That also raises the stakes and encourages others to arm themselves, thereby triggering a preemptive strike: "I better get him before he gets me."[73]

In fact, the correlation between access to guns and juvenile homicide rates is striking. The juvenile arrest rate for weapons violations doubled between 1987 and 1993. By 1994, 82 percent of all homicides committed by juveniles involved a handgun. Then, as the homicide rate began to drop, so did the arrest rate for weapons offenses, and many experts believe that the downward trend in juvenile homicide arrests can be traced largely to a decline in firearm usage.[74]

Despite these encouraging trends, guns are still widespread in youth culture. Research conducted by H. Naci Mocan, now of Louisiana State University, and Erdal Tekin of Georgia State University found that 13 percent of juveniles in urban areas and 32 percent of juveniles in suburban and rural areas have access to guns at home. This troubling reality contributes to several school shootings each year.[75] According to the Centers for Disease Control, 9.8 percent of male students and 1.7 percent of female students will carry a gun at least once during any given year.[76] About 22,500 juveniles were arrested for weapons violations in 2010, the majority of which involved firearms.[77]

Discussion Tip: Have students debate the role that guns play in juvenile offending. Ask students if they believe that controlling youth access to weapons will significantly decrease violent crime in this population?

SELFASSESSMENT

Fill in the blanks and check your answers on page 532.

Criminologists have identified a number of _____ factors that increase the probability of juvenile misbehavior. One is youth. Studies of a process called _____ _____ show that children commit fewer offenses as they grow older. According to two researchers, _____ _____ at the hands of parents or guardians doubles the chances of delinquency. Youth who become involved in _____ _____ are also more likely to engage in criminal activity than those who do not.

FIRST CONTACT: THE POLICE AND PRETRIAL PROCEDURES

Until recently, most police departments allocated few resources to dealing with juvenile crime. The number of violent crimes committed by youths under the age of eighteen has, however, provided a strong incentive for departments to set up special services for children. The standard bearer for these operations is the *juvenile officer,* who operates either alone or as part of a juvenile unit within a department. The initial contact between a juvenile and the criminal justice system is, however, usually handled by a regular police officer on patrol who either apprehends the juvenile while he or she is committing a crime or answers a call for service. (See Figure 15.7 below for an overview of the juvenile justice process.) The youth is then passed on to the juvenile officer, who must decide how to handle the case.

> ⊘ The **National Center for Juvenile Justice** is a valuable source for juvenile delinquency information and data. Find its Web site by visiting the *Criminal Justice CourseMate* at **cengagebrain.com** and selecting the *Web links* for this chapter.

POLICE DISCRETION AND JUVENILE CRIME

Police arrest about 1.3 million youths under the age of eighteen each year. In most states, police officers must have probable cause to believe that the minor has committed an offense, just as they would if the suspect was an adult. Police power with regard to juveniles is greater than with adults, however, because police can take youths into custody for status

FIGURE 15.7 The Juvenile Justice Process

This diagram shows the possible tracks that a young person may take after her or his first contact with the juvenile justice system (usually a police officer).

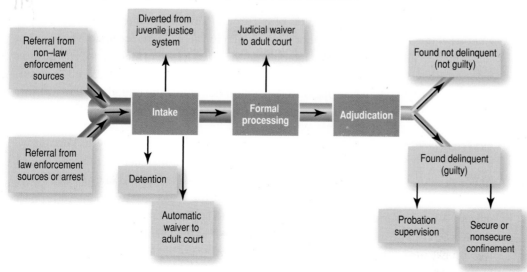

Source: Office of Juvenile Justice and Delinquency Prevention.

offenses, such as possession of alcohol or truancy. In these cases, the officer is acting *in loco parentis,* or in the place of the parent. The officer's role is not necessarily to punish the youths, but to protect them from harmful behavior.

LOW-VISIBILITY DECISION MAKING Police officers also have a great deal of discretion in deciding what to do with juveniles who have committed crimes or status offenses. Juvenile justice expert Joseph Goldstein labels this discretionary power low-visibility decision making because it relies on factors that the public is not generally in a position to understand or criticize. When a grave offense has taken place, a police officer may decide to formally arrest the juvenile, send him or her to juvenile court, or place the youth under the care of a social-service organization. In less serious situations, the officer may simply issue a warning or take the offender to the police station and release the child into the custody of her or his parents.

LO 6 In making these discretionary decisions, police generally consider the following factors:

*   The nature of the child's offense.
*   The offender's past history of involvement with the juvenile justice system.
*   The setting in which the offense took place.
*   The ability and willingness of the child's parents to take disciplinary action.
*   The attitude of the offender.
*   The offender's race and gender.

Law enforcement officers notify the juvenile court system that a particular young person requires its attention through a process known as a referral. Anyone with a valid reason, including parents, relatives, welfare agencies, and school officials, can refer a juvenile to the juvenile court. The vast majority of cases in juvenile courts, however, are referred by the police.[78]

ARRESTS AND MINORITY YOUTHS As in other areas of the criminal justice system, members of minority groups are disproportionately represented in juvenile arrests. The violent crime arrest rate for African American juveniles is about four times that for white juveniles, and the property arrest crime rate for black juveniles is double that of whites. Furthermore, African American juveniles are referred to juvenile court twice as often as their white peers.[79]

A great deal of research, much of it contradictory, has been done to determine whether these statistics reflect inherent racism in the juvenile justice system or whether social factors are to blame.[80] The latest large-scale study, performed by federal government crime researchers Carl E. Pope and Howard Snyder using the National Incident-Based Reporting System (see pages 78–79), found that nonwhite offenders were no more likely than white offenders to be arrested for the same delinquent behavior.[81]

FAILING THE "ATTITUDE TEST" In general, though, as Figure 15.8 on the facing page shows, police officers do seem more likely to arrest members of minority groups. Although this may be partially attributed to the social factors discussed in Chapter 2, it also appears that minority youths often fail the "attitude test" during interactions with police officers. After the seriousness of the offense and past history, the most important factor in the decision of whether to arrest or release appears to be the offender's attitude. An offender who is polite and apologetic generally has a better chance of being released. If the juvenile is hostile or unresponsive, the police are more likely to place him or her in custody for even a minor offense.[82]

Low-Visibility Decision Making A term used to describe the discretionary power police have in determining what to do with misbehaving juveniles.

Referral The notification process through which a law enforcement officer or other concerned citizen makes the juvenile court aware of a juvenile's unlawful or unruly conduct.

Teaching Tip: Ask students to list and explain the circumstances under which a police officer can take a juvenile into custody. How does this differ from police interaction with adult suspects? (LO 6)

Furthermore, police officers who do not live in the same community with minority youths may misinterpret normal behavior as disrespectful or delinquent and act accordingly.[83] This "culture gap" is of crucial importance to police-juvenile relations and underscores the community-oriented policing goal of having law enforcement agents be more involved in the communities they patrol, as we discussed in Chapter 6.

JUVENILES AND *MIRANDA* RIGHTS

The privacy and *Miranda* rights of juveniles are protected during contact with law enforcement officers, though not to the same extent as for adults. In most jurisdictions, the Fourth Amendment ban against unreasonable searches and seizures and Fifth Amendment safeguards against custodial self-incrimination apply to juveniles. In other words, juvenile court judges cannot use illegally seized evidence in juvenile hearings, and police must read youths their *Miranda* rights after arrest.

In *Fare v. Michael C.* (1979),[84] the Supreme Court clarified law enforcement officials' responsibilities with regard to *Miranda* warnings and juveniles. The case involved a boy who had been arrested on suspicion of murder. After being read his rights, the youth asked to speak to his probation officer. The request was denied. The boy eventually confessed to the crime. The Court ruled that juveniles may waive their right to protection against self-incrimination and that admissions made to the police in the absence of counsel are admissible.

Then, in 2004, the Court seemed to blur any constitutional distinction between juveniles and adults for *Miranda* purposes. That year, it ordered trial courts to ignore a defendant's age when determining whether the defendant had acted reasonably in believing himself or herself to be "in custody" for purposes of arrest.[85] (See pages 237–240 to review the *Miranda* procedure.) Juvenile status is not completely irrelevant in these situations, however. Remember that any statement to the police must be given voluntarily. Thus, courts can look at the defendant's age in determining whether he or she was unfairly coerced into speaking.[86] As can be seen in the feature *A Question of Ethics—Interrogating Children* on the following page, police may be taking a chance if they rely on the testimony of young suspects and witnesses.

INTAKE

As noted earlier, if, following arrest, a police officer feels the offender warrants the attention of the juvenile justice process, the officer will refer the youth to juvenile court. Once this step has been taken, a complaint is filed with a special division of the juvenile court, and the **intake** process begins. Intake may be followed

LO 7

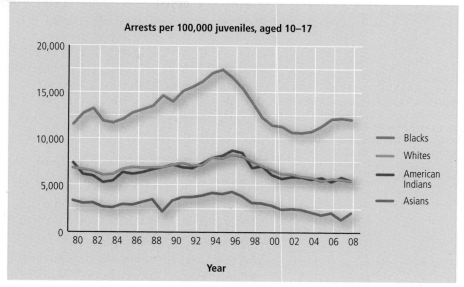

FIGURE 15.8 Juvenile Arrest Rates by Race, 1980 to 2008
Using the FBI's Uniform Crime Report, statisticians can determine the rates of arrest for persons aged ten to seventeen in the United States. As you can see, the rate of arrests per 100,000 juveniles remains considerably higher for African Americans than for other racial groups.

Arrests per 100,000 juveniles, aged 10–17

- Blacks
- Whites
- American Indians
- Asians

Source: Office of Juvenile Justice and Delinquency Prevention, "Juvenile Arrest Trends," at **www.ojjdp.ncjrs.org/ojstatbb/crime/JAR_Display.asp?ID=qa05260&text=yes**.

Critical Thinking Skill Analysis: In a written assignment, ask students to decide whether juveniles should have the ability to waive their *Miranda* rights.

Intake The process by which an official of the court must decide whether to file a petition, release the juvenile, or place the juvenile under some other form of supervision.

by diversion to a community-based program, transfer to an adult court, or detention to await trial in juvenile court. Thus, intake, diversion, transfer, and detention are the four primary stages of pretrial juvenile justice procedure.

During intake, an official of the juvenile court—usually a probation officer, but sometimes a judge—must decide, in effect, what to do with the offender. The intake officer has several options during intake.

Teaching Tip: In a short writing assignment, have students consider the intake process. What are the advantages of this early screening process? Are there any disadvantages?

1. Simply dismiss the case, releasing the offender without taking any further action.
2. Divert the offender to a social-services program, such as drug rehabilitation or anger management.
3. File a petition for a formal court hearing. The petition is the formal document outlining the charges against the juvenile.
4. Transfer the case to an adult court, where the offender will be tried as an adult.

With regard to status offenses, judges have sole discretion to decide whether to process the case or *divert* the youth to another juvenile service agency.

Petition The document filed with a juvenile court alleging that the juvenile is a delinquent or a status offender and requesting that the court either hear the case or transfer it to an adult court.

PRETRIAL DIVERSION

In the early 1970s, Congress passed the first Juvenile Justice and Delinquency Prevention (JJDP) Act, which ordered the development of methods "to divert juveniles from the traditional juvenile justice system."[87] Within a few years, hundreds of diversion programs had been put into effect. Today, diversion refers to the process of removing low-risk offenders from the formal juvenile justice system by placing them in community-based rehabilitation programs.

A QUESTION OF ETHICS: *Interrogating Children*

THE SITUATION The body of an eleven-year-old girl named Ryan Harris has been found in a lot behind an empty building. Evidence shows that Ryan was beaten and sexually assaulted before her death. Chicago police believe that a seven-year-old boy has knowledge of the circumstances surrounding the murder. Two detectives isolate the boy in an empty room at the police station and ask him if he knows what a lie is. "You should never lie," the boy answers.

Each of the detectives takes one of the boy's hands and asks him about Harris. The seven-year-old admits to throwing a brick at the girl and knocking her off her bicycle, and then dragging her body into the weeds with the help of an eight-year-old friend. After corroborating the story with this accomplice, the police detain the boys and classify the case of Ryan Harris as "Cleared/Closed by Arrest."

THE ETHICAL DILEMMA The law allows police to interrogate a juvenile of any age without a parent or guardian being present. In these situations, the police must only make a "reasonable attempt" to contact the parents, after which they can question the child. Indeed, as we saw in the text, the rules for interrogating juveniles are almost indistinguishable from those that apply to adults. Police questioning of children does, however, raise ethical and practical questions. How can children as young as the ones involved in this case understand the concept or consequences of waiving their *Miranda* rights, as both boys did? Isn't any situation in which police officers are alone in a room with a child inherently coercive?

WHAT IS THE SOLUTION? How reliable do you consider the statements of juveniles, especially those as young as the boys in the Harris murder? Regardless of the law, how should police approach the interrogation of children who may not fully understand the concept of constitutional rights? (In this case, although the police did not break any rules, their strategy backfired. After a forensic examination found semen—which boys so young could not have produced—on the girl's torn underwear, the suspects were immediately released and the investigation reopened.)

Diversion programs vary widely, but fall into three general categories:

1. *Probation.* In this program, the juvenile is returned to the community, but placed under the supervision of a juvenile probation officer. If the youth breaks the conditions of probation, he or she can be returned to the formal juvenile system.
2. *Treatment and aid.* Many juveniles have behavioral or medical conditions that contribute to their delinquent behavior, and many diversion programs offer remedial education, drug and alcohol treatment, and other forms of counseling to alleviate these problems.
3. *Restitution.* In these programs, the offender "repays" her or his victim, either directly or symbolically through community service.[88]

Proponents of diversion programs include many labeling theorists (see Chapter 2), who believe that contact with the formal juvenile justice system "labels" the youth a delinquent, which leads to further delinquent behavior.

TRANSFER TO ADULT COURT

One side effect of diversionary programs is that the youths who remain in the juvenile courts are more likely to be seen as "hardened" and thus less amenable to rehabilitation. This, in turn, increases the likelihood that the offender will be transferred to an adult court, a process in which the juvenile court waives jurisdiction over the youth. As the American juvenile justice system has shifted away from ideals of treatment and toward punishment, transfer to adult court has been one of the most popular means of "getting tough" on delinquents.

Critical Thinking Skill Development: Ask students to work in small groups to answer "Questions for Critical Analysis" number two on page 533, in which they consider the issue of transfer to adult court.

METHODS OF TRANSFER There are three types of transfer laws, and most states use more than one of them depending on the jurisdiction and the seriousness of the offense. Juveniles are most commonly transferred to adult courts through judicial waiver, in which the juvenile judge is given the power to determine whether a young offender's case will be waived to adult court. The judge makes this decision based on the offender's age, the nature of the offense, and any criminal history. All but five states employ judicial waiver.

Twenty-nine states have taken the waiver responsibility out of judicial hands through automatic transfer, also known as *legislative waiver.* In these states, the legislatures have designated certain conditions—usually involving serious crimes such as murder and rape—under which a juvenile case is automatically "kicked up" to adult court. In Rhode Island, for example, a juvenile aged sixteen or older with two prior felony adjudications will automatically be transferred on being accused of a third felony.[89]

Fifteen states also allow for prosecutorial waiver, in which prosecutors are allowed to choose whether to initiate proceedings in juvenile or criminal court when certain age and offense conditions are met. In twenty-five states, criminal court judges also have the freedom to send juveniles who were transferred to adult court back to juvenile court. Known as *reverse transfer* statutes, these laws are designed to provide judges with a measure of discretion even when automatic transfer takes place.

Judicial Waiver The process in which the juvenile judge, based on the facts of the case at hand, decides that the alleged offender should be transferred to adult court.

Automatic Transfer The process by which a juvenile is transferred to adult court as a matter of state law. In some states, for example, a juvenile who is suspected of murder is automatically transferred to adult court.

Prosecutorial Waiver A procedure used in situations in which juvenile and adult courts each have jurisdiction over certain offenses, depending on the age of the offender, and the prosecutor decides which court will hear the case.

INCIDENCE OF TRANSFER Each year, about 8,500 delinquency cases are waived to adult criminal court—less than 0.5 percent of all cases that reach juvenile court.[90] As we saw earlier in the chapter, those juveniles who commit the most violent felonies are the most likely to be transferred. For example, when he was fifteen years old, Vernon Bartley raped and murdered a neighbor, Karen Ertell, who was scheduled to testify against him

during a burglary trial in Ewa Beach, Hawaii. Given the "gruesome, violent, detestable" nature of his crimes, there was little doubt that a judge would waive Bartley to adult court. In 2010, he was tried as an adult, found guilty of second degree murder, and sentenced to life in adult prison (see the photo alongside).

DETENTION

Once the decision has been made that the offender will face adjudication in a juvenile court, the intake official must decide what to do with him or her until the start of the trial. Generally, the juvenile is released into the custody of parents or a guardian—most jurisdictions favor this practice in lieu of setting money bail for youths. The intake officer may also place the offender in detention, or temporary custody in a secure facility, until the disposition process begins. Once a juvenile has been detained, most jurisdictions require that a detention hearing be held within twenty-four hours. During this hearing, the offender has several due process safeguards, including the right to counsel, the right against self-incrimination, and the right to cross-examine and confront witnesses.

In justifying its decision to detain, the court will usually address one of three issues:

1. Whether the child poses a danger to the community.
2. Whether the child will return for the adjudication process.
3. Whether detention will provide protection for the child.

The Supreme Court upheld the practice of preventive detention (see Chapter 9) for juveniles in *Schall v. Martin* (1984)[91] by ruling that youths can be detained if they are deemed a "risk" to the safety of the community or to their own welfare. Partly as a result, the number of detained juveniles increased by 48 percent between 1985 and 2007.[92]

What factors are taken into consideration when deciding whether juveniles such as Vernon Bartley, right, who have been charged with violent crimes should be tried as adults?
AP Photo/Richard Ambo, *The Honolulu Advertiser*

Detention The temporary custody of a juvenile in a secure facility after a petition has been filed and before the adjudicatory process begins.
Detention Hearing A hearing to determine whether a juvenile should be detained, or remain detained, while waiting for the adjudicatory process to begin.

SELFASSESSMENT

Fill in the blanks and check your answers on page 532.
If the circumstances are serious enough, a police officer can formally _____ an offending juvenile. Otherwise, the officer can _____ the juvenile to the juvenile court system or place her or him in the care of a _____-service organization. During the _____ process, a judge or juvenile probation officer decides the immediate fate of the juvenile delinquent. One of the options is _____, in which low-risk offenders are placed in community rehabilitation programs. If the judge believes that the seriousness of the offense so warrants, he or she can transfer the juvenile into the adult court system through a process called judicial _____.

Teaching Tip: If possible, invite a correctional officer from a local juvenile detention center to visit the classroom. Ask her or him to describe a typical day in juvenile detention. How would she or he describe the population of the juvenile facility?

JUVENILES ON TRIAL

Over the past forty years, the one constant in the juvenile justice system has been change. Supreme Court rulings in the wake of *In re Gault* (1967) have increased the procedural formality and the overriding punitive philosophy of the juvenile court.

Diversion policies have worked to remove many status offenders from the juvenile court's jurisdiction, and waiver policies ensure that the most violent juveniles are tried as adults. Some observers feel these adjustments have "criminalized" the juvenile court, effectively rendering it indistinguishable both theoretically and practically from adult courts.[93] Just over half of the states, for example, permit juveniles to request a jury trial under certain circumstances. As the *Mastering Concepts* feature below explains, however, juvenile justice proceedings may still be distinguished from the adult system of criminal justice, and these differences are evident in the adjudication and disposition of the juvenile trial.

ADJUDICATION

LO 8 During the adjudication stage of the juvenile justice process, a hearing is held to determine whether the offender is delinquent or in need of some form of court supervision. Most state juvenile codes dictate a specific set of procedures that

Critical Thinking Skill Development: In a writing assignment, ask students to discuss how the juvenile justice system has become more like the adult court system. How are the two systems still different?

MASTERINGCONCEPTS

THE JUVENILE JUSTICE SYSTEM VERSUS THE CRIMINAL JUSTICE SYSTEM

AP Photo/Columbus Dispatch, James D. DeCamp

When the juvenile justice system was first established in the United States, its participants saw it as being separate from the adult criminal justice system. Indeed, the two systems remain separate in many ways. There are, however, a number of similarities between juvenile and adult justice. Here, we summarize both the similarities and the differences.

SIMILARITIES	DIFFERENCES		
		Juvenile System	**Adult System**
• The right to receive the *Miranda* warnings.	**Purpose**	Rehabilitation of the offender.	Punishment.
• Procedural protections when making an admission of guilt.	**Arrest**	Juveniles can be arrested for acts (status offenses) that are not criminal for adults.	Adults can be arrested only for acts made illegal by the relevant criminal code.
• Prosecutors and defense attorneys play equally important roles.	**Wrongdoing**	Considered a "delinquent act."	A crime.
• The right to be represented by counsel at the crucial stages of the trial process.	**Proceedings**	Informal; closed to public.	Formal and regimented; open to public.
• Access to plea bargains.	**Information**	Courts may NOT release information to the press.	Courts MUST release information to the press.
• The right to a hearing and an appeal.	**Parents**	Play significant role.	Play no role.
	Release	Into parent/guardian custody.	May post bail when appropriate.
• The standard of evidence is proof beyond a reasonable doubt.	**Jury trial**	In some states, juveniles do NOT have this right.	All adults have this right.
• Offenders can be placed on probation by the judge.	**Searches**	Juveniles can be searched in school without probable cause.	No adult can be searched without probable cause.
• Offenders can be held before adjudication if the judge believes them to be a threat to the community.	**Records**	Juvenile's record is sealed at age of adult criminal responsibility.	Adult's criminal record is permanent.
	Sentencing	Juveniles are placed in separate facilities from adults.	Adults are placed in county jails or state or federal prisons.
• Following trial, offenders can be sentenced to community supervision.	**Death penalty**	No death penalty.	Death penalty for certain serious crimes under certain circumstances.

must be followed during the adjudicatory hearing, with the goal of providing the respondent with "the essentials of due process and fair treatment." Consequently, the respondent in an adjudicatory hearing has the right to notice of charges, counsel, and confrontation and cross-examination, and the privilege against self-incrimination. Furthermore, "proof beyond a reasonable doubt" must be established to find the child delinquent. When the child admits guilt—that is, admits to the charges of the initial petition—the judge must ensure that the admission was voluntary.

At the close of the adjudicatory hearing, the judge is generally required to rule on the legal issues and evidence that have been presented. Based on this ruling, the judge determines whether the respondent is delinquent or in need of court supervision. Alternatively, the judge can dismiss the case based on a lack of evidence. It is important to remember that finding a child delinquent is *not* the same as convicting an adult of a crime. A delinquent does not face the same restrictions imposed on adult convicts in some states, such as limits on the right to vote and to run for political office (discussed in Chapter 13).

DISPOSITION

Once a juvenile has been adjudicated delinquent, the judge must decide what steps will be taken toward treatment and/or punishment. Most states provide for a *bifurcated* process in which a separate disposition hearing follows the adjudicatory hearing. Depending on state law, the juvenile may be entitled to counsel at the disposition hearing.

SENTENCING JUVENILES In an adult trial, the sentencing phase is primarily concerned with the needs of the community to be protected from the convict. In contrast, a juvenile judge uses the disposition hearing to determine a sentence that will serve the needs of the child. For assistance in this crucial process, the judge will order the probation department to gather information on the juvenile and present it in the form of a predisposition report. The report usually contains information concerning the respondent's family background, the facts surrounding the delinquent act, and interviews with social workers, teachers, and other important figures in the child's life.

JUDICIAL DISCRETION In keeping with the rehabilitative tradition of the juvenile justice system, juvenile judges generally have a great deal of discretion in choosing one of several disposition possibilities. A judge can tend toward leniency, delivering only a stern reprimand or warning before releasing the juvenile into the custody of parents or other legal guardians. Otherwise, the choice is among incarceration in a juvenile correctional facility, probation, or community treatment. In most cases, the seriousness of the offense is the primary factor used in determining whether to incarcerate a juvenile, though history of delinquency, family situation, and the offender's attitude are all relevant.

Further indication of the treatment goals of juvenile courts can be found in the indeterminate sentencing practices that, until recently, dominated disposition. Under this system, correctional administrators were given the freedom to decide when a delinquent had been sufficiently rehabilitated and could be released. Today, nearly half of the states have enacted determinate or minimum mandatory sentencing laws that cover convicted juvenile offenders. Such statutes shift the focus of disposition from the treatment needs of the delinquent to society's desire to punish and incapacitate.

JUVENILE CORRECTIONS

In general, juvenile corrections are based on the concept of graduated sanctions—that is, the severity of the punishment should fit the crime. Consequently, status and first-time offenders are diverted or placed on probation, repeat offenders find themselves in intensive community supervision or treatment programs, and serious and violent offenders are placed in correctional facilities.[94]

As society's expectations of the juvenile justice system have changed, so have the characteristics of its corrections programs. In some cities, for example, juvenile probation officers join police officers on the beat. Because the former are not bound by the same search and seizure restrictions as other law enforcement officials, this interdepartmental teamwork provides more opportunities to fight youth crime aggressively. Juvenile correctional facilities are also changing their operations to reflect public mandates that they should both reform and punish. Also, note that about 7,500 juveniles are in adult jails and another 25,000 are serving time in adult prisons.[95]

Graduated Sanctions The practical theory in juvenile corrections that a delinquent or status offender should receive a punishment that matches in seriousness the severity of the wrongdoing.

JUVENILE PROBATION

The most common form of juvenile corrections is probation—33 percent of all delinquency cases disposed of by juvenile courts result in conditional diversion. The majority of all adjudicated delinquents (nearly 60 percent) will never receive a disposition more severe than being placed on probation.[96] These statistics reflect a general understanding among juvenile court judges and other officials that a child should normally be removed from her or his home only as a last resort.

The organization of juvenile probation is very similar to adult probation (see Chapter 12), and juvenile probationers are increasingly subjected to electronic monitoring and other supervisory tactics. The main difference between the two programs lies in the attitude toward the offender. Adult probation officers have an overriding responsibility to protect the community from the probationer, while juvenile probation officers are expected to take the role of a mentor or a concerned relative in looking after the needs of the child.

Teaching Tip: Invite a juvenile probation officer to visit the classroom. Ask her or him to describe how juvenile probation differs from adult probation.

CONFINING JUVENILES

About 92,000 American youths (up from 30,000 at the end of the 1970s) are incarcerated in public and private juvenile correctional facilities in the United States.[97] Most of these juveniles have committed crimes against people or property, but a significant number (about 15 percent) have been incarcerated for technical violations of their probation or parole agreements.[98] After deciding that a juvenile needs to be confined, the judge has two sentencing options: nonsecure juvenile institutions and secure juvenile institutions.

CAREERS IN CJ

Photo Courtesy of Carl McCullough, Sr.

CARL McCULLOUGH, SR.
SENIOR YOUTH WORKER

I was born and raised in Amarillo, Texas. My dad was murdered when I was a little kid. So, it was just me and my mom, and I was always into something. All my uncles were in and out of prison; I was pretty much raised by my grandmother. By the time I was thirteen, I already had a juvenile record. I had one uncle, who was stationed in the army in Minnesota, and he knew what Amarillo was all about; it was basically a trap. So, he moved me to Minnesota, and that was when my life changed.

SCHOOL DAYS When I came to Minnesota, there were a number of people who were placed in my life, who made a difference and who helped me over that hump. I eventually went to the University of Wisconsin on a football scholarship. While at school, I caught the attention of one of my academic tutors. He noticed that I had a gift for building relationships with kids and suggested that I volunteer with the Dane County Juvenile Detention Center. I checked it out and felt an instant connection. Dealing with these kids, and hearing their stories—it was all just like what I went through. I had a shot in the NFL, playing for the Buffalo Bills and the Minnesota Vikings, but that lasted only a short time. Even when I was still a student, I knew that I wanted to work with kids again one day. So I majored in Afro-American studies, and I also took a lot of courses in sociology.

THE HEART OF THE MATTER Today, I work at the Hennepin County (Minnesota) Juvenile Detention Center where I'm responsible for a group of twelve young men, aged thirteen to eighteen, who are awaiting trial, waiting for placements, or just being held in a secure place due to the high-profile nature of their cases. I'm with the kids every day and every other weekend from 6:30 A.M. to 2:30 P.M. I do everything from helping with homework to supervising their leisure time, running group programs, and just being a positive, caring adult with whom to talk. Having the NFL experience is a huge icebreaker with the residents. "Why are you here?" they always ask me, and I tell them I am here because I care about them, because I want to see a change, and because I'd like to help them believe that something better is possible. To do this job well, you have to be good at building relationships. It helps to know how to work with different cultures as well. Then you have to have patience; without it you won't last long. You know they are going to test you, to see what they can and can't get away with. You also have to be willing to learn a few things from them. You have to be a good listener.

MAKING A DIFFERENCE This is not a field where you're going to get rich, but you have good benefits and a great retirement plan. This job is all about making a difference in someone's life, the same way that someone came along and made a difference in mine.

FAST FACTS

JUVENILE CORRECTIONAL OFFICER JOB DESCRIPTION:

- Provide safety, security, custodial care, discipline, and guidance. Play a critical role in the rehabilitation of youth and, as a result, have a potentially great impact on a youth's success during and after his or her incarceration.

WHAT KIND OF TRAINING IS REQUIRED?

- A bachelor's degree in human services, behavioral science, or a related field.
- Professional and respectful verbal communication skills.
- Commitment and dedication to the needs of adolescent offenders and their families.
- Ability to recognize and respect cultural differences and provide culturally appropriate services. Fluency in English and one of the following languages a plus: Spanish, Somali, Hmong, Russian.

ANNUAL SALARY RANGE AND BENEFITS?

- $33,000–$52,000
- Full benefit package includes health, vision, dental, and life insurance, retirement benefits, education and professional development resources.

For additional information on a career as a resident youth worker, visit:
www.corrections.com/jobs/show/3429.

Chris Scredon/iStockphoto

NONSECURE CONFINEMENT Some juvenile delinquents do not require high levels of control and can be placed in **residential treatment programs.** These programs, run by either probation departments or social-services departments, allow their subjects freedom of movement in the community. Generally, this freedom is predicated on the juveniles following certain rules, such as avoiding alcoholic beverages and returning to the facility for curfew. Residential treatment programs can be divided into four categories:[99]

1. *Foster care programs,* in which the juveniles live with a couple who act as surrogate parents.
2. *Group homes,* which generally house between twelve and fifteen youths and provide treatment, counseling, and education services by a professional staff.

LO 9
3. *Family group homes,* which combine aspects of foster care and group homes, meaning that a single family, rather than a group of professionals, looks after the needs of the young offenders.
4. *Rural programs,* which include wilderness camps, farms, and ranches where between thirty and fifty children are placed in an environment that provides recreational activities and treatment programs.

SECURE CONFINEMENT Secure facilities are comparable to the adult prisons and jails we discussed in Chapters 13 and 14. These institutions go by a confusing array of names depending on the state in which they are located, but the two best known are boot camps and training schools.

Boot Camps A **boot camp** is the juvenile variation of shock probation. As we noted in Chapter 12, boot camps are modeled after military training for new recruits. Boot camp programs are based on the theory that by giving wayward youths a taste of the "hard life" of military-like training for short periods of time, usually no longer than 180 days, they will be "shocked" out of a life of crime. New York's Camp Monterey Shock Incarceration Facility is typical of the boot camp experience. Inmates are grouped in platoons and live in dormitories. They spend eight hours a day training, drilling, and doing hard labor, and also participate in programs such as basic adult education and job skills training.[100]

Recently, the boot camp industry has come under heavy criticism from parents, criminal justice experts, and government regulators for harsh living conditions and inhumane treatment of its juvenile charges. Several years ago, the federal Government Accountability Office released a report detailing ten deaths and thousands of cases of abuse in these camps. According to investigators, teenagers were starved, left to wallow in their own excrement and vomit, and forced to eat dirt to survive.[101] Along with studies showing that boot camps have little, if any, positive impact on recidivism, this kind of publicity has raised serious questions about the benefits of this form of juvenile confinement.[102]

Training Schools No juvenile correctional facility is called a "prison." This does not mean they lack a strong resemblance to prisons. The facilities that most closely mimic the atmosphere at an adult correctional facility are **training schools,** alternatively known as youth

This support class for fathers at the Hogan Street Regional Youth Center in St. Louis, Missouri, is one of many group-counseling classes offered at the juvenile facility. Why would the Missouri juvenile justice system, as well as juvenile justice systems in other states, emphasize rehabilitation and therapeutic intervention for young offenders rather than adult-style punitive incarceration?
Dilip Vishwanat/*New York Times*/Redux

Residential Treatment Program A government-run facility for juveniles whose offenses are not deemed serious enough to warrant incarceration in a training school.

Boot Camp A variation on traditional shock incarceration in which juveniles (and some adults) are sent to secure confinement facilities modeled on military basic training camps instead of prison or jail.

Training School A correctional institution for juveniles found to be delinquent or status offenders.

Discussion Tip: Ask students to debate boot camps as a form of "shock" probation. What are the advantages and disadvantages of boot camp programs for juvenile offenders?

camps, youth development centers, industrial schools, and several other similar titles. Whatever the name, these institutions claim to differ from their adult countparts by offering a variety of programs to treat and rehabilitate the young offenders. In reality, training schools are plagued by many of the same problems as adult prisons and jails, including high levels of inmate-on-inmate violence, substance abuse, gang wars, and overcrowding.

AFTERCARE Juveniles leave correctional facilities through an early release program or because they have served the length of their sentences. Juvenile corrections officials recognize that many of these children, like adults, need assistance readjusting to the outside world. Consequently, released juveniles are often placed in aftercare programs. Based on the same philosophy that drives the prisoner reentry movement (discussed in the previous chapter), aftercare programs are designed to offer services for the juveniles, while at the same time supervising them to reduce the chances of recidivism. The ideal aftercare program includes community support groups, aid in finding and keeping employment, and continued monitoring to ensure that the juvenile is able to deal with the demands of freedom.

Aftercare The variety of therapeutic, educational, and counseling programs made available to juvenile delinquents (and some adults) after they have been released from a correctional facility.

TRANSFER AND ADULT CORRECTIONS Proponents of transferring juveniles to the adult justice system point out that violent juvenile offenders pose a risk to nonviolent offenders in juvenile detention centers. Thus, their removal makes the juvenile justice system safer. Critics of the practice point out that, by the same token, adult prisons and jails can be very dangerous places for young offenders. Research shows that juveniles in jails have the highest suicide rates of all inmates and suffer disproportionate levels of physical and sexual abuse.[103]

Data also suggest that juveniles transferred to adult correctional facilities have higher recidivism rates than those who remain in the juvenile justice system.[104] Experts have several theories to explain this pattern, including the negative effect of labeling juveniles as "felons" (to review labeling theory, see pages 46 and 48) and the decreased opportunities for family support in adult correctional facilities.[105] Furthermore, the criminogenic effect, discussed at the end of Chapter 8, holds that younger inmates will gain knowledge of the criminal lifestyle from older, more experienced prisoners. "You can learn a whole lot more bad things in here than good," said one juvenile inmate from his cell in an Arizona adult prison.[106]

> "Here, it was me against the world, and out of necessity I was transformed into a rough creature. There was nowhere to run and nowhere to hide and deep down inside I knew I was walking in hell."
>
> **—Will,** describing his experience as a juvenile in an adult jail (2007)

SELFASSESSMENT

Fill in the blanks and check your answers on page 532.
The most common form of juvenile corrections is _____. If the judge decides that the juvenile needs more stringent supervision, he or she can sentence the offender to a _____ facility such as a residential treatment program. If the juvenile's offense has been particularly serious, she or he will most likely be sent to a secure confinement facility such as a _____ camp or a _____ school.

CJ IN ACTION

LIFE WITHOUT PAROLE FOR JUVENILES

In 2010, when the United States Supreme Court prohibited sentences of life without parole (LWOP) for juveniles convicted of nonhomicide crimes (see pages 508–509), Kenneth Young was hopeful. Ten years earlier, a Hillsborough County (Florida) judge had sentenced Young, then fourteen years old, to LWOP for participating in a series of armed robberies. The Court's *Graham* ruling, Young and his attorneys assumed, would provide him an avenue to freedom. But they were wrong. Florida officials refused to even consider Young's early release. Indeed, as this *CJ in Action* feature will explore, the *Graham* decision may have served to intensify the debate over the controversial practice of LWOP sentences for juveniles.

LWOP VERSUS THE DEATH PENALTY

The United States has nearly 2,500 inmates serving LWOP sentences for crimes committed before they turned eighteen years old—by far the highest tally in the world (Israel, in second place, has seven). The vast majority of these inmates were convicted of homicides, and thus do not qualify for resentencing under the *Graham* decision.[107] Even those who do qualify are only given the *chance* for parole. As Kenneth Young found out, this opportunity can be denied by state corrections officials. Consequently, the practical impact of the Court's recent ruling appears to be limited.

Although many juvenile justice insiders have consistently attacked LWOP sentences as being overly punitive for teenagers, their protests had little effect on U.S. courts until 2005. In that year, the Supreme Court handed down its ruling in *Roper v. Simmons,* which held that the death penalty was unconstitutional for offenders who were under the age of eighteen when they committed their offense. The Court concluded that juveniles' lack of maturity hinders them from making rational decisions and causes them to take risks that older persons would know to avoid. Therefore, said the Court, justifications for the death penalty such as retribution and deterrence do not apply to adults and juveniles equally.[108] The ruling led critics of LWOP sentences to ask why the same rationale does not apply to LWOP, a fate many consider "death in prison" for young and old offenders alike.[109]

THE CASE FOR SENTENCING JUVENILES TO LIFE WITHOUT PAROLE

- LWOP is a rational and moral response to the worst of criminal acts. Dennis Hurwitz, whose daughter Karen was killed by a sword-wielding juvenile, thinks that if someone is capable of extreme violence, "even in the teenage years, it's best that they not be on the streets in a position to do that again."[110]

- LWOP spares victims and families of victims the hardships of going through parole hearings and the devastating possibility that the offender will be set free.

- Prior to the *Graham* ruling, thirty-seven states and the federal government had laws that allowed for LWOP sentences for juveniles convicted of nonhomicide offenses. Thus, there is no national consensus against LWOP.

THE CASE AGAINST SENTENCING JUVENILES TO LIFE WITHOUT PAROLE

- In the *Roper* decision, Justice Anthony Kennedy wrote, "From a moral standpoint, it would be misguided to equate the failings of a minor with those of an adult, for a greater possibility exists that a minor's character deficiencies will be reformed."[111] If this reasoning precludes capital punishment for juveniles, it should apply to LWOP sentences as well.

- The United States is the only country in the world that routinely sentences juveniles to LWOP.

- Life in adult prison is particularly cruel for young offenders, who are subjected to a great deal of physical, mental, and even sexual abuse, and are not offered treatment programs because they are considered "lost causes."

YOUR DECISION— WRITING ASSIGNMENT

In general, what is your opinion of LWOP sentences for juvenile offenders? If you support such sentences, do you think they should be reserved for only the most violent young offenders, for those over the age of fourteen who commit murder, or for some other category of offenders? Support your answer. Before responding, you can review our discussions in this chapter concerning:

- The traditional principles underlying the juvenile justice system (pages 503–504).
- The culpability question (pages 508–509).
- The transfer of juveniles to adult court (pages 523–524).

Your answer should include at least three full paragraphs.

CHAPTER SUMMARY

LO 1
Describe the child-saving movement and its relationship to the doctrine of _parens patriae._ Under the doctrine of _parens patriae,_ the state has a right and a duty to care for neglected, delinquent, or disadvantaged children. The child-saving movement, based on the doctrine of _parens patriae,_ started in the 1800s. Its followers believed that juvenile offenders require treatment rather than punishment.

LO 2
List the four major differences between juvenile courts and adult courts. (a) No juries, (b) different terminology, (c) limited adversarial relationship, and (d) confidentiality.

LO 3
Identify and briefly describe the single most important Supreme Court case with respect to juvenile justice. The case was _In re Gault,_ decided by the Supreme Court in 1967. In this case a minor was arrested for allegedly making an obscene phone call. His parents were not notified and were not present during the juvenile court judge's decision-making process. In this case, the Supreme Court held that juveniles are entitled to many of the same due process rights granted to adult offenders, including notice of charges, the right to counsel, the privilege against self-incrimination, and the right to confront and cross-examine witnesses.

LO 4
Describe the one variable that always correlates highly with juvenile crime rates. The older a person is, the less likely he or she will exhibit criminal behavior. This process is known as aging out. Thus, persons in any at-risk group will commit fewer crimes as they get older.

LO 5
Indicate some of the reasons why youths join gangs. Some alienated teenagers join gangs for the social relationships and the sense of identity that gangs can provide. Youths living in high-crime neighborhoods join gangs as a form of protection. The excitement of belonging to a gang is another reason to join.

LO 6
List the factors that normally determine what police do with juvenile offenders. The arresting police officers consider (a) the nature of the offense, (b) the youthful offender's past criminal history, (c) the setting in which the offense took place, (d) whether the parents can take disciplinary action, (e) the attitude of the offender, and (f) the offender's race and gender.

LO 7
Describe the four primary stages of pretrial juvenile justice procedure. (a) Intake, in which an official of the juvenile court engages in a screening process to determine what to do with the youthful offender; (b) pretrial diversion, which may consist of probation, treatment and aid, and/or restitution; (c) jurisdictional waiver to an adult court, in which case the youth leaves the juvenile justice system; and (d) some type of detention, in which the youth is held until the disposition process begins.

LO 8
Explain the distinction between an adjudicatory hearing and a disposition hearing. An adjudicatory hearing is essentially a "trial." Defense attorneys may be present during the adjudicatory hearing in juvenile courts. In many states, once adjudication has occurred, there is a separate disposition hearing that is similar to the sentencing phase in an adult court. At this point, the court, often aided by a predisposition report, determines the sentence that serves the "needs" of the child.

LO 9
List the four categories of residential treatment programs. Foster care, group homes, family group homes, and rural programs such as wilderness camps, farms, and ranches.

SELF ASSESSMENT ANSWER KEY

Page 507: i. _parens patriae;_ **ii.** status offenses; **iii.** delinquency

Page 509: i. state; **ii.** state; **iii.** impulsive; **iv.** peer; **v.** death penalty

Page 513: i. declining; **ii.** girls; **iii.** School; **iv.** Bullying

Page 519: i. risk; **ii.** aging out; **iii.** child abuse/child neglect; **iv.** youth gangs

Page 524: i. arrest; **ii.** refer; **iii.** social; **iv.** intake; **v.** diversion; **vi.** waiver

Page 527: i. adjudicatory; **ii.** disposition; **iii.** predisposition

Page 530: i. probation; **ii.** nonsecure; **iii.** boot; **iv.** training

KEY TERMS

QUESTIONS FOR CRITICAL ANALYSIS

1. What is the difference between a status offense and a crime? What punishments do you think should be imposed on juveniles who commit status offenses?

2. Several years ago, eight Florida teenagers ranging in age from fourteen to eighteen beat a classmate so badly that she suffered a concussion. According to law enforcement officials, the teenagers recorded the assault so that they could post it on the Internet. If you were a prosecutor and could either waive these teenagers to adult court or refer them to the juvenile justice system, which option would you choose? What other information would you need to make your decision?

3. Forty-four states have enacted parental responsibility statutes, which make parents responsible for the offenses of their children. Seventeen of these states hold parents criminally liable for their children's actions, punishing the parents with fines, community service, and even incarceration. What is your opinion of these laws—particularly those with criminal sanctions for parents?

4. Do you think that bullying should be punishable as a felony along the same lines as assault? (For the definition of assault, see page 7.) Why or why not?

5. Research shows that judges in adult criminal courts impose a "juvenile penalty" during the sentencing process. That is, they tend to punish juveniles who have been transferred to adult court more harshly than young adults (nineteen- and twenty-year-olds) who have been convicted of similar crimes. Why do you think judges behave in this manner?

CourseMate *For Online Help*

For online help and access to resources that accompany *Criminal Justice Today,* go to www.cengagebrain.com/shop/ISBN/1111835578. Click "Access Now," where you will find flashcards, an online quiz, and other helpful study aids. If you have an access code for CourseMate, log in and go to the chapter of your choice for additional online study aids.

NOTES

1. Quoted in Rafael Olmeda, "'I'm a Monster' Treacy Laments in Confession," *Sun Sentinel (Ft. Lauderdale, FL)* (June 4, 2010), 1A.

2. Quoted in Rafael Olmeda, "In Jail Recordings, Suspect Talks about Beating Student," *Charleston (WV) Gazette* (June 18, 2010), 4C.

3. Jennifer M. O'Connor and Lucinda K. Treat, "Getting Smart about Getting Tough: Juvenile Justice and the Possibility of Progressive Reform," *American Criminal Law Review* 33 (Summer 1996), 1299.

4. Eric K. Klein, "Dennis the Menace or Billy the Kid: An Analysis of the Role of Transfer to Criminal Court in Juvenile Justice," *American Criminal Law Review* 35 (Winter 1998), 371.

5. "Attitudes toward the Treatment of Juveniles Who Commit Violent Crimes," *Sourcebook of Criminal Justice Statistics 2003,* Table 2.48, at www.albany.edu/sourcebook/pdf/t248.pdf.

6. *In re Gault,* 387 U.S. 1, at 15 (1967).

7. Samuel Davis, *The Rights of Juveniles: The Juvenile Justice System,* 2d ed. (New York: C. Boardman Co., 1995), Section 1.2.

8. Quoted in Anthony Platt, *The Child Savers* (Chicago: University of Chicago Press, 1969), 119.

9. 383 U.S. 541 (1966).

10. *Ibid.*, 556.

11. 387 U.S. 1 (1967).

12. 397 U.S. 358 (1970).

13. 421 U.S. 519 (1975).

14. 403 U.S. 528 (1971).

15. Quoted in Sadie Gurman, "Hearing to Focus on Boy's Rehab Possibilities," *Pittsburgh Post-Gazette* (March 12, 2010), B1.

16. Sadie Gurman, "Boy Faces Murder Trial as Adult," *Pittsburgh Post-Gazette* (March 30, 2010), A1.

17. Gary B. Melton, "Toward 'Personhood' for Adolescents: Autonomy and Privacy as Values in Public Policy," *American Psychology* 38 (1983), 99–100.

18. Research Network on Adolescent Development and Juvenile Justice, *Youth on Trial: A Developmental Perspective on Juvenile Justice* (Chicago: John D. & Catherine T. MacArthur Foundation, 2003), 1.

19. Richard E. Redding, "Juveniles Transferred to Criminal Court: Legal Reform Proposals Based on Social Science Research," *Utah Law Review* (1997), 709.

20. Howard N. Snyder and Melissa Sickmund, *Juvenile Offenders and Victims: A National Report* (Washington, D.C.: U.S. Department of Justice, 1995), 47.

21. 543 U.S. 551 (2005).

22. *Ibid.*, 567.

23. 560 U.S. ____ (2010).

24. *Ibid.*

25. *Surveillance Summaries: Youth Risk Behavior Surveillance—United States, 2001* (Washington, D.C.: Centers for Disease Control and Prevention, June 28, 2002).

26. Federal Bureau of Investigation, *Crime in the United States, 2010* (Washington, D.C.: U.S. Department of Justice, 2011), at **www.fbi.gov/about-us/cjis/ucr/crime-in-the-u.s/2010/crime-in-the-u.s.-2010/tables/10tbl38.xls.**

27. Office of Juvenile Justice and Delinquency Prevention, *Juvenile Arrests 2008* (Washington, D.C.: U.S. Department of Justice, December 2009).

28. Alfred Blumstein, "Youth Violence, Guns, and Illicit Drug Markets," *NIJ Research Journal* (Washington, D.C.: National Institute of Justice, 1995).

29. David McDowell, "Juvenile Curfew Laws and Their Influence on Crime," *Federal Probation* (December 2006), 58.

30. *Crime in the United States, 2010,* at **www.fbi.gov/about-us/cjis/ucr/crime-in-the-u.s/2010/crime-in-the-u.s.-2010/tables/10tbl38.xls.**

31. Office of Juvenile Justice and Delinquency Prevention, "Community Prevention Grants Program," at **www.ojjdp.gov/cpg.**

32. Kimberly Kempf-Leonard and Lisa Sample, "Disparity Based on Sex: Is Gender-Specific Treatment Warranted?" *Justice Quarterly* 17 (2000), 89–128.

33. Melissa Sickmund, *Delinquency Cases in Juvenile Court, 2005* (Washington, D.C.: Office of Juvenile Justice and Delinquency Prevention, June 2009), 1.

34. *Crime in the United States, 2010,* at **www.fbi.gov/about-us/cjis/ucr/crime-in-the-u.s/2010/crime-in-the-u.s.-2010/tables/10tbl33.xls.**

35. Margaret A. Zahn *et al.*, "The Girls Study Group—Charting the Way to Delinquency Prevention for Girls," *Girls Study Group: Understanding and Responding to Girls' Delinquency* (Washington, D.C.: Office of Juvenile Justice and Delinquency Prevention, October 2008), 3.

36. Melissa Sickmund and Howard N. Snyder, *Juvenile Offenders and Victims: 1999 National Report* (Washington, D.C.: Office of Juvenile Justice and Delinquency Prevention, 1999), 58.

37. Meda Chesney-Lind, *The Female Offender: Girls, Women, and Crime* (Thousand Oaks, CA: Sage Publications, 1997).

38. National Center for Education Statistics and Bureau of Justice Statistics, *Indicators of School Crime and Safety: 2010* (Washington, D.C.: U.S. Department of Justice, November 2010), 6.

39. *Ibid.*, 10–15.

40. *Ibid.*, 62.

41. *Ibid.*, v.

42. Jessica Bennett, "From Lockers to Lockup," *Newsweek* (October 11, 2010), 39.

43. Adam J. Speraw, "No Bullying Allowed: A Call for a National Anti-Bullying Statute to Promote a Safer Learning Environment in American Public Schools," *Valparaiso University Law Review* (Summer 2010), 1151–1198.

44. Quoted in Dionne Walker, "Bullying Laws Give Scant Protection," *Associated Press* (September 14, 2009).

45. Marvin E. Wolfgang, *From Boy to Man, from Delinquency to Crime* (Chicago: University of Chicago Press, 1987).

46. Gary Sweeten, Shawn D. Bushway, and Raymond Paternoster, "Does Dropping Out of School Mean Dropping into Delinquency?" *Criminology* (February 2009), 47–88.

47. Quoted in John H. Laub and Robert J. Sampson, "Understanding Desistance from Crime," in *Crime and Justice: A Review of Research* (Chicago: University of Chicago Press, 2001), 6.

48. Travis Hirschi and Michael Gottfredson, "Age and the Explanation of Crime," *American Journal of Sociology* 89 (1982), 552–584.

49. Robert J. Sampson and John H. Laub, "A Life-Course View on the Development of Crime," *Annals of the American Academy of Political and Social Science* (November 2005), 12.

50. David P. Farrington, "Offending from 10 to 25 Years of Age," in *Prospective Studies of Crime and Delinquency,* ed. Katherine Teilmann Van Dusen and Sarnoff A. Mednick (Boston: Kluwer-Nijhoff Publishers, 1983), 17.

51. Office of Juvenile Justice and Delinquency Prevention, *Juveniles in Court* (Washington, D.C.: U.S. Department of Justice, June 2003), 29.

52. "State Estimates of Underage Alcohol and Self-Purchase of Alcohol," *The NSDUH Report* (Rockville, MD: Office of Applied Studies, Substance Abuse and Mental Health Services Administration, April 2010), 1.

53. Gary McClelland, Linda Teplin, and Karen Abram, "Detection and Prevalence of Substance Abuse among Juvenile Detainees," *Juvenile Justice Bulletin* (Washington, D.C.: Office of Juvenile Justice and Delinquency Prevention, June 2004), 10.

54. Arrestee Drug Abuse Monitoring Program, *Preliminary Data on Drug Use and Related Matters among Adult Arrestees and Juvenile Detainees* (Washington, D.C.: National Institute of Justice, 2003).

55. National Mental Health Association, "Mental Health and Adolescent Girls in the Justice System," at **www.nmha.org/children/justjuv/girlsjj.cfm.**

56. David Finekhor *et al.*, *Children's Exposure to Violence: A Comprehensive National Survey* (Washington, D.C.: Office of Juvenile Justice and Delinquency Prevention, October 2009), 1.

57. Kimberly A. Tyler and Katherine A. Johnson, "A Longitudinal Study of the Effects of Early Abuse on Later Victimization among High-Risk Adolescents," *Violence and Victims* (June 2006), 287–291.

58. Grover Trask, "Defusing the Teenage Time Bombs," *Prosecutor* (March/April 1997), 29.

59. Cathy Spatz Widom, *The Cycle of Violence* (Washington, D.C.: National Institute of Justice, October 1992).

60. Janet Currie and Erdal Tekin, *Does Child Abuse Cause Crime?* (Atlanta: Andrew Young School of Policy Studies, April 2006), 27–28.

61. *National Gang Threat Assessment 2009* (Washington, D.C.: National Gang Intelligence Center, January 2009), iii.

62. "Race/Ethnicity of Gang Members," *National Youth Gang Survey Analysis* (Institute for Intergovernmental Research/National Youth Gang Center, 2009), at **www.iir.com/nygc/nygsa.**

63. Rachel A. Gordon, Benjamin B. Lahey, Eriko Kawai, Rolf Loeber, and Magda Stouthamer-Loeber, "Antisocial Behavior and Youth Gang Membership: Selection and Socialization," *Criminology* (February 2004), 55–89.

64. National Alliance of Gang Investigators Associates, *2005 National Gang Threat Assessment* (Washington, D.C.: Bureau of Justice Assistance, 2005), 10–11.

65. *National Gang Threat Assessment 2009,* 12.

66. Anthony Pinizzotto, Edward Davis, and Charles Miller, "Street-Gang Mentality: A Mosaic of Remorseless Violence and Relentless Loyalty," *FBI Law Enforcement Bulletin* (September 2007), 1–6.

67. Sara R. Battin, Karl G. Hill, Robert D. Abbott, Richard F. Catalano, and J. David Hawkins,

"The Contribution of Gang Membership to Delinquency beyond Delinquent Friends," *Criminology 36* (1998), 93–115.

68. "Number of Gang Related Homicides," *National Youth Gang Survey Analysis* (Institute for Intergovernmental Research/ National Youth Gang Center), at **www. iir.com/nygc/nygsa/measuring_the_ extent_of_gang_problems.htm**.

69. *National Gang Threat Assessment 2009,* 8–9.

70. Karl G. Hill, Christina Lui, and J. David Hawkins, *Early Precursors of Gang Membership: A Study of Seattle Youth* (Washington, D.C.: Office of Juvenile Justice and Delinquency Prevention, December 2001).

71. Joseph F. Sheley and James D. Wright, *In the Line of Fire: Youth, Guns, and Violence in Urban America* (Hawthorne, NY: Aldine De Gruyter, 1995), 100.

72. Beth Bjerregaard and Alan J. Lizotte, "Gun Ownership and Gang Membership," *Journal of Criminal Law and Criminology* 86 (1995), 49.

73. Quoted in Gracie Bond Staples, "Guns in School," *Fort Worth Star-Telegram* (June 3, 1998), 1.

74. Office of Juvenile Justice and Delinquency Prevention, *1999 National Report Series: Juvenile Justice Bulletin—Kids and Guns* (Washington, D.C.: U.S. Department of Justice, March 2000), 4.

75. H. Naci Mocan and Erdal Tekin, "Guns and Juvenile Crime," *Journal of Law and Economics* (October 2006), 507.

76. Centers for Disease Control and Prevention, "Youth Risk Behavior Surveillance—United States, 2009," *Morbidity and Mortality Weekly Report* (June 4, 2010), 5.

77. *Crime in the United States, 2010,* at **www. fbi.gov/about-us/cjis/ucr/crime-in-the- u.s/2010/crime-in-the-u.s.-2010/tables/ 10tbl36.xls**.

78. Charles Puzzanchera, Benjamin Adams, and Melissa Sickmund, *Juvenile Court Statistics 2006–2007* (Washington, D.C.: National Center for Juvenile Justice, March 2010), 31.

79. Neelum Arya and Ian Augarten, *Critical Condition: African-American Youth in the Justice System* (Washington, D.C.: Campaign for Youth and Justice, 2008), 17–20.

80. Carl E. Pope and Howard N. Snyder, *Race as a Factor in Juvenile Arrests* (Washington, D.C.:

Office of Juvenile Justice and Delinquency Prevention, April 2003), 1.

81. *Ibid.,* 4.

82. National Institute of Justice, *The Code of the Street and African-American Adolescent Violence* (Washington, D.C.: U.S. Department of Justice, February 2009), 7, 10, 14.

83. George S. Bridges and Sara Steen, "Racial Disparities in Official Assessments of Juvenile Offenders," *American Sociological Review* 63 (1998), 554.

84. 422 U.S. 23 (1979).

85. *Yarborough v. Alvarado,* 541 U.S. 652 (2004).

86. *Schneckloth v. Bustamonte,* 412 U.S. 218 (1973).

87. 42 U.S.C. Sections 5601–5778 (1974).

88. S'Lee Arthur Hinshaw II, "Juvenile Diversion: An Alternative to Juvenile Court," *Journal of Dispute Resolution* (1993), 305.

89. Rhode Island General Laws Section 14-1-7.1 (1994 and Supp. 1996).

90. Office of Juvenile Justice and Delinquency Prevention, *Delinquency Cases in Juvenile Court, 2007* (Washington, D.C.: U.S. Department of Justice, June 2010), 3.

91. 467 U.S. 253 (1984).

92. Puzzanchera, Adams, and Sickmund, 32

93. Barry C. Feld, "Criminalizing the American Juvenile Court," *Crime and Justice* 17 (1993), 227–254.

94. Eric R. Lotke, "Youth Homicide: Keeping Perspective on How Many Children Kill," *Valparaiso University Law Review* 31 (Spring 1997), 395.

95. Bureau of Justice Statistics, *Jail Inmates at Midyear 2010—Statistical Tables* (Washington, D.C.: U.S. Department of Justice, April 2011), Table 6, page 7; and Bureau of Justice Statistics, *Prisoners in 2009* (Washington, D.C.: U.S. Department of Justice, December 2010), Appendix table 13, page 27.

96. Sarah Livsey, "Juvenile Delinquency Probation Caseload, 2005," *OJJDP Fact Sheet* (Washington, D.C.: Office of Juvenile Justice and Delinquency Prevention, June 2009), 1.

97. Office of Juvenile Justice and Delinquency Prevention, *Juvenile Residential Facility Census, 2006: Selected Findings* (Washington, D.C.: U.S. Department of Justice, December 2009), 2.

98. Howard N. Snyder and Melissa Sickmund, *Juvenile Offenders and Victims: 2006 National*

Report (Washington, D.C.: National Center for Juvenile Justice, March 2006), 98.

99. Sickmund and Snyder, 182.

100. Dean John Champion, *The Juvenile Justice System: Delinquency, Processing, and the Law,* 5th ed. (Upper Saddle River, NJ: Pearson Prentice Hall, 2007), 581–582.

101. U.S. Government Accountability Office, "Residential Treatment Programs: Concerns Regarding Abuse and Death in Certain Programs for Troubled Youth," at **www.gao. gov/new.items/d08146t.pdf**.

102. Jamie E. Muscar, "Advocating the End of Juvenile Boot Camps: Why the Military Model Does Not Belong in the Juvenile Justice System," *University of California at Davis Journal of Juvenile Law and Policy* 12 (Winter 2008), 2–50.

103. *Jailing Juveniles: The Dangers of Incarcerating Youth in Adult Jails in America* (Washington, D.C.: Campaign for Youth Justice, November 2007).

104. Richard E. Redding, *Juvenile Transfer Laws: An Effective Deterrent to Delinquency?* (Washington, D.C.: Office of Juvenile Justice and Delinquency Prevention, June 2010), 4.

105. Richard E. Redding, "Juvenile Transfer Laws: An Effective Deterrent to Delinquency?" *Juvenile Justice Bulletin* (Washington, D.C.: Office of Juvenile Justice and Delinquency Prevention, August 2008), 7.

106. Judi Villa, "Adult Prisons Harden Teens," *Arizona Republic* (November 14, 2004), A27.

107. Nathan Koppel, "Judges Forced to Revisit Juveniles' Life Sentences," *Wall Street Journal* (October 29, 2010), at **online.wsj.com /article/SB1000142405270230344390457 5578444151929822.html**.

108. *Roper v. Simmons,* 543 U.S. 551, at 571–572.

109. *Cruel and Unusual: Sentencing 13- and 14-Year-Old Children to Die in Prison* (Montgomery, AL: Equal Justice Initiative, November 2007).

110. Quoted in Chris Togneri, "Pa. Leads Nation in Sentencing Minors to Life," *Pittsburgh Tribune Review* (December 17, 2007), A1.

111. *Roper,* at 570.

CHAPTER

16

Homeland Security

Scott Goldsmith/Aurora Photos

LEARNING OBJECTIVES

After reading this chapter, you should be able to . . .

LO 1 Describe the concept of *jihad* as practiced by al Qaeda and its followers.

LO 2 Identify three important trends in international terrorism.

LO 3 Compare WMDs and CBERN.

LO 4 Explain why the Antiterrorism and Effective Death Penalty Act of 1996 (AEDPA) is an important legal tool against terrorists.

LO 5 Describe the primary goals of an intelligence agency and indicate how it differs from an agency that focuses solely on law enforcement.

LO 6 Explain how American law enforcement agencies have used "preventive policing" to combat terrorism.

LO7 List the primary duties of first responders following a terrorist attack or other catastrophic event.

LO 8 Explain why unregulated border entry is a homeland security concern.

LO 9 Explain how the Patriot Act has made it easier for federal agents to conduct searches during terrorism investigations.

The nine learning objectives labeled LO 1 through LO 9 are designed to help improve your understanding of the chapter.

WRONG NUMBER

"Do you remember when 9/11 happened, when those people were jumping from the skyscrapers?" asked nineteen-year-old Mohamed Osman Mohamud. "I thought that was awesome." These are strong, even shocking, words, but Mohamud, a Somali American who had recently dropped out of Oregon State University at Corvallis, was willing to back them up. On July 30, 2010, Mohamud met for the first time with a person he knew only as "Abdulhadi" in nearby Portland to plan his own terrorist attack. When the two met again three weeks later, Mohamud had chosen his target: the city's annual Christmas tree–lighting ceremony in Pioneer Square, held the day after Thanksgiving. "I want whoever is attending that event to leave . . . dead or injured," he said.

Abdulhadi, along with several associates, helped Mohamud work toward this goal. They provided him with nearly $3,000 to rent an apartment and purchase bomb components. They took him to a remote location near the Oregon coast for an operational dry run. Then, on November 26, Abdulhadi and Mohamud loaded a white van with six 55-gallon drums of explosives and diesel fuel, parked it near Pioneer Square, and retired to a safe distance. At 5:40 P.M., as thousands of people gathered in the downtown plaza to see a tall Douglas fir tree laced with tiny Christmas lights, Mohamud took out his cell phone and dialed a number. He thought he was going to detonate the huge bomb in the van.

Nothing happened. As it turned out, Abdulhadi was a federal agent, and the detonator was a fake designed by Federal Bureau of Investigation (FBI) specialists. When Mohamud tried to dial a second time, he was arrested. Eventually, authorities charged him with attempted use of a weapon of mass destruction, which carries a maximum sentence of life in prison. Told of his exploits, friends were astounded that "Mo," a suburban teen who liked to play video games, was capable of such behavior. "When you think of someone doing what he did, you think of some crazy kind of guy," said one. "He wasn't like that. He was just like everybody else."

Before being apprehended by federal law enforcement agents, Mohamed Osman Mohamud planned to attack Portland's annual Christmas tree lighting ceremony with a car bomb.
ZUMA Press/Newscom

Discussion Tip: Before beginning the chapter, have students share their views on terrorism. Ask the class its opinion on the likelihood of another large-scale terrorist attack on American soil. How should the criminal justice system address threats of this nature?

Mohamed Osman Mohamud is only one in a series of recent American terrorists who seemed "just like everybody else." In June 2009, Abdulhakim Muhammad, born Carl Bledsoe, opened fire on a military recruiting center in Little Rock, Arkansas, killing one soldier and wounding another. On November 5 of that year, U.S. Army major Nidal Malik Hasan fatally shot thirteen people during a surprise rampage at Fort Hood in Texas. In February 2011, Colleen LaRose, a blonde Pennsylvania woman who called herself "JihadJane," pleaded guilty to plotting the death of a Swedish cartoonist whose work had offended some Muslims.

These "homegrown" extremists present a grave new challenge for law enforcement. Because they have been raised in the United States, they know how to operate on American soil. Because they possess U.S. passports, they can move freely in and out of the country. Unless they draw attention to themselves by posting their views on the Internet—which is how the FBI was first alerted to Mohamud—they can go unnoticed until they take action. Consequently, the old terrorist profile has been "broken," according to Bruce Hoffman, a terrorism expert at Georgetown University in Washington, D.C.: "It's women as well as men, it's lifelong Muslims as well as converts, it's college students as well as jailbirds."[1]

Such unpredictability is one of the most striking, and unnerving, aspects of life in the United States, post–September 11. Terrorism and its uncertainties have been a constant theme throughout this textbook, and we have seen many instances in which law enforcement, the courts, and corrections have had to evolve to meet the challenge. In this chapter, we will focus solely on the criminal justice system's role in *homeland security,* defined by the federal government as

> a concerted national effort to prevent terrorist attacks within the United States, reduce America's vulnerability to terrorism, and minimize the damage and recover from attacks that do occur.[2]

We start with a discussion of the phenomenon that has driven the homeland security movement in the United States since September 11, 2001—terrorism.

THE CHANGING GLOBAL CONTEXT OF TERRORISM

Relatively speaking, the term *terrorism* has had a short history. In the political context, its birth can be traced to the time during the French Revolution (1789–1799), when the French legislature ordered the public executions of nearly 18,000 "enemies" of the new government. As a result of this *régime de la terreur* (reign of terror), terrorism was initially associated with state-sponsored violence against the people. By the dawn of the twentieth century, this dynamic had shifted. Terrorists had evolved into nonstate actors, free of control by or allegiance to any nation, who used violence to further political goals such as the formation or destruction of a particular government.

> **Nonstate Actor** An entity that plays a role in international affairs but does not represent any established state or nation.

   Today, the dominant strain of terrorism mixes political goals with very strong religious affiliations. Modern terrorism is also characterized by extreme levels of violence. The January 24, 2011, suicide bombing at Russia's busiest airport in Moscow killed at least 35 people and injured 150 more. The three-day November 2008 raid on the financial district of Mumbai, India, left 173 dead and more than 300 wounded. And, of course, the September 11, 2001, attacks on New York and Washington, D.C., claimed nearly 3,000 lives. Indeed, the power of terrorism is a direct result of the fear caused by this violence— not only the fear that such atrocities will be repeated, but also that next time, they will be much worse.

DEFINING TERRORISM

Terrorism has always had a subjective quality, summed up by the useful cliché "one person's terrorist is another person's freedom fighter." Because it means different things to different people in different situations, politicians, academics, and legal experts alike have long struggled to determine which acts of violence qualify as terrorism and which do not. One observer has even compared these efforts to the legendary quest for the Holy Grail, stating, "periodically, eager souls set out, full of purpose, energy and self-confidence, to succeed where so many others before have tried and failed."[3]

> **Critical Thinking Skill Development:** Ask students to generate a short written assignment in which they respond to "Questions for Critical Analysis" number one on page 571, which asks them to define terrorism.

   The Federal Bureau of Investigation (FBI) defines terrorism as

> the unlawful use of force or violence against persons or property to intimidate or coerce a government, the civilian population, or any segment thereof, in furtherance of political or social objectives.[4]

This definition is useful for our purposes because it is relatively straightforward and easy to understand. It is inadequate, however, in that it fails to capture the wide scope of international terrorism in the twenty-first century. Today, many observers are asking whether the state should consider terrorist violence merely "unlawful," as in the FBI definition, or

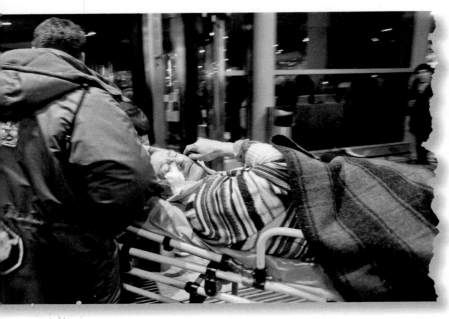

Rescue workers tend to a victim of the suicide bomber who struck Moscow's Domodevo International Airport on January 24, 2011. Russian officials blamed the attack, which killed at least thirty-seven and wounded nearly 200 more, on militant Islamists. How are such acts of terrorism distinguished from acts of war?

AP Photo/Ivan Sekretarev

an act of war? The answer is crucial in the homeland security context because, as we shall see later in the chapter, our rules for preventing crimes and fighting a war are markedly different.

Generally, wars are considered military actions undertaken by one state or nation against another. This would seem to remove terrorism from the realm of war, given that its instigators are nonstate actors, as mentioned earlier.

Professor David A. Westbrook of the State University of New York at Buffalo points out, however, that the large scale and financial resources of some modern terrorist organizations make them as powerful as many nations, if not more so. In addition, the high body counts associated with the worst terrorist acts seem better described in terms of war than of crime, which in most cases involves two people—the criminal and the victim.[5] Thus, as we see in Figure 16.1 on the facing page, perhaps the most satisfying, if not the most concise, definition of terrorism describes it as a "supercrime" that incorporates many of the characteristics of warfare.

AL QAEDA VERSUS THE UNITED STATES

On May 1, 2011, a team of U.S. Navy Seals in helicopters descended on a three-story house in Abbottabad, a town located about thirty miles northeast of Islamabad, the capital of Pakistan. Forty minutes later, they left with the body of Osama bin Laden, whom they had killed after a shootout with his bodyguards. "Justice has been done," said President Barack Obama, echoing the sentiments of many Americans for whom the event marked a symbolic triumph in the struggle against international terrorism.[6] Experts, however, doubted that bin Laden's death would have much practical impact. Al Qaeda, the movement he had helped to start, seemed already to be moving on without him.

OSAMA BIN LADEN AND AL QAEDA Just as there has been some trouble coming up with a useful definition of terrorism, there has been a great deal of confusion concerning the terrorists themselves. To start with, the Arabic term *al Qaeda*, which can be roughly translated as "the base," has two meanings. One alludes to a diffuse, general anti-Western global social movement, while the other refers to a specific organization responsible for the September 11 attacks and numerous other terrorist activities over the past two decades.[7]

Osama bin Laden's al Qaeda organization grew out of a network of volunteers who migrated to Afghanistan in the 1980s to rid that country of its Communist occupiers. (Ironically, in light of later events, bin Laden and his comrades received significant American financial aid.) For bin Laden, these efforts took the form of *jihad*, a controversial

LO 1

term that also has been the subject of much confusion. Contrary to what many think, *jihad* does not mean "holy war." Rather, it refers to three kinds of struggle, or exertion, required of the Muslim faithful: (1) the struggle against the evil in oneself, (2) the struggle against the evil outside oneself, and (3) the struggle against nonbelievers.[8] Many Muslims believe that this struggle can be achieved without violence and denounce the form of *jihad* practiced by al Qaeda. Clearly, however, bin Laden and his fol-

FIGURE 16.1 The "Supercrime" of Terrorism

To accommodate the idea of terrorism as a "supercrime," Professor George Fletcher of the Columbia University School of Law has devised eight variables that often—though not always—capture the essence of what we think about when we consider terrorism.

New York City, September 2001
Beth A. Keiser/AFP/Getty Images

1. **The violence factor.** First and foremost, terrorism is an expression of violence.

2. **The intention.** Just as the goal of bank robbers is to get the cash, terrorists have an objective each time they act. In some instances, the very act of violence or destruction fulfills this intent.

3. **The victims.** Terrorist acts generally target civilians or "innocent" persons rather than military personnel.

4. **The wrongdoers.** Similarly, terrorists operate outside any military command structure.

5. **A "just cause."** Those who decide to use terror to further their aims believe that the ends justify the often-violent means.

6. **Organization.** Generally, terrorists act in concert with other like-minded individuals. The solo terrorist is only now becoming more common.

7. **Theater.** For a terrorist act to be truly effective, it must be dramatic. One expert has even said, "Terrorism is theater."

8. **The absence of guilt.** Terrorists are so certain of the righteousness of their cause that they act without feeling guilt or remorse.

Source: George P. Fletcher, "The Indefinable Concept of Terrorism," *Journal of International Criminal Justice* (November 2006), 894–911.

lowers rejected the notion that *jihad* can be accomplished through peaceable efforts. (The feature *Myth versus Reality—Terrorists Represent the "True" Islam* on the following page further explores the differences between Islamic extremists and the Muslim majority.)

AN EVOLVING THREAT In the 1990s, bin Laden began to turn his attention to the United States, and al Qaeda set its sights on American interests abroad. In 1998, for example, the organization bombed two U.S. embassies in Africa, killing 231 people. Two years later, al Qaeda agents launched a suicide attack on the U.S.S. *Cole*, a Navy destroyer docked in Aden, a port in the small Middle Eastern country of Yemen, during which seventeen U.S. sailors died. About a year after the September 11, 2001, attacks, bin Laden wrote a letter to the American people outlining the reasons behind al Qaeda's opposition to our government. These included American support for Israel, which is widely seen as an enemy to Muslims, and U.S. exploitation of Islamic countries for their oil. Furthermore, bin Laden criticized the presence of U.S. military forces in the Middle East, "spreading your ideology and thereby polluting the hearts of our people."[9]

According to bin Laden, terrorism could be either "commendable" or "reprehensible." He maintained that terrorism is "reprehensible" only when it is aimed at innocent people, while "terrorizing oppressors and criminals and thieves and robbers is necessary." Not surprisingly, bin Laden considered the terrorism he practiced against the United States to be "commendable" because it was "directed at the tyrants and aggressors and the enemies of Allah."[10]

A CONTINUING THREAT Two years before his death, Osama bin Laden boasted that his disciples would "continue *jihad* for another seven years, seven years after that,

Critical Thinking Skill Development: Ask students to contrast the definition of terrorism provided in the beginning of the chapter with the definition used by Osama bin Laden. How did bin Laden justify his organization's repeated attacks against U.S. interests?

Several months after the September 11 terrorist attacks, the so-called bin Laden videotape was released. It showed an interviewer congratulating al Qaeda leader Osama bin Laden for his "great work" in the name of Allah. Bin Laden responded that one of his goals was to foster understanding of the "true" Islam. "[The attacks] made people think about [the true Islam], which benefited them greatly," he said.

THE MYTH Muslims committed the September 11 attacks, as well as numerous other deadly acts of terrorism over the past two decades. Consequently, there is a causal link between Islam—the religious faith of Muslims—and terrorism. Furthermore, traditional Islamic teachings support and even encourage such violence.

THE REALITY The defining characteristic of terrorism is extremism in the pursuit of a political goal, not the religion of those who carry out terrorist acts. For al Qaeda and other Islamic terrorist organizations, religion provides a powerful tool for recruiting adherents and convincing them that their cause is just. Male suicide bombers, for example, are told that their deaths, or "martyrdoms," will be rewarded by an automatic place in a heavenly Paradise where they will enjoy the "fleshy delights" of seventy-two virgins. In fact, the Qur'an (Koran) expressly prohibits suicide because it implies a lack of trust in God. Moreover, the Prophet Muhammad, who founded Islam in the seventh century, taught that any person who brings about death "hurriedly" is denied entrance to Paradise. Indeed, many passages in the Qur'an seem to disallow terrorism. The text instructs Muslims not to "take any human being's life" and to avoid war except for self-defense. According to Islamic scholars, other taboo acts include killing women, children, the aged, and other Muslims (several hundred of whom perished on September 11).

The vast majority of the world's 1.2 billion Muslims reject Islamic extremism. In the wake of September 11, for example, Los Angeles County Sheriff Lee Baca said he was "overwhelmed" by the number of American Muslims in Southern California who offered to work with police to "help keep the peace." Indeed, according to the Triangle Center on Terrorism and Homeland Security, of the 120 Muslims suspected of domestic terrorism in the United States between 2001 and 2011, 48 were identified to law enforcement by fellow Muslims.

FOR CRITICAL ANALYSIS The Qur'an forbids the taking of human life "otherwise than in [the pursuit] of justice." The text also states "that if anyone slays a human being—unless it be [in punishment] for murder or spreading corruption on earth—it shall be as though he has slain all mankind." Can you see how Islamic fundamentalists find justification in these passages for their violent actions against nonbelievers?

---

and even seven years more after."[11] Two days after his death, al Qaeda posted a statement on the Internet that echoed this prediction. "Sheik Osama didn't build an organization to die when he dies," it said. "The soldiers of Islam will continue in groups and united, plotting and planning . . . with determination, without giving up until striking a blow."[12] Indeed, as we shall see later in the chapter, although smaller in numbers, shorter on funds, and less capable of executing large-scale attacks than a decade ago, al Qaeda still has a great deal of influence over radical Islamic extremists around the world. "Bin Laden is dead. Al Qaeda is not," warns Leon Panetta, director of the Central Intelligence Agency.[13]

DOMESTIC TERRORISM

Domestic Terrorism Acts of terrorism that take place within the territorial jurisdiction of the United States without direct foreign involvement.

Following September 11, 2001, America's counterterrorism strategies proceeded under the assumption that there were two distinct strands of terrorism. First—and most dangerous—was international terrorism, represented by bin Laden and al Qaeda and possessing the resources to carry out massive, coordinated attacks. Second was **domestic terrorism,** which involves acts of terrorism that are carried out within one's own country, against one's own people, and with little or no direct foreign involvement. Recently, these two strands have intermeshed to create the worst of both worlds—homegrown terrorists with international support.

ALIENATED AND ONLINE In the homeland security context, a domestic terrorist is often an alienated individual who becomes emboldened after meeting others who share his or her extreme views. Often these views involve outrage over American military excursions against Muslims in the Middle East, as well as contempt for Western cultural norms at home. Invariably, American radicals find encouragement on pro-*jihadist* Web sites, which offer training manuals, audio and video propaganda, and communication with like-minded individuals through chat rooms.

A good example of the "plugged-in" domestic terrorist is Mohamed Osman Mohamud, whose attempt to bomb a Portland tree-lighting ceremony was discussed at the beginning of this chapter. Mohamud first caught the attention of federal law enforcement authorities when he began trading e-mails with a friend who had moved to Waziristan, an al Qaeda stronghold in northwestern Pakistan. Mohamud also wrote numerous articles for online extremist magazines, including one article entitled "Getting in Shape without Weights" that aimed to help readers prepare "physically for *jihad*" using Pilates.[14]

Critical Thinking Skill Development: In a short written assignment, have students discuss the melding of international terrorism and domestic terrorism. How does this development impact American anti-terrorism efforts?

RADICALIZED AMATEURS As occurred with Mohamed Osman Mohamud, the process of self-radicalization can result in a plan to carry out a terrorist attack on U.S. soil. Given would-be domestic terrorists' lack of experience, when these plots do materialize, they are often haphazard and amateurish. On May 1, 2010, for example, Faisal Shahzad packed a Nissan Pathfinder with ten gallons of gasoline, sixty gallons of propane, 250 pounds of fertilizer, and hundreds of M-88 fireworks, and parked the car in New York City's Times Square. Shahzad, a U.S. citizen born in Pakistan who lived in Bridgeport, Connecticut, lit a fuse connected to the fireworks and walked away, expecting the ensuing explosion to create a fireball of destruction. His plan failed, though, because he used the wrong type of fertilizer and the firecrackers were not powerful enough to detonate the containers of propane and gasoline.[15] Instead, a street vendor noticed suspicious white smoke coming from the vehicle and alerted officials before the makeshift bomb could do any damage.

"Consider me the first droplet of the blood that will follow."

—**Faisal Shahzad,** the failed Times Square bomber, to a federal judge during his sentencing hearing (2010)

THE INTERNATIONALIZATION OF DOMESTIC TERRORISM After Faisal Shahzad (see photo alongside) was apprehended at New York's John F. Kennedy Airport, he told interrogators that he had received five days of explosives training and $15,000 from the Pakistani Taliban, an extremist group that also operates out of Waziristan. (The Pakistani Taliban is not the same as the Taliban groups that the U.S. military is fighting in Afghanistan.) This confession was notable for two reasons: (1) it involved a terrorist organization other than al Qaeda operating in the United States, and (2) Shahzad's American citizenship and connections to a foreign enemy indicated that there was no longer a clear line between international and domestic terrorism.

A Different al Qaeda Because of successful U.S. military operations against al Qaeda bases and worldwide law enforcement efforts to cut off its supply of funds, al Qaeda

Who helped Faisal Shahzad, shown here on Al-Arabiya TV, prepare for his failed plot to set off a car bomb in New York City in May 2010? Why was this support significant?
AP Photo/Al-Arabiya via AP Television Network

is no longer as powerful as it was in the late 1990s and early 2000s. It now relies more on a loose organization of affiliates—it is "more of a McDonald's . . . than a General Motors," in the words of one expert.[16] Today, diffuse al Qaeda cells create their own strategies and pick their own targets. Even before Osama bin Laden's death, these groups tended to see him more as an inspirational figure than a hands-on leader.[17]

Indeed, the threat from a franchise called al Qaeda in the Arabian Peninsula (AQAP), based in Yemen, seems to have eclipsed the dangers posed by al Qaeda's core fighters in Afghanistan. AQAP was responsible for training Umar Farouk Abdulmutallab, a Nigerian who attempted to detonate a bomb hidden in his underwear on a Northwest Airlines flight as it landed in Detroit on December 25, 2009. Then, in October 2010, two packages containing bombs were shipped from Yemen to Jewish religious centers in Chicago. These packages were intercepted only because of a tip from Saudi Arabian law enforcement agents. Finally, the writings of al Qaeda associate Anwar al-Awlaki, a radical U.S.-born cleric hiding in Yemen (until his 2011 death), are known to have influenced Abdulmutallab, Major Nidal Malik Hasan (who, as mentioned earlier, killed thirteen people at Fort Hood, Texas, in 2009), and the Oregon teenager Mohamed Osman Mohamud.[18]

Recruiting Strategies Al Qaeda franchises such as AQAP, lacking the resources or the desire to execute large-scale operations such as the 9/11 attacks, have recently focused on smaller jobs using American-born operatives, both in the United States and abroad. In August 2010, federal officials charged fourteen people involved in enlisting potential recruits from immigrant neighborhoods in Minnesota to join an extremist rebel group with al Qaeda ties in the African country of Somalia. Other terrorist organizations seem to be following a similar strategy. After Faisal Shahzad, the Times Square suspect, was arrested, an Afghan Taliban leader bragged that with "all this new technology, it's not difficult to recruit people in the West." He also claimed to have received hundreds of e-mails from potential homegrown American terrorists who "want to join us."[19]

TERRORISM TRENDS FOR THE FUTURE

LO 2 "It's pretty clear that while al Qaeda would still love to have home runs, they will take singles and doubles if they can get them," one terrorism expert said. "And that makes the job of counterterrorism much, much harder."[20] Smaller operations involving American-born terrorists influenced by international sources reflect several trends identified by homeland security expert Brian M. Jenkins, each of which de-emphasizes the importance of any single, dominant organization such as al Qaeda:[21]

1. *Terrorists have developed more efficient methods of financing their operations* through avenues such as Internet fund-raising, drug trafficking, and money laundering schemes.
2. *Terrorists have developed more efficient organizations* based on the small-business model, in which individuals are responsible for different tasks including recruiting, planning, propaganda, and social services such as supporting the families of suicide bombers. These "employees" do not answer to a single leader but rather function as a network that is quick to adjust and difficult to infiltrate.
3. *Terrorists have exploited new communications technology to mount global campaigns,* relying on the Internet for immediate, direct communication among operatives and as a crucial recruiting tool. Furthermore, large numbers of "jihobbyists" are operating online, disseminating extremist writings and videos and using social media to spread the terrorist message in cyberspace.

Discussion Tip: Ask students to discuss how the al Qaeda threat has changed in recent years. What is al Qaeda in the Arabian Peninsula (AQAP) and what threat to the United States does this group pose? (LO 2)

Critical Thinking Skill Development: Ask students to take a few minutes in class to write about Jenkins's trends in international terrorism. Have students identify the trend they find the most disturbing and then brainstorm methods of addressing that trend. If time allows, have students discuss their work with the class. (LO 2)

As you may have noted, each of these trends favors the global terrorism movement. Indeed, Jenkins finds that today's *jihadists* are dangerous, resilient survivors who have achieved some strategic results and are determined to continue attacking their enemies. "Destroying their terrorist enterprise," he concludes, "will take years."[22]

> "Terrorism cannot be 'defeated,' because it is a tactic and not an enemy."
>
> —**Nora Bensahel,**
> political scientist

SELF ASSESSMENT

Fill in the blanks and check your answers on page 570.

Terrorists are _____ actors, meaning that they are not affiliated with any established nation. The FBI defines terrorism as the use of violence to further _____ or social objectives. Until recently, _____ terrorists have attempted to meet these objectives without direct aid from international sources. Recently, however, homegrown American terrorists are more likely to have received support from international extremists, either by traveling abroad for training or communicating via the _____.

THE WEAPONRY OF TERRORISM

On January 6, 2011, two packages containing incendiary devices were sent to state government offices in Maryland. The next day, a similar parcel addressed to Homeland Security Secretary Janet Napolitano ignited briefly in a Washington, D.C., mail annex. Although nobody was injured, the incidents brought back unpleasant memories of the anthrax mail scare of 2001. Anthrax is a dangerous infectious disease transmitted by bacteria so small that a thousand spores would not reach across the thin edge of a dime.[23] In the weeks after the September 11 attacks, a batch of envelopes containing several grams of anthrax powder infiltrated the U.S. Postal Service, eventually killing seven people, including two Washington, D.C., postal workers.

Although the images and memories of September 11, 2001, remain part of the national psyche, the anthrax mailings have largely been forgotten. For the most part, however, homeland security experts are more concerned about the dangers presented by minuscule bacteria than by the threat posed by two-hundred-ton airplanes. Robert Mueller, the director of the FBI from 2001 to 2011, said that "the biggest threat faced by the United States in the counterterrorism arena . . . is [a] WMD in the hands of terrorists."[24] WMD is the acronym for weapons of mass destruction, a term used to describe a wide variety of deadly instruments that represent significant security challenges for the United States and other targets of international terrorism. Anthrax is considered a WMD because a very small amount of it has the potential to cause a massive amount of destruction, killing and sickening thousands of people.

TYPES OF WMDs

WMDs come in four categories: (1) *biological* weapons, (2) *chemical* weapons, (3) *nuclear* weapons, and (4) *radiological* weapons. Biological weapons are living organisms such as bacteria, viruses, and other microorganisms such as anthrax that cause disease and death. Because these weapons are "alive," they have unique capabilities to reproduce and spread undetected through large populations of humans, animals, and plants. In contrast, chemical weapons are manufactured for the purpose of causing harm or death. They can be inhaled or ingested, and they can seep into the body through the

Technology Tip: Have students go online and learn more about anthrax from the Centers for Disease Control at **www.bt.cdc.gov/agent/anthrax**.

Weapons of Mass Destruction (WMDs) A term that describes nuclear, radiological, chemical, or biological weapons that have the capacity to cause large numbers of casualties or do significant property damage.

Biological Weapon Any living organism, such as a bacterium or virus, used to intentionally harm or kill adversaries in war or targets of terrorist attacks.

Chemical Weapon Any weapon that uses a manufactured chemical to harm or kill adversaries in war or targets of terrorist attacks.

Discussion Tip: Ask students to discuss the various types of WMDs and the concerns surrounding their use. Which of the WMDs discussed in the text do students feel poses the greatest threat to Americans? (LO 3)

In March 2010, federal agents arrested several members of Hutaree, the Michigan Christian militia group shown here in full regalia. Hutaree had planned to use IEDs to kill law enforcement officers. Why do many terrorist groups favor IEDs?

AP Photo/United States District Court, Eastern District of Michigan, Southern Division

skin or eyes. Specialists at the Centers for Disease Control and Prevention in Atlanta, Georgia, have identified sixty-five known chemical agents that can be used as weapons. Three—cyanide, ricin, and sarin—are considered to be particularly well suited for terrorist purposes.[25]

The true "doomsday" terrorist attack scenario involves nuclear weapons. The destructive force of these bombs is caused by the massive release of heat and energy that accompanies their detonation. Only two such bombs have ever been used—by the U.S. military against the Japanese cities of Hiroshima and Nagasaki in August of 1945. About 70,000 people in Hiroshima and 40,000 people in Nagasaki were killed instantly. Adding to the devastating impact of these weapons is the radiation that is released following detonation. Radiological material destroys human cells, and exposure to high levels of radiation can lead to immediate death. Exposure to lower levels of radiation is also dangerous, greatly increasing the risk of long-term health problems such as cancer.

CONVENTIONAL EXPLOSIVES

For all the concern over WMDs, conventional explosives and improvised explosive devices (IEDs), created by amateurs rather than professionally manufactured, are still

LO 3 the dominant type of weapon used in terrorist attacks. IEDs are easy to obtain and to use, and instructions for their assembly are readily available on the Internet. Many can be prepared by mixing chemicals available in common household items. By one estimate, more than 70 percent of all terrorist attacks involve these sorts of devices.[26] In law enforcement and military circles, therefore, the different terrorist threats are summarized with another acronym, CBERN, which stands for "chemical, biological, explosive, radiological, and nuclear."

CBERN experts have also begun to recognize that the different categories of weaponry can be "mixed and matched" for greater effect. For example, a significant amount of radiological material is found in hospitals, universities, and other research institutions. If such material is stolen, it can be used in a "dirty bomb," the popular term for radiological dispersion devices (RDDs) that employ conventional explosives rather than nuclear weapons to spread harmful radiation waves. According to one study, an RDD detonated in downtown New York City would kill two thousand people and expose thousands more to severe radiation poisoning.[27]

THE INCIDENCE OF WMDs

As mentioned earlier, for all the nightmarish possibilities, WMDs have been more a threat than a reality on American soil. Besides the anthrax mailings already discussed, only one instance of bioterrorism has occurred in the United States. In 1984, members of the Rajneesh cult spread salmonella bacteria through supermarkets and restaurants in The Dalles, Oregon, as part of an effort to influence local elections. About 750 residents fell ill, none fatally. Terrorist attacks using chemical agents have been rare throughout the world, and there have been no nuclear or radiological terrorism incidents.

There are a number of reasons why WMDs have rarely been used. The biological agents most appropriate for terrorist attacks are short lived and easily destroyed, so there is no guarantee that they will be effective. The materials needed to carry out a chemical, nuclear, or radiological attack are heavily regulated by the world's governments, and their theft or purchase in significant amounts is likely to set off alarm bells. Furthermore, once a threat has been identified, governments respond by lessening the risks associated with that threat. Within two years of the anthrax scare, for example, U.S. post offices began installing alarm systems designed to detect the presence of anthrax spores in mail-handling facilities.[28]

SELFASSESSMENT

Fill in the blanks and check your answers on page 570.

WMDs is an acronym for "weapons of _____ _____." These weapons, which have the potential to do significant damage, include (1) _____ weapons, which are living organisms; (2) _____ weapons, which are manufactured to cause great harm; and (3) _____ weapons, whose destructive power comes from their massive release of heat and energy. Despite the attention given to WMD threats, most terrorist attacks feature _____ explosives, which are cheaper and easier to hide and transport.

THE HOMELAND SECURITY RESPONSE

On September 12, 2001, President George W. Bush made a public promise that the "United States of America will use all our resources to conquer this enemy."[29] About seven and a half years later, as Barack Obama assumed the presidency, he warned "those who seek to advance their aims by inducing terror and slaughtering innocents" that "[o]ur spirit is stronger and cannot be broken; you cannot outlast us, and we will defeat you."[30]

So far in this chapter we have concentrated on the nature of terrorism and the threat that it poses. Now we turn our attention to the "resources" that the United States has at its disposal to "defeat" this threat. Eventually, this discussion will lead us to an examination of the tactics used by law enforcement agents and other government actors to combat terrorism, along with the controversies that these tactics have sparked. We start, however, with an examination of the rules governing counterterrorism and the agencies and individuals that are bound by them.

THE ANTITERRORISM AND EFFECTIVE DEATH PENALTY ACT

Signed into law by President Bill Clinton on April 24, 1996, the Antiterrorism and Effective Death Penalty Act (AEDPA) was passed in response to the 1995 truck bomb-

LO 4

ing of the Alfred P. Murrah Federal Building in Oklahoma City, Oklahoma. The primary goal of the AEDPA is to hamstring terrorist organizations by cutting off their funding from outside sources. The law prohibits persons from "knowingly providing material support or resources" to any group that the United States has designated a "foreign terrorist organization," or FTO.[31] Each year, the U.S. secretary of state is required to provide Congress with a list of these FTOs, loosely defined to cover organizations that (1) are foreign, (2) engage in terrorist activity, and (3) threaten the security of U.S. citizens or the United States itself.[32] The latest edition of this list included forty-four such organizations, most of them based in the Middle East.[33]

"Material support" is defined very broadly in the legislation, covering funding, financial services, lodging, training, expert advice or assistance, communications

Antiterrorism and Effective Death Penalty Act of 1996 (AEDPA) Legislation giving law enforcement officers the power to arrest and prosecute any individual who provides "material support or resources" to a "foreign terrorist organization."

Critical Thinking Skill Development: In a written assignment, ask students to reflect on the importance of the AEDPA in the fight against terrorism. What is the primary benefit of this legislation from the government's point of view? (LO 4)

A fighter with the extremist group Al-Shabab trains at a camp outside Mogadishu, the capital of Somalia. How does Al-Shabab's designation as a "foreign terrorist organization" by the American government limit the group's ability to raise funds in the United States?

AP Photo, File

Patriot Act Legislation passed in the wake of the September 11, 2001, terrorist attacks that greatly expanded the ability of government agents to monitor and apprehend suspected terrorists.

⊗ The **U.S. Department of Justice** maintains a Web site dedicated to providing information on the Patriot Act. To visit this site, click on the *Criminal Justice CourseMate* at **cengagebrain.com** and select the *Web links* for this chapter.

equipment, transportation, and other physical assets.[34] The "knowingly" requirement applies to all material support except for direct monetary donations to FTOs—this act is a strict liability crime (see pages 110–111). Consequently, even if a person is unaware that the recipient of charitable giving is involved in terrorist activity, he or she can be prosecuted under the AEDPA.[35]

THE PATRIOT ACT

The original AEDPA did not include the provision making a donation to an FTO a strict liability crime. This amendment was part of the far-reaching scope of the Patriot Act, signed into law by President George W. Bush on October 26, 2001, just six weeks after the September 11 terrorist attacks.[36]

"LEVELING THE PLAYING FIELD" As we have seen throughout this textbook, the emphasis on the rights of the accused in the American criminal justice system often makes it difficult to arrest and convict suspected criminals. The Patriot Act is the result of a strong impulse in Washington, D.C., and elsewhere to "level the playing field" when it comes to terrorists. The legislation makes it easier for law enforcement agents to collect information about those suspected of committing terrorist acts or having knowledge of terrorist activity and then detain them based on that information. It enhances the power of the federal government to keep noncitizens under suspicion of having terrorist sympathies from entering the United States, and, as we have seen, it targets the fund-raising of terrorist enterprises.

A massive piece of legislation, the Patriot Act is difficult to summarize. Selected aspects are listed here, however, to provide a general idea of the statute's goals, as well as its methods of achieving them.[37]

- The act relaxes restrictions on information sharing between various U.S. law enforcement agencies and other governmental departments concerning suspected terrorists.
- It creates the crime of knowingly harboring a terrorist.
- It allows law enforcement agents greater freedom in seizing the e-mail records of suspected terrorists.
- It authorizes funds to triple the number of border patrol agents, customs inspectors, and immigration enforcement officers along the United States' northern border with Canada.
- It allows the federal government to detain non-U.S. citizens suspected of terrorist activity for up to seven days without informing them of the charges on which they are being held.
- It eliminates the statute of limitations (see page 322) for prosecution of the most serious terrorism-related crimes.

RENEWING PROVISIONS OF THE PATRIOT ACT Most of the Patriot Act is permanent law. Three of its provisions, however, were enacted with expiration dates because of concerns over their impact on the civil rights of all Americans, not just suspected terrorists. One provision allows federal agents to use "roving wiretaps" to monitor terrorist suspects who switch phone numbers, and another enables agents to obtain court-approved access to business records pertinent to terrorism investigations. The third, known as the "lone wolf" provision, permits agents to monitor non-U.S. citizens without having to show a connection between the target and a specific terrorist organization.

The last time these provisions came up for renewal, in 2011, several members of Congress tried to block their passage, arguing that they violated constitutional guarantees of privacy.[38] The Obama administration, however, countered that the provisions were crucial tools for investigating terrorist plots on U.S. soil. Eventually, in May the president signed a four-year extension of the disputed sections.[39] Nevertheless, as we will see later in the chapter, the Patriot Act continues to be criticized by civil rights advocates for its supposed abuses of the U.S. Constitution.

THE DEPARTMENT OF HOMELAND SECURITY

While the Patriot Act transformed the legal landscape of America's counterterrorism efforts, the Homeland Security Act of 2002 had a similar effect on the inner workings of the U.S. government.[40] Prior to this legislation, disaster management at the federal level was primarily the responsibility of the Federal Emergency Management Agency (FEMA). The Patriot Act placed FEMA, as well as twenty-one other federal agencies, under the control of the Department of Homeland Security (DHS). Descriptions of those agencies within the DHS that have traditionally been oriented toward law enforcement can be found in Chapter 5, and we will not repeat that discussion here. Instead, this section will focus on the DHS's organizational structure, shown in Figure 16.2 below.

Technology Tip: Have students learn more about the Department of Homeland Security online at **www.dhs.gov**.

FIGURE 16.2 U.S. Department of Homeland Security

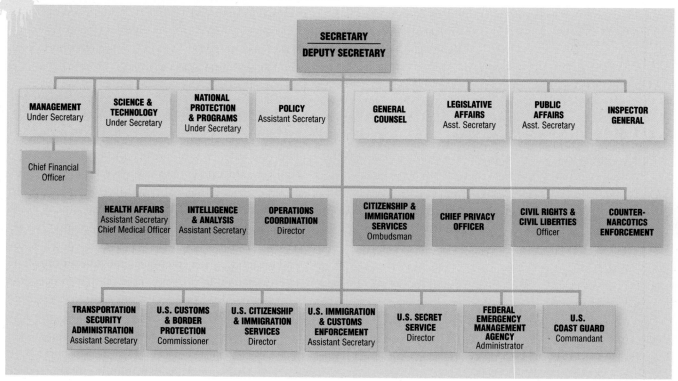

THE OFFICE OF THE SECRETARY As you saw in Figure 16.2, at the top of the DHS "totem pole" is the secretary of homeland security, a cabinet-level public servant who reports directly to the president. The current DHS secretary is Janet Napolitano, who served as governor of Arizona before being named to the post by President Barack Obama.

A wide variety of federal agencies answer directly to the secretary of homeland security. The Office of Health Affairs, for example, coordinates all the medical activities of the DHS, including preparation for and response to the health effects of a WMD attack. The Directorate of Science and Technology partners with private companies, national laboratories, universities, and domestic and foreign government agencies to develop counterterrorism technologies. The Office of the Inspector General audits the entire DHS to ensure that its budget—nearly $50 billion in 2012—is spent efficiently and with a minimum of waste.

THE AGENCIES OF THE DHS The seven agencies lined up across the bottom rung of Figure 16.2 on the previous page represent the front line of the DHS's anti-terrorism efforts. The responsibilities of U.S. Customs and Border Protection (CBP), U.S. Immigration and Customs Enforcement (ICE), the U.S. Secret Service, and the U.S. Coast Guard were explained earlier (see pages 155–156). The others, though not considered law enforcement agencies, play a crucial role in preventing and responding to terrorist-related activity.

- The *Transportation Security Administration (TSA)* is responsible for the safe operation of our airline, rail, bus, and ferry services.
- *U.S. Citizenship and Immigration Services (USCIS)* handles the "paperwork" side of U.S. immigration law. The agency processes the more than 20 million applications made each year by individuals who want to visit the United States or reside or work in this country.
- *FEMA* retains its position as the lead federal agency in preparing for and responding to disasters such as hurricanes, floods, terrorist attacks, and *infrastructure* concerns. Infrastructure includes all of the facilities and systems that provide the daily necessities of modern life such as electric power, food, water, transportation, and telecommunications.

FEDERAL AGENCIES OUTSIDE THE DHS

The DHS does not directly control all federal efforts to combat terrorism. Since September 11, 2001, the FBI, a branch of the Department of Justice, has been the "lead federal agency" for all terrorism-related matters. Its Strategic Information Operations Center serves as an information clearinghouse for federal, state, and local law enforcement agents who want to share information on terrorism-related matters. Indeed, the agency now lists "protecting the United States from terrorist attack" as its highest organizational priority.[41]

The *intelligence* agencies of the U.S. government also play an important role in anti-terrorism efforts. In contrast to

LO 5

Infrastructure The services and facilities that support the day-to-day needs of modern life, such as electricity, food, transportation, and water.

A resident of Hueytown, Alabama, speaks with a FEMA agent atop the remains of his home, which was destroyed by a tornado in April 2011. What are FEMA's responsibilities as part of this country's homeland security apparatus?
Nicholas Kamm/AFP/Getty Images/Newscom

a law enforcement agency, which works to solve crimes that have already occurred, an **intelligence agency** works to prevent crimes or other undesirable acts by gathering information, or intelligence, on potential wrongdoers and stopping the illegal conduct in the planning stage. Intelligence operations rely on the following strategies to collect information:

1. *Electronic surveillance* of phone and e-mail communications, as well as advanced recording devices placed on satellites, aircraft, and land-based technology centers.
2. *Human-source collection*, which refers to the recruitment of foreign agents and interviews with people who have particular knowledge about areas of interest.
3. *Open-source collection,* or close attention to "open" data sources such as books, newspapers, radio and television transmissions, and Internet sites.
4. *Intelligence sharing* with friendly foreign intelligence services.
5. *Counterintelligence,* which involves placing undercover agents in a position to gain information from hostile foreign intelligence services.[42]

In particular, two intelligence agencies are integral to American anti-terrorism efforts. The first is the **Central Intelligence Agency (CIA),** which is responsible for gathering and analyzing information on foreign governments, corporations, and individuals, and then passing that information on to the upper echelons of our federal government. The second, the **National Security Agency (NSA),** is also in the business of gathering and analyzing information, but it focuses primarily on communications. NSA agents eavesdrop on foreign conversations, whatever form they might take, while at the same time working to ensure that sensitive messages sent by the U.S. government are not subjected to similar scrutiny.

STATE AND LOCAL ANTI-TERRORISM EFFORTS

Even with the significant resources of the DHS and the extensive expertise of organizations such as the FBI and the CIA, the federal government cannot effectively protect the United States against terrorism without help. To provide such aid, over the past decade almost every state law enforcement agency and about a quarter of local law enforcement agencies (primarily in the most populated municipalities) have formed specialized units to combat terrorism.[43] As we discussed in Chapter 5, local and state law enforcement officers are often in a much better position than their federal counterparts to notice something out of the ordinary "on the beat." Also, they are better positioned to make a low-level arrest that could have homeland security implications.

In the past, the various law enforcement agencies have struggled to share counterterrorism intelligence effectively with one another. To alleviate these problems, the federal government has established seventy-two **fusion centers** throughout the country. Serving as clearinghouses for terrorism-related information, these centers are designed to convey threat data from federal agencies to local ones and vice versa.[44] Furthermore, fusion centers work in tandem with the network of more than one hundred Joint Terrorism Task Forces (JTTFs) that operate in the United States. JTTFs are made up of teams of state and local law enforcement officers, FBI agents, and other federal agents who cooperate to investigate and prevent terrorist attacks.

INTERNATIONAL COUNTERTERRORISM EFFORTS

In 2005, after the hunt for Osama bin Laden had grown cold, the CIA launched a new effort called Operation Cannonball to track down the elusive al Qaeda leader. One of the key initiatives of Operation Cannonball was to put more CIA agents on the ground

Discussion Tip: Have students work together to discuss the differences between law enforcement agencies and intelligence agencies. (LO 5)

Intelligence Agency An agency that is primarily concerned with gathering information about potential criminal or terrorist events to prevent those acts from taking place.

Central Intelligence Agency (CIA) The U.S. government agency that is responsible for collecting and coordinating foreign intelligence operations.

National Security Agency (NSA) The intelligence agency that is responsible for protecting U.S. government communications and producing intelligence by monitoring foreign communications.

Fusion Center A collaborative effort involving local, state, and federal law enforcement agencies that focuses on sharing information related to terrorist activity.

Teaching Tip: To ensure that students can clearly distinguish between the Central Intelligence Agency and the National Security Agency, have them work together to research both agencies and compare and contrast their functions.

Special counterterrorism police train in Dubai, the largest city in the United Arab Emirates (UAE). Why is it important for the United States to have Middle Eastern partners such as the UAE in its fight against global and domestic terrorism?
Marwan Naamani/AFP/Getty Images

in Pakistan, where bin Laden was believed to be hiding. Working with local informants, one of these agents succeeded in learning the family name of one of bin Laden's key employees, a trusted courier. Using intercepted phone calls and e-mails, the NSA refined this crucial piece of intelligence, ultimately determining the man's full identity.

The CIA quickly placed a tail on the courier, who eventually led them to the Abbottabad compound where U.S. Navy Seals killed bin Laden in May 2011. Notably, the Pakistani government did not aid American intelligence in the search for bin Laden, raising suspicions that local officials were protecting the world's most wanted terrorist.[45] In many other instances, however, international cooperation with foreign partners—including Pakistan—has been crucial to American counterterrorism efforts.

COOPERATIVE EFFORTS As nonstate actors, terrorists often operate on a global scale. The September 11 hijackers, for example, trained in the Middle East, developed their plans in western Europe, and carried out their attacks in New York and the Washington, D.C., area. Consequently, *coalitions,* or alliances between different nations, play a crucial role in the fight against terrorism.

In July 2010, for example, three Norwegian immigrants were arrested—two in Norway and one in Germany—on suspicion of building a series of IEDs with which to commit terrorist acts. The three suspects had been under surveillance for a year after being traced to a group of al Qaeda operatives operating out of Pakistan. The operatives had, a year earlier, attempted to bomb New York's subway system and a shopping center in Manchester, England. Counterterrorism officials from England, Germany, Norway, and the United States shared information to ensure that none of these plots were able to succeed.[46]

JURISDICTIONAL RESTRAINTS In February 2009, American and Pakistani law enforcement agents teamed up to arrest al Qaeda operative Sufyan al-Yemeni in Quetta, Pakistan, one of several joint operations between the two countries.[47] Because of jurisdictional rules (see pages 257–260), such operations are relatively rare. Most countries will not allow U.S. agents to operate on their soil. Moreover, the jurisdiction of American courts rarely extends to non-U.S. citizens captured in other countries, even if they are alleged to have committed crimes involving the United States or its citizens. In 2007, a German court sentenced Mounir el-Motassedeq to fifteen years in prison for his role in planning the September 11, 2001, attacks. Motassedeq would probably have received a harsher punishment had he been convicted in the United States, but, having been arrested in Germany, he was under the jurisdiction of the German court system.

COUNTERTERRORISM CHALLENGES AND STRATEGIES

Nearly a decade ago, the chair the 9/11 Commission, an independent congressional panel established to investigate the September 11 attacks, said that the "most important failure" of the nation's leaders prior to the attacks was "one of imagination."[48] In other words, because our criminal justice and intelligence experts could not imagine such an attack, they were powerless to prevent it.

Today, no such imagination is necessary. With memories of the falling towers and a smoldering Pentagon still potent, the U.S. homeland security apparatus has developed a wide variety of methods to protect America from terrorist activity. These methods, it seems, have been successful. From 2008 to 2010, law enforcement and intelligence agencies foiled at least fifteen domestic terrorist plots,[49] and the likelihood of a U.S. citizen dying at the hands of a terrorist is minuscule. Keeping in mind the ever-present possibility of a successful terrorism operation, in this section we will examine the various strategies that have been devised to detect terrorist plots and prevent another attack.

Critical Thinking Skill Development: In a written assignment, ask students to respond to the statement that the most important failure prior to 9/11 was "one of imagination." How have counterterrorism efforts changed since that time? (LO 6)

Why were the arrests of Mohamed Mahmood Alessa, shown here, and his partner Carlos Almonte in June 2010 an example of preventive policing? AP Photo/U.S. Marshals Service

PREVENTIVE POLICING

Twenty-year-old Mohamed Mahmood Alessa may not have been a criminal mastermind, but he was an expert braggart. "He's not better than me. I'll do twice what he did," Alessa, an American citizen of Palestinian descent, said of Major Nidal Hasan, who killed thirteen people at Fort Hood, Texas, in 2009.[50] "My soul cannot rest until I shed blood," Alessa exclaimed on another occasion. "I wanna, like, be the world's best known terrorist."[51] Unfortunately for Alessa, when he made these claims he was talking to an undercover officer working for the New York Police Department. Consequently, in June 2010, Alessa and his friend Carlos Eduardo Almonte were arrested as they tried to board a flight to Africa and were charged with conspiring to join the Somali terrorist group al-Shabaab. (See the photo alongside.)

LO 6

TAKING NO CHANCES In Chapter 4, we saw that criminal law generally requires intent and action. A person must have both intended to commit a crime and taken some steps toward doing so. In most cases, criminal law also requires that a harm has been done and that the criminal act caused the harm. According to federal officials, however, no evidence showed that either Mohamed Mahmood Alessa or Carlos Eduardo Almonte had made any successful contacts with established terrorist groups. The only weapons the two men possessed were folding knives, and they appeared to have spent most of their time lifting weights, playing violent video games, and watching *jihadist* videos on the Internet.

The case of Alessa and Almonte represents a growing trend in the criminal justice system brought about by the new challenges of fighting terrorism. The goal for many law enforcement agencies is no longer to solve crimes after they have occurred, but rather to prevent them from happening in the first place. Even though Alessa and Almonte did not pose any "known immediate threat to the public,"[52] federal authorities were not willing to take the risk that these men might eventually develop into something dangerous to U.S. citizens. Although some observers claim that law enforcement officials are exaggerating the threat posed by many of these accused plotters, the government points to a record of successes to justify this new approach (see Figure 16.3 below).

INFORMANTS AND ENTRAPMENT To infiltrate homegrown terrorist cells, law enforcement relies heavily on intelligence provided by informants. Because these makeshift cells often need help to procure the weaponry necessary for their schemes, they are natural targets for well-placed informants and undercover agents (both discussed in Chapter 6). Because of their amateur approach to terrorist activities, these suspects also are natural targets for well-placed "insiders." According to the Center on Law and Security at New York University, 62 percent of the federal government's most significant terrorism prosecutions have relied on evidence provided by informants.[53] As you may recall from the beginning of this chapter, FBI agents gave Mohamed Osman Mohamud funds to purchase explosive material and even provided him with a fake bomb to use to carry out an attack in Portland, Oregon.

Critical Thinking Skill Development: Have students respond to "Questions for Critical Analysis" number three on page 571, concerning the role ordinary citizens can play in counterterrorism efforts.

FIGURE 16.3 Preventive Policing: The Age of the Foiled Plot

Testifying before Congress in 2001, then attorney general John Ashcroft succinctly outlined the nation's new law enforcement strategy regarding domestic terrorists: "Prevent first, prosecute second." This blueprint has led to dozens of "quick strikes" against alleged terrorists, including the three examples listed here.

Facebook Farce December 2010	Targeting the Military October 2010	Terrorism Camp July 2009
The Plot: Antonio Martinez, a recent American convert to Islam, tried to blow up a U.S. military recruitment center in Catonsville, Maryland. On his Facebook page, Martinez wrote that all he "thinks about is *jihad*."	**The Plot:** Farooque Ahmed, a U.S. citizen born in Pakistan, planned on detonating several bombs in the Washington, D.C., Metro subway system to "kill as many military personnel as possible."	**The Plot:** A group of North Carolinians, apparently led by a man named Patrick Boyd, prepared to travel to the Middle East to wage "holy war" against the United States and its allies.
How Far It Got: Martinez loaded an SUV with barrels of explosives and parked the vehicle next to the recruitment center. He then dialed a cell phone number that he believed would detonate the bombs, but they were actually fakes provided by an FBI undercover agent.	**How Far It Got:** Ahmed, who lived in nearby Ashland, Virginia, spent six months casing Metro stations near the Pentagon, the headquarters of the U.S. Department of Defense. Ahmed also met several times with undercover federal agents disguised as al Qaeda operatives to discuss possible contributions to worldwide *jihad*.	**How Far It Got:** Boyd ran a kind of terrorist training camp on private property in rural Caswell County, North Carolina. He trained his charges in the use of Kalashnikov AK-47 rifles and other weapons used in various Middle East conflicts. Four of the suspects planned to "meet up" in Israel to begin their violent *jihad*.
The Result: Martinez was charged with attempted use of weapons of mass destruction and attempted murder of federal officers. If convicted, he faces life behind bars.	**The Result:** Ahmed was charged with attempting to provide material support to a foreign terrorist organization and planning a terrorist attack on a transit facility. If found guilty, he could spend fifty years in prison.	**The Result:** In February 2011, Boyd pleaded guilty to charges of conspiring to provide support to terrorists and conspiring to murder, kidnap, maim, and injure potential victims. He could be sentenced to a lifetime in prison for his crimes.

These tactics have drawn criticism from some quarters. Following Mohamud's apprehension, for example, one commentator wrote an article entitled "The FBI Successfully Thwarts Its Own Terrorist Plot."[54] Stephen R. Sady, Mohamud's defense attorney, asserted that the FBI was "basically grooming" his client to commit a terrorist act.[55] As you learned in Chapter 4, entrapment is a possible defense for criminal behavior when a government agent plants the idea of committing a crime in a defendant who would not have considered it on his or her own. Although the entrapment defense has often been raised in terrorism cases involving informants or undercover agents, it has yet to succeed. In every instance, judges and juries have found that the defendant was predisposed to terrorist behavior without any help from the government.[56]

THREE MODELS: CRIMINAL JUSTICE, INTELLIGENCE, AND MILITARY

The various tactics used in preventive policing are supported by anti-terrorism legislation. As noted earlier in the chapter, both the AEDPA and the Patriot Act contain provisions making it illegal to offer "material support" to terrorist organizations. Thus, these laws permit law enforcement agents to arrest suspects even though no crime, in the traditional sense of the word, has taken place and no evident harm has been caused. The AEDPA and the Patriot Act are crucial aspects of America's criminal justice model response to terrorism. Under this model, terrorism is treated like any other crime, and the law enforcement, court, and correctional systems work together to deter terrorist activity through the threat of arrest and punishment.

THE CRIMINAL JUSTICE MODEL Before September 11, 2001, the criminal justice model was our primary response to terrorist activity on American soil. In 1993, for example, a car bomb exploded in the basement of the World Trade Center in New York City, killing six people and injuring more than one thousand. Following an intense investigation, law enforcement agents were able to identify and apprehend the members of the fundamentalist Islamic group responsible for the act. Foreign governments provided aid in the worldwide search for the suspects. In fact, police in Pakistan arrested Ramzi Yousef, who planned the bombing, and extradited him to the United States to stand trial. Though one suspect remains at large, the remaining perpetrators were tried, convicted, and sentenced in the U.S. District Court for the Southern District of New York.[57]

Since the September 11 attacks, the criminal justice system has, as we have seen throughout this textbook, been very active in apprehending, prosecuting, and convicting terrorist suspects. Between 2001 and 2009, federal prosecutors brought nearly 850 terrorism-related charges against suspects, winning a conviction nearly 90 percent of the time.[58] On entering office in 2009, President Barack Obama voiced his commitment to using the criminal justice system as the primary weapon against terrorism, announcing that all terrorist suspects would be tried in civilian criminal court, regardless of their nationality or where they were apprehended.[59] The public, however, remains wary of the criminal justice model,[60] and in March

On entering office, President Barack Obama favored the criminal justice model of combating terrorism. What are the primary tools of the criminal justice model when it comes to anti-terrorism efforts? Martin H. Simon-Pool/Getty Images

2011, the Obama administration announced plans to revive the practice of military trials—which we will discuss later in the chapter—for certain terrorist suspects.

THE INTELLIGENCE AND MILITARY MODELS In some ways, the criminal justice system is at a disadvantage in the "war" against terrorism. It offers little protection against large-scale attacks, especially when terrorists are willing to commit suicide in the process and are therefore impervious to deterrence. After-the-fact punishment, no matter how harsh, of someone who may be responsible for hundreds or thousands of deaths also strikes many as an irrelevant response to damage that has already been done.

Because of these drawbacks, many experts believe that the intelligence model, rather than the criminal justice model, should be the nation's blueprint for combating terrorism. The intelligence model regards terrorist activities as threats to the security of the state rather than as criminal acts.[61] Instead of attempting to deter wrongdoing with the threat of arrest and punishment, the goal of an intelligence investigation, as we have seen, is to gather information that will keep the wrongdoing from happening in the first place.

Local Intelligence "Intelligence used to be a dirty word" for local police departments, according to David Carter, a professor of criminal justice at Michigan State University.[62] Today, however, financial support from the U.S. Departments of Justice and Homeland Security has helped create more than one hundred nonfederal police intelligence units, with at least one in every state.[63] The New York Police Department, in a class by itself, has more than one thousand personnel assigned to homeland security and has stationed agents in six foreign countries. As mentioned earlier in the chapter, thanks to fusion centers and the FBI Joint Terrorism Task Forces, local police departments have more opportunities to share intelligence with their federal counterparts.

Indeed, intelligence gathered by local police is playing a crucial role in the FBI's continuing efforts to build a massive database of potential wrongdoers. As of December 2010, this database already contained the names and personal information of more than 160,000 U.S. citizens who were the subjects of suspicious activity reports (SARs) provided by local police officers.[64] These reports are designed to alert federal analysts of behavior that is not illegal but may indicate "pre-operational planning" related to terrorism.[65] For example, a local police officer in Southern California filed an SAR concerning a "suspicious subject" who was "taking photographs of the Orange County Sheriff's Department Fire Boat . . . with a cellular phone camera."[66]

Although few SARs lead to investigations, civil liberties experts worry about the existence of such a massive law enforcement database of as-yet innocent persons. "If we want to get to the point where we connect the dots, the dots have to be there," explains Richard A. McFeely, special agent in charge of the FBI's office in Baltimore, Maryland.[67]

Military Solutions From 2001 to 2009, the administration of President George W. Bush made it clear that, besides the criminal justice model and the intelligence model, there is a third response to the terrorist threat: the *military model.* Although the scope of this textbook does not include U.S. military actions in Afghanistan, Iraq, and other global "hot spots," the militarization of the fight against terrorists did lead to several developments with repercussions for the criminal justice system.

Under President Bush, the U.S. Department of Defense was authorized to designate certain terrorist suspects detained during the course of military operations as *enemy combatants.* According to the policy at the time, this designation allowed a suspect to be "held indefinitely until the end of America's war on terrorism or until the military determines on a case-by-case basis that the particular detainee no longer poses a threat to the United States or its allies."[68] As a result, more than eight hundred "enemy combatants" were transferred to the U.S. Naval Base at Guantánamo Bay, Cuba. The Bush administration also followed the rules of war rather than the rules of the criminal justice system when interrogating terrorist suspects, an extremely controversial decision that we will examine in the *CJ in Action* feature at the end of the chapter.

CJ&TECHNOLOGY *Predator Drones*

Oleg Yarko/Shutterstock

As CIA officials watched from an office at the agency's headquarters in Langley, Virginia, Baitullah Mehsud relaxed on the rooftop of his father-in-law's house in Zanghara, Pakistan. The live video feed of Mehsud, a leader of the Pakistani Taliban, was being provided by the infrared camera of a Predator drone. This remotely controlled, unmanned aircraft was hovering about two miles above the target. "It was a perfect picture," said one observer. Suddenly, an explosion filled the screen. In Langley, one of the CIA officials had launched two Hellfire missiles from the Predator, obliterating the house and instantly killing Mehsud and eleven others, including his wife and in-laws. According to many terrorism experts, the CIA's Predator program is America's most effective weapon against al Qaeda and other terrorist groups in Pakistan and Afghanistan.

Between 2008 and 2011, Predators were used to kill more than five hundred terrorism-related targets in those countries. Although American law prohibits political assassinations, the Predator program is considered legal because it is an extension of U.S. military operations on foreign soil.

THINKING ABOUT PREDATOR DRONES

A critic of the Predator drone program argues that "it's almost always better to arrest terrorists than to kill them. You get intelligence then. Dead men tell no tales." A proponent counters that the drones are the only way to "stop dangerous terrorists who hide in remote parts of the world, inaccessible to U.S. troops, law enforcement, or any central government." Which argument do you find more convincing? Why?

EMERGENCY PREPAREDNESS AND RESPONSE

Several years ago, the federal government asked a branch of the military known as the United States Northern Command (NORTHCOM) to develop plans for responding to multiple terrorist attacks on the United States. NORTHCOM officials contemplated a "worst-case scenario"—three simultaneous strikes—and concluded that about three thousand military troops, including members of the National Guard, would need to be sent to the site of each attack.[69] Such planning, as part of an overall strategy of *preparedness,* is an integral part of homeland security.

The White House defines **preparedness** as the "existence of plans, procedures, policies, training, and equipment necessary at the federal, state, and local level to maximize the ability to prevent, respond to, and recover from major events."[70] The term has come to describe a wide variety of actions taken at different governmental levels to protect a community not only against terrorist attacks, but also against natural disasters such as

Technology Tip: Ask students to go online and research preparedness and response initiatives in your area. How well is your community prepared to respond to a terrorist incident or natural disaster? (LO 7)

Preparedness An umbrella term for the actions taken by governments to prepare for large-scale catastrophic events such as terrorist attacks or environmental disasters.

Members of a hazardous material team wear protective suits as they respond to a 2008 anthrax scare in Centennial, Colorado. Why are these emergency personnel called *first responders*? What role do first responders play in homeland security?

John Moore/Getty Images

First Responders Those individuals, such as firefighters, police officers, and emergency medical technicians, who are responsible for the protection and preservation of life and property during the early stages following a disaster.

Visa Official authorization allowing a person to travel to and within the issuing country.

Teaching Tip: Take a few moments to provide some background for your students as you begin the lecture on border security. Many students do not consider border security a homeland security issue. Explain to students how border security can influence the likelihood of a terrorist attack on U.S. soil. (LO 8)

hurricanes, tornadoes, and floods. The Oakland County (Michigan) Emergency Operations Center, for example, combines the contributions of thirty-four different local agencies, each one organized and prepared for a different type of emergency.

A necessary correlate to preparedness is *response,* or the actions taken after an incident has occurred. Because the federal government is usually unable to respond rapidly to any single incident, the burden of response initially falls on local emergency personnel such as police officers, firefighters, and emergency medical technicians. These aptly named **first responders** have several important duties, including the following:

LO 7

- Securing the scene of the incident by maintaining order.
- Rescuing and treating any injured civilians.
- Containing and suppressing fires or other hazardous conditions that have resulted from the incident.
- Retrieving those who have been killed.[71]

First responders often show great bravery in carrying out their duties under extremely dangerous circumstances. On September 11, 2001, 343 firefighters and 75 police officers were killed in the line of duty.

BORDER SECURITY

In its final report on the events that led up to September 11, 2001, the 9/11 Commission had plenty of blame to spread around. Poor preparation for a terrorist attack, poor performances by the FBI and other domestic law enforcement agencies, and poor intelligence gathering by the CIA were all highlighted as causes for concern. The commission seemed particularly disturbed, however, at the ease with which proven and potential terrorists could enter the United States. "Protecting borders was not a national security issue before 9/11," the report remarked, with more than a hint of disbelief.[72] The protection of our national borders has certainly become an issue since the commission published its report, though questions remain as to whether homeland security has significantly improved as a result.

REGULATED POINTS OF ENTRY People and goods legally enter the United States through checkpoints at airports, seaports, and guarded land stations. At these regulated points of entry, government agents check documents such as passports and *visas* and inspect luggage and cargo to ensure compliance with immigration and trade laws. (A **visa** is a document issued by the U.S. State Department that indicates the conditions under which a holder can enter and travel within the United States.) The task is immense. Close to 90 million foreign visitors arrive at America's more than one hundred international airports each year, with millions more passing through patrol stations along our borders with Mexico and Canada.

Increased Scrutiny One of the hard lessons of the September 11 attacks was that regulation of points of entry does not ensure security. Every one of the nineteen hijackers involved in those attacks entered the United States legally—that is, with a valid visa. They were also able to easily board the airplanes that they used as flying bombs. Consequently, one of the hallmarks of homeland security has been increased scrutiny at points of entry—particularly airports. The DHS Transportation Security Administration (TSA) has overseen significant changes in the way airports screen passengers, luggage, and cargo. Border personnel, both at home and abroad, have been trained to scrutinize all foreigners entering the United States for "terrorist risk factors." The FBI's Terrorist Screening Center has also compiled a "no fly" list of individuals who are deemed to pose a risk of terrorist activity and therefore are not allowed to board flights leaving or entering the United States.

Success and Failure Sometimes port-of-entry strategies succeed, and sometimes they fail. Two of the risk factors mentioned above are the purchase of a one-way plane ticket with cash and failure to check any luggage for a long flight. These behavior patterns may indicate a traveler who wishes to keep his or her identity hidden and has no plans for a return flight. One troubling aspect of the "Christmas bomber" case that was discussed previously in this chapter is that Umar Abdulmutallab followed this pattern exactly. Yet, he was still allowed to board Northwest Flight 253 in Amsterdam and fly to Detroit. At the same time, Faisal Shahzad, the attempted Times Square bomber, would have successfully fled the country had his name not been on the "no fly" list. Federal agents arrested him while his airplane destined for the Middle East was still at the gate in New York.[73]

UNREGULATED BORDER ENTRY Every year hundreds of thousands of non-U.S. citizens, unable to legally obtain visas, enter the country illegally by crossing the large, unregulated stretches of our borders with Mexico and Canada. Securing these **LO 8** border areas has proved problematic, if not impossible, for the various homeland security agencies. As a result, the border areas provide a conduit for illegal drugs, firearms and other contraband, illegal immigrants, and, possibly, terrorists and WMDs to be smuggled into the country.

A Logistical Nightmare The main problem for the U.S. Border Patrol and local law enforcement agents in trying to stem this flow is logistics. The U.S.-Canadian border extends for 3,957 miles (not counting Alaska), and the border with Mexico stretches for 1,954 miles. Much of the borderland consists of uninhabited plains and woodland to the north and desert and scrubland to the south. To compensate, the homeland security presence on the Mexican border has never been greater. Today, approximately 21,500 Border Patrol agents are monitoring the area, up from 9,000 in 2001.

Even with this small army of agents and physical barriers such as checkpoint stations, barbed-wire fences, and roadblocks in the most populous areas, effectively policing this immense expanse of land is nearly impossible. Furthermore, in 2011 the Department of Homeland Security canceled a project to build a "virtual fence"—consisting of sensors, cameras, and other surveillance technology—along the border because of high costs and low efficiency.

Terrorist Crossings Many national security officials worry that the porous nature of America's borders will

The topic of immigration is heavily debated on the Internet. Web pages managed by the **Immigration Policy Center** and the **Brookings Institution** offer a great deal of information on the subject. To visit these sites, visit the *Criminal Justice CourseMate* at **cengagebrain. com** and select the *Web links* for this chapter.

Discussion Tip: Ask students to consider the difficulties in securing the U.S.-Mexican border. What goals are behind American efforts to secure this border? What are the most effective ways of achieving these goals? (LO 8)

A Border Patrol agent examines a tunnel that leads from Mexico into the sewage system under the streets of Nogales, Arizona. Why do foreign citizens who cannot procure a visa choose to take such drastic measures as crawling down a long, cramped tunnel to get into the United States?

A.E. Araiza/*Arizona Daily Star*

CAREERS IN CJ

Photo Courtesy Paul Morris

FASTFACTS

CUSTOMS AND BORDER PROTECTION AGENT JOB DESCRIPTION:

- Make sure that laws are observed when goods or people enter the United States. Work at ports of entry and all along the border to prevent smuggling and the entrance of illegal immigrants.

- Conduct surveillance along the border, using electronic sensors, infrared scopes, low-light television systems, and aircraft.

- Must be willing to use and carry firearms, work overtime, and work in shifts under arduous conditions. Subject to random drug testing. May also be sent on temporary assignments on short notice and on permanent reassignments to any duty location.

WHAT KIND OF TRAINING IS REQUIRED?

- Be under age 40, be a U.S. citizen and resident of the United States, and possess a valid state driver's license.

- Be fluent in Spanish or be able to learn the Spanish language.

- Pass a thorough background investigation, medical examination, fitness test, and drug test.

ANNUAL SALARY RANGE?

- $36,600–$46,500

For additional information on a career as a CBP agent, visit: **www.cbp.gov.**

PAUL MORRIS
CUSTOMS AND BORDER PROTECTION AGENT

After finishing nineteen weeks at the Federal Law Enforcement Training Center in Glynco, Georgia, I reported to my new post in Uvalde, Texas, which is about one hundred kilometers from the Mexican border. On my first day, my mentor, a crusty old agent named Jim, started to show me the ropes. With his help, I began to learn the signs of my trade—the clues left behind by persons who had illegally entered the United States and were traveling through the desert toward jobs and perhaps family members. From that first day, I loved what I was doing.

A "SEA CHANGE" The most memorable day of my career was, without a doubt, September 11, 2001. That morning, as I watched the fall of the Twin Towers, I knew that things were going to be different. Personally, the attacks left me with a resolve to ensure, to the maximum extent possible, that nothing similar ever happens again. Professionally, that day marked a sea charge with respect to how the federal border agencies viewed border security. Ever since, our anti-terrorism mission has been elevated above our other responsibilities, such as controlling illegal immigration, protecting our agricultural interests, and stopping the flow of illegal narcotics into this country.

To be sure, as each of these tasks is crucially important, the extra burdens of anti-terrorism pose a significant challenge. With the volume of vehicles, cargo, and persons crossing our borders, there can be no guarantees that a potential terrorist or weapon of mass destruction cannot slip across the border. Nevertheless, with advanced identification technology, increased personnel, and a more efficient infrastructure, I am confident that the possibility of such a breach is low.

VIOLENCE BORN OF DESPERATION Ports of entry along our shared border with Mexico have seen an increase in violent incidents in recent years. In my opinion, this shows that we are doing our jobs. As it becomes harder for illegal immigrants and narcotics smugglers to make their way across the border, they get desperate and turn to violence. As we continue to improve our operations, these criminal organizations will try to find ways to circumvent us. I am confident, however, that no matter where they go, we are going to be there to stop them.

CAREER ADVICE A high school diploma or equivalent is necessary to apply for a position with U.S. Customs and Border Protection (CBP), and applicants must successfully pass an intensive background investigation. Capable and ambitious officers who are geographically mobile and especially those who may have pursued graduate degrees in management, business, or government administration will have outstanding opportunities to advance quickly through the grades and to work in land border, airport, or seaport ports of entry.

The federal government is a marvelous opportunity for those wishing to pursue a career in law enforcement, and CBP provides a multitude of opportunities in a wide variety of areas. Because of the broad scope of our authority and because we have more than three hundred ports of entry in and outside the United States, the possibilities for responsibilities and locations are endless. And the work is extremely rewarding.

prove too tempting for terrorist organizations to resist. These fears have led to increased homeland security measures along the U.S.-Canadian border, which had previously received much less attention than southern crossing routes. Still, smugglers have little problem getting marijuana, Ecstasy, and methamphetamine (heading south) and tax-free cigarettes, weapons, and cocaine (heading north) across the divide.[74] A 2011 U.S. Government Accountability Office report, citing the threat of "known terrorist organizations" operating in Canada, determined that just thirty-two miles of the northern border have an acceptable level of security.[75] Despite these worries, as of late 2011 no high-level terrorist suspects are known to have taken an illegal land route into the United States.

Teaching Tip: Ask students why homeland security concerns relating to the U.S.-Canadian border have been receiving more attention. What kind of issues are associated with our northern border?

SELFASSESSMENT

Fill in the blanks and check your answers on page 570.
Since September 11, 2001, law enforcement agencies have been taking steps to _____ terrorist-related wrongdoing before it gets beyond the planning stage. To do so, they often rely on _____ operations to gather information about terrorist plots. In the unlikely event of a large-scale terrorist attack, local emergency personnel such as police officers and firefighters, otherwise known as first _____, are called on to maintain order. To control the flow of people into the United States, the U.S. State Department requires most foreign visitors to obtain a _____ before entering this country.

THE DOUBLE-EDGED SWORD: SECURITY VERSUS CIVIL LIBERTIES

Several years ago, a group called "Keep America Safe" questioned the patriotism of seven lawyers who had represented foreign terrorist suspects detained by the U.S. military. In an Internet video, the group criticized the U.S. Department of Justice, where these lawyers had taken positions, as the "Department of *Jihad*" and demanded to know "whose values do they share?"[76] Defenders of the "al Qaeda seven" pointed out that the Sixth Amendment guarantees the right to counsel for criminal defendants. One commentator said that the lawyers were not "fighting to protect *jihadist* murderers" but rather "defending the U.S. Constitution."[77]

The role of the Constitution in the struggle against terrorism has been a topic of constant debate over the past decade. Often, the debate is quite public, as in the "Keep America Safe" campaign and the controversy over *Miranda* rights for terrorist suspects, discussed in Chapter 7. The issue is a private one as well, both for criminal justice professionals and for other citizens. Magistrate Judge H. Kenneth Schroeder, Jr., who oversaw the trial of six young "wannabe" terrorists in Lackawanna, New York, several years ago, said he spent "some pretty restless, sleepless nights" trying to "balance the rights of the people of the community to be safe and the rights of the defendants."[78] In a 2011 poll, 34 percent of those questioned about the Patriot Act felt that the law "goes too far and poses a threat to civil liberties" while 42 percent considered it "a necessary tool that helps the government fight terrorists."[79] As we have seen throughout this textbook, the need to balance the rights of society and the rights of the individual is a constant in the criminal justice system. As we will see in this section, nowhere is this challenge more fraught with difficulty than in the struggle against terrorism.

> **"As terrible as 9/11 was, it didn't repeal the Constitution."**
>
> **—Rosemary S. Pooler,**
> U.S. circuit judge

Teaching Tip: Take a informal poll of your students. Which rights, if any, are students willing to sacrifice for increased security?

FREEDOM OF SPEECH

Critical Thinking Skill Development: Ask students to respond to "Questions for Critical Analysis" number four on page 571, regarding free speech.

"Ours is the most outspoken society on earth," writes journalist Anthony Lewis. "Americans are freer to think what we will and say what we think than any other people."[80] The rights to be "outspoken" and to "think what we will and say what we think" are enshrined in the First Amendment, which protects freedom of speech. This freedom is not without its limits, however, and continuing efforts to determine those limits have intensified under the pressures of fighting terrorism. (See the *Mastering Concepts* feature below for an overview of the pressures on personal freedoms in the era of homeland security.)

TERRORIST INCITEMENT More than forty years ago, a Ku Klux Klan leader in Hamilton County, Ohio, broadcast a speech in which he threatened to take "revengance [sic]" on the president, Congress, and the United States Supreme Court if those institutions continued to "suppress the white, Caucasian race."[81] He was arrested and convicted under a state law that made it illegal to advocate crime or violence. Despite the defendant's antipathy toward it, the Supreme Court overturned the state law and set the standard for regulating "advocacy of the use of force." Such speech cannot be punished,

MASTERINGCONCEPTS
THE BILL OF RIGHTS IN THE AGE OF TERRORISM

In this section, we examine the tensions between civil liberties and the counterterrorism tactics adopted by the federal government. To help you better understand these conflicts, this Mastering Concepts feature focuses on the aspects of the First, Fourth, Fifth, and Sixth Amendments that require the government to balance the constitutional rights of the individual with the realities of counterterrorism.

	PROVISION	THE CONSTITUTIONAL BALANCING ACT
First Amendment	The government shall not abridge the "freedom of speech."	The government cannot punish speech unless it causes "imminent lawless action and is likely to incite or produce such action." To what extent does this allow criminal sanctions for those who support terrorist action, particularly on the Internet, or contribute funds to terrorist causes?
Fourth Amendment	Individuals have the right to be "secure in their persons" against "unreasonable searches and seizures."	To get a search warrant, government agents must provide a judge with probable cause that criminal activity has been or is being committed. To prevent terrorist acts, investigators often need to take action before a criminal act has occurred. How can law enforcement agents reconcile this contradiction in their anti-terrorism efforts?
Fifth Amendment	No one can be deprived of life, liberty, or property without due process of law.	Government officials cannot indefinitely detain criminal suspects without providing them a chance to prove their innocence. Many terrorist suspects, however, pose a constant threat to U.S. troops based abroad and civilians at home. How can the U.S. government justify the indefinite detention of these suspects without a trial?
	No person can be required to incriminate himself or herself.	Any information gained from a suspect as the result of improper coercion is inadmissible in criminal court. Military and intelligence agents, however, often employ "whatever means necessary" when interrogating terrorist suspects. How can this information eventually be used to gain a conviction?
Sixth Amendment	An accused person is guaranteed a speedy and public trial before an impartial jury.	Criminal trials are, by definition, public affairs. Consequently, open trials and rules of evidence make it very difficult to protect "classified information" critical to counterterrorism intelligence operations. How can security concerns be balanced against the free flow of information so crucial for a fair criminal trial?
	A suspect has a right to counsel.	Government-provided counsel must protect the confidentiality of all attorney-suspect communications. With terrorist suspects, however, these communications might include important information about future terrorist attacks. Under what circumstances can attorney-client confidentiality be breached in the interest of national security?

the Court ruled, unless the speech produces a danger of "imminent"—likely to happen at any moment—illegal activity *and* makes it "likely" that the imminent activity will take place.[82]

Promoting *Jihad* In its decision concerning the Ohio Ku Klux Klan leader, the Supreme Court supported the view that even speech that one disagrees with or finds abhorrent should be protected unless it poses a clear threat. Practically, however, the Ku Klux Klan leader posed little threat to his named targets. Courts tend to be less idealistic when the danger is more concrete. Five days after the September 11 attacks, for example, an American Islamic scholar named Ali al-Timimi told a group of young men in Virginia that they had a duty as Muslims to defend Afghanistan in the event of a U.S. military invasion. Four of the men did, in fact, fly to Pakistan and train for several weeks at a camp operated by the terrorist group Lashkar-e-Taiba. They then returned to the United States without further action.

Given the Supreme Court's guidelines, al-Timimi's speech would seem to be protected by the First Amendment. He did not specifically advise the young men to go to Pakistan and train with Lashkar-e-Taiba. Furthermore, at the time he spoke with the young men, none of the steps they took in the weeks to come were considered illegal by the U.S. government. Nonetheless, al-Timimi was convicted of, among other crimes, levying war against the United States and sentenced to life in prison.[83]

Members of the Kurdistan Workers' Party (PKK) wave to supporters during a parade in southeastern Turkey. In 2010, the U.S. Supreme Court banned Americans from providing technical support to foreign terrorist groups such as the PKK, even if that support is not directly connected to violent acts. What is your opinion of this ruling?
STR/AFP/Getty Images

Online Support Ali al-Timimi gave his speech in person, but the true breeding ground for speech that incites terrorism is found online. The Department of Homeland Security monitors several thousand radical or extremist Web sites and calls the Internet "an area of relative security exploited by terrorists to indoctrinate, recruit, coalesce, train, and regroup, as well as prepare and support their operations."[84] Although these Web sites are considered "speech" and are protected by the U.S. Constitution, the Patriot Act criminalizes any use of the Internet that provides "material support" to terrorists by offering "training" or "expert advice or opinion."[85]

In 2004, Sami Omar Al-Hussayen, a citizen of Saudi Arabia studying at the University of Idaho, was charged with violating the Patriot Act by providing material support to terrorists. He was accused of helping design several Web sites for the Islamic Assembly of North America. The Web sites contained four *fatwas,* or religious edicts issued by Muslim clerics, that advocated "martyrdom attacks" such as crashing airplanes into enemy targets. Federal prosecutors did not claim that Al-Hussayen wrote any of the offending material or even that he supported the causes. Instead, his alleged crime was providing his expertise to create the Web sites. An Idaho jury, however, acquitted al-Hussayen because, in the words of one juror, in the United States "people could say whatever they want . . . provided it would not cause imminent action."[86]

> The **American Civil Liberties Union** dedicates a Web page to the issue of homeland security and constitutional rights. To visit this site, go to the *Criminal Justice CourseMate* at **cengagebrain.com** and select the *Web links* for this chapter.

SEARCHES, SURVEILLANCE, AND SECURITY

The Fourth Amendment protects against unreasonable searches and seizures. According to the United States Supreme Court, the purpose of this amendment is to "prevent arbitrary and oppressive interference by enforcement officials with the privacy and personal security of individuals."[87] In practice, this has meant that a "neutral and detached" judge must, in most circumstances, decide whether a search or surveillance of a suspect's person or property is warranted. Law enforcement has often chafed against these restrictions, and this tension has only been exacerbated by the demands of counterterrorism search and surveillance strategies.

THE PATRIOT ACT AND SEARCHES The case of Zacarias Moussaoui is "Exhibit A" for those who feel that the Fourth Amendment, as interpreted by the courts, is incompatible with homeland security. During the summer of 2001, FBI agents in Minnesota arrested Moussaoui for immigration violations and sought a warrant to search his apartment and laptop computer. Because their superiors felt the agents had not established Moussaoui's involvement in terrorist activities, they refused to ask a judge for the necessary search warrant until after the September 11 attacks. (For a review of these procedures, see pages 227–229.) According to a congressional report, the information on Moussaoui's computer would have helped provide a "veritable blueprint for 9/11."[88]

Addressing these concerns, several sections of the Patriot Act make it easier for law enforcement agents to conduct searches. Previously, to search a suspect's apartment and examine the contents of his or her computer, they needed a court order based on probable

LO 9 cause that a crime had taken place or was about to take place. The Patriot Act amends the law to allow the FBI or other federal agencies to obtain warrants for "terrorism" investigations, "chemical weapons" investigations, or "computer fraud and abuse" investigations as long as agents can prove that such actions have a "significant purpose."[89] In other words, no proof of criminal activity need be provided.

THE PATRIOT ACT AND SURVEILLANCE Even before September 11, 2001, the Foreign Intelligence Surveillance Act of 1978 (FISA), which we first discussed in Chapter 7, had made it easier for intelligence agents to practice surveillance. Under FISA, the Foreign Intelligence Surveillance Court (FISC) would issue a warrant (technically known as a "special court order") without probable cause as long as the "primary purpose" of the document was to investigate foreign espionage and not to engage in criminal law enforcement.[90]

The Patriot Act gives federal agents even more leeway. It amends FISA to allow for searches and surveillance if a "significant purpose" of the investigation is intelligence gathering or any other type of antiterrorist activity.[91] The statute also provides federal agents with "roving surveillance authority," allowing them to continue monitoring a terrorist suspect on the strength of the original warrant even if the suspect moves to another jurisdiction.[92] Furthermore, the Patriot Act makes it much easier for law enforcement agents to avoid the notification requirements of search warrants. This means that a person whose home has been the target of a search and whose voice mails or computer records have been seized may not be informed of these activities until weeks after they have taken place.[93]

Following a series of controversies concerning the ability of the National Security Agency (NSA) to monitor telephone and e-mail communications of terrorism suspects, several years ago Congress passed an amended version of FISA.[94] The new law allows the NSA to wiretap any person "reasonably believed" to be outside the United States for seven days without a court order if necessary to protect national security. It also permits the wiretapping of Americans for seven days without a court order if the attorney general has probable cause to believe that the target is linked to terrorism. Supporters of the amendments claim that the average American has nothing to fear from the law "unless you have al Qaeda on your speed dial." Critics, however, see it as a further erosion of Fourth Amendment protections in the name of homeland security.[95]

PRIVACY VERSUS SECURITY

As far as many members of the general public are concerned, the most intrusive searches in the name of homeland security are taking place at airports. Complaints focus on body scanners, which enable screeners to see passengers' bodies underneath their clothing, and aggressive pat-downs, which include checking areas such as the groin and breasts for signs of explosives or weapons. The backlash against such techniques was neatly captured in a 2010 YouTube video showing a traveler named John Tyner refusing a pat-down while telling TSA employees, "You touch my junk, and I'm going to have you arrested!"

Reports that the federal government had been secretly collecting the phone call records of millions of American citizens caused a great deal of controversy and led to numerous protests.
Charles Dharpak/AP Photo

Necessary Intrusions Despite the threat of airline passenger boycotts and lawsuits, federal officials insist that the security measures are necessary. "We know through intelligence that there are . . . terrorists who are trying to kill not only Americans but innocent people around the world," warns John Pistole, head of the TSA.[96] In particular, the measures are designed to detect an explosive powder called PETN, which was sewn into the underwear of Umar Abdulmutallab as he boarded Flight 253 for Detroit on December 25, 2009. This white powder was also packed by al Qaeda operatives into computer printer cartridges and shipped to Chicago in October 2010. PETN does not trigger metal detector alarms and is easily hidden. Furthermore, only a small amount is needed to cause a serious explosion. With the body scanners and pat-down searches, security personnel hope to detect the devices needed to detonate PETN, which are more difficult to conceal.

"**We cannot depend on dumb luck, incompetent terrorists, and alert citizens to keep our families safe.**"

—**Missouri Senator Kit Bond** (2010)

Terrorist Profiling Criticizing the more invasive security measures at airports, Jason Chaffetz, a Republican congressman from Utah, said, "We don't need to look at naked eight-year-olds and grandmothers to secure airplanes."[97] If not, who do we "need to look at"? Polls have found that a relatively high percentage of Americans favor using Muslim identity as a trigger for government surveillance and preflight boarding interrogations.[98] Indeed, when collecting domestic intelligence, FBI agents are permitted to use race or religion as a factor—though not the only factor—in choosing targets for investigation.[99]

These strategies raise concerns of racial and cultural profiling. In Chapter 7, you learned that because of the Fourth Amendment, law enforcement agents cannot legitimately stop a suspect unless they have a reasonable suspicion of illegal behavior. Is a person's race or religion ever sufficient to create reasonable suspicion? The question has yet to be directly addressed by U.S. courts in the context of homeland security. As the poll cited above shows, however, because of the connection between Islamic extremists and international terrorism, the public does seem somewhat comfortable discriminating against Muslims based on their religious beliefs. For its part, the American Muslim community expects the federal government to protect its members against such attitudes. "We're not asking for special treatment, just equal treatment," said Agha Saeed of the

Critical Thinking Skill Development: In a written assignment, ask students to answer the question: "Is a person's race or religion alone ever sufficient to create reasonable suspicion?"

Council of American-Islamic Relations.[100] (To learn about a country where Arabs and Muslims do receive special treatment, see the feature *Comparative Criminal Justice—The Not-So-Friendly Skies* below.)

DUE PROCESS AND INDEFINITE DETENTION

Discussion Tip: Ask students to discuss the Fifth Amendment in the context of homeland security. Does the Fifth Amendment apply only to U.S. citizens? Why or why not?

The Fifth Amendment provides that no *person* shall be deprived of life, liberty, or property without due process of law. (See page 123 for a review of due process.) More than a century ago, the United States Supreme Court ruled that, because the amendment uses the word *person* and not *citizen,* due process protections extend to non-U.S. citizens under the jurisdiction of the U.S. government.[101] Immediately after the September 11, 2001, attacks, however, the Office of the U.S. Attorney General set forth regulations that allowed homeland security officials to detain non-U.S. citizens of "special interest" without first charging them with any crime. The new rules also allowed for the indefinite detention of such suspects in the event of "emergency or other extraordinary circumstance."[102]

As noted earlier in the chapter, more than eight hundred of these "enemy combatants" were eventually sent to a U.S. military detention center at the U.S. Naval Base in Guantánamo Bay, Cuba (GTMO). At the time, American officials insisted that, because these al Qaeda and Taliban operatives had been captured during military operations, they could be held indefinitely without being charged with any wrongdoing.[103] The detainees were denied access to legal representation or family members and were subjected to harsh interrogation tactics such as waterboarding, sleep and food deprivation, physical stress positions, and isolation.[104] As a result of the conditions at GTMO, the U.S. government came under a great

COMPARATIVE CRIMINAL JUSTICE

THE NOT-SO-FRIENDLY SKIES

El Al, the national airline of Israel, has an impressive security record. Despite Israel's near-constant state of war with one or more of its neighbors in the Middle East, and the country's status as a favored target for terrorist attacks, no El Al airplane has been hijacked in three decades. The Israeli government credits this success to its profiling strategy, which is based on the principle that it is "essential to focus on a very small percentage of passengers with terrorist intent."

Wheras American security procedures are designed to find weapons, the Israelis focus on finding terrorists. At Ben Gurion International Airport, outside Tel Aviv, travelers are stopped several times before they reach their gate. During these encounters, airport security personnel ask a series of questions and evaluate the security risk of each passenger. In doing so, screening agents take into account a traveler's country of origin and skin color. Most Jewish Israeli citizens are waived through this process rather quickly. Arab Israelis and other non-Jewish passengers, however, are generally taken aside for lengthy questioning, as well as a thorough luggage check and physical examination.

Saleh Yaaqubi, an Arab Israeli student, called the security check at Ben Gurion "the most offensive and humiliating experience I have ever had." Americans, too, are often surprised by the experience. Writer Matthew Yglesias noted that the one African American traveling with his group was singled out for intense scrutiny, and criticized Ben Gurion staff for "the most unpleasant encounter I've had with airport security in a decade." Israeli terrorism experts dismiss such complaints as shortsighted. "How many blonde, blue-eyed ladies have brought down planes in the last twenty years?" asked one security consultant. "They were all fanatic Muslims. So, if you are a Muslim, we have to find out if you are a fanatic or not."

FOR CRITICAL ANALYSIS

Would you be in favor of instituting Israeli screening methods in American airports? Why or why not?

deal of international criticism, particularly from Arab and Muslim countries and from those non-Muslim nations, such as Australia and Great Britain, whose citizens were being held at the detention center.

DOWNSIZING GTMO The Obama administration has indicated a preference for eventually closing down GTMO. The primary challenge in doing so, however, is finding a way to disperse its remaining detainees without risking the safety of the American public. Many of the prisoners participated in significant terrorist incidents, including the September 11 attacks, and homeland security officials believe they still pose a threat. Furthermore, about one in seven of the detainees released from GTMO has returned, or is suspected of having returned, to terrorist activity.[105] One former prisoner, Said Ali al-Shihri, became the deputy leader of al Qaeda operations in Yemen.[106] Nevertheless, the Bush administration managed to release about 500 GTMO detainees, and by the fall of 2011, the Obama administration had reduced the number of prisoners on the base to about 170.

Detainees in orange jumpsuits sit in a holding area at the U.S. Naval Base at Guantánamo Bay, Cuba. Do you think non-U.S. citizens who are in the custody of the U.S. military should be protected by our Constitution? Why or why not?
Reuters NewMedia, Inc./Corbis

MILITARY JUSTICE For those who remain incarcerated at GTMO, the Obama administration appears to have two options for trying them: a civilian criminal court or a *military tribunal.* In a civilian court on U.S. soil, the detainees would enjoy all of the rights available to any criminal defendant, as described in Chapter 10. By contrast, military tribunals, located at GTMO, offer a more limited set of protections. In a tribunal, the accused does not have the right to a trial by jury, as guaranteed by the Sixth Amendment. Instead, a panel of at least five military commissioners acts in place of the judge and jury and decides questions of both "fact and law." Only two-thirds of the panel members need to agree for a conviction, in contrast to the unanimous jury required by criminal trials. Furthermore, evidence that would be inadmissible in criminal court, such as some forms of hearsay testimony (pages 336–337) and "fruit of the poisoned tree" from unreasonable searches and seizures (page 219), is allowed before these tribunals.[107] (See Figure 16.4 on the following page for an overview of the rules that govern military trials.)

Military Tribunal A court that is operated by the military rather than the criminal justice system and is presided over by military officers rather than judges.

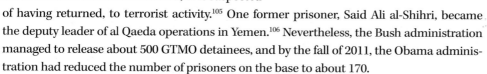

The Ghailani "Failure" As of September 2011, more than two dozen GTMO detainees had been brought before military commissions, and six had been convicted and sentenced. The first trial of a GTMO detainee in civilian court took place in 2010, when Ahmed Khalfan Ghailani faced charges relating to the bombing of two U.S. embassies in East Africa twelve years earlier. As we saw in Chapter 10, even though Ghailani was convicted of one count of conspiracy and sentenced to life in prison, the trial was perceived as something of a failure. Ghailani was acquitted of more than 280 other counts of conspiracy and murder, and the rules of evidence of criminal court prohibited crucial evidence from being presented to the jury.

Critical Thinking Skill Development: Have students respond to "Questions for Critical Analysis" number five on page 571, concerning civilian trials versus military tribunals.

Risk Reduction Because of the negative reaction to the Ghailani trial, as well as political maneuvering by Congress, the Obama administration has decided that military tribunals will be the primary means for trying GTMO detainees, even though this decision will not further the president's goal of shutting down GTMO. The military tribunals will

FIGURE 16.4 Military Trials for Terrorist Suspects

The guidelines for military tribunals can be found in the Military Commissions Act of 2009. Several basic questions concerning the procedures used in such tribunals are answered below.

Who is eligible to appear before a military tribunal?

Only "unprivileged enemy belligerents" can be tried by a military tribunal. A person is considered an "unprivileged enemy belligerent" if he or she

A. Has engaged in hostilities against the United States or one of its military allies;

B. Has purposefully and materially supported hostilities against the United States or one of its military allies; or

C. Was a member of al Qaeda at the time of the offense.

Who decides the suspect's guilt or innocence?

A suspect's fate will be decided by a tribunal of at least five military officers. The vote will be conducted in secret, and a two-thirds majority is necessary to find the suspect guilty.

What procedural protections will the suspect be granted during military tribunals?

The military tribunals provide the following procedural protections:

A. The right of the accused to present witnesses in his or her defense and cross-examine hostile witnesses.

B. Protection against self-incriminating statements (see pages 323–324).

C. A ban on statements obtained through cruel, inhuman, or degrading treatment.

D. The ability to offer the affirmative defense of mental disease or defect (pages 114–116).

In this drawing Binyam Muhammad, right, sits with his unidentified defense council in the U.S. military courtroom in Guantánamo Bay, Cuba. Muhammad is accused of plotting to blow up apartment buildings and gas stations in the United States.

AP Photo/Janet Hamlin, Pool

Source: Military Commissions Act of 2009, Public Law No. 111-84, Sections 1801–1807, 123 Stat. 2190 (2009).

Technology Tip: Have students go online and read the FBI's inquiry into the treatment of GTMO detainees at **vault.fbi.gov/ Guantanamo%20**.

operate out of a $12 million, high-tech courtroom located at the Guantánamo Bay facility. Furthermore, the administration has identified at least fifty GTMO detainees who will not be tried at all because they are considered too dangerous to risk their release. Federal officials will review the status of these detainees periodically, but in theory they could be held indefinitely.[108] At present, no alternative incarceration site for these men has been identified. Thus, despite the administration's stated preference, GTMO appears likely to remain open and operational for the foreseeable future.

SELFASSESSMENT

Fill in the blanks and check your answers on page 570.

According to the United States Supreme Court, the _____ Amendment protects speech, even incitement to terrorism, unless it creates a danger of _____ terrorist activity. Under the Patriot Act, government agents no longer need to show _____ cause to obtain warrants for terrorist investigations. Rather, they only need to show that their actions have a "_____ purpose." President Barack Obama has resumed the use of _____ tribunals to try prisoners held at the U.S. military detention center in Guantánamo Bay, Cuba, and has raised the possibility of _____ detention for certain dangerous detainees.

CJ IN ACTION

INTERROGATING TERRORISTS

Abu Zubaydah was in bad shape, feverish and suffering from bullet wounds in his groin and abdomen, but conditions were about to get worse for the al Qaeda operative. The CIA agents who had detained him in a Thai safehouse in the spring of 2002 were certain that he had information "that could save innocent lives." To get this information, the interrogators stripped Zubaydah naked and then adjusted the air-conditioning until he turned blue with cold. Meanwhile, they blasted him with deafening rock music from bands such as the Red Hot Chili Peppers.[109] The CIA agents also, unwittingly, contributed to the debate that is the subject of this *CJ in Action* feature: How far should the United States go in interrogating suspected terrorists?

TORTURE LITE

Under U.S. criminal law, it is a crime for any person inside or outside the country to commit torture.[110] Actions taken by U.S. agents to secure counterterrorism intelligence have, however, skirted the generally accepted definition of torture—the infliction of severe physical or mental pain or suffering on a person in custody. At the Guantánamo Bay military prison in Cuba, for example, detainees were subjected to "waterboarding," a technique that involves repeatedly pouring water down the throat of a subject to reproduce the feeling of drowning.[111] In Iraq, American military officers authorized twenty-nine "aggressive" interrogation techniques, including isolation, stress positions, sensory and sleep deprivation, and the use of canines to exploit "Arab fear of dogs."[112]

Defenders of these coercive interrogation methods, often known as "torture lite," argue that they do not meet the definition of torture because no actual harm is done to the subject. Critics reject this stance as both disingenuous and untrue. On taking office in 2009, President Barack Obama stopped U.S. agents from implementing "enhanced" interrogation techniques. Debate on the subject was rekindled in 2011, however, when some sources claimed that "torture lite" provided information that led the U.S. military to Osama bin Laden. At best, said CIA Director Leon Panetta, the usefulness of such techniques is "always going to be an open question."[113]

THE CASE FOR COERCIVE INTERROGATION

- In a number of instances (such as with the aforementioned Abu Zubaydah, who provided detailed information about al Qaeda's organizational strategies), coercive interrogation has produced vital information that has helped disrupt terrorist plots and save lives.
- The rules of U.S. criminal law do not apply to these methods because they are used to gather intelligence, not to provide evidence in a criminal trial.
- The far greater brutality and blatant torture tactics used by many terrorist organizations justify the use of these methods.

THE CASE AGAINST COERCIVE INTERROGATION

- These methods are immoral and abhorrent. "It's not about the terrorists," says Senator John McCain (R., Ariz.). "It's about us. It's about what kind of country we are."[114]
- Research has shown that confessions made under duress are unreliable, as the subject will "say anything" to avoid further pain.
- If terrorism cases are tried in criminal courts, any "coerced" statements made by subjects will be inadmissible under the rules of evidence.

AP Photo/Saurabh Das

WRITING ASSIGNMENT—YOUR OPINION

Several years ago, the U.S. Justice Department released a series of memos describing the "enhanced" interrogation methods used by the CIA. The authors of these documents justified the methods by referring to the "ticking bomb" situation. In this hypothetical scenario, the suspect is known to have knowledge of an extreme danger—such as a "ticking bomb"—and he or she must be persuaded to part with this knowledge immediately to save innocent lives.

What rules should govern the "ticking bomb" scenario? Where would you draw the line on coercive interrogations of terrorist suspects in general? Before responding, you can review our discussions in this chapter concerning:

- The definition of terrorism (pages 539–540).
- The difference between the criminal justice model and the intelligence model of combating terrorism (pages 555–557).
- Civil rights and terrorism (page 561).

Your answer should include at least three full paragraphs.

CHAPTER SUMMARY

LO 1 **Describe the concept of *jihad* as practiced by al Qaeda and its followers.** *Jihad* is a term for the struggle against evil that the Muslim faith demands of its adherents. As practiced by al Qaeda and other religious extremist groups, the tenets of *jihad* require violent action against "evil" nonbelievers, a viewpoint that is rejected by the majority of Muslims.

LO 2 **Identify three important trends in international terrorism.** (a) Terrorists have developed more efficient methods of financing their operations. (b) Terrorists have developed more efficient organizations based on the small-business model. (c) Terrorists have exploited new communications technology to mount global campaigns.

LO 3 **Compare WMDs and CBERN.** WMDs is an acronym for "weapons of mass destruction," which include nuclear, radiological, chemical, and biological weapons with the capacity to do great damage. CBERN, a term favored by the military, stands for "chemical, biological, explosive, radiological, and nuclear"—adding "explosive" because of the threat posed by conventional explosives.

LO 4 **Explain why the Antiterrorism and Effective Death Penalty Act of 1996 (AEDPA) is an important legal tool against terrorists.** The AEDPA allows federal law enforcement officials to prosecute those suspected of providing "material support or resources" to any group that the U.S. government has designated a "foreign terrorist organization." The legislation permits the arrest of a suspect who has not yet committed a crime, thereby allowing for preventive measures not usually available under criminal law.

LO 5 **Describe the primary goals of an intelligence agency and indicate how it differs from an agency that focuses solely on law enforcement.** The primary goal of an intelligence agency is to prevent crime by gathering information on potential illegal acts before they occur. In contrast, a law enforcement agency devotes its resources to solving crimes that have already occurred and bringing those who committed those crimes to justice.

LO 6 **Explain how American law enforcement agencies have used "preventive policing" to combat terrorism.** American law enforcement agencies are no longer willing to take the chance that nascent terrorist plots will develop into significant security threats. Therefore, they are taking steps to stop these plots in the planning stages, even if the dangers posed by the conspirators are minimal.

LO 7 **List the primary duties of first responders following a terrorist attack or other catastrophic event.** (a) Secure the scene of the incident, (b) rescue and treat any injured civilians, (c) contain fires or other hazardous conditions that may have resulted from the event, (d) and retrieve the dead.

LO 8 **Explain why unregulated border entry is a homeland security concern.** Each year, hundreds of thousands of non-U.S. citizens enter the country illegally. Illegal drugs, firearms, and other contraband also easily flow across America's borders with Mexico and Canada. Homeland security officials worry that the porous nature of these borders provides an opportunity for terrorists and WMDs to be smuggled into the country.

LO 9 **Explain how the Patriot Act has made it easier for federal agents to conduct searches during terrorism investigations.** In requesting a search warrant for investigations of terrorism, federal agents no longer need to provide probable cause of wrongdoing. They must only prove that their actions have a "significant purpose," which means that no proof of criminal activity need be provided.

SELF ASSESSMENT ANSWER KEY

Page 545: **i.** nonstate; **ii.** political; **iii.** domestic; **iv.** Internet

Page 547: **i.** mass destruction; **ii.** biological; **iii.** chemical; **iv.** nuclear; **v.** conventional

Page 553: **i.** material; **ii.** Patriot; **iii.** Homeland Security; **iv.** intelligence

Page 561: **i.** prevent; **ii.** intelligence; **iii.** responders; **iv.** visa

Page 568: **i.** First; **ii.** imminent; **iii.** probable; **iv.** significant; **v.** military; **vi.** indefinite

KEY TERMS

Antiterrorism and Effective
Death Penalty Act of 1996
(AEDPA)   **547**

biological weapon   **545**

Central Intelligence Agency
(CIA)   **551**

chemical weapon   **545**

domestic terrorism   **542**

first responders   **558**

fusion center   **551**

improvised explosive devices
(IEDs)   **546**

infrastructure   **550**

intelligence agency   **551**

military tribunal   **567**

National Security Agency
(NSA)   **551**

nonstate actor   **539**

nuclear weapon   **546**

Patriot Act   **548**

preparedness   **557**

radiation   **546**

visa   **558**

weapons of mass destruction
(WMDs)   **545**

QUESTIONS FOR CRITICAL ANALYSIS

1. Using your own words, what is the definition of *terrorism?*

2. Why do defendants charged with acts of domestic terrorism often present the entrapment defense at trial? Why is this strategy likely to be unsuccessful?

3. In 2011, a North Carolina chemical supply company told the FBI about an unusual order by a twenty-year-old college student from Saudi Arabia. The student was eventually arrested for planning to bomb various targets in the United States. Do you think that citizens or companies have a duty to report suspicious activity to the authorities? What might be some of the drawbacks of this practice?

4. Amal, a Muslim American, becomes angry after watching coverage of U.S. military operations in Afghanistan on CNN. He immediately sends out a tweet that reads, "I hate this country. I think someone should blow up the White House." Has Amal committed the crime of inciting terrorism? Do you need any other information to answer the question?

5. According to Donna Marsh, whose pregnant daughter was killed on September 11, 2001, in New York City, it is "unconscionable" to hold terrorism suspects for nearly a decade without trial, and it "demeans the United States' justice system" to say these suspects cannot be tried in civilian courts. What is your opinion of these statements?

CourseMate *For Online Help*

For online help and access to resources that accompany *Criminal Justice Today*, go to www.cengagebrain.com/shop/ISBN/1111835578. Click "Access Now," where you will find flashcards, an online quiz, and other helpful study aids. If you have an access code for CourseMate, log in and go to the chapter of your choice for additional online study aids.

NOTES

1. Quoted in Richard A. Serrano, "'JihadJane' Indictment Unsealed," *Los Angeles Times* (March 10, 2010), 1.

2. *National Strategy for Homeland Security* (Washington, D.C.: Office of Homeland Security, 2002), 2.

3. Geoffrey Levitt, "Is 'Terrorism' Worth Defining?" *Ohio Northern University Law Review* 13 (1986), 97.

4. "Domestic Terrorism Program," at **baltimore.fbi.gov/domter.htm**.

5. David A. Westbrook, "Bin Laden's War," *Buffalo Law Review* (December 2006), 981–1012.

6. Quoted in Kimberly Dozier and David Espo, "U.S. Kills Osama bin Laden Decade after 9/11 Attacks," *Associated Press* (May 2, 2011).

7. Marc Sageman, "Understanding Al-Qaida Networks," in *The McGraw-Hill Homeland Security Handbook*, ed. David G. Kamien (New York: McGraw-Hill, 2006), 53–54.

8. Ahmed S. Hashim, "Al-Qaida: Origins, Goals, and Grand Strategy," in *The McGraw-Hill Homeland Security Handbook*, ed. David G. Kamien (New York: McGraw-Hill, 2006), 24.

9. Quoted in *ibid.*, 9.

10. "Interview: Osama bin Laden," May 1998, at **www.pbs.org/wgbh/pages/frontline/shows/binladen/who/interview.html**.

11. Quoted in "The Growing, and Mysterious, Irrelevance of al Qaeda," *The Economist* (January 24, 2009), 64.

12. Quoted in Maggie Michael, "Al-Qaida Confirms Osama bin Laden's Death," *Associated Press* (May 6, 2011).

13. Quoted in Dozier and Espo.

14. Bob Drogin and April Choi, "Oregon Man, 19, Is Held in Plan to Bomb Tree-Lighting," *Los Angeles Times* (November 29, 2010), A24.

15. Evan Thomas and Mark Hosenball, "53 Hours in the Life of a Near Disaster," *Newsweek* (May 17, 2010), 27.

16. Quoted in Josh Meyer, "Small Groups Seen as Biggest Threat in U.S.," *Los Angeles Times* (August 16, 2007), 1.

17. Evan F. Kohlmann, "'Homegrown' Terrorists: Theory and Cases in the War on Terror's Newest Front," *Annals of American Academy of Political and Social Science* (July 2008), 95–99.

18. Robert F. Worth, "Yemen: U.S.-Born Cleric Is Sentenced," *New York Times* (January 19, 2011), A7.

19. Quoted in Thomas and Hosenball, 29.

20. Quoted in Lolita C. Baldor, "Success of Lone Gunmen May Shift al-Qaida Strategy," *Associated Press* (March 11, 2010).

21. Brian Michael Jenkins, "The New Age of Terrorism," in *The McGraw-Hill Homeland Security Handbook*, ed. David G. Kamien (New York: McGraw-Hill, 2006), 117–129.

22. *Ibid.,* 128.

23. Leonard A. Cole, "WMD and Lessons from the Anthrax Attacks," in *The McGraw-Hill Homeland Security Handbook*, ed. David G. Kamien (New York: McGraw-Hill, 2006), 167.

24. Quoted in David Cook, "Robert Mueller," *Christian Science Monitor* (May 10, 2007), 25.

25. Jane A. Bullock *et al., Introduction to Homeland Security*, 2d ed. (Burlington, MA: Butterworth-Heinemann, 2006), 156–157, 160–163.

26. *Ibid.,* 153.

27. Terrorism Project, "What If the Terrorists Go Nuclear?" at **www.cdi.org/terrorism/ nuclear-pr.cfm**.

28. Cole, 169.

29. Quoted in Jim Lobe, "Nation Girds for War with Unidentified Enemy" (September 12, 2001), at **ipsnews.net/news. asp?idnews=34634**.

30. "Transcript: President Obama's Inaugural Address," *New York Times* (January 21, 2009), P2.

31. 18 U.S.C. Section 2339B(a)(1) (1996).

32. 8 U.S.C. Section 1182(a)(3)(B) (Supp. I 2001); and 8 U.S.C. Section 1189(a)(1)(C) (Supp. I 2001).

33. U.S. Department of State, "Country Reports on Terrorism," at **www.state.gov/s/ct/rls/ crt/2008/122449.htm**.

34. 18 U.S.C. Section 2339A(b) (Supp. I 2001).

35. 8 U.S.C. Section 1182(a)(3)(B)(iv)(VI) (Supp. I 2001), amended by the Patriot Act of 2001, Pub. L. No. 107-56, Section 411(a), 115 Stat. 272.

36. Uniting and Strengthening America by Providing Appropriate Tools Required to Intercept and Obstruct Terrorism Act of 2001, Pub. L. No. 107-56, 115 Stat. 272 (2001).

37. Bullock *et al.,* 41–42.

38. Jim Abrams, "Congress Sends Terrorism-Fighting Bill to Obama," *Associated Press* (May 26, 2011).

39. Jim Abrams, "Obama, in Europe, Signs Patriot Act Extension," *Associated Press* (May 27, 2011).

40. Pub. L. No. 107-296, 116 Stat. 2135.

41. Federal Bureau of Investigation, "Facts and Figures: FBI Priorities," at **www.fbi.gov/ priorities/priorities.htm**.

42. Bullock *et al.,* 198.

43. Lois M. Davis *et al., When Terrorism Hits Home: How Prepared Are State and Local Law Enforcement?* (Santa Monica, CA: RAND Corporation, 2004), 8.

44. Lois M. Davis *et al., Long Term Effects of Law Enforcement's Post-9/11 Focus on Counterterrorism and Homeland Security* (Santa Monica, CA: RAND Corporation, 2011), 39–56.

45. Farah Stockman, "Ambassador Fends Off Doubts about Pakistan's Role," *Boston Globe* (May 8, 2011), 1.

46. Scott Shane and Eric Schmitt, "Norway Announces Three Arrests in Terrorist Plot," *New York Times* (July 9, 2010), A4.

47. Eric Schmitt and Mark Mazzetti, "U.S. Relies More on Aid of Allies in Terror Cases," *New York Times* (May 24, 2009), A1.

48. National Commission on Terrorist Attacks upon the United States, *The 9/11 Commission Report: Executive Summary* (Washington, D.C.: National Commission on Terrorist Attacks upon the United States, 2004), 9.

49. Shane and Schmitt.

50. Quoted in Bruce Shipkowski and Matt Apuzzo, "N.J. Man Held at JFK: 'I'll Outdo Fort Hood Killer,'" *Associated Press* (June 7, 2010).

51. *Ibid.*

52. U.S. Attorney, District of New Jersey, "Two New Jersey Men Arrested and Charged with Conspiring to Kill Persons outside the United States," press release, at **www.state. nj.us/njhomelandsecurity/press-room/ press-releases/2010/06-06-10-alessa-mohamed-and-almont-carlos-arrest-complaint-pr.pdf**.

53. Center on Law and Security, *Terrorist Trial Report Card: September 11, 2001–September 11, 2009* (New York: New York University School of Law, January 2010), 42–44.

54. Glenn Greenwalk, "The FBI Successfully Thwarts Its Own Terrorist Plot," *Salon. com* (November 28, 2010), at **www. salon.com/news/opinion/glenn_ greenwald/2010/11/28/fbi**.

55. Quoted in Bob Drogin and April Choi, "Defense Takes Aim at FBI," *Los Angeles Times* (November 30, 2010), A10.

56. Eric Schmitt and Charlie Savage, "In U.S. Sting Operations, Questions of Entrapment," *New York Times* (November 30, 2010), A22.

57. *United States v. Salameh,* 152 F.3d 88 (2d Cir. 1998).

58. Center on Law and Security, i–ii.

59. Josh Meyer, "FBI Planning a Bigger Role in Terrorism Fight," *Los Angeles Times* (May 28, 2009), 1.

60. Jane Mayer, "The Trial," *The New Yorker* (February 15/22, 2010), 57.

61. Arunabha Bhoumik, "Democratic Responses to Terrorism: A Comparative Study of the United States, Israel, and India," *Denver Journal of International Law and Policy* (Spring 2005), 285.

62. Quoted in "Spies among Us," *U.S. News & World Report* (May 8, 2006), 43.

63. *Ibid.,* 41–43.

64. Dana Priest and William M. Arkin, "Monitoring America," *Washington Post* (December 20, 2010), A1.

65. James E. Steiner, "More Is Better: The Analytic Case for a Robust Suspicious Activity Reports Program," *Homeland Security Affairs* (September 2010), 1.

66. Priest and Arkin.

67. Quoted in *ibid.*

68. *In re Guantánamo Detainee Cases,* 535 F.Supp.2d 443, 447 (D.D.C. 2005).

69. Bradley Graham, "War Plans Drafted to Counter Terror Attacks in U.S.: Domestic Effort Is Big Shift for Military," *Washington Post* (August 8, 2005), A1.

70. "Homeland Security Presidential Directive/ HSPD-8," at **www.fas.org/irp/offdocs/ nspd/hspd-8.html**.

71. Bullock *et al.,* 315.

72. National Commission on Terrorist Attacks upon the United States, 14.

73. Thomas and Hosenball, 30.

74. Chris Hawley, "Border Agents in North Fight Drug War on Ice," *Associated Press* (February 15, 2011).

75. *Border Security: Enhanced DHS Oversight and Assessment of Interagency Coordination Is Needed for Northern Border* (Washington, D.C.: U.S. Government Accountability Office, December 2010), 2, 10.

76. Quoted in "Justice Smeared," *Los Angeles Times* (March 9, 2010), 12.

77. Dahlia Lithwick, "More than Words," *Slate* (March 5, 2010), at **www.slate.com/ id/2246903**.

78. Quoted in Susan Sachs, "Murky Lives, Fateful Trip in Buffalo Terrorism Case," *New York Times* (September 20, 2002), A1.

79. Pew Research Center for the People and the Press, "Public Remains Divided over the Patriot Act" (February 15, 2011), at **pewre-search.org/pubs/1893/poll-patriot-act-renewal**.

80. Anthony Lewis, *Freedom for the Thought That We Hate* (New York: Basic Books, 2008), ix.

81. *Brandenburg v. Ohio,* 395 U.S. 444, 445 (1969).

82. *Ibid.*, at 447.

83. Eric Lichtblau, "Scholar Is Given Life Sentence in 'Virginia Jihad' Case," *New York Times* (July 14, 2005), A21.

84. Department of Homeland Security, "Country Reports on Terrorism 2005," at **www. state.gov/documents/organization/ 65466.pdf**.

85. 18 U.S.C. Sections 2384 and 2385 (2000).

86. Quoted in Richard B. Schmitt, "Acquittal in Internet Terrorism Case Is a Defeat for the Patriot Act," *Los Angeles Times* (June 11, 2004), 20.

87. *INS v. Delgado,* 466 U.S. 215 (1983).

88. Quoted in Philip Shenon, "Senate Report on Pre-9/11 Failure Tells of Bungling at FBI," *New York Times* (August 28, 2002), A14.

89. Pub. L. No. 107-56, Section 201-2-2, 115 Stat. 272, 278 (2001).

90. 50 U.S.C. Section 1803 (2000).

91. Patriot Act, Section 203(d)(1), 115 Stat. 272, 280 (2001).

92. Patriot Act, Section 206, amending Section 105(c)(2)(B) of the Foreign Intelligence Surveillance Act.

93. Patriot Act, Section 213.

94. FISA Amendments Act of 2008, Pub. L. No. 110-261, 122 Stat. 2436 (2008).

95. Eric Lichtblau, "Senate Approves Bill to Broaden Wiretap Powers," *New York Times* (July 10, 2008), A1.

96. Quoted in Jim Puzzanghera, "TSA Won't Back Off on Pat-Downs," *Los Angeles Times* (November 22, 2010), A8.

97. Quoted in David G. Savage, "Scanners Pit Privacy against Security," *Los Angeles Times* (January 13, 2010), 11.

98. "Anti-Muslim Sentiments Fairly Commonplace," *Gallup Poll* (August 10, 2006), at **www.gallup.com/poll/24073/ antimuslim-sentiments-fairly- commonplace.aspx**.

99. Charlie Savage, "Wider Authority for FBI Agents Stirs Concerns," *New York Times* (October 29, 2009), A1.

100. Quoted in Samantha Henry, "Some Muslims Rethink Close Ties to Law Enforcement," *Associated Press* (May 4, 2009).

101. *Wong Wing v. United States,* 163 U.S. 228 (1896).

102. 66 *Federal Register* 48334 (September 20, 2001).

103. Richard M. Pious, *The War on Terrorism and the Rule of Law* (Los Angeles: Roxbury Publishing Co., 2006), 165–166.

104. Michael Greenberger, "You Ain't Seen Nothin' Yet: The Inevitable Post-Hamdan Conflict between the Supreme Court and the Political Branches," *Maryland Law Review* 66 (2007), 805, 807.

105. "One in 7 Who Leave Guantanamo Involved in Terrorism," *Reuters* (May 26, 2009).

106. Brian Bennett, "Former Detainees Now Plot in Yeman," *Los Angeles Times* (November 2, 2010), A1.

107. Military Commission Act of 2009, Pub. L. No. 111-84, Sections 1801–1807, 123 Stat. 2190 (2009).

108. Charlie Savage, "U.S. Prepares to Lift Ban on Guantanamo Cases," *New York Times* (January 20, 2011), A1.

109. David Johnston, "At a Secret Interrogation, Dispute Flared over Tactics," *New York Times* (September 10, 2006), A1.

110. 18 U.S.C. Section 2340A (1994).

111. Memorandum from Donald Rumsfeld, Secretary of Defense, U.S. Department of Defense to Commander, U.S. Southern Command, "Counter-resistance Techniques" (January 15, 2003).

112. Major General George R. Fay, "AR 15-6 Investigation of the Abu Ghraib Detention Facility and 205th Military Intelligence Brigade 8 (2004)," at **news.findlaw.com/ hdocs/docs/dod/fay82504rpt.pdf**.

113. Quoted in Matt Apuzzo and Adam Goldman, "Bin Laden Death Reignites Debate over CIA Tactics," *Associated Press* (May 7, 2011).

114. Quoted in "Do We Use Torture?" *Los Angeles Times* (June 18, 2007), 16.

CHAPTER 17

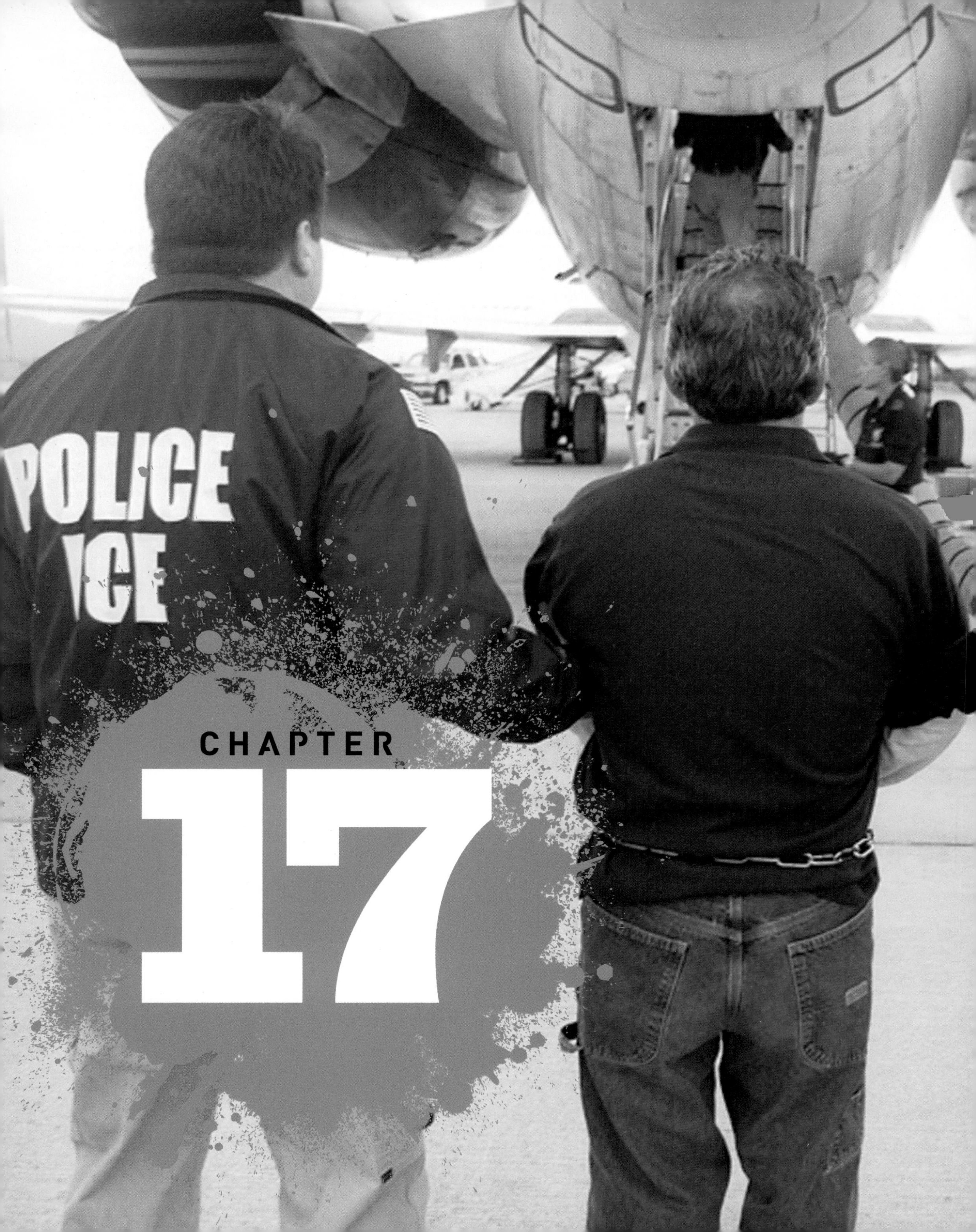

AP Photo/ICE

Today's Challenges:

Immigration, Cyber Crime, and White-Collar Crime

LEARNING OBJECTIVES

After reading this chapter, you should be able to . . .

LO 1   Explain the difference between a temporary visa and a green card.

LO 2   Indicate how local and federal law enforcement agencies cooperate under the Secure Communities program.

LO 3   Distinguish cyber crime from "traditional" crime.

LO 4   Describe the three following forms of malware: (a) botnets, (b) worms, and (c) viruses.

LO 5   Explain how the Internet has contributed to piracy of intellectual property.

LO 6   Outline the three major reasons why the Internet is conducive to the dissemination of child pornography.

LO 7   Indicate some of the ways that white-collar crime is different from violent or property crime.

LO 8   Explain the concept of corporate violence.

The eight learning objectives labeled LO 1 through LO 8 are designed to help improve your understanding of the chapter.

A LONG WAY FROM HOME

On April 14, 2010, Antonio Perez was taking a break from his day job at a Webcrafters in Madison, Wisconsin, when four young men approached him. "Are you C-14?" one of them asked, referring to the name of a local street gang. "Yes," Perez answered. In fact, he had founded the Madison branch of C-14, whose name comes from the intersection of two streets in Los Angeles. A few minutes later, Perez was dead, shot by Ivan Mateo-Lozenzo, who, like the other three men, was a member of the rival South Side Carnales gang.

Madison police quickly arrested five people in connection with Perez's murder. Mateo-Lozenzo managed to escape, probably to his native Mexico, but local law enforcement authorities had other worries. C-14 members were reportedly stockpiling weapons in preparation for retaliatory strikes against the South Side Carnales. "Family members, babies, were not off limits," said Captain James Wheeler of the Madison Police Department. To head off a full-scale gang war, the department's antigang unit, made up of only six officers, was going to need outside help.

Several months after Perez's death, help did come—from the federal government. In August, five teams of U.S. Immigration and Customs Enforcement (ICE) agents, working with Madison police, took eleven "key" C-14 gang members into custody. Even though five of the eleven detainees had prior convictions for crimes including carrying a concealed weapon and theft, it was unlikely that any of them would be tried in an American criminal court or spend time in an American jail or prison. None of the C-14 gang members was a U.S. citizen. Indeed, none had permission to be in the United States. Consequently, ICE would interview and fingerprint them, and then return them to their home country of Mexico.

Karen Giron-Cruz, an illegal immigrant, is one of five people charged with murdering Antonio Perez as part of a gang dispute in Madison, Wisconsin. Steve Apps/*Wisconsin State Journal*

The C-14 situation was not the first time the Madison police had asked federal agents to intervene in a local gang matter. Two years before Antonio Perez's death, the South Side Locos had made a death threat against detective George Chavez, then a member of the city's antigang unit. In response, local law enforcement and ICE joined forces to dismantle the gang. "It got pretty hairy there for a while," remembers Madison police officer Lester Moore,[1] but within six months the operation had succeeded, in large part because of ICE's ability to arrest gang members for immigration law violations.

As you learned in Chapter 15, street gangs have plagued the United States for most of the nation's history. Only recently, however, have law enforcement authorities turned to immigration law as a tool to disrupt gang activity and reduce gang-related crime. In this final chapter of this textbook, we will address several "hot topics" in the field, starting with the increasingly blurred—and controversial—distinction between immigration law and criminal law. Next, we will examine the various types of crimes that take place in cyberspace and the efforts of law enforcement agencies to combat them. Finally, we will discuss a form of criminal activity that has received part of the blame for the United States' worst economic downturn since the Great Depression of the 1930s—white-collar crime.

THE CRIMINALIZATION OF IMMIGRATION LAW

At the outset, it is important to understand two crucial aspects of immigration law:

1. It is a *civil* regulatory system. Violations of immigration law are civil infractions, not criminal infractions. America's criminal justice and immigration systems are separate entities.

2. The U.S. Constitution gives the power to admit, exclude, or expel non-U.S. citizens to the *federal* government, not the state governments.[2]

Historically, then, immigration law has generally been considered a civil and federal matter. In recent decades, however, a process labeled "crimmigration" by some observers has drastically changed the immigration landscape. According to its critics, this process has resulted in a hybrid system in which non-U.S. citizen civil law violators are treated as criminals while state and local law enforcement officers increasingly take on immigration law enforcement responsibilities.[3] For supporters of crimmigration measures, such developments are not only welcome but also long overdue.

Teaching Tip: In a short reaction paper, have students ponder the idea of "crimmigration." How is this new trend inconsistent with the traditional U.S. response to illegal immigration?

IMMIGRATION LAW BASICS

Fundamentally, immigration law acts as a screening process. It determines which non-U.S. citizens may come into this country, how long they can stay, and when they must leave. People violate immigration law in two ways: by entering the United States without proper authorization from the federal government or by staying in the country after that authorization becomes invalid.

VISA BASICS An **alien** is someone who is not a citizen of the country in which he or she is located. As we saw in the previous chapter, proper authorization for an alien to enter the United States usually comes in the form of a *visa*. The most common types of visas allow aliens to visit this country for purposes of employment, tourism, education, or medical treatment. Such visas are *temporary* and allow only a limited stay in the United States. When a visa expires, the non-U.S. citizen must either renew it or leave the country immediately. (As the feature *Anti-Terrorism in Action—Illegal Presence* on the following page shows, certain loopholes in the visa system have become a national security concern.)

LO 1

Nontemporary visas are also available to certain foreign citizens who want to live in the United States on a permanent basis. Most of those who succeed in obtaining a nontemporary visa—known as a **green card** even though the document itself is no longer green—do so with the help of a U.S. citizen family member or an American employer. Green card holders, or **permanent residents,** enjoy many of the same rights as U.S. citizens to live and work in this country. Permanent residents are still aliens, however, and must carry their green cards with them at all times.[4] Furthermore, they are subject to *removal* from the United States if they violate the terms of their visas.

Alien A person who is not a citizen of the country in which he or she is found and therefore does not enjoy the same rights as a citizen of that country.

Green Card A document—no longer green—that indicates the holder's status as a lawful permanent resident of the United States.

Permanent Resident An alien who has been granted permission by the U.S. government to live and work in the United States on a permanent basis.

Removal The process used by the federal government to expel an alien from the United States.

REMOVAL BASICS As we noted in Chapter 16, hundreds of thousands of non-U.S. citizens enter the United States each year without first obtaining a visa, mostly by crossing the U.S. border with Mexico. By definition, these aliens are inadmissible (illegal) and can be removed by American immigration authorities at any time. **Removal** is a legal proceeding in which the U.S. government formally declares that a legal or illegal alien has violated immigration law and therefore does not enjoy the

Teaching Tip: Ask students to explain the differences between a temporary visa, a green card, and U.S. citizenship. Under what circumstances is an individual subject to removal? (LO 1)

right to stay in the United States. Generally, removal results in the alien being returned to his or her home country.

The mere presence of an illegal alien on U.S. soil, if detected by immigration authorities, will almost always lead to his or her removal. In contrast, a permanent resident must have violated immigration law in a specific way to become eligible for deportation, another form of removal. Examples of such violations include lying to a federal immigration agent or encouraging another alien to enter the United States illegally. Criminal convictions also put permanent residents in danger of being removed.[5] Indeed, of the nearly 400,000 aliens removed by ICE in 2010, about 35 percent had criminal convictions.[6] Keep in mind that removal proceedings are separate from the criminal court proceedings you have been studying in this textbook. When an alien faces removal, she or he is involved in a civil process with its own courtrooms, judges, and opportunities for appeal.

ANTI-TERRORISM IN ACTION

ILLEGAL PRESENCE

The September 11 plot exposed a weakness in America's homeland defenses: an inability to track foreigners who fail to conform to the terms of their visas and are therefore illegally present in the United States. For example, Nawaf Alhazmi, one of the hijackers and a Saudi Arabian citizen, had entered the country on a B-2 tourist visa on January 15, 2000. Because B-2 visas are valid for only six months, he had already been in the country illegally for more than a year when the attacks occurred. Another hijacker, Saudi Arabian Hani Hanjour, was given permission to attend classes at a language center in Oakland, California, on an F-1 student visa in December 2000. By failing to show up for his classes, he also had annulled his permission to be in the United States. In total, five of the hijackers had violated their visas—and were therefore eligible for removal from the country—before the attacks occurred.

To remedy this situation, the Department of Homeland Security created the United States Visitor and Immigrant Status Indicator Technology (US-VISIT) program. Under US-VISIT, which started in 2004, most foreigners entering the United States on visas are subject to fingerprinting and a facial scan using digital photography. Their names are also checked against criminal records and watch lists for suspected terrorists. Although the program has been effective in recording the entry of foreigners, it has been less successful in following their movements once in the United States. Furthermore, without the cooperation of the visitor, US-VISIT is unable to confirm when, or if, she or he has left the country. As

a result, about 200,000 non-U.S. citizens intentionally overstay their visas each year.

Argus/Shutterstock

Unwelcome Visitor

This security loophole was exposed again several years ago, when federal authorities arrested Hosam Maher Husein Smadi for plotting to bomb a Texas skyscraper. Smadi, a nineteen-year-old

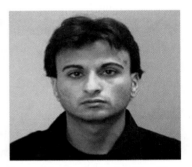

According to federal authorities, Hosam Maher Husein Smadi planned to destroy a skyscraper in Dallas, Texas.
AP Photo/Dallas County Sheriff

Jordanian citizen, had entered the United States on a six-month tourist visa. He broke the terms of his visa several times, first by enrolling in high school and then by getting a job. Finally, a year after his visa expired, the Federal Bureau of Investigation detained Smadi for plotting to blow up the Fountain Palace office building in downtown Dallas. After Smadi's arrest, one expert pointed out that aliens who become radicalized after entering the United States are the responsibility of local and federal law enforcement, adding, "You can't ask the immigration system to do everything."

FOR CRITICAL ANALYSIS Why do you think the airline industry has refused the federal government's requests to photograph and fingerprint foreigners as they depart the United States? How might this procedure help immigration officials track visa holders?

ENFORCING IMMIGRATION LAW

About 11.2 million illegal aliens are living in the United States, according to research conducted by the nonpartisan Pew Hispanic Center.[7] The vast majority of these aliens are law-abiding individuals who have come to this country for no other reason than to make a better life for themselves and their families. Nevertheless, some aliens— both legal and illegal—do commit crimes, and American law enforcement has developed strategies to combat this criminal behavior. Increasingly, these strategies have focused on a particular vulnerability of criminal illegal aliens: their immigrant status.

In March 2011, ICE agents and local law enforcement officers teamed up as part of Project Southern Tempest. The operation resulted in the arrests of more than 400 non-U.S. citizen gang members throughout the nation. What advantages do ICE agents have when apprehending gang members who are in the country illegally?
Belmarie Campos/Senior Forensic Photographer/Medical Examiner Dept./ Miami-Dade County/ICE

DIFFERENT STANDARDS In matters of criminal justice, the U.S. Constitution does not differentiate on the basis of citizenship. Before, during, and after a criminal trial, both U.S. citizens and non-U.S. citizens are protected by the Fourth, Fifth, and Sixth Amendments.[8] This "equality principle" does not apply to the enforcement of immigration law, however. For example, an ICE agent can arrest a person for violating immigration law even if no probable cause exists. The agent needs to have only an "articulable," or explainable, suspicion of a violation for the arrest to be valid.[9] Immigration law violators also have no right to receive the *Miranda* warning before custodial interrogations and have no right to an attorney when appearing before an immigration judge.[10]

Furthermore, an alien can face criminal and immigration charges at the same time. In the last chapter, we reviewed the case of Sami Omar Al-Hussayen, the Saudi Arabian citizen and University of Idaho student who was acquitted of providing material support to terrorists (see page 563). Before Al-Hussayen's acquittal, an immigration judge ordered that he be deported because he had accepted payment for computer work in violation of the terms of his student visa. Though Al-Hussayen avoided prison time, he was forced to return to Saudi Arabia after his trial. Thus, the immigration system sometimes acts as a "safety valve" for its more unpredictable criminal justice counterpart.

Teaching Tip: Immigration law is quite different from criminal law. Invite an immigration attorney to visit the classroom and discuss which elements of due process apply when an individual faces immigration charges.

OPERATION COMMUNITY SHIELD As we have seen, the probable cause requirement places significant restrictions on law enforcement's ability to arrest suspects (see pages 218–219). Facing no such restraints when it comes to immigration law, federal agents can prove valuable partners for their counterparts in local law enforcement. The benefits of such a partnership are evident in Operation Community Shield, launched in 2005 by ICE to "target violent transnational street gangs" by arresting and removing alien gang members.[11] The mechanics of Operation Community Shield are fairly simple. First, local police officers identify street gang members who are also in the country illegally. Then, ICE agents use immigration law to remove these gang members, a process that, as we have noted, is much quicker and easier than criminal prosecution.

> **"We will not tolerate those who come [to the United States] to take to a life of crime."**
>
> —**John Morton,** director, U.S. Immigration and Customs Enforcement

In the opening to this chapter, we saw how Madison (Wisconsin) police officers and ICE agents combined forces under Operation Community Shield to dismantle the local branch of the C-14 gang. Overall, in its first five years, Operation Community Shield resulted in the arrest of more than 17,500 gang members.[12] Although about 70 percent of

FIGURE 17.1 Criminal History of Suspects Arrested under Operation Community Shield

During the first two years of Operation Community Shield, 40 percent of the suspects arrested by U.S. Immigration and Customs Enforcement agents had committed violent crimes or weapons-related offenses.

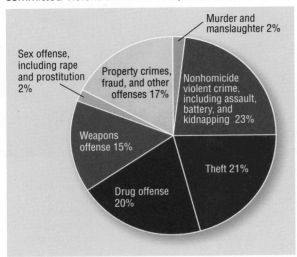

- Murder and manslaughter 2%
- Sex offense, including rape and prostitution 2%
- Property crimes, fraud, and other offenses 17%
- Nonhomicide violent crime, including assault, battery, and kidnapping 23%
- Weapons offense 15%
- Theft 21%
- Drug offense 20%

Source: Jon Freere and Jessica Vaughan, "Taking Back the Streets: ICE and Local Law Enforcement Target Immigrant Gangs," Center for Immigration Studies, September 2008, at **www.cis.org/immigrantgangs**.

Detainer A document that gives U.S. Immigration and Customs Enforcement custody of an immigration law violator following the disposition of that person's case by the criminal justice system.

these aliens were ultimately removed because of immigration law violations,[13] a significant number of them had violent criminal histories, as Figure 17.1 alongside shows.

SECURE COMMUNITIES The most ambitious cooperative effort between the federal government and state and local law enforcement is the Secure Communities initiative. Under this program, started in 2008, information on every suspect arrested by state and local police officers is transmitted electronically to the Department of Homeland Security (DHS) during the booking process. If this instant background check shows that the suspect has a history of criminal or immigration law violations that makes him or her eligible for removal, ICE will issue a **detainer.** This document allows ICE to take custody of the suspect at the conclusion of his or her contact with the criminal justice system, usually after the suspect has been released by police or has completed a jail or prison sentence.

LO 2

In July 2010, for example, the Baton Rouge Police Department arrested an individual for burglary and possession of stolen property. A Secure Communities check revealed that he had previously been removed from the United States for a drug conviction and was therefore in the country illegally. Consequently, ICE issued a detainer, ensuring that federal agents would take this defendant into custody at some point.[14] As of February 2011, just over a thousand state and local law enforcement agencies had access to Secure Communities software, and the program had resulted in the removal of about 58,000 aliens.[15]

CJ & TECHNOLOGY — Immigration Biometrics

James Tourtellotte/Department of Homeland Security/cbp.gov

Each year, state and local law enforcement officers arrest approximately 1 million non-U.S. citizens who may be eligible for removal. Traditionally, it has been very difficult to identify these aliens and determine their immigration status and possible criminal backgrounds. Police have had to rely on biographical information such as name and date of birth, which they would submit to ICE's Law Enforcement Support Center (LESC). Even if this biographical information was correct—and often it was not—LESC personnel would have to go through the complicated and lengthy process of manually checking it against the agency's records. Today, however, biometrics—which we first encountered in Chapter 1 of this textbook (see page 23)—have transformed these background checks. Using fingerprint biometrics, state and local police have almost instant access to the criminal history (via the Federal Bureau of Investigation) and immigration records (via the DHS) of every suspect they book.

THINKING ABOUT IMMIGRATION BIOMETRICS

This process applies to all persons arrested and booked, not just those suspected of being illegal aliens. Consequently, according to federal authorities, it protects against the possibility of racial profiling by local police officers, first discussed in Chapter 7 (see pages 220–221) and addressed again below. Do you agree with this assessment? Why or why not?

IMMIGRATION AND STATE LAW

Partnerships such as those encouraged by Operation Community Shield and Secure Communities have not received universal approval. Critics point out that such programs give law enforcement agents an incentive to arrest suspected aliens on minor charges, thereby exposing them to removal even if they are not violent criminals. For example, after authorities in Irving, Texas, began checking the immigration status of jail inmates, local police began arresting Hispanics for petty misdemeanor offenses at a significantly higher rate than whites or African Americans.[16] In New York and New Jersey, past Operation Community Shield initiatives seem to have targeted immigration law violators to a much greater extent than violent criminals.[17] For similar reasons, Hans Meyer of the Colorado Immigration Rights Coalition called Secure Communities an "overbroad dragnet that will end up destroying communities and families."[18]

Given that Hispanics make up the majority of both legal and illegal immigrants in the United States, this demographic has received the most attention when it comes to the criminalization of immigration law. As we noted in Chapter 13, Hispanics are the fastest growing group among federal inmates, mostly as a result of immigration offenses.[19] On the state level, recent attempts to criminalize immigration have spurred debate and outrage far beyond the borders of the jurisdictions involved.

LEGISLATIVE ACTION Approximately half of all illegal border crossings in this country take place along Arizona's border with Mexico.[20] As a result, Arizona has a significant illegal alien population. In response to a perceived lack of federal attention to this problem, in 2010 Governor Jan Brewer signed legislation to "protect the state of Arizona."[21] Known as S.B. 1070, this law, among other things:

- Requires state and local police officers to check the immigration status of a person they have stopped for other reasons. This check should occur only when "there exists a reasonable suspicion that the suspect is an alien and is unlawfully present."
- Makes the failure of a non-U.S. citizen to carry federally issued documentation such as a green card or a visa a state criminal offense.
- Creates a new state crime for illegal immigrants trying to find employment.[22]

Following the passage of S.B. 1070, a number of other state legislatures took similar steps, with Alabama, Georgia, and New Mexico passing bills like Arizona's.[23]

THE "REASONABLE SUSPICION" CONTROVERSY As we saw in Chapter 7, many observers reacted harshly to Arizona's S.B. 1070. Critics of the law believe that, combined with the police's ability to make pretextual stops, also discussed in Chapter 7, S.B. 1070 and the other state laws will result in increased incidents of racial profiling. For example, in an interview with the Georgia American Civil Liberties Union, a Hispanic

Critical Thinking Skill Development: Have students respond to "Questions for Critical Analysis" number two on page 602, in which they consider Alabama's 2011 immigration control bill.

Technology Tip: Have the students visit the Arizona legislature online to read the contents of S.B. 1070 at **www.azleg.gov/legtext/49leg/2r/summary/s.1070pshs.doc.htm**.

A Mexican citizen tries to enter the United States illegally by climbing over a wall on Arizona's border with Mexico. Describe the Arizona legislature's legal response to the presence of illegal immigrants within state borders.
REUTERS/Alonso Castillo

woman said she had been pulled over by a police officer for having an expired license plate tag. When she was not able to present a driver's license, the officer arrested her and passed her immigration information to the federal government. The woman claimed that she was targeted because of her skin color and that a white driver would not have attracted law enforcement attention for such a petty initial offense.[24]

What factors, besides skin color, provide "reasonable suspicion" that a person is violating immigration law? "We know how to determine whether these guys are illegal," insists one Arizona law enforcement officer. "The way the situation looks, how they are dressed, where they are coming from."[25] Still, the perception that local police officers, not trained in the fine points of immigration law, will inevitably rely on race and ethnicity in determining "reasonable suspicion" has dominated public debate over S.B. 1070. (In the *CJ in Action* feature at the end of this chapter, we will discuss whether local police departments can effectively carry out duties related to immigration law.)

JUDICIAL DECISIONS From our discussion of pretextual stops in Chapter 7, we know that the police officer's actions regarding the Hispanic woman in Georgia described above were constitutional. As long as the reason for the initial stop—the expired tags—was supported by probable cause, the officer's "true" motivation in making the stop is not relevant.[26] Furthermore, Arizona's S.B. 1070 and the other state laws prohibit stopping a suspect solely on the basis of race and ethnicity.

Consequently, when a federal judge issued an *injunction* against the more controversial aspects of S.B. 1070 in July 2010, keeping them from going into effect, she did not do so because of concerns over racial profiling. Instead, the judge decided that Arizona's immigration policy was in conflict with federal immigration regulation.[27] Remember that when federal law and state law are in conflict, federal law takes precedence. Arizona authorities contested the judge's ruling, and in all likelihood, the fate of these controversial state immigration laws will ultimately be decided by the United States Supreme Court.

SELFASSESSMENT

Fill in the blanks and check your answers on page 601.

Immigration violations are a matter of _____, rather than criminal, law, and such violations have traditionally come under the jurisdiction of the _____ government, not the states. When the holder of a green card, also known as a _____ resident, violates immigration law, then he or she is subject to _____. Arizona and several other states recently passed laws requiring state and local police officers to check the _____ status of a crime suspect if the officer has a _____ _____ that the suspect is in the United States illegally.

CYBER CRIME

On September 19, 2010, Dharun Ravi set up a hidden Webcam in his Rutgers University dorm room. He then joined his friend Molly Wei in her room, and the pair allegedly watched a live stream of Tyler Clementi, Ravi's roommate, having a romantic encounter with another man. As was briefly mentioned in Chapter 15, Clementi was so distressed by the incident that, three days later, he jumped to his death from the George Washington Bridge. In the eyes of many, the blame for Clementi's suicide belonged not just to Ravi and Wie but to a third "player" as well—the Internet. "Just as an assault rifle facilitates mass murder," wrote one commentator, "the Internet facilitates mass character assassination."[28]

At the least, the Internet provided Ravi and Wei with both the means to illegally record Clementi's private behavior and a false sense of security that they would not be caught doing so. Access and anonymity are two of the hallmarks of this technology, which has transformed daily life in the twenty-first century. Nearly three-fourths of all American households now own a computer, and the proliferation of handheld Internet devices has made it possible to be online at almost any time or "place." Furthermore, nearly every business in today's economy relies on computers to conduct its daily affairs and to provide consumers with easy access to its products and services. In short, the Internet has become a place where large numbers of people interact socially and commercially. As in any such environment, wrongdoing has an opportunity to flourish.

COMPUTER CRIME AND THE INTERNET

The U.S. Department of Justice broadly defines **computer crime** as "any violation of criminal law that involves a knowledge of computer technology for [its] perpetration, investigation, or prosecution."[29] More specifically, computer crimes can be divided into three categories, according to the computer's role in the particular criminal act:[30]

1. The computer is the *object* of a crime, such as when the computer itself or its software is stolen.
2. The computer is the *subject* of a crime, just as a house is the subject of a burglary. This type of computer crime occurs, for example, when someone "breaks into" a computer to steal personal information such as a credit-card number.
3. The computer is the *instrument* of a crime, as when Dharun Ravi and Molly Wei used a computer to invade Tyler Clementi's privacy.

In this chapter, we will be using a broader term, **cyber crime**, to describe any criminal activity occurring via a computer in the virtual community of the Internet. It is very difficult, if not impossible, to determine how much cyber crime actually takes place. Often, people never know that they have been the victims of this type of criminal activity. Furthermore, businesses sometimes fail to report such crimes for fear of losing customer confidence. Nonetheless, in 2010, the Internet Crime Complaint Center (IC3), operated as a partnership between the Federal Bureau of Investigation (FBI) and the National White Collar Crime Center, received more than 300,000 complaints.[31] Furthermore, the United States appears to have gained the unwanted distinction of being the world's leader in cyber crime: 19 percent of all global computer attacks originate in this country, and America is the target of nearly one-quarter of all illegal Internet activity.[32]

CYBER CRIMES AGAINST PERSONS AND PROPERTY

LO 3

Most cyber crimes are not "new" crimes. Rather, they are existing crimes in which the Internet is the instrument of wrongdoing. In March

"You know, you can do this just as easily online."

P.C. Vey/Conde Nast Publications/www.cartoonbank.com

Discussion Tip: Have students discuss the differences between traditional crime and cyber crime. What are the challenges of combating crimes that occur via the Internet? (LO 3)

Computer Crime Any wrongful act that is directed against computers and computer parts or that involves wrongful use or abuse of computers or software.

Cyber Crime A crime that occurs online, in the virtual community of the Internet, as opposed to in the physical world.

2010, for example, a religious fanatic named Norman Leboon posted a YouTube video in which he threatened to kill U.S. congressman Eric Cantor, a Republican from Virginia, and Cantor's family. Federal authorities charged Leboon with communicating threats in interstate commerce, the same charge that would have been filed if Leboon had used a telephone or even the mail to make his menacing remarks.

The challenge for law enforcement is to apply traditional laws, which were designed to protect persons from physical harm or to safeguard their physical property, to crimes committed in cyberspace. This challenge is made all the greater by two aspects of the Internet that may aid the perpetrators of cyber crimes—the anonymity it provides and the ease with which large amounts of information may be transferred quickly. Here, we look at several types of activity that constitute "updated" crimes against persons and property—online consumer fraud, cyber theft, and cyberstalking.

CYBER CONSUMER FRAUD The expanding world of e-commerce has created many benefits for consumers. It has also led to some challenging problems, including fraud conducted via the Internet. In general, fraud is any misrepresentation knowingly made with the intention of deceiving another person. Furthermore, the victim must reasonably rely on the fraudulent information to her or his detriment. Cyber fraud, then, is fraud committed over the Internet. Scams that were once conducted solely by mail or phone can now be found online, and new technology has led to increasingly more creative ways to commit fraud. Several years ago, for example, online advertisements featuring adorable photos of "free" English bulldog puppies began appearing on the Internet. A number of respondents paid close to $1,000 in "shipping fees" (from West Africa), "customs costs," "health insurance," and other bogus charges before realizing that no puppy would be forthcoming.

As you can see in Figure 17.2 below, two widely reported forms of cyber crime are *online retail fraud* and *online auction fraud*. In the simplest form of online retail fraud, consumers order and pay for items that are never delivered. Online auction fraud is also fairly straightforward. A person puts up an item for auction, on either a legitimate or a fake auction site, and then refuses to send the product after receiving payment. As a variation, the wrongdoer may send the purchaser a forgery or an item that is worth less than the one offered in the auction. Several years ago, for example, the FBI broke up an international crime organization that sold about $5 million worth of fake paintings by well-known artists including Andy Warhol and Marc Chagall, mostly on eBay.[33]

CYBER THEFT In cyberspace, thieves are not subject to the physical limitations of the "real" world. A thief can steal data stored in a networked computer with network access from anywhere on the globe. Only the speed of the connection and the thief's computer equipment limit the quantity of data that can be stolen.

Identity Theft This freedom from physical limitations has led to a marked increase in identity theft, which occurs when the wrongdoer steals a form of identification—such as a name, date of birth, or Social Security number—and uses the information to access the victim's financial resources. In 2010, about 8 million Americans reported being victims of identity theft.[34]

This crime existed to a certain extent before the widespread use of the Internet. Thieves would "steal" calling-card numbers by watching

Cyber Fraud Any misrepresentation knowingly made over the Internet with the intention of deceiving another and on which a reasonable person would and does rely to his or her detriment.

Identity Theft The theft of personal information, such as a person's name, driver's license number, or Social Security number.

FIGURE 17.2 **Criminal Activities Online**
In 2010, the Internet Crime Complaint Center (IC3) received about 303,000 complaints of online criminal behavior. This graph shows the percentage breakdown of the complaints that the IC3 considered serious enough to refer to law enforcement.

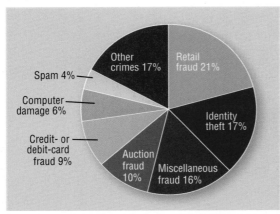

Other crimes 17%
Retail fraud 21%
Spam 4%
Computer damage 6%
Credit- or debit-card fraud 9%
Auction fraud 10%
Miscellaneous fraud 16%
Identity theft 17%

Source: Internet Crime Complaint Center, *IC3 2010 Internet Crime Report* (Glen Allen, VA: National White Collar Crime Center, 2011), Table 4, page 9.

people using public telephones, or they would rifle through garbage to find bank account or credit-card numbers. The identity thief would then use the calling-card or credit-card number or withdraw funds from the victim's account until the theft was discovered.

The Internet has provided even easier access to personal data. Frequent Web surfers surrender a wealth of information about themselves without knowing it. Many Web sites use "cookies" to collect data on those who visit their sites. The data can include the areas of the site the user visits and the links the user clicks on. Furthermore, Web browsers often store information such as the consumer's name and e-mail address. Finally, every time a purchase is made online, the item is linked to the purchaser's name, allowing Web retailers to amass a database of who is buying what. (See Figure 17.3 below for information on how to avoid being the target of identity theft.)

Discussion Tip: Ask students to discuss online fraud. Why is it difficult to prevent and control this form of cyber crime? (LO 3)

Phishing A distinct form of identity theft known as phishing has added a different wrinkle to the identity theft. In a phishing attack, the perpetrators "fish" for financial data and passwords from consumers by posing as a legitimate business such as a bank or credit-card company. The "phisher" sends an e-mail asking the recipient to "update" or "confirm" vital information, often with the threat that an account or some other service will be discontinued if the information is not provided. Once the unsuspecting target enters the information, the phisher can use it to masquerade as the person or to drain his or her bank or credit account. In 2010, dozens of companies, including Amazon.com, AT&T, and Zappos.com, were forced to warn consumers that fraudulent e-mails asking for personal and financial information had been sent in the companies' names.

Phishing Sending an unsolicited e-mail that falsely claims to be from a legitimate organization in an attempt to acquire sensitive information such as passwords or credit-card details from the recipient.

Phishing scams have also spread to other areas, such as text messaging and social-networking sites. Nearly 13 percent of all phishing, for example, takes place using Facebook alerts.[35] A new form of this fraud, called spear phishing, is much more difficult

Technology Tip: Have students learn more about cyber crime and the recommended safety practices for computer users from the National Cyber Security Alliance online at **www.staysafeonline.org**.

FIGURE 17.3 Eight Steps toward Preventing Identity Theft

1. **Share information only when necessary.** Make sure that you give out your credit-card number and/or Social Security number only to a trustworthy party that has a legitimate need for this information.

2. **Be cautious about providing identity information in public.** Be on the lookout for "shoulder surfers" when entering account information at an automated teller machine. Also, do not put private information on something that can be easily observed, such as a key chain.

3. **Do not carry unnecessary identification in a purse or wallet.** Thieves can easily gain personal information after stealing these items.

4. **Secure your mailbox.** Thieves can also obtain personal information through stolen mail.

5. **Secure information on your personal computer.** Again, specific information such as credit-card or Social Security numbers should be given out only to legitimate enterprises on the Internet. Also, you should ensure that your hard drive is protected by firewall software that isolates your computer system from the rest of the Internet, thus preventing unauthorized access to personal data.

6. **Shred all nonessential material containing identity information.** Any material with your personal information, such as credit-card statements, canceled checks, bank statements, or even junk mail, should be destroyed before it is placed in the trash.

7. **Remove your name from mailing lists.** This reduces the number of commercial entities with access to your identity information. To opt out of many direct-mail lists, visit the DMAchoice Web site of the Direct Marketing Association at **www.dmachoice.org**.

8. **Review financial statements.** Review all credit-card statements, bank account statements, and other personal financial reports for accuracy. Also, pay attention to billing cycles. A missed bill may mean that the document has been stolen.

Source: Office of the United States Attorney.

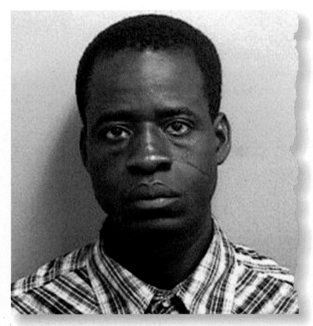

In May 2011, police arrested Patenema Ouedraogo outside the Palm Beach, Florida, home of Serena Williams. Ouedraogo had been following the tennis star for several months, relying on Williams's Twitter updates to learn about her whereabouts. Why would this behavior lead to Ouedraogo being charged with cyberstalking?

Booking Photo/*PacificCoastNews/* Newscom

> ## "Reply to my e-mail or you will die."
>
> —E-mail message sent by a male University of San Diego undergraduate to a female classmate

Cyberstalking The crime of stalking, committed in cyberspace through the use of e-mail, text messages, or another form of electronic communication.

Critical Thinking Skill Development: Have students respond to "Questions for Critical Analysis" number four on page 602, in which they consider the difficulties in prosecuting cyberstalking cases across multiple jurisdictions.

to detect because the messages seem to have come from co-workers, friends, or family workers. "It's a really nasty tactic because it's so personalized," explains security expert Bruce Schneier. "It's an e-mail from your mother saying she needs your Social Security number for the will she's doing."[36]

CYBER AGGRESSION AND THE NEW MEDIA Megan Meier's suicide was a watershed moment in how many people perceived the dangers lurking on the Internet. Several years ago, Meier killed herself after being taunted online by a neighbor's mother pretending to be a teenage boy. Even though the mother, Lori Drew, was eventually acquitted of criminal charges, public outrage surrounding the case led nearly twenty states to pass new laws criminalizing aggressive behavior perpetrated through technology. For the most part, these laws focus on *cyberbullying,* which we discussed in the context of school crime in Chapter 15 (see pages 512–513) and *cyberstalking.* Both of these activities are examples of relatively common offline behavior that has been exacerbated by e-mail, social networking, instant and text messaging, and the far reach of the Internet.

In 2009, the U.S. Department of Justice released a landmark study that shed light on the high incidence of stalking in the United States. Defined as a "credible threat" that puts a person in reasonable fear for her or his safety or the safety of the person's immediate family, stalking, according to the study, affects approximately 3.4 million Americans each year.[37] About one in four of these victims experiences a form of cyberstalking, in which the perpetrator uses e-mail, text messages, or some other form of electronic communication to carry out his or her harassment.[38] Even before Megan Meier's suicide, forty-five states and the federal government had legislation to combat cyberstalking.

The only limitations on a cyberstalker's methods are computer savvy and imagination. Social-networking sites such as Facebook and Google Plus have become particularly tempting for online stalkers. In 2010, for example, Travis Allen Davis of New Castle, Indiana, created a fake Facebook profile with the name of an ex-girlfriend. Using this falsified account, Davis, pretending to be the ex-girlfriend, contacted *another* of his ex-girlfriends and threatened to post images of the second girlfriend having sex with Davis online if she did not resume her relationship with him. Davis was charged with stalking, among other crimes. In 2011, Mitchell Hill was arrested and charged with extortion and video voyeurism for using a fake Facebook identity to pressure Louisiana State University sorority pledges to send him nude pictures of themselves over the Internet.

CYBER CRIMES IN THE BUSINESS WORLD

Just as cyberspace can be a dangerous place for consumers, it presents a number of hazards for businesses that wish to offer their services on the Internet. The same circumstances that enable companies to reach a wide number of consumers also leave them vulnerable to cyber crime. For example, in 2011 Rogelio Hackett, Jr., of Lithonia, Georgia, pleaded guilty to fraud and identity theft for stealing more than 675,000 credit-card accounts from online businesses. Hackett would sell these accounts for as little as $20 to third parties, who used them to make fraudulent charges of more than $36 million.

HACKERS Rogelio Hackett, Jr., is a particular type of cyber criminal known as a *hacker*. Hackers are people who use one computer to illegally access another. The danger posed by hackers has increased significantly because of botnets, or networks of computers that have been appropriated by hackers without the knowledge of their owners. A hacker will secretly install a program on thousands, if not millions, of personal computer "robots," or "bots," that allows him or her to forward transmissions to an even larger number of systems. The program attaches itself to the host computer when someone operating the computer opens a fraudulent e-mail.

LO 4

The Zeus Trojan, or Zbot, for example, employs a technique called *keystroke logging* to embed itself in a victim's computer and then record user names and passwords. Using this "banking Trojan," cyberthieves stole $4 million from American bank accounts in 2010.[39] Computer security experts also worry that fake apps containing botnets will find their way onto the increasingly popular smartphones and tablet computers, allowing hackers to harvest personal information from those devices.

MALWARE Programs that create botnets are one of the latest forms of *malware*, a term that refers to any program that is harmful to a computer or, by extension, a computer user. A worm, for example, is a software program that is capable of reproducing itself as it spreads from one computer to the next. A virus, another form of malware, is also able to reproduce itself, but must be attached to an "infested" host file to travel from one computer network to another. Worms and viruses can be programmed to perform a number of functions, such as prompting host computers to continually "crash" and reboot, or otherwise infect the system.

On any given day in 2010, the Koobface worm infected 500,000 computers in the United States, spreading through social-networking outlets such as Facebook, Myspace, and Twitter.[40] The Koobface worm allows its creators to steal usernames and passwords, along with any other personal or financial data entered in the affected computer. The Ponemon Institute, a private research organization, estimates that individual American businesses lose an average of $5.9 million a year because of malware and other cyber crime.[41]

THE SPREAD OF SPAM Businesses and individuals alike are targets of spam, or unsolicited "junk e-mails" that flood virtual mailboxes with advertisements, solicitations, and other messages. Considered relatively harmless in the early days of the Internet, by 2010 nearly 300 billion spam messages were being sent each day, accounting for about 97 percent of all e-mails. Far from being harmless, the unwanted files can wreak havoc with computer systems. Bot networks, described earlier, are responsible for about 90 percent of spam e-mail.[42] To rectify this situation, in 2003 Congress passed the Controlling the Assault of Non-Solicited Pornography and Marketing Act (CAN-SPAM), which requires all unsolicited e-mails to be labeled and to include opt-out provisions and the sender's physical address.[43]

In December 2010, federal authorities in Wisconsin charged Oleg Y. Nikolaenko with violating CAN-SPAM. According to prosecutors, the twenty-three-year-old Russian used botnets to send out one of every three unwanted e-mails in the world. The prosecution and incarceration of spammers such as Nikolaenko seem to be having some effect. According to networking giant Cisco Systems, the amount of spam on the World Wide Web declined for the first time in 2010.[44] Another reason for this trend may be that consumers are turning from personal computers to mobile devices, which are harder—so far—for criminals to target.[45]

PIRATING INTELLECTUAL PROPERTY ONLINE Most people think of wealth in terms of houses, land, cars, stocks, and bonds. Wealth, however, also includes

Hacker A person who uses one computer to break into another.

Botnet A network of computers that have been appropriated without the knowledge of their owners and used to spread harmful programs via the Internet; short for *robot network*.

Worm A computer program that can automatically replicate itself over a network such as the Internet and interfere with the normal use of a computer. A worm does not need to be attached to an existing file to move from one network to another.

Virus A computer program that can replicate itself over a network such as the Internet and interfere with the normal use of a computer. A virus cannot exist as a separate entity and must attach itself to another program to move through a network.

Spam Bulk e-mails, particularly of commercial advertising, sent in large quantities without the consent of the recipient.

Critical Thinking Skill Development: Given the far reaching and potentially severe consequences of hacking, what do students think the penalties should be for this offense?

Teaching Tip: Take a few moments to talk with students about the consequences of malware. While students perceive viruses as being inconvenient, some have a hard time framing this as a criminal issue. (LO 4)

Several years ago, a team of FBI agents arrested Gilberto Sanchez at his New York apartment for uploading an unfinished copy of the film *Wolverine* onto the Internet. After pleading guilty to one count of copyright violation in 2011, Sanchez faced a possible penalty of three years in prison and/or a $250,000 fine. Do you think this punishment would be too harsh? Why or why not?

Librado Romero/*New York Times*/Redux Pictures

Intellectual Property
Property resulting from intellectual, creative processes.

> "The argument that I hear a lot, that 'music should be free,' must then mean that musicians should work for free. Nobody else works for free. Why should musicians?"

—Drummer **Lars Ulrich** of the rock group Metallica, testifying before Congress on the illegal downloading of music

intellectual property, which consists of the products that result from intellectual, creative processes. The government provides various forms of protection for intellectual property, such as copyrights and patents. These protections ensure that a person who writes a book or a song or creates a software program is financially rewarded if that product is sold in the marketplace.

Intellectual property such as books, films, music, and software is vulnerable to "piracy"—the unauthorized copying and use of the property. In the past, copying intellectual products was time consuming, and the quality of the pirated copies was clearly inferior. In today's online world, however, things have changed. Simply clicking a mouse can now reproduce millions of unauthorized copies,

LO 5 and pirated duplicates of copyrighted works obtained via the Internet are often exactly the same as the original, or close to it.

The Business Software Alliance estimates that 29 percent of all business software is pirated, costing software makers more than $59 billion in 2010.[46] In the United States, digital pirates can be prosecuted under the No Electronic Theft Act[47] and the Digital Millennium Copyright Act.[48] In 2005, the entertainment industry celebrated the United States Supreme Court's decision in *MGM Studios v. Grokster.*[49] The ruling provided film and music companies with the ability to file piracy lawsuits against file-sharing Web sites that market software used primarily to illegally download intellectual property. In the near future, however, such "peer-to-peer" transmission may be the least of the entertainment industry's problems. With the advent of Internet TV and "cyberlocker" Web sites that store illegal content for computer viewing on demand, some industry insiders predict that these streaming pirate sites will surpass peer-to-peer use by 2013.[50]

CYBER CRIMES AGAINST THE COMMUNITY

One of the greatest challenges cyberspace presents for law enforcement is how to enforce laws governing activities that are prohibited under certain circumstances but are not always illegal. Such laws generally reflect the will of the community, which recognizes behavior as acceptable under some circumstances and unacceptable under others. Thus, while it is legal in many areas to sell a pornographic video to a fifty-year-old, it is never legal to sell the same item to a fifteen-year-old. Similarly, placing a bet on a football game with a bookmaker in Las Vegas, Nevada, is legal, but doing the same thing with a bookmaker in Cleveland, Ohio, is not. Of course, in cyberspace it is often impossible to know whether the customer buying porn is age fifty or fifteen, or if the person placing the bet is in Las Vegas or Cleveland.

ONLINE PORNOGRAPHY The Internet has been a boon to the pornography industry. Twelve percent of all Web sites have pornographic content, and these sites generate $4.2 billion in revenue a year.[51] Though no general figures are available, the Internet has undoubtedly also been a boon to those who illegally produce and sell material depicting sexually explicit conduct involving a child— child pornography. As we have seen with other cyber crimes, the Internet is conducive to child pornography for a number of reasons:

• *Speed.* The Internet is the fastest means of sending visual

LO 6 material over long distances. Child pornographers can deliver their material faster and more securely online than through regular mail.

- *Security.* Any illegal material that passes through the hands of a mail carrier is inherently in danger of being discovered. This risk is significantly reduced with e-mail. Furthermore, Internet sites that offer child pornography can protect their customers with passwords, which keep random Web surfers (or law enforcement agents) from stumbling on the site of chat rooms.
- *Anonymity.* Obviously, anonymity is the most important protection offered by the Internet for sellers and buyers of child pornography, as it is for any person engaged in illegal behavior in cyberspace.[52]

Because of these three factors, courts and lawmakers have had a difficult time controlling the dissemination of illegal sexual content via the Internet. In 2008, however, the United States Supreme Court upheld a federal law known as the Protect Act. This legislation makes it a crime to exchange "any material or purported material" online that would cause "another to believe" it depicted a minor engaged in sex, whether "actual or simulated."[53] Essentially, this new law gives prosecutors the power they need to arrest purveyors of virtual child pornography, which uses computer images—not real children—to depict sexual acts.

GAMBLING IN CYBERSPACE In general, gambling is illegal. All states have statutes that regulate gambling—defined as any scheme that involves the distribution of property by chance among persons who have risked something of value for the opportunity to receive the property. In some states, certain forms of gambling, such as casino gambling or horse racing, are legal. Many states also have legalized state-operated lotteries, as well as lotteries, such as Bingo, conducted for charitable purposes. A number of states also allow gambling on Native American reservations.

In the past, this mixed bag of gambling laws has presented a legal quandary: Can citizens in a state that does not allow gambling place bets to a Web site located in a state that does? After all, states have no constitutional authority over activities that take place in other states. Complicating the problem was the fact that many Internet gambling sites are located outside the United States in countries where Internet gambling is legal, and no state government has authority over activities that take place in other countries. In 2006, Congress, concerned about money laundering stemming from online gambling, the

Even though it is technically illegal, more than 10 million Americans, including this one, regularly play online poker. What are the arguments for and against allowing states to pass their own online poker laws?
Rich Frishman/Getty Images/*Sports Illustrated*

Discussion Tip: Ask students to consider the topic of online gambling. Is online gambling an illegal activity? Should it be? What issues are involved in the regulation of online gambling Web sites?

problem of addiction, and underage gambling, passed legislation that greatly strengthened efforts to reduce online gaming. The Unlawful Internet Gambling Enforcement Act of 2006 cuts off the money flow to Internet gambling sites by barring the use of electronic payments, such as credit-card transactions, at those sites.[54]

FIGHTING CYBER CRIME

Simply passing a law does not guarantee that the law will be effectively enforced. While the Unlawful Internet Gambling Enforcement Act may reduce visible Internet gambling, few believe that it will stop the practice altogether. "Prohibitions don't work," says Michael Bolcerek, president of the Poker Player's Alliance. "This [legislation] won't stop anything. It will just drive people underground."[55] In fact, despite the efforts of lawmakers and law enforcement, the United States is the largest online betting market in the world, with some $6 billion wagered illegally each year.[56]

As we have already seen in this chapter, the Internet provides an ideal environment for the "underground" of society. With hundreds of millions of users in every corner of the globe, transferring unimaginable amounts of information almost instantaneously, the Internet has proved resistant to government regulation. In addition, although a number of countries have tried to "control" the Internet (see the feature *Comparative Criminal Justice—The Great Firewall of China* on the facing page), the U.S. government has generally adopted a hands-off attitude to better promote the free flow of ideas and encourage the growth of electronic commerce. Thus, in this country cyberspace is, for the most part, unregulated, making efforts to fight cyber crime all the more difficult.

Teaching Tip: If possible, invite a law enforcement agent who specializes in the area of cyber crime to speak to the class. What are the most common cyber crimes? Which cases are considered the highest priority? How does the investigative process differ from that of a traditional criminal offense?

CHALLENGES FOR LAW ENFORCEMENT In trying to describe the complexities of fighting cyber crime, Michael Vatis, former director of the FBI's National Infrastructure Protection Center, imagines a bank robbery during which the police arrive just as "the demand note and fingerprints are vanishing, the security camera is erasing its own images, and the image of the criminal is being erased from the mind of the teller."[57] The difficulty of gathering evidence is just one of the challenges that law enforcement officers face in dealing with cyber crime.

Cyber Forensics Police officers cannot put yellow tape around a computer screen or dust a Web site for fingerprints. The best, and often the only, way to fight computer crime is with technology that gives law enforcement agencies the ability to "track" hackers and other cyber criminals through the Internet. But, as Michael Vatis observed, these efforts are complicated by the fact that digital evidence can be altered or erased even as the cyber crime is being committed. In Chapter 6, we discussed forensics, or the application of science to find evidence of criminal activity. Within the past two decades, a branch of this science known as **cyber forensics** has evolved to gather evidence of cyber crimes.

The main goal of cyber forensics is to gather **digital evidence,** or information of value to a criminal investigation that is stored on, received by, or transmitted by an electronic device such as a computer.[58] Experts in cyber forensics often rely on software that retraces a suspect's digital movements. Such software works by creating a digital duplicate of the targeted hard drive, enabling cyber sleuths to break access codes, determine passwords, and search files.[59] "Short of taking your hard drive and having it run over by a Mack truck," says one expert, "you can't be sure that anything is truly deleted from your computer."[60]

Jurisdictional Challenges Regardless of what type of cyber crime is being investigated, law enforcement agencies are often frustrated by problems of jurisdiction (explained

Cyber Forensics The application of computer technology to finding and utilizing evidence of cyber crimes.

Digital Evidence Information or data of value to a criminal investigation that is either stored or transmitted by electronic means.

THE GREAT FIREWALL OF CHINA

The typical Internet café in China bears little resemblance to its American counterpart. Each *wangren,* or Web surfer, must register using a real name before logging on. The government requires that each computer feature spyware called Internet Detective, which records all online activities. Any suspicious activity, such as viewing pornography or the use of the words *freedom* or *democracy,* is immediately transmitted via the spyware to computers at the local police station. Furthermore, several security guards sit in a back room, monitoring each computer to ensure that no banned content appears.

In the United States, the issue of whether the government should regulate the Internet—and, if so, how much—is hotly debated. In China, the question was answered long before the Internet was even imagined. Since the 1950s, the Chinese Communist Party has exercised strict control over all forms of information, including newspapers, television, radio, movies, and books. Today, under the auspices of the Ministry of Information Industry, that control has been extended to the World Wide Web.

Under broad laws that prohibit, among other things, "destroying the order of society" and "making falsehoods or distorting the truth," Chinese censors have free rein to limit the flow of information through government-controlled Internet service providers. The "Great Firewall," as this system is sometimes called, has traditionally focused on blocking entry to "politically sensitive sites," including the Web pages of the *New York Times* and the human rights organization Amnesty International.

In recent years, however, Chinese censors have also blocked access to such popular sites as Flickr, Wikipedia, YouTube, and Myspace. These steps have angered many Chinese citizens and inspired an Internet-based evasion campaign. Chinese programmers are creating software that evades the government restrictions, and a number of Web sites and blogs in the country are dedicated to "tearing down" the Great Firewall. "I don't know if it's better to speak out or keep silent, but if everyone keeps silent, the truth will be buried," wrote a seventeen-year-old blogger from Guangdong Province who posted instructions on how to access YouTube. "I don't want to be silent, even if everyone else shuts up."

FOR CRITICAL ANALYSIS

How would China-style Internet censorship affect cyber crime in the United States? Under what circumstances, if any, would Americans accept such levels of Internet control by the government?

---

more fully in Chapter 8). Jurisdiction is primarily based on physical geography—each country, state, and nation has jurisdiction, or authority, over crimes that occur within its boundaries. The Internet, however, destroys these traditional notions because geographic boundaries simply do not exist in cyberspace.

To see how this can affect law enforcement efforts, let's consider a hypothetical cyberstalking case. Phil, who lives in State A, has been sending e-mails containing graphic sexual threats to Stephanie, who lives in State B. Where has the crime taken place? Which police department has authority to arrest Phil, and which court system has authority to try him? To further complicate matters, what if State A has not yet added cyberstalking to its criminal code, while State B has? Does that mean that Phil has not committed a crime in his home state, but has committed one in Stephanie's?

The federal government has taken to answering this question by stating that Phil has committed a crime wherever it says he has. The Sixth Amendment to the U.S. Constitution states that federal criminal cases should be tried in the district in which the offense was committed.[61] Because the Internet is "everywhere," the federal government has a great deal of leeway in choosing the venue in which an alleged cyber criminal will face trial. In January 2011, for example, FBI agents arrested Anthony Steven Rodriguez in Georgia for sexually exploiting a ten-year-old boy in Helena, Montana, via the Internet. Although Rodriguez never set foot in Montana while allegedly committing this crime, he

Discussion Tip: Ask students to discuss the challenge of determining jurisdiction in cyber crime cases. How does the federal government decide the issue of jurisdiction?

CAREERS IN CJ

Photo Courtesy Dr. Melinda Merck

DR. MELINDA MERCK
FORENSIC ANIMAL DOCTOR

After Georgia passed a new felony animal cruelty law in 2000, I joined a group called the Georgia Legal Professionals for Animals. Our mission was to hold free educational seminars on animal cruelty for various criminal justice practitioners such as law enforcement agents, judges, and attorneys. As a veterinarian, my role was to provide information on a vet's perspective of a crime scene investigation. At the time, nobody was doing this, so as I was lecturing, I was also learning from local forensic experts on how to apply their techniques to animal crimes. Now, when I arrive on a crime scene, I take photographs, test for blood, look for weapons and bodily fluids, and generally collect any evidence that might link a suspect to a victim.

THE MICHAEL VICK CASE In the summer of 2007, I was asked by the U.S. Attorney's office to assist in executing a search warrant on Michael Vick's property in Virginia. It was hardly an ideal day—hot and muggy and smelly! In all, I supervised the exhumation of two mass graves, working with an FBI forensics unit. I had to make sure that the commingled remains of the dogs were removed separately and correctly. I also supervised the sifting of the dirt—we were looking for any type of evidence, including entomology evidence (that is, insects) to determine the time of burial. I looked over all the property, including where the dogs were housed and trained. Blood spatter, including expired blood (blown out of the lungs or mouth), could be seen on the walls where the dogs were fought.

When I am working a case, I have to remain objective and keep any emotional response to a minimum. Of course, I find acts of animal cruelty to be depraved and a threat to society. I believe that Vick's punishment was appropriate for the applicable law and sentencing guidelines. I was amazed and gratified by the public's reaction—not only were people disgusted by the acts but negative public opinion has been sustained for a long time. I think this new awareness by the public and politicians will help strengthen current laws.

CAREER ADVICE I am a veterinarian who works in the field of forensics. To do veterinary animal forensics you do not need to be a vet, as this is a newly emerging field. A bachelor's degree in forensic science, crime scene investigation training, experience in animal cruelty investigation, training in animal handling and disaster work—all of these are helpful in pursuing a career in animal forensics.

This career is not just about loving animals and wanting to be their voice—it is about helping society. It is also about being part of a team with law enforcement agents and prosecutors, all of us working toward the same goal. To be good at this job, you need to be a problem solver who refuses to rest until every piece of the puzzle is in its proper place and the case is closed.

FAST FACTS

FORENSIC ANIMAL DOCTOR JOB DESCRIPTION:

- Visit crime scenes and work closely with law enforcement.
- Collect forensic evidence and maintain the chain of custody to protect evidence.
- Testify in court on behalf of victims.

WHAT KIND OF TRAINING IS REQUIRED?

- Bachelor's degree in forensic science, plus training in crime scene investigation.
- A degree in veterinary medicine with a specialty in pathology is highly desirable.
- Additional experience in animal cruelty investigation, animal handling, and/or disaster relief work is a bonus.

ANNUAL SALARY RANGE?

- $50,000–$82,000

For additional information on a career as an animal CSI professional, visit: **www.aspca. org/fight-animal-cruelty**

Eric Isselee/Shutterstock

will face trial in federal court there because the victim (and his computer) was located in that state.

FEDERAL LAW ENFORCEMENT AND CYBER CRIME Because of its freedom from jurisdictional restraints, the federal government has traditionally taken the lead in law enforcement efforts against cyber crime. This is not to say that little cyber crime prevention occurs on the local level. Most major metropolitan police departments have created special units to fight cyber crime. In general, however, only a handful of local police and sheriffs' departments have the resources to support a squad of cyber investigators.

As the primary crime-fighting unit of the federal government, the FBI has taken the lead in law enforcement efforts against cyber crime. The FBI has the primary responsibility for enforcing all federal criminal statutes involving computer crimes. In 1998, the Bureau added a Cyber Division dedicated to investigating computer-based crimes. The Cyber Division and its administrators coordinate the FBI's efforts in cyberspace, specifically its investigations into computer crimes and intellectual property theft. The division also has jurisdiction over the Innocent Images National Initiative (IINI), the agency's online child-pornography subdivision. In addition, the FBI has developed several Cyber Action Teams (CATs), which combine the skills of some twenty-five law enforcement agents, cyber forensics investigators, and computer programming experts. Today, cyber crime is the FBI's third-highest priority (after counterterrorism and counterintelligence), and each of the bureau's fifty-six field divisions has at least one agent who focuses solely on crimes committed on the Internet.

PRIVATE EFFORTS TO COMBAT CYBER CRIME Several years ago, Jody Buell met a man on an online dating service who called himself Claude Eichmann and described himself as a Maryland businessman. Over the course of three months, Buell, who lives in Burnsville, Minnesota, sent Eichmann $10,000 worth of equipment to start a new business in the African nation of Ghana. As it turned out, both Eichmann and his business were frauds. Instead of feeling sorry for herself, Buell started working with **romancescams.org**, a Web site dedicated to helping victims of online dating fraud.[62] For all of the government's efforts, its ability to combat fraud and protect the integrity of all, or even most, computers and computer users is limited. It must rely on the efforts of the private sector and individuals such as Buell to make the Internet a safer place.

Online Security The fear of being hacked has spurred a billion-dollar industry that helps clients—either individuals or corporations—protect the integrity of their computer systems. Because every computer connected to the Internet is a potential security breach, cyber security companies help devise elaborate and ever-changing password systems to ensure that only authorized users can access data. These companies also install protective software and antivirus programs, which can limit outside access to a computer or a network. Such measures are credited with a positive development in one of the most troublesome areas of cyber crime: according to one Internet security company, the amount of identity theft in the United States fell 28 percent in 2010.[63]

> **"The Internet is a scary place. It can really hurt you."**
>
> —**Sabrina Spatz,** eighth grader (2010)

Technology Tip: Ask students to go online and explore the FBI's Cyber Division. If time allows, ask them to share what they learned about this crime-fighting unit.

Cyber Angels is an organization designed to assist people who need help online—whether they are being cyberstalked, harassed, or otherwise victimized by cyber criminals. To visit this Web site, click on the *Criminal Justice CourseMate* at **cengagebrain. com** and select the *Web links* for this chapter.

A special agent with U.S. Immigration and Customs Enforcement (ICE) poses in front of the agency's Cyber Crimes Center in Fairfax, Virginia. Why are federal agencies such as ICE generally better positioned to fight cyber crime than local law enforcement agencies?
Richard Clement/Reuters/Landov

Passwords and Encryption For anybody who uses a wireless router, the most important step to help maintain security is password protection. Otherwise, such routers can be accessed and used to commit crimes. In 2011, for example, an innocent man in Buffalo, New York, was arrested for downloading thousands of images of child pornography. Eventually, investigators determined that a neighbor had been using the man's unprotected wireless signal (Wi-Fi) to access the material.[64]

Another effective way to protect computer information is to encrypt it. Through **encryption**, a message (plaintext) is transformed into something (ciphertext) that only the sender and receiver can understand. Unless a third party is able to "break the code," the information will stay secure. Encryption is particularly useful in protecting the content of e-mails. The main drawback of this technology is the rate at which it becomes obsolete. As a general rule, computing power doubles every eighteen months, which means that programs to break the "latest" encryption code are always imminent. Consequently, those who use encryption must ensure that they update their systems at the same rate as those who would abuse it.

Encryption The process by which a message is transmitted into a form or code that the sender and receiver intend not to be understandable by third parties.

SELFASSESSMENT

Fill in the blanks and check your answers on page 601.
One common cyber crime is online _____ fraud, which occurs when a consumer pays for a product that is not delivered. Web thieves have opportunities to practice _____ theft because of the large amount of personal financial information that is stored on the Internet. A _____ is someone who gains illegal access to one computer using another computer. These wrongdoers sometimes use _____, or networks of hijacked computers, to carry out various improper online activities, including the illegal spread of junk e-mails known as _____.

WHITE-COLLAR CRIME

A woman in Huntsville, Alabama, squanders $60,000 in student loans on house bills and "entertainment." The owners of the Glory Pharmacy in Hernando County, Florida, knowingly accept 1,400 fake prescriptions for the painkiller oxycodone. A New Jersey defense contractor sells the U.S. Army faulty helicopter parts. A onetime presidential candidate is indicted for illegally spending nearly $1 million in campaign funds to cover up an affair with his pregnant mistress.

These court cases, all from the spring of 2011, represent a variety of criminal behavior with different motives, different methods, and different victims. Yet they all fall into the category of *white-collar crime,* an umbrella term for wrongdoing marked by deceit and scandal rather than violence. As we mentioned in Chapter 1, white-collar crime has a broad impact on the global economy, causing American businesses alone approximately $300 billion in losses each year.[65] Despite its global and national importance, however, white-collar crime has consistently challenged a criminal justice system that struggles to define the problem, much less effectively combat it.

"My morals were for sale."

—**Justin Paperny,** who served eighteen months in prison for misleading investment clients (2010)

WHAT IS WHITE-COLLAR CRIME?

White-collar crime is not an official category of criminal behavior measured by the federal government in the Uniform Crime Report. Rather, it covers a broad range of illegal acts involving "lying, cheating, and stealing," according

LO 7

to the FBI's Web site on the subject.[66] To give a more technical definition, white-collar crimes are financial activities characterized by deceit and concealment that do not involve physical force or violence. Figure 17.4 below lists and describes some common types of white-collar crime.

DIFFERENT TECHNIQUES To differentiate white-collar crime from "regular" crime, criminologists Michael L. Benson of the University of Cincinnati and Sally S. Simpson of the University of Maryland focus on technique. For example, in an ordinary burglary, a criminal uses physical means, such as picking a lock, to get somewhere he or she should not be—someone else's home—to do something that is clearly illegal. Furthermore, the victim is a specific identifiable individual—the homeowner. In contrast, white-collar criminals usually (1) have legal access to the place where the crime occurs; (2) are spatially separated from the victim, who is often unknown; and (3) behave in a manner that is, at least superficially, legitimate.[67]

Benson and Simpson also identify three main techniques used by white-collar criminals to carry out their crimes:[68]

1. *Deception.* White-collar crime almost always involves a party who deceives and a party who is deceived. For example, in 2009 Congress passed legislation giving first-time home buyers an $8,000 tax credit. By 2010, federal agents had uncovered more than 100,000 instances of deception involving this benefit—applicants were lying about being first-time home buyers or were misusing the funds.[69]

2. *Abuse of trust.* A white-collar criminal often operates in a position of trust and misuses that trust for personal benefit. Dishonest stockbrokers, for example, may steal funds from clients rather than investing those funds in the stock market as promised.

⊘ The **Federal Bureau of Investigation** maintains a Web site with information concerning its ongoing efforts to fight white-collar crime. To find this site, visit the *Criminal Justice CourseMate* at **cengagebrain. com** and select the *Web links* for this chapter.

Critical Thinking Skill Development: In a written assignment, ask students to differentiate white-collar crimes from property crimes. What are the most common white-collar crimes? (LO 7)

FIGURE 17.4 White-Collar Crimes

Embezzlement
Embezzlement is a form of employee fraud in which an individual uses his or her position within an organization to *embezzle,* or steal, the employer's funds, property, or other assets. Pilferage is a less serious form of employee fraud in which the individual steals items from the workplace.

Tax Evasion
Tax evasion occurs when taxpayers underreport (or do not report) their taxable income or otherwise purposely attempt to evade a tax liability.

Digital Vision CD

PhotoDisc/Getty Images

Credit-Card and Check Fraud
Credit-card fraud involves obtaining credit-card numbers through a variety of schemes (such as stealing them from the Internet) and using the numbers for personal gain. Check fraud includes writing checks that are not covered by bank funds, forging checks, and stealing traveler's checks.

Mail and Wire Fraud
This umbrella term covers all schemes that involve the use of mail, radio, television, the Internet, or a telephone to intentionally deceive in a business environment.

Securities Fraud
Securities fraud covers illegal activity in the stock market. Stockbrokers who steal funds from their clients are guilty of securities fraud, as are those who engage in *insider trading,* which involves buying or selling securities on the basis of information that has not been made available to the public.

Bribery
Also known as *influence peddling,* bribery occurs in the business world when somebody within a company sells influence, power, or information to a person outside the company who can benefit. A county official, for example, could give a construction company a lucrative county contract to build a new jail. In return, the construction company would give some of the proceeds, known as a *kickback,* to the official.

Consumer Fraud
This term covers a wide variety of activities designed to defraud consumers, from selling counterfeit art to offering "free" items, such as electronic devices or vacations, that include a number of hidden charges.

Insurance Fraud
Insurance fraud involves making false claims in order to collect insurance payments. Faking an injury in order to receive payments from a workers' compensation program, for example, is a form of insurance fraud.

Digital Vision CD

In June 2011, onetime presidential candidate John Edwards was arrested for using $1 million in campaign contributions to hide his pregnant mistress from the public and media. Why would this wrongdoing, if proven, fall into the category of white-collar crime? AP Photo/U.S. Marshals Service

3. *Concealment and conspiracy.* To continue their illegal activities, white-collar criminals need to conceal those activities. In *odometer fraud,* for example, an automobile dealership "rolls back" the odometers of used cars so that a higher price can be charged for the vehicles. As soon as the fraud is discovered, the scheme can no longer succeed.

VICTIMS OF WHITE-COLLAR CRIME

As the above examples show, sometimes the victim of a white-collar crime is obvious. A fraudulent stockbroker is stealing directly from his or her clients, and odometer fraud denies consumers the actual value of their purchased automobiles. But who was victimized when the tax credit for first-time home buyers was fraudulently claimed? In that instance, the "victims" were the U.S. taxpayers, who collectively had to cover the cost of the unwarranted benefits. Often, white-collar crime does not target individuals but rather large groups or even abstract concepts such as "society" or "the environment."

CORPORATE WHITE-COLLAR CRIME The lack of a single, easily identifiable victim often complicates the prosecution of white-collar crime. For instance, the Deepwater Horizon oil spill off the coast of Louisiana in April 2010 caused a great deal of obvious harm. Eleven workers were killed in the oil rig explosion that caused the spill, and the Louisiana coastline suffered immense ecological damage, threatening the livelihoods of thousands of seafood suppliers. Yet, eighteen months after the incident, no punishment for BP, the corporation that operated Deepwater Horizon, or any of its employees was forthcoming. Because so many different individuals and several companies besides BP might have contributed to the disaster, the federal government could not easily determine who bore ultimate responsibility.

By the time this textbook is published, however, it is likely that BP will have been criminally charged in connection with the oil spill. For legal purposes, a corporation can be treated as a person capable of forming the intent necessary to commit a crime. In 2010, Guidant Corporation was found guilty of deliberately selling flawed heart defibrillators, which employ electric energy to correct irregular heart rhythms. Because six people who used the faulty devices died, Guidant was fined nearly $300 million and placed on three years' probation, during which time its operations would be subject to regular government inspections.[70]

REGULATING AND POLICING WHITE-COLLAR CRIME

LO 8 The deaths of six people because of Guidant Corporation's heart defibrillators are an example of *corporate violence.* In contrast to assaults committed by individual people, **corporate violence** is a result of policies or actions undertaken by a corporation. In the United States, parallel regulatory and criminal systems have evolved to prevent corporate violence and other forms of white-collar crime.

Corporate Violence Physical harm to individuals or the environment that occurs as the result of corporate policies or decision making.

THE REGULATORY JUSTICE SYSTEM Although most white-collar crimes cause harm, these harms are not necessarily covered by criminal statutes. Indeed, more often they are covered by *administrative* laws, which we first encountered in Chapter 4 (see page 103). Such laws make up the backbone of the U.S. regulatory system, through which the government attempts to control the actions of individuals, corporations, and other institutions. The goal of regulation is not prevention or punishment as much as compliance, or the following of regulatory guidelines.[71] For example, as part of their efforts to clean up the massive oil spill of 2010, BP and government agencies used dispersants, which cause oil to disintegrate in water. Agents from the Environmental Protection Agency (EPA) monitored levels of these chemicals to ensure that further damage was not done to the Gulf of Mexico (see the photo alongside).[72]

The EPA—which regulates practices relating to air quality, water quality, and toxic waste—is one of the federal administrative agencies whose compliance oversight brings them into contact with white-collar crime. Another, the Occupational Safety and Health Administration (OSHA), enforces workplace health and safety standards. In 2011, OSHA cited Taft Grain and Elevator for noncompliance and fined the company $188,000 after one of the its employees was killed in a grain bin accident.[73] In addition, the Federal Trade Commission regulates business interactions, and the Securities and Exchange Commission (SEC) ensures that financial markets such as the New York Stock Exchange operate in a fair manner.

LAW ENFORCEMENT AND WHITE-COLLAR CRIME In general, when officials at a regulatory agency find that criminal prosecution is needed to punish a particular violation, they will refer the matter to the U.S. Department of Justice. Either through such referrals or at their own discretion, federal officials prosecute white-collar crime using the investigatory powers of several different federal law enforcement agencies. The FBI has become the lead agency when it comes to white-collar crime, particularly in response to the recent financial scandals, as we shall soon see. The U.S. Postal Inspection Service is also quite active in such investigations, as fraudulent activities often involve the U.S. mail. In addition, the Internal Revenue Service's Criminal Investigative Division has jurisdiction over a wide variety of white-collar crimes, including tax fraud, and operates perhaps the most effective white-collar crime lab in the country.[74]

Local and state agencies also investigate white-collar crimes, but because of the complexity and costs of such investigations, most are handled by the federal government. Federal prosecutors are also in a unique position to enforce the federal Racketeer Influenced and Corrupt Organizations Act (RICO), which we discussed briefly in Chapter 12. Originally designed to combat organized crime, RICO makes it illegal to receive income through a pattern of *racketeering*.[75] The definition of racketeering is so inclusive—basically covering any attempt to earn illegal income involving more than one person—that it can be used against a broad range of white-collar wrongdoing. In 2011, for example, federal prosecutors used RICO to convict eleven tobacco companies for misleading the American public about the addictive qualities of cigarettes.

WHITE-COLLAR CRIME IN THE 2000s

The decade that ended in 2010 was marked by two periods of financial scandal. First, in 2001 and 2002, fraudulent accounting practices led to the demise of giant corporations such as Enron and Worldcom, costing investors tens of billions of dollars. Then, near the end of the decade, the collapse of the subprime mortgage market caused millions of Americans to lose their homes to foreclosure and led to the collapse of major financial institutions such as Lehman Brothers and Washington Mutual. In the latter period,

What role did the Environmental Protection Agency (EPA) play in monitoring efforts to clean up the oil slick from the Deepwater Horizon oil spill in the spring of 2010? Why is the EPA considered a regulatory agency and not a law enforcement agency?

Ted Jackson/*The Times-Picayune*/Landov

Regulation Governmental control of society through rules and laws that is generally carried out by administrative agencies.

Compliance The state of operating in accordance with governmental standards.

Racketeering The criminal action of being involved in an organized effort to engage in illegal business transactions.

Critical Thinking Skill Development: Have students work together to respond to "Questions for Critical Analysis" number five on page 602, concerning antiracketeering laws such as RICO.

During the 1980s, the nation was rocked by a series of financial scandals including the "savings and loan crisis." As a result of this debacle, dozens of financial institutions failed, eventually costing American taxpayers more than $160 billion. To the outrage of many, the high-profile white-collar criminals from the era received relatively light prison sentences for their fraudulent behavior. Corrupt Louisiana financier Herman K. Beebe spent less than a year in prison. Michael Milken, "the junk bond king" who pleaded guilty to violating securities laws, was released after twenty-two months. Bank president Charles Keating, Jr., whose actions wiped out the savings of more than 20,000 customers, served four and a half years.

THE MYTH White-collar criminals, with their high-priced lawyers and friends in high places, receive light penalties. Even though their wrongdoing causes a great deal of suffering, they are not treated as harshly by the criminal justice system as petty thieves or low-level drug dealers.

THE REALITY The political response to the financial scandals of the early 2000s focused on increasing penalties for white-collar criminals. In November 2001, the U.S. Sentencing Commission increased its recommended punishments for businesspersons who commit fraud, particularly when the misdeeds involve losses in excess of $100 million. Then, in 2002, Congress passed the White Collar Crime Penalty Enhancement Act, which doubled the maximum sentences for some corporate frauds.

The results have been striking. In 2009, Edward Hugh Okun was sentenced to 120 years for stealing $126 million from clients, and Richard Harkless received 100 years for defrauding investors out of nearly $40 million. In March 2010, a U.S. district judge sentenced Robert Thompson to 309 years in prison for targeting the elderly in a series of scams.

That same year, Bernie Madoff, discussed in the text, received a 150-year prison term. Although judges still have great leeway to depart from the guidelines when sentencing white-collar criminals, public outrage at white-collar crime has apparently created an environment in which harsh punishments are the rule rather than the exception.

FOR CRITICAL ANALYSIS What are some of the justifications for punishing white-collar criminals such as Robert Thompson and Bernie Madoff so harshly? Are there any reasons to be lenient with those whose crimes do not physically harm their victims?

Bernie Madoff, left center, was sentenced to 150 years in prison for stealing tens of billions of dollars from investment clients.
Timothy A. Clary/AFP/Getty Images

headlines focused on widespread *mortgage fraud,* or dishonest practices relating to home loans, along with the misdeeds of Bernard Madoff. Before his 2008 arrest, Madoff managed to defraud thousands of investors out of approximately $65 billion.

As has often occurred in U.S. history, these scandals and the concurrent economic downturns led to greater regulation and criminalization of white-collar crime. In 1934, for example, in the wake of the Great Depression, Congress established the SEC to watch over the American economy.[76] Similarly, in 2002 Congress passed legislation which, among other things, enhanced the penalties for those convicted of white-collar crimes.[77] (See the feature *Myth versus Reality—Soft Time for White-Collar Crime* above.) In response to the "Great Recession" of 2008 and 2009, the FBI created the National Mortgage Fraud Team and began to crack down on a variety of white-collar crimes. Indeed, FBI agents are increasingly using aggressive tactics such as going undercover, planting wiretaps, and raiding offices—tactics previously reserved for drug dealers, mobsters, and terrorists—against white-collar criminals.[78]

SELFASSESSMENT

Fill in the blanks and check your answers on page 601.

According to the FBI, white-collar crimes are economic activities characterized by _____ and concealment that do not involve _____. Administrative agencies such as the _____ Protection Agency make up the backbone of the U.S. regulatory system, which combats white-collar crime by requiring _____ with certain guidelines. A powerful tool for law enforcement in combating white-collar crimes, _____ can be used against groups or organizations that attempt to earn income illegally.

In 2011, the FBI arrested Tim Durham, center, for using funds given to him by investors to buy expensive homes, a 100-foot yacht, and travel on a personal jet. Why has the economic downturn of recent years put pressure on the FBI to crack down on white-collar crime? ZUMA Press/Newscom

CJ IN ACTION

POLICING ILLEGAL IMMIGRANTS

Several years ago, Francis Hernandez ran a red light and raced into a busy intersection in Aurora, Colorado, where his SUV hit a pickup truck that in turn smashed into an ice cream parlor. The accident caused three deaths, including that of a three-year-old boy. Community outrage over the incident was aggravated by the fact that Hernandez was an illegal immigrant from Guatemala who had been arrested more than a dozen times. Had a police officer checked Hernandez's immigration status during one of these arrests, he could have been reported to federal authorities and removed from the country. In this *CJ in Action* feature, we look at the question of whether local and state law enforcement agencies should take on the responsibility—and burden—of helping to enforce our nation's immigration laws.

NEW LEVELS OF COOPERATION

Before 1996, local police officers were rarely, if ever, given immigration law responsibilities. That year, Congress created the 287(g) program.[79] Essentially, this program allows for partnerships between federal immigration authorities and local law enforcement agencies. Under the auspices of 287(g), federal agents train local police officers in the specifics of immigration law, and the certified officers are then able to enforce federal immigration laws. In practical terms, the program gives local officers the ability to notify Immigration and Customs Enforcement (ICE) when they encounter illegal aliens as part of their daily law enforcement routine.

The 287(g) program does *not* give local police officers the ability to apprehend someone they suspect is an illegal alien. Rather, the officers run a background check to determine immigration status after they come in contact with the suspect for another reason, such as an arrest or a traffic stop. By July 2010, seventy-one state and local law enforcement agencies had signed 287(g) agreements with ICE, and more than 1,200 local officers had been certified under the program.[80] Between 2006 and 2010, more than 172,000 aliens were removed by ICE after being identified by these local officers.[81]

THE CASE FOR HAVING LOCAL POLICE OFFICERS ENFORCE IMMIGRATION LAW

- Using local police would help prevent crimes committed by illegal aliens who should not be living in the United States, such as the one described in the first paragraph of this feature.

- The assistance is badly needed. The federal government has only about 11,000 immigration agents, compared with an estimated 11 million illegal immigrants in the United States.

- Arrests for immigration violations are an important part of law enforcement efforts against terrorism and violent criminal gangs. Local police lose the opportunity to apprehend suspects in both areas because they cannot detain them for being in the United States illegally.

THE CASE AGAINST HAVING LOCAL POLICE OFFICERS ENFORCE IMMIGRATION LAW

- If members of the immigrant community identify local police with federal immigration authorities, they will be much less likely to report crimes and cooperate with criminal investigations, either as witnesses or victims.[82]

- Immigration law is complex and, inevitably, will be misapplied by inexperienced police officers. "The fear is that if you put it in the discretion of local law enforcement, you will have situations where they go outside of the law," said one observer.[83]

- The new duties would be a poor use of scarce law enforcement resources, diverting local police from crime fighting and other responsibilities. "I don't think any of us delight in the idea of becoming immigration officers," said one Arizona sheriff.[84]

Creative Commons

WRITING ASSIGNMENT—YOUR OPINION

In some jurisdictions, the political establishment has chosen to reject the cooperation offered by ICE by passing so-called sanctuary laws. Generally speaking, these laws *prohibit* local law enforcement agencies from inquiring about the immigration status of residents or enforcing immigration law in any way.

In January 2011, soon after taking office, New Mexico governor Susana Martinez issued an executive order to discontinue a sanctuary law that had previously covered the entire state. Do you agree or disagree with Martinez's decision? What is your opinion of policies allowing local law enforcement officers to enforce immigration laws? Before responding, you can review our discussions in the chapter concerning:

- Immigration law basics (pages 577–578).

- Enforcing immigration law (pages 579–580).

- Immigration and state law (pages 581–582).

Your answer should include at least three full paragraphs.

CHAPTER SUMMARY

LO 1 Explain the difference between a temporary visa and a green card.

A temporary visa is a document that gives a non-U.S. citizen permission to visit the United States for a limited amount of time and for a limited purpose. A green card, or nontemporary visa, confers on the holder the status of permanent resident, and he or she enjoys many of the same rights as U.S. citizens to live and work in this country.

LO 2 Indicate how local and federal law enforcement agencies cooperate under the Secure Communities program.

When a suspect is arrested, the local police send information about the suspect electronically to the Department of Homeland Security. If this instant background check shows that the suspect has violated criminal or immigration law in a way that makes him or her removable from the United States, the federal government will issue a detainer that allows U.S. Immigration and Customs Enforcement eventually to take custody of the suspect.

LO 3 Distinguish cyber crime from "traditional" crime.

Most cyber crimes are not "new" types of crimes. Rather, they are traditional crimes committed in cyberspace. Perpetrators of cyber crimes are often aided by certain aspects of the Internet, such as its ability to cloak the user's identity and its effectiveness as a conduit for transferring—or stealing—large amounts of information very quickly.

LO 4 Describe the three following forms of malware: (a) botnets, (b) worms, and (c) viruses.

(a) A botnet is a network of computers that have been hijacked without the knowledge of their owners and used to spread harmful programs across the Internet. (b) A worm is a damaging software program that reproduces itself as it moves from computer to computer. (c) A virus is a damaging software program that must be attached to an "infested" host file to transfer from one computer to the next.

LO 5 Explain how the Internet has contributed to piracy of intellectual property.

In the past, copying intellectual property such as films and music was time consuming, and the quality of the pirated copies was vastly inferior to that of the originals. On the Internet, however, millions of unauthorized copies of intellectual property can be reproduced at the click of a mouse, and the quality of these items is often the same as that of the original, or close to it.

LO 6 Outline the three major reasons why the Internet is conducive to the dissemination of child pornography.

The Internet provides (a) a quick way to transmit child pornography from providers to consumers; (b) security such as untraceable e-mails and password-protected Web sites and chat rooms; and (c) anonymity for buyers and sellers of child pornography.

LO 7 Indicate some of the ways that white-collar crime is different from violent or property crime.

A wrongdoer committing a standard crime usually uses physical means to get somewhere he or she legally should not be in order to do something clearly illegal. Also, the victims of violent and property crimes are usually easily identifiable. In contrast, a white-collar criminal usually has legal access to the crime scene where he or she is doing something seemingly legitimate. Furthermore, victims of white-collar crimes are often unknown or unidentifiable.

LO 8 Explain the concept of corporate violence.

Corporate violence occurs when a corporation implements policies that ultimately cause harm to individuals or the environment.

SELF ASSESSMENT ANSWER KEY

Page 582: i. civil; **ii.** federal; **iii.** permanent; **iv.** removal; **v.** immigration; **vi.** reasonable suspicion

Page 594: i. retail; **ii.** identity; **iii.** hacker; **iv.** botnets; **v.** spam

Page 599: i. deceit; **ii.** violence/physical force; **iii.** Environmental; **iv.** compliance; **v.** RICO/antiracketeering laws

KEY TERMS

QUESTIONS FOR CRITICAL ANALYSIS

1. Guy, who was born in Haiti, has lived in Miami, Florida, for fifteen years and is a permanent resident, meaning that he has a green card. One night Guy gets in a fight with a neighbor and is eventually convicted of simple assault. Even if a judge sentences him to probation rather than jail time, how might this conviction affect Guy's ability to continue living in the United States legally?

2. Alabama's 2011 immigration control bill makes it a crime to knowingly rent housing to an illegal immigrant. What is your opinion of this provision?

3. Why does the nature of online communication make it difficult to identify and prosecute those who commit cyber crimes?

4. Consider the following situation: Melissa Chin is the sheriff of Jackson County, Missouri, population 1,434. Sheriff Chin has only two deputies at her disposal. Mae Brown, a resident of Jackson County, is receiving threatening e-mails from someone who has the cyberspace name of johndoe1313. Mae is certain that the sender is actually Matthew Green, her ex-husband. Matthew lives in Wilson County, Louisiana. What are some of the jurisdictional problems Sheriff Chin may face in investigating Matthew's possible involvement in cyberstalking? What are some of the practical problems Sheriff Chin may encounter? How might she solve these problems?

5. Law enforcement agencies have extensively employed antiracketeering laws such as RICO in combating drug dealers and criminal gangs. (To review RICO, go to page 597.) Why would such legislation be useful in prosecuting these non-white-collar criminals?

CourseMate *For Online Help*

For online help and access to resources that accompany *Criminal Justice Today*, go to www.cengagebrain.com/shop/ISBN/1111835578. Click "Access Now," where you will find flashcards, an online quiz, and other helpful study aids. If you have an access code for CourseMate, log in and go to the chapter of your choice for additional online study aids.

NOTES

1. Quoted in Sandy Cullen, "City Gangs: Low-Key but Dangerous," *Wisconsin State Journal* (September 5, 2010), A1.

2. *The Chinese Exclusion Case*, 130 U.S. 581 (1889).

3. Teresa A. Miller, "Lessons Learned, Lessons Lost: Immigration Enforcement's Failed Experiment with Penal Severity," *Fordham Urban Law Journal* (November 2010), 217.

4. 8 U.S.C.A. Section 1304(e).

5. 8 U.S.C.A. Section 1227(a).

6. Suzanne Gamboa, "Homeland Security Touts Record Criminal Removals," *Associated Press* (October 6, 2010).

7. John S. Passel and D'Vera Cohn, "Unauthorized Immigrant Population: National and State Trends, 2010," *Pew Hispanic Center* (February 1, 2011), at **pewhispanic.org/reports/report.php?ReportID=133**.

8. *Wong Wing v. United States*, 163 U.S. 228 (1895).

9. 8 C.F.R. Section 287.3(a)-(b).

10. *Ibid.*; and *Samayoa-Martinez v. Holder*, 558 F.3d 897, 901–902 (9th Cir. 2009).

11. U.S. Immigration and Customs Enforcement, "Operation Community Shield/Transnational Gangs," at **www.ice.gov/community-shield**.

12. James Walsh, "Feds Arrest Eighteen Gang Members," *Star Tribune (Minneapolis–St. Paul)* (July 9, 2010), 4B.

13. Jon Freere and Jessica Vaughan, "Taking Back the Streets: ICE and Local Law Enforcement Target Immigrant Gangs,"

Center for Immigration Studies, September 2008, at **www.cis.org/immigrantgangs**.

14. David J. Venturella, "Secure Communities: Identifying and Removing Criminal Aliens," *The Police Chief* (September 2010), 44.

15. Julia Preston, and Kirk Semple, "Taking a Hard Line: Immigrants and Crime," *New York Times* (February 18, 2011), A20.

16. Trevor Gardner II and Aarti Kohli, *The C.A.P Effect: Racial Profiling in the ICE Criminal Alien Program* (Berkeley, CA: The Chief Justice Earl Warren Institute on Race, Ethnicity, and Diversity, 2009), 1–8.

17. Bess Chui *et al.*, *Constitution on ICE: A Report on Immigration Home Raid Operations* (New York: Cardozo Immigration Justice Clinic, 2009), 1–44.

18. Quoted in Dan Frosch, "In Colorado, a Debate over Program to Check Immigration History of the Arrested," *New York Times* (July 30, 2010), A14.

19. Amanda Lee Myers, "More Hispanics Go to Federal Prison," *Associated Press* (June 7, 2011).

20. Federation for American Immigration Reform, "Immigration in Arizona: Fact Sheet," at **www.fairus.org/site/News2/78 4178954?page=NewsArticle&id=22901&s ecurity=1601&news_iv_ctrl=1761**.

21. State of Arizona, Office of the Governor, "Statement by Governor Jan Brewer" (April 23, 2010), at **azgovernor. gov/dms/upload/PR_042310_ StatementByGovernorOnSB1070.pdf**.

22. S.B. 1070, 2010 Arizona Session Laws 0113, amended by 2010 Arizona Session Laws 0211 (H.B. 2162, 49th Legislature, 2d Session (Arizona 2010).

23. Julia Preston, "Immigrants Are Focus of Harsh Bill in Alabama," *New York Times* (June 4, 2011), A10.

24. Azadeh Shashahani, *Terror and Isolation in Cobb: How Unchecked Police Power under 287(g) Has Torn Families Apart and Threatened Public Safety* (Atlanta: American Civil Liberties Union Foundation of Georgia, October 2009), 9–10.

25. Quoted in Howard Witt, "Does Crackdown Cross Line?" *Chicago Tribune* (May 26, 2008), 1.

26. *Whren v. United States,* 517 U.S. 806 (1996).

27. Randal C. Archibold, "Judge Blocks Arizona's Immigration Law," *New York Times* (July 29, 2010), 1.

28. Sally Kalson, "Bad Intentions: The Rutgers Suicide Shows the Ugly Side of 'Sharing,'" *Pittsburgh Post-Gazette* (October 10, 2010), B3.

29. National Institute of Justice, *Computer Crime: Criminal Justice Resource Manual* (Washington, D.C.: U.S. Department of Justice, 1989), 2.

30. *Ibid.*

31. Internet Crime Complaint Center, *IC3 2010 Internet Crime Report* (Glen Allen, VA: National White Collar Crime Center, 2011), 6.

32. *Symantec Global Internet Security Threat Report: Trends for 2009* (Mountain View, CA: Symantec, April 2010), 16.

33. Stephen Brookes, "Fooled, Fleeced, and Forgotten," *Washington Times* (June 8, 2011), C8.

34. *2011 Identity Fraud Survey Report* (Pleasanton, CA: Javelin Strategy and Research, 2011), 1.

35. Benny Evangelista and Alejandro Martinez-Cabrera, "Big Jump in Number of People on Twitter," *San Francisco Chronicle* (September 4, 2010), D2.

36. Quoted in Matt Richtel and Verne G. Kopytoff, "E-Mail Fraud Hides behind Friendly Face," *New York Times* (June 3, 2011), A1.

37. Bureau of Justice Statistics, *Stalking Victimization in the United States* (Washington, D.C.: U.S. Department of Justice, January 2009), 1.

38. *Ibid.*

39. Geraldine Baum and Stuart Pfeifer, "Dozens Charged in Bank Thefts," *Los Angeles Times* (October 1, 2010), B1.

40. Byron Acohido, "An Invitation to Crime," *USA Today* (March 2010), 1A.

41. *Second Annual Cost of Cyber Crime Study: Benchmark Study of U.S. Companies* (Traverse City, MI: Poneman Institute, August 2011), 1.

42. *Symantec Global Internet Security Threat Report: Trends for 2009,* 16.

43. 15 U.S.C. Sections 7701–7713 (2003).

44. *Cisco 2010 Annual Security Report* (San Jose, CA: Cisco Systems, 2010), 2.

45. *Ibid.,* 30.

46. *Eighth Annual BSA and IDC Global Software Piracy Study* (Washington, D.C.: Business Software Alliance, May 2011), 2.

47. 17 U.S.C. Section 23199(c) (1998).

48. 17 U.S.C. Sections 2301 *et seq.* (1998).

49. 545 U.S. 913 (2005).

50. Dawn C. Chmielewski, "A New Wave of Piracy Feared," *Los Angeles Times* (September 21, 2010), B3.

51. "The Internet Porn 'Epidemic': By the Numbers," *The WEEK* (June 17, 2010), at **theweek.com/article/index/204156/the-internet-porn-epidemic-by-the-numbers**.

52. William R. Graham, Jr., "Uncovering and Eliminating Child Pornography Rings on the Internet," *Law Review of Michigan State University Detroit College of Law* (Summer 2000), 466.

53. *United States v. Williams,* 533 U.S. 285 (2008). In the act's name, "Protect" stands for "Prosecutorial Remedies and Other Tools to end the Exploitation of Children Today."

54. 31 U.S.C. Sections 5361 *et seq.* (2006).

55. Quoted in Michael McCarthy, "Feds Go After Offshore Online Betting Industry," *USA Today* (July 19, 2006), 6C.

56. Steve Chapman, "More Freedom Is a Sound Bet," *Chicago Tribune* (August 1, 2010), 21.

57. Quoted in Richard Rapaport, "Cyberwars: The Feds Strike Back," *Forbes* (August 23, 1999), 126.

58. National Institute of Justice, "What Is Digital Evidence?" in *Electronic Crime Scene Investigation: A Guide for First Responders,*

2d ed. (Washington, D.C.: U.S. Department of Justice, April 2008), ix.

59. Matthew Boyle, "The Latest Hit: *CSI* in Your Hard Drive," *Fortune* (November 14, 2005), 39.

60. Quoted in "Cybersleuths Find Growing Role in Fighting Crime," *HPC Wire*, at **www.hpc-wire.com/hpc-bin/artread.pl?direction= Current&articlenumber=19864**.

61. Laurie P. Cohen, "Internet's Ubiquity Multiplies Venues to Try Web Crimes," *Wall Street Journal* (February 12, 2007), B1.

62. James Eli Shiffer, "Online Scams Break Hearts, Bank Accounts," *Arizona Daily Star* (February 5, 2011), A11.

63. Javelin Strategy and Research, "Identity Fraud Fell 28 Percent in 2010 According to New Javelin Strategy & Research Report" (February 8, 2011), at **www. javelinstrategy.com/news/1170/92/ Identity-Fraud-Fell-28-Percent-in-2010-According-to-New-Javelin-Strategy-Research-Report/d,pressRoomDetail**.

64. Carolyn Thompson, "NY Case Underscores Wi-Fi Privacy Dangers," *Associated Press* (April 24, 2011).

65. The Federal Bureau of Investigation, Seattle Division, "What We Investigate," at **www.fbi.gov/seattle/about-us/what-we-investigate/priorities**.

66. The Federal Bureau of Investigation, "White-Collar Crime" at **www.fbi.gov/about-us/ investigate/white_collar/whitecollar crime**.

67. Michael L. Benson and Sally S. Simpson, *White-Collar Crime: An Opportunity Perspective* (New York: Routledge, 2009), 79–80.

68. *Ibid.,* 81–87.

69. Anton R. Valukas, "White-Collar Crime and Economic Recession," *University of Chicago Legal Forum* (2010), 5.

70. U.S. Department of Justice, "Medical Device Manufacturer Guidant Sentenced for Failure to Report Defibrillator Safety Problems to FDA" (January 12, 2011), at **www.justice. gov/opa/pr/2011/January/11-civ-035. html**.

71. Benson and Simpson, 189.

72. Raffi Khatchadourain, "The Gulf War," *The New Yorker* (March 14, 2011), 51–53.

73. Occupational Safety & Health Administration, "US Labor Department's OSHA Cites Grain Elevator Operator with Safety Violations Following Worker Death in Taft, Texas" (May 9, 2011), at **www.osha.gov/pls/ oshaweb/owadisp.show_document?p_ table=NEWS_RELEASES&p_id=19764**.

74. David O. Friedrichs, *Trusted Criminals: White Collar Crime in Contemporary Society,* 4th ed. (Belmont, CA: Wadsworth Cengage Learning, 2010), 278–283.

75. Lawrence Salinger, *Encyclopedia of White-Collar and Corporate Crime,* 2d ed. (Thousand Oaks, CA: Sage, 2004), 361.

76. 15 U.S.C. Sections 78a *et seq.*

77. White-Collar Crime Penalty Enhancement Act of 2002, 18 U.S.C. Sections 1341, 1343, 1349–1350.

78. Peter Lattman and William K. Rashbaum, "A Trader, an F.B.I. Witness, and Then a Suicide," *Reuters* (June 2, 2011).

79. 8 U.S.C. Section 1357(g) (2006).

80. U.S. Immigration and Customs Enforcement, "New Release: 26 Law Enforcement Officers Trained by ICE to Enforce Immigration Law" (July 23, 2010), at **www.ice.gov/news/releases/1007/100723charleston.htm**.

81. *Ibid.*

82. Anita Khashu, *The Role of Local Police: Striking a Balance between Immigration Enforcement and Civil Liberties* (Washington, D.C.: The Police Foundation, April 2009).

83. Quoted in Jenny Jarvie, "Citizenship Checks Strain Trust in Police," *Los Angeles Times* (July 29, 2007), 16.

84. Quoted in Giovana Dell'orto, "Feds Seek Enforcement Help," *Richmond Times-Dispatch* (May 5, 2006), A4.

APPENDIX A THE CONSTITUTION OF THE UNITED STATES

PREAMBLE

We the People of the United States, in Order to form a more perfect Union, establish Justice, insure domestic Tranquility, provide for the common defence, promote the general Welfare, and secure the Blessings of Liberty to ourselves and our Posterity, do ordain and establish this Constitution for the United States of America.

ARTICLE I

Section 1. All legislative Powers herein granted shall be vested in a Congress of the United States, which shall consist of a Senate and House of Representatives.

Section 2. The House of Representatives shall be composed of Members chosen every second Year by the People of the several States, and the Electors in each State shall have the Qualifications requisite for Electors of the most numerous Branch of the State Legislature.

No Person shall be a Representative who shall not have attained to the Age of twenty five Years, and been seven Years a Citizen of the United States, and who shall not, when elected, be an Inhabitant of that State in which he shall be chosen.

Representatives and direct Taxes shall be apportioned among the several States which may be included within this Union, according to their respective Numbers, which shall be determined by adding to the whole Number of free Persons, including those bound to Service for a Term of Years, and excluding Indians not taxed, three fifths of all other Persons. The actual Enumeration shall be made within three Years after the first Meeting of the Congress of the United States, and within every subsequent Term of ten Years, in such Manner as they shall by Law direct. The Number of Representatives shall not exceed one for every thirty Thousand, but each State shall have at Least one Representative; and until such enumeration shall be made, the State of New Hampshire shall be entitled to chuse three, Massachusetts eight, Rhode Island and Providence Plantations one, Connecticut five, New York six, New Jersey four, Pennsylvania eight, Delaware one, Maryland six, Virginia ten, North Carolina five, South Carolina five, and Georgia three.

When vacancies happen in the Representation from any State, the Executive Authority thereof shall issue Writs of Election to fill such Vacancies.

The House of Representatives shall chuse their Speaker and other Officers; and shall have the sole Power of Impeachment.

Section 3. The Senate of the United States shall be composed of two Senators from each State, chosen by the Legislature thereof, for six Years; and each Senator shall have one Vote.

Immediately after they shall be assembled in Consequence of the first Election, they shall be divided as equally as may be into three Classes. The Seats of the Senators of the first Class shall be vacated at the Expiration of the second Year, of the second Class at the Expiration of the fourth Year, and of the third Class at the Expiration of the sixth Year, so that one third may be chosen every second Year; and if Vacancies happen by Resignation, or otherwise, during the Recess of the Legislature of any State, the Executive thereof may make temporary Appointments until the next Meeting of the Legislature, which shall then fill such Vacancies.

No Person shall be a Senator who shall not have attained to the Age of thirty Years, and been nine Years a Citizen of the United States, and who shall not, when elected, be an Inhabitant of that State for which he shall be chosen.

The Vice President of the United States shall be President of the Senate, but shall have no Vote, unless they be equally divided.

The Senate shall chuse their other Officers, and also a President pro tempore, in the Absence of the Vice President, or when he shall exercise the Office of President of the United States.

The Senate shall have the sole Power to try all Impeachments. When sitting for that Purpose, they shall be on Oath or Affirmation. When the President of the United States is tried, the Chief Justice shall preside: And no Person shall be convicted without the Concurrence of two thirds of the Members present.

Judgment in Cases of Impeachment shall not extend further than to removal from Office, and disqualification to hold and enjoy any Office of honor, Trust, or Profit under the United States: but the Party convicted shall nevertheless be liable and subject to Indictment, Trial, Judgment, and Punishment, according to Law.

Section 4. The Times, Places and Manner of holding Elections for Senators and Representatives, shall be prescribed in each State by the Legislature thereof; but the Congress may at any time by Law make or alter such Regulations, except as to the Places of chusing Senators.

The Congress shall assemble at least once in every Year, and such Meeting shall be on the first Monday in December, unless they shall by Law appoint a different Day.

Section 5. Each House shall be the Judge of the Elections, Returns, and Qualifications of its own Members, and a Majority of each shall constitute a Quorum to do Business; but a smaller Number may adjourn from day to day, and may be authorized to compel the Attendance of absent Members, in such Manner, and under such Penalties as each House may provide.

Each House may determine the Rules of its Proceedings, punish its Members for disorderly Behavior, and, with the Concurrence of two thirds, expel a Member.

Each House shall keep a Journal of its Proceedings, and from time to time publish the same, excepting such Parts as may in their Judgment require Secrecy; and the Yeas and Nays of the Members of either House on any question shall, at the Desire of one fifth of those Present, be entered on the Journal.

Neither House, during the Session of Congress, shall, without the Consent of the other, adjourn for more than three days, nor to any other Place than that in which the two Houses shall be sitting.

Section 6. The Senators and Representatives shall receive a Compensation for their Services, to be ascertained by Law, and paid out of the Treasury of the United States. They shall in all Cases, except Treason, Felony and Breach of the Peace, be privileged from Arrest during their Attendance at the Session of their respective Houses, and in going to and returning from the same; and for any Speech or Debate in either House, they shall not be questioned in any other Place.

No Senator or Representative shall, during the Time for which he was elected, be appointed to any civil Office under the Authority of the United States, which shall have been created, or the Emoluments whereof shall have been increased during such time; and no Person holding any Office under the United States, shall be a Member of either House during his Continuance in Office.

Section 7. All Bills for raising Revenue shall originate in the House of Representatives; but the Senate may propose or concur with Amendments as on other Bills.

Every Bill which shall have passed the House of Representatives and the Senate, shall, before it become a Law, be presented to the President of the United States; If he approve he shall sign it, but if not he shall return it, with his Objections to the House in which it shall have originated, who shall enter the Objections at large on their Journal, and proceed to reconsider it. If after such Reconsideration two thirds of that House shall agree to pass the Bill, it shall be sent together with the Objections, to the other House, by which it shall likewise be reconsidered, and if approved by two thirds of that House, it shall become a Law. But in all such Cases the Votes of both Houses shall be determined by Yeas and Nays, and the Names of the Persons voting for and against the Bill shall be entered on the Journal of each House respectively. If any Bill shall not be returned by the President within ten Days (Sundays excepted) after it shall have been presented to him, the Same shall be a Law, in like Manner as if he had signed it, unless the Congress by their Adjournment prevent its Return in which Case it shall not be a Law.

Every Order, Resolution, or Vote, to which the Concurrence of the Senate and House of Representatives may be necessary (except on a question of Adjournment) shall be presented to the President of the United States; and before the Same shall take Effect, shall be approved by him, or being disapproved by him, shall be repassed by two thirds of the Senate and House of Representatives, according to the Rules and Limitations prescribed in the Case of a Bill.

Section 8. The Congress shall have Power To lay and collect Taxes, Duties, Imposts and Excises, to pay the Debts and provide for the common Defence and general Welfare of the United States; but all Duties, Imposts and Excises shall be uniform throughout the United States;

To borrow Money on the credit of the United States;

To regulate Commerce with foreign Nations, and among the several States, and with the Indian Tribes;

To establish an uniform Rule of Naturalization, and uniform Laws on the subject of Bankruptcies throughout the United States;

To coin Money, regulate the Value thereof, and of foreign Coin, and fix the Standard of Weights and Measures;

To provide for the Punishment of counterfeiting the Securities and current Coin of the United States;

To establish Post Offices and post Roads;

To promote the Progress of Science and useful Arts, by securing for limited Times to Authors and Inventors the exclusive Right to their respective Writings and Discoveries;

To constitute Tribunals inferior to the supreme Court;

To define and punish Piracies and Felonies committed on the high Seas, and Offenses against the Law of Nations;

To declare War, grant Letters of Marque and Reprisal, and make Rules concerning Captures on Land and Water;

To raise and support Armies, but no Appropriation of Money to that Use shall be for a longer Term than two Years;

To provide and maintain a Navy;

To make Rules for the Government and Regulation of the land and naval Forces;

To provide for calling forth the Militia to execute the Laws of the Union, suppress Insurrections and repel Invasions;

To provide for organizing, arming, and disciplining, the Militia, and for governing such Part of them as may be employed in the Service of the United States, reserving to the States respectively, the Appointment of the Officers, and the Authority of training the Militia according to the discipline prescribed by Congress;

To exercise exclusive Legislation in all Cases whatsoever, over such District (not exceeding ten Miles square) as may, by Cession of particular States, and the Acceptance of Congress, become the Seat of the Government of the United States, and to exercise like Authority over all Places purchased by the Consent of the Legislature of the State in which the Same shall be, for the Erection of Forts, Magazines, Arsenals, dock-Yards, and other needful Buildings;—And

To make all Laws which shall be necessary and proper for carrying into Execution the foregoing Powers, and all other Powers vested by this Constitution in the Government of the United States, or in any Department or Officer thereof.

Section 9. The Migration or Importation of such Persons as any of the States now existing shall think proper to admit, shall not be prohibited by the Congress prior to the Year one thousand eight hundred and eight, but a Tax or duty may be imposed on such Importation, not exceeding ten dollars for each Person.

The privilege of the Writ of Habeas Corpus shall not be suspended, unless when in Cases of Rebellion or Invasion the public Safety may require it.

No Bill of Attainder or ex post facto Law shall be passed.

No Capitation, or other direct, Tax shall be laid, unless in Proportion to the Census or Enumeration herein before directed to be taken.

No Tax or Duty shall be laid on Articles exported from any State.

No Preference shall be given by any Regulation of Commerce or Revenue to the Ports of one State over those of another: nor shall Vessels bound to, or from, one State be obliged to enter, clear, or pay Duties in another.

No Money shall be drawn from the Treasury, but in Consequence of Appropriations made by Law; and a regular Statement and Account of the Receipts and Expenditures of all public Money shall be published from time to time.

No Title of Nobility shall be granted by the United States: And no Person holding any Office of Profit or Trust under them, shall, without the Consent of the Congress, accept of any present, Emolument, Office, or Title, of any kind whatever, from any King, Prince, or foreign State.

Section 10. No State shall enter into any Treaty, Alliance, or Confederation; grant Letters of Marque and Reprisal; coin Money; emit Bills of Credit; make any Thing but gold and silver Coin a Tender in Payment of Debts; pass any Bill of Attainder, ex post facto Law, or Law impairing the Obligation of Contracts, or grant any Title of Nobility.

No State shall, without the Consent of the Congress, lay any Imposts or Duties on Imports or Exports, except what may be absolutely necessary for executing its inspection Laws: and the net Produce of all Duties and Imposts, laid by any State on Imports or Exports, shall be for the Use of the Treasury of the United States; and all such Laws shall be subject to the Revision and Controul of the Congress.

No State shall, without the Consent of Congress, lay any Duty of Tonnage, keep Troops, or Ships of War in time of Peace, enter into any Agreement or Compact with another State, or with a foreign Power, or engage in War, unless actually invaded, or in such imminent Danger as will not admit of delay.

ARTICLE II

Section 1. The executive Power shall be vested in a President of the United States of America. He shall hold his Office during the Term of four Years, and, together with the Vice President, chosen for the same Term, be elected, as follows:

Each State shall appoint, in such Manner as the Legislature thereof may direct, a Number of Electors, equal to the whole Number of Senators and Representatives to which the State may be entitled in the Congress; but no Senator or Representative, or Person holding an Office of Trust or Profit under the United States, shall be appointed an Elector.

The Electors shall meet in their respective States, and vote by Ballot for two Persons, of whom one at least shall not be an Inhabitant of the same State with themselves. And they shall make a List of all the Persons voted for, and of the Number of Votes for each; which List they shall sign and certify, and transmit sealed to the Seat of the Government of the United States, directed to the President of the Senate. The President of the Senate shall, in the Presence of the Senate and House of Representatives, open all the Certificates, and the Votes shall then be counted. The Person having the greatest Number of Votes shall be the President, if such Number be a Majority of the whole Number of Electors appointed; and if there be more than one who have such Majority, and have an equal Number of Votes, then the House of Representatives shall immediately chuse by Ballot one of them for President; and if no Person have a Majority, then from the five highest on the List the said House shall in like Manner chuse the President. But in chusing the President, the Votes shall be taken by States, the Representation from each State having one Vote; A quorum for this Purpose shall consist of a Member or Members from two thirds of the States, and a Majority of all the States shall be necessary to a Choice. In every Case, after the Choice of the President, the Person having the greater Number of Votes of the Electors shall be the Vice President. But if there should remain two or more who have equal Votes, the Senate shall chuse from them by Ballot the Vice President.

The Congress may determine the Time of chusing the Electors, and the Day on which they shall give their Votes; which Day shall be the same throughout the United States.

No person except a natural born Citizen, or a Citizen of the United States, at the time of the Adoption of this Constitution, shall be eligible to the Office of President; neither shall any Person be eligible to that Office who shall not have attained to the Age of thirty five Years, and been fourteen Years a Resident within the United States.

In Case of the Removal of the President from Office, or of his Death, Resignation or Inability to discharge the Powers and Duties of the said Office, the same shall devolve on the Vice President, and the Congress may by Law provide for the Case of Removal, Death, Resignation or Inability, both of the President and Vice President, declaring what Officer shall then act as President, and such Officer shall act accordingly, until the Disability be removed, or a President shall be elected.

The President shall, at stated Times, receive for his Services, a Compensation, which shall neither be increased nor diminished during the Period for which he shall have been elected, and he shall not receive within that Period any other Emolument from the United States, or any of them.

Before he enter on the Execution of his Office, he shall take the following Oath or Affirmation: "I do solemnly swear (or affirm) that I will faithfully execute the Office of President of the United States, and will to the best of my Ability, preserve, protect and defend the Constitution of the United States."

Section 2. The President shall be Commander in Chief of the Army and Navy of the United States, and of the Militia of the several States, when called into the actual Service of the United States; he may require the Opinion, in writing, of the principal Officer in each of the executive Departments, upon any Subject relating to the Duties of their respective Offices, and he shall have Power to grant Reprieves and Pardons for Offenses against the United States, except in Cases of Impeachment.

He shall have Power, by and with the Advice and Consent of the Senate to make Treaties, provided two thirds of the Senators present concur; and he shall nominate, and by and with the Advice and Consent of the Senate, shall appoint Ambassadors, other public Ministers and Consuls, Judges of the supreme Court, and all other Officers of the United States, whose Appointments are not herein otherwise provided for, and which shall be established by Law; but the Congress may by Law vest the Appointment of such inferior Officers, as they think proper, in the President alone, in the Courts of Law, or in the Heads of Departments.

The President shall have Power to fill up all Vacancies that may happen during the Recess of the Senate, by granting Commissions which shall expire at the End of their next Session.

Section 3. He shall from time to time give to the Congress Information of the State of the Union, and recommend to their Consideration such Measures as he shall judge necessary and expedient; he may, on extraordinary Occasions, convene both Houses, or either of them, and in Case of Disagreement between them, with Respect to the Time of Adjournment, he may adjourn them to such Time as he shall think proper; he shall receive Ambassadors and other public Ministers; he shall take Care that the Laws be faithfully executed, and shall Commission all the Officers of the United States.

Section 4. The President, Vice President and all civil Officers of the United States, shall be removed from Office on Impeachment for, and Conviction of, Treason, Bribery, or other high Crimes and Misdemeanors.

ARTICLE III

Section 1. The judicial Power of the United States, shall be vested in one supreme Court, and in such inferior Courts as the Congress may from time to time ordain and establish. The Judges, both of the supreme and inferior Courts, shall hold their Offices during good Behaviour, and shall, at stated Times, receive for their Services a Compensation, which shall not be diminished during their Continuance in Office.

Section 2. The judicial Power shall extend to all Cases, in Law and Equity, arising under this Constitution, the Laws of the United States, and Treaties made, or which shall be made, under their Authority;—to all Cases affecting Ambassadors, other public Ministers and Consuls;—to all Cases of admiralty and maritime Jurisdiction;—to Controversies to which the United States shall be a Party;—to Controversies between two or more States;—between a State and Citizens of another State;—between Citizens of different States;—between Citizens of the same State claiming Lands under Grants of different States, and between a State, or the Citizens thereof, and foreign States, Citizens or Subjects.

In all Cases affecting Ambassadors, other public Ministers and Consuls, and those in which a State shall be a Party, the supreme Court shall have original Jurisdiction. In all the other Cases before mentioned, the supreme Court shall have appellate Jurisdiction, both as to Law and Fact, with such Exceptions, and under such Regulations as the Congress shall make.

The Trial of all Crimes, except in Cases of Impeachment, shall be by Jury; and such Trial shall be held in the State where the said Crimes shall have been committed; but when not committed within any State, the Trial shall be at such Place or Places as the Congress may by Law have directed.

Section 3. Treason against the United States, shall consist only in levying War against them, or, in adhering to their Enemies, giving them Aid and Comfort. No Person shall be convicted of Treason unless on the Testimony of two Witnesses to the same overt Act, or on Confession in open Court.

The Congress shall have Power to declare the Punishment of Treason, but no Attainder of Treason shall work Corruption of Blood, or Forfeiture except during the Life of the Person attainted.

ARTICLE IV

Section 1. Full Faith and Credit shall be given in each State to the public Acts, Records, and judicial Proceedings of every other State. And the Congress may by general Laws prescribe the Manner in which such Acts, Records and Proceedings shall be proved, and the Effect thereof.

Section 2. The Citizens of each State shall be entitled to all Privileges and Immunities of Citizens in the several States.

A Person charged in any State with Treason, Felony, or other Crime, who shall flee from Justice, and be found in another State, shall on Demand of the executive Authority of the State from which he fled, be delivered up, to be removed to the State having Jurisdiction of the Crime.

No Person held to Service or Labour in one State, under the Laws thereof, escaping into another, shall, in Consequence of any Law or Regulation therein, be discharged from such Service or Labour, but shall be delivered up on Claim of the Party to whom such Service or Labour may be due.

Section 3. New States may be admitted by the Congress into this Union; but no new State shall be formed or erected within the Jurisdiction of any other State; nor any State be formed by the Junction of two or more States, or Parts of States, without the Consent of the Legislatures of the States concerned as well as of the Congress.

The Congress shall have Power to dispose of and make all needful Rules and Regulations respecting the Territory or other Property belonging to the United States; and nothing in this Constitution shall be so construed as to Prejudice any Claims of the United States, or of any particular State.

Section 4. The United States shall guarantee to every State in this Union a Republican Form of Government, and shall protect each of them against Invasion; and on Application of the Legislature, or of the Executive (when the Legislature cannot be convened) against domestic Violence.

ARTICLE V

The Congress, whenever two thirds of both Houses shall deem it necessary, shall propose Amendments to this Constitution, or, on the Application of the Legislatures of two thirds of the several States, shall call a Convention for proposing Amendments, which, in either Case, shall be valid to all Intents and Purposes, as part of this Constitution, when ratified by the Legislatures of three fourths of the several States, or by Conventions in three fourths thereof, as the one or the other Mode of Ratification may be proposed by the Congress; Provided that no Amendment which may be made prior to the Year One thousand eight hundred and eight shall in any Manner affect the first and fourth Clauses in the Ninth Section of the first Article; and that no State, without its Consent, shall be deprived of its equal Suffrage in the Senate.

ARTICLE VI

All Debts contracted and Engagements entered into, before the Adoption of this Constitution shall be as valid against the United States under this Constitution, as under the Confederation.

This Constitution, and the Laws of the United States which shall be made in Pursuance thereof; and all Treaties made, or which shall be made, under the Authority of the United States, shall be the supreme Law of the Land; and the Judges in every State shall be bound thereby, any Thing in the Constitution or Laws of any State to the Contrary notwithstanding.

The Senators and Representatives before mentioned, and the Members of the several State Legislatures, and all executive and judicial Officers, both of the United States and of the several States, shall be bound by Oath or Affirmation, to support this Constitution; but no religious Test shall ever be required as a Qualification to any Office or public Trust under the United States.

ARTICLE VII

The Ratification of the Conventions of nine States shall be sufficient for the Establishment of this Constitution between the States so ratifying the Same.

AMENDMENT I [1791]

Congress shall make no law respecting an establishment of religion, or prohibiting the free exercise thereof; or abridging the freedom of speech, or of the press; or the right of the people peaceably to assembly, and to petition the Government for a redress of grievances.

AMENDMENT II [1791]

A well regulated Militia, being necessary to the security of a free State, the right of the people to keep and bear Arms, shall not be infringed.

AMENDMENT III [1791]

No Soldier shall, in time of peace be quartered in any house, without the consent of the Owner, nor in time of war, but in a manner to be prescribed by law.

AMENDMENT IV [1791]

The right of the people to be secure in their persons, houses, papers, and effects, against unreasonable searches and seizures, shall not be violated, and no Warrants shall issue, but upon probable cause, supported by Oath or affirmation, and particularly describing the place to be searched, and the persons or things to be seized.

AMENDMENT V [1791]

No person shall be held to answer for a capital, or otherwise infamous crime, unless on a presentment or indictment of a Grand Jury, except in cases arising in the land or naval forces, or in the Militia, when in actual service in time of War or public danger; nor shall any person be subject for the same offence to be twice put in jeopardy of life or limb; nor shall be compelled in any criminal case to be a witness against himself, nor be deprived of life, liberty, or property, without due process of law; nor shall private property be taken for public use, without just compensation.

AMENDMENT VI [1791]

In all criminal prosecutions, the accused shall enjoy the right to a speedy and public trial, by an impartial jury of the State and district wherein the crime shall have been committed, which district shall have been previously ascertained by law, and to be informed of the nature and cause of the accusation; to be confronted with the witnesses against him; to have compulsory process for obtaining witnesses in his favor, and to have the Assistance of Counsel for his defence.

AMENDMENT VII [1791]

In Suits at common law, where the value in controversy shall exceed twenty dollars, the right of trial by jury shall be preserved, and no fact tried by jury, shall be otherwise reexamined in any Court of the United States, than according to the rules of the common law.

AMENDMENT VIII [1791]

Excessive bail shall not be required, nor excessive fines imposed, nor cruel and unusual punishments inflicted.

AMENDMENT IX [1791]

The enumeration in the Constitution, of certain rights, shall not be construed to deny or disparage others retained by the people.

AMENDMENT X [1791]

The powers not delegated to the United States by the Constitution, nor prohibited by it to the States, are reserved to the States respectively, or to the people.

AMENDMENT XI [1798]

The Judicial power of the United States shall not be construed to extend to any suit in law or equity, commenced or prosecuted against one of the United States by Citizens of another State, or by Citizens or Subjects of any Foreign State.

AMENDMENT XII [1804]

The Electors shall meet in their respective states, and vote by ballot for President and Vice-President, one of whom, at least, shall not be an inhabitant of the same state with themselves; they shall name in their ballots the person voted for as President, and in distinct ballots the person voted for as Vice-President, and they shall make distinct lists of all persons voted for as President, and of all persons voted for as Vice-President, and of the number of votes for each, which lists they shall sign and certify, and transmit sealed to the seat of the government of the United States, directed to the President of the Senate;—The President of the Senate shall, in the presence of the Senate and House of Representatives, open all the certificates and the votes shall then be counted;—The person having the greatest number of votes for President, shall be the President, if such number be a majority of the whole number of Electors appointed; and if no person have such majority, then from the persons having the highest numbers not exceeding three on the list of those voted for as President, the House of Representatives shall choose immediately, by ballot, the President. But in choosing the President, the votes shall be taken by states, the representation from each state having one vote; a quorum for this purpose shall consist of a member or members from two-thirds of the states, and a majority of all states shall be necessary to a choice. And if the House of Representatives shall not choose a President whenever the right of choice shall devolve upon them, before the fourth day of March next following, then the Vice-President shall act as President, as in the case of the death or other constitutional disability of the President.—The person having the greatest number of votes as Vice-President, shall be the Vice-President, if such number be a majority of the whole number of Electors appointed, and if no person have a majority, then from the two highest numbers on the list, the Senate shall choose the Vice-President; a quorum for the purpose shall consist of two-thirds of the whole number of Senators, and a majority of the whole number shall be necessary to a choice. But no person constitutionally ineligible to the office of President shall be eligible to that of Vice-President of the United States.

AMENDMENT XIII [1865]

Section 1. Neither slavery nor involuntary servitude, except as a punishment for crime whereof the party shall have been duly convicted, shall exist within the United States, or any place subject to their jurisdiction.

Section 2. Congress shall have power to enforce this article by appropriate legislation.

AMENDMENT XIV [1868]

Section 1. All persons born or naturalized in the United States, and subject to the jurisdiction thereof, are citizens of the United States and of the State wherein they reside. No State shall make or enforce any law which shall abridge the privileges or immunities of citizens of the United States; nor shall any State deprive any person of life, liberty, or property, without due process of law; nor deny to any person within its jurisdiction the equal protection of the laws.

Section 2. Representatives shall be apportioned among the several States according to their respective numbers, counting the whole number of persons in each State, excluding Indians not taxed. But when the right to vote at any election for the choice of electors for President and Vice President of the United States, Representatives in Congress, the Executive and Judicial officers of a State, or the members of the Legislature thereof, is denied to any of the male inhabitants of such State, being twenty-one years of age, and citizens of the United States, or in any way abridged, except for participation in rebellion, or other crime, the basis of representation therein shall be reduced in the proportion which the number of such male citizens shall bear to the whole number of male citizens twenty-one years of age in such State.

Section 3. No person shall be a Senator or Representative in Congress, or elector of President and Vice President, or hold any office, civil or military, under the United States, or under any State, who having previously taken an oath, as a member of Congress, or as an officer of the United States, or as a member of any State legislature, or as an executive or judicial officer of any State, to support the Constitution of the United States, shall have engaged in insurrection or rebellion against the same, or given aid or comfort to the enemies thereof. But Congress may by a vote of two-thirds of each House, remove such disability.

Section 4. The validity of the public debt of the United States, authorized by law, including debts incurred for payment of pensions and bounties for services in suppressing insurrection or rebellion, shall not be questioned. But neither the United States nor any State shall assume or pay any debt or obligation incurred in aid of insurrection or rebellion against the United States, or any claim for the loss or emancipation of any slave; but all such debts, obligations and claims shall be held illegal and void.

Section 5. The Congress shall have power to enforce, by appropriate legislation, the provisions of this article.

AMENDMENT XV [1870]

Section 1. The right of citizens of the United States to vote shall not be denied or abridged by the United States or by any State on account of race, color, or previous condition of servitude.

Section 2. The Congress shall have power to enforce this article by appropriate legislation.

AMENDMENT XVI [1913]

The Congress shall have power to lay and collect taxes on incomes, from whatever source derived, without apportionment among the several States, and without regard to any census or enumeration.

AMENDMENT XVII [1913]

Section 1. The Senate of the United States shall be composed of two Senators from each State, elected by the people thereof, for six years; and each Senator shall have one vote. The electors in each State shall have the qualifications requisite for electors of the most numerous branch of the State legislatures.

Section 2. When vacancies happen in the representation of any State in the Senate, the executive authority of such State shall issue writs of election to fill such vacancies: *Provided,* That the legislature of any State may empower the executive thereof to make temporary appointments until the people fill the vacancies by election as the legislature may direct.

Section 3. This amendment shall not be so construed as to affect the election or term of any Senator chosen before it becomes valid as part of the Constitution.

AMENDMENT XVIII [1919]

Section 1. After one year from the ratification of this article the manufacture, sale, or transportation of intoxicating liquors within, the importation thereof into, or the exportation thereof from the United States and all territory subject to the jurisdiction thereof for beverage purposes is hereby prohibited.

Section 2. The Congress and the several States shall have concurrent power to enforce this article by appropriate legislation.

Section 3. This article shall be inoperative unless it shall have been ratified as an amendment to the Constitution by the legislatures of the several States, as provided in the Constitution, within seven years from the date of the submission hereof to the States by the Congress.

AMENDMENT XIX [1920]

Section 1. The right of citizens of the United States to vote shall not be denied or abridged by the United States or by any State on account of sex.

Section 2. Congress shall have power to enforce this article by appropriate legislation.

AMENDMENT XX [1933]

Section 1. The terms of the President and Vice President shall end at noon on the 20th day of January, and the terms of Senators and Representatives at noon on the 3d day of January, of the years in which such terms would have ended if this article had not been ratified; and the terms of their successors shall then begin.

Section 2. The Congress shall assemble at least once in every year, and such meeting shall begin at noon on the 3d day of January, unless they shall by law appoint a different day.

Section 3. If, at the time fixed for the beginning of the term of the President, the President elect shall have died, the Vice President elect shall become President. If the President shall not have been chosen before the time fixed for the beginning of his term, or if the President elect shall have failed to qualify, then the Vice President elect shall act as President until a President shall have qualified; and the Congress may by law provide for the case wherein neither a President elect nor a Vice President elect shall have qualified, declaring who shall then act as President, or the manner in which one who is to act shall be selected, and such person shall act accordingly until a President or Vice President shall have qualified.

Section 4. The Congress may by law provide for the case of the death of any of the persons from whom the House of Representatives may choose a President whenever the right of choice shall have devolved upon them, and for the case of the death of any of the persons from whom the Senate may choose a Vice President whenever the right of choice shall have devolved upon them.

Section 5. Sections 1 and 2 shall take effect on the 15th day of October following the ratification of this article.

Section 6. This article shall be inoperative unless it shall have been ratified as an amendment to the Constitution by the legislatures of three-fourths of the several States within seven years from the date of its submission.

AMENDMENT XXI [1933]

Section 1. The eighteenth article of amendment to the Constitution of the United States is hereby repealed.

Section 2. The transportation or importation into any State, Territory, or possession of the United States for delivery or use therein of intoxicating liquors, in violation of the laws thereof, is hereby prohibited.

Section 3. This article shall be inoperative unless it shall have been ratified as an amendment to the Constitution by conventions in the several States, as provided in the Constitution, within seven years from the date of the submission hereof to the States by the Congress.

AMENDMENT XXII [1951]

Section 1. No person shall be elected to the office of the President more than twice, and no person who has held the office of President, or acted as President, for more than two years of a term to which some other person was elected President shall be elected to the office of President more than once. But this Article shall not apply to any person holding the office of President when this Article was proposed by the Congress, and shall not prevent any person who may be holding the office of President, or acting as President, during the term within which this Article becomes operative from holding the office of President or acting as President during the remainder of such term.

Section 2. This article shall be inoperative unless it shall have been ratified as an amendment to the Constitution by the legislatures of three-fourths of the several States within seven years from the date of its submission to the States by the Congress.

AMENDMENT XXIII [1961]

Section 1. The District constituting the seat of Government of the United States shall appoint in such manner as the Congress may direct:

A number of electors of President and Vice President equal to the whole number of Senators and Representatives in Congress to which the District would be entitled if it were a State, but in no event more than the least populous state; they shall be in addition to those appointed by the states, but they shall be considered, for the purposes of the election of President and Vice President, to be electors appointed by a state; and they shall meet in the District and perform such duties as provided by the twelfth article of amendment.

Section 2. The Congress shall have power to enforce this article by appropriate legislation.

AMENDMENT XXIV [1964]

Section 1. The right of citizens of the United States to vote in any primary or other election for President or Vice President, for electors for President or Vice President, or for Senator or Representative in Congress, shall not be denied or abridged by the United States, or any State by reason of failure to pay any poll tax or other tax.

Section 2. The Congress shall have power to enforce this article by appropriate legislation.

AMENDMENT XXV [1967]

Section 1. In case of the removal of the President from office or of his death or resignation, the Vice President shall become President.

Section 2. Whenever there is a vacancy in the office of the Vice President, the President shall nominate a Vice President who shall take office upon confirmation by a majority vote of both Houses of Congress.

Section 3. Whenever the President transmits to the President pro tempore of the Senate and the Speaker of the House of Representatives his written declaration that he is unable to discharge the powers and duties of his office, and until he transmits to them a written declaration to the contrary, such powers and duties shall be discharged by the Vice President as Acting President.

Section 4. Whenever the Vice President and a majority of either the principal officers of the executive departments or of such other body as Congress may by law provide, transmit to the President pro tempore of the Senate and the Speaker of the House of Representatives their written declaration that the President is unable to discharge the powers and duties of his office, the Vice President shall immediately assume the powers and duties of the office as Acting President.

Thereafter, when the President transmits to the President pro tempore of the Senate and the Speaker of the House of Representatives his written declaration that no inability exists, he shall resume the powers and duties of his office unless the Vice President and a majority of either the principal officers of the executive department or of such other body as Congress may by law provide, transmit within four days to the President pro tempore of the Senate and the Speaker of the House of Representatives their written declaration that the President is unable to discharge the powers and duties of his office. Thereupon Congress shall decide the issue, assembling within forty-eight hours for that purpose if not in session. If the Congress, within twenty-one days after receipt of the latter written declaration, or, if Congress is not in session, within twenty-one days after Congress is required to assemble, determines by two-thirds vote of both Houses that the President is unable to discharge the powers and duties of his office, the Vice President shall continue to discharge the same as Acting President; otherwise, the President shall resume the powers and duties of his office.

AMENDMENT XXVI [1971]

Section 1. The right of citizens of the United States, who are eighteen years of age or older, to vote shall not be denied or abridged by the United States or by any State on account of age.

Section 2. The Congress shall have power to enforce this article by appropriate legislation.

AMENDMENT XXVII [1992]

No law, varying the compensation for the services of the Senators and Representatives, shall take effect, until an election of Representatives shall have intervened.

APPENDIX B YOU BE THE JUDGE: THE COURTS' ACTUAL DECISIONS

1.1 In 2009, New York Senator Charles Schumer introduced the Avoiding Life-Endangering and Reckless Texting by Drivers Act (ALERT), which would deny federal highway funds to states that fail to ban texting while driving. As of December 2011, Congress has failed to pass ALERT, and states continue to have the freedom to decide this issue without federal intrusion.

4.1 The appellate court refused to throw out the charges. Although Emil was unconscious at the time his car struck the schoolgirls, he had made the initial decision to get behind the wheel despite the knowledge that he suffered from epileptic seizures. In other words, the *actus reus* in this crime was not Emil's driving into the girls, but his decision to drive in the first place. That decision was certainly voluntary and therefore satisfies the requirements of *actus reus*. Note that if Emil had never had an epileptic seizure before, and had no idea that he suffered from that malady, the court's decision would probably have been different.

6.1 The situation described in this example is a composite of numerous interactions that Michele Okin had with members of the Village of Cornwall-on-Hudson, New York, Police Department. Okin claimed that she complained repeatedly to police officers about domestic violence she suffered at the hands of Roy Sears, her live-in boyfriend. Sears was never arrested or even detained. Police officials agreed that Okin had made numerous reports of abuse, but asserted that she was unreliable in her claims and had repeatedly refused to file a complaint against Sears. She sued the police department for its inaction, and during the trial the presiding judge criticized the department for failing to protect Okin or advise her of her rights as a domestic violence victim. To win the lawsuit, however, Okin needed to prove that the Village police's behavior was "so egregious" and "so outrageous" that it would "shock the contemporary conscience." In other words, the police officers' decision-making with regard to Okin could not just be wrong or misguided—they had to have known that she was being repeatedly abused and deliberately chose to ignore this fact. This is a very difficult standard to meet, and in the end the court decided against Okin, yet another instance of a judge's unwillingness to question the discretion of police officers.

6.2 As these events actually played out, fifteen Cincinnati law enforcement officers had surrounded a suspect named Lorenzo Collins when he brandished the brick, and the two officers closest to Collins fatally shot him. The two officers were cleared of any wrongdoing, given that a reasonable officer in their position could have seen the brick as an instrument that could cause death or serious bodily harm. The court of public opinion, however, was against the police officers, who were accused by members of the community of needlessly killing a mentally unstable man who was carrying a brick, not a knife or a gun.

7.1 The judge did provide a search warrant and the detective found numerous illegal substances in the house, leading to the arrest of the defendant. Eventually, however, an appeals court ruled that a search warrant should not have been given. The court held that the anonymous tip, plus the small amount of marijuana found in the defendant's trash, did not support a reasonable conclusion that the defendant was dealing drugs. Rather, the small amount of drugs showed personal use—not trafficking. Interestingly, the same Florida court came to a different conclusion in another case where probable cause was established by a "trash pull." In that instance, the law enforcement officer found a large quantity of cocaine in the garbage bag, which was enough probable cause for a valid search warrant.

9.1 The North Carolina prosecutor in this case charged Judy Norman with first degree murder, reasoning that self defense did not apply because Judy did not face any *imminent* danger from her husband, John. Despite his threats and the years of abuse, John was, at the time of his murder, asleep and thus incapable of harming her. A jury in the case, however, found Judy guilty of voluntary manslaughter only, and she was sentenced to six years in prison. This case gained national attention because the trial court refused to allow evidence of *battered woman syndrome (BWS)* to be presented to the jury. The term describes the psychological state a person descends into following a lengthy period of physical abuse. In a courtroom, an expert might argue that anyone suffering from this syndrome is in a constant, and reasonable, fear for their lives. Some states do allow evidence of BWS to support the defendant's claim of self-defense in these sorts of cases, and it has been effective. A New York woman who shot her abusive husband as he slept, for example, was acquitted after a jury accepted her self-defense claims, bolstered by expert testimony on BWS.

10.1 In defending Daniel Aguilar against charges regarding Christopher Ash's murder, defense attorney Antonio Bestard's primary argument was that his client did not know that Ash was going to be killed in the garage. After all, they were best friends. Along the same lines, Bestard argued that Aguilar was forced to lure his friend to the garage by older gang members, who would have killed Aguilar had he refused. Bestard also attacked the credibility of the main witness, José Covarrubias, who not only was under the influence of drugs on the night of the murder and sleeping with the victim's sister, but also had received a lighter sentence of twenty-two years in return for testifying against fellow gang members. Bestard suggested that Covarrubias had an incentive to lie to law enforcement officials to get a lighter sentence. In the end, however, the jury found Aguilar guilty of first degree murder, and he was sentenced to life in prison without parole.

11.1 A Connecticut jury eventually decided that the mitigating circumstances outweighed the aggravating circumstances, and recommended a life sentence in prison for Jonathan Mills. It should be noted, however, that Connecticut juries are somewhat reluctant to impose the death penalty. At the time of Mills's trial, the state had not carried out an execution since 1960, and only ten prisoners are currently residing on Connecticut's death row.

12.1 Alain LeConte's probation officer did not take any steps to revoke his probation. The issue became moot, however, when LeConte was arrested for killing a gas station attendant during an armed robbery in Norwalk, Connecticut. The crime took place between his first and second failed drug tests. LeConte's probation officer came under a great deal of criticism for failing to revoke his probation, but she received support from her supervisor. "We can only do so much," he said. "[LeConte's] probation officer went out of her way to assist this young man, but unfortunately it wasn't successful." The supervisor also pointed out that LeConte has no known history of violent behavior and had been a generally cooperative probationer when it came to getting treatment. This case underscores the difficult aspects of a probation officer's job. A misjudgment, even if it was based on a reasonable evaluation of the situation, can end in tragedy.

14.1 Susan Atkins was a disciple of cult leader Charles Manson and, in the summer of 1969, participated in one of the most sensationalized mass murders in American history. The woman Atkins stabbed sixteen times was Sharon Tate, an actress and the wife of film director Roman Polanski. On September 2, 2009, the California Board of Parole unanimously denied compassionate release for Atkins, marking the eighteenth time she had been refused parole. Three months later, Atkins died of brain cancer. Her case highlights the extent to which parole boards are often swayed by the nature of the crime above all other considerations.

APPENDIX C   TABLE OF CASES

GLOSSARY

A

acquittal A declaration following a trial that the individual accused of the crime is innocent in the eyes of the law and thus is absolved from the charges.

actus reus (pronounced *ak*-tus *ray*-uhs). A guilty (prohibited) act. The commission of a prohibited act is one of the two essential elements required for criminal liability, the other element being the intent to commit a crime.

adjudicatory hearing The process through which a juvenile court determines whether there is sufficient evidence to support the initial petition.

administrative law The body of law created by administrative agencies (in the form of rules, regulations, orders, and decisions) in order to carry out their duties and responsibilities.

adversary system A legal system in which the prosecution and defense are opponents, or adversaries, and present their cases in the light most favorable to themselves. The court arrives at a just solution based on the evidence presented by the contestants and determines who wins and who loses.

affidavit A written statement of facts, confirmed by the oath or affirmation of the party making it and made before a person having the authority to administer the oath or affirmation.

affirmative action A hiring or promotion policy favoring those groups, such as women, African Americans, or Hispanics, who have suffered from discrimination in the past or continue to suffer from discrimination.

aftercare The variety of therapeutic, educational, and counseling programs made available to juvenile delinquents (and some adults) after they have been released from a correctional facility.

age of onset The age at which a juvenile first exhibits delinquent behavior.

aggravating circumstances Any circumstances accompanying the commission of a crime that may justify a harsher sentence.

aging out A term used to explain the fact that criminal activity declines with age.

alien A person who is not a citizen of the country in which he or she is found and therefore may not enjoy the same rights as a citizen of that country.

Allen Charge An instruction by a judge to a deadlocked jury with only a few dissenters that asks the jurors in the minority to reconsider the majority opinion.

anomie A condition in which the individual suffers from the breakdown or absence of social norms. According to this theory, this condition occurs when a person is disconnected from these norms or rejects them as inconsistent with his or her personal goals.

Antiterrorism and Effective Death Penalty Act (AEDPA) Legislation giving law enforcement officers the power to arrest and prosecute any individual who provides "material support or resources" to a "foreign terrorist organization."

appeal The process of seeking a higher court's review of a lower court's decision for the purpose of correcting or changing this decision.

appellate courts Courts that review decisions made by lower courts, such as trial courts; also known as *courts of appeals*.

arraignment A court proceeding in which the suspect is formally charged with the criminal offense stated in the indictment. The suspect enters a plea (guilty, not guilty, *nolo contendere*) in response.

arrest To take into custody a person suspected of criminal activity.

arrest warrant A written order, based on probable cause and issued by a judge or magistrate, commanding that the person named on the warrant be arrested by the police.

assault A threat or an attempt to do violence to another person that causes that person to fear immediate physical harm.

attempt The act of taking substantial steps toward committing a crime while having the ability and the intent to commit the crime, even if the crime never takes place.

attendant circumstances The facts surrounding a criminal event. With some crimes, these facts must be proved to convict the defendant of the underlying crime. With other crimes, proving these facts can increase the penalty associated with the underlying crime.

attorney-client privilege A rule of evidence requiring that communications between a client and his or her attorney be kept confidential, unless the client consents to disclosure.

attorney general The chief law officer of a state; also, the chief law officer of the nation.

authority The power designated to an agent of the law over a person who has broken the law.

automatic transfer The process by which a juvenile is transferred to adult court as a matter of state law. In some states, for example, a juvenile who is suspected of murder is automatically transferred to adult court.

B

bail The dollar amount or conditions set by the court to ensure that an individual accused of a crime will appear for further criminal proceedings.

bail bond agent A businessperson who agrees, for a fee, to pay the bail amount if the accused fails to appear in court as ordered.

ballistics The study of firearms, including the firing of the weapon and the flight of the bullet.

ballot initiative A procedure in which the citizens of a state, by collecting enough signatures, can force a public vote on a proposed change to state law.

battery The act of physically contacting another person with the intent to do harm, even if the resulting injury is insubstantial.

bench trial A trial conducted without a jury, in which a judge makes the determination of the defendant's guilt or innocence.

beyond a reasonable doubt The degree of proof required to find the defendant in a criminal trial guilty of committing the crime. The defendant's guilt must be the only reasonable explanation for the criminal act before the court.

Bill of Rights The first ten amendments to the U.S. Constitution.

biological weapon Any living organism, such as a bacterium or virus, used to intentionally harm or kill adversaries in war or targets of terrorist attacks.

biology The science of living organisms, including their structure, function, growth, and origin.

blue curtain A metaphorical term used to refer to the value placed on secrecy and the general mistrust of the outside world shared by many police officers.

body armor Protective covering that is worn under a police officer's clothing and designed to minimize injury from being hit by a fired bullet

booking The process of entering a suspect's name, offense, and arrival time into the police log following her or his arrest.

boot camp A variation on traditional shock incarceration in which juveniles (and some adults) are sent to secure confinement facilities modeled on military basic training camps instead of prison or jail.

botnet A network of computers that have been appropriated without the knowledge of their owners and used to spread harmful programs via the Internet; short for *robot network*.

***Boykin* form** A form that must be completed by a defendant who pleads guilty. The defendant states that she or he has done so voluntarily and with full comprehension of the consequences.

broken windows theory Wilson and Kelling's theory that a neighborhood in disrepair signals that criminal activity is tolerated in the area. Thus, by cracking down on quality-of-life crimes, police can reclaim the neighborhood and encourage law-abiding citizens to live and work there.

bullying Overt acts taken by students with the goal of intimidating, harassing, or humiliating other students.

bureaucracy A hierarchically structured administrative organization that carries out specific functions.

burglary The act of breaking into or entering a structure (such as a home or office) without permission for the purpose of committing a felony.

burnout A mental state that occurs when a person suffers from exhaustion and has difficulty functioning normally as a result of overwork and stress.

C

capital punishment The use of the death penalty to punish wrongdoers for certain crimes.

case attrition The process through which prosecutors, by deciding whether to prosecute each person arrested, effect an overall reduction in the number of persons prosecuted.

case law The rules of law announced in court decisions. Case law includes the aggregate of reported cases that interpret judicial precedents, statutes, regulations, and constitutional provisions.

caseload The number of individual probationers or parolees under the supervision of a probation or parole officer.

causation The relationship in which a change in one measurement or behavior creates a recognizable change in another measurement or behavior.

Central Intelligence Agency (CIA) The U.S. government agency that is responsible for collecting and coordinating foreign intelligence operations.

challenge for cause A *voir dire* challenge for which an attorney states the reason why a prospective juror should not be included on the jury.

charge The judge's instructions to the jury following the attorneys' closing arguments. The charge sets forth the rules of law that the jury must apply in reaching its decision, or verdict.

chemical weapon Any weapon that uses a manufactured chemical to harm or kill adversaries in war or targets of terrorist attacks.

child abuse Mistreatment of children by causing physical, emotional, or sexual damage without any plausible explanation, such as an accident.

child neglect A form of child abuse in which the child is denied certain necessities such as shelter, food, care, and love.

choice theory A school of criminology that holds that wrongdoers act as if they weigh the possible benefits of criminal or delinquent activity against the expected costs of being apprehended. When the benefits are greater than the expected costs, the offender will make a rational choice to commit a crime or delinquent act.

chronic offender A delinquent or criminal who commits multiple offenses and is considered part of a small group of wrongdoers who are responsible for a majority of the antisocial activity in any given community.

circumstantial evidence Indirect evidence that is offered to establish, by inference, the likelihood of a fact that is in question.

citizen oversight The process by which citizens review complaints brought against individual police officers or police departments.

civil confinement The practice of confining individuals against their will if they present a danger to the community.

civil law The branch of law dealing with the definition and enforcement of all private or public rights, as opposed to criminal matters.

civil rights The personal rights and protections guaranteed by the Constitution, particularly the Bill of Rights.

classical criminology A school of criminology based on the belief that individuals have free will to engage in any behavior, including criminal behavior. To deter criminal behavior, society must hold wrongdoers responsible for their actions by punishing them.

clearance of an arrest For crime-reporting purposes, occurs when the arrested suspect is charged with a crime and handed over to a court for prosecution.

clearance rate A comparison of the number of crimes cleared by arrest and prosecution with the number of crimes reported during any given time period.

closing arguments Arguments made by each side's attorney after the cases for the plaintiff and defendant have been presented.

coercion The use of physical force or mental intimidation to compel a person to do something—such as confess to committing a crime—against her or his will.

cold case A criminal investigation that has not been solved after a certain amount of time

cold hit The establishment of a connection between a suspect and a crime, often through the use of DNA evidence, in the absence of an ongoing criminal investigation.

common law The body of law developed from custom or judicial decisions in English and U.S. courts and not attributable to a legislature.

community policing A policing philosophy that emphasizes community support for and cooperation with the police in preventing crime. Community policing stresses a police role that is less centralized and more proactive than reform-era policing strategies.

competency hearing A court proceeding to determine whether the defendant is mentally well enough to understand the charges filed against him or her and cooperate with a lawyer in presenting a defense. If a judge believes the defendant to be incompetent, the trial cannot take place.

compliance The state of operating in accordance with governmental standards

computer crime Any wrongful act that is directed against computers and computer parts or that involves wrongful use or abuse of computers or software.

concurrent jurisdiction The situation that occurs when two or more courts have the authority to preside over the same criminal case.

concurring opinions Separate opinions prepared by judges who support the decision of the majority of the court but who want to make or clarify a particular point or to voice disapproval of the grounds on which the decision was made.

Conducted Energy Devices (CED) A less lethal weapon designed to disrupt a target's central nervous system by means of a charge of electrical energy.

confidential informant (CI) A human source for police who provides information concerning illegal activity in which he or she is involved.

conflict model A criminal justice model in which the content of criminal law is determined by the groups that hold economic, political, and social power in a community.

confrontation clause The part of the Sixth Amendment that guarantees all defendants the right to confront witnesses testifying against them during the criminal trial.

congregate system A nineteenth-century penitentiary system developed in New York in which inmates were kept in separate cells during the night but worked together in the daytime under a code of enforced silence.

consensus model A criminal justice model in which the majority of citizens in a society share the same values and beliefs. Criminal acts are acts that conflict with these values and beliefs and that are deemed harmful to society.

consent searches Searches by police that are made after the subject of the search has agreed to the action. In these situations, consent, if given of free will, validates a warrantless search.

constitutional law Law based on the U.S. Constitution and the constitutions of the various states.

control theory A series of theories that assume that all individuals have the potential for criminal behavior, but are restrained by the damage that such actions would do to their relationships with family, friends, and members of the community. Criminality occurs when these bonds are broken or nonexistent.

coroner The medical examiner of a county, usually elected by popular vote.

corporate violence Physical harm to individuals or the environment that occurs as the result of corporate policies or decision making.

corpus delicti The body of circumstances that must exist for a criminal act to have occurred.

correlation The relationship between two measurements or behaviors that tend to move in the same direction.

courtroom work group The social organization consisting of the judge, prosecutor, defense attorney, and other court workers. The relationships among these persons have a far-reaching impact on the day-to-day operations of any court.

crime An act that violates criminal law and is punishable by criminal sanctions.

crime control model A criminal justice model that places primary emphasis on the right of society to be protected from crime and violent criminals.

crime mapping Technology that allows crime analysts to identify trends and patterns of criminal behavior within a given area.

criminal justice system The interlocking network of law enforcement agencies, courts, and corrections institutions designed to enforce criminal laws and protect society from criminal behavior.

criminal model of addiction An approach to drug abuse that holds that drug offenders harm society by their actions to the same extent as other criminals and should face the same punitive sanctions.

criminologist A specialist in the field of crime and the causes of criminal behavior.

criminology The scientific study of crime and the causes of criminal behavior.

cross-examination The questioning of an opposing witness during trial.

cultural deviance theory A branch of social structure theory based on the assumption that members of certain subcultures reject the values of the dominant culture through deviant behavior patterns.

custodial interrogation The questioning of a suspect after that person has been taken into custody. In this situation, the suspect must be read his or her *Miranda* rights before interrogation can begin.

custody The forceful detention of a person, or the perception that a person is not free to leave the immediate vicinity.

cyber crime A crime that occurs online, in the virtual community of the Internet, as opposed to in the physical world.

cyber forensics The application of computer technology to finding and utilizing evidence of cyber crimes.

cyber fraud Any misrepresentation knowingly made over the Internet with the intention of deceiving another and on which a reasonable person would and does rely to his or her detriment.

cyberstalking The crime of stalking, committed in cyberspace though the use of e-mail, text messages, or another form of electronic communication.

D

dark figure of crime A term used to describe the actual amount of crime that takes place. The "figure" is "dark," or impossible to detect, because a great number of crimes are never reported to the police.

day reporting center (DRC) A community-based corrections center to which offenders report on a daily basis for treatment, education, and rehabilitation.

deadly force Force applied by a police officer that is likely or intended to cause death.

defendant In a civil court, the person or institution against whom an action is brought. In a criminal court, the person or entity who has been formally accused of violating a criminal law.

defense attorney The lawyer representing the defendant.

delegation of authority The principles of command on which most police departments are based in which personnel take orders from and are responsible to those in positions of power directly above them.

"deliberate indifference" A standard that must be met by inmates trying to prove that their Eighth Amendment rights were violated by a correctional facility. It occurs when prison officials are aware of harmful conditions of confinement but fail to take steps to remedy those conditions.

departure A stipulation in many federal and state sentencing guidelines that allows a judge to adjust his or her sentencing decision based on the special circumstances of a particular case.

deprivation model A theory that inmate aggression is the result of the frustration inmates feel at being deprived of freedom, consumer goods, sex, and other staples of life outside the institution.

desistance The process through which criminal activity decreases and reintegration into society increases over a period of time.

detainer A document that gives U.S. Immigration and Customs Enforcement custody of an immigration law violator following the disposition of that person's case by the criminal justice system.

detective The primary police investigator of crimes.

detention The temporary custody of a juvenile in a secure facility after a petition has been filed and before the adjudicatory process begins.

detention hearing A hearing to determine whether a juvenile should be detained, or remain detained, while waiting for the adjudicatory process to begin.

determinate sentencing A period of incarceration that is fixed by a sentencing authority and cannot be reduced by judges or other corrections officials.

deterrence The strategy of preventing crime through the threat of punishment.

deviance Behavior that is considered to go against the norms established by society.

differential response A strategy for answering calls for service in which response time is adapted to the seriousness of the call.

digital evidence Information or data of value to a criminal investigation that is either stored or transmitted by electronic means.

directed patrol A patrol strategy that is designed to focus on a specific type of criminal activity at a specific time.

direct evidence Evidence that establishes the existence of a fact that is in question without relying on inference.

direct examination The examination of a witness by the attorney who calls the witness to the stand to testify.

direct supervision approach A process of prison and jail administration in which correctional officers are in continuous personal contact with inmates during the day.

discovery Formal investigation prior to trial.

discretion The ability of individuals in the criminal justice system to make operational decisions based on personal judgment instead of formal rules or official information.

discretionary release The release of an inmate into a community supervision program at the discretion of the parole board within limits set by state or federal law.

discrimination The illegal use of characteristics such as gender or race by employers when making hiring or promotion decisions.

disposition hearing Similar to the sentencing hearing for adults, a hearing in which the juvenile judge or officer decides the appropriate punishment for a youth found to be delinquent or a status offender.

dissenting opinions Separate opinions in which judges disagree with the conclusion reached by the majority of the court and expand on their own views about the case.

diversion In the context of corrections, a strategy to divert those offenders who qualify away from prison and jail and toward community-based and intermediate sanctions.

DNA fingerprinting The identification of a person based on a sample of her or his DNA, the genetic material found in the cells of all living things.

docket The list of cases entered on a court's calendar and thus scheduled to be heard by the court.

domestic terrorism Acts of terrorism that take place within the territorial jurisdiction of the United States without direct foreign involvement.

domestic violence The act of willful neglect or physical violence that occurs within a familial or other intimate relationship.

double jeopardy To twice place at risk (jeopardize) a person's life or liberty. The Fifth Amendment to the U.S. Constitution prohibits a second prosecution in the same court for the same criminal offense.

double marginality The double suspicion that minority law enforcement officers face from their white colleagues and from members of the minority community to which they belong.

drug Any substance that modifies biological, psychological, or social behavior; in particular, an illegal substance with those properties.

drug abuse The use of drugs that results in physical or psychological problems for the user, as well as disruption of personal relationships and employment.

Drug Enforcement Administration (DEA) The federal agency responsible for enforcing the nation's laws and regulations regarding narcotics and other controlled substances.

dual court system The separate but interrelated court system of the United States, made up of the courts on the federal (national) level and the courts on the state level.

due process clause The provisions of the Fifth and Fourteenth Amendments to the Constitution that guarantee that no person shall be deprived of life, liberty, or property without due process of law. Similar clauses are found in most state constitutions.

due process model A criminal justice model that places primacy on the right of the individual to be protected from the power of the government.

duress Unlawful pressure brought to bear on a person that causes the person to perform an act that he or she would not otherwise perform.

duty The moral sense of a police officer that she or he should apply authority in a certain manner.

duty to retreat The requirement that a person claiming self-defense prove that she or he first took reasonable steps to avoid the conflict that resulted in the use of deadly force. Generally, the duty to retreat (1) applies only in public spaces and (2) does not apply when the force used in self-defense was nondeadly.

E

electronic monitoring A technique of probation supervision in which the offender's whereabouts are kept under surveillance by an electronic device.

electronic surveillance The use of electronic equipment by law enforcement agents to record private conversations or observe conduct that is meant to be private.

encryption The process by which a message is transmitted into a form or code that the sender and receiver intend not to be understandable by third parties.

entrapment A defense in which the defendant claims that he or she was induced by a public official—usually an undercover police officer—to commit a crime that he or she would otherwise not have committed.

ethics The rules or standards of behavior governing a profession; aimed at ensuring the fairness and rightness of actions.

evidence Anything that is used to prove the existence or non-existence of a fact.

exclusionary rule A rule under which any evidence that is obtained in violation of the accused's rights under the Fourth, Fifth, and Sixth Amendments, as well as any evidence derived from illegally obtained evidence, will not be admissible in criminal court.

exigent circumstances Situations that require extralegal or exceptional actions by the police. In these circumstances, police officers are justified in not following procedural rules, such as those pertaining to search and arrest warrants.

expert witness A witness with professional training or substantial experience qualifying her or him to testify on a certain subject.

expiration release The release of an inmate from prison at the end of his or her sentence without any further correctional supervision.

extradition The process by which one jurisdiction surrenders a person accused or convicted of violating another jurisdiction's criminal law to the second jurisdiction.

F

Federal Bureau of Investigation (FBI) The branch of the Department of Justice responsible for investigating violations of federal criminal law. The bureau also collects national crime statistics and provides training and other forms of aid to local law enforcement agencies.

federalism A form of government in which a written constitution provides for a division of powers between a central government and several regional governments. In the United States, the division of powers between the federal government and the fifty states is established by the Constitution.

felony A serious crime, usually punishable by death or imprisonment for a year or longer.

felony-murder An unlawful homicide that occurs during the attempted commission of a felony. Regardless of the actor's intent or the circumstances surrounding the death, the homicide is automatically considered first degree murder.

field training The segment of a police recruit's training in which he or she is removed from the classroom and placed on the beat, under the supervision of a senior officer.

finality The end of a criminal case, meaning that the outcome of the case is no longer susceptible to challenge by prosecutors or the defendant.

first responders Those individuals, such as firefighters, police officers, and emergency medical technicians, who are responsible for the protection and preservation of life and property during the early stages following a disaster.

forensics The application of science to establish facts and evidence during the investigation of crimes.

forfeiture The process by which the government seizes private property attached to criminal activity.

frisk A pat-down or minimal search by police to discover weapons. It is conducted for the express purpose of protecting the officer or other citizens, rather than finding evidence of illegal substances for use in a trial.

fruit of the poisoned tree Evidence that is acquired through the use of illegally obtained evidence and is therefore inadmissible in court.

furlough Temporary release from a prison for purposes of vocational or educational training, to ease the shock of release, or for personal reasons.

fusion center A collaborative effort involving local, state, and federal law enforcement agencies that focuses on sharing information related to terrorist activity.

G

general patrol A patrol strategy that relies on police officers monitoring a certain area with the goal of detecting crimes in progress or preventing crime due to their presence. Also known as *random* or *preventive patrol*.

genetics The study of how certain traits or qualities are transmitted from parents to their offspring.

"good faith" exception The legal principle, established through court decisions, that evidence obtained with the use of a technically invalid search warrant is admissible during trial if the police acted in good faith when they sought the warrant from a judge.

"good time" A reduction in time served by prisoners based on good behavior, conformity to rules, and other positive actions.

graduated sanctions The practical theory in juvenile corrections that a delinquent or status offender should receive a punishment that matches in seriousness the severity of the wrongdoing.

grand jury The group of citizens called to decide whether probable cause exists to believe that a suspect committed the crime with which she or he has been charged.

green card A document—no longer green—that indicates the holder's status as a lawful permanent resident of the United States.

gun control Efforts by a government to regulate or control the sale of guns.

H

habeas corpus An order that requires correctional officials to bring an inmate before a court or a judge and explain why he or she is being held in prison.

habitual offender laws Statutes that require lengthy prison sentences for those who are convicted of multiple felonies.

hacker A person who uses one computer to break into another.

halfway house A community-based form of early release that places inmates in residential centers and allows them to reintegrate with society.

"hands-off" doctrine The unwritten judicial policy that favors noninterference by the courts in the administration of prisons and jails.

hate crime law A statute that provides for greater sanctions against those who commit crimes motivated by bias against an individual or a group based on race, ethnicity, religion, gender, sexual orientation, disability, or age.

hearsay An oral or written statement made by an out-of-court speaker that is later offered in court by a witness (not the speaker) concerning a matter before the court. Hearsay usually is not admissible as evidence.

home confinement A community-based sanction in which offenders serve their terms of incarceration in their homes.

homeland security A concerted national effort to prevent terrorist attacks within the United States and reduce the country's vulnerability to terrorism.

hormone A chemical substance, produced in tissue and conveyed in the bloodstream, that controls certain cellular and body functions such as growth and reproduction.

hot spots Concentrated areas of high criminal activity that draw a directed police response.

hung jury A jury whose members are so irreconcilably divided in their opinions that they cannot reach a verdict.

hypothesis A possible explanation for an observed occurrence that can be tested by further investigation.

I

"identifiable human needs" The basic human necessities that correctional facilities are required by the Constitution to provide to inmates.

identity theft The theft of personal information, such as a person's name, driver's license number, or Social Security number.

illicit drugs Certain drugs or substances whose use or sale has been declared illegal.

impeachment The formal process by which a public official is charged with misconduct that could lead to his or her removal from office.

improvised explosive devices (IEDs) Explosive charges created using nonmilitary or nontraditional components, often used by terrorists or other nonstate actors without access to standard weapons training.

incapacitation A strategy for preventing crime by detaining wrongdoers in prison, thereby separating them from the community and reducing criminal opportunities.

inchoate offenses Conduct deemed criminal without actual harm being done, provided that the harm that would have occurred is one the law tries to prevent.

incident-driven policing A reactive approach to policing that emphasizes a speedy response to calls for service.

indeterminate sentencing An indeterminate term of incarceration in which a judge determines the minimum and maximum terms of imprisonment. When the minimum term is reached, the prisoner becomes eligible to be paroled.

indictment A charge or written accusation, issued by a grand jury, that probable cause exists to believe that a named person has committed a crime.

"inevitable discovery" exception The legal principle that illegally obtained evidence can be admitted in court if police using lawful means would have "inevitably" discovered it.

infancy A condition that, under early American law, excused young wrongdoers of criminal behavior because presumably they could not understand the consequences of their actions.

information The formal charge against the accused issued by the prosecutor after a preliminary hearing has found probable cause.

infraction In most jurisdictions, a noncriminal offense for which the penalty is a fine rather than incarceration.

infrastructure The services and facilities that support the day-to-day needs of modern life such as electricity, food, transportation, and water.

initial appearance An accused's first appearance before a judge or magistrate following arrest. During the appearance, the defendant is informed of the charges, advised of the right to counsel, told the amount of bail, and given a date for the preliminary hearing.

insanity A defense for criminal liability that asserts a lack of criminal responsibility. According to the law, a person cannot have the requisite state of mind to commit a crime if she or he did not know at the time of the act that it was wrong, or did not know the nature and quality of the act.

intake The process by which an official of the court must decide whether to file a petition, release the juvenile, or place the juvenile under some other form of supervision.

intellectual property Property resulting from intellectual, creative processes.

intelligence agency An agency that is primarily concerned with gathering information about potential criminal or terrorist events in order to prevent those acts from taking place.

intelligence-led policing An approach that measures the risk of criminal behavior associated with certain individuals or locations so as to predict when and where such criminal behavior is most likely to occur in the future.

intensive supervision probation (ISP) A punishment-oriented form of probation in which the offender is placed under stricter and more frequent surveillance and control than in conventional probation by probation officers with limited caseloads.

intermediate sanctions Sanctions that are more restrictive than probation and less restrictive than imprisonment.

internal affairs unit (IAU) A division within a police department that receives and investigates complaints of wrongdoing by police officers

interrogation The direct questioning of a suspect to gather evidence of criminal activity or gain a confession.

intoxication A defense for criminal liability in which the defendant claims that the taking of intoxicants rendered him or her unable to form the requisite intent to commit a criminal act.

involuntary manslaughter A negligent homicide, in which the offender had no intent to kill his or her victim.

irresistible-impulse test A test for the insanity defense under which a defendant who knew his or her action was wrong may still be found insane if he or she was unable, as a result of a mental deficiency, to control the urge to complete the act.

J

jail A facility, usually operated by the county government, used to hold persons awaiting trial or those who have been found guilty of misdemeanors.

judicial misconduct A general term describing behavior—such as accepting bribes or consorting with known felons—that diminishes public confidence in the judiciary.

judicial reprieve Temporary relief or the postponement of a sentence on the authority of a judge.

judicial review The power of a court—particularly the United States Supreme Court—to review the actions of the executive and legislative branches and, if necessary, declare those actions unconstitutional.

judicial waiver The process in which the juvenile judge, based on the facts of the case at hand, decides that the alleged offender should be transferred to adult court.

jurisdiction The authority of a court to hear and decide cases within an area of the law or a geographic territory.

jury nullification An acquittal of a defendant by a jury even though the evidence presented and the judge's instructions indicate that the defendant is guilty.

jury trial A trial before a judge and a jury.

just deserts A sanctioning philosophy based on the assertion that criminals deserve to be punished for breaking society's rules. The severity of the punishment should be determined only by the severity of the crime.

justice The quality of fairness that must exist in the processes designed to determine whether individuals are guilty of criminal wrongdoing.

juvenile delinquency Behavior that is illegal under federal or state law that has been committed by a person who is under an age limit specified by statute.

L

labeling theory The hypothesis that society creates crime and criminals by labeling certain behavior and certain people as deviant. The stigma that results from this social process excludes a person from the community, thereby increasing the chances that she or he will adopt the label as her or his identity and engage in a pattern of criminal behavior.

larceny The act of taking property from another person without the use of force with the intent of keeping that property.

lay witness A witness who can truthfully and accurately testify on a fact in question without having specialized training or knowledge; an ordinary witness.

learning theory The hypothesis that delinquents and criminals must be taught both the practical and emotional skills necessary to participate in illegal activity.

liability In a civil court, legal responsibility for one's own or another's actions.

licit drugs Legal drugs or substances, such as alcohol, caffeine, and nicotine.

life course criminology The study of crime based on the belief that behavioral patterns developed in childhood can predict delinquent and criminal behavior later in life.

lockdown A disciplinary action taken by prison officials in which all inmates are ordered to their quarters and nonessential prison activities are suspended.

low-visibility decision making A term used to describe the discretionary power police have in determining what to do with misbehaving juveniles.

M

magistrate A public civil officer or official with limited judicial authority within a particular geographic area, such as the authority to issue an arrest warrant.

mala in se A descriptive term for acts that are inherently wrong, regardless of whether they are prohibited by law.

mala prohibita A descriptive term for acts that are made illegal by criminal statute and are not necessarily wrong in and of themselves.

malice aforethought A depraved state of mind in which the offender's behavior reflected a wanton disregard for the well-being of his or her victim.

mandatory arrest policy Requires a police officer to detain a person for committing a certain type of crime as long as there is probable cause that he or she committed the crime.

mandatory release Release from prison that occurs when an offender has served the full length of his or her sentence, minus any adjustments for good time.

mandatory sentencing guidelines Statutorily determined punishments that must be applied to those who are convicted of specific crimes.

master jury list The list of citizens in a court's district from which a jury can be selected; compiled from voter-registration lists, driver's license lists, and other sources.

maximum-security prison A correctional institution designed and organized to control and discipline dangerous felons, as well as prevent escape; characterized by intense supervision, cement walls, and electric, barbed wire fences.

medical model A model of corrections in which the psychological and biological roots of an inmate's criminal behavior are identified and treated.

medical model of addiction An approach to drug addiction that treats drug abuse as a mental illness and focuses on treating and rehabilitating offenders rather than punishing them.

medium-security prison A correctional institution that houses less dangerous inmates and therefore uses less restrictive measures to prevent violence and escapes.

mens rea (pronounced *mehns ray*-uh). Mental state, or intent. A wrongful mental state is as necessary as a wrongful act to establish criminal liability.

methamphetamine (meth) A synthetic stimulant that creates a strong feeling of euphoria in the user and is highly addictive.

military tribunal A court that is operated by the military rather than the criminal justice system and is presided over by military officers rather than judges.

minimum-security prison A correctional institution designed to allow inmates, most of whom pose low security risks, a great deal of freedom of movement and contact with the outside world.

Miranda rights The constitutional rights of accused persons taken into custody by law enforcement officials, such as the right to remain silent and the right to counsel.

misdemeanor A criminal offense that is not a felony; usually punishable by a fine and/or a jail term of less than one year.

Missouri Plan A method of selecting judges that combines appointment and election. Under the plan, the state governor or another government official selects judges from a group of nominees chosen by a nonpartisan committee. After a year on the bench, the judges face a popular election to determine whether the public wishes to keep them in office.

mitigating circumstances Any circumstances accompanying the commission of a crime that may justify a lighter sentence.

M'Naghten rule A common law test of criminal responsibility, derived from *M'Naghten's* Case in 1843, that relies on the defendant's inability to distinguish right from wrong.

Model Penal Code A statutory text created by the American Law Institute that sets forth general principles of criminal responsibility and defines specific offenses. States have adopted many aspects of the Model Penal Code, which is not itself a law, into their criminal codes.

morals Principles of right and wrong behavior, as practiced by individuals or by society.

motion for a directed verdict A motion requesting that the court grant judgment in favor of the defense on the ground that the prosecution has not produced sufficient evidence to support the state's claim.

murder The unlawful killing of one human being by another.

N

National Security Agency (NSA) The intelligence agency that is responsible for protecting U.S. government communications and producing intelligence by monitoring foreign communications.

necessity A defense against criminal liability in which the defendant asserts that circumstances required her or him to commit an illegal act.

negligence A failure to exercise the standard of care that a reasonable person would exercise in similar circumstances.

neurotransmitter A chemical that transmits nerve impulses between nerve cells and from nerve cells to the brain.

new-generation jail A type of jail that is distinguished architecturally from its predecessors by a design that encourages interaction between inmates and jailers and that offers greater opportunities for treatment.

night watch system An early form of American law enforcement in which volunteers patrolled their community from dusk to dawn to keep the peace.

noble cause corruption Knowing misconduct by a police officer with the goal of attaining what the officer believes is a "just" result.

nolo contendere Latin for "I will not contest it." A criminal defendant's plea, in which he or she chooses not to challenge, or contest, the charges brought by the government. Although the defendant may still be sentenced or fined, the plea neither admits nor denies guilt.

nonpartisan elections Elections in which candidates are presented on the ballot without any party affiliation.

nonstate actor An entity that plays a role in international affairs but does not represent any established state or nation.

nuclear weapon An explosive device that derives its massive destructive power from the release of nuclear energy.

O

opening statements The attorneys' statements to the jury at the beginning of the trial. Each side briefly outlines the evidence that will be offered during the trial and the legal theory that will be pursued.

opinions Written statements by the judges expressing the reasons for the court's decision in a case.

oral arguments The verbal arguments presented in person by attorneys to an appellate court. Each attorney presents reasons why the court should rule in his or her client's favor.

organized crime Illegal acts carried out by illegal organizations engaged in the market for illegal goods or services, such as illicit drugs or firearms.

P

pardon An act of executive clemency that overturns a conviction and erases mention of the crime from the person's criminal record.

parens patriae A doctrine that holds that the state has a responsibility to look after the well-being of children and to assume the role of parent if necessary.

parole The conditional release of an inmate before his or her sentence has expired.

parole board A body of appointed civilians that decides whether a convict should be granted conditional release before the end of his or her sentence.

parole contract An agreement between the state and the offender that establishes the conditions under which the latter will be allowed to serve the remainder of her or his prison term in the community.

parole grant hearing A hearing in which the entire parole board or a subcommittee reviews information, meets the offender, and hears testimony from relevant witnesses to determine whether to grant parole.

parole guidelines Standards that are used in the parole process to measure the risk that a potential parolee will recidivate.

parole revocation When a parolee breaks the conditions of parole, the process of withdrawing parole and returning the person to prison.

Part I offenses Crimes reported annually by the FBI in its Uniform Crime Report. Part I offenses include murder, rape, robbery, aggravated assault, burglary, larceny, and motor vehicle theft.

Part II offenses All crimes recorded by the FBI that do not fall into the category of Part I offenses. These crimes include both misdemeanors and felonies.

partisan elections Elections in which candidates are affiliated with and receive support from political parties. The candidates are listed in conjunction with their party on the ballot.

Patriot Act Legislation passed in the wake of the September 11, 2001, terrorist attacks that greatly expanded the ability of government agents to monitor and apprehend suspected terrorists.

patronage system A form of corruption in which the political party in power hires and promotes police officers, receiving job-related "favors" in return.

penitentiary An early form of correctional facility that emphasized separating inmates from society and from each other.

peremptory challenges *Voir dire* challenges to exclude potential jurors from serving on the jury without any supporting reason or cause.

permanent resident An alien who has been granted permission by the U.S. government to live and work in the United States on a permanent basis.

petition The document filed with a juvenile court alleging that the juvenile is a delinquent or a status offender and requesting that the court either hear the case or transfer it to an adult court.

phishing Sending an unsolicited e-mail that falsely claims to be from a legitimate organization in an attempt to acquire sensitive information such as passwords or credit-card details from the recipient.

plaintiff The person or institution that initiates a lawsuit in civil court proceedings by filing a complaint.

plain view doctrine The legal principle that objects in plain view of a law enforcement agent who has the right to be in a position to have that view may be seized without a warrant and introduced as evidence.

plea bargaining The process by which the accused and the prosecutor work out a mutually satisfactory conclusion to the case, subject to court approval.

podular design The architectural style of new generation jails. Each "pod" consists of between twelve and twenty-four one-person cells and a communal dayroom to allow for social interaction.

police corruption The abuse of authority by a law enforcement officer for personal gain.

police cynicism The suspicion that citizens are weak, corrupt, and dangerous. This outlook is the result of a police officer being constantly exposed to civilians at their worst and can negatively affect the officer's performance.

police subculture The values and perceptions that are shared by members of a police department and, to a certain extent, by all law enforcement agents.

policy A set of guiding principles designed to influence the behavior and decision making of police officers.

positivism A school of the social sciences that sees criminal and delinquent behavior as the result of biological, psychological, and social forces. Because wrongdoers are driven to deviancy by external factors, they should not be punished but treated to lessen the influence of those factors.

precedent A court decision that furnishes an example of authority for deciding subsequent cases involving similar facts.

predisposition report A report prepared during the disposition process that provides the judge with relevant background material to aid in the disposition decision.

preliminary hearing An initial hearing in which a magistrate decides if there is probable cause to believe that the defendant committed the crime with which he or she is charged.

preparedness An umbrella term for the actions taken by governments to prepare for large-scale catastrophic events such as terrorist attacks or environmental disasters.

preponderance of evidence The degree of proof required to decide in favor of one side or the other in a civil case. In general, this requirement is met when a plaintiff proves that a fact more likely than not is true.

prescription drugs Medical drugs that require a physician's permission for purchase.

presentence investigative report An investigative report on an offender's background that assists a judge in determining the proper sentence.

pretrial detainees Individuals who cannot post bail after arrest or are not released on their own recognizance and are therefore forced to spend the time prior to their trial incarcerated in jail.

pretrial diversion program An alternative to trial offered by a judge or prosecutor, in which the offender agrees to participate in a specified counseling or treatment program in return for withdrawal of the charges.

preventive detention The retention of an accused person in custody due to fears that she or he will commit a crime if released before trial.

prisoner reentry A corrections strategy designed to prepare inmates for a successful return to the community and to reduce their criminal activity after release.

prison gang A group of inmates who band together within the corrections system to engage in social and criminal activities.

prisonization The socialization process through which a new inmate learns the accepted norms and values of the prison culture.

prison programs Organized activities for inmates that are designed to improve their physical and mental health, provide them with vocational skills, or simply keep them busy while incarcerated.

prison segregation The practice of separating inmates based on a certain characteristic, such as age, gender, type of crime committed, or race.

private prisons Correctional facilities operated by private corporations instead of the government and, therefore, reliant on profits for survival.

private security The practice of private corporations or individuals offering services traditionally performed by police officers.

proactive arrests Arrests that occur because of concerted efforts by law enforcement agencies to respond to a particular type of criminal or criminal behavior.

probable cause Reasonable grounds to believe the existence of facts warranting certain actions, such as the search or arrest of a person.

probation A criminal sanction in which a convict is allowed to remain in the community rather than be imprisoned as long as she or he follows certain conditions set by the court.

probationary period A period of time at the beginning of a police officer's career during which she or he may be fired without cause.

problem-oriented policing A policing philosophy that requires police to identify potential criminal activity and develop strategies to prevent or respond to that activity.

procedural criminal law Rules that define the manner in which the rights and duties of individuals may be enforced.

procedural due process A provision in the Constitution that states that the law must be carried out in a fair and orderly manner.

professionalism Adherence to a set of values that show a police officer to be of the highest moral character.

professional model A style of policing advocated by August Vollmer and O. W. Wilson that emphasizes centralized police organizations, increased use of technology, and a limitation of police discretion through regulations and guidelines.

property bond An alternative to posting bail in cash, in which the defendant gains pretrial release by providing the court with property valued at the bail amount as assurance that he or she will return for trial.

prosecutorial waiver A procedure used in situations in which juvenile and adult courts each have jurisdiction over certain offenses, depending on the age of the offender, and the prosecutor decides which court will hear the case.

psychoactive drugs Chemicals that affect the brain, causing changes in emotions, perceptions, and behavior.

psychoanalytic theory Sigmund Freud's theory that attributes our thoughts and actions to unconscious motives.

psychology The scientific study of mental processes and behavior.

public defenders Court-appointed attorneys who are paid by the state to represent defendants who are unable to hire private counsel.

public order crime Behavior that has been labeled criminal because it is contrary to shared social values, customs, and norms.

public prosecutors Individuals, acting as trial lawyers, who initiate and conduct cases in the government's name and on behalf of the people.

R

racial profiling The practice of targeting members of minority groups for police stops based solely on their race, ethnicity, or national origin.

racketeering The criminal action of being involved in an organized effort to engage in illegal business transactions.

radiation Harmful energy that is transmitted outward from its source through rays, waves, or particles following the detonation of a nuclear device.

reactive arrests Arrests that come about as part of the ordinary routine of police patrol and responses to calls for service.

real evidence Evidence that is brought into court and seen by the jury, as opposed to evidence that is described for a jury.

"real offense" The actual offense committed, as opposed to the charge levied by a prosecutor as the result of a plea bargain.

reasonable force The degree of force that is appropriate to protect the police officer or other citizens and is not excessive.

rebuttal Evidence given to counteract or disprove evidence presented by the opposing party.

recklessness The state of being aware that a risk does or will exist and nevertheless acting in a way that consciously disregards this risk.

recruitment The process by which law enforcement agencies develop a pool of qualified applicants from which to select new officers.

referral The notification process through which a law enforcement officer or other concerned citizen makes the juvenile court aware of a juvenile's unlawful or unruly conduct.

regulation Governmental control of society through rules and laws that are generally carried out by administrative agencies.

rehabilitation The philosophy that society is best served when wrongdoers are provided the resources needed to eliminate criminality from their behavioral pattern.

reintegration A goal of corrections that focuses on preparing the offender for a return to the community unmarred by further criminal behavior.

relative deprivation The theory that inmate aggression is caused when freedoms and services that the inmate has come to accept as normal are decreased or eliminated.

release on recognizance (ROR) A judge's order that releases an accused from jail with the understanding that he or she will return for further proceedings of his or her own will; used instead of setting a monetary bond.

relevant evidence Evidence tending to make a fact in question more or less probable than it would be without the evidence. Only relevant evidence is admissible in court.

removal The process used by the federal government to expel an alien from the United States.

repeat victimization The theory that certain people and places are more likely to be subject to criminal activity and that past victimization is therefore a valuable crime prevention tool because it is a strong indicator of future victimization.

residential treatment program A government-run facility for juveniles whose offenses are not deemed serious enough to warrant incarceration in a training school.

response time The rapidity with which calls for service are answered.

restitution Monetary compensation for damages done to the victim by the offender's criminal act.

restorative justice An approach to punishment designed to repair the harm done to the victim and the community by the offender's criminal act.

retribution The philosophy that those who commit criminal acts should be punished based on the severity of the crime and that no other factors need be considered.

robbery The act of taking property from another person through force, threat of force, or intimidation.

rule of four A rule of the United States Supreme Court that the Court will not issue a writ of *certiorari* unless at least four justices agree to hear the case.

S

search The process by which police examine a person or property to find evidence that will be used to prove guilt in a criminal trial.

searches and seizures The legal term, as found in the Fourth Amendment of the U.S. Constitution, that generally refers to the searching for and the confiscating of evidence by law enforcement agents.

searches incidental to arrests Searches for weapons and evidence of persons who have just been arrested. The fruit of such searches is admissible if any items found are within the immediate vicinity or control of the suspect

search warrant A written order, based on probable cause and issued by a judge or magistrate, commanding that police officers or criminal investigators search a specific person, place, or property to obtain evidence.

security threat group (STG) A group of three or more inmates who engage in activity that poses a threat to the safety of other inmates or the prison staff.

seizure The forcible taking of a person or property in response to a violation of the law.

self-defense The legally recognized privilege to protect one's self or property from injury by another. The privilege of self-defense covers only acts that are reasonably necessary to protect one's self or property.

self-reported survey A method of gathering crime data that relies on participants to reveal and detail their own criminal or delinquent behavior.

sentencing discrimination A situation in which the length of a sentence appears to be influenced by a defendant's race, gender, economic status, or other factor not directly related to the crime he or she committed.

sentencing disparity A situation in which those convicted of similar crimes do not receive similar sentences.

sentencing guidelines Legislatively determined guidelines that judges are required to follow when sentencing those convicted of specific crimes. These guidelines limit judicial discretion.

separate confinement A nineteenth-century penitentiary system developed in Pennsylvania in which inmates were kept separate from each other at all times, with daily activities taking place in individual cells.

sex offender notification law Legislation that requires law enforcement authorities to notify people when convicted sex offenders are released into their neighborhood or community.

sexual assault Forced or coerced sexual intercourse (or other sexual act).

sexual harassment A repeated pattern of unwelcome sexual advances and/or obscene remarks in the workplace. Under certain circumstances, sexual harassment is illegal and can be the basis for a civil lawsuit.

sheriff The primary law enforcement officer in a county, usually elected to the post by a popular vote.

shock incarceration A short period of incarceration that is designed to deter further criminal activity by "shocking" the offender with the hardships of imprisonment.

social conflict theories A school of criminology that views criminal behavior as the result of class conflict. Certain behavior is labeled illegal not because it is inherently criminal, but because the ruling class has an economic or social interest in restricting such behavior to protect the status quo.

social disorganization theory The theory that deviant behavior is more likely in communities where social institutions such as families, schools, and the criminal justice system fail to exert control over the population.

socialization The process through which a police officer is taught the values and expected behavior of the police subculture.

social process theories A school of criminology that considers criminal behavior to be the predictable result of a person's interaction with his or her environment. According to these theories, everybody has the potential for wrongdoing. Those who act on this potential are conditioned to do so by family members or peer groups, or institutions such as the media.

social reality of crime The theory that criminal laws are designed by those in power to help them keep power at the expense of those who do not have power.

spam Bulk e-mails, particularly of commercial advertising, sent in large quantities without the consent of the recipient.

specialty courts Lower courts that have jurisdiction over one specific area of criminal activity, such as illegal drugs or domestic violence.

split sentence probation A sentence that consists of incarceration in a prison or jail, followed by a probationary period in the community.

stare decisis (pronounced *ster*-ay dih-*si-ses*). A common law doctrine under which judges are obligated to follow the precedents established under prior decisions.

status offender A juvenile who has been found to have engaged in behavior deemed unacceptable for those under a certain statutorily determined age.

statute of limitations A law limiting the amount of time prosecutors have to bring criminal charges against a suspect after the crime has occurred.

statutory law The body of law enacted by legislative bodies.

statutory rape A strict liability crime in which an adult engages in a sexual act with a minor. The difference in age between the two participants automatically criminalizes the behavior of the older participant, regardless of whether the younger one consented.

stop A brief detention of a person by law enforcement agents for questioning. The agents must have a reasonable suspicion that a crime has taken place before stopping a suspect.

strain theory The assumption that crime is the result of frustration felt by individuals who cannot reach their financial and personal goals through legitimate means.

street gang A group of people, usually three or more, who share a common identity and engage in illegal activities.

stressors The aspects of police work and life that lead to feelings of stress.

strict liability crimes Certain crimes, such as traffic violations, in which the defendant is guilty regardless of her or his state of mind at the time of the act.

subculture A group exhibiting certain values and behavior patterns that distinguish it from the dominant culture.

substantial-capacity test (ALI/MPC test) From the Model Penal Code, a test that states that a person is not responsible for criminal behavior if when committing the act "as a result of mental disease or defect he [or she] lacks substantial capacity either to appreciate the wrongfulness of his [or her] conduct or to conform his [or her] conduct to the requirements of the law."

substantive criminal law Law that defines the rights and duties of individuals with respect to one another.

substantive due process The constitutional requirement that laws used in accusing and convicting persons of crimes must be fair.

supermax prison A correctional facility reserved for those inmates who have extensive records of misconduct in maximum-security prisons; characterized by extremely strict control and supervision over the inmates, including extensive use of solitary confinement.

suspended sentence A judicially imposed condition in which an offender is sentenced after being convicted of a crime, but is not required to begin serving the sentence immediately. The judge may revoke the suspended sentence and remit the offender to prison or jail if he or she reoffends.

sworn officer A law enforcement agent who has been authorized to make arrests and use force, including deadly force, against civilians

system A set of interacting parts that, when functioning properly, achieve a desired result.

T

technical violation An action taken by a probationer that, although not criminal, breaks the terms of probation as designated by the court.

ten percent cash bail An alternative to traditional bail in which defendants may gain pretrial release by posting 10 percent of their bond amount to the court instead of seeking a bail bondsperson.

terrorism The use or threat of violence to achieve political objectives.

testimony Verbal evidence given by witnesses under oath.

testosterone The hormone primarily responsible for the production of sperm and the development of male secondary sex characteristics such as the growth of facial and pubic hair and the change of voice pitch.

theory An explanation of a happening or circumstance that is based on observation, experimentation, and reasoning.

time served The period of time a person denied bail (or unable to pay it) has spent in jail prior to his or her trial. If the suspect is found guilty and sentenced to a jail or prison term, the judge will often shorten the duration of the sentence based on the amount of time served as a pretrial detainee.

total institution An institution, such as a prison, that provides all of the necessities for existence to those who live within its boundaries.

trace evidence Evidence such as a fingerprint, blood, or hair found in small amounts at a crime scene.

training school A correctional institution for juveniles found to be delinquent or status offenders.

trial courts Courts in which most cases usually begin and in which questions of fact are examined.

truth-in-sentencing laws Legislative attempts to assure that convicts will serve approximately the terms to which they were initially sentenced.

U

Uniform Crime Report (UCR) An annual report compiled by the FBI to give an indication of criminal activity in the United States. The FBI collects data from local, state, and federal law enforcement agencies in preparing this report.

U.S. Customs and Border Protection (CBP) The federal agency responsible for protecting U.S. borders and facilitating legal trade and travel across those borders.

U.S. Immigration and Customs Enforcement (ICE) The federal agency that enforces the nation's immigration and customs laws.

U.S. Secret Service A federal law enforcement organization with the primary responsibility of protecting the president, the president's family, the vice president, and other important political figures.

utilitarianism An approach to ethical reasoning in which the "correct" decision is the one that results in the greatest amount of good for the greatest number of people affected by that decision.

V

venire The group of citizens from which the jury is selected.

verdict A formal decision made by the jury.

victim impact statement (VIS) A statement to the sentencing body (judge, jury, or parole board) in which a victim or a victim's family member is given the opportunity to describe how the crime has affected her or him.

victimology A school of criminology that studies why certain people are the victims of crimes and the optimal role for victims in the criminal justice system.

victim surveys A method of gathering crime data that directly surveys participants to determine their experiences as victims of crime.

virus A computer program that can replicate itself over a network such as the Internet and interfere with the normal use of a computer. A virus cannot exist as a separate entity and must attach itself to another program to move through a network.

visa Official authorization allowing a person to travel to and within the issuing country.

voir dire The preliminary questions that the trial attorneys ask prospective jurors to determine whether they are biased or have any connection with the defendant or a witness.

voluntary manslaughter A homicide in which the intent to kill was present in the mind of the offender, but malice was lacking. Most commonly used to describe homicides in which the offender was provoked or otherwise acted in the heat of passion.

W

warden The prison official who is ultimately responsible for the organization and performance of a correctional facility.

warrantless arrest An arrest made without first seeking a warrant for the action. Such arrests are permitted under certain circumstances, such as when the arresting officer has witnessed the crime or has probable cause that the suspect has committed a felony.

weapons of mass destruction (WMDs) A term that describes nuclear, radiological, chemical, or biological weapons that have the capacity to cause large numbers of casualties or do significant property damage.

"wedding cake" model A wedding cake–shaped model that explains how different cases receive different treatment in the criminal justice system. The cases at the "top" of the cake receive the most attention, while those cases at the "bottom" are disposed of quickly and largely ignored by the media.

white-collar crime Nonviolent crimes committed by business entities or individuals to gain a personal or business advantage.

widen the net The criticism that intermediate sanctions designed to divert offenders from prison actually increase the number of citizens who are under the control and surveillance of the American corrections system.

work release program Temporary release of convicts from prison for purposes of employment. The offenders may spend their days on the job, but must return to the correctional facility at night and during the weekend.

worm A computer program that can automatically replicate itself over a network such as the Internet and interfere with the normal use of a computer. A worm does not need to be attached to an existing file to move from one network to another.

writ of certiorari A request from a higher court asking a lower court for the record of a case. In essence, the request signals the higher court's willingness to review the case.

wrongful conviction The conviction, either by verdict or by guilty plea, of a person who is factually innocent of the charges.

Y

youth gang A self-formed group of youths with several identifiable characteristics, including a gang name and other recognizable symbols, a geographic territory, a leadership structure, and participation in illegal activities.

Clemmer, Donald, 463
Clemons, Maurice, 301
Clerk of the court, 274
Clinton, Bill, 434, 547
Closed-circuit television (CCTV) cameras, 235–236
Closing arguments, 340–341
Coast Guard, 154
Cobbins, Letalvis, 334
Cocaine, 72–73, 74
   crack, 83
   crime trends and, 83
Cockfighting, 105
Code of Hammurabi, 99
Code of Israelites, 99
Code of Justinian, 99
CODIS, 184
Coercion
   confession and, 237
   inherent, 238
Coffee, John C., 372
Cohen, Larry, 52–53
Cold cases, 322
   databases and cold hit, 184
   defined, 182
Cold hit, 184
Cole, David, 220
Cole, Samuel Roshard, 184
Cole, U.S.S., bombing of, 540
Collective incapacitation, 359–360
Collier, Acurie, 411
Collins, Audrey, 273
Commission on Law Observance and Enforcement, 139
Common law, 99–100
   defined, 99
   English, 99–100
   statutory law and, 101–102
Community corrections, 398–421
   cost of, 400
   diversion, 399–400
   intermediate sanctions, 411–419
   justification for, 399–400
   low-cost alternative, 400
   number of people in, 398
   paradox of, 420
   probation, 401–442
   reintegration, 399
Community policing, 22, 136
   challenges of anti-terrorism and, 142–143
   criticism of, 191
   defined, 191
   historical perspective on, 141
Community service
   as form of punishment, 365
   provided by police, 177
Competency hearing, 116
Compliance, 597
Comprehensive Drug Abuse Prevention and Control Act, 74
CompStat, 189
Computer axial tomography, 40
Computer crime. *See also* Cyber crimes
   defined, 583
Concealment, white-collar crime and, 596
Concurrence, 111
Concurrent jurisdiction, 257–258
Concurring opinions, 267
Conditioning strategy, 241
Conducted energy devices (CEDs), 200
Confessions
   attorney-client privilege and, 295
   coercion and, 237
   recording, 243
   as self-incrimination, 237
Confidential informant, 181
Conflict model, 5–6
Confrontation clause, 337
Congregate system, 430
Conroy, Jeffrey, 127
Consensus model, 5

Consent
   electronic surveillance and, 235
   searches with, 230–231
Consent decree, 148
Consent searches, 230–231
Conspiracy, white-collar crime and, 596
Constitutional law, 101
Constitution of United States. *See also* specific amendments
   amending, 122
   arrests, 223–226
   Bill of Rights, 122–123
   choice of defense attorney, 293
   cruel and unusual punishment, 122
   double jeopardy, 122
   due process, 123–126
   excessive bail and fines, 122
   exclusionary rule, 219–220
   Fourth Amendment, 217–220
   identification process and, 244–245
   illegal immigrants and, 579
   interrogation process, 237–243
   juveniles and, 505–506, 520
   Miranda warning, 237–243
   prisoners' rights, 476
   private prisons, 447
   probable cause, 218–219
   public trial, 122
   racial profiling and, 246
   reasonableness, 217
   right to bear arms, 20, 27
   right to lawyer, 122
   search and seizure, 226–236
   as source of American criminal law, 101
   speedy trial, 122
   stops and frisks, 220–223
   Supreme Court as interpreter of, 266
   unreasonable searches and seizures, 122
   warrants for searches, 122
   witness incrimination, 122
Constitutions, state, 101
Consumer fraud, 595
   as cyber crime, 584
Continuity theory of crime, 52
Controlled Substances Act (CSA), 74, 157
   schedule of narcotics as defined by, 74
Controlling the Assault of Non-Solicited Pornography and Marketing Act (CAN-SPAM), 587
Control theory, 46, 55
Cooksey, Kazi, 71
Cooper, Jessica, 307
Cordner, Gary W., 177
Coroner, 153
Corporate violence, 596
Corpus delicti (body of crime), 107, 112, 336
Correctional officers, 472–478
   discipline, 474–476
   discretion and, 15, 16
   duties of, 473
   female, 476
   legitimate security interests, 475
   malicious and sadistic standard, 475–476
   rank of, 473–474
   salary, 161
   sanctioning prisoners, 474–475
   use of force, 475–476
Corrections
   juvenile, 527–530
   role in criminal justice system, 14
Corrections Corporation of America (CCA), 445, 446
Correlation, theory of criminology, 35
Corruption. *See* Police corruption
Cotton, Jeffrey, 200
Counterfeiting, 77
Counterintelligence, 551
County attorney, 287
County sheriff, 11
Court reporters, 274
Courtroom work group, 274–278
   assembly-line justice, 276, 278

docket, 269
   formation of, 275
   impact of excessive caseloads, 276, 278
   incentives to cooperate, 276
Courts
   bureaucratic function, 256
   crime control function, 256
   drug courts, 412–413
   dual system of, 14
   due process function, 255–256
   federal court system, 260–261, 264–267
   functions of, 255–256
   jurisdiction of, 257–260
   legitimacy of, 255
   rehabilitation function, 256
   specialty, 263
   state court system, 261–263
   Supreme Court, 264–267
   work group in, 274–278
Courtyard style, 439
Couture, Jake, 111
Cox, Winston, 134
Crack cocaine, 83
   juvenile delinquency and, 510
   sentencing and, 371
Crank, John P., 205
Creach, Wayne Scott, 288
Credit-card fraud, 585–586, 595
Crew, Keith, 372
Crime(s). *See also* Crime theories; specific types of crimes
   age and, 82–83
   attendant circumstances, 112–113
   brain and, 38
   causation, 112
   class and, 86–87
   classification of, 69–75
   concurrence, 111
   conflict model of, 5–6
   consensus model of, 5
   controlling, 10
   criminal act of, 107–108
   cyber crime, 8–9
   decline and leveling off of, 84–85
   defined, 5, 6–7
   degree of, 7, 70–71
   vs. deviance, 7
   drop in crime rate, 20, 25
   drug-crime relationship, 56–58
   drugs and, 21, 54–58
   economy and, 83
   education and, 86
   elements of, 107–113
   ethnicity and, 87, 89
   fear of, 20
   gangs and, 22
   genetics and, 38–39
   guns and, 20–21
   harm, 113
   mala in se, 72–75
   mala prohibita, 72–75
   measuring, 75–81
   mental state and, 108–111
   organized crime, 8
   prevention of, 10, 136–137
   property crime, 7–8
   psychology and, 41–42
   public order crime, 8
   race and, 85–89
   seduction of, 38
   seriousness of, and sentencing, 367
   strict liability, 110–111
   theories of (*See* Crime theories)
   trends in, 82–89
   types of, 7–9
   victimless, 8
   violent crime, 7
   violent video games and, 60
   white-collar crime, 8
   women and, 89